UNIVERSITY LIBRARY
UW-STEVENS POINT

W9-AOV-809

69.95
6x

UNIVERSITY LIBRARY
UNIVERSITY OF ...

Handbook of
AGING
AND THE
SOCIAL
SCIENCES

THE HANDBOOKS OF AGING

Consisting of Three Volumes:

Critical comprehensive reviews of
research knowledge, theories,
concepts, and issues

Editor-in-Chief: **James E. Birren**

Handbook of the Biology of Aging

Edited by Caleb E. Finch and Edward L. Schneider

Handbook of the Biology of Aging

Edited by James E. Birren and K. Warner Schaie

Handbook of Aging and the Social Sciences

Edited by Robert H. Binstock and Ethel Shanas

Handbook of
AGING AND THE SOCIAL SCIENCES

Second Edition

Editors
Robert H. Binstock
Ethel Shanas

With the assistance of Associate Editors

George L. Maddox
George C. Myers
James H. Schulz

VNR VAN NOSTRAND REINHOLD COMPANY
————————————————— **New York**

Copyright © 1985 by Van Nostrand Reinhold Company Inc.

Library of Congress Catalog Card Number: 84–25729
ISBN: 0-442-26480-1

All rights reserved. Certain portions of this work copyright © 1976 by Van Nostrand Reinhold Company Inc. No part of this work covered by the copyright hereon may be reproduced or used in any form or by any means—graphic, electronic, or mechanical, including photocopying, recording, taping, or information storage and retrieval systems—without permission of the publisher.

Manufactured in the United States of America

Published by Van Nostrand Reinhold Company Inc.
135 West 50th Street
New York, New York 10020

Van Nostrand Reinhold Company Limited
Molly Millars Lane
Wokingham, Berkshire RG11 2PY, England

Van Nostrand Reinhold
480 Latrobe Street
Melbourne, Victoria 3000, Australia

Macmillan of Canada
Division of Gage Publishing Limited
164 Commander Boulevard
Agincourt, Ontario M1S 3C7, Canada

15 14 13 12 11 10 9 8 7 6 5 4 3 2 1

Library of Congress Cataloging in Publication Data
Main entry under title:

Handbook of aging and the social sciences.
  (The Handbooks of aging)
  Includes indexes.
  1. Gerontology—Addresses, essays, lectures.
2. Aging—Social aspects—Addresses, essays, lectures.
I. Binstock, Robert H.   II. Shanas, Ethel.
HQ1061.H336 1985   305.2′6   84–25729
ISBN 0–442–26480–1

HQ
1061
.H336
1985

CONTRIBUTORS

W. Andrew Achenbaum, Ph.D.
Associate Professor, Department of History, Carnegie-Mellon University, Pittsburgh, Pennsylvania

Toni C. Antonucci, Ph.D.
Associate Research Scientist, Institute for Social Research, Assistant Professor, Department of Family
Practice, Adjunct Associate Professor, Department
of Psychology, The University of Michigan, Ann Arbor, Michigan

David L. Baumer, Ph.D., J.D.
Assistant Professor, North Carolina State University,
Raleigh, North Carolina

Vern L. Bengtson, Ph.D.
Professor of Sociology, Director, Gerontology Re-
search Institute, University of Southern California,
Los Angeles, California

Robert H. Binstock, Ph.D.
Henry R. Luce Professor of Aging, Health, and So-
ciety; Senior Fellow, Center on Aging and Health;
Professor of Epidemiology and Community Health,
School of Medicine; Professor of Nursing, School of
Nursing; Case Western Reserve University, Cleve-
land, Ohio

Richard T. Campbell, Ph.D.
Associate Professor of Sociology and Senior Fellow,
Center for the Study of Aging and Human Devel-
opment, Duke University, Durham, North Carolina

Marjorie Cantor, M.A.
Brookdale Professor of Gerontology, Graduate
School of Social Service, Fordham University, New
York, New York

Yung-Ping Chen, Ph.D.
Frank M. Engle Professor in Economic Security Research; Research Director of McCahan Foundation,
and Professor of Economics, The American College,
Bryn Mawr, Pennsylvania

Robert Clark, Ph.D.
Professor, Department of Economics and Business,
North Carolina State University, Raleigh, North Car-
olina

Sally Coberly, Ph.D.
Senior Staff Associate, Employment and Retirement
Division, Andrus Gerontology Center, University of
Southern California, Los Angeles, California

Neal E. Cutler, Ph.D.
Professor of Political Science, Research Associate in
Gerontology, University of Southern California, Los
Angeles, California

Karen Davis, Ph.D.
Chairman and Professor, Department of Health Policy and Management, School of Hygiene and Public
Health; Professor of Political Economy in the Faculty of Arts and Sciences, The Johns Hopkins University, Baltimore, Maryland

Howard Eglit, J.D.
Professor, IIT Chicago-Kent College of Law, Chicago, Illinois

Carroll L. Estes, Ph.D.
Professor and Chair, Department of Social and Be-
havioral Sciences; Director, Aging Policy Center,
University of California, San Francisco, California

Howard E. Freeman, Ph.D.
Professor of Sociology, University of California, Los
Angeles, California

Jack Habib, Ph.D.
Director, Brookdale Institute of Gerontology and
Adult Human Development in Israel; Senior Lec-
turer, Department of Economics, School of Social
Work, Hebrew University, Jerusalem, Israel

Gunhild O. Hagestad, Ph.D.
Assistant Professor of Human Development, Pennsylvania State University, University Park, Pennsylvania

Robert B. Hudson, Ph.D.
Associate Professor of Social Policy, Graduate School
of Social Service, Fordham University, New York,
New York

Jacquelyne Johnson Jackson, Ph.D.
Professor, Department of Human Development,
School of Human Ecology, Howard University,
Washington, D.C.

365316

Richard A. Kalish, Ph.D.
Director, Adult Development: Education and Consultation; Clinical Professor, Department of Psychiatry, University of New Mexico, Santa Fe, New Mexico

Jennie Keith, Ph.D.
Professor of Anthropology, Swarthmore College, Swarthmore, Pennsylvania

Peter Laslett, Ph.D.
Co-founder and Consultant Director, Cambridge Group for the History of Population and Social Structure; Fellow of Trinity College, Cambridge, England

M. Powell Lawton, Ph.D.
Director, Behavioral Research, Philadelphia Geriatric Center, Philadelphia, Pennsylvania

Martin A. Levin, Ph.D.
Associate Professor of Politics, Brandeis University, Waltham, Massachusetts

Virginia C. Little, Ph.D., ACSW
Professor, The University of Connecticut, School of Social Work, West Hartford, Connecticut

George L. Maddox, Ph.D.
Professor of Sociology and of Medical Sociology (Psychiatry); Senior Fellow, Center for the Study of Aging and Human Development; Chairman, University Council on Aging and Human Development, Duke University, Durham, North Carolina

David J. Mangen
Executive Vice President, Mangen & Namakkal, Human Resource Evaluation and Allocation System, Minneapolis, Minnesota

Victor W. Marshall, Ph.D.
Associate Professor, Department of Behavioural Science, University of Toronto, Toronto, Canada

George C. Myers, Ph.D.
Professor of Sociology and Director Center for Demographic Studies, Duke University, Durham, North Carolina

Bernice L. Neugarten, Ph.D.
Professor of Education and Sociology, Northwestern University, School of Education, Evanston, Illinois

Robert J. Newcomer, Ph.D.
Associate Professor, Department of Social and Behavioral Sciences; Deputy Director, Aging Health Policy Center, University of California, San Francisco, California

Carolyn E. Paul, Ph.D.
Senior Staff Associate, Employment and Retirement Division, Andrus Gerontology Center, University of Southern California, Los Angeles, California

Matilda White Riley, D.Sc.
Associate Director, Behavioral Sciences Research, National Institute on Aging, Bethesda, Maryland

Pauline K. Robinson, Ph.D.
UPS Foundation Research Professor of Gerontology, Andrus Gerontology Center, University of Southern California, Los Angeles, California

Irving Rosow, Ph.D.
Professor of Medical Sociology, Langley Porter Institute, University of California, San Francisco, California

Ethel Shanas, Ph.D.
Professor of Sociology, Emerita, University of Illinois at Chicago, Chicago, Illinois

John Strate, Ph.D.
Research Associate, Center for Survey Research, University of Massachusetts, Boston, Massachusetts

Gordon F. Streib, Ph.D.
Graduate Research Professor, Department of Sociology, University of Florida, Gainesville, Florida

Marvin H. Sussman, Ph.D.
Unidel Professor of Human Behavior, Department of Individual and Family Studies with joint appointments in the College of Urban Affairs and Public Policy and the Department of Sociology, University of Delaware, Newark, Delaware

Richard A. Weatherley, Ph.D.
Associate Professor, School of Social Work, University of Washington, Seattle, Washington

365316

PREFACE

The purposes of this Second Edition of the *Handbook of Aging and the Social Sciences* are to provide comprehensive information, major reference sources, and central issues for further research on aging. To achieve these purposes the *Handbook* presents knowledge about aging through the systematic perspectives of a variety of social sciences, broadly conceived: anthropology, demography, economics, history, the humanities, law, political science, social policy analysis, social psychology, social work, and sociology. Building upon the First Edition, it encompasses in one volume the enormous growth of ideas, information, and research literature on the social aspects of aging that has taken place during the last decade.

The scope of the volume is broader than that of the First Edition, and its content is substantially different. Six chapters are on new subjects. Seven topics that were included in the earlier volume have been treated by different authors who bring their own perspectives to bear upon the subject matter. The remaining chapters have been revised and brought up-to-date, and in many cases enriched by the contributions of additional co-authors. Of the 40 authors and co-authors in this new edition, 17 were represented in the first edition. All of the authors are in the top echelon of specialists in their respective subject areas.

The *Handbook* is intended for use by researchers, professional practitioners, and students in the field of aging. It is also expected to serve as a basic reference tool for scholars, professionals, and others who are not presently engaged in research and practice directly focused on aging and the aged. The book has been prepared with sensitivity to an international audience, and whenever possible chapters have been written with a cross-national perspective.

This edition retains the approach to the subject that was used in the earlier volume, an approach that was new then and remains unique. The book is designed to reflect the editors' belief that knowledge about the social aspects of aging can be best understood and developed within the framework of the social science disciplines. Each discipline approaches the study of aging and the aged in terms of its own constructs and subject matter, contributing its unique strengths to an understanding of the topic. This multidisciplinary focus, we believe, substantially enriches the intellectual resources available for understanding the social dimensions of aging. Accordingly, the volume has been planned so as to include all of the relevant disciplines, and the content has been divided into chapters that can be treated on a disciplinary basis. In some cases where subjects might be treated equally well but differently by authors from alternative disciplines, we have enlisted an author to address a topic in the Second Edition who is from a different discipline than the author who addressed it in the First Edition.

The 26 chapters of the *Handbook* are organized in five major sections: I. *The Study of Aging;* II. *The Social Aspects of Aging;* III. *Aging and Social Structure;* IV. *Aging and Social Systems;* and V. *Aging and Social Intervention.* Each chapter was conceived and written specifically for this volume. The book includes a thorough subject-matter index and a comprehensive bibliography on the social aspects of aging. All of the research literature cited throughout the volume is also indexed by author.

The contributors to this Second Edition successfully met a number of challenges. They organized their chapters in terms of analytical constructs that enabled them to sift through a great deal of literature bearing upon their topics. They provided historical perspectives on these topics, drawing upon classic and contemporary references in the field, and constructed their presentations so as to ensure that the usefulness of the volume would not be limited by specific time referents. Most impressively, they were able to present their knowledge and viewpoints succinctly and to relate their treatments to those of their fellow authors.

In developing the subject matter for this volume and in the selection of contributors, the Editors were greatly assisted by three Associate Editors: George L. Maddox, George C. Myers, and James H. Schulz. These Associate Editors also helped substantially in the process of editorial review. Successive drafts of each chapter were read and critically reviewed by at least one Associate Editor and one Editor. Comments and suggestions from these readings were organized and forwarded to the authors for their consideration in undertaking revised drafts. Throughout this process the participation of the Associate Editors was indispensable and we are grateful to them.

If this volume has any special merit it is due to the seriousness with which the chapter authors accepted their assignments and to the good will with which they responded to editorial criticism and suggestions. To these colleagues, the Editors and Associate Editors would like to express their special appreciation. We also wish to acknowledge the dedicated and competent technical assistance of Kathryn O'Connell, Susan Lanspery, Amanda Vaughan, Stephanie Kalfayan, and Shirley Whitfield.

ROBERT H. BINSTOCK
Cleveland, Ohio

ETHEL SHANAS
Evanston, Illinois

CONTENTS

PART FOUR

Aging and Social Systems

PART FIVE

Aging and Social Intervention

Handbook of
AGING
AND THE
SOCIAL
SCIENCES

PART 1 THE STUDY OF AGING

1
SCOPE, CONCEPTS, AND METHODS IN THE STUDY OF AGING

George L. Maddox
and
Richard T. Campbell
Duke University

Since the first edition of this *Handbook* was published, social scientific interest in adult development has intensified, and, on balance, recent research reflects increasing methodological and theoretical sophistication. Investigators now understand, although they have not solved, "the age/period/cohort problem." They now understand, but have not solved, the problem of triangulating testable propositions derived from theory with available techniques of analysis and with strategic populations or sites for exploring life course development in the adult years.

Several longstanding general characterizations of social scientific studies of aging and older adults in recent decades remain current. These studies continue to reflect to a marked degree an appreciation of and commitment to multidisciplinary and interdisciplinary approaches to life course development in adulthood. And they continue to reflect an appreciation of and commitment to both basic and applied research interests: solving the practical social problems of aging populations remains as important as understanding the theory and methodology of studying aging.

While this chapter builds on the chapter in the first edition, we will concentrate on updating rather than repeating the material there. Our intention is to summarize the issues identified earlier and to concentrate on whether and how our understanding has changed. The earlier chapter does constitute a record and an assessment of social scientific thought and research in 1976, and should be read by those who are unfamiliar with the recent history of social scientific studies of aging and older adults.

This chapter, unlike the earlier one, will provide only a very brief discipline-by-discipline review, highlighting current theory, methodology, and research findings. The extensiveness of current social scientific research on aging and older adults defies a more detailed review. Moreover, other *Handbook* chapters deal with a variety of subjects that are recognizably the principal domains of one or another social scientific discipline. Those chapters are the proper location of extensive bibliographies and critiques of disciplinary performance.

In this edition relatively more attention will be given to international developments

3

in social scientific research on aging and older adults than was given in the earlier volume. We cannot hope to be adequate in our coverage. But our shortcomings will not reflect intellectual parochialism so much as limitations of space and simple lack of information about social scientific research on aging worldwide, particularly outside Western Europe and in Japan.

Finally, our treatment of research methods will stress basic issues in methodology rather than research techniques. We continue to take for granted that the elements of sound research design and knowledge of available techniques of data analysis are fundamental in social scientific studies of aging and older adults. This chapter is not intended to provide a manual of research techniques. Our discussion of recent developments in research methodology will highlight issues selectively. Specifically, attention will focus on current understanding of the interaction of age, period, and cohort in research on aging; the adequacy of current and developing data bases in the United States and abroad; and the potential and limitations of longitudinal methodology.

AGING AS SOCIAL PROBLEM AND SCIENTIFIC ISSUE REVISITED

Kuhn (1970) argued persuasively that science as it is normally pursued is a strenuous and devoted attempt to force nature into the conceptual boxes supplied by professional education. The propositions presented in the paradigms of science identify significant facts, match fact and theory, and organize the perspectives that purport to describe and explain various aspects of reality. Scientific research does not ordinarily aim to produce conceptual or phenomenal novelty and, when successful, produces neither one. Rather, scientists are essentially puzzle-solvers whose paradigms suggest which puzzles are interesting and solvable and which are not. Hence, prevailing paradigms of a scientific community often tend, Kuhn argues, to isolate scientists from problems that are not reducible to puzzle form and that do not have

a definitive solution. Unlike engineers or physicians, scientists need not choose problems because they need solution or choose their problems without regard to the availability of the concepts and techniques necessary to solve them. Social scientists are more likely than others, Kuhn suggests, to defend the choice of problems in terms of their social significance, but this is not common even among them.

Kuhn's observations are relevant to understanding the study of aging. Recognition of aging as a social problem is recent; recognition of aging as a social scientific problem is more recent still. The social scientific study of aging needs, but currently lacks, widely shared paradigms that would provide common conceptualization of issues, standard measurements, and clearly defined agendas for the systematic testing of hypotheses derived from theory. Applied, problem-oriented studies of the societal consequences of aging predominate; but increasingly sophisticated theory and research techniques are now available to social scientists for use in describing, monitoring, and forecasting social issues posed by an aging population. No single theoretical perspective organizes substantive research on the social aspects of aging. In fact, methodological issues have dominated the attention of social scientists in recent years. We will assess some signs of progress subsequently, particularly in regard to recent developments in data analysis that link substantive and theoretical issues with appropriate research design.

A recent critical review of the implications of Kuhn's work by Eckberg and Hill (1979), addressed explicitly to sociology, has general relevance for all social scientific disciplines, particularly those interested in adult development. Kuhn's concept of science organized around consensual paradigms of related theoretical propositions and methods for confirming these propositions has been interpreted variously, and, according to Eckberg and Hill, interpreted incorrectly. The heart of the matter, they argue, involves the recognition that Kuhnian paradigms (exemplars) are essentially never discipline-wide but concentrate on particular substantive areas of disciplinary research. Moreover, vital paradigms are the property of communities of scientific practitioners who coalesce around them and are used both to generate and to solve puzzles; cumulatively, research concerning the shared paradigms generates a visible research tradition. Scientific revolutions, or more modestly, significant theoretical advances, occur when a community of scientists recognizes new puzzles it believes to be solvable and worth solving. The puzzles in aging that have received the most attention in recent years have focused on scientific issues of theory (e.g., disengagement and modernization) and methodology (e.g., cohort analysis in longitudinal research design) rather than on the social problem aspects of aging (e.g., income maintenance and housing) that dominated earlier studies.

From this perspective, some of the puzzles in aging attacked by social scientists in the last decade or two warrant comment. A few illustrations will suffice. Consider disengagement theory as a paradigm proposing to explain life satisfaction in the later years. We know the paradigm proposed was faulty, and we also know why (Hochschild, 1975). In brief, the propositions of disengagement theory (i.e., disengagement of individuals from society and vice versa reflects intrinsic, universal forces and hence is inevitable) were conceptualized in ways that made them unfalsifiable. Worse, the theory tended toward biological reductionism and hence dealt inadequately with both the social context of aging and the personal meaning of aging. Hochschild's critique was on target. Unfortunately her proposal, which emphasized the necessity to identify and measure social structural in addition to personal variables, has not been systematically pursued. The failure to pursue a useful proposal is explained, at least in part, by the inability of social scientists, even in 1975, to attack a puzzle that required the simultaneous study of macroscopic (structural) and microscopic (personality) variables. This failure reflects both lack of an adequate data base with suf-

ficient variation in macrosocial variables and lack of adequate strategies for data analysis.

Another community of interests in research on aging is illustrated by research on the interaction of age, period, and cohort. This puzzle emerged as a central concern of methodologists in aging during the decade 1965–75 and currently remains a major preoccupation of social scientists. While this preoccupation appears to be methodological rather than substantive, it suffuses almost every substantive issue of importance in the study of aging. In fact, the age/period/cohort puzzle is quite germane to Hochschild's critique of disengagement theory. An adequate test of the theory in her view requires an understanding of the complex interaction of personal and social variables over time and the comparative study of aging within and between societies.

The substantive implications of the age/period/cohort perspective are now widely understood, and the evidence lies in applications of the perspective to a growing variety of studies organized around the concept of life course. This concept has been applied with considerable vigor to research on families, work, education, and health (Demos and Boocock, 1978; Hareven, 1978; Riley, 1979; Hess and Bond, 1981). Each of the edited volumes cited provides extensive bibliographies of current research that, cumulatively, constitute a record of an emerging community of social scientists who share convergent paradigms with respect to transitions into and through adulthood.

One more illustration of a Kuhnian community of scientific perspective among social scientists studying aging will suffice. Interest in the relationship between societal change and aging produced one of the earliest and most persistent gerontological paradigms (Cowgill and Holmes, 1972; Palmore and Manton, 1974; Bengtson et al., 1975; Maddox, 1978). Simply stated, the issue was whether societal change as indexed by industrialization, urbanization, and related modifications such as formal education predictably lowered the social status and welfare of older adults. Before modernization, the paradigm proposed, the status and welfare of older adults tends to be high; after modernization, their status and welfare are low. While the available evidence is far from definite, the evidence against the hypothesis as originally stated is reasonably convincing.

Some common themes and issues emerge from these illustrations. The implicit or explicit paradigms developed by scholars working on each of the illustrated puzzles posed by aging people or populations have not been perceived—or could not easily be perceived, for that matter—as the province of a single discipline. Quite the contrary. Adequate explication of well-being—either the perceived well-being of disengagement theory or the objective social and economic well-being of modernization theory—benefits from, probably requires, the theoretical insights and evidence of social psychologists, sociologists, anthropologists, economists, political scientists, and historians. And the shared understanding by all scholars of the methodological implications of the intersection of age, period of measurement, and cohort will reduce if not obviate in the future inadequate time-bound, culture-bound, and cohort-bound propositions about human aging.

The implications of these illustrations for psychosocial theories of aging warrant particular comment. Both disengagement and modernization theory offered relatively comprehensive approaches to the study of aging, but were markedly different in the outcome they proposed to explain and the basic causal mechanism for explaining observed outcomes. Disengagement theory proposed to explain *subjective* well-being and identified the causal mechanism as fundamentally intrinsic and hence inevitable psychobiological age-related processes. In contrast, modernization theory proposed to explain *objective* well-being and identified the causal mechanism as structural modification of economic and social institutions. One of the criticisms of disengagement theory posed by Hochschild, as noted above, was the failure to consider the necessary intersection and interaction of psychobiological and social structural variables. Further, she criticized both disengagement theory (explicitly) and modernization theory (implicitly) for failing to consider the meaning of the experience of aging for purposive actors.

A more comprehensive paradigm of psychosocial aging is obviously called for, and is in fact implied by the age/period/cohort perspective on aging processes. The outline of an appropriate and potentially useful theoretical perspective for future research has been proposed by Hernes (1976) and illustrated in Figure 1. Hernes's model of change identifies the logical components of an adequate theoretical orientation. As such, it is an orientation rather than a set of interrelated, testable propositions.

Hochschild's fundamental complaint against disengagement theory can be clearly illustrated from the perspective of Hernes. Disengagement theory as proposed initially not only focused on microlevel variables but also focused primarily on one property of actors—their changed capacities—and

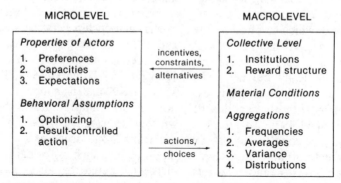

Figure 1. The relationship between microlevel and macrolevel variables. SOURCE: Hernes, 1976.

secondarily on derived changes in prefer- ences and expectations. Macrolevel factors that produce various social incentives, con- straints, and alternatives were ruled out by assumption rather than demonstration. Early criticisms of disengagement theory, var- iously and imprecisely expressed as activity theory or continuity theory, considered but typically did not make explicitly the argu- ment suggested by Hernes; that is, that so- cietal context provides different incentives, constraints, and alternatives that affect choices and actions. Modernization theory provided an equally truncated, reductionis- tic, and mechanical perspective on aging. No significance was attached to, nor was pro- vision made for the mediating effects of mi- crolevel variables. Both disengagement and modernization theory proposed to describe *the* state of affairs of *the* aged. In the case of disengagement theory, behavior in the later years was explained by an intrinsic process that would be observed universally; variance in the process was treated as devi- ance rewarded by low life satisfaction. Mod- ernization theory postulated various out- comes for individuals in different societies at different levels of modernization but did not encourage the exploration of variation in the subjective or objective status of older adults within a society or potential alternative out- comes of social change within or between so- cieties.

The differences among older adults within societies and differences in the same society over time are documented facts with which psychosocial and structural theories of aging must deal. Clearly, research that reflects the age/period/cohort perspective would re- quire a theoretical framework like that out- lined by Hernes. The observed and potential differences between cohorts of older adults within a society and changes in the charac- teristics of cohorts over time imply a com- plex interaction between microlevel and macrolevel variables.

While a comprehensive theoretical frame- work for the study of psychosocial aging is not the equivalent of a psychosocial theory of aging, the framework proposed by Hernes

assists in specifying the logical requirements of theories of societal or developmental change and the strategic considerations in the construction of such theories. This is notably the case for an emerging community of in- terests described as "life course analysis" (e.g., Riley, 1979). A relatively recent syn- thesis of developmental, life events, and adult socialization models—life course anal- ysis—includes a number of emphases that are related to Hernes's recommended frame- work (see e.g, George, 1982). Life course, as distinct from life cycle, has a distinctly social emphasis. Divisions of the life course, the events related to life course transitions, and adaptation to movement over the life course are substantially social constructs. The par- ticular manifestations of growing older, therefore, are the products of microlevel (per- sonal) and macrolevel (social) factors that interact, and this interaction can and does produce both stability and change in pref- erences, capacities, expectations, and behav- ior.

Recognition that micro- and macrolevel interaction can and does produce change is precisely what underlies interest in the lon- gitudinal, comparative study of aging proc- esses and in the observed differential probabilities of stability and change among cohorts of older adults over the life course. Further, life course analysis has another dis- tinguishing feature consistent with Hernes's framework. Different age cohorts are differ- entially at risk for life events, the timing of events, and the social interpretation of events. Moreover, personal changes over the adult life course and the composition of ag- ing cohorts (capacities, preferences, expec- tations) affect the material conditions of society, its reward structures, and its insti- tutional arrangements. This is a distinctive departure from the assumption of one-way effects of social structure on individuals.

The emerging life course perspective takes a broad view of aging among adults, and in- itial applications of the perspective in re- search displayed relatively more interest in younger than older adults (Maddox, 1979), a truncated view that recent work has tended to correct (Hess and Bond, 1981; George, 1982). In any case, an emphasis on the adult life course, broadly defined, appropriately stresses continuity and change in adulthood in a useful way. Seeing later life as integrally related to adulthood is theoretically and conceptually appropriate. Further, the dominant current interest of life course analysts in the family (e.g., Elder, 1978) and work (e.g., Zuckerman and Merton, 1972; Spilerman, 1977) is germane to the interests of those who study older adults within the traditions of social gerontology and the sociology of aging.

Productive Tension between Basic and Applied Research

Productive tension between scientists and practitioners in aging regarding the relative importance of investigating human aging and of advocacy and action in behalf of the aged continues. Kuhn correctly observed that scientists generally do not undertake to solve problems simply because the problems are socially significant and warrant solving; they certainly do not respond when the concepts and tools required for the solution are obviously missing or when the solutions involve, to a substantial degree, political preferences and political action. Nevertheless, in the past decade significant signs of resolving some of the tensions between research and social action are evident.

First, conceptualization of issues has been clarified. Consider again Hernes's framework for analysis (Figure 1, above) and the related discussion of disengagement and modernization theory. The aging of individuals and of populations generates personal and societal problems that can be specified within Hernes's framework as both microlevel (e.g., individual capacities) and macrolevel (e.g., social role resource allocation). Further, we know that interaction of variables at both levels generates problems for aging individuals and societies and is, therefore, appropriately and necessarily involved in the solution of these problems. As noted in the first edition of this *Handbook,* prob-

lems of aging individuals and populations involve the biology of senescence, societal values and public policies that encourage discrimination on the basis of age in the allocation of resources, and the interaction of both types of factors. Scientific research has contributed significantly to the identification and conceptualization of age-related problems and to the clarification and evaluation of options for responding, as documented in Part IV of this *Handbook.* Further, chapters throughout this volume will discuss the actual and potential contribution of research to the analysis of age-related problems and to evaluative research in the interest of assessing options. However, while it has become increasingly clear that science can provide the tools for thinking about and dealing with age-related social problems, science can provide neither the value preferences nor the political consensus necessary to solve these problems. Societal values have, so far, encouraged basic and applied research on aging. The implementation of what we know to transform the future of aging will require the development of a political consensus to identify and implement new goals and new strategies for dealing with personal and societal aging. Chapters in this volume on political aspects of population aging and societal strategies for responding will identify salient issues.

DISCIPLINARY PERSPECTIVES

As noted above, this introductory chapter will not review in detail and by discipline developments in the social scientific study of aging. Readers with specific disciplinary interests will find familiar theoretical, methodological, and substantive issues in the following chapters as they review literature reporting recent work on various topics. Selected disciplinary developments, however, warrant brief highlighting and comment. If there is a dominant theme in social scientific studies of aging currently, it is renewed interest in multidisciplinary and interdisciplinary research, which is a distinctive hallmark of research on aging over the past three decades.

In sociology, the historically dominant emphasis in the social psychology of adaptation (House and Robbins, 1983) is being balanced by a strong emphasis on social structure and social change (Maddox, 1978, 1979; Riley, 1979; Hess and Bond, 1981). The macrolevel emphasis on societal structure and processes of social change in sociology has activated demographers (Winsborough, 1979; Siegel, 1981; Myers, 1982) on the one hand, and spurred interest in the collaboration of historians and sociologists on the other (illustrated, e.g., in Demos and Boocock, 1978; Hareven, 1978). The activation of demographers follows both from an increasing appreciation of Norman Ryder's conceptualization of cohort as a key concept in demographic analysis, which anticipated as well as contributed to research on age, period, and cohort problems, and from increasing interest on the aging of populations worldwide. The involvement of historians follows logically from increased awareness of the relevance of variations in the social meaning of life course segments and transitions over time.

Comparative sociologists and anthropologists have been involved in research on aging (Cowgill and Holmes, 1972; Kiefer, 1974; Palmore, 1975; Palmore and Manton, 1974; Foner and Kertzer, 1978; Keith, 1980; Vatuk, 1980). According to Keith (1980), age as a principle of social organization has not received detailed attention in anthropology. Older people have frequently served as informants in anthropological research, and there is increasingly a literature on the anthropology of old age. The prospects and outline for an anthropology of age will be reviewed in a later chapter of this volume. Another comparative interest, the study of minority and ethnic populations, is now receiving systematic attention (Jackson, 1980; Gelfand, 1981) and is reviewed in a chapter of this volume.

While historians have collaborated productively with sociologists, they have made a contribution in their own right (see, Fischer, 1977; Demos and Boocock, 1978; Hareven, 1978; Achenbaum, 1978), particularly in regard to the history of aging in the United States. Sociological analysis in the United States has been distinctly ahistorical (Zaret, 1980), and social scientists have tended to be out of touch with historical methodology (see, e.g., Boocock, 1978). However, the substantive topics approached through historical analysis that are obviously relevant for research on social change and the comparative analysis of aging in different societies over time are now getting systematic attention. A new chapter on historical research on aging is, therefore, a welcome addition to this volume.

Economists and sociologists have continued to describe the economic status and well-being of older adults with increasing precision. Of particular importance is improved conceptualization of the sources of income, measurement of net worth (Henretta and Campbell, 1976, 1978; Campbell and Henretta, 1981) clarification of income levels, and understanding of how income maintenance and income transfer systems operate (e.g., Clark and Menefee, 1981). Several distinctive emphases in economics of aging are worth noting. First, there is interest in comparative economics systems (Schulz et al. 1974; Espenshade and Braun, 1981), a reassertion of the connection between demographic transitions that transform societal age structure and related economic consequences (Easterlin, 1980; Espenshade and Braun, 1981). Economists and sociologists have an intersection of interest in life course problems that relate careers, incomes, and retirement over time and in relation to the structure of the labor market (Spilerman, 1977).

Social scientists interested in the politics of aging have continued to focus their attention on age as a variable in political behavior and on governmental responses to population aging, particularly the evolution of public policy (see Chapter 19 of this *Handbook*). Much of the research has concentrated on the United States (e.g., Estes, 1979; Vladeck, 1980), although interest in the politics of aging societies is evident in Canada (e.g., Marshall, 1980b) and France (e.g., Guillemard, 1980). Available evidence continues to document continued interest and involvement in politics among older adults and the relative absence of age-polarization in political behavior (e.g., Dowd, 1975; Cutler et al., 1980; Miller et al., 1980). But new interest has been expressed in the potential for age-polarization in political responses to perceived increasing scarcity of societal resources and the concomitant weakening of broad-based political parties by fragmentation of political issues defined by a large variety of special-interest groups. The previous conclusion that an age-polarized political environment was possible but improbable, at least in the United States, may be tested by the current high visibility of age-related special-interest organizations, problems associated with rapid population aging, and perceived scarcity of societal resources.

An International Perspective

The International Association of Gerontology has convened 12 multidisciplinary congresses in recent decades. Proceedings of these conferences provide an overview of scientific theory and research worldwide. Several dominant impressions emerge from a review of the proceedings of these congresses. First, the biomedical sciences, and to some degree psychology, have produced theoretical paradigms for research on aging and standardized research techniques that provide for relatively universal discourse among an international community of scholars investigating cells, organ systems, and cognitive processes. This is not the case for the social scientists who exhibit relatively little community of scientific interests in theory or methodology to deal with the obvious variety of societal differences in the context of aging or in the manifestations of aging in various contexts. Consequently, social scientific research on aging presented in international meetings tends to be atheoretical, descriptive, and national rather than comparative.

The major systematic, comparative, social scientific research of the 1960s—*Older People in Three Industrial Societies* (Shanas et al., 1968)—remains an exception to the general rule. Disengagement theory, which invited comparative research, generated very little interest among social scientists. Modernization theory, which has a distinctly comparative emphasis, has not generated as much research as one would expect. However, current interest in aging in developing countries, stimulated by preparation for the 1982 United Nations World Assembly on Aging, will probably increase interest in comparative social scientific study and the potential of such research. Two expressions of this interest which review research on aging in both developed and developing countries are volumes commissioned explicitly for the World Assembly, one by the United Nations Fund for Population Activities (Binstock et al., 1982) and the other by the International Association of Gerontology (Thomae and Maddox, 1982).

Among social scientists, demographers tend to be interested in cross-national comparisons, and recent applications of this interest are found in Myers (1982; see also Chapter 7 in this *Handbook*) and Siegel (1981). The capacity of demographers to work with increasing effectiveness is enhanced by the availability of appropriate international data now generated systematically and routinely for many countries through the United Nations and the World Health Organization. These data sources permit useful characterizations of populations by country and region, current estimates and projections of future population growth and distribution, changing age composition in populations, death rates, and longevity. Data are increasingly available in the detail necessary to permit disaggregation of populations by marital status, household composition, geographic location, and migration status. At the same time, epidemiological research is generating information worldwide on the functional status of aging populations which, while more obviously relevant for planners and policy analysts, will be increasingly useful to social scientists (Maddox, 1982; Mahler, 1980). Being aware of potential experienced collaborators in other countries is an important condition in assessing the feasibility of future comparative, cross-national research. On a similar note, later in this chapter we identify compilations of longitudinal studies in Europe that summarize the state of affairs abroad and identify active research investigators.

A recent international handbook on aging (Palmore, 1980) summarizes research on aging in 28 countries. The coverage in this survey volume is relatively complete for economically developed countries; the summaries provide illustrative demographic information, outline governmental programs, and, in some instances, report research, research findings, and bibliographies. A useful illustration from Palmore's handbook is the chapter on Austria, which includes a history of the development of gerontological and geriatric research in that country. Of interest to social scientists, a succinct review of most recent demographic characteristics of the Austrian population (14.2 percent 65 and older in 1971) is followed by an overview of sociological research and findings on intergenerational interaction, living arrangements, and functional capacity. The chapter ends with a summary of research at the L. Boltzmann Institute for Social Gerontology and Life Span Research in Vienna under the leadership of Leopold Rosenmayr. Rosenmayr's research that is reviewed in the chapter, supplemented by an article in a new European journal *Aging and Society* (Rosenmayr, 1981), is a convenient introduction to the social scientific study of aging in Europe.

In a recent review of sociological and, more broadly, social scientific research on aging in Canada, Victor Marshall (1980a; see also 1980b) presents a critical analysis of activities in that country which parallel the scientific issues noted at the outset of this chapter. Social scientific studies of aging in Canada, as in the United States, lack widely shared paradigms that provide common conceptualization, measurement, and a research agenda around which a community of scholars can rally. Marshall is critical of what he calls ''gerontological orthodoxy'' in the United States and in Canada which has con-

tinued to focus on social psychological (microlevel) studies of individual adaptation to the neglect of structural (macrolevel) research on modernization, demographic transitions, and, more generally, analysis that concentrates on the consequences of the timing of life course events. Further, he makes a particularly strong recommendation for political/sociological studies of power and conflict in understanding aging and societal responses to aging populations. This interest, which has waxed and waned in the general sociology of the United States, has not been particularly evident in gerontological research (Estes, 1979, is an exception) but has been a focus in Europe (see, e.g., Guillemard, 1980).

While social scientists in the United States, in Europe, and increasingly in Japan have developed and maintained an exchange of information, this is much less true for Latin American social scientists. A recent comprehensive review by Finley (1981; see also Delgado and Finley, 1978) will help correct this deficiency. The bulk of past work on aging in Latin America, Finley concludes, has been in anthropology and medicine. And even in the case of anthropology, interest has focused on older adults as useful informants rather than on aging processes and the life course. Only a few sociological studies of aging in Latin America are identifiable, and, in general, findings tend to be demographic and descriptive. Nevertheless, Finley's bibliography will be a useful point of departure for social scientists interested in comparative study of aging populations in Latin America. Further, he notes that awareness of population aging is increasing in Latin America, and that nations in this area may be prime candidates for studies of the effects of modernization.

THEMES AND ISSUES IN THE STUDY OF AGING

In the first edition, this introductory chapter highlighted and interpreted selected themes and issues in social scientific research on aging from the published literature. In preparation for this revised introduction, we asked colleagues in the United States, Canada, Europe, and Japan to comment on the continuing relevance of these issues and to suggest additional ones. On balance, our colleagues concluded that the themes identified earlier continue to be reasonably current, although specific suggestions were made for clarification of certain points. Therefore, we will use the earlier chapter as a point of departure for the sake of continuity and add additional interpretative comments as appropriate. Specifically, we will focus on: (a) aging and social integration; (b) successful adaptation; (c) age as a variable in social scientific research; (d) society as a succession of cohorts; (e) environment as a variable in understanding behavior; and (f) the continuing search for a unified perspective for the social scientific study of aging. We will also, as in the first edition, conclude with a section on methodology. The earlier edition highlighted two methodological issues of particular relevance for the social scientific study of aging: the disentangling of age, period, and cohort effects in data analysis and the methodological implications of selecting the life course as a unit of analysis. We will not repeat the detailed discussion of these issues here. Instead, the concluding section of this chapter will focus on three problems in research on aging: the status of the age/period/cohort problem; the emerging data base for life course research; and the potential and limits of longitudinal research on the life course of adults.

Aging and Social Integration

Four decades ago the projected rapid increase in the proportion of older persons in industrialized urban societies was viewed with concern by observers who understood the relationships among population aging, the probability of increasing dependency with age, and the demands of dependent individuals on societal resources. In such societies, social differentiation and specialization characterized both individuals and social institutions; productivity tended to be valued and to provide an important basis for

assessing individual merit. Older people, defined primarily as retired from productive roles, were therefore perceived to be very vulnerable in modern societies. The social integration of older persons appeared to be problematic on both theoretical and evidential grounds to many social scientists (e.g., Cowgill and Holmes, 1972). Effective social integration of older persons continues to seem problematic to some social scientists, particularly observers of or in developing countries (Maddox, 1982). The values of modern industrial urban societies do appear to favor youthfulness; important social roles in late life do appear to be ambiguously defined, inviting the inference that late life is roleless; and access to important social goods and services does appear to be comparatively restricted for many older persons (see, e.g., Rosow, 1974; Dowd, 1975; Estes, 1979).

But evidence of the social integration of older persons in urban industrial societies has now been well documented in the chapters of this *Handbook* on social structure, social systems, and social interventions, which review, for example, evidence on the allocation of social resources such as income, housing, and health and social services by age. Further, both legislation and participation in political processes by older persons have created a favorable climate for an optimistic view that age-related inequities in the distribution of resources, once identified, are subject to debate and modification. On balance, evidence of integration outweighs evidence of isolation (e.g., Shanas et al., 1968; Palmore and Manton, 1974). While no one would argue that older persons are exempt from discrimination, few would argue that older persons are singular targets of social inequity. Basic legal rights of older persons have been maintained; political participation of older citizens is not strikingly different from that of other adults; most older persons live in private households; kinship relationships between generations demonstrably exist at a level that is higher than prevailing theory and conventional wisdom would have suggested; and social and economic security in the later years, while problematic for a substantial minority, is achieved to a tolerable degree for the majority. We do not argue that late life is universally an unproblematic or a socially and personally attractive period of life. Rather, we argue that current evidence indicates that older persons are more likely to be socially integrated than not. Chronological age per se is not an adequate predictor of social integration.

The agenda for future research in aging, we believe, should concentrate on identifying personal and social factors that facilitate or impede social integration. Even if chronological age, or age-related characteristics such as disability and poverty, were demonstrably an impediment to social integration in a given society, one would still need to explore the transience and modifiability of these characteristics. It is particularly relevant in analyzing the status and well-being of older populations in a society to compare the distribution of these characteristics for the same persons over the life course as well as their differential distribution among persons of various ages (Henretta and Campbell, 1976). Surely some individuals become disadvantaged when they are older as a result of reduced capacity, social discrimination, or both. But with equal certainty, some individuals are disadvantaged throughout their lives and take those disadvantages into old age. We see no necessary connection between age per se and actual or potential social integration on either theoretical or evidential grounds.

The capacity of the great majority of older persons in economically developed countries to achieve a satisfactory level of social integration tends to be taken for granted currently in the United States (Harris Poll, 1977). If failure to achieve this outcome occurs, it is treated as a problem but a modifiable one. Observers in and of developing countries tend to be less certain of this outcome, at least in the short run (Maddox, 1982). This concern may be well placed and is certainly an occasion for systematic comparative research in which both the social and individual characteristics affecting the occurrence of social change are specified, and the differential outcomes associated with social change are explained.

Successful Adaptation

The relationship between aging and successful adaptation (variously "morale" or "life satisfaction" or "well-being") is perhaps the oldest, most persistently investigated issue in the social scientific study of aging (Nydegger, 1977). The consensus which has emerged is impressively consistent: Successful adaptation in late life is demonstrably the rule, not the exception, in a wide range of societies. Consensus does not exist about why this is the case.

In the 1960s it was popular to pit activity theory against disengagement theory (Hochschild, 1975, provides a convenient summary of issues) as alternative and contradictory explanations; the one purportedly emphasized social integration and involvement as the explanation of life satisfaction and the other, withdrawal of affective attachment and withdrawal from conventional involvement in social roles. Both perspectives, however, predicted successful adaptation as the expected outcome. And both perspectives were partially correct.

What we have learned from longitudinal studies of successful adaptation in late life is that there are multiple pathways to this common outcome. While, on balance, research documents that the relatively more socially involved members of a cohort of older persons are more likely to report satisfaction, a disengaged life-style can also be found, but not commonly; moreover, a disengaged lifestyle, when observed, appears to be continued from adulthood into late life and is not a product of late life (Maddox, 1968). The capacity to maintain life satisfaction in the face of decreasing social involvement is an interesting phenomenon warranting study.

Research on subjective adaptation over the life course has become progressively more sophisticated in recent years. This sophistication is reflected in more adequate conceptualization, better measurement, and an increased awareness of differential response from subgroups within aging populations.

Campbell and his colleagues in *The Quality of American Life* (1976) and Andrews and Withey (1976) contributed significantly to the understanding of the conceptual complexity involved in measuring subjective well-being, noting particularly the importance of distinguishing at least between feeling or mood (happiness) and assessment of one's situation (satisfaction). Further, they anticipated correctly not only that the mix of happiness and satisfaction could vary over the life course but also that satisfaction with various dimensions of life (e.g., income, health, family, neighborhood) could vary in complex, situationally responsive ways. Noting that this cross-sectional study suggested that, on average, reported happiness tended to decrease but satisfaction tended to increase with age (see also Fernandez and Kulik, 1981), they suggested a possible theoretical explanation. Reported satisfaction tends to reflect the relative congruence between personal expectations and achievement, a congruence that realistically could be expected for most adults.

While it is possible that reports of general satisfaction in later life might be explained alternatively by lowered expectations rather than achievement, a recent Harris Poll (1981) is useful. Older adults (65 and over) and younger adults (18–64) tend to give very similar responses to inquiries about their personal problems in regard to fear for personal safety or the availability of health care. And, in fact, more younger people than older ones complained of inadequate income and housing, conclusions not demonstrably contradicted by available evidence. A life course perspective is particularly useful and necessary in undertaking study of perceived well-being of older adults vis-à-vis other adults within a society and over time. The factors that explain well-being over a lifetime are not uniformly favorable to the young (see, e.g., Easterlin, 1980).

Critiques of past research on perceived well-being and useful suggestions for improving the adequacy and interpretability of future research in this area are increasingly common (see, e.g., George, 1981; Fernandez and Kulik, 1981). Further, social psychological theory and research, in which adaptation in adulthood is a major issue, are integrating models derived in useful ways from developmental theory, analysis of life events, and adult socialization to specify how personal characteristics and social conditions interact to produce observed changes and continuities in behavior and patterns of adaptation (Bengtson, 1975; George, 1980, 1982). An extensive systematic review of relevant current theory and research that relates individual development to the changing context in which that development occurs is found in Part II of this *Handbook*.

Age as a Research Variable

Over three decades ago, Otto Pollak (1948) called attention to definitions of age that alternatively reference aspects of biological maturation, psychosocial development, and location in the age structure of society. He concluded that, while chronological age can and does provide a convenient marker for locating individuals in social space, the meaning of "age" is in important ways a dependent rather than an independent variable. The meaning of "old" varies by social and cultural context and is, at best, a relatively crude marker of biological, psychological, and social capacity. A decade later James Birren (1959) noted there is an "aura of inelegance" surrounding research on aging, particularly in social scientific research. This is so because relationships between chronological age and related variables of interest rarely exhibit invariant properties. Anticipating later discussions of necessary distinction among age, period, and cohort, Birren concluded that apparent age effects tend to be confounded with the effects of other variables correlated with age. Consequently, observed age differences may reflect different environmental histories of age cohorts rather than invariant intraindividual processes indexed by chronological age. This line of argument suggests that, as the immediate and continuing effects of environments on relatively malleable individuals are specified with increasing precision, chronological age will progressively have less and less utility as a variable in research.

Social and behavioral scientists have responded in a variety of ways to the imprecise denotations of chronological age as a research variable. Chronological age continues to be used by demographers and actuaries in the construction of life tables and by sociologists in multivariate regression analyses (e.g., Fernandez and Kulik, 1981) to assess direct and indirect effects on one or another dependent variable. Social scientists, following the tradition of demographers, also use age categories, typically but not necessarily covering five years. The resulting "cohorts" of persons "born about the same time" presumably index individuals who are exposed to similar environmental circumstances that affect behavior (Riley, 1972; see also Chapter 13 in this *Handbook*). Cohorts may be of different size, may have different social characteristics (e.g., years of education or health), and may have been exposed to distinctive environmental events (e.g., war or economic depression) that affect subsequent experience over the life course (see, e.g., Elder, 1974; Uhlenberg, 1978; Easterlin, 1980). In the tradition of age/period/cohort analysis, therefore, cohort becomes a concept that is intended to index potentially distinctive and continuing effects of the interaction between individuals of approximately the same age and environments in which they are located. In this sense, cohort effects are presumably potentially different from age effects; further, *cohort* is a higher-order concept than age because it indexes person/environment interaction and therefore tends to be more interesting than age as an explanatory factor in social scientific research. The importance of this distinction is reinforced by the repeated observation in social scientific research that chronological age is typically a weak explanatory variable. An additional conceptual distinction is necessary; *generation,* used most appropriately to differentiate the procreational sequence in kinship groups, is not simply interchangeable either with chronological age or cohort (see, e.g., Bengtson, 1975, and Chapter 11 in this *Handbook*).

A substantial portion of current social scientific research on aging consequently tends to subordinate chronological age to locating adults within institutionally defined sequences of roles, within cohorts, or within generations. This is particularly the case for investigators who utilize a life course perspective to study the careers of individuals within families (Bengtson, 1975; Elder, 1978) and the workplace (Spilerman, 1977), and to study status attainment and maintenance (Henretta and Campbell, 1976). Chronological age also plays a relatively insignificant role in life course research that concentrates on the behavioral and social consequence of events (e.g., early marriage or childbearing for women) or the sequenced pattern of events in early adulthood such as completion of education, first job, and marriage (Hogan, 1978, 1980). In research on "event structure," the events of interest in fact concentrate in early adulthood, but chronological age per se figures only incidentally, as when these events occur relatively earlier or later or occur over longer or shorter periods of time. Exposure to various historic periods and events (such as war or depression) is considered more relevant in the analysis than chronological age per se (see also Elder, 1978).

In current social scientific literature on aging, consequently, one no longer expects to find, and in fact rarely does find, an uncritical or casual use of chronological age as an explanatory or control variable. There is widespread appreciation of the early observation of Pollak that a significant component of age among adults is its social meaning, and that this social meaning includes what we now understand to be the interaction of persons and environmental contexts we attempt to index with the concept cohort. This does not mean that chronological age is an irrelevant variable; it does mean that the denotations and connotations of chronological age must be more carefully specified if age is to be retained as a distinct variable in future social scientific research.

Failure to achieve an adequate degree of specification has continued to cloud the discussion of the confounding of age, period, and cohort effects in research on adult development.

As documented in Parts I and II of this *Handbook*, cultural and social preferences and the structure of social relationships have rather clearly affected age status and related age norms variously over time in the same society and from one society to another. The demonstrated tenuousness in the relationship between chronological age and adult behavior underlies the now common distinction between age differences and age changes and more recently the significance attached to age cohorts. Age norms observed in a society are intended to constrain behavior and presumably do so; one consequence of this is that behavior displayed at a particular chronological age cannot be assumed to be a totally reliable indicator of the range of possible behavioral responses. Observed differences in behavior among persons of various ages, therefore, cannot confidently be attributed to changes that inevitably occur over time. Discussions of society as a succession of age cohorts exposed to the events of various periods also suggest why the demonstration of changes in behavior unambiguously attributable to chronological age is quite difficult. The documented variability and potential for individual change in later life in response to changes in social environments underlie the basically optimistic view, illustrated in Part V of this *Handbook*, that interventions designed to restructure social institutions and environments can have beneficial effects on older adults.

Society as a Succession of Age Cohorts

While the methodological implications of age cohort analysis in studies of aging will be addressed specifically in the last section of this chapter, a brief substantive comment is appropriate here. Individuals born at approximately the same time constitute a cohort of persons that, at least figuratively, moves through time together. We call attention to the phrase "born at approximately the same time." The decision of investigators to define a cohort in terms of a single year or some longer period appears to be based primarily on practical rather than theoretical considerations. Cohorts differentiated by year of birth are conventional in the construction of life tables. Cohorts differentiated by five-year age spans are conventional in social scientific research in which census data are used. Even in its most specific form (e.g., cohort as specific year of birth), the term cohort is quite crude. There is no theoretical or evidential reason for believing that a population aggregate defined by year of birth, even if exposed to known historical events, is composed of members affected in exactly the same way by these events.

At any point in time, a given society can be described as a collection of cohorts succeeding one another as they move from birth to death. If, for instance, we define a cohort simply in terms of a particular chronological age, such as 65, we would observe that a new cohort achieves this age each year. Over a period of time we might observe that successive cohorts achieving age 65 are numerically larger or smaller, make different demands on available societal resouces, have completed more or fewer years of education, are in better or worse health, or are more or less homogeneous in a variety of ways. If we observed this succession for, say, 20 years, the collection of survivors in the various cohorts would constitute a collectivity we might call "the elderly between the ages of 65 and 85." However, our continuous observations would have made us quite aware of inter- and intracohort differences at age 65. Unless we were willing to treat the observed differences at age 65 for the various cohorts as irrelevant or as likely to be negated by the passage of time after age 65, we would be very reluctant to explain any differences in behavior observed between a 65-year-old and an 85-year-old adult simply in terms of changes related to age. This is yet another reason for caution in using age to explain adult behavior.

The significance of viewing society as a succession of cohorts has been discussed at length by Riley (1972; see also Chapter 13 in this *Handbook*). Some of the theoretical, methodological, and practical implications of this perspective warrant emphasis. Theoretically, the awareness of potential cohort differences calls attention to the significance of explaining and interpreting as well as describing observed differences. This kind of explication and interpretation necessarily intersects with the general social scientific interest in understanding social change (Maddox, 1978, 1979) and its multiple causes, which cross-cut the domains of theory in all the social sciences, including history.

A life course perspective within gerontological research emphasizes distinctly not only the changing composition of cohorts but also the comparative (cross-cultural) and historical dimensions of change. Methodologically, the study of society as a succession of cohorts necessarily confronts the issues posed by distinguishing and accounting for age, period, and cohort effects and is necessarily comparative in its emphasis. Practically, viewing society as a succession of cohorts severely limits the utility of conceptualizing persons 65 years of age and older as *the* elderly. Older adults included in such a broad category would include persons in five or six five-year age cohorts that on neither theoretical nor empirical grounds could be appropriately interchanged as though the oldest cohort predicted the fate of the youngest or on the basis that the oldest cohort was characterized similarly to the youngest at an earlier date. Conceptualizing differential cohorts as successive in a society obviously presents a considerable challenge for social planners, who would necessarily have to plan for the future with specified cohorts in mind and not for *the* elderly.

Environment

If successive cohorts arriving at the same chronological age are different in ways that affect their behavior and subsequent life course, then we must entertain the hypothesis that the environments in which members of successive cohorts matured were different in some consequential ways. It is plausible to believe that the effects of environments in the distant past of individuals on their experience as members of a cohort affect their experience of, and response to, subsequent environments.

While there is consensus among social scientists regarding the importance of both distant and immediate environmental effects on behavior, no consensus is apparent regarding the conceptualization and measurement of environments. Efforts to conceptualize and measure environments have been complicated further by continuing uncertainty about how to assess the relative importance of perceived vis-à-vis objective aspects of environment.

Behavioral scientists have, in recent years, been increasingly willing to concede the limitations of explaining behavior in terms of personality traits and to stress the importance of interaction among personal preferences, predispositions or traits, and environmental stimuli. Social scientists, while pleased with this concession to the relevance of their perspective, have not developed the conceptualization and measurement of environments to the extent that psychologists have developed the conceptualization and measurement of personality. The limited capacity to conceptualize and measure environment is a serious impediment to further social scientific research on behavior in late life that is suggested by sociological models of change (e.g., Hernes, 1976) and ecological models of person/environmental interaction in psychology (Lawton and Nahemow, 1973; Moos, 1974).

Continuing difficulty in the conceptualization and measurement of environments is evident in discussions of how to unconfound age, period, and cohort effects in analyzing adult development. The problem can be illustrated and partially explained by the kinds of data used in age/period/cohort analysis which have typically been provided by large social surveys, particularly surveys that have been repeated over a number of years or decades. The probabilistic sampling procedures most frequently used in such surveys tend to

ensure that individuals are drawn from social contexts that are not measured specifically. Consequently, information about
environmental contexts is limited to individual perceptions of largely unspecified contexts and/or is indexed by time of measurement. In such situations *time of measurement* as an index of *period* characteristics is
usually devoid of substance, and, at most,
these period characteristics are intended to
reference potentially significant social, economic, or political events such as wars, new
legislation, economic conditions, or political
controversies (see, e.g., Elder, 1974; Spilerman, 1977; Uhlenberg, 1978; Cutler et al.,
1980).

Research investigators in aging have similar reasons to be concerned about the conceptualization and measurement of time of
measurement or period. If one assumes that
period in fact indexes socially significant social conditions and events, then it would not
be surprising that a period effect might be
reflected variously in the characteristics of
different cohorts observed in or after that
period. But this relatively crude indexing
would obviously result in substantial error
variance. And in the absence of specifying
the variable impact of the indexed period
characteristics on individuals and specifying
the mechanisms of these effects, explication
and interpretation of period effects would
necessarily be quite limited.

The problems of measuring environments
and relating contextual variation to behavior
are beginning to be understood better, and
there are some promising developments in
this area. Elder (1974) has demonstrated the
utility of specifying and measuring the macrolevel economic characteristics of a particular period of economic depression relative
to the microlevel characteristics of a sample
of families and, in turn, to the implications
of these contextual characteristics to individual family members. Fernandez and Kulik
(1981) demonstrate a procedure for using
survey data to relate the contextual characteristics of neighborhoods to differences in
reported life satisfaction. Further, an older
tradition in social scientific research—per-

son–environment fitting and more generally
the impact of context on individual behavior—continues as a strategy for assessing the
interactions of personal and contextual variables (e.g., Kahana et al., 1980; Lemke and
Moos, 1981; Cole, 1979; Long and Mc-
Ginnis, 1981).

Toward a Theoretical Perspective

The social scientific study of aging has long
been properly described as atheoretical and
descriptive. Exceptions to this generalization
have been disengagement theory and modernization theory, both discussed above. But
today there is a better appreciation of why
useful comprehensive theories of adult development, given current limitations of theory and methods, still constitute an agenda
for the future. The task will be formidable,
but the probable course of theory development in social scientific research on aging can
be outlined.

Theory construction in the social scientific
study of aging will, we believe, concentrate
not on particular theories of adult development but on the logical requirements of such
theories and strategic considerations in con-
structing such theories. For this reason we
attach particular significance to the theoretical perspective of Hernes (1976) on structural change in social processes discussed
earlier, and the perspective of George (1982)
that outlines the convergence of multiple
theoretical models in the social psychology
of adult development. Hernes and George,
we believe, are fundamentally correct in emphasizing the necessary and continuing interaction of multiple variables at both the
microlevel and the macrolevel. Several implications of these perspectives for the social
scientific study of aging warrant special emphasis.

First, these perspectives do not preclude
the utility of descriptive research designed to
document the variability of social contexts
of adult development or of intra- or interindividual differences in development. But
they both imply that explaining and interpreting observed differences in individuals or

cohorts in the absence of considering both microlevel and macrolevel factors simultaneously will be seriously if not fatally flawed. Understanding this is at the heart of current discussions of the necessary interaction of age, period, and cohort effects in adult development processes.

Second, the construction of better theories of adult development will necessarily be multidisciplinary and comparative. No single discipline currently has the theory, methodology, and analytic techniques necessary to apply Hernes's and George's perspectives in attacking significant problems of adult development in a definitive way. Further, defensible generalizations about adult developmental processes—even within a particular society, much less between societies—require research comparing social change over time within and between societies and different subgroups within societies.

Third, current evidence suggests there is substantial variation in social definitions of age and related normative expectations, the social outcomes of aging, and the personal experience of aging. This does not indicate necessarily that orderly, sequential processes of development do not underlie the observed variability. It does imply that these processes involve the complex interaction of multiple personal, social, and environmental variables that may produce a variety of personally and socially viable outcomes. In this connection it is useful to recall the critiques of disengagement and modernization theory discussed above. We know, for example, that successful adaptations in adulthood appear to be possible for most individuals with different personal and social characteristics in a variety of social contexts. Apparently some congruence between individual and contextual characteristics is required to achieve a viable outcome; but a tolerable fit between persons and environments may take various forms. If this is the case, research would be profitably directed not toward identification of the sole determinants of a particular outcome—for example, life satisfaction or well-being—but toward the specification of the limits of tolerable fitting of individual and contextual factors that produce viable outcomes, and of the combinations of variables that produce these outcomes.

If both individuals and social contexts are malleable—as they appear to be to a significant degree—then another implication follows. It is possible to imagine, as the authors of the chapters in Part V of this *Handbook* do, the modification of social context in potentially beneficial ways. The processes of adult aging reflect relatively less what one may assume that nature requires and relatively more what social groups prefer and are able to achieve through purposive social and political action.

Finally, our observations about the severe limitations on theory construction in the social scientific study of aging lead us to expect in the near term what we in fact observe currently—attention to partial theoretical perspectives rather than to comprehensive theory. It is not surprising, we believe, that social scientists currently are attracted to life course analysis. Life course analysis is not a theory but a perspective that incorporates both theoretical and methodological elements traditionally found in social gerontological and aging research (Maddox, 1979). It is a perspective that focuses primarily on two institutional contexts—the family and work—and on adulthood rather than the entire life course. What is attractive about this perspective is, in part, derivable from its congruence with what we believe to be the essential emphasis of the broader theoretical perspective suggested by Hernes and George. Life course analysis stresses the interaction of micro- and macrolevel factors, is distinctly comparative in emphasis, articulates well with the theoretical and methodological perspectives focusing on the interaction of age, period, and cohort, and focuses on selective dimensions of aging rather than the totality of aging processes.

The need to pay attention to multiple levels of analysis and several different kinds of influences on the life course requires careful consideration of methodological matters. While methods must never become an end in themselves, the past decade has of necessity been preoccupied with conceptual issues involving the proper articulation of theory, data, and analysis. In particular, the age/period/cohort (APC) problem has required and received a great deal of attention. Many of the more difficult conceptual and statistical issues in APC analyses now seem to be resolved, at least to the extent that researchers have a common understanding of them. The following section reviews the technical aspects of the APC problem and then turns to a discussion of the data base that will be required to implement the rather complex statistical procedures that have been developed.

METHODOLOGY

One of the more intriguing coincidences in the history of social research was the concurrent publication in 1965 of Warner Schaie's careful elaboration of the age, period, and cohort issue in the study of development and Norman Ryder's seminal paper on the role of cohorts in social change. In many respects, these papers defined a research agenda for the next decade, and the first edition of this *Handbook* devoted a good deal of its energy to an appreciation of the issues that Schaie and Ryder raised and to tracing out their methodological implications. Whereas early approaches to the APC problem focused primarily on statistical issues, more recent work has concentrated on the substantive ramifications of proposed solutions. It is clear that these solutions require data that are only now becoming available.

The Age/Period/Cohort Issue

Schaie (1965) illustrated the relationship among age, time of measurement, and date of birth as shown in Table 1. The table describes a hypothetical data set that would provide life course data on a succession of birth cohorts, and it makes clear that, if one knows the date of measurement (*P*) and year of birth (*C*), then age (*A*) is unequivocally defined; that is, $A = P - C$. Put differently, if age and time of measurement are known, birth cohort follows; hence any two factors determine the third. Palmore (1978) provided several excellent examples of this kind of confounding and suggests ways to deal with the problem. Schaie saw this table within the framework of the analysis of variance (ANOVA) and attempted to lay out an analysis paradigm that permitted one to distinguish among age, period, and cohort in terms of main effects for two of the dimensions (e.g., age and period) and the interaction between them. It soon became clear, however, that, both conceptually and statistically, attempting to deal with a three-factor problem in a two-factor framework presented insurmountable obstacles.

A careful examination of Table 1 makes it clear that age appears on the diagonal of the table. All 20-year-olds appear on a diagonal, all 40-year-olds on the next diagonal up, and so forth. The two-variable table could be rewritten as a three-variable (age by period by cohort) table, one that would contain a great many empty cells but a three-dimensional table nonetheless. Thus we have a choice. We can conceptualize age as the interaction of

TABLE 1. Ages of Selected Cohorts Available to an Investigator in 1960 at 20-Year Intervals.

Date of birth	DATE OF MEASUREMENT										
	1860	1880	1900	1920	1940	1960	1980	2000	2020	2040	2060
1860	0	20	40	60	80	100	—	—	—	—	—
1880	—	0	20	40	60	80	100	—	—	—	—
1900	—	—	0	20	40	60	80	100	—	—	—
1920	—	—	—	0	20	40	60	80	100	—	—
1940	—	—	—	—	0	20	40	60	80	100	—
1960	—	—	—	—	—	0	20	40	60	80	100

Source: Adopted from Schaie (1965), p. 93.

period and cohort, or we can treat it as a main effect. Note that if age is thought of as an interaction, it is an interaction of a specific kind; there is one effect associated with each diagonal of the table. Various other $P \times C$ interactions remain. This is the aspect of the analysis with which Schaie was unable to deal successfully in an ANOVA paradigm.

Mason et al. (1973) suggested an analysis of Table 1 that is sufficiently important to warrant a detailed description. Within a general linear model framework, they propose writing an equation in which dummy variables represent the various rows (cohort), columns (period), and diagonals or layers (age) of the table. These dummy variables are coded "1" if an observation is in a particular row, column, or layer and "0" otherwise. A table of this form can be analyzed using a multiple regression equation of the following form:

$$Y = K + \sum_{i=1}^{I-2} a_i A_i + \sum_{j=1}^{J-1} p_j P_j + \sum_{k=1}^{K-1} c_k C_k$$

where A is a set of I dummy variables indexing age categories; P is a set of J dummy variables for time of measurement and C is a set of K dummy variables for cohort; a, p, and c are regression coefficients; and K is a constant. As is conventional in such analyses, one begins by arbitrarily eliminating one of the dummy variables within each set from the equation; in this case the dummy variable for the oldest age cohort and the earliest period do not appear. There are, in other words, as many dummy variables for each effect as degrees of freedom associated with it, and each dummy variable coefficient represents a particular contrast (cf. planned comparison in ANOVA terminology). Dropping a dummy variable sacrifices no information and provides the exact equivalent of a three-way analysis of variance. For a particularly clear mathematical exposition of these issues, see Hagenaars and Cobben (1978).

Unfortunately, even with this approach, one cannot get unique estimates of the a_i, p_j,

and c_k precisely because age is "determined by" cohort and period; that is, for each cohort–period combination there is only one age group available for analysis. As a result, there is a confound among the three variables, and a unique variance decomposition into A, P, and C components is not possible, nor can the coefficients be estimated. Mason et al. (1973) show, however, that with one further restriction a complete analysis is possible. The complete APC model can be estimated if one is willing to assume that any two specific ages, cohorts, or periods have the same impact on the dependent variable; that is, that the contrasts (regression coefficients) associated with them are equal. The model is "restricted" in that within one of the dummy variable sets, A, P, and C, we estimate, say, not $A - 1$ coefficients, but $A - 2$. It will typically be the case that the specific effects chosen are adjacent (e.g., that the two oldest age groups have similar effects), but this is not required. Moreover, the solution is more general. One need not specify exact equalities; a constant inequality (e.g., that one effect is twice another) will suffice. Note also that if one is willing to specify that two adjacent ages have the same effect (thus eliminating not one but two dummy variables for age from the equation), then all $C - 1$ cohort and $P - 1$ period effects can be estimated; that is, the restriction is required within only one set of dummy variables. Thus a willingness of the part of an analyst to specify a particular restriction "solves" the APC problem, at least from the standpoint of statistical analysis.

The Mason et al. approach is an "accounting mechanism"—that is, it provides estimates of differences among age groups, period, and cohorts, but does not specify in detail the source of the observed differences. To do that would require one to operationalize specifically the presumed causal variables associated with, say, a cohort effect in terms of cohort size, nutritional milieu, or whatever. Nonetheless, the technique represents a significant breakthrough. It has been extended to categorical outcomes with good results (Feinberg and Mason, 1979) and has been applied to several interesting substantive problems (e.g., Knoke and Hout, 1974; Mason and Smith, 1984). However, the method has been criticized, and a recent exchange in the *American Sociological Review* puts the issues in a particularly clear light (Rogers, 1982a,b; Smith et al., 1982, see also Glenn, 1976 and Mason, et al., 1976). In these various commentaries, debates, and rejoinders, three basic issues emerge, as follows.

1. Definition of Age, Period, and Cohort Effects. Conventional definitions of what one means by age, period, or cohort effect can be found in many sources (e.g., Ryder, 1965; Schaie, 1965; Baltes et al., 1979); however, in actual practice distinctions tend to blur. To take one example, the introduction of vitamin D into milk supplies, now a routine procedure, can be thought of as a period effect in that at the time of the innovation it cut across all age groups and was a fairly instantaneous transition. On the other hand, certain cohorts of newborns received the benefits of this innovation almost immediately from birth, while preceding cohorts were exposed to it beginning no earlier than their age at the date of introduction. The period effect thus impacted cohorts differentially; some cohorts received the vitamin supplement all of their lives (assuming they drank milk) while others, depending on date of birth, were exposed to the innovation during a smaller proportion of their childhood years. Do we think of this nutritional innovation as a period effect, a cohort effect, or both? As Maddox and Wiley noted in the first edition of this *Handbook,* a complete specification of APC effects necessitates the inclusion of lagged effects which may or may not diminish over time. Nutritional innovations, for example, may manifest effects early in the life cycle and again very late in life but have relatively little impact at midlife. The conventional APC model does not permit such lags, although it would be relatively easy, given appropriate data, to estimate such models.

2. Specification of Appropriate Models. In order to obtain estimates of the coefficients in an APC model, one must assert in advance that at least two effects within one of the three sets (i.e., two age effects, period effects, or cohort effects) are equal. On the surface, this appears to be a fairly trivial assumption; however, it is easy to demonstrate both analytically (Clogg, 1984) and with simulated data (Rogers, 1982a) that if the analyst makes a wrong choice of restrictions, the resulting estimates can be significantly biased. In their defense, Mason and his colleagues argue (Smith et al., 1982) that their approach, like any other causal model, requires a careful theoretical approach to model specification. The APC equations are, in fact, a model for the data, a model not different from any of the other hundreds of causal models that have appeared in the social science literature over the past 15 years. The logical status of deleting a particular effect from the model by constraining assumptions is not different from assuming that a particular path model is recursive rather than reciprocal. Thus the issue needs to be debated in theoretical terms (are the constraints correct?) rather than technical terms (does the model "work"?).

3. Specification of Additional Interactions. As noted above, an APC table can be conceived as a three-dimensional table with numerous empty cells. Representing such a table in terms of an additive model assumes, for example, that the effects of period do not vary across ages and cohorts. It is possible, of course, to represent other interactions in the analysis; for instance, one could include interactions between age and cohort, thus implying that certain period effects differ depending on the cohort involved. Period effects are not purely additive, and representation of interactions is tantamount to dealing in a particular way with the issue of lagged effects discussed above. Again, the issue here is not primarily statistical but theoretical. The issue is not whether one *must* include this or that interaction term in the model but whether inclusion is appropriate given an investigator's theoretical approach to a problem.

All of these issues are nicely demonstrated in a recent paper by Mason and Smith (1984), which provides an elaborate example of the techniques and a careful discussion of the estimation issues. They analyze two time series of data on tuberculosis mortality, one from Massachusetts spanning the period 1860 to 1970 and the other for the United States as a whole from 1935 to 1975. In their analysis, Mason and Smith are able to obtain plausible estimates of age, period, and cohort differences in mortality rates by assuming that two adjacent age categories (5–9 and 10–14) demonstrate similar effects. In choosing their restrictions, the authors make use of a great deal of additional information including known dates of chemotherapeutic innovation, rates of migration, proportions of young men in the armed forces at particular times, percent foreign-born by cohort, and other data. Finally, in order to get reasonable estimates, Mason and Smith must include an interaction term for being 18–35 in 1945, thereby representing the effects of World War II on tuberculosis mortality.

In summary, a great deal of progress has been made in resolving APC issues. It is clear that the problem is theoretical and conceptual, not simply statistical; it is also clear that, with appropriate assumptions, unique estimates for age, period, and cohort can be generated. While the problem is by no means "solved"—and indeed cannot be in any general sense, since a particular problem requires its own substantive rationale—experience with estimation procedures has produced increasing confidence in how the APC problem can be resolved. Ideally, however, one would prefer not merely to index ages, period, and cohorts, but rather to include in one's models direct measures of the presumed causal variables. Doing so, however, requires access to a very sophisticated macro- and microlevel time series and cross-national data bases that are only now beginning to emerge. We turn now to a discussion of recent developments in the availability of adequate data for social scientific research on aging processes and their outcomes.

The Emerging Data Base

In an earlier section of this chapter, we reviewed Hernes's model of social change, noting his insistence that the process of change must be seen in terms of both macro- and microlevel variables and in terms of the reciprocal relationship between the two. The particular microlevel choices that individuals make in terms of education, occupation, marriage, and fertility, for example, are constrained by macrolevel social phenomena such as cohort size, labor markets, sex ratios, and investment decisions. Microlevel choices of individuals, in turn, affect the macrostructure of society; high fertility, for example, tends to reduce rates of female labor force participation. To analyze age, period, and cohort effects operationalized directly in terms of presumed causal variables rather than accounting (dummy) variables, requires detailed information on myriad variables at various levels of aggregation. It is important to realize that, although any APC table with at least three levels of one of the variables (e.g., two ages, two cohorts, three periods) can be analyzed within the regression-based accounting scheme reviewed above, serious attempts to operationalize APC effects directly in terms of presumed causes will require substantial variation in those variables. That is, a single time period will not suffice. Many of the variables in which one would be most interested change rather slowly, and often in parallel, over the short run. Following World War II, for example, a wide variety of economic and social variables (e.g., gross national product, fertility, consumption, quality of health care) showed parallel incremental change over a 10- to 15-year period. If these increments are primarily linear, they will be confounded with each other, and any one variable will serve as a proxy for them all; they will be so collinear that analysis of specific effects is impossible. To the extent that one has cross-cultural variation and a long time series, the confounding will be less severe. In general, however, an adequate solution of the APC problem requires a comprehensive data base, which is just beginning to emerge.

The absence of comprehensive data is by no means an indictment of current research investigators; it reflects primarily the developmental status of social scientific disciplines. Although various surveys on older populations were carried out in the 1940s and 1950s, adequate machine-readable social survey or biomedical data for secondary analysis were not available until the early 1960s. Data collected on older persons in 1960 provided information on birth cohorts dating back to perhaps 1880; however, reasonably adequate sampling occurred only from 1890 (persons who were 70 years old in 1960) onward because of the very few persons above age 70 likely to be found in earlier survey samples. Now, in the 1980s, data from persons born between 1900 and 1920 are available. Thus, most of what we know in any systematic way about aging is available for cohorts born during a rather narrow window in time.

Concentrating on the United States, we note that the cohorts for whom we have useful information experienced quite different historical events, and they experienced certain events in common (e.g., World War II) at very different life stages ranging from age 20 through about 40 or 50. Thus, studies being done now on persons who are 70 and above deal with very different cohorts from studies of 70 year olds carried out 20 years ago. While this is a commonplace observation, our point is that cross-cohort replication of life course data is both necessary and desirable. A recent compilation of survey data by Taeuber and Rockwell (1982), which concentrates on repeated cross-sectional or longitudinal surveys, documents these assertions more completely.

Projecting forward to the turn of the century, we can see how the value of our growing catalog of data will increase tremendously as we begin to compare the birth cohorts of 1910, 1920, 1930, and 1940 as they adapt to aging. It is probably fair to say, for example, that cohorts entering the sixth decade of life at the beginning of this century until the present time, with the possible exception of those aged 60 at the beginning of the depression, faced increasingly favorable social conditions for the aged. We are now entering an era in which the relative condition of the newly aged cohorts may be substantially less favorable. A comparable observation about the changing experience of young adults has been made by Easterlin (1980). Variation in the social, economic, and political response to changing societal conditions on the part of older persons themselves will tell us much about how aging processes are affected by period and cohort factors.

The amount of data potentially available to study these processes staggers the imagination. In the United States we have carefully collected time series on a wide variety of social and economic indicators over more than a century. We have long series of routinely collected institutional data on such things as disability applications, tax records, ability and achievement tests, and a wide variety of other data from national and state-level governmental agencies. The federal government has conducted surveys and censuses of the population at large for decades. Siegel and Taeuber (1982) provide a compilation and a useful discussion.

The Current Population Survey (CPS) began shortly after World War II and is gradually being reconstructed in machine-readable form, as are public use samples of the 1940 and 1950 censuses. In addition to governmental surveys, long series of general surveys of the civilian population conducted for various purposes, such as presidential election surveys dating back to the fifties and a long series of consumer surveys, now exist. There are also various longitudinal surveys designed to study aging processes including the Social Security Administration's Retirement History Survey (LRHS) (Irelan, 1972) and various longitudinal studies of local populations (Palmore, 1970, 1974).

All this information is potentially available. The process of placing these data in the public domain, in the sense that they are stored in a central location in machine-readable form, is taking place with remarkable speed. The Inter-university Consortium for Political and Social Research (ICPSR) now has hundreds of data sets available that can be used by researchers with fairly minimal technical training in computerized data management (ICPSR, 1982). Both ICPSR and the Duke University Center for the Study of Aging and Human Development Data Archives provide data sets to users at minimal cost. While start-up costs involved in using available data sets tend to be high, they are trivial compared to the cost of securing new data. Increasingly, distributing agencies such as the Duke Archives also provide technical support to less experienced investigators.

As the number of studies increases, and as variability in time and population covered continues to increase, we will find ourselves with an increasingly powerful data base on which to test sophisticated theories of how age, environment, and cohort affect the life course. The data will be used initially in simple cross-cohort comparisons of findings. We can imagine a monograph on ''The Children of Affluence'' (see, e.g., Easterlin, 1980) to match Elder's *Children of the Great Depression* (1974). More rigorous analyses will be possible as data sets are actually combined. For example, the original *National Longitudinal Studies (NLS) of Labor Force Mobility* (Parnes, 1975), in which young people 14 to 24 years old in 1966 were studied longitudinally, are now being replicated using samples of persons who were those same ages in 1980. Once individual-level data gathered on persons of equivalent age at different time periods are available, it will be necessary to supplement the data with information on social structure and cultural conditions (the ''environment'').

While no systematic effort has been un-

dertaken to gather comprehensive life course data on sequential cohorts in the United States (although there are several cross-sectional time series such as the CPS), an increasingly rich data base is becoming available. Migdal et al. (1981) describe nearly 50 longitudinal studies of the life course done in the United States which focus on middle and old age. Undoubtedly, the list is not complete. These studies, combined with numerous repeated cross-sectional surveys such as the ICPSR election studies and the NORC General Social Surveys, constitute an emerging archive of unprecedented power. Data sets originally collected at great cost are now routinely available for nominal fees. The quality of documentation and the ease of transition from one computer to the next continue to increase. It is now possible, for example, to examine the economic status of widows using as many as 20 different data sets, each of which has particular strengths and weaknesses in terms of sample and item coverage. Increasingly, it is also possible to supplement these data with national (macro)-level information on social and economic variables. For example, if one were examining changes in perceived well-being over the life cycle, using a sequence of surveys in which the appropriate questions had been asked, one might supplement individual (micro)-level observations with societal (macro) information pertaining to inflation, interest rates, unemployment, crime rates, and other social and economic indicators for the year in which the question was asked (ICPSR, 1982). Machine-readable economic and social time series are now available. Recent developments in statistical software (e.g., SAS and the forthcoming SPSS-X) make the merging of new information into an existing data file a relatively simple exercise.

With respect to data from outside the United States, the picture is not quite so encouraging, although here also we have good reason to be optimistic about emerging possibilities. Migdal et al. (1981) describes more than 20 longitudinal data sets pertaining to middle- and old-age respondents from outside the United States. All of them are from Europe, and many come from the Scandanavian countries. Mednick and Baert (1981) provide descriptive information on more than 60 longitudinal data sets focusing on mental health, most of which do not appear in the list provided by Migdal et al. Mednick and Baert consider studies of all ages, and their volume reviews studies of samples taken from birth cohorts from as far back as 1850 to samples taken of newborns in the past few years. These various studies show tremendous variation in sample coverage, content, data quality, and every other respect, of course; but the possibilities for comparative research are clearly taking shape. At the same time, a series of sequential cross-sectional surveys conducted in various European countries has become available. The Euro-Barometer series of surveys (ICPSR, 1982), which provide information on various topics from the mid-1970s to the present for many European countries, can be used in aging research in the same way that similar data sets have been used in the United States (e.g., the NORC General Social Surveys in machine-readable form). Machine-readable macro-level time series for Great Britain, Germany, and France are also now available.

The Role of Longitudinal Studies

Our discussion of secondary data resources has blurred the distinction between those that are longitudinal (in the sense that they follow a particular group of individuals through time) and those that are sequential cross sec-

tions (in that they sample cohorts across time, but sample different individuals in those cohorts). The latter design provides, of course, a longitudinal study of a cohort at the aggregate level, but not of individuals. Longitudinal studies at the microlevel, often called panel studies, have been assumed to be the *sine qua non* of aging research. What one might call the "classic design" consists of taking a group of individuals selected on the basis of age (58–63 in the case of the Social Security Administration's Longitudinal Retirement History Survey; 45–59 in the case of the National Longitudinal Survey of Labor Market Experiences) and following them on an annual or semiannual basis. This design is so much a part of our thinking about research on aging that its logical basis has rarely been questioned. However, use of panel designs of this kind is only one of many ways that one can obtain data, and they have various weaknesses and ambiguities that are just beginning to be understood. While no comprehensive discussion of these issues can be offered here, a few basic points should be emphasized.

Many authors have provided detailed rationales for longitudinal studies, among them Wohlwill (1973) and Wall and Williams (1970). However, the most cogent discussion of issues, in our opinion, is that offered by Baltes and Nesselroade (1979), whose approach is summarized in Figure 2. The columns of this two-by-two table distinguish between descriptive or normative studies and those that have causal analysis as a goal; the rows distinguish between differences that are

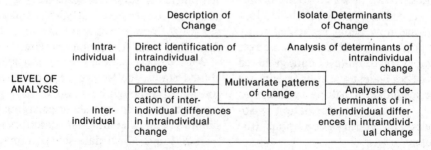

PURPOSE OF RESEARCH

		Description of Change	Isolate Determinants of Change
LEVEL OF ANALYSIS	Intra-individual	Direct identification of intraindividual change	Analysis of determinants of intraindividual change
		Multivariate patterns of change	
	Inter-individual	Direct identification of interindividual differences in intraindividual change	Analysis of determinants of interindividual differences in intraindividual change

Figure 2. A rationale for longitudinal research. Based on Baltes and Nesselroade (1979).

interindividual (between individuals) and intraindividual (within individuals). Thus, a longitudinal study may focus on studying the changes of individuals over time on a descriptive basis. In this case we would be interested, for example, in how an individual's income or life satisfaction varies over time. The same study might be concerned with how much variation there is in patterns of individual variation: Does every individual follow an essentially parallel curve, or are there differences in the income paths of individuals? In addition to description, a study might be concerned with explanation. What are the determinants of variation in an individual's income stream? The search for determinants might be broadened to include a search for determinants of interindividual variability in income and change over time. Finally, the box in the center of the table reminds us that we are often searching for multivariate patterns of change, seeking to find at the intraindividual level particular characteristic profiles and at the interindividual level characteristic patterns of differences.

One might conclude that all longitudinal studies must do all these things. After all, longitudinal studies are extremely expensive; and unless one can get maximum use from the data, they can hardly be justified. Although many existing studies have been used for multiple purposes, we argue that a research investigator who wishes a particular study to serve multiple masters is inevitably forced into compromises in design that reduce the integrity of the study for any one purpose. In particular, a study that attempts to obtain broad normative data at the same time it attempts to explain the determinants of a particular phenomenon is not likely to accomplish both objectives and may accomplish neither. Basically, there are four closely related design issues to be faced, as outlined below. Space considerations prohibit an extended discussion of these issues, although to the best of our knowledge they have received only limited systematic attention in the literature. The linkage of analysis and design needs to be explored in much greater detail.

Study Content. As the discussion of Figure 2 (above) concludes, a clear decision is required at the beginning of a study regarding objectives. Is the study intended to provide descriptive/normative information on broad classes of variables related to aging processes or to provide information on the determinants of a particular outcome? Each objective is legitimate. Experience suggests that the achievement of both objectives simultaneously is unlikely.

Sample Selection. As a rule, the broader the objectives of a study, the more difficult it is to define the sampling frame. Descriptive/normative studies typically require repeated measurement of key variables at relatively precise, theoretically specified intervals. Moreover, such studies require either a carefully drawn sample from contiguous birth cohorts or a sample based on a cohort-defining event (e.g., all women experiencing widowhood in a particular year). If a study is intended to be broadly descriptive of aging processes, a birth cohort sample is preferred; if it is intended to describe the concomitants and consequences of age-related events, then sampling for the event is indicated. Within reasonable limits of time and sample size, it is unlikely that the sample of a single study can achieve both objectives.

Retrospective versus Prospective Data. It is useful to define a longitudinal study generally as one in which, for example, stability and change in roles, statuses, events, and attitudes can be located with respect to time and in time with respect to each other. In principle, there is no reason why this goal cannot also be accomplished retrospectively. For example, a complete occupational history can be gathered by asking someone to list all jobs held or by asking a person once a month to list the current job. Depending on the use to which the data are to be put, either method of data collection might suffice, although the analytic problems they present are rather different. Clearly, however, recall of one's entire occupational career is likely to be difficult or impossible for many respondents. Moreover, some subjective variables, like morale, are almost impossible to measure retrospectively because the report of past status is likely to be biased by current status. Nonetheless, as Featherman (1977) points out, retrospective studies are extremely inexpensive and efficient relative to prospective panel studies and ought always to be considered as an alternative.

Timing of Measurement. Some variables of interest in longitudinal studies of aging change relatively slowly and typically in a linear fashion (e.g., income); such variables may be assessed conveniently, say, once a year. Other variables may change rapidly and in a nonlinear form (e.g., morale) in response to some life event such as illness or widowhood. The greater the number and variety of variables, the more difficult the decision regarding intervals between measurement.

Studies intended to explore determinants of an outcome face two special problems: When should the baseline observation be made, and how long should the interval between measurement be? While the answer to these questions tends to be made on practical rather than theoretical grounds, this compromise usually ensures substantial difficulty in interpreting findings. In sum, we recommend resisting the temptation to attempt too much at once in longitudinal studies.

SUMMARY AND CONCLUSION

The history of research on aging has demonstrated a continual tension between the need to understand the aging process and its potential problems of illness, social isolation, and poverty, and a desire to see the life course whole with the end of life having no greater demand on our attention than the beginning. While the two perspectives are by no means antithetical, they do have somewhat different theoretical traditions, research perspectives, and scholarly communities. Within the past decade we have seen

more emerging unity between the two perspectives than in the past.

Increasingly, we have abandoned attempts to explain the "life cycle" in terms of some overarching unifying concept like disengagement theory or Eriksonian stages and instead have attempted to understand how individual lives are played out in particular historical, cultural, and economic circumstances, and how variation in these circumstances affects the model of adaptation to late life. Hernes's (1976) paper draws our attention to how macro- and microlevel variables are related in reciprocal fashion. The environment offers various alternatives and constraints, and individuals responding to them change the environment in ways that alter the alternatives available to successive cohorts.

The concern with age, period, and cohort analyses on the part of researchers in aging reflects this understanding. Early attempts to sketch time-invariant curves (e.g., for intellectual ability) were contradicted by clear cohort differences (Baltes et al., 1979). Similar examples can be found in the study of tuberculosis rates, as outlined above, and elsewhere. While we are now basically at an accounting stage in terms of specifying age, period, and cohort phenomena, from a theoretical perspective it is increasingly desirable and possible to express directly those aspects of the environment (broadly defined) and those aspects of biological aging that affect human behavior; merely indexing them is inadequate. To do so obviously requires measures of such variables, and measurement is increasingly possible.

We are the beginning stages of a data collection process that will eventually yield cross-cultural, cross-temporal, and cross-cohort comparative data on whole lives, or at least on large segments of whole lives with macrolevel time series data to supplement them. Certainly, the form that these data sets take will be motivated in part by the theoretical concerns of those who do the data collection, but much of the data will come from a more or less random process of administrative and academic concerns. To forward research in aging, investigators concerned with aging will need to help shape that process.

REFERENCES

Achenbaum, A. 1978. *Old Age in a New Land*. Baltimore: The Johns Hopkins Press.

Andrews, F. M., and Withey, S. B. 1976. *Social Indicators of Well-being*. New York: Plenum Press.

Baltes, P. B., and Nesselroade, J. R. 1979. History and rationale of longitudinal research. *In* J. R. Nesselroade and P. B. Baltes (eds.), *Longitudinal Research in the Study of Behavior and Development*, pp. 1–40. New York: Academic Press.

Baltes, P. B., Cornelius, S. W., and Nesselroade, J. R. 1979. Cohort effects in developmental psychology. *In* J. R. Nesselroade and P. B. Baltes (eds.), *Longitudinal Research in the Study of Behavior and Development*, pp. 61–87. New York: Academic Press.

Bengtson, V. 1975. Generational and family effects in value socialization. *Am. Soc. Rev.* 40:358–371.

Bengtson, V., Dowd, J., Smith, D., and Inkeles, A. 1975. Modernization, modernity, and perspectives of aging. *J. Geront.* 30:688–695.

Binstock, R., Chow, W., and Schulz, J. (eds.). 1982. *International Perspectives on Aging: Population and Policy Challenges*. New York: United Nations Fund for Population Activities.

Birren, J. 1959. Principles of research in aging. *In* J. Birren (ed.), *Handbook of Aging and the Individual: Psychological and Biological Aspects*, pp. 3–42. Chicago: University of Chicago Press.

Boocock, S. 1978. Historical and sociological research on the family and the life cycle: Methodological alternatives. *In* J. Demos and S. Boocock (eds.), *Turning Points*. Chicago: University of Chicago Press.

Campbell, A., Converse, P., and Rodgers, W. 1976. *The Quality of American Life*. New York: Russell Sage Foundation.

Campbell, R., and Henretta, J. 1981. Status claims and status attainments: The determinants of financial well-being. *Am. J. Soc.* 86:618–629.

Clark, R., and Menefee, J. 1981. Federal expenditures for the elderly: Past and future. *Gerontologist* 21(2):132–137.

Clogg, C. C. 1984. A note on the identification problem in age period cohort model for archival data. *In* W. M. Mason and S. E. Feinberg (eds.), *Cohort Analysis in Social Research: Beyond the Identification Problem*. New York: Springer-Verlag.

Cole, S. 1979. Age and scientific productivity. *Am. J. Soc.* 84(4):958–977.

Cowgill, D., and Holmes, L. (eds.). 1972. *Aging and Modernization*. New York: Appleton-Century-Crofts.

Cutler, S., Lentz, S., Muha, M., and Riter, R. 1980. Aging and conservation: Cohort changes in attitudes toward legal abortion. *J. Geront.* 35(1):115–123.

Delgado, M., and Finley, G. 1978. The Spanish-speaking elderly: A bibliography. *J. Geront.* 18(4):387–394.

Demos, J., and Boocock, S. (eds.). 1978. *Turning Points: Historical and Sociological Essays on the Family*. Chicago: The University of Chicago Press.

Dowd, J. 1975. Aging as exchange: A preface to theory. *J. Geront.* 30:584–94.

Easterlin, R. A. 1980. *Birth and Fortune*. New York: Basic Books.

Eckberg, D., and Hill, L. 1979. The paradigm concept and sociology: A critical review. *Am. Soc. Rev.* 44 (Dec.):925–937.

Elder, G. 1974. *Children of the Great Depression*. Chicago: University of Chicago Press.

Elder, G. 1978. Approaches to social change and the family. *In* J. Demos and S. Boocock (eds.), *Turning Points*. Chicago: University of Chicago Press.

Espenshade, T., and Braun, R. 1981. Economic aspects of an aging population and the material well-being of older persons. *In* B. Hess and K. Bond (eds.), *Leading Edges*. Washington, D.C.: National Institutes of Health.

Estes, C. 1979. *The Aging Enterprise*. San Francisco: Jossey-Bass.

Featherman, D. L. 1977. Retrospective longitudinal research: Methodological considerations. *J. Econ. & Bus.* 32(2):152–169.

Feinberg, S. E., and Mason, W. M. 1979. Identification and estimation of age–period–cohort models in the analysis of discrete archival data. *In* K. F. Schuessler (ed.), *Sociological Methodology*, pp. 1–67. San Francisco: Jossey-Bass.

Fernandez, R., and Kulik, J. 1981. A multilevel model of life satisfaction: Effects of individual characteristics and neighborhood composition. *Am. Soc. Rev.* 46 (Dec.):840–850.

Finley, G. 1981. Aging in Latin America. *Spanish-Language Psychology* 1:223–248.

Fischer, D. H. 1977. *Growing Old in a New Land*. New York: Oxford University Press.

Foner, A., and Kertzer, D. 1978. Transitions over the life course: From age-set societies. *Am. J. Soc.* 83 (Mar.):1081–1104.

Gelfand, D. E. 1981. Ethnicity and aging. *In* C. Eisdorfer (ed.), *Annual Review of Gerontology and Geriatrics*, Vol. 2, pp. 91–117. New York: Springer Publishing Co.

George, L. K. 1980. *Role Transitions in Later Life*. Monterey, Calif.: Brooks/Cole.

George, L. K. 1981. Subjective well-being: Conceptual and methodological issues. *In* C. Eisdorfer (ed.), *Annual Review of Gerontology and Geriatrics*, Vol. 2, pp. 345–384. New York: Springer Publishing Co.

George, L. K. 1982. Models of transition in middle and later life. *Ann. Am. Acad. Polit. Soc. Sci.* 464: 22–37.

Glenn, N. D. 1976. Cohort analyst's futile quest: Statistical attempts to separate age, period, and cohort effects. *Am. Soc. Rev.* 41:900–904.

Guillemard, Anne-Marie, 1980. *La viellesse et l'état*. Paris: Presses Universitaires de France.

Hagenaars, J. A., and Cobben, N. P. 1978. Age, cohort

and period: A general model for the analysis of social change. *Neth. J. Soc.* 14:55–91.

Hareven, T. (ed.). 1978. *Transitions: The Family and Life Course in Historical Perspective.* New York: Academic Press.

Harris Poll. 1977. *The Myth and Reality of Aging in America.* Washington, D.C.: National Council on the Aging.

Harris Poll. 1981. *Aging in the 80s: America in Transition.* Washington, D.C.: National Council on the Aging.

Henretta, J., and Campbell, R. 1976. Status attainment and status maintenance: A study of satisfaction in old age. *Am. Soc. Rev.* 41:981–992.

Henretta, J., and Campbell, R. 1978. Wealth vs. income in status attainment models. *Am. J. Soc.* 83:1204–1223.

Hernes, G. 1976. Structural change in social processes. *Am. J. Soc.* 82 (Nov.):513–547.

Hess, B., and Bond, K. (eds.). 1981. *Leading Edges: Recent Research on Psychosocial Aging.* Washington, D.C.: National Institutes of Health.

Hochschild, A. 1975. Disengagement theory: A critique and a proposal. *Am. Soc. Rev.* 40 (Oct.):553–569.

Hogan, D. 1978. The variable order of events in the life course. *Am. Soc. Rev.* 43:573–586.

Hogan, D. 1980. The transition to adulthood as a career contingency. *Am. Soc. Rev.* 45 (Apr.): 261–276.

House, J., and Robbins, C. 1983. Age, psychosocial stress, and health. *In* M. W. Riley, B. B. Hess, and K. Bond (eds.), *Aging in Society,* pp. 175–197. Hillsdale, N.J.: Lawrence Erlbaum Associates.

Inter-university Consortium for Political and Social Research. 1982. *Guide to Resources and Services, 1981–1982.* Ann Arbor: Institute for Social Research.

Irelan, L. M. 1972. Retirement history study: Introduction. *Soc. Sec. Bull.* 35:3–9.

Jackson, J. J. 1980. *Minorities and Aging.* Belmont, Calif.: Wadsworth Publishing Co.

Kahana, E., Liang, J., and Felton, B. 1980. Alternative models of person–environment fit: Predicting morale in three homes for the aged. *J. Geront.* 35:4, 584–595.

Keith, J. 1980. "The best is yet to be": Toward an anthropology of age. *In* B. J. Seigel (ed.), *Annual Review of Anthropology.* Palo Alto, Calif.: Annual Reviews, Inc.

Kiefer, C. 1974. *Changing Cultures, Changing Lives.* San Francisco: Jossey-Bass.

Knoke, D., and Hout, M. 1974. Social and demographic factors in American political party affiliation, 1952–1972. *Am. Soc. Rev.* 39:700–713.

Kuhn, T. S. 1970. *The Structure of Scientific Revolutions,* 2nd ed. Chicago: University of Chicago Press.

Lawton, M. P., and Nahemow, L. 1973. Ecology and the aging process. *In* C. Eisdorfer and P. Lawton (eds.), *The Psychology of Adult Development and Aging,* pp. 619–674. Washington, D.C.: American Psychological Association.

Lemke, S., and Moos, R. 1981. The suprapersonal environments of sheltered care settings. *J. Geront.* 36(2):233–243.

Long, S., and McGinnis, R. 1981. Scientific productivity and the reward structure, *Am. Soc. Rev.* 46 (Aug.):422–442.

Maddox, G. L. 1968. Persistence of lifestyle among the elderly. *In* B. Neugarten (ed.), *Middle Age and Aging.* Chicago: University of Chicago Press.

Maddox, G. L. 1978. Sociology, aging and guided social change. *In* M. Yinger and S. Cutler (eds.), *Major Social Issues: A Multidisciplinary View.* New York: Free Press.

Maddox, G. L. 1979. Sociology of later life. *In* A. Inkeles (ed.), *Annual Review of Sociology,* Vol. V, pp. 113–135. Palo Alto, Calif.: Annual Reviews, Inc.

Maddox, G. L. 1982. Challenge for health policy and planning. *In* R. Binstock, W. Sun Chow, and J. Schulz (eds.), *International Perspectives on Aging: Population and Policy Challenges.* New York: United Nations Fund for Population Activity.

Mahler, H. 1980. People. *Sci. Am.* 243(3):67–77.

Marshall, V. (ed.). 1980a. *Aging in Canada: Social Perspectives.* Toronto: Fitzhenry and Whiteside.

Marshall, V. 1980b. The sociology of aging. Paper presented to the 9th annual meeting of The Canadian Assoc. of Gerontology, Saskatoon, Saskatchewan, Oct.

Mason, K. O., Mason, W. M., Winsborough, H. H., and Poole, W. K. 1973. Some methodological issues in the cohort analysis of archival data. *Am. Soc. Rev.* 38:242–258.

Mason, W. M., and Smith, H. L. 1984. Age-period-cohort analysis and the study of deaths from pulmonary tuberculosis. *In* W. M. Mason. and S. E. Feinberg (eds.). *Cohort Analysis in Social Research: Beyond the Identification Problem.* New York: Springer-Verlag.

Mason, W. M., Mason, K. O., and Winsborough, H. H. 1976. Reply to Glenn. *Am. Soc. Rev.* 41(5):904–905.

Mednick, S. A., and Baert, A. E. (eds.). 1981. *Prospective Longitudinal Analysis: An Empirical Basis for Primary Prevention of Psychological Disorders.* New York: Oxford University Press.

Migdal, S., Abeles, R. P., and Sherrond, L. R. 1981. *An Inventory of Longitudinal Studies of Middle and Old Age.* New York: Social Science Research Council.

Miller, A., Gurin, P., and Gurin, G. 1980. Age consciousness and the political mobilization of older Americans. *Gerontologist* 20(6):691–700.

Moos, R. H. 1974. *Evaluating Treatment Environments.* New York: Wiley.

Myers, G. 1982. The aging of populations. *In* R. Binstock, W. Sun Chow, and J. Schulz (eds.), *International Perspectives on Aging: Population and Policy Challenges.* New York: United Nations Fund for Population Activity.

Nydegger, C. (ed.) 1977. *Measuring Morale: A Guide to Effective Assessment.* Washington, D.C.: Gerontological Society.

Palmore, E. (ed.) 1970. *Normal Aging: Reports from the Duke Longitudinal Studies, 1955-1969.* Durham, N. C.: Duke University Press.

Palmore, E. (ed.) 1974. *Normal Aging II: Reports from the Duke Longitudinal Studies, 1970-1973.* Durham, N. C.: Duke University Press.

Palmore, E. 1975. *The Honorable Elders.* Durham, N. C.: Duke University Press.

Palmore, E. 1978. When can age, period, and cohort be separated? *Soc. Forces* 57:282-295.

Palmore, E. 1980. *International Handbook on Aging.* Westport, Conn.: Greenwood Press.

Palmore, E., and Manton, K. 1974. Modernization and the status of the aged. *J. Geront.* 16:504-507.

Parnes, H. S. 1975. The national longitudinal studies: New vistas for labor market research. *Am. Econ. Rev.* 65:224-249.

Pollak, O. 1948. Social adjustment in old age. A research planning report. New York: Social Science Research Council.

Riley, M. 1972. The succession of cohorts. *In* M. Riley, M. Johnson, and A. Foner (eds.), *Aging and Society.* New York: Russell Sage Foundation.

Riley, M. (ed.). 1979. *Aging from Birth to Death: Interdisciplinary Perspectives.* Washington, D.C.: American Association for the Advancement of Science.

Rogers, W. L. 1982a. Estimable functions of age, period, and cohort effects. *Am. Soc. Rev.* 47:774-787.

Rogers, W. L. 1982b. Reply to Mason, Smith and Feinberg. *Am. Soc. Rev.* 47:783-796.

Rosenmayr, L. 1981. Objective and subjective perspectives of life span research. *Aging and Society* 1(1) (Mar.):29-49.

Rosow, I. 1974. *Socialization to Old Age.* Berkeley, Calif.: Univ. of California Press.

Ryder, N. B. 1965. The cohort as a concept in the study of social change. *Am. Soc. Rev.* 30:843-861.

Schaie, K. W. 1965. A general model for the study of developmental problems. *Psych. Bull.* 64:92-107.

Schulz, J., Carrin, G., Krupp, H., Peschke, M., Sclar, E., and Van Steenberge, J., 1974. *Providing Adequate Retirement Income.* Hanover, N. H.: The University Press of New England.

Shanas, E., Townsend, P., Wedderburn, D., Friis, H., Milhøj, P., and Stehouwer, J. 1968. *Old People in Three Industrial Societies.* New York: Atherton.

Siegel, J. 1981. Demographic background for international gerontology. *J. Geront.* 36:93-102.

Siegel, J. S., and Taeuber, C. M. 1982. The 1980 census and the elderly: New data available to planners and practitioners. *Gerontologist* 22:144-150.

Smith, H. L., Mason, W. M., and Feinberg, S. E. 1982. More chimeras of the age-period-cohort accounting framework: Comments on Rogers. *Am. Soc. Rev.* 47:787-793.

Spilerman, S. 1977. Careers, labor market structure, and socioeconomic achievement. *Am. J. Soc.* 83(3):551-593.

Taeuber, R. C., and Rockwell, R. C. 1982. National social data series: A compendium of grief descriptions. *Rev. Public Data Use* 10:23-111.

Thomae, H., and Maddox, G. L. 1982. *New Perspectives on Old Age.* New York: Springer Publishing Co.

Uhlenberg, P. 1978. Changing configurations of the life course. *In* T. Hareven (ed.), *Transitions,* pp. 65-97. New York: Academic Press.

Vatuk, S. 1980. Withdrawal and disengagement as a cultural response to aging in India. *In* C. Fry (ed.), *Aging in Culture and Society,* pp. 126-148. New York: J. F. Bergin Publishers.

Vladeck, B. C. 1980. *Unloving Care: The Nursing Home Tragedy.* New York: Basic Books.

Wall, W. D. and Williams, H. L. 1970. *Longitudinal Studies and the Social Sciences.* London: Heinemann.

Winsborough, H. 1979. Changes in the transition to adulthood. *In* M. Riley (ed.), AAAS Selected Symposium 30, *Aging from Birth to Death: Interdisciplinary Perspectives,* pp. 137-152. Boulder, Colo.: Westview Press.

Wohlwill, J. F. 1973. *The Study of Behavioral Development.* New York: Academic Press.

Zaret, D. 1980. From Weber to Parsons and Schutz: The eclipse of history in modern social theory. *Am. J. Soc.* 85(5):1180-1201.

Zuckerman, H., and Merton, R. 1972. Age, aging and age structure in science. *In* M. Riley, M. Johnson, and A. Foner (eds.), *Aging and Society: A Sociology of Age Stratification,* Vol. III, pp. 292-356. New York: Russell Sage Foundation.

PART 2 THE SOCIAL ASPECTS OF AGING

2
AGE AND THE LIFE COURSE

Gunhild O. Hagestad
Pennsylvania State University
and
Bernice L. Neugarten
Northwestern University

This chapter examines the social creation of life paths in modern society and ways in which scholars have approached the study of the life course. First, we take a brief look at the intellectual roots of a life course perspective. A second section gives an overview of social age systems in modern society and ways in which they have been studied. The next three sections discuss empirical work in three areas: the cultural phenomenology of age, social age norms, and age-related transitions. In a final section, we point to some critical issues raised by past work on the life course.

THE CONCEPT OF THE LIFE COURSE

Since the first edition of this *Handbook* was prepared, the term life course has become widely used by social scientists. Both in North America and in Europe, several new edited volumes (e.g., Back, 1980; Demos and Boocock, 1978; Hareven, 1978; Hareven and Adams, 1982; Kohli, 1978; Riley, 1979) and many research papers have addressed patterns of the life course. Some authors leave the term undefined, but more often the definition varies with the disciplinary background of the investigator. Psychologists usually speak of life span development, and sociologists speak of life course; yet some authors use these terms interchangeably as if they refer to the same underlying concept.

In our view, a life span orientation in psychology and a life course perspective differ in their key intellectual concerns. Whereas the former focuses a good deal of attention on intrapsychic phenomena (George, 1982), the latter emphasizes turning points when the "social persona" undergoes change. In particular, a life course approach concentrates on age-related transitions that are *socially created, socially recognized,* and *shared*.

The social and personal significance of the passage of life time is shaped by cultural age systems. All societies divide the life span into recognized seasons of life (Fry and Keith, 1982; Schütz, 1932; Zerubavel, 1981). The cultural segmentation of life time takes several forms. The periods of life are defined; people are channeled into positions and roles according to age criteria; and privileges, rights, and obligations are based on culturally shared age definitions. Finally, populations are divided into age groups whose interactions are socially structured and regulated (Fry, 1980b; Hagestad, 1982; Neugarten and Hagestad, 1976).

Age systems create predictable, socially recognized turning points that provide roadmaps for human lives and outline life paths. In this sense, the life course can be seen as a heuristic concept (Atchley, 1975), useful in describing pathways along an age-differentiated, socially created sequence of transitions (Cain, 1964; Clausen, 1972; Elder, 1975, 1978a, 1981). Thus, the life course perspective is linked to the sociology of age and age stratification (Cain, 1964, Elder, 1981; Neugarten and Moore, 1968; Riley et al., 1972; Chapter 13 of this *Handbook*). Indeed, German scholars discuss life course as a part of social structure—a social institution (e.g., Kohli et al., 1983; Meyer, 1981).

The focus on socially shaped and socially recognized turning points distinguishes life course analysis from many of the issues of concern to life-span developmental psychologists. It also sets it apart from much of the recent research on life events (for overviews see Brim and Ryff, 1980; Danish et al., 1980; Filipp, 1981; Hultsch and Plemons, 1979) because events selected for study may not be those that are culturally meaningful in the sense dicussed here. Finally, because of the emphasis on social transitions, life course analysis by necessity has to consider historical time, as changes in society lead to changes in the social structuring of individual life time (e.g., Elder, 1981; Hareven, 1981).

Although the life course approach is linked to the sociology of age, it has its roots in a different intellectual tradition: ethnographic work on age grading. It was the anthropologists who first examined how societies create age-related social transitions and thereby assign social meaning to the passage of life time (e.g., Van Gennep, 1908). Anthropological studies pointed to the dual nature of age grading: its social-structural and social-psychological dimensions (Fry and Keith, 1982). In the first instance, age is a key dimension of social structure, providing, along with gender, the basis for assigning people to roles and for distributing valued resources. The social segmentation of life time ensures the continuity and stability of society. It channels new generations into statuses and roles, ensuring that key societal functions are being met, and that human capacities are being appropriately utilized. From this societal perspective, age grading provides a normative system that reflects the social meanings and values of the society.

On a social-psychological level, age systems constitute cognitive constructions, what LeVine (1978b) calls a "cultural phenomenology of the life course," and what Plath (1982) refers to as an "ethnotheory of the life cycle." Members of a society have a common way of thinking about the changes that occur from birth to death and the significance of these changes, views that reflect broader cultural interpretations of the relations of man to nature and the supernatural.

Cultural age systems also comprise norms that regulate status and role occupancy across the span of life. For the individual, such norms provide a scheduled set of transitions. Along with other cultural constructions regarding age, they create a sense of what lies ahead—"the normal predictable life cycle" (Neugarten, 1969). If we share the assumption that "the impulse to define the predictability of life is a fundamental and universal principle of human psychology" (Marris, 1975, p. 3), then the social structuring of life time fills a compelling human need. Plath (1982) suggests that in our efforts to make sense out of the passage of individual life time, "the most nourishing ideas that we feed upon are those contained in our cultural schedules, ideas that help us plot where we are in the confused currents of time so that we can project where we yet may go" (p. 9).

SOCIAL AGE SYSTEMS

A comprehensive review of anthropological research on age grading will not be presented here (such reviews can be found in Cain, 1964; Eisenstadt, 1956; Foner and Kertzer, 1978; Gulliver, 1968; and Neugarten and Hagestad, 1976), nor does the present chapter deal with cross-cultural studies of aging (see Chapter 9 in this *Handbook*). In the present context, some major insights should be noted that come from nearly a century of scholarly work by anthropologists on the social segmentation of individual life time.

Three important themes emerge from this work: the nature of social transitions, the interrelatedness of life careers, and systematic variations in life course patterns.

The Nature of Transitions

All societies recognize a sequence of life periods and "punctuations of the life line" (Neugarten and Peterson, 1957). Members of a given society are able to name the periods of life and to describe the demarcations between them. Passing from one age grade to another in a traditional society marks multiple changes in social identity. Persons are perceived as having entered a new phase of life that has its distinctive characteristics, with different access to valued social and economic resources, and with new social roles, rights, and obligations (Foner and Kertzer, 1978; Fry, 1980b). For some transitions, elaborate rites of passage mark what Van Gennep (1908) described as social "ceasings and becomings," points in life when the individual becomes a "new" person (Fry, 1980b). Such ceremonies and rituals also signify that transitions are socially shared. Individuals have peers with whom they share the significant transition experience, and who provide social support. Sometimes these transition peers are distinguished by a special term (Gulliver, 1968; Stewart, 1977). A transition is socially recognized also by non-peers, who reorient their perceptions and expectations of those who have made the new transition (Berger and Luckman, 1966; Strauss, 1959; Young, 1965).

Interrelated Careers

Anthropological accounts of age grading provide ample illustrations of the interrelatedness of life careers. Two kinds of interconnections are described. First, transitions often cut across a number of different "institutional careers," and the individual moves simultaneously to new family, military, and religious roles. In some cases, a transition in one sphere of life is contingent on a transition in another. Second, transitions for one individual are often contingent on those of other persons, primarily kin (e.g., Prins, 1953).

Examples of both types of interdependence are provided by Whiting (1981) in his description of the Kikuyu of Kenya. The life course for men in traditional Kikuyu society had five age grades: junior warrior, senior warrior, junior elder, senior elder, and ritual elder. Puberty rites marked the entry into junior warrior status. Men could not marry, however, until they had gone through the two warrior grades. After marriage, they graduated to junior elder, a status in which domestic responsibilities were central. Senior elder, which entailed ritual and political functions, could not be reached until the men's oldest sons were initiated as junior warriors. Similarly, the highest and last status, that of ritual elder, was not open to men until their last sons were circumcised. According to Prins's (1953) description of the Kikuyu, this last transition was also contingent on wives' having passed menopause.

Variations in Life Course Patterns

Few ethnographic accounts describe contrasting or competing cultural constructions of age within a single society. This is not surprising, given the fact that most such accounts are based on folk societies—stable, small, homogeneous, and characterized by primary group relations. Thus, this literature reflects little attention to what in today's terminology is referred to as "intracohort variation" in life patterns, a topic to be discussed in detail below.

There is one notable exception to this trend. For variations within a group of individuals who were born into a society at the same time, the key factor identified by anthropologists is gender (Linton, 1942; LaFontaine, 1978; Parsons, 1942). Van Gennep (1908) stated that rites of passage always apply to one sex only. Seventy years later, in discussing adulthood and aging in a variety of non-Western cultures, a group of scholars concluded that descriptions of life patterns must be differentiated by sex:

The cultural vocabulary and normative structure of age-related behavior is so different for men and women . . . that no single description of the ideal or typical life course would suffice. It seems clear that even in the simplest societies, men and women measure their lives against radically different standards. (LeVine, 1978a, p. 3)

Young (1965), in a social-psychological perspective on initiation rites, suggests that not only do men and women encounter different transitions, they may also orient themselves to different levels of group membership. He argues that women's lives are typically structured by the immediate social environment, particularly kin groups, whereas men's lives are more typically shaped by a wider, more macrolevel social unit.

Although recent cross-cultural studies describe what happens to age status systems when traditional societies encounter modernization and Westernization (e.g., Cowgill and Holmes, 1972; Finley, 1982; Press and McKool, 1972), most descriptions of age grading have been ahistorical. They generally assume a stable society in which successive generations pass through the same set of age grades. When historical change is incorporated in such discussions, it tends to be in reference to particular historical events. For example, Whiting (1981) mentions that the Kikuyu had an age set named "Shillingi" who went through initiation rites in the year the British introduced shillings as currency. How wars and famines, with their associated demographic changes, influence transition patterns in successive cohorts has also been described (Foner and Kertzer, 1978). However, anthropological studies do not provide adequate models for incorporating the dimension of historical time into the study of the life course—a necessary dimension in describing societies characterized by complex processes of social and cultural change.

Age Systems and the Life Course in Modern Society

Like any other society, that of the United States recognizes socially defined periods of life, and assigns rights, duties, and privileges on the basis of social age. Life course transitions, however, lack the uniformity, stability, and synchrony that are characteristic of many traditional societies. Demarcations between the periods of life are not clear-cut, nor are they necessarily tied to major status and role changes.

Plural systems of age-grading are differentiated in relation to particular social institutions, and they vary in the extent to which they are explicit and formal (e.g., the school system is much more formally age-graded than the family). Furthermore, movement in one subsystem is not necessarily synchronous with movement in another (Cain, 1964). Persons reach adulthood in the political system when they reach 18 and are given the right to vote, but many reach adulthood in the economic system later, when they become full-time workers. At the same time, a more generalized age system also exists; and whether or not persons make the role transitions in family or work, they are recognized as adolescents and then as young adults on the basis of chronological age alone. For these reasons, the models of a single age stratification structure and of movement from one cross-cutting stratum to another do not capture the complexities of age systems or of age-related transitions in our society. Because people follow multiple pathways in different institutional spheres, they are often "age-status inconsistent" at various points in their lives (Cain, 1964; Elder, 1975; Neugarten and Moore, 1968).

Another source of complexity stems from the fact that in a pluralistic society, subgroups may have their own age systems. In addition to gender, factors such as ethnicity, socioeconomic status, and geographic region may create systematic variations in the definitions of age-statuses and produce variations in life paths (Clausen, 1972; Elder, 1975; Hogan, 1981; Neugarten and Peterson, 1957; Youmans, 1971). Finally, social change creates ongoing changes in age systems, so that different cohorts age in different ways (Riley et al., 1972). Thus the study of the life course in modern societies has become a complex, multifaceted enterprise.

Recent studies of the age systems and the life course in modern societies have taken three main directions. The first is the cultural phenomenology of age, where researchers have attempted to map shared perceptions of the periods of life, their characteristics, and the demarcations between them. A second line of research has focused on age norms and on the presence of normatively controlled timetables. A third body of work—by now the largest—has examined role transitions, mostly their timing and sequencing.

These three lines of inquiry have been only loosely linked up to now. The search for a conceptual framework that is appropriate to the study of age systems and the life course in modern societies, one that relates them to other phenomena such as historical change and subgroup differences, is still under way. (See Chapter 13.)

THE CULTURAL PHENOMENOLOGY OF AGE AND LIFE PERIODS

A number of researchers have asked how members of American society view the segmentation of individual life time. Three kinds of questions have been pursued: What are the perceived periods of life and the boundaries between them? What are the typical characteristics of individuals in the different life periods? How are the various periods evaluated (Hagestad, 1982)?

Empirical studies have shown considerable public consensus regarding four major phases of adult life: young adulthood, maturity, middle age, and old age, and their chronological boundaries (Cameron, 1969; Drevenstedt, 1976; Fry, 1976; National Council on Aging, 1975; Neugarten and Peterson, 1957; Shanas, 1962). Like Neugarten and Peterson in their earlier study (1957), Fry (1980a) found that changes in family or work roles and shifting obligations are commonly used dimensions for differentiating life phases.

For middle age and old age, there are common views of the "typical" person with regard to physical appearance or personality characteristics. There is a sizable literature, for example, on perceptions of older people (McTavish, 1982). Research methods used in exploring these perceptions have included various types of interview schedules, checklists, and attitude scales, among them, the "semantic differential" used by Rosencranz and McNevin (1969) and an often-used adjective checklist created by Tuckman and Lorge (1953).

In related studies, respondents have been asked to compare individuals in different life periods on such indicators as attitude and outlook (Bengtson, 1971), opportunity for happiness (Cameron, 1972), general well-being (National Council on Aging, 1975), and power (Youmans, 1971). Back and Bourque (1970), building on Frenkel-Brunswik's (1963) earlier conceptualizations, explored subjective evaluations of different ages through the use of "life graphs."

Sex Differences

In most of the research on perceptions of different life phases, respondents have been asked to react to such general categories as "the middle-aged" or "people over 65." There are strong indications, however, that each age period is defined differently for each sex. Indeed, some authors who have looked at the emergence of distinct life phases from an historical perspective, suggest that sometimes a phase is first recognized for one sex only. For example, in his classic study of the concept of childhood, French historian Aries (1962) argues that when, in the seventeenth and eighteenth centuries, childhood was recognized as a life phase with a distinct set of charcteristics and needs, there was only recognition of boyhood. Girls were still seen as "miniature women." Along the same lines, it has recently been suggested that a social awareness of middle age as a distinct phase came first in the case of women, whose lives were dramatically changed by altered rhythms of family events as well as by increased life expectancy.

In the Kansas City study of adult life, it was found that men and women saw rather different "punctuation points" across the life span (Neugarten and Peterson, 1957).

Men reported a succession of dividing points, with age 30 mentioned most often as an important point of transition. Women saw one major dividing point that outweighed the others in significance, and tended to describe adult life in terms of two somewhat disconnected lives, one before and one after 40.

In a more recent study, clear sex differences emerged concerning the onset of middle age and old age, both among those who were judging and those who were being judged (Drevenstedt, 1976). Both sexes indicated that women enter middle age and old age earlier than men do. The same trend was reported by Shanas (1962) who asked respondents about the age at which a man or a woman is old. However, women in the Drevenstedt study differentiated less between the sexes than did men and also gave higher ages for both life phases. Thus, women were likely to be labeled "middle-aged" or "old" at an earlier age by men than by women. Similar findings are reported in a recent study by Kogan (1979), who found that perceived age boundaries separating young adult from middle-aged, and middle-aged from elderly, were lower for women than for men.

In general, research findings seem to support the claim that our culture has a double standard of aging (Bell, 1970; Sontag, 1972): Age-related physical changes have more detrimental social consequences for women than for men, and they occur earlier in the lives of women. A study by Laurence (1964) showed men's ratings of women to be particularly "harsh" for middle age; and based on his own similar findings, Kogan (1979) concluded:

> There is a strong reason to believe on the basis of the present data that age is a more salient and value-laden dimension for males than for females. . . . Females appear to be more relaxed and tolerant about age differences, and make no distinctions between males and females on an age-linked basis. (p. 365)

In an innovative comparison of age–sex categories among the African Nyakusa and those found in Swedish children's books, Liljeström (1971) reached a similar conclusion:

> Boys/men are taught to give priority to the norms of their own age and sex group. Girls/women are taught flexibility by shifting of reference categories, i.e., by adjusting their behavior to the norms of several categories of norm senders. (p. 19)

Recently, several authors have urged that we pay attention to differences between time perspectives of men and women (e.g., Cottle, 1976); such contrasts may be related to different life course strategies (e.g., Skrede, 1982).

Other Systematic Variations

Research on the cultural phenomenology of age in our society is still quite limited. Very few investigators have explored the effects of socioeconomic status, ethnicity, or regional background on people's perceptions of the life span. In the Kansas City study, Neugarten and Peterson (1957) found lower age boundaries for middle age and old age reported by working class respondents than by the middle class. They suggest that this may be related to the earlier peak in occupational status and earnings for blue collar workers than for white collar workers. To our knowledge, no researcher has examined perceptions of life periods in population subgroups with life expectancies significantly different from the general population, such as inner city blacks and American Indians. There is also a lack of longitudinal studies on perceptions of life phases. Cross-sectional comparisons suggest that older respondents report higher age boundaries for the periods of later adulthood and give less negative views of old age than do younger respondents. Possible cohort shifts in views of the life span have not been explored, nor have possible age and cohort biases in the measurements used to assess age-related perceptions. Overall, one important shortcoming is that recent research on the cultural phenomenology of age has tended to disregard historical time.

AGE NORMS AND AGE CONSTRAINTS

As mentioned, social age systems entail cultural norms. Three kinds of age norms have been discussed in studies of industrialized societies: "the three P's" (permission, proscription, and prescription) with regard to role entries and exits, timetables, (Roth, 1963) and norms regarding other kinds of age-appropriate behavior.

In their conceptual model of age stratification, Riley et al. (1972) applied the three P's in describing how age criteria function to channel cohorts of persons into various social roles; and Cain (1974, 1976) has described how formalized age norms (i.e., laws), have functioned to define the status of older people. Here, however, the discussion of role entries and exits will be limited to social-psychological studies.

Building on earlier work at the University of Chicago, Wood and her co-workers (Wood, 1973; Pincus et al., 1974) developed a set of items asking when a person is "old enough" or "too old" to occupy specific roles in three spheres: political/legal, education/work, and family/friendship. They found that both young and old respondents showed greater consensus on when persons should enter a role than when they should exit; that older respondents delineated appropriate age limits more clearly than did college students; and that the highest degree of consensus was in the sphere of family and friendship roles.

Researchers from the University of Chicago conducted the first research on awareness of age norms in American society. In the Kansas City Study of Adult Life, interviews included questions about timetables and the optimal timing of major role transitions (Neugarten and Peterson, 1957). Over 80 percent of the respondents agreed that the best age to finish school and start work was 20 to 22; and nearly two-thirds agreed that men should hold their top jobs between age 45 and 50. In more recent studies, norms regarding the spacing and sequencing of transitions have been explored. Hogan (1982a) has found that adolescents have shared ideas on the ideal order of young adult transitions. Nydegger's (1981) recent work on the timing of fatherhood found little concensus among men regarding the appropriate age for starting a family, but considerable consensus that a two- to three-year interval should ensue between marriage and the first child.

It has been found that respondents are aware of their own positions within social timetables and describe themselves as "off-time" or "on-time" (Neugarten et al., 1965; Sofer, 1970). As Strauss (1959) stated: "When paths are institutionalized, a candidate can easily mark his progress, note how far he has come and how far he has yet to go." Thus, social clocks become internalized, and age norms operate to keep people "on the time-track," to use Lyman and Scott's (1970) terms.

Both timetables and other age-related expectations create a sense of what lies ahead as life progresses. Major stresses often arise when events upset the expected sequence and rhythm, while "scheduled" transitions do not appear correlated with significant psychological change (Pearlin, 1982). Two explanatory factors have been suggested for the fact that being on schedule reduces stress. First, persons go through anticipatory socialization, or rehearsal, for scheduled events. Second, when a transition occurs on time, the person has a set of peers who can provide social support and a sense of "all in the same boat at the same time" (Brim and Ryff, 1980; Seltzer, 1975). When the event is off-time, both these factors are changed, and therefore stress can occur. Blau (1961) found that women who were widowed relatively early, as well as men who retired early, had greater disruptions in their social relationships than did those for whom the events occurred at the expected time.

Not all predictable role changes are normatively scheduled, nor are all age-related regularities produced through normative control. Widowhood is an example: Although most women become widowed in their sixties, the timing of this transition is not regulated by cultural norms, and accordingly the event is not "normative" in the sense in which most students of the life course use the term.

Thus far this discussion has focused on age norms that regulate role occupancy; but not all age norms are tied to roles. The studies first initiated at the University of Chicago also explored informal norms regarding how to "act one's age." Neugarten et al. (1965) devised a series of items probing approved and disapproved behaviors for men and women of different ages, and then developed an overall "age constraint score" based on the extent to which respondents agree on an "appropriate," "marginal," or "inappropriate" age for each of various behaviors. The same approach has recently been used with a Japanese sample (Plath and Ikeda, 1975) and with several American samples (Fallo-Mitchell and Ryff, 1982; Passuth and Maines, 1981; Wood, 1971; Zepelin et al., 1982).

The study of Passuth and Maines (1981) was a direct replication of the earlier Chicago study, and the study of Plath and Ikeda (1975) followed the same procedures. Figure 1 presents findings from these three studies, comparing age constraint scores for respondents' own personal opinions and for opinions attributed to "most other people." As the figure shows, there are distinct similarities across the three studies. First, respondents attributed more age constraints to "other people's opinions" than to their own

opinions, and the gap between the two scores were the most marked among young adults. Second, personally perceived age constraint was positively related to the age of respondents, but "other people's" views showed somewhat lower constraint scores among old respondents than among young adults. These trends in combination produce a third pattern: a convergence of personal opinion and other people's views among respondents over 65, a pattern that was remarkably similar across the three studies. It appears that we are observing a true age-related phenomenon, since it was found in two different cohorts of American respondents, as well as in a Japanese sample. Fourth, in all three samples, men perceived greater age constraint in themselves as well as in "other people" than did women. The only exception to this trend was young adulthood. It may be that young women see greater time pressures in young adulthood because the timing of parenthood has biological "ceilings" for them.

Both Plath and Ikeda (1975) and Passuth and Maines (1981) examined the relationship between educational levels and perceived age constraint. They found different patterns. In

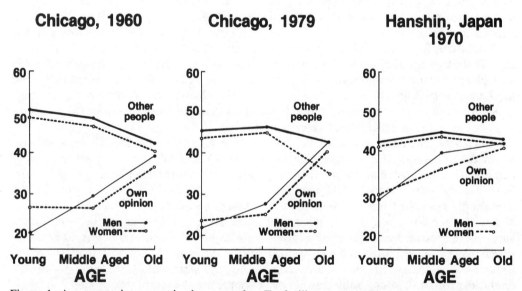

Figure 1. Age constraint scores in three samples. To facilitate comparisons, raw mean scores have been converted to standard ratios i.e., percentage of total possible scores), a procedure followed by Plath and Ikeda. SOURCES: Neugarten, Moore, and Lowe, 1965; Passuth and Maines, 1981; Plath and Ikeda, 1975.

the Japanese sample, there appeared to be a positive relationship between education and perceived age-constraint, whereas the Chicago respondents showed the inverse pattern: the higher their education, the lower their age constraint scores.

Much work remains to be done on systematic variations in informal age norms, on both an inter- and an intracohort level. No study has systematically explored changes in such norms during recent history. The work by Passuth and Maines (1981) suggests that we may have witnessed a decrease in overall age constraint in the United States between 1960 and the late 1970s. There is the problem, however, that the identical questions asked of two different cohorts may take on somewhat different social meaning in light of the social changes that have intervened. For example, in comparing the two Chicago samples, nearly 90 percent of respondents agreed in 1960 that age 19–24 was the appropriate time for women to marry, but only 40 percent agreed in 1980. As is well known, the proportion of American women who remained single beyond age 24 showed an all-time low in the 1950s, but increased dramatically in the 1970s. This exemplifies one of the underlying problems in carrying out "repeat" studies of social perceptions with different birth cohorts: The meaning of the questions themselves may change, thereby obscuring the extent to which normative consensus has increased or decreased. All in all, our understanding of historical shifts in age-related normative constraints is very limited. Another significant limitation of past work on age norms is that it has totally neglected sanctions attached to such norms. For example, no study has included questions on perceived benefits of conforming to social timetables, the consequences of being off-time or having a disorderly sequence of transitions, or the sources of positive and negative sanctions.

We return to conceptual problems in the study of age norms and possible pitfalls in the uses of normative explanations later in the chapter. First, it is useful to review some of the research carried out on transition patterns, since this work illustrates problems raised by a normative framework.

PATTERNS OF ROLE TRANSITIONS

So far, we have examined work exploring the cultural phenomenology of age and the existence of age-related norms in our society. The third body of work on age systems and the life course in modern societies has concentrated on patterns of role transitions. A number of issues have been pursued with regard to such turning points. Some researchers have concentrated on the timing, duration, spacing, and sequencing of transitions. Some have explored the interrelationships of transitions in different institutional spheres, whereas others have examined long-term consequences of particular transition patterns. Finally, there has been some work on the social psychology of transitions, the personal significance of life course changes and their associated decisions. Across all of these issues, a number of efforts have been made to contrast patterns of men and women. The issues listed have also been pursued with a variety of research approaches, using several units and levels of analyses.

Our discussion will fall in four sections. First, we review recent work that has focused on intercohort variations in transition patterns. Most of this research has concentrated on the timing and sequencing of role changes. Second, we turn to studies of intracohort patterns of transitions. A main theme in this work is the interrelations of transitions, across institutional spheres and across phases of individual life time. Third, we present work on life course patterns of men and women. Fourth, we discuss how transitions are interrelated across individual lives.

Intercohort Comparisons

Possible changes in transition patterns across historical time have been explored through comparisons of different birth cohorts. Such work has addressed four aspects of role transitions: timing, duration, spacing, and order

(Elder, 1978b). Timing refers to when in the life course a given transition occurs. Duration is typically conceptualized as the amount of time it takes a cohort to complete a transition. Modell et al. (1976, 1978) refer to the latter as "spread." Spacing is the length of time occurring between two or more transitions, as, for example, the time between entry into the work force and marriage. Order refers to the sequencing of role changes. So far, the aspect that has received the most attention in intercohort comparisons is timing.

A significant development in the study of the life course has been the interest shown by family historians, exemplified in two recent collections of papers, one edited by Demos and Boocock (1978), the other by Hareven (1978). In both books, transitions are discussed from an historical perspective. Other scholars have also addressed historical changes in life patterns (e.g., Cherlin, 1981; Glick, 1977; Hogan, 1981; Uhlenberg, 1974, 1978), usually by examining aggregate cohort patterns of role transitions in different periods of recent history.

As might have been anticipated, there are demonstrable historical differences. For example, Glick and his colleagues (e.g., Glick, 1977) have focused on family transitions and compared median ages for the timing of role changes such as first marriage, birth of first child, birth of last child, and widowhood. They have described a changed rhythm of these events over successive decades, with a quickening of family transitions in young adulthood and a slowing in late adulthood. Other investigators have focused on the duration of transitions, studying the number of years it takes quartiles or deciles of given birth cohorts to complete them. This is the approach taken by Hogan (1981), Modell et al. (1976, 1978), and Winsborough (1978, 1979) in studying transitions in early adulthood. All these researchers conclude that young adult transitions have become more compressed; that is, members of recent cohorts make a set of transitions in a shorter span of years than was the case in earlier periods of American history. Winsborough

(1980) uses a similar approach in studying a later-life transition, that which occurs with the death of parents. He shows that not only does the transition now occur later in life than in earlier periods of history, it has also become more predictable insofar as it is encountered by members of a cohort over a shorter number of years. Cherlin (1981) examines the timing of first marriage for cohorts in the nineteenth and twentieth centuries. By contrasting cohort quartiles, he demonstrates that the age of those who marry early has remained remarkably stable, and that for nearly a century, the first 25 percent of birth cohorts have married by age 19. Recently, the overall age at marriage has increased mostly because members of the third quartile of successive cohorts have married later.

Several authors have described combinations of transitions. Uhlenberg (1980) delineated a set of transition patterns and then asked what percentage of different birth cohorts followed each pattern. For example, he examined the proportion of women in different cohorts who followed a "normal" life course pattern of marriage and parenthood and found that the proportion rose dramatically when he compared cohorts of women born from 1870 to 1930 (Uhlenberg, 1974, 1978). An interesting variant of such an approach has been used in the Norwegian Occupational History Study. Ramsöy (1978) suggests that one can conceptualize patterns of role investments across the life course as time use profiles, which can then be compared across cohorts. (See also Skrede, 1982; Uhlenberg, 1983.) Abeles et al. (1980) analyzed data from the large-scale longitudinal study called Project TALENT by using an elaborate path model to show the variety of career patterns now being followed by late adolescents and young adults. Hogan (1981) studied the sequencing of role changes by focusing on three major transitions for young men: finishing school, starting work, and marrying. Treating the order just mentioned as "the presumed normative order," and comparing cohorts born early in this century to those born after 1930, he found a decrease in the proportion of men who followed that order.

Several authors have suggested that the next few decades will be characterized by less clear patterns of sequencing, both within and across institutional spheres. Sarason (1977), among others, argues that we are moving away from what he calls "the one life/one career imperative" in the domain of work, and suggests that a growing number of individuals will have not one orderly, linear career but multiple and sequential careers. Hirschorn (1977) argues that we are moving away from a "lock-step" pattern of education first, work second. He suggests that in postindustrial society, school and work will be interspersed, with greater demands for flexibility stemming in part from the changing careers in a third sphere, the family. Best (1980) makes a similar point and suggests that retirement will also change as a result of more flexible life schedules.

A few investigators have also studied duration and spacing together. In Hogan's (1981) study it was found that the early adult transitions for men are made in shorter periods of time than in previous eras. A dramatic difference appears between men born in 1907 and those born in 1947. In the former group, the transitions took 17.8 years, but in the most recent cohort, they took only 7.8 years. Hogan, like Chudacoff (1980), Modell et al. (1976, 1978), and Winsborough (1978, 1979), concludes that the first part of adulthood appears to be more clearly age-graded now than was the case in the nineteenth century.

With regard to late life, several authors have suggested that lives are socially unstructured in old age and that there are few social expectations of how older people should invest time and energy (e.g., Blau, 1973; Rosow, 1976; Treas and Bengtson, 1982). This may be one reason why there have been few studies of late-life transitions. Another reason may be that only recently have large numbers of cohort members survived to old age. Some transitions in the second half of life have become more predictable, as shown in Winsborough's (1980) study of the role change that accompanies death of parents, but to our knowledge, no investigator has examined, either in a single cohort or in successive cohorts, the sequencing or spacing of late-life transitions. For instance, how common is it for grandparenthood to precede retirement, and how many people experience the two transitions within a five-year period? In a recent volume on retirement, Szinovacz (1982a) points to how the empirical and theoretical separation of retirement and widowhood in past research has severly limited our understanding of either phenomenon.

In general, the major problem with most intercohort comparisons (and it is a very major problem) is that life sequences themselves have seldom been the object of study. Investigators have focused on birth cohorts and on central tendencies, and we do not know how many of the individuals who were at the median age on one transition are among those at the median age on the next. Notable exceptions are the studies mentioned here by Abeles et al. (1980) and Hogan (1981), where the data were organized by accumulating individual patterns of transitions.

The metaphor of a life course as a pathway means a linking of successive roadmarkers as the traveler progresses. However, pathways cannot be charted from most intercohort studies; and in this sense, much of the research that has been labeled life course analysis does not analyze lives. Rather, it presents the statistical histories of birth cohorts (Winsborough, 1978). At best, such work allows for what Modell et al. (1978) call "contrived life course analysis."

Most of the studies of intercohort differences have concentrated on the description of transition patterns, but not on ways of explaining those patterns. We recognize that the collective biography of a birth cohort is shaped by the societal context—historical events, economic conditions, cultural change, and the size and other characteristics of cohorts themselves (Easterlin, 1980; Waring, 1975). Yet few researchers have attempted to identify which of these factors are most influential. Cohort is an "empty" variable (e.g., Rosow, 1978). To put meaning behind the term cohort is a large research enterprise that requires understanding of history and the mechanisms by which historical events are translated into changes in life patterns. Several authors have argued that in order to build such understanding, we need to consider the interaction of intercohort and intracohort factors (Elder, 1978b, 1984; Hogan, 1981; Moen et al., 1982; Rosow, 1978; Schaie, 1982). The next section examines work that has focused on patterns within birth cohorts.

Studies of Intracohort Patterns

Intracohort Variation. In attempting to account for either intra- or intercohort differences, there are two major issues: First, what are the social forces that shape life patterns? Second, because factors that operate at intermediate social levels buffer, transform, or reinforce effects of the wider societal context, at what levels of social groupings are the effects best observed?

The work by Elder (1978b, 1981) has repeatedly pointed to the interplay of historical change, individual phases of development, gender, and family context. His study of *Children of the Great Depression* (1974) shows that the depression did not affect all subgroups of a given cohort equally. Only in those individuals whose families experienced marked deprivation (i.e., a drop in income of one-third or more) were long-term life course effects observable. Furthermore, the long-term consequences were different for families who were originally at different social class levels; and family interaction patterns themselves served as a lens that sometimes magnified, sometimes reduced the effects on the life course of the individual.

Because of its large sample size, Hogan's (1981) study of men's transition patterns allowed the examination of variability within cohorts. He considered three intracohort factors: ethnic background, social class, and contrasts between urban and rural commu-

nities, and found, for instance, that in patterns of transition timing and ordering, to live in a rural area operated in much the same way as being black or Hispanic. He demonstrated also that intercohort changes in timing and sequencing can be accounted for by intracohort factors such as the proportion of individuals from poorer SES backgrounds who are able to seek a college education. Recently, a number of scholars have pointed to the importance of focusing on intermediate levels of social context if we want to understand the social structuring of lives (Hogan, 1982a,b; Kohli, 1982; Kohli et al., 1983). In particular, some recent work points to the importance of work settings (Kohli et al., 1983; Rosenbaum, 1980; Schrank and Waring, 1983). These authors argue that not only do work settings reflect a societal system of age stratification (Schrank and Waring, 1983), they may also create their own, individual systems. Kohli et al. (1983) suggest that "we have to move to the level of the enterprise, and to examine its strategies of organizing the life course of its workers." Rosenbaum's (1980) work has taken such an approach. He argues that the extent to which workers will experience a midlife period of reassessment may depend on the system of promotion used in work organizations. Drawing a parallel between promotion systems and "tracking" in high schools (Rosenbaum, 1979), he discusses how the rigidity of such systems limits life course flexibility, especially for women. Schrank and Waring (1983) also point to the fact that age structures within firms often operate differently for men and women. For example, it is not uncommon to find women of a wide range of ages in entry-level positions. A number of authors have recently discussed how women's patterns of "disorderly careers" and late career entry make the retirement transition different from common patterns found among men (e.g., Atchley, 1982; O'Rand and Henretta, 1982; Szinovacz, 1982b). The recent volume edited by Szinovacz contains several papers concluding that women are less likely than men to have formal retirement planning programs available in their work settings. Such retirement planning has been found to be related to subsequent retirement adjustment.

It is clear that much additional work is needed on how various social contexts structure adult transitions. Rosenbaum (1980) warns that relying on survey research that asks people's *perceptions* of context will not do, but that social scientists need to do direct observation of social settings, such as the workplace. Both he and Kohli et al. (1983) are indeed suggesting that we need to do some anthropological field work on the age structure in settings of everyday life. The latter authors make the bridge to an anthropological approach more explicit, by reminding the reader that there is an intimate connection between the structure of economic activity and the social construction of personal "life worlds."

Interrelations among Transitions. In studying the interrelations among transitions, some investigators have taken a synchronic perspective. Bertaux and Bertaux-Wiame (1981), in their study of French bakers, provide an interesting example. Traditionally, it was impossible for a man to succeed in a small bakery shop without the help of a wife. Some of the bakers, when asked about their work histories, equated getting married with starting a business, and had trouble separating the two transitions in their own minds.

A few studies present a picture of what might be called "transition domino effects." A good example is how adolescent parenthood often leads to early marriage and early exit from school, with the result that all three transitions occur off-time. Card and Wise (1978) compared persons who became parents in their adolescence with those who became parents after age 24, controlling for such factors as academic ability and family background, and found that the early parents were much less likely ever to attain a college education. In a diachronic view of interrelated transitions, some research has examined how early transitions affect subsequent life changes.

In their longitudinal study, Howell and Freeze (1982) examined three transitions in adolescents and young adults: parenthood, marriage, and exit from school. With a sample size that permitted comparisons between blacks and whites, and between men and women, these investigators found the highest degree of association among the three transitions among white women; the lowest, among black men. They conclude, as have others (e.g., Hofferth and Moore, 1979; Waite and Moore, 1978), that there are greater pressures against being off-time and against disorderly sequenced transitions among whites than among blacks. They point also to the importance of gender. Young white women who were early parents had a 90 percent chance of also being school dropouts. The corresponding figure for young black men was 20 percent.

Some investigators have examined long-term consequences of transition timing. Studies of age at marriage have shown it to be positively related to marital stability (Elder et al., 1979; Otto, 1979); and age at marriage predicts socioeconomic attainment later in life (Hogan, 1981). In examining the consequences of deviations from the normal sequence of school exit, work, and marriage, Hogan also found that the men who did not follow that order were more likely to have their marriages terminated by divorce.

If attention is shifted from the family sphere to the work sphere, few researchers have asked about the long-term consequences of early work transitions, as, for instance, the relationship between the timing of work entry and the timing of retirement, or how a period of being unemployed affects subsequent work transitions, or the effects of the interrupted or "disorderly" work careers described by Wilensky (1961, 1981) on the timing of retirement.

The effects of interrupted work careers on subsequent family transitions have also been neglected, although Goodwin's (1972) longitudinal study of unemployed men suggests that prolonged joblessness increases the chance of marital disruption. Reciprocally, we have little information regarding how disrupted marital careers affect work histories, with the exception that there are data showing that divorce rates are positively related to work force participation by women (Johnson, 1980; Moen, 1985).

Other Social Psychological Perspectives. Within a synchronic approach, investigators have asked about the association between timing of transitions and, say, the sense of competence in a given life period. For instance, the consequences of the "compression" of transitions in early adulthood may produce a sense of overload. Pearlin and co-workers (Pearlin, 1982; Pearlin and Lieberman, 1979), using data from a longitudinal study of transitions, concluded that because of the cumulative pressures of multiple transitions and uncertainties, young adults are more vulnerable to psychological stress then are older adults. In the Michigan studies of how Americans view their well-being and mental health (Veroff et al., 1981), similar findings were reported. Riley et al. (1972) discussed the erratic work performance of young workers, suggesting that it may reflect role overload because of the simultaneous transitions young workers are experiencing in other spheres of their lives.

Several authors have suggested that military service has provided men with a social mechanism for taking "time out," and for entering adulthood gradually (Hogan, 1981; Sharp and Krasenor, 1968). Others have examined the possible benefits of being late in one transition and of thereby reducing overall role strains. For example, Nydegger (1973) showed that men who were late fathers were more comfortable in the parental role than either early or on-time fathers, indicating that men were more effective fathers if parenthood did not coincide with the demands of early career building in the work area. A study of first-time mothers (Daniels and Weingarten, 1982), however, found that women in their early twenties had an easier time adjusting to parenthood than women in their late twenties. Rossi (1980a), in her studies of midlife women, found that the older a woman had been at the birth of her first child, the more difficult childrearing was

all through the child's adolescence. In considering such findings, women's employment patterns (Presser, 1975), as well as their cohort membership, would seem important factors.

Another study of the possible consequences of timing is Lowe's (1964) study of U.S. Army officers, which showed systematic differences between men who were on-time and off-time in their army careers. The two groups differed not only with regard to evaluations of their careers, but also with regard to self-esteem, mobility aspirations, anticipated adjustment to retirement, perception of status in the civilian community, and degree of social integration in the community. Similar findings were reported in Sofer's (1970) study of British managers.

Few if any such studies of the personal meaning of the timing or sequencing of transitions have been carried out for persons in the later half of life under the rubric of life course analysis. It is particularly noteworthy that students of the life course have given little attention to individual decision-making with regard to the timing of transitions. A few historians, as will be mentioned below, have discussed this general question in the context of waning family influences on the timing of the individual's transitions, but we have no systematic studies of how persons explain their own timing patterns or the significance they attach to them.

Sex Differences

As Fiske and her coworkers have demonstrated (1980; Lowenthal et al., 1975), it is imperative that studies of transition patterns and their consequences consider differences between men and women. Yet, recent research seldom allows for systematic comparisons between the sexes. Studies of the timing of family transitions (e.g., Glick, 1977; Spanier and Glick, 1980) have concentrated on women's patterns. Hogan's study (1981) dealt only with men's patterns.

Two themes have emerged, however, in discussions of men's and women's life paths. First is the relative salience of different institutional spheres and what Fiske (1980) calls "hierarchies of commitment." Specifically, it has been argued that the family is the main force shaping the course of women's adult lives, while work is the key influence on men's lives. Second is the question of how much regularity and continuity are found in life careers. It has been argued that women's lives are characterized by discontinuity and form no "orderly" patterns like those generally found in men's lives.

Van Dusen and Sheldon (1976), in an often-cited article, reviewed the changing roles of women in the spheres of education, family, and work. Their key argument was that if life course patterns of men and women are converging, this convergence is due to a decrease in the salience of family roles in shaping women's lives. Lopata and Norr (1980) refer to this phenomenon as the "decrystallization" of women's life patterns. Since the Van Dusen and Sheldon article appeared, a number of investigators have examined what Pleck (1977) calls "the work–family role system" (e.g., Gutek et al., 1981; Masnick and Bane, 1980; Moen et al., 1982; Moen, 1985; Waite, 1980; Young, 1978), and many of these investigators have come to a different conclusion: that family transitions still are more critical in shaping the life course patterns of women than of men. Despite such facts as the unprecedented rise in labor force participation among married mothers of young children (U. S. Department of Commerce, 1980), most authors still describe family roles as primary for women, and work roles as secondary. Moen (1982, 1983), for example, contends that a true "double track" pattern of parenthood and continuous employment outside the home is still the exception among young women. The same author warns that generalizations about women's career paths are typically based on cross-sectional rather than longitudinal studies, and that such data do not capture women's patterns of entries and exits from the labor force over the course of their lives.

A number of authors have argued that men's work careers have more of a clockwork character than those of women. Dun-

can and Featherman (1982) have suggested that for men educational level predicts career attainment only in the early stages, but that in later stages previous work experience becomes the more important predictor. For women, however, education predicts attainment throughout because women's work patterns do not show the regular progression that is characteristic of men's. Sanguiliano (1978) claims that women lead serial lives, with little continuity, an argument also made by Kline (1975). In such a view, it is women's family orientation that provides whatever continuity there may be from early to late life (Hagestad and Marshall, 1980).

Many questions go unanswered about life course patterns of men and women because observers often proceed on assumptions rather than on empirical findings. For example, very little is known about the interaction of family roles and work careers in the lives of men (Bronfenbrenner and Crouter, 1982; Presser, 1975; Uhlenberg, 1983). Or, to take a different example, knowledge about women's retirement is limited because, as Beeson (1975) has said, it has been viewed as a non-event. Pampel (1981) has argued that in part, the lack of knowledge regarding women's retirement reflects the fact that until very recently, the role of retiree was not common among women. Szinovacz (1982a), in a volume on women's retirement, reports that until 1975 the annual meetings of the Gerontological Society had little or no discussion of female retirement. However, she finds that the last few years have had a growing number of papers comparing men's and women's exits from the work force. Most important is the changing nature of work for both sexes. Will there be greater similarities between men's and women's work careers because economic factors have made occupational careers less orderly and predictable (Moen, 1985)?

In seeking to understand the complex interactions of family and work transitions, the unit of analysis should be changed. Men and women have been studied as separate statistical aggregates rather than as dyads. To paraphrase Plath (1982), attention should be given to "the bumping and grinding of time-tables in interaction" for husbands and wives. Such interaction among lives has recently been discussed by numerous authors.

Interwoven Lives

A number of investigators have recently pointed to the importance of studying lives, not as monads or single entities but as co-biographies. For example, a collection of papers by scholars from different countries and different disciplinary backgrounds (Bertaux, 1981) calls for a co-biographical approach in pursuing various sociological and historical questions, as, for instance, analyzing the life "stories" of groups of interrelated individuals. Plath (1980), in considering smaller social units, uses Schütz's term *consociates,* "those around us whose lives run close and parallel to ours"; and he points out that the individual's opportunities and constraints hinge on the uncertain progress of others in their own life-stage tasks. Consociates are usually family members, but they can also be found in other long-term relationships formed by friendship or work roles. For instance, work and family careers are often significantly shaped by life course choices of work superiors; many workers have had their lives dramatically altered when a department head decided to retire early or move.

A number of authors have suggested that, in studying how individual life time is patterned, we need to consider its embeddedness not only in historical time but also in family time (Aldous, 1978; Elder, 1978; Hareven, 1977; Hareven and Adams, 1982; Watkins, 1980). Hareven (1981) and Modell et al. (1976), among others, contend that the demarcations between family time and individual life time are clearer now than in earlier historical periods. They suggest that transitions used to be "a family affair," not a matter of individual choice. Hareven (1981) says that "the essential aspect of the timing of a transition was not the age at which a person left home, married, or became a parent, but rather how this transition was re-lated to those that other family members were undergoing" (p. 160).

Such arguments rest on the view that in the past, timing was a critical factor in controlling the ebb and flow of the family's economic resources; but that now, when adult family members are no longer bonded by economic necessity, transitions become more a matter of individual actions guided by general societal age norms (Treas and Bengtson, 1982). As the locus of control for individual transitions has shifted from family economic constraints to general normative constraints imposed by society, the result is clearer modalities in the timing of transitions across large groups of persons (Modell et al., 1976).

The arguments presented by these family historians raise a host of research issues: first, the need to examine further the past and present patterns of interdependence among the lives of family members; second, the need to study families as normative and symbolic units in their own right; third, the need to study the limitations of societal norms as the explanatory factors in the patterning of lives.

Interdependence among Family Members

World literature provides ample descriptions of how the lives of family consociates are interwoven; but social scientists studying the life course in modern societies have neglected this topic. Three kinds of individual life career interconnections, or what Klein et al. (1979) call developmental reciprocities, deserve attention: career contingencies, countertransitions, and shared life chances (Hagestad and Dixon, 1980).

As mentioned earlier in this chapter, anthropologists have reported on life transitions that are contingent on those of other family members. American society does not have formal norms regarding such interdependencies, but informal expectations have important influences, not only on the individual's transitions but on the meanings attached to the transitions of others. For example, parents build life course expectations regarding their children. Recent studies of the transition to "the empty nest" suggest that it is when children do not leave home on time (and thus do not "turn out right") that parents are left with a sense of strain and personal failure (Harkins, 1978; Nydegger and Mitteness, 1979; Wilen, 1979). Or, another example, most adults anticipate rhythms of generational turnover, expecting to spend some time in a middle generation between aged parents and young adult offspring. If death of parents comes too early, it upsets such expectations (Marshall and Rosenthal, 1982).

The family is also an arena for what Riley and Waring (1976) called counterpoint transitions, or, to shorten the term, countertransitions. Marriage by one member creates the in-law role for other members. Parenthood creates grandparenthood and great-grandparenthood. Family "ripple effects" are also evident. The timing of parenthood in the two preceding generations influences the probability that the third generation will grow up knowing their grandparents (Troll, 1971). When men marry women who are substantially younger than themselves, it will often result in off-time widowhood and children who grow up without a paternal grandfather.

Divorce and remarriage can be studied with regard to life course interdependencies. Long-term consequences of such transition events might also be studied cross-generationally. For example, as pointed out by Kulka and Weingarten (1979), little is known about the influence of parental divorce on adult children, although there are indications that adults whose parents were divorced have a somewhat increased probability of experiencing marital disruption themselves (Greenberg and Nay, 1982; Pope and Mueller, 1976). So far, most studies have concentrated on the psychological effects of marital break-up on young children, but in a few studies the interconnections between the lives of parents and older children have been explored. For example, Weiss (1975, 1979) found that adolescents whose parents were divorced showed accelerated independence and maturity. A study of divorce in middle age (Hagestad et al., 1984) suggested that a break-up of the parents' marriage may delay the adult child's transitions into adult roles. In a number of cases, middle-aged mothers relied on a young adult child for support, and a number of those young people moved back home to provide emotional and financial help. There have been no systematic studies of how children's divorce affects the life course of parents. How often does it happen, for instance, that the divorce of a daughter who has young children to support will influence her parents' decision to postpone their own retirement?

The family is still significant in shaping the life chances (i.e., the availability of material resources) of its adult members as well as of its young children. Oppenheimer (1974, 1981) speaks of "life cycle squeezes," times when family income is out of step with the needs of parents and children. This may occur not only when parents are young, but when parents are middle-aged and face increased expenditures for their children's education at the same time that they make financial plans for their own retirement. Along the same line, Oppenheimer (1981) and others have suggested that there has been a historical shift from adolescent children to wives as the family's "life course earnings stabilizers." Modell et al. (1976) remark that in 1880 Philadelphia, young men and women typically contributed to the family income for a period of seven years. Today, their educations and even their first years of marriage may be partly subsidized by their working mothers.

Families as Cultural Units. A second significant question concerns how families transmit or modify societal normative expectations in shaping the life course of their members. As mentioned, Elder's (1974) study of the effects of the depression has shown that families are units in which historical events are given interpersonal and personal meaning. Families are also the first social units in which individuals are exposed to age norms.

From a very early age, children are told how to act their age and are taught that activities, rights, and privileges are tied to age. In one view of family socialization, it is assumed that families are the transmitters and reinforcers of the norms of the wider society. In another view, family socialization is a process of negotiation through which shared expectations emerge (Bengtson and Black, 1973). The latter perspective allows for the existence of different norms in different families and for these differences to persist across generations. Despite the fact that parents are commonly seen as the transmitters of general societal norms, there have been few studies of age norms in the family context.

In the Howell and Freeze (1982) study of adolescent parenthood, the authors compared the adolescents' expectations regarding educational attainment with their mothers' expectations, and found that departure from school affected the mother's aspirations for the child more than the child's own aspirations. Howell and Freeze suggest that parents communicate the society's norms and the view that deviation from such norms has negative consequences. In this instance, parents conveyed the message that early parenthood and early school departure represent an irreversibly disrupted life course. In his study of more than 6000 high school students' plans regarding timing of early adult transitions, Hogan (1982b) also had data on parents' expectations. He found strong evidence for parental influence on their children's plans. His data also pointed to some marked contrasts by sex and race. Women's plans regarding transitions were more influenced by parents than were those of men. Furthermore, women were more likely than men to count on family help and encouragement in making the transitions. Contrasting black and white students, Hogan found a trend that has been reported in work on family patterns: a greater reliance on kin for help, such as housing and financial help, among blacks (Cantor, 1979; Jackson, 1981; Sussman, 1976). Much further work is needed to explore similarities in life

course patterns of parents and children, or among siblings (Hagestad, 1981). In large data sets, such as those produced by the Bureau of the Census, individuals or households are the typical units of analysis. Based on such data, we are told the age at first marriage or the proportion of a given cohort who never married or who married but remained childless; but we are not told how often these individuals had siblings or children who took the same life course route. Are there families who for generations are early or late in such role transitions as job entry, marriage, and parenthood? In his classic article on cohort analysis, Ryder (1965) cites an Arab proverb: "A man resembles his times more than his father." To what extent is this true in modern society, and how do cohort membership and family membership together shape life course patterns?

LIMITATIONS OF PAST WORK ON LIFE COURSE TRANSITIONS

The Issue of Norms

In much of the recent work on transition patterns, variability has been examined across and within birth cohorts. It is typically assumed that when uniformities and regularities are observed, they can be accounted for by societal age norms. As several authors have argued recently (e.g., Abeles et al., 1980; Marini, 1981), researchers have treated norms as givens. Indeed, we may have *reified* social norms. Such assumptions and practices need critical evaluation, with attention given to theoretical as well as empirical problems.

Norms are socially shared expectations that represent "shoulds" or "oughts" for behavior (Gibbs, 1965; Parsons, 1937). They act as what Davis and Blake (1964) called "the cutting edge of social control." Attached to such expectations are positive and negative sanctions. Udry (1982), like others before him, has identified two aspects of norms: consensus and sanctions. As described above, there have been scattered research efforts addressed to the first dimension, consensus, but to our knowledge, no investigator has explored the sanctions attached to the kinds of norms discussed in this chapter. For instance, what are the perceived benefits or rewards for conforming to social timetables; what happens to persons who are off-time or who have a disorderly sequence of transitions; what kinds of sanctions are perceived; who does the sanctioning? With regard to the three studies described above (Figure 1), in which there was increasing convergence with age between respondents' personal opinions and "other people's opinions," does this repeated finding mean that young people see older people as sanctioners, but that older people see their age-peers as sanctioners?

Social scientists make a distinction between statistical norms and sociocultural norms. In the sociology of age, age-related life changes are of interest only if they hold social significance and are assigned meaning through cultural symbols and norms. From such a perspective, the timing of events can be "nonnormative" or "anormative." The former represent a breach of social norms; the latter are not subject to normative regulation.

In much of the research on life course transitions, it has been overlooked that some life changes can be normative in the statistical sense but not in the sense that their timing is normatively controlled. An example would be widowhood. Transitions that show statistically normative patterns give rise to shared expectations with regard to when in the individual's life they are likely to occur, even though such expectations are not social "oughts" accompanied by sanctions. Such regularities allow for anticipatory socialization and group support from transition peers. At the same time, for investigators interested in the extent to which individuals at different ages experience culturally provided opportunities and constraints, it is important to separate normative from anormative transitions.

Researchers interested in uniformity and variability in the ways cohorts are channeled into social roles need to consider alternatives to normative explanations. If transition patterns show statistical regularity, it is not to be automatically inferred that the regularity was produced by cultural norms (Marini, 1981; Udry, 1982); if patterns show increasing variability over time, it is not to be inferred that the variability was produced by a "weakening" of the norms. For example, age at first marriage has increased for a significant proportion of the cohorts that reached adulthood in the last decade. Does this phenomenon reflect changing age norms, or is it produced by other factors, such as changes in opportunity structures? A recent paper by Modell (1980) explores such questions in considerable detail, through innovative use of past opinion polls, census data, and the popular press. A major part of his paper compares views on timing of marriage and the actual age at marriage in two decades, the 1930s and the 1940s. As is well known, the Depression Era led to delayed entry into marriage, while World War II brought a marked reduction in age at marriage. However, in comparing opinion polls on the ideal timing of marriage, Modell found few differences between views in the two decades. He concludes that "the data I present do not argue that norms generally explain observed changes in the ages at which individuals marry." Rather, he suggests that "values regarding marital timing are in part codifications of one's own and others' prior behavior" (Modell, 1980, p. 212). Modell suggests that *economic* change, rather than altered norms freed young adults in the 1940s and 1950s to enter marriage earlier.

The extent to which different ethnic and socioeconomic groups show subcultural differences in normative expectations regarding the life course is also a question that needs clarification. Some authors have suggested that greater similarity between parents and children in their patterns of adult transitions occurs when there is little or no intergenerational mobility. For instance, Ankarloo (1978) has noted that when parents and offspring have similar social status, they are more likely to marry at the same age than when the children are upwardly mobile. Do we account for such findings by assuming that parents and children of similar socio-economic status share normative timetables, or is it that material resources and life-long projected earnings are the critical factors, as emphasized by Oppenheimer (1981)? In his work on early adult transitions, Hogan (1981; 1982a,b) recognizes the tension between norms and available resources as alternative explanations for subgroup variations in the observed patterns. The same type of tension is evident in a recent exchange between two authors who discuss ethnic variations in patterns of aging (Holzberg, 1982a,b; Markides, 1982, 1983). The first author emphasizes ethnicity as shared culture; the latter links ethnic background with minority status and unequal access to "life chances."

Careful attention to the relative impact of cultural norms and social and economic resources would not only greatly enhance our understanding of how lives are socially structured; it would also focus on an area in which the study of lives could make a significant contribution to disciplines such as anthropology, social psychology, and sociology.

The Problem of Levels

As we stated in the beginning of the chapter, a life course approach examines the social structuring of individul life time and its interaction with historical time. What does such a research focus imply about the level at which we study life patterns? As should be clear from the above reviews of past work on transitions, researchers have chosen different levels and units of analysis. On a macrolevel, the dimension of historical time has been approached through intercohort comparisons. In such work, the dimension of individual time is not addressed directly because the unit of observation is the birth cohort. Changes in lives over historical time are inferred by comparing aggregate patterns of transitions in different cohorts. In a recent article on midlife transitions, O'Rand and Henretta (1982b) describe a life course approach as using the birth cohort, rather

than the individual, as the unit of analysis. A number of authors quite likely would take issue with such a view, arguing that if we truly want to study life paths, the unit of observation must be the individual. The problem is, of course, that in seeking to account for historical change, we seldom have data that allow us to trace individuals across transitions and then compare common life trajectories in different birth cohorts. Watkins (1980) is quite correct when she states that with the data and data analysis techniques currently at our disposal, we cannot really do the kind of life course analysis we ideally would like to do. Given this state of affairs, the critical factor is an awareness of limitations in different approaches. For many research questions, there is considerable value in comparing "life structures" as they emerge in the description and comparisons of "statistical histories of birth cohorts" (Winsborough, 1978) as long as we are careful not to translate such knowledge into statements about the structure of individual lives. The concepts of timing and sequencing can refer to individuals' transitions, or they can describe aggregate cohort patterns. On the other hand, transition "spread" or duration can only characterize cohort aggregates. Recent discussions of transition patterns have not always recognized such rather fundamental distinctions. Furthermore, in making inferences from empirical data, it is an easy fallacy to assume that a series of "cohort transition snapshots" provides us with pictures of individuals' life progress through key transition roadmarkers.

Among researchers who insist on the individual as the unit of observation in the study of the life course, views differ on the importance of subjective accounts of life paths. Back (1980), in the introduction to a collection of papers on the life course, states that we are faced with an apparent paradox. "The study of the life course is a search for systematic regularities in events of unique meaning" (Back, 1980, p. 2). The same volume includes a provocative essay by Olney (1980), who ponders "inside" and "outside" views of human lives: "What we see in ourselves is life; what we see in another is the course of a life; what we see in generalized others is the life course" (p. 36). He goes on to suggest that as we move from the first to the third view of lives, we also move from art to science, from autobiography to biography to sociology and psychology.

Because of the nature of much recent work on life course patterns, we may have overestimated the clarity of distinctions between "subjective" and "objective" views of human lives. As we discussed earlier in this chapter, anthropological work on the meanings of age made some important points about the nature of age-related transitions. It pointed to the intimate connection between the social and personal meanings of such turning points. Transitions that are socially created, socially recognized and shared, reflect the very cultural fabric in which they are embedded, its symbols, beliefs, and values. The personal meaning of life course transitions, therefore, is in its very nature also interpersonal and social. In developing a complex understanding of turning points in human lives, and how they change through history, we will benefit from truly interdisciplinary work, where biographers, students of life history, and social scientists join forces.

REFERENCES

Abeles, R. P., Steel, L., and Wise, L. L. 1980. Patterns and implications of life-course organization: Studies from Project TALENT. In P. Baltes and O. G. Brim (eds.), Life-Span Development and Behavior, Vol. 3, pp. 307–337. New York: Academic Press.

Aldous, J. 1978. Family Careers: Developmental Change in Families. New York: John Wiley.

Ankarloo, B. 1978. Marriage and family formation. In T. K. Hareven (ed.), Transitions: The Family and Life Course in Historical Perspective. New York: Academic Press.

Aries, P. 1962. Centuries of Childhood. New York: Alfred A. Knopf.

Atchley, R. C. 1975. The life course, age grading, and age-linked demands for decision making. In N. Datan and L. H. Ginsberg (eds.), Life-Span Developmental Psychology. New York: Academic Press.

Atchley, R. C. 1982. Retirement: Leaving the world of work. Annals of the Academy of Political and Social Science 464:120–131.

Back, K., and Bourque, L. B. 1970. Life graphs: Aging and cohort effect. Journal of Gerontology 25:249–255.

Back, K. W. 1980. (ed.), Life Course: Integrative Theories and Exemplary Populations. Boulder, Colo.: Westview Press.

Beeson, D. 1975. Women in studies of aging: A critique and suggestion. Social Problems 23:52–59.

Bell, I. P. 1970. The double standard. Trans-Action 8:75–80.

Bengtson, V. L. 1971. Inter-age differences in perception and the generation gap. The Gerontologist 11(4, Part 2):85–90.

Bengtson, V., and Black, O. 1973. Intergenerational relations: Continuities in socialization. In P. Baltes and W. Schaie (eds.), Life Span Developmental Psychology. New York: Academic Press.

Berger, P. L., and Luckman, T. 1967. The Social Construction of Reality: A Treatise in the Sociology of Knowledge. Garden City, N. Y.: Doubleday.

Bertaux, D. 1981 (ed.) Biography and Society: The Life History Approach in the Social Sciences. Beverly Hills, Calif.: Sage Publications.

Bertaux, D., and Bertaux-Wiame, I. 1981. Life stories in the bakers' trade. In D. Bertaux (ed.), Biography and Society: The Life History Approach in the Social Sciences. Beverly Hills, Calif.: Sage Publications.

Best, F. 1980. Flexible Scheduling: Breaking the Education–Work–Retirement Lockstep. New York: Praeger.

Blau, Z. S. 1961. Structural constraints on friendships in old age. American Sociological Review 26:429–439.

Blau, Z. S. 1973. Old Age in a Changing Society. New York: New Viewpoints.

Brim, O. G., Jr., and Ryff, C. D. 1980. On the properties of life events. In P. B. Baltes and O. G. Brim, Jr., (eds.), Life-Span Development and Behavior, Vol. 3. New York: Academic Press.

Bronfenbrenner, U. and Crouter A. C. 1982. Work and family through time and space. In S. Kammerman and D. Hayes (eds.), Families that Work: Children in a Changing World. Washington, D.C.: National Academy of Sciences.

Cain, L. D., Jr. 1964. Life course and social structure. In R. F. Faris (ed.), Handbook of Modern Sociology. Chicago: Rand McNally.

Cain, L. D., Jr. 1974. The growing importance of legal age in determining the status of the elderly. The Gerontologist 14(2):167–174.

Cain, L. D. 1976. Aging and the law. In R. H. Binstock and E. Shanas (eds.), Handbook of Aging and the Social Sciences, 1st ed., pp. 342–368. New York: Van Nostrand Reinhold Company.

Cameron, P. 1969. Age parameters of young adult, middle-aged, old, and aged. Journal of Gerontology 24:201–202.

Cameron, P. 1972. Stereotypes about generational fun and happiness versus self-appraised fun and happiness. The Gerontologist 12:120–123.

Cantor, M. 1979. The informal support system of New

York's inner city elderly: Is ethnicity a factor? *In* D. Gelfand and A. Kutzik, (eds.), *Ethnicity and Aging: Theory, Research, and Policy.* New York: Springer.

Card, J. J., and Wise, L. L. 1978. Teenage mothers and teenage fathers. The impact of early childbearing on the parents' personal and professional lives. *Family Planning Perspectives* 10:199–205.

Cherlin, A. 1981. *Marriage, Divorce, Remarriage.* Cambridge, Mass.: Harvard University Press.

Chudacoff, H. P. 1980. The life course of women: Age and age consciousness, 1865–1915. *Journal of Family History* 5:274–292.

Clausen, J. A. 1972. The life course of individuals. *In* M. W. Riley, M. Johnson, and A. Foner (eds.), *Aging and Society: A Sociology of Age Stratification,* Vol. 3. New York: Russell Sage Foundation.

Cottle, T. J. 1976. *Perceiving Time: A Psychological Investigation With Men and Women.* New York: Wiley-Interscience.

Cowgill, D. O., and Holmes, L. D. 1972. *Aging and Modernization.* New York: Appleton-Century-Crofts.

Daniels, P., and Weingarten, K. 1982. *Sooner or Later: The Timing of Parenthood in Adult Lives.* New York: Norton.

Danish, S. J., Smyer, M. A., and Nowak, C. A. 1980. Developmental intervention: Enhancing life-event processes. *In* P. B. Baltes and O. G. Brim, Jr. (eds.), *Life-Span Development and Behavior,* Vol. 3. New York: Academic Press.

Davis, K., and Blake, J. 1964. Norms, values, and sanctions. *In* R. E. L. Faris (ed.), *Handbook of Modern Sociology.* Chicago: Rand McNally.

Demos, J., and Boocock, S. 1978 (eds.), *Turning Points: Historical and Sociological Essays on the Family.* Chicago: University of Chicago Press.

Drevenstedt, J. 1976. Perceptions of onsets of young adulthood, middle age, and old age. *Journal of Gerontology* 31:53–57.

Duncan, N., and Featherman, D. L. 1982. Social mobility through marriage and careers: Achievement over the life course. *In* J. Spence (ed.), *Achievement and Achievement Motivation: Psychological and Sociological Perspectives.* San Francisco: Freeman.

Easterlin, R. A. 1980. *Birth and Fortune: The Impact of Numbers on Personal Welfare.* New York: Basic Books.

Eisenstadt. S. N. 1956. *From Generation to Generation: Age Groups and Social Structure.* New York: Free Press.

Elder, G. H., Jr. 1974. *Children of the Great Depression.* Chicago: University of Chicago Press.

Elder, G. H., Jr. 1975. Age differentiation and the life course. *In* A. Inkeles, J. Coleman, and N. Smelser (eds.), *Annual Review of Sociology I.* Palo Alto: Annual Reviews.

Elder, G. H., Jr. 1978a. Family history and the life course. *In* T. K. Hareven (ed.), *Transitions: The Family and the Life Course in Historical Perspective.* New York: Academic Press.

Elder, G. H., Jr. 1978b. Approaches to social change and the family. *In* J. Demos and S. S. Boocock (eds.) *Transitions. American Journal of Sociology* Supplement.

Elder, G. H., Jr. 1981. History and the life course. *In* D. Bertaux (ed.), *Biography and Society: The Life History Approach to the Social Sciences.* Beverly Hills, Calif.: Sage Publications.

Elder, G. H., Jr. 1984. Family and kinship in sociological perspective. *In,* R. Parke (ed.), *Review of Child Development Research,* Vol. 7; *The Family.* Chicago: University of Chicago Press.

Elder, G. H., Jr., Rockwell, R. C., and Ross, D. J. 1979. Psychological patterns in marital timing and divorce. *Social Psychology Quarterly* 42(4):399–404.

Fallo-Mitchell, L., and Ryff, C. D. 1982. Preferred timing of female life events: Cohort differences. *Research on Aging* 4:249–267.

Filipp, S. H. (ed.) 1981. *Kritische Lebensereignisse.* Munich: Urban & Schwarzenberg.

Finley, G. E. 1982. Modernization and aging. *In* T. M. Field, A. Huston, H. C. Quay, L. Troll, and G. E. Finley (eds.), *Review of Human Development.* New York: John Wiley.

Fiske, M. 1980. Changing hierarchies of commitment in adulthood. *In* N. J. Smelser and E. H. Erikson (eds.), *Themes of Work and Love in Adulthood.* Cambridge, Mass.: Harvard University Press.

Foner, A., and Kertzer, J. 1978. Transitions over the life course: Lessons from age-set societies. *American Journal of Sociology* 83:1081–1104.

Frenkel-Brunswik, E. 1963. Adjustments and reorientation in the course of the life span. *In* R. G. Kuhlen and G. G. Thompson (eds.) *Psychological Studies of Human Development.* New York: Appleton-Century-Crofts.

Fry, C. L. 1976. The ages of adulthood: A question of numbers. *Journal of Gerontology* 31:170–177.

Fry, C. L. 1980a. Cultural dimensions of age: A multidimensional scaling analysis. *In* C. L. Fry (ed.), *Aging in Culture and Society: Comparative Viewpoints and Strategies.* New York: Praeger.

Fry, C. L. 1980b. Toward an anthropology of aging. *In* C. L. Fry (ed.), *Aging in Culture and Society: Comparative Viewpoints and Strategies.* New York: Praeger.

Fry, C. L., and Keith, J. 1982. The life course as a cultural unit. *In* M. W. Riley, R. P. Abeles, and M. S. Teitelbaum (eds.), *Aging From Birth to Death,* Vol. 2, *Sociotemporal Perspectives.* Boulder, Colo.: Westview Press.

George, L. K. 1982. Models of transitions in middle and later life. *Annals of the Academy of Political and Social Science* 464:22–37.

Gibbs, J. P. 1965. Norms: The problem of definition and classification. *American Journal of Sociology* 70:586–594.

Glick, P. C. 1977. Updating the family life cycle. *Journal of Marriage and the Family* 39:5–13.

Goodwin, L. 1972. *Do the poor want to work?* Washington, D.C.: Brookings Institute.

Greenberg, E. F., and Nay, W. R. 1982. The intergenerational transmission of marital instability reconsidered. *Journal of Marriage and the Family* 44(2):335–347.

Gulliver, P. H. 1968. Age differentiation. *International Encyclopedia of the Social Sciences* 1:157–161.

Gutek, B., Nakamura, C., and Nieva, V. 1981. The interdependence of work and family roles. *Journal of Occupational Behavior* 2:1–16.

Hagestad, G. O. 1981. Problems and promises in the social psychology of intergenerational relations. *In* R. W. Fogel, E. Hatfield, S. B. Kiesler, and E. Shanas (eds.), *Aging: Stability and Change in the Family.* New York: Academic Press.

Hagestad, G. O. 1982. Life-phase analysis. *In* D. J. Mangen and W. Peterson (eds.), *Clinical and Social Psychology,* Vol.1, *Research Instruments in Social Gerontology.* Minneapolis, Minn.: University of Minnesota Press.

Hagestad, G., and Dixon, R. 1980. Lineages as units of analysis: New avenues for the study of individual and family careers. Paper presented at the NCFR Theory Construction and Research Methodology Workshop, Portland, Oreg.

Hagestad, G. O., and Marshall, V. W. 1980. Discontinuity versus flexibility: The need for a social psychological approach to men's and women's adult roles. Paper prepared for the Annual Meeting of the Gerontological Society, San Diego, Calif. Nov.

Hagestad, G. O., Smyer, M. A., and Stierman, K. L. 1984. The impact of divorce in middle age. *In* R. S. Cohen, B. J. Cohler and S. H. Weissman (eds.) *Parenthood: A Psychodynamic Perspective.* New York: Guilford Press.

Hareven, T. K. 1977. Family time and historical time. *Daedalus* 106:57–70.

Hareven, T. K. (ed.). 1978. *Transitions: The Family and the Life Course in Historical Perspective.* New York: Academic Press.

Hareven, T. K. 1981. Historical changes in the timing of family transitions: Their impact on generational relations. Ch. 7 in R. W. Fogel, E. Hatfield, S. B. Kiesler, and E. Shanas (eds.), *Aging: Stability and Change in the Family.* New York: Academic Press.

Hareven, T. K., and Adams, K. J. (eds.). 1982. *Aging and Life Course Transitions: An Interdisciplinary Perspective.* New York: Guilford Press.

Harkins, E. B. 1978. Effects of empty nest transition on self-report of psychological and physical well-being. *Journal of Marriage and the Family* (Aug.):549–556.

Hirschhorn, L. 1977. Social policy and the life cycle: A developmental perspective. *Social Service Review* 51:434–450.

Hofferth, S. L., and Moore, K. A. 1979. Early childbearing and later economic well-being. *American Sociological Review* 44 (Oct.):784–815.

Hogan, D. P. 1981. *Transitions and Social Change: The Early Lives of American Men.* New York: Academic Press.

Hogan, D. P. 1982a. Adolescent expectations about the sequencing of early life transitions. Unpublished manuscript, University of Chicago.

Hogan, D. P. 1982b. Parental influences on the timing of early life transitions. Unpublished manuscript, University of Chicago.

Holzberg, C. S. 1982a. Ethnicity and aging: Anthropological perspectives on more than just the minority elderly. *The Gerontologist* 22:249–257.

Holzberg, C. S. 1982b. Ethnicity and aging: Rejoinder to a comment by Kyriakos S. Markides. *The Gerontologist* 22:471–472.

Howell, F., and Freeze, W. 1982. Adult role transition, parental influence, and status aspirations early in the life course. *Journal of Marriage and the Family* 44:35–49.

Hultsch, D., and Plemons, J. 1979. Life events and lifespan development. *In* P. B. Baltes and O. G. Brim (eds.), *Life-Span Development and Behavior,* Vol. 2. New York: Academic Press.

Jackson, J. 1981. Urban black Americans. *In* A. Harwood (ed.), *Ethnicity and Medical Care.* Cambridge, Mass.: Harvard University Press.

Johnson, B. 1980. Marital and family characteristics of the labor force, March, 1979. *Monthly Labor Review* (Apr.):48–52.

Klein, D. M., Jorgensen, S. R., and Miller, B. 1979. Research methods and developmental reciprocity in families. *In* R. M. Lerner and G. B. Spanier (eds.), *Child Influences on Marital and Family Interaction: A Life-Span Perspective.* New York: Academic Press.

Kline, C. 1975. The socialization of women. *The Gerontologist* 15:485–492.

Kogan, N. 1979. A study of age categorization. *Journal of Gerontology* 34(3):358–367.

Kohli, M. (ed.). 1978. *Soziologie des Lebenslaufs.* Darmstadt: Hermann Luchterhand Verlag BmbH & Co.

Kohli, M. 1982. Social organization and subjective construction of the life-course. Paper presented at for the International Conference on Life-Course Research on Human Development, Berlin, Sept. 16–21.

Kohli, M., Rosenow, J., and Wolf, J. 1983. The social construction of aging through work: Economic structure and life-world. *Aging and Society* 3(1, Mar.):23–42.

Kulka, R. A., and Weingarten, H. 1979. The long-term effects of parental divorce in childhood on adult adjustment. *Journal of Social Issues* 35(4):50–78.

LaFontaine, J. S. 1978. *Sex and Age as Principles of Social Differentiation.* London: Academic Press, Inc.

Laurence, M. W. 1964. Sex differences in the perception of men and women at four different ages. *Journal of Gerontology* 19:343–348.

LeVine, R. A. 1978a Adulthood and aging in cross-cultural perspective. Social Science Research Council: *Items* 31–32, 4:1–5.

LeVine, R. A. 1978b. Comparative notes on the life

course. *In* T. Hareven (ed.), *Transitions: The Family and the Life Course in Historical Perspective.* New York: Academic Press.

Liljestrom, R. V. 1971. On vertical differentiation of sex roles: Age classes among the Nyakusa and patterns of interaction in Swedish children's books. *Acta Sociologica* 14:13–23.

Linton, R. A. 1942. Age and sex categories. *American Sociological Review* 7:589–603.

Lopata, H. Z., and Norr, K. F. 1980. Changing commitments of American women to work and family roles. *Social Security Bulletin* 43:3–13.

Lowe, J. 1964. A study of the psychological and social impact of age-expectations on an age-graded career—the army officer. Unpublished paper on file, Committee on Human Development, University of Chicago.

Lowenthal, M. F., Thurnher, M., Chiriboga, D., et al. 1975. *Four Stages of Life.* San Francisco: Jossey-Bass.

Lyman, S. M., and Scott, M. B. 1970. *A Sociology of the Absurd.* New York: Appleton-Century-Crofts.

Marini, M. M. 1981. Age and sequencing norms in the transition to adulthood. Paper presented at the annual meeting of the American Sociological Association, Toronto, Canada.

Markides, K. S. 1982. Ethnicity and aging: A comment. *The Gerontologist* 22:467–470.

Markides, K. S. 1983. Minority aging. *In* M. W. Riley, B. B. Hess, and K. Bond (eds.), *Aging in Society: Selected Review of Recent Research,* Hillsdale, N. J.: Lawrence Erlbaum Associates.

Marris, P. 1975. *Loss and Change.* New York: Doubleday.

Marshall, V. W., and Rosenthal, C. J. 1982. Parental death: A life course marker. *Generations,* Winter, 30–31.

Masnick, G., and Bane, M. J. 1980. Labor force participation of married women: A study of labor supply. *In* Bureau of Research (ed.), *Aspects of Labor Economics.* Princeton: Princeton University Press.

McTavish, D. G. 1982. Perceptions of old people. *In* D. J. Mangen and W. A. Peterson (eds.), *Clinical and Social Psychology,* Vol. 1, *Research Instruments in Social Gerontology.* Minneapolis: University of Minnesota Press.

Meyer, J. W. 1981. The institutionalization of the life course and its effects on the self. Paper prepared for the Oct. meetings of the SSRC-Committee on Life-Course Perspectives.

Modell, J. 1980. Normative aspects of American marriage timing since World War II. *Journal of Family History* 5:210–234.

Modell, J., Furstenberg, F. F., Jr., and Hershberg, T. 1976. Social change and transitions to adulthood in historical perspective. *Journal of Family History* 1:7–32.

Modell, J., Furstenberg, F. F., and Strong, D. 1978. The timing of marriage in the transition to adulthood: Continuity and change, 1860-1975. *In* J. De-

mos and S. S. Boocock (eds.), *Turning Points.* *American Journal of Sociology* Supplement, 84. 120–150.

Moen, P. 1985. Continuities and discontinuities in women's labor force activity. In G. H. Elder, Jr. (ed.), *Life Course Dynamics: Transitions and Trajectories 1968 to 1980s.* Ithaca, N.Y.: Cornell University Press.

Moen, P., Kain, E. L., and Elder, G. H., Jr. 1982. Economic conditions and family life: Contemporary and historical perspectives. *In* R. Nelson and Skidmore, F. (eds.), *American Families and the Economy.* Washington, D.C.: National Academic Press.

National Council on the Aging. 1975. *The Myth and Reality of Aging in America.* Washington, D.C.: National Council on the Aging.

Neugarten, B. L. 1969. Continuities and discontinuities of psychological issues into adult life. *Human Development,* 12:121–130.

Neugarten, B. L., and Hagestad, G. O. 1976. Age and the life course. *In* R. H. Binstock and E. Shanas (eds.), *Handbook of Aging and the Social Sciences,* 1st ed., pp. 35–55. New York: Van Nostrand Reinhold Company.

Neugarten, B. L., and Moore, J. W. 1968. The changing age status systems. *In* B. L. Neugarten (ed.), *Middle Age and Aging.* Chicago: University of Chicago Press.

Neugarten, B. L., and Peterson, W. A. 1957. A study of the American age grading system. *Proceedings* of the Fourth Congress of the International Association of Gerontology.

Neugarten, B. L., Moore, J. W., and Lowe, J. C. 1965. Age norms, age constraints, and adult socialization. *American Journal of Sociology* 70:710–717.

Nydegger, C. N. 1973. Late and early fathers. Paper presented at the Annual Meeting of the Gerontological Society, Miami Beach.

Nydegger, C. N., and Mitteness, L. 1979. Role development: The case of fatherhood. Paper presented at the Annual Meeting of the Gerontological Society, Washington, D.C.

Olney, J. 1980. Biography, autobiography and the life course. *In* K. W. Back (ed.), *Life Course: Integrative Theories and Exemplary Populations.* Boulder, Colo.: Westview Press.

Oppenheimer, V. K. 1974. The life cycle squeeze: The interaction of men's occupational and family life cycles. *Demography* 11:227–245.

Oppenheimer, V. K. 1981. The changing nature of the life-cycle squeezes: Implications for the socioeconomic position of the elderly. *In* R. W. Fogel, E. Hatfield, S. B. Kiesler, and E. Shanas (eds.), *Aging: Stability and Change in the Family.* New York: Academic Press.

O'Rand, A. M., and Henretta, J. C. 1982a. Delayed career entry, industrial pension structure and retirement in a cohort of unmarried women. *American Sociological Review* 47:365–373.

O'Rand, A. M., and Henretta, J. C. 1982b. Women at

middle age: Developmental transitions. *Annals of the Academy of Political and Social Science* 464:57–64.

Otto, L. 1979. Antecedents and consequences of marital timing. *In* W. R. Burr, R. Hill, R. I. Nye, and I. L. Reiss (eds.), *Contemporary Theories About the Family,* Vol. 1. New York: The Free Press.

Pampel, F. C. 1981. *Social Change and the Aged.* Lexington, Mass.: Lexington Books.

Parsons, T. 1937. *The Structure of Social Action.* New York: McGraw Hill Book Company.

Parsons, T. 1942. Age and sex in the social structure of the United States. *American Sociological Review* 7:604–616.

Passuth, P. M., and Maines, D. R. 1981. Transformations in age norms and age constraints: Evidence bearing on the age-irrelevancy hypothesis. World Congress on Gerontology, Hamburg, 1981.

Pearlin, L. I. 1982. Discontinuities in the study of aging. *In* T. K. Hareven and K. J. Adams (eds.), *Aging and Life Course Transitions: An Interdisciplinary Perspective.* New York: The Guilford Press.

Pearlin, L. I. and Lieberman, M. A. 1979. Social sources of emotional distress. In R. Simmons (Ed.), *Research in community and mental health,* pp. 217–248. Greenwich, Conn.: JAI Press.

Pincus, A., Wood, V., and Kondrat, R. 1974. Perceptions of age appropriate activities and roles. Paper presented to the 27th Annual Meeting of the Gerontological Society, Portland, Oreg., Nov. 5–9.

Plath, D. W. 1980. Contours of consocation: Lessons from a Japanese narrative. *In* P. B. Baltes and O. G. Brim, Jr. (eds.), *Life-Span Development and Behavior,* Vol. 3. New York: Academic Press.

Plath, D. W. 1982. Arcs, circles and spheres: Scheduling selfhood. Presented at Midwest Regional Seminar on Japan, Earlham College, Richmond, Ind., Apr.

Plath, D., and Ikeda, K. 1975. After coming of age: Adult awareness of age norms. *In* T. R. Williams (ed.), *Socialization and Communication in Primary Groups.* Mouton: The Hague.

Pleck, J. 1977. The work-family role system. *Social Problems* 24:417–427.

Pope, H., and Mueller, C. W. 1976. The intergenerational transmission of marital instability: Comparisons by race and sex. *Journal of Social Issues* 32(1):49–66.

Press, I., and McKool, M. 1972. Social structure and status of the aged: Toward some valid cross-cultural generalizations. *Aging and Human Development* 3:297–306.

Presser, H. B. 1975. Age differences between spouses: Trends, patterns and social implications. *American Behavioral Scientist* 19(2):190–205.

Prins, A. H. J. 1953. *East African Age-Class Systems.* Groningen, Djakarta: J. B. Wolters.

Ramsöy, N. R. 1978. Life histories as time use profiles: Experience from the Norwegian occupational history study. Working paper, INAS, Oslo.

Riley, M. W. (Ed.). 1979. *Aging from birth to death* (Vol. 1). Boulder, CO: Westview Press.

Riley, M. W., and Waring, J. 1976. Age and aging. *In* R. K. Merton and R. Nisbet (eds.), *Contemporary Social Problems,* 4th ed. New York: Harcourt, Brace and Jovanovich.

Riley, M. W., Johnson, M. E., and Foner, A. (eds.). 1972. *Aging and Society: A Sociology of Age Stratification,* Vol. 3. New York: Russell Sage Foundation.

Riley, M. W., Abeles, R. P., and Teitelbaum, M. S. (eds.), 1979. *Aging from Birth to Death,* Vol. II, *Sociotemporal Perspectives.* Boulder, Colo.: Westview Press.

Rosenbaum, J. E. 1979. Tournament mobility: Career patterns in a corporation. *Administrative Science Quarterly* (June):220–241.

Rosenbaum, J. E. 1980. Organizational careers and life-cycle stages. Paper presented at the Annual Meeting of the American Sociological Association, New York City, Aug. 30.

Rosencranz, A. A., and McNevin, T. E. 1969. A factor analysis of attitudes toward the aged. *The Gerontologist* 9:55–59

Rosow, I. 1976. Status and role change through the life span. *In* R. H. Binstock and E. Shanas (eds.), *Handbook of Aging and the Social Sciences,* 1st ed., pp. 457–482. New York: Van Nostrand Reinhold Company.

Rosow, I. 1978. What is a cohort and why? *Human Development* 21:65–75.

Rossi, A. S. 1980a. Aging and parenthood in the middle years. *In* P. B. Baltes and O. G. Brim, Jr. (eds.), *Life-Span Development and Behavior,* Vol. 3. New York: Academic Press.

Rossi, A. S. 1980b. Life-span theories and women's lives. *Signs. Journal of Women in Culture and Society* 6(1):4–32.

Roth, J. A. 1963. *Timetables.* Indianapolis: Bobbs-Merrill.

Ryder, N. 1965. The cohort as a concept in the study of social change. *American Sociological Review* 30:843–861.

Sanguiliano, I. 1978. *In Her Time.* New York: William Morrow and Company.

Sarason, S. B. 1977. *Work, Aging and Social Change.* New York: Free Press.

Schaie, K. W. 1982. Historical time and cohort effects. Paper presented at the West Virginia University Conference on Life-Span Developmental Psychology, Morgantown, W. Va.

Schrank, H. T., and Waring, J. M. 1983. Aging and work organizations. *In* M. W. Riley, B. B. Hess, and K. Bond (eds.), *Aging in Society: Selected Reviews of Recent Research,* Ch. 4. Hillsdale, N. J.: Lawrence Erlbaum Associates.

Schütz, A. 1932. *Der Sinnhafte Aufbau Der Sozialen Welt.* Wien.

Seltzer, M. M. 1975. Suggestions for the examination of time disordered relationships. In J. F. Gubrium (ed.), *Time, Role, and Self in Old Age.* New York: Behavioral Publications.

Shanas, E. 1962. *The Health of Older People: A Social Survey.* Cambridge, Mass.: Harvard University Press.

Sharp, L., and Krasenor, R. 1968. College students and military service: The experience of an earlier cohort. *Sociology of Education* 41:380–400.

Skrede, K. 1982. Fate, fortune or plans? The intersection of the productive and reproductive life cycle of women: Timing of events and adjustment to paid work in the early stages of child-rearing. Paper presented at the Tenth World Congress of Sociology, Mexico City, Mexico, Aug.

Sofer, C. 1970. *Men in Mid-Career.* New York: Cambridge University Press.

Sontag, S. 1972. The double standard of aging. *Saturday Review,* 23, 29–38 (Sept.).

Spanier, G. B., and Glick, P. C. 1980. The life cycle of American families: An expanded analysis. *Journal of Family History* (Spring):97–111.

Stewart, F. H. 1977. *Fundamentals of Age-Group Systems.* New York: Academic Press.

Strauss, A. L. 1959. *Mirrors and Masks: The Search for Identity.* New York: Free Press of Glencoe.

Streib, G. F., and Schneider, C. J. 1971. *Retirement in American Society: Impact and Process.* Ithaca, N. Y.: Cornell University Press.

Sussman, M. B. 1976. The family life of old people. *In* R. H. Binstock and E. Shanas (eds.), *Handbook of Aging and the Social Sciences,* 1st ed., pp. 218–243. New York: Van Nostrand Reinhold.

Szinovacz, M. 1982a. Introduction: Research on women's retirement. *In* Szinovacz, M. (ed.), *Women's Retirement.* Beverly Hills, Calif.: Sage Publications.

Szinovacz, M. (ed.) 1982b. *Women's Retirement.* Beverly Hills, Calif.: Sage Publications.

Treas, J., and Bengtson, V. L. 1982. The demography of mid- and late-life transitions. *Annals of the Academy of Political and Social Science* 464:11–21.

Troll, L. E. 1971. The family of later life: A decade review. *Journal of Marriage and the Family* 33:263–290.

Tuckman, J., and Lorge, I. 1953. Attitudes toward old people. *Journal of Social Psychology* 37:249–260.

Udry, J. R. 1982. The effect of normative pressures on fertility. *Population and Environment* 5:1–18.

Uhlenberg, P. 1974. Cohort variations in family life cycle experiences of United States females. *Journal of Marriage and the Family* 36:284–292.

Uhlenberg, P. 1978. Changing configurations of the life course. *In* T. K. Hareven (ed.), *Transitions: The Family and the Life Course in Historical Perspective,* pp. 65–97. New York: Academic Press.

Uhlenberg, P. 1980. Death and the family. *Journal of Family History* 5:313–320.

Uhlenberg, P. 1983. Men's lives and family change: 1960–1980. Unpublished manuscript.

U.S. Department of Commerce. 1980. *A Statistical Portrait of Women in the United States: 1978.* Washington, D.C.: U.S. Government Printing Office.

Van Dusen, R. A., and Sheldon, E. B. 1976. The changing status of American women: A life cycle perspective. *American Psychologist* 31(2):106–116.

Van Gennep, A. 1908. The *Rites of Passage.* 1908 Reprint. Chicago: University of Chicago Press. 1960.

Veroff, J., Douvan, E., and Kulka, R. 1981. *The Inner American: A Self-Portrait from 1957 to 1976.* New York: Basic Books.

Waite, L. J. 1980. Working wives and the family life cycle. *American Journal of Sociology* 86(2):272–294.

Waite, L. J., and Moore, K. A. 1978. The impact of an early first birth on young women's educational attainment. *Social Forces* 56(Mar.):845–865.

Waring, J. M. 1975. Social replenishment and social change: The problem of disordered cohort flow. *American Behavioral Scientist* 2:237–255.

Watkins, S. C. 1980. On measuring transitions and turning points. *Historical Methods* 13(3):181–186.

Weiss, R. S. 1975. *Marital Separation.* New York: Basic Books.

Weiss, R. S. 1979. *Going It Alone: The Family Life and Social Situation of the Single Parent.* Basic Books.

Whiting, J. W. M. 1981. Aging and becoming an elder: A cross-cultural comparison. *In* R. W. Fogel, E. Hatfield, S. B. Kiesler, and E. Shanas (eds.), *Aging: Stability and Change in the Family.* New York: Academic Press.

Wilen, J. B. 1979. Changing relationships among grandparents, parents, and their young adult children. Paper presented at the Annual Meeting of the Gerontological Society, Washington, D.C.

Wilensky, H. L. 1961. Orderly careers and social participation in the middle mass. *American Sociological Review* 24:836–845.

Wilensky, H. L. 1981. Family life cycle, work, and the quality of life: Reflections on the roots of happiness, despair, and indifference in modern society. *In* B. Gardell and G. Johansson (eds.), *Working Life.* New York: John Wiley and Sons.

Winsborough, H. H. 1978. Statistical histories of the life cycle of birth cohorts: The transition from schoolboy to adult male. *In* K. E. Taeuber, L. L. Bumpass, and J. A. Sweet (eds.), *Social Demography.* New York: Academic Press.

Winsborough. H. H. 1979. Changes in the transition to adulthood. *In* M. W. Riley (ed.), *Aging from Birth to Death: Interdisciplinary Perspectives.* Boulder, Colo.: Westview Press.

Winsborough, H. H. 1980. A demographic approach to the life cycle. *In* K. W. Back (ed.), *Life Course: Integrative Theories and Exemplary Populations.* Boulder, Colo.: Westview Press.

Wood, V. 1971. Age-appropriate behavior for older persons. *The Gerontologist* 11(4, Part 1):74–78.

Wood, V. 1973. Role allocation as a function of age. Paper presented to the 26th Annual Meeting of the Gerontological Society, Miami Beach, Nov.

Youmans, E. G. 1971. Generation and perceptions of old age: An urban–rural comparison. *The Gerontologist* 11(4, Part 1):284–288.

Young, F. W. 1965. *Initiation Ceremonies*. Indianapolis: Bobbs-Merrill.

Young, C. M. 1978. Work sequences of women during the family life cycle. *Journal of Marriage and the Family* 40(2):401–411.

Zepelin, H., Sills, R. A., and Heath, M. W. 1982. Age norms: The influence of age, sex, and occupational level. Paper presented to the Section on Behavioral and Social Sciences at the 35th Annual Meeting of the Gerontological Society of America, Boston, Nov.

Zerubavel, E. 1981. *Hidden Rhythms: Schedules and Calendars in Social Life*. Chicago: University of Chicago Press.

3
STATUS AND ROLE CHANGE THROUGH THE LIFE CYCLE

Irving Rosow*
University of California, San Francisco

You should live so long.
—Ancient Chinese valediction

After a meticulous review of the relevant literature, John Clausen recently concluded that we have no comprehensive theory of the adult life cycle. He wrote (1972, pp. 498, 412):

> If we have been able to discern certain links and certain patternings . . . in life course lines, they are by no means a basis for a general theory of the life course. . . . They remain largely unintegrated insofar as a general theory of the life course is concerned. Perhaps it is unrealistic to think of a theory of the life course. Perhaps we can only look forward to more limited theories relevant to aspects of the life course.

Clausen's implicit call for modest middle-range theories is sound. Its basis warrants a skeptical view of the prospect for any comprehensive theory of the life cycle in the near future. Clearly, any possible overall theory is complicated by at least two factors: (1) The empirical and normatively appropriate patterns at each life-stage are diverse. When these variations *within* life-stages are compounded into sets of permutations *across all*

life-stages, their variety and complexity are quickly exponentialized. They simply become too many patterns to handle. To be sure, these permutations are neither random nor completely independent, but have some correlation between stages. However, there is enough independence and slippage across stages for the number of patterns to become unmanageable, exceeding the capacity of any comprehensive theory to deal with them economically, if at all. (2) Also, social change itself compounds this problem insofar as it imposes on life-stage differences additional generational differences with selective effects. This cohort problem simply underscores the importance of efforts to distinguish developmental from social change effects (Rosow, 1978).

For similar reasons, it is hardly surprising that, despite some preliminary groundwork (Riley et al., 1972), we also have no viable theory or conceptual schema for status and role change through the life span.

But before a coherent theory of this process will even be possible, especially one that includes aging, the notions of status and role themselves must be clarified. For these concepts are fraught with ambiguities that are problematic enough to vitiate any comprehensive theory of role change through the life span. Insofar as age is a major status and age-grading involves roles, any discussion of

*I am indebted to my colleague, Dr. Corinne Nydegger, for her thoughtful, searching review of the draft of this chapter.

62

their change in the course of life is subject to the same ambiguities that obscure the basic concepts and require clarification. This is especially true whenever old age is involved (Rosow, 1974).

Therefore, in this chapter, I wish to address one underlying confusion that has plagued social scientists since the 1930s: *the assumption that status and role are invariably complementary.* For as I will propose, the relationship between the twin concepts is *not* constant, it probably varies along lines that I will indicate, and this variation is consequential. Accordingly, in this chapter, I want to: (1) trace the source of confusion about status and role; (2) clarify the ambiguity by *separating* the two concepts; (3) construct a set of role types based on their independence of one another; and (4) examine some changes in the life cycle in terms of this typology.

STATUS-ROLE CONFUSION

The concepts of status and role have recently been judged to accommodate much of sociology's substantive concern (Komarovsky, 1973). They are fundamental to social structure and to many of its processes. As primary social units, status and role become organizing concepts in the analysis of most norms, relationships, conformity and deviance, and stability and change. Accordingly, as basic elements of social intercourse, they are essential to the analysis of group and institutional functioning and to the formulation of diverse problems.

The two concepts are presently quite adequate for most workaday sociological discourse. Informally, they are treated as synonymous and interchangeable; typically the two terms are even alternated in professional writing to avoid the stylistic awkwardness of repetition. Occasionally they are even fused, as in "status-role." Colloquially, the terminology suffices for routine professional dialogue.

The basis for this usage lies in Linton's (1936) classic formulation that made them not simply complementary concepts, but opposite sides of a single coin that were irrevocably and indissolubly bound together. Status and role were treated as conceptual Siamese twins, one structural and the other functional. Their complementarity presumably made them inseparable. This is abundantly clear from Linton's definition and explication of the concepts (1936, pp. 113–114; italics of *complete sentences* inserted):

> The polar positions in such patterns of reciprocal behavior are technically known as *statuses*. The term *status,* like the term *culture,* has come to be used with a double significance. A *status,* in the abstract, is a position in a particular [interaction] pattern. It is thus quite correct to speak of each individual as having many statuses, since each individual participates in the expression of a number of patterns. However, unless the term is qualified in some way, *the status* of any individual means the sum total of all the statuses which he occupies. It represents his position with relation to the total society . . . .
>
> A status, as distinct from the individual who may occupy it, is simply a collection of rights and duties . . . .
>
> A *role* represents the dynamic aspect of a status. The individual is socially assigned to a status and occupies it with relation to other statuses. When he puts the rights and duties which constitute the status into effect, he is performing a role. *Role and status are quite inseparable, and the distinction between them is of only academic interest. There are no roles without statuses or statuses without roles.* Just as in the case of *status,* the term *role* is used with a double significance. Every individual has a series of roles deriving from the various patterns in which he participates and at the same time *a role,* general, which represents the sum total of these roles and determines what he does for his society and what he can expect from it.

Here, status is treated as a position in a social structure and role as the pattern of activity intrinsic to that position and expected of one who occupies it. The distinction is perfectly familiar, and this usage has certainly been standard since Linton's time.

Sociologists will readily see that Merton's later concept of *status set* assimilates Linton's notion of a person's many statuses; but Merton also appreciated that each specific status involves multiple relationships, and he formulated this in his concept of *role set* (Merton, 1957, pp. 368–370). His deceptively simple refinement opened up an array of complex new issues about differentiation within roles. In itself, this qualification of only the one rather than both concepts belies Linton's view that the distinction between status and role is always unimportant.

Linton's analysis was clear enough and a major advance when it appeared. But this is not to say that all difficulties suddenly vanished, for some other problems remained that subsequent efforts have still not resolved (Biddle and Thomas, 1966). Linton's formulation ultimately proved to be incomplete, leaving in its wake various undefined issues (viz., Merton's role set) and a residue of haziness. It predictably gave rise to the familiar problem of single terms with multiple referents and multiple terms for single referents, as well as a host of other difficulties (Biddle and Thomas, 1966, pp. 3–19). It blurred some vital distinctions that are necessary in certain analyses, notably noninstitutionalized roles and other significant phenomena. Accordingly, there has been an intermittent, but abiding confusion when the heart of a problem has been focused specifically on status and role or has involved *atypical* role activity. Where precision is needed, the terminology is wanting.

FOUR PROBLEMS

The most important ambiguities involve four major role issues, those of: (1) presence, (2) boundary criteria, (3) interaction, and (4) levels. We will consider them briefly.

1. The *presence* problem: *Is there a role?* Roles are not always delineated sharply enough to establish "when" there is a role, to identify its type, and to indicate clearly when behavior is actual role activity. Consequently, certain roles that are integral to group structure and process have not been related to role theory, but to personality or other factors. Noninstitutional and deviant roles have particularly suffered from such disregard.

2. The *boundary criteria* problem: *What is the role?* Given the fact that there is a role, we cannot always set its boundaries sharply enough to distinguish role from non-role behavior, particularly around the edges. We have not been able to judge clearly what is intrinsic and what is extrinsic to the role, what is specifically role activity and what is residual or idiosyncratic. The central elements have been less problematic. But beyond them, vagueness quickly sets in, and precision bleeds off at the boundaries. Merton's (1957, p. 133) treatment of the constraints on and options open to the actor provides some entree to the distinction between central and peripheral requirements. But subsequent work has not appreciably developed such leads. Neither the most ambitious role taxonomy yet devised (Biddle and Thomas, 1966, pp. 23–63) nor one of the leading role theorists (Sarbin and Allen, 1968; Sarbin, 1968) has made significant inroads on the criteria of setting boundaries.

3. The *interaction* problem: *Roles affect each other.* This might also be called the "permutations" issue. The total status set provides the context of its specific parts, and the norms of a given position are affected by those of a person's other statuses. Although some positions are rather segregated from others, few are hermetically sealed. So various roles spill over to modify the norms of other roles. In other words, there is an interaction effect within the status set that qualifies the norms for any particular position (cf. Rosow, 1974, pp. 42–50).

This interaction effect may be either of two kinds: (a) Sometimes it is a *simple* qualification of other roles. In that case, for example, the sexual norms for an adolescent daughter might differ if her father were a minister or a psychologist, an engineer or an artist, not to mention a devout Catholic or an atheist. (b) In other cases, the statuses in a set may be ordered in a *hierarchy* of importance so that some roles have more pervasive effects than others. Then the interaction effects are asymmetrical, with more central roles taking clear precedence and coloring others more strongly than they are affected in return. These effects may reflect sheer subcultural influences, as in the case of the proverbial middle-class Jewish mother in the United States. With *all* other things being equal, the norms of strong maternal nurturance, solicitude, and control over children are significantly greater for such a stereotypical Jewish mother than for a Protestant of comparable social class and position.

However, the basic point is that for any particular status set, the relation among its components may significantly modify the norms for any specific role. To illustrate again, the normative expectations for widowhood may differ drastically as variations occur in other factors, such as the actor's sex, race, social class, religion, family situation, and residence. Thus, the role of widowhood is quite different for a black Baptist cleaning woman living with her adult children in Tuscaloosa from that for a retired white Jewish businessman without any family who lives alone in Miami Beach. Thus, the interaction effects within status sets may diversify and obscure the norms for any particular role across a sample of respondents. While these norms may appear as a set of variations on a common theme, the situation is not always clear. The unequal weights of the different statuses in a series of role permutations may blur the specific norms in question. And if we consider the full range of contexts, the common elements of a role may even account for less behavior than the differences that arise from varying status sets. In other words, it remains unclear how the basic norms of a particular role are infused and qualified by the diversity of *other* roles across a series of cases.

This problem certainly confounds the study of age and sex positions. The reciprocal effects make it difficult to refine the pure age factor from a person's other statuses or to see clearly how age operates differently in various status sets. In the analysis of data, there is now no practical alternative to holding these other status patterns constant while trying to abstract the distinctive age factor cleanly (Rosow, 1974). The tremendous variation among status sets makes this extremely difficult. And at best, this is only an interim expedient that may blur precisely those interaction effects that might be the most crucial for age roles (cf. Clausen, 1972).

4. The *levels* problem: *overall status and role.* This is the most general form of the interaction problem, requiring the integration of Linton's specific and general levels. It goes beyond simple reciprocal influences between roles and poses the problem of how to translate an actor's entire status set or all his roles into a single, *general* social status or role. How does one systematically combine his many separate statuses into *one* abstract social status? How does one convert a person's many role complexes at a concrete level into *the* role at a comprehensive level? The criterion issue is formidable. This problem may press somewhat harder on anthropologists and analysts of small communities where status consistency and convergence may be fairly common, with the same people continually interacting in different status capacities. But the role segregation of larger, more complex societies, with separate groups of actors in interaction, does not clarify the conceptual difficulty. The specific and general levels reflect the pervasive problem of diverse status patterns and role combinations in a person's life.

Obviously this chapter cannot even begin to address all four of these problems. We will concentrate only on the first as the logical starting point. This analysis will mainly concern the presence problem, of "when" there is a role and its type. But it will not consider the last three: the boundary criteria problem (what is included in the role); the interaction problem (the reciprocal effects of various roles within status sets); and the levels problem (synthesizing a discrete status set into a general social status or an array of roles into an overall social role).

We must readily concede that as basic as they are, status and role may ultimately prove to be the kind of sensitizing concepts (such as "culture") that help to orient theory, but which in themselves are resistant to precise, rigorous application, free of any ambiguity. However, the limits on such precision cannot be established without efforts at clarification, even by chipping away at one problem at a time. Certainly the four problems mentioned here are not exhaustive, but they do indicate some basic dilemmas in determining what does or does not qualify as role behavior, whether in terms of age or other factors.

NONINSTITUTIONALIZED ROLES: THE EXCLUDED CASES

The deviant cases of noninstitutionalized roles are extremely awkward, if not embarrassing. As residual cases, they reflect Linton's lack of closure. What does one do with them? Where do they fit? In the course of actual analysis, they are usually handled in one of two ways. They are often arbitrarily excluded from consideration and effectively ignored. Or else they are consigned to some residual category, such as symbolic interaction or ethnomethodology, that typically lies outside the perspective of conventional structural analysis.

Both these alternatives are succinctly mooted in the Presidential Address at the 1973 annual meeting of the American Sociological Association. On that occasion, Mirra Komarovsky included in her introductory remarks several apposite caveats (1973; italics inserted):

> The substantive content of roles would appear to span much of the subject matter of sociology . . . [and] any theoretical propositions concerning the normative content of these roles would hardly be distinguishable from the general fields of political, economic, or family sociology. . . . [Accordingly,] I shall deal only with *institutionalized roles, linked to recognized social statuses.* Excluded, then, are many "regularities in interpersonal relationships" (Newcomb, 1966) or forms of interaction like the "family scapegoat," "the big wheel," or "the rebel," lacking the normative content of institutionalized roles (Popitz, 1972). Moreover, the emphasis will be primarily on social structural analysis rather than on symbolic interactionism of the descendants of Cooley and Mead.

It is quite legitimate, of course, to address only a selected set of problems. But in terms of role theory, where do such patterned social relationships of the family scapegoat, the big wheel, the rebel, or others actually fit in? It may be comforting to prejudge them all as lacking in social norms, but surely this is an empirical issue. It is arbitrary, if not cavalier, to dismiss by definition what must at least be regarded as a legitimate, open question. In view of competing reference groups, conflicting expectations, and various role options, it is rather foolhardy to foreclose the possibility of normative content in these atypical cases. For even much deviance, especially in marginal groups, is heavily normative.

The regrettable fact is that we still lack a frame of reference that can accommodate the atypical forms of status and role that arise in noninstitutionalized contexts. Many of these are relevant to role theory, though in terms that remain to be clarified. But aside from their more general significance, they are also germane to various age roles and norms (cf. Neugarten et al., 1965), particularly for the elderly who systematically lose major institutionalized roles simply with the passage of time.

THE CENTRAL PROBLEM

Clearly, Linton cannot be held responsible for all the ambiguities of role theory, for many difficulties were not appreciated before they gradually crystallized in later work. But the heart of our immediate problem is his treatment of status and role as inseparable twins. His most basic premise was that status and role must occur together and cannot vary independently: if there is a status, there must be some significant role; if there is a role, there must be some specifically related status position. If status, then role; if role, then status. This is the essence of their complementarity.

But this formulation is not exhaustive. That is, the coexistence of status and role is not the only form in which they occur. While their inseparability is integral to most institutionalized roles, this is not invariant, and, as we have seen, it does not apply to the difficult classes of deviant cases. For some statuses and roles do *not* neatly correspond; each does not have its "natural" complement in a binary pair, but *may appear by itself*. Significant discrepancies and anomalies recur with disquieting persistence, usually but not exclusively with nonmajor statuses. In these cases, status and role simply unravel and come unbound.* But the assumption of their necessary and invariant linkage, as in Siamese twins or binary stars, cannot accommodate such separation.

Yet the severing of this tie is necessary, and this chapter undertakes to examine its implications. The separation of status and role will cast role change through the life span into a fresh perspective.

Therefore, we want to treat status and role as independent, to formulate an inclusive typology of their variations, and then to relate these variations to the life cycle. If one is willing to abandon Linton's restrictive premise, a simple, exhaustive schema is readily available. Accordingly, we will waive Linton's proviso and assume instead that status and role may occur separately, regardless of the relative frequency of their different combinations. If we regard the concept as independent, all patterns can be distinguished and classified in an inclusive typology. This provides for not only the major institutionalized roles but also the deviant and noninstitutionalized.

ASSUMPTIONS

But before presenting the typology, we should make several assumptions clear, not as a token genuflection, but as a set of premises on which the analysis is based. Hopefully this will defer some premature secondary questions that would distract from

*In a similar vein, Alice Rossi (1968, especially pp. 36–39) criticized the careless assumption that the actual relationship of paired concepts, such as instrumental-expressive or authority-support, is necessarily as given. She showed that their occurrence and effects were empirical issues that could only be verified if the concepts were treated as independent factors rather than constrained by definition.

and vitiate the main point. In other words, we want to examine the forest, not the trees.

Now to our premises. First, in the matter of definitions, our use of the concepts is fairly conventional in Linton's terms. *Status* represents a formal office or social position that can be designated by name or a clear term of reference. This classifies and locates a person in a social structure and *may* denote "a collection of rights and duties" for that position—although this prospect is moot and at the very crux of our problem. *Role* consists of the expected behavior considered appropriate to *any* set of rights and duties. This involves the activity and interaction connected with a position *or* a set of relationships for which the person is held responsible or which he is accorded.

Second, we will speak of the "presence" or "absence" of status and role *in relative, not absolute terms*. Some normative expectations, as in many institutionalized roles, are reasonably explicit and commonly understood by the actor and his associates. But in other roles, including some of the noninstitutionalized, expectations are often limited, superficial, and vague. We shall regard a role as *developed* (+) if the following conditions are met: if the expectations refer to a definite status or person and if they are normative, shared, and reasonably consensual within some significant reference group. But we shall regard a role as diffuse or *minimal* (−) when expectations are vague, limited, variable, or unpatterned, with negligible consensus or normative elements. That is, it is minimal if the norms are few, weak, amorphous, or subject to little accord. Therefore, as a convention of terminology, the following typology will classify status and role simply as "developed" (+) or "minimal" (−), with the proviso that this dichotomy is only a gross distinction between those that are significant and clear and those that are relatively limited and amorphous.

Finally, the designation of role types in the following framework is purely arbitrary. The names are simply convenient labels for purposes of discussion, no more and no less. They are not evaluative, nor are they literal concepts; they are only convenient terms of reference. They are not to be burdened with gratuitous inferences.

THE TYPOLOGY

With these caveats firmly in mind, the typology of status–role permutations in which the two concepts are treated as independent appears in Figure 1.

What do these respective types portray and include? The Institutional represent statuses with roles; the Tenuous, statuses without roles; the Informal, roles without statuses; and the Non-Role, neither statuses nor roles. We will consider them seriatim.

Institutional: + +

These represent the major institutionalized statuses *with* roles to which Komarovsky (1973) referred. They are the least problematic prototypes of the most commanding sociological importance and interest. They involve the central positions of occupation, family, social class, race, ethnicity, religious affiliation, sex, for the most part age, and so on. These factors are neither exhaustive nor homogeneous, for the Institutional include diverse offices, positions, and statuses—formal and informal, ascribed and achieved. But the Institutional roles are all those in which normative expectations are clearly linked with definite positions or attributes: men, women, professionals, manual workers, parents, children, Catholics, Baptists, public officials, organizational members, race, ethnicity, and so on.

Aside from the interaction effects among statuses, the basic problem in Institutional age roles is the delineation of age norms.

Role Types	Status	Role
1. Institutional	+	+
2. Tenuous	+	−
3. Informal	−	+
4. Non-Role	−	−

Figure 1. Status–role combinations of various role types.

These have come under focal study only infrequently (Havighurst and Albrecht, 1953; Neugarten et al., 1965; Rosow, 1974), and their social meanings and functions have yet to be intensively examined. Most important is the extent to which age norms are *a matter of agreement, for this may eventually compel a careful reexamination of the concept "institutionalized."* Age norms may vary in clarity and consensus, and these remain to be explicated. For many norms that are now *assumed* to be commonly held may prove to be nothing of the kind; they may actually conceal widespread ignorance about a great diversity of underlying views. Or some norms, as in the abortion issue, may be subject to great conflict. Therefore, any significant variation in the *degree of agreement* about proper norms would oblige us to specify a "consensual" threshold, a minimal level that would be necessary before we would regard a pattern as "institutionalized." This is, of course, a generic problem of social structure that transcends the sheer issue of Institutional roles.

Empirically, Institutional roles may well be the modal type of all roles. Following Linton, this is the dominant frame of reference for role analysis and the least problematic category in our types. It provides one basis for examining a diversity of roles. However, the key point *for our problem* is that in Institutional roles, expectations are directly linked to definite social statuses. The main difficulties arise in the remaining types which do not meet this condition.

Tenuous: + −

This is the case that consists of definite social positions *without* roles or with only vague, insubstantial ones. Ernest Burgess (1950) pointed out long ago that the position of the aged is essentially roleless, an observation occasionally resurrected for ritual acknowledgment by gerontologists, but whose implications have been largely ignored by old age specialists and role theorists alike. The effects of role attrition for the aged have been amply demonstrated in many contexts: the results are to divert them from the mainstream of social participation, to undermine their group integration, and commonly to demoralize them (Riley and Foner, 1968; Rosow, 1967). But the elderly are only prototypical of the Tenuous, and others belong here as well.

In general, the Tenuous consist of several basic subtypes, including: (A) those in *titular* positions or offices, whether honorific or nominal; (B) the genuinely *amorphous* of several kinds. (Members of a third possible subtype, pariahs and outcasts, are not properly roleless, for they are hedged in with powerful sanctions that are quite clear and to which compliance can readily be judged.)

(A) Among the titular, (A1) the *honorific* involve statuses in which high prestige is publicly bestowed for valued characteristics or achievements. The prototypes here include Nobel laureates or members of the British peerage who are *not* invited to participate actively in the House of Lords. The honors are symbolic, and no specific role activities beyond the most token are associated with the position. This does not minimize the collective social values that such honors represent, but simply recognizes that each involves an extremely limited role. (A2) The *nominal* positions or offices are also basically token, whether in organizational or personal terms. Many public and even private bureaucracies harbor divisions, departments, or posts that are literally obsolete and have no essential functions, but nonetheless continue to survive. In these instances, vacuous roles take on a group quality. In other cases, people are effectively disposed of by token promotion or by being "kicked upstairs" in a face-saving gesture that gracefully removes them from positions of power or consequence to ones where their influence is reduced. [The process of face-saving in such situations has long been a concern of Erving Goffman (1958b).] Such procedures are not limited to formal organizations; they also occur in families or informal groups where others sharply curtail a person's ac-

tual functions, but maintain a facade of deference to him. The basic condition is that such roles are shorn of effective resources and significant activities.

Whereas honorific positions symbolically reward valued attributes or performance and thereby constitute social "promotions," nominal positions represent "demotions" that signify loss, obsolescence, superannuation, or exclusion from influence or authority. Role functions are drastically stripped away or limited.

(B) The genuinely amorphous are the most problematic of the Tenuous types. They include many who are devalued, both deviants and others who exemplify social loss, failure, stigma, or marginality. Though commonly deprecated as deviant, people who are "failures" typically are *not* assimilated into those coherent subcultures that afford them significant group support and clear behavioral expectations. Rather, these roles tend to occur under conditions that provide the actor with few normative guidelines and often, though not invariably, oblige him to face his role dilemmas privately.

Aside from the aged, to whom we shall presently return, there are at least four forms of amorphousness. (B1) Goode (1956) described a classic *ambiguous* situation in his 1948 study of younger divorced mothers. For these women, there were virtually no significant norms by which they could restructure their lives as divorcees in most institutional contexts: in relation to their children, exhusbands, other men, work, leisure, social life, friendships, and the potential remarriage arena. Divorce has been increasing steadily over recent decades, including the period of Goode's research. By 1950, the divorce rate for married women 15 years and older had reached 10.3, and during the fifties, the ranks of divorces were swelled by almost 400,000 per year (Bureau of the Census, 1973, p. 90). But for our problem, the crucial factor is that so many women were then entering this marital status—in a central institution—without clear norms about their appropriate role and their proper relations with others. Indeed, the very composition of suitable role sets remained equivocal. We may also note that, except in countries where illegitimacy has been reasonably institutionalized (Goode, 1960a), similar ambiguities mark the position of the unwed mother.

(B2) A second form of amorphousness is *de facto,* exemplified by the chronically unemployed, the jobless high school dropout, and similar individuals. In this type, the person retains obligations (to work and support his family), but objective circumstances deny him the opportunity to perform. The effects of long-term unemployment during the depression have been well documented (Bakke, 1934, 1940a,b; Ginzberg, 1943; Jahoda et al., 1971; Komarovsky, 1940; Sletto and Rundquist, 1936). Millions of men lost jobs. As household heads, they were still financially responsible for their families, but their economic effectiveness was destroyed. They were technically role failures, but in circumstances for which they were not personally responsible. Without work, their financial functions were nil, and their occupational role was empty. They had no economic activities, and their authority within the family was often undermined. Their main obligation became to seek jobs unremittingly in a stagnant labor market that had effectively disappeared. Even this unemployment status became virtually roleless, for those who daily pounded the pavements and conscientiously pursued the few ads that appeared usually finished their rounds early and quickly exhausted any prospects. In this process, many men underwent the corrosive conversion from the unemployed to the unemployable. Yet, whether or not they suffered this particular fate, all the chronically unemployed exemplified men with financial responsibilities, but without corresponding economic activities. In our usage, they had status obligations, but their economic roles were de facto Tenuous. While the literature has described their situation, it has not analyzed the data systematically in relation to role theory or abstracted the appropriate propositions in those terms.

(B3) Amorphousness is also expressed in two forms of *role attrition.* (B3a) The first may be called *role emptying,* in which the responsibilities and normative expectations of a position gradually dwindle away. This is seen to a large extent in old age when there is significant shrinkage *within* roles. It is also particularly reflected in some incarcerated populations. Some inmates of total institutions have contrived to develop adaptive survival mechanisms (Goffman, 1958a, 1961), but this has by no means applied to all. Particularly relevant in this sense are long-term state mental hospital patients, primarily the burnt-out chronic schizophrenics and the senile dementias, who have wasted away for decades in the back wards of custodial institutions. Commonly admitted in an emergency to the "front wards," they often received some treatment and were given time to recover, with some guidelines and expectations of them as patients. However, if they were not well enough to leave the hospital within a year, they seldom left at all, but were transferred to the chronic wards. Once consigned to these back wards, they were perceived and labeled as lifelong institutional patients. Processes of degradation and depersonalization effectively wrote them off as human beings and rendered them socially invisible. Nothing further was expected of them, including even the rudiments of personal hygiene, and any rights that they might have formerly claimed were virtually forfeit. The process of institutionalization to the chronic back wards rapidly shriveled their status to one of an empty role, with no residue of rights and duties.

(B3b) The second type of role attrition and the final case of the amorphous Tenuous is that of *status loss.* This is the contraction of the status set that results in the loss of roles. It is exemplified by the most problematic aged, those who have lost central institutional positions in the family, the labor force, and so on, whose social participation has become marginal, and whose life-styles have been vitiated by the various decrements of aging. Their major status losses start with retirement, widowhood, failing health, and drastically reduced income, and then they spread to other areas as their social contacts and activities dwindle.

As their statuses diminish, roles of the elderly tend to become increasingly Tenuous, for these sociological decrements are largely irreversible and not compensated by substitutes. Few of the widowed remarry, few of the retired return to full-time work, few of the ill recover their health, and reduced income is almost never restored. Unlike previous life transitions, losses in old age are seldom replaced. Thus, there is an interruption of two normal earlier processes: status *accretion* in which new positions are added to those already held, and status *succession* in which new roles replace those that are outgrown or left behind. For the aged, such losses are usually irreversible, and the attrition leaves their roles Tenuous.

Why is this? In a rapidly changing technology, the older worker may become obsolete, but economic utility is not invariably an exhaustive value. Vacuous roles are not simply a function of *personal* incompetence, obsolescence, or worthlessness. Rather, the problem lies in judgments of people's *social* utility. Sociologically, the loss of roles reflects a steady decline in major *responsibilities* and thereby the possibility that old people's actions and performance can affect others significantly. As long as they are not unusually dependent, whether through incapacity or deprivation, their behavior has relatively little effect on other persons and is thus *socially inconsequential*. If they create no trouble and perform few functions on which the social system depends, then they have little impact on that system. By the same token, if the system has replacements to take over their previous functions, then there is little social stake in their decisions and behavior as long as these are not particularly problematic. Thus, even though the elderly do have an age status, the loss of responsibility and functions is the basis of their role limitation. The loss of statuses leaves them with few normative expectations, with lives that are unstructured by significant *social* prescriptions and guidelines (Rosow, 1974). Society simply has little stake in establishing

special requirements and standards for those in positions with little social effect and few consequences.

I have examined various aspects of this problem in several different contexts (Rosow, 1962, 1967, 1974). But because the aged are the subject of this *Handbook* and the major exemplars of the amorphous Tenuous, the concomitants of their status (here, also role) loss warrant more detailed attention than has been devoted to the other role types. I have previously analyzed their case in the following terms (Rosow, 1973):

First, *the loss of roles excludes the aged from significant social participation and devalues them.* It deprives them of vital functions that underlie their sense of worth, their self-conceptions and self-esteem. In a word, they are depreciated and become marginal, alienated from the larger society. Whatever their ability, they are judged invidiously, as if they have little of value to contribute to the world's work and affairs. In a society that rewards men mainly according to their economic utility, the aged are arbitrarily stigmatized as having little marginal utility of any kind, either economic or social. On the contrary, they tend to be tolerated, patronized, ignored, rejected, or viewed as a liability. They are first excluded from the mainstream of social existence, and because of this nonparticipation, they are then penalized and denied the rewards that earlier came to them routinely.

Second, *old age is the first stage of life with systematic status loss for an entire cohort.* All previous periods—childhood, adolescence, and various phases of adulthood; from education through marriage, parenthood, raising and educating a family; from modest occupational beginnings through successively higher positions—all are normally marked by steady social growth. This involves gains in competence, responsibility, authority, privilege, reward, and prestige. But the status loss of old age represents the first systematic break in this pattern of acquisition. Not only are the gains and perquisites disrupted, but the sheer loss of [prestige] actually reverses the trend. People pass through a vague period of transition in which they are redefined as old and obsolete. The norms applied to them change quickly from achievement to ascription, from criteria of performance to those of sheer age regardless of personal accomplishment. People who were formerly judged as individuals are then bewilderingly treated as members of an invidious category. They are dismissed as superannuated, peculiarly wanting in substance and consequence, almost in character, and thereby lacking any moral claim on the normal social values available for distribution.

To be sure, there are other patterned [social] losses in our society, but none uniquely connected with age. People do have illegitimate children, go to prison, get divorced, wind up in mental hospitals, or otherwise fall from grace. But they are deviants who are in the minority; age has nothing to do with their status. They are construed as personal failures in some fundamental sense. Yet the losses of old age ultimately overtake everybody, not because they have significantly failed, but only because they have survived. This raises perplexing problems of social justice for the aged: to comprehend a loss of [esteem] when there has been no personal failure.

Third, *persons in our society are not socialized to the fate of aging.* This, too, is a major discontinuity from previous experience. Usually people are rather systematically, if not always formally, trained for their next stage of life. They are indoctrinated about future roles and expectations, about the values and norms that will govern them. While the role losses of old age are institutionalized, the socialization to them is not [Rosow, 1974]. People must adapt to the strains and develop a way of life without clear definitions, expectations, and standards [Lipman, 1961]. Our society generally does not prepare people for defeats and losses of status and certainly not for those of old age.

Fourth, *because society does not specify an aged role, the lives of the elderly are socially unstructured.* Even though people are classified as old, they have almost no duties. Shorn of roles, their responsibilities and obligations are minimal. Their position is part of no division of social labor and does not mesh with any definite group of others that sociologists call a "role set" (Merton, 1957). Consequently, they tend to live in an imperfect role vacuum with few standards by which to judge themselves and their behavior. Others have few expectations of them and provide no guides to appropriate activity. They have no significant norms for restructuring their lives. There are no meaningful

prescriptions for new goals and experience, no directions to salvation as occasionally accompany sin, loss, or failure at younger ages [Rosow, 1974]. There are only platitudes: take care of yourself, stay out of drafts, keep active, hold onto the banister, find a hobby, don't overdo, take your medicine, eat. The very triviality of these bromides simply documents the empty *social* role of the aged, the general irreversibility of their losses, and their ultimate solitude in meeting their existential declines.

In this sense, it is virtually impossible for them to be literal role failures. This is not necessarily reassuring, however, for psychologists know that unstructured situations generate anxiety. Certainly with a broad horizon of leisure and few obligations, many old people feel oppressively useless and futile. They are simply bored—but not quite to death.

Although freedom from responsibility may sound heavenly to the young, it actually demands strong personal interests and motivation. In earlier periods, life is mainly structured by social duties. People's social positions and role obligations largely govern their general activities and time budgets. This is not true in old age for, *within objective constraints,* life is essentially shaped by individual choice and personal initiative. Because many people lack the interest and initiative to fashion a satisfying existence independently (Hunter and Maurice, 1953), life patterns range from the highly active and imaginative to passive vegetation. To be sure, almost the entire spectrum of possible styles is socially acceptable (Rosow, 1967). But this broad range of permissible alternatives simply documents the role vacuum: there are few prescriptions, norms, and expectations; weak definitions of what an old person should be like and how he should spend his time; and only a clouded picture of the good life in old age.

Finally, *role loss deprives people of their social identity.* This is almost axiomatic, for sociologists define the social self as the totality of a person's social roles. These roles identify and describe him as a social being and are central to his very self-conceptions. The process of role loss steadily eats away at these crucial elements of social personality and converts what is to what was—or transforms the present into the past. In psychological terms, this is a direct, sustained attack on the ego. If the social self consists of roles, then role loss erodes self-conceptions and sacrifices *social* identity.

These then are the social inputs of the crisis of aging. For the first time in life, the elderly are excluded from the central functions and social participation on which self-conceptions and self-esteem are based. They systematically lose perquisites and [value] solely on the basis of age. Social pressures that they are powerless to dispel result in invidious judgments of them, and their personal efforts cannot significantly affect their various losses. Because they lack major responsibilities, society does not specify a role for the aged, and their lives become socially unstructured. This is a gross discontinuity for which they are not socialized, and role loss deprives them of their very social identity.

Clearly, the aged are not the only amorphous Tenuous in our society, but they do represent the largest prototypical case. Analytically, they expose one of the key factors that govern the social position of most others of this type: the loss of major responsibility and authority. Hence, the retention of statuses without functions (including old age) earmarks many of those who have little substance or consequence in the normal operation of the system, who are generally depreciated.

Informal: − +

This type represents role behavior that is *not* connected with any particular status or position, but which *serves significant group functions,* whether positive or negative. Such informal roles are not invariably present, but when they do occur, they involve patterned activities that have perceptible consequences for a group and the relations among its members. While they are neither required nor indispensable to its operation—and their absence certainly signifies no vacant positions—informal roles do affect group processes, if not structure. To this extent, they have social functions that are associated with a particular person or subgroup. As a definite pattern of conduct or relations, such regularities of behavior in a relatively stable group may even become semi-institutionalized, with incipient expectations and norms crystallizing about the actor(s). The basic conceptual distinction of this type is that its

functions are not intrinsic to a status, to the "collection of rights and duties" that are integral to a social position.

Who may be included in this category? Certainly all of Komarovsky's (1973) casual examples: the family scapegoat, the big wheel, the rebel. There are also numerous others: heroes, villains, and fools (Klapp, 1962), rabblerousers, charismatic figures, and other symbolic leaders (Klapp, 1965), roués, playboys and boulevardiers, tough guys, manipulators and operators, mediators, patsies, blackmailers, prima donnas, confidants, gossips, informal leaders and influentials, shills, ratebusters, scabs, locals and cosmopolitans, earth mothers and nymphomaniacs, stool pigeons, certainly homosexuals, flirts, and "gold diggers." Such examples can be extended considerably, but these suffice to make the point.

This category provides a place for many of the "residual" cases that have embarrassed role theorists. Because they could not be linked with institutionalized statuses, they have been treated almost as a form of sociological detritus or as a conceptual dandruff to be hastily brushed away before anyone took notice. Yet how can sociologists conscientiously ignore what Newcomb (1966) properly termed "regularities in interpersonal relationships"? To which we might add, regularities of social function.

The general point can be emphasized with several examples of formal influence, though they will be balanced by other cases as a reminder that the issue is not limited to influence. Kitchen cabinets and executive confidants are inner circles of advisors often without (or independent of) any position. Among community influentials, power groups may coalesce around specific problems and then dissolve when the problems are resolved; or, relatively stable power elites commonly function purely informally, without the sanction of public office. Locals and cosmopolitans may have quite different orientations and reference groups, though these are not necessarily built into their formal statuses, including their social class positions. Crisis situations may cry out for charismatic leadership that may not always be forthcoming, for those waiting in the wings do not always have the symbolic and personal qualities that can effectively capture the popular imagination and retrieve the situation. One may advertise in the want ads with fair assurance of success for a competent accountant, but it is quite another matter to advertise successfully for one with charisma (or "hustle"), no matter how desirable this might seem. For charismatic qualities cannot be required and built into an institutional (much less an official) status, no matter what the imperatives, any more than happiness can be required of a spouse or the incumbent of any other position. Similarly, an old widow might well have an old next-door neighbor, but not necessarily one whom she could trust as a confidante who would be so important for her stability and integration (Lowenthal and Haven, 1968).

Clearly, all informal roles without statuses are not equally significant, for some are obviously more consequential than others. They exist at different institutional levels and have quite different scope. Those at the primary or small group level certainly have more limited effects than those in large groups, organizations, or broader institutions. The pool hall hustler and the village gossip affect far fewer people than a Bernard Baruch quietly conferring with a president, but their informal roles within their spheres are equally amenable to analysis, probably in similar analytic terms.

Informal roles assimilate what appear in Sarbin and Allen's (1968) taxonomy as "character roles." Other psychologists who enter this arena commonly refer to them as *psychological types*. They assume that social behavior and relationships result from individual personality characteristics or predispositions that are reflected in personal styles or adaptations to given situations. This may be quite true, but obviously questions about the *psychological causes* of action are quite different from those about behavior's *social effects*. Self-selection may cast the actors in informal roles, but the social consequences of their activity are quite a separate matter.

On the other hand, various sociologists, among them Goffman, Klapp, Becker, and Strauss, discuss such figures in the rhetoric of *social types*. Aside from his interest in the informal mechanisms within bureaucracies, Goffman has been mainly concerned with the face-work and social psychology of interpersonal relations. Klapp's (1962, 1965) interest in social types has focused on their symbolic reflection of prevailing and changing social values. Becker (1963) and Strauss (1959) have dealt with the emergence and maintenance of social identities. While these various issues are not the same, they share a common core of interest and afford a reasonably similar basis of discourse.

Both the psychological and the social perspectives have been legitimately concerned with various problems of personality or social psychology. Clearly, personality factors do operate in individual adaptations and in various other sociological contexts. This appears to be so not only in problems of social structure and personality, but also in such processes as leadership, decision making, self-selection procedures, social perception, stereotyping, and others. But neither the psychological nor the social tradition has tried to integrate its social psychological concerns systematically with role theory as such.

Our immediate problem is not the personality aspects or social psychology of unusual roles. Our interest in Informal roles concerns their consequences for various groups or systems; that is, their effects on the social units in which they occur. The typology proposed here constitutes a framework for the classification of various status–role patterns and offers one possible entrée to their integration with role theory. (It may even provide one base of a bridge between role theory and work in other traditions, such as symbolic interactionism.)

Non-Role: – –

This is a logical, but irrelevant "type" that is extraneous to role problems. It is a miscellany of such elements as idiosyncratic behavior, personality factors, personal style, and so on, that have *no* significant patterned social consequences. Accordingly, though we note the category here for the sake of logical closure, it has no importance for our problem. Because Non-Role behavior is peripheral to our interests, it should not distract us, and we will simply exclude it from the rest of the analysis.

DISCUSSION

The preceding considerations make it clear that Linton's premise of the necessary complementarity of status and role is too restrictive. While the concepts are linked in the Institutional type, this does not cover all important social relationships, nor does it exhaust the problems of role theory. Our analysis shows that status and role do not invariably occur together, but may arise separately—a point that was previously disregarded by treating the Tenuous and Informal types as conceptually deviant. Tenuous roles empty statuses of functions, whereas Informal roles invoke processes that are independent of social positions. These types pose significant problems for role theory in any structural analysis.

The Tenuous include many of the "unsuccessful" and the social "misfits." Ours is a competitive society whose ideology of progress is reinforced by values of personal striving, acquisition, and success. Accordingly, theory has been absorbed with problems of aspiration, growth, mobility, and success. But there has been no equal attention to the analysis of the unsuccessful, to those on the fringe and in vacuous roles. When such analytic categories are provided, as in the present typology, it is not surprising that so many of the social "failures" appear among the Tenuous. Except for the honorific, the Tenuous contain several varieties of role loss, ineptitude, and deprivation, before and during old age.

The later years approximate *social* "failure" in many respects. Particularly with the decrements of retirement, widowhood, and declining health and income, the aged commonly move on to fewer and emptier roles.

They drop out of organizations, see less of their friends and neighbors, and their social world outside the family shrinks significantly, often drastically. While disengagement theorists have arbitrarily interpreted the shrinkage as a function of a normal social psychological process, they have not articulated this view with a coherent theory of adult development. Yet there are more economic explanations of reduced social participation: role loss and devaluation. In both role emptying and status loss, people often withdraw and fail to exercise options that would provide alternatives, such as joining voluntary associations. In other words, social decline and failure are invidious, and, as a consequence, people frequently restrict their public participation.

The common element here is the social definition of failure, whether by omission or commission, by obsolescence or inadequacy, by performance or ascription. On a *societal* level, *we do not socialize people to deviance or failure*. Nor do we accord them any but the most limited claims on available social values when their responsibilities and consequential actions are minimal. Therefore, when major problems of disruption or social control are not involved (as exemplified perhaps by criminals or contagious sanatoria patients), those who no longer perform socially productive roles or are devalued in ascriptive terms are often stigmatized and cut off from conventional opportunities. In either case, the roles presumably connected with their statuses (or expected sequences) are usually limited and may even become vacuous (cf. Veevers, 1972, 1973). Among the aged, these pressures systematically push them toward the Tenuous category.

As far as Informal roles are concerned, whether positive or negative, their implications for future work in role theory become almost axiomatic, and we can present them briefly without elaborate discussion. (1) Informal roles without statuses operate within and outside the formal system. (2) They are heterogeneous and exist at virtually all levels of the social structure. (3) They are not inconsequential, but have significant functions, whether positive or negative, within their respective groups or institutional spheres. (4) While some may be correlates of or supplements to various positions, *Informal roles are neither intrinsic to nor Implicit in these statuses.* One cannot readily infer role from status or vice versa. (5) Their social functions in various contexts usually have either been related to a given substantive field or analyzed in conventional institutional or systemic terms. But they have seldom been addressed specifically as role problems or systematically related to role theory. Their significance for role theory warrants attention, but has been overlooked.

Finally, (6) Informal roles represent a large, diverse range of second-order activities and patterned relationships. They provide essential functions that the major Institutional roles do not cover, filling gaps in the processes by which a social structure operates—especially as it becomes more differentiated and complex. Thus, they flesh out the functions of the skeletal structure. Clearly, they may supplement, overlap with, or deviate from the Institutional roles in any group or level of the system. Thus, their possible functions are understandably diverse: to innovate or improvise, to compensate for inadequate provisions of Institutional roles, to help moderate role conflicts, to meet crises and accommodate strains, to integrate or disrupt groups, to lubricate or create frictions in various systems, to generate or mediate personal conflicts, and so on.

Indeed, the analogy between Informal roles and informal systems becomes almost inescapable. In this sense, one can express the conceptual correspondence with systems analysis in the following terms:

$$\frac{\text{Informal roles}}{\text{Institutional roles}} = \frac{\text{Informal systems}}{\text{Formal systems}}$$

That is, Informal roles bear the same relationship to Institutional roles that informal systems do to formal systems. The development and elaboration of Informal roles are integral to the status structure, but are not provided by it. Institutional status positions generate the most essential roles of a system, but ultimately, even in the central institutions, these roles tend to be incomplete. They certainly represent the necessary, but not sufficient (much less optimal) conditions of operation. The bare bones need fleshing out. Just as a structure requires the development of an informal system for flexibility, so are its processes virtually dependent on the elaboration of Informal roles that are not inherent in Institutional statuses. A central problem for future theory remains the explication of these relationships in role terms and the refinement of existing theory in light of such analysis.

EN PASSANT: AN ILLUSTRATIVE APPLICATION

To illustrate the generality of our schema, we can apply it to selected elements of a particular model. In this case, a most suitable example is that of Riley et al. (1972, p. 9), which describes the channeling of cohort members into age roles. From their complete flow chart, we can select three key components on which our respective role types are differentially processed—not only for age roles, but more generally as well. This is illustrated by Figure 2, where the notations of the column headings refer to the original diagram of Riley et al., and examples of subtypes are footnoted.

The contents of Figure 2 are straightforward and can be read accordingly. For our immediate purposes, certain qualifications that would be necessary in a refined analysis (viz., the actual variation in socialization to different Institutional roles) need not divert us here. What is more to the point is that the various role types may be allocated differently, but this is not invariably consequential for their subsequent processing. For example, even though the Amorphous aged (+) are allocated by ascription and the divorced (−) are recruited by choice, their normative expectations and socialization patterns are similarly vague and diffuse. On the other hand, among the Informal roles, the normative expectations and socialization processes differ according to whether they are

Role Types	Social Allocation (P3)	Normative Expectations (4)	Socialization (P4)
1. Institutional	+	High	+
2. Tenuous			
Titular	+	Low	−
Amorphous[a]	+/−	Low	−
3. Informal			
Group-selected[b]	+	Moderate	±
Self-selected	−	Variable	−

[a] Viz.: + (aged) and − (divorced)
[b] Viz.: scapegoat

Figure 2. Allocation, norms, and socialization of role types.

filled by group designation or by self-selection.

These details warrant a more refined, systematic analysis than we can undertake here. But the central point is that the role typology offers some new perspective on the Riley–Johnson–Foner model and affords leads for deeper examination of its elements. To this extent, it provides an entrée to the more systematic analysis of particular role problems that have been neglected but warrant careful study.

Our immediate interest is simply to indicate this rather than to pursue its complex implications here. But we will presently apply the typology to variations in role activity through the life span.

THE MEANINGS OF ROLE CHANGE

The concept of role change has several different usages that should be distinguished prior to any discussion. All are legitimate, but their referents and implications differ. So, before applying our typology to the life span, we should indicate which of the meanings concern us here. I hope that this clarification will avoid some troublesome misunderstanding.

Role change involves at least five different temporal connotations. (1) The first is that of the *simple movement* between two positions that one holds simultaneously. This is clearly illustrated by a person's moving between family and work roles. Or, within each

sphere, by movement between being a father (to a child) and being a son (to an older parent); or between being a supervisor and a subordinate to different people at work. These changes involve routine shifts between different role relationships in a short time, but the remaining changes involve significantly longer time perspectives.

The next pair entail important *internal* role alterations. (2) Roles may be modified and redefined as a function of *social change*. Thereby, they are transformed in their content, normative expectations, and so on, in response to historical events. The changing position of American women in the family, the labor force, and other institutions illustrates such a fundamental restructuring of these roles in scope, quality, and focus.

(3) There are also comparable changes within roles that are correlated with age, essentially as functions of different *life-stages*. For example, being a son or a daughter involves progressive role changes as a person traverses the life cycle, growing from childhood through adolescence to adulthood and on through the successive stages of maturity. Clearly, different normative standards govern the expectations and reciprocities of a daughter and her parents when she is a child, an adolescent, a young woman, a wife, a mother, a matron, and a grandmother. She remains a daughter during all these periods, but her role and its content are steadily modified. Such changes within a role may be construed in human developmental or socio-

logical frames of reference. They also have both qualitative and quantitative aspects. The nature of a role may alter during the life span, as in the case of filiality mentioned above. And a role can expand or contract in volume, as was indicated earlier in the emptying of amorphous roles. The essential factor in all these cases is that specific role expectations and relationships vary by life-stages and implicitly by age-appropriate norms (Neugarten et al., 1965). So roles may change internally according to both history and stage of life.

The final two connotations involve alteration of the *status set* by the acquisition of new roles or the loss of existing ones. (4) A status set may simply be enlarged by *accretion* or reduced by *attrition*. The person adds or loses a role by joining or leaving a group or association, whether formal or informal. While the activity or membership he acquires or drops is usually quite voluntary, this certainly is not a requisite. But the particular character of such changes is often age-related. Thus, people's roles may fluctuate *in number* by joining or leaving a church, the Girl Scouts, a union, the PTA, a bowling team, the local Democratic party, a Little League team, a bridge club, a professional society, or a social circle. The age relationship is commonly linked to life-stages, and it may vary from attendance at nursery school to senior citizens clubs. Such roles may be added or dropped singly. But the processes of accretion and attrition are often integral to life-styles evolving at different periods, with several new roles being acquired or lost during a rather limited period. These changes commonly involve role complexes (correlated, if not integrated, multiple roles) that are related to expanding or contracting life-stages.

(5) Finally, a change of role may also refer specifically to *status passage,* the transition between positions that are sequentially ordered. This invariably involves the relinquishment of one status and the acquisition of the succeeding one, for the two positions are mutually exclusive within a status succession, and their order is usually irreversible.

In the prototypical case, such as the professional career ladder, the statuses are often hierarchically arranged, with the preceding stage a prerequisite of the succeeding one. The classic formulation of status passage was set forth by Van Gennep (1960), who traced the three-step process of separation–transition–induction. Clear illustrations of such role change include getting married, graduation from school and entrance to a profession, having a child, and so on. To be sure, not all statuses are arranged in sequential chains. Even when they are, deviations from the typical pattern of role succession occasionally do occur (as in an annulment of a marriage, with the parties reverting to the "single" status). However, in the life cycle, despite the wonders of cosmetology and surgery, age is progressive and not reversible. The crucial element here is that in these status passages, the transition occurs between mutually exclusive, successive roles.

Now for the caveat. In this chapter on the life span, we are mainly interested in statuses and roles that change as functions of new *life-stages*. Therefore, we are concerned only with the relevant variations, those pertaining to the last three connotations of role change: (3) *modifications of single roles* between age grades or periods, (4) *accretion and attrition,* and (5) *sequential status passages.* So we will *not* deal with the two other referents of role change: routine movement between current roles and the alteration of roles by social change.

CHANGES THROUGH THE LIFE SPAN

We will trace the different status–role types as they fluctuate over the life cycle, tentatively proposing their gross profiles as they wax and wane in relative importance through time. We should also like to distinguish the role changes according to their kind: modification across periods, accretion–attrition, or status passage. Then, ideally, we could assess the relative salience of the three kinds of change in different life-stages.

But this poses some difficulty, for the *relative importance* of the role types is not simply reducible to *quantitative* terms, to their respective shares of the person's total role activity. The Tenuous type emphasizes role attrition and contraction, in a word, loss or inactivity. The conception of role as activity does not accommodate the notion of role as *in*activity. In quantitative terms, as Tenuous roles increase, their activity values come to approximate zero. Yet, the *relative importance* of Tenuous roles is increasing. So there is a contradiction between their declining activity and mounting importance. There is no meaningful way to express this growing *qualitative* importance in a declining *numerical* index. Hence, this precludes the possible equation of importance with sheer amount of role activity.

Accordingly, the gross profiles of change throughout the life cycle must reflect the prominence of the three types in some other fashion. For the moment, we will simply leave this as an arbitrary judgment. I will express their relative importance schematically as *hypothetical curves in a model of comparative change*. This will indicate their shifting significance at different life-stages without regard to the particular sources of change. While these sources (role modification, accretion–attrition, and status passage) may vary considerably across periods, their relative salience and relation to role types remain problems for future research. Therefore, this model will simply trace the tentative curves of our three role types as I conceive their shifting importance throughout life. In this presentation, the profile of the major Institutional roles will be the basic frame of references to which the others will be compared.

To simplify the model, we will assume that the life span is divided into the most basic, fundamental stages—with clear understanding that all of them can be embellished, subdivided, and refined much further. Obviously, "young adulthood" can be broken down into completion of school, starting work, getting married, having children, and so on, even with courtship inserted somewhere along the way. Or "middle age" can simultaneously involve sex differences in a waxing career line for men and the waning of an emptying nest for women as children grow up and successively leave home. By the same token, "old age" may similarly be subdivided. An excellent summary of the substantive trends is readily available in Clausen's (1972) fine treatment of this difficult, nebulous subject. But in this chapter, we will assume such substages and take them for granted without further consideration, for at the moment it is the principle rather than the details that concerns us.

Furthermore, there is an important difference in the clarity of movement within and between major life-stages: transitions between larger life-stages are often more indefinite and blurred than changes within them. The ostensibly "lesser" movements tend to be the most specific, sharpest, and clearest. This is most apparent in those based on sheer age criteria, as when another birthday qualifies one to enter school, secure a driver's license, vote, or buy liquor, or forces one to retire. These are scheduled and legalistic. Other specific status changes, role acquisitions, and losses are also often punctuated by public or private rites of passage that sharply denote the transition. For example, ceremonies of baptism, bar mitzvah, graduation, engagement, marriage, funerals, and the like, signify not only an actor's status change, but also his new reciprocal relationships with significant others. Status changes such as these are typically sequential, very specific, and clear-cut. But they do not invariably and automatically delineate major life-stages in social terms. Widowhood or retirement may change one's status drastically, but *not* necessarily one's lifestage.

Other role changes tend to be vaguer and more blurred. They are not so clearly tied to any specific sequence of statuses, yet they are linked, if only loosely, to major life periods. They tend to be one of two kinds: The first marks the *gradual* changes within a role through time, such as the evolving roles of parents as their children grow from infancy to adulthood, or conversely those of adult children as their parents pass from middle age to old age and into senility. These modifications tend to develop somewhat slowly and gradually. Though they are sometimes precipitated by immediate events, the changes are not scheduled (Glaser and Strauss, 1971), they are usually independent of any particular status passages, and they may cover several stages of the life cycle.

The second set concerns the *timing* of role changes in relation to age-appropriate norms. Certain status transitions and other behavior tend to be judged by what is suitable at given ages. In other words, there are informal but definite expectations that reflect age-appropriate norms (Neugarten et al., 1965). These do not incorporate a precise deadline or cut-off point, but rather a loose period of time whose flexibility varies with the particular change in question. While the marriage ceremony itself signifies a sharp status change, the period during which a person is normatively expected to get married is relatively flexible before informal social pressures are brought to bear (Veevers, 1972). Other examples of such flexible periods that tend to stiffen at their boundaries include: family and other role timing (Nydegger, 1973, 1980, 1981a), other family changes (Olson, 1969), progress along career lines (Huyck, 1970), and the timing of different status changes in related institutional contexts (Huyck, 1973). Both types of change, modification within roles and normative timing, may emerge within life-stages, but in relatively loose, blurred transition zones. Yet the normative shifts are extremely significant.

Finally, the demarcations that distinguish one major life-stage from another may be the vaguest of all. Here the transitional periods are the broadest and their boundaries the most ambiguous. Legal criteria, individual attributes, and social definitions are often so disparate that few meaningful cutting points can be established. Indeed, the definition of life-stages may vary more by people's lifestyle (viz., social class) than by the stages themselves. Therefore, it is wisest at this point simply to acknowledge the ordering of the life cycle, with the full understanding that

its phases are not always sharply separated from one another so much as buffered by broad zones of transition. For purposes of this chapter, this implies that at present too precise or refined a division of major life-stages is premature and unwarranted, an invitation to misplaced concreteness.

Accordingly, we will construe the basic life-stages in quite simple terms, such as infancy/childhood, adolescence, youth/adulthood, middle age, and old age. We will not pin them to specific chronological ages. Also, these various stages obviously cover different intervals of time, but no matter. This is not crucial for our immediate problem.

With these assumptions, we can now consider how our role types shift in relative importance during the course of life. This is schematized in Figure 3.

Institutional: + +

Changes in the relative importance of the major Institutional roles show a clear profile across the life span. Elsewhere, I have indicated that significant status transitions *before* old age are marked by basic role continuity, net social gains, and various rites of passage; but the movement *into* old age reverses these patterns, with major role discontinuity, systematic social losses, and few rites of passage. Such discontinuities and

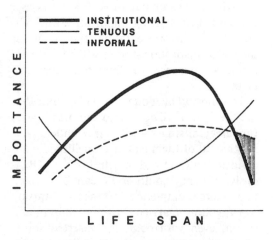

Figure 3. Relative importance of role types in the life span.

losses often precede rather than follow the change in status (Rosow, 1974, Ch. 2).

For our purposes, the key factor is the asymmetry of the Institutional curve. (This is the heavy reference line in Figure 3.) There is a fairly steady increase in importance and in social gains that reach their peak and level off in late middle age and then decline with the losses of old age. These social gains and decrements are basically a function of the changing dependence and responsibilities of a person as he traverses the life course. The sequence of roles and their increase in number generally involve growing responsibilities, both within and among roles. These new obligations also involve correlates of greater social resources: power and authority, privileges and rewards, a diversity of options, and so on. While these prerogatives are usually valued by the actor, this is not always the case. They are not necessarily an unmixed blessing, and they are not always psychologically welcome. On balance though, they usually are construed as gains and advantages. But in terms of status and role structure, the curve of responsibility and its social gains generally grows steadily and relatively smoothly into late middle age. This obtains in virtually all major institutional spheres, notably the family, education, and work; in civic, religious, political, and community affairs; in formal and informal groups; in voluntary organizations; and even in leisure activities. The pattern of growth marks both single roles and role complexes as well.

In this growth curve, then, the person moves from stages and positions of lower responsibility and privilege to higher ones. In childhood, this starts with the reduction of dependency and the acquisition of skills that reduce the necessity for his care and supervision. With greater independence, the person is expected to be more responsible for himself and to attain greater autonomy. Eventually he moves on to roles where he assumes increasing responsibility for others who are socially less competent, typically younger persons. This profile of change occurs within and between life-stages, that

within them being a dampened version of the larger curve of gain across stages.

This correspondence with social maturation is reflected in the succession of statuses. An actor's movement through most of life shows a growing share of available values. He has larger spheres of decision, greater recognition, rewards, and prerogatives; his span of authority increases as the number of people exercising authority over him declines. These gains are age-related and integral to life-stages. Because successive phases impose greater responsibility, they are accorded greater authority. And, because such obligations are socially consequential, systematic incentives and prerogatives are provided. Accordingly, during the life-stages of social gain, the major Institutional roles increase in relative importance until late middle age.

After the leveling off of social gains in late middle age, the declines of old age begin to set in. There is a steady attrition of statuses and some emptying of roles, with the major Institutional ones clearly declining in importance. But this process will be discussed in the next section.

We must remember, of course, that the slope of this curve varies somewhat, not only for individuals, but also for different institutional spheres and subgroups in the population: sex, occupation, social class, and so on. But here we are concerned only with the generic profile through life-stages.

Tenuous: + −

The relationship between the Tenuous and major Institutional roles can be succinctly summarized. They are moderately, but inversely correlated throughout the life span. Thereby, the relative importance of the Tenuous type presents a contrary profile to the Institutional curve, but not its precise opposite because of the modifying influence of the Informal roles. Clearly, the interaction effects among the three curves remain a problem for future research that the gross schematization of Figure 3 can only reflect.

Obviously, minimal roles are most conspicuous and important at the extremes of the life span, early and late in life. In infancy and childhood, a person is being socialized into the most basic elements of his culture and is being weaned from a position of extreme dependence. In the preschool period, his roles are few and limited, almost confined to the family and play group and perhaps nursery school. With the start of school, he begins to take on a few more roles with gradually increasing responsibility as he moves into a slowly expanding social world. This increase in roles, life space, membership groups, and responsibilities continues steadily throughout adolescence and as he approaches maturity. Each social gain reflects his diminishing dependence and greater competence in the adolescent transition from childhood to adulthood. As he moves into new institutional spheres, especially in education, sex, and work, two things occur: his existing activities *expand* and he also *acquires* new roles. So there is both a growth within roles and an increase in their number. Correlatively, his role restriction has declined steadily since childhood, it reaches a rather low point during adolescence, and it remains relatively unimportant for the decades of adulthood until late middle age and the onset of old age. In effect, role limitation lies dormant during most of adulthood.

The first stirrings of a revival of the Tenuous appear well into middle age. The obverse of the adolescent pattern is gradually set into motion, involving both decline of activity within roles (despite the retention of statuses) and reduction in their number. This is reflected in both the titular (honorific and nominal) and the amorphous subtypes. Later middle age is the main period when possible adult honors start to arrive and also when some persons are deflected into relatively empty positions. The amorphous varies somewhat by category. The ambiguous (viz., divorcee) and the de facto (viz., chronically unemployed) are less sensitively geared to life-stages than are the two forms of role attrition (role emptying and status loss); but though they are subject to objective market factors and other institutional forces, they

still do display a perceptible relationship to life-stage. In our immediate examples, for instance, the probability of divorce is greater in early adulthood, and extended unemployment is more likely in middle and old age. But the two forms of role attrition definitely make their incipient appearance in most cases in the heart of middle age, by the midforties. For women, role contraction begins domestically when the first child leaves home and continues into the so-called empty-nest stage when the last child departs. The decline of mothering and managing a ménage reflects the reduction of role activity, although the status is retained. During this period, some men who are well established begin to relax a bit at work and shift into a lower gear. At the same time, a few secondary activities may even be given up. These, however, are simply the first harbingers of future trends. The relative importance of the Tenuous in middle age is not yet great, for many Institutional roles remain viable and are actively maintained.

But the Tenuous begins to grow steadily with the onset of old age and the increase of role attrition, in both the emptying and the loss of roles. With retirement, widowhood, illness, failing income, and their correlates in the lapse of organizational memberships and so on, the person loses roles and enters a stage of reduced activity, a contracting social world, more marginal social participation, and possibly greater dependency. This involves the normal decrements of aging that have been so amply documented in the gerontological literature and are brought up to date in other chapters of the *Handbook*.

What is crucial is that during old age, people lose Institutional roles in most spheres, and this loss increases precipitously after age 75. That the age status of the elderly is evaluated in ascriptive rather than performance terms (Rosow, 1973) testifies to both forms of role attrition, particularly the loss of Institutional and other statuses. But, we will suggest that Informal roles may well be retained longer than the Institutional.

In summary, the relative importance of the Tenuous type in the course of life describes a U-shaped curve, biased toward the late stages. It is high at the extremes of childhood and old age, and it is relatively low and flat during most of adulthood and maturity. During childhood and adolescence, it declines steadily in importance with the acquisition of statuses and the expansion of roles. Conversely, it begins to revive again by later middle age; its importance grows increasingly with the progressive attrition of old age. In general, gradual role contraction may be somewhat more typical of late middle age and both contraction and status loss of old age.

Informal: − +

The Informal roles present a novel perspective and are more interesting in some respects than the others, whether they exemplify integrative or disruptive functions. Though smoothed in Figure 3, Informal roles usually describe an irregular, fluctuating curve that is flatter than either of the other types. And, for most life-stages, those between childhood and old age, their relative importance tends to fall between the other two curves. Then, in the later years, when the Tenuous increase as Institutional roles are lost, the Informal type changes significantly less than either of the others.

Figure 3 shows that the profile of the Informal roles starts low and slightly later than the Institutional curve. By adolescence, it rises to intermediate levels. Then it fluctuates irregularly through adulthood and middle age as a constrained, flattened, muted echo of the Institutional profile. In other words, there is a loose, moderate correlation between the two types prior to old age.

But at that point, there is a sharp divergence between them. When the Institutional curve declines quickly with the attrition of major roles, the relative importance of Informal roles drops off much less. It does drop to some extent because of older people's generally lower social participation. But of the three types, the relative importance of the Informal roles changes least from the earlier life-stages and remains the most sta-

ble throughout life. This is probably true whether the persons involved are self-selected or group-selected, although this is subject to future research.

The flatter profile of the Informal curve probably involves four main factors, as outlined in the following paragraphs.

1. Informal roles encompass a broader range of contexts than the Institutional type. They occur in both the major and lesser institutional spheres, in formal and informal settings, in organized and more amorphous groups. But regardless of setting, they belong to the *informal* system. To this extent, they may operate within formal structures to supplement and modify Institutional roles and adapt them to the particular local context. This is the basis for their moderate correlation with the Institutional curve. However, insofar as they also operate within informal groups that are not so institutionalized, this tends to reduce their correlation with the Institutional profile. Therefore, their straddling of purely informal social groups and the informal subsystems of major institutions tend to have contrary effects that operate in somewhat different directions. Because there are two loci of activity, one with major Institutional roles and the other without them, Institutional roles can account for only part of the variance. This reduces the possible correlation between them.

However, insofar as Informal roles appear in purely informal settings that remain viable spheres of participation in the later years, they are not subject to the sharp attrition that characterizes the loss of major Institutional roles. Therefore, even in retirement and widowhood, people may continue to operate in their informal groups of friends and neighbors, preserving some significant basis of their Informal roles. Thereby, these roles may remain more stable and decline less than the Institutional.

2. These considerations also make it clear that Informal roles are *less* correlated than the Institutional type with social responsibility. Therefore, the Informal curve should not vary so sensitively as the Institutional

through the life-stages with the ebb and flow of social duties and obligations. This factor alone would prevent these roles from reaching the relative importance of the Institutional type. To the extent that the Informal occur in major institutionalized contexts, they may echo the other profile, but only partially and with considerable modulation. Accordingly, the Informal curve is relatively flatter.

3. The sheer number of persons with Informal roles is fewer than those with Institutional roles. For any particular individual, the ratio of his Informal/Institutional roles is almost certainly lower prior to old age than when he is elderly. During most of adulthood, people's lives are basically structured by their Institutional role obligations (Goode, 1960b), and these almost invariably take precedence over other considerations. That is, regardless of the deviant minority (viz., the never married, the imprisoned, and so on), virtually all adults have major status and role commitments. But within any given group or setting, only some members, not all, have significant Informal roles. Not all are leavening jokesters or scapegoats serving to unify other group members. Not all have special functions for the group that distinguish them from other members, whether in formal or informal settings. Therefore, in contrast to the Institutional type, fewer persons perform Informal roles, and there are fewer of these in any actor's total role repertoire. This also limits the correlation between the two curves and keeps the relative importance of the Informal type below that of the Institutional prior to old age. By the same token, because fewer people are involved, the overall Informal profile may vary irregularly, but within a narrower, flatter range, over the life course.

4. Finally, Informal roles are also the major repository of people's more stable personal styles. These may evolve from and reflect personality characteristics that are refined in adolescence and adulthood into fairly regular attributes that confer individual tone and flavor to people's social identities. As nominal personal qualities, they may set a common manner in which the person fills different roles. The actor develops a style that may be perceived in personality terms and evokes similar reactions across situations and groups. His relatively basic, stable style may underlie his similar relation to these groups and the nature of his Informal roles. The sheer fact that such particular patterns may develop from personality characteristics may reflect a selection process in the casting of characters. But otherwise, personality may have little further effect on the social functions that these styles may serve. From the group perspective, it may make little difference *who* performs certain functions. On the other hand, the personal styles may also affect what functions are served. Needless to say, such styles are not always expressions of personality, for many are purely socially or culturally determined, as the women's liberation movement has insisted and other professional literature has borne out (Clausen, 1968; Inkeles and Levinson, 1968; Lieberman, 1950; Goslin, 1969). But at the moment, regardless of source and their reinforcing interaction, personal styles may play themselves out in similar ways across groups and situations. So an individual may develop a style—as a kittenish coquette, as an irascible grouch, as a pollyanna *Luftmensch,* as a braggart, as a cynic, or whatever—that colors his relations to others and his participation in diverse groups. In the process, his personal style may well predispose him or others to cast him in various Informal roles. To the extent that these inhere in relatively settled, well-developed forms, they should help to stabilize the curve of Informal roles throughout a person's life.

These four factors, then—the straddling of Institutional and Informal contexts, lower social responsibility, fewer persons, and personal styles—seem to be the key variables that account for the profile of the Informal type: its relatively greater stability than the other two in the course of life, its lower overall importance than the Institutional type before old age, and its greater importance during old age when the loss of major roles becomes significant.

POLICY IMPLICATIONS

As an added note, the theory underlying these curves contains one implication for the aged that policy makers and practitioners might consider. This is illustrated by the shaded section in Figure 3, after the Institutional and Informal curves intersect in old age. If we assume that one major social policy objective is the maintenance of roles for the elderly, then the curves in later life in Figure 3 shed some light on the possible resources for this. The shaded area shows the relatively greater stability of Informal over Institutional roles. The blank area between the Informal and Tenuous profiles represents an effective role "deficit." The policy objective of role maintenance would be to minimize this role deficit. Under different conditions—certainly in another social system, or perhaps in a less imperfect or a more idealistic, sentimental world—one might try to preserve the rights, duties, and participation of the aged by maintaining their Institutional roles and thereby reducing their Tenuous posture. But there is little prospect for this in modern, advanced societies, for our social organization systematically undermines the position of the elderly and deprives them of major institutional functions (Rosow, 1962). So it is fatuous to hope that policy makers can preserve these central roles simply through goodwill and ingenuity. Other drastic social changes in our institutional structure and its dominant values would be necessary. And such fortuitous developments cannot simply be taken for granted. Under these conditions, the maintenance of Institutional roles presents no viable alternative to the reduction of the Tenuous–Informal gap.

If an alternative policy and a possible resource for it exist, they must be sought in enlarging the shaded area of Informal roles. Any prospective flexibility must be found there. This has two major implications:

1. Attention would have to be focused primarily on the *informal* social system, mainly on the networks of friendship, neighboring, and similar links that develop from spontaneous associations and voluntary activities that generate cohesive social groups. The problem is not simply to contrive artificial programs to be imposed from above in an effort to induce old people to participate. Rather, it would be necessary to recognize and work with those conditions that stimulate *spontaneous* social ties and provide natural opportunities for informal roles within our present institutional structure. Then social policy could undertake to support and strengthen those favorable conditions. In other words, from a strategic standpoint, there is less likelihood of a significant *role* payoff in direct service programs for the aged than there might be in those efforts that address the social context of their lives, their environment, and the world in which they live and move. This means very simply to optimize those normal social forces that are conducive to spontaneous relationships, voluntary groups, and Informal roles. Once these favorable conditions have been strengthened and contextual obstacles to association minimized, the factors that are congenial to interaction could then come into play and operate more freely. Thereby, the chances of increasing Informal roles at the expense of the Tenuous would be enhanced.

2. Furthermore, the prospective success of such intervention would increase to the extent that it mobilized and capitalized on old people's *status similarity*. This would ideally rest not simply on age alone, but generally on as many other shared statuses as possible: sex, marital position, race, ethnicity, social class, religion, and other aspects of common social background. This reflects the fact that insofar as people share a similar cultural heritage, history, social position, life-style, experience, and fate, the prospect of their spontaneous interaction and group stability is enhanced. In other words, the closer one approximates social homogeneity, the greater the likelihood of informal group life, continued participation, and the development of Informal roles.

Such integration has viable prospects when based on old people's other voluntary associations or formal organizations, even if membership or participation has lapsed. The success of many enterprises for the aged is greatly enhanced when there is self-selectivity (or even eligibility) based on other shared statuses or identities. For this reason, senior citizens programs attached to an established church or ethnic center are more successful than those organized by agencies with which old people have not been previously affiliated. The same principle applies to various retirement housing or communities that limit recruitment to selected groups, such as Florida's Salhaven (upholsterers' union) and Moosehaven (the Moose Lodge), the retired teachers' apartment in Omaha, and others. Arlie Hochschild's (1973) study provides an excellent example of the solidary effects of common background, shared statuses, and social homogeneity in providing continuity of life-style and generating informal roles. Formal organizations and voluntary associations afford an entrée to persons of similar identity and status, both past and present. To the extent that such former memberships were salient and meaningful, they retain a significant status potential that could be mobilized with imaginative contextual management. Thus, shared statuses, both current and previous, including formal organizational affiliations, could well be capitalized upon in the maintenance and even increase of informal roles in old age. But clearly, regardless of how common statuses may be used, the essential leverage remains within the system of Informal roles.

SOME PENULTIMATE THOUGHTS

Before concluding, it is useful to clarify how the present formulation is related to other perspectives in the literature. Here we are not concerned with theories of personality development or technical issues of developmental psychology; nor with that life review (Butler, 1963) whereby individuals continue to "process" residual problems from earlier life stages; nor with those subjective evaluations of events, periods, or stage transitions of the life history that generate "satisfaction profiles" or "stress curves" (Lowenthal et al., 1975). These global perspectives are oriented to the life span, but they are not systematically concerned with role problems per se.

Though her interests were certainly peripheral to ours, a general debt must be acknowledged to Charlotte Buehler's early attention to the life course as a psychological problem (1933). Her profound concern with personal growth and "self-realization" eventually came to settle on processes of goal setting and the determinates of changing goals throughout life (Buehler and Massarik, 1968). Yet her central interests remained psychological; so her work was not readily commensurate with a role perspective, even though institutional factors were recognized as significant variables in goal setting (Buehler and Massarik, 1968, Part IV).

But her earlier work is somewhat more relevant here. Buehler developed a simple technique to profile individual lives. It distributed the relative activity of a person in different spheres ("dimensions") that were salient at some point during the life span—spheres such as marriage, housekeeping, social activity, work, avocational interests, or whatever significantly depicted the person's life at any stage (Frenkel-Brunswik, 1968). It traced the constancy and change in the activity profiles over an individual's life course. From our perspective, these activity spheres do not correspond to status–role types, though many do represent Institutional or Informal roles. But the degree of correspondence per se is not crucial. The significance of Buehler for our formulation is her concern with a range of potential role activity beyond sheer Institutional roles.

One of the foremost sociological role theorists has recently produced a definitive volume on role theory that attempts an integrative theoretical statement (Biddle, 1979). This is an impressive book in many respects, but one that does not cast roles in a temporal framework of role timing, role change, roles in the life span, or role sequences, in age or other terms. The only attention to change is related to occupations (pp. 312–321): at the system level, social change alters work roles, and at the individual level, the person can be changed by socialization to work and by conforming to job expectations (as in any given role performance). But Biddle does not deal with the analytic problem of status types addressed here or with role change in a life span perspective.

Other scholars, however, have been specifically concerned with roles in various contexts of time or change. A major stimulus to modern sociological interest in role chronology was Paul Glick's work on the family cycle, begun in the late forties and periodically updated (Glick, 1947; Glick et al., 1963; Glick and Parke, 1965; Glick, 1977). He divided the family history into stages marked by the spouses' ages at the time of selected role changes or transitions, such as marriage, birth and marriage of children, and death of spouse. Others extended the principle to encompass a broader range of status successions (Neugarten and Moore, 1968). These interests were paralleled by increased attention to stages or "trajectories" in other contexts, including career mobility (Glaser, 1968), hospital courses (Roth, 1963), or other transitions (Glaser and Strauss, 1973).

But it remained for Bernice Neugarten to highlight the special problem of role timing in status sequences (Neugarten, 1968; Neugarten and Moore, 1968; Neugarten and Datan, 1973). She postulated that entry to and exit from various roles was regulated by social norms of age appropriateness, and that deviation from them tended to have adverse consequences. Subsequent research confirmed the operation of normative timing in family (Olson, 1969) and career (Huyck, 1970) stages. But the predicted effects of off-timing proved uneven, being negative in some contexts (Nydegger, 1973; Veevers, 1972), but surprisingly favorable in others (Nydegger, 1973).

This work basically concentrated on role timing *within* single institutions: major roles in family or career sequences. The next logical step was to examine timing *between* institutional roles, the synchronized or asynchronous loading of different positions. This

proved at least as consequential as the timing of single institutional successions (Huyck, 1973). Nydegger's (1981b) research on fathers found that early fatherhood tends to penalize career development by concentrating the conflicting demands of job and family in the early career stages, sometimes with long-term reverberations. On the other hand, late fatherhood reduces role conflict by ordering major demands in these spheres serially, thereby facilitating performance in both areas.

In this vein, Hogan (1981) examined the transition of American men to adulthood in the timing and sequence of three major events: completion of education, start of first job, and getting married. He found that the time taken to complete these three steps is contracting. But more important, the succession of education, work, and marriage is socially normative, and men who change the sequence of these steps suffer in their subsequent career mobility, earnings, and marital disruption. In this respect, while Nydegger's late fathers were significantly off-time, they did not violate the institutional sequencing that Hogan projected. The normative ordering of these major roles apparently confers an advantage in our society.

Another valuable perspective appears in Spence and Lonner's (1978–79) treatment of motherhood as a "career"—somewhat in my sense of role change as the modification of a single role between age periods (though they do not consider stages). They speak of such careers as having developmental thrust, trajectory, awareness of the timing of sequential events, long-term planning, and expectations based on those plans. They suggest that breakdown in the planned development of one role will disrupt other role trajectories—implicitly as a projection of role conflict through time. Yet their discussion is illustrative, not systematic, and it is blurred by inconsistencies and ambiguities, viz., "Beyond the motherhood career, women have wifehood and selfhood careers . . . . Career set is the balance of these various careers at any point in time" (Spence and Lonner, 1978–79). While the notion of multiple roles is cast in a time framework, its articulation and analysis are vague.

But Spence and Lonner introduce the novel view that a collection of changing roles can be conceptualized as a "career set" that complements Merton's (1957) notion of status set. Career set places several simultaneous roles squarely in a dynamic framework. It implicitly poses the problem of how to relate their respective patterns to one another. The means of integrating several profiles of role change is an extremely subtle problem. It is even more complicated than that of status crystallization: the reconciliation of people's disparate positions on Weber's three classic stratification orders of class, status, and power. The problem of career set is more complex because it requires the analysis of multiple change profiles and the conceptualization of their temporal relations, including matters of relative timing, phasing, harmony, resonance, dissonance, and so on. These issues are also involved in my status-role profiles. In this sense, Spence and Lonner's concept of career set taps common theoretical ground, but in terms of discrete roles (however vague at times) rather than the more general role typology of this chapter. Career set is an important concept awaiting more systematic development.

Other empirical and conceptual work, however, is only tangentially related to these problems, tangential insofar as work that potentially concerns any aspect of role change might conceivably become germane. Such research abounds. As an illustration, Videbeck and Knox (1965) report on changes in the levels and types of "non-sustenance" activities in an aging subsample (50+ years) of a representative sample of 1500 adult Nebraskans. Their major findings emphasize the familiar continuity of middle-age patterns into the later years, particularly when there is no major change of life or roles, such as retirement, widowhood, residential move, and so on. However, the data were gathered for another purpose than that of this chapter, so they are cast in quite different terms. This is typical of the current gerontological treatment of roles which has only limited relevance for our typology.

To summarize the foregoing review, this chapter is part of an increasing body of temporal thought about problems of role change in adult life. It is distinguished by a life-span perspective and conceptualization of roles as analytic types rather than discrete entities. Both aspects have generality and provide a framework for the integration of changes in different types of roles across life-stages. This is a long-neglected problem area that warrants substantial research and development.

No other work has proposed a comparable analytic framework for the study of role change through the life span. But in recent years, several strands of research have begun to crystallize around issues of role timing and role sequences (Nydegger, 1980). Most have concentrated on major Institutional roles rather than the range of types addressed in this chapter. While some have involved longer time perspectives, such as the extended effects of deviant role timing, most have tended to examine proximate questions. None has been set in the larger framework of the adult life course. The general concern with the timing of Institutional status sequences is significant and bodes well for the development of an important body of middle-range theory.

The concept of career set is also potentially rich and promising. It continues Buehler's broad concern with changing lives, expanding the scope of pertinent roles beyond the Institutional, and adopting a longer-term perspective than that of most timing/sequencing research. It evokes the problem of how several discrete profiles of changing roles can be conceptualized, analyzed, and integrated—the original problem posed at the beginning of this chapter (Clausen, 1972). Career set obviously provides no analytic framework for this integration, but it does offer a useful concept to identify and locate the problem, also serving as a constant reminder of its presence. Giving a distinctive name to such an unresolved problem is not to be despised.

On another matter, the status–role curves delineated in Figure 3 are not molded in concrete. Just as discrete roles and role types are subject to life-stage changes, so are the change profiles themselves subject to shifts from historical circumstances. As the force of their governing variables changes, the curves may be tugged and pushed in different directions, even though the same variables remain in charge. Pressures of change are constantly at work, especially on Institutional roles, that may slightly displace the curves in one direction or another, particularly if they reinforce each other. Thereby, for example, earlier marriage, parenthood, or retirement would independently push the Institutional curve to the left, whereas deferring these events would press it to the right. Or, the drastic increase in longevity during this century would have had major effects on these curves. Similarly, the growing disparity in men's and women's longevity should have different effects on these profiles. Also, changes in the timing of widowhood would shift the right edge of both the Institutional and Tenuous curves in the same direction—to the left if widowhood came earlier, to the right if it came later. Or several forces of change that push in opposite directions could cancel each other and leave the curve relatively unaffected. Or role sequences that substitute one Institutional role for another (viz., finishing school and starting work) would not particularly move the Institutional curve either way or alter its shape. So sheer role successions within or even between institutional spheres do not necessarily have strong effects on the location or shape of the curve.

On the whole, the main pressures on the curves in recent years center in the Institutional sphere. During the 1960s and 1970s—before inflation became a massive problem—affluence and improved retirement incomes fostered a significant trend toward early retirement, and this clearly shifted the right edge of the Institutional and Tenuous curves to the left.

By the same token, an economy of greater scarcity promises several counteracting effects on work and retirement in old age, especially if deepening scarcity is a long-term prospect. The key factors are the rising costs of social security and the pressure of public policy to reduce them by eliminating compulsory retirement, discouraging retirement altogether, and promoting longer work life. Another aspect of such scarcity is a reduction in economic growth and the rate of capital investment. The lower capitalization promises to reduce productivity and, with deterioration of plant and equipment, places some premium on labor to replace the production of worn-out equipment—the obverse process of technological displacement. In this case, lower productivity may sustain a limited market for labor. To the extent that older workers command scarce skills, they might enjoy a market advantage. Maintaining some demand for older workers and preserving their jobs would make the Institutional curve bulge to the right.

On the other hand, there is no assurance that older workers would have any advantage. Other forces might severely undermine them. A scarcity economy immediately implies a depressed if not contracting market. This would limit the demand for labor, creating a labor surplus and extensive unemployment. Hence, intense competition would probably arise for the few available jobs. Unless older workers could offer especially scarce skills or experience, the prospect of their successful competition against younger workers would be unpromising. Their chances would be even dimmer if residual unions or other labor contractors were to give priority for jobs to young and middle-aged workers with heavier family responsibilities than the old. The net effect would reduce the general demand for workers, particularly the old, excluding them from the labor force earlier and imposing on everybody a shorter (employed) work life. While major economic change could drastically alter the entire structure of the labor market, it would necessarily alter the factors and thrust of this analysis.

Which set of these forces would ultimately prevail is quite unpredictable, for that would depend on many immediate conditions that cannot be foretold. So the outcome would be an empirical issue, one directly pertinent to the shape of future role curves.

If demographic and resource pressures

promise increasing economic scarcity into the twenty-first century as many analysts predict (cf. Rosow, 1975), then other shifts in the Institutional curve might be projected on the basis of short- versus long-term trends in health and longevity. The cohort born between the two world wars represents a significant transitional generation, a major beneficiary of modern public health and medicine as well as the unprecedented bounty of the 1950s and 1960s. Now on the threshold of retirement, this transitional generation may prove to be the healthiest and longest-lived of any older cohort yet observed. If this should be true, it could defer the onset of widowhood in the near term (until the end of the century) and press the right edges of the Institutional and Tenuous curves toward the right. But if an economy of scarcity should be well established by the end of the century, these health and longevity gains would be difficult to maintain. And in the long term, our transitional healthy cohort might be succeeded by shorter-lived generations in poorer health. Accordingly, earlier mortality and widowhood would then tend to displace the Institutional and Tenuous curves back to the left.

This discussion clearly illustrates the dynamic nature of the role curves in adult life, their responsiveness to forces of history and social change. The curves have sufficient ballast not to be easily deflected by ephemera or chance breezes. But they do reflect the basic institutional forces in social organization, and they will shift as these change.

I have also been asked to comment on the current state of norms for older people in light of my observations in the earlier edition of this chapter (p. 463). These were predicated on work done for my *Socialization to Old Age* (Rosow, 1974), in which a meticulous review of the literature revealed only weak evidence of social norms for the aged. With minor normative expectations, there were no significant elements of age roles. Since that time, my graduate students and I have continued to monitor the literature, and the situation remains essentially unchanged. We have been unable to locate research that clearly documents changing age norms as *so-*

cial norms for older people, of significant new prescriptions or proscriptions for them. Perhaps the closest approach to a new norm—in Miami and possibly other retirement centers—is the apparent easing of the strong proscription against unmarried older couples living together, presumably a response to the marriage penalty for social security benefits and an extension to the older populace of the casual contemporary mores and life-styles. But aside from this, there is little. Despite all the airy assumptions to the contrary, there are still no significant research data on emergent age norms for the elderly, no new sets of normative expectations.

If this is the case, why do these assumptions persist? There seem to be two related reasons. First, as Wrong (1961) noted, there is an uncritical generalization of the socialization process and its effects. Wrong criticized the almost indiscriminate readiness to attribute so many personal characteristics to socialization. This tendency may operate virtually as a reflex, tautologically ascribing to socialization things that have nothing whatever to do with it. Because many phenomena are so commonly assumed to be the outcome of socialization, their very presence is taken as its confirmation—indeed, tautology with a vengeance. Actually, the results of socialization are often very problematic and uncertain, so they require unequivocal demonstration, not blithe assertion.

The second reason for the unwarranted assumption about age norms is the careless abuse of the notion of social norms. This is a technical concept. In terms of the elderly, *social norms involve valued beliefs and behavior generally regarded as desirable and proper for older people because of their age.* As normative expectations, social norms can always be formulated as "should" or "ought" statements. Insofar as age roles are shaped by *shared* views on age-appropriate behavior, social norms specify what is proper for older persons. Inculcation of such norms is the object of socialization.

This sense of social norms is rigorous, but pefectly conventional—and it is regularly forgotten. Confusion arises with an oblivious shift from *social* to *statistical* norms. Where social norms specify the oughts, statistical norms independently describe what is, whether or not that is valued (Rosow, 1974). When the two are not carefully distinguished, there is a tendency to blur and then to equate them, unwittingly sliding into another tautology: the "is-es" signify the "oughts." Or statistical tendencies putatively express social norms. Obviously this is not necessarily so. As I have elsewhere suggested, old people's typically straitened finances are by no means desirable, nor, by any stretch of the imagination, is the modality of widowhood (Rosow, 1974). Some modalities do express social norms, but many do not, and the terms of their correspondence or independence is a major theoretical problem. Statistical tendencies may reflect many social factors beside norms: common characteristics, objective problems/circumstances that give rise to similar adaptations without any social value attached, the persistence of various social patterns without reference to age, and so on.

So the frequent assumption of significant social norms and age roles for older persons reflects an overgeneralization of socialization processes and a misuse of the concept of social norms. Most casual assertions about norms do not refer to genuine social norms. Despite the subtle difficulties in explicating norms for any role, the scientific literature still reveals no firm evidence of significant social norms or age roles for the elderly.

CONCLUSION

We have offered here an inclusive taxonomy of status and role types to incorporate the deviant cases that Linton's formulation failed to take into account. This enabled us to clarify several abiding ambiguities associated with these concepts, notably the Tenuous and Informal types in which status and role occur separately rather than together. This made these atypical cases more amenable to analysis within a role framework, and eventually we proposed separate profiles of role change through the life cycle.

The aged represent the prototype of Ten-uous roles in which statuses are emptied of functions. While the Tenuous describe a U-shaped curve in the course of life, their relative importance is biased toward the later stages. Role contraction typifies late middle age, and both contraction and status loss mark old age.

The declining social responsibility and role attrition of the elderly are reflected in their shrinking social world. Sociologically, they display the decrements of retirement, widowhood, declining health and income, reduced group memberships and social interaction. This involves the loss and emptying of roles, in both number and content. For women, the contraction of domestic roles begins well into middle age when the first child leaves home and continues into old age, especially after widowhood. For men, role attrition starts about the same time with an easing of work activity and continues after retirement. In the vestibule to old age during the preretirement period, people enter a phase of declining social activity, including formal organizational memberships, and a gradually contracting social world. This reflects their increasingly marginal social participation. Institutional roles wither away, and other decrements rise precipitately after age 65.

This general pattern appears in the inverse relationship between the curves of Institutional and Tenuous roles. In later life, the Institutional decline in relative importance, and the Tenuous correspondingly increase. Indeed, this process makes such residual ascribed statuses as age more prominent and, in the social evaluation of the elderly, supports the shift from standards of role performance to ascriptive criteria.

Although Informal roles have significant group and individual functions, they are neither integral nor reducible to particular status positions. In contrast to Institutional and Tenuous roles, the Informal curve through the life span varies less and is relatively flatter. In old age, its comparative importance decreases much less than the Institutional and does not rise as the Tenuous does. This relatively greater stability inheres in the facts that Informal roles are not closely linked with social responsibility, they straddle formal and informal contexts, and the absorb personal styles across situations. Accordingly, as we have seen, Informal roles afford the most viable prospect for role maintenance in the face of the Institutional deficits of later life, particularly if this capitalizes on status homogeneity among the aged and on continuities from their earlier life-stages.

The present formulation is an interim refinement of current perspectives on status and role, hopefully one that will stimulate further research and theoretical development, not only on the elderly per se but on a sociology of the life course where aging properly belongs.

REFERENCES

Bakke, E. W. 1934. *The Unemployed Man.* New York: E. P. Dutton.

Bakke, E. W. 1940a. *Citizens Without Work.* New Haven: Yale University Press.

Bakke, E. W. 1940b. *The Unemployed Worker.* New Haven: Yale University Press.

Becker, Howard, 1963. *Outsiders: Studies in the Sociology of Deviance.* New York: The Free Press.

Biddle, Bruce. 1979. *Role Theory: Expectations, Identities, and Behaviors.* New York: Academic Press.

Biddle, Bruce, and Thomas, Edwin (eds.). 1966. *Role Theory: Concepts and Research.* New York: John Wiley.

Buehler, Charlotte, 1933. *Die Menschliche Lebenslauf als psychologisches Problem* (The Human Life Course as Psychological Problem). Leipzig: S. Hirzel. (1959. 2nd ed. Goettingen: Verlag fuer Psychologie).

Buehler, Charlotte, and Massarik, Fred (eds.). 1968. *The Course of Human Life: A Study of Goals in Humanistic Perspective.* New York: Springer Publishing.

Bureau of the Census. 1973. *Statistical Abstract of the United States, 1973.* Washington, D.C.: Department of Commerce.

Burgess, Ernest. 1950. Personal and social adjustment in old age. *In* Milton Derber (ed.), *The Aged and Society,* pp. 138–156. Champaign, Ill.: Industrial Relations Research Association.

Butler, Robert. 1963. The life review: An interpretation of reminiscence in the aged. *Psychiatry* 26:65–76.

Clausen, John (ed.). 1968. *Socialization and Society.* Boston: Little, Brown.

Clausen, John. 1972. The life course of individuals. *In* Matilda Riley, Marilyn Johnson, and Anne Foner, *Aging and Society,* Vol. 3, *A Sociology of Age Stratification,* pp. 457–514. New York: Russell Sage Foundation.

Frenkel-Brunswik, Else. 1968. Adjustments and reorientation in the course of the life span. *In* Bernice Neugarten (ed.), *Middle-Age and Aging,* pp. 77–84. Chicago: University of Chicago Press.

Ginzberg, E. 1943. *The Unemployed.* New York: Harper and Brothers.

Glaser, Barney, 1968. *Organizational Careers.* Chicago: Aldine Publishing.

Glaser, Barney, and Strauss, Anselm. 1971. *Status Passage.* Chicago: Aldine-Atherton.

Glick, Paul. 1947. The family cycle. *Am. Soc. Rev.* 12:167–174.

Glick, Paul. 1977. Updating the life cycle of the family. *J. Marr. & Fam.* 39:5–13.

Glick, Paul, Heer, David, and Beresford, John. 1963. Family formation and family composition. *In* Marvin Sussman (ed.), *Sourcebook in Marriage and the Family,* 2nd ed. Boston: Houghton Mifflin.

Glick, Paul, and Parke, Robert, Jr. 1965. New approaches in studying the life cycle of the family. *Demography* 2:187–202.

Goffman, Erving. 1958a. The characteristics of total institutions. *In: Symposium on Preventive and Social Psychiatry,* pp. 43–84. Washington, D.C.: Walter Reed Army Institute of Research.

Goffman, Erving. 1958b. *Presentation of Self in Everyday Life.* Edinburgh: University of Edinburgh.

Goffman, Erving. 1961. *Asylums.* Garden City, New York: Doubleday.

Goode, William. 1956. *After Divorce.* New York: The Free Press.

Goode, William. 1960a. Illegitimacy in the Caribbean social structure. *Am. Soc. Rev.* 25:21–30.

Goslin, David (ed.). 1969. *Handbook of Socialization Theory and Research.* Chicago: Rand McNally.

Havighurst, Robert, and Albrecht, Ruth. 1953. *Older People.* New York: Longmans.

Hochschild, Arlie. 1973. *The Unexpected Community.* Englewood Cliffs, N. J.: Prentice-Hall.

Hogan, Dennis. 1981. *Transitions and Social Change.* New York: Academic Press.

Hunter, Woodrow, and Maurice, Helen. 1953. *Older People Tell Their Story.* Ann Arbor: University of Michigan, Division of Gerontology.

Huyck, Margaret. 1970. Age norms and career lines in the careers of military officers. Unpublished Ph.D. thesis, University of Chicago.

Huyck, Margaret. 1973. Social class and age cohort patterns in timing of education, family and career. Paper delivered at the 26th Annual Meetings of the Gerontological Society, Miami Beach.

Inkeles, Alex, and Levinson, Daniel. 1968. National character: The study of modal personality and sociocultural systems. *In* Gardner Lindzey and Elliot Aronson (eds.), *Handbook of Social Psychology,* 2nd ed., Vol. 4, pp. 418–506. Reading, Mass.: Addison-Wesley.

Jahoda, Marie, Lazarsfeld, Paul, and Zeisel, Hans. 1971. *Marienthal: The Sociography of an Unemployed Community.* Chicago: Aldine-Atherton.

Klapp, Orrin. 1962. *Heroes, Villains and Fools.* Englewood Cliffs, N. J.: Prentice-Hall.

Klapp, Orrin. 1965. *Symbolic Leaders: Public Dramas and Public Men.* Chicago: Aldine.

Komarovsky, Mirra. 1940. *The Unemployed Man and His Family.* New York: Dryden.

Komarovsky, Mirra. 1973. Some problems in role analysis. *Am. Soc. Rev.* 38:649-662.

Lieberman, Seymour. 1950. The effects of changes in roles on the attitudes of role occupants. *Hum. Rel.* 9:385-403.

Linton, Ralph. 1936. *Study of Man.* New York: Appleton-Century.

Lipman, Aaron. 1961. Role conceptions and morale of couples in retirement. *J. Geront.* 16:267-271.

Lowenthal, Marjorie, and Haven, Clayton. 1968. Interaction and adaptation: Intimacy as a critical variable. *Am. Soc. Rev.* 33:23-30.

Lowenthal, Marjorie, Thurnher, Majda, Chiriboga, David, et al. 1975. *Four Stages of Life.* San Francisco: Jossey-Bass.

Merton, Robert. 1957. *Social Theory and Social Structure,* rev. ed. New York: The Free Press.

Neugarten, Bernice. 1968. Adult personality: Toward a psychology of the life cycle. *In* Bernice Neugarten (ed.), *Middle Age and Aging,* pp. 137-147. Chicago: University of Chicago Press.

Neugarten, Bernice, and Datan, Nancy. 1973. Sociological perspectives on the life cycle. *In* Paul Baltes and K. Warner Schaie (eds.), *Life Span Developmental Psychology: Personality and Socialization,* pp. 53-69. New York: Academic Press.

Neugarten, Bernice, and Moore, Joan. 1968. The changing age-status system. *In* Bernice Neugarten (ed.), *Middle Age and Aging,* pp. 5-21. Chicago: University of Chicago Press.

Neugarten, Bernice, Moore, Joan, and Lowe, John. 1965. Age norms, age constraints and adult socialization. *Am. J. Sociol.* 70:710-717.

Newcomb, Theodore. 1966. Foreword. *In* Bruce Biddle and Edwin Thomas (eds.), *Role Theory,* pp. v-vi. New York: John Wiley.

Nydegger, Corinne. 1973. Timing of fatherhood: Role perception and socialization. Unpublished Ph.D. thesis. The Pennsylvania State University.

Nydegger, Corinne. 1980. Role and age transitions: A potpourri of issues. *In* Christine Fry and Jennie Keith (eds.), *New Methods for Old Age Research,* pp. 127-145. Chicago: Loyola University Press.

Nydegger, Corinne. 1981a. On being caught up in time. *Hum. Dev.* 24:1-12.

Nydegger, Corinne. 1981b. Social class and paternal salience. Paper delivered at American Anthropological Association annual meeting, Los Angeles, Dec.

Olson, Kenneth. 1969. Social class and age-group differences in the timing of family status changes. Unpublished Ph.D. thesis, University of Chicago.

Popitz, Heinrich. 1972. The concept of social role as an element in sociological theory. *In* John Jackson (ed.), *Role,* pp. 11-39. New York: Cambridge University Press.

Riley, Matilda, and Foner, Anne. 1968. *Aging and Society,* Vol. 1, *An Inventory of Research Findings.* New York: Russell Sage Foundation.

Riley, Matilda, Johnson, Marilyn, and Foner, Anne. 1972. *Aging and Society,* Vol. 3, *A Sociology of Age Stratification.* New York: Russell Sage Foundation.

Rosow, Irving, 1962. Old age: One moral dilemma of an affluent society. *Gerontologist* 2:182-191.

Rosow, Irving. 1967. *Social Integration of the Aged.* New York: The Free Press.

Rosow, Irving. 1973. The social context of the aging self. *Gerontologist,* 13:82-87.

Rosow, Irving. 1974. *Socialization to Old Age.* Berkeley: University of California Press.

Rosow, Irving. 1975. The aged in post-affluent society. *Gerontology* (Israel) 1(4):3-16.

Rosow, Irving. 1978. What is a cohort and why? *Hum. Dev.* 21:65-75.

Rossi, Alice. 1968. Transition to parenthood. *J. Marr. & Fam.* 30:26-39.

Roth, Julius. 1963. *Timetables.* Indianapolis: Bobbs-Merrill.

Sarbin, Theodore. 1968. Notes on the transformation of social identity. *In* Leigh Roberts, Norman Greenfield, and Milton Miller (eds.), *Comprehensive Mental Health,* pp. 97-115. Madison: University of Wisconsin Press.

Sarbin, Theodore, and Allen, Vernon. 1968. Role Theory. *In* Gardner Lindzey and Elliot Aronson (eds.), *Handbook of Social Psychology,* 2nd ed., Vol. 1, pp. 488-567. Reading, Mass.: Addison-Wesley.

Sletto, Raymond, and Rundquist, E. 1936. *Personality in the Depression.* Minneapolis: University of Minnesota Press.

Spence, Donald, and Lonner, Thomas. 1978-79. Career-set: A resource through transitions and crises. *Int. J. Aging & Hum. Dev.* 9:51-65.

Strauss, Anselm. 1959. *Mirrors and Masks: The Search for Identity.* New York: The Free Press.

Van Gennep, Arnold. 1960 (1908). *Rites of Passage.* Chicago: University of Chicago Press.

Veevers, J. E. 1972. The violation of fertility mores: Voluntary childlessness as deviant behavior. *In* Craig Boydell, Carl Grindstaff, and Paul Whitehead (eds.), *Deviant Behavior and Societal Reaction,* pp. 571-592. Toronto: Holt, Rinehart & Winston.

Veevers, J. E. 1973. Voluntarily childless wives. *Sociol. & Soc. Res.* 5:356-366.

Videbeck, Richard, and Knox, Alan. 1965. Alternative participatory responses to aging. *In* Arnold Rose and Warren Peterson (eds.), *Older People and Their Social World,* pp. 37-48. Philadelphia: F. A. Davis.

Wrong, Dennis. 1961. The oversocialized conception of man. *Am. Soc. Rev.* 26:183-193.

4
PERSONAL CHARACTERISTICS, SOCIAL SUPPORT, AND SOCIAL BEHAVIOR*

Toni C. Antonucci
University of Michigan

Although the importance of formal and informal relationships has long been recognized, social scientists have recently become increasingly interested in the ways in which interpersonal ties contribute to the health and well-being of the individual. In this chapter the importance of these interpersonal relationships is explored with specific attention given to older adults.

It is the purpose of this chapter to update material presented on these issues in the first edition of this *Handbook,* especially the chapters by Lowenthal and Robinson on "Social Networks and Isolation" and Kurt Back on "Personal Characteristics and Social Behavior." First, conceptual and methodological issues are considered in some detail. Next, a model is proposed to facilitate the organization of the literature. A review of the literature follows with a focus on consistent trends and contradictory findings. Finally, suggestions for future research goals are presented.

*Preparation of this chapter was supported in part by grants AG01632 and AG02746 from the National Institute on Aging. I would like to express appreciation to my colleagues for their support during the preparation of this chapter. Special thanks to James S. Jackson and Robert L. Kahn.

CONCEPTUAL ISSUES

Because the terms social support, social networks, and convoys of social support are central to this chapter, a discussion of the most common and useful definitions of these terms follows.

Social Support: Definitions

The task of defining social support has been approached in a variety of ways. Some have defined support on the basis of the individual's perception of social support; others have focused on types of support, that is, categories of behaviors or actions that are considered supportive; and still others have suggested that support be defined in terms of its positive or negative effects.

One of the earliest gerontological studies of social support was reported by Lowenthal and Haven (1968), who focused on the role of intimacy as a critical resource in the lives of older people. The Lowenthal and Haven study used a subjective definition allowing each individual to decide what he or she considered an intimate relationship. Tolsdorf (1976) defined social support as any action or behavior that functions to assist the focal person in meeting his or her personal goals or in dealing with the demands of the particular situation. The focal individual generally makes this subjective evaluation. Similarly, Norbeck (1981) talks about "supportive interactions."

Another group of researchers has attempted to define social support more specifically in terms of types of social support. In this effort there have been some surprising consistencies. Cobb (1976, 1979) represents an early example of this tradition. He defined social support as information that prompts the individual to believe that he or she is cared for and loved, esteemed and valued and belongs to a network of common and mutual obligation. Caplan and Killilea (1976) define social support in a similar manner, suggesting that it improves adaptive competence through emotional mastery, guidance, and feedback. More recently, researchers have focused on three or four different types of support somewhat related to the information emphasis outlined by Cobb and the competence effect suggested by Caplan and Killilea. For example, Gottlieb (1981) refers to four types of support: those that are emotionally sustaining, are problem-solving-oriented, involve indirect personal influence, or involve environmental action. Lopata (1975) and Wellman (1981) have included emotional, informational, and material types of support as important. Cohen and Hoberman (1983) specify four types of support: appraisal, self-esteem, belonging, and tangible support. House (1981) suggests four different types: emotional (involving empathy, love, caring), appraisal (information relevant to self evaluation), informational (to aid coping), and instrumental (tangible aid or help). And, finally, in our own research (Kahn, 1979; Kahn and Antonucci, 1980), we have found the trichotomy of aid (instrumental support), affect (emotional support), and affirmation (acknowledgment or agreement with another's statement or act) most useful.

Support has also been defined in terms of outcomes, especially positive outcomes. Cohen and McKay (1984) define social support as interpersonal processes presumed to result in positive outcomes and to buffer stress. Lin, Ensel, Simeone, and Kuo (1979) suggest that support is that which is accessible to an individual through social ties to other individuals, groups, or the larger community. And recently, Beels (1981), addressing the role of social support in health promotion, defined it as "those factors there are in the environment that promote a favorable course of an illness." These definitions highlight a problem with this construct. Consensual validity is assumed but may not be present. Each of these outcome-oriented definitions, though relatively nonspecific, seems to define support tautologically; that is, support is that which has a positive outcome. Although sometimes sufficient, such a definition may be problematic, for example, in those instances where intent is positive but outcome is not.

The discussion thus far has assumed that the intent and the outcome of the social interaction or social support are each always positive. This assumption can be questioned. In the ideal case, a supportive transaction involves the intent of an actor to be supportive of another, a behavior that expresses that intent, and a supportive effect (i.e., the other person feels supported, and the effect of that support is some objectively ascertainable positive outcome). A complication develops when one or more of these components is inconsistent with the others. For example, A "intends" to act supportively but does not do so, or A acts supportively (according to his or her intent and an objective observer), but the effect on B is negative (i.e., B does not feel supported, or the effect on B's behavior is negative). There may be maladaptive forms of support, for example, overprotection, reinforcement of health-damaging behaviors, or assistance given on demeaning and debilitating terms. For these reasons, it is important that a distinction between intention and outcome be made. It is very possible that the intent of the "supporter" is positive, but the outcome for the recipient of that support is negative.

To summarize this brief review, support has been defined in terms of the individual's perceptions, the types of support provided, and the effect or outcome of the supportive interchange. Most definitions assume that social support is based on supportive social interactions and that the effect of this interaction is favorable. The circularity of these assumptions has been noted (Thoits, 1982). In an effort to avoid this problem in this chapter, social support is defined as interpersonal transactions involving key elements such as aid, affect, or affirmation. However, positive outcomes are not assumed. Consequently apparently negative results of supportive behaviors must also be considered (Heller, 1979).

Social Networks: Definitions

Social networks can be conceived of as vehicles through which social support is distributed or exchanged. The structure of the network has been assessed by counting the individuals who provide certain supports or perform support functions; by mapping formal relationships, for example, between spouses, or supervisor and employee; and by eliciting nominations from the individual about the people he or she feels close to or who are important to him or her. Networks consist of points (sometimes called nodes or positions) and bonds (also called ties, arrows, etc.) indicating connections between points. A network of social support would thus consist of a set of persons and the specified ties of support—the giving and receiving among them (Barnes, 1972; Mitchell, 1969). Perhaps the simplest way to distinguish social support from social networks is to describe social networks as consisting of those people who provide social support. Indeed this has been one of the most frequent approaches taken by researchers. Respondents are asked who would perform specific activities or functions for them, such as take care of them when sick, lend them money, give them advice about a problem. Fischer (1982a,b; Fischer et al., 1977), Phillips (1981), Stephens et al. (1978), and Wellman (1981), among others, have successfully used this approach. Walker et al. (1977) define so-

cial networks as "the set of personal contacts through which the individual maintains his social identity and receives emotional support, material aid and services, information about new social contacts." Most people have focused on the social connectedness of social networks and consider those people who exchange supportive interactions as network members (Fischer et al. 1977; Hammer, 1981; Hirsch, 1981; Israel, 1982; Phillips, 1981; Wan, 1982).

Still another common approach to defining social networks is formal relationship. Lin et al. (1981) describe social networks as the direct and indirect ties linking a group of individuals over definable criteria such as kinship or friendship. This definition introduces a structural or categorical component that deserves attention. By virtue of specific relationships with an individual, that is, being related to the person or labeled by the person as friend or co-worker, one would qualify as a member of his or her social network. Following these lines some researchers have used living arrangements, household composition, and marital status as criteria for network membership (Berkman and Syme, 1979; Brody et al., 1978; Langlie, 1977; Lin, Dean, and Ensel, 1979; Shanas, 1979a,b). Some researchers have allowed respondents to define their social network by naming those people with whom they feel close and with whom they maintain or exchange social interactions and resources. Hirsch (1981), Kahn and Antonucci (1983), Sokolovsky and Cohen (1981a), and Tolsdorf (1976) have used this approach successfully. Social networks are commonly defined in terms of structural properties such as size, stability, homogeneity, symmetry, complexity, and connectedness. It is critical to be aware of the network definition utilized by the researcher, since the operational definition employed will have a significant influence on the type of network data acquired (Antonucci and Depner, 1982). In general, it seems useful to think of social networks as structures and social support as functional behaviors. The critical research question with regard to both structure and function remains: what is their effect on the support exchanged and how do they, either directly or indirectly, affect individual well-being?

Convoys of Social Support: Definitions

The definition of social network as the structure within which support is given, received, and exchanged is rooted in the present and represents a static model. The term Convoy of social support is used to describe the dynamic concept of social networks over the life course (Kahn, 1979). Kahn and Antonucci (1980) visualized the individual as surrounded from early childhood by a variety of network members who are sources of social support. Beginning with the well-documented phenomenon of attachment to primary caregivers, the individual develops a variety of interpersonal relationships that become the bases for the support Convoy. Many of the members continue to maintain a relationship with the focal person. As the individuals involved grow and mature, the nature of their relationships develops and changes. At different points in the life course, members of the Convoy may be lost either through death or through less radical changes. At the same time, as the individual matures, experiencing different life events and transitions, new Convoy members are added.

Thus the child maintains significant though constantly changing relationships with parents but might lose childhood friends who have moved away. With marriage, the individual acquires at minimum one significant new Convoy member who will be a central member until death or perhaps divorce. The elderly widow may have lost many important members of her Convoy, but there still may be some members who have been important to her as a source of social support for 50 years or more. At the same time, she may develop new friendships with other widowed women. These friendships may be short in terms of years but very significant in terms of sharing present life experiences. The term Convoy of social support is designed to emphasize this dynamic aspect of

social interactions. It seems important especially with older people to know the history of a relationship of support exchanges to be able to understand the support relationship in the present. Thus, for example, an older widow may feel perfectly comfortable accepting support or help from one member of her Convoy but not another. With person A she has a "support reserve" having nursed this friend through a severe illness ten years ago, but with person B she has no such support reserve and therefore feels uncomfortable accepting help. We offer the term Convoy, borrowed from the anthropologists (Plath, 1975), to capture this life course dynamic interchange (Kahn and Antonucci, 1980).

METHODOLOGICAL ISSUES

The specific words used to formulate the measurement instrument have a significant impact on the assessment of a construct such as social support or social network (Antonucci and Depner, 1982). Several researchers have used a subjective approach to the definition of social support, asking to whom does the respondent feel close or who is important to the respondent (Kahn and Antonucci, 1983; Lowenthal and Haven, 1968; Pattison et al., 1979). This approach has the advantage of allowing the respondent maximum participation in the assessment. Because subjective assessment has been shown to be an important component of the supportive relationship (Conner et al., 1979), this is an advantage. The obvious disadvantage of this approach is the possible lack of consistency across respondents. To some, "close" might mean geographically close; to others, "important" might mean powerful or influential. Some respondents might feel that such terms as close and important should be reserved only for family members and thereby nominate a social network devoid of friends or non-relatives.

Another common approach to social support assessment has relied on categorical memberships. This approach, used by Berkman and Syme (1979) and Shanas (1979b), assumes that by virtue of a formal relationship the individual is a member of the focal person's network and is engaged in supportive interchanges with that person. There are several advantages to this approach and several limitations. The listing of supporters by category has the potential to be more complete. Thus it is less likely that the respondent will unintentionally structure his network according to a closed set (e.g., all relatives, only non-professionals). If the researcher specifically asks about network members or sources of support from a variety of different sources, it is considerably more likely that the result will be a more complete assessment. On the other hand, this benefit may also be a limitation. If this categorical approach is used, the support sources are limited only to those categories of support mentioned. A major source of support might not be acknowledged because he or she does not fit into any of the offered categories. Experience with both approaches (Antonucci, 1981; Kahn and Antonucci, 1978; Kahn and Antonucci, 1983) indicates that providing categories generally results in more varied network membership that includes people to whom the respondent feels both very close and not too close. Another advantage to the categorical approach is that it increases the likelihood that network members are nominated regardless of the presence of occasional negative as well as positive interactions.

A third measurement approach is to ask respondents who performs certain activities or functions for them and vice versa. Examples of this approach include questions such as who would watch your house if you were out of town for a week, who would lend you money if you needed it, who would take care of you if you were sick. Fischer (1982a), Kahn and Antonucci (1983), Wellman (1981), and Lowenthal et al. (1975) have used this approach with national and regional samples. This approach samples a wide variety of support behaviors, is relatively specific, and provides information that is generalizable. However, these function questions assess very different levels or types of social support. One might feel comfortable asking a neighbor who is practically a stranger to look after one's house while one is out of town but be very unlikely to ask that person for help when sick. In this case the advantage of assessing a wide variety of support behaviors is balanced by the probability of receiving an inflated picture of the number of people the respondent really feels are an important part of his or her social network.

The support network data acquired can be quite different across measures. For example, the support network obtained when asking people who provide a variety of supports is likely to be much larger than that obtained when people are asked to whom they feel close. This difference is apparent in the average number of network members obtained through the two methods. Fischer (1982a), generally using the functional approach of asking who provides specific supports, obtained networks with an average of 18 people in them, whereas Kahn and Antonucci (1983) using the "close and important" definition obtained an average of only 9. Even considering regional and age differences in the two studies, it is clear that some of this discrepancy is due to differences in the measurement techniques. In addition, in some situations (e.g. among the institutionalized elderly) there may be very little overlap between people who are close and important to you and people who perform certain tasks for you. Family and friends may be close and important to the institutionalized elderly, but institutional staff are responsible for their sick care. Longino and Lipman (1981) and Lopata (1979) in particular have noted the possibility of different types of support systems. Longino and Lipman distinguish the provision of support from the appropriation of support, while Lopata discusses emotional, social, economic, and service support systems.

In summary, there are several different types of measurement approaches that have been used successfully to assess social support and social networks. Support can be measured in terms of the individual's perceptions, the type of support provided, and the result or outcome of the "supportive behavior." Networks can be assessed on the basis of formal relationships (e.g., family, friends, co-workers) or on the basis of the performance of supportive acts. Measurement of the former will perhaps be most helpful for an understanding of the mechanisms of support, while the latter should help with an understanding of the process through which support operates.

Network Analysis

Much of the conceptualization of networks is due to the work of Barnes (1972), Bott (1955), Mitchell (1969), and Moreno (1934). In recent years a great deal of attention has been paid to the analysis of networks (Burt, 1980; Marsden, 1982; Wellman, 1981). Analytic strategies tend to focus on network structural characteristics such as size, connectedness, homogeneity, stability, complexity, and symmetry. These terms refer respectively to the number of people in the network; network members who know each other; age, sex, occupational, and other similarities among network members; the average number of years of network membership; the number of different roles or types of relationships shared with another member (uniplex or multiplex); and the reciprocity existing in the relationship in terms of providing and receiving different types of support. In addition, dyadic property links have been utilized and then extended to examine the relationship among network pairs. These dyadic links can be explored in terms of frequency of interactions or number of interactions during a specified time period; initiative or the proportion of interactions initiated by the focal person; complexity, the variety of areas or life domains around which the interaction is based; and duration, the length of time the relationship has endured. It is sometimes helpful to characterize network analysis as being of first or second order. First order analyses involve variables directly available from the raw data (e.g., number of people in the network). Second

order data analyses, on the other hand, involve index construction, that is, variables derived from several sources and considered together. Examples of a second order level variable might include network homogeneity. It would be necessary to consider several characteristics such as age, sex, and race of the network as a whole in order to assess network homogeneity. In recent years there has been a plethora of books and articles on different techniques for network analysis (Alba and Kadushin, 1976; Boorman and White, 1976; Burt, 1980; Fennema and Schijf, 1978/79; Leinhart, 1977; Marsden, 1982; Schwartz and Jacobson, 1977; Tichy, 1980; Wellman, 1981; White et al., 1976). A complete review of these analytic strategies is recommended for the researcher planning to undertake analysis of network data. New techniques being developed should permit exciting discoveries in network research.

A MODEL: THE CONVOY OF SOCIAL SUPPORT

The Convoy of Social Support is a model of social networks over the life course. In this chapter the Convoy, with the older person as the focal point, is used as the organizing theme. In particular, the determinants of the individual's Convoy, the characteristics of the structure and function of the Convoy, and the effects of these on the individual are considered. In principle, this model is longitudinal and, as indicated earlier, refers to a lifetime pattern of support relationships. In fact, much of the research that is reviewed in the context of this model is based upon cross-sectional data. It will be possible to explicate the model more fully when longitudinal data become available.

The basic outline of the model and the hypotheses generated by it are presented in Figure 1. The determinants of Convoy Structure and Functions are related to Personal and Situational Properties. Both types of properties include stable and dynamic characteristics.

Properties of the Person. These properties include age, sex, income, marital status, and

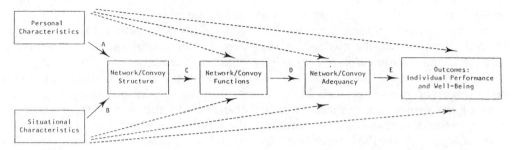

Figure 1.   Hypothetical determinants and effects of network/Convoy properties.

other demographic characteristics, personality, and abilities. Over the life course some characteristics (e.g., gender) will be stable, and others (e.g., age) will change. The majority of these personal properties, however, will vary idiosyncratically. Some people may have stable demographic characteristics, whereas others may experience considerable variability, (e.g., the individual who is middle class throughout his or her lifetime vs. an upwardly mobile counterpart who moves from lower to middle to upper class over a lifetime). Similarly, some personality characteristics are considered stable, others dynamic (e.g., temperament vs. morality—as in moral reasoning). Since individuals vary in terms of their abilities, they may excel in some areas and fail in others. These differences can be stable over time (e.g., the mathematician vs. the linguist), or they may change over time as in the case of the novice who becomes an expert.

Properties of the Situation. Situational Properties involve more objective, externally oriented aspects of the environment. Role expectations, opportunities, demands, resources, residence, organizational membership, and life events are examples of situational characteristics. They generally include the roles one occupies throughout one's life. The research on role theory, in particular role stress, is helpful in this context (House and Wells, 1978; Kahn, 1974). Roles generally incorporate expectations, limitations, opportunities, and requirements, each of which may be influential in activating the Support Convoy. Additionally external factors such as place of residence, organiza-

tional membership and activity, both positive and negative life experiences, and geographical location (urban vs. rural) constitute Properties of the Situation for the individual. As arrows A and B in Figure 1 indicate, Properties of both the Person and the Situation affect the Structure of the Convoy.

Convoy Structure. Convoy Structure refers to network composition over the life course. Among the structural characteristics most commonly assessed are size, connectedness, stability, symmetry, complexity, and homogeneity. These properties have been referred to previously in the discussion of network analysis. However, two points are of special interest. Convoy Structure refers to network structure over the life course. Thus, the ways in which these properties change over time are thought to have significant impact on the person's perception of his/her Convoy and the operation of that Convoy. In addition, Convoy Structure as indicated by arrow C in Figure 1, is hypothesized to influence Convoy Functions directly.

Convoy Functions. Convoy Functions are the actual support given, received, or exchanged by members of the Convoy. Also of importance to the understanding of Convoy Functions is the distribution of supports given, received, and reciprocated. Although research is only now beginning to address this issue, there is reason to believe that giving support only or receiving support only has a more negative effect on an individual than does the exchanging of support. Additionally, the life-span framework of the Convoy concept emphasizes the need to examine these exchange patterns over time. Thus, persons may be only receiving support at this time but may have provided it at an earlier time, and therefore feel they are drawing from a "support reserve."

Convoy Adequacy. All of the components considered thus far, the Properties of the Person and the Situation, and Convoy Structure and Functions, combine to determine the Adequacy of the Convoy, as indicated in Figure 1 by arrow D. This aspect of the model has been interpreted as a subjective component; that is, whether the focal person perceives his or her network as adequate. Thus far we have measured Convoy Adequacy in terms of the individual's perception of the Convoy. If the individual reports that the Convoy is too demanding, not understanding, becoming less important, or consisting of too few people, these are assumed to be indications of Convoy Inadequacy. In some cases Convoy Adequacy might best be considered an outcome itself (see below).

Outcomes. It is our assumption that the individual's sense of Convoy Adequacy is directly related to and a determinant of individual well-being. This relationship is indicated by arrow E in Figure 1. Examples of broad categories of Outcome variables include productive behavior, role performance, self development, health, and overall well-being. Specific Outcome measures commonly employed include health satisfaction, life satisfaction, additional domains of satisfaction, happiness, positive and negative affect. These variables are known to be important indicators of life quality. With the proposed model it is assumed that the Convoy of Social Support helps the individual to adapt and develop over the life course, and thus has an important influence on well-being.

It should be noted that this model is a modified version of that previously presented by Kahn and Antonucci (1980). For convenience the direct influence of each of the separate components of the model on each other has been ignored. Thus, Properties of the Person might influence not only Convoy Structure and through Structure, influence Functions, Adequacy, and Well-

being, but also directly influence Convoy Functions as well as Convoy Adequacy and Well-being. Since the focus of this chapter is on the role of social support and support networks on the individual's behavior and well-being, those aspects of the model that have social support as the central focus have been emphasized. In addition, although the model appears to assume unidirectionality, this assumption is one of convenience. It is recognized that other configurations are possible.

RECENT FINDINGS AND LITERATURE REVIEW

In this section available data are reviewed in terms of the proposed model. The specific variables discussed in this chapter are presented within the context of the model in Table 1.

Properties of the Person

Age. A recent national study of noninstitutionalized adults ($N = 718$) (Kahn and Antonucci, 1983) involved an in-depth assessment of the social networks of people 50 years of age and older. There were no differences among the three age groups (50–64; 65–74; 75–95) in size of network (see Table 2).

In addition to questions about the size of respondents' networks, they were asked about the types of support they received from and provided to their network members. Specifically, people were asked about six types of support: confiding, reassurance, respect, care when sick, talking with when upset, and talking about health. There were few age differences in the amount of support people report receiving from others, although older people compared to younger people report that they provide support to fewer persons.

Responses concerning network adequacy indicate that the younger, not older, respondents wished that they had more people in their network and that their network members were more dependable. As noted previously, however, there were no significant age differences in size of network. It would

TABLE 1. Specific Convoy Variables to be Reviewed.

Personal Characteristics	Network Function
age	confide
sex	reassure
marital status	respect
parental status	sick care
income	talk about health
education	talk when upset
ethnicity	
personality	
frailty	
Situational Characteristics	Network Adequacy
type of residence	doesn't understand
retirement	too demanding
organizational member- ship and activity	network satisfaction network changed
urban/rural living	
Network Structures	Outcomes
size	life satisfaction
connectedness	well-being
homogeneity	domain satisfaction
stability	happiness
complexity	
symmetry	

be intriguing to collect longitudinal data from these people to help determine if this is a cohort or an age effect. Related to this point, a recent study by Veroff et al. (1981) comparing national data from 1957 and 1976 found that younger people (beginning with people 21 years old) report wanting more friends than older people (their oldest age group was categorized as 65+). This trend was evident for both years. However, people in 1976 overall were likely to report wanting more friends than people in 1957. Thus, the data of Veroff et al. along with our own, suggest that older people in the United States do not want more personal contacts and do not feel that they are suffering from insuf-

TABLE 2. Size of Network by Age and Sex.[1]

	50–64	65–74	75–95	Total
Men	8.71	7.13	8.00	7.9
Women	10.06	9.51	9.04	9.5
Total	9.39	8.32	8.52	

[1] Kahn and Antonucci, 1983.

ficient social networks, although a cohort effect seems to also be present.

Our older respondents (Kahn and Antonucci, 1983) also reported greater feelings of network adequacy. They reported less negative feelings about their network than their younger counterparts and more satisfaction with both family and friends.

The assumption is generally made, however, that older people suffer from severe losses in their social networks and that they are both dissatisfied and unhappy with their personal networks. Indeed, Harris (1975) found that while the elderly, especially among the poor, sometimes report feelings of loneliness and rejection, most elderly have fairly extensive social contacts and clearly are not isolated from family and friends. It appears that much of the research evidence used to substantiate the claim of the unattached elderly is based on biased, institutionalized, and/or unhealthy samples. Much less research has been conducted that examines noninstitutionalized, relatively healthy older adults.

However, research evidence on the general elderly population has begun to accumulate. In addition to the results from the Kahn and Antonucci study outlined above, other research findings have indicated similar results. Babchuk (1978–79) conducted an investigation of the primary relations of a large (N = 800) noninstitutionalized Nebraska sample. He found no age differences in the number of primary and confidant relatives cited by both the younger (45–54) and the older (55–64; 65–74) respondents. On the other hand, age differences did appear in the number of primary and confidant friends reported by his respondents. Those in the younger age group tended to claim more network friends than those in either of the older age groups. Stephens et al. (1978) in a large telephone survey in Texas (N = 2604) found that people in their older group (70 and over) were more likely than those in the younger groups to report that they had no one to perform various supportive functions or services for them. However, aside from the experience of this small group of isolates, the three age groups they examined (55–64; 65–69; 70+) were about equally likely to have from two to five people available as supports. Campbell's (1980) data from a national probability sample of adults 20 years of age and older also indicate that there is similarity across age in network size but that older people tended to have fewer confidants. Fischer (1982a) reports a study of the personal networks of adults in Northern California ($N = 1050$). This study, using a functional approach to defining networks, found that people under 40 report more non-kin in their networks than older people. And Cantor (1975), focusing on the urban elderly of New York City, indicates a large informal network among the elderly that does not significantly decrease with age.

In summary, although many persons continue to think that people become increasingly isolated with age, available data simply do not demonstrate this phenomenon. This is not to suggest that there are no isolated aged or that people do not find themselves old and alone. However, as Shanas and Streib reported years ago (1965), the bulk of the data suggest that old people are surrounded by a support network of family and friends (Lebowitz, 1978; Sussman, 1979). The isolated elderly may be continuing a lifelong pattern of isolation as indicated by the studies of people living in single room occupancy hotels (Cohen and Rajkowski, 1982; Felton et al., 1977). In other words, their lifetime Convoy of social support has always been relatively limited. Although there is little change in network size with age, there does appear to be a significant change in the amount of social support exchanged among network members with age. A consistent finding is that people report providing fewer supports to their network members as they get older. Kahn et al. (in press) have noted that the oldest respondents report less frequent contact with network members. However, there is relatively little change in the number of people from whom they receive support. The Convoy notion of social support suggests that the effect of these differences in support received and provided with

age will be dependent upon previous history. Thus, if people are now receiving support from Convoy members to whom they have previously provided a great deal of support, the apparent imbalance will be minimized. On the other hand, if there has been no period when the individual has provided support to a Convoy member, the present imbalance is likely to be experienced more acutely.

Sex. There are differences in the social networks of men and women. As the data from the Kahn and Antonucci (1983) study illustrate (see Table 2), women have significantly larger networks than men. Women also report providing more support than men. An interesting pattern of sex differences is evident, however, for support exchanged, depending upon the designation of support giver and/or support receiver. For example, women overall report providing more support to others than men, but husbands say they provide more support to their spouses than wives report they provide to husbands (Depner and Ingersoll, 1983; Kahn and Antonucci, 1983; Ingersoll, 1982). Women compared to men also report being significantly more satisfied with their friends, but there are no differences in reported satisfaction with family. When asked specifically about marital satisfaction, men report higher levels of satisfaction than women (Antonucci, 1982), and both men and women generally report higher levels of marital satisfaction with age (Kahn and Antonucci, 1983).

In general women have larger and more multifaceted social networks than men. These data are corroborated by several national surveys of the adult population (Campbell, 1980; Harris, 1975; Veroff et al., 1981). The nature of the social ties of women seems to be different from that of men. Men turn to their wives for support, whereas women turn not only to their husbands but also to children, other family members, and friends. This may be a distinction that has far-reaching ramifications for the social relationships of the elderly. Hess (1979; Hess and Markson, 1980) and others (Block et al.,

1981; Candy et al., 1981; Cool, 1981; Depner and Ingersoll, 1983; Powers and Bultena, 1976; Troll et al., 1979; Troll and Turner, 1979) have argued that women have better interpersonal skills than men, and that these skills become important and highly functional in old age. Women can use this interpersonal advantage and their multifaceted networks to achieve greater flexibility with their support Convoys. This becomes increasingly important as the Convoy changes over the life course and network members become unavailable through death, illness, frailty, or geographical distance. Wright (1982) has disagreed with this reasoning, arguing that the friendships of men are different from, not inferior to women's. Nevertheless, these differences might be less adaptive for men than for women in old age.

Relevant data are available. Babchuk's (1978–79) study indicated no differences in the number of primary relations reported by men and women, but there were differences in the number of confidant relatives. Specifically men were more likely to list only one confidant, whereas women more commonly listed more than one. If the prime confidant, most likely the spouse, is available, minimal problems should accrue. However, when that confidant is unavailable, as is the case among widows and widowers, the greater flexibility of a larger network including several confidants is extremely advantageous. Indeed, Antonucci and Wethington (1983) found that the negative effects of marital dissatisfaction were decreased for people who had larger networks and who reported confiding in their network members. This interpretation is consistent with the findings of Hirsch (1981), McKinlay (1980), and Mitchell and Trickett (1980) that size and density are related to mental health, coping, and adaptation.

Marital and Family Status. Marital status definitely affects network membership. In the Kahn and Antonucci study (1983) married people had larger networks than people who were separated and divorced, widowed, or never married. However, there are sex differences within the larger networks of married persons. Wives are less likely than husbands to report receiving support from their spouses, but wives are also less likely than husbands to say that they provide their spouse with support (Depner and Ingersoll, 1983). Women report providing and receiving more support from their children than do men.

Other researchers have also begun to explore variations in social networks among people of different marital and family statuses. Overall, results comparing the social networks of married people with those of people who are not married find married people at an advantage. Babchuk (1978–79) found that married men and women had larger social networks than people who were single, divorced, or widowed. Longino and Lipman (1981), comparing people of different marital statuses, found that married women had the largest support networks and unmarried males the smallest. They also found that unmarried women had better support networks than unmarried men. Ward (1979a) specifically investigated people who had never been married and found that although they reported less happiness than people who were married, they were slightly better off than people who were widowed or divorced. Childlessness seemed to have a minimal effect on the well-being of married people, although childless widows were negatively affected. Johnson and Catalano (1981) report an interesting comparison between childless marrieds and childless unmarrieds. They found that childless married people tended to be more isolated and to rely fairly exclusively on each other. Childless unmarrieds, on the other hand, were more resourceful and had greater diversity in their social networks.

Recent research has addressed the special situation of widowed women. Lopata (1975, 1978, 1979) conducted a large study of the support networks of women in the Chicago area. She found that widows were generally involved in extensive support networks and that the role of children, particularly daughters, was crucial. She also noted the absence of men in the support networks of women.

Gibbs (1981), in a smaller study of the support networks of widows, was also impressed that the women in her sample mentioned no men as network members. And, although Petrowsky (1976) reported that widows were more isolated from kin and friends than were marrieds, Kohen (1983) found that widows do more visiting with others, compared to married people. However, Ferraro and Barresi (1982), using longitudinal data, found no reduction in family interaction until four years after widowhood. And in a recent study, Beckman and Houser (1982) found that widows reported lower levels of well-being than marrieds. These apparent contradictions in interaction patterns may be clarified when examined within the context of social support Convoys over the life course, that is, in terms of consistency and change over time.

Seelback (1977) gives us some insight by examining parents' beliefs about filial responsibility. He found that women had much higher expectations for personal care from children than men. Apparently these expectations are met by the children of widows, since they seem to be considerably more involved in the social networks of widowed mothers than in the networks of widowed fathers.

It should be noted that parent–child interaction patterns are not likely to emerge in late life. Data suggest (Campbell, 1980; Veroff et al., 1981) that, on the contrary, life-long patterns are present, and these patterns simply become more evident with years. For example, Leigh (1982) reports that there are no differences over the family life cycle in the amount of interaction between parents and children. And Troll and Smith (1976), in a three-generation sample of women, found that family bonds override distance and separation regardless of age or generation placement. The pattern of relationships does not seem to emerge with old age but rather appears to be present at different ages and among different generations.

As noted earlier, women have greater diversity than men in their social networks. They are more likely to include both family and friends in their network, and appear to have generally more close relationships or confidants than men. Chiriboga's (1982b) finding that divorce in late life is harder on men than on women lends further support to this notion of the greater social adaptability of women. The Convoy notion should be helpful in understanding the effects of changes in the support network over time. Bengtson and Cutler's (1976) concept of developmental stake suggesting that the generations have differential commitments to intergenerational relationships should also be considered within this context.

Siblings and Grandchildren. Two additional areas of family life have been explored to some limited degree, relations with siblings and relations with grandchildren. As with other family patterns there appear to be sex differences in the nature of sibling relationships. Cicirelli (1977) reports that women provide more emotional support to their siblings than men. Sisters appear to be closer than brothers. However, Lee and Ihinger-Tallman (1980) report no relationship between sibling interaction and morale in older people, and Leigh (1982) found no difference in the amount of interaction among siblings over the family life cycle.

Relationships with grandchildren and the role of grandparents have also recently begun to be explored (Troll et al., 1979; Wood and Robertson, 1976). The findings indicate that the role of grandparent is valued in this society, particularly by older people (Kivnick, 1982). However, interaction with grandchildren does not seem to be correlated with increased well-being or morale among grandparents (Stephens et al., 1978; Wood and Robertson, 1978).

The data on interaction with siblings suggest relative stability over the life course, indicating that the role of siblings in an individual's Convoy is consistent. The role of grandparent, which emerges in middle and late life, is less clear, especially since it appears to be unrelated to well-being. Being a grandparent may best be understood in terms of other relationships over the life course, such as relationships with children and other family members.

Socioeconomic Status, Income, and Education. Personal characteristics of the individual also include other demographic variables such as socioeconomic status, income, and education. These three variables are grouped together because the pattern of network characteristics is similar and consistent. People who have lower socioeconomic status, lower income, and less education tend to have smaller networks that consist mainly of family members. Members of these networks naturally know each other, and network membership is stable. Relationships tend to be multiplex; that is, the same people exchange a variety of different types of supports. People from higher socioeconomic statuses, with higher incomes, and with more education generally report larger networks with a diverse membership consisting of both family and friends. Network members of these latter groups are less likely to know each other, are likely to have known each other for less time, and are more likely to involve uniplex or single support exchanges. A review of recent research in this area is presented below.

Fischer (1982a) reports that people with more education have network relationships that are broader and possibly richer, compared to less educated individuals. The networks of these persons are less dense, and they are more likely to include non-kin. Using household income as the criterion, he found that higher income was associated with more non-kin in the network. In addition, poorer people reported having fewer friends than relatives in their networks and, compared to middle class people, also reported fewer family members in their networks. A national survey (Harris, 1975) found that older people with less education and less income were more likely to report feelings of loneliness, compared to those with more education and income.

Other studies confirm these general findings. Babchuk (1978–79) found that higher levels of education and occupation are as-

sociated with less isolation and with larger networks. Spakes (1979) reports from a national sample of people 55 years of age and over that higher income and education are associated with greater levels of community involvement. Kernodle and Kernodle (1979), in a smaller regional study in the South, found that elderly individuals of lower socioeconomic status had fewer contacts with both family and friends. On the other hand, Cantor (1979) reports that while both the poor and middle class elderly of New York City have extensive contacts with family and friends, the content of their interaction is different. Middle class families are more likely to exchange gifts and money, whereas poorer people exchange instrumental, day-to-day help. Elwell and Maltbie-Crannell (1981) found that men and women with fewer personal resources such as income, had lower levels of social support. Levitt et al. (in press) compared an older, less affluent, uneducated, migrant, Jewish sample in the South Beach section of Miami with a national sample of the elderly using an identical and extensive assessment of their support networks. The discrepancy between the support networks of the two samples was remarkable, with the Miami sample reporting decidedly smaller networks and the exchange of far fewer supports.

Parks and Pilisuk (1981) in their study of 50 older Southern Californians indicated that lower income and less education are associated with increased contact with formal networks (e.g., doctors, clergy, social workers, etc.). In a related study, Pilisuk and Froland (1978) indicated that people in tightly knit networks, such as those characterized by a predominance of family members, are more likely to seek professional support than individuals with loosely knit networks. Since loosely knit networks are associated with characteristics such as high income and education, one could infer that people with higher income and more education are less likely to seek certain types of formal support. Heltsley and Powers (1975) reported a very interesting relationship between socioeconomic status and (a) the amount of contact with family and friends and (b) the perception of that contact. Individuals with higher socioeconomic status had a much more positive perception of their contact with family and friends, although there were no differences in the actual amount of contact.

Some findings point to the special effects of these variables on widows. Lopata (1979) reports that widows with more education have more social interaction with friends and are generally more socially integrated than less educated widows. This effect is stronger for the elderly widows in her sample than for the younger. Little information is available concerning income because this sample was restricted to former or current social security beneficiaries. Two anomalous findings are also worth mentioning. Ferraro and Barresi (1982), examining low-income disabled widows, found no difference in the isolation reported by males and females (i.e., widowers and widows). Dunckley and Lutes (1979) also report that men and women in their Southwestern sample of very poor people had the same number of confidants. These two studies are unusual, since they indicate a lack of sex difference in number of close network members. The possibility exists, given the nature of these two samples, that men and women do not differ markedly in support network characteristics under certain stressful conditions such as poverty. Cohen and Sokolovsky (1980), for example, found that among single room occupancy hotel (SRO) residents, people with less money had fewer family contacts, and that overall SRO inhabitants had a dearth of intimate relations. It may be that poverty both changes the makeup of the social network, such as proportion of family to friends, and also possibly eliminates the sex differences observed in more advantaged groups by reducing network membership of both men and women to an absolute minimum.

Ethnicity. Investigators have explored the possibility of ethnic differences in social support. Gelfand (1980; Gelfand and Kutzik, 1979) noted that some ethnic groups seem to have a more positive view of the elderly than is usual in the United States. This difference may have an important impact upon the quality of life and the social supports older people enjoy. Butler and Lewis (1982), for example, have suggested that some ethnic groups such as blacks and Mexican Americans have stronger family ties than other ethnic groups. A variety of data offer some support for this hypothesis. Cantor's (1979) study of the social support exchanged by inner city elderly in New York City included blacks, whites, and Hispanics, in about equal numbers. These data indicate Hispanics interact with their children more than blacks or whites. Bengtson and his associates (Bengtson, 1979; Bengtson et al., 1981; Dowd and Bengtson, 1978) reported on a large sample ($N = 1269$) from Los Angeles county, including blacks, whites, and Mexican Americans. They, too, found that Mexican Americans have more contact with family than blacks or whites. They also found that whites have more contact with non-kin or friends. Their data suggest that the differences in frequency of contact among family members levels off and begins to disappear with increasing age. In addition, Cantor (see Chapter 26 in this *Handbook*) speculates that these differences might be eradicated when controls for socioeconomic status and education are introduced.

Martineau (1977) reported that informal social participation among blacks in South Bend, Indiana ($N = 530$) was high for both family and friends and considered very important. Kernodle and Kernodle (1979) reported similar findings for blacks with a small Florida sample, but found no differences in the amount of interaction blacks and whites have with friends. They also reported that people with lower socioeconomic status, both blacks and whites, have less contact with friends than people of higher socioeconomic status. In another study in Florida, Linn et al. (1979) compared blacks, whites and Cubans ($N = 283$). They found that women in all three ethnic groups reported more social participation and activity than men, and that Cubans had the least amount of social involvement, whereas blacks had the most. A few studies have examined other ethnic minorities. Johnson (1978) reported that Italians engage in high levels of social contact with family but that this begins to dissipate as intermarriage occurs. Weeks and Cuellar (1981) examined ten different ethnic groups in San Diego ($N = 1139$) and found that immigrants of all ethnic groups were more likely to have closer family ties than American-born generations. As the literature accumulates, however, it begins to appear that ethnic differences in social support are not so pronounced once demographic controls are introduced. Mutran and Skinner (1981) found no race differences in social support but rather found differences in family and friendship contact based upon need. They suggest that the high proportion of negative life events likely to be experienced by the black elderly may account for "the strong bonds of extending help." They argue that blacks receive more help from their families, but that this is because they are in greater need than whites.

The National Study of Black Americans (NSBA) (Jackson et al., 1982) provides the first national data on a probability sample of blacks. Taylor et al. (1982) summarize the support received from family members by older blacks (55 +). Interestingly, they report no sex difference in the amount of support received by men and women. Contrary to the need hypothesis, respondents with less income report receiving support less often than respondents with higher incomes, and, similarly, people with less education report receiving less support from family than people with more education. It may be that the need hypothesis works only within limits; that is, if one is too needy for too long, the support Convoy may disassociate. Along these lines, blacks report a positive relationship between the amount of contact they have with family and the frequency of receiving help from their family. In addition, people report greater feelings of closeness with family members from whom they receive informal support. These NSBA data suggest that a high degree of informal support is exchanged among blacks, but that this is affected by demographic variables such as age, income, and education. In summary, there seem to be ethnic differences in social support, but the nature of these differences is influenced by both demographic and structural factors.

Personality. Another relevant personal characteristic related to social support is personality. It seems clear that an individual's personality will have an important impact upon the type of social support he or she experiencs. Indeed, personality might be seen as a causal attribute in the very development of one's Convoy of support over the life course. Kaplan et al. (1977) have suggested that a Person–Environment (P–E) fit is sought between the individual's personality and his or her support needs. Since individuals differ in their need for and interest in interaction with others, French's (1974) P–E fit perspective may provide an explanatory framework.

In general, personality has not been a main focus of gerontology research. Fortunately, several studies have been conducted with relatively consistent findings that inform our understanding of the relationship between personality and social support. Thomae (1980) recently reviewed this literature which includes several major longitudinal studies of personality. He reports widespread continuity in personality type across the lifespan. This is relevant to the present discussion in that he included among personality characteristics such attributes as activity, social participation, and interaction with family and friends. Studies by Britton and Britton (1972), Costa and McCrae (1976), Maas and Kuypers (1974), Neugarten (1978), Palmore and Kivett (1977), Pierce and Chiriboga (1979), and Schaie and Parham (1976) all point to a relatively high degree of consistency in personality traits. These traits, of course, are subject to variability with extreme changes in circumstances, such as major changes in health or environment.

The personality literature relates to social

support in several ways. The relationship between personality and morale or life satisfaction has been examined, and it seems clear that some personality types are more likely than others to have high morale and life satisfaction (Chiriboga, 1982a; Costa and McCrae 1976; Knapp 1976; Rundall and Evashwick 1982). George (1978) reports that personality factors are related to well-being, but that activity per se is not. Filsinger and Sauer (1978) found no difference in formal or informal organization membership or activity level among different personality clusters. One interpretation of these findings is that for some personality types high interaction or activity with others will be positively related to positive outcomes, but that for other types this relationship does not hold. An important distinction may be necessary here between actual frequency of interaction versus satisfaction with that frequency. As one might predict, the latter is more important than the former, and is not always objectively related to the former. However, in general, some caution is advised in consideration of the assumed relationship between personality and social activity.

Schulz (1982) has explored the "emotionality" of the aged, what some might consider a personality characteristic. He too reports a great deal of similarity in characteristics of the aged and non-aged but some differences. Although variability in emotional states is somewhat reduced with age, there is an increased tendency for negative emotional experiences among older people, including death and illnesses of family and friends. This, of course, has implications for the role and importance of the support network. People experiencing greater negative emotional experiences may have increased need for supportive interactions. However, it is informative to note that Leon et al. (1981) have found that previous knowledge of personality characteristics does not necessarily lead to better prediction of present functioning in response to current life events.

Three somewhat tangential bodies of research might also be considered within the context of personality characteristics: the research on self and mutual help groups; the research on single room occupancy hotels; and late-life movers. Although each of these literatures also clearly relates to situational characteristics and will be mentioned again in that context, it seems relevant to note that the people involved in these three types of organizations or situations are likely to have certain personality characteristics. For example, people involved in self help or mutual help groups (Butler et al., 1979–80; Caplan and Killilea, 1976; Katz, 1981) are capable of deriving support and help from themselves and others. Although research on SRO residents suggests that they are more social than had previously been assumed, it is clear that their level of social involvement and social activity is different from and less than that of people in the general population (Felton et al., 1977; Sokolovsky and Cohen, 1981b).

And finally, people, especially older people, who move away from their families may have a certain type of personality. It seems probable that people who leave close family ties to relocate at such a distance from their families are somewhat different from the majority of people who remain with or return in old age to their children and other relatives. The implications of these personality characteristics and their impact on the social support available to or exchanged by such individuals are not well understood and are only now becoming a focus of research (Sullivan and Stevens, 1982; Wiseman, 1980).

In summary, the Person-Environment (P–E) fit paradigm would suggest that people with different personalities have differing environmental needs and will seek out those environments. Mutual and self help group members, SRO residents, and late-life movers may represent three such P–E fit resolutions.

Frailty. Health is an important personal characteristic that both affects and is affected by supportive interchanges. (See Berkman and Syme, 1979; Cobb, 1979; DiMatteo and Hays, 1981; House et al., 1982; Kaplan et al., 1977; Schaefer et al.,

1981; Wan, 1982; Wantz and Gay, 1981.) Sauer and Coward (in press) are exploring the relationship between support networks and the care of the elderly. This chapter focuses on the illustrative case of social support and the frail elderly who need help with activities of daily living. The needs of the frail elderly pose a special demand on the support network. Cantor (1981) reports that the frail elderly are typically cared for by spouse, children, and other family and friends. The support provided often determines whether the older person will be able to maintain independent living quarters and avoid institutionalization (Branch and Jette, 1983; Gross-Andrew and Zimmer, 1978; Lindsey and Hughes, 1981; Wan and Weissert, 1981). Research evidence also indicates that the frail elderly prefer to obtain support from these informal sources. However, practicalities sometimes intervene. For example, Crossman et al. (1981) have noted that the most typical situation is that of a frail older man being cared for by an only slightly less frail older female. Frail parents often have aging children (Schmidt, 1980). The provision of constant support to the frail elder can become a life-threatening strain for the support provider. Similarly, Brody (1981) has discussed the problem of women in the middle, that is daughters who are called upon to provide care for their aging parents and meet the needs of their growing children while increasingly maintaining outside employment. These women are feeling the strain of providing support to a frail elder (Eckels, 1981; Finch and Groves, 1982; Lang and Brody, 1983; Schmidt, 1981).

Research evidence suggests that for the most part the frail elderly receive either formal or informal supports, but not both. Evidence thus far indicates that people with good informal supports are often blocked from access to formal services by their well-meaning informal network (O'Brien and Wagner, 1980; Pilisuk and Froland, 1978). However, available formal services can provide a needed respite for informal caregivers. Since outcomes tend to be less positive with the receipt of formal resources, it seems clear that a combination of formal and informal supports would optimize outcomes while relieving the strain on the informal provider. Indeed several researchers have suggested that federal and community services be redesigned to complement and temporarily relieve the informal supports (Eggert et al., 1977; Friedman and Kaye, 1979; Froland et al., 1981; Meyers and Drayer, 1979). The community outreach program of Toseland et al. (1979) suggests that such a goal can be successfully obtained.

The support interactions of the frail elderly follow several predictable patterns. The frail older man is cared for by his wife. If she becomes frail, she is likely to turn to her children for help. It is when the older woman herself becomes too frail to care for her spouse or is unable to care for herself that the extended family becomes involved. As Longino and Lipman (1982) have shown, the childless older woman is at a much greater disadvantage than the spouseless older woman. The extended family wants to help (Shanas, 1979a,b; Streib, 1983) but sometimes cannot. The decision to institutionalize is a difficult one (Koff, 1982) but sometimes serves to strengthen family ties (Smith and Bengtson, 1979). The experience of coping with a frail elder, choosing the long-term care facility, and making the decision to institutionalize the older relative can draw the family closer together. Unfortunately the strength of this informal support network is generally not taken advantage of by the formal system. Thus, the frail elderly tend to disproportionately use either the formal or the informal support system, overburdening the single system and minimizing its effectiveness. The frail elder who has maintained independence and is no longer capable of doing so is at a significant disadvantage when confronted with institutionalization in a long-term care facility, separation from family, and loss of independence. The effects are likely to be very negative (Altergott and Eustis, 1981; Brody et al., 1978). This type of all-or-none situation, with either all-formal or all-informal support, is, of course, counterproductive.

Personal Characteristics, Social Support and Well-Being. There are some data available that directly document the relationship between specific personal characteristics, social support, and well-being. An interesting series of epidemiological findings not generally cited in the gerontological literature documents the relationship between social support and morbidity/mortality. Berkman and Syme (1979), House et al. (1982), and Kasl and Berkman (1981) have reported significant relationships between fairly gross measures of social support and mortality. Berkman and Syme (1979) studied residents of Alameda County, California, and found that men and women who were married and reported high amounts of social interaction with family and friends were less likely to die within the nine years of the study than those who were unmarried and reported few social contacts. House et al. (1982) found a similar relationship for men in an eleven-year longitudinal study of residents of Tecumseh, Michigan. The pattern of relationships was the same though not significant for women. Kobrin and Hendershot (1977) report that family ties reduce mortality. And, Blazer (1982) found that mortality was related to social support in a longitudinal sample of people over 65. On a more individual level, Chappell (1983; Strain and Chappell, 1982) suggests that social relationships with nonfamily peers are critical, and that the confidant relationship may be more important to quality of life than the quantity of interactions with either family or friends.

In a series of secondary analyses of several large data sets, Antonucci (1982) reported a positive relationship between perceived support measures such as marital satisfaction, frequency of meeting with friends and relatives, feelings of closeness with family and enjoyment of friends, and well-being, especially happiness and life satisfaction. This relationship was particularly strong with age and among women.

Research evidence is limited and contradictory on the impact of consistency versus change in support networks over time. For example, Cohler (1983) notes that older people, especially women with continued family responsibilities, show decreased morale and increased psychological distress. On the other hand, Mancini (1980) reports little continuity over the life course with regard to either interdependence or autonomy with family as determinants of high morale and positive adjustment.

The research relating personal characteristics, social support, and well-being is provocative but still somewhat inconsistent. Future research of course, must, address these issues. However, the work of Heller (1979) and Reis (1984) suggests a possible explanation. These researchers propose that social competence is distinctly related to the use and misuse of social support. The person who is socially competent is more likely either to acquire support network members or to be able to activate their aid in problem solving. Hence such persons will experience a better quality of life and fewer negative outcomes than less socially competent individuals. The available data could certainly be interpreted as supportive. However, thus far, such a hypothesis with its life course emphasis involving the development and continuity of the support Convoy has not been directly tested.

Situational Characteristics

The characteristics considered thus far (e.g., age, sex, personality, and frailty) have predominately focused on the individual. The Convoy model suggests that situational characteristics are also important factors affecting the structure and function of social support. Several situational characteristics have been considered in the literature. In this chapter research is reviewed concerning environmental factors such as institutional living and retirement communities; role changes and life events such as retirement; organizational membership and activity, for example, church and civic groups; and place of residence, that is, urban versus rural living.

Living Arrangements. A wide array of living arrangements are available to the elderly.

The majority of older people live either alone or with a spouse. Some live independently within the larger community, others live within specified communities (e.g., retirement or religious communities). Older people are also likely to live with other relatives, particularly children. Institutional arrangements can vary from relative independence with perhaps communal dining and recreation facilities to skilled nursing care (Carp, 1976; Lawton, 1980a,b; Mindel and Wright, 1981; Moos, 1981). It is clear that the type of living situation is directly related to the amount and kind of social interchange experienced by the individual. Carp and Carp (1980), Rosow (1976), and Teaff et al. (1978) found that a high proportion of older people in the immediate residence (e.g., apartment house) increases the amount of social interchange among the elderly. Studies that examine the social networks of the elderly should take note of residential variations (e.g., elderly vs. non-elderly communities), and how these change over time, since such variations have an impact on the individual's social interactions. For example, much of the work reported by Babchuk (1978–79) and Longino and Lipman (1982) represents data collected from older people living in retirement communities. The social interactions of persons in their samples therefore may be somewhat inflated as compared with other older people. Residents of these communities are likely to be in good health, financially secure, married, and living in an age-homogenous situation. Of course, these sample biases indicate self-selection; the more gregarious and people with fewer service needs are likely to choose a retirement community over a skilled care facility.

Those studies that examine the preferred living arrangements of elderly people living in the community find that the first preference of most older people is to live with a spouse, next, to live alone, and only last to live with an adult child. Older men, people who are divorced, and those with higher incomes are most likely to live in non-family arrangements (Kobrin, 1981). It is interesting that the first two of these groups are likely to be experiencing problematic relations with their Convoy of social support. Older men without a spouse are without the usual female liaison to interpersonal and support interactions. Divorced people often experience a major crisis within their support network or Convoy. And finally, only a certain degree of financial resources will permit independent living.

It is clear that certain housing preferences such as that for independent living are relatively constant. However, many factors intervene and sometimes determine actual housing choices. For the elderly in the community, health, finances, and informal supports play an important role in determining how long the individual will be able to maintain preferred living arrangements. Lindsey and Hughes (1981) followed people who had requested but been denied entry into an institution. These people used their family as sources of informal support to help them maintain independent living situations. Similarly, Branch and Jette (1983) found that elderly people in the community used informal sources of support to help with daily tasks. A support Convoy is obviously very useful in this context, particularly if people have a "support reserve" upon which to draw.

Several investigators have commented on the existence of informal supports in the community and the need to bolster them. Ehrlich (1979) suggests that informal support providers be used to help incorporate the noninteractive community elderly into a mutual help mode. Petty et al. (1976) have argued that self and mutual help groups for the elderly reduce anxiety, while Pilisuk and Minkler (1980) have documented the variety of support groups that now exist specifically to meet the needs of older persons (e.g., Gray Panthers, Widow to Widow, etc.). Butler et al. (1979–80) have also discussed the role of self care and self help in the lives of the elderly.

Single Room Occupancy Hotels. It is important to note whether the present interactive patterns of the elderly represent life-long patterns and personal choice (Toseland et al., 1979). In this vein a series of studies have recently been conducted examining the support networks of single room occupancy hotel residents (Cohen and Rajkowski, 1982; Cohen and Sokolovsky, 1980; Felton et al., 1977; Sokolovsky and Cohen, 1981a,b). These studies found that SRO hotel residents have life-long patterns of minimal entrenchment in Convoys of social support. They are likely to have lived alone for a long time, over 25 years, and either to have never been married or to have been married for only brief periods. They have minimal interaction with family; tend to compartmentalize or separate their social exchanges, that is, have uniplex rather then multiplex relationships; and generally show a dearth of feelings of intimacy toward anyone. These people seem to be relative isolates by general standards and to have had a life-long pattern of such behavior. They should be considered quite differently from the elderly person who has had a rich and vibrant social network from which he or she somehow becomes separated or which is disintegrating.

The SRO residents maintain unique support networks that are different from the general population, tend to show consistency over time, and involve the exchange of supportive acts. These exchanges are more likely to be instrumental and less likely to involve affection or love (Cohen and Rajkowski, 1982). It does seem noteworthy that even this population maintains a consistent pattern of social exchanges. Though their Convoys of support may not be typical, they do have life span continuity.

Institutional Settings. In many ways the most important issues with regard to residential arrangements of the elderly have to do not with community settings but with institutional settings. Fortunately, a great deal of research has been conducted in this area, and some specific data are now available. Recently the effects of the controllability, predictability, and understandability of the environment on the institutionalized individual's morale have received a great deal of attention. These findings show that the greater the perception of control among institutionalized residents, the more positive the outcome (Langer and Rodin, 1976; Moos, 1981; Parmelee, 1982; Schulz and Brenner, 1977).

In many cases the positive outcome reported is an increase in social interaction or the maintenance of previous pre-institution levels of social interaction. For example, Moos and associates (Lemke and Moos, 1981; Moos, 1981; Moos and Igra, 1980) have compared three different types of residential settings: congregate care facilities, residential care facilities, and skilled nursing care facilities. They have shown that the greater perceived control the residents have, the more likely they are to maintain high levels of social interaction and to perceive the social environment positively. Congregate care facility residents in the Moos studies are likely to have the most control over their environment, and residents of skilled nursing care facilities the least.

These findings are important, but it should be remembered that they are grossly confounded by the health selection bias involved. However, this research is relevant to social support, since it is apparent that perceptions of control, understanding, and predictability also affect the individual's social interaction. Research has yet to determine the relationship among these variables over the life course.

Another body of research has been reported recently that provides insight into the perceptions of the institutional resident concerning staff and other residents and the effects of social interaction on adaptation to various aspects of institutional living. Tesch et al. (1981) report that institutional residents receiving frequent visits from people outside the home became less impaired. Kahana et al. (1980) have noted that personal characteristics, including affect, are important in explaining the institutionalized elder's morale. Similarly, Wells and MacDonald (1981) indicate that among relocated institutionalized elderly, those who reported greater support ties with the staff and greater ties outside the institution to family and friends made better adjustments. Thus it appears that social interaction contributes to the adjustment of older people in institutions, and that some interactions, (e.g., with staff and people outside the home) are more advantageous than others.

In this light a recent study by Noelker and Poulshock (in press) seems particularly relevant. In examining the social relationships among institutional residents, they report that older people feel that intimacy is denied, avoided, and in some cases regulated against. Judgments or ratings of the degree of intimacy and social interaction reported by residents and staff are widely discrepant. The staff, compared to the residents, felt there was much more social interaction. At the same time Walsh and Kiracoff (1979–80) report changes in significant other relationships, that is, with central members of one's Convoy of social support, during the course of extended institutionalization.

In summary, the relationship between social support and residential environment is both important and complicated. The better the social interaction and support the resident perceives, the better the adjustment and morale of the individual (Noelker and Harel, 1983). For example, age-segregated community dwellings and retirement communities are more conducive to the exchange of informal supports than age-heterogeneous settings. These effects are the result of both the characteristics of the living environment and the selection bias that predisposes certain types of people to inhabit these residences.

Role Changes-Retirement. Over the life course an individual experiences a number of role changes and life events that might be considered situational characteristics influencing his or her Convoy of social support. An increasingly large body of research has begun to examine the stress precipitated by these life events and role changes (Atchley, 1982; Dohrenwend and Dohrenwend, 1977; Fiske, 1980; George, 1980; House, 1981; Kahn, 1981; Kessler, 1979; Lowenthal et al., 1975; Pearlin et al., 1981). There are characteristic role changes that occur with age, and many of them involve role loss. Examples include widowhood, the loss of the role

of spouse; retirement, the loss of the working role; relocation, the loss of the family home and associated role requirements. Although each of the above-mentioned role changes is a situational characteristic, the role of retirement is considered in some detail here as exemplary. It has previously been documented that social support can be quite successful in mitigating the negative effects of work stress and job loss (Gore, 1978; House, 1981; Kahn, 1981; LaRocco et al., 1980). It seems probable that social support can similarly mitigate the sometimes negative effects of retirement. Considerable research has explored the adjustment of the older worker to retirement (Kasworm and Wetzel, 1981; McCluskey and Borgatta, 1981; Szinovacz, 1982). Beck (1982) reports that the best predictors of positive adjustment to retirement are health and income, whereas recent widowhood is the most significant negative predictor. Elwell and Maltbie-Crannell (1981) found that role loss (such as retirement) had both a direct and an indirect effect on coping resources and life satisfaction, especially for men. They found that people experiencing feelings of role loss were likely to have poorer health and less money, which, in turn, were related to less social support and lower levels of life satisfaction. Examining factors that contribute to life satisfaction and adjustment in retirement, Walker et al. (1980–81) found that retirement styles in essence match preretirement behaviors. Some retirees are active and organized, substituting non-work activities for work activities once retired, while others become "rocking chair" types and choose to reduce their level of activity as a result of retirement.

These findings suggest that although health and income are known to affect retirement (Mutran and Reitzes, 1981), other variables also have an impact. Social support appears to be such a variable. It is interesting that despite the voluminous amounts of research that have focused on retirement, very little has actually considered social support in depth. The Walker et al. (1980–81) study suggests that for the most part people will maintain previous levels of social activity. People who have maintained an extensive Convoy of support will substitute retirement social interactions for work social interactions. However, Atchley (1976) found that women were more work-oriented than men and took longer to adjust to retirement. He found that men often assumed that they would experience an increase in social interaction with retirement, whereas women feared they would have less. Although Atchley's sample of working women is unusual for that age cohort (i.e., a disproportionate number of women who are unmarried or never married and who were employed outside the home for a significant number of years), he did find that loneliness was more prevalent among older women than older men. This finding is somewhat contrary to other results that suggest that women have more versatile networks that do not necessarily suffer with retirement. Cool (1981) has argued that women's lifetime flexibility permits better adaptation to role changes, especially role loss, in old age. Gorton (1979) reports that retired women in North Carolina had an average of 17.8 members of their network. And Holahan (1981), reporting on the women now over 65 from the Terman Gifted Children sample, found that retirement often triggered an increase in social activities. It seems as though these women were using their newly acquired leisure time to engage in social interactions that their previous working status did not permit. Indeed, Keating and Spiller (1981) report that retired women define leisure as "freedom to do what you like." In the main, the research examining the contribution of social support to retirement adjustment has relied on relatively global measures of social support such as frequency of interaction with family and friends. This might account for the somewhat inconsistent findings.

Recently more detailed data have become available. Depner and Ingersoll (1982) have examined the structure and function of support networks among retired men and women. Using the national sample described previously (Kahn and Antonucci, 1983), they report that retired women have an average of 9.3 people in their networks, whereas retired men have about 7.6. Depner and Ingersoll (1982) report that women consider more people close and important to them (3.68 vs. 2.75). This suggests that retired men have fewer close relationships than retired women, a finding that corroborates the more general finding that women have several close friends or confidants, but men have only one, their spouse. General network membership is fairly similar for retired men and women, consisting of spouse, children, other family, and friends.

Depner and Ingersoll (1982) also examined six types of supports given and received: confiding, reassurance, respect, sick care, and talk about health and when upset. Despite a general similarity in the exchange of support, retired women report that they confide in and are reassured by more people, and that they talk with others more about their health problems and when they are upset. There were no differences, however, in the amount and kind of support retired men and women report providing to others.

In general, there appears to be lifetime continuity in patterns of social support (i.e., pre- and post-retirement). Sex differences are apparently also present although the data are somewhat contradictory as to the exact nature of the sex differences.

Organizational Membership and Activity. Organizational membership and activity is another important situational characteristic. There are a variety of types of organizations: civic, political and work-related groups sports and hobby groups; service and religious organizations. Each type of organization involves different levels of commitment and seems to affect social interaction and the exchange of social support. Some research on social support and organizational membership among the elderly is available.

There is clearly a link between organizational membership and number of people in one's network. This may seem obvious, since as a member of an organization the individual is likely to have the opportunity to meet many people within that organization. This is true. However, Fischer (1982a) reports that the more organizations an individual belongs to, not only the more fellow members does he or she know, but also the more nonmembers that person is likely to know. Thus it appears that people who belong to organizations are more likely to be involved and interact with people. Other recent data (Kahn and Antonucci, 1983) also corroborate this finding.

Babchuk et al. (1979) explored organizational membership among 125 older people. Most people in their sample were affiliated with some type of organization, and over half were involved in multiple organizations. Women belonged to more groups than men, and people who belonged to more than one group were more likely to be active in the groups. They also report an apparent sex difference in the types of organizations to which people belonged. Women were more likely to belong to church or social-expressive groups, whereas men were more likely to belong to work or service-related groups. Cutler (1976) provides age-related information about organization membership using a national sample of 2974 individuals. He notes a linear age pattern with fraternal groups such as lodges and church groups; curvilinear age pattern for work-related and service groups; and absolutely no age differences in farm, political, hobby, or national groups. An additional interesting finding is that of Trela (1976), who found that people with higher socioeconomic status were more likely to be involved with age-graded organizations. Others report that the number of groups and frequency of attendance at group meetings is related to income, occupation, education, and health (Fischer, 1982a; Ward, 1979b).

Several types of information are available concerning religion and religious involvement. Depner et al. (1982) found that the clergy are often an important source of social support for the elderly during times of stress. Longino and Kitson (1976) examined the role and attitude of clergy toward the aged and report neither positive nor negative

age bias. However, they do note that clergy who consider ministering an expressive (supportive) occupation, are especially responsive to the needs of the elderly.

Heisel and Faulkner (1982) found that among blacks, women were more religious than men, and Taylor (1983) reports that religious involvement represents a primary source of social support for many blacks. In summary, there are definite demographic characteristics that influence organizational involvement. In general, such involvement has the effect of increasing social participation and the perception of social support.

Place of Residence.   Like residential environment, place of residence (i.e., urban vs. rural living) is an important situational characteristic that has direct impact upon the individual's social experiences. Harbert and Wilkenson (1979) and Rodgers-Siregar et al. (1981) report that rural communities have elaborate support systems. Kahn and Antonucci (1983) found that rural dwellers have larger networks than urban dwellers. An additional interesting finding, reported by Keating and Marshall (1980), indicates that among rural farm and rural non-farm couples there is a great deal of continuity in the frequency of social interactions with family and friends from the pre- to post- retirement period.

Although this question has not been widely addressed through comparative studies, Fischer's (1982a) study in Northern California was specifically designed to examine the differences in urban and rural settings. Urban respondents compared to rural residents have fewer relatives among their network members. Urbanites tend to have networks that are less dense than is commonly the case among rural residents. This is consistent with the fact that fewer members of the city dweller's network are relatives. Urbanites are also very likely to have uniplex relationships with their network members; that is, different friends occupy different support roles rather than the same network members occupying multiple support roles. This too is consistent with the friends versus family distinction. Fischer's study involved adults of all ages. He reports several clear indications of selection bias in terms of residential choice. Young people tend to choose big cities, whereas older people prefer small towns.

These findings should be considered in conjunction with Cantor's (1979) New York City data. She reports that the large numbers of ethnic elderly in New York City have extensive networks consisting primarily of family but also of friends and neighbors. Clearly there are important differences. But Fischer notes, among other selection-biasing factors, the fact that people who immigrate are likely to settle in big cities, as are people looking for jobs or improved conditions. He also notes that cities by their nature tend to attract the untraditional, since they are more supportive of nontraditional values and lifestyles. The meaning of these findings may be different from coast to coast, but the implication is clear that there is an effect of geographical location at least on the structure and possibly on the functions of social support. Levitt et al. (in press), comparing a national sample of older Americans with a select sample of less affluent twice-migrated (from Russia to New York, and then to Miami) Jewish immigrants, found very few relatives and a generally depressed social network among the Miami sample. These people too should be compared with Cantor's New York sample. Cantor's sample involved less affluent people, frequently migrants from other countries, but they remained near their family and report well-developed support networks. The Miami sample either has no family or has purposefully moved away from that family. It is perhaps therefore to be expected that their network profiles are different even though both samples represent urban environments.

In sum, a few facts about the social networks of urban and rural residents are available. Structural characteristics of the support network tend to be different. However, it is not clear that the actual support functions performed by network members are substantially different. Deimling and Huber (1981), comparing urban and rural caregivers of the elderly, report that there were no differences in the availability of care among the two, although urban caregivers were more likely to be single, whereas rural caregivers were more likely to be married. Apparently conflicting data recording both limited and extensive social networks of urban residents suggest that other factors in addition to urban life may attenuate the effects of place of residence on the exchange of social support. The scattered data do seem to indicate, nevertheless, that the composition of one's Convoy of social support is different in rural versus urban settings.

Migration and Return Migration. One additional item will be addressed under the rubric of structural characteristics: the migration and return migration of the elderly (Longino and Jackson, 1980). Data have clearly documented the migration of the elderly to sun belt states (Biggar, 1980). These people tend to be younger, have more money, and be in better health than most other elderly. A second pattern of return migration is also apparent. The Florida return immigrants (people who have moved from the North to Florida and back North) are older, have less money, are in poorer health, and are in need of support from family (Longino, 1979). Although very little research has explored the Convoy of social support of people in each of these migration situations, it seems like an important and relevant question. What type of person would leave life-long friends and family to move to a more attractive climate? It may be that people who are willing to make this major break with their support network simply have had a Convoy of support over their life-course that has been less than optimal and therefore is easy to leave behind. Other explanations are also viable; for example, people have more money, or communications and transportation are so improved as to make the distance manageable. Important family members, such as children, may have already moved, reducing the attraction of the hometown. Or people in the young-old category may simply want a period of obligation-free recreation while at the same time relieving their family, at least temporarily, of the burden of their care or responsibility. These alternatives suggest different interpretations of the Convoy of social support. Return migration of the elderly frequently occurs when the older person or spouse has developed health problems and requires support from family and old friends. Thus far, we have barely collected demographic information concerning people involved in these moves. Important social interactive dynamics are also involved, and research needs to be focused on these questions. For example, how do the elderly and their support network members feel about their return? Does their support network welcome them, or are they in the position of reasserting themselves upon an unsympathetic or perhaps ambivalently supportive network?

Situational Characteristics, Social Support, and Well-being. Research is available that directly addresses the question of the relationship between situational characteristics, social support, and well-being. Studies examining the morale of elderly people living in various residential environments find that morale is directly related to housing preferences; it is highest for elderly people living with their spouse, somewhat less for people living alone, and still less for people living with their children (Mindel and Wright, 1981). Kivett and Learner (1982) have noted that among older rural adults who share housing with their children and people who felt their income was adequate, blacks and married people had higher levels of morale. Even among institutionalized elderly, morale has been found to be related to environmental characteristics and satisfaction (Dooghe et al., 1980). Noelker and Harel (1978) report that the best predictors of well-being and survival among the institutionalized elderly are their subjective perceptions of the facility and their preference for living in it or elsewhere.

Some data are also available that examine the relationship between giving and receiving support among retired men and women. In-gersoll (1982) reports that receiving rather than providing support is more predictive of quality of life and well-being for both men and women. Interestingly, providing support is not predictive of quality of life for either retired men or women. It appears that well-being is more affected by what one receives from others than by what one provides to others (Ingersoll, 1982; Kahn et al., in press).

A positive relationship has also been documented between organizational membership and activity and overall well-being. Palmore and Kivett (1977), using three waves of the Duke Longitudinal data, report that organizational activity is second only to health in predicting life satisfaction in their sample. Similarly, Hoyt et al. (1980) found that organizational involvement was associated with feelings of zest as opposed to apathy. And Duff and Hong (1982) report that frequent church attenders experience higher levels of life satisfaction than infrequent attenders.

Several studies have found a relationship between religious involvement and well-being, especially among blacks (Neighbors et al., 1983), suggesting that this can be an important element in the Convoy of social support. Heisel and Faulkner (1982) found religious affiliation and church attendance to be positively related to life satisfaction among blacks regardless of age and sex. The overall impression seems clear: involvement with organizations and organizational activity positively influences one's Convoy of social support and well-being.

And finally, urban versus rural living seems to differentially influence both social support and subjective well-being. There appear to be different priorities involved for the urban and the rural resident. Lee and Lassey (1980) compared rural and urban elderly and found that the urban elderly were often better off according to objective indicators. However, subjective evaluations by the rural elderly often find them giving higher subjective evaluations of their condition and higher levels of overall well-being than the urban elderly. Along these lines, Windley and Scheidt (1982) examined 989 rural Kansans over 65 and found that environmental conditions, satisfaction with dwelling, and satisfaction with the community were the best predictors of well-being for this population, whereas activity, security, and contact with friends and relatives were not predictive. For the rural aged, then, environmental characteristics appear to have a significant impact on well-being. Fengler and Jensen (1981) compared ($N = 1405$) urban and nonurban Vermonters. They, too, like Lee and Lassey (1980) report that objective conditions are not significant indicators of well-being among the nonurban, although disadvantaged conditions are important predictors of the level of life satisfaction among the urban residents. Sauer (1977) examined the morale of the urban elderly and found that social support was an important factor. In addition, Herzog and Rodgers (1981a,b) have consistently shown that the factor structure of life satisfaction and its components is similar across different age groups.

In summary, although the research findings on situational characteristics are somewhat scattered, they seem to indicate a relatively consistent positive relationship among situational characteristics, social support, and well-being.

PRESENT KNOWLEDGE—FUTURE GOALS

As this chapter attests, research evidence concerning the nature and effects of social support is rapidly accumulating. It is clear that personal and situational characteristics have a major impact on both the structure and function of social networks, and that they probably influence the eventual effects of support on individual outcome variables. However, as this research accumulates, certain major findings raise significant questions. These issues are briefly outlined below.

1. One important issue concerning social support can best be summarized as distinguishing between quality and quantity of support (e.g., Duff and Hong, 1982; Porritt, 1979). Evidence thus far suggests that quality is a better indicator of positive outcomes, but the data are equivocal. It should be noted, however, that this distinction may reflect a methodological artifact. Almost all studies of social support are based on self-report, and self-reported quality may be more vulnerable to bias than self-reported quantity (numbers of friends, frequency of contact, and the like). It might be better to summarize the data thus far as indicating that the subjective assessment of the quality of support is the best predictor of positive outcomes; that is, perceived adequacy of social support best predicts subjective well-being. However, this statement may be dangerously near to tautology. In addition, quality of support cannot be considered alone, since it seems clear that some minimum quantity is necessary. Support Convoys must include at least one person as provider, and one may suffice. For example, many men seem to rely on one member of their support network, their spouse. This is adequate under most conditions. When the sole source of support or link with others becomes ill or is unable to maintain that support role, this minimum level of quantity or lack of depth in the support network becomes a detriment. In short, the relationship between quality and quantity needs to be further explicated.

2. The importance of reciprocity in support relations has been highlighted by several investigators (Mindel and Wright, 1982; Satariano et al., 1981; Wentowski, 1981). It appears that opportunity to both give and receive is critical to the individual's assessment of and satisfaction with his or her network. In general, people appear to prefer to engage in reciprocal interactions. However, much more information is necessary for us to fully understand this phenomenon. For example, we do not know to what extent it is important for people to reciprocate in kind (e.g., you lend me money, and I lend you money) and to what extent reciprocity can be achieved across functions (e.g., you fix my faucet, and I bake you a cake). Wentowski's data suggest that the answer depends upon the degree of intimacy one feels with the other person. Among relative strangers reciprocity should be in kind, but among close friends and family this is not necessary.

3. Similarly, the question of time arises. If

support is provided, what are the time limits within which reciprocity must be accomplished? This difference too is probably related to levels of intimacy; with close friends and family, accounting might be more loose or long-term. One does not need to pay back immediately or with exactly the same type of support. It is expected that the account will be paid over the life course. For example, a "support bank" or "support reserve" could be hypothesized to explain the feeling of many elders that children should provide support for their parents, since they, the children, had previously received support from their parents. This notion of a "support bank" into which one makes deposits and from which one makes withdrawals should be explored within a life course framework.

4. It is also important to note that work in social support thus far has generally ignored the question of etiology. It is not clear why some people have better Convoys of social support than others, or why people with objectively similar Convoys vary in their subjective interpretation of those Convoys and the resultant effect on well-being. Is it a prior experience/condition/phenomenon such as social competence (cf. Heller and Swindle, in press) that accounts for this variability? And if so, the question becomes, what influences the development of social competence? That is, what is its etiology? There has been a considerable array of descriptive research; some explains notably little variance, whereas some yields contradictory results. It may be that looking to a prior causal factor will help explicate the relationship between social support and well-being. This possibility seems to indicate an important avenue of future research.

5. Methodological and analytic issues are particularly critical at this point, since they influence the results that are accumulating. Several people have asked, "Does help help?" (Lieberman and Mullan, 1978) and "What's supportive about social support?" (Depner et al., 1982). The answers to these questions depend directly upon the measures used and the methods. Similarly we must begin to explore causal relationships. For ex-

ample, to what extent are people who are well-supported more satisfied, and to what extent are people who are satisfied more likely to be supported? Inferences are commonly made from limited data.

6. Consistent sex differences have been documented in the support networks of men and women. Women have larger and more multifaceted networks than men. Future research should focus on this difference and determine if men, or possibly women, are at a disadvantage in late life. If there is a disadvantage, investigators should explore those methods that will help compensate for the experienced deficiencies.

7. The role of family versus friends as support providers has received some attention (e.g., Arling, 1976; Wood and Robertson, 1978). The results of studies comparing the two are intriguing, suggesting that support from friends makes a larger contribution to the individual's well-being than support from family. In some ways this result is counter-intuitive. Why should one be more satisfied by supports from a stranger (relatively speaking) than from a spouse or child? I propose a somewhat complicated explanation that warrants future investigation. Support from family is a minimal level of support without which one would suffer. Its absence is detrimental, but its presence may have very little positive impact. On the other hand, support from friends is seen as optional, rather than obligational. Its absence is not detrimental, but its presence has a more significant and positive impact on well- being than support from family.

8. Much of what we now know about the role of social support is based on a unique cohort of older adults. The experiences of older Americans are changing, and this is likely to have a significant effect on their Convoys of social support. To take just one example, although Wood and Robertson (1976) reported that grandparenthood was an empty role that lacked many prescribed behaviors, the new generation of grandparents are finding that they have the opportunity to take an important and very active role in the lives of their grandchildren. As the divorce

rate increases and as two-career families become more common, many single and overburdened parents are turning to their parents for help. These grandparents occupy important and significant roles in the lives of their children and the care of their grandchildren. Such cohort differences in experience are important and must be documented. They are likely to have a significant impact on Convoys of social support over the life course.

REFERENCES

Alba, R. D., and Kadushin, C. 1976. The intersection of social circles: A new measure of social proximity in networks. *Sociological Methods and Research* 5(1): 77–102.

Altergott, K., and Eustis, N. A. 1981. Evaluation of everyday life: The impact of relationships, decrements of age, and service environment. Paper presented at the annual meeting of the Gerontological Society of America, Toronto.

Antonucci, T. C. 1981. Frontiers in aging: Attachment and social support across the life span. *In* A. Lee (ed.), *Frontiers in Aging.* Pullman: Washington State University.

Antonucci, T. C. 1982. Attachment in the aging process: A life span framework. Final report to the National Institute on Aging.

Antonucci, T. C., and Depner, C. E. 1982. Social support and informal helping relationships. *In* T. A. Wills (ed.), *Basic Processes in Helping Relationships.* New York: Academic Press.

Antonucci, T. C., and Wethington, E. 1983. The potentiating effects of social support. (Unpublished.)

Arling, G. 1976. The elderly widow and her family, neighbors, and friends. *Journal of Marriage and the Family* 38:757–768.

Atchley, R. C. 1976. Selected social and psychological differences between men and women in later life. *Journal of Gerontology* 31(2):204–212.

Atchley, R. C. 1982. Retirement as a social institution. *Annual Review of Sociology* 8:263–287.

Babchuk, N. 1978–79. Aging and primary relations. *International Journal of Aging and Human Development* 9(2):137–151.

Babchuk, N., Peters, G. R., Hoyt, D. R., and Kaiser, M. A. 1979. The voluntary associations of the aged. *Journal of Gerontology,* 34(4):579–587.

Barnes, J. A. 1972. *Social Networks.* New York: Addison-Wesley.

Beck, S. H. 1982. Adjustment to and satisfaction with retirement. *Journal of Gerontology* 37(5):616–624.

Beck, S. H. 1982. Adjustment to and satisfaction with retirement, *Journal of Gerontology* 37(5):616–624.

Beckman, L. J., and Houser, B. B. 1982. The consequences of childlessness on the social-psychological well-being of older women. *Journal of Gerontology* 37(2):243–250.

Beels, C. C. 1981. Social support and schizophrenia. *Schizophrenia Bulletin* 4(1):59–72.

Bengtson, V. L. 1979. Ethnicity and aging: Problems and issues in current social science inquiry. *In* D. E. Gelfand and A. J. Kutzik (eds.), *Ethnicity and Aging.* New York: Springer.

Bengtson, V. L., and Cutler, N. E. 1976. Generations and intergenerational relations: Perspectives on age groups and social change. *In* R. H. Binstock and E. Shanas (eds.), *Handbook of Aging and the Social Sciences,* 1st ed., pp. 130–159. New York: Van Nostrand Reinhold.

Bengtson, V. L., Burton, L., and Mangen, D. 1981. Family support systems and attribution of responsibility: Contrasts among elderly blacks, Mexican-Americans, and whites. Paper presented at the annual meeting of the Gerontological Society of America, Toronto.

Berkman, L. S., and Syme, S. L. 1979. Social networks, host resistance, and mortality: A nine year follow-up study of Alameda County residents. *American Journal of Epidemiology* 109(2):186–204.

Biggar, J. C. 1980. Re-assessing elderly sunbelt migration. *International Research on Aging* 2(2):177–190.

Blazer, D. G. 1982. Social support and mortality in an elderly population. *American Journal of Epidemiology* 115:684–694.

Block, M. R., Davidson, J. L., and Grambs, J. D. 1981. *Women Over Forty: Visions and Realities.* New York: Springer.

Boorman, S. A., and White, H. C. 1976. Social structure from multiple networks: Role structures. *American Journal of Sociology* 81(6):1384–1446.

Bott, E. 1955. Urban families: Conjugal roles and social networks. *Human Relations* 18:345–384.

Branch, L. G., and Jette, A. M. 1983. Elder's use of informal long-term care assistance. *The Gerontologist* 23(1):51–56.

Britton J., and Britton J. O. 1972. *Personality Changes in Aging: A Longitudinal Study of Community Residents.* New York: Springer.

Brody, E. M. 1981. Women in the middle and family help to older people. *The Gerontologist* 21(5):471–480.

Brody, S. J., Poulshock, S. W., and Masciocchi, C. F. 1978. The family caring unit: A major consideration in the long-term support system. *The Gerontologist* 18(6):547–555.

Burt, R. 1980. Models of network structure. *Annual Review of Sociology* 6:79–141.

Butler, R. N., and Lewis, M. I. 1982. *Aging and Mental Health: Positive Psychosocial and Biomedical Approaches.* St. Louis: C. V. Mosby.

Butler, R. N., Gertman, J. S., Oberlander, D. L., and Schindler, L. 1979–80. Self-care, self-help, and the elderly. *International Journal of Aging and Human Development* 10(1):95–117.

Campbell, A. 1980. *A Sense of Well-Being in America,* New York: McGraw-Hill.

Candy, S. G., Troll, L. E., and Levy, S. G. 1981. A developmental exploration of friendship functions in women. *Psychology of Women Quarterly* 5(3):456–472.

Cantor, M. H. 1975. Life space and the social support system of the inner city elderly of New York. *The Gerontologist* 15(1):23–27.

Cantor, M. H. 1979. The informal support system of New York's inner city elderly: Is ethnicity a factor? *In* D. E. Gelfand and A. J. Kutzik (eds.), *Ethnicity and Aging.* New York: Springer.

Cantor, M. H. 1981. Factors associated with strain among family, friends and neighbors, caring for the frail elderly. Paper presented at the annual meeting of the Gerontological Society of America, Toronto.

Caplan, G., and Killilea, M. (eds.), 1976. *Support Systems and Mutual Help: Multidisciplinary Explorations.* New York: Grune and Stratton.

Carp, F. M. 1976. Housing and living environments of older people. *In* R. H. Binstock and E. Shanas (eds.), *Handbook of Aging and the Social Sciences,* 1st ed., pp. 244–271. New York: Van Nostrand Reinhold.

Carp, F. M., and Carp, A. 1980. Person–environment congruence and sociability. *Research on Aging* 2(4): 395–415.

Chappell, N. A. 1983. Informal support networks among the elderly. *Research on Aging* 5(1):77–100.

Chiriboga, D. A. 1982a. An examination of life events as possible antecedents to change. *Journal of Gerontology* 37(5):595–601.

Chiriboga, D. A. 1982b. Adaptation to marital separation and later and earlier life. *Journal of Gerontology* 37(1):109–114.

Cicirelli, V. G. 1977. Relationship of siblings to elderly person's feelings and concerns. *Journal of Gerontology* 32(3):317–322.

Cobb, S. 1976. Social support as a moderator of life stress. *Psychosomatic Medicine* 38(5):300–314.

Cobb, S. 1979. Social support and health through the life course. *In* M. W. Riley (ed.), *Aging from Birth to Death.* Boulder, Colo.: Westview Press.

Cohen, C. I., and Rajkowski, H. 1982. What's in a friend? *The Gerontologist* 22(3):261–266.

Cohen, C. I., and Sokolovsky, J. 1980. Social engagement versus isolation: The cost of the aged in SRO hotels. *The Gerontologist* 20(1):36–44.

Cohen, S., and Hoberman, H. M. 1983. Positive events and social supports as buffers of life change stress. *Journal of Applied Social Psychology.* 13(2):99–125.

Cohen, S., and McKay, G. 1984. Social support, stress, and the buffer hypothesis: A theoretical analysis. *In* A. Baum, J. E. Singe, and S. E. Taylor (eds.), *Handbook of Psychology and Health,* Vol. 4, 253–267. Hillsdale, N.J.: Erlbaum.

Cohler, B. J. 1983. Autonomy and interdependence in the family of adulthood: A psychological perspective. *The Gerontologist* 23(1):33–39.

Conner, K. A., Powers, E. A., and Bultena, G. L. 1979.

Social interaction and life satisfaction: An empirical assessment of late-life patterns. *Journal of Gerontology* 34(1):116–121.

Cool, L. E. 1981. Role continuity or crisis in later life? A Corsican case. *International Journal of Aging and Human Development* 13(3):169–181.

Costa, P. T., Jr., and McCrae, R. R. 1976. Age differences in personality structure: A cluster analytic approach. *Journal of Gerontology* 31(5):564–570.

Crossman, L., London, C., and Barry, C. 1981. Older women caring for disabled spouses: A model for supportive services. *The Gerontologist* 21(5):464–470.

Cutler, S. J. 1976. Age profiles of membership in 16 types of voluntary organizations. *Journal of Gerontology* 31(4):462–470.

Deimling, G. T., and Huber, L. W. 1981. The availability and participation of immediate kin in caring for rural elderly. Paper presented at the Gerontological Society of America annual meeting, Toronto, Nov.

Depner, C., and Ingersoll, B. 1982. Employment status and social support: The experience of the mature woman. *In* M. Szinovacz (ed.), *Women's Retirement, Policy Implications of Recent Research* Vol. 6, pp. 61–76, Sage Yearbooks on Women's Policy Studies. Beverly Hills, Calif.: Sage.

Depner, C., and Ingersoll, B. 1983. Conjugal social support: Patterns in later life. (Unpublished.)

Depner, C., Antonucci, T., and Wethington, E. 1982. What makes social support supportive? Paper presented at the 35th Annual Scientific Meeting of the Gerontological Society of America, Boston.

DiMatteo, M. R., and Hays, R. 1981. Social support and seniors' illness. *In* B. N. Gottleib, *Social Networks and Social Support.* Beverly Hills, Calif.: Sage.

Dohrenwend, B. P., and Dohrenwend, B. S. 1977. The conceptualization and measurement of stressful life events: An overview. *In* J. S. Strauss et al. (eds.), *Proceedings of the Conference on Methods of Longitudinal Research in Psychopathology.* New York: Plenum.

Dooghe, G., Vanderleyden, L., and VanLoon, F. 1980. Social adjustment of the elderly residing in institutional homes: A multivariate analysis. *International Journal of Aging and Human Development,* 11(2): 163–176.

Dowd, J. J., and Bengtson, V. L. 1978. Aging in minority populations: an examination of the double jeopardy hypothesis. *Journal of Gerontology* 33: 427–436.

Duff, R. W., and Hong, L. K. 1982. Quality and quantity of social interactions in the life satisfaction of older Americans. *Sociology and Social Research,* 66(4):418–434.

Dunckley, R. A., and Lutes, C. J. 1979. Confidant relationships among the aged poor as a function of age, sex and race. Paper presented at the annual meeting of the Gerontological Society of America, Washington, D.C.

Eckels, E. T. 1981. Negative aspects of family relationships for older women. Paper presented at the Joint Annual Meeting of the Gerontological Society of America and the Canadian Association of Gerontology, Toronto.

Eggert, G. M., Granger, C. V., Morris, R., and Pendleton, S. F. 1977. Caring for the patients with long-term disability. *Geriatrics* 32(10):102–114.

Ehrlich, P. 1979. Service delivery for the community elderly: The mutual help model. *Journal of Gerontological Social Work* 2(2):125–136.

Elwell, F., and Maltbie-Crannell, A. D. 1981. The impact of role loss upon coping resources and life satisfaction of the elderly. *Journal of Gerontology* 36(2):223–232.

Felton, B., Lehmann, S., Adler, A., and Burgio, M. 1977. Social supports and life satisfaction among old and young. Paper presented at the meeting of the Gerontological Society, San Francisco, Nov.

Fengler, A. P., and Jensen, L. 1981. Perceived and objective conditions as predictors of the life satisfaction of urban and non-urban elderly. *Journal of Gerontology* 36(6):750–752.

Fennema, M., and Schijf, H. 1978/79. Analyzing interlocking directorates: Theory and methods. *Social Networks* 1:297–33a.

Ferraro, K. F., and Barresi, C. 1982. The impact of widowhood on the social relations of older persons. *Research on Aging* 4(2):227–248.

Filsinger, E., and Sauer, W. J. 1978. An empirical typology of adjustment to aging. *Journal of Gerontology* 33(3):437–445.

Finch, J., and Groves, D. 1982. By women for women: Caring for the frail elderly. *Women Studies International Forum* 5(5):427–438.

Fischer, C. S. 1982a. *To Dwell Among Friends, Personal Networks in Town and City*. Chicago: University of Chicago Press.

Fischer, C. S. 1982b. What do we mean by "friend"? An inductive study. *Social Networks* 3(4):287–306.

Fischer, C. S., Jackson, R. M., Stueve, C. A., Gerson, K., Jones, L. M. and Baldassre, M. 1977. *Networks and Places: Social Relations in the Urban Setting*. New York: Free Press.

Fiske, M. 1980. Tasks and crises of the second half of life and the interrelationship of commitment, coping and adaptation. *In* J. E. Birren and R. B. Sloane (eds.), *Handbook of Mental Health and Aging*, Englewood Cliffs, N.J.: Prentice-Hall.

French, J. R. P., Jr., 1974. Person-role fit. *In* Alan McLean (ed.), *Occupational Stress*, pp. 71–79. Springfield, Ill.: Chalres C. Thomas.

Friedman, S. R., and Kaye, L. W. 1979. Homecare for the frail elderly: Implications for an interactional relationship. *Journal of Gerontological Social Work* 2(2):109–124.

Froland, C., Pancoast, D. L., Chapman, N. J., and Kimboko, P. J. 1981. Linking formal and informal supportive systems. *In* B. H. Gottleib (ed.), *Social Networks and Social Support*. Beverly Hills, Calif.: Sage.

Gelfand, D. E. 1980. Ethnicity, aging, and mental health. *International Journal of Aging and Human Development* 10(3):289–298.

Gelfand, D. E., and Kutzik, A. J. (eds.). 1979. *Ethnicity and Aging*. New York: Springer.

George, L. K. 1978. The impact of personality and social status factors upon levels of activity and psychological well-being. *Journal of Gerontology* 33(6): 840–847.

George, L. 1980. *Role Transitions in Later Life*. Monterey, Calif.: Brooks/Cole.

Gibbs, G. M. 1981. Significant other relationships: Their location and importance for the older widow. Paper presented at the 34th Annual Scientific Meeting of the Gerontological Society of America, Toronto, Nov.

Gore, S. 1978. The effect of social support in moderating the health consequences of unemployment. *Journal of Health and Social Behavior* 19 (June):159–165.

Gorton, A. 1979. A network analytic approach to assess social support systems of retired women. Paper presented at the meeting of the Gerontological Society.

Gottlieb, B. H. 1981. Preventive interventions involving social networks and social support. *In* B. H. Gottleib (ed.), *Social Networks and Social Support*. Beverly Hills, Calif.: Sage.

Gross-Andrew, S., and Zimmer, A. H. 1978. Incentives to families caring for the disabled elderly: Research and demonstration project to strengthen the natural supports system. *Journal of Gerontological Social Work* 1(2):119–134.

Hammer, M. 1981. Social supports, social networks, and schizophrenia. *Schizophrenic Bulletin* 7(1):45–57.

Harbert, A., and Wilkenson, C. 1979. Growing old in rural America. *Aging*, 291–292:36–40.

Harris, L. 1975. *The Myth and Reality of Aging in America*. Washington, D.C.: The National Council on Aging.

Heisel, M. A., and Faulkner, A. O. 1982. Religiosity in an older black population. *Gerontologist* 22(4):354–358.

Heller, K. 1979. The effects of social support: Prevention and treatment implications. *In* A. P. Goldstein and F. H. Kanfer (eds.), *Maximizing Treatment Gains: Transfer Enhancement in Psychotherapy*. New York: Academic Press.

Heller, K., and Swindle, R. W. In press. Social networks, perceived social support and coping with stress. *In* R. D. Felner, L. A. Jason, J. Montsugu, and S. S. Farber (eds.), *Preventive Psychology: Theory, research and practice in community intervention*. Elmsford, N.Y.: Pergamon Press.

Heltsley, M. E., and Powers, R. C. 1975. Social interaction and perceived adequacy of interaction of the rural aged. *The Gerontologist* 15(6):533–536.

Herzog, A. R., and Rodgers, W. L. 1981a. Age and satisfaction: Data from several large surveys. *Research on Aging* 3(2):142–165.

Herzog, A. R., and Rodgers, W. L. 1981b. The structure of subjective well-being in different age groups. *Journal of Gerontology* 36(4):472–479.

Hess, B. B. 1979. Sex roles, friendship and the life course. *Research on Aging* 1(4):494–515.

Hess, B. B., and Markson, E. W. 1980. *Aging and Old Age.* New York: Macmillan.

Hirsch, B. J. 1981. Social networks and the coping process: Creating personal communities. *In* B. H. Gottleib (ed.), *Social Networks and Social Support.* Beverly Hills, Calif.: Sage.

Holahan, C. K. 1981. Lifetime achievement patterns, retirement and life satisfaction of gifted aged women. *Journal of Gerontology* 36(6):741–749.

House, J. S. 1981. *Work Stress and Social Support.* Reading, Mass.: Addison-Wesley.

House, J. S., and Wells, J. A. 1978. Occupational stress, social support, and health. *In* Alan McLean, Gilbert Black, and Michael Colligan, (eds.), *Reducing Occupational Stress: Proceedings of a Conference.* U.S. Department of Health, Education and Welfare, HEW(NIOSH) Publication No. 78-140.

House, J. S. Robbins, C., and Metzner, H. C. 1982. The association of social relationships and activities with mortality: Perspective evidence from the Tecumseh community health study. *American Journal of Epidemiology* 116(1):123–140.

Hoyt, D. R., Kaiser, M. A., Peters, G. R., and Babchuk, N. 1980. Life satisfaction and activity theory: A multidimensional approach. *Journal of Gerontology* 35(6):935–941.

Ingersoll, B. N. 1982. Gender differences in social support and quality of life among retirees. Unpublished doctoral dissertation, The University of Michigan.

Israel, B. A. 1982. Social networks and health status: Linking theory, research and practice. *Patient Counselling and Health Education,* 4(2):65–79.

Jackson, J. S., Tucker, M. Belinda, and Bowman, P. J. 1982. Conceptual and methodological problems and survey research on black americans. *Methodological Problems in Minority Research,* P/AAMHRC Occasional Paper Series No. 7, 11–40.

Johnson, C. L. 1978. Family support systems of elderly Italian Americans. Paper presented at the Gerontological Society Annual Scientific Meeting, Dallas, Tex.

Johnson, C. L., and Catalano, D. J. 1981. Childless elderly and their family supports. *The Gerontologist* 21(6):610–618.

Kahana E., Liang, J., and Felton, B. J. 1980. Alternative models of person–environment fit: Prediction of morale in three homes for the aged. *Journal of Gerontology* 35(4):584–595.

Kahn, R. L. 1974. Conflict ambiguity and overload: Three elements in job stress. *In* A. McLean (ed.), *Occupational Stress.* Springfield, Ill.: Charles C. Thomas.

Kahn, R. L. 1979. Aging and social support. *In* M. W. Riley (ed.), *Aging from Birth to Death,* Boulder, Colo.: Westview Press.

Kahn, R. L. 1981. *Work and Health.* New York: John Wiley.

Kahn, R. L., and Antonucci, T. C. 1978. Social support networks among new teachers. Technical proposal to The National Institute of Education.

Kahn, R. L., and Antonucci, T. C. 1980. Convoys over the life course. Attachment, roles and social support. *In* P. B. Baltes and O. G. Brim (eds.), *Life-Span Development and Behavior.* New York: Academic Press.

Kahn, R. L., and Antonucci, T. C. 1983. Social supports of the elderly: Family/friends/professionals. Final report to the National Institute on Aging.

Kahn, R. L., Wethington, E., and Ingersoll, B. N. In press. Social networks: Determinants and Effects. In R. Abeles (ed.), *Implications of the Life-span Perspective for Social Psychology,* New York: Lawrence Erlbaum Associates.

Kaplan, B. H. Cassell, J. C., and Gore, S. 1977. Social support and health. *Medical Care* 15(5) Supplement: 47–58.

Kasl, S. V., and Berkman, L. F. 1981. Some psychosocial influences on the health status of the elderly: The perspective of social epidemiology. In J. L. McGaugh and S. B. Kiesler (eds.), *Aging: Biology and Behavior.* New York: Academic Press.

Kasworm, C., and Wetzel, J. W. 1981. Women and retirement: Evolving issues for future research and education intervention. *Educational Gerontology: An International Quarterly,* 299–314.

Katz, A. H. 1981. Self and mutual aid: An emerging social movement? *Annual Review of Sociology* 7: 129–155.

Keating, N., and Marshall, J. 1980. The process of retirement: The rural self employed. *The Gerontologist* 20(4):437–443.

Keating, N. C., and Spiller, L. J. 1981. Retired women's definitions of leisure. Paper presented at the annual meeting of the Gerontological Society of America, Toronto.

Kernodle, R. W., and Kernodle, R. L. 1979. A comparison of the social networks of blacks and whites. Paper presented at the Gerontological Society 32nd Annual Scientific Meeting, Washington, D.C., Nov.

Kessler, R. C. 1979. Stress, social status, and psychological stress. *Journal of Health and Social Behavior* 20(2):259–272.

Kivett, V. R., and Learner, R. M. 1982. Situational Influences on the morale of older rural adults in child-shared housing: A comparative analysis. *The Gerontologist* 22(1):100–106.

Kivnick, H. Q. 1982. Grandparenthood: An overview of meaning and mental health. *The Gerontologist* 22(1):59–66.

Knapp, M. R. J. 1976. Predicting the dimensions for life satisfaction. *Journal of Gerontology* 31(5):595–604.

Kobrin, F. E. 1981. Family extension and the elderly:

Economic, demographic and family cycle factors. *Journal of Gerontology* 36(3):370–377.

Kobrin, F. E., and Hendershot, G. E. 1977. Do family ties reduce mortality? Evidence from the United States 1966–1968. *Journal of Marriage and the Family* 39:737–746.

Koff, Theodore H. 1982. *Long-Term Care: An Approach to Serving the Frail Elderly.* Boston, Mass.: Little, Brown.

Kohen, Janet A. 1983. Old but not alone: Informal social supports among the elderly by marital status and sex. *The Gerontologist* 23(1):57–63.

Lang, A. M., and Brody, E. M. 1983. Characteristics of middle-aged daughters and help to their elderly mothers. *Journal of Marriage and the Family,* 45(1):193–202.

Langer, E. J., and Rodin, J. 1976. The effects of choice and enhanced personal responsibility for the aged: A field experiment in an institutional setting. *Journal of Personality and Social Psychology* 34:191–198.

Langlie, J. K. 1977. Social networks, health beliefs, and preventive health behavior. *Journal of Health and Social Behavior* 18(3):244–260.

LaRocco, J. M., House, J. S., and French, J. R. P., Jr. 1980. Social support, occupational stress and health. *Journal of Health and Social Behavior* 21:202–218.

Lawton, M. P. 1980a. *Environment and Aging.* Monterey, Calif.: Brooks-Cole.

Lawton, M. P. 1980b. Environmental change: The older person as initiator and responder. *In* N. Datan and N. Lohmann (eds.), *Transitions of Aging.* New York: Academic Press.

Lebowitz, B. 1978. Old age and family functioning. *Journal of Gerontological Social Work* 1(2):111–118.

Lee, G. R., and Ihinger-Tallman, N. 1980. Sibling interaction and moral: The effects of family relations on older people. *Research on Aging* 2(3):367–391.

Lee, G. R., and Lassey, M. L. 1980. Rural–urban differences among the elderly: Economic, social and subjective factors. *Journal of Social Issues* 36(2):62–74.

Leigh, G. K. 1982. Kinship interaction over the family life span. *Journal of Marriage and the Family,* 44(1):197–208.

Leinhart, S. (ed.) 1977. *Social Networks: A Developing Paradigm.* New York: Academic Press.

Lemke, S., and Moos, R. H. 1981. The suprapersonal environments of sheltered care settings. *Journal of Gerontology* 36(2):233–243.

Leon, G. R., Kamp, J., Gillum, R. and Gillum B., 1981. Life stress and dimensions of functioning in old age. *Journal of Gerontology* 36(1):66–69.

Levitt, M., Antonucci, T. C., Clark, M. C., Rotton, J., and Finley, G. E. In press. Social support and well-being: Preliminary indicators based on two samples of the elderly. *International Journal of Aging and Human Development.*

Lieberman, M. A., and Mullan, J. T. 1978. Does help

help? The adaptive consequences of obtaining help from professionals and social networks. *American Journal of Community Psychology* 6(5):499–517.

Lin, N., Dean, A., and Ensel, W. M. 1979. Development of social support scales. Paper presented at the Third Biannual Conference on Health Survey Research Methods, Reston, Va.

Lin, N., Dean, A., and Ensel, W. M. 1981. Social support scales: A methodological note. *Schizophrenia Bulletin* 7(1):73–89.

Lin, N., Ensel, W. M., Simeone, R. S., and Kuo, W. 1979. Social support, stressful life events and illness: A model and an empirical test. *Journal of Health and Social Behavior* 20 (June):108–119.

Lindsey, A. M., and Hughes, E. M. 1981. Social support and alternatives to institutionalization for the at-risk elderly. *Journal of The American Geriatrics Society* 29(7):308–315.

Linn, M. W., Hunter, K. I., and Perry, P. R. 1979. Differences by sex and ethnicity in the psychosocial adjustment of the elderly. *Journal of Health and Social Behavior* 20(3):273–281.

Longino, C. F., Jr. 1979. Going home: Aged return migration in the United States 1965–1970. *Journal of Gerontology* 34(5):736–746.

Longino, C. F., Jr. and Jackson, D. J. (eds.), 1980. Migration and the aged. Special edition of *Research on Aging* 2(2):131–280.

Longino, C. F., Jr. and Kitson, G. C. 1976. Parish clergy and the aged: Examining stereotypes. *Journal of Gerontology* 31(3):340–345.

Longino, C. F., Jr. and Lipman, A. 1981. Married and spouseless men and women in planned retirement communities: Support network differentials. *Journal of Marriage and the Family* 43(Feb.):169–177.

Longino, C. F., Jr. and Lipman, A. 1982. The married, the formerly married and the never married: Support system differentials of older women in planned retirement communities. *International Journal of Aging and Human Development* 15(4):285–297.

Lopata, H. Z. 1975. Support systems of elderly urbanites: Chicago of the 1970's. *The Gerontologist* 15(1):35–41.

Lopata, H. Z. 1978. Contributions of extended families to the support systems of metropolitan area widows: Limitations of the modified kin network. *Journal of Marriage and the Family* 40:355–364.

Lopata, H. Z. 1979. *Women as Widows: Support Systems.* New York: Elsevier-North Holland.

Lowenthal, M. F., and Haven, C. 1968. Interaction and adaptation: Intimacy as a critical variable. *American Sociological Review* 33:20–30.

Lowenthal, M. F., Thurnher, M. and Chiriboga, D. A. 1975. *Four Stages of Life.* San Francisco: Jossey-Bass.

Maas, H. J., and Kuypers, J. A. 1974. *From Thirty to Seventy.* San Francisco: Jossey-Bass.

Mancini, J. A. 1980. Friend interaction, competence and morale in old age. *Research on Aging* 2(4):416–431.

Marsden, P. V. 1982. *Social Structure and Network Analysis.* Beverly Hills, Calif.: Sage.

Martineau, W. H. 1977. Informal social ties among urban black Americans: Some new data and a review of the problem. *Journal of Black Studies* 8(1):83–104.

McCluskey, N. G., and Borgatta, E. F. 1981. *Aging and Retirement,* Beverly Hills, Calif.: Sage.

McKinlay, J. B. 1980. Social network influences on morbid episodes and the career of help seeking. In L. Eisenberg and A. Kleinman (eds.), *The Relevance of Social Science For Medical Practice.* Boston, Ma.: D. Reidel Publishing Company.

Meyers, J. M., and Drayer, C. S. 1979. Support systems and mental illness in the elderly. *Community Mental Health Journal* 15(4):277–287.

Mindel, C. H., and Wright, R., Jr. 1981. Living arrangements of elderly and morale. Paper presented at the 34th Annual Meeting of the Gerontological Society of America, Toronto.

Mindel, C. H., and Wright, R. Jr. 1982. Satisfaction in multigenerational households. *Journal of Gerontology* 37(4):483–489.

Mitchell, J. C. (ed.) 1969. *Social Networks and Urban Situations.* Manchester: Manchester University Press.

Mitchell, R., and Trickett, E. 1980. Social networks as mediators of social support: An analysis of the effects and determinants of social networks. *Community Mental Health Journal* 16:27–44.

Moos, R. H. 1981. Environment choice and control in community care settings for older people. *Journal of Applied Psychology* 11(1):23–43.

Moos, R. H., and Igra, A. 1980. Determinants of the social environments of sheltered care settings. *Journal of Health and Social Behavior,* 21:88–98.

Moreno, J. L. 1934. *Who Shall Survive?* Washington, D.C.: Nervous and Mental Disease Publishing Co.

Mutran, E., and Reitzes, D. C. 1981. Retirement, identity and well-being: Realignment of role relationships. *Journal of Gerontology* 36(6):733–740.

Mutran, E., and Skinner, G. 1981. Family support and the well-being of widowed: Black–white comparisons. Paper presented at the 34th Annual Meeting of the Gerontological Society of America, Toronto.

Neighbors, H. W., Jackson, J. S., Bowman, P. J., and Gurin, G. Spring. 1983. Stress, coping and black mental health: Preliminary findings from a national study. *Prevention and Human Services* 2(3):5–29.

Neugarten, B. L. 1978. The future and the young-old. In Jarvik, L. F. (ed.), *Aging into the 21st Century,* pp. 137–152. New York: Gardner Press.

Noelker, L., and Harel, Z. 1978. Predictors of well-being and survival among institutionalized aged. *Gerontologist* 18(6):562–567.

Noelker, L., and Harel, Z. 1983. The integration of environment and network theories in explaining the aged's functioning and well-being. *Interdisciplinary Topics in Gerontology* 17(8):

Noelker, L. S., and Poulshock, S. W. In press. Intimacy: Factors affecting its development among members of a home for the aged. *International Journal of Aging and Human Development.*

Norbeck, J. S. 1981. Social support, a model for clinical research and application. *Advances in Nursing Science,* 3(4):43–59.

O'Brien, J. E., and Wagner, D. L. 1980. Help seeking by the frail elderly: Problems in network analysis. *The Gerontologist* 20(1):78–83.

Palmore, E., and Kivett, V. 1977. Change in life satisfactions: A longitudinal study of persons aged 46–70. *Journal of Gerontology* 32(3):311–316.

Parks, S. H., and Pilisuk, M. 1981. Social ties and health status in an elderly population. Paper presented at the Annual Meetings of the American Psychological Association, Los Angeles.

Parmelee, P. A. 1982. Social contacts, social instrumentality and adjustment of institutionalized aged. *Research on Aging,* 4(2):269–280.

Pattison, E. M., Llamas, R., and Hurd, G. 1979. Social network mediation of anxiety. *Psychiatric Annals* 9:56–57.

Pearlin, L. I., Menaghan, E. G., Lieberman, M. A., and Mullan, J. T. 1981. The stress process. *Journal of Health and Social Behavior* 22:237–356.

Petrowsky, M. 1976. Marital status, sex and the social networks of the elderly. *Journal of Marriage and the Family* 38:749–756.

Petty, B. J., Tamerra, P. M., and Campbell, R. Z. 1976. Support groups for elderly persons in community. *The Gerontologist* 16(6):522–528.

Phillips, S. L. 1981. Network characteristics related to the well-being of normals: A comparative base. *Schizophrenia Bulletin* 7(1):117–124.

Pierce, R. C., and Chiriboga, D. A. 1979. Dimensions of adult self-concept. *Journal of Gerontology* 34(1):80–85.

Pilisuk, M., and Froland, C. 1978. Kinship, social networks, social support and health. *Social Science and Medicine* 12:273–280.

Pilisuk, M., and Minkler, M. 1980. Supportive networks: Life ties for the elderly. *Journal of Social Issues* 36(2):95–116.

Plath, D. 1975. Aging and social support. A presentation to the Committee on Work and Personality in the Middle Years, Social Science Research Council.

Porritt, D. 1979. Social support in crises: Quality or quantity? *Social Science and Medicine* 13(6A):715–722.

Powers, E., and Bultena, G. 1976. Sex differences in intimate friendships of old age. *Journal of Marriage and the Family* 38:739–747.

Reis, H. T. 1984. Social interaction and well-being. In S. Duck (ed.), *Personal Relationships V: Repairing Personal Relationships.* London: Academic Press.

Rodgers-Siregar, S., Shelly, R. K., and Sutherland, D. 1981. Kinship structure and the rural elderly: An anthropological and sociological synthesis. Paper presented at the Gerontological Society of America meeting, Toronto, Nov.

Rosow. I. 1976. Status and role change through the life span. In R. H. Binstock and E. Shanas (eds.), *Handbook of Aging and the Social Sciences*, 1st ed. pp. 457–482. New York: Van Nostrand Reinhold.

Rundall, T. G., and Evashwick, C. 1982. Social networks and help-seeking among the elderly. *Research on Aging* 4(2):205–226.

Satariano, W. A., Minkler, M. A., and Langhauser, C. 1981. Supportive exchange: A missing link in the study of social networks and health status in the elderly. Paper presented at the annual meeting of the American Gerontological Society, Toronto.

Sauer, W. 1977. Morale of the urbanized: A regression and analysis by race. *Journal of Gerontology* 32:600–608.

Sauer, W., and Coward, R. Forthcoming. *Social Support Networks and the Care of the Elderly: Theory Research, Practice and Policy*. New York: Springer.

Schaefer, C., Coyne, J., and Lazarus, R. 1981. Health-related functions of social support. *Journal of Behavioral Medicine* 4(4):381–406.

Schaie, K. W., and Parham, I. A. 1976. Stability of adult personality traits: Facts or fable? *Journal of Personality and Social Psychology* 34:146–158.

Schmidt, M. G. 1980. Failing parents, aging children. *Journal of Gerontological Social Work* 2(3):259–268.

Schmidt, M. G. 1981. Personal networks. Assessment, care and repair. *Journal of Gerontological Social Work* 3(4):65–76.

Schulz, R. 1982. Emotionality and aging: A theoretical and empirical analysis. *Journal of Gerontology* 37(1):42–51.

Schulz, R., and Brenner, G. 1977. Relocation of the aged: A review and theoretical analysis. *Journal of Gerontology* 32(3):323–333.

Schwartz, D. F., and Jacobson, E. 1977. Organizational communication network analysis: The liaison communication role. *Organizational Behavior and Human Performance* 18:158–174.

Seelbach, W. C. 1977. Gender differences in expectations for filial responsibility. *Journal of Gerontology* 17(5):421–425.

Shanas, E. 1979a. Social myth as hypothesis: The case of the family relations of old people. *The Gerontologist* 19:3–9.

Shanas, E. 1079b. The family as a social support system in old age. *The Gerontologist* 19(2):169–174.

Shanas, E., and Streib, G. (eds.), 1965. *Social Structure and the Family Generational Relations*. Englewood Cliffs, N.J.: Prentice-Hall.

Smith, K. F., and Bengtson, V. L. 1979. Positive consequences of institutionalization: Solidarity between elderly and their middle-aged children. *The Gerontologist* 19(5):438–447.

Sokolovsky, J., and Cohen, C. I. 1981a. Toward a resolution of methodological dilemmas in network mapping. *Schizophrenia Bulletin* 7(1):109–116.

Sokolovsky, J., and Cohen, C. I. 1981b. Measuring social interaction of the urban elderly: A methodolog-ical synthesis. *International Journal of Aging and Human Development* 13(3):233–244.

Spakes, P. R. 1979. Family, friendship and community interaction as related to life satisfaction of the elderly. *Journal of Gerontological Social Work* 1(4):279–294.

Stephens, R. C., Blau, Z. S., Oser, G. T., and Miller, M. D. 1978. Aging, social support systems, and social policy. *Journal of Gerontological Social Work* 1(1):33–45.

Strain, L. A., and Chappell, N. A. 1982. Confidants: Do they make a difference in quality of life? *Research and Aging* 4(4):479–502.

Streib, G. F. 1983. The frail elderly: Research dilemmas and research opportunities. *The Gerontologist* 23(1):40–44.

Sullivan, D. A. and Stevens, S. A. 1982. Snowbirds: Seasonal migrants to the Sunbelt. *Research on Aging* 4(2):159–178.

Sussman, M. B. 1979. Social economic supports and family environments for the elderly. Final report. Washington, D.C.: Administration on Aging.

Szinovacz, M. 1982. *Women's Retirement Policy Implications of Recent Research*. Vol. 6. Beverly Hills, Calif.: Sage.

Taylor, R. J. 1983. The informal social support networks of the black elderly: The impact of family, church members and best friends. Unpublished dissertation, The University of Michigan.

Taylor, R. J., Jackson, J. S., and Quick, A. D. 1982. The frequency of social support among black Americans: Preliminary findings from the national survey of black Americans. *Urban Research Review* 8(2):1–4, 11.

Teaff, J. D., Lawton, M. P., Nahemow, L., and Carlson, D. 1978. Impact of age integration on the well-being of elderly tenants in public housing. *Journal of Gerontology* 33(1):126–133.

Tesch, S., Whitbourne, S. K., and Nehrke, M. F. 1981. Friendship, social interaction and subjective well-being of older men in an institutional setting. *International Journal of Aging: Human Development* 13(4):317–328.

Thoits, P. A. 1982. Conceptual, methodological, and theoretical problems in studying social support as a buffer against life stress. *Journal of Health and Social Behavior* 23:145–149.

Thomae, H. 1980. Personality and Adjustment to Aging. In J. E. Birren and R. B. Sloane (eds.), *Handbook of Mental Health and Aging*. Englewood, N. J.: Prentice-Hall.

Tichy, N. M. 1980. Networks in organizations. In P. C. Nystrom and W. H. Starbuck (eds.), *Handbook of Organizational Design*, Vol. 2, *Remodeling Organizations and Their Environments*. London: Oxford University Press; Englewood Cliffs, N.J.: Prentice-Hall.

Tolsdorf, C. 1976. Social networks, support, and coping: An exploratory study. *Family Process* 15:407–417.

Toseland, R. W., Decker, J., and Bliesner, J. 1979. A community outreach program for socially isolated older persons. *Journal of Gerontological Social Work* 1(3):211–224.

Trela, J. E. 1976. Social class and association membership: An analysis of age graded and non-graded voluntary participation. *Journal of Gerontology* 31(2):198–203.

Troll, L. E., and Smith, J. 1976. Attachment through the life-span: Some questions about dyadic bonds among adults. *Human Development* 19(3):156–170.

Troll, L., and Turner, B. 1979. Sex differences in problems of aging. *In* E. Gombert and V. Franks (eds.), *Gender and Disordered Behavior*. New York: Bruner/Maze.

Troll, L., Miller, S. J., and Atchley, R. C. 1979. *Families in Later Life*. Belmont, Calif.: Wadsworth.

Veroff, J., Douvan, E., and Kulka, R. 1981. *The Inner American*. New York: Basic Books.

Walker, J. W., Kimmel, D. C., and Price, K. F. 1980–81. Retirement style and retirement satisfaction: Retirees aren't all alike. *International Journal of Aging and Human Development* 12(4):267–281.

Walker, K., Macbride, A., and Vachon, M. 1977. Social support networks and the crisis of bereavement. *Social Science and Medicine* 11:35–41.

Walsh, J. A., and Kiracoff, N. M. 1979–80. Change in significant other relationships and life satisfaction in the aged. *International Journal of Aging and Human Development* 10(3):273–281.

Wan, T. T. H. 1982. *Stressful Life Events, Social-Support Network and Gerontological Health*. Lexington, Mass.: D. C. Heath.

Wan, T. T. H., and Weissert, W. G. 1981. Social support networks, patient status and institutionalization. *Research on Aging* 3:240–256.

Wantz, Molly S., and Gay, John E. 1981. *The Aging Process: A Health Perspective*. Cambridge, Mass. Winthrop.

Ward, R. A. 1979a. The never married in later life. *Journal of Gerontology* 34(6):861–869.

Ward, R. A. 1979b. The meaning of voluntary association participation to older people. *Journal of Gerontology* 34(3):438–445.

Weeks, J. R., and Cuellar, J. B. 1981. The role of family members in the helping networks of older people. *The Gerontologist* 21(4):388–394.

Wellman, B. 1981. Applying network analysis to the study of support. *In* B. H. Gottlieb (ed.), *Social Networks and Social Support*, pp. 171–200, Sage Studies in Community Mental Health 4. Beverly Hills and London: Sage.

Wells, L., and MacDonald, G. 1981. Interpersonal networks and post-relocation adjustment of the institutionalized elderly. *The Gerontologist* 21(2):177–183.

Wentowski, G. J. 1981. Reciprocity and the coping strategies of older people: Cultural dimensions of network building. *The Gerontologist* 21(6):600–609.

White, H. C., Boorman, S. A., and Breiger, R. L. 1976. Social structure from multiple networks: Block models of roles and positions. *American Journal of Sociology* 81(4):730–780.

Windley, P. G., and Scheidt, R. J. 1982. An ecological model of mental health among small-town rural elderly. *Journal of Gerontology* 37(2):235–242.

Wiseman, R. F. 1980. Why older people move: Theoretical issues. *Research on Aging* 2(2):141–154.

Wood, V., and Robertson, J. F. 1976. The significance of grandparenthood. *In* J. Gubrium (ed.), *Time, Roles, and Self in Old Age*. New York: Human Science Press.

Wood, V., and Robertson, J. F. 1978. Friendship and kinship interaction: Differential effect on the morale of the elderly. *Journal of Marriage and the Family* 40(2):367–375.

Wright, P. H. 1982. Men's friendships, women's friendships, and the alleged inferiority of the latter. *Sex Roles* 8(1):1–20.

5
SOCIETAL PERCEPTIONS OF AGING AND THE AGED

W. Andrew Achenbaum

Carnegie-Mellon University

INTRODUCTION

Significance of Topic

Perceptions of the aging and aged—those congeries of ideas, images, and stereotypes about growing older and being elderly—have always had a profound impact on the ways people individually and collectively define and grapple with the potentials and limitations of the human condition.

Attitudes toward senescence, in fact, are something of a cultural prism. They are not simply the result of personal experiences. The ways different age groups "see" each other and themselves are not biologically predetermined. Nor are they mainly a function of some balance of power or socioeconomic relationship. Rather, the origins and manifestations of our perceptions have been largely determined by ideas and conditions prevailing in society over time.

Gerontologists long have been aware of the importance of understanding the nature and dynamics of our ideas about becoming old(er). They influence the choices men and women make about sexual activity, for example, or living arrangements or retirement behavior. They help to shape the opinions people at all ages express about their current self-worth or concerning their future selves. The manner in which researchers and practitioners deal with "age" reflects norms in areas as diverse as work, property, longevity, and parent–child relations.

Despite the fundamental importance of identifying and understanding the structure and dynamics of societal perceptions of aging and the aged, very little work has been done thus far. (This is hardly surprising, given the educational backgrounds, research interests, and professional experiences of those who have been active in gerontology since its formative years.) Much of the existing literature is riddled with unsystematic, even anecdotal, observations and is couched in untested assumptions.

There are notable exceptions. Leo Simmons's *The Role of the Aged in Primitive Societies* (1945) remains indispensable reading. Dr. Joseph T. Freeman's bibliography (1979) greatly enhanced our understanding of continuities and changes in attitudes toward the old in Western society. Social scientists such as Cowgill and Holmes (1972) and Hendricks and Hendricks (1981), moreover, have exposed serious flaws in earlier theories about the impact of modernization upon the aged's actual and perceived social status. David Guttmann (1977) documented the powers and weaknesses ascribed to older people when they are viewed as "The Other" by the neighbors.

Though one might have expected historians, philosophers, artists, literary critics, and ethicists to have done most of the spade-work, very few humanistic perspectives on aging actually were published before the late 1970s. Even these were not always helpful in identifying and extirpating erroneous ideas about aging. For instance, Simone de Beauvoir's *The Coming of Age* (1972), probably the best-known work on the subject by a contemporary humanist, regrettably echoes and exaggerates fears about the numbing sense of worthlessness, decline, and alienation in old age.

Nevertheless, important humanistic research on the range of images and ideas reflected in a variety of media has become available during the past decade. Humanists have begun to account for the diversity in attitudes about being old within specific segments of the population at various points in time.

To date, historians have done the most interesting work of these researchers. Histories of age relations and the evolution of the human life cycle in the United States and western Europe since early modern times are being published. Scholars have uncovered layers of sociohistorical and ideological screens interposed between views of the elderly and responses of the aged to developments that affect(ed) their lives.

Before assessing this new body of information, it is important to highlight some of the sources, methodological assumptions, and research strategies from which it has been derived. I will take an explicitly historical approach for two reasons. Intellectually, this is the most effective way to introduce gerontologists to questions and issues shaping this subfield. Methodologically, because history serves as a bridge between the social sciences and the humanities (Hughes, 1975; Kammen, 1980), surveying the humanists' findings from a historian's perspective will expose opportunities and challenges in doing cross-disciplinary research.

Humanistic Orientations and Procedures

Most humanists interpret thoughts and feelings about senescence embodied in all forms of human expression, including folklore, myths, magic, rituals, religion, art, poetry, songs, medical diagnoses and therapies, proverbs, social mores and customs, legal codes, novels, essays, jokes, movies, and television programs. Having identified major themes, ambiguities, ironies, contradictions, and paradoxes within a particular document, investigators then try to differentiate what is universal and unvarying about the meanings and experiences of growing old(er) from what is particular and time-bound (Philibert, 1974, 1979; Van Tassel, 1979; Moody, 1981; Achenbaum, 1981). Thus far, their concerns have clustered around four broad issues:

1. *Definitions of aging:* Over time and across cultures, has aging embraced the entire life course, or has it been limited to the last stage(s) of existence? Why has our conceptualization of the life course itself changed? What is the relationship between aging and dying? Has the inevitability of death typically augmented or diminished the value of late life?

2. *The dynamics of aging:* Has senescence been viewed as a decremental process? Under what circumstances has this theme been counterbalanced by notions that aging provides an opportunity for renewal and growth? How have people traditionally explained and rationalized the pains and problems of growing older? What efforts have they made to modify the vicissitudes of living?

3. *Variations of aging:* What are the universal features of aging? To what extent have divergent meanings and experiences of aging been shaped by culture? historical circumstances? gender? class? race? changes in life expectancy at birth and at other points in the life cycle? Do self-perceptions of aging shift as a consequence of specific rites-of-passage or life crises? Have the universals of age been more salient than the variations? Does the multiplicity of variations preclude broad generalizations?

4. *The independent significance of perceptions:* To what extent have ideas, images, and stereotypes corresponded to the physical

"realities" of the human condition? Conversely, how do they reflect and result from the concatenation of forces shaping a particular society? How have prevailing ideas about the assets and liabilities of specific life stages influenced the allocation of social roles, functions and power? How do new notions about aging become rooted in a culture? What causes the rise and fall of stereotypes about senescence?

As the preceding set of questions suggests, humanistic gerontology emphasizes the extent to which the *modes* of conceptualizing and expressing ideas perennially have shaped people's viewpoints of age and influenced their behavior as they age(d). Philibert (1968) has shown, for instance, that much of the richness—and ambiguity—in definitions of "age" stem from the manifold connotations associated with the word in daily parlance.

Sometimes, the terms we use to describe the aged are colored by our perceptions of the aging process. For example, Genesis 24:9 in the Revised Standard Version of the Bible reads, "Now Abraham was old, well advanced in years." Other texts tell us that Abraham was "stricken" in years. In the first instance, Abraham's age is a matter of fact; in the latter case, an ageist connotation is introduced. Different translations of ancient texts thus can change the interpretation of particular words to conform to contemporary sensibilities.

Needless to say, ideas about age and aging are not shaped just by words. What people "see" affects their perspectives. Unconsciously or deliberately, their images of age become embodied with symbolic meaning. Consider the following illustration. Among the most easily discerned features of the process of aging are the progressive wrinkling and roughening of skin and the restructuring of memory in later years. Berg and Gadow (1978, p. 86) suggest a positive interpretation of these phenomena: "It is as though, through these changes, body and mind express the greater intricacies, the finer articulations that are possible in the person for whom reality has become many-layered." A less positive vision is possible: telltale signs of age may symbolize the loss of vitality and clarity of expression manifested during the earlier stages of a person's life.

Both readings of the same physiological phenomena are plausible. They would be valid in a variety of settings. The complexity and contrarieties in our individual and societal images of age and aging thus are a function of the manner in which we perceive and attempt to make sense of the world around us. The meanings and experiences of growing old(er) cannot be grasped without grounding our analysis in as deep and broad a context as possible.

Humanistic perspectives, accordingly, place special emphasis on understanding how various parts of the specific subject matter under investigation hang together (and fall apart) within a particular sociohistorical milieu. Comprehending the ways that human beings in past and present times observe(d), characterize(d), evaluate(d), and interpret(ed) the aged and the aging—whether as literary characters or artistic images, as subjects of scientific curiosity or figures encountered in everyday experiences, or as objects of social welfare or social control—presupposes some sense of how particular groups of people established and altered their prevailing conceptual categories, classificatory schema, explanatory frameworks, and moral criteria over time (Snow, 1969; Geertz, 1973; Berkhofer, 1978).

Such methodological assumptions affect the ways humanists and historians do their work. Any interpretive history of age relations and of specific stages of life must be presented as an aspect of the larger historical evolution of society and culture itself. Scholars need to acknowledge that as people's ways of behaving and viewing themselves shifted from one generation to the next, so too did their perceptions of senescence, though not necessarily in the same ways or to the same degree or at the same time (Achenbaum and Stearns, 1978).

What follows is an overview of continuities and changes in ideas, images, and stereotypes about senescence. The Western bias in this essay is unavoidable. It reflects gaps in our knowledge, and a broader cultural myopia: Western perceptions have not been profoundly affected by Oriental traditions, philosophy, and imagery. The summary of trends in Western civilization presented here is incomplete. The corpus of relevant materials has not yet been systematically surveyed. Yet despite the arbitrariness and selectivity of its focus, this essay can trace the persistence of a complex range of attitudes toward age and aging, and assess the impact of modernization on our contemporary societal perceptions of senescence.

THE LEGACY OF WESTERN CIVILIZATION

We begin with societal perceptions of aging and the aged in the Bible for two reasons. First, the oral traditions of the great Patriarchs (ca. 2000–1500 B.C.), the Pentateuch, the psalms and proverbs of the early Hebraic culture, the recorded visions of the Prophets and the written documents of the fledgling Christian church provide a rich vein of ideas and imagery concerning the human condition and its relationship to the divine order. Second, the powerful classics of the Judeo–Christian tradition have exercised a profound impact on the development of Western thought and ethics. The events, actors, and texts of this early period have set crucial standards by which believers and non-believers alike have judged themselves and sought to understand their times (Tracy, 1981). Many of the beliefs and attitudes toward senescence expressed by "modern" people build upon orientations recorded in Scripture.

Perceptions of Age in Ancient Hebraic Culture

The Old Testament abounds in positive images of old age: "A hoary head is a crown of glory; it is gained in a righteous life" (Proverbs 16:31). The special status ascribed to late life is viewed as one of God's blessings (Psalm 91:16; see also, Proverbs 9:11). Longevity is the Lord's reward for prior service (Deuteronomy 4:40), adherence to all of His commandments (Deuteronomy 5:33,

11:21, 22:7), steadfastness in belief and faith in Israel's special mission (Exodus 23:26; Proverbs 10:27), and "humility and fear of the Lord" (Proverbs 22:4).

While the gift of a ripe old age could be bestowed only by God, the elderly's favorable position in Hebraic culture was also a function of three vital roles they played. The aged made intercessions to the Lord and often were instruments of His will. Considerable emphasis is placed on the heroes' advanced ages. Noah was 600 years old when the Lord commanded him to prepare for the deluge; he died at the age of 950 (Genesis 7:6, 9:29). Though most biblical scholars doubt the literal accuracy of this chronology, there can be little doubt that Noah was considerably older than his peers. The old, moreover, wielded considerable political power (Numbers 11:16–18). Above all, the elderly were custodians of the collective wisdom of the years (Job 12:12, 32:7; see also, Knapp, 1976).

Respect for age affected the tenor of Hebraic parent–child relations. The Fifth Commandment—"Honor your father and your mother, as the Lord your God commanded you; that your days may be prolonged, and that it may go well with you, in the land which the Lord your God gives you" (Deuteronomy 5:16)—provides the most familiar guidelines. Note that the second dependent clause makes the younger generation's own well-being conditional upon ensuring the personal and social security of those who are presently aged. Several Old Testament stories, particularly Ruth 4:13–17, illustrate the benefits of mutual support.

The Fifth Commandment's importance is underscored, conversely, in the magnitude of punishments levied if parental orders were not obeyed or if a child cursed his or her parent (Leviticus 20:9; see also Exodus 21:17, Deuteronomy 21:18–21). Clearly, the Old Testament was written for and in a world in which ideals were not always realized, and parents were not invariably obeyed. Promulgating laws to protect the aged presupposes that growing older could be disadvantageous.

Ecclesiastes 12:1–8 graphically details the

physical woes of senescence. Its metaphorical catalog of trembling arms, stooping legs, missing and worn-down teeth, failing vision, white hair, swollen stomachs, and diminished sexual desire contrasts sharply with the physical ideal personified by youthful David in I Samuel 18:24. Old Testament writers recognized, moreover, that the aged were not always guiltless, much less paragons of virtue.

The fear of rejection—"Do not cast me off in the time of old age; forsake me not when my strength is gone"—is evoked poignantly in Psalm 71:9. While respect for old age and a concern for harmonious relations between the generations are clearly dominant themes, they were neither easily attainable nor motivated solely by human altruism and compassion. But the central commandment to honor and fear the Lord colored all relations. The juxtaposition between honoring the face of an old man and fearing the Lord expressed in Leviticus 19:32 could not be more unequivocal.

Far from being anomalous situations, suffering and even death were seen as part of a cosmic order that only the Almighty could divine. Thus Jewish tradition prepared believers to tolerate the foibles of age in others and, if necessary, accept pain as their own lot in life. Those who failed to provide the aged with care and support had to be prepared to face the consequences.

There is some evidence that the attitudes toward old age and aging set forth in Scripture have remained a salient feature of Jewish culture. The corpus of Talmudic literature and traditions elucidates and amplifies prescriptions concerning the respect due age (Blech, 1975). The course of Jewish history has underscored the importance of family solidarity, adherence to religious teachings and practices, and one's responsibility to succor the sick, needy, and aged. Even today, many traditional family rituals and customs are passed down from one generation to the next by the elders of the household. A few researchers have attributed the quality of care and range of services in Jewish old-age centers to deeply engrained religious attitudes (Maves, 1960; Myerhoff, 1978). Sub-stantiating this point, however, will require systematic investigation.

Early Christian Views

The earliest Christian perspectives on age and aging built on Old Testament precedents. Different writers rehearsed the commandment to honor thy mother and thy father (Mark 7:11-13; Matthew 15:1-20; Colossians 3:20). They repeated the longstanding principle that honoring the older generation is a way of being obedient to God (Ephesians 6:1-4).

In certain respects, New Testament perspectives on senescence parallel Eastern religious thought. The image of Jesus as one who "emptied himself, taking the form of a servant, being born in the likeness of men" (Philippians 2:7) resembles the ascetical notion of *sunyata* in Madhyamika Buddhism and the role of "emptiness" in Taoism. The spiritual discipline of letting go has special significance for the aging and elderly in both traditions (Whitehead, 1978). The liabilities of old age, no less than its advantages, are part of the divine order; learning to cope with trouble enables one to understand better the ultimate meanings of the human condition.

Distinctively "Christian" views of age and aging in the New Testament arise from the ways that the early church conceived of the personhood of Christ:

> But grace was given to each of us according to the measure of Christ's gift. . . . until we all attain to the unity of the faith and of the knowledge of the Son of God, to mature manhood, to the measure of the stature of the fulness of Christ; so that we may no longer be children, tossed to and fro and carried about with every wind of doctrine. . . . Rather, speaking the truth in love, we are to grow up in every way into him who is the head, into Christ, from whom the whole body, joined with which it is supplied, when each part is working properly, makes bodily growth and upbuilds itself in love. (Ephesians 4:7,13-16)

This image of aging goes beyond the parameters of Old Testament thought and differs from all other religions insofar as it posits that the goal of human development is to grow into the "mature manhood" of

Christ. Whereas the Old Testament emphasizes qualitative differences among the various age groups, the New Testament accentuates the theme of continuity. Growth begins at birth, stretches through the course of human life, and ends when one becomes fully incorporated into the Body of Christ.

According to this metaphor, the child lives on in the man. The image of childhood invoked differs from childishness; a Christian is to grow in spontaneity and in faith, and to reject fads and passing fancies (Bouwsma, 1978). Nor does the image violate the injunction to honor "gray hairs," but it does put the commandment in a more transcendent context. No Christian, no matter how advanced in years, can attain full maturity in this world. Perhaps this explains why no older person in the New Testament is portrayed as vividly as the Patriarchs of the Old Testament; the central figure is a vigorous middle-aged Christ (O'Brien, 1981).

Normative New Testament attitudes toward age thus are deeply bound up in the eschatological framework that undergirded the thinking and doctrines of the early church. When Christian doctrine repeats Old Testament teaching, it is presumed that the basis for understanding the original Jewish laws and insights has been transformed by Christ's death, resurrection, and ascension.

The relationship between death and aging described in the Bible also depends on how and where one is reading the text. The Old Testament offers little comfort or consolation for the reality of death in terms of belief in immortal life (Choron, 1963; LeFevre and LeFevre, 1981). The New Testament, on the other hand, proclaims victory over death, though biblical scholars have shown that various Christian sects visualized the afterlife in divergent ways (Pagels, 1979).

The differences between Jewish and Christian views on the course and destiny of human existence, however, are less significant than their similarities. Views of the human condition in the Old and New Testaments are not oblivious to considerations of economic productivity and social usefulness, yet, ultimately, they are independent of them. Precisely because biblical images are rooted in theological presuppositions, in beliefs about the realms of the natural and supernatural, the sacred and the profane, and good and evil, they have acquired levels of religious meanings and points of reference that diverge profoundly from secular opinions.

Graeco-Roman Perspectives

Graeco-Roman culture provides the other major wellspring of perceptions about aging and old age. Its philosophy, drama, mythology, and folklore contain some of the most profound ideas about growing older and becoming elderly ever expressed. The images in these classical sources are poignant, heroic, satiric, and tragic.

In his *Treatise on Rhetoric,* for instance, Aristotle describes youth and age as antithetical stages of life. The errors of youth, he suggests, arise from young people's extravagances and excessive earnestness. The faults of age, he claims, are far more serious. Among other things, the elderly "are apt to be suspicious from distrust, and they are distrustful from their experience. And on this account, they neither love nor hate with great earnestness . . . they both love as though about to hate, and hate as though about to love. . . . And they live more by calculation than by moral feeling; for calculation is of expediency, but moral feeling is of virtue" (Book 2, Ch. 13). Elsewhere, Aristotle contends that the elderly should be barred from political office, since they growth increasingly inflexible and small-minded with years (*Politics,* Book 2, Ch. 9). Aristophanes suggests in his satires, moreover, that those who wielded economic, political, and social power past the age of 60 frequently abused it through covetousness, greed, lechery, and arrogance (Ehrenberg, 1951).

The vulnerabilities of late life constitute a prominent theme in classical legends and literature. Even Homer, whose epics often parallel Hebraic thought in their allusions to the wisdom of experience and the honor that should be ascribed to the aged, has Aphrodite proclaim at one point that "the gods too detest old age" (de Beauvoir, 1972, p. 99). Homer attributes momentous acts of valor and decisive victories to men in their prime. Elderly Nestor is characterized as the supreme counselor but not the one who saves the day. Decrepit Laertes must abdicate in favor of Ulysses in order to save his kingdom. Hector is nurtured by Priam but in the end must take precedence over him. In Homeric thought, older men who are hampered by mounting weakness should yield their place and power to the rising generation.

Indeed, an omnipresent threat of generational discord arises when the old do not make way for the young. Stories about major characters in the Greek pantheon prominently feature intergenerational patterns of hatred and distrust. They include appalling episodes such as the castration of Uranus as an act of revenge by his own children whom he earlier had cast out, and the sorry account of Cronus eating the progeny that he has come to despise.

Perhaps the most compelling archetypes of the gruesomeness of old age emerge from Greek myth. Descriptions of Geras, the god who personified old age, portray him as a malevolent force. Geras was a dreaded and dreadful monster, despite his wrinkles, thinning hair, dwarflike stature, and emaciated, enfeebled body. Furthermore, the story of Tithonus underscores the important difference between adding years to life and life to years. According to legend, Aurora (the goddess of dawn) asked Zeus to bestow the gift of eternal life upon Tithonus (a Trojan warrior who had gained her affection). Zeus granted her request, and the couple lived together blissfully for a while. But because Aurora failed to ask that her lover's life retain its youthful vitality, Tithonus was condemned to endure forever, wracked by increasing pain and decrepitude. The sad tale ends in one version with Aurora shutting the wretched fellow away in a dark room; in another rendition, Tithonus is turned into a grasshopper. The Tithonus theme subsequently inspired Juvenal, Swift, Wilde, and Huxley (Gruman, 1966; Stahmer, 1978).

Other features of Greek antiquity indicate, however, that some older people, especially those who retained their mental faculties and commanded influence, were genuinely honored for their past accomplishments and present services. Seniority counted. The laws of Solon gave considerable political and economic power to the eldest members of the ruling families. Richardson's (1933) exhaustive analysis of old age in ancient Greece indicates that many of the orators, historians, lawyers, poets, and thinkers who achieved fame at the time did some of their most important work after the age of 60. Older men and women sometimes were thought to possess supernatural powers.

Even after the old aristocratic order gave way to more democratic impulses, the aged retained the prerogative of speaking first in Hellenic council. They continued to serve as judges in cases involving disputes between parents and children. In Sparta, men over 60 were exempted from military service, but they hardly were relegated to the barracks. Twenty-eight Spartans, called from the ranks of the oldest and richest, constituted the *gerusia,* a body that made the truly important decisions. Such instances counterbalance the negative imagery of old age derived from Greek mythology, epics, and drama.

Roman politicians, essayists, critics, dramatists, and poets amplified Greek notions about the assets and liabilities of growing older. The prerogatives enjoyed and influence exercised by elderly Attica landowners, for example, find their counterpart in the Roman concept of *pater familias.* As in ancient Athens and in Sparta, the eldest spoke first in the Roman Senate.

Probably the most glorious paean to the worth of old age ever written comes from Roman literature. *De Senectute,* composed by Cicero in his sixty-third year, proclaims that "the crowning glory of old age is influence . . . . when the preceding part of life has been nobly spent, old age gathers the fruits of influence at last." Such influence is derived mainly from the elderly's success in weathering the physical, emotional, and moral dangers of youth and middle age. Diminishing physical strength, in Cicero's view, pales in importance when compared to the opportunities advancing years provide for the mature ripening of mind and soul. Indeed, the disagreeable features of being old are described as manifestations of long-standing character defects. By continuing to acquire wisdom and living virtuously, Cicero claims, the elderly are able to maintain themselves in an ideal position. They can afford to be tranquil, for they have freed themselves from the brash and relentless drive for success that preoccupies younger people. They can at last put their affairs in order. Above all, they can approach death with stoic resignation.

We should not infer from all this, however, that classical Rome provided a bucolic elysium for the elderly. The phrase *sexagenarius de ponte,* after all, refers to the primitive practice of drowning decrepit senior citizens in the Tiber River. And it is important to remember that *De Senectute* was written with Cicero's senatorial peers in mind: the essayist acknowledged that poor people found old age difficult to endure. The greatest Roman essayists, poets, and dramatists dealt harshly with the physical decay associated with old age. Hence Lucian addresses an elderly woman in this epigram illustrated by allusions to Greek mythology: "You may dye your locks, but you can never dye your years; you will never make the wrinkles vanish from your cheeks . . . . Never will white lead or vermilion turn Hecuba into Helen" (quoted in de Beauvoir, 1972, p. 112). Seneca concluded that *senectus morbidus est*—old age is a disease. Plutarch's essays and plays by Terence and Plautus contain savage references to the foibles, buffoonery, and lechery of aged men and women. "A common pleasure at the discomfiture of the *Senex*," suggests the literary critic Leslie Fiedler (1979), drew laughs in ancient times and has inspired stock plots through the ages.

This cursory survey of ancient Judeo-Christian and Graeco-Roman perceptions reveals that diversity is not the exclusive hallmark of the contemporary era. Records from Western civilization's most venerable traditions abound in a wide range of images of senescence. Equally revealing are those cases in which the aged and the aging are presented as The Other—as objects from which observers can dissociate themselves and onto which they can project their fears and hopes. A staggering variety of emotions and thoughts, moreover, are to be found within specific ideographs themselves. Sometimes, multiple meanings are caused by the refractions of class, gender, mental aptitude, or physical condition. In other cases, they reflect a disparity between rhetoric and reality, or differences in the various points of view directly or indirectly suggested by the image.

Developments during the Middle Ages

Our understanding of concepts of senescence between the decline of the Roman empire and the rise of the early modern era is far from satisfactory. Nonetheless, two fairly obvious but important generalizations seem warranted. No single image of (old) age and aging dominated elite or popular culture. Furthermore, writers and artists during the period relied heavily on Judeo-Christian and Graeco-Roman prototypes in shaping their ideas and images.

To document the esteem accorded age during the period, for instance, one need only refer to the rise of the papacy in the religious realm and the influence of presbyters and aldermen in the affairs of state. The titles of these positions bespeak age-specific connotations surrounding fatherhood (the papacy) or being elderly ("presby" and "alder" are cognates of "old"). Except in the case of the Venetian doges, not every incumbent of these important offices was invariably advanced in years, but the symbols of these offices reflected the dress and instruments of power associated at the time with late life. Furthermore, the wisdom and courage of age are extolled in stories about Charlemagne and in various renditions of *Le Mort d'Arthur.*

Women past the age of 50 rarely possessed much political power or economic control, but historians have uncovered some evidence indicating places and instances in which they were treated with more respect and affection than were men. In the French village of Montaillou, for instance, age often was more important than sex in determining power and authority. Older women dominated younger men frequently enough to qualify the prevailing patriarchal order, thereby underscoring the rich complexity of relationships at the time (LeRoy Ladurie, 1979).

Medieval literature and society are replete with negative as well as positive images of old age. Satirizing cuckolds and the foolish lust of older women reaches ribald heights in the works of Chaucer and Boccaccio as well as the *commedia dell'arte*. The physical ugliness and disgusting behavior of the aged were frequently mentioned in Villon's poetry and Grimm's fairy tales.

Few authors have surpassed William Shakespeare's ability to convey the conflicting emotions and contrasting masks associated with old age. His interpretation of King Lear transformed a popular medieval legend about a dispossessed father ill-treated by his heirs into a brilliant commentary about the darkly ambivalent textures of the human condition. By incarnating humanity in the persona of a wretched yet sympathetic protagonist, a raving yet profound old man who attains sublimity precisely at the moment of his collapse, Shakespeare transmogrified the assets and liabilities of age into powerful symbols of the isolated and alienating creativity of late life.

Possibly the most original contributions to images of aging during the Middle Ages were created by portraitists and folk artists. In high culture, icons of age are rarely found in the paintings of wealthy merchants, princes of the church, or members of nobility: these are generally reflections of the awesome power devolving from social rank and riches rather than the cumulative experiences of a long life. Rather, new levels of understanding can be obtained in the self-presentations of geniuses who engaged in a brutally honest life-review in pictorial form.

The portrait of the artist as an older person, observes Erich Neumann (1974), "no longer relates either consciously or unconsciously to any historical time; the solitary monologue of these 'extreme' words is spoken, as it were, into the void. And one cannot quite tell whether it is a monologue or a dialogue between man and the ultimate." Consider Rembrandt's unflattering self portraits, which did not disguise the ravages of age on his visage. Yet the Dutch master continually reaffirmed his sense of dignity amid personal tragedy. He conveyed the numinous luminance of a creative life in the face of encroaching shadows caused by limitations inherent in the human condition (Moody, 1979; for a broader statement concerning art as a medium for conveying one's completion of being, see O'Connor, 1979).

Folk artists, moreover, incorporated new ideas about human biology in depicting fresh views of the stages of life. Intellectuals at the time sought correspondences among the symbolism of numbers, physical "facts," theological tenets, astrological speculations, and different ways of conceiving the stages of life. Some invoked the Trinity as their rationale for suggesting that the life course could be divided into three broad periods. Others claimed that there were four major stages. This made some sense, since there were four seasons to the calendar year and, according to Hellenic scientific principles, four basic elements that made up the universe. Because the numbers 7 and 9 were embued with symbolic power, still others believed that "the grand climacteric" of human existence occurred at 63, an age derived by multiplying the two numbers.

Renditions of the "steps of ages" in which figures progressed from birth up stairs and then descended another set to death became commonplace (Ariès, 1962; de Beauvoir 1972). From the fourteenth through the eighteenth centuries, the relationship among chronological age, biological stage, and social function can readily be adduced: babes played with toys; at the next stage, boys carried books and girls learned to spin; then came the ages of love and war and chivalry, and finally the sedentary duties of late life. Lawyers thus are portrayed as old men with beards, certainly not because there were no young barristers, but because in popular imagery learning was perceived to be an old man's vocation.

From such evidence, historians and literary critics have drawn some tantalizing inferences about shifts in popular thinking concerning the relationship between age and death. Iconographic changes occurred in the portrayal of Father Time. Artists after 1400 accentuated the devastating effect of the passage of years on the human frame. The sickle, an agricultural tool symbolizing fertility, became an instrument of destruction. These changes have lead Stannard (1977) and de Beauvoir (1972) among others to speculate about the increasing association drawn between old age and death—independent of any major shift in age-specific mortality rates. Until more work is done, however, it would be inappropriate to say any more. Instead, we should consider the impact of modernization on perceptions of age and aging, a topic about which far more is known.

THE IMPACT OF MODERNIZATION

The Main Lines of Transformation

Modernization began to transform the structure and dynamics of Western civilization no later than the eighteenth century. Initially, the process had a greater impact on Europe than on the United States. To different degrees and at divergent rates, various factors—industrialization, technological innovation, bureaucratization, professionalization, urbanization, internal and international migration, as well as new scientific and philosophical orientations—altered the demographic, economic, political, social, and cultural features of Western civilization. These broad-scale forces profoundly changed the meanings and conditions of people's lives.

Demographically, there has been a long-term drop in the birth rate across all major ethnic and racial lines and a remarkable increase in life expectancy at birth, stemming from gains in infant and childhood mortality during the nineteenth century. Advances in

medical technology, new etiologies and therapeutic interventions, better public health practices, improved personal hygiene and diet enhanced the quantity and quality of life. Declining fertility rates and changes in mortality rates contributed to a widespread aging of population structures themselves (Bogue, 1958; Grabill et al., 1958; Vinovskis, 1978; Hendricks and Hendricks, 1981).

Economically, the shift from an agrarian to an industrial society is one of the most familiar components of modernization (Stearns, 1975; Chandler, 1977). First in Great Britain, next in the United States, France, and Germany, and then rapidly in other northern and southern European nations, one can see the diminishing importance of farming as an occupation, the rise of middle class professionalism, and the growing number of women gainfully employed outside the home. From the interplay of all these developments emerged a mature industrial economy, which was responsive to new consumption patterns, the flowering of mass culture, and the rising demands for special services.

Politically, the process of modernization has involved the extension of suffrage, the rise of parliamentary and cabinet styles of government, and the immense growth of official apparatus. Alterations in government's overall functions and levels of responsibilities increased its scope, cost, and importance in everyday life (Janowitz, 1978; Keller, 1977; Lindblom, 1977). Over time, its power to collect taxes and revenues, regulate the economy, direct civilian and military endeavors, and intervene in human affairs through the courts and its welfare system has vastly increased. Concurrently, the balance of power shifted steadily upward to national capitals: responsibilities for education, health care, social welfare, and commerce centralized.

Socially, as countries urbanized and the national political economy touched more and more citizens' lives, mass consumption, mass production, and mass media transformed people's tastes and relationships (Rodgers, 1978; Tilly and Scott, 1978). Cities' lures and discomforts—the urbanity and opportunities combined with the prejudices and inequalities, the advantages of technology juxtaposed with the inadequacies of public service—increasingly defined the "standard of living" by which Europeans and Americans measured their collective progress and set their personal goals.

Other factors were intimately connected to this spreading urban nexus. For instance, there have been fundamental changes in the nuclear family's size, structure, and allocation of power and resources over time. The institution no longer serves as society's basic unit of productivity and social control, but its images as a "haven" of affection has proved remarkably resilient to the pressures of divorce and new sexual mores as well as the tensions between work and play, career and homelife. The need to be part of fads and trends reshaping "modern" life, moreover, magnified a cultural paradox deeply rooted in the Western experience: as middle class life became more ubiquitous and homogenous, the gap between the haves and have-nots widened.

Modernization and (Old) Age

Rates of change within given societies and across major subdivisions differed widely. Consequently, the impact of modernization on various segments of the population was neither uniform nor unidirectional. Different *age* groups historically "modernized" in divergent ways and with varying degrees of adaptive success. The timing of certain major life transitions—the age of leaving school or the age at marriage—became more uniform in the life courses of successive generations. At the same time, however, divergences in life experiences—especially those encountered in old age—became more pronounced as age groups became modernized.

For instance, upper class households in Europe "discovered" children before the onset of the Industrial Revolution. Ariès (1962) contends that changes in household arrangements, economic patterns, and ideas prompted this new outlook. Instead of viewing the very young as little adults who worked and played with older people, parents began to dress their young in special clothing and develop new attitudes about the meanings and functions of family life, which were oriented around the child's socialization. This new orientation quickly pervaded all ranks of society; understanding and attending to the special needs of children as well as preparing them for their future roles in society have become a major preoccupation and priority, not just of parents but also of public and private institutions (Wishy, 1968; Hunt, 1972).

The spread of and rising importance placed on higher education aptly illustrate the point. Parents and officials increasingly appreciated the role that schools played in enhancing chances for upward mobility. Consequently, enrollments grew, and the educational experience itself became more age-graded and monitored. Those who did not or could not obtain a secondary education found their options also determined by structures and notions associated with "modernization." They increasingly worked as apprentices in factories or sought lowly employment in cities.

Furthermore, the concept of "adolescence" took on new meanings on both sides of the Atlantic during the nineteenth century. Gillis (1974) and Kett (1977) among others have argued that modernization greatly affected the options and challenges associated with transition from childhood to adulthood. The rising importance of middle class professionalism, democratic–capitalist structures, and urban mores are typically cited as causal factors. These forces popularized new images of this stage of life. Youth, claimed commentators, were in the best position to grapple with the challenges, surmount the problems, and capitalize on new opportunities transforming society.

The elderly were among the last to be affected by the process of modernization. Historical studies of the elderly in Western civilization prior to the 1800s reveal the persistence from earlier times of favorable, disparaging, conflicting, ambiguous, and ambivalent attitudes toward the aged. Researchers have found no evidence that the wide range of self-images among older Europeans or Americans changed significantly over time.

Furthermore, the elderly's economic and social status were not greatly altered by the initial stages of modernization. Throughout the nineteenth century, workers past the age of 60 engaged in agriculture, politics, most professions, and traditional crafts. Working and saving for one's declining years, relying on kith and kin and (as a last resort) local charity remained the predominant way of dealing with dependency in late life. The striking modifications in behavioral patterns among the young and middle-aged in the United States and France were not paralleled by revolutionary shifts among the old in household arrangements, marital patterns, or property relationships (Dahlin, 1980; D. S. Smith, 1978; Stearns, 1980).

Historians disagree about the relationship between modernization and the rise of new perceptions about age and aging. Few argue that "once upon a time" older men and women invariably enjoyed immense prestige and respect in Western society, or that their status has deteriorated sharply as a result of the emergence of a new urban–industrial political economy. Such a simplistic scenario ignores the extent to which people in every European society as well as in the United States acknowledged and bemoaned the liabilities of growing older long before the onset of any causal factors that might be associated with the process of modernization (Fischer, 1978).

Nor can monolithic, two-stage interpretations adequately account for the notable cross-cultural differences in early modern attitudes. The French well into the nineteenth century looked upon old age with pity and scant respect (Stearns, 1977). Gerontophobic comments abound in the satiric works of eighteenth century English writers (Freedman, 1978). This gloomy perspective pervaded British society and culture, though its more unpleasant features were mitigated as long as the aged possessed power, money,

and/or social position (Laslett, 1976; Stone, 1977a; S. R. Smith, 1978). No "golden age" flourished in colonial America. Data drawn primarily from seventeenth- and eighteenth-century New England church records, court proceedings, census materials, and literature suggest, nonetheless, that most older people (though not widows, slaves, or paupers) enjoyed a greater measure of respect and deference than their European counterparts (D. S. Smith, 1978; Demos, 1978).

The timing and precise nature of change in attitudes in the United States and western Europe during the past two centuries remain debatable. Fischer's (1978) provocative thesis has attracted the widest attention. Being old, Fischer argued, conferred an authority that grew steadily stronger during the first 150 years of the colonial experience. Then, suddenly, this age-bias was reversed as part— but only one aspect—of a fundamental transformation in the new republic's polity, economy, and comity. The "deep change" in American culture and society, according to this interpretation, was caused by the social and intellectual forces unleashed by revolutions in America and in France. After a fairly brief transitional period, a progressively stronger bias in favor of youth developed in the United States. Fischer believes that a second transition occurred in the twentieth century, with the discovery of old age as a "social problem," and unprecedented efforts to address the situation. The recent countermovement against the cult of youth, he suggests by way of a conclusion, might presage a new era in age relations.

Most of the controversy centers on the "revolution in age relations" that presumably occurred between 1770 and 1830. Historians and gerontologists have questioned whether there really was as dramatic and sudden a transition from gerontophilia to gerontophobia as implied here—precisely because of the constancy of some attitudes toward age and aging. They have suggested that the age-bias/youth-bias schema misses the pivotal role played by the middle-aged throughout American history. Fischer's research design, while praised for its ingenuity, has come under sharp attack (Stone, 1977b; Comfort, 1977; Stearns, 1978; Achenbaum, 1978a). Other pivotal decades—the antebellum period, the last quarter of the nineteenth century, the Progressive period, the Great Depression, and the period since World War II—seem as significant as the Revolutinary era.

Even without a compelling consensus regarding the "modern" history of the elderly in Western civilization, scholars concur that novel images of age and aging have emerged since the American and French revolutions. Some appear to have been reworkings of earlier notions; others demonstrably were products of the times. The development of new perspectives and images of (old) age reflect and result from broad changes in society. The impact of science and technology, of industrial innovations and bureaucratization, and of heightened age-consciousness and age-grading were considerable.

The Impact of Science and Technology

Before 1800, most people believed that chronic ailments and acute diseases in late life were inevitable ravages of Nature. Scientists classified and explained the decrements of age in terms of an imbalance of humors or loss of "vital forces." The best therapy for the elderly was to observe elementary rules of sensible living. During the nineteenth century, prevailing views began to change. Researchers in this country and overseas were influenced by the theories and findings of French, German, Russian, and British scientists who believed that the maladies of old age could be understood by investigating structural lesions. Case studies of senile gangrene, senile chorea, and a senile bronchitis were reported in medical journals. "Senility," which once had simply been a synonym for old age, acquired pathological connotations. These developments had a striking if paradoxical impact on medical opinions and popular thinking. On the one hand, since the elderly's infirmities were diagnosable, many hoped that they might also be treatable. On the other hand, nihilism

flourished among those who doubted that old age could be cured, ironically because it was a progressively debilitating disease.

In the latter decades of the nineteenth century and first third of the twentieth century, there were notable efforts but only modest progress made in unraveling the mysteries of senescence (Achenbaum, 1978b). Despite all the technological and conceptual advances in medicine itself, scientists did not discover a remedy for the problems associated with growing older. Those who believed that heroic therapies could perform miracles remained convinced that "modern" medicine would someday find a remedy for being old. Pessimists within and beyond professional circles remained skeptical. Experts and the public at large thus disagreed among themselves and with each other about whether old age ultimately could be "cured." Regrettably for the elderly, the "therapeutic revolution" proved less successful in treating older patients than in dealing with the ailments and diseases of younger people.

Simultaneously, new perceptions of the relationship between age and death took hold. Advances in science and technology surely did not eliminate the fear of dying, but they did lessen the risk of dying young. More favorable mortality rates for all but the elderly resulted. This led to a reformulation of previously held notions about death and dying, which reinforced negative images of age.

The respect ascribed to the aged has been partly based on the image of old age as that transitional stage between life on earth and life in a world-to-come. People still could have argued that the elderly's proximity to death put them in the best position to understand the phenomenon. But, ironically, this did not happen. Precisely because the aged *did* have the last word about the inevitability of death, they were excluded (conceptually and otherwise) from a world awed by the vitality of youth. They became victims of a worldview that increasingly chose to deny the existence of death (Becker, 1973; Kastenbaum, 1979). More and more, people overcame death by ignoring it in youth and associating it with old age.

Impact of Industrial Innovation and Bureaucratization

Science was not the only factor shaping new ideas about aging. The experiences and expectations of an ever-growing proportion of the labor force were altered as efficiency and impersonality in functions and procedures, not particular employees, were deemed indispensable. In this milieu, managers gradually disesteemed the wisdom of age. "Gray hair has come to be recognized as an unforgivable witness of industrial imbecility," observed an anonymous American editor in 1913.

Historians have been careful not to exaggerate the novelty of the situation. They note that disability and illness in late life has always diminished the likelihood of finding and maintaining gainful employment. "Superannuation" predates the "modern" period. Nor did the initial phases of industrialization suddenly cause all older workers to be demoted or discharged, or completely overturn every previously held favorable opinion about their current and potential performances. According to the best available estimates, the percentage of older men and women in the nineteenth-century labor force declined very little.

Nevertheless, the new practice of requiring employees to retire after they had attained a certain age, or giving them the option to do so, provides the clearest indication that ideas about older people's usefulness were changing. Even though a very small proportion of the work force was covered initially by such policies, "retirement" increasingly signaled that people had reached a stage in their careers at which they were no longer qualified for gainful employment (Achenbaum, 1974; Haber, 1979, 1983; Graebner, 1980). From management's viewpoint, retirement systems improved efficiency and morale by removing obsolescent workers.

During most of the twentieth century, a variety of factors contributed to the continued devaluation of age in the marketplace and a marked decline in the proportion of older workers in the labor force (Achen-baum, 1983). Evidence gathered after World War I presumably demonstrated that workers became inefficient as they grew older. (Studies during the past three decades have undermined the scientific basis for such a presumption; the notion that older people are not dependable or "competent" nonetheless remains quite prevalent.) Firms with advanced or rapidly changing technologies generally preferred to hire inexperienced workers rather than retrain those familiar with outmoded techniques.

Other factors accelerated the withdrawal of older people from the labor force in the twentieth century. Considerations of cost and efficiency induced personnel managers to favor youth and discriminate against age in hiring and firing practices. Most surveys of retirees and early retirees found that ill health was a major reason why older employees stopped working before they were forced to do so (Shanas et al., 1968). And as retirement packages in the public and private sector became more universal and generous in coverage, the aged themselves preferred to pursue recreational activities rather than stay on the job, a choice encouraged (and in many instances dictated) by society at large. Middle class elderly men and women seemed well on the way to becoming the "modern" era's new leisured class.

Impact of Age-Consciousness and Age-Grading

Age-consciousness and age-grading are not byproducts of the process of modernization. Ascribing distinctive assets and liabilities to particular age groups is not new. Allocating social roles, responsibilities, qualifications, and prerogatives according to such distinctions has long traditions in Western civilization (Eisenstadt, 1956; Maddox and Wiley, 1976; Neugarten and Hagestad, 1976).

Nevertheless, the nature and dynamics of age-consciousness and age-grading have changed dramatically in advanced industrial societies. The sheer population growth since the 1800s, the broadening scope and magnitude of governmental bureaucracies, as well as the increasing complexity of macro-economic structures, have engendered more discontinuities and greater systemic disarticulation in the United States and western Europe than had been the case in less developed nation-states. Major changes in the elderly's prescribed status in the United States during the past two centuries illustrate the point.

Early American history offers a striking example of how the elderly were once treated in what might be described as an "age-integrated" society. Essayists and other commentators identified the specific strengths and weaknesses of late life. But old age per se neither bestowed any special privileges nor legitimized social discrimination. With remarkably few exceptions, an older person had the same rights and responsibilities that were accorded to individuals of his or her sex, race, ethnic group, occupation, or station.

Yet the physical and economic woes associated with being old were viewed as individual hardships rather than societal problems. Consequently, the needy aged generally had to rely upon their own resources and resourcefulness, kith and kin, and those individuals and institutions charged with aiding the poor in local communities. To be sure, there were a few private old-age homes; the federal government provided small pensions for superannuated, indigent veterans and their dependents. But in contrast to orphans, the blind, and the deaf—those groups whose particular plight aroused considerable concern that led in turn to the enactment of categorical legislation and institutional support during the first half of the nineteenth century—the needy aged were often victims of benign neglect, or they were forced to seek help from people and agencies often unwilling or unable to deal with their special needs (Trattner, 1979; Rosenkrantz and Vinovskis, 1978).

The situation gradually changed after the Civil War. Evidence was gathered to "prove" that the physical decay, mental decline, economic uselessness, and personal isolation brought on by advancing years, coupled with the elderly's growing numbers and deteriorating socioeconomic position, were rapidly making the plight of older men and women more visible and acute (Achenbaum, 1978b; Gruman, 1978). Old age was no longer seen as just a personal misfortune: it was fast becoming a serious national dilemma. The Great Depression confirmed that most elderly people were in desperate straits, and that some sort of categorical assistance was necessary.

Redefining the elderly's position to be problematic led to a search for new "solutions." Psychologists, social workers, and educators devised schemes to "salvage" old age. The elderly themselves steadily joined forces to provide mutual support and aid as well as to press for special relief legislation (Holtzman, 1963; Pratt, 1976; Calhoun, 1978; Williamson et al., 1982). Gradually, business groups, labor unions, state officials, and eventually the federal government sought new economic programs to help those who were old and poor.

With the enactment of Social Security in 1935, the United States joined other Western countries in providing a nationwide institutional structure to assist those Americans who had attained a particular age (Brown, 1972; Heclo, 1974; Roebuck, 1978; Roebuck and Slaughter, 1979). In the process, prevailing definitions of old age were altered: Age 65, for example, was established as the bench mark for the onset of socioeconomic old age. As governmental bureaucracies, private agencies, and professional bodies have created and expanded categorical programs at the national level, chronological age increasingly has been used to define older people's position in society and to determine their options.

PERCEPTIONS OF AGE AND AGING IN CONTEMPORARY CULTURE

Prevailing societal values and circumstances demonstrably affect the quality of life and well-being of older persons, as the contemporary situation of the elderly in the United States demonstrates. There surely has been a transformation of the normative and structural foundations that once contributed to a sense of dignity and meaning in the lives of the aged. The prejudice against age as well as the discomforts and disappointments associated with growing older, it has been argued, seem all the more difficult to bear in our present "culture of narcissism" (Lasch, 1978). Yet, at the same time, the proliferation of opportunities for leisure, education, culture, and self-realization often improve the value of late life, multiplying the possibilities of growth, especially for the "young-old" (Neugarten and Havighurst, 1977). Being old in the United States today thus has positive and negative features that result from the interplay of broad historical vectors, which are themselves independent of any intrinsic features of senescence.

No single image, or cluster of ideas, in short, sufficiently embraces our contemporary understanding of the meanings and experiences of growing older and being old. New efforts at redefinition are under way, but none prevails. Although it is beyond the scope of this chapter to offer predictions about future perceptions about age and aging, several generalizations are in order by way of conclusion.

Large-scale changes in individual expectations and life-styles, cultural norms, economic conditions, political arrangements, societal processes, and international relations have created a new set of parameters enveloping the rhetoric and reality of old age (Achenbaum, 1983; Tibbitts, 1979). Despite the fact that Western society itself has grown increasingly age-graded, describing and explaining the salient characteristics of subsets of the population in terms of some age-specific construct often mask the wide range of variations *within* groupings. Continuing to view old age as a "problem" has become problematic (see Part V of this *Handbook*).

Students of aging, moreover, have become particularly sensitive to stereotypes about the conditions of the aged in contemporary society: More than a hundred major studies have been published since the 1940s (Seltzer and Atchley, 1971; L. Harris et al., 1975; Ansello, 1977; Harris and Feinberg, 1977; Wingard, 1980; Palmore, 1981; Thomas, 1981). "Ageism can be seen as a systematic stereotyping of and discrimination against people because they are old," asserts Robert Butler, who coined the term in 1968, "just as racism and sexism accomplish this with skin color and gender" (Butler, 1975, p. 12). Ageism deprives many senior citizens, particularly those from low-income and minority groups, of access to health care, social services, and self-enrichment activities. It exacerbates the financial difficulties and reduces the employment prospects of those whose savings and other assets have become inadequate. Ageism needlessly magnifies fears about growing older.

Stereotypic, inconsistent, and erroneous perceptions of aging pose practical problems and raise ethical issues that have enormous implications for all age groups (Binstock, 1983). They complicate decisions about long-term care, alternatives to institutionalization, social security benefits and private pensions, worker productivity, technological intervention, and prolongevity. These difficulties are compounded, in turn, by the current distrust and lack of confidence in "experts" and "bureaucrats" (Janowitz, 1978).

Few public officials in the United States or western Europe ignore the presumed political clout of the so-called gray lobby, or doubt that the economics of health care and income support will continue to loom large in the political arena. Yet they must also contend with an overwhelming number of other issues and disparate interest groups. Pluralistic political processes, for better and for worse, do not and cannot sort out competing claims according to some universally agreed upon ideological formulae or unequivocal set of values. Thus in order to respond to controversial issues and justify their decisions amid diffuse political pressures, officials need to be able to decide when chronological age or life stage is (and is not) a suitable criterion for dealing with present societal problems and for anticipating future ones.

The time has come, it appears, for being

more precise in talking about and distinguishing between images of aging and images of (old) age. Ideally, we should keep those historically conditioned perspectives on senescence that remain valid and discard the rest. This in turn requires devising and applying an explicit and rigorous set of criteria by which, on the one hand, we acknowledge that all age groups have certain basic rights and responsibilities and face common problems, and, on the other hand, we recognize that the cumulative experiences of living dictate that people at different stages of life may have divergent priorities, desires, hopes, and needs.

To accomplish this task will entail much more research in a variety of areas. Scholars must investigate continuities and changes in self-image(s) over the life cycle, gender-specific differences in ideas of age, as well as the complex relationship between human values and social policies in an aging society. Above all, systematic inquiries into the nature and dynamics of perceptions of age and aging, especially in the "modern" period, are needed.

This survey of major themes in Western civilization attests to the perennial mixture of salutary, sobering, conflicting, erroneous, indifferent, and ambiguous perspectives on senescence. The diversity of ideas and imagery that exists today, therefore, is not merely the product of our pervasive cultural pluralism and relativism. Prevailing perceptions of age and aging are manifestations of the richness and contradictions in the human condition, at once amazingly resilient and yet simultaneously molded by the interplay of historical forces and varying societal circumstances. We can manipulate ideas and images of age to fit new conditions, but there are limits to our ability to create perceptions that have no foundation in historical traditions or current realities.

For this reason, continually scrutinizing our assumptions about the nature and dynamics of growing old(er) is imperative. Because the values and society in which we live are constantly changing, perceptions of the aged and aging will never be static. Our views may echo previous sentiments or parallel longstanding beliefs, but they will never fully resemble them, because the normative foundations and sociocultural milieu that sustain the realm of ideas and imagery are constantly evolving. Thus if we truly hope to address people's real needs and help them satisfy their desires, then we must be prepared to challenge prevailing verities and alter our preconceptions to conform more accurately to changing circumstances.

REFERENCES

Achenbaum, W. A. 1974. The obsolescence of old age in America, 1865–1914. *J. Soc. Hist.* 8:45–64.

Achenbaum, W. A. 1978a. From womb through bloom to tomb. *Rev. in Am. Hist.* 6:178–184.

Achenbaum, W. A. 1978b. *Old Age in the New Land: The American Experience since 1790.* Baltimore: The Johns Hopkins Press.

Achenbaum, W. A. 1981. The humanities and aging America. *In* 1981 White House Conference on Aging, *The Arts, the Humanities, and Older Americans,* pp. 53–76. Washington, D.C.: National Council on the Aging.

Achenbaum, W. A. 1983. *Shades of Gray: Old Age, American Values, and Federal Policies since 1920.* Boston: Little, Brown.

Achenbaum, W. A., and Stearns, P. N., 1978. Old age and modernization. *The Gerontologist* 18:307–313.

Anonymous. Aug. 28, 1913. Independent opinions. *Independent* 75:504.

Ansello, E. 1977. Age and ageism in children's first literature. *Ed. Gerontology* 2:255–274.

Ariès, P. 1962. *Centuries of Childhood,* trans. R. Bardick. New York: Knopf.

Aristotle. 1883. *Treatise on Rhetoric,* trans. Theodore Buckley. London: George Bell & Sons.

Aristotle. 1942. *Politics,* trans. Benjamin Jowett. New York: Modern Library.

Becker, E. 1973. *The Denial of Death.* New York: Free Press.

Berg, G., and Gadow, S. 1978. Toward more human meanings of aging: Ideals and images from philosophy and art. *In* S. F. Spicker, K. M. Woodward, and D. D. Van Tassel (eds.), *Aging and the Elderly,* pp. 83–92. Atlantic Highlands, N.J.: Humanities Press.

Berkhofer, R. F., Jr. 1978. *The White Man's Indian.* New York: Knopf.

The Holy Bible, Revised Standard Version. 1953. New York: Thomas Nelson & Sons.

Binstock, R. H. 1983. The aged as scapegoat. *The Gerontology.* 23:136–143.

Blech, B. 1981. Judaism and gerontology. *In,* C. Le-

Fevre and P. LeFevre (eds.), *Aging and the Human Spirit,* pp. 4–33. Chicago: Exploration Press.

Bogue, D. 1958. *Principles of Demography.* Chicago: University of Chicago Press.

Bouwsma, W. J. 1978. Christian adulthood. *In* E. Erikson (ed.), *Adulthood,* pp. 81–97. New York: W. W. Norton.

Brown, J. D. 1972. *An American Philosophy of Social Security.* Princeton: Princeton University Press.

Butler, R. N. 1975. *Why Survive?: Being Old in America.* New York: Harper & Row.

Calhoun, R. B. 1978. *In Search of the New Old: Redefining Old Age in America, 1945–1970.* New York: Elsevier.

Chandler, A. D., Jr. 1977. *The Visible Hand.* Cambridge, Mass.: Harvard University Press.

Choron, J. 1963. *Death and Western Thought.* New York: Collier.

Cicero. 1923. *De Senectute,* trans. William A. Falconer. London: William Heinemann.

Comfort, A. Apr. 17, 1977. The way we treat the old is new. *In* The New York Times, *New York Times Book Review,* pp. 7, 30.

Cowgill, D., and Holmes, L. 1972. *Aging and Modernization.* New York: Appleton-Century-Crofts.

Dahlin, M. 1980. Perspectives on the family life of the elderly in 1900. *The Gerontologist* 20:99–107.

de Beauvoir, S. 1972. *The Coming of Age.* New York: G. P. Putnam's Sons.

Demos, J. 1978. Old age in colonial New England. *In* M. Gordon (ed.), *The Family in Social-Historical Perspective,* 2nd ed., pp. 220–257. New York: St. Martin's Press.

Ehrenberg, V. 1951. *The People of Aristophanes: The Society of Old Attic Comedy.* Cambridge, Mass.: Harvard University Press.

Eisenstadt, S. N. 1956. *From Generation to Generation.* New York: The Free Press.

Fiedler, L. A. 1979. Eros and thanatos: Old age in love. *In* D. D. Van Tassel (ed.), *Aging, Death, and the Completion of Being,* pp. 235–254. Philadelphia: University of Pennsylvania Press.

Fischer, D. H. 1978. *Growing Old in America,* expanded ed. New York: Oxford University Press.

Freedman, R. 1978. Sufficiently decayed: Gerontophobia in English literature. *In* S. F. Spicker, K. M. Woodward, and D. D. Van Tassel (eds.), *Aging and the Elderly,* pp. 49–61. Atlantic Highlands, N.J.: Humanities Press.

Freeman, J. T. 1979. *Aging: Its History and Literature.* New York: Human Sciences Press.

Geertz, C. 1973. *The Interpretation of Cultures.* New York: Basic Books.

Gillis, J. R. 1974. *Youth and History.* New York: Academic Press.

Grabill, W. H. et al. 1958. *The Fertility of American Women.* New York: John Wiley and Sons.

Graebner, W. 1980. *A History of Retirement: The Meanings and Function of an American Institution, 1885–1978.* New Haven: Yale University Press.

Gruman, G. J. 1966. *A History of Ideas about the Pro-*

longation of Life. Philadelphia: The American Philosophical Society.

Gruman, G. J. 1978. Cultural origins of present-day "age-ism": The modernization of the life cycle. *In* S. F. Spicker, K. M. Woodward, and D. D. Van Tassel (eds.), *Aging and the Elderly,* pp. 359–387. Atlantic Highlands, N.J.: Humanities Press.

Guttmann, D. 1977. The cross-cultural perspective: Notes toward a comparative psychology of aging. *In* J. E. Birren and K. W. Schaie (eds.), *Handbook of the Psychology of Aging,* pp. 302–326. New York: Van Nostrand Reinhold.

Haber, C. 1979. Mandatory retirement in 19th century America. *J. Soc. Hist.* 12:77–97.

Haber, C. 1983. *Beyond Sixty-Five.* New York: Cambridge University Press.

Harris, A., and Feinberg, J. F. 1977. Television and aging. *The Gerontologist* 17:464–469.

Harris, L., and Associates. 1975. *The Myth and Reality of Aging in America.* Washington, D.C.: National Council on the Aging.

Heclo, H. 1974. *Modern Social Politics in Britian and Sweden.* New Haven: Yale University Press.

Hendricks, J., and Hendricks, C. D. 1981. *Aging in Mass Society,* 2nd ed. Cambridge, Mass.: Winthrop Publishing.

Holtzman, A. 1963. *The Townsend Movement.* New York: Bookman Associates.

Hughes, H. S. 1975. *History as Art and Science.* New York: Harper & Row.

Hunt, D. 1972. *Parents and Children in History.* New York: Harper & Row.

Janowitz, M. 1978. *The Last Half-Century.* Chicago: University of Chicago Press.

Kammen, M. (ed.) 1980. *The Past Before Us.* Ithaca: Cornell University Press.

Kastenbaum, R. 1979. Exit and existence: Society's unwritten script for old age and death. *In* D. D. Van Tassel (ed.), *Aging, Death and the Completion of Being,* pp. 69–94. Philadelphia: University of Pennsylvania Press.

Keller, M. 1977. *Affairs of State.* Cambridge, Mass.: Harvard University Press.

Kett, J. 1977. *Rites of Passage: Adolescence in America, 1790 to the Present.* New York: Basic Books.

Knapp, K. R. 1976. Respect for age in Christianity: The base of our concern in Scripture and Tradition. *In* C. LeFevre and P. LeFevre, (eds.), *Aging and the Human Spirit.* Chicago: Exploration Press.

Lasch, C. 1978. *The Culture of Narcissism.* New York: W. W. Norton Co.

Laslett, P. 1976. Societal development and aging. *In* R. H. Binstock and E. Shanas (eds.), *Handbook of Aging and the Social Sciences,* 1st ed., pp. 87–116. New York: Von Nostrand Reinhold.

LeFevre, C., and LeFevre, P. 1981. *Aging and the Human Spirit.* Chicago: Exploration Press.

LeRoy Ladurie, E. 1979. *Montaillou.* New York: Vintage Press.

Lindblom, C. E. 1977. *Politics and Markets.* New York: Basic Books.

Maddox, G. L., and Wiley, J. 1976. Scope, concepts and methods in the study of aging. *In* R. H. Binstock and E. Shanas (eds.), *Handbook of Aging and the Social Sciences,* 1st ed., pp. 3–34. New York: Von Nostrand Reinhold.

Maves, P. B. 1960. Aging, religion and the church. *In* C. Tibbitts (ed.), *Handbook of Social Gerontology.* Chicago: University of Chicago Press.

Moody, H. R. 1979. Portrait of the artist as an old man: The late self portraits of rembrandt. Unpublished paper prepared for the 1979 Gerontological Society meeting, Washington, D.C.

Moody, H. R. 1981. Aging and cultural policy. *In* White House Conference on Aging, *The Arts, The Humanities and Older Americans,* pp. 3–32. Washington, D.C.: National Council on the Aging.

Myerhoff, B. 1978. *Number Our Days.* New York: Simon and Schuster

Neugarten, B. L., and Hagestad, G. O. 1976. Age and the life course. *In* R. H. Binstock and E. Shanas (eds.), *Handbook of Aging and the Social Sciences,* 1st ed., pp. 35–57. New York: Von Nostrand Reinhold.

Neugarten, B. L., and Havighurst, R. J. (eds.), 1977. *Social Ethics, Social Policy and the Aging Society.* Washington, D.C.: Government Printing Office.

Neumann, E. 1974. Art and time. *In* Bolligen Series, number 61, *Art and the Creative Consciousness.* Princeton: Princeton University Press.

O'Brien, M. 1981. Ageism in the New Testament. (Unpublished.)

O'Connor, F. V. 1979. Albert Berne and the completion of being. *In* D. D. Van Tassel (ed.), *Aging, Death and the Completion of Being,* pp. 255–289. Philadelphia: University of Pennsylvania Press.

Pagels, E. 1979. *The Gnostic Gospels.* New York: Basic Books.

Palmore, E. 1981. Social values and attitudes toward aging and the aged: stereotypes. Unpublished position paper prepared for the National Institute on Aging, National Research Plan on Aging.

Philibert, M. 1968. *L'echelle des ages.* Paris: Le Seuil.

Philibert, M. 1974. The phenomenological approach to images of aging. *Soundings* 57:3–24.

Philibert, M. 1979. Philosophical approach to aging. *In* J. Hendricks and C. D. Hendricks (eds.), *Dimensions of Aging,* pp. 379–395. Cambridge, Mass.: Winthrop Publishing.

Pratt, H. J. 1976. *The Gray Lobby.* Chicago: The University of Chicago Press.

Richardson, B. E. 1933. *Old Age among the Greeks.* Baltimore: The Johns Hopkins Press.

Rodgers, D. 1978. *The Work Ethic in Industrial America.* Chicago: University of Chicago Press.

Roebuck, J. 1978. When does old age begin? The evolution of the English definition. *J. Soc. Hist.* 12:416–428.

Roebuck, J., and Slaughter, J. 1979. Ladies and pensioners. *J. Soc. Hist.* 13:105–114.

Rosenkrantz, B. G., and Vinovskis, M. A. 1978. The invisible lunatics: Old age and insanity in mid-nineteenth-century Massachusetts. *In* S. F. Spicker, K. M. Woodward, and D. D. Van Tassel (eds.), *Aging and the Elderly,* pp. 95–125. Atlantic Highlands, N.J.: Humanities Press.

Seltzer, M. and Atchley, R. C. 1971. The concept of old. *The Gerontologist* 11:226–230.

Shanas, E., Townsend, P., Wedderburn, D., Friis, H., Milhoj, P., and Stehouwer, J. 1968. *Old People in Three Industrial Societies.* New York: Atherton Press.

Simmons, L. 1945. *The Role of the Aged in Primitive Societies.* New Haven: Yale University Press.

Smith, D. S. 1978. Old age and the "great transformation." *In* S. F. Spicker, K. M. Woodward, and D. D. Van Tassel (eds.), *Aging and the Elderly,* pp. 285–302. Atlantic Highlands, N.J.: Humanities Press.

Smith, S. R. 1978. Death, dying and the elderly in seventeenth-century England. *In* S. F. Spicker, K. M. Woodward, and D. D. Van Tassel (eds.), *Aging and the Elderly,* pp. 201–219. Atlantic Highlands, N.J.: Humanities Press.

Snow, C. P. 1969. *The Two Cultures: And a Second Look.* Cambridge: At the University Press.

Stahmer, H. M. 1978. The aged in two ancient oral cultures: The ancient Hebrews and Homeric Greece. *In* S. F. Spicker, K. M. Woodward, and D. D. Van Tassel (eds.), *Aging and the Elderly,* pp. 23–36. Atlantic Highlands, N.J.: Humanities Press.

Stannard, D. E. 1977. *The Puritan Way of Death.* New York: Oxford University Press.

Stearns, P. N. 1975. *European Society in Upheaval.* New York: Macmillan Co.

Stearns, P. N. 1977. *Old Age in European Society.* New York: Holmes and Meier.

Stearns, P. N. 1978. Toward historical gerontology. *J. Interdisc. Hist.* 8:737–746.

Stearns, P. N. 1980. Modernization and social history. *J. Soc. Hist.* 14:189–209.

Stone, L. 1977a. Walking over Grandma. *N.Y. Rev.* 24 (May 12):26–29.

Stone, L. 1977b. Growing old: An exchange. *N.Y. Rev.* 24 (Sept. 15):48–49.

Thomas, W. R. 1981. The expectation gap and the stereotype of a stereotype. *The Gerontologist* 21:402–407.

Tibbitts, C. 1979. Can we invalidate negative stereotypes of aging? *The Gerontologist* 19:10–20.

Tilly, L., and Scott, J. 1978. *Women, Work and Family.* New York: Holt, Rinehart & Winston.

Tracy, D. 1981. *The Analogical Imagination.* New York: Crossroad.

Trattner, W. I. 1979. *From Poor Law to Welfare State,* 2nd ed. New York: Free Press.

Van Tassel, D. D. (ed.) 1979. *Aging, Death, and the Completion of Being.* Philadelphia: University of Pennsylvania Press.

Vinovskis, M. A. 1978. Recent trends in American historical demography: Some methodological and conceptual considerations. *Ann. Rev. Soc.* 4:603–627.

Whitehead, E. E. 1978. Religious images of aging: An examination of themes in early Christian thought. *In* S. F. Spicker, K. M. Woodward and D. D. Van Tassel (eds.), *Aging and the Elderly,* pp. 37–48. Atlantic Highlands, N.J.: Humanities Press.

Williamson, J. B., Evans, L., and Powell, L. A. 1982. *The Politics of Aging: Power and Policy.* Springfield, Ill.: Charles C. Thomas.

Wingard, J. 1981. Measures of attitudes toward the elderly. *Exper. Aging Res.* 6:229–313.

Wishy, B. 1968. *The Child and the Republic.* Philadelphia: University of Pennsylvania Press.

6
THE SOCIAL CONTEXT OF DEATH AND DYING

Richard A. Kalish

University of New Mexico

What is death? The answers are numerous, varying according to culture, age, health, cognitive capacities, one's life situation, perhaps sex, the nature of dependents, projects finished and unfinished. Death means different things to the same person at different times; and it means different things to different persons at the same time.

Death is a biological event, a rite of passage, an inevitability, a natural occurrence, a punishment, extinction, the enforcement of God's will, absurd, separation, reunion, and time for judgment. It is a reasonable cause for anger, depression, denial, repression, guilt, frustration, relief, absolution of self, increased religiousness, and diminished religiousness. It is a disruption of the social fabric by removing a significant person from the scene; it strengthens the social fabric by removing those less capable of doing their tasks and by permitting others, who otherwise chafe at being restricted, to move into more demanding roles. It has one set of meaning for the dying person, another for those who love that individual, yet another for those responsible for his or her health care, and still another set of meanings for those involved with funerals, legal documents, insurance, estates and trusts, public health statistics, wars, and executions.

The one invariant of the meaning of death for both the individual and the society is that

death matters. And so does the process of dying. The event of death and the process of dying have immense impact on individuals and on the community, whether judged by emotional feelings, social relationships, spiritual well-being, financial stresses, or changes in daily living.

Death itself is an abstraction, probably best defined as "the transition from the state of being alive to the state of being dead" (Kass, 1971, p. 699). By definition death is irreversible; it is determined by the cessation of the vital functions of the organism, particularly the circulatory and respiratory systems. However, more recently, medical technology has enabled these systems to continue to function, even after all forms of cognitive behavior have irreversibly ceased. As a result, the Ad Hoc Committee to Examine the Definition of Brain Death of Harvard Medical School proposed that cessation of brain function, recorded for 24 hours, take precedence as a criterion for death; a similar approach has developed in Europe, where determinations may be made by angiography, radioisotopes, or sonic techniques that evaluate circulation in the brain (Veatch, 1976).

The term "dying" is properly used when the process eventuates in death. This needs to be clearly differentiated from the process of aging. The familiar statements "Well, we

149

are all dying" or "To be born is to begin to die" may be logically or even physiologically true, but they can only obscure the phenomenological significance of dying and death in the real world.

AGING, MEANINGS, AND ATTITUDES

The relationship between age and death has altered greatly over the centuries. During prehistoric times, life expectancy from birth was probably around 18 years; this increased to roughly 20 in the Greco-Roman period, then to 35 by the Middle Ages (Dublin, 1965). At the turn of this century, Americans could anticipate living for nearly 50 years.

Not only was life expectancy much lower in earlier times, but death was not nearly so predictable a function of age as it now is. Infant mortality was extremely high, and many women died in childbirth, presumably somewhere between their midteens and mid-thirties; inadequate health care, poor nutrition, insufficient sanitation, and poor housing and working conditions combined to increase susceptibility to illness at all ages; medical technology had not yet found proper treatments for the so-called childhood diseases or for such adult diseases as tuberculosis and pneumonia.

In recent decades, however, especially in much of the Western world and Japan, death has become highly predictable as a function of age. Because of the close association between old age and death in modern industrial societies, the individual and social concerns relating to death are in some ways individual and social concerns of aging. Being elderly may not only generate concerns as to what limited finitude means, but even working with or living with older persons may make these issues more salient. We may certainly hypothesize that one of the significant reasons that the old are sometimes avoided and isolated is that their proximity to death leaves others feeling anxious.

The Meanings of Death

How is the human condition affected by the fact that death exists? Further, what is the influence of the changes described above, in which death has become primarily the province of the elderly?

It seems logical that the meanings of death, as well as attitudes toward death, change with both chronological age and anticipated future length of life. Thus, Ariès (1981) noted that people in earlier centuries could not anticipate a long life and were, therefore, pressed to live each day to the fullest. He speculates that the lengthy futurity of most non-elderly in the world today has permitted them to postpone many things they wished to do until late in life, when they may lack the health or vigor for the tasks.

Marshall (1975) also emphasizes that it is likely to be anticipated finitude, rather than chronological age per se, that influences the meaning of impending death. In seeking predictors of anticipated futurity, he found that not only present age but also the age at which family members died were useful predictors. Anticipated futurity in a life-span developmental context is certainly worthy of additional research, both in its role as an outcome variable and as a predictor of how each person faces the world each day.

It seems probable that the human being is the only living creature that can anticipate and, therefore, plan for its own death. This awareness of death, however, arises from experiencing, either directly or indirectly, the deaths of others, and it is through these interactions that the meaning of death develops. Since, at least theoretically, each individual confronts the possibility of personal death at any moment, albeit with changing probabilities, death has meaning for persons of all ages.

There are many ways to view the meanings of death. In the following paragraphs, I will discuss four of them: death as an organizer of time, death as a punishment for sins, death as a transition to another form of existence or perhaps to extinction, and death as loss.

Death as an Organizer of Time. Our awareness that life is finite alters the meaning of the way in which we use time. If time were infinite, we could have time to do many things and we would not need to establish priorities or give up desirable options. For the elderly, death is a clearly perceived parameter that directly limits their personal futurity. Older persons projected themselves into a much briefer futurity than younger persons when asked to what age they expected to live (Reynolds and Kalish, 1974) and when asked to report important future events in their lives and the timing of these events (Kastenbaum, 1966b). They were not differentiated from younger persons, however, on their ability to use the concept of time to organize and interpret experience in general.

In a more recent study, chronological age was again found the best predictor of perceived distance from death, even among a population of elderly, aged 72 to 99. The multiple-regression analysis for women in this study showed that age-group identification (self-ratings and "middle-age" or "elderly") and health status followed chronological age as predictors; for men, the availability of social-support persons was next to chronological age in importance (Keith, 1981–82).

Retrospective time seems to pass with increasing rapidity with age, while ongoing experienced time varies not so much with age as with the nature of the experience, mood, fatigue, and anticipation. A graphic illustration of this was an 80-year-old man who made the following two comments within the same interview: "When you're as old as me, you'll learn that time devours you"; "(Even if I had more, there is) nothing I could do with the time" (Kastenbaum, 1966a).

Thus, on the one hand, the coming of death speeds up the feeling of being "devoured" by time when contemplated retrospectively in weeks and months; on the other hand, death makes the moments and minutes creep by because there is nothing meaningful to do, since whatever is attempted may be transient or left unfinished.

Over 400 Los Angeles County respondents were asked what they would do if they knew they had only six months to live. Of those 60 and over, 37 percent indicated they would spend their time in reading, contemplation, prayer, or other activities reflecting inner life, spiritual needs, or withdrawal; this was well over twice as high a proportion as found among the two younger-adult age groups. Similarly, only 9 percent of the older adults indicated they would undergo a marked change in their lives, while 31 percent stated that they would make no real changes; about 20 percent of the others would undergo a marked change, and 23 percent would not change at all (Kalish and Reynolds, 1976).

These findings might arise from (a) physical and health changes, (b) the pressure of disengagement, or (c) preference for inward-directed rather than interpersonal involvements, for focusing on changing the self rather than changing others and the environment. Still, death seems to organizes time differently for people of different ages. It is, of course, possible that the age-related differences are a function of the age-cohort effect. Additional research in this area is certainly warranted.

Death as Punishment. Death is seen simultaneously as a punishment for sins, as release from pain, and as reward through being a transition to a better existence. In fact, even the existence of death, in Christian theology, is as a punishment for sin. Many cultures share the view that one's own sins contribute to a briefer life. The Hopi believed that kindness, good thoughts, and peace of mind led to a long life; among the Berber, deceit was punished by a shorter life (Simmons, 1945).

Death as Transition. "It is the prospect of not being any more that makes most men abhor death" (Choron, 1964, p. 10). When asked "Regardless of your belief about life after death, what is your wish about it?," 73 percent of a sample of older adults said they wanted some kind of life after death, while only 10 percent would prefer no kind of life after death (Kalish and Reynolds, 1976). Comparable data from another study are 71 percent and 6 percent (Wass et al., 1978–79). About three out of four people in the United States believe in life after death (Argyle and Beit-Hallahmi, 1975). And while the elderly are more likely to believe in life after death than younger persons (e.g., Kalish and Reynolds, 1976), it is uncertain whether this is an age-cohort or a developmental effect.

Death as Loss. With death come numerous losses: the loss of experiencing, of people and places and things, of control and competence, of the capacity to complete projects and carry out plans, and of one's body and physicalness. None of these is unique to death; each of these losses can occur in response to circumstances other than physical death. However, death is the only event involving such losses that itself (a) leads directly to these circumstances and (b) is experienced by everyone.

Gerontologists are well aware that the above losses are usually continuous processes, not discrete events, although the trajectory that describes each form of loss may be more or less steep for different individuals. Thus the decline of an institutionalized older person dying from lung cancer is often a much more gradual, downhill trajectory than the decline of the healthy older person who dies of a heart attack and who remains alert until shortly before death.

Some of the losses in the trajectory toward death are commonly experienced throughout the life span, usually accelerating in the later years. For example, we all lose people who are important in our lives well before we are elderly. Other losses normally don't occur until near the end of life (e.g., the inability to complete projects). And still others usually occur only with death: the permanent and irreversible loss of experiencing.

Well over two decades ago, 563 persons were asked to rank in terms of personal importance seven "values lost by death" (Diggory and Rothman, 1961). The final rankings were: (1) cause grief to family and friends, (2) end of projects and plans, (3) fear of painful dying process, (4) inability to continue having experiences, (5) inability to care for dependents, (6) uncertainty as to what occurs after death, and (7) fear of what happens to one's body. The relatively small sample of persons over age 55 ($N = 30$) and a somewhat larger sample between age 40 and

54 ($N = 85$) placed "inability to care for dependents" as their greatest concern, but otherwise showed little deviation from the considerably larger younger population.

A later study, using a better age distribution with less dependency on younger respondents, found that respondents over age 60 were more fearful of what would happen to their bodies after death than the younger (age 20–39) and middle-aged (age 40–59) groups, and they were less concerned about caring for dependents and bringing grief to others, undoubtedly because people in this age group have fewer significant survivors and also recognize that their deaths are more anticipated (Kalish and Reynolds, 1976).

Attitudes toward Death: Some Conceptual and Measurement Problems

The previous section looked at meanings of death, or how people are affected by the existence of death. The following pages are concerned with attitudes toward death, which refers to how individuals think, feel, and behave in favorable or unfavorable ways regarding death. The two terms will be occasionally applied in overlapping ways, but they are conceptually different nonetheless.

Undoubtedly, more studies have been conducted on attitudes toward death than any other issue concerning death, dying, and grief. Numerous instruments have been developed, although a scale carefully validated by Templer (1970) has probably received the greatest research use. (See also Marshall, 1982.)

Perhaps the most important conceptual problem in studies of death attitudes is the implicit assumption that people say what they mean. This is a problem of attitude research in general and certainly of death-attitude research in particular. It is assumed that a person who states he or she is unafraid of death is, thereby, unafraid of death. Moreover, to the extent that such fear or lack of fear exists, researchers have tended to ignore the issue of what aspects of death may engender fear.

One exception is the work by Feifel and

his associates, who attempted to probe death concerns at different levels of awareness. The initial study investigated reactions to death at the conscious level, fantasy level, and below the level of awareness. "The dominant conscious response to fear of death is one of repudiation (of the *fear*); that of the fantasy or imagery level, one of ambivalence; and at the nonconscious level, one of outright negativity" (Feifel and Branscomb, 1973, p. 286). A subsequent study confirmed the usefulness of his conscious and fantasy level instruments (measured by semantic differential and metaphors, respectively) for improving the prediction of death fear, but found the nonconscious instrument (a time latency measure of responding to death-related words presented in differing colors) ineffective (Feifel and Nagy, 1981).

A second conceptual problem in death-attitude research is the inaccurate use of terms and the confusion caused by inappropriate labeling of measurement scales. For example, the concepts "meaning of death" and "process of dying" are certainly quite distinct, as are the concerns with death-of-self and death-of-others. Thus, Collett and Lester (1969) developed a questionnaire based on four conceptual factors: fear of death of self, fear of death of others, fear of dying of self, fear of dying of others. The factors were not only conceptually distinguishable, but could be distinguished through their research as well.

For the most part, however, measures of death attitudes combine two or more factors into the same scale, which is then assumed to measure a general factor of death fear/anxiety/concern. A related conceptual tangle occurs in the blurring of boundaries between such terms as *fear, anxiety, avoidance, denial,* and *not wanting to die.* An individual who states he or she does not want to die may be scored "plus" for "fear of death," which may be a distortion of the respondent's intent.

Factor analysis has offered some help in clarifying these conceptual tangles. An early study found four death-attitude factors (among others that are less relevant to our present pursuits): avoidance of contact with death, lack of death concern, desire to avoid dying and personal death, and overt death anxiety (Kalish, 1963). A later factor analytic study resulted in four dimensions of death fear/anxiety: death fear ("Everyone in his right mind is afraid to die."); death denial ("I want the best casket available so that my body would be well protected."); death avoidance ("I couldn't sleep in a room with a dead body."); and reluctance to interact with the dying ("I would mind working with dying persons.") (Nelson and Nelson, 1975).

A more recent study factor analyzed 15 measures of death attitudes, derived from eight instruments, and emerged with five factors. These were titled (1) Negative Evaluation of Personal Death, (2) Reluctance to Interact with the Dying, (3) Negative Reaction to Pain, (4) Reaction to the Reminders of Death, and (5) Preoccupation with Thoughts of Dying (Durlak and Kass, 1981–82). Rigdon and Epting (1981–82), using the same data but a different form of factor analysis, came up with three factors: (1) General Negative Response to Personal Death, (2) Avoidance of the Dying and of Death Reminders, and (3) Preoccupation with Thoughts of Death.

The similarities among the four analyses suggest that underlying constructs are fairly consistent from population to population. "Lack of death concern" reemerges as "preoccupation with thoughts of death"; "avoidance of contact with the dead" returns as "death avoidance" and then as "avoidance of the dying and of death reminders"; the remaining two factors from the earlier study merge to form "death fear" and "general negative response to personal death" in the latter two.

Factor analytic studies inevitably suffer from being able to get out only what was put in in the first place. For instance, both Nehrke et al. (1981) and Kalish (1963) found a factor describing concern with existence after death. This was missing from the other studies because relevant items were not initially included. Nonetheless, these factor analytic studies have not received sufficient attention, and research is still published that ignores the possibilities of building on the base of previous work.

The Influences of Aging on Attitudes toward Death

With advancing age, people are increasingly likely to have certain experiences, awarenesses, and health concerns that appear to affect their attitudes regarding death. Like the matter of losses described earlier, some of these changes occur at a fairly steady rate throughout the adult life span, while others accelerate in their frequency, likelihood, and/or impact in the later years, and a few are probably inconsequential for most people until the later years.

For the most part, older people have had many more death-related experiences than younger people. They have virtually always experienced the deaths of both parents; they have experienced the deaths of more family members and friends; they have attended more funerals and visited more people who were dying; and they are more likely to have had one or more personal encounters with their own possible death and are more likely to be suffering from a life-threatening health condition.

Five aspects of death awareness may be said to develop as age increases. First, as already indicated, the anticipated life span is foreshortened, and the future seems finite rather than virtually infinite. This requires ongoing restructuring in the allocation of time, effort, and other resources; the closer we get to death, the more we shift our priorities and reallocate our energies (Marshall, 1980).

Second, older persons often reflect the familiar societal value that they do not have sufficient futurity to deserve a major investment of the resources of others: the state, the family, the community, the work organization (Glaser, 1966).

Third, desirable roles are closed to them, although other desirable roles may emerge. On balance, however, the future is likely to be seen as requiring increasing effort in order to maintain the status quo or a minimal decline.

Fourth, when people face the imminence of their own deaths at a later age than they anticipated, they often feel that they have received their entitlement; when they face their own foreseeable death in advance of that time, they may feel deprived. In fact, Rosenfeld (1978) suggests that the greatest challenge to the elderly men in her longitudinal study was not that of facing death, but of using the "bonus years," the years after retirement and the deaths of most age peers, to good advantage. This certainly parallels Erikson's (1963) last stage of ego integrity versus despair.

Fifth, as more and more persons in their age cohort die, the surviving elderly cannot help but be affected, perhaps by a combination of loneliness, sadness, fear and anxiety, and the pleasure and accompanying guilt that arises from "It wasn't me."

Changing health status in old age also seems to have a considerable effect on attitudes toward death. Many older persons receive increasing reminders of impending death through signals from within their bodies and through restrictions and increasing dependency on medication.

Another health-related influence on death attitudes as people age is that of the conditions that lead to their death, which change with advancing age. Among younger persons, these conditions are much more likely to be accidents, suicides, homicides, and acute illnesses; among the elderly, death is likely to come from a chronic condition. The condition that causes the elderly individual's death presumably interacts with general feelings about death to influence the overall behavior pattern that occurs at this time. Even people who do not suffer from a life-threatening health condition will often fantasize about how they will die, and these fantasies serve much the same function as actual illness serves for those with serious or critical prognoses.

Greater Salience, Less Fear, and Some Disengagement

To the extent that the foregoing represents an accurate representation and interpretation of what occurs, we could offer three hypotheses: first, that death, being closer in time and intruding more into their lives, would be of greater salience to older persons than to younger persons; second, that in the later years, the values lost through death are less important, and therefore, death is less frightening; and third, that the imminence of death leads to greater isolation from society, imposed both by the person who is dying and those in that person's milieu, which reflects a type of disengagement (Cumming and Henry, 1961).

Several studies have compared death attitudes of the elderly with those of other age groups. These show, with fair consistency, that the elderly think and talk more about death, whether asked to respond in terms of the frequency with which they contemplate death (Kalish and Reynolds, 1976; Riley, 1970) or in terms of having had such a thought during the previous five minutes (Cameron et al., 1973). Nonetheless, death appears less frightening for those who are older, a finding that has appeared for a variety of groups and using a variety of instruments and procedures (Bengtson et al., 1977; Feifel and Branscomb, 1973; Kalish and Reynolds, 1976; Kogan and Wallach, 1961; Martin and Wrightsman, 1965).

Further confirmation comes from two other studies, one in India (Sharma and Jain, 1969) and one in the United States (Rosenfeld, 1978). In describing the participants in the latter study, all of whom were men who had been studied intensively, the author comments that "few were found to be overtly afraid of death, and those who were seemed to have attitudes formed early which were deeply characteristic of their entire lives" (p. 16).

One issue that appears to come through in the foregoing discussion is that, to the extent that disengagement occurs, it is in part due to awareness of death and diminishing finitude. If despair is a partial function of feeling that the future is insufficient in both quantity and quality, and if the result of despair for any given person is diminished ego integrity, then one might infer that the end stage would be withdrawal and depression.

The work of Kübler-Ross (1969) has tended to support this position and also has supported the position that, when death is imminent, disengagement is adaptive. Her final stage of dying, *acceptance*, is described as pertaining to a dying person who is well advanced in reducing attachments to people, groups, material possessions, and ideas. This course of action will permit focusing the remaining energy on only those attachments that are most vital. The dying individual's sense of loss diminishes as attachments diminish in importance. That this stage closely resembles disengagement is seldom acknowledged (Kalish, 1984).

Apparently the pressures for disengagement that so often confront the elderly individual also confront the dying person at any age. These pressures encourage a turning inward, contemplation of meaning of the present and the future, and pulling back from the emotional pain that occurs when attachments are lost or broken. When the elderly enter their terminal phase, they may have already begun to disengage as a function of being old, and the additional detachment that is apparently induced by an imminent death encounter may be easier for them to cope with than for younger persons facing the same circumstance. Therefore, we might hypothesize that the death of an older person would be less stressful than the death of an individual whose disengagement only began in response to the dying process itself. While this hypothesis remains in need of empirical testing, Neugarten (1977) has shown that life-cycle events and crises are more stressful when they occur well outside of their usual time position.

Correlates of Older Persons' Attitudes toward Death

In addition to obvious individual differences among the elderly in reactions to death and dying, numerous differences have been observed as a function of such factors as sex, religious affiliation and religious belief systems, ethnic identification, age (within the elderly population), and personality qualities.

Comparisons of sex differences have shown conflicting results. In some studies, the self-ratings of elderly women have indicated a higher fear level than the self-ratings of elderly men (e.g., Wass and Sisler, 1978); other studies have shown no sex differences (e.g., Dickstein, 1972; Nehrke et al., 1977–78).

Two recent studies suggest that a more complex interpretation of the data may be needed. Wittkowski (1981), investigating 109 middle- and upper-middle-class adults in Germany (mean age was slightly over 50), found that both fear of death and dying *and* acceptance of death correlated with being female. As part of a much larger study, Keith (1979) presented 600 older men and women a questionnaire consisting of 12 items to reflect positive or negative attitudes toward death. More women (57%) than men (44%) scored above the mean for the entire group. However, Keith's items combined those that measured fear with those that measured perceptions of life after death and those that measured general acceptance. Integrating these two studies with the earlier literature, it would appear possible that women find the prospect of their own death to be more fear-arousing than men find it to be, but that women simultaneously have a greater acceptance of their own death. Acceptance of death and fear of death have usually been assumed to be antithetical, but this may not be the case.

Feelings about death and dying also vary as a function of religiousness as operationalized either in terms of being a churchgoing, denomination-affiliated person or in terms of adhering to a traditional religious belief system. The results of numerous studies of persons of various ages have shown that the greater the extent of religious feeling, the less the fear of death (Feifel and Nagy, 1981; Jeffers et al., 1961; Martin and Wrightsman, 1965; Templer, 1972). Other studies found a curvilinear relationship, with the fear of death being least among both the deeply religious and the deeply irreligious, while persons who were uncertain or uncommitted exhibited the greatest anxiety (Gorer, 1967; Kalish, 1963; Nelson and Nelson, 1973). Perhaps in these latter studies, the major independent variable was a confused and uncertain belief system rather than specific religious views.

Research that has successfully isolated religious belief systems from other aspects of life is virtually nonexistent, but one ethnographic study of the Amish shows that the integration of intrinsic religious beliefs and a strong, supportive family and community can indeed encourage an acceptance of death. Within this community, communication among family members about an impending death is common and accepted; a dying person is provided with as much autonomy as possible, including encouragement to make plans for the coming death and the related rituals and ceremonies; and both the dying and bereaved are given effective community and family support (Bryer, 1979).

Studies of ethnicity and death attitudes are not common, but a few have been conducted. Myers et al. (1980) found that elderly black respondents in a Southern state indicated a higher level of death fear than white respondents. Bengtson et al. (1977) observed a declining fear of death with age among the three ethnic communities they were studying (blacks, Mexican Americans, and whites), but the rates of age-related change did not differ significantly from group to group. These investigators also found that elderly blacks were much more likely to anticipate a long life expectancy than either Mexican Americans or whites, which confirmed previous findings of Reynolds and Kalish (1974).

Several studies have attempted to relate fear of death and personality variables. High scores on depression measures seem to correlate with overt fear of death, as do measures of hypochondriasis, impulsivity, and hysteric disorders (Magni, 1972; Rhudick and Dibner, 1961; Templer, 1971). However, two reviews of the numerous studies probing this issue emphasize that results are inconsistent, and that most findings fall short of statistical significance (Pollak, 1979–80; Schulz, 1978).

An entirely different, and potentially more

valuable, kind of study comes from England, where Hinton (1975) worked with 60 terminally ill cancer patients and their spouses (age was not stated). He obtained ratings of the patients' reactions to their impending death from the patients themselves, their senior nurses, and their spouses, along with numerous personality measures. Terminally ill patients who were rated as normally capable of coping with their problems were also rated as less angry and less withdrawn in their general mood compared to other such patients; those who had previously had high life satisfaction were now seen as less depressed, anxious, and angry by their spouses and by themselves; those rated as having high marital harmony were also less depressed, anxious, and angry, as well as more accepting of death. Although Hinton emphasizes that many correlations were too low for significance, his results suggest that those terminally ill patients who function most successfully are those who had previously shown high coping skills, high life satisfaction, and good marital relationships. Both Hinton's procedures and his results appear promising for future studies.

THE PROCESS OF DYING

The process of dying is a stage in the life of every individual, although only a moment for some. A major task addressed by professionals and others who work with the dying is that of finding ways to enrich the remaining life of those who have been defined as "terminal." To accomplish that, it is necessary to understand more about the process itself and the meaning of the process to those who are affected by it, especially the dying person, family members and close friends, and the health professionals.

The Dying of Older Persons

In some ways, the dying process of the elderly differs from the dying process of younger persons, at least in terms of trends. First and perhaps foremost, the causes of death and, therefore, the dying trajectories differ. As observed earlier, the elderly are most likely to die from chronic disease that develops over a period of time; younger people are relatively more likely to die from accidents.

Because of the higher incidence of certain medical conditions, frequent use of medications, and increased likelihood of organic brain conditions, older people are more likely than younger people to be confused or comatose during the period leading up to their deaths. This directly affects the person's options for social relationships with family members and others. Communication becomes difficult or impossible, and the decision-making processes are taken over by others.

The matter of dying in the later years also influences who is available to provide support relationships. It is not unusual for an older person, especially an extremely old person, to have no available family members who are both willing and capable of providing physical care or even offering personal warmth and social visits.

Also, with age the social value of life diminishes (Glaser, 1966), and people in the community explicitly consider the death to be less tragic (e.g., Kalish and Reynolds, 1976). Thus, even assuming equivalent cognitive powers and equivalent family relationships, the elderly are less likely to elicit the investment of time, energy, money, and personal affect from their family members or from the health-care professionals. This is exacerbated by the familiar assumption that if the elderly do not die of these conditions sooner, they will die of those conditions later.

Two major considerations in the dying process are (1) the degree to which the five stages proposed by Elisabeth Kübler-Ross (1969) actually occur, and (2) the ways in which the denial process is utilized. Numerous stage theories of the dying process have been advanced, but only Kübler-Ross's has received significant attention, and none of the stage theories has been evaluated as to its applicability to elderly dying persons.

Kübler-Ross's model consists of five stages that, she contends, not only frequently *do* occur in the described sequence, but *should* occur in that sequence in order that the dying persons attain the final and adaptive stage. The five stages are denial and isolation, anger and resentment, bargaining and an attempt to postpone, depression and sense of loss, and acceptance.

How have these stages held up under scrutiny? As indicated earlier, there has not been any important research to determine whether these stages are normative or whether they are adaptive, or whether they exist at all. Kübler-Ross (1974) herself pointed out that the stages are not rigidly adhered to: "Most of my patients have exhibited two or three stages simultaneously and these do not always occur in the same order" (pp. 25–26). Shneidman (1973) has insisted that the dying with whom he has worked are more likely to alternate between acceptance and denial, than to move through all five stages in regular sequence. Schulz and Aderman (1974), drawing on the existing literature, have concluded that Kübler-Ross's model was not confirmed by the experience or research of others, and that depression is the dominant mood of most dying persons during the duration shortly before their death.

Dying an Appropriate Death

Kübler-Ross exhorts us to enable dying people to accept their death and to meet it calmly; innumerable others exhort us to create a milieu where dying people can retain their dignity. In order to avoid the implicit value assumptions of the first statement and the vagueness of the second statement, Weisman (1972) proposed that we endeavor to permit each person to die an *appropriate death,* which means to permit each individual to die as he or she wishes to die, at least to the extent that this is possible.

Some people, fearing that they will not be able to die appropriately, express the desire to die sooner than their health condition indicates. This is especially true for elderly persons who fear that a protracted illness will prevent them from having an appropriate death (Weisman, 1972). As Marshall's (1980)

research has suggested, death is often preferable to (1) inactivity, (2) loss of ability to be useful, (3) becoming a burden, (4) loss of mental faculties, and (5) living with progressively deteriorating physical health and suffering physical discomfort and pain.

Three factors have been suggested as paramount in enabling people to die an appropriate death, assuming their health and cognitive condition permit: (1) a warm and intimate personal relationship, preferably with a family member or friend, but if necessary with a health caretaker; (2) an open awareness context (Glaser and Strauss, 1965), in which the dying person and the important people in that person's social environment are aware of the prognosis and can relate to each other in terms of the terminal condition; and (3) a belief system that provides for meaning. These three circumstances can be integrated with each other to provide a sense of transcendence that permits dying persons to retain self-esteem and the belief that their future—however, brief—and their lives in general have significant meaning (Augustine and Kalish, 1975).

Knowledge of the Prognosis

The issue of open awareness and communication with the dying person has been an especially significant one for persons who care for the dying, since an appropriate death is apparently enhanced by providing optimal levels of communication without engendering unnecessary depression or feelings of hopelessness. The predominant position of both experienced practitioners and scholars is that, with few exceptions, the dying not only have a right to know their prognosis, but they usually know what is happening anyway, even without having been told directly. To develop a *mutual pretense* context (Glaser and Strauss, 1965), in which both the dying person and those relating to that person pretend they do not know the prognosis, serves to isolate both parties from each other, since neither can then discuss what is uppermost in his or her mind.

The "When" of Death

In talking about appropriate dying, two factors are often mentioned by both professionals in the field and interested persons in general: the extent to which the death is sudden and unexpected and the setting in which the dying occurs.

For the most part, neither the dying person nor those in his or her milieu have any control over the suddenness of the death. Sudden deaths, which are often also unexpected deaths, tend to be preferred by young and middle-aged adults, while elderly persons are more divided on the issue (Kalish and Reynolds, 1976). Those desiring sudden (and perhaps unexpected) death probably wish to avoid physical pain and suffering, as well as emotional stresses for themselves and their survivors. However, this kind of death can be more brutal for the survivors, since there has been no opportunity for them to prepare, nor does it permit the dead person to get affairs in order, to try to finish important projects, or to participate in the grieving process with loved ones. In many ways, a sudden and unexpected death has less impact on the survivors of an elderly person, where the rehearsal for death has probably been in process for some time and where preparations for death are more probably already made (Lipman and Marden, 1966; Kalish and Reynolds, 1976).

The "Where" of Dying

Unlike the "when" of death, the "where" of dying is much more under the control of individuals. Most people die in health care institutions, in the United States (Lerner, 1970), in Canada (Marshall, 1980), and in England (Cartwright et al., 1973), and by far the greater proportion of these persons die in general hospitals. Although only about 5% of the elderly are in a long-term care facility at any given time, upwards of 20% of death certificates for persons 65 years of age and older stipulate that such a facility was the residence at the time of death (Kastenbaum and Candy, 1973; Palmore, 1976).

When asked where they want to die, most people of all ages would prefer to die at home; in one study, over three times as many elderly wanted to die at home as wanted to die in a hospital (Kalish and Reynolds, 1976). At the same time, in a British study, the majority of family members of those who did die at home were glad that the death took place where it did; however, the burden of the caretakers was found to be very heavy, and fully one-third of the respondents were subsequently either uncertain of the wisdom of the decision or felt a hospital would have been preferable (Cartwright et al., 1973).

The opportunity to have significant interactions with others not only offers the dying older person some pleasure; it may also be life-sustaining by providing stimulation. The general living arrangement is certainly important, but so is the specific location within the facility. Watson (1976) noted that one facility was structured so that elderly patients with low mental status scores were placed in rooms farthest from the nursing station and were visited least often. Patients were moved to these facilities for the "near-dead" when they ceased to indicate that their condition was temporary or when they were unresponsive to or rejecting of staff attempts to treat them.

Although for many dying persons and under many circumstances, home provides a far better place for the dying process to occur than a hospital or other institution, this is not always the case. Dying at home is most appropriate when the individual is reasonably alert and capable of interaction with others; when his or her health condition is either beyond effective treatment, or effective treatment is possible at home; when being home will provide something important, such as more frequent or more meaningful personal relationships or familiarity or privacy; and when death is imminent and the final weeks, days, or hours are most fruitfully spent in familiar surroundings with loving people. For some people, none of these conditions can be met, and this is more likely to be the case for the elderly than for younger persons. The hospice program (to be discussed later) offers another alternative.

Rights of the Dying

It is impossible to discuss the idea of appropriate death without commenting on the rights of individuals to determine the time and conditions of their own deaths. Medical technology has increased the length of existence, but not always the quality of that existence. In many instances individuals are incapacitated physically through a stroke or advanced cancer or are incapacitated psychologically through cognitive losses, yet lack the potential for any active form of self-euthanasia (actually a euphemism for what some would consider to be an appropriate suicide).

In recent years, the "living will" has become either legally enforceable or, at least, an advisory document. The living will states the conditions under which an individual, in good health and cognitively alert at the time of signature, requests that no medically heroic methods be used to sustain his or her existence; the request can be extended to the elimination of life-sustaining equipment and medications.

Although these living wills, as presently written into law, will affect relatively few individuals, the fact that they exist is a source of consolation to some elderly people who greatly fear a lengthy period of incapacitation and the immense burden that this would place on their children. Little research has developed regarding this issue, in spite of its significance, and the flurry of media discussions of living wills seems to have subsided since the mid-1970s. However, there is every reason to believe that the issue will retain its importance during the coming decade, especially as medical costs rise and as the prospect of existence without meaningful life or of life with immense pain and incapacitation becomes more a part of public consciousness (Kalish, 1984; Veatch, 1976).

GRIEF, BEREAVEMENT, AND MOURNING

This chapter began with a discussion of the various meanings of death and of attitudes regarding death, then moved to a description of the dying process. The present section is concerned with the survivors of the deaths of others.

Once again, we find that terms with somewhat overlapping meanings are frequently used interchangeably. *Grief* refers to the feelings engendered by loss; *bereavement* is the status of being deprived by loss; *mourning* is the expression of grief and bereavement through behavior that is, in varying degrees, determined by custom and expressed through ritual. However, the extent of overlap among these concepts does justify some interchangeable usage.

Rituals and Ceremonies

Almost every death sets into motion a series of rituals, customs, and ceremonies. Some of these affect the individual survivors, while others affect the broader society as well.

Every society prescribes certain kinds of behavior for grieving individuals and proscribes other kinds of behavior. Consider some of the forms of behavior that are restricted in Western societies if the grieving person is to be viewed as mourning appropriately: certain kinds of clothing cannot be worn; certain social events need to be avoided; absence from work and other events is countenanced; laughter and joy should be exhibited only in moderation; sexual behavior—or at least its appearance—should be avoided. Although such customs differ greatly from culture to culture, and even from subculture to subculture within cultures, and although these customs do change over time, all societies have some role expectations for persons in mourning. The punishment for violating these customs is primarily social disapproval and, if extreme, social ostracism, albeit usually temporary, depending on the presumed seriousness of the offense.

Certainly there are few ceremonies in our society that are more significant than the funeral. This is simultaneously a rite of passage for the dead person and a show of support for the survivors. It is also purported to have a therapeutic value for the survivors by permitting them to grieve openly and to advance their acceptance of the reality of the death (Pine, 1975).

Five phases in the funeral and subsequent burial process in the United States have been outlined: (1) removal of the body or the separation of the dead from the living; (2) the visitation period—attending a wake or a scripture service, or sitting shiva; (3) the funeral rite itself; (4) the procession from the place where the funeral is held to the place of burial or disposal of the body; and (5) the committal of the body to its final disposal (Raether and Slater, 1977). Although the specific nature of this procedure varies considerably from society to society, the basic procedure is found in many societies. One difference among societies is the form of body disposal. In most of the world, disposal is through land (burial) and fire (cremation); however, water and air are also used in some cultures.

One major function of the funeral and related rituals is to provide the support of the extended family and the community for those who have suffered the loss. In the early stages of dealing with such loss, the bereaved are not always capable of effective functioning, and they require the resources given by others so that they can deal with the shock, distress, depression, and other feelings engendered by the severance of ties. "The wake and the funeral reaffirm the group identity of the survivors, often with the help of religious collective representations extending all members into afterlife" (Lopata, 1973, p. 53). Lopata describes the need of the survivors to develop some sense of transcendence or transcendent meaning for both their loved one and for themselves. The sharing of ritual and of food and drink is an affirmation of family and community ties during a time of stress.

The graveyard is also part of this ritual, serving simultaneously the sacred function of providing appropriate religious symbols of continuity for the deceased and the secular or public health function of disposing of the corpse (Warner, 1959). Whatever the method of disposal, both sacred and secular

functions are involved. When the body is unobtainable, as occurs in some wartime deaths or in airplane or boat accidents or drownings, some symbolic alternative is often utilized.

There seems little doubt that traditional death-related rituals are in a state of transition today. In some societies people frequently request that charitable donations be made in lieu of sending flowers; some desire cremation, with the ashes sprinkled over a mountain or in the ocean, instead of land burial. Neither money donations (which also have long served in many cultures and American subcultures to help the survivors get through what is often a period of acute financial crisis) nor sprinkling of ashes suggests a secularization of death. Rather, they point to the development of new kinds of sacred rituals.

Some people donate their bodies for medical research and teaching, while others have made arrangements to donate organs, such as eyes and hearts, to those who may continue to use them. In instances in which such donations are made without the knowledge of surviving family members, tensions may result.

Stages of Grief

Whether identifiable stages of grief exist is still a matter of controversy. Parkes (1970) has identified four phases of grief: (1) numbness, during which the loss is partially disregarded; (2) yearning, during which the desire to recover the lost object is paramount and leads to searching behavior; (3) disorganization and despair, when the permanence of loss is accepted and searching ceases; and (4) reorganization of behavior. Three of these stages appear to have counterparts with Kübler-Ross's stages of dying: numbness as denial, despair as depression, and reorganization as acceptance. And most certainly the expression of anger is not uncommon among grieving persons.

Bowlby (1974) has also proposed stages of grieving: yearning and desire for the dead person, often with anger; apathy and disorganization; and recovery. Since Bowlby and Parkes have worked together, the similarity between their models is not surprising. However, Bowlby has focused largely on children, and Parkes has focused on nonelderly adults. There has been little if any attempt to explore differences between the grieving processes of different age groups, which suggests that this is a fruitful avenue for future research.

One stage in the grieving process actually occurs prior to the death. Termed *anticipatory grief*, it describes the initiating of grief and mourning in anticipation of an impending death (Lindemann, 1944), and it appears to permit the bereaved to cope with their loss with less emotional and social upset (Carey, 1979–80). However, a careful analysis of the research data indicates that there is still considerable uncertainty as to whether anticipatory bereavement is adaptive for survivors who are in their middle years or older (Marshall, 1980). Perhaps the younger widows who were observed, being less accustomed to death and less likely to have participated in the *rehearsal for widowhood*, required more time to deal with the idea of their spouse's death, while the older widows responded more negatively to the exhausting physical and emotional demands of providing care for a dying spouse over an extended time period.

The Individual Survivor

Many kinds of physiological changes accompany grief, although there is no single pattern that is universally observed. Lindemann (1944) describes the characteristics of a person suffering acute grief as including "sensations of somatic distress occurring in waves lasting from twenty minutes to an hour at a time, a feeling of tightness in the throat, choking with shortness of breath, need for sighing, an empty feeling in the abdomen, lack of muscular power, and an intense subjective distress described as tension or mental pain" (p. 187). In addition, he found changes in respiration, especially when the person was discussing his grief, and in phys-

ical strength and digestion. These, it must be emphasized, are normal grief reactions.

The behavioral responses to the loss are also numerous:

—Anger, often accompanied by expressions of blame directed against others who might or might not have had any objective role in the death (e.g., physicians and other health caretakers, God, another member of the family).
—Guilt, based on real or fantasized responsibility for the death or on real or fantasized inadequacies in the course of the relationship, increased by the realization that it is too late to make amends.
—Depression, described by Parkes (1972) as being episodic and acute rather than chronic and prolonged.
—Anxiety and restlessness, inability to sit still, but all actions accomplished without zest (Parkes, 1972, mentions that 18 out of 22 nonelderly widows reported restlessness and increased muscular tension during the first month following their loss).
—Preoccupation with the image of the deceased, often so vivid, real, and immediate that those suffering recent losses frequently feel they have encountered the dead person in reality, while simultaneously knowing it is "impossible" (Lindemann, 1944; Parkes, 1972).

When a death does occur, ". . . the newly bereaved person is often treated by society much in the same way as a sick person. Employers expect him to miss work, he stays at home, and relatives visit and talk in hushed tones. For a time, others take over responsibility for making decisions and acting on his behalf" (Parkes, 1972, p. 5).

The suggestion that the bereaved person is like a sick person can be carried beyond the perception of his role by others. People who have suffered a recent loss of a loved one show a higher level of both morbidity and mortality than actuarially predicted (e.g., Maddison and Viola, 1968; Parkes, 1972). These findings may result from a combination of (1) the psychological stress produced by the period preceding the death and the impact of the loss itself, and (2) the physical stress induced by the caretaking process which often leads to inadequate sleep, lack of exercise, and poor eating habits. Interestingly, only nonelderly people are found to have rising illness and death rates following a loss; the elderly appear unaffected in these aspects (Rees and Lutkins, 1967). However, Clayton (1973) feels that little if anything definitive can be stated beyond recognizing that physician visits and the prescribing of tranquilizers and sedatives sharply increase after bereavement.

Widows and Widowers

In most countries a substantial proportion of older persons are widows and widowers, the former tending to outnumber the latter. In the United States, for example, just over half of all women over age 65 are widows, and the proportion goes up to 70 percent among women over 75; widows outnumber widowers six to one among those 65 to 75, and the ratio is nearly five to one for those over 75 (Brotman, 1982). This leads to the development of a "society of widows," that is, a group of widows, most of whom are elderly, who serve as an informal social network for each other and bring newly widowed women into their membership.

Marshall (1980) points out one ramification of this society of widows that is often ignored. These elderly widows often become seriously or terminally ill at a time when their adult children are themselves coping with impending retirement or, not infrequently, are already retired, their husbands having died when the children were in their active middle years. Thus, women are much more likely than men to be the first generation in a four-generation family. The tendency is for the dying elderly man to have a wife to take care of him; when his widow becomes terminally ill, she has greater difficulty in finding a caretaker in the family. Further, if the husband survives his wife, there are innu-

merable younger widows, as well as women his own age, who might be available for companionship, sexual intimacy, and living-together or marriage; whereas for the older widow, the pool of available men is quite small. Perhaps because of this imbalance, widows are considerably more likely to live alone (Cartwright et al., 1973).

Lopata (1979) has suggested that one way widows cope with their loss is through "sanctifying" their deceased husbands, that is, through idealizing both the person and the past relationship. This would appear to give meaning to the previous life of the widow, while simultaneously justifying any tendency she might have to avoid the risk of new relationships. Whether this attitude dissipates with time is not certain.

The major problem of widows is loneliness. When 119 widows and widowers were queried, 54 percent of the women and 27 percent of the men cited loneliness as their key difficulty after their spouse's death. Widows are also more likely to mention problems in making decisions alone and in doing things by themselves. Widowers expressed greater concern about the practical problems of running a household (Carey, 1979–80).

Another major problem of widows is finances. In one study a group of widows overwhelmingly agreed that acquiring financial knowledge was the most important way to prepare for widowhood (Barrett, 1978). Another study found that 71 percent of the husbands of 1700 women widowed before they were elderly had not made wills; in these cases, the average family income dropped to just above half of what it had been before the husband's death (Nuckols, 1973).

Nor do the problems of widows and widowers seem to diminish much over the years. Working with 193 widows and widowers, Barrett and Schneweis (1980–81) looked at six durations of widowhood, ranging from under 3 years to over 20 years, and addressed such issues as changes in morale, participation in activities, physical health, and optimism about the future. Their results were extremely pessimistic, and they concluded that "We give time too much credit as a healer" (p. 102).

THE IMPACT OF DEATH ON THE COMMUNITY

The previous discussion has centered around the meanings of death, the process of dying, and grief and bereavement in regard to the individual in a social context. The present section covers the issues of death, dying, and loss from the viewpoint of community and family structures.

Community Structure

The social implications of the deaths of older persons for the community structure differ considerably from the deaths of the non-elderly. As Blauner (1966) has pointed out, the socially disruptive quality of a death is a direct function of the extent to which the dead person has been important in the vital functions of society: giving birth to and socializing the young, producing sustenance, and maintaining the ceremonies and rituals. In most communities in Western culture, the elderly have already ceased to function in these roles or, at the very least, have reduced their participation considerably.

Another approach is listing the important institutions in which people function: work, family, education, politics, religious groups, and social organizations. Most older people have long since halted their involvement in educational institutions; retirement has usually removed them from the work force; and their family responsibilities, if any, are primarily to their spouse, with only limited responsibilities for children and grandchildren. Although their involvement in political, religious, and social organizations does continue, even this diminishes as they enter the old-old phase of life, and their leadership roles in these institutions are minimal.

Not only do institutions tend to remove older people from important positions well before their dying process, but the tendency of the elderly to die from long-term chronic disease means that their deaths can be anticipated well in advance, and they can be phased out from even the few remaining roles they have. As a result, the death of an older person does not upset the institutional operation to the extent that the death of a younger person often does.

One exception is the organizations specifically geared to older persons, where their roles are frequently highly significant: in the United States, for instance, senior centers, the Gray Panthers, the American Association of Retired Persons, the Retired Senior Volunteer Program (RSVP), and so on. Except in such situations, however, and except occasionally for the death of an elderly officeholder, church leader, creative artist, or organization executive, very few elderly are in positions of community power when they die.

Such institutions as retirement homes and communities, long-term health-care facilities, and other age-segregated programs have the effect of adding to the isolation of the elderly and further diminishing the impact of their death. And even the transfer of property is usually accomplished through a legal system and sometimes controlled by an impersonal trust officer, rather than being a direct negotiation between the elderly and their heirs.

Family Structure

Death affects the family structure in several important ways. First, it removes a person from the family system. Some of that person's roles may require replacement; sometimes, in fact, the dead individual is replaced directly, along with many of his or her roles, as occurs when a recent widow remarries. On other occasions, the roles are distributed. For example, the 40-year-old son whose father has just died may feel he can or should participate more actively in his mother's life, but he also looks to the local senior center and to his mother's brother to take on additional responsibilities. His mother, of course, may view the lost relationship quite differently; she may wish a man in her life for companionship, sex, and affection, while not perceiving any significant changes in her relationships to her son, her brother, or the senior center.

Some recent writing adds another dimension to the impact of the removal of the dead person from the family system. It has been noted that the existential reality of the dead person often continues meaningfully in the lives of the survivors; sometimes the deceased is even seen, heard, felt, or otherwise sensed by the survivors (Gorer, 1967; Parkes, 1972). Moss and Moss (1980) have now proposed that the tie with the deceased spouse is much more durable and powerful than has been assumed, and the same authors (1983–84) have also initiated examination of the enduring tie between deceased parents and their middle-aged children. The themes of the connection between a bereaved person and his or her dead spouse include caring, intimacy, commitment, family feeling, and reciprocal identity support (Moss and Moss, unpublished). This appears to be a most promising avenue for research by family sociologists as well as gerontologists.

The second way in which death affects the family structure is that the family system must reorganize without the dead person, while the lingering presence of the deceased still influences the re-forming structure. Thus, the widowed mother's search for male companionship is inhibited by a middle-aged daughter who has idealized her dead father and strongly disapproves of her mother's actions. Or a recent widower moves in with his widowed older sister, while his attachment to his dead wife precludes formation of new relationships with other women.

Third, the economic effects of the death may influence the wealth and the income of the survivors. However, this effect is not spread evenly over all the survivors, nor is it spread evenly over time. Thus, the surviving spouse may accumulate more money immediately through insurance and other benefits, but his or her long-term income may diminish so that over a period of years the death leads to a net decrease in wealth and in income. Also, adult children may not receive what each considers a fair allocation of the deceased person's wealth; this can lead to tension among them. Further, in many instances, the loss of income for the surviving spouse leads to a redistribution of income from the adult children so that the widow(er) receives money from his or her children.

Fourth, the death of an older person may free survivors, both elderly and younger, to pursue goals that had been set aside, either because of the health problems of the dead person or because caretaking was required. Thus, the daughter whose mother's death requires her, at least in her own thinking, to remain with her father is freed from this obligation when her father dies.

Fifth, the death sets into motion several series of prescribed events that affect both the family and the general community. One series may be funeral arrangements–wake–funeral–burial ceremony; another series of events involves transfer of property; another concerns the possibility of autopsy, issuance of the death certificate, and recording the death. Others may involve contacting family members around the country, informing employers or other relevant persons, and finally deciding about living-arrangement changes for surviving household members.

EDUCATIONAL, SOCIAL, HEALTH, AND MENTAL HEALTH PROGRAMS

Numerous programs have been developed for those who are dying and those who will survive them, as well as for the general population. Some of these programs are primarily educational, while others have a social, health, and/or mental health orientation.

The Hospice Program

By far the best known of the health-care programs for the dying is the hospice (Koff, 1981). The present hospice model, developed in Great Britian by Dr. Cicely Saunders (1977), emphasizes care for persons who physicians believe are beyond curative powers of medicine and for whom further hospital-based treatment is inappropriate. In the

United States and Canada, the hospice movement has emphasized the use of outpatient care and volunteer services, and it has focused on the cancer patient.

Hospice programs have been developed in many parts of the world, and innumerable models are available. Some hospices are housed on wards of existing hospitals, while others are freestanding; some link into other community health services, while others have created their own autonomous care system; some have (or have plans for) elaborate physical plants, while others restrict themselves to outpatient services and follow-ups on patients in whatever hospitals or other institutions they go to (see Special Issue on Hospice, *Death Education,* 1978). Hospices can be viewed as a philosophy of health care for the terminally ill rather than as a specific building or facility (Koff, 1981).

For the most part, hospices underserve the elderly population in comparison to other age groups. This may result from their programs being geared to people who are cognitively intact, who are living with someone who could provide at-home care with help, and whose dying trajectory is not long and drawn out. Leaders of the hospice movement have acknowledged this situation and have expressed the desire to serve a larger number of older persons (based on author's observations and on informal communications).

Very little research exists regarding hospice effectiveness, but an initial study in England showed hospice patients to be less anxious and less depressed than comparable hospital patients; the hospice patients also approved warmly of the opportunity for open communication concerning their terminal status, and they rated the staff and treatment program higher in general than persons dying in hospitals rated theirs (Hinton, 1979).

Another study compared a group of patients cared for at home under the auspices of the New Haven, Connecticut hospice with a control group that received no hospice support. The hospice home-care patients were significantly better off in terms of anxiety,

depression, and hostility, and their family members also appeared more satisfied (Lack and Buckingham, 1978). However, Parkes (1980) has pointed out that home care, in comparison to hospital care, may increase stress on patients who are concerned about burdening family members and on the family members themselves. Home care may provide more life satisfaction to the patient, but simultaneously more stress to the caregivers during the final days and weeks of life.

Given the potential for improving both cost-effectiveness of health care and the personal well-being of terminally ill patients and their family members, the hospice is a prime candidate for a variety of kinds of research. These include a determination of which models of hospice care function most effectively under specified community-health arrangements; the most appropriate methods of reducing staff burn-out; optimum staff-selection criteria; the extent to which hospice care is, in fact, cost-effective and conducive to improved feelings of personal well-being for the dying persons and their family members; and how hospice services and philosophy can be appropriately extended to encompass care for more terminally-ill older people.

Representative Examples of Other Programs

One kind of program that focuses more on the general population than those with immediate stress is exemplified by the death education movement. This is represented by the hundreds of courses on death found in college and university catalogues; by the founding of the Forum of Death Education and Counseling, a membership organization of some 800 interested professionals; by the establishment of the journals *Death Education* and *Omega;* and by the countless educational programs sponsored by churches, health institutions, social agencies, and educational institutions.

A second form of program consists of personal support services for people who are dying or who are bereaved. One such program is Make Today Count, which brings together, in chapters throughout the United States, people who are seriously ill with cancer (Kelly, 1977). This is essentially a self-support group, with chapters having extensive autonomy.

Compassionate Friends is an organization in the United States that brings together parents of children who have died. Like Make Today Count, it is a self-support group operation, with nearly 400 chapters around the country, and it is highly dependent on its membership for local programming and financial support (from materials supplied by Compassionate Friends, 1984).

A totally different kind of program, now available in many hospitals, consists of counseling services for terminally ill patients, often conducted by a chaplain or social worker who has had specific training for this purpose. This may take the form of psychotherapy, but it is more commonly a kind of supportive counseling, perhaps for brief periods on a more-or-less ad hoc basis.

For the most part, these programs—whether for the dying, the bereaved, or the general community—are not geared to the elderly. Little information is available as to the proportion of relevant services that are provided to older persons, but the author's general impression is that they remain underserved, not only in an absolute sense but also in comparison to other age groups. This would appear to be an appropriate setting for both research and advocacy.

FUTURE PRIORITIES

Although the status of knowledge concerning death, dying, and bereavement has moved ahead only moderately during the past decade, the status of services for the dying and the bereaved and the status of death education and counseling have moved ahead substantially. The major task for the coming decade is improving the knowledge base in the field, while continuing to forge ahead with services.

Numerous pressing research issues remain. The stage theory of Kübler-Ross has not yet been carefully tested through empir-

ical research, either as to the frequency with which it occurs or as to its value as an effective way of adapting to the dying process and imminent death. We have learned more about effective communication with dying persons, the importance of open awareness, the desire of terminally ill patients to die in familiar surroundings and among those they love, and numerous other matters. However, our knowledge tends to be global and based on a plurality of responses of research populations; we know little about factors that differentiate persons who fit the modal response and those who do not.

We also need to add to our knowledge of what the fear/terror/anxiety of death actually is, what it is that is unique to the dying process and death, and how to predict and understand responses of people who actually confront their own death. In spite of the numerous studies on death attitudes, we have a long way to go in order to develop a cohesive picture of this issue. For example, what is the role of religious belief systems for death attitudes? What are the predictors that will enable us to understand which people will become more anxious as they age and approach death and which people will become calmer and more accepting?

We also need desperately to evaluate our newly developing services and service models: death education courses, counseling the dying, hospice and palliative care units, dying at home, and open awareness contexts. And we must also be cautious of our own rhetoric. For example, is "death with dignity" in danger of becoming a catch-phrase to permit people to die sooner than they need to, because the rest of us have trouble coping with their presence? Is the present attention to death and the dying process merely a fad or fashion that is simply another indirect form of denying the real terror caused by the overriding awareness that someday "*I* will die!"?

This is a topic that not only permits, but virtually calls out for, interdisciplinary research and what might be termed multiple-methodology research. The strongly quantitative psychologist needs to coordinate research efforts with the skillfully qualitative anthropologist; they might then both team up with the social historian and finally integrate their findings with the experienced service-provider. While it is true that many researchers in this field do utilize the research and writing of people from other disciplines, the research models themselves have remained, for the most part, narrow.

And finally, each of the previous comments requires testing for its relevance to older persons and to persons as they get older. There are now a substantial number of individuals around the world who have conducted research, taught courses, and provided services on these issues for several years or more. There is a vast array of written materials in many languages. The difficult task of integrating this information and extracting its relevance for the elderly is still waiting to be accomplished.

REFERENCES

Ariès, P. 1981. *The Hour of Our Death*. New York: Knopf.

Argyle, M., and Beit-Hallahmi, B. 1975. *The Social Psychology of Religion*. London: Routledge & Kegan Paul.

Augustine, M. J., and Kalish, R. A. 1975. Religion, transcendence, and appropriate death. *Journal of Transpersonal Psychology* 7:1–13.

Barrett, C. J. 1978. Strategies for preventing the stresses of widowhood. Presentation at the Southwestern Psychological Association, New Orleans.

Barrett, C. J., and Schneweis, K. M. 1980–81. An empirical search for stages of widowhood. *Omega* 11:97–104.

Bengtson, V. L., Cuellar, J. B., and Ragan, P. K. 1977. Stratum contrasts and similarities in attitudes toward death. *Journal of Gerontology* 32:76–88.

Blauner, R. 1966. Death and social structure. *Psychiatry* 29:378–394. Reprinted 1968. *In* B. Neugarten (ed.), *Middle Age and Aging*, pp. 531–540. Chicago: University of Chicago Press.

Bowlby, J. 1974. *Separation*. New York: Basic Books.

Brotman, H. B. 1982. *Every Ninth American*. An Analysis for the Chairman, Select Committee on Aging, U.S. House of Representatives. Washington, D.C.: Government Printing Office.

Bryer, K. B. 1979. The Amish way of death. *American Psychologist* 34:255–261.

Cameron, P., Stewart, L., and Biber, H. 1973. Consciousness of death across the life-span. *Journal of Gerontology* 28:92–95.

Carey, R. G. 1979–80. Weathering widowhood: Problems and adjustment of the widowed during the first year. *Omega* 10:135–145.

Cartwright, A., Hockey, L., and Anderson, J. L. 1973. *Life Before Death*. London: Routledge and Kegan Paul.

Choron, J. 1964. *Modern Man and Mortality*. New York: Macmillan.

Clayton, P. J. 1973. The clinical morbidity of the first year of bereavement: A review. *Comprehensive Psychiatry* 14:151–157.

Collett, L., and Lester, D. 1969. Fear of death and fear of dying. *Journal of Psychology* 72:179–181.

Cumming, E., and Henry, W. E. 1961. *Growing Old*. New York: Basic Books.

Death Education. 1978. Special issue on hospice. 2 (1 & 2); entire issue.

Dickstein, L. S. 1972. Death concern: Measurement and correlates. *Psychological Reports* 30:563–571.

Diggory, J. C., and Rothman, D. Z. 1961. Values destroyed by death. *Journal of Abnormal and Social Psychology* 63:205–210.

Dublin, L. I. 1965. *Factbook on Man*. New York: Macmillan.

Durlak, J. A., and Kass, R. A. 1981–82. Clarifying the measurements of death attitudes: A factor analytic evaluation of fifteen self-report scales. *Omega* 12:129–141.

Erikson, E. 1963. *Childhood and Society*, 2nd ed. New York: Norton.

Feifel, H., and Branscomb, A. B. 1973. Who's afraid of death? *Journal of Abnormal Psychology* 81:282–288.

Feifel, H., and Nagy, V. T. 1981. Another look at fear of death. *Journal of Consulting and Clinical Psychology* 49:278–286.

Glaser, B. G. 1966. The social loss of aged dying patients. *The Gerontologist* 6:77–80.

Glaser, B. G., and Strauss, A. L. 1965. *Awareness of Dying*. Chicago: Aldine.

Gorer, G. 1967. *Death, Grief, and Mourning*. New York: Doubleday, Anchor Books.

Hinton, J. M. 1975. The influence of previous personality on reactions to having terminal cancer. *Omega* 6:95–111.

Hinton, J. M. Jan. 6, 1979. Comparison of places and policies for terminal care. *Lancet* 8106:29–32.

Jeffers, F. C., Nichols, C. R., and Eisdorfer, C. 1961. Attitudes of older persons toward death: A preliminary study. *Journal of Gerontology* 16:63–56.

Kalish, R. A. 1963. An approach to the study of death attitudes. *American Behavioral Scientist* 6:68–80.

Kalish, R. A. 1984. *Death, Grief and Caring Relationships*. 2nd edition Monterey, Calif.: Brooks/Cole.

Kalish, R. A., and Reynolds, D. K. 1976. *Death and Ethnicity: A Psychocultural Study*. Los Angeles: University of Southern California Press. Republished 1981. Farmingdale, N.Y.: Baywood Publishing Co.

Kass, L. R. 1971. Death as an event: A commentary on Robert Morison. *Science* 173:698–702.

Kastenbaum, R. 1966a. As the clock runs out. *Mental Hygiene* 50:332–336.

Kastenbaum, R. 1966b. On the meaning of time in later life. *Journal of Genetic Psychology* 109:9–25.

Kastenbaum, R., and Candy, S. E. 1973. The 4% fallacy: A methodological and empirical critique of extended care facility population statistics. *Aging and Human Development* 4:15–22.

Keith, P. M. 1979. Life changes and preceptions of life and death among older men and women. *Journal of Gerontology* 6:870–878.

Keith, P. M. 1981–82. Perceptions of time remaining and distance from death. *Omega* 12:307–318.

Kelly, O. E. 1977. Make Today Count. *In* H. Feifel (ed.), *New Meanings of Death*. New York: McGraw-Hill.

Koff, T. H. 1981. *Hospice: A Caring Community*. Cambridge, Mass.: Winthrop Publishers.

Kogan, N., and Wallach, M. 1961. Age changes in values and attitudes. *Journal of Gerontology* 16:272–280.

Kübler-Ross, E. 1969. *On Death and Dying*. New York: Macmillan.

Kübler-Ross, E. 1974. *Questions and Answers on Death and Dying*. New York: Macmillan.

Lack, S. A., and Buckingham, R. W. 1978. *The First American Hospice: Three Years of Home Care*. New Haven, Conn.: Hospice, Inc.

Lerner, M. 1970. When, why, and where people die. *In* O. G. Brim, Jr., H. E. Freeman, S. Levine, and N. A. Scotch (eds.), *The Dying Patient*, pp. 5–29. New York: Russell Sage Foundation.

Lindemann, E. 1944. Symptomatology and management of acute grief. *American Journal of Psychiatry* 101:141–148. Reprinted 1965. *In* R. Fulton (ed.), *Death and Identity*, pp. 186–201. New York: John Wiley.

Lipman, A., and Marden, P. 1966. Preparation for death in old age. *Journal of Gerontology* 21:426–431.

Lopata, H. Z. 1973. *Widowhood in an American City*. Cambridge, Mass.: Schenkman.

Lopata, H. Z. 1979. *Women as Widows: Support Systems*. New York: Elsevier-North Holland.

Maddison, D., and Viola, A. 1968. The health of widows in the year following bereavement. *Journal of Psychosomatic Research* 12:297–306.

Magni, K. G. 1972. The fear of death. *In* A. Godin (ed.), *Death and Presence*, pp. 125–138. Brussels: Lumen Vitae Press.

Martin, D. S., and Wrightsman, L. 1965. The relationship between religious behavior and concern about death. *Journal of Social Psychology* 65:317–323.

Marshall, V. W. 1975. Age and awareness of finitude in developmental gerontology. *Omega* 6:113–129.

Marshall, V. W. 1980. *Last Chapters: A Sociology of Aging and Dying*. Monterey, Calif.: Brooks/Cole.

Marshall. V. W. 1982. Death and dying. In D. J. Mangen and W. A. Peterson (eds.), *Research Instruments in Social Gerontology. Volume 1, Clinical and Social Psychology*. Minneapolis: University of Minnesota Press.

Moss, M. S., and Moss, S. Z. 1980. The image of the deceased spouse in remarriage of elderly widow(er)s. *Journal of Gerontological Social Work* 3:59–69.

Moss, M. S., and Moss, S. Z. 1983–84 The impact of parental death on middle-aged children. *Omega* 14:65–75.

Moss, M. S., and Moss, S. Z. Some aspects of the elderly widow(er)s persistent tie with the deceased spouse. (Unpublished.)

Myers, J. E., Wass, H., and Murphey, M. 1980. Ethnic differences in death anxiety among the elderly. *Death Education* 4:237–244.

Nehrke, M. F., Bellucci, G., and Gabriel, S. J. 1977–78. Death anxiety, locus of control, and life satisfaction in the elderly: Toward a definition of ego-integrity. *Omega* 8:359–368.

Nehrke, M. F., Hulicka, I. M., Turner, R. R., Morganti, J. B., Whitbourne, S. K., and Cohen, S. H. 1981. Factor analysis of death anxiety. Presentation to Gerontological Society of America, Toronto.

Nelson, L. D., and Nelson, C. C. 1973. Religion and death anxiety. Presentation to the annual joint meeting, Society for the Scientific Study of Religion and Religious Research Association, San Francisco.

Nelson, L. D., and Nelson, C. C. 1975. A factor analytic inquiry into the multidimensionality of death anxiety. *Omega* 6:171–178.

Neugarten, B. L. 1977. Personality and aging. *In* J. E. Birren and K. W. Schaie (eds.), *Handbook of the Psychology of Aging*. New York: Van Nostrand Reinhold.

Nuckols, R. 1973. Widows study. *JSAS Catalog of Selected Documents in Psychology* 3:9.

Palmore, E. 1976. Total chance of institutionalization among the aged. *The Gerontologist* 16:504–507.

Parkes, C. M. 1970. "Seeking" and "finding" a lost object. *Social Science and Medicine* 4:187–201.

Parkes, C. M. 1972. *Bereavement*. New York: International Universities Press.

Parkes, C. M. 1980. Terminal care: Evaluation of an advisory domiciliary service at St. Christopher's Hospice. *Postgraduate Medical Journal* 56:685–689.

Pine, V. R. 1975. *Caretaker of the Dead: The American Funeral Director*. New York: Irvington.

Pollak, J. M. 1979–80. Correlates of death anxiety: A review of empirical studies. *Omega* 10:97–121.

Raether, H. C., and Slater, R. C. 1977. Immediate post-death activities in the United States. *In* H. Feifel (ed.), *New Meanings of Death*. New York: McGraw-Hill.

Rees, W. D., and Lutkins, S. G. 1967. Mortality of bereavement. *British Medical Journal* 4:13–16.

Reynolds, D. K., and Kalish, R. A. 1974. Anticipation of futurity as a function of ethnicity and age. *Journal of Gerontology* 29:224–231.

Rhudick, P. J., and Dibner, A. S. 1961. Age, personality and health correlates of death concerns in normal aged individuals. *Journal of Gerontology* 16:44–49.

Rigdon, M. A., and Epting, F. R. 1981–82. Reclarifying the measurement of death attitudes. *Omega* 12:143–146.

Riley, J. W., Jr. 1970. What people think about death. *In* O. G. Brim, Jr., H. E. Freeman, S. Levine, and N. A. Scotch (eds.), *The Dying Patient,* pp. 30–41. New York: Russell Sage Foundation.

Rosenfeld, A. H. 1978. *New Views on Older Lives.* Washington, D.C.: Government Printing Office.

Saunders, C. 1977. Dying they live: St. Christopher's Hospice. *In* H. Feifel (ed.), *New Meanings of Death.* New York: McGraw-Hill.

Schulz, R. 1978. *The Psychology of Death, Dying and Bereavement.* Reading, Mass.: Addison-Wesley.

Schulz, R., and Aderman, D. 1974. Clinical research and the stages of dying. *Omega* 5:137–143.

Sharma, K. L., and Jain, U. C. 1969. Religiosity and fear of death in young and retired persons. *Indian Journal of Gerontology* 1:110–114.

Shneidman, E. S. 1973. *Deaths of Man.* New York: Quadrangle/New York Times.

Simmons, L. W. 1945. *The Role of the Aged in Primitive Society.* New Haven: Yale University Press.

Templer, D. I. 1970. The construction and validation of a death anxiety scale. *Journal of General Psychology* 82:165–177.

Templer, D. I. 1971. Death anxiety as related to depression and health of retired persons. *Journal of Gerontology* 26:521–523.

Templer, D. I. 1972. Death anxiety in religiously very involved persons. *Psychological Reports* 31:361–362.

Veatch, R. M. 1976. *Death, Dying, and the Biological Revolution.* New Haven: Yale University Press.

Warner, W. L. 1959. The city of the dead. *In* W. L. Warner, *The Living and the Dead.* New Haven: Yale University Press.

Wass, H., Christian, M., Myers, J., and Murphey, M. 1978–79. Similarities and dissimilarities in attitudes toward death in a population of older persons. *Omega* 9:337–354.

Wass, H., and Sisler, H. 1978. Death concerns and views on various aspects of dying among elderly persons. International Symposium on the Dying Human, Tel Aviv, Israel.

Watson, W. H. 1976. The aging sick and the near dead: A study of some distinguishing characteristics and social effects. *Omega* 7:115–123.

Weisman, A. D. 1972. *On Dying and Denying.* New York: Behavioral Publications.

Wittkowski, J. 1981. Attitudes toward death and dying in older persons and their dependence on life satisfaction and death-related experiences. Presented to the International Congress of Gerontology, Hamburg, Germany.

PART **3** AGING AND SOCIAL STRUCTURE

7
AGING AND WORLDWIDE POPULATION CHANGE

George C. Myers

Duke University

INTRODUCTION

Demography, the scientific study of population, represents a fundamental and long-standing approach to the understanding of human society. The importance of age has been recognized within the discipline as an underlying structural feature of populations and a variable that is involved intrinsically in the demographic dynamics of fertility, mortality, and spatial movement. In the past decade, however, increasing attention has been given to specific consideration of the *demography of aging,* a subfield of general demography that relates in important ways to the concerns of social gerontologists. As Siegel (1980) notes, "The demography of aging brings demographers to focus holistically on a population group, the elderly, and a demographic process, aging." The demography of aging, therefore, is concerned with determining (1) the state of the older population, (2) changes in the numbers, proportionate size, and composition of this subpopulation that have occurred in the past and are likely to occur in the future, and (3) the determinants and consequences of these developments.

Unlike much of our knowledge of social gerontology, which is of fairly recent origin, consideration of population aging has a somewhat longer history. This is under-standable when we consider that relatively large numbers of older persons are virtually a prerequisite for generating major concern with issues relating to the aged and the aging process (Kiesler, 1981). The first attention to population aging emerged in France at the close of the nineteenth century. The proportion of older persons aged 65 years and over in the population of France exceeded 5 percent as early as 1800 and gradually increased to 8 percent by 1900 (United Nations, 1956). This was a major consequence of the decline of fertility to replacement levels during the century, which aroused dire concerns about potential depopulation of the country, its threatened position of power vis-à-vis its rapidly growing neighbors, and the possible decline of French "culture" (Spengler, 1979). This debate surged on and off for decades and, interestingly, still evokes considerable heated discussion (Wulf, 1982).

The demographic situation in Sweden, another country that experienced considerable population aging in the nineteenth century, was examined in detail by Sundbärg (1894). In comparing the population composition of Sweden and a number of other countries, Sundbärg (1900) found that the proportion of the population between the ages of 15 and 50 constituted roughly 50 percent of the total for each of these countries, even though they might have quite divergent fertility, mortal-

173

ity, and rates of growth. However, the proportions of the population under age 15 and age 50 and over were found to differ considerably both among countries and over time. Thus, Sundbärg was led to a classification of countries on the basis of the relative proportions found in the youthful and older age categories. The groups were entitled progressive (young), stationary (balanced), and regressive (old). Apart from the pejorative connotations that might be attached to these terms, Sundbärg was the first demographer to note systematic differences in age composition among countries and, by implication, the shift that takes place over time toward an aging population structure.

Whereas France and Sweden led the way in population aging, for most other "Western" countries the aging of population has been a distinctly twentieth-century phenomenon. Concerted demographic attention to the aging process in the United States can be noted as early as the 1920s in the work by Dublin (1928). By the 1930s increasing concern was expressed as the fertility declines of the depression period promised rapid changes in the age structure of the population (Thompson and Whelpton, 1930, 1933; Dublin and Lotka, 1937; Pearl, 1940). The prophetic title of Thompson and Whelpton's 1930 article in the *American Mercury,* "A Nation of Elders in the Making," presaged the growing interest of demographers in capturing the dimensions of this phenomenon. The post–World War II era was marked by a steadily expanding body of literature on population aging, especially by United States, French, and United Nations demographers. At present, there are few Western countries for which studies of the demographic aspects of aging have not been made.

There is increasing awareness that population aging will be an important issue, as well, for third-world countries that are currently in the process of social and economic development (Siegel, 1981; Siegel and Hoover, 1982; Myers, 1982). It can truly be said that population aging is now recognized as a worldwide phenomenon that commands immediate attention if effective societal responses are to be made to changing demographic realities. The United Nations World Assembly on Aging (United Nations, 1982c) highlighted the global issues that have emerged with the rapid growth in the number of older persons and the consequent shifting of the population structure of many of the world's countries. Many of these issues relate to the degree to which nations are likely to make commitments to the health, economic, and social welfare of the aged in light of other priorities they face in resource allocation for social and economic development.

In this chapter, major perspectives of the demography of aging are examined, with particular emphasis placed on contemporary research issues. Initially some conceptual issues are discussed that relate to the ways in which demographers view the field. The remainder of this chapter is organized around three concepts that can serve to guide our understanding of population aging—population *momentum,* population *metabolism,* and population *diversity.* These are concepts that demographers have used on occasion to focus on structural properties and on dynamic elements of total populations. In using these dimensions for studying population aging, we draw attention to the fact that the population of older persons can be viewed as a distinctive component of a total population. This is not to suggest that less attention should be given to the aged population as a product of the dynamics that affect the total population or to the so-called *aging* of other subpopulations, such as the labor force, the population of veterans, or the electorate, to mention a few groups that have been studied. A focus on the aged population, however, deals directly with a wide variety of issues that have central meaning for gerontologists.

Dimensions of Aging

It has been traditional to distinguish between aging as an individual phenomenon and aging as an aggregative process through which population structure is modified. In considering the former, it is important to emphasize that human aging is a multifaceted phenomenon that begins at birth and follows varied timetables depending on whether one is tracing biological, cognitive, or social parameters. Although demographers are less concerned with the aging of individuals per se, there may be some senses in which such a perspective is appropriate, as, for example, in the elaboration of life expectancy or survival functions at specified ages. For the most part, major demographic attention has been given to population aging, in terms of average age of a population, the size and proportion of various age categories of the population, and ratios between different age categories (see, e.g., Rosset, 1964). These are mainly static conceptions, but take on additional meaning when examined over time. For example, a distinction is often drawn between "aging at the apex" and "aging from the base" (United Nations, 1956). Although these processes may not be mutually exclusive, the former can be said to occur when the proportion of older persons in a population increases, whereas the latter refers to situations in which the proportion of younger persons in a population declines. Although strictly adhering to a definition that relates to the relative proportions of population found in certain age groups may have certain advantages, we prefer to view the aging of population in a less restrictive way by also considering the change in the absolute *number* of older persons in a population.

There is another active field of gerontological study, amply demonstrated in other contributions to this *Handbook,* that focuses on the rate and timing of events in the entire life course, using chronological age as a reference scale upon which important social transitions can be identified. For examining the status of older persons, earlier events obviously assume great importance in understanding the structure and behavior of the aged. The demographer's concern with these processes is generally directed to a consideration of cohorts—that is, aggregates of individuals who typically are classified by common age, measured from birth (Wins-

borough, 1980). Thus, we can also speak of the aging of cohorts, which seems to offer an intermediate formulation between the aging of individuals and the aging of populations. This conceptualization is particularly well suited for demographic analysis (Ryder, 1964, 1965; Riley, 1973).

Another consideration which adds further complexity concerns the various definitions that may be used for delineating old age and, thereby, the aged population. The demographer commonly uses a fixed age such as 60 or 65 as a boundary point because it facilitates standardized analyses and is grounded in legal and conventional practice (e.g., in social security provisions, retirement decisions, etc.). It is interesting to note, however, that the practice of designating the age of 60 or the age of 65 may vary even among different agencies within the same parent organization. The United Nations Population Division, for example, typically has used age 65 for defining the aged, whereas other United Nations agencies have used 60. In the United States, the National Institute on Aging has used 65, but the Administration on Aging has used 60 or 62. These varying procedures illustrate the desire on the part of agencies to emphasize the numerical importance of the constituency to which programs are directed, and, in part, it is recognition of the fact that different definitions may be appropriate in certain contexts. This may be especially true in cross-national investigations, which include countries in which life expectancy is low and the numbers of aged persons are relatively small. For the sake of consistency, age 65 is used in this chapter for defining the aged population.

The Aged As A Subpopulation

A demographic focus on older persons as a subpopulation calls attention to certain features that are dissimilar to those characterizing the total population or the aged as merely one segment of that population, as well as other features that are similar. A closer examination of these matters is useful.

First, we can consider the demographic

factors that produce changes in the size of the aged population, namely, fertility, mortality, and migration. While the forces that produce rapid growth in the number and proportion of older persons are necessarily a reflection of the prior mortality and fertility trends experienced by a total population, an emphasis on the aged population itself directs attention specifically to matters of increment and decrement.

Increment occurs through entrance of persons to this subpopulation at some specified age—for example, 65 years of age. This represents a form of birth, although clearly not in the sense of reproduction. For example, in the United States it is estimated that older persons who reach age 65 each year currently comprise about 7.4 percent of the extant aged population.

Decrement, on the other hand, occurs through the death of older persons. A high proportion of the deaths in a total population occurs to persons over the age of 65, but the number of deaths is generally less than the number of entrants to the aged population. In the United States, about 5.1 percent of the total aged, including those who have turned 65 and those already at the older ages, die each year. Considering both these forces, we can state that the aged population is subject to high population *turnover,* a topic of importance that is examined further in this chapter. This contrasts with the total population, where turnover is relatively low—only a fifth as much.

The final factor, migration, is a relatively minor factor in considering direct changes to the size of the aged population on a national level, but it may be locally important and have profound implications for those older persons who move or for those who do not.

Second, there is growing recognition that the aged population is a heterogeneous category of the total population in terms of such characteristics as age, sex, race and ethnic composition, marital status, socioeconomic status, and so on. This diversity is often not emphasized sufficiently when the older population is merely considered as a single category of the population consisting of persons 65 years of age and over. Thus, there is a clear-cut need for considering the disaggregation of the aged population, a population that includes persons who range over a span of some 30 to 35 years. Explicit attention to the composition of the aged population itself leads to recognition of important changes that are taking place to modify this structure, such as the high relative increase in numbers of extremely old persons, declining sex ratios, and shifts in marital status, living arrangements, and ethnic status, to mention only a few major alterations. These changing properties of the subpopulation can result from differences in the demographic and social characteristics of (a) new cohorts entering old age, (b) survivors resulting from differential attrition of those already aged, and (c) older persons experiencing changes in status (either through biological processes, such as adding years to life, or through mainly volitional changes such as retirement, remarriage, migration, etc.).

Third, a focus on the aged as a subpopulation serves to emphasize the needs that arise from the number and differing types of older persons, as well as from their proportion in the total population. This is particularly important for those charged with public policy and program implementation, for it explicitly recognizes the differential demands on public and private services that arise from the growth and changing composition of the aged population. In a somewhat different sense, this perspective has drawn increasing attention to the "demographics" of an aged population—that is, the way in which the changing size and composition of the aged population modify consumer demand, political constituencies, economic conditions, and social structures. These issues are the result of a range of demographic factors that command interdisciplinary attention from other social scientists, private and public officials, and the general public.

Finally, it should be acknowledged that some features of the aged population are quite unlike those of total populations or, for that matter, unlike those of other subpopulations. The aged population is not geographically delimited and, therefore, is not exposed to common external or environmental effects. It also lacks certain group properties that other subpopulations may possess, although the extent to which the aged identify themselves as a distinctive grouping is a subject of considerable discussion. Because the growth of the aged population is determined in part through entry into old age, the forces producing change are a function of past experiences in the population as a whole. As a result, the size and composition of the aged population is subject to less unforeseen change in terms of most characteristics. Thus, it can be said that policies relating to population aging are properly viewed as "population-responsive" rather than "population-influencing." In contrast, population control measures directed to the total population, such as policies aimed at reducing fertility, can have a more immediate impact on the growth of that population than would be true for any policies that might be designed to influence the size and structure of the aged population.

To summarize, the position taken in this chapter is to focus attention on the aged population as a distinctive subpopulation that is both heterogeneous and continually changing over time. To grasp why these changes take place we need to appreciate the long-term dynamics of the population as a whole, as well as factors directly operating at the later ages. In the sections to follow, this broadened perspective of the demography of aging will be examined.

POPULATION MOMENTUM

Population momentum refers to the fact that the characteristics of a population, such as its age or sex structure and growth conditions, at any point of time are a product not only of the current forces producing change but its historical past. It also implies that future characteristics are necessarily a reflection in part of present conditions. This can be understood clearly by considering birth and death phenomena, the dynamic factors producing population change (leaving aside

consideration of migration for the present). The distribution of births and deaths by age varies in patterned ways. Thus, births occur to women exclusively in the reproductive ages and provide a total population with replacement or increments at the earliest age. Deaths viewed as decrements to a population may occur at any age, but are more frequent at birth, or shortly thereafter, and at older ages. Thus, the rates of increment and decrement vary by age, and their impact is intrinsically tied to the structure of a population. When changes in population structure occur, corresponding changes can be expected in mortality and fertility. So, too, mortality and fertility changes modify population structure.

Demographers have devoted considerable attention to the formal properties of this demographic process of renewal. For example, high fertility at time t produces a large number of women who reach childbearing ages at $t + n$. Even if fertility rates decline over the interval, the large cohorts of women will produce high numbers of children, and the growth rate will be influenced. As Keyfitz (1977, p. 155) notes, "the age distribution of a rapidly increasing population is favorable to increase" in the future. When mortality declines, and fertility declines follow, as they do typically in the demographic transition, growth rates are high and continue to be elevated for some time thereafter. In more formal terms, this population momentum depends on the annual decline in rates, and the length of the time that it takes for the decline to occur. Ryder (1975) has also examined the effect of population momentum for cohorts. These formulations have played an important role in forecasting the possible, but always uncertain, size and structure of future populations, especially those populations moving toward a stationary state of zero population growth and basically fixed age structure (Frejka, 1981).

Demographic Transition

Population aging can be examined as a special case of population momentum. To do so, we can examine the features of the so-called demographic transition. Four stages of this transition are usually distinguished, which characterize the main developments that most Western countries have experienced and which are considered likely to occur for countries that are currently developing (Bourgeois-Pichat, 1979).

1. An initial stage with high levels of fertility and mortality and, consequently, very slow and fluctuating growth of total population. Such populations have a "young" population profile with large proportions of younger persons and relatively few older persons.

2. A second stage in which mortality levels decline while fertility remains high. Natural increase is large, and the size of a population increases rapidly. The population structure may actually become younger during this stage, with very low proportions of older persons.

3. A third stage in which fertility levels fall and the rate of population growth starts declining. The proportion of older population slowly increases during this stage.

4. A final stage in which fertility and mortality are in equilibrium, as in the first stage, but at considerably lower rate levels. Population growth is negligible, if not zero, and the population structure is stabilized, with relatively high proportions of older population. While population size could conceivably decline in this stage, a long-term depopulation is not considered likely.

This is a generalized pattern that no population fits precisely, but it does provide an overall perspective on the history of population. The size of the total population in this transition is greatly increased, depending on the rapidity of change and the levels of fertility and mortality at different stages. It is estimated that European countries that have passed through this transition have populations currently five to six times as large as they had in 1750, a convenient time point preceding the transition (Bourgeois-Pichat,

1965). Population projections for countries presently developing suggest that these countries could experience even greater growth because of rapid mortality declines and persistence of fertility at relatively high levels.

Population aging, in the two senses we have defined it in this chapter (as the number and as the proportion of the total population 65 years of age and over), occurs in different ways at each stage of the demographic transition. As a proportion of the population, aging does not set in until the third stage, whereas some growth in the numbers of the aged population may occur in the second stage in conjunction with growth of the population in general. This depends on whether mortality declines, which characterize the second stage, occur over all ages. In general, however, the declines are more pronounced at younger ages, especially reductions in infant mortality. It is fair to say that the growth of the total population is very responsive initially to declining mortality, whereas the growth of aged persons, especially in their proportionate share of the total population, mainly occurs when fertility falls (Coale, 1957, 1964).

Figure 1 provides a stylized depiction of the demographic transition showing the curves for birth and death rates. In addition, a curve is super-imposed to show how the population increases. It should be noted that the amount of growth depends on the factors mentioned previously, the annual declines in rates and the length of time for the transition to be accomplished. A curve indicating the aged population also is included (not drawn to scale with respect to total population) to show the lag in the increase of this aged segment of the population. Thus, there is a momentum in the growth of a population and its age structure that is built into the population structure at time t but is not evinced in the size of the older population until a later date, time $t + n$. The demographic transition that brings about a population explosion due to change in fertility and mortality also effects a transition in the population structure—one major feature of which is population aging.

STAGES

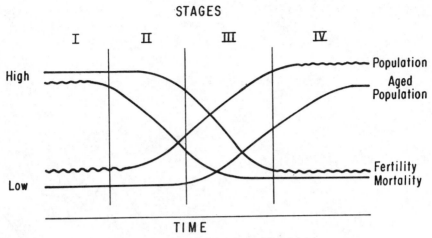

Fig. 1.   Schema of demographic transition.

Figure 2 provides an indication of the varying lengths of time that it has taken for population aging to take place within countries. The two countries that showed aging tendencies during the nineteenth century, France and Sweden, still had barely over 8 percent of their total population consisting of persons 65 years of age and over in the year 1900. These countries may be described as Type I countries in terms of this early trend in population aging and in the steady increase in their proportion of aged, which, even today, ranks them as the two countries with the highest aging levels.

Three other types of countries can be identified in terms of their chronological trajectory of population aging. The United States and Greece are countries that can be classified as Type II countries (Bulgaria is another), which experienced rather sharp increases in the proportion aged beginning after 1900. Two countries exemplifying Type III, Argentina and Japan, have mainly experienced population aging in the post–World War II period. Whereas the trends for Japan and Argentina have been roughly comparable to the present, strikingly different patterns between the two countries are expected in the future. Argentina's aging will flatten out toward the end of this century, but Japan will experience a spectacular growth in the aged proportion of the population well into the first quarter of the twenty-first century. In fact, by the year 2025 Japan will have the highest proportion of aged persons in the world, according to recent projections (Nihon University, 1982). This unprecedented rise is attributable to steep declines in mortality rates and curtailed fertility in the post–World War II period. Two examples of a Type IV pattern have been selected, Sri Lanka and the Republic of Korea, to characterize developing countries in which mortality has declined sharply and some fertility reductions also can be noted.

There are similarities in growth patterns for all four types of countries. Growth is slow at first, then accelerates, and finally levels off somewhat. For Type I and II countries there is a flattening of the curve, reflecting the proportion of aged persons around the year 2000, followed by another period of acceleration. This reflects the large "baby-boom" cohorts reaching old age in the second decade of the next century. There are limits, of course, to how high these ratios of the aged population might go, given certain assumptions about mortality and fertility; but tracing forecasted developments to the year 2025 leads to the conclusion that there will be considerable momentum toward levels greatly elevated over the present in the proportion of aged. Recent United Nations projections for the world and major

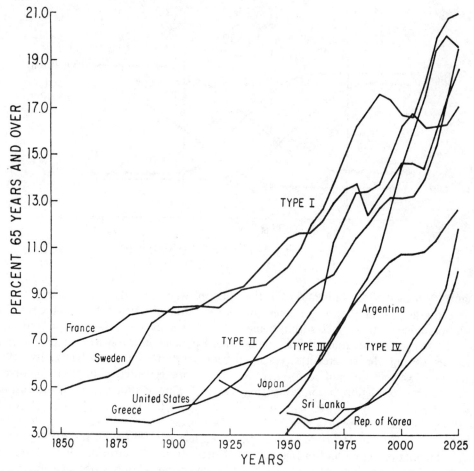

Fig. 2.   Trends in percentage of population 65 years of age and over, selected countries, 1850–2025.
SOURCE: Center for Demographic Studies, Duke University.

regions allow us to review these trends in a broader perspective.

World and Regional Trends

Table 1 shows the number of aged persons in the world and major regions, and the increase to the year 2025, using a base of 100 for the 1980 population. The global aged population of 761 million in 2025 is nearly three times the size of this population in 1980, according to these latest United Nations (1982a) projections. Earlier, more extended projections by the United Nations estimated that there would be 1.2 billion older persons by 2050 and, by the end of the twenty-first century, a further increase to 1.9 billion. It should be noted that nearly all of the persons who will be in the older ages in 2050 have already been born, so the sole factor affecting the number of global aged population in these projections is the mortality assumptions that are introduced over the period.

The growth in the number of older persons is by no means evenly distributed over the countries or regions of the world. A classification used by the United Nations differentiates countries as currently more and less developed. The latter category includes all the countries of Africa, Asia (excluding Japan), Latin America, and Oceania (excluding Australia and New Zealand). In 1980 the number of older persons in the more devel-

TABLE 1. Population 65 Years of Age and Over, Population Increase, and Percent Aged of Total Population, for World and Major Regions 1980-2025.

	Population (in Millions)			Increase (1980 as base = 100)			Percent Aged		
	1980	2000	2025	1980	2000	2025	1980	2000	2025
World	259.4	402.9	760.6	100	155	293	5.8%	6.6%	9.3%
More developed	127.8	166.0	230.3	100	130	180	11.3	13.0	16.7
Less developed	131.7	236.9	530.4	100	180	403	4.0	4.9	7.8
Africa	14.3	27.3	65.9	100	192	462	3.0	3.2	4.3
Latin America	15.5	27.9	61.9	100	179	398	4.3	4.9	7.2
Northern America	26.2	33.1	54.8	100	126	209	10.6	11.1	15.9
East Asia	68.2	116.0	232.4	100	170	340	5.8	7.9	13.6
South Asia	43.8	84.2	195.1	100	192	445	3.1	4.1	6.9
Europe	63.0	74.4	94.9	100	118	151	13.0	14.3	18.2
Oceania	1.8	2.6	4.5	100	147	250	7.9	8.9	12.5
U.S.S.R.	26.6	37.3	51.2	100	140	192	10.0	12.0	14.4

SOURCE: United Nations, *Population Projections Based on Data Assessed in 1980*, Tape Files.

oped countries was quite similar to the figure for less developed countries. In fact, the 1970s are sometimes referred to as a "decade of transition," in which parity was experienced in the distribution of the older persons in each region. However, in the decades ahead the share of the world's total elderly population living in less developed countries will increase markedly. By the year 2025 nearly 70 percent of the world's older population will be found in the developing countries.

This dramatic growth in the aged population is highlighted when one considers the projected trends for major regions. The numerical increase is especially large in East and South Asia. However, the percentage gain is expected to be greatest for Africa. These are all regions that are included under the category of less developed (except for Japan). Among the countries in these regions, it is estimated that China will have 195 million and India 92 million persons 65 years of age and over by the year 2025.

In contrast, the more developed regions, which had quite high growth before 1980, do not show the levels of numerical increase that are expected for less developed regions. Nonetheless, Northern America, Oceania (mainly Australia and New Zealand), and the Soviet Union will have over or close to twice as many older persons in 2025 as in 1980. Even Europe will experience a 50 percent increase in the aged over this period. Within the more developed regions, it is estimated that in 2025 the Soviet Union will have 51 million, and Japan 26 million older persons. Recent projections for the United States forecast 58.6 million older persons by the year 2025 (United States, Bureau of the Census, 1982). This is a considerably larger figure than that incorporated in the United Nations series, which is based on earlier Bureau of the Census calculations.

From the standpoint of the numerical growth of older persons, the aging of the world's population is expected to progress at an impressive rate of over 2 percent a year over the next 55 years. Much of this overall increase is due to the accelerating pace of growth rates for the less developed countries. For less developed countries as a whole, the growth reflects the population momentum produced by sustained high fertility and improved survival in past decades for cohorts of persons who will reach older ages during the first quarter of the twenty-first century—a trend that will continue, incidentally, for some time thereafter. Thus, the annual rates of growth of 2.9 percent for the period 1980–2000 will rise to 3.2 percent per annum between the years 2000 and 2025.

The more developed region will experience a growth rate of 1.3 percent per annum in both periods according to these projections, reflecting in large measure the effect of cohorts of children born in the post–World War II period, who will reach old age after 2012. Only in the Soviet Union does the rate of growth decline between 1980 and the year 2000, from 1.7 to 1.3 percent per annum in the next 25-year period. It is such figures that lend substance to statements that aging has become a worldwide phenomenon that commands attention both in countries now considered developed and in the developing nations of the third world. While the main impact of growing numbers of older persons in less developed countries will be faced in the twenty-first century, the virtual certainty of these developments is well established. Policies to implement the provision of economic and social support to the older population in light of the manifold societal changes that alterations in population structure bring about must be an emerging concern for future generations (Binstock et al., 1982).

The percentage of older persons in the total population, the most frequently used measure to describe the aging of a population, provides a somewhat contrasting view for the more and less developed countries. The figures provided in Table 1 indicate that the proportion of aged persons is nearly three times higher in the set of more developed countries than in the less developed. Moreover, there is a trend toward higher levels in the more developed category, which indicates that 16.7 percent of its total population will be aged by the year 2025. Even the less developed countries, as a whole, will experience nearly a twofold increase in the proportion of aged persons, from 4.0 percent to 7.8 percent over this period.

By region, Europe will continue to lead the way in structural aging, but the most spectacular increase will be in East Asia, from 5.8 percent in 1980 to 13.6 percent in 2025. Africa and South Asia are expected to experience the least change in the proportion of aged, even though, as noted earlier, the two regions will experience the highest relative growth in the numbers of older persons. This seeming paradox can be explained by the fact that the total population in Africa and South Asia is expected to grow at a rapid rate, which makes the sharp increase in the numbers of older persons much less significant in altering the overall distribution toward greater population aging. Thus, the number of older persons can show considerable increase, and even the proportion of aged can rise somewhat, while the total population is growing at very high rates of natural increase. It is in this sense of population momentum that both the total population and the aged population continue to progress by time lags that were depicted in Figure 1.

Determinants of Population Change

The major demographic forces that change the size of a population and its age composition are basically levels of fertility and mortality. These, in turn, directly determine the rates of change, either positively, as they have typically done, or negatively. Measures frequently used to reflect fertility and mortality are the general fertility rate, the annual number of births per 1000 women in the reproductive ages, and the life expectancy at birth. The values shown in Table 2 refer to the levels used in the medium variant projections of the United Nations as assessed in 1980. It should be noted that the parameter

values incorporated into the high or low variant projections would be considerably different from the medium variant, which is often referred as the "best guess" forecast.

The world figures shown here reflect an assumption of sharply declining fertility and increasing survival to the year 2025. The changes forecasted bring about a reduction in total population rates of growth to a level of 1 percent annually. Even with a level of 1 percent, total populations double in a period of 35 years if that level is maintained. The decline in fertility is projected to be very substantial for the less developed set of countries, cutting the prevailing levels almost in half. For these countries, life expectancy gains are anticipated to be very large over this period. For the more developed countries, some decline in fertility is projected for the period up to the year 2000. A modest rise is forecasted thereafter, so that the levels are nearly the same in 2025 as at present. A steady improvement in life expectancy is anticipated, but the change will be much less than for the less developed countries.

Reductions in fertility and gains in overall survival are expected to be particularly large in Africa and South Asia, although the levels for these two regions will still be lower than for other developing regions. The patterns for Latin America are interesting in that less fertility decline and mortality improvement is foreseen, with resulting rates of growth that exceed those in all regions except Africa. What emerges from these figures, which represent one scenario of population change, is increasing convergence among the major regions of the world in terms of both fertility and mortality. Whether fertility and mortality declines of such proportions can be anticipated in less developed regions is a subject of much dispute, especially with respect to the rapidity of change (United Nations, 1982b; Office of Technology Assessment, 1982). Coale (1982) has noted that levels and trends of fertility in less developed countries show great diversity, with examples of both surprisingly little change and of rapid change. On the other hand, the assumptions

TABLE 2. Measures of Fertility, Mortality, and Annual Rates of Growth for World and Major Regions, 1980–2025.

	General Fertility Rate*			Life Expectancy at Birth			Annual Rate of Growth*		
	1980	2000	2025	1980	2000	2025	1980	2000	2025
World	119.4	93.9	71.6	57.5	63.9	70.4	1.7	1.5	1.0
More developed	62.8	58.1	61.5	71.9	73.7	75.4	.7	.5	.2
Less developed	141.0	103.2	73.4	55.0	62.4	69.6	2.1	1.7	1.1
Africa	203.0	174.0	98.1	48.6	57.8	67.2	2.9	2.9	1.9
Latin America	143.5	106.5	84.9	62.5	68.1	71.8	2.4	2.0	1.5
Northern America	64.1	56.4	60.5	73.0	74.0	75.1	.9	.7	.4
East Asia	86.9	62.6	56.5	67.6	72.7	74.8	1.4	1.0	.4
South Asia	160.2	105.6	65.7	50.6	59.4	68.6	2.2	1.7	.9
Europe	59.6	54.0	59.5	72.0	74.3	75.7	.4	.2	.0
Oceania	91.0	74.7	66.8	65.6	70.2	73.8	1.5	1.2	.6
U.S.S.R.	69.8	66.4	65.7	69.6	71.5	74.6	.9	.6	.5

* Rates are averages for the five-year period preceding dates shown.
SOURCE: United Nations, *Population Projections Based on Data Assessed in 1980*, Tape Files.

about the leveling off of life expectancy in more developed regions would seem to represent a more pessimistic outlook than would be held by some investigators (Myers, 1981; Manton, 1982). This is particularly the case for mortality declines at older ages, which tend to increase life expectancy at birth only to a modest extent, but nonetheless would have important effects on the composition of the aged population (Lopez and Hanada, 1982).

Our purpose in providing such overall measures of the demographic factors producing population change is not only to provide descriptive detail, but also to focus attention on the complex interaction of factors that produce the aging of populations. Demographers have examined these phenomena in depth through the application of formal mathematical models of the process (e.g., United Nations, 1954; Coale, 1957, 1964; Hauser, 1976), but it is important to establish empirically that the rapid aging of populations is more than a possibility—it is a reality in the world today and demands an understanding of salient demographic factors that are operative at present and are likely to shape the future.

POPULATION METABOLISM

The second major concept that provides a perspective for the demography of aging concerns the *dynamic* properties that operate to produce the long-term growth of the aged population—a process that we have described previously in terms of population momentum. The central notion of metabolism is drawn from the concept used in biology and physiology to express the sum of processes in the building up and destruction of protoplasm. The analogy to population processes has been most explicitly treated by Ryder in several articles (1964, 1965, 1975), but without explicit reference to the population of older persons. Earlier uses of the concept of "demographic metabolism" were made by the eminent Italian biostatistican and demographer Gini in his 1929 Harris Lectures at the University of Chicago (Gini,

1930), and, a little later, by Sorokin and Anderson (1931). In the first uses of the concept, however, it was applied to the process of cyclical shifts in the social class structure of societies and other social organizations, largely determined, in the case of Gini, through the negative effects of social mobility on fertility.

Applied to a total population, the concept refers to the renewal or replacement process by which a population is modified over time in size and composition. Changes in fertility levels and, to a somewhat lesser extent, mortality levels affect the sizes of different cohorts. These, in turn, may directly influence the future numbers of births and deaths and/or indirectly influence the social contexts that serve to modify behavior. Easterlin (1980) has devoted considerable attention, for example, to the effects of cohort size on fertility and related demographic behavior. The increasing attention to age, period, and cohort effects in the field of social gerontology can be viewed as an extension of the analyses of structural changes upon behavior that have been most thoroughly examined in terms of demographic behavior (e.g., fertility behavior—see Hobcraft et al., 1982).

A consideration of population metabolism for the aged population calls attention to the increments and decrements over time that serve to modify its size and composition. This section considers two aspects of the phenomenon, with the U.S. population used as an example. First, the annual net changes that are projected to occur to the year 2050 are examined. Second, an analysis is undertaken of the components of change and the turnover of the aged population experienced in the intercensal period 1970-80.

Net Change in the Aged Population

A graphic illustration is made in Figure 3 of the annual *net* changes in the older population that are projected for the United States to the year 2050. The shape of the curves reveals the changing sizes of future cohorts of persons as they reach age 65, which are mainly a reflection of fertility levels in the

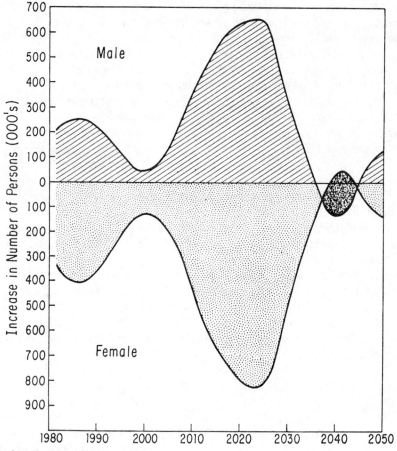

Fig. 3.   Projected annual increase of population aged 65 and over, by sex United States, 1982–2050 (middle series projections). SOURCE: U.S. Bureau of the Census, 1982.

past. Survival also plays a role, however, in terms of mortality levels through the life course as well as in the later ages. These emerging patterns have led some analysts to refer to its "hourglass" form or, in less genteel terms, to a pattern that could result from a pig being ingested by a python.

At the present time a growing number of persons are being added each year to the aged population, but by the mid-1980s a decline in the net addition will have set in. From an annual increase of approximately 600,000 older persons currently, the number will reach a nadir of about 150,000 in 1999. This will be followed by a steady gain in the net additions after the year 2000, a trend that will continue through the early decades of the next century. The smoothed curves pre-

sented here obscure the marked increase in the year 2012 as the first cohorts from the post–World War II baby boom reach age 65, but they do serve to emphasize that the trend is clearly upward as early as the year 2000. For a seven-year period in the early 2020s, over 1.4 million persons will be added each year to the aged population. Thereafter, declining net additions are expected until net deficits are reached in the last years of the 2030s. These deficits will persist for nearly a decade. The projections also reveal that the net increases are greater for females than males throughout this period, reflecting the differentials in mortality that produce higher survival for females than males.

The graph shows the fluctuations in the growth of the aged population that are projected for the United States. These patterns also will be characteristic of most of the more developed countries of the world. The dynamic patterns are of critical importance in gaining an understanding of the process of demographic metabolism. An examination of these "moving waves of population growth," as noted by Grier (1979), provides a necessary and complementary view of the aggregative process of secular growth of the aged population. The societal responses that are made to the demands generated by the size and composition of the aged population, therefore, must be flexible and take into account the short-term as well as the long-term changes.

Turnover

A further step in examining the metabolism of a population is to view the operation of the incremental and decremental elements, as well as the net effect that they have on the *size* of the aged population. The extensive literature on turnover, especially as it is found in organizations, has been reviewed by

Price (1977), with particular attention to the ubiquity of the phenomenon and its implications for social effectiveness. This same theme is noted by Ryder (1975, p. 21): "Every society, and every group within a society, experiences continual turnover of its personnel. From one standpoint that process of demographic metabolism represents a challenge to the preservation of order and stability; from another standpoint it provides a mode of aggregate flexibility and adaptation to change . . . ." Although the specific example that Ryder uses is that of the working-age population, his perspective is one that also can be applied meaningfully to the aged population, a population that as we have suggested is extremely dynamic and subject to significant growth.

In a series of U.S. Bureau of the Census reports (1973, 1976, 1984), Siegel and his associates have presented data on intercensal changes in the aged population of the United States. Table 3 presents the components of change that have been estimated for the United States during the period between 1970 and 1980. It should be noted that the figures

TABLE 3. Estimates of the Demographic Components of Change in the Population 65 Years of Age and Over, United States 1970–80 (Numbers in Thousands).

	Number	Rate (percent)
Population		
July 1, 1980	25,707	
July 1, 1970	20,107	
Change*	5,600	21.8%
Components		
Gains	17,950	89.3
Persons reaching age 65	17,897	
Net migrants	53	
Losses	12,442	61.9
Deaths to 1970 population	10,051	50.0
Deaths to persons reaching age 65	2,391	13.4
Change		
Gross	30,393	
Net to gross		18.4

*Estimate based on census counts. Does not include "errors of closure" that may arise from enumeration discrepancies from both censuses.
SOURCE: Adapted from U.S. Bureau of the Census, "Demographic and Socioeconomic Aspects of Aging in the United States" by Jacob S. Siegel and Maria Davidson, *Current Population Reports,* Series P-23, 1984.

do not precisely balance as they are estimates drawn from two different sources, vital statistics and censuses, the latter being subject to differences in the precision of the enumerations. Nonetheless, they provide important insights into the changes that are occurring within the aged population.

The population 65 years of age and over increased by nearly 22 percent in the ten-year period 1970–80, which added 5.6 million persons to the aged population. This net change resulted from both incremental and decremental forces. The gains amounted to almost 18 million persons, or 90 percent of the 20.1 million older persons found at the beginning of the period. The overwhelming share of the gains came from the entrants, that is, persons who reached the age of 65 during the period. Net migration contributed only an estimated 53,000 persons, reflecting the fact that immigration of older persons accounts for only a small fraction of all immigrants, most of whom are at much younger ages.

Losses to the aged population are the result of deaths occurring to persons who were 65 and over in 1970 and to entrants who reached 65 during the period. The combined death losses represented nearly 62 percent of the initial population. Exactly half of that initial population died in the period, which indicates the high attrition among the aged, who were distributed, of course, at various ages in 1970. In addition, 13.4 percent of the entrants also died in the ten-year period. Thus, even though the average length of stay within the aged population is roughly 16.7 years, as measured by current life tables (United States, National Center for Health Statistics, 1982a), the decrements over a ten-year period are still extremely large.

The gross change accounted for over 30 million "events" of gain and loss, some of which are not independent. This figure greatly exceeds the total aged population at both its initial and terminal points. The "efficiency" of these changes, the ratio of net to gross change, was only 18.4 percent. That is, over five increments and decrements occurred to produce a change of one net addition. From these figures, we can readily grasp the high turnover that characterizes the aged population, even over a ten-year interval.

Another way to determine the rate of turnover is to examine the proportion of the total population who are 65–74 years of age at the end point of the period. These survivors of the total entrants represented 60.9 percent of the total aged population in 1980. This means that only 39.1 percent of the older persons in 1970 survived to the end of the period. The percentage of total entrants has been declining for the United States (in 1960 it was 66.4 percent), even though the numbers reaching age 65 years have increased and their survival to that age improved. The decline also reflects the rather rapid reduction of mortality at the older ages, especially above 74 years of age (United States, National Center for Health Statistics, 1982b). This has resulted in a dramatic increase of the old-old population, especially at extreme ages. Thus, although the rate of turnover has declined somewhat over time, it still remains at a rather high level.

The dynamic change in the older population also can be examined by noting increments and decrements that occur over shorter periods of time than the ten-year intercensal period used in Table 3. For example, it is estimated that each day 5200 persons celebrate their 65th birthday and 3600 older persons die (Brotman, 1982). The net result, exclusive of net migration, is about 1600 persons added to the aged population. As we noted in the earlier section, this number will fluctuate over time, but the growth is still substantial.

In this section, we have examined the dynamic properties of change in the aged population that reflect on population metabolism. The emphasis has been on the numbers of persons entering and exiting from the aged population, but it also is important to consider the characteristics of these persons and the aggregate changes in composition that emerge through this process of metabolism.

POPULATION DIVERSITY

The last concept to be considered is diversity, which has been widely used in a number of disciplines and contexts, but with little rigorous specification. As Patil and Taillie (1982) point out in a recent review, "a common theme is that of the apportionment of some quantity into a number of well-defined categories" (p. 548). This is analogous to the demographer's concern with examining the composition of a population. A consideration of population diversity, therefore, calls attention to how a population is differentiated on a range of demographic and social characteristics, calling particular attention to the relative distribution among categories.

The term seems especially appropriate for application to the aged population, for the aged are often viewed as becoming more heterogeneous over time. It may be as important to consider the disaggregative properties of this population, therefore, as to consider the gross increase in their number and proportion. It also is possible to examine diversity in terms of how the aged differ from the total population of younger persons, but in this section the focus is on variation within the older population itself. This is in keeping with our intent to regard the aged as a subpopulation. However, acknowledgment also should be given to the fact that intercohort factors, arising from the full life course, are crucial in determining the characteristics of persons who survive to the older ages and may serve, thereby, to change the overall characteristics of the total aged population.

The diversity is a clear manifestation of population metabolism through which the composition of the aged population may change over time as a result of entering cohorts having different characteristics from those characteristics of persons in preceding cohorts who are dying (Uhlenberg, 1977). It is also the case, as noted earlier, that some characteristics may be altered through changes occurring among older persons themselves. These may be due both to biological factors, such as individual aging or selective mortality of related persons (e.g., spouses), and to behavioral factors (e.g., remarriage and other changes in status). It is interesting to note that many of the compositional factors are most influenced by changes in mortality levels, whereas the size and proportion of the aged population is more deeply affected by changes in fertility levels.

There is a vast array of demographic and social characteristics of the aged population that are both possible and important to study. In this section, a number of characteristics have been selected to demonstrate important changes in the population composition of the aged that have taken place in the past and are likely to continue in the future. Uhlenberg (1977) and Winsborough (1980) have called attention to the transitional nature of many trends that tend to alter population composition. Trends measured as proportions or other descriptive aggregate measures often follow an s-shaped distribution, in much the same fashion as the growth curves presented earlier—slowing rising, then accelerating, and finally leveling off as they reach an asymptote. For example, the percent of population living in urban places, differences in educational levels between generations, and mortality are often cited in this regard. The leveling-off of trends influencing the composition of the aged population may be true, particularly for countries in which socioeconomic development and the demographic transitions have proceeded for some time.

Age

In preceding sections, we have documented the increasing growth of the aged population and the aging of total populations. It also is the case that most aged populations are themselves growing older. These changes are most notable among the very old, or what might be termed the old-old or extreme aged (Neugarten, 1974). On a global level, nearly 14 percent of the *older* population is estimated to be 80 years of age and over. In more developed countries, the figure is 16.8 percent, compared with 11.1 percent in less developed countries (Myers, 1982). The trend has been upward in both more and less developed regions, and it is projected that the share of the aged population at extreme ages will continue to increase in the future.

The changing age distribution of the aged population can be readily grasped in the projected figures for the United States that are presented in Table 4. From 1980 to the year 2000, the numbers of older persons are expected to increase across all age categories, but the numerical gains are particularly large in the 80–84 and 85-and-over intervals. The percentage distribution that results shows a decline in the first two categories, ages 65–69 and 70–74, and increasing proportions of persons 75 years of age and over. It has been suggested by some writers (e.g., Uhlenberg, 1979) that the relatively slow growth of the total aged population to the year 2000 should

allow a "breathing spell" period in which constructive institutional responses can be made to some of the current problems produced by past rapid growth of the aged population. These figures make it clear, however, that considerable aging within the subpopulation will be experienced during this period, which may give rise to additional issues not foreseen by a focus on the aged population as a whole.

In the ensuing 25-year period up to the year 2025, the large cohorts noted previously will reach older ages and swell the size of the young-old intervals, but numerical gains also are projected for all age intervals, including the extreme aged. Under assumptions adopted for these projections, the two oldest age intervals will experience very large growth to the midpoint of the next century. At that time nearly a quarter of the aged population will be 85 years of age and over.

These projections show the trend toward

TABLE 4. Selected Statistics on Population 65 Years of Age and Over, United States (Middle Series Projections to Year 2050) (Numbers in Thousands).

	1980*	2000	2025	2050
Total population	25,708	35,036	58,636	67,060
Percent aged	11.3	13.1	19.5	21.1
Ages—Number				
65–69	8,805	9,110	18,314	16,591
70–74	6,843	8,583	13,774	13,431
75–79	4,815	7,242	11,103	11,352
80–84	2,972	4,965	6,767	9,624
85 +	2,274	5,136	7,678	16,063
Ages—Percent	100.0	100.0	100.0	100.0
65–69	34.2	26.0	31.2	24.7
70–74	26.6	24.5	25.2	20.0
75–79	18.7	20.7	18.9	16.9
80–84	11.6	14.2	11.5	14.4
85 +	8.8	14.6	13.1	24.0
Sex ratio	67.5	64.5	70.3	67.6
65–69	80.0	82.1	87.4	89.6
70–74	72.4	74.2	79.6	82.6
75–79	62.7	64.3	69.8	73.4
80–84	53.0	54.0	58.2	62.4
85 +	43.6	37.2	36.9	40.4
Percent nonwhite of total aged	9.3	10.9	14.5	19.0

* July 1, 1980 Estimates.
SOURCE: U.S. Bureau of the Census, Projections of the population of the United States: 1982 to 2050 (advance report), *Current Population Reports,* Series P-25, No. 922, Oct. 1982.

increasing diversity by age among the older population. There are fluctuations, to be sure, but the tendency is for a considerably older population. A major implication of these changes is the increasing survival of persons to ages that usually entail elevated levels of disability, ill-health, and general support needs.

Sex

A major variation that has accompanied the aging of population has been the increasing proportion of females at older ages. This has resulted from sex differentials in mortality that favor females at all ages, thus producing higher proportions of females than males surviving to old age and passing through the later years of life. The current sex ratio (the ratio of males to females) for the world's aged population is estimated to be 75.0—that is, three males for every four females (Myers, 1982). The relative share of women is particularly imbalanced in the world's more developed countries (62.4) compared with the less developed countries (89.6). The trends in both regions, however, have been toward lower sex ratios.

Table 4 also provides a view of the trends anticipated for the United States, based on current official projections. From a current level of 67.5, ratios are expected to decline further through the end of the century, then rise somewhat as large entry cohorts, in which sex ratios are higher, enter the aged population. A decline to the same sex ratio level as in 1980 is forecasted for the year 2050, as some convergence for mortality levels is introduced into the projections. There is considerable controversy among demographers as to whether such a convergence can be expected, for the trend has certainly been in the other direction—toward increased divergence, as mortality rates have fallen for both sexes, but at a faster pace for females (Siegel, 1980; Kitagawa, 1977).

A closer examination of variations in sex ratios by age within the aged population itself reveals sharp declines in the ratio with increasing age. In 1980, among persons 80 years of age and over, there were two females for every male. Moreover, there is a decline projected in the sex ratio for the oldest age category up to at least the year 2025, although all other age intervals show progressively higher levels. In short, in the United States, and in most other developed countries, the aged population has shown a strong tendency in the past to become more comprised of females. While the sex ratios for the total aged are expected to continue declining well into the next century, there may be some slight convergence in all but the most extreme age interval. As noted earlier, this is also the age interval in which the greatest proportionate growth will be experienced.

Race and Ethnicity

The extent to which societies are homogeneous with respect to race and ethnicity depends largely on such historical factors as immigration and subsequent levels of fertility and mortality. This is particularly true for the aged population, as prior conditions play a central role in determining population composition for these ascribed characteristics.

In the United States the major waves of immigration occurred in the nineteenth and early twentieth centuries, although significant movement of persons from the Western Hemisphere and Asia has occurred recently. In terms of foreign-born persons, Uhlenberg (1977) notes that the percentage of white foreign-born persons in the age category 60–64 has dropped from a third of the population in 1900 to about 6 percent in 1980. However, this percentage is expected to increase to nearly 8 percent by the year 2000. The nativity composition of the aged population has clearly become less diverse in this century, but some tendency in the opposite direction is expected to occur in subsequent decades as cohorts of more recent immigrants (e.g., Vietnamese, Cubans) reach the older ages.

The proportion of nonwhites in the United States at older ages generally has been smaller than the proportion for whites (blacks, incidentally, represent about 88 percent of these nonwhites at older ages). In 1980, 11.9 percent of the total white population was at older ages, compared with only 7.8 of the nonwhite population. The trend over time has been toward increasingly higher proportions of aged persons among nonwhites, just as it has been for whites. The proportions of nonwhites who are aged are projected to continue increasing in the future. In conjunction with relatively larger cohorts of nonwhites than whites reaching old age, the proportion that nonwhites constitute of the aged population also will continue to rise. Table 4 presents these figures as the percentage of the total aged population that is nonwhite. A slight increase is projected between 1980 and 2000, but thereafter marked upward shifts are expected. By the year 2050, nearly a fifth of all aged persons will be nonwhite. Thus, with respect to race and ethnicity, the trend clearly is toward greater diversity of the aged population.

Marital Status

Another characteristic that can be examined in terms of diversity is the marital status of older persons. The importance of this characteristic rests not only on its meaning for individuals, but also on its impact upon the family status, living arrangements, and support systems of older persons. The composition of the aged population with respect to marital status is influenced by complex patterns of family formation and dissolution that vary cross-culturally, as well as by the important constraints imposed by differential mortality of males and females (Myers and Nathanson, 1982).

In the process of the demographic transition, most Western societies have experienced trends toward universal marriage and marriage at younger ages, patterns that ironically characterize most less developed countries at present. The reduced mortality that distinguishes the transition brings about greatly lengthened durations of marriage, as the joint survival of both males and females is extended (Ryder, 1975). However, the widening gap in survival between the sexes, which we noted earlier in this section, also creates a situation in which widowhood for females becomes common at older ages. Under the less favorable mortality conditions found in less developed countries, the likelihood of experiencing widowhood before reaching old age tends to be high; whereas in more developed countries higher proportions survive to older ages in intact family situations, but eventually become widows. Marital dissolution through divorce or separation, and remarriage in later life, are additional factors that must be considered. The net effect of these forces, in concert with changes in the number of older persons as a whole and at different ages, is a subject that has recently started to attract demographic attention (Goldman and Lord, 1983; Espenshade and Braun, 1982).

Myers (1982) has found that there is general similarity between the distributions by marital status for both older males and females among a large number of countries, including those less and more developed. For older males, between 65 and 80 percent are currently married, while another 10 to 20 percent are widowed. In contrast, the overall proportion of older females who are married ranges between 25 and 30 percent and those widowed between 50 to 65 percent. In a number of European countries and many countries in the Western Hemisphere the proportions of never-married males and females are quite high (10 to 20 percent). The proportion of older persons who are divorced is invariably less than 5 percent for this period of time.

Between 1950 and 1970, the trend for virtually every country was toward higher proportions of both older males and older females married, especially males, and lower proportions widowed. In general, the relative levels of never-married persons declined, while the proportion of divorced persons increased slightly. When age is considered, there are clear increases by age for both males and females, as might be expected, but the trends still follow the general patterns noted above. Finally, it should be noted that remarriage at older ages plays a relatively small part in modifying the marital status distributions, especially for females, although remarriage at earlier ages can have an important bearing on those reaching age 65 and, subsequently, being enumerated as currently married.

Masnick and Bane (1980) report on U.S. projections of marital status by age and find that little change can be expected in the proportions of older persons never-married and widowed to 1990. However, they provide clear evidence that cohorts reaching the older ages after 1990 will be more likely to be divorced or separated and less likely to be married with spouse present. Because of the substantially higher proportions of divorced or separated persons in younger cohorts who will reach the older ages in subsequent periods, considerably more diversity will characterize the aged population in the future with respect to marital status.

A dimension of family life that is closely related to marital status is the extent to which trends in mortality and fertility affect kin relations and multigenerational families for older persons. Shanas and Hauser (1974) and Shanas and Sussman (1981) have pointed out the emerging development of the four-generation family with the lengthening of life, especially in more developed countries. Even with regimes of replacement-level fertility that lead to a stationary population, it is anticipated that the expected number of living siblings will increase in the next few decades for persons in the older ages and, correspondingly, the number of living parents also will increase (Hammel et al., 1981). Wolf (1983) has estimated that 91 percent of males aged 65–69 in the year 2000 will have a living child and 22 percent at least one living parent. Although there is agreement that these trends are not likely to lead to any reversal in the pattern of independent living arrangements, the aged population in the decades ahead should have more living relations of different generations and, therefore, greater potential sources of social and material support (Soldo, 1981). However, the long-term trend at a point of population sta-

tionarity may well result in more restricted availability of kin of various types for a high proportion of the population (Pullum, 1982). Thus, there is considerable evidence for more diverse patterns of family life that will emerge in the future, given continuation of present demographic trends.

Geographic Patterns and Movement

In this final section on population diversity, consideration is given to the spatial characteristics of older persons and the factors that are operating to modify existing patterns. On a worldwide level, rural areas have tended to have higher proportions of older persons than urban areas (Myers, 1982). This is particularly true in less developed countries of Asia and Africa, but, interestingly, it is not the case in Latin American countries. The same pattern holds for more developed countries, although the differentials are rather small. These patterns are thought to reflect the "aging-in-place" phenomenon, in which selective outmigration of younger persons to urban areas leaves a considerably older population behind.

When these broad categories of rural and urban are disaggregated, however, other patterns of concentration emerge. In rural areas, it is found that small towns compared with rural-farm areas contain considerably higher proportions of the aged. An explanation for this no doubt lies in the movement of older persons from farms into towns in close geographic proximity after farm labor becomes too onerous for them. In the case of urban areas, it is often noted that central cities contain higher concentrations of older persons than suburban areas. This undoubtedly reflects the movement of younger families from central cities, which correspondingly serves to raise the proportions of aged persons in central cities. Thus, a primary element shaping these distributions lies in the migratory behavior of the younger segment of the population, which produces characteristic patterns of geographic distribution for less mobile older persons.

There is recent evidence, however, that the

residential movement of older persons is also a phenomenon of considerable importance in understanding the distributional patterns of the aged population, especially for areas of substantial in- or outmigration. In addition, movement has a major impact on older persons themselves, far greater than we might be led to expect from the percentage moving among this age group. Although it is frequently noted that rates of movement for older persons are lower than for other age categories of the population, the rates are not insignificant. For example, in the United States 28 percent of persons aged 65 years and over in 1970 changed their residence at least once between 1965 and 1970 (Wiseman, 1980). Not only does the relative amount of movement differ between younger and older categories of the population; but the types of moves, the determinants of mobility, and the consequences may also be quite different. These distinctive features of movement among the aged have recently served to generate several concerted research efforts in the United States, France, and England (see, e.g., Longino and Jackson, 1980; Warnes, 1982a; Cribier, 1980).

Lee (1980) points out that the likelihood of residential movement is strongly tied to points in the life course in which important events occur. In a real sense, movement can be viewed as a "coping response of an individual seeking an environment more congruent with stage-in-life related goals or needs" (Golant, 1980). Mobility rates are high during childhood, when family formation necessitates housing shifts; fall during the teens; then rise again in the late teens and early twenties as schooling ends and employment and family formation occur. A steady decline in rates appears to occur in most societies from about age 25 through to age 65, when the rates rise in connection with retirement. A decline follows, but is followed by rising levels after age 75 during the terminal phase of life. Thus, two of the three periods of increasing movement, in fact, are found at older ages, which suggests dynamic properties affecting the elderly that result in movement.

With growing numbers of older persons, the amount of movement among the aged has naturally grown, and there are even signs that the proportion moving also is increasing (Lee, 1980). Much of this movement accompanies retirement, a time in which locational restraints arising from employment are relaxed. Changes in the extent of retirement movement are tied to retirement at earlier ages, the increasing proportion of intact husband–wife families at older ages resulting from increasing joint survival, and the improved financial status of older persons.

A number of studies in the United States and other countries have pointed to the fact that movement over longer distances has been characteristic of recent migration patterns of the elderly. This movement may represent a return to areas of origin, an opportunity to be closer to relatives or friends, or a shift in residence to more suitable environmental circumstances, as, for example, in the case of migration of so-called snowbirds to areas with warmer climates (Serow, 1978; Warnes, 1982b). This longer-distance movement is often out of urban industrial centers toward nonmetropolitan areas, a phenomenon in part responsible for the remarkable growth of nonmetropolitan regions in the past decade that has been observed in many Western countries—France, Great Britain, and the United States, for example. In the United States, recent studies have revealed that older persons not only participated in the significant movement from metropolitan to nonmetropolitan areas that began in the late 1960s, but actually may have led the way in that movement (Longino, 1982; Lichter et al., 1981).

Thus, these developing trends in the movement of older persons are bringing a greater diversity in their patterns of residence. The result is the redistribution of the aged to areas that are more suitable environmentally, a shift that calls attention to emerging needs for new amenities and services. Although these are patterns that mainly characterize more developed, industrialized societies, the increasing mobility of older persons, even in developing countries, is a phenomenon that demands close investigation.

SUMMARY

This review of the nascent field of demography of aging has drawn attention to selected aspects of this complex topic. The intent has been to present not only a view of the accelerating population aging that is characteristic of both more and less developed countries, but to examine the dynamic forces that have shaped this growth in the past and are likely to operate in the future. By concentrating attention on the aged population as a distinctive subpopulation, additional insights are provided for studying its heterogeneous nature and the continuing need for disaggregative analyses. Thus, it would appear that an appropriate conceptual framework is in place for furthering research on salient issues in the demography of aging. A similar judgment can be made of the necessary methodological approaches for research in the field, which include formal demographic methods, such as life table, stable population, projection techniques, and other mathematical models, as well as multivariate analytic methods that can be used for examining microdata sets from censuses and surveys.

However, a major limitation for research developments in the field has been the relative paucity of suitable data, especially with sufficient specificity at older ages. This is being overcome, in part, by the increasing use of computerized microdata sets, which provide detailed information on individuals and, therefore, provide more disaggregated data than typically has been the case in published data reports. Examples are the public-use sample tapes from censuses, periodic national sample surveys (e.g., the United States Current Population Survey and the Federal Republic of Germany's Microcensus), and detailed mortality records. Another interesting development has been the promise of greater availability of data from linked records, such as from the National Death Index, longitudinal study files, and other integrated data systems. There also is evidence that a systematic cross-national database will be established to supplement the rather meager population data on the aged that are now collected by the United Nations and published in the Demographic Yearbooks.

The availability of more extensive demographic data must be accompanied by greater attention to assessment of the quality of data, especially in terms of age accuracy. For example, considerable attention has been given in the past to the number of centenarians in a population, particularly in certain areas of the world where it is believed that there exist large proportions of extremely longevous persons (e.g., Vilcabamba in southern Ecuador, Abkhazia in the Caucasus of the Soviet Union). Careful data assessment and life table analyses for these areas have demonstrated convincingly that reports of extreme longevity are greatly exaggerated and that little evidence can be substantiated for such claims (Mazess and Mathisen, 1982; Palmore, 1984). Apart from the issue relating to centenarians, there is clearly a need to examine the effects of age misstatement for older persons more generally. Horiuchi and Coale (1982) have addressed this issue with respect to the estimation of life expectancy at older ages and reach the conclusion that substantial adjustments are required for intercountry comparisons, especially for less-developed countries. In addition to the question of age accuracy, there also exists the matter of the undercoverage of persons of older age in census enumerations and death reporting. Careful consideration of these methodological topics is a particularly appropriate field of interest for persons engaged in the demography of aging.

Finally, we have drawn attention in this review to the importance of projections of the aged population, not only in terms of total size but also in terms of other characteristics of older persons. An expanded data base will permit ''interactive projections'' that will enable analyses to be made of the social and economic implications of demographic developments implicit in the aging process. This will have an important bearing on public policy decision-making that is needed for constructive responses to be made for an aging society. Thus, the research agenda for the demography of aging must be expanded to include consideration of the *demographics* of aging—the consequences of future population changes.

As the demography of aging emerges as an established disciplinary focus, it should provide alternative opportunities for demographers to apply both substantive and methodological formulations, developed for other purposes, to the study of aging and the aged population. To date, most demographers have come to study these phenomena as simply another aspect of general demography. The field of the demography of aging will be enriched by integrated and concerted efforts at developing training and research in both social gerontology and demography.

REFERENCES

Binstock, R. H., Chow, W. S., and Schulz, J. H. (eds.). 1982. *International Perspectives on Aging: Population and Policy Challenges.* New York: United Nations Fund for Population Activities.

Bourgeois-Pichat, J. 1965. The general development of the population of France since the eighteenth century. *In* D. V. Glass and D. E. C. Eversley (eds.), *Population in History: Essays in Historical Demography,* pp. 474–493. Chicago: Aldine.

Bourgeois-Pichat, J. 1979. La transition demographique: Vieillissement de la population (The demographic transition: Aging of population). *In: Population Science in the Service of Mankind,* pp. 211–239. Liege: International Union for the Scientific Study of Population.

Brotman, H. B. 1982. *Every Ninth American (1982 Edition).* An analysis for the chairman of the Select Committee on Aging, House of Representatives Comm. Pub. No. 97–332. Washington, D.C.: U.S. Government Printing Office.

Coale, A. J. 1957. How the age distribution of a human population is determined. *Cold Spring Harbor Symposia on Quantitative Biology* 22:83–89.

Coale, A. J. 1964. How a population ages or grows younger. *In* R. Freedman (ed.), *Population: The Vital Revolution.* New York: Doubleday & Company.

Coale, A. J. 1982. A reassessment of world population trends. *Population Bulletin of the United Nations* ST/ESA/SER.N/14:1–16.

Cribier, F. 1980. A European assessment of aged migration. *Research on Aging* 2:255–270.

Dublin, L. I. 1928. *Health and Wealth: A Survey of the Economics of World Health,* Ch. VII, The problem of old age, pp. 149–168. New York and London: Harper and Brothers.

Dublin, L. I., and A. J. Lotka. 1937. *Length of Life: A Study of the Life Table.* New York: Ronald Press.

Easterlin, R. A. 1980. *Birth and Fortune: The Impact of Numbers on Personal Welfare.* New York: Basic Books.

Espenshade, T. J., and Braun, R. E. 1982. Life course analysis and multistate demography: An application to marriage, divorce, and remarriage. *Journal of Marriage and the Family* 44:1025–1036.

Frejka, T. 1981. Long-term prospects for world population growth. *Population and Development Review* 7:489–511.

Gini, C. 1930. The cyclical rise and fall of population. *In: Population,* pp. 3–140. Chicago: University of Chicago Press.

Golant, S. M. 1980. Future directions for elderly migration research. *Research on Aging* 2:271–280.

Goldman, N., and Lord, G. 1983. Sex differences in life cycle measures of widowhood. *Demography* 20:177–195.

Grier, G. 1979. *Aging in the Future: The Changing Societal Environment.* Washington, D.C.: International Center for Social Gerontology Symposium on White House Conferences as Agents of Social Change.

Hammel, E. A., Wachter, K. W., and McDaniel, C. K. 1981. The kin of the aged in A.D. 2000: The chickens come home to roost. *In* S. B. Kiesler, J. N. Morgan, and V. K. Oppenheimer (eds.), *Aging: Social Change,* pp. 11–39. New York: Academic Press.

Hauser, P. M. 1976. Aging and world-wide population change. *In* R. H. Binstock and E. Shanas (eds.), *Handbook of Aging and the Social Sciences,* 1st ed., pp. 58–86. New York: Van Nostrand Reinhold.

Hobcraft, J., Menken, J., and Preston, S. 1982. Age, period, and cohort effects in demography: A review. *Population Index* 48:4–43.

Horiuchi, S., and Coale, A. J. 1982. A simple equation for estimating the expectation of life at old ages. *Population Studies* 36:317–326.

Keyfitz, N. 1977. *Applied Mathematical Demography.* New York: John Wiley.

Kiesler, S. B. 1981. The aging population, social trends, and changes of behavior and belief. *In* S. B. Kiesler, J. N. Morgan, and V. K. Oppenheimer (eds.), *Aging: Social Change,* pp. 41–74. New York: Academic Press.

Kitagawa, E. 1977. On mortality. *Demography* 14:381–389.

Lee, E. S. 1980. Migration of the aged. *Research on Aging* 2:131–135.

Lichter, D. T., Fuguitt, G. V., Heaton, T. B., and Clifford, W. B. 1981. Components of change in the residential concentration of the elderly population: 1950–1975. *Journal of Gerontology* 36:480–489.

Longino, C. F., Jr. 1982. Changing aged nonmetropolitan migration patterns, 1955 to 1960 and 1965 to 1970. *Journal of Gerontology* 37:228–234.

Longino, C. F., Jr. and Jackson, D. J. (eds.). 1980. Migration and the aged. Special Issue of *Research on Aging* 2:131–280.

Lopez, A. D., and Hanada, K. 1982. Mortality patterns and trends among the elderly in developed countries. *World Health Statistics Quarterly*. 35:203–224.

Manton, K. G. 1982. Changing concepts of morbidity and mortality in the elderly population. *Milbank Memorial Fund Quarterly/Health and Society* 60:183–244.

Masnick, G., and Bane, M. J. 1980. *The Nation's Families: 1960–1990*. Cambridge, Mass.: Joint Center for Urban Studies of MIT and Harvard University.

Mazess, R. B., and Mathisen, R. W. 1982. Lack of unusual longevity in Vilcabamba, Ecuador. *Human Biology* 54:517–524.

Myers, G. C. 1981. Future age projections and society. *In* A. J. J. Gilmore et al. (eds.), *Aging: A Challenge and Social Policy*, Vol. II, pp. 248–260. Oxford: Oxford University Press.

Myers, G. C. 1982. The aging of populations. *In* R. H. Binstock, W. S. Chow, and J. H. Schulz (eds.), *International Perspectives on Aging: Population and Policy Challenges*, pp. 1–39. New York: United Nations Fund for Population Activities.

Myers, G. C. 1982. Cross-national variations in marital patterns among the elderly. Paper presented at Gerontological Society annual meeting, Boston, Mass.: November, 1982.

Myers, G. and Nathanson, C. 1982. Aging and the Family. *World Health Statistics Quarterly* 35:225–238.

Neugarten, B. L. 1974. Age groups in America, society and the rise of the young-old. *In* F. R. Eisele (ed.), *Political Consequences of Aging. The Annals of the American Academy of Political and Social Sciences*, 415:187–198.

Nihon University. 1982. *Population in Aging in Japan: Problems and Policy Issues in 21st Century*. Report for International Symposium on an Aging Society: Strategies for the 21st Century Japan, Tokyo.

Office of Technology Assessment. 1982. *World Population and Fertility Planning Technologies: The Next 20 Years*. Washington, D.C.: U.S. Government Printing Office.

Palmore, E. B. 1984. Longevity in Abkhazia: A reevaluation. *The Gerontologist*. 24:95–96.

Patil, G. P., and Taillie, C. 1982. Diversity as a concept and its measurement. *Journal of the American Statistical Association* 77:548–561.

Pearl, R. 1940. The aging of populations. *Journal of the American Statistical Association* 209:277–297.

Price, J. L. 1977. *The Study of Turnover*. Ames, Iowa: Iowa State University Press.

Pullum, T. W. 1982. The eventual frequencies of kin in a stable population. *Demography* 19:549–565.

Riley, M. W. 1973. Aging and cohort succession: Interpretations and misinterpretations. *Public Opinion Quarterly* 37:35–49.

Rosset, E. 1964. *Aging Process of Population*. New York: Macmillan.

Ryder, N. 1964. Notes on the concept of a population. *American Journal of Sociology* 69:447–463.

Ryder, N. 1965. The cohort as a concept in the study of social change. *American Sociological Review* 30:843–861.

Ryder, N. 1975. Notes on stationary populations. *Population Index* 41:3–28.

Serow, W. J. 1978. Return migration of the elderly in the USA: 1955–1960 and 1965–1970. *Journal of Gerontology* 33:288–295.

Shanas, E., and Hauser, P. M. 1974. Zero population growth and the family life of old people. *Journal of Social Issues* 30:79–92.

Shanas, E., and Sussman, M. B. 1981. The family in later life: Social structure and social policy. *In* R. W. Fogel et al. (eds.), *Aging: Stability and Change in the Family*, pp. 211–231. New York: Academic Press.

Siegel, J. S. 1980. On the demography of aging. *Demography* 17:345–364.

Siegel, J. S. 1981. Demographic background for international gerontological studies. *Journal of Gerontology* 36:93–102.

Siegel, J. S. and Hoover, S. L. 1982. Demographic aspects of the health of the elderly to the year 2000 and beyond. *World Health Statistics Quarterly*. 35:133–202.

Soldo, B. J. 1981. The living arrangements of the elderly in the near future. *In* S. B. Kiesler, J. N. Morgan, and V. K. Oppenheimer (eds.), *Aging: Social Changes*, pp. 491–512. New York: Academic Press.

Sorokin, P. A. and Anderson, C. A. 1931. Metabolism of different strata on social institutions and institutional continuity (Comitato Italiano per lo studio dei problemi della populazione). Rome: Instituto Poligrafico dello Stato.

Spengler, J. J. 1979. *France Faces Depopulation: Postlude Edition, 1936–1976*. Durham, N.C.: Duke University Press.

Sundbärg, G. 1894. *Grundragen Af Befolkningslaren*. Stockholm.

Sundbärg, G. 1900. Sur la repartition de la population par age et sur les taux de mortalite (On the separation of the population by age and the rates of mortality), *Bulletin of the International Institute of Statistics* 12:89–94.

Thompson, W. S., and Whelpton, P. K. 1930. A nation of elders in the making. *American Mercury* 19:385–397.

Thompson, W. S., and Whelpton, P. K. 1933. *Population Trends in the United States*. New York: McGraw-Hill.

Uhlenberg, P. 1977. Changing structure of the older

population of the USA during the twentieth century. *The Gerontologist* 17:197–202.

Uhlenberg, P. 1979. Demographic change and problems of the aged. *In* M. W. Riley (ed.), *Aging from Birth to Death: Interdisciplinary Perspectives,* AAAS Selected Symposium Series No. 30, pp. 153–166. Boulder, Colo.: Westview Press.

United Nations. 1954. The cause of the aging of populations: Declining mortality or declining fertility? *Population Bulletin of the United Nations* ST/SOA/SER.N/4:30–38.

United Nations. 1956. *The Aging of Populations and Its Economic and Social Implications,* ST/SOA/SER.A/26. New York: United Nations.

United Nations. 1982a. *Demographic Indicators of Countries: Estimates and Projections as Assessed in 1980,* ST/ESA/SER.A/82. New York: United Nations.

United Nations. 1982b. *Levels and Trends of Mortality Since 1950,* ST/ESA/SER.A/74. New York: United Nations.

United Nations. 1982c. *Report of the World Assembly on Aging,* A/CONF.113/31. New York: United Nations.

United States, Bureau of the Census. 1973. Some demographic aspects of aging in the United States, *Current Population Reports,* Series P-23, No. 43. Washington, D.C.: U.S. Government Printing Office.

United States, Bureau of the Census. 1976. Demographic aspects of aging and the older population in the United States, *Current Population Reports,* Series P-23, No. 59. Washington, D.C.: U.S. Government Printing Office.

United States, Bureau of the Census. 1982. Projections of the population of the United States: 1982 to 2050 (advance report), *Current Population Reports,* Series

P-25, No. 922. Washington, D.C.: U.S. Government Printing Office.

United States, Bureau of the Census. 1984. Demographic and socioeconomic aspects of aging in the United States, J. S. Siegel and M. Davidson, *Current Population Reports,* Series P-23. Washington, D.C.: U.S. Government Printing Office.

United States, National Center for Health Statistics. 1982a. Annual summary of births, deaths, marriages, and divorces: United States, 1981, *Monthly Vital Statistics Report,* Vol. 30, No. 13. Washington, D.C.: U.S. Government Printing Office.

United States, National Center for Health Statistics. 1982b. Changes in mortality among the elderly: United States, 1940–78, L. Fingerhut, *Vital and Health Statistics, Analytical Studies,* Series 3, No. 22. Washington, D.C.: U.S. Government Printing Office.

Warnes, A. M. (ed.). 1982a. *Geographical Perspectives on the Elderly.* London: John Wiley.

Warnes, A. M. (ed.). 1982b. The destination decision in retirement migration. *In: Geographical Perspectives on the Elderly,* pp. 53–81. London: John Wiley.

Winsborough, H. H. 1980. A demographic approach to the life cycle. *In* K. W. Back (ed.), *Life Course: Integrative Theories and Exemplary Populations,* AAAS Selected Symposium 41. Boulder, Colo.: Westview Press.

Wiseman, R. F. 1980. Why older people move: Theoretical issues. *Research on Aging* 2:141–154.

Wolf, D. A. 1983. *Kinship and the Living Arrangements of Older Americans.* Washington, D.C.: The Urban Institute.

Wulf, D. 1982. Low fertility in Europe: A report from the 1981 IUSSP meeting. *Family Planning Perspectives* 14:264–270.

8
SOCIETAL DEVELOPMENT AND AGING

Peter Laslett
Cambridge Group for the History of Population and Social Structure

INTRODUCTORY, HISTORICAL SOCIOLOGY IN RELATION TO AGING

Historical sociology is the study appropriate to the examination of societal development and aging, that is, the question of how the process of aging and the position of the aged have changed over time. But historical sociology is the newest and least developed of the social sciences, first emerging as a distinct study in the mid-1960s. Little can yet be expected, therefore, in the way of considered conclusions; the area of knowledge is still small, and theoretical principles are scanty and mostly untried. What is advanced in this chapter must be very tentative and subject to rapid obsolescence.

There are three sources of historical information on aging:

1. Running records of births, marriages, and deaths.
2. Census documents of the statistical era and census-type documents from earlier times.
3. Literary and plastic materials.

Literary and Plastic Data on Aging in the Past

The third of these sources has easily the greatest chronological span and goes as far back as the earliest representation of human individuals whose state of maturity can be recognized—the cave paintings of southern Europe, perhaps, or the iconography of the Egyptian treatment of the dead. But little can be made of such evidence until the epoch is reached when written materials survive in sufficient quantity to give meaning to pictures, statues, and monuments and to provide a representation of aging and the aged that can be both interesting and revealing, though it is usually fragmentary. The span of centuries open to examination, therefore, is confined for practical purposes in the case of Europe to the 2500 years that have elapsed since surviving Greek and Hebrew writings were first set down, and for Asia presumably since the Chou dynasty in China, going some 500 years further back. This is an exceedingly shallow tract of time from which to make assertions about human development.

Until the recent growth of historical demography, literary and plastic materials were virtually the only sources consulted when questions of aging were considered, and the class of evidence for the past most favored by the sociologist, the psychologist, or the gerontologist was probably what might be called high literature. Appeal was made, therefore, to Cicero's *De Senectute,* or to Vasari's life of Titian, or to Shakespeare's *King Lear,* or even to Jane Austen's Mr.

Woodhouse, when a contrast was to be drawn between what happens now and what used to happen, or when some particular recommendation was thought to need historical legitimation. When this subject was pursued outside the European arena, similar use was made of similar materials, such as, for example, the early Japanese novel. These tales were apparently just as realistic in their portrayal of the old, their attitudes, and attitudes toward them, as any of the classics of our own cultural tradition, perhaps even more so.

But high literature is only a small part, and in some ways a rather deceptive part, if taken on its own, of materials of this kind. If, however, diaries, letters, poems, sermons, plays, novels, and so on, are supplemented by medical observations, legal regulations, and court cases, by recordings made for economic and political purposes, and by funerary practices and funerary iconography as well as by works of art, it is notable how much relevant evidence can be assembled. There are attractive instances of this in the writings of the French historian Philippe Ariès (see, e.g., his work on childhood and family life, 1962; and especially his study of Western attitudes towards death since the Middle Ages, 1974). These sources are, of course, the only ones capable of yielding any information on the *attitudes* of persons toward the aged and aging and on the outlook of aging individuals for any period in the past.

Our experiences as historical sociologists, however brief if may be, has taught us to be wary of all inferences from literary and plastic evidence, unless it can be checked from evidence outside itself, especially numerical evidence. This brings us to sources 1 and 2.

Numerical Data on the History of Aging

From running records of births, marriages, and deaths (source 1), we can now recover, under rather special circumstances, fairly reliable estimates of rates of mortality at various ages; hence the expectation of life and (by the use of demographic theory) proportions of various age groups in the population can be estimated. These estimates are frequently made for small populations, and are somewhat approximate; but in the 1980s the first set of figures for a whole nation (i.e., for England) has become available, going back nearly 450 years to the 1540s. Good approximations for expectation of life and for proportions of the population aged over 60 have been published for that country at five-year intervals over that length of time (Wrigley and Schofield, 1981). The running records making such estimates possible are ordinarily those attached to baptism, marriage celebration, and burial rather than to the vital events themselves. English national birth rates and marriage rates are also available, together with rates of remarriage and ages at marriage and remarriage, which can be recovered with considerable reliability for individual villages. To be able to reckon these vital statistics for as long ago as this for the English population and for English villages, or from the late seventeenth century for French villages, is an open invitation to examine the effect of societal development on aging since those earlier generations, from the demographic point of view. Now that exactly similar results are appearing for other countries, even for Japan in the "late feudal" era of her social development (i.e., Tokugawa times, from our early seventeenth to our late nineteenth centuries), we can at last make a beginning in the direction of two-dimensional comparison, across time and between cultures, in the matter of vital statistics.

In order to study the personal and familial situation of older persons in former times as distinct from their expectation of life and so on, it is necessary to go to our second numerical source, census and census-type documents. These also exist for dates as early as the mid–sixteenth century for England and for other countries as well—in some, like Italy, Sweden, or Japan, in much larger quantities. Some examples, all unfortunately imperfect, are already known for the Middle Ages and from earlier times, including one from the second century A.D. in Roman

Egypt (Hammel and Laslett, 1974). Where repetitive listings of high quality are available, the life course of individuals with its horizons can, in principle, be accurately determined. These have to be inferred from cross-sectional data, that is, individual listings giving ages (examples of this exercise are Berkner, 1972; Hammel, 1972). If repetitive detailed listings can be found along with vital registration, and other materials of a "literary" and a plastic kind joined to them, then the historical sociologist has his or her best opportunity for analyzing aging in the past, and indeed for examining the whole nexus of familial and kin relationships. In the 1980s this demanding task is being tackled by several research centers in various countries, but results have yet to become at all plentiful. The examination of social development actually altering the position of the aged can of course only be undertaken if bodies of revealing data of this kind are gathered from before and after the significant change. The one change so far envisaged as likely to have an effect of this order has been industrialization. It will be insisted here that this is a mistake. The "demographic transition" is a more important change from the point of view of the social structural position of the elderly; and although it is sometimes contemporaneous with industrialization, the two are analytically distinct.

Limitations on Historical Sociology as to Aging

The most telling opportunities for carrying out such definitive exercises in historical sociology are likely to occur within the statistical era (i.e., since about the year 1800 in European countries) in which the state has been recording births, marriages, and deaths, as well as carrying out regular censuses. Unfortunately, however, when our interest is in the transition between preindustrial and industrial, the process of industrialization itself usually includes the initiation of these centralized, official and reliable statistics. Unfortunately also, from the point of view of historical sociology, more recent history is becoming more and more difficult to reconstruct because the state in most developed countries is denying access to the relevant records in the cause of personal privacy.

The drastic restrictions as to the capacities of historical sociology to tackle such a subject as aging should now be clear, both those which arise from its youth as a study and those which are inherent in all historical enterprises. They can never create their own data, but merely discover what has been left behind by our human predecessors.

The reader must be left in no doubt on one capital point. The sustained and detailed work just described as being possible has not yet been done. We report here on much more preliminary outcomes.

SOCIETAL DEVELOPMENT AND AGING, THE CURRENT THEORETICAL SITUATION

Absence of Formal Theory

There appears to be a lack of formal theory specifically devoted to societal development and aging, which stands in sharp contrast to the wealth of theoretical speculation on some subjects in the social sciences. This is no doubt to be expected because of the primitive state of historical sociology and because of the quite recent development of gerontology itself. There nevertheless seems to exist a series of quasi-theoretical assumptions, which may affect the outlook of those responsible for welfare policies as well as that of gerontologists. These assumptions correspond to popular attitudes to a large extent, and if they are not those of experts on aging, they seem often to be believed by the aging and the aged themselves. What follows is an attempt to write out this existent body of informal theorization in a dogmatic form.

Informal Existent Dogmatic Theory

Four sets of propositions are taken here to constitute this body of existent informal theory of a dogmatic kind on societal development and aging: historical propositions, normative propositions, functional propositions, and domestic propositions. The major historical dogma, the most important because the subject itself is historical, is that there has been a *before* and an *after* in the matter of aging, and that the transition between the two has been from one uniform situation to another. This transition is associated with industrialization, modernization, and/or (following Marxist historical theory) the rise of the bourgeoisie and of capitalist social forms. It may be noted that in Marxist historical analysis, capitalist productive arrangements and ideology existed well before industrialization, which raises issues as to where in past social development the division between *before* and *after* is to be placed. A more formidable complication is the tendency to equate the *historical* distinction between a given society at a time when industrialization was absent and at a time when it was present with the *geographical* distinction between nonindustrial societies in our contemporary world and industrial ones. However conceived, the assertion is that aging was different in the *before* from what it became in the *after,* and as has been said, the role of a demography in the two contrasted phases of social development has been played down.

The second set of dogmatic propositions, the normative ones, lays down that in the *before,* aging was an accepted part of the system of belief, and the aged themselves were both entitled to respect and were universally accorded it. In the *after,* aging has been rejected as unworthy of any note: the aged are allotted no prestige, and society tends to proceed as if the aged did not exist, or as if it would be better if they did not exist. These informal, normative dogmatic claims follow closely as might be expected, upon a number of dogmas under our third head, the function of the aged.

In these functional propositions it is maintained that in the *before,* the aged had specified and valued economic and emotional roles, which particularly attached to grandparents, and the multigenerational house-

hold was an approved institution that had important, even indispensable, functions. In the *after,* however, according to this presumed series of dogmatic assertions, neither aged persons, nor surviving ancestors, grandparents, or otherwise, have any obvious function as representatives of the approved and traditional; and in fact they have become obstacles to the adoption of "modern" ways of life. Compulsory retirement, universal in high industrial society, typifies the relegation of older people to a position of inactive insignificance. The aged decidedly lack any economic utility, and the multigenerational household has no advantage of any kind; it has no welfare functions, for these are now undertaken by political agencies.

The fourth set of dogmatic generalizations, the domestic, begins by asserting that in the *before,* the constitution of the domestic group was specified by universally accepted social assumptions, and the group was expected to allot membership to all senior persons within the kin network of its head, including parents and siblings of his spouse. These beliefs about the *before* are of considerable importance to gerontology as a whole and seem to be capable of some elaboration, even providing an order of priority to the duties that the household had to perform toward surviving members of generations preceding that of its head, or toward members of the head's generation, if they happened to be old.

The first priority was to ensure that the head's own parents, or his wife's, should be accorded full support, including membership in the domestic group, if this became necessary for any reason, such as widowhood, debility, or economic decline. The elderly parent accordingly always had a right to live in the household of one of his or her sons or daughters, though it seems to be conceded that it might have been a matter of negotiation as to which of the children would undertake the responsibility. This prime obligation operated on sons and daughters when they were grown-up. It might well require that instead of forming his own household at marriage, or on succession to the active direction of the family farm or "business," one son should stay at home with his wife and with their children as they arrived in order to maintain the parental household, whether or not that parent remained the household head. This domestic regulation would completely dictate the decisions of an only son.

The same duty might require a daughter to bring her husband into the parental household. In both cases it seems to be contemplated that if an independent household had been set up elsewhere, the child might be expected to return to the domestic group of his or her aging parents if necessary, bringing spouse and children. Further implications are that marriage might have to be postponed in reference to these duties, especially for daughters, who indeed might be compelled to put off or even abandon their prospects of having their own families in order to stay at home and look after aging and/or infirm parents, and who might even have to return home for this purpose from a position of independence elsewhere, whether or not they were married.

The principle that every surviving member of an earlier generation in the *before* had to be provided with a place in the family of one or other surviving offspring could be defeated if no surviving offspring existed. This brought the second order of obligation on the domestic group into play, which (in this set of dogmatic assertions) required that the household should fit in aging members of the kin other than the parents of the head or of his spouse, beginning perhaps with aunts and uncles, but not stopping at great aunts and great uncles and including second cousins and so on. For the extreme form of the dogmatic principle at issue is that in the *before,* no aging relatives, least of all an aging parent, should have to live alone, or with inadequate company, or, perhaps worst of all, in an institution.

Though the provisions included in this fourth, domestic, set of dogmatic quasi-theoretical assertions can become quite complicated as they apply to the *before,* they are quite straightforward in the *after.* Nowadays, in capitalist, bourgeois, postindustrial, or high industrial society, no doubt also in post-Revolutionary socialist societies, the domestic group has been drastically redefined, and its earlier principles have been abandoned. In the *after,* a family (the notion of household becomes less and less appropriate) consists exclusively of a man, his wife, and their children, if present, living alone and independently. No one else has any right of any kind to belong to it. The right to marry at will and to leave home for that purpose is also absolute. Members of former generations and older persons generally, therefore, have no expectation that offspring will ever bring a spouse to live in their families rather than leaving to establish another family; they cannot hope to become a member of any offspring family under any circumstances, least of all to be received within the family of more distant connections. Aged persons and grandparents live with each other, if they can, or they live alone, or they go into institutions. The duties of caring for them, insofar as they are recognized at all, are fulfilled by economic assistance or by visiting and being visited, never by permanently changing the strictly specified shape of the domestic group.

Comment on Existent, Informal Dogmatic Theory

The unifying concept of this body of dogma, insofar as it can be said to have one, is that of a transition between a *before,* which existed at some time in the past (or "our past," the past presumably of the national society to which the speaker belongs, since the possibility that traditional societies may have differed in respect of aging does not seem to be contemplated), and an *after,* which exists today. This transition is deeply interfused with a sense of loss: society has been impoverished by ceasing to take account of aging, and the aged themselves have been brutally deprived.

The historical sociologist has come to recognize these sentiments as belonging to what has been identified as *the world we have lost syndrome,* in which the deficiencies of the present are referred to the destruction of an idealized society at some point in the past. (See Laslett, 1965, 3rd ed. 1983, a work in which the phrase "the world we have lost" is taken in several senses, though never intentionally in a recommendatory or sentimental one.) The parallel and connected belief, or misbelief, in the universality of the large household in the past may be taken as another instance of this tendency. This is a dogma that historical sociologists are not finding easy to expose to reasoned reassessment (see Laslett, 1972b). The location of this will to construct a compensatory ideal projected backward in time in the minds of people not given to critical analysis, and its presence in fairy tales, journalism, television scripts, and fantasy material of other kinds, are presumably reasons for its persistent vitality.

A discovery that helped to show up the belief in the universal presence of the complex household as misplaced in respect of the past, was that few households in the northwestern area of preindustrial Europe contained more than two generations. The figure was 5.7 percent (± 1.45 percent) in 61 English communities at various dates between 1599 and 1821. Moreover kin of all kinds were rare in these households; in 44 places in England between the same dates, 3.4 percent of the population (± 0.3 percent) consisted in resident relatives other than the immediate family, living in 11.7 percent (± 0.8 percent) of the family groups (Laslett, 1977, Tables 1.2 and 1.5). In the whole of rural Denmark in 1787 and 1801 there were only 2.6 percent resident relatives (Hajnal, 1983, quoting Johansen, 1976). These facts themselves cast doubt on any supposition that there was ordinarily an easy, familiar, and familial relationship between the aged and the young, especially as it can be shown that if these peasants and townsfolk had wanted to live in multigenerational households, they could easily have established many more than seem to have existed among them. It also implies that the multigenerational household can hardly have been an institution universally valued for its functions.

The smaller relative numbers of the elderly in past demographic regimes ensured that there would be fewer candidates for placement in households in their later dependent years. A fair proportion therefore were so accommodated even though multigenerational households were uncommon.

Elementary demography in fact asserts that in the societies of the past, as in all other "underdeveloped" or "preindustrial" societies, old people must have been rarer and the experience of aging less common than in industrial societies today. High fertility and high mortality brought this about, the first ensuring that the numbers of the old should have been small in relation to the population as a whole, and the second that expectation of life should have been lower. (See Pressat, 1972, Ch. 9, especially pp. 277–282, for a demonstration that a growth in the proportion of the elderly in a population is almost entirely due to a decline in fertility, and not, to any extent, due to a rise in the expectation of life.) Aging, therefore, is unlikely ever to have been a problem, except perhaps locally, in the societies of the past, and the aged cannot often have represented a burden, in spite of the very much lower levels of production and social resources that then prevailed. The consequence may well have been that the comparative rarity of old men and old women, and the exceptional character of their experiences, gave a value to them in earlier times that they no longer possess and entitled them to a respect that has disappeared.

It is a commonplace of literary surveys of the literary and plastic evidence, especially when such material is drawn indiscriminately from the past of cultivated societies and from "primitive" societies in the contemporary world, that this value and respect was supposed to have been attached to aged persons for a whole range of familial, social, and even religious reasons. There are conspicuous and interesting exceptions, though, where quite the reverse is indicated by the sources (see, e.g., de Beauvoir, 1970). In these contexts, aged people are neglected, despised, and sometimes even disposed of.

The ambiguity and contrariness of sources of this kind finally become exasperating to the interpreter. We are unlikely to get much nearer the truth about older people by counting and comparing contexts in which aging seems to be respected and those in which it seems to be condemned. But we can begin to appreciate the actual experience of old people in the past if we try to establish numerically, as far as we can, how much less common they were than they are now, and so how much less likely to be felt as a burden and how much more likely to be valued for their rarity. We shall find that in European societies of the past the elderly were not so small a proportion of the population as has been assumed. Those over 60 have never to our knowledge formed less than 6.5 percent of the English population, and reached 10 percent early in the eighteenth century. Expectation of life was rarely below 30, never as low as 25, and usually nearer 40.

We can go rather further in our examination if we direct our attention to circumstances that may have been of greater consequence to the security and welfare of the aged, that is, the extent to which they continued to live in a familial situation. This means discovering how often they retained their spouses and children, and how likely it was that they would otherwise be accepted as members of the families of their children, their kinsfolk, and their juniors in general. Rough statistics of this kind can now be recovered from a selection of our exiguous sources.

Nevertheless, with even the limited numerical evidence in hand, we are in a better position to make a choice between the favorable and unfavorable elements in the literary materials and to pronounce on the informal dogmatic theory of the aged in relation to societal development that has been sketched out above. I shall be so bold as to preface our survey of such numerical data

with an alternative general theory of societal development and aging.

AN ALTERNATIVE GENERAL THEORY OF SOCIETAL DEVELOPMENT AND AGING

Revision and Rejection of Stereotyped Assumptions

A revised hypothetical general theory of aging and societal development in recent centuries begins with the historical dogma about a *before* and *after*. The notion of a single transition is wholly too simple, especially when it is identified with that overall, predominantly economic development through which traditional societies become modern, advanced societies. It is true that some traditional societies have in fact undergone a process during which modernization was accompanied by a crucial change in the proportion of the aged in the social structure. Several of the many ethnic and economic regions which constitute the present Soviet Union are possible examples, as well as others in central and eastern Europe. Japan is another. In none of these countries, it may be noted, was the coincidence at all precise, and in the case of Western societies, as in that of Britain, particularly, the two developments have been almost entirely separate in time.

In France, in the United States, and especially in Britain the crucial alteration in the proportions of the aged in the population and in expectation of life took place a century or more after the onset of industrialization. This was so because the demographic transition, during which the regime of high fertility and high mortality characteristic of traditional society gives way to the regime of low fertility and low mortality characteristic of a modern industrial society, was not contemporaneous in these societies with the start of industrialization, but occurred later, in Britain much later. Another way of describing the development when it did arrive in the middle 50 years of the twentieth century—between 1925 and 1975—is as a transition between a "modernized" and a "post modern," or an "industrial" and a "post industrial" society (see Smith, 1981). These titles, cumbersome and even illogical as they may seem, have the advantage of insisting that the transformation has been in social structure and in attitude as well as in demography. It is a fact of outstanding interest that certain characteristics of the familial life of these and of other highly developed societies (e.g., Japan, or Yugoslavia), characteristics of first importance to the elderly, seem to have survived the transformation (see, Smith, 1981). I shall use "high industrial" to refer to countries like the United States, Britain, Japan, and France.

In England and Wales, if it is legitimate to make assumptions about a *before* and an *after* at all, it is on the understanding that something like a century and a half or more of intricate change took place before the one gave way to the other. If we are to talk of transformation, moreover, it is very recent times that we must have in mind, not the notorious years of early industrialization associated with the young Queen Victoria, and least of all the time when capitalism or bourgeois attitudes and practices first became established.

We shall also observe, to make matters more complicated, that England cannot be taken as necessarily typical of Western experience, except during the final stages; it certainly is not indicative in detail of what happened in France. Indeed, we shall consider indications that the actual behavior of old people in respect of residence may have differed from area to area in traditional European society, and that England may have been somewhat exceptional in its uniformity. In what follows it must be borne in mind that English conditions are being discussed.

Although it might be worth retaining in a highly modified form the notion of a *before* and an *after* in respect of the history of societal development in relation to aging, in England and among English speakers, very little of the remainder of the informal dogmatic theory we have set out can enter into a revised hypothetical general theory. It is

true that the fragmentary though suggestive evidence we shall cite indicates that the aged in preindustrial England were more frequently to be found surrounded by their immediate family than is the case in the England of today, even taking account of their different demographic situations. It is possible that they were given access to the families of their married offspring more readily than is now the case. This may be thought surprising in view of the infrequent occurrence of multigenerational and of complicated households of all kinds. But we shall find that these circumstances can be persuasively accounted for without having to suppose that in traditional England deliberate provision was made for the physical, emotional, or economic needs of aged persons, aged relations, or aged parents in a way that was in any sense superior to the provisions being made by the children, the relatives, and the friends of aged persons in our own day, not to speak of the elaborate machinery of an anxiously protective welfare state.

As for the rest of the informal dogmatic theory, it is for the most part illusory as far as England and the English past are concerned, and in its pure form perhaps for the whole of the West. There is little need to remind readers of this *Handbook* that the majority of aged persons in these areas today are not found in fact to be in the position described above as characteristic of the *after,* whatever the stereotypes. Retirement may be widespread and peremptory in high industrial society, but its effect varies with the interest of the job that has to be abandoned, the skill and effectiveness of the individual concerned, his health, and his economic position. It is certainly not always felt as a deprivation, or even as a diminution of consequence. Nor are the old so drastically bereft of prestige and respect; they do have recognized functions, especially in respect of their families and their children; they are supported, emotionally and otherwise, by their offspring, sometimes by their siblings, and even by more distant kin. These supportive kin relationships are, of course, subject to demographic vicissitude, but the much better health of the late twentieth century modulates this to an extent inconceivable in a wholly undeveloped society (see Wachter et al., 1978).

Elderly and aged persons may live apart from their close relatives in our society, but they very often manage to live near enough to them to be in intimate contact. This is an arrangement they are known to appreciate because it combines interchange with independence (see the relevant chapters of this *Handbook;* Tunstall, 1966; Shanas et al., 1968). We must not be led to suppose that the sufferings of some of the aged and the miseries of the minority of the anomic amongst them who come into contact with the welfare services are a proper indication of the conditions of old people generally in contemporary high industrial society. So much for the *after*.

The *domestic* generalizations of the informal dogmatic theory as to the *before,* while not all inaccurate, cannot be confirmed as a whole from the available English historical evidence and certainly do not bear the interpretation that has been put upon them. Some of the assumptions can be rejected out of hand. It can be shown, for example, that the second order obligations of the family supposed above to have existed in traditional English society, which would require it to give succor and even family membership to aged relatives other than the parents of the head, were entirely absent as a recognized social duty. The famous Elizabethan Poor Law of 1601 specifically confined responsibility for the relief of the elderly to their children alone. In spite of the supposedly bilateral character of English kinship, moreover, the case law developed by the judges on this basis succeeded in confining all such duties to "natural" connections, and thus excluded all affinal kin, even stepfathers and stepmothers.

The behavior of children in the matter of marriages affecting the welfare of their own parents can also be shown to have been very different from the dogmatic assumptions. Family reconstitution demonstrates that

English children had no traceable disposition to wait until the parents died before they took spouses; in fact, the marriage of orphaned children appears to have been later than that of those whose parents were alive. No doubt most daughters and some sons did conduct themselves so as to assure the comfort and security of their aging parents as far as they could, but we have found it difficult to confirm that they would return home for that purpose from their jobs or their holdings in other localities. Movement of failing fathers and mothers into the households of their married offspring certainly did go on, but it ws not a very widespread occurrence in the evidence we have so far surveyed, and it was certainly not a universal pattern.

Two General Principles in an Alternative Theory

The first general principle in an alternative theory is a negative one and has implications that go far beyond the issue of aging. It presumes that in the traditional English social order, at least at its final stages, the membership of the coresident domestic group, as we now call it, was never specified in such a way that any person other than the head or spouse of the head had a right to belong to it.

It is not even clear that the offspring of the head lived by right in his domestic group, although up to the age of seven they were regarded as "nurse children" and could not be separated from their parents. The inference can be made, and there is evidence for it in the surviving data, that, after seven years, children might be removed from the domestic group, with no right to be restored to the parental family. If this were so, how could it be supposed that elderly parents rightfully belonged to the households of their mature children, married or unmarried, or that such children could be required by social custom and neighborly opinion to live with those parents if necessary?

The authority of the father in traditional England was real enough, especially amongst the elite. But if he could command his children whether or when to marry, or where to live, and even do so successfully, this was evidently not effected on the ground that the approved shape of the coresident domestic group itself demanded it. In practice, as we have said and shall try to demonstrate numerically here, English parents showed little disposition to keep children at home after marriage or to require them to return after marriage or after being launched in the world elsewhere. They could certainly not appeal to norms of household composition in order to effect such things; all the evidence indicates that these conventions favored quite opposite actions and attitudes. The ordinary story of the family-household after the child-rearing stage was of offspring leaving successively, though not necessarily in order of age, until the parents finally found themselves alone if they survived. There is a telling contrast here with the traditional familial system of an area like South China, for example, where no child left the parental household except under clearly specified conditions because the recognized rules of familial behavior required coresidence wherever possible, and where no father or mother of grown offspring would ever live alone. Some part at least of what has been called the "world we have lost syndrome" must be attributed to English and English-speaking peoples being led to believe that their familial past has been the same as that of people like the Chinese.

If the stem family arrangements so widely assumed, at least until recently, to have been common or even universal in traditional Europe had in fact been so in England, then the patriarch in charge, or even his widow, might have had the sanctions at hand to require a grown and often married child to live at home, and to provide a supporting circle of family members when retirement arrived (see Berkner, 1974, 1977). But this form of the domestic group seems to have been of singularly little importance amongst the English in the generations just before traditional society began the process of transformation.

Where membership of the domestic group was conferred upon solitary, necessitous, or infirm parents or kinfolk in England in earlier times, therefore, it may be supposed to have been done because of the advantages of the presence of elderly relatives, or because married children chose to fulfill their public duty to support their parents in this way, and for reasons of affection and loyalty. As for the advantages, they must have existed even before the rise of the factory took the working mother some distance away from the home during the whole of the day and created the need for perpetual child minders (see Anderson, 1971). All that we know as yet tends to confirm what common sense suggests, that the older generation were of use in child rearing.

Careful distinction is necessary here. Since a child had a socially recognized and even a legally enforceable obligation to support a parent in need, it is understandable that this duty should frequently be fulfilled by offering house room, especially when such a move might be useful to the household. But these circumstances do not of themselves create a right of elderly parents to coreside with married children. So little was this the case that we sometimes find such coresidents described as "lodgers" rather than as family members, and even as a "lodger, receiving parish relief" (Laslett, 1972a, p. 35, footnote p. 50: the lodger concerned was the aged father of the head of the household). We may notice in these cases that the poor law authorities were in a sense paying people to do their work, for paupers would have had to be publicly supported in any case. In the one or two sets of data where we can follow such vicissitudes in peasant England, we find examples of sons succeeding to the family occupation (perhaps even to the family cottage) and actually leaving their widowed mothers and their sisters to live in the poor law institutions. The extreme poverty of such persons as these must be borne in mind before judging such cases, but it must not be overlooked that the legal duty of a child to assist his parents never seems to have been construed as an obligation to receive or maintain him or her in the household. The wider kin, moreover, were never required to support the necessitous elderly. We may say that society, rather than the kin network—that is, the family in its nonresidential sense—was primarily responsible for the financial support of old persons in traditional, western European society (Laslett, 1982).

Nevertheless, this general theoretical proposition about aging and societal development should not be taken to imply that children usually did little or nothing to assist or to entertain their aging parents out of love and respect, when and as they could, in traditional English society. There are good grounds for supposing that in fact they aided them in this way, although we are certainly not yet in a position to estimate how much money was transferred to their parents, how often they visited them, and how frequently and strenuously then exerted themselves to live near them or to find accommodations that would enable the parents themselves to come within easy reach. The wisps of evidence we have suggest that in some families elderly persons and children did live in close proximity, in others not. But we cannot hope to decide from the present state of our knowledge how successful our ancestors were in making such provisions, taking account of the very different situation of younger, independent people in that era of exiguous resources, poor communications, and widespread illiteracy, which made keeping in touch with home and relations generally so much more difficult. The most likely conjecture from what we do know is that they behaved very much as we behave now in this respect, no better and no worse.

The second general principle in an alternative hypothetical theory about aging, in relation to social development in England and in the Western world generally, is that the position of the elderly in the late twentieth century social structure is historically novel. If the increased expectation of life and the great numbers of the aged present us with a "problem to be solved," it is a "problem" that has never been solved in the past because it did not exist in what has been called the *before*. Although the notion of the elderly as a "problem" is dubious and mis-

leading, since it mistakes the whole for the part, the dependent part, it makes it possible to offer a generalization about the past in relation to the present that is of some importance to gerontology. The value of historical sociology to the creation of policy in the present is in denoting how far we differ from past people and how much we and they are the same. With respect to aging, the theory is that we are in an unprecedented situation—we shall have to invent appropriate social forms, for they cannot be recovered from our history. It follows that elderly people and the gerontologists who help to create policy for them are at a serious disadvantage while they continue to accept a world we have lost, a world that it would make sense to try to restore. Our situation remains irreducibly novel; it calls for invention rather than imitation.

The rest of this chapter will be given over to the presentation of some of the evidence on which this tentative alternative general theory of aging and societal development has been based, and a remark or two will be made of a comparative kind, hinting at the rather different general view that might have emerged if our evidence had been equally derived from non-Western as well as from English sources. The preliminary and uncertain character even of the English data themselves will be apparent to the reader, and the status of our general hypothesis must be judged accordingly.

HISTORICAL DATA FOR A TENTATIVE THEORY OF AGING AND SOCIETAL DEVELOPMENT

The painfully recovered facts that underlie the statements made in the previous three sections about the *before* in contrast to the *after* will be presented in the form of eight tables, one figure, and commentary. In view of what has been asserted about the differing dates of modernization and of demographic transition, it will be appreciated why there has been difficulty about dates before which the societies in question could be justly said to be "traditional" or "preindustrial," and after which they could be said to be "modern," or in full progress towards modernization. This has led to some discrepancies between the various sets of figures, but it is to be hoped that the message of these statistics has not been obscured.

Life Expectation and Proportion of the Elderly in Traditional Societies in the Past

A selection of the few available estimates of the expectation of life in some traditional so-cieties in the past is presented in Table 1. The variations in these estimates from period to period are sometimes surprising to those to whom the demography of earlier societies is unfamiliar. It is now a commonplace in historical sociology, however, that in the same village, county, or even country, fertility, nuptiality, and mortality can be expected to change quite drastically between generation and generation, up and down. No single figure for life expectation in preindustrial times generally would make sense.

TABLE 1. Expectation of Life in Some Traditional Societies of the Past.

Country	Date	Expectation of life at birth (years)	Expectation of life at (years)	
England			1690s	1980s
National sample	1541	33.7	(women only)	
[Figures for five-	1601	35.6	(0) c.35	over 70
year periods	1661	35.9	(30) c.30	c.44
centered at cited	1721	32.5	(50) c.18	c.26
date]	1781	34.7	(60) c.12	c.18
	1841	40.3	(70) c.8	c.11
Colonial America				
Massachusetts and	18th century	28.15		
New Hampshire	(Wigglesworth)			
			(10) 49.23	
			(20) 34.21	
			(30) 30.24	
			(50) 21.16	
			(60) 15.43	
			(70) 10.06	
France				
Paris Basin	Late 17th century		(20) c.32	
Whole Country	Late 18th century	28.8		
	1821	c.41 (women only)		
Switzerland	Late 18th century	20–30		
Spain	Before 1797	26.8		
Germany				
Breslau	1690s	27.5	(10) 40.2	
Japan				
One Village	1671–1725		(10) 50.0 (males)	
			38.3 (females)	
	1726–1775		(10) 49.9 (males)	
			48.1 (females)	
Another Village	1717–1830		(1) 46.9 (males)	
			50.7 (females)	
Italy				
Verona	1761–1766	28		
Milan	1804–1805	30		
Bologna	1811–1812	26		
India	1891–1901	23.8		
	1901–1911	22.9		
	1911–1921	20.15		

On the whole, figures for the duration of life are higher rather than lower than might be thought probable, and this is particularly the case with estimates for later ages. It will be observed that although an Englishwoman at birth in the 1690s had less than half of the expectation of life of an Englishwoman in the 1980s, by age 30 the discrepancy had fallen to less than a half, and by age 70 was not much more than a third, 8 years as compared with 11 (compare Laslett, 1965, 3rd ed. 1983). This is important to the question of aging in relation to social change not only because it may mean that the experience of being old came to more people—that is, to persons no longer children—than might be supposed, but also because it implies that the family group lasted rather better. The duration of marriage in preindustrial England was of the order of 25 to 27 years for most couples, but it could last for 35 years or more for a fifth or a quarter of them (see Laslett, 1975, in criticism of the view of Ariès that married life was too brief to ensure familial stability). A lost spouse did not necessarily mean solitude in any case, since remarriage was so frequent, at least before 1700. These circumstances in turn improved the chances that old people who were made solitary or helpless would have the home of one or another of their children to go to and stay in.

At the time of this writing (June 1982), the Cambridge Group for the History of Population and Social Structure is not in a position to provide any very useful figures for elderly persons, of 60 years and over, or aged persons, of 65 and over, who had at least one married son or a married daughter alive to go and live with, given marriage ages, number of children, and so on, prevailing in preindustrial times. Clearly, there must have been considerable variability from family to family, place to place, time to time, and even greater variability when England is contrasted with other cultural areas. Neither can we say how many relatives of any kind such people would have had—how often, for example, an elderly or aged spinster would have had a similar sister or brother she could live with; the numbers of old people with no living relatives, or even with no living child,

married or unmarried, must have been small at all times. Without larger more precise knowledge of this kind, our evidence is less useful than it might be, especially when we compare the situation then with the situation now. The intention, however, is to make such estimates for varying demographic rates, and so on, with the use of microsimulation.*

Even with this information at hand, however, we shall still have to try to determine, or to guess, how many of the surviving children of an elderly person would be in contact with him or her, in a position to give house room, with the resources to do so, and with a motive as well, of a child-minding character or of any other. These circumstances underline, once more, how preliminary our present knowledge is, and how much there is yet to do to get any *precise* notion of the situation of the aged today in comparison with the situation in earlier times. This is so even in the case of late nineteenth century America, for which, however, considerably superior information has already become available (see, e.g., Smith, 1979; Chudacoff and Hareven, 1979).

Tables 2a and 2b contain a collection of figures that have been recovered from lists of inhabitants for individual cities, towns, or villages, together with those from several national or provincial censuses, and one outcome from palaeodemography—the estimation of the ages of the skeletons excavated from an eleventh century graveyard. To these have been added national estimates for six quinquennia between the 1540s and the 1870s recently published by the Cambridge Group for the History of Population and Social Structure (Wrigley and Schofield, 1981). A noteworthy feature of the results of calculating the proportions in the higher age groups of the populations concerned is that they are also nearly all relatively high in relation to what one might expect in traditional societies. Only 8 of the 58 figures for

*At the time of final proof (June 1984), these microsimulation results had become available and were in course of publication. They show surprisingly little difference in many respects between the eighteenth and twentieth century and they do not contradict the message of the present contribution.

TABLE 2a. PROPORTIONS OF AGED PERSONS (BY SEX) IN SOME TRADITIONAL SOCIETIES IN THE PAST.

	Population	AGED 60 AND ABOVE				AGED 65 AND ABOVE				AGED 70 AND ABOVE				AGED 75 AND ABOVE				AGED 80 AND ABOVE			
		M	F	Both	Sex ratio	M	F	Both	Sex ratio	M	F	Both	Sex ratio	M	F	Both	Sex ratio	M	F	Both	Sex ratio
England																					
(national 1541				8.5																	
sample) 1601				8.3																	
1661				9.7																	
1721				9.7																	
1781				8.2																	
1821				6.6																	
S.E. Europe																					
11th Century								2.5													
(Excavated Graveyard)																					
Italy																					
Arezzo 1427				9.9																	
Venice 1601–10		15.9	15.9	15.9	104	10.0	10.2	10.1	105	8.1	8.6	8.4	109								
1691–1700				10.7																	
				11.6																	
France																					
Mostejols 1690	439	9.6	8.9	9.3	123	5.7	6.9	6.1	93	4.3	3.9	4.1	126	1.8	1.8	1.8	100	1.3	1.5	1.4	100
Longuenesse 1778	332	8.5	9.7	9.1	76	5.9	8.0	7.0	104	2.0	5.1	3.7	25								
1790	387	10.2	5.5	7.7	173	6.4	4.5	5.4	133	3.2	3.0	3.1	100								
Belgium																					
Lisswege 1739	796	4.5	5.1	4.8	100																
1748	702	3.6	3.4	3.9	117																
Denmark																					
Bjorre Is. 1650	1,032			7.7																	
Zealand Prov. 1650	129,000			7.0																	
(Natl Census) 1787		8.0	9.3	8.7	85					2.6	3.4	3.0	74					0.4	0.7	0.6	56
1801		8.8	9.8	9.4	87					2.9	3.6	3.2	79					0.5	0.8	0.7	69
Iceland																					
(Natl Census) 1703		5.8	9.2	7.7	52	3.6	6.1	4.6	48	2.2	4.1	3.3	44	1.2	2.5	1.9	40	0.8	1.6	1.2	45
1729		12.4	16.7	14.7	82	9.0	12.7	11.0	60	5.8	8.6	7.3	57	3.2	4.9	4.2	55	1.4	2.2	1.9	54
1787		6.5	8.7	7.8	58					1.6	2.5	2.1	48								
Germany																					
Löffingen Gemeinde 1777	2,500			8.7																	

Place	Date	Size															
Switzerland																	
Meltmenstetten	1634				5.1												
Zürich, S. Peter	1637				7.2												
Albisrieden Zumiken	1634				3.4												
Wiesendangen	1721				6.3												
(Ober-u Unter)	1764				9.9												
Bern	1764				10.3												
Austria																	
Abtenau	1632	4,000+			5.4												
Estonia																	
(Village Census)	1782		6.8	5.7	6.3	118											
	1795		4.3	4.7	4.8	89											
Hungary																	
Kölked	1816	638	5.7	4.6	5.0	113	2.8	3.3	3.1	82	2.2	2.1	2.2	100	1.3	0.9	1.1
Serbia																	
Belgrade	1733	1,357	5.2	3.4	4.7	133	2.6	1.5	2.1	77	1.8	1.3	1.5	137			
Japan																	
15 places	1671–90		6.7	6.8	6.7	100											
15 places	1711–40		8.9	8.4	8.7	115											
	1761–90		11.5	11.8	11.7	107											
	1811–40		8.6	9.7	9.1	93											
Nishinomiya	1713	653	9.2	9.9	9.7	106	6.3	6.9	6.6	104	4.3	3.6	4.0	136			
Colonial U.S.A.																	
Bedford and New Rochelle	1698	385			5.7				1.8				0.8				

TABLE 2b. PROPORTIONS OF AGED PERSONS (BY SEX) IN CERTAIN PLACES IN ENGLAND BEFORE 1800.

	Year	Population	AGED 60 AND ABOVE				AGED 65 AND ABOVE				AGED 70 AND ABOVE				AGED 75 AND ABOVE				AGED 80 AND ABOVE			
			M	F	Both	Sex ratio	M	F	Both	Sex ratio	M	F	Both	Sex ratio	M	F	Both	Sex ratio	M	F	Both	Sex ratio
Ealing	1599	427	7.0	4.5	5.9	133	1.7	1.0	1.4	130	0.4	1.0	0.7	175								
Chilvers Coton	1684	780	6.6	6.7	6.7	104	3.6	2.4	3.0	61	1.9	1.0	1.4	71								
Lichfield	1695	2,861	6.4	9.4	8.1	160	3.4	4.6	4.1	86	2.1	2.5	2.3	66								
Stoke-on-Trent	1701	1,627	8.2	9.1	8.6	87	5.0	5.3	5.2	100	2.6	3.6	3.1	98								
Corfe Castle	1790	1,239	9.8	9.5	9.7	100	6.6	6.3	6.4	133	3.4	3.5	3.3	127								
Ardleigh	1796	1,126	7.2	4.4	5.9	215	3.4	1.8	3.1	81	2.4	2.0	2.2									
Grasmere	1683	310	8.4	10.3	9.4	81	3.9	7.1	5.5		3.2	5.2	4.2									
Buckfastleigh	1698	1,111	6.4	5.7	6.0	116	2.6	2.4	2.5	75	1.6	1.7	1.6									
Ringmore	1698	188	19.3	19.4	19.1	80	10.8	11.6	11.2		6.0	7.8	6.9									
Trent	1748	375	6.6	10.3	8.0	60				75	1.7	3.6	2.7	43								
Shrewsbury	1770	1,046											5.6				2.7				1.6	
	1780	1,113											3.6				2.0				0.8	
Ackworth	1757	603	10.3	8.5	9.1	150					2.5	2.8	2.6	100					1.3	0	0.6	
	1767	728	8.5	11.0	9.9	67					2.6	3.8	3.3	60					0.6	1.3	1.0	
	1772	678	8.5	12.7	10.6	21					2.6	4.4	3.5						0.6	1.4	1.0	
Ashton-Under-Lyne	1773	7,956			5.9								1.7								0.3	
Chester	1774	14,713											4.3									
Sandwich	1776	609	14.2	12.2	13.1	100					6.0	4.6	5.5	113					1.4	0.6	1.0	
Carlisle	1780	7,677			9.1																	
	1788	8,677			9.1																	
Manchester	1773	13,786			3.4								1.9									
Maidstone	1782	5,755									4.2	5.9	5.1								0.6	
Taunton	1791	5,472											4.7									
Wigton	1791	1,650			16.3						3.0	4.8	4.0	50								
Bocking	1793	2,943									3.3	2.1	2.6								1.5	

the percentage of persons aged 60 and above are as low as the percentage reported in Tunisia in 1966 or in Brazil in 1970, two contemporary industrializing societies (compare with Table 5—only 3 are as low as the figure for Indonesia in 1964–65). The variation from place to place, though noticeable, is certainly rather less than might be expected. These variations do not seem to be entirely the result of the smallness of the population studied, since that of Venice was in the tens of thousands. England, with the interesting exception of Manchester in 1773 in the very dawn of the factory era, seems always to have had quite a high proportion of the elderly.

These statistics, then, might be held to confirm the impression given by the estimates of the expectation of life; that is, that a fair number of people reached the higher ages in historic times, and that fertility may have been consistently lower than the levels now reached in underdeveloped societies in our day. The probable reasons are not without significance to the overall contrast in marital habits that has been proposed as distinguishing western European areas from other areas of the world—later age of first marriage for women (see Hajnal, 1965; Laslett, 1977, Ch. 1). They tend to modify the contrast between the *before* and the *after* in a somewhat surprising way, as well as the assertion that the aged were not likely to have been a burden in preindustrial society, an assertion not easily maintained in the case of, say, Arezzo in 1427.

It should be insisted, however, that the absolute reliability of all the figures in Tables 2a and 2b is questionable, since they come from societies where the reckoning of ages must have been much less accurate than it is today in advanced societies, or even in countries like Indonesia or Tunisia. Older people are known to have exaggerated their ages when they talked to the list-takers of the past, and to have declared themselves at the decadal years to a great extent. This undoubtedly had the effect of inflating the numbers over 60 and probably even more at the advanced ages.

Social Development in the Past and Sex Ratio, Marital Status, and Proportion of the Elderly and Aged

In Tables 3a and 3b are set out a small selection of figures for the proportion of married, widowed, and single among the older age groups, by males and females. The reason why the number of communities is so few, even fewer than in Tables 2a and 2b, is that for England and Wales a concerted search over a decade and more has so far failed to uncover further documents giving the relevant information. In the case of other countries (e.g., Italy and Germany), it is known that a great deal more evidence exists, but it has not yet been analyzed. Comments on these data therefore must be even more tentative than on the other sets of figures presented here. Nevertheless, it may be worthwhile to draw attention to some of the features of these data.

Variability is clearly considerable in these statistics, as must be expected for such minute numbers. But the indications are, for what they are worth, that elderly and aged women were no less liable to be widowed then than they are in Western countries in our own day. In 1960, 50 percent of all women were widowed above the age of 65 in Britain, 53 percent in the United States, and 43 percent in Denmark (Shanas et al., 1968, p. 12). The same effect is observable for men, if a little less pronounced; the contemporary figures for widowers above 65 are 22 percent in Britain, 19 percent for the United States, and 23 percent for Denmark. There is evidently little ground here for believing that living in a state of widowhood was less common in the English past, in spite of a tendency toward remarriage.

It is interesting, however, that the really sharp contrasts come in Table 3b and for two places outside the European west, Belgrade and Nishinomiya, where over 80 percent of women of 65 and above are given as widowed. A mere 13 percent of the men lack spouses in Belgrade, and this is a result of earlier marriage for women and proscription

TABLE 3a. MARITAL STATUS OF ELDERLY AND AGED PERSONS BY SEX AND AGE CATEGORY IN CERTAIN PLACES IN ENGLAND BEFORE 1800, IN PERCENTAGES.

		AGED 60 AND ABOVE		AGED 65 AND ABOVE		AGED 70 AND ABOVE	
		Male	Female	Male	Female	Male	Female
Ealing, Middlesex	Married	62	70	33	33	0	50
1599, pop. 427 (16 males,	Widowed	19	20	67	67	100	50
12 females aged 60 and above)	Single	19	10	0	0	0	0
Chilvers Coton, Warws.	Married	74	58	75	40	71	50
1683, pop. 780 (24 males, 23	Widowed	19	42	25	60	29	50
females aged 60 and above)	Single	5	0	0	0	0	0
Grasmere, Wstmrld.	Married	75	41	80	50	75	60
1683, pop. 310 (11 males,	Widowed	16	58	20	40	25	40
12 females aged 60 and above)	Single	8	0	0	0	0	0
Lichfield, Staffs.	Married	80	41	81	23	76	19
1695, pop. 2,861 (79 males,	Widowed	12	58	19	77	24	81
131 females aged 60 and above)	Single	8	1	0	0	0	0
Stoke-on-Trent, Staffs.	Married	62	37	58	25	45	20
1701, pop. 1,627 (65 males,	Widowed	27	55	31	70	40	73
75 females aged 60 and above)	Single	11	8	11	5	15	7
Corfe Castle, Dorset	Married	58	40	60	37	57	32
1790, pop. 1,239 (60 males,	Widowed	34	48	38	55	38	68
77 females aged 60 and above)	Single	8	12	2	8	5	0
Ardleigh, Essex	Married	67	50	75	64	70	57
1796, pop. 1,126 (43 males,	Widowed	33	45	25	36	30	43
20 females aged 60 and above)	Single	0	5	0	0	0	0

NOTE: Not all individuals in these places have marital status recorded. Those of uncertain status have been classified as single.

TABLE 3b. MARITAL STATUS OF ELDERLY AND AGED PERSONS BY SEX AND AGE CATEGORY IN CERTAIN PLACES OUTSIDE ENGLAND BEFORE 1800, IN PERCENTAGES.

		AGED 60 AND ABOVE		AGED 65 AND ABOVE		AGED 70 AND ABOVE	
		Male	Female	Male	Female	Male	Female
Longuenesse, N. France	Married	64	44	67	31	33	12
1778, pop. 333 (11 males,	Widowed	27	56	22	69	33	88
16 females aged 60 and above)	Single	9	0	11	0	33	0
1790, pop. 387 (18 males,	Married	61	54	67	56	67	50
11 females aged	Widowed	22	46	25	44	33	50
60 and above)	Single	6	0	8	0	0	0
Belgrade, Serbia	Married	69	7	80	7	70	14
1733–4, pop. 1,357 (28 males,	Widowed	12	90	13	86	20	72
50 females aged 60 and above)	Single	19	3	7	7	10	14
Nishinomiya, Japan	Married	67	17	50	16	46	0
1713, pop. 653 (32 males,	Widowed	33	83	50	84	54	100
30 females aged 60 and above)	Single	0	0	0	0	0	0

NOTE: Not all individuals in these places have marital status recorded. Those of uncertain status have been classified as single.

of remarriage of women, together with the greater gap between spouses (see Laslett, 1972a, pp. 52–53; Laslett, 1977, p. ii). In Japan, the remarriage of widows was perhaps even less common. Almost nothing can be learned from the tables about the probability of being a bachelor or a spinster in later life at these places. This is so because the evidence so often leaves unclear the distinction between the unmarried and the widowed. It is known that the proportion never married was variable, but surprisingly high in English society at all relevant ages.

Table 4, with its accompanying figure, provides an account of the actual course of change in the proportion of the elderly in the population for England and Wales on the one hand, and France on the other. This covers the whole period of industrial life from the eighteenth century until 1971, together with a conspectus of comparative figures from other Western, industrialized countries. The pattern presented by these data is conspicuous and interesting.

The singular constancy of the proportions of the elderly in England and Wales up until

TABLE 4. PROPORTIONS OF ELDERLY PERSONS IN ENGLAND AND WALES AND IN FRANCE (BOTH SEXES) SINCE THE LATE 18TH CENTURY (WITH SOME FIGURES FROM OTHER COUNTRIES FOR AGED PERSONS).

		ENGLAND AND WALES			FRANCE		
Date	% 60 and above	Men	Women	Both	Men	Women	Both
1776					7.2	7.3	7.3
1786					7.8	8.1	7.9
1796					8.6	8.7	8.6
1801					8.7	8.8	8.7
1811					9.0	9.0	9.0
1821		7.3	7.6		9.6	9.8	9.7
1831					9.5	10.4	10.0
1841		6.8	7.4	7.2	9.2	10.4	9.9
1851		6.9	7.8	7.4	9.2	11.1	10.1
1861		7.0	7.8	7.3	9.9	11.4	10.7
1871		6.6	7.8	7.4	11.0	11.9	11.7
1881		6.9	7.8	7.3	11.7	12.5	12.1
1891		6.8	7.9	7.2	12.0	13.2	12.6
1901		6.8	8.0	7.3	12.3	13.5	13.0
1911		7.3	8.6	7.9	11.6	13.5	12.6
1921		8.7	10.0	9.3	11.5	14.5	13.7
1931		10.7	12.3	11.5	12.7	15.1	14.0
1936					13.4	16.0	14.7
1946					13.8	17.9	15.9
1951		14.6	17.7	15.9	13.5	18.8	16.2
1961		15.3	17.9	16.2			
1968					15.7	21.6	18.8
1971		15.9	21.9	18.7			

AGED PERSONS (% 65 AND ABOVE, BOTH SEXES)

Date	England and Wales	France	Germany	Italy	The Netherlands	Sweden	U.S.A.	Canada
1850	4.6	6.5			4.7	4.8		
1900	4.7	8.2	4.9	6.2	6.0	8.4	4.1	5.1
1930	7.4	9.3	7.4		6.2	9.2	5.4	5.6
1950	10.8	11.8	9.7		7.7	10.3	8.1	7.8
1969/70	13.0	13.0	14.0	11.0	10.0	14.0	10.0	8.0

the year 1901 should first be noted, together with the indication that these proportions were lower during those three generations than they had been in traditional times. But charge, when it did begin, soon became extraordinarily marked, and it could justly be said that the proportions of the aged were completely transformed in the 60 years after 1911. Change was greatest in the 1940s, 1950s, and 1960s.

There is a close resemblance in this development over time to the course of mean household size in England, which was noticeably constant over the period of industrialization: in fact, from the seventeenth century until 1901 (see Laslett, 1972b, pp. 139–144, Figures 4.3, 4.4). Between the 1920s and the 1970s, the elderly in England became markedly more numerous, and the dispro-

portion in the numbers of old women as compared with old men, consistently small in the nineteenth century, suddenly grew. Meanwhile, household size was becoming smaller, so that the percentage of those living in households of one or two persons more than tripled, many of these solitaries and pairs being older people. It might be said that action in the story of societal development and aging in England and Wales was long in coming, but when it did arrive, in the lifetime of the aged people still with us today, it was swift and fundamental.

This may be thought to be a surprisingly dramatic story for such a subject as this, and since it is apparently the first time that such a story has been told, it might be natural to suppose that what happened in English society would be typical. The parallel series of

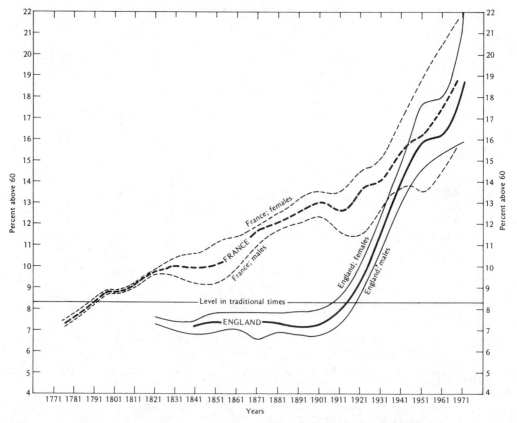

Figure 1. Proportions of elderly persons (aged 60 and above) in England and Wales and in France since the eighteenth century. The rise between the 1830s and the 1840s in the English estimates may be due to the difference between the figures of Wrigley and Schofield (1981) and official figures.

figures from France and the scattered numerical details from other countries in Europe and North America show that this cannot be so.

In France, the proportion of the elderly in the population was not so consistent during the nineteenth century, over the years when industrialization was beginning, as it was in England and Wales, and it was noticeably higher. The difference in the ratio of the proportion of the elderly by sex varied too. There was a curious rise in this statistic during the years 1821–51, when it could be claimed that France first began to industrialize on any scale, since in that country the process came later than in England. And so the different story continued until the 1950s, when development coincided completely in England and in France for the first time. Meanwhile, it is evident that neither country could be taken as a representative of western Europe, though England and Wales may have been at one extreme, where, as in Germany, the proportion of older people remained low until the end of the nineteenth century, and France at the other extreme, where, as in Sweden, the proportion was already high by 1900. The body of evidence from very recent decades as to proportions of the elderly and aged, sex ratios, and so on, shows a tendency toward convergence in what we have called high industrial societies, especially and perhaps paradoxically between England and France.

Table 5 has been inserted to show how different the situation can be now, in countries at various stages of the demographic transition and of industrialization as well.

Household Position of the Widowed, the Elderly, and the Aged in Traditional English Society

The three final tables attempt to portray the domestic situation of elderly and aged persons in one country, the first to undergo both modernization and industrialization and the first to be studied from the point of view of the present chapter. The great difficulty here is to get enough data to illustrate the prin-

ciples already laid down about this, the most important part of our subject. Accordingly, we have begun with a table drawn from lists of inhabitants that do not specify ages. While we possess these in tens, we have less than a dozen English documents in all with data that provide useful age statistics. Table 6 sets out the household position of widowed persons (age not given) in 61 English settlements. Although it is not advisable to use widowhood as a reliable indicator of age—indeed, up to half the women aged 45–49 could be widowed in an Elizabethan village—these figures indicate an interesting and important principle. This is that once a man or woman had become a householder or a householder's wife in England in traditional times, he or she tended to stay at the head of the family, in spite of the vicissitudes of life in that insecure world.

Even these figures are dubious, of course, because of the problem of identification by sex and situation; all men and women living with their children and without a spouse in the household, for example, have to be counted as widowed, so that some numbers of deserted spouses, especially deserted wives, must be present in the data of the table. Still we may attach some importance to these indications of how few "widowed" persons were living alone, or in institutions; to indications that having a married son or daughter living in the family was rare; and to implications that living in a household headed by such married offspring was considerably commoner, but still only affected about a tenth of all "widowed" people. The "other" persons in whose households the widowed are found were a miscellaneous lot, and included a good proportion of unrelated people with whom they were simply lodging. But some amongst them may have been married daughters unrecognized by us.

These uncertainties, it seems to me, cannot disguise the message of Table 6. Widows and widowers in preindustrial England lived for the most part where they were before they became widowed. The loss of a spouse did not always or even usually lead to the break-up of the household and certainly not to its

TABLE 5. PROPORTIONS OF ELDERLY AND AGED PERSONS IN CERTAIN INDUSTRIALIZED, INDUSTRIALIZING, AND NONINDUSTRIAL COUNTRIES IN THE 1960'S AND '70'S.

		AGED 60 AND ABOVE				AGED 65 AND ABOVE				AGED 70 AND ABOVE				AGED 75 AND ABOVE				AGED 80 AND ABOVE			
		M	F	Both	Sex ratio	M	F	Both	Sex ratio	M	F	Both	Sex ratio	M	F	Both	Sex ratio	M	F	Both	Sex ratio
United Kingdom	1971	15.9	21.7	18.9	69	10.3	15.7	11.1	62	5.8	10.0	8.2	55	3.2	6.1	4.6	46	1.4	3.1	2.3	41
United States	1970	12.6	15.6	14.1	81	8.5	11.2	9.7	72	5.3	7.5	6.3	68	3.0	4.5	3.7	64	1.4	2.3	1.6	60
Poland	1971	11.1	14.9	13.1	70	6.9	10.1	8.5	65	3.7	6.1	5.0	51	1.7	3.2	2.5	51				
Brazil	1970	5.0	5.1	5.1	96									1.7	1.9	1.8	87				
India	1971	6.1	6.0	5.9	110	3.3	3.4	3.3	106	2.1	2.1	2.1	104	1.0	1.1	1.0	100	0.6	0.6	0.6	96
Tunisia	1966	5.8	5.3	5.6	115	3.7	3.3	3.5	116	2.1	2.0	2.1	112	1.2	1.1	1.2	116	0.6	0.6	0.6	108
Indonesia (September 1964–February 1965)		4.8	4.2	4.5	110	2.3	2.2	2.3	103	1.5	1.4	1.4	100	0.6	0.7	0.6	93				

TABLE 6. HOUSEHOLD POSITION OF WIDOWED PERSONS BY SEX IN 61 PLACES IN ENGLAND BEFORE 1821.

	HEADING HOUSEHOLDS CONTAINING					IN HOUSEHOLDS HEADED BY						
	Unmarried offspring	Married or widowed son	Married or widowed daughter	Only those not offspring	Sub-total	Son or daughter	Son- or daughter-in-law	Other kin	Other persons	Solitary	In institutions	Total
Widowers												
Number	120	9	5	24	158	12	2	9	18	12	0	211
Percent	57%	4%	2%	11%	74%	6%	1%	4%	9%	6%	0	100%
Widows												
Number	243	7	5	50	305	48	17	19	41	65	6	501
Percent	49%	1%	1%	10%	61%	10%	3%	4%	8%	13%	1%	100%
Both												
Number	363	16	10	74	463	60	19	28	59	77	6	712
Percent	51%	2%	1%	10%	65%	8%	3%	4%	8%	11%	1%	100%

being absorbed into another household. We know that those who administered the Elizabethan Poor Law would assist a widow in keeping her family together, though we do not know how often this venture failed. There may, for instance, have been widowed persons present in these 61 English communities concealed from us because they lived as servants.

Table 6 is of value also because it gives a comparative context and some very welcome confirmation of the numerous facts about the household position of the aged persons in preindustrial England that have been marshaled in Tables 7a, 7b, and 7c. If, for instance, 6 percent of all widowers and 13 percent of all the widows can be supposed from the figures in Table 6 to have been living alone, it is reasonable that we should find that 5 percent of the widowers over 60 years old in Table 7c, and 16 percent of the widows of that age, should also be found to be solitary.

The difference in living arrangements between men and women was no doubt due to the greater facility with which widowers remarried, and this is one of a number of interesting contrasts between the sexes among the elderly in historical communities. Though we find three-quarters or so of persons above 60 to be living as heads of households, and so establish the principle that the old as well as the widowed were left to continue in their families as before, it transpires that over four-fifths of old men were in that position and only some two-thirds of old women. This was so because more widows than widowers were solitary, in earlier times, as indeed they are now, and because more widows lived with their married children although they did not quite so frequently form a household with their unmarried offspring as widowers did.

Old men, on the other hand, showed a slightly greater tendency to live as lodgers and in institutions if they lacked spouses. Here we must recognize that some of the individuals were certainly bachelors. Indeed, one 80-year-old inhabitant of the hospital at Lichfield was called "maidenly Harry" in the listing document.

The interest of the array of figures in Table 7 lies in the contrast between the domestic situation of the elderly in preindustrial society and their domestic situation in the England and Wales of our own day. We have found it difficult to establish comparison in just the terms that would be most revealing, and the best we can do for the time being is to be found in Table 8. Here the ages are higher, 65 and above, and only five settlements can be included from traditional England. The resemblances and differences are so interesting that it is hoped that these places are in fact reasonably representative. We shall rather rashly refer to the aged persons in this little group of places as "traditional English society," and the carefully selected sample (from Shanas et al., 1968, see Tables VI.16, VI.17) studied in the 1960s as "England today."

While two-thirds of married couples over the age of 65 live on their own with each other in England today, in traditional England this was not the case. Half of the married women were in that position, but rather fewer of the married men. In England today only a quarter of aged married persons of either sex have their "families" of children still at home.

Here we reach the same important point again, that, in the traditional world, full family life, defined in this way, lasted proportionately longer for most persons than it does in the present world, for those who got married and for those who became widowed as well. We may dwell a little, with these tables in front of us, on the probable reasons for these important circumstances, although at the present time we cannot be very precise in our discussion or entirely confident in the conclusions.

Under the demographic conditions and with the familial rules that prevailed in preindustrial England, numbers of children were quite large, if variable—completed family sizes varying, at different times and places, from four or five to six, seven, or eight. Offspring were born relatively late in the childbearing stage, both of the husband and of the wife, in contrast, that is to say,

TABLE 7a. HOUSEHOLD POSITION BY SEX AND MARITAL STATUS OF PERSONS AGED 60 AND ABOVE IN SIX PLACES IN ENGLAND BEFORE 1800: NUMBERS AND PROPORTIONS OF ELDERLY MARRIED PERSONS LIVING:—

	As head (or his spouse) with unmarried children		Not as head with unmarried children		As head (or his spouse) with married children		Not as head with married children		As head (or his spouse) with grandchildren		As head (or his spouse) with servants		As head (or his spouse) with spouse only		As head (or his spouse) with kin and/or lodgers		Not as head with kin of any kind		As lodger or in unclear status or position in the household		In institutions	
	M	F	M	F	M	F	M	F	M	F	M	F	M	F	M	F	M	F	M	F	M	F
Ealing, 1599	9	1	0	0	0	0	0	0	0	0	1	2	4	3	0	0	0	0	0	0	0	0
Chilvers Coton, 1684	5	8	0	0	2	0	0	0	1	1	0	1	5	1	2	2	0	0	0	0	0	0
Lichfield, 1695	27	20	0	0	4	5	0	1	0	0	2	2	13	15	4	4	0	0	0	0	0	1
Stoke-on-Trent, 1701	22	14	0	1	2	1	0	0	2	1	3	3	10	9	0	0	0	0	0	0	0	0
Corfe Castle, 1790	13	10	0	0	0	0	0	0	6	7	0	0	6	7	4	1	0	0	0	0	0	0
Ardleigh, 1796	11	4	0	0	0	0	0	0	3	1	1	1	6	4	2	1	0	0	1	0	0	0
Total	87	57	0	1	8	6	0	1	12	10	7	9	44	39	12	8	0	0	1	0	0	1
Proportion	51%	43%	0%	1%	5%	5%	0%	1%	7%	8%	4%	7%	26%	29%	7%	6%	0%	0%	1%	0%	0%	1%

222

TABLE 7b. HOUSEHOLD POSITION BY SEX AND MARITAL STATUS OF PERSONS AGED 60 AND ABOVE IN SIX PLACES IN ENGLAND BEFORE 1800: NUMBERS AND PROPORTIONS OF ELDERLY WIDOWED PERSONS (INCLUDING DESERTED SPOUSES AND NEVER MARRIED) LIVING:—

	As head with unmarried children		Not as head with unmarried children		As head with married children		Not as head with married children		As head with grandchildren		As head with servants		Solitary		As head with kin and/or lodgers		Not as head with kin of any kind		As lodger or in unclear status or position in the household		In institution	
	M	F	M	F	M	F	M	F	M	F	M	F	M	F	M	F	M	F	M	F	M	F
Ealing, 1599	0	1	0	0	0	1	0	0	0	0	1	0	0	1	0	0	0	3	1	0	0	0
Chilvers Coton, 1684	6	3	0	0	0	2	0	2	0	1	2	0	0	1	1	0	0	0	1	1	0	0
Lichfield, 1695	9	30	0	0	0	2	0	8	0	0	0	2	1	13	4	10	0	0	4	4	11	14
Stoke-on-Trent, 1701	7	13	0	0	1	2	0	7	1	0	1	2	3	6	1	4	1	1	6	13	0	0
Corfe Castle, 1790	6	1	0	0	2	2	1	3	1	2	2	1	1	7	2	8	1	1	10	4	0	0
Ardleigh, 1796	6	1	0	0	2	0	1	1	0	0	1	0	0	1	0	1	0	0	4	3	5	2
Total	34	49	0	0	5	9	2	21	2	3	7	5	5	29	8	23	2	5	26	25	16	16
Proportion	32%	26%	0%	0%	5%	5%	2%	11%	2%	2%	7%	3%	3%	15%	7%	12%	2%	5%	24%	13%	15%	9%

223

TABLE 7c. HOUSEHOLD POSITION BY SEX AND MARITAL STATUS OF PERSONS AGED 60 AND ABOVE IN SIX PLACES IN ENGLAND BEFORE 1800: PROPORTIONS OF THE ELDERLY HEADING HOUSEHOLDS, OR LIVING OTHERWISE.

| | MARRIED | | WIDOWED | | | | |
	Male	Female	Male	Female	All males	All females	All persons
Heads or spouses of heads	100%	98%	52%	48%	82%	69%	75%
In household headed by others	0 ⎫		28%	27%	10%	17%	14%
Alone	0 ⎬	2%	5%	16%	2%	9%	6%
In institution	0 ⎭		15%	9%	6%	5%	5%
Total	100%	100%	100%	100%	100%	100%	100%

with parts of the world where the European marriage pattern did not prevail. Although they finally left home with remorseless promptness, if not necessarily in age-order, these children went on arriving until well into the forties of the life span of their mothers. Therefore, some of them would still be in the parental household when the parents entered into old age.

Many of the families would be broken by death, but the children would remain with their widowed parents; remarriage, as we shall see, was frequent, especially for fathers widowed during the childbearing stage (see Laslett, 1977, Ch. 4 on orphans—a quarter or a third of all orphans were living with re-married parents). As old age proceeded, solitary couples and solitary widowed people grew more common, and living as lodgers or even in institutions began to be the fate of a few of the senescent. But three additional circumstances helped to ensure that these conditions were confined to a few. First there was the tendency for a proportion of the surviving grandparents, especially widowed grandmothers, to be taken into the families of their married offspring. Second was the fact that the expectation of life of the old in that society was lower than it is today, as is shown in Table 1. Third was the existence of retirement arrangements, at least for property holders, ensuring that for them the end of the life cycle did not mean poverty even if it did mean living in a reduced household, or even as a solitary. (See Wall, in Ch. 1 of Wall et al., 1983; and Spufford, 1974).

In the above rather dogmatic general account of the domestic situation of the old in preindustrial England, nothing has been said of those who never married, but these individuals, as will be seen, make no appearance in our tables because we cannot identify them adequately.

There are contrasts between the position now and the position then that are evident and clearly marked. According to Table 8, we have twice as many widowed persons living alone in our day as they had in preindustrial times. But some parts of the pattern described have to be extracted from our tabular information by comparison and inference. Table 7a shows, for example, that 30 percent of married males and 36 percent of married females over 60 were living with spouses only (4 and 7 percent, respectively, with servants as well). Table 8 reveals that by age 65, 44 percent and 49 percent of married men and women were living with spouses alone. We can therefore infer that, during the five years that elapsed as their parents passed from 60 years to 65 years old, the numbers of last remaining children went down quite sharply, and that this left their fathers and mothers on their own. Nevertheless at 65, as Table 8 makes plain, half as many again were living alone in England in the 1960s. And by the 1980s the numbers of solitary elderly persons had grown considerably.

The contrast between the contemporary world and the traditional world is well marked in these respects in Table 8, but there are interesting resemblances as well as dif-

TABLE 8. HOUSEHOLD POSITION BY SEX AND MARITAL STATUS OF AGED[a] PERSONS IN ENGLAND IN FIVE PLACES BEFORE 1800 COMPARED WITH BRITAIN IN THE 1960'S.

	CHILVERS COTON 1684		LICHFIELD 1695		STOKE-ON-TRENT 1701		CORFE CASTLE 1790		ARDLEIGH 1796		TOTAL		PER-CENTAGES		BRITAIN, 1960'S PER-CENTAGES	
	Men	Women	Men	Women	Men	Women	Men	Women	Men	Women	Men	Women	Men	Women	Men	Women
Married persons Living with:—																
spouse and unmarried children	3	2	8	6	12	2	7	2	5	4	35	16	46%	37%	24%	24%
spouse and married children	1	0	3	0	1	1	0	1	0	0	5	2	7%	5%	5%	1%
spouse only	5	2	8	5	4	3	11	9	3	2	31	21	44%	49%	67%	68%
others	0	0	1	2	0	1	2	0	2	1	5	4	7%	9%	4%	7%
Widowed, etc. persons Living with:—																
unmarried children	1	0	3	14	5	8	4	1	0	1	13	24	23%	20%	18%	20%
married children	0	2	1	10	3	13	2	7	2	2	8	34	14%	28%	23%	17%
others	1	1	9	16	5	8	7	11	5	5	27	41	48%	34%	22%	18%
Living alone	0	1	1	10	4	8	3	4	0	0	8	23	14%	19%	37%	45%

[a] Aged 65 and above.

ferences. Married persons over 65 were only very little more likely, it would seem from this evidence, to be living with their married, as distinct from the unmarried, children, than is the case today. With such wavering statistics, in fact, it may well be that there was no difference at all, especially for the males. So much, once again, for the outmoded stereotype of two or more married couples usually being present in the same domestic group in the *before* but not in the *after*.

In traditional England elderly married persons seem to have resembled their successors in another important respect. They were members of the households of persons other than their children just about as often as they are today. The heading "others" in Table 8 is inclusive and covers lodging and being in institutions as well as being present as a member of a family household.

A few, we cannot unfortunately say how many, of the "others" were kinsfolk and represent the whole sum of the *residential* responsibility that related persons, apart from members of the immediate family, undertook for the care of old people. In the case of the "widowed" (which covers the never married and those deserted by their spouses), the proportions living with these others are quite high, much higher than today. A comparison with Table 7, which in a sense breaks down this category for the over-60s, seems to imply that it represented lodging to a rather greater extent than living with kin (though, which is exasperating to the researcher, we have already seen that the two situations, lodging and living with kin, may not have been always distinguished in that society).

The deserted, and those who had never married, were perhaps the most likely to be living as lodgers, a form of residence that seems to have become more common for people of this sort as they grew older. To find that up to one-half of all spouseless old men—that is, "widowed, etc." males in Table 8—were in this (presumably) entirely *unfamilial* situation, and one-third of the

women too, is somewhat surprising, even after what has been claimed here about the lack of any responsibility upon the household in that social order to give shelter to distant relatives in need.

It could be said, on the other hand, that one was much less likely to be solitary as an aged widow or widower in earlier times. This may have been so because of the lodging arrangements we have just described as well as because of a greater propensity for widowed people to live with their own children, married, or unmarried. Sharing a household with married children compares in a rather complicated way between the traditional world and our own. Widows now are in this position considerably less often than they were then, but widowers today are actually much more frequently found with their married children than they were in the *before*. A comparison with Table 7 shows that this practice also seems to have grown as age advanced.

Little then seems to be left in favor of any prejudice against the contemporary English family for expelling the really old, or for failing to take them in, at least when the comparison is made with the English familial past. Even the advantage, in general, reckoned for widows and widowers in traditional England in Table 6, and for those over 60 in Table 7—that is, the advantage of being left to live with unmarried children—seems from Table 8 to have been eroded by age 65. Not many more of the spouseless had such offspring still resident than they do in our own contemporary world. When we are able to allow for the difference between the preindustrial situation and our own in respect of the numbers of children surviving to the old age of their parents, we will be able to make a more realistic comparison between the two epochs in respect of the aged, even with the present unsatisfactory data. It is possible that in this way a case might finally be made for believing that the aged would then have been less alienated from the family group than they are observed to be today, given that the same residential conventions had survived from traditional times. But I doubt if any such attempt at demonstration would be convincing.

We have described the old in preindustrial England as having in general been left as they were, and where they were, watching their children grow up and leave home never to return, and not receiving into their households their own elderly relatives for company, nor joining those relatives for the same reason. The crude, cross-sectional data on which our tables are based cannot tell us about the previous experience of the individuals described, and we do not know how many of the few found living with their married children had allowed, or encouraged, those children to bring their spouses into the house, or how many had joined those children in their households, abandoning their own family homes. We can, however, form a provisional if not a numerical impression of what usually happened in the study of change over periods of years in village society. This is an exercise that is occasionally possible in historical or traditional English communities (see, e.g., Laslett, 1977, Ch. 2).

These materials seem to bear out what has been claimed. None of the parents as they grew older between 1676 and 1688 in Clayworth, for example, seem to have been rejoined by a son or a daughter, married or unmarried, coming home to help them as their health and their strength failed. Quite a number of these aging heads of households were being denuded of their children during this period of time, and one or two were actually reduced to living on parish relief, or even in the Poor Law institution, while their children set up home for themselves in the village. The handful of instances in which married children did live with their parents seem to have come about because a son brought his wife, or a daughter brought her husband, into the house for a year or two or a month or two after marriage. Except for the unfortunates who had to go into institutions, the rule of continued independent residence by the old seems by and large to have been maintained.

There are two other possible resources against loneliness amongst the elderly in such a familial system: the introduction, perhaps by adoption, of young children into the household, and remarriage. Grandchildren are sometimes found in English households in traditional times, without their own parents being present, and very occasionally other children too. But we do not yet know how often the motive was indeed to provide companionship, and some personal service, to elderly persons, or how often it was brought about by parental loss. Indeed it may sometimes have happened that the English Poor Law authorities, who took responsibility for orphans, placed them with their grandparents and paid for their keep. Adoption was not a recognized, legally sanctioned practice until the twentieth century, though it occurred. Remarriage, we have now had to recognize, was not an expedient to provide companionship for the elderly widowed. Frequent as it was, and particularly so at Clayworth, until the eighteenth century, it took place largely among those capable of procreation.

Historical Data and Aging: Commentary and Conclusion

It has been insisted that the notion of a *before* covering both contemporary and historical preindustrial society is entirely misleading. So also is any assumption about uniformity in respect of the position of old people in the societies that represent our own past, the past, that is, of English-speaking peoples and especially of late twentieth century North Americans. Whereas the English, of English descent, can look back on what seems to have been a uniform past in respect of aging, other Europeans can do so to a lesser extent, and North Americans least of all. Before we conclude this essay in the preliminary analysis of aging and societal change, we may glance at a little of the newly available evidence from one or two other past societies, to get some idea of how variable they have been in their treatment of the widowed and the old. Further evidence will be found in Smith (1981).

Beginning with France in the seventeenth century, there is, for example, the village of Montplaisant in 1644, with some 350 inhabitants situated in the Dordogne (South Central). There were only 12 widowed persons there, and 11 of these were heading their own households; the twelfth was a solitary widow. All four of the widowers and four of the eight widows were, in fact, the first named in households that contained their married sons, households that seem to have been complex, some indeed very complex. All this is in sharp contrast to the English pattern we have examined, though when we reach 1836 we find in Montplaisant fewer multiple households than in 1644. In that later year, however, a singular circumstance appeared: the widowers, four out of five of them, were living with their married sons, but the widows, five out of nine, with their married daughters; no widower is found with his daughter, no widow with her son. Perhaps a chance effect of small numbers this, but indicating nevertheless how these practices might differ from small community to small community. In northern France at the same time, the aged were in the English situation, which (as far as we can yet tell) was by no means confined to England.

If we go on to take a German village, in the Baltic area in 1795 (Grossenmeer with 880 people), we find no solitary widowed persons at all, and a conspicuous difference between the sexes: 10 widowers to 44 widows. Two-thirds of these persons were living with their married children, equally divided between married sons and married daughters, but only two of them as heads.

Going outside the boundaries of western Europe, we can find villages with even fewer widowed persons, and with even lower levels of residence with unmarried children. At Vändra in Estonia in 1683 (population 967), the only widower recorded was at the head of a household of a married son, and all the eight widows were living as members, not as heads, in the households of married sons as well. Households, if household is quite the

word, were huge in that settlement and often very complicated. The situation was the same in villages in Latvia in the eighteenth century.

For the settlement of Kölked, in Transdanubian Hungary, in 1816, we have age evidence. There were 13 males and 17 females over 60 amongst the population of 636, less than 5 percent, of whom 6 of the men and 13 of the women were widowed. All the elderly males, married and widowed, were at the heads of the households of married sons, as well as one of the widows; five of the other widows were living in the families of married sons, and the rest of the elderly women were variously disposed. Only five of the women were in the "English" position, that is, in charge of a household containing their unmarried children. Once more, households were often complex in Kölked, but in settlements not far away they were as simple as they have been found to have been almost everywhere in England, with the aged in much the same position as we have described for the English.

The one cultural area outside Europe from which information on the old is beginning to be available for the past is Japan. Here we find examples of a situation which occurs very seldom in our own European data, the situation in which old people, and especially widows, have yielded the headship of the household to their *unmarried* children. Widowhood was commoner in Japan than might have been expected, and remarriage seems to have stopped altogether at the later ages; most old people evidently lived with their married sons. Some of these sons were adopted rather than offspring in the European sense.

We do not yet know enough to say whether local variation was common in Japan. Indeed, it must be clear that the sum of our present information goes only to the stage of providing a little of a comparative framework in which to place the English and the western European pattern of aging. Our own ancestors lived in their own distinctive way in this respect, but it will be a long time before we can say quite how much they differed from the rest of the world. We cannot yet pass any judgment at all on the *common situation* of the aged in nonindustrial society generally, among humanity as a whole, as has often been done by those who have previously pronounced on aging in relation to social development.

It has been convention in discussions of aging and the household in the European past, as far as these things have been systematically discussed at all, to insist on two features so far scarcely mentioned here, the stem family form of the household, and the tradition of retirement. It has recently been shown, for example, that in certain eighteenth century areas of Austria and Germany, a stem family arrangement prevailed among a sizable minority of households, allotting to the old a familial situation that gave to retirement an institutional form (see Berkner, 1972, 1974). These arrangements meant demotion from the headship and even, in a sense, expulsion from the family group. This might be said to be a less "familial" way of treating the aged, or even a more inhumane one, than the practices described for traditional England. But this pattern, which has also been found in twentieth century Ireland, did succeed in allotting a position in space to the outdated farmer or laborer, a space given the name "the west room" on Irish farms. In European areas where stem family tendencies were present to any extent, areas in Germany, Austria, and elsewhere between the Western and Eastern poles of familial organization (see Laslett in Wall et al., 1983), retirement arrangements were widespread and could be complicated (Mitterauer and Sieder, 1981, Ch. 8).

This is not the place to pursue the controversy about the extent to which social scientists have exaggerated the prevalence and importance of stem family arrangements. The "west room" of the Irish is now treated with some scepticism by the social scientists, for example. Nor have we the space to survey the evidence now being assembled about the position and role of the aged during the long generations that elapsed between the *before* and the *after* in English historical de-velopment. The aged, it has been commonly assumed, acquired a new role in the early factory era, a role as child-minder. It is becoming known, however (Anderson, 1971), that it was not always the parents and parents-in-law of the mill-girl wives who kept the home going during the long shifts at the loom, but friends and neighbors as well, not all of them old.

One further question only can be broached. How far was it an advantage to the widowed and the old in the traditional world to be kept in the familial situation? Did they in fact have the same appreciation of independence as their successors in our day?

We have one stray result to present in this connection from our English evidence. Amongst the privileged, widowed persons were less, not more, likely to be living with their married children than amongst those below them in the social scale (Back, 1974). Those who could afford to do just what they wanted about their aged parents did not have them at home. They seem to have set them up with their own servants in their own households. Or was it rather that the old gentlemen and old ladies themselves amongst the rich and powerful saw to it that they did not have to live with their married sons and daughters, but maintained their own establishments with their own staffs? This detail is the more significant in that the English gentry, like all privileged classes, were more and not less likely to have their relatives of other kinds living with them in extended or in multiple households. But the practice was not entirely confined to the gentry. We can see much more modest people providing servants for their aging parents in the evidence from those English villages that can be studied over time.

The conclusion might be that then, as now, a place of their own, with help in the house, with access to their children, within reach of support, was what the elderly and the aged most wanted for themselves in the preindustrial world. This was difficult to secure in traditional England for any but fairly substantial people. It must have been almost impossible in many other cultural areas of the world.

REFERENCES

Anderson, M. 1971. *Family structure in 19th Century Lancashire.* Cambridge: Cambridge University Press.

Ariès, P. 1962. *Centuries of Childhood,* translated by Robert Baldick. London: Cape, 2nd ed., 1973.

Ariès, P. 1974. *Western Attitudes Towards Death.* Baltimore: The Johns Hopkins Press.

Back, Kurt, 1974. Class differentials in the household position of widowed persons in traditional English society. Typescript.

Berkner, L. 1972. The stem family and the development cycle of the peasant household. *Am. His. Rev.* 77:398–418.

Berkner, L. 1974. Inheritance, land tenure and family structure at the end of the 17th century. Paper read at the International Conference of Economic History, Copenhagen.

Berkner, L. 1977. Inheritance, land tenure and peasant family structure. *In* J. Goody, J. Thirsk, and E. P. Thompson (eds.), *Family and Inheritance in Rural Western Europe.* Cambridge: Cambridge University Press.

Chudacoff, H. and Hareven, T. K. 1978. Family transitions into old age. *In* T. K. Hareven (ed.), *Transitions: The Family and the Life Course in Historical Perspective.* New York and London: Academic Press.

Chudacoff, H., and Hareven, T. K. 1979. From the empty nest to family dissolution: Life course transitions into old age. *Journal of Family History* 4(1):69–83.

de Beauvoir, Simone. 1970. *La Vieillesse.* Paris. Translated by Patrick O'Brian as *Old Age,* 1972.

Hajnal, J. 1965. European marriage patterns in perspective. *In* D. Glass and D. Eversley (eds.), *Population in History.* London: Arnold.

Hajnal, J. 1983. Two pre-industrial household formation systems. *In* R. Wall with P. Laslett and J. Robin (eds.), *Family Forms in Historic Europe.* Cambridge: Cambridge University Press.

Hammel, E. A. 1972. The Zadruga as process. *In* P. Laslett and R. Wall (eds.), *Household and Family in Past Time.* Cambridge: Cambridge University Press.

Hammel, E. A., and Laslett, P. 1974. Comparing household structure over time and between cultures. *Comparative Studies in Society and History.* 16(1):73–109.

Hareven, T. K. (ed.). 1978. *Transitions: The Family and the Life Course in Historical Perspective.* New York and London: Academic Press.

Johansen, H. C. 1976. *Befolkningsudvikling og familiestruktur i det 18 århundrete.* Odense: Odense University Press.

Laslett, Peter. 1965. *The World We Have Lost.* London: Methuen. New York: Scribner, 3rd ed., 1983.

Laslett, Peter. 1972a. Introduction. *In* P. Laslett and R. Wall (eds.), *Household and Family in Past Time.* Cambridge: Cambridge University Press.

Laslett, Peter. 1972b. Mean household size in England since the 16th century. *In* P. Laslett and R. Wall (eds.), *Household and Family in Past Time.* Cambridge: Cambridge University Press.

Laslett, Peter. 1977. *Family Life and Illicit Love in Earlier Generations.* Cambridge: Cambridge University Press. (See especially Chs. 1, 2, and 4.)

Laslett, Peter. 1983. Family and household as work group and kin group; areas of traditional Europe compared. In Wall et al. (eds.), *Family Forms in Historic Europe,* Cambridge: Cambridge University Press.

Mitterauer, M., and Sieder, R. 1981. *The European Family: Patriarchy to Partnership.* Oxford: Blackwell.

Pressat, R. 1972. *Demographic Analysis.* Chicago: Aldine-Atherton; London: Arnold.

Shanas, E., Townsend, P., Wedderburn, D., Milhøj, P., Friis, H., and Stehouwer, J. 1968. *Old People in Three Industrial Societies.* New York: Atherton Press; London: Routledge and Kegan Paul.

Smith, D. S. 1979. Life course norms and the family systems of older Americans in 1900. *Journal of Family History* 4(3):285–298.

Smith, D. S. 1981. Historical change in the household structure of the elderly in developed countries. *In* R. Fogel, E. Hatfield, S. Kiesler, and E. Shanas (eds.), *Aging: Stability and Change in the Family.* New York and London: Academic Press.

Spufford, M. 1974. *Contrasting Communities: English Villages in the 16th and 17th Centuries.* Cambridge: Cambridge University Press.

Tunstall, Jeremy. 1966. *Old and Alone.* London: Routledge.

Wachter, K., Hammel, E. A., and Laslettt, P. 1978. *Statistical Studies in Historical Social Structure.* New York and London: Academic.

Wall, R., Laslett, P., and Robin J. (eds.). 1983. *Family Forms in Historic Groups.* Cambridge: Cambridge University Press.

Wrigley, E. A., and Schofield, R. S. 1981. *The Population History of England: A Reconstruction.* Cambridge, Mass.: Harvard University Press; London: Arnold.

9
AGE IN ANTHROPOLOGICAL RESEARCH

Jennie Keith
Swarthmore College

INTRODUCTION

Old age is new territory for anthropological exploration.* Although old people have been essential partners in most ethnographic encounters (they have both time and information), the topic of conversation has seldom been old age or aging. In the last 20 years, however, a characteristically anthropological approach to age and aging has developed, moving from what Margaret Clark has called the ethnographic veto of gerontological generalizations ("My people don't disengage.") toward more systematic efforts to discover patterns of aging in various cultural contexts. Characteristic anthropological questions and strategies appear in this development. Most important, the scope of both questions and search for answers is broadly cross-cultural. In addition, the focus is "emic," that is, on insiders' organizations of meaning within the cultural contexts considered and among the old themselves. Finally, the anthropological view tends to be holistic. A large slice of social reality is considered in order to place individual experience in cultural context. (See Fry and Keith,

1980, for the application of anthropological research strategies in gerontology.)

In relation to other social sciences, the characteristic role of anthropology has been that of curator. In gerontology, as in other fields, anthropologists have often been purveyors of exotic examples and anecdotes that researchers from other disciplines put to their own uses. As anthropological work on age develops, however, we are becoming more active participants in the gerontological enterprise by proposing what cross-cultural data should be collected and how they should be used. In this chapter, I will assume both traditional and modern anthropological roles. Exotic tidbits will be offered, but there will also be the more solid fare of hypotheses about patterns of aging and the significance of age in cross-cultural perspective.

The familiar signs of an emerging specialty—edited volumes, workshops, review articles, a new organization—now signal the focusing of an anthropological approach to aging and old age (Amoss and Harrell, 1981; Fry, 1980, 1981; Fry and Keith, 1980; Keith, 1980, 1982c; Sokolovsky, 1983). This chapter reviews the questions, strategies, and results of that approach under three broad headings: "Old People in Society" reviews the status and treatment given old people by others, and the consequences of social change for their participation in society.

*This chapter was written with Swarthmore College sabbatical support and while the author was a Lang Faculty Fellow. I am also grateful to Alice Brodhead, Roy G. Fitzgerald, Christine L. Fry, and Etta Zwell for their comments on the manuscript.

"Aging and Culture" shifts to questions about cultural definitions of the life course, including the requirements of "functionality" at various life stages, definition of careers in various domains of life, rituals and symbols associated with age, and the impact of cultural values on the aging experience. "Age in Society" considers the broadest issues: conditions and consequences of various uses of age as a principle of social organization. When, for instance, is age particularly emphasized as a basis of social differentiation; for example, in formal "age-grading" or in separate old-age communities? How is age as a principle of social organization related to others, such as kinship or social class?

OLD PEOPLE IN SOCIETY

Comparison of the roles, status, and treatment of old people in various societies has led from the overgeneralization that all people did better in the "good old days" of traditional societies to more refined propositions about conditions under which some old people do better in some societies and during certain types of social change. To comprehend sources of the status and treatment of the old, the essential questions are, first, what are these sources for anyone in the community, not only the elderly, and, second, are there any features of this context that either obstruct old people's access to these sources, or give them privileged opportunity? Refinements to generalizations about the status and treatment of the old result both from progress beyond the use of secondhand information to the use of firsthand data, and from more sophisticated sampling and analytic techniques that extract better information from the existing ethnographic reports. More precision in analysis also results from more careful distinctions on several dimensions. These include distinctions: between status and treatment, or norms and behavior, and between what old people get and what they want; among various meanings of status; between young-old and old-old; among types of societies; among social categories within societies, such as men and women or members of different social classes. There is also one distinction that must be erased, that between old people and the other people in their societies. Our understanding of old people in society has been obscured by viewing them in isolation from other age groups.

The earliest work on status and treatment of the aged was secondary analysis of ethnographic reports not originally centered on aging or old age. These earlier studies suffer from the difficulties characteristic of secondary analysis. First, the information available had not been collected in order to answer the questions of the later investigators. Consequently, an adequate sample for analysis was difficult to obtain, and inferences had to be made from fairly sketchy reports. In addition, because the whole society is typically the unit of analysis, in these ethnographic reports, intrasociety variation is underestimated. The tentative generalizations of these reviews of existing literature, however, have become an important springboard for anthropologists who now go to the field in order to collect information about aging and the old.

The anthropological pioneer in cross-cultural studies of roles and status of the aged is Leo Simmons, whose *The Role of the Aged in Primitive Society* was published in 1945. Simmons compared the position of the old in 71 societies using the then new Human Relations Area Files at Yale University. Simmons reported that higher status for old people was derived from traditional skills and knowledge; security from property rights, civil and political power; food from communal sharing and exemptions from taboos; and general welfare from routine services performed by old people, for example, baby sitting, cooking, mending (1945, reprinted 1970). More recent comparative studies using similar quantitative techniques have identified information control as a key factor in explaining the position of old people (Maxwell and Silverman, 1970), and increasing social and economic heterogeneity, nonhousehold economic activity, or early turnover of resources to the young as threats to the status of the elderly (Press and McKool, 1972). The broad conclusion of all the early secondary analyses of older people's status is summed up by Cowgill and Holmes (1972): "The status of the aged is high in pre-literate societies and lower and more ambiguous in modern societies."* As reports from more recent firsthand fieldwork and from more sophisticated secondary analyses become available, they reinforce the broad outlines of conditions promoting high status for the elderly identified by Simmons and his descendants. The refinements to the earlier hypotheses result mainly from the recognition that these conditions for high status do not always apply.

Status versus Treatment

The first of the new distinctions derive from an "unpacking" of the concept of status. Significant illumination of the positions of old people in traditional society has resulted from the simple untangling of status or prestige from treatment. Examining the status and treatment of old people in a careful probability sample of 60 nonindustrial societies, Glascock and Feinman discovered a sharp distinction between the prestige of the old and the way they were actually treated. Over 80 percent of the societies in their sample had some form of nonsupportive treatment (ranging from insults to killing) for the old. However, in every case, societies with negative treatment for their older members also were reported to respect them (Glascock and Feinman, 1980, 1981).

What people say versus what they do, or social norms versus behavior, is one possible

source for these apparent contradictions. Most societies have norms enjoining good treatment for the old, but there is more variety in what people practice than in what they preach. Reports of variability in actual treatment of the old people in China and Taiwan are particularly significant because of the idealization of their status in Confucian ethics and, perhaps even more dramatically, in the wistful eyes of Western observers. Both fieldwork and historical research reveal that filial piety is not and was not always manifested even in rural and traditional settings, but is affected by factors such as family resources and number of living children (Ikels, 1980). Another quantitative survey of 95 societies found that lack or loss of children was the most important explanation of contempt toward old people (Maxwell and Maxwell, 1980). Intensive study of small communities in Appalachia points to additional factors that promote enforcement of norms about good treatment for the old. Treatment of old people must be visible and must have some salience to other members of the community (Lozier and Althouse, 1974). These two features of a small, rural community may be absent in larger and more transient urban or suburban populations. However, the salience dimension raises questions about possible effects of increasing numbers and increasing official recognition of older Americans. How Americans manage relationships with their aging parents may become as significant a basis for their evaluation by others, as the way they manage relationships with their growing children already is.

Norms about treatment of old people may also offer manipulative strategies to the elderly. Black Carib women in Belize, for example, were observed to publicize their children's neglect or generosity in attempts to rally the children's peers in maintaining pressure to uphold the norms (Kerns, 1980, 1983).

The concept of status must be further unraveled to distinguish what old people get from what they want, and support or care of the elderly from their power and active com-

*Their volume *Aging and Modernization* brought the interpreters a step closer to the data (Cowgill and Holmes, 1972). The book is derived from a session at the Central States Anthropology meetings in which Cowgill and Holmes posed questions about the status of old people to ethnographers familiar with various societies. Although the anthropologists answering their questions are reporting on societies they themselves studied, they are still limited to collecting information from their field notes rather than from their respondents—and the societies are not a systematic sample.

munity participation. In rural Taiwan, for example, although old men are well cared for by their sons, once the family property has been divided among these sons and the father is no longer head of the household, he is powerless and finds most of his social activity among other old male cronies (Harrell, 1981). The Sherpa of Nepal provide an example of old people who seem to have everything that could be included under the heading of high status and yet are unsatisfied with their situation. They live in a Buddhist society that idealizes old age, they own their situation. They live in a Buddhist society that idealizes old age, they own their own homes, and are in strikingly good physical condition. However, they bemoan the absence of the youngest sons with whom they would traditionally have shared their households, as these young men have left rural areas in search of mountaineering or construction jobs. Although other children are nearby, living with one of them is culturally defined as dependence. As older sons leave the parental household, each is given land. The youngest traditionally stayed with the parents and inherited his share, and theirs, only at their death. Living with an older son therefore requires the old people to leave their own home and become dependents in the child's household.

Categories of Old. Young-old and old-old in Neugarten's terms may be the universal distinction that at least partially explains the co-existence of high status and bad treatment for old people in many traditional societies. Glascock and Feinman in their comparative studies discovered a differentiation they label "intact" versus "decrepit." Their research, based on a more adequate sample than was available to Simmons, provides more systematic evidence for the two categories he was the first to identify, reporting terms such as the "overaged," the "useless state," "sleeping period," the "age grade of the dying," for the decrepit or old-old age category. In all but one of the sample societies in which the intact–decrepit distinction is made, different treatment is directed to-

ward old people in the two different categories. A more positive behavioral orientation toward the young-old consonant with positive attitudes persists until the individuals become decrepit, when various forms of nonsupportive or even "death-hastening" behavior appear, such as abandonment or murder; in 19 percent of these societies killing of the old was reported. Consistent with the positive attitudes toward the old in many societies in which they also recieve nonsupportive treatment, is the fact that in all cases where gericide occurs, it is done at the direction of the old person and by a close relative, usually a son (Glascock and Feinman, 1980, 1981).

Although these data make clear that the good old days were not always so good for all old people, they leave open questions about which types of traditional society were more or less likely to permit nonsupportive treatment of their older members. Both the Glascock and Feinman study and other ethnographic reports suggest two factors influencing the treatment of old people. First, communities in which old people receive nonsupportive treatment are most likely to be located in harsh climates, and they are likely to have no or only shifting horticulture as opposed to advanced agriculture. Second, they are likely not to have class stratification. For example, the Eskimo of the Canadian Arctic who were hunters were sometimes forced to abandon the old, but the sedentary Eskimo of St. Lawrence Island were not obliged to leave their old people to die. Other hunters and gatherers, such as the !Kung or the Asmat of New Guinea, did not experience the subsistence stress of the Eskimo, and their old men were able to maintain positions of leadership (Amoss and Harrell, 1981). Looking back to Simmons's original propositions, both the means of subsistence and the presence or absence of stratification are mechanisms affecting the ability of old people to acquire resources to protect their position in old age. In Maxwell and Maxwell's sample of 95 societies, for example, loss of wealth did not explain contempt for the old, probably because the possibility of extensive resource control was not present in many of these societies (Maxwell and Maxwell, 1980). When this possibility is absent, then *if* subsistence becomes marginal, old people are likely to be abandoned or killed, unless their cultural expertise has fostered a tradition of protecting them. (See Halperin, 1984, for a discussion of age and levels of economic complexity.)

Class and Sex Differences. Strategies and consequences of aging are consistently different for individuals of different social classes as well as for men and women. Reporting on her research into realization of norms of filial piety in traditional rural China, for example, Ikels (1980) concludes that "what limited evidence there is suggests that the image of the venerated elder surrounded by numerous progeny is essentially a depiction of the aspirations of the well-to-do." Demographic variables of fertility, morbidity, mortality, and migration combine to reduce the likelihood that any old person would have a large number of surviving children. Especially in southern China, many families possessed only fragments of land and supported themselves with difficulty. Consequently, adult sons have left South China for work in Southeast Asia, the United States, Europe, and Hong Kong for over a hundred years (Ikels, 1980, p. 82).

There is considerable agreement in the anthropological literature that old women age with less difficulty than do old men but less consensus on why. Both in descriptive reports and in more systematic studies, women in many traditional societies appear to weather both physical and psychological challenges of aging better than men (Cool and McCabe, 1983). Continuity is the reason, according to one set of hypotheses; discontinuity, according to another. "Both" is probably the right answer.

Because women in most societies play out their entire lives within the domestic domain, some researchers argue that women are therefore faced with less dramatic and difficult transitions in old age. Physical requirements of tasks performed by women in many

societies are also more adaptable to the constraints of aging. Hunting or heavy agricultural work may be difficult for old men to perform and their efficiency noticeably less than that of younger men. Old women may more easily continue food preparation and child care and, in addition, by performing these domestic jobs, free younger, stronger women for gathering or gardening. The hours and years invested in child care pay off for women in another way as well. The affectionate bonds created between women and their children and between women and their grandchildren are often a guarantee of both material and emotional comfort in later years. Men's power in earlier years may ensure them support to the letter of the law, but not foster the emotional ties that encourage care beyond the call of duty and are a satisfaction in themselves (e.g., Harrell, 1981).

In societies as distant as Corsica and Taiwan, the successful old woman is a powerful director of household affairs, an important source of advice to her affectionate and respectful sons, and the object of gratitude and love from her grandchildren. An old man is more likely to have transferred his household authority to his son, to be excluded by his earlier authoritarianism from intimacies with children and grandchildren, and to find most social satisfactions among a few male age-mates (Cool and McCabe, 1983; Harrell, 1981).

Another argument suggests that emphasis on the continuity of women's household activity underestimates its diversity both at any one moment and, in particular, over time. In many Mediterranean societies famed for "keeping women in their place," such as Greece, Lebanon, Corsica, and Spain, women in fact change places both spatially and socially in significant ways (Campbell, 1964; Cool and McCabe, 1983; Denich, 1974). Because most of these societies are patrilocal, young brides leave their family households to move to those of their husbands. Here, as subserviant and timid new arrivals, they are dominated by a mother-in-law who heads the household. Very gradually, the young bride pursues her own career through motherhood toward household headship of her own. These patterns are the basis of an interpretation of women as successful agers based on their lifelong experience in role change and adjustment to the requirements of various statuses and social situations.

Women are also experienced at adjusting to constraints imposed by physical conditions such as pregnancy, lactation, and menstruation. The need to adjust to bodily changes with aging may therefore produce less shock and outrage in women than in men. In many more complex societies, women are also more accustomed then men to a type of social identity that prepares them for roles in later life. When the repertory of social identities in a social context includes those that are ascribed, or acquired at birth, and those that are achieved, or acquired through individual experiences, old age may represent a surprising and unpleasant return to ascriptive identity for men who have spent their adult lives acting primarily through achieved roles in occupational and political domains. Women, even when they enter more public realms, are rarely in situations where their ascriptive identity as females is irrelevant. Underlying both arguments about women's successful aging is the premise that discontinuity is difficult. Women are seen as likely to adjust more easily to aging either because they experience less discontinuity or because they experience more and therefore are more skilled than men at adjusting to it.

"Which way does the discontinuity go?" is an obvious but often ignored distinction, as Rosow (1963) observed early in this debate. In many societies, women may be both more satisfied in old age than old men and more satisfied than they were themselves as young women, because their social position improves with age. The shift from timid, dominated bride to powerful household head provides not only experience of discontinuity but also a clear-cut increase in power and status. Feisty older women who perform bawdy dances and assert their opinions in

male councils are notorious in ethnographic reports (see Brown, 1982, for a review). Postmenopausal women are often allowed both freedom and influence. The key question is, why in some societies are women more severely constrained in earlier years?

The reviews of the literature done so far suggest, first, that some improvement in women's lives in their post-reproductive years occurs very widely, and, second, that there is variation in the degree of this improvement. Two kinds of hypotheses have been suggested by cross-cultural researchers, one to explain the variation and one the universality. Variation in degree of female role change in late life is related to degree of constraint in earlier years. Such restriction may have various sources. For example, if property ownership is linked to women's reproductivity, as in many complex stratified societies where inheritance goes to both men and women, women are strictly controlled before marriage and during early marriage. Their sexuality must be properly channeled in order to protect family prestige and property. The chaperoned courtship and obsession with virginity of societies all around the Mediterranean are examples of this pattern (see Cool and McCabe, 1983, on Corsica and Lebanon). When a woman is no longer fertile, her sexuality is no longer a social danger, and she may take her turn as a powerful supervisor of daughters and daughters-in-law (see Brown, 1982; Goody, 1976). Another type of contraint on women in child-bearing years is the "aloofness" required of husbands and wives in societies where all young adult men are warriors. The daring and aggressiveness required of warriors are supported by the separation of husbands and wives, who do not eat, sleep, or relax together and do not share child-rearing tasks (Whiting and Whiting, 1975).

A reasonable general hypothesis about variation in life improvement for older women, therefore is that the greater the distinctiveness of domestic and public spheres (for whatever reason), the sharper the behavioral shift toward freedom and visible influence in women's community participation after menopause. (See Rosaldo, 1974, for discussion of the domestic/public distinction.)

Moroccan folklore presents a hypothesis about universal male–female "cross-over" that has received considerable support from cross-cultural psychological studies. Fifty jinns, say the Moroccans, are born with every male child, none with a female. However, every year one jinn jumps from the head of a male to the head of a female, so that women become more assertive, clever, and malicious as they age, while these qualities decline in men. Projective tests of men in Druze (Israel), Navaho, Mayan, and American communities have been interpreted as revealing a shift with age from active to passive mastery (Gutmann, 1977). A cross-over shift toward a more active orientation is hypothesized for women (Neugarten and Gutmann, 1968). At least two other studies, however, offer evidence counter to Gutmann's hypothesis of a universal "cross-over" toward passivity for men and activity for women (Cohler and Lieberman, 1979; Werner, 1981; and see discussion in Fry, 1984). The findings of these studies could still be consistent with a deeper "return of the repressed" pattern, however, which is Gutmann's explanation of the male-female personality shifts he observed. If he is correct that men become more passive and women more masterful in a release from the repression of earlier years, then variation in early gender socialization would produce patterns other than "cross-over." To evaluate this broader hypothesis, it will be necessary to combine cross-cultural data on early gender socialization with data on personality in later life. Even if personality shifts with aging are universal, of course, role structures congruent with them are not, as the discussion of variation in role shift indicates. As Gutmann points out, for example, among the Druze, ritual roles are available to men whose more passive orientations in old age are appropriate for "passive affiliation with supernatural power (which) tends to replace the control and deployment of individual strength" (Gutmann, 1977, p. 308).

Social Change

"Where is it going and how fast?" are the central questions about social change and the relationship of old people to it. The generally gloomy view of this relationship portrayed by modernization theory has been criticized by historians for its unidimensionality, its flaws of timing, and its homogenization of the old (Fischer, 1977; Laslett, 1976). Cross-cultural evidence complicates the picture in similar ways (N. Foner, 1984). Like the historical record, the cross-cultural information reveals many reasons why the old may suffer from rapid social change, which includes urbanization, increased literacy, and technological development. Young people may leave communities; they may acquire alternative economic opportunities that undermine seniority and the authority of the old; information may be stored more efficiently than in the human brain; experience may become irrelevant, supernatural sanctions less threatening. However, these consequences of social change are not inevitable, and there are conditions under which the old may benefit from even rapid social changes. The distinctions to be considered include the level of modernization, its source, who is affected, what is the starting point, and what reactions old people display. First of all, reconsiderations of the modernization theory by some of its original proponents show that the asserted negative effects reverse at higher levels when the supports of the welfare state may reinforce the position of the old (Cowgill, 1974). During the depression in the United States, elderly who received pensions were important sources of revenue and accordingly valued household members. Similar effects of pensions are described more recently in the contemporary Soviet Union (McKain, 1972). Colonization as a source of social change sometimes froze old men in positions of power from which they would in more traditional circumstances have been obliged to retire sooner, that is, by redefinition of a traditional political role to a position in the new colonial administrative structure. Independence movements, on the other hand, were more likely to promote power for the young (N. Foner, 1984; Wilson, 1977). Various categories of people in a society are of course likely to be affected differently by social change because they start out in different positions. Men and women at older ages may experience modernization differently because men are more vulnerable to changes in the public domain of community life, while women may be more able to retain favorable positions in the domestic arena.

Members of different birth cohorts are also likely to experience social change differently (Mannheim, 1952). Many societies offer poignant examples of those who are both young and old at the wrong time: young when it is the old who are favored, and old when modernization has shifted the balance of power toward the young (e.g., Simic, 1978, on Yugoslavia). However, the threat to the old may be quite narrowly directed toward specific birth cohorts, as those young who are initially favored by social change may be able to maintain their strong position into old age. Flooding from a major dam built in the homeland of the Gwembe Tonga forced relocation that cost many old people their exclusive control over land resources. However, the young who acquired attractive land at that time are well on their way to powerful elder status based on their control of land (Colson and Scudder, 1981). In this case, the traditional connection between land ownership and power has not changed, though for one birth cohort the likelihood that the combination would be achieved in old age was threatened. In some cases the changes of modernization may threaten the source of authority, as well as permanently or temporarily reshuffle access to it. Land as a basis of power seems more resistant to change, for example, than supernatural sanctions. Old people also react to change in ways that may maintain or improve their position. Among the Sherpa described above,

for example, the motto seems to be, "If you are not going to be venerated, then hang on to the real estate." As younger sons move away from the community and are not available to share households and care for the old, the old resist the traditional division of property and are tending to keep the younger sons' shares for themselves. The old Sherpa also assert that small families are preferable to large these days, since the share of land left for the aged parents needs to be larger to compensate for the unreliability of support from children (Goldstein and Beall, 1981).

Modernization is not the only type of change. Revivalistic change oriented back toward a newly valued past may increase the status of old people who have the skills and information needed to facilitate the revival. Among the Coast Salish Indians, for example, a religious renaissance has shored up the position of the elderly Indians initially threatened by exposure to modernization. The old Salish are the only ones who know the words and the dance steps required in the recent revival of Indian religion (Amoss, 1981; Amoss and Harrell, 1981).

Summary

In conclusion, old people in society are affected by the same conditions that constrain or promote status and treatment of other members of their communities. We must then ask if there is any basis for asking questions specifically about the old at all. Put another way, are there any special features of old age present, and therefore potentially influential on participation and access to resources, in any setting? Yes—on the negative side age increases the probability of physical frailty; on the positive side, age increases seniority, and the probability of cultural expertise acquired through experience. The task of cross-cultural, comparative study of the status and treatment of the aged is to reveal features of various contexts that compensate for possible physical decline and/or reward seniority and experience. The results of research so far show the characteristic human situation: a dynamic interweave of physical, social, and cultural context shaping and shaped by human action. Security of subsistence base, including its vulnerability to environmental stress, constrains any society's capability of maintaining members who are not physically strong. However, the impact of subsistence marginality on the old is mediated by the degree of accepted social differentiation, which may or may not permit accumulation of resources, which in turn make it possible for some or all old to assume a powerful and protected social position. If all goes well, egalitarianism and lack of social differentiation may provide weaker old people the opportunity to participate and access to resources. However, if the subsistence base is squeezed, then weaker old people may be vulnerable to death or abandonment unless they can support themselves by control of significant property. Old people's control of less material assets, such as cultural expertise, may, on the other hand, make their support worthwhile for other members of the community. If the group's adaptation is stable enough over time to make experience a significant source of expertise, some old people may be especially useful in just the kind of stress situations that would otherwise threaten their maintenance. Respect and support for old people might then become part of a cultural adaptation giving both the wider community and its older members protection in times of ecological pressure.

AGING AND CULTURE

Culture is a "design for living," the shared understandings underlying a shared way of life—cognitive and precise as well as symbolic and ambiguous. Culture is a central concept in anthropology, and, like many well-worn tools, it has become a bit smooth and slippery over time. The essential attribute of culture is that it is shared: culture is both used and transmitted socially. Recently, anthropologists have given more attention to variation around a core of shared understanding: variation between males and females, or between members of different classes or ethnic groups, as well as variation across situations. Awareness has also increased that culture is less a template than a filter, and, at that, a filter made of elastic fibers and constantly stretched and reshaped by its users (see also Fry, 1984).

Consideration of the relationships between culture and aging raises issues of mutual influence. First of all, the life course itself is a cultural unit. Its definition and evaluation are part of a cultural map. Key features in cultural influence on old age appear to be: definitions of age, number and content of life careers, rites of passage, other ritual roles available to the old, valuation of cultural distinctiveness by community members, bases of personal evaluation. On the other hand, the processes of human aging present both constraints and potential for the transmission of culture from one generation to the next. In evolutionary terms, researchers speculate that this interweaving of culture and aging may be a significant part of human history. From this perspective, culture both requires and makes possible the presence of old people in human groups. Cultural artifacts such as weapons for defense and tools for food preparation make possible the maintenance of older and probably frailer individuals, as inability to run fast or chew meat are no longer death sentences. Older members of a group may in return offer care for the young and wisdom in the face of crisis that promote the survivial of their younger relatives. Some support of these speculations comes from recent observations of older nonhuman primates such as apes and monkeys. Among the macaque and langur monkeys, for instance, old females are important defenders and caretakers for infants. Old monkeys have also been observed to provide information derived from long experience (e.g., the location of a formerly used water hole). Their experience of the environment may rescue younger members of the troop from the effects of a natural crisis such as drought (Hrdy, 1981). This section will examine first, the influence of culture on aging and old age, and then the influence of aging and of old people on culture.

Definitions of Age and the Life Course

The most obvious cultural influence on age is its definition. Age is calculated differently in various cultural systems, with varying emphases on chronology (number of years lived) versus function (what a person is capable of doing), with varying numbers of categories in the life course, and with varying indications of age identity. Descriptions of each of these types of variation must then face the "so what" question: what are the consequences for the old of the various patterns? In worldwide terms, the most common way of measuring age is by functionality; chronology comes second; and the two sometimes occur together. There is not, in spite of the stereotypes, a clear-cut split between traditional and modern societies in functional versus chronological calculations of age. There are preindustrial societies such as Fulani (West Africa) in which years are counted, and individuals assigned to age categories on that basis. In a national survey, on the other hand, half of the American respondents used a functional definition for old age in response to the question "At what age does the average man or woman become old?" (NCOA, 1976, pp. 22–25). In addition, the Americans who did define old age in years also typically referred to the reasons why people are old at that point, for instance, retirement, physical decline, or change in mental attitude. The kind of function referred to in nonchronological definitions of old age is usually more social than physical, for instance, change in work responsibility or the adult status of children. In Glascock's sample of traditional societies, the least used definition of age is a change in physical capability such as senility or invalidism (Glascock and Feinman, 1981). Physical capability may be the marker for old age only rarely because most people are classified as old *before* they become physically impaired.

What are the consequences of different ways of counting? They may be a matter of life and death, as the differential treatment of "intact" and "decrepit" old people shows. At the least, they offer very different opportunities for individual negotiation of the aging process. The transition to old age may be more gradual and more voluntary when function rather than chronology is the indicator. Chronological definitions of age may also affect attitudes toward aging. When time is measured accurately and the point at which people should retire and die is calculated, individuals may feel anxiety about aging (Smith, 1961). It is more likely that attitudes will be crystallized into stereotypes about a category of old people when reckoning is chronological, as individual distinctiveness is more obvious when age categories are based on what people can do. Again, a clear traditional–modern split does not occur. More positive attitudes toward the old occur with functional definitions of age among Quecha Indians, Greenland Eskimos, Japanese, Burmese, and North Indians, and in the same national sample of contemporary Americans mentioned above (Kleemeier, 1961; NCOA, 1976). Those Americans who feel that people over 65 are very useful members of their community are less likely to define old age in numbers of years than those who feel that people over 65 are not very useful members of their community (NCOA, 1976, p. 24).

Functionality. There is great variation in the definition of functionality in different cultures as the requirements for full participation vary across communities. However, an explicit distinction between those who are and are not functional community members may be universal, as suggested by the "intact–decrepit" study described above (Glascock and Feinman, 1980, 1981).

What is required for participation in a community varies widely. The "activities of daily living" required for an old person to be perceived as functional are by no means universal. Physical anthropologists are beginning to create strategies for discovering the bases of functionality in various settings.

Extension of the comparative study of human physical development beyond adulthood into old age is a new enterprise for this field. As they have already done for child to adult development, physical anthropologists are now trying to discover relationships among biological age (e.g., skeletal or dental development), chronological age, and functionality for older adults in various cultures (Beall, 1981, 1984). It is not only what is required of the old person to be seen as "functioning" that must be taken into account, but also what culturally acceptable supports are available. For example, if a grandchild is a usual part of the old person's household, many physically demanding chores may be performed by the child with no implication of dependency for the old person. Physical requirements of appropriate community participation of course may also vary over time. Environmental stress may transform a marginally intact individual to someone defined as decrepit in a very short time. Again, this combination of environmental stress, available supports, and definitions of functionality transcends the traditional–modern distinction. The preliminary step in research on functionality must be discovery of its indicators. The often time-consuming effort involved in this initial discovery of measures, which typically requires the anthropological technique of participant observation, is as necessary for minority populations of modern societies as it is across traditional cultural boundaries (Eckert and Beall, 1980).

Life Course Categories. However the old age category is defined, it is in every culture embedded in a broader set of categories defining the entire life course. The number of age categories ranges from the minimal distinction of young, adult, and old through the intricacies of systems with ten or more named grades, or even two systems, one based on age and one based on generation. There is great variation in the number of age grades defined in various cultures. In a comparative study of 60 traditional societies (the same sample as used by Glascock and Feinman), the range was from 3 to 11 age grades for men, from 2 to 8 for women (Keith, unpublished). Among the St. Lawrence Eskimo, for example, age is used simply to separate boys from men, girls from women. Men and women as they mature "continue doing what (they have) always done as long as possible," then finally enter old age (Hughes, 1961). The Arusha of Kenya are near the opposite extreme of age differentiation. Members of this agricultural tribe recognize six formal age statuses or grades, youths, junior warriors, senior warriors, junior elders, senior elders, and retired elders. Approximately every five years an age set is created, including all the young men circumcised together in initiation ceremonies during that period. Public rites of passage move members of an age set through the progression of age grades.

The finer the degrees of differentiation in life-course categories, the more closely they can correspond to the continuous variation of actual aging. Two societies, alike in every way but their age categories, provided a natural experiment in the consequences. The Mesakin (Sudan) view the life course as tripartite, and men enter the eldest category while still in their thirties. As being "old" requires renunciation of attractive activities and also relinquishment of some resource control to younger relatives, the transition is difficult, and intergenerational conflict intense. The greater number of age categories in neighboring Korongo communities channels the natural life course less violently. Men are physically older when they are required to "act their age," and intergenerational conflict, as measured by witchcraft accusations, is less problematic than in the Mesakin (Nadel, 1952).

The most extensive research on perceptions of life course categories has used the techniques of ethnoscience or cognitive anthropology. The goal of these techniques is to discover the way people think about some domain of reality. The evidence used is linguistic: labels are elicited and then used as the counters in a code-breaking search for underlying dimensions that organize the differentiation indicated by the labels. Two studies, one in Lafayette, Indiana, and one among the Masai in Tanzania, used ethnoscientific methods and multidimensional scaling analyses to investigate age categorization, its conditions and consequences.

Fry (1976) presented informants a set of 34 cards each carrying the description of an individual in terms of sex, marital status, status of children, residential status, educational and career position; for example, "male, recently promoted at work, married, living with wife and children," or "female, married, has two school children and is working." Respondents were asked to sort the cards into age categories, then to assign a chronological age or range of ages to each grouping of cards, and if possible, to give a name to the age bracket that would describe the people in that category. First results are a reminder of how unwieldy a unit "American culture" is in a comparative study. The random sample of 242 adults in a midwestern city identified from 2 to 15 categories and assigned their age groupings over 200 different labels. However, a closer look at this intracultural variation does reveal some patterns. First, the number of age grades distinguished is affected by the marital and parental status of respondents as well as by their age. Fry argues that the people who make the most distinctions are those who need them most. She links number of age categories created by her respondents to their stage in the domestic cycle. When there are more individuals of different ages in people's immediate kinship network, in other words, when they have children of their own at home or when they become grandparents, she suggests that they will sort the cards into a greater number of categories. The basic premise that people use more labels when a domain is more salient could also underlie an explanation focused more directly on age. Heightened sensitivity to age boundaries may occur with more age-homogeneous social networks at certain points in the life course, such as the transitions in and out of social maturity around adolescence and retirement. In the middle adult years, when occupational and other social roles are the most numer-

ous, age has more "competition" and is likely to be less significant in individuals' categorizations of their social environment. On these grounds, age categorizations should be more significant and the number of categories consequently more numerous before and after the middle years of most intense work, child rearing, and community activity, exactly what Fry reports.

Another source of order in the multiplicity of names these Americans used for life course stages is on the deeper level of the principles according to which they were classifying the hypothetical individuals on the cards. Analysis by multidimensional scaling techniques revealed four major dimensions along which individuals were being scored, although the number of categories and their labels varied. The first dimension, not surprisingly, is chronological age; the others are labeled by Fry as engagement–responsibility, reproductive cycle, and encumberment, or the extent to which an individual is constrained or burdened. The most parsimonious analysis uses only the two dimensions of engagement–responsibility and reproductive cycle (Fry, 1980, 1981).

A second study carried out independently among the Masai of Tanzania began with the age categories established by the formal Masai age-grade system and proceeded to elicit the personality attributes of individuals in the various age statuses (Kirk and Burton, 1978). Multidimensional scaling was used to discover dimensions underlying these expectations. Both Masai and Americans categorize individuals by age in terms of their responsibilities and their domestic situation. However, their life courses assume different shapes because the underlying dimensions are related differently. In the United States because the engagement–responsibility dimension and the reproductive dimension overlap, people are expected to be most responsible at the time in the middle of their lives when they are married and raising a family. The relationship between marriage, childbearing, and responsibility is more complex among the Masai. First of all, the two dimensions do not overlap in the sense that peaks of intensity appear at different points on these two distinct life lines. In addition, male and female patterns are more sharply distinguished among the Masai than by the American respondents (Fry, 1980).

The idea that the life course may assume different contours in various cultures evokes the recent shift in gerontological usage from life cycle to life course. Cross-cultural study reinforces the empirical as well as stylistic basis for this distinction. There are cultures whose norms for aging make life cycle the most appropriate label. Among the Akwe-Shavante of Brazil, for instance, men who live long enough see their age set "recycle" from the most senior to the most junior age grade. The long-lived members of the set consequently participate once again in the activities expected of the junior grade, and old men may be seen helping the very young to build their huts (Maybury-Lewis, 1984). A linear life course is a better image for American aging than a circle. However, a close look at that line in comparison to some other cultural images also reveals further American assumptions about aging. A long, graying line descending into decrepitude is not the only alternative to life cycles; many lines is another option. As revealed in the American–Masai contrast discussed above, dimensions underlying age categorizations are more distinct in some cultural systems than in others.

Careers. Another way to consider the consequences of these distinctions between different domains of living is through the concept of career. A career may be viewed objectively as a series of statuses (occupational career, reproductive career) or subjectively as any chain of life events perceived by an individual to be connected and distinctive (career as alcoholic, spiritual career). Anthropologists have been collecting information about careers in both senses primarily through the life history. (See Langness and Frank, 1981, for a review of anthropological approaches to biography, including an extensive bibliography; Frank, 1980; Holzberg, 1982b; Myerhoff and Tufte, 1975, on life history as used by anthropologists in gerontological research.) Variation appears cross culturally in the number, content, interrelationship, and timing of careers, as well as in the major "themes" integrating individual lives (see Kaufman, 1981, for discussion of this concept and techniques for eliciting themes from life histories). It is well recognized that the overlapping of marital, reproductive, and occupational careers is a source of stress for many Americans, since responsibilities and accompanying tensions typically occur simultaneously in the various domains. This is not universally true, so that life stages perceived as particularly difficult for Americans may not be so for physiological, but rather for cultural reasons, as Mead (1928) suggested about adolescence long ago. For example, the timing of reproductive and subsistence careers is more differentiated among the Masai than for urban Americans (Fry, 1980, and discussed earlier in this section). The content of various careers and their relationship to physical aging obviously have important consequences for the old.

Careers exist in some cultures that do not appear at all in others. Ritual participation, for example, is a significant part of life in many societies and often offers increasing opportunities for participation and influence to the old as their reproductive and subsistence activities decline. It is a common pattern among the Bantu of sub-Saharan Africa for social participation to continue after death (Sangree, 1974). Ancestors are perceived as influential forces in living communities, and the old are viewed as powerful because they are the most effective communicators with the influential dead. African societies also provide many examples of the fact that men and women do not have the same options for maintaining reproductive careers. This is less obvious in a monogamous society, but polygyny emphasizes the fact that a man may continue the reproductive role longer than a woman. Increasing divorce rates in the United States, sometimes described as creating serial polygamy, may produce a sharpening distinction between male and female reproductive careers similar to that found where polygamy is more explicit.

Life careers are variable in another, more basic way: the concept of career itself may be more or less culturally relevant. For example, LeVine contrasts the intense attention to fertility history among Gusii farmers with comparative lack of interest in reproductive careers among Bushmen hunter-gatherers. LeVine's hypothesis about this difference focuses on subsistence activity. The Gusii are agricultural and consequently sedentary, while the Bushmen are hunter-gatherers (LeVine, 1978). The mechanism involved would be the importance of reproductive history in assigning individuals to kinship groups and consequently to relationships of property ownership. Among the Bushmen property is minimal, and social groups are fluid; so precise monitoring of reproductive careers perhaps has less social consequence for them.

In addition to differences in its contours and its content, a life may also be put to different uses as a conceptual unit in various cultures. Movement through life may be more or less explicitly choreographed; more or less spontaneity and innovation may be appropriate. A life may or may not be used as a unit for planning or for evaluation of persons. The Nepalese see a life of individual development with many branches for choice and the continuing possibility of personal change. Tahitians, by contrast, view life as a known path traveled by individuals who are completely defined beings when very young (LeVine, 1978). The possibility that these differences are at least partly due to the contrast between a small-scale and undifferentiated society and one that is complex, urban, and highly differentiated is reinforced by research. In Guatemala in the village of Atchatlan, Indians perceive life more like Tahitians, as having a well-worn path that all should follow as closely as possible. Mestizos in the same village, however, participate in wider Guatemalan society and perceive many possible paths through life (Fry and Keith, 1982; Moore, 1973). These differences obviously have implications both for planning and for evaluation of how people make use of their lives.

In the broadest possible sense, a life may or may not even be the relevant unit for calculating either achievements or responsibilities. If an entire life is the balance sheet, for example, care for older persons seems likely to be seen as reciprocity for their own efforts in earlier years. The view of old people as burdens on middle-aged children seems in this sense shortsighted to those from cultures with a longer view. An entire life can only be used as a unit, of course, when it is known. The stability of face-to-face groups—in turn affected by patterns of residential mobility—is consequently likely to have an important influence on salience and sanctioning of care for the old.

Ritual

In the context of the life course, as elsewhere, ritual is essentially a bridge—across the unknown or beyond the unimaginable. Ritual behavior, so highly patterned that it acquires an aura of the sacred, provides something for humans to do in those situations where in more practical terms there is nothing to be done. Old people in many societies play a special role in ritual, and, in addition, ritual has particular meaning for old people in certain times and places.

Rites of Passage. Whether it is perceived as a course or a cycle, the life span implies movement. The greater the discontinuity in behavior required by transition from one category to another, the more elaborate the ritual road map is likely to be. The classic definition of a rite of passage includes three stages: separation, marginality, and reincorporation. These stages may be collapsed into a few minutes or hours or spread out over weeks and months. Initiates are often dressed or decorated in special ways to indicate their temporary transitory position outside of normal society and day-to-day events. Old people in many traditional settings have a special role in rituals of passage. They are the teachers or the directors of the ritual production. In nonliterate societies, the old are the ones who know the words and remember the movements. In societies where old age is a distinct period in the life course, there are also rituals of transition into an older status. Such rituals are more common for men than for women, as nature provides a clear signal of status change for individual women at menopause (see Brown 1982, p. 146).

The existence of ritual formulae is no guarantee that all transitions will go smoothly. When to perform the ritual may be a topic of considerable conflict. In many cases, it is the younger who, like the Mad Hatter, press for a "clean place" while the elders resist retirement. In a study of 21 African societies with formal age-grade systems, those with fixed timing for transition rituals were rare and also the only ones without conflict between younger and older over timing (Foner and Kertzer, 1978). The hypothesis derived from this study, that conflict over the retirement transition increases as its timing is less fixed, appears to contradict the proposition discussed earlier that a larger number of age categories will reduce cross-age conflict by providing a better fit between social expectation and physical capability.

Looked at in terms of these generalizations, mandatory retirement laws could be seen as both sources of conflict and means of alleviating it. More flexible retirement should provide a better social–physical congruity. On the other hand, indeterminacy of retirement timing may promote repeated conflicts across age lines. One major difference between many traditional systems and the retirement process in the United States is the collective aspect of age transition in the former. Collective experience of ritualized transition may reinforce peer ties that become a resource in adjusting to the new circumstances.

Research in communities of old people suggests that the reverse may also be true. The availability of peers may promote creation of rituals of passage. Age-homogeneous communities of the old in modern society are a reminder that old people may be active participants in social change, and that the effects of change upon their social position are not always negative. In terms of ritual roles, it is true that modernization may undermine the exclusive role of older people as living archives of ritual. However, the age-homogeneous communities show us old people still as ritual experts, although now in a creative rather than a maintenance role. Old people in these settings have created rituals of passage with the classic phases of separation, marginality, and reincorporation. In the wider society, only the exit signs are obviously provided: the retirement dinner, the gold watch. However, the creativity demonstrated in the more extreme age-homogeneous community setting suggests it would be worth looking among informal networks of old people for such new rituals of passage as travel after retirement and changes in dress, hair style, housing, or car.

Margaret Mead (1970) observed that in times of rapid change learning may become "pre-figurative," that is, the young may teach the old; but in the particular domain of aging, the young do not know what they are talking about. In particular, at a time when what it means to be old is changing in itself, it must be the old who create and transmit responses, including rituals of transition, into the old-age society. Although such rituals are likely to be more defined and dramatic in collective situations such as old-age communities, more diffuse collective understandings may develop in natural communities and be experienced or played out by old people as individuals or in smaller groups. Social change may have positive effects on the ritual role of old people in another sense also. Particular expertise that is revalued is characteristically located in ritual domains. As we noted above in the case of the Salish Indians, revivalistic change may have positive consequences for the old who are experts in the past.

Significance of Ritual for the Old. Ritual viewed more broadly also offers important roles to the old in many societies where they are seen as ritual experts beyond the realm of age. In Hindu communities, as in communities of the Israeli Druze, prescribed ritual careers offer old people a path to influence and participation distinct from those of production or reproduction. Gutmann (1974) points out the congruence between such ritual careers and the personality shifts toward passive rather than active mastery that he hypothesizes as universal for males. Such ritual roots to social participation offer alternatives less dependent on physical vigor to old people and maximize the advantages of lifelong experience, especially in preliterate societies.

Because the old are especially likely to have experienced discontinuity, ritual tends to have a special significance for them. The aging process itself involves change on an individual level. Because ritual by definition is relatively unchanging compared to other kinds of behavior, ritual participation provides a thread of continuity through the life span. Ritual performance may evoke earlier ages in a powerful way, reaffirming the persistence of the self in spite of bodily change (Myerhoff, 1984). Ritual explicitly requiring the integrative reminiscence that Butler (1968) calls the "life review" also appears in traditional societies. Among the Kenya Boran, men moving into the retired age-grade are required to recite in public all the exploits of their lives (Legesse, 1973). Old people are also likely to feel most poignantly the discontinuity of change on the social level either as immigrants moving into a new social setting or as survivors in a social setting that changes around them. In either case, the old are likely to be active participants in rituals that offer a lifeline of continuity with the past.

Ritual as a bridge across many types of discontinuity, both personal and social, consequently has several kinds of special significance for old people. Rites of passage ease transitions into new age categories for the old as for others, but, in addition, the old are often influential guides in these ceremonies. In the societies where such rituals do not exist in later years, the old have often become guides in another sense, creating rites of passage for themselves and possibly for others who will follow them. As ritual is by definition one of the least changing aspects of a culture, it is a domain where seniority and experience are most likely to be honored. Finally, because aging itself is an experience of discontinuity, the continuities of ritual may have special meaning to the old.

Values

It is impossible to discuss the relationship between culture and aging without finally confronting the concept of values or cultural themes. These nonmaterial elements of culture are most difficult to capture for systematic comparison. The invocation of values as an explanation for the position of older people, as for anything else, is usually in the form of extensive case description. Such explanations offer satisfaction or frustration, depending on one's methodological point of view. The challenge is to raise such residual interpretations in terms of values or cultural themes up one level from the descriptive case to hypotheses about more general patterns.

Ethnicity. Value placed positively and explicitly on a culture itself is the first of these general patterns that promote a strong position for the old. As the "goldfish don't discover water" principle suggests, culture is often not explicitly acknowledged and consequently not explicitly valued. Its edges of distinctiveness are likely to be perceived and possibly defended through contrast with something different. When awareness of such distinctiveness is shared, and attributed to a common origin, the result is ethnic identity or ethnicity. Since ethnicity is a recognition of diversity, its relationship to any experience should be variable. There is considerable quantitative evidence that old people of different ethnic backgrounds have distinct experiences in basic aspects of life such as household arrangements, health maintenance, and income (e.g., Gelfand, 1982; Jackson, 1980; University Center on Aging, 1981). However, it has been the contribution of anthropology to discover the mechanisms through which ethnicity, as opposed to poverty or discrimination, has its effects. (See Holzberg, 1982a, for a critical review of ethnic research in gerontology.) Long-term, in-depth study of ethnic communities in the United States and other complex societies reveal the influence of traditional behaviors and values on the situations of old people (Cool, 1980, 1981; Cuellar, 1978; Kiefer, 1974). These effects are mediated both by the feedback between these traditions and changing social contexts as experienced by new generations, *and* by the active manipulation of the traditional resources by older individuals in response to these changes (see Amoss, 1981; Amoss and Harrell, 1981). The traditional culture is neither a guarantee of satisfaction nor a writ of doom for older members of ethnic groups. Like any human cultural repertory, an ethnic tradition offers compensations and/or constraints that its older participants may manipulate with varying degrees of skill.

In Boston, for example, traditional kinship and inheritance patterns affect care of elderly Irish and Chinese. In both groups, the child living nearest is likely to become the major caretaker when one becomes necessary. However, among the Irish, this is likely to be a daughter, among the Chinese a daughter-in-law. Strategies for ensuring care among aging Chinese consequently include encouraging a son's marriage, while Irish may wish a daughter to delay or even avoid marriage (Ikels, 1982). Research among Japanese-Americans in San Francisco reveals three major Japanese cultural themes—intense cooperation, situational ethics, and shame—that combine to produce a strong emphasis on sensitivity to others' reactions and the careful fostering of social ties. Individuals are consequently evaluated in terms of their skill at building human bonds. A person's success in life is judged by social as well as material productivity (Kiefer, 1974).

When the creation and nurturance of a living web of social relationships are significant bases for prestige, the position of older community members is bolstered. Positive valuation of interdependence also should foster both supportive care of older members in the community and their willingness to accept such support from the young. Clark and Anderson (1967) eloquently describe the dilemma of older Americans whose culture prescribes independence but does not always provide the means for maintaining it. Interdependence is not only not valued in our society, but often not even recognized. The scale and complexity of social relationships in a modern industrial society easily obscure interpersonal dependencies that are obvious in small, face-to-face communities. What is defined as dependence also varies. The Sherpa (discussed earlier in this chapter) consider support from the youngest son as appropriate and not indicative of dependence, whereas assistance from any other child is unacceptable because it means loss of independence (Beall and Goldstein, 1981; Goldstein and Beall, 1981). One unfortunate consequence of overgeneralization about the content and the salience of ethnic cultures in the United States, for example, is that all elders with obvious ethnic identities are assumed to be sheltered in the bosoms of extended families, and therefore not in need of services (see Cuellar, 1978; Maldonado, 1979, for discussion of this problem among Chicanos).

A second appropriate generalization about ethnicity and old age identifies one circumstance in which ethnic identity does seem to be universally positive in effect on the old. When younger members of an ethnic group value this identity, for whatever reason, the position of older members is likely to be strengthened. Promotion of ethnic identities may be more or less overt, depending on legal or tactical constraints in various social contexts. When overt ethnic association is a less promising strategy, a shift to the ritual domain often occurs as an alternative means of maintaining ethnic distinctiveness (Cohen, 1969, 1981).

Either overt ethnic organization or a ritual alternative is likely to increase opportunities for influential social participation by the old. When ethnic organization is overt, the old are technical experts in customs that mark distinctiveness. Their favored role may even in itself be an indicator of ethnic difference. When ethnic unity is maintained by less overt means, such as Lions' Club membership among East Asians in Kenya or Masonic Lodges among Creoles of Sierra Leone, elder community members are still likely to benefit from seniority principles and emphases on ritual rather than material prowess (Cohen, 1981).

Overt ethnic association also offers a focus and a location for sociability among older peers who might otherwise be isolated in modern urban settings. As Corsican identity has become a political basis for demands on the French government, for example, older Corsicans in Paris are a significant source of technical information for the young. In addition, good treatment of one's old relatives is considered a badge of Corsican identity (see Hendel-Sebestyen, 1979, for a similar example among Sephardic Jews in the United States). The Maison Corse is also an important meeting place for the old. Portuguese residents of the western United States attempt to emphasize their ethnic identity in order to distinguish themselves from Mexican-Americans who suffer economic and social discrimination. Their associations in California offer similar status and opportunity for sociability to the old (Cool, 1981). Native Americans, fighting for resources assigned on the basis of tribal identity, may turn to the elders in a similar way. The catch is that to take advantage of these opportunities to be cultural experts, the old must have the necessary experience. For some cohorts of Native Americans that experience is not available. Historical moment will consequently have important effects both on the likelihood that the young will turn to the old and on the way in which the old can respond (Williams, 1980).

Finally, regardless of its evaluation by young people, shared ethnicity may facilitate creation of age groups by old people if they have access to each other. Cuellar (1978) describes the opportunities for vigorous social participation shared by Chicano members of "El Senior Citizens Club" in Los Angeles.

Old Japanese immigrants offer each other a similarly intense but less formalized community in San Francisco (Kiefer, 1974).

Summary

The influences of culture and aging are mutual. Evidence from other primates and from contemporary hunters and gatherers suggests that old people have been significant in the evolution of a cultural adaptation that requires learning and therefore social transmission of a shared way of life. On the other hand, human culture per se makes possible, and in many of its manifestations also normative, the care of physically frail individuals. Variation in the position of old people in different societies can be partly understood through the constraints and compensations negotiable within the cultures of their communities. Finally, value placed on the distinctiveness of any culture is likely to reinforce the position of older people as its symbols and/or specialists.

AGE IN SOCIETY

Retracing the steps of anthropological research on age in society, I will begin with the formal age systems of grade and sets that were the first focus of ethnographic attention, probably because they symbolically contain physical aging most firmly within cultural channels. These formal age systems present most clearly the contrast between the two faces of age, the external and hierarchical relations across age lines and the internal, egalitarian bonds among age mates. The second major focus of ethnographic work on age and society is on the creation of age-homogeneous communities and informal support networks in modern Western contexts. Parallels between the relationships among age mates in these communities and in the traditional age systems suggest some generalizations about the conditions and consequences of age-peer grouping. Finally, the relationship of age as a principle of social organization to other characteristics such as kinship is now being considered in light of evidence from a range of societies crossing the traditional–modern distinction.

Formal Age Systems

Formal age systems present the extreme case of explicit age differentiation and maximal use of age as a basis for social action. The systems appearing in the societies often referred to as age-set or age-grade societies include grades, sets, and groups. Age grades are statuses, such as youth, junior warrior, and junior and senior elder, with associated roles and expected styles of behavior. An age set is a category of persons, often recruited over a period of years, so that the set is described as opening and closing. Age sets are not always corporate groups but may include large numbers of people from many communities and meet together, if ever, only for internal business and rituals of the age organization. Local age groups of men initiated together in one neighborhood are more likely to form a corporate entity and to share specific community tasks as well as strong social and emotional ties. The distinction among age grades, sets, and groups is parallel to the difference among the American concepts of senior year in high school (grade), the graduation class of a particular year (set), and the individuals who were seniors together in a particular high school in a given year (group). (See Radcliffe-Brown, 1929; Gulliver, 1968; Stewart, 1977; Kertzer, 1978, for discussion of terminology; and Baxter and Almagor, 1978, for a review of empirical research.)

Recent interpretations have placed formal age systems both under more refined scrutiny and in a broader comparative context. Often described as exclusive to East Africa—in spite of counterexamples (e.g., Jones, 1962)—and as military and political in function, age systems in fact have appeared in North and South America, in East Asia, and in western Europe, and more commonly specialize in ritual than in politics more narrowly construed. One side effect of recent empirical research correcting stereotypic views of gerontocratic authority and coeval

egalitarianism has been to give more plausibility to comparisons of age differentiation that cross the modern–traditional distinction.

Male and Female Age Systems. Most specific examples of age-set activity refer to men. In a recent quantitative cross-cultural study, almost half of the 60 sample societies had male age sets, whereas less than 20 percent had age sets for women (Keith, unpublished). In the few cases that have been reported, women's sets seem to have less significance and to share fewer and less-elaborate rituals than men's. They are sometimes described as more like ladies auxiliaries to the male organizations than distinct women's systems (see Gessain, 1971; Kertzer, Oker, and Madison, 1981; Maybury-Lewis, 1984; Ottenberg, 1971, for examples of female age sets in East and West Africa and Brazil). It is not yet clear whether the apparent lack of women's age sets is real, or created by the same lack of attention to women's lives that has characterized ethnography more generally. There are several speculations about reasons for the apparent absence of women's age organizations in many societies. First, women are more tightly integrated into familial roles than men, and these ties of kinship may override age commonality (Gulliver, 1968; Kertzer, Oker, and Madison, 1981). If women spend a greater proportion of their lives in the domestic sphere, they may also be less likely to participate in age groups that in some societies offer in more public spheres a counterweight to the ties of kinship (this complementarity will be discussed more fully below). Among the Ibo of Nigeria, for instance, women are organized into age groups that play an important part in women's trading activities in the public market. Ottenberg also reports that women's age sets have become more significant since precolonial times as women have become more active and independent outside the home. The priority of male–female distinction over age differences among women may be especially likely in patrilocal communities where a woman moves into her husband's territory and lives with many other unrelated women in a network of male kin (Kertzer, Oker, and Madison, 1981). Women may also be less likely to participate in elaborate age organizations because they do not need them. Transitions in the female life course are more neatly marked on an individual basis and by nature, so that age setting could be seen as a compensatory cultural development among men.

The significant dimensions of age differentiation include, first, the number of age grades and how clear their definitions are; that is, how much consensus is there about age-grade characteristics, and how specific are the attributes and functions associated with each grade? Second, how many age sets are there? Do they have specific social functions? How many? How central to the community? Three, are there age groups? Is membership universal? How relevant are they for how much of the life span? ["Comprehensive" age organization encompasses the entire life span; "transitory" does not (Gulliver, 1968).] Of course, the significance of age-group membership may fade in and out at various stages of the life course, so that the points of greatest relevance may not be continuous. Fourth, how are transitions from one age to another managed? How many of them are recognized? How much cultural elaboration does each receive, for instance, in ritual and other types of symbolic signaling such as clothing, speech, hair style change? What is the extent of accepted behavior change? Are the transitions recognized individually or collectively?

Such complete mapping of age as a principle of social organization has so far been done only for the most extreme cases in either traditional or modern settings: on the traditional side, explicit grades and comprehensive sets and groups; on the modern side, separate, age-homogeneous communities of the elderly. However, working with the material we have, it is possible to preview the insights of a broader comparison with initial contrasts between these examples of explicit age differentiation in modern and traditional contexts.

Societies such as Masai that have many clearly marked grades as well as comprehensive sets and groups are easily recognized as societies that "have age systems." Such classic cases also have other common features: egalitarian relationships among those in junior age grades, gerontocratic control by those in senior age grades, and separation of certain age groups from the rest of the community for a substantial amount of time. A first step toward comparison is to point out that both age-mate equality and gerontocratic control have been stereotypically exaggerated. Both assume more realistic proportions in a life-span perspective. The famous egalitarianism of age mates, extended to wife sharing and extolled in metaphors of brotherhood, is characteristic only of certain age grades. Most commonly, the grades whose occupants stress equality are those who have little access to the material resources or political influence that might make them unequal. The youths ease their exclusion from power and resources with an insulation of "sour grapes" egalitarianism that weakens as they move into higher ranks and enjoy access to property, women, and political influence. Age is a symbol rather than a source of equality.

The gerontocratic power of the old has also been overdrawn. If gerontocratic control is strictly defined to refer to power based on the ascriptive criterion of age, then it is quite rare. Even in those examples such as Samburu where members of older age grades have powerful ritual reinforcements of their authority, there are important distinctions among old men based on their individual achievements in domains such as polygynous marriage and creation of cattle herds. The important logical distinction is between what one anthropologist has called achieved gerontocracy and ascribed gerontocracy (Almagor, 1978a). In many societies, where the old exercise important resource control, their acquisition of a disproportionate amount of valued things is not ascribed on the basis of age. Their seniority, rather, has given them a head start in accumulating resources that take time to acquire and a broad web of social relationships that also takes time to create. Among the Tiwi of Australia, for instance, the pathway to power and influence is polygynous marriage. Wives are acquired in exchange for sisters and daughters, and a long career of alliances and exchanges is required before a man can be head of a large polygamous household. Old age does not guarantee that position, but it is impossible to achieve as a young man (Goodale, 1971; Hart and Pilling, 1960). In other systems, both achieved and ascribed gerontocratic principles operate. Among the Dassanetch of Ethiopia, for example, the senior members of the senior generation set are the official decision makers in the community. However, leadership of this group is elected, so that the leaders within the decision-making grade are chosen on the basis of individual achieved qualities. In addition, the leaders in more local arenas of decision making and conflict resolution emerge solely on the basis of achieved distinction among senior men without the ritually reinforced ascribed legitimation of authority reserved for those in the senior generation set; however, the position of these men may wane if their fortunes change (i.e., if their herds diminish or their network of social connections is weakened) (Almagor, 1980).

The hierarchical face of age is most often seen as smiling upon the old in traditional contexts. However, in recent years old people in modern industrial societies have achieved dubious promotion to a position where they do have resources to lose, and consequently to protect, on the basis of age. In the gerontocratic societies, old people attempt to maintain their privilege by ritual and symbolic reinforcement of ascriptive access to resources. Old people in the United States are now threatened, for example, by reorganization of Social Security, in ways that may elicit similar responses. The veteran who fought for us, the discrimination of mandatory retirement, the previous lifetimes of hard work, even the mother who made us apple pie, are likely to appear in justification of maintained support for older Americans. If benefits for old people begin to be perceived by younger Americans as costly

privileges, then a symbolic smokescreen may be necessary in older people's political activity, as it is for other categories of political participants who need temporarily to obscure special benefits to which they have exclusive access (Edelman, 1964).

Age-Homogeneous Communities and Social Networks

The two faces of age, hierarchy and equality, emphasized in the extreme cases of "age-grade and age-set" societies, illuminate some modern phenomena that originally appeared bizarre. True communities based on old age were initially viewed as at least improbable, and usually undesirable as well. Anthropologists working inside these settings gradually discovered a reasonable and positive view that has much in common with transitory age groups in the traditional context. Using the most distinctive of anthropological methods, ethnographic participant observers have done their characteristic "inside job" in a variety of age-homogeneous living arrangements (Keith 1979, 1980b, 1982c). Retirement communities, public housing, and mobile home parks, in the United States and western Europe, were the first sites of intensive anthropological research focused on old age.

The major finding about communities of the old is that they exist. Collectivities of old people, popularly viewed as "geriatric ghettos" in which worn-out people were put by their cold-hearted children, were revealed as active, complex social worlds. Both dimensions of community, the affective and the structural, are present in force. "We feeling" is strong, and social structure is distinctive. Strong "we feelings," typically verbalized in references to "we old people" or "we residents," promote both positive and so-called negative behaviors. On the positive side, mutual aid is extensive. In every community of old people yet studied, patterns of social support are one of the most striking characteristics. The old people create routines for checking up on one another using signals such as raised curtains or scheduled phone calls to make sure that friends and neighbors are alive and well each day. One or several stronger individuals often care for someone who is more frail. Even people with handicaps as severe as blindness may be helped through their daily lives by neighbors they met only inside the old age community. As precious as the material support itself is its low cost in self image. Both the observer and the old people consistently point to the lack of dependency stigma attached to these helping relationships. Help between friends, often referred to in familial metaphors, does not impose the cost of admitted dependency feared by many old people if they accept support from children or the state.

The superficially more negative side of the strong feelings residents have about the old age communities we have observed is the high level of conflict typically found there [Fry, 1979; Hendel-Sebestyen, 1979; Hochschild, 1973; Ross, 1977 (Keith, 1982c)]. The surface trappings of those waging battle are to an anthropologist's eyes delightfully diverse: French political factions, American Baptist churches, Turkish and Greek Sephardim. However, a high level of factional conflict is characteristic of these new old age communities. Why so much conflict? The newness rather than the old age of these communities is the answer. In a new community there is a great deal of undefined social territory to fight about. If the residents perceive little alternative to living in this setting and consequently have an "all in the same life boat" level of commitment to it, the scene is set for vigorous conflict. Although the persistent skirmishes may be a nuisance for administrators, they should be viewed as significant vital signs by the residents.

Distinctiveness. The boundaries of old age communities are also defined by the distinctiveness of their social structure. Both norms and behavior patterns are markedly different from those of the world outside. Distinctive norms about death and sexuality have not surprisingly made a forceful impression on younger observers. Open admission of the existence of these two facts of life—the one generally denied and the other denied more specifically to the old—is the first distinctive feature of the old people's normative system. Community members help each other prepare for death. There are characteristically recognized ways of "dying with your boots on." Discussion of funeral and financial arrangements is an acceptable topic among peers, in contrast to the "Oh, Mother, don't talk about that" response old people often report from their middle-aged children. The bereaved are supported and helped back into community participation. Recognition of death in ways appropriate to the particular cultural context are also reassuring to those who will follow. The bungled attempts by the administration at minimizing the first death in the French retirement residence I studied were greeted with comments of "I don't want that to happen to me," quickly glossed for the anthropologist as "I don't mean I don't want to die. I mean I don't want my funeral minimized and mismanaged." In that politically prickly context, the next step was a list of specific demands for future recognition of residents' death.

Sexual activity is also recognized as an appropriate part of life for those who want it. Old people in various communities both act like sexual beings and make comments about the increased possibilities of doing so among their peers. Fears of shocking children or of being ridiculed or patronized are expressed, as is wonder at the beginning of a "second life" with a partner met in the new community. Although for older women it would be unfair to suggest that partners become plentiful, still the opportunities for romantic and sexual relationships are greater in an age-homogeneous setting. Part of the normative understanding in these communities is a basis for distinguishing couples from promiscuous matings, although legal marriage is unusual. One of the distinctive elements in the social organization of the French retirement residence I studied was the recognition as married pairs, of individuals who did not fulfill the requirements of the outside legal system.

Behavior patterns, as well as norms, define a boundary between these age-homogeneous worlds and the society outside. Ethnicity, sex roles, social status all acquire new significance. In several American public housing projects, for instance, ethnic relations are more harmonious than in the cities beyond. Common age, in other words, assumes some priority over ethnic difference. Conditions promoting these eased ethnic relations include desirable formal organized activities (e.g., hot meals or trips), opposition to an external opponent (e.g., the perceived patronizing attitude of bureaucratic officials), and the presence of individual "culture brokers" who have personality characteristics and previous experiences to facilitate this role (Wellin and Boyer, 1979; Kandel and Heider, 1979). Sex roles in some cases become less differentiated in age-homogenous communities. More commonly reported is the redefinition of these roles. Men and women continue to do different things, in other words, but those things are not differentiated in the same ways as in the wider society. For example, the pottery class in the French retirement residence was a female activity in spite of vigorous staff efforts to integrate it. Particular tables in the lounge, on the other hand, were a preserve for male card players. Although both men and women did volunteer work in the kitchen, specific tasks became defined as male or female.

Egalitarianism. "We're all old people here. Who does she think she is?" is a statement made in various accents and in various languages in every old age community we have studied. The most distinctive aspect of their social organization is the rejection of external status and the stress on egalitarian values. Elected officers who revel too obviously in their recognition by outsiders, retired executives who cannot stop talking about their former power, even well-intentioned individuals who use former business contacts in at-

tempts to benefit the community, are punished by formal removal from office or by informal critique. As in the youthful age grades of traditional societies, status differentiation grounded in present-tense activities internal to the group is more acceptable than that based on the past and on links to the world outside. The parallel stress upon egalitarianism among the youthful age grades in many traditional societies and among old age mates in modern retirement communities derives not from the fact that both are age groups but from the situation of both as age mates excluded from power and access to resources. Predictably, it is the opposition forces with less access to whatever resources are at issue who are most likely to invoke equality within an age-homogeneous group. In addition, there is a slight amount of evidence that the egalitarian emphasis is more vehement when the age mates share a lower class status in external terms (Byrne, 1971, 1974). The general pattern, however, is that among the old age peers, as among the young warriors, age does not produce equality but may symbolize, evoke, and protect it among peers. Age, in its egalitarian aspects, is most attractive to those who have the most to lose by acceptance of hierarchy or competition.

Liminality. The transition into retirement and old age is not facilitated in modern societies by a ritual of passage with the three stages of separation, marginality (liminality), and reincorporation. The exit signs are numerous, but the individuals moving out of social participation as mature adults are stranded without a pathway to reincorporation. In response to this passage without a ritual, old people as individuals have created such marginal and reincorporation phases as extended travel after retirement and a plunge into volunteer activities on return. In retirement communities there is a collective creativity in two senses. First of all, the move to an age-homogenous setting is in itself a ritual of passage with both marginal and reincorporation stages. In addition, entrance into the new community itself repeats the three phases in a more nuanced way. As the new arrival learns to redefine outside identities, whether occupational, political, or ethnic, into their appropriate significance in the new context, marginal and then integrated phases are marked by, for instance, frequent table changes and finally a permanent place in the dining room (see Keith, 1982c).

In another sense, suggested by parallels between the old age communities and the separate age camps of many youthful age grades in traditional contexts, the entire age-homogeneous setting is marginal or liminal. Liminality is derived from the Latin word for threshold. It refers to the in-between state of transition from one social position to another (Turner, 1969). Couples on a honeymoon, military recruits entering training camp, pilgrims en route from profane to sacred space, initiates suspended between non-membership and belonging, are all in liminal states. Liminality not only exists between more structured states of existence; it is also an antithesis of normal structure. Most ordinary roles are "neutralized" in liminal periods. If hair styles represent social position, for instance, then initiants' heads are shaved. Special secret argots are often acquired and used during liminal experiences such as those of young men temporarily placed in isolated camps during their initiation period. The marginal or liminal phase is a fallow field for communality and creativity, as it offers temporary respite from status differentiation and normative structure. Learning with and from peers is a central aspect of the liminal phase of many rituals of passage. Individuals who share experiences of the liminal often share feelings of *communitas*—unstructured, spontaneous communal feeling. The logical and empirical link between liminality and age peers is that the "social clocks" of many cultures move age mates through liminal states together so that the egalitarian potentialities of age are accentuated in the combination of celebration and ordeal typical of most rites of passage. Liminality both evokes and is eased by solidarity with others in the same circumstances. Given their visibility, the col-

lective experiments in social creativity carried out by old people in age-homogeneous housing may have an influence well out of proportion to their numbers on an eventual definition of a reincorporation phase defining appropriate channels for social participation by the old in modern industrial contexts.

On the broadest comparative level, then, there are many reasons why old people might take advantage of the availability of peers to develop strong informal ties with an egalitarian emphasis. First of all, peer ties develop as an egalitarian or horizontal balance to the vertical strains of hierarchy among those whose position in the status ladder is low. Material as well as social needs may be met by peers in a spirit of reciprocity that does not require admission of dependence. A world of age mates insulates from external ranking members of an age grade temporarily or permanently excluded from power. The sometimes painful equality of shared status transitions also bonds peers together as co-learners and co-teachers. Shared experience of liminality is a powerful source of communal feeling in a context that goes beyond negation of ranking to a temporary irrelevance of all structure. In liminal circumstances there may be, in addition, a spontaneous ferment of social creativity. Old people in many modern societies are exposed to all of these conditions. When peers are available, we should therefore expect that old people, like other people, will be linked to these age mates in informal networks that provide both tangible and intangible support. In the study of old age, as in many other domains, the failing of anthropology has been to restrict research to the small bonded domains that were the easiest to study, retirement communities and other age-homogeneous housing in the case of old people. Questions about conditions and consequences of age bonding must be extended into more naturalistic situations.

A first step in this direction is exemplified by recent research among the elderly in single-room-occupancy (SRO) hotels of several

American cities. The insights of participant observers, combined with formal interviewing, are essential in these contexts. When asked about their social relationships, many SRO dwellers reply that they have none. Anthropologists who have followed these individuals through their daily lives discover, by contrast, extensive networks of social support that in fact permit these lifelong loners to remain independent. Once again, we hear that help from peers is not perceived as entailing the dependence feared in support from kin or institutions (Sokolovsky and Cohen, 1978, 1981).

A further step is taken in the only existing attempt at a complete ethnography of age in a natural community. In her study of a small southern town in the United States, Fennell discovered that age-graded women's organizations provide an avenue into the community of "Curlew Point" for the many retired women who move there. Once members of these formal groups, women can move into more age-heterogeneous relationships through introductions by two types of intermediaries: a "peer link," a person no more than five to eight years distant in age from either of the two strangers and therefore considered a peer by both; or a "familial peer link," a relative of one of the strangers whose participation in a cross-generational relationship acquires through kinship a legitimacy that is extended to the new pair (Fennell, 1981, p. 135).

Relationship of Age to Other Principles of Social Organization

Age systems were originally interpreted as war machines, or when flagrantly unmilitaristic, as either cultural survivals of previously militaristic organization or cultural flourishes with no obvious function. More recent analysis questions the relationship of age to other aspects of social organization, in particular, kinship. Although the usage of terms such as "generation gap" in modern Western societies places the onus of conflict between young and old on age difference per se, cross-cultural comparison reminds us that the nexus of intergenerational conflict is the family. Analyses of the interrelationships of age and kinship as social principles tend to identify kinship as divisive and award the peace-making role to age. The "Oedipal knot," as Fortes has called it—that is, the stressful fact that children replace parents—is universal. The issue raised by cross-cultural comparisons is whether the same generational relationship writ large into formalized age organizations might relieve some of the strain within the kin group, or contain family conflicts so that they cannot extend through a community. Among several pastoral groups in East Africa, for example, the age organization is a channel for avoidance or management of conflict focused on the parent–child knot in the rope of generational succession. The Arusha (Tanzania) value land as their most precious resource. Land conflicts, which typically occur across generations within a kin group, are kept out of the "parish" assemblies of the age organizations. In the arena of the age system that links the entire community, competition between adjacent generations is constrained. For the Samburu (Kenya) the scarcest prize is wives, for whom polygynous fathers and sons are in direct competition. Among the Samburu, authority over a man's sons is shifted within the age organization into another's hands. He is not allowed to be a powerful "firestick elder" over his own sons. The Masai (Kenya and Tanzania) also prize women, over whom competition also may occur within families. When an oldest son enters the warrior grade among the Masai, his mother and her other sons move with him into a separate warrior village. Father and adult sons are consequently distanced in space and also in the formalization of relationships within the age system (Spencer, 1976).

A general theme of kinship as conflictual and the age organization as harmonious counterweight also appears in Indian communities of Central Brazil. In these villages the world view emphasizes duality. Male-female distinctions are extensively elaborated, and villages are divided into central and peripheral areas. The entire universe is perceived as pushed and pulled toward equilibrium by opposing forces of strife and harmony. The complementarity of kinship and age affiliations merges these various qualities. Although specifics differ, typically village centers are male spheres where formal public activities occur. The center is the domain of ritual, and issues reach the community agenda via the men's forum there. The female world of domestic private life occurs on the periphery where households are located. Age organization operates in the center, sometimes in opposition to kinship at the periphery, sometimes (in patrilineal groups when kinship is consequently more male-centered) as a balance to kinship groups also in the center (Maybury-Lewis 1984).

A spatial dimension to the formalization of relations among generations is common around the world. Probably the most famous instance is the age villages of the Nyakyusa of Tanzania. In the traditional Nyakyusa communities, boys at about the age of ten set up their own small village, to which they eventually brought their wives. Finally, in a great retirement ceremony, the young men replaced their elders in the center of the community, while the old leaders moved to the outskirts. Nyakyusa view the age villages where age mates eat and sleep together throughout their lives as a means of avoiding conflicts between fathers and sons, who might otherwise compete over the young women attached to polygynous older men (Wilson, 1951). Separate quarters or sections of villages for different age groups also occur in several West African societies (Paulme, 1969). In a recent cross-cultural quantitative analysis, 28 percent of the societies had separate housing arrangements for men of a certain age category at some point during the life course, 18 percent for women (Keith, unpublished).

Conflict across age lines is by no means a modern invention. It occurs, and bitterly, around the world (LeVine, 1965). What is perhaps more distinctive to the traditional

settings are the techniques developed for conflict management. Remarkably, one of these, spatial separation of adjacent age categories, tends to be identified in modern Western societies as a source of conflict. Age-homogeneous communities such as retirement residences are feared as seed-beds of conservativism and negative political action by the old. Although there are examples of old people in the United States fighting legal battles for their right to live in age-homogeneous communities, I know of no evidence that living with age mates is a source of intergenerational conflict. The cross-cultural comparisons suggest first, that more formal age differentiation may ease conflict across the generations, and, second, that negative views of such formalization may result from particular American responses to age and to emphasis of social differentiation of any kind.

The ethnographic community studies give strong evidence that living among other old people is neither caused by nor a cause of unsatisfactory family relations. Relationships to children are an important part of the activity and value system of age-homogeneous communities. These relationships are an important topic of discussion. Children and grandchildren are included in many community activities. Community celebrations are rescheduled so that residents may participate in family holiday observances. Like same-sex friends scouting a party, old friends often agree to "fade" if children appear unexpectedly [Hochschild, 1973; Jonas, 1979; Ross, 1977 (Keith, 1982c)]. There is also evidence that age-homogeneous residence may parallel the traditional age organizations as a tension deflecter. Disagreements about norms and life-styles can be battled in a more formal and collective way between residents and directors or between tenants' councils and representatives of formal bureaucracies. Rules about noise, dress, or use of recreational facilities are less conflictual when imposed by a collectivity of older people on all their young visitors. Financial arrangements between the generations for shelter, food, and care are also formalized between strangers, protecting a more voluntary and affective atmosphere for the intimate intergenerational relations of the family.

Sources of Emphasis on Age. The broadest hypotheses about conditions for extreme emphasis on age, as in maximal age systems, refer to the significance of age at transition points and to age as a "residual" characteristic most significant when other social principles are least. Eisenstadt (1956) proposed that age groups appeared when the household was not an adequate locus for socialization or when members of the household actively impeded a young man's access to social maturity. In either case, the age group, he argued, served as a transitional sphere between the domestic and public domains when the household itself was not adequate as a launch. In his analysis, focused on socialization, Eisenstadt measured the degree of inconsistency between household and public domains in terms of styles of social interaction. Since relationships within the household are particularistic, ascribed and expressive (focused on individual attributes acquired at birth, and on means as well as ends), they are adequate preparation for mature participation in societies that are organized in terms of these principles. In those social settings, however, where more public domains are organized by achieved, universalistic, and instrumental relationships, the household is not an adequate site for socialization, and age groups are likely to appear. The exception to this generalization is the basis for Eisenstadt's second hypothesis: in some societies in which bases of social relations inside and outside the household are parallel, members of the household may still impede a young man's access to maturity, for example, by withholding resources needed for his marriage. In a polygynous society, these resources may be a focus of conflict between young men wanting to marry for the first time and older men hoping to acquire additional wives. Age groups are likely to serve as a lever for the young men against their more powerful seniors.

Almagor (1980) in a more recent analysis of East African age systems, makes a structurally similar argument with an emphasis on resource allocation rather than on socialization into modes of interaction. Almagor proposes that in pastoral societies where men own these portable resources as individuals, the age system provides a transition from the collective social base of the household to more individualized and flexible resource acquisition in the wider society.

The "residual" hypothesis about age relations states that age ties should be most significant when other bonds are less strong. Put this baldly, the argument does not seem particularly insightful. However, in more abstract comparative terms, it offers some illumination of conditions promoting comprehensive, rather than transitory, age groups. In a life-span perspective, it proposes that certain life stages are more likely to foster significant age ties than others. In structural and comparative terms, comprehensive age-group systems are likely to operate where significant roles and social functions are not determined by kinship or by the state, either because there is no political specialization and only a limited kinship system, as among the Masai or the Plains Indians, or because age-group activities are strictly separated from other spheres, as among the Jie of Uganda where the age groups are ritual specialists or among the Arusha of Tanzania where the age-group system is local and kinship nonlocal (Gulliver, 1968). Transitory age-group systems, on the other hand, appear when social roles are defined in a centralized political system and/or a well-developed kinship system, especially one that involves corporate kin groups.

The residual hypothesis can be extended slightly to place a more positive interpretation on age bonds, in particular, from a life-course perspective. It is not simply that age ties are significant by default when nothing else is available, but that links to coevals offer an especially powerful response to an exclusionary status system. Common age is not a guarantee of equality, in other words, but a most effective symbolization of it for those who benefit by evoking egalitarianism from their lowly position in a hierarchy. The broad cross-cultural hypotheses about age systems as transitional and residual suggest that from a life-span view age ties should be most significant in life stages that require important transitions, and during which there are fewer cross-cutting ties and reduced access to resources.

Comparative analysis of age systems also highlights the elaboration of rituals of transition. A general hypothesis is that rituals of transition will be most elaborate when the greatest behavioral change is required by the shift in roles. At the gerontocratic end of age systems, senior groups are invoking age as a means of maintaining power and access to resources. The strategies used commonly involve ritual and manipulation of symbols. The entire system of age setting with its ritual choreography for moving groups of individuals through time in calculated jerks has been interpreted as a means for the old to maintain power as long as possible by collective invocation of ritual reinforcements for their seniority. The elders manage to delay competition from young men through the rules of age setting (Baxter and Almagor, 1978).

Age is likely to be elaborated as a principle of mediation across two kinds of discontinuities: the vertical flow of generations and the horizontal transition from domestic to public spheres of social action. It is aging that carries individuals up the generational ladder and moves them from the household into more public arenas. Cultural elaboration—and consequently tighter control—of this time flow is most likely when the transitions are particularly problematic. Formal age associations, age-grouping, and/or extensive rituals of passage are likely to occur when the gap between modes of social participation inside and outside the household is great and when resource transmission down the generations is conflictual. (Conflict over resource transmission is affected by factors such as amount of property ownership permitted, specificity of inheritance rules, timing of inheritance at death or before.) Age groups provide social support in a community of fellow sufferers and co-learners. Formalization of relations and their symbolization in transition rituals may bridge difficult discontinuities by placing the flow of time under tighter cultural control: making the rules more explicit, shifting conflict up from the individual level. This displacement of unresolvable conflicts, such as those of generational placement, up to a ritual sphere is another example of ritual as the human response to situations when, in more tangible terms, there *is* no effective response. Social theory itself may be viewed as a ritualized domain in which contemporary instances of this level-shifting appear in the timing of major theoretical work on age relations. Severe social dislocations, stimulating feelings of cohort distinctiveness and inter-age conflicts, have also inspired the most elaborate studies of age relations: Mannheim's after World War I; that of Davis and Parsons after World War II; and the most recent surge after the civil rights and Vietnam issues of the late 1960s and early 1970s (Bengtson and Cutler, 1976; Laufer and Bengtson, 1974).*

CONCLUSION

In summary, comparison of the "extreme-case" reports of age differentiation now available from traditional age sets and modern age-homogeneous communities has produced many hypotheses that should both guide and be refined by more thorough comparative study of the uses of age in society. Nothing less than complete maps of age as a feature of life in various types of communities will do. Comparisons so far point to

*Anthropologists have participated in two ways in the debates about generation and cohort terminology. On the one hand, from their interest in the emic or "inside" perspective, anthropologists emphasize that a cohort may be a cultural unit, acquiring reality from shared feelings of individuals that they share a distinctive experience of history (e.g., Eckert, 1978; Nydegger, 1977; and cf. Rosow, 1978). On the other hand, anthropologists hoping to clarify cross-cultural comparison plead for a consistent use of generation only in its genealogical sense (e.g., Kertzer, 1982). See also Fortes (1984) on the appropriateness of generation as a metaphor.

life transitions, liminality, and the relation of age to other bases of differentiation as particularly promising entry points.

Ask an anthropologist about old age and what do you learn? That old people are people is the most succinct answer. Old people, like all members of human communities, exist in a social and cultural context that shapes and responds to their lives. Although audiences are sometimes annoyed by this undramatic summary of cross-cultural research, it is a necessary correction for over differentiation of old people from others in their communities, of old people in modern societies from old people in traditional societies, of old age from age per se as a principle of social structure. Translating proper names into variables is major progress in research on any topic. Cross-cultural research on aging and age has just reached this stage. As the hypotheses in each section demonstrate, we have moved beyond "old people do better in China than in the United States," or "Masai warriors are egalitarian" to identification of mechanisms through which interwoven physical, social, and cultural contexts interact with aging in any setting: for example, subsistence stress, residential stability, definitions of the life course, age structure of social networks, degree and bases of social stratification and economic specialization, rate and direction of social change. Variables make variation easier to observe—so far, so good. The next phase of cross-cultural research, now in progress, is the systematic observation and eventual comparison that will evaluate and refine the hypotheses through worldwide "ethnographies of age."

REFERENCES

Almagor, Uri. 1978a. Gerontocracy, polygyny and scarce resources. In J. S. La Fontaine (ed.), Sex and Age as Principles of Social Differentiation. London: Academic Press.

Almagor, Uri. 1978b. Equality among Dassanetch agepeers. In P. T. W. Baxter and Uri Almagor (eds.), Age, Generation and Time. London: Hurst.

Almagor, Uri. 1980. Coevals and Competitors. Jerusalem: Hebrew University (mimeo).

Amoss, Pamela, 1981. Coast Salish elders. In Pamela Amoss and Stevan Harrell (eds.), Other Ways of Growing Old. Palo Alto, Calif.: Stanford University Press.

Amoss, Pamela, and Harrell, Stevan. 1981. Introduction: an anthropological perspective on aging. In Pamela Amoss and Stevan Harrell (eds.), Other Ways of Growing Old. Palo Alto, Calif.: Stanford University Press.

Baxter, P. T. W., and Almagor, Uri. 1978. Introduction. In P. T. W. Baxter and Uri Almagor (eds.), Age, Generation and Time. London: Hurst.

Beall, Cynthia. 1981. Introduction. Social Science and Medicine. Special Issue: Biocultural Studies of Aging.

Beall, Cynthia. 1984. Theoretical dimensions of a focus on age in physical anthropology. In David Kertzer and Jennie Keith (eds.), Age and Anthropological Theory. Ithaca, N. Y.: Cornell University Press.

Beall, Cynthia, and Goldstein, Melvyn C. 1981. Work, aging and dependency in a Sherpa population in Nepal. Social Science and Medicine. Special Issue: Biocultural Studies of Aging.

Bengtson, Vern, and Cutler, Neal. 1976. Generations and intergenerational relations: Perspectives on age groups and social change. In Robert H. Binstock and Ethel Shanas (eds.), Handbook of Aging and the Social Sciences, 1st ed. New York: Van Nostrand Reinhold.

Brown, Judith K. 1982. Cross-cultural perspectives on middle-aged women. Current Anthropology 23(2): 143–156.

Butler, Robert. 1968. The life review: An interpretation of reminiscence in the aged. In Bernice Neugarten (ed.), Middle Age and Aging. Chicago: University of Chicago Press.

Byrne, Susan. 1971. Arden, an adult community. Ph.D. dissertation, University of California, Berkeley.

Byrne, Susan. 1974. Arden, an Adult Community. In George Foster and Robert Kemper (eds.), Anthropologists in Cities. Boston: Little, Brown.

Campbell, J. K. 1964. Honour, Family and Patronage. New York: Academic Press.

Clark, Margaret, 1972. Cultural values and dependency in later life. In Donald Cowgill and Lowell D. Holmes (eds.), Aging and Modernization. New York: Appleton-Century-Crofts.

Clark, Margaret, and Anderson, Barbara. 1967. Culture and Aging: an Anthropological Study of Older Americans. Springfield, Ill.: Charles C. Thomas.

Cohen, Abner. 1969. Custom and Politics in Urban Africa. Berkeley: University of California Press.

Cohen, Abner. 1981. The Politics of Elite Culture. Berkeley: University of California Press.

Cohler, B., and Lieberman, Morton. 1979. Personality change across the second half of life: Findings from a study of Irish, Italian and Polish-American Men and Women. In Donald Gelfand and A. Kutzik (eds.), Ethnicity and Aging. New York: Springer.

Colson, Elizabeth, and Scudder, Thayer. 1981. Old age

in Gwembe District, Zambia. *In* Pamela Amoss and Stevan Harrell (eds.), *Other Ways of Growing Old*, pp. 125–154. Palo Alto, Calif.: Stanford University Press.

Cool, Linda. 1980. Ethnicity and aging: Continuity through change for elderly Corsicans. *In* Christine L. Fry (ed.), *Aging in Culture and Society*. New York: Praeger (a James Bergin Book).

Cool, Linda. 1981. Ethnic identity: A source of community esteem for the elderly. *Anthropological Quarterly* 54(4):179–189.

Cool, Linda, and McCabe, Justine. 1983. The "scheming hag" and the "dear old thing": The anthropology of aging women. *In* Jay Sokolovsky (ed.), *Growing Old in Different Cultures*, Belmont, Calif.: Wadsworth.

Cowgill, Donald. 1974. Aging and modernization: A revision of the theory. *In* Jaber F. Gubrium (ed.), *Late Life: Communities and Environmental Policy*. Springfield, Ill.: Charles C. Thomas.

Cowgill, Donald, and Holmes, Lowell. 1972. *Aging and Modernization*. New York: Appleton-Century-Crofts.

Cuellar, Jose. 1978. El Senior Citizens Club. *In* Barbara Myerhoff and Andrei Simic (eds.), *Life's Career: Aging*. Beverly Hills, Calif.: Sage.

Davis, Kingsley. 1940. The sociology of parent–youth conflict. *Am. Soc. Rev.* 5:523–534.

Denich, Bette. 1974. Sex and power in the Balkans. *In* Michelle Rosaldo and Louise Lamphere (eds.), *Women, Culture and Society*. Palo Alto, Calif.: Stanford University Press.

Eckert, J. Kevin. 1978. Experimental cohorts among American men. Paper presented to the Gerontological Society Annual Meeting, Dallas, Texas.

Eckert, J. Kevin. 1980. *The Unseen Elderly*. San Diego, Calif.: The Campanile Press.

Eckert, J. Kevin, and Beall, Cynthia. 1980. Approaches to measuring functional capacity cross culturally. *In* Christine L. Fry and Jennie Keith (eds.), *New Methods for Old Age Research*. Chicago: Center for Urban Policy, Loyola University of Chicago. (2nd, expanded ed. 1984, South Hadley, MA: Bergin and Garvey).

Edelman, Murray. 1964. *The Symbolic Uses of Politics*. Urbana: University of Illinois Press.

Eisenstadt, Shmuel N. 1956. *From Generation to Generation: Age Groups and Social Structure*. New York: The Free Press.

Fennell, Valerie. 1981. Older women in voluntary organizations. *In* Christine L. Fry (ed.), *Dimensions: Aging, Culture and Health*. New York: Praeger (A James Bergin Book).

Fischer, David. 1977. *Growing Old in America*. New York: Oxford University Press.

Foner, Anne, and Kertzer, David. I. 1978. Transitions over the life course: Lessons from age-set societies. *Am. J. Sociol.* 83:1081–1104.

Foner, Nancy, 1984. Age and social change. *In* David Kertzer and Jennie Keith (eds.), *Age and Anthropological Theory*. Ithaca, N. Y.: Cornell University Press.

Fortes, Meyer. 1984. Age, generation and social structure. *In* David Kertzer and Jennie Keith (eds.), *Age and Anthropological Theory*. Ithaca, N. Y.: Cornell University Press.

Frank, Gelya. 1980. Life histories in gerontology: The subjective side to aging. *In* Christine L. Fry and Jennie Keith (eds.), *New Methods for Old Age Research*. Chicago: Center for Urban Policy, Loyola University of Chicago. (2nd, expanded ed. 1984, New York: Praeger.)

Fry, Christine L. 1976. The ages of adulthood: A question of numbers. *Journal of Gerontology* 31:170–177.

Fry, Christine L. 1979. Stuctural conditions affecting community formation among the aged. *In* Jennie Keith (ed.), *The Ethnography of Old Age*, Special Issue. *Anthropological Quarterly* 52:19–28.

Fry, Christine L. 1980. Cultural dimensions of age: A multidimensional scaling analysis *In* Christine L. Fry (ed.), *Aging in Culture and Society*. New York: Praeger (A James Bergin Book).

Fry, Christine L. (ed.). 1981. *Dimensions: Aging, Culture and Health*. New York: Praeger (A James Bergin Book).

Fry, Christine L. 1984. Culture and aging. *In* James Birren (ed.), *Handbook of Aging and Psychology*, 2nd ed. New York: Van Nostrand Reinhold.

Fry, Christine L., and Keith, Jennie. 1982. The life course as a cultural unit. *In* Matilda W. Riley (ed.), *Aging from Birth to Death: Sociotemporal Perspectives*. Boulder, Colo.: Westview Press.

Fry, Christine L., and Keith, Jennie (eds.). 1980, 1984. *New Methods for Old Age Research: Anthropological Alternatives*. Chicago: Center for Urban Policy, Loyola University of Chicago (2nd, expanded ed. 1984, South Hadley, MA: Bergin and Garvey).

Gelfand, Donald. 1982. *Aging: the Ethnic Factor*. Boston: Little, Brown.

Gessain, Monique. 1971. Les classes d'age chez les Vassari d'Etyolo. *In* Denise Paulme (ed.), *Classes et Associations d'Age en Afrique de l'Ouest*. Paris: Plon.

Glascock, Anthony, and Feinman, Susan. 1980. Toward a comparative framework: Propositions concerning the treatment of the aged in non-industrial societies. *In* Christine L. Fry and Jennie Keith (eds.), *New Methods for Old Age Research*. Chicago: Center for Urban Policy, Loyola University of Chicago. (2nd, expanded ed. 1984, South Hadley, MA: Bergin and Garvey).

Glascock, Anthony, and Feinman, Susan. 1981. Social asset or social burden: An analysis of the treatment for the aged in non-industrial societies. *In* Christine L. Fry (ed.), *Dimensions: Aging, Culture and Health*. New York: Praeger (A James Bergin Book).

Goldstein, Melvyn C., and Beall, Cynthia M. 1981. Modernization and aging in the third and fourth world: Views from the rural hinterland in Nepal. *Human Organization* 40(1):48–55.

Goodale, Jane. 1971. *Tiwi Wives*. Seattle: University of Washington Press.

Goody, Jack. 1976. *Production and Reproduction: a Comparative Study of the Domestic Domain*. New York: Cambridge University Press.

Gulliver, Philip, 1968. Age differentiation. *International Encyclopedia of the Social Sciences*. New York: The Free Press.

Gutmann, David. 1974. Alternatives to disengagement: The old men of the highland Druze. *In* Robert LeVine (ed.), *Culture and Personality: Contemporary Readings*. Chicago: Aldine.

Gutmann, David. 1977. The cross-cultural perspective: Notes towards a comparative psychology of aging. *In* James E. Birren and K. Warner Schaie (eds.), *Handbook of the Psychology of Aging*, pp. 302–326. New York: Van Nostrand Reinhold.

Halperin, Rhoda. 1984. Age and cultural economics. *In* David Kertzer and Jennie Keith (eds.), *Age and Anthropological Theory*. Ithaca, N.Y.: Cornell University Press.

Harrell, Stevan. 1981. Growing old in rural Taiwan. *In* Pamela Amoss and Stevan Harrell (eds.), *Other Ways of Growing Old*. Palo Alto, Calif.: Stanford University Press.

Hart, C. W. M., and Pilling, A. R. 1960. *The Tiwi of Northern Australia*. New York: Holt, Rinehart & Winston.

Hendel-Sebestyen, Giselle. 1979. Role diversity: Toward the development of community in a total institutional setting. *In* Jennie Keith (ed.), *The Ethnography of Old Age*. Special Issue, *Anthropological Quarterly* 52:19–28.

Hochschild, Arlie. 1973. *The Unexpected Community*. Englewood Cliffs, N.J.: Prentice-Hall.

Holzberg, Carol. 1982a. Ethnicity and aging: Anthropological perspectives on more than just the minority elderly. *The Gerontologist* 22(3):249–257.

Holzberg, Carol. 1982b. Anthropology, life histories and the aged: The Toronto Baycrest Center. *International Journal of Aging and Human Development*.

Hrdy, Sarah Blaffer. 1981. "Nepotists" and "altruists": The behavior of old females among macaques and langur monkeys. *In* Pamela Amoss and Stevan Harrell (eds.), *Other Ways of Growing Old*, pp. 59–76. Palo Alto, Calif.: Stanford University Press.

Hughes, Charles C. 1961. The concept and use of time in the middle years: The St. Lawrence Island Eskimo. *In* Robert W. Kleemeier (ed.), *Aging and Leisure*. New York: Oxford University Press.

Ikels, Charlotte. 1980. The coming of age in Chinese society. *In* Christine L. Fry (ed.), *Aging in Culture and Society*. New York: Praeger (A James Bergin Book).

Ikels, Charlotte. 1982. Final progress report on "cultural factors in family support for the elderly." Mimeo.

Jackson, Jacquelyne. 1980. *Minorities and Aging*. Belmont, Calif.: Wadsworth.

Jonas, Karen. 1979. Factors in development of community in age-segregated housing. *In* Jennie Keith (ed.), *The Ethnography of Old Age*. Special Issue, *Anthropological Quarterly* 52(1):29–38.

Jones, G. I. 1962. Ibo age organization. *Journal of the Royal Anthropological Institute of Great Britain and Ireland* 92:191–211.

Kandel, Randy, and Heider, Marian. 1979. Friendship and factionalism in a tri-ethnic housing complex. *In* Jennie Keith (ed.), *The Ethnography of Old Age*. Special Issue, *Anthropological Quarterly* 52(1):49–60.

Kaufman, Sharon. 1981. Cultural components of identity in old age. *Ethos* 9(1):51–87.

Keith, Jennie (ed.) 1979. *The Ethnography of Old Age*. Special Issue, *Anthropological Quarterly* 52(1):1–69.

Keith, Jennie. 1980a. The best is yet to be: Toward an anthropology of age. *Annual Review of Anthropology*, Vol. 9. Palo Alto, Calif.: Annual Reviews, Inc.

Keith, Jennie. 1980b. Old age and community creation. *In* Christine L. Fry (ed.), *Aging, Culture, and Society*. New York: Praeger (A James Bergin Book).

Keith, Jennie. 1982a. Old age and age differentiation: Anthropological speculation on age as a social border. *In* Sara B. Kiesler, James N. Morgan, and Valerie Kincade Oppenheimer (eds.), *Aging: Social Change*. New York: Academic Press.

Keith, Jennie. 1982b. *Old People as People: Social and Cultural Influences on Aging and Old Age*. Boston: Little, Brown.

Keith, Jennie. 1982c. *Old People, New Lives: Community Creation in a Retirement Residence*. Chicago: University of Chicago Press (Phoenix ed. of Ross, 1977).

Kerns, Virginia. 1980. Aging and mutual support relations among the black Carib. *In* Christine L. Fry (ed.), *Aging in Culture and Society*. New York: Praeger (A James Bergin Book).

Kerns, Virginia. 1983. *Women and Ancestors*. Champaign: University of Illinois Press.

Kertzer, David. 1978. Theoretical developments in the study of age-group systems (review of Stewart, 1977). *American Ethnologist* 5:368–374.

Kertzer, David. 1982. Generation and Age in Cross-Cultural Perspective. *In* Matilda W. Riley, Ronald Abeles, and Michael Teitelbaum (eds.), *Aging from Birth to Death: Sociotemporal Perspectives*. Boulder: Westview Press.

Kertzer, David, Oker, B., and Madison, B. 1981. Women's age-set systems in Africa: the Latuka of Southern Sudan. *In* Christine L. Fry (ed.) *Dimensions: Aging, Culture and Health*. New York: Praeger (A James Bergin Book).

Kiefer, Christie. 1974. *Changing Cultures, Changing Lives*. San Francisco: Jossey-Bass.

Kirk, Lorraine, and Burton, Michael. 1977. Meaning and context: A study of contextual shifts in meaning of Masai personality descriptions. *American Ethnologist* 4:734–761.

Kleemeier, Robert. 1961. *Aging and Leisure*. New York: Oxford University Press.

Langness, L. L. and Frank, Gelya. 1981. *Lives: An An-*

thropological Approach to Biography. Novato, Calif.: Chandler and Sharp.

Laufer, Robert S., and Bengtson, Vern. 1974. Generations, aging and social stratification: On the development of generational units. *Journal of Social Issues* 30:181-206.

Laslett, Peter. 1976. Societal development and aging. *In*, Robert H. Binstock and Ethel Shanas (eds.), *Handbook of Aging and the Social Sciences,* 1st ed. pp. 87-116. New York: Van Nostrand Reinhold.

Legesse, Asmarom. 1973. *Gada.* New York: The Free Press.

LeVine, Robert. 1965. Intergenerational tensions and extended family structures in Africa. *In* Ethel Shanas and Gordon F. Streib (eds.), *Social Structure and the Family,* p. 188-204. Englewood Cliffs, N.J.: Prentice-Hall.

LeVine, Robert. 1978. Aging and adulthood in crosscultural perspective. *Items* 31/31:1-5.

Lozier, John, and Althouse, Ronald. 1974. Social enforcement of behavior toward elders in an Appalachian mountain settlement. *Gerontologist* 14:69-80.

Maldonado, D. 1979. Aging: the Chicano context. *In* Donald Gelfand and A. Kutzik (eds.), *Ethnicity and Aging.* New York: Springer.

Mannheim, Karl. 1952. The problem of generations. *In: Essays on the Sociology of Knowledge,* pp. 276-320. New York: Oxford University Press.

Maxwell, Robert, and Maxwell, Eleanor Krassen. Explanations for contempt expressed toward old people. (Unpublished.)

Maxwell, Robert, and Silverman, Philip. 1970. Information and esteem. *Aging and Human Development* 1:361-392.

Maybury-Lewis, David. 1984. Age and kinship: A structural view. *In* David Kertzer and Jennie Keith (eds.), *Age and Anthropological Theory.*

McKain, Walter. 1972. The Aged in the U.S.S.R. *In* Donald Cowgill and Lowell Holmes (eds.), *Aging and Modernization,* pp. 151-165. New York: Appleton-Century-Crofts.

Mead, Margaret. 1928. *Coming of Age in Samoa.* New York: William Morrow and Co.

Mead, Margaret. 1970. *Culture and Commitment: A Study of the Generation Gap.* Garden City, N.Y.: Doubleday.

Moore, Alexander. 1973. *Life Cycles in Atchatlan: The Diverse Careers of Certain Guatemalans.* New York: Teachers College, Columbia University.

Myerhoff, Barbara. 1984. Rites and signs of ripening. *In* David Kertzer and Jennie Keith (eds.), *Age and Anthropological Theory.* Ithaca, N.Y.: Cornell University Press.

Myerhoff, Barbara, and Tufte, Virginia. 1975. Life history as integration. *Gerontologist* 541(Dec.):544.

Nadel, S. F. 1952. Witchcraft in four African societies. *American Anthropologist* 54:18-29.

National Council on Aging (NCOA). 1976. *The Myth and Reality of Aging in America.* Washington, D.C.: National Council on Aging.

Neugarten, Bernice, and Gutmann, David. 1968. Age-sex roles and personality in middle age. A thematic apperception study. *In* Bernice Neugarten (ed.), *Middle Age and Aging,* pp. 58-71. Chicago: University of Chicago Press.

Nydegger, Corinne. 1977. Multiple cohort membership. Paper presented to Gerontological Society Annual Meeting, San Francisco.

Ottenberg, Simon. 1971. *Leadership and Authority in an African Society: The Afikpo Village-Group.* Seattle: University of Washington Press.

Parsons, Talcott. 1942. Age and Sex in the Social Structure of the United States. *American Sociological Review.* 7:604-616.

Paulme, Denise (ed.). 1969. *Classes et Associations d'Age en Afrique de l'Ouest.* Paris: Plon.

Paulme, Denise. 1973. Blood pacts, age classes and caste in black Africa. *In* Pierre Alexandre (ed.), *French Perspectives in African Studies.* London: Oxford University Press.

Press, Irwin, and McKool, Michael. 1972. Social structure and status of the aged. *Aging and Human Development* 3:297-306.

Radcliffe-Brown, A. R. 1929. Age and organization terminology. *Man* 29:21.

Rosaldo, Michelle Z. 1974. Women, culture and society: A theoretical overview. *In* Michelle Z. Rosaldo and Louise Lamphere (eds.), *Women, Culture and Society.* Palo Alto, Calif.: Stanford University Press.

Rosow, Irving. 1963. Adjustment of the normal aged. *In* R. Williams, Clark Tibbitts, and Wilma Donahue (eds.), *Processes of Aging,* Vol. II, pp. 195-223. New York: Atherton Press.

Rosow, Irving. 1978. What is a cohort and why? *Human Development* 21:65-75.

Ross, Jennie-Keith. 1977. *Old People, New Lives: Community Creation in a Retirement Residence.* Chicago: University of Chicago Press. (Phoenix paperback ed., Keith, 1982c).

Sangree, Walter. 1974. Youths as elders and infants as ancestors: The complementarity of alternate generations, both living and dead, in Tiriki, Kenya, and Irigwe, Nigeria. *Africa* 44:65-70.

Simic, Andrei. 1978. Winners and losers: Aging Yugoslavs in a changing world. *In* Barbara Myerhoff and Andrei Simic (eds.), *Life's Career—Aging: Cultural Variations on Growing Old,* pp. 77-105. Beverly Hills, Calif.: Sage Publications.

Simmons, Leo. 1945. *The Role of the Aged in Primitive Society.* New Haven: Yale University Press. (Reprinted Archon Books, 1970.)

Skinner, William. 1961. Integenerational conflict among the Mossi. *Journal of Conflict Resolution* 5:55-60.

Smith, Robert. 1961. Cultural differences in the life cycle and the concept of time. *In* Robert Kleemeier (ed.), *Aging and Leisure.* New York: Oxford University Press.

Sokolovsky, Jay. (ed.) 1983. *Growing old in Different Societies,* Belmont, Calif.: Wadsworth.

Sokolovsky, Jay, and Cohen, Carl. 1978. The cultural

meaning of personal networks for the inner city elderly. *Urban Anthropology* 7:323–342.

Sokolovsky, Jay, and Cohen, Carl. 1981. Being old in the inner city: Support systems of the SRO aged. *In* Christine L. Fry (ed.), *Dimensions: Aging, Culture and Health*. New York: Praeger.

Spencer, Paul. 1976. Opposing streams and the gerontocratic ladder: Two models of age organization. *Man* 11:153–174.

Stewart, Frank. 1977. *Fundamentals of Age-Group Systems*. New York: Academic Press.

Turner, Victor. 1969. *The Ritual Process*. Chicago: Aldine.

University Center on Aging. 1981. *Minority Aging Codification Project Bibliography*. San Diego, Calif.: University Center on Aging, San Diego State University.

Wellin, Edward, and Boyer, Eunice. 1979. Adjustment of black and white elderly to the same adaptive niche. *In* Jennie Keith (ed.), *The Ethnography of Old Age*. Special Issue, *Anthropological Quarterly* 52(1):39–48.

Werner, Dennis. 1981. Gerontocracy among the Mekranoti of Central Brazil. *Anthropological Quarterly* 54:15–27.

Whiting, John W. M., and Whiting, Beatrice. 1975. Aloofness and intimacy of husbands and wives: A cross-cultural study. *Ethos* 3:183–207.

Williams, Gerry C. 1980. Warriors no more: A study of the American Indian elderly. *In* Christine L. Fry (ed.), *Aging in Culture and Society*. New York: Praeger (A James Bergin Book).

Wilson, Monica. 1951. *Good Company: Study of Nyakyusa Age Villages*. London: Oxford University Press.

Wilson, Monica. 1977. *For Men and Elders*. New York: Holmes and Meier.

10
RACE, NATIONAL ORIGIN, ETHNICITY, AND AGING

Jacquelyne Johnson Jackson

Duke University

INTRODUCTION AND SCOPE

For many years prior to the mid-1960s, most social gerontologists in the United States limited their research to white subjects and ignored racial and cultural variations in aging. Their typical exclusion of nonwhites (Jackson, 1967) suggested that they then believed that race and culture affect aging, but that they rarely explored that topic, which is now the subject matter of ethnogerontology, the newest and perhaps the most undeveloped field of social gerontology.

During the late 1950s and on into the 1960s, a small, but growing number of gerontological publications focused on racial or cultural differences and on the social statuses of aged minorities. The most prominent of these publications included Talley and Kaplan (1956), the National Urban League (1964), Clark and Anderson (1967), Jackson (1967), Youmans (1967), and Carp (1968). Gerontologic concentration on race and culture has increased since then, with opinions now abounding about the effects of race and culture on aging. But the accumulation of "scientific generalizations concerning ethnicity as a mediator in problems of aging" is just beginning (Bengston, 1979, p. 10).

This chapter is primarily concerned with the current and the prospective status of eth-

nogerontology. It does *not* contain a comprehensive review of all of the research findings in ethnogerontology, *owing primarily to their largely descriptive and inconclusive nature.* Its three major foci are (1) the emergence of ethnogerontology and its key concepts, (2) sociodemographic comparisons of black, Hispanic, and white aged, and (3) the two major ethnogerontologic issues of double jeopardy and of the racial crossover in mortality. The discussion of these three foci is followed by brief sections that treat public policies and the current and the prospective status of ethnogerontology. The aged are defined conventionally as people over 65 years of age, even though the feasibility of that definition for some racial minorities has long been questioned (see, e.g., White House Conference on Aging, Special Concerns Session on Aging and Aged Blacks, 1972). The main concern here is with minority, as opposed to majority, aged in the United States, despite the fact that the majority aged contain various groupings of ethnic aged.

The first section discusses the emergence of ethnogerontology and its key concepts, with the exception of the concept of double jeopardy, which is considered in the third section. Stressed here are the need for conceptual clarity between *ethnic group* and *minority group* and the possibility of regarding ethnicity as a continuum instead of as a discrete concept. Also considered in this section is whether ethnicity and culture are synonymous or are conceptually different dimensions of social differentiation of groups.

The second section describes and analyzes some recent demographic trends of blacks, Hispanics, and whites, mostly for the aged. Data about American Indians, Eskimos, and Aleuts (hereafter, generally Indians) and Asian and Pacific islanders (hereafter, generally Asians) have typically been lacking, although data from the 1980 United States Census of Population should remedy some of these omissions. The concentration on demographic trends reflects the fact that many ethnogerontologic studies deal primarily with sociodemographic comparisons, often using data collected by the U.S. Bureau of the Census (see, e.g., Pacific Asian Elderly Research Project, 1977; Hill, 1978; Jackson, 1980; Manuel and Reid, 1982; Berger, 1983). Other ethnogerontologic studies, of course, have used primary or secondary data that were not collected by federal agencies, and these studies have often extended their analyses beyond sociodemographic data to include sociocultural and psychological data (see, e.g., Jackson and Wood, 1976; Kalish and Reynolds, 1976; Bengtson et al., 1977; Dowd and Bengtson, 1978; Holley, 1978; Jackson and Walls, 1978; Eve and Friedsam, 1979; Cuellar and Weeks, 1980; Pieper, 1981; Gibson, 1982a,b).

The third section deals specifically with the two dominant issues of double jeopardy and the racial crossover in mortality (for the first, see, e.g., Talley and Kaplan, 1956; National Urban League, 1964; Henderson, 1965; Jackson, 1967; National Council on the Aging, 1971; Jackson, 1971a; Lindsay, 1971; Daly, 1976; Bell et al., 1976; Fujii, 1976a; Jackson and Wood, 1976; Dowd and Bengston, 1978; Crandall, 1980; Jackson, 1980; Cuellar and Weeks, 1980; M. Jackson et al., 1982; Manuel, 1982a—and for the second, see, e.g., Demeny and Gingrich, 1967; Thornton and Nam, 1968; Manton and Poss, 1977; Manton et al., 1979; Jackson, 1980; Manton, 1980; Jackson, 1982; Manton,

1982). The discussion in this section will also facilitate the consideration of the current and the prospective status of ethnogerontology.

In a brief fourth section, there is a discussion of certain public policies that have been proposed by some ethnogerontologists in order to improve the quality of life for aged minorities in the United States and to reduce the existing inequities between the dominant and the minority aged. This discussion, while brief, is significant because much of the ethnogerontologic literature deals with the delivery of public services or applicable public policies (see, e.g., Davis, 1939; Jackson, 1965; Lipman, 1965; Carp, 1968, 1969, 1971; Dominick and Stotsky, 1969; Gordon and Rehr, 1969; Gregory, 1970; Solomon, 1970; Kent and Hirsch, 1971; Reynoso and Coppelman, 1972; Davis, 1973; Wu, 1974; Anderson, 1975; Ishikawa and Archer, 1975; McCaslin and Calvert, 1975; Bell et al., 1976; Fujii, 1976b; Kart and Beckham, 1976; Eribes, 1977; Kasschau, 1977; Williams, 1977; Eribes and Bradley-Rawls, 1978; German et al., 1978; Hunt, 1978; Smith, 1978; Colen and Soto, 1979; Zambrana et al., 1979; Chen, 1980; Cuellar and Weeks, 1980; Guttmann, 1980, Hawkins, 1980; Waring and Kosberg, 1980; Hawkins, 1982; Jacobson, 1982; Lacayo, 1982). Most of the reviewed policies or proposed policies are available in documents or reports prepared for the 1971 and 1981 White House Conferences on Aging, the Older Americans Act of 1965, as amended (see U.S. House of Representatives, 1982) and the National Commission on Social Security Reform (1983).

A brief fifth section reviews the current status of ethnogerontology, and leads to a discussion of its prospects.

ETHNOGERONTOLOGY AND KEY CONCEPTS

Ethnogerontology is the study of the causes, processes, and consequences of race, national origin, and culture on individual and population aging. The failure of most aging specialists to distinguish clearly between race, national origin, and culture is illustrated by

Bechill (1979, pp. 137, 140), who referred similarly "to the needs of minority and ethnic aged," to "cultural, racial, and ethnic factors," and to ethnic factors, followed shortly by a listing of "Black, Hispanic, Polish American, or Italian American." Agreeing, however, that aging is both a biological and a cultural process (Wylie, 1976), Bechill (1979, pp. 140–141) noted that "Culture invests the aging process with particular meanings and defines the appropriate relationships of the aged to themselves" and to their environments.

Bechill (1979) also followed Wylie (1976) in noting that disappointing and frustrating results often occur when human service programs designed for middle-class, white urbanites are applied unchanged to minorities. But here we do not know if Bechill means that such programs are always inapplicable to middle-class, minority urbanites merely because they are minorities, or that no minorities are middle-class. This kind of confusion can be reduced through clear differentiations between race, national origin, and culture and through more information about racial similarities within social classes (see, e.g., Dollard, 1937; Seelbach and Sauer, 1977; Blau et al., 1979). Based upon their review of the literature about aged blacks, Bell et al. (1976) felt that the findings in that literature did not support the delivery of services on the basis of race, largely because they regarded the apparent racial differences as being instead socioeconomic differences.

Markson (1979), who defined ethnicity narrowly as referring only to foreign-born, in her study of referrals of aged people to New York City hospitals, found that the hospitals rarely met the needs of these ethnics. Her conclusion that institutionalized adjustments could be fostered by grouping aged foreigners on the basis of national origin also raises the important question of distinguishing clearly between the effects of ethnicity on aging and the effects of being foreign-born and aged on institutionalized persons. Cuellar and Weeks (1980, p. 42) proposed that foreign-born elderly of the same ethnic group may have different needs for public services, depending on whether they are "pioneer minority elders" who were young when they immigrated to the United States, or "followers of children." Cain (1983) noted the relatively new phenomenon, beginning after World War II, of older parents following their children, as well as of older immigrants arriving alone in the United States.

The concerns of Bechill (1979), Markson (1979), Cuellar and Weeks (1980), and Cain (1983) help to highlight a prevalent issue in ethnogerontology. Should ethnogerontology be restricted to minority groups based upon ethnicity, or should it be expanded to include all ethnic or cultural groups? Our definition of ethnogerontology stated earlier supports the latter view. But, notwithstanding the expansive views, for example, of Kalish (1971), Kaplan (1975), Fandetti and Gelfand (1976), Gelfand and Kutzik (1979a), Guttmann (1979), and Mostwin (1979), ethnogerontology is still primarily confined to racial and national origin minorities. But, expansion seems to be the wave of the future.

The Emergence of Ethnogerontology

When ethnogerontology first emerged in the late 1960s, it concentrated mostly on racial comparisons of blacks and whites. Combined sociodemographic, academic, and civil-rights patterns abetted its emergence and subsequent development. Those patterns include the numerical growth of minority aged, the increase of minority academicians interested in social gerontology, and the upsurge of theses and dissertations related to aged minorities during the late 1960s and the 1970s, as well as a growing interest in white ethnics (for minorities see Davis, 1966; Ball, 1967; Dhaliwal, 1967; Harper, 1967; Crocker, 1968; Lambing, 1969; Rodriguez, 1970; Stojanovic, 1970; Walker, 1970; Blum, 1972; Moriwaki, 1972; Rubenstein, 1972; Chen, June, and Tu, 1973; Stewart, 1973; Bielefeld, 1974; Davis, 1974; Votau, 1974; Wu, 1974; Anderson, 1975; Bailey, 1975; Sauer, 1977; Yelder, 1975;

Beard, 1976; Hawkins, 1976; Torres-Gil, 1976; Washington, 1976; Cuellar, 1977; Gray, 1977; Reilly, 1977; Seelbach, 1977; Williams, 1977; Chen, 1978; Curran, 1978; Holley, 1978; Huling, 1978; Hunt, 1978; Korte, 1978; Miranda, 1978; Pollard, 1978; Smith, 1978; and for white ethnics see, e.g., Gelfand and Kutzik, 1979a). The impact of the National Caucus on the Black Aged (a group formed in 1970 largely through the efforts of Hobart C. Jackson, the black administrator of the Stephen Smith Home for the Aged in Philadelphia, Pennsylvania, the oldest home for aged blacks in the United States today, and Robert J. Kastenbaum, a white psychologist of aging) on the 1971 White House Conference on Aging and on the United States Administration on Aging was also a critical factor in the development of ethnogerontology. Further, William Oriol, as the director of the United States Senate Special Committee on Aging, was extremely instrumental in generating hearings pertaining to aged minorities and in disseminating information about aged minorities during the late 1960s and early 1970s.

The inclusion of black subjects in the first longitudinal study of older people by the Duke University Center for the Study of Aging and Human Development also focused interest on minority aging. When Heyman and Jeffers (1964), Jackson (1971b), and Jericho (1977) analyzed social data about blacks from that longitudinal study, they all found some variations among aged blacks that were influenced by sex or social class factors. When Nowlin (1979) examined certain data from the longitudinal study, he concluded that the medically determined health statuses of older blacks and whites were generally similar. His conclusion is very important in light of the argument about the comparative health statuses of older blacks and whites. Shanas (1962) included blacks in her nationally representative sample of the health patterns of older Americans, but she did not analyze her data by race. In a later national survey, Shanas (1977) analyzed her data by race, with some controls for socioeconomic status, and reported racial differ-

ences in health or disability statuses. The Hispanic Health and Nutrition Examination (HHANES), launched by the National Center on Health Statistics in July, 1982, may also provide useful data about the medically determined health statuses of Mexican Americans, Cuban Americans, and Puerto Ricans.

The longstanding anthropological interest in ethnic groups in the United States, dating back at least to Franz Boas and his associates in the early 1900s, to Herskovits (1928), to Warner (1936), and to Warner and Srole (1945), may also have contributed, at least indirectly, to the emergence of ethnogerontology, as seen, for instance, in the later work of Koenig et al. (1971), Wylie (1971), Trela and Sokolovsky (1979), and Wellin and Boyer (1979). Also, the recent resurgence of the women's movement may have prompted an increased interest in ethnogerontology with respect to minority or ethnic women (see, e.g., Hamlett, 1959; Himes and Hamlett, 1962; Jenkins, 1971; Jackson, 1972a, 1976, 1979; Walls and Jackson, 1977; Holden, 1978; Bremer and Ragan, 1979; Cantor et al., 1979; Cohler and Lieberman, 1979; Hunter et al., 1979; Cohler, 1982; Gibson, 1982a). However, the interest of black women in their often discouraging social status also has a long and famous history, as evidenced, for example, by Sojourner Truth's now famous statement "'. . . and ain't I a woman'" in 1851, Cooper (1892), and Williams (1898). Undoubtedly, similar kinds of data exist for other minority women who are not black.

The growth of ethnogerontologic literature, apparent, for example, in the overlapping bibliographies of Jackson (1967, 1971c, 1980), Suzuki (1975), Dancy (1977), Ragan and Simonin (1977), Delgado and Finley (1978), Gelfand and Kutzik (1979a), Davis (1980), the University Center on Aging, San Diego State University (1981), and Butler (1982), and in various professional journals, such as *The Gerontologist* or the *Journal of Gerontology,* is a healthy developmental sign. The further accumulation of such largely descriptive literature can help in the promotion of disciplinary maturity. Most disciplines initially were generally descriptive and atheoretical, and "a substantial body of descriptive information about a phenomenon" is needed for theoretical development (Shock, 1977, p. 103).

Social Aging

The general absence of racial and ethnic minorities in cross-sequential or longitudinal studies prevents the accumulation of knowledge about their social aging. A concept related to social age, culture, and social structure, *social aging* refers "to the changing statuses and roles of aging persons, the conditions influencing those changes, and their individual and societal consequences" (Jackson, 1980, p. 118) or to "the characteristic sequence of changes in the status, roles, and relationships to other persons which the individual experiences along with chronological age" (Glenn, 1977, p. 18). The key feature of social aging is the investigation of age changes in statuses and roles.

For instance, most analysts comparing widows assume that widowhood is associated with monetary losses (see, e.g., Lopata, 1979). But, in a study of income changes and midlife widowhood, Morgan (1981) used data from the National Longitudinal Surveys cohort of older women to demonstrate convincingly that most low-income widows entered widowhood with already low incomes. The total family income of black, but not of white, widows tended to drop after widowhood and then rise. Morgan's (1981) data do not permit a careful analysis of the factors generating that racial difference, but the subsequent rise in the income of black widows may be related either to an increase in the widow's earned or unearned income or to an increase in the number of income recipients in her family.

Ethnic Group and Minority Group

Conceptual clarity between *ethnic group* and *minority group* is needed because every ethnic group is not a minority group, and a minority group is not necessarily confined to a single ethnic group. Further, conceptual agreement is sorely needed about the definition of an ethnic group, primarily because, as suggested earlier, the term is used too loosely in referring variously to racial groups, nationalistic groups, and cultural groups.

Schermerhorn's (1970) distinction between an ethnic group and a minority group may be helpful. A "collectivity within a larger society," an ethnic group has "real or putative common ancestry, memories of a shared historical past, and a cultural focus on one or more symbolic elements defined as the epitome of their peoplehood" (Schermerhorn, 1970, p. 12). Illustrative symbolic elements are "kinship patterns, physical contiguity (as in localism or sectionalism), religious affiliation, language or dialect forms, tribal affiliation, nationality, phenotypical features, or any combination of these" (Schermerhorn, 1970, p. 12). In contrast, a minority group, *a numerical minority,* "is an appreciable subsystem with limited access to roles and activities central to the economic and political institutions of the society" (Schermerhorn, 1970, p. 14).

Thus, under Schermerhorn's definitions, women and Hispanics are improperly classified as ethnics or minorities. For example, Argentines, Cubans, Mexicans, and Puerto Ricans fall short with respect to common ancestry and shared historical memories. Hispanics *qua* Hispanics have no appreciable subsystem. Blacks are only an ethnic group when ethnicity is limited solely to race. When ethnicity refers instead to national origin, then various black ethnic groups in the United States include Haitian Americans, Jamaican Americans, and Nigerian Americans, a point often overlooked. Some Nigerian Americans might even argue that they should be characterized on the basis of their tribal affiliation, and not simply lumped together as Nigerians. Cuellar and Weeks (1980), for example, did not distinguish among their black subjects, several of whom were foreign-born, by nationality. Moreover, the racially ethnic group of blacks contains many different cultural groups (Green, 1981). Akin to Schermerhorn (1970), Gelfand and Kutzik (1979b) view all persons as ethnics by their racial, religious, or nationalistic membership, thereby not limiting ethnicity to minorities.

Guttmann (1979, p. 248) defines ethnicity "as the cultural bond of a given social group," a definition that matches Berry's (1958, p. 54) conception of an ethnic group as "a human group bound together by ties of cultural homogeneity." Further, American Negroes, a racial and not an ethnic group, "have no unique culture of their own" (Berry, 1958, p. 55). Gelfand and Kutzik (1979b) suggest the use of the concept of *ethclass* (Gordon, 1964) as a substitute for the separate concepts of ethnicity and social class because they believe that the effects of the compound of ethnicity and social class are unitary. Berry's conception of an ethnic group that stresses cultural homogeneity is the most useful one for ethnogerontologists because it does not combine racial and cultural groups.

With respect to conceptions of a minority group, Manuel (1982b, p. 24) differs from Schermerhorn (1970) in that he conceptualizes a minority group as "a special type of ethnic group, subsuming racial criteria," with such unique features as prejudicial or discriminatory victimization, fewer power resources than "the implied majority," and "a sense of consciousness" that foments marital and social endogamy. Manuel claimed that he based his identification of Asians, blacks, Hispanics, and Indians as the current minority groups in the United States on his definition of a minority group. But his classification simply follows the current federal pattern of protected groups (where, incidentally, Asians, blacks, and Indians are often grouped as "all other races").

Cain (1983) goes even further in stretching the concept of minority group to include "those with predictably reduced life expectancies" and with "life shortening diseases," such as Down's syndrome or Tay-Sachs disease. Moreover, following Barron (1953), some few gerontologists have stretched the concept of a minority group to include the aged (see, e.g., Palmore, 1969; Palmore and Whittington, 1970; Cuellar and Weeks, 1980), a position that has been rejected by Streib (1965, 1976) and Jackson (1980).

Berry (1958, p. 52) suggested that sociologists had substituted the term *minority* for *race,* and had "restricted the term to certain kinds of groups," "divested it of all statistical meaning," and "looked upon discrimination and exclusion from full social participation as the essential characteristics." Berry (1958, p. 52) then cited Wirth's (1945) definition of a minority as "'a group of people who, because of physical or cultural characteristics, are singled out from the others in the society in which they live for differential and unequal treatment, and who therefore regard themselves as objects of collective discrimination.'" Wirth's definition differs from that of Schermerhorn in at least three important ways. In addition to their difference about the relative size of a minority group, Schermerhorn defining a minority group always as a numerical minority, Wirth's definition includes the element of discrimination, whereas the limited access in Schermerhorn's definition need not be due to discrimination. Further, under Wirth's definition, a minority group exists only when the people singled out for differential and unequal treatment so define themselves.

Dominant-Minority Groups

The existence of any minority group demands the presence of one dominant group that is an *actual* majority through power. The dominant group "has the preeminent authority to function both as guardians and sustainers of the controlling value system, and as prime allocators of rewards in the society" (Schermerhorn, 1970, pp. 12–13). But many ethnogerontologists simplistically categorize *all* whites as dominant group members. Equating whiteness with dominance reflects the pervasiveness of the doctrine of white superiority. Under that doctrine, white Cubans in the United States would be members of the dominant group and *not* members of the Hispanic minority. A contrary view, of course, is that membership within a dominant or minority group is not permanent or absolute, but may shift according to the definition of the situation involving the specific person and his relevant others.

Dominant group membership is not determined solely by race. Many whites also have limited "access to roles and activities central to the economic and political institutions." The faulty perception of all whites as dominant group members is a major flaw of many ethnogerontologic studies undertaken to determine the effects of minority group membership on old age (see, e.g., Bengtson et al., 1977). Just as flawed is the automatic bestowal of minority group membership upon whites whose remote ancestors spoke Spanish, while their native tongue and that of their parents is English.

Behavioral and Ideological Ethnicity

Unlike dominant and minority groups, ethnicity is a neutral concept that does not connote prejudice, discrimination, oppression, or power. In a useful investigation of relationships between medical care and ethnicity, where the investigator did *not* restrict the concept of ethnicity to cultural homogeneity as we would have done, Harwood (1981) expanded the concept of ethnicity by positing it as a continuum whose polar opposites are behavioral and ideological ethnicity.

Behavioral ethnicity refers to the "distinctive values, beliefs, behavioral norms, and languages" that ethnics acquire through socialization, with those standards forming the basis for their intragroup and interethnic group interaction and affecting their "participation in mainstream social institutions" (Harwood, 1981, p. 4). It is especially typical of blacks, Hispanics, and Indians (but not of Asians) because they were "systematically excluded from mainstream educational and political institutions" (Harwood, 1981, p. 4).

More fragmented, situational, and voluntary than behavioral ethnicity, ideological ethnicity is "based largely on customs that are neither central to a person's social life nor necessarily learned from early sociali-

zation" (Harwood, 1981, p. 4). Functioning principally as interest groups, ideological ethnics represent "'invisible organizations' which have materialized at a particular moment in American history to advance certain political and economic interests" (Harwood, 1981, p. 5).

White's (1982) analysis of ethnic groups by their recent political behaviors nationally suggests the wisdom of the concept of ideological ethnics, but it does not support the polar opposition of behavioral and ideological ethnicity. Instead, ideological ethnics are probably subgroups of behavioral ethnics. For example, the black members of the original National Caucus on the Black Aged formed an ideological ethnic group on the basis of customs acquired during their occupational socialization and from other experiences that were not generally derived from their early socialization. Involved in a voluntary and situational effort that was not central to the totality of their lives, they did not function as a behavioral ethnic group merely on the basis of being black.

Missing from Harwood's (1981) work is a detailed typology of the points of the continuum of ethnicity. If the continuum of behavioral–ideological ethnicity is plausible, it must await the accumulation of sufficient empirical data. More useful now, perhaps, is the development of a typology of ideological ethnics as a behavioral ethnic subgroup. Minority aging organizations as ideological ethnic groups could also be classified by their distance from the major sociocultural norms and values of their groups. The National Center and Caucus for Black Aged is probably much more distant from such norms and values than is the Asociacion Nacional Pro Persones Mayores or the National Indian Council on Aging.

Ethnic and Minority Group Identification

The vexing question of basing ethnic or minority group membership on racial or linguistic background or on self-identification is especially apparent in the 1980 United States Census of Population. The reduction in the proportion of persons of Spanish origin classified as white between the 1970 and the 1980 censuses resulted in part from a decision made by the U.S. Bureau of the Census *not* to count Mexicans, Venezuelans, Latinos, and the like as white if they did not self-designate themselves as being white (U.S. Bureau of the Census, 1980a).

An even more vexing question is whether minority group membership, as opposed to minority group status, is a function of a person's recognition that he is victimized by discrimination, as well as his personal identification with people he views as being similarly victimized. A further problem in determining the effects of ethnicity and culture on aging, then, is the adequate placement of research subjects by objective and by subjective identification. Determining the extent to which Puerto Rican black aged in New York City deviate from dominant cultural norms about the aged requires some knowledge about the cultural norms these Puerto Ricans follow. It simply cannot be assumed, a priori, that they follow "Hispanic" norms because they or their forebears spoke Spanish, or "black" norms because, by race, they are black (see also Matsumoto et al., 1970; Beard, 1976; Clark et al., 1976; Washington, 1976; Guttman, 1979).

Defining ethnic identity as "the subjective or emblematic use by a group of any aspect of culture in order to differentiate themselves from others," Trela and Sokolovsky (1979, p. 129) continued by distinguishing between groups with high, moderate, and low levels of ethnic distinctiveness. Sometimes treating culture and ethnicity synonymously (to which we would not object), they placed such groups as the Amish, Hasidic Jews, Navaho, and Zuni on the high level; Asian and Hispanic Americans, Orthodox Jews, and certain black subgroups on the moderate level; and Italian, Polish, Jewish, and Irish Americans on the low level. In addition to comparing group norms and the treatment of the aged in each group, Trela and Sokolovsky (1979) examined the importance of ethnic differences that are related to the role-sets of older people as they age, the control those older people have of the significant physical and educational resources

within their societies, and the relationship between the concept of self-esteem and self-reliant individualism within the value system of their society. Since cultural differences between nonaged ethnics affect their aged, a strong sense of ethnic identification may be highly important in replacing occupational identification among the aged. "Perhaps most important is that a positive valuation of ethnicity as a nondenigrating component of identity can be a more continuous basis of self-esteem than an occupational identity, which suffers greatly through retirement" (Trela and Sokolovsky, 1979, p. 129).

Manuel (1982c) developed an ethnic minority identification scale which he tested on a nonrepresentative sample of black residents of Washington, D.C., who were between 50 and 102 years of age. He then tended to equate blacks with other minorities.

The further development of unidimensional and multidimensional scales for adequate measurement of at least ethnic, minority, and cultural identification could benefit ethnogerontology. Such scales would be helpful in comparing younger and older family members, for example, to see if movements toward ethnic pluralism lead to greater identificational congruence intergenerationally. Arce and his associates (IRS Newsletter, 1982, p. 7) reported that their older Chicano subjects found "it perfectly natural and normal to identify themselves as Mexicanos, and among the younger people the data show a movement toward ethnicity and away from the 'melting pot.'" Manuel, Arce, and other ethnogerontologists should be encouraged to perfect an ethnic identification scale on a multidimensional level.

DEMOGRAPHIC COMPARISONS

Population Sizes and Age Distributions

Table 1 shows the population sizes of Asians, blacks, Hispanics, Indians, and whites under 15 and over 65 years of age, by sex, in the United States in 1980. About 83 percent of the total population of all ages was white in 1980. Much smaller percentages were black

TABLE 1. Sizes of Selected Population Groups, by Sex and Age, United States: 1980*

Sex and Age	Whites N	%	Blacks N	%	Spanish Origin N	%	Asian and Pacific Islanders N	%	American Indians Eskimos & Aleuts N	%
Female										
All ages	96,671,164	100.0	13,972,286	100.0	7,327,624	100.0	1,807,294	100.0	717,188	100.0
Under 15 years	19,547,715	20.2	3,772,091	27.0	2,297,087	31.3	429,951	23.8	222,521	31.0
65+ years	13,723,735	14.2	1,239,569	8.9	403,640	5.5	107,837	6.0	41,948	5.8
65–69 years	4,329,974	4.5	445,113	3.2	148,156	2.0	40,543	2.2	15,475	2.2
70–74 years	3,542,234	3.7	329,100	2.4	108,668	1.5	27,081	1.5	11,068	1.5
75–79 years	2,659,386	2.8	234,565	1.7	77,449	1.1	19,501	1.1	7,658	1.1
80–84 years	1,761,745	1.8	124,910	0.9	39,094	0.5	12,061	0.7	4,190	0.6
85+ years	1,430,396	1.5	105,881	0.8	30,273	0.4	8,651	0.5	3,557	0.5
Male										
All ages	91,669,626	100.0	12,515,932	100.0	7,278,259	100.0	1,693,342	100.0	701,007	100.0
Under 15 years	20,574,782	22.4	3,826,679	30.6	2,377,437	32.7	445,664	26.3	228,577	32.6
65+ years	9,220,298	10.0	846,257	6.8	305,145	4.2	103,997	6.1	32,840	4.7
65–69 years	3,481,097	3.8	331,484	2.6	115,542	1.6	39,180	2.3	12,781	1.8
70–74 years	2,551,944	2.8	234,277	1.9	84,748	1.2	30,961	1.8	8,818	1.2
75–79 years	1,649,900	1.8	152,666	1.2	58,927	0.8	19,653	1.2	6,084	0.9
80–84 years	923,048	1.0	74,850	0.6	27,371	0.5	9,000	0.5	2,862	0.4
85+ years	614,309	0.7	52,980	0.4	18,557	0.2	5,203	0.3	2,295	0.3

SOURCE: U.S. Bureau of the Census, *Supplementary Reports, 1980 Census of Population*, "Age, Sex, Race, and Spanish Origin of the Population by Regions, Divisions, and States: 1980," PC80–S1–1, Washington, D.C.: U.S. Government Printing Office, 1980a, Table 1, p. 3. In U.S. Bureau of the Census, *Current Population Reports*, Series P–25, No. 917, "Preliminary Estimates of the Population of the United States by Age, Sex, and Race: 1970 to 1981," Washington, D.C.: U.S. Government Printing Office, 1982a, higher population sizes are given for blacks (roughly increasing the aged females by almost 12,500 and the aged males by over 4,700), but similar data were not available for all of the other groups shown here. Percentage rounding of the age subgroups under 65+ years of age was undertaken above.

(11.5%), Hispanic (6.4%), Asian (1.5%), Indian (0.6%), or other (3.0%). Among the aged, almost 26 million persons in 1980, the white percentage (89.8%) was also higher than those of blacks (8.2%), Hispanics (2.8%), Asians (0.6%), and Indians (0.3%). Different age distributions of these groups reflect variations in their fertility, mortality, and immigration rates.

The sum of the specific percentages reported above will never round off to approximately 100 percent if a Hispanic percentage is included. The reason for this anomaly is that the U.S. Bureau of the Census does not treat the Hispanic category as one that is mutually exclusive from the racial categories. Thus, the Hispanic data are also included within each of the racial categories. This treatment of the Hispanic data by the U.S. Bureau of the Census may highlight the importance of the need to define clearly the concepts of race, national origin, and language as they relate to the formation of statistically aggregated groups.

The total population of the United States increased by 11.5 percent between 1970 and 1980, with far larger increases for Asians (129.3%), Indians (86.5%), Hispanics (57.1%), and blacks (17.5%) than for whites (5.7%). The population of people over 65 years of age also grew more rapidly between 1970 and 1980 (27.1%) than did the total population. The increases in the aged populations were also larger for Asians (110.1%), Indians (71.4%), Hispanics (53.9%), and blacks (31.4%) than for whites (25.0%). Among people over 65 years of age, the percentages in the 65–74-year-old group decreased slightly between 1970 and 1980 for Hispanics (67.6 to 64.5%), blacks (66.4 to 64.2%), Asians (66.0 to 65.0%), Indians (65.3 to 64.4%), and whites (61.4 to 60.6%). Thus, each of these aged populations grew older between 1970 and 1980.

Sex Ratios

Table 2 shows the sex ratios (or the number of males per every 100 females) for Asians, Hispanics, Indians, whites, and blacks in

1970 and 1980, by all ages and by age-specific groups for those over 65 years. The general trend is the growing presence of females in each of these populations. The excess of females compared to males for persons under 70 years of age was most pronounced among blacks, after which it was typically highest among whites.

A major difference between blacks and whites is the greater presence of females among younger adults (Jackson, 1971e). But, in the older years, a *sex ratio crossover* occurs between blacks and whites. In 1970, for persons between 65 and 69 years of age, the white sex ratio was higher; the black sex ratio was higher for persons who were 70 or more years of age. In 1980, however, for persons between 65 and 74 years of age, the white sex ratio was higher; for ages over 74 it was higher for blacks. The increasing age for the sex ratio crossover between blacks and whites is similar to the increasing age for the racial crossover in mortality between blacks and whites (Jackson, 1982).

Geographical Location

Geographical dispersion of the aged is much greater for whites than for blacks, Hispanics, Asians, and, undoubtedly, Indians. In 1980, about 79 percent each of Hispanic and Asian aged were concentrated in six and five states, respectively. About 92 percent of aged blacks lived in 20 states and the District of Columbia, concentrated most heavily in New York (7.8%) and Texas (6.9%).

By geographical region, in 1980, most aged blacks (61.7%) and whites (51.7%) lived in the South, as did 40.1 percent of aged Hispanics, but only 6.0 percent of aged Asians. In the near future, most black and white aged will probably still be in the South, as will growing proportions of Hispanics and Asians.

George Myers (1983) has suggested that the correspondence between the concentration of aged whites and of minorities of all ages in certain geographical areas, such as major cities, could expose those areas to double jeopardy. This is certainly a testable hypothesis,

TABLE 2. Sex Ratios of Selected Population Groups, All Ages and over 65 Years of Age, United States, 1970 and 1980*

Age and Year	Asians**	Hispanics	Indians	Whites	Blacks
All ages					
1970	98.7	98.0	96.5	95.2	90.7
1980	93.7	99.3	97.7	94.8	89.6
65–69 years					
1970	141.0	94.9	92.8	80.1	79.3
1980	96.6	78.0	82.6	80.4	74.5
70–74 years					
1970	119.5	94.8	92.4	73.2	80.2
1980	114.3	78.0	79.7	72.0	71.2
75–79 years					
1970	91.7	85.1	95.4	68.8	78.7
1980	100.8	76.1	79.4	62.0	65.1
80–84 years					
1970	118.4	82.2	91.6	61.6	69.4
1980	74.6	70.0	68.3	52.4	59.9
85+ years					
1970	118.1	71.8	80.5	55.2	63.9
1980	60.1	61.3	64.5	42.9	50.0

* SOURCES of raw data: U.S. Bureau of the Census, *Census of Population, 1970, Detailed Characteristics,* Final Report PC(1)–D1, United States Summary, Washington, D.C.: U.S. Government Printing Office, 1973, Table 190, pp. 1-593–1-594, and Table 191, pp. 1-596–1-597, and U.S. Bureau of the Census, *Supplementary Reports, 1980 Census of Population,* "Age, Sex, Race, and Spanish Origin of the Population by Regions, Divisions, and States: 1980," PC80-S1-1, Washington, D.C.: U.S. Government Printing Office, 1980a, Table 1, p. 3.

** In 1970, Japanese, Chinese, Filipino, Korean, and Hawaiian groups were combined to produce the Asian category.

but, in the absence of any specific studies concentrated upon that problem, Table 3 simply shows the geographical locations of blacks and whites in metropolitan and non-metropolitan areas in 1980, as well as the percentages of each group residing inside poverty areas. Within each racial group, the aged were less likely to reside in metropoli-tan areas and more likely to reside inside poverty areas. Future studies about the economic and political consequences of double jeopardy as they relate to the concentrated mixes of the aged and of minority groups in major cities may be useful in the formation or modification of public policies, such as those that seek to match the employment

TABLE 3. Geographic Locations of Blacks and Whites by Metropolitan and Poverty Areas, by Age, United States, 1980*

Geographical and Poverty Area	Under 65 years of age		65+ years of age	
	Blacks	Whites	Blacks	Whites
Total number (thousands)	24,354	170,587	2,054	22,325
% in metropolitan areas	78.4	66.3	67.3	62.7
% inside central cities	57.0	22.8	52.7	27.0
% inside poverty areas	24.2	2.2	29.6	2.8
% outside central cities	21.5	43.5	14.6	35.7
%inside poverty areas	5.4	1.7	6.2	1.7
% in nonmetropolitan areas	21.6	33.7	32.7	37.3
% inside poverty areas	14.7	10.5	26.1	12.9

* SOURCE of raw data: U.S. Bureau of the Census, *Current Population Reports,* Series P-60, No. 133, "Characteristics of the Population Below the Poverty Level: 1980," Washington, D.C.: U.S. Government Printing Office, 1982b, Table 9, pp. 38–43.

needs of younger people with the service needs of older people.

Educational Levels

Table 4 shows the median number of years of formal education for each sex for blacks, Hispanics, and whites who were over 25 years of age, and for later age-specific groups in 1970 and 1979. The educational level of each group rose over time, except for Hispanic men and women over 70 years of age, a decrease that may be due to the greater presence of recent and older immigrants in that group. On the average, whites were better educated than blacks and Hispanics, and blacks were better educated than Hispanics. Within each group, women were also typically better educated than men, but less so among Hispanics.

Using the white male median educational level as the standard, between 1970 and 1980 the educational gap for all people over 25 years of age narrowed between white men and black men, white men and black women, and white men and Hispanic women, while

remaining stationary between white and Hispanic men, and widening slightly between white men and women.

Economic Levels

Table 5 shows the poverty levels based on money income by sex and familial status of blacks, Hispanics, and whites over 65 years of age in four recent years. *A family contains two or more persons related by birth, marriage, or adoption who reside together. An unrelated individual lives with no relatives, but may live in a household with nonrelatives or in group quarters. In 1970 and 1975, a husband who lived with his wife was always designated as the familial head, but not so in 1980 or 1981.* But poverty remained most pronounced among unrelated individuals, and especially so among black female unrelated individuals. Among others, Snyder (1979) contends that both cash *and* noncash benefits should be used to compute poverty statuses, a position with which we agree.

The median money income of individuals

TABLE 4. Median Years of Formal Education of Blacks, Hispanics, and Whites over 25 Years of age, by Sex and Age, United States, 1970 and 1979*

Population Group and Year	Age (in years)					
	25 +	55–59	60–64	65–69	70–74	75 +
1970						
Hispanic women	9.3	7.8	6.7	6.2	5.9	5.4
Black men	9.8	7.6	6.9	6.0	5.6	5.1
Hispanic men	9.9	8.2	7.0	6.1	5.9	4.9
Black women	10.1	8.4	7.9	7.0	6.7	6.1
White men	12.1	11.0	10.0	8.9	8.7	8.4
White women	12.1	11.6	10.7	9.5	8.9	8.7
1979						
Hispanic women	10.2	8.1	8.2	6.6	5.3	5.1
Hispanic men	10.4	8.6	8.5	6.7	—	4.2
Black men	11.9	8.9	8.2	7.6	6.3	5.1
Black women	11.9	9.7	8.8	8.5	7.6	7.3
White women	12.5	12.4	12.2	12.0	11.0	9.0
White men	12.6	12.5	12.2	11.1	10.2	8.8

* Sources of data: U.S. Bureau of the Census, *Census of Population: 1970, Detailed Characteristics*, Final Report PC(1)-D1, United States Summary, Washington, D.C.: U.S. Government Printing Office, 1973, Table 199, pp. 1-628–1-629, and U.S. Bureau of the Census, *Current Population Reports,* Series P-20, No. 356, "Educational Attainment in the United States: March 1979 and 1978," Washington, D.C.: U.S. Government Printing Office, 1980b, Table 1, pp. 11–13.

— = no available data.

TABLE 5. Percentages of Aged Blacks, Hispanics, and Whites below the Poverty Level, by Sex and Familial Status, United States, 1970-1981*

Familial Status and Year	Black		Hispanic		White	
	Female	Male	Female	Male	Female	Male
Total, all statuses						
1970	53.2	41.3	—	—	26.5	17.0
1975	40.2	31.0	36.0	28.2	16.1	9.5
1980	42.6	31.4	34.3	27.0	16.1	9.0
1981	43.5	32.2	27.3	23.6	16.2	8.5
Family householder						
1970	45.5	39.2	—	—	15.8	13.8
1975	36.9	26.0	39.4	29.5	7.4	7.1
1980	34.4	25.0	36.8	21.1	9.5	6.9
1981	30.9	29.2	34.0	22.4	11.5	6.4
Spouse of householder						
1970	41.8	0.0	—	0.0	14.0	0.0
1975	23.8	0.0	32.0	0.0	7.2	0.0
1980	23.5	40.0	25.5	25.0	7.0	7.1
1981	28.9	25.0	21.3	14.3	6.4	10.6
Other family member						
1970	25.6	11.3	—	—	7.5	6.5
1975	10.2	10.5	8.6	0.0	3.4	2.8
1980	19.2	19.5	16.7	32.1	5.1	5.7
1981	17.6	9.1	9.6	12.0	5.5	3.2
Unrelated individual						
1970	79.2	59.7	—	—	47.5	36.0
1975	65.8	51.8	60.3	35.3	29.1	23.8
1980	66.5	45.1	64.1	56.9	29.3	21.1
1981	64.3	46.0	48.3	35.4	28.2	19.7

*SOURCES: U.S. Bureau of the Census, *Current Population Reports,* Series P-60, No. 133, "Characteristics of the Population Below the Poverty Level: 1980," Washington, D.C.: U.S. Government Printing Office, 1982b, Table 3, pp. 17-18, and U.S. Bureau of the Census, *Current Population Reports,* Series P-60, No. 138, "Characteristics of the Population Below the Poverty Level: 1981," Washington, D.C.: U.S. Government Printing Office, 1983, Table 3, pp. 13-14.
— = no available data.

in 1980 remained higher among people between 25 and 64 years of age than among people who were 65 or more years of age, respectively being $5,479 and $2,879 for Hispanic women, $6,233 and $4,399 for white women, $6,404 and $3,149 for black women, $11,186 and $4,469 for black men, $12,187 and $4,772 for Hispanic men, and $18,048 and $7,671 for white men. The widest income gap by age was that for white men ($10,377) and the least that for white women ($1,834).

The relationship between education and income among aged people differs by race-sex groups. The positive relationship for white men is generally duplicated for black men and white women, but not for black women. For example, poverty is almost as high among black women with less than six years of schooling as among those who attended high school. Also, college education does not preclude poverty in old age: in 1980, 16.1 percent of black and 5.7 percent of white aged of both sexes who had at least some college attendance were poor.

The total money income of householders 55-64 years of age tends to be higher than that of those 65 or more years of age. Regardless of age, however, total money income is also higher among married couples with a wife in the paid labor force than among married couples without a wife in the paid labor force. Further, total money income is typically higher for white than for black married couples, also regardless of age. The difference in total money income between married couples with an aged householder where the wife is and is not employed is also much greater for whites than for blacks. In 1979, the difference in familial income in white families between those with a working and nonworking wife where she was aged or her husband was aged was $6,601. The comparable difference between their black counterparts was $1,057, substantially less. Thus, among aged couples, the contribution of the working wife to the familial income is much higher for white than for black wives.

Almost all of the aged had some kind of income. Table 6 shows income sources for black and white families with a householder over 65 years of age and for unrelated individuals who were over 65 years of age in 1980, by poverty level status. The percentage of those with earnings was highest among black families with an aged householder who was above the poverty level, and lowest among the aged whites who were living as unrelated individuals and who were below the poverty level.

The overwhelming majority of the aged received Social Security payments. The mean income received from Social Security in 1980 by people over 65 years of age, by race, familial status, and income level, is shown in Table 7. In general, the Social Security benefits received by the aged whites exceeded those of the aged blacks.

Marital Status

Table 8 shows the marital statuses of blacks, Hispanics, and whites who were over 55 years of age in the United States in 1970 and 1981, by sex. In each group, men were much more likely than women to be married and much less likely to be widowed or divorced. These sex differences in marital status are linked to sex differences in mortality, since women commonly outlive men. The differences also reflect the usually higher age of a groom than a bride, and higher male than female remarriage rates.

TABLE 6. Percentages of Types of Income Received by Aged Blacks and Whites, by Familial Status and Poverty Level, United States, 1980*

Type of Income	Black Family**		Black Unrelated		White Family**		White Unrelated	
	Poverty Level		Poverty Level		Poverty Level		Poverty Level	
	Above	Below	Above	Below	Above	Below	Above	Below
% with earnings	60.4	39.4	29.2	6.4	45.4	20.4	17.9	5.1
% with wage & salary income	58.0	38.5	27.8	6.2	39.9	15.6	15.6	3.7
% with other income	98.0	96.4	97.6	98.2	99.6	95.4	99.4	97.9
% with Social Security	88.9	80.5	89.9	84.7	93.9	85.2	94.7	88.6
% with Public Assistance	6.2	21.7	1.0	5.5	1.1	4.5	1.2	4.3
% with Supplemental Security	21.2	51.1	12.4	47.3	3.7	27.4	4.0	24.0
% with Unemployment workers' compensation, and veterans payments	14.6	9.0	12.1	9.4	9.1	4.6	8.6	7.3
% with dividends, interest, and rent	35.5	10.0	40.6	12.3	82.7	38.6	79.3	41.7
% with private pensions, government employee pensions, alimony, annuities, etc.	34.8	6.3	32.9	4.8	50.1	8.3	37.0	6.3
% with no income	0.0	1.8	0.0	0.9	0.0	3.6	0.0	1.2

*SOURCE: U.S. Bureau of the Census, *Current Population Reports,* Series P-60, No. 133, "Characteristics of the Population Below the Poverty Level: 1980," Washington, D.C.: U.S. Government Printing Office, 1982b, Table 35, pp. 137, 140.
**The familial householder is over 65 years of age.

TABLE 7. Mean Social Security Income Received by People Over 65 Years of Age, by Race, Familial Status, and Income Level, United States, 1980*

Familial and Income Status	Mean Social Security Income	
	Black	White
All families	$4,432	$6,059
Below the poverty level	3,104	3,336
Female householder, no husband present	3,455	4,863
Below the poverty level	(B)	2,971
All other families	4,851	6,217
Below the poverty level	3,432	3,404
All unrelated individuals	3,126	3,736
Below the poverty level	2,457	2,605
Male unrelated individuals	3,529	4,042
Below the poverty level	2,639	2,611
Female unrelated individuals	2,916	3,664
Below the poverty level	2,390	2,604

* SOURCE: U.S. Bureau of the Census, *Current Population Reports,* Series P-60, No. 133, "Characteristics of the Population Below the Poverty Level: 1980," Washington, D.C.: U.S. Government Printing Office, 1982b, Table 35, pp. 143–148. (B) = data base less than 75,000; mean income not computed.

TABLE 8. Marital Statuses of Older Blacks, Hispanics, and Whites, by Sex and Age, United States: 1970 and 1981*

Marital Status & Age	Black				Hispanic				White			
	Female		Male		Female		Male		Female		Male	
	1970	1981	1970	1981	1970	1981	1970	1981	1970	1981	1970	1981
Never married												
55–64 years	6.4	5.3	7.4	7.2	6.7	5.8	6.0	6.9	6.8	4.1	6.3	5.0
65–74 years	5.7	4.9	7.6	6.5	7.1	7.5	8.3	5.4	7.7	5.5	7.1	4.4
75+ years	6.8	5.4	8.9	2.6	8.8	8.3	9.8	4.1	9.1	6.3	7.9	3.5
Married, with spouse												
55–64 years	47.1	43.9	67.7	62.6	55.7	55.6	78.9	78.6	66.2	69.6	83.6	83.4
65–74 years	32.1	33.5	59.8	62.7	37.9	43.0	69.3	74.2	45.0	49.8	76.5	82.7
75+ years	14.6	14.4	46.9	58.0	17.6	27.3	52.0	58.8	19.0	22.5	57.2	70.9
Married, without spouse												
55–64	10.7	11.1	10.5	10.9	7.8	10.3	6.3	6.8	2.8	2.4	2.9	2.4
65–74 years	6.9	6.2	9.1	7.7	4.9	5.5	5.4	5.8	2.4	1.3	3.1	1.8
75+ years	4.3	4.5	9.8	6.8	3.5	0.2	6.4	2.8	3.6	1.2	4.4	1.6
Divorced												
55–64 years	6.5	10.2	5.5	10.4	7.0	10.5	4.1	5.3	4.9	6.8	3.6	5.7
65–74 years	4.3	6.8	4.2	6.8	4.7	7.0	3.9	6.1	3.7	4.2	3.2	3.6
75+ years	2.7	3.5	1.6	3.8	2.3	1.4	2.7	4.8	1.0	2.2	2.5	2.3
Widowed												
55–64 years	29.3	29.5	8.9	8.9	22.8	17.9	4.7	2.4	19.3	17.0	3.6	3.6
65–74 years	51.0	48.6	19.3	16.3	45.4	36.9	13.1	8.5	41.2	39.2	10.1	7.5
75+ years	71.6	72.2	32.8	28.7	67.8	62.7	29.1	29.5	67.3	67.8	28.0	21.6

* SOURCES: U.S. Bureau of the Census, *Census of Population, 1970, Detailed Characteristics,* Final Report PC(1)-D1, United States Summary, Washington, D.C.: U.S. Government Printing Office, 1973, Table 203, pp. 1-641–1-643, and U.S. Bureau of the Census, *Current Population Reports,* Series P-20, No. 372, "Marital Status and Living Arrangements: March 1981," Washington, D.C.: U.S. Government Printing Office, 1982c, Table 1, pp. 7–9.

Among older women, white and Hispanic women were more likely to be married than black women. The percentages of women living with their husbands declined between 1970 and 1980 for black women who were between 55 and 64. There was also a decline among Hispanic women 55–64 years of age. Widowhood rates remained fairly stable for both black and white women while decreasing for all age groups among Hispanics. Between 1970 and 1980, among men the only significant decline in the proportion of married men with a spouse present occurred among black men 55–64 years of age. The divorce rates of each group of men rose, as did the rates for married black men who were not living with their wives. A lesser proportion of both black and white men over 65 years of age and Hispanic men over 55 years of age reported being widowed.

The marital statuses of the aged generally showed increased diversity by race between 1970 and 1980, and especially so when measured by the presence of a spouse. The current patterns of marital statuses among younger adults portend widening gaps in the marital statuses of aged blacks and whites in the years ahead, as suggested some years ago by Jackson (1970). A consideration of the marital statuses of younger adults as they age is important because marital status is often linked to the economic security of older persons, and particularly so for black women.

Living Arrangements

Table 9 contains data about various patterns of living arrangements among black, Hispanic, and white householders, 65–74 years of age and 75 or more years of age, in 1982. With the exception of both black and white householders who were over 75 years of age, the majority of the aged householders headed families, as defined by the U.S. Bureau of the Census. A plurality or majority of the black householders and the white householders in the older age group did not head families. These kinds of data help to dispel any prevailing myth that aged black householders are far more likely than are aged white householders to head families. Women among aged blacks, Hispanics, and whites,

TABLE 9. Selected Household and Familial Characteristics of Aged Black, Hispanic, and White Householders, United States, 1982*

Characteristics	Blacks		Hispanics		Whites	
	65–74 years	75+ years	65–74 years	75+ years	65–74 years	75+ years
Total number of households**	959	547	230	122	9,292	6,323
% family household	52.9	46.8	64.4	62.6	61.5	44.2
% married-couple family	37.2	27.4	48.6	41.2	54.2	35.2
% other family, male householder	2.5	3.1	3.3	7.0	1.4	1.9
% other family, female householder	13.2	16.3	12.5	14.4	6.0	7.1
% not family households	47.1	53.2	35.6	37.4	38.5	55.8
% male householder	13.9	13.6	12.1	12.5	7.4	10.4
% female householder	33.2	39.6	23.4	24.9	31.0	45.4
Total number of families**	507	256	148	76	5,718	2,793
% in owner-occupied dwellings	71.4	75.4	73.0	63.2	88.4	85.0
% living with only one other person	59.0	73.4	60.1	72.4	82.1	88.9
% living with only two other persons	19.1	13.3	16.2	19.7	13.2	7.8
% with any members under 18 years of age	30.4	16.4	27.0	7.9	4.9	2.1
% with own children of any age	35.5	30.9	40.5	43.4	17.4	18.5

* SOURCE: U.S. Bureau of the Census, *Current Population Reports,* Series P-20, No. 381, "Household and Family Characteristics: March 1982," Washington, D.C.: U.S. Government Printing Office, 1983b, Table 3, pp. 34, 38, and 42, and Table 22, pp. 201–205.

** Numbers in thousands.

are more likely than men not to live in families.

A comparison of the living arrangements of blacks, Hispanics, and whites who were over 65 years of age and unmarried (i.e., those who were never married, or who were divorced or widowed) in 1980, showed that living alone occurred more often among the widowed or divorced aged than among the never married aged for both sexes in each group. Further, a majority of the following groups lived alone in 1980: widowed black women, 65–74 years of age; never married, widowed, and divorced black men, 75 or more years of age; never married, divorced, and widowed white women, 65 or more years of age; widowed and divorced white men, 65 or more years of age, and never married white men, 75 or more years of age; divorced Hispanic women, 65–74 years of age; and widowed and divorced Hispanic men, 65–74 years of age.

Most aged blacks, Hispanics, and whites who lived in families resided in owner-occupied dwellings with only one other person. Only a minority of them lived with any minor child or with any of their own children of any age. Their household composition, however, varied by at least the age, sex, and income status of the aged householder. The presence of a related child under 18 years of age was most likely when the household was headed by a poor, aged female, and especially by a poor, aged female who was black.

In general, the presence of own children of any age in households headed by an aged person is lower for whites than for blacks or Hispanics (see, e.g., Cantor, 1979), but most aged blacks, Hispanics, and whites do not live with their children. In 1982, black, Hispanic, and white families whose householders were over 65 years of age differed somewhat by the presence of one or more of their own children within their households. Among the married-couple families, whites were the least likely, and Hispanics the most likely, to have one or more children dwelling with them. But, in families with a female householder, Hispanics and whites were generally much more likely than blacks to have at least one child living with them. More spe-

cifically, in 1982, among the other families (i.e., not a married-couple family) where the female householder was between 65 and 74 years of age, at least one child of the householder lived with 55.2 percent of the Hispanics, 51.8 percent of the whites, and 50.8 percent of the blacks. The differences were more substantial for the female householders over 75 years of age: 83.3 percent for Hispanics, 66.7 percent for whites, and 51.7 percent for blacks (U.S. Bureau of the Census, 1983b, Table 3). The sharing of a household by aged parents and their children is a function of such factors as age, marital status, and health of the parent and/or child (Shanas et al., 1968), and not just of race.

Comparative Pitfalls

The kind of demographic data presented above is useful in comparing the structural patterns and trends of broadly defined older populations and subpopulations, but aging specialists and advocates should remain well aware of the limitations and pitfalls of these data, four of which are listed below.

1. There is often a lack of correspondence between the groups classified by the U.S. Bureau of the Census for whom data are provided and the groups of special interest to ethnogerontologists. Ethnogerontologists can avoid this problem when they collect primary data; but, owing to the enormous costs of primary data, they must typically rely upon the U.S. Bureau of the Census for data collected from periodic national censuses. The U.S. Bureau of the Census could be urged to oversample adult populations of the smaller ethnic or minority groups, such as the Japanese, and, where necessary, the oldest age groups of the larger ethnic or minority groups, such as blacks. Ideally, of course, treating each such group as a separate population would provide even better data.

2. Classificatory shifts made by the U.S. Bureau of the Census in its grouping of people by race as "white," "black," or "other" affect the accumulation of trend data. For example, Indians from India, who were returned as "white" for many years, are now classified as Asians and returned as members

of the "other race." The category "other race" was also swelled between 1970 and 1980 by the reclassification of "persons of Spanish origin." *In 1970, 93 percent of the Hispanics were white, and 1 percent were "other"; in 1980, 56 percent were white, and 40 percent were "other"* (U.S. Bureau of the Census, 1980a). Futher, the U.S. Bureau of the Census often reports data separately for "persons of Spanish origin," but, nevertheless, as previously indicated, still includes their data in the racial categories of white, black, or "other," thereby providing a troublesome overlap, as in comparisons of blacks, Hispanics, and whites.

3. Some aging specialists and advocates reify the "statistical person" by attributing group characteristics to each member of the group. They also misinterpret racially comparative findings. For example, when given the demographic fact that poverty is disproportionately higher among black than white aged, they believe that all aged blacks are poor and then interact with affluent aged blacks as if they were poor.

4. The ethnogerontologic concentration on politically or statistically defined dominant and minority groups by fiat or by inference has led to an almost singular lack of concentration on empirical studies of racial and ethnic relationships. Demographic data, of course, cannot depict power relationships. They may, for instance, point toward significant racial differences in the institutionalization of the aged, provided that the data are accurate (Wershow, 1976), but they cannot pinpoint the causes and effects of those racial differences. Thus, demographic results must ultimately be used by ethnogerontologists to design and implement studies that will describe and explain those causes and effects, as well as provide data about the effects of race and ethnicity on the changing statuses, roles, and interpersonal relationships of people as they age.

FINDINGS AND ISSUES

A comprehensive review of the ethnogerontologic literature in this chapter is impracticable because that literature appears to be largely descriptive, atheoretical, and heavily weighted with sociodemographic comparisons that rarely provide longitudinal data about multiple birth cohorts. This section, then, deals mostly with the issues of double jeopardy and of the racial crossover in mortality, including a limited discussion of findings related to those issues.

Double Jeopardy

Double or multiple jeopardy (hereafter, generally double jeopardy) is often regarded as *the* central concept of ethnogerontology, perhaps because many ethnogerontologists have emphasized the inferior socioeconomic statuses of the minority aged populations relative to the majority aged population. Manuel (1982a) regards double jeopardy as the landmark inquiry about minority aged. Its dominant focus has remained on sociodemographic differences, whether emphasis is placed on being old *and* a minority, or whether reference is made to its presumably opposing hypothesis of the leveling effects of advancing age (Kent, 1971; Bengston, 1979).

Talley and Kaplan (1956), who first applied the concept of double jeopardy to social gerontology, referred specifically to the jeopardizing status of being simultaneously Negro *and* old. The National Urban League's pamphlet, *Double Jeopardy—The Older Negro in America Today* (1964), generated under Hobart C. Jackson's leadership, perceived older Negroes as being doubly jeopardized merely because they were Negro *and* old. They were doubly jeopardized because they carried into old age "a whole lifetime of economic and social indignities" caused by racial prejudice and discrimination (National Urban League, 1964, p. 2). Thus, double jeopardy focused solely upon the lifetime effects of racism that were compounded by old age, and it also treated all Negroes as if they were alike.

Following Smith's (1967) characterization of rural aged blacks as being in multiple jeopardy and Jackson's (1967) focus on double jeopardy, the concept was soon expanded or modified to include such variants as triple jeopardy (see, e.g., National Council on the Aging, 1971), and quadruple jeopardy (see, e.g., Jackson, 1971d; Daly, 1976; Gibson, 1982b). A cooperative effort between the National Caucus on the Black Aged (which primarily involved Hobart C. Jackson and Jacquelyne J. Jackson) and the U.S. Senate Special Committee on Aging led to Lindsay's (1971) emphasis on multiple jeopardy. The further expansion of the concept to include nonblack racial minorities, such as Chinese, was accompanied by an extension to *white* Hispanics, thereby dropping the criterion of the immutable trait of race. Crandall's (1980) application of double jeopardy to individuals who possess two or more traits that are societally undesirable, thereby subjecting them to prejudice and discrimination, also discards the aforementioned criterion. Moreover, in addition to his failure to distinguish between permissible and impermissible discrimination, Crandall (1980) drops the inherent notion in the original conception of double jeopardy of lifelong vicitimization due to *racial discrimination,* as does the age-as-leveler hypothesis proposed by Kent (1971) and supported by Dowd and Bengston (1978). The mere fact that the racial gaps in socioeconomic indicators may narrow for birth cohorts in their old age, as compared to their younger years, does not invalidate the presence of double jeopardy.

Contrasting views exist about the theoretical value of double jeopardy. Jackson, Kolody, and Wood (1982) believe that the concept is advantageous in going beyond description to organize facts about the heterogeneity of minority aged, and that it may lead to a theory of minority aging and even of aging. Jackson and Wood (1976) operationalized double jeopardy as existing whenever blacks are more disadvantaged than are whites in the same birth cohort. Jackson, Kolody, and Wood (1982), who redefined double jeopardy as occurring when blacks over 65 years of age were more disadvantaged than were whites between 18 and 39 years of age, used self-assessment of physical health as a measure of double jeopardy. Jackson, Kolody, and Wood (1982) pro-

vided no explicit definition of *disadvantage.* Instead, it seems apparent that they considered disadvantage to exist whenever the values of the variables they employed were lower (in a negative direction) for one group than for another group. For example, if the aggregated group of aged blacks considered their health to be more of a serious problem than did the aggregated group of much younger whites, then the aged blacks were disadvantaged.

Jackson, Kolody, and Wood (1982), as well as Dowd and Bengston (1978) and Cuellar and Weeks (1980), do not restrict their measures of double jeopardy to objective factors. They all used the subjective factor of life satisfaction to measure double jeopardy. But their conclusions about older blacks, Mexican Americans, or minority women being in double jeopardy based on life satisfaction differ, probably because of conceptual and methodological variations in their studies, including the use of different samples.

But consistent results do not always occur when independent investigators use the same data set, as did Jackson and Walls (1978), Register (1981), Jackson, Kolody, and Wood (1982), and Ward and Kilburn (1983) in their comparisons of the life satisfaction scores of blacks and whites in the 1974 Harris data set (Harris and Associates, 1975). Unlike Jackson, Kolody, and Wood (1982), Jackson and Walls (1978), Register (1981), and Ward and Kilburn (1983) appropriately weighted the sample size for aged blacks in their analyses because blacks were oversampled in the survey. They also did not measure double jeopardy, nor did they indicate in any manner that they intended to measure double jeopardy. Jackson, Kolody, and Wood (1982) and Register (1981) did not control for socioeconomic status. Jackson and Walls (1978) controlled for socioeconomic status, albeit only by 1973 household income. Ward and Kilburn (1983) controlled their data by income and by health.

Jackson and Walls (1978) found insignificant differences in the mean life satisfaction scores of low-income blacks and whites, as well as of high-income blacks and whites, all of whom were 65 or more years of age. Ward and Kilburn (1983) also found insignificant differences between the life satisfaction scores of blacks and whites over 65 years of age. The findings of Jackson and Walls (1978) and Ward and Kilburn (1983) are consistent with results obtained from different samples by Bradburn (1969), Sauer (1977), and Harris and Associates (1981). Register (1981), who tested for the significance of racial differences in the low, medium, and high levels of life satisfaction of blacks and whites who were over 65 years of age, found that the black scores were significantly lower. He indicated that his results might have been different had he controlled for socioeconomic status. Jackson, Kolody, and Wood (1982), who used the two levels of high and low life satisfaction, concluded that blacks over 65 years of age were in double jeopardy by life satisfaction, as compared to whites between 18 and 39 years of age, because a much larger proportion of the latter than the former had high life satisfaction scores.

Whenever double jeopardy is perceived as carrying into old age "a whole lifetime of economic and social indignities" caused by racial prejudice and discrimination (National Urban League, 1964, p. 2), the mere use of cross-sectional data is grossly ineffective in measuring double jeopardy, largely because investigators using this method typically focus only upon differences by race or national origin. This does not mean, however, that investigators cannot use cross-sectional data to identify the correlates of life satisfaction for particular samples, as did Smith (1978), Markides (1980a), and Ward and Kilburn (1983).

Schaie et al. (1982, p. 229) used life satisfaction data from blacks and whites, 30–73 years of age, in the 1973 and 1977 surveys of the National Opinion Research Center, to demonstrate convincingly that "research on aging and social change affecting minority communities, or the study of differences between ethnic groups, needs to consider the interacting effect of race not only with age, but also with cohort and period effects."

Their cross-sequential and time-sequential analyses indicated that the black scores were significantly lower in both years, but that the white scores remained relatively stable over time, while those of the blacks increased.

In contrast, then, to the view of Jackson, Kolody, and Wood (1982) about the efficacy of double jeopardy, Jackson (in press) argues that the current confusion surrounding the concept reduces its theoretical and methodological value. This confusion is most conspicuous in the absence of ethnogerontologic agreement about the concept's conceptual and operational elements. In short, if double jeopardy is to be the central concept of ethnogerontology, it needs to be developed in the form of an ideal type. Further, in its present use, double jeopardy may well be time-bound, owing largely to major social and political changes in the statuses of minorities. For example, because marital history affects income statuses, the higher income level of old white compared to old black women is not a function solely of racial differences, but also of marital stability and occupational and wage histories of women and men in different birth cohorts. Thus, an operationalized definition of double jeopardy must either be freed from period effects, or different operational definitions of double jeopardy must be devised for different birth cohort or generational groupings.

Gibson's (1982a) longitudinal investigation of the work and retirement patterns of black and white householders over 45 years of age, by sex, in the Panel Study of Income Dynamics (Institute for Social Research, University of Michigan), helps to identify some economic indignities that black women, in comparison to black men and white women and men, may carry into old age. Her research design may be a good model for testing double jeopardy if the longitudinal period of observation is extended and if it can be demonstrated clearly that any unearthed indignities are at least due to racial or racial and sexual discrimination occurring prior to old age, where the adverse consequences are carried into old age. Also,

Gibson's (1982a) research could be readily supplemented by the studies that seek to identify the specific factors that may influence the possibility of double jeopardy in old age or the satisfaction of minority groups with their lives (see, e.g., Jackson et al., 1977).

It remains to be determined if double jeopardy is or should be *the* central concept of ethnogerontology. We think not. This determination is especially important because investigators who have attempted to test double jeopardy have rarely, if ever, provided any useful information about age changes, as opposed to age differences, in the statuses, roles, interpersonal relationships, attitudes, and values of adult minority individuals or populations as they age in their later years. In particular, Jackson and Wood (1976), Dowd and Bengston (1978), and Jackson, Kolody, and Wood (1982) have *not,* contrary to their assertions, ever tested the specific hypothesis of double jeopardy. Consequently, the question of the effects of minority group status on age changes in the later years remains wide open.

Further, the theories that underlie jeopardy and the age-as-leveler hypotheses must be distinguished. For example, the fact that the socioeconomic gaps between blacks and whites may narrow as they age in their later years, is not a sufficient substitute for denying the presence of double jeopardy. Contrary also to the suppositions of Kent (1971) and Dowd and Bengston (1978), these are not opposing conceptions. Double jeopardy evokes the notion of "what might have been" were it not for racial discrimination. The age-as-leveler hypothesis has no such connotation. Ethnogerontologists who consider double jeopardy as the landmark concept must define it carefully and consider seriously the theoretical soundness of any competing hypothesis.

Racial Crossover in Mortality

The racial crossover in mortality of the age-specific crude death rates of blacks or non-whites and whites, apparent in the United States for many years (see, e.g., Calloway, 1967; Thornton and Nam, 1968; Kitagawa and Hauser, 1973; Manton and Poss, 1977; Nam and Ocay, 1977; Manton et al., 1979; Manton, 1982), is not unique to the United States (Manton, 1982). But ethnogerontologic interest in this issue in the United States has usually been confined to attempts to explain it (including its relationship to the racial crossover in life expectancy values) or to consider it tangentially by focusing upon comparative health statuses of majority and minority aged.

Jackson's (1982) study of the death rates of blacks and whites, 65 or more years of age, in the United States between 1964 and 1978, showed that the crude death rate for white women 65–79 years of age was consistently higher than the comparable rate for black women, with the racial crossover occurring in the 80–84-year-old group. The white male rate was also consistently higher than the rate for black men in the 65–74-year-old group in each year between 1964 and 1978. The black male advantage in the 75–79-year-old group between 1964 and 1969 was extinguished by 1970, after which the racial crossover in mortality occurred among men within the 80–84-year-old group, thereby approximating the female pattern. Also between 1964 and 1978, the racial gaps in the crude death rates decreased for both sexes for the 80–84-year-old age group, while widening for the 85-or-more-years-of-age group. Moreover, in 1980, the crude death rates for each sex were *only* higher for blacks than for whites in the latter age group.

Manton et al. (1979), who assumed that the racial crossover in mortality was not an artifact of data due to errors in the reporting of age or enumerations of the population sizes and deaths, considered genetic and environmental models in their attempts to explain the black/white crossover in mortality in the United States. Their comparisons of 1969 data about deaths due to ischemic heart disease, stroke, generalized arteriosclerosis, hypertensive heart disease, and cancer did not lead to definitive conclusions about the biological or environmental factors that might be related to the significant racial differences in those death rates. They did, however, stress the need to determine when a death should be attributed to disease or to aging, an important distinction if the crossover is explicable by racial differences in aging rates.

Manton (1982) categorized the existing explanations of the racial crossover in mortality or life expectancy as census enumeration errors, socioeconomic and familial factors, population and individual dynamics (e.g., mortality selection), and differential rates of aging (see Morgan, 1968; McPherson et al., 1978). He leaned heavily toward the last explanation, provided that the crossover is not an artifact of enumerative errors. Rives (1977) believes that enumerative errors have a minimal impact on black life expectancy values, suggesting thereby that the crossover exists. Otherwise, the supposition would be that the undercount unduly inflates the mortality rates, which, in turn, are used in the computation of life expectancy values.

Most of the investigators of the racial crossover in mortality have been primarily concerned with its documentation as opposed to its explanation. The actual existence of the crossover is now relatively well established, but the cause of the crossover is not yet known. Although such investigators as Manton et al. (1979) and Manton (1982) favor the theory of differential rates of aging between racial groups, we tend to agree with Calloway (1967) that the black/white crossover in mortality rates in the United States is largely, if not entirely, a function of differential environmental exposures and resources available to various racial or ethnic groups.

We agree with Manton (1982), however, that our understanding of the crossover requires more research about the relative differences in the age-related health statuses of blacks and whites. Substantial improvements in morbidity data (analyzable by such variables as age, sex, marital status, social class, and migration) are essential for comparisons of the health statuses of ethnic or dominant and minority populations (see,

e.g., Jackson, 1981; Manton, 1982). But, unlike the research design used by Manton et al. (1979), tests of the theory of differential rates of aging will definitely require the grouping of research subjects by local races who share the same genetic pool, as opposed to the traditional use of geographical races that are based upon phenotypical or social definitions of race (see especially Garn and Coon, 1955; Estel, 1956).

PUBLIC POLICIES

A growing and perhaps increasingly controversial issue is whether or not federal statutes and rules of public programs designed to deliver services to older people should typically be minority-specific (see Jackson, 1980), so as to reduce social inequities between the aged of dominant and minority groups, or to increase the participation of minority and non-minority ethnic aged in those programs (see, e.g., Jackson 1968, 1971a; White House Conference on Aging, 1972, 1981; McCaslin and Calvert, 1975; Bechill, 1979; Biegel and Sherman, 1979; Federal Council on Aging, 1979; Guttmann, 1979; Holmes et al., 1979; Markson, 1979; Cuellar and Weeks, 1980; Newton, 1980; U.S. Commission on Civil Rights, 1982a,b; Cain, 1983).

This issue has been raised most often by minority aging specialists, minority aging organizations, minority participants in the 1971 and 1981 White House Conferences on Aging, and by ethnogerontologic investigators of non–Anglo-Saxon white native-born and immigrant ethnics in the United States. Jackson's (1968) proposal that the age standards for black primary beneficiaries of Social Security's Old Age and Survivors Insurance program (OASI) should be lowered to reflect the earlier death rates of black than white OASI contributors was subsequently adopted by the then–ad hoc National Caucus on the Black Aged in 1970. This proposal was restricted to old-age pensions.

Jackson's (1968) idea was extended by various ethnogerontologic advocates to a number of nonblack minority groups (see, e.g., White House Conference on Aging,

1972, 1981). Also, following Ryder's (1975) proposal that the determination of old age should be based on counting backward from the projected data of death, presumably based upon life expectancy values, Cain (1978) further pursued the idea of counting backward. The National Tribal Chairmen's Association, Inc. (1976) also sanctioned the use of life expectancy differentials by race as the basis for determining the age standards for Indian participants in public programs for the aged.

Later, however, Jackson (1980, 1982, in press) generally opposed any minority-specific provisions in federal statues and regulations for aging programs for at least several reasons, including the fact that life expectancy values are never determined for an individual. Allowing a major exception for Indians due to their historically unique relationship with the federal government, Jackson's opposition was also due to her strong belief that Social Security's Old Age and Survivors Insurance program should be transformed from being a largely social welfare program, as it now is, into a true insurance program (see Ferrara, 1980). Such a transformation could have monetary benefits for the estates of blacks who were covered under the system and who died before they became old enough to receive any substantial benefit from the system.

The National Commission on Social Security Reform (1983) restricted its scope of study to the retirement or old-age pension section of Social Security. It did not deal with the disability or health components of Social Security. The Commission devoted no attention to the specific question of the existence of racial inequities in the old-age pension system. A minority report, however, contains some views about discrimination against women in the Social Security system. This lack of attention to blacks or other racial minorities may be due to the absence of any racial minority member on the 15-member Commission. Robert Myers (1983), the executive director of that Commission, also believes that Social Security is an inappropriate vehicle to use for remedying social dis-

crimination against blacks, a view we do not share.

The American public probably does not believe that Social Security discriminates against blacks and women. In her telephone interview survey of a random sample of black and white residents of Washington, D.C., who were between 20 and 64 years of age, Weaver (1984) found that only a minority of her respondents felt that the old-age pension section of Social Security discriminated against blacks (19.5%) or women (23.0%), while a numerically low minority in each instance reported that they did not know if any such discrimination occurred. These attitudes were similar among respondents of different races and each sex with respect to discrimination against women, but not against blacks. Black women and white men were significantly more likely than were black men and white women to think that Social Security discriminated against blacks.

Perhaps Jackson's (1980) distinction between institutionalized victimization and systematic discrimination (see also Cuellar and Weeks, 1980) is useful here. Simply put, most of Weaver's respondents may have thought that the racial or sexual discrepancies in monthly benefits from the old-age pension section of Social Security are due only to institutionalized victimization during the working years of the primary beneficiaries, such as being the result of racial and sexual discrepancies in wages, but that the actual benefits now received are based upon a neutral formula that does not take into account the earlier discriminatory factors in the market place. In short, then, according to them, Social Security does not discriminate against blacks or women. But Weaver's (1984) data also showed that a majority of her respondents were generally unaware of the financial or operating structure of Social Security. Harris and Associates (1981) indicated that their nationwide survey showed that blacks and Hispanics were less knowledgeable than whites about the financing component of Social Security.

The need for minority-specific provisions in aging programs, however, could be supported partially by Rosow's (1976) view that participation in socially homogeneous groups (such as by race or nationality) enhances the informal support networks of the aged. Chen (1980) found that most of her Chinese (78.0%) and Mexican (61.7%), but not her black (16.7%) subjects (each of whom participated in a racially or ethnically identifiable, federally funded nutrition site for the elderly in Los Angeles, California) felt that it was important that their friends shared their racial or ethnic membership. Chen's data about her Chinese and Mexican subjects partially support Rosow's view.

The recent surge of older legal and illegal immigrants who do not speak English must also be considered. As pointed out, for example, by Cuellar and Weeks (1980) and the U.S. Commission on Civil Rights (1982a,b), perhaps the federal government should recognize and respond to the special needs of these groups for information about federally sponsored programs for which they are eligible on the basis of their age or some other criteria, for multilingual staffing of those programs, and even for the establishment of linguistic-specific or interpreter programs in local areas, especially since the proper goal of public programs should be the effective delivery of services to all eligible persons (Butler, 1975). But, as a practical matter, the provision of widespread multilingual information or staff could be enormously costly. The use of multilingual staff could also promote the separation by national origin or race of the aged in on-site, federally funded programs.

Ethnogerontologic advocates of equitable or preferential treatment for minorities need to distinguish clearly between their sociological, anthropological, and political definitions of (1) racial and ethnic groups, (2) minority and non-minority aged, (3) equitable and preferential treatment, and (4) permissible and impermissible preferential treatment. We also agree with White (1982), who restricts the concept of minorities to the federally protected classes, that the U.S. Congress is obligated to define and justify precisely its special entitlement groups for

federal programs on the basis of race, nationality, or whatever. Otherwise, for example, "The 'Hispanics' so entitled may be fresh out of Spain from Barcelona; or Argentines, whom we, as Americans, never wronged. They may be Sephardic Jews whose names end with 'ez,' as in Lopez, or a vowel, as in Cardozo—entitled to rights not extended to Jews of European heritage whose names end with a 'sky' or an 'ovitz'" (White, 1982, pp. 366–367). Such a legislative clarification could be very helpful to ethnogerontologists who engage in political research, including evaluations of racial or ethnic equity in the staffing patterns of aging programs using federal funds.

Many ethnogerontologists are properly worried about the barriers to minority participation in programs for the aged that are created by negative attitudes of dominant-group staff members toward minority participants (see, e.g., Bell et al., 1976; Schneider, 1979; Cuellar and Weeks, 1980; U.S. Commission on Civil Rights, 1982a,b). Thune's (1967) focus on the negative attitudes of white participants toward black participants in the on-site programs for the aged suggests another barrier to the participation of aged minorities in certain settings. The issue has also arisen in a different way with respect to the negative effects of the use of minority-group staff in predominantly white, on-site programs for the aged, such as in nursing homes (see, e.g., Weinstock and Bennett, 1968).

Much of the ethnogerontologic literature seems to favor the matching of staff and clients by racial or national origin background in on-site programs for the aged (see, e.g., Rosow, 1976; Cuellar and Weeks, 1980; U.S. Commission on Civil Rights, 1982a,b). But there also tends to be much support for the equal employment provisions of the Civil Rights Act of 1964, thereby creating a dilemma that is exacerbated by economic and political competition between dominant-group and minority-group members of the labor force (see Jackson, 1983). This persistent dilemma needs to be resolved through a balancing of constitutional and statutory rights involving equity in employment and in services for the aged.

THE CURRENT STATUS
OF ETHNOGERONTOLOGY

The existing ethnogerontologic literature may be subdivided by five major areas, the first of which is *aging images and attitudes,* such as a focus on subjective perceptions about the importance of religion, the definition of old age, life satisfaction, morale, fear of death, or the expected number of years of remaining life (see, e.g., Sherman, 1955; Stone, 1959; Heyman and Jeffers, 1964; Roberts, 1964; Dovenmuehle and McGough, 1965; Lipman and Marden, 1966; Berrien et al., 1967; Harper, 1967; Messer, 1968; Weinstock and Bennett, 1968; Moore, 1970; Stojanovic, 1970; Koenig et al., 1971; Blum, 1972; Crouch, 1972; Gobetz, 1972; Kalish and Moriwaki, 1973; Brand and Smith, 1974; Clemente and Sauer, 1974; Reynolds and Kalish, 1974; Hutchinson, 1975; Sauer, 1977; Gitelman, 1976; Kalish and Reynolds, 1976; Watson and Kivett, 1976; Bengston et al., 1977; Golden, 1977; Jackson et al., 1977; Seelbach and Sauer, 1977; Holley, 1978; Korte, 1978; Miranda, 1978; Bremer and Ragan, 1979; Chapman, 1979; Creecy and Wright, 1979; Hunter et al., 1979; Cuellar and Weeks, 1980; Markides, 1980b; Markides et al., 1980, 1981; Orchowsky and Parham, 1981; Pieper, 1981; Register, 1981; Register and Mitchell, 1981–82; Kivett, 1982, 1983; Ball, 1983).

The second area is *aging activities,* such as reading, watching television, attending church, babysitting, being gainfully employed, doing volunteer work, participating as a member of an officer in formal organizations, voting, or "just sitting and thinking" (see, e.g., Heyman and Jeffers, 1964; Davis, 1966; Ball, 1967; Dhaliwal, 1967; Rubenstein, 1971; Lambing, 1972; Bielefeld, 1974; Clemente et al., 1975; Jericho, 1977; Torres-Gil and Becerra, 1977; Cuellar, 1978; Jackson and Walls, 1978; Rogers and Gallion, 1978; Cuellar and Weeks, 1980; Harris and Associates, 1981; Gibson, 1982a).

The third area is *aging problems,* such as the presence and severity of problems that the aged experience with income, health, housing, and loneliness, including the presence of a confidant (see, e.g., Clark, 1959; Ellis, 1962; Fenz, 1962; Niebank and Pope, 1965; Aiken and Ferman, 1966; Crocker, 1968; Clark and Mendelson, 1969; Fisher, 1970; Walker, 1970; Richeck et al., 1971; Fox and Faine, 1973; Moriwaki, 1973; Gaitz and Scott, 1974; Bourg, 1975; Boykin, 1975; Faulkner, 1975; Anderson, 1975; Cantor and Mayer, 1976; Carp and Kataoka, 1976; Abbott, 1977; Nowlin, 1977; Ragan, 1977; Walls and Jackson, 1977; Carter, 1978; Chen, 1978; Cheng, 1978; Garcia and Juarez, 1978; Ishikawa, 1978a,b; McCoy and Brown, 1978; Blau et al., 1979; Candy, 1979; Eve and Friedsam, 1979; Federal Council on Aging, 1979; Finley and Delgado, 1979; Nowlin, 1979; Rorick and Crimshaw, 1979; McMurray, 1981; Carter, 1982; J. S. Jackson et al., 1982; Ozawa, 1982; Taylor, 1982; Berger, 1983).

The fourth area of *supportive networks* is generally confined to kinship and friendship circles, but occasionally extended to include the providers of services in aged programs, such as the frequency and satisfaction of contact with relatives and friends, the type and amount of instrumental and affective exchanges between the aged and their relatives and friends, and, less often, the degree of support that the aged receive through voluntary associations that are specifically focused upon their particular illnesses or stages in their individual or familial life cycles, including terminal illnesses or widowhood (see, e.g., Barnett, 1960; Jackson, 1971a, 1972a; Barg and Hirsch, 1972; Mindel and Hays, 1973; Cantor, 1975; Kim and Condon, 1975; Lopata, 1975; Yelder, 1975; Petrowsky, 1976; Anderson, 1978; Curran, 1978; Evans and Northwood, 1978; Gerber et al., 1978; German et al., 1978; Murphy, 1978; Stephens et al., 1978; Woehrer, 1978; Bastida, 1979; Cantor et al., 1979; Martinez, 1979; Manuel, 1980; Sauer et al., 1980; Seelbach, 1980; Dilworth-Anderson, 1981; Manson et al., 1981; Cohler, 1982; Colen, 1982; Taylor et al., 1982).

The fifth and final area is *need, access, and use of aging programs,* such as Medicaid, nursing homes, food stamps, and subsidized housing (see, e.g., Davis, 1939; Jackson, 1965; Lipman, 1965; Carp, 1969; Dominick and Stotsky, 1969; Gordon and Rehr, 1969; Gregory, 1970; Solomon, 1970; Benedict, 1971; Carp, 1971; DeGeynot, 1971; Kent, and Hirsch, 1971; Reynoso and Coppelman, 1972; Davis, 1973; Sue and Kitano, 1973; Wu, 1974; Anderson, 1975; Ishikawa and Archer, 1975; Kim and Condon, 1975; McCaslin and Calvert, 1975; Bell et al., 1976; Farris, 1976; Fujii, 1976b; Kart and Beckham, 1976; Eribes, 1977; Kasschau, 1977; Williams, 1977; Eribes and Bradley-Rawls, 1978; Hunt, 1978; Murdock and Schwartz, 1978; Red Horse et al., 1978; Smith, 1978; Colen, 1979; Maldonado, 1979; Montero, 1979; Carpenter and Bollman, 1980; Chen, 1980; Hawkins, 1980, 1982; Manuel, 1980; Red Horse, 1980; Taylor, 1980; Waring and Kosberg, 1980; Jacobson, 1982; Lacayo, 1982). An increasing tendency in this type of literature is an emphasis that the widespread myth about racial minorities always residing in highly supportive and caring, extended families is invalid. This tendency seems to be buttressed by relatively strong and growing attitudes that the government should be responsible for the welfare of elderly people. Thus, the ethnogerontologists do not welcome a shield that may limit the receipt of public benefits by aged minorities.

As indicated earlier, the current status of ethnogerontology is fragile, largely because it is extremely descriptive, fragmented, inconclusive, and uncertain about its specific scope or subject matter. The existing literature generally documents well the major sociodemographic differences between aged blacks and whites and, to a lesser extent, between dominant and minority aged. Most of the comparisons of cultural norms related to the aged (e.g., definitions of when a person is old, or the frequency of contact between aged parents and their adult children) focus solely on racial or national origin groups, and typically only on blacks, Hispanics, and whites.

Comparisons that are restricted to cultur-

ally homogeneous groups are almost totally absent in the literature, but there has been some increase in intraracial comparisons. Most of the available data here or elsewhere are cross-sectional data from surveys that are not supplemented by in-depth interviews or by ethnographic investigations. Cuellar and Weeks, for example, sought to correct the ethnographic oversight in their 1979–80 field study of racial and national origin groups in San Diego, California. Also, James S. Jackson and his associates are studying kinship relationships between three generations of blacks. Both of these kinds of studies should help to illuminate ethnogerontology.

Most of the recent research in ethnogerontology concentrates heavily upon the single area of need, access, and use of services by aged minorities, owing largely, we suspect, to the influence of research priorities of the Administration on Aging, a major funding source for research by minority ethnogerontologists.

The existing literature contains little information about social aging, such as age changes in adult statuses and roles. Some of the anecdotal data of Coles (1974) and Salber (1983) about Mexican Americans and blacks, respectively, could stimulate systemic examinations of age changes in statuses and roles. Davis's (1980) annotated bibliography focuses partially upon the changing work roles of black slaves as they aged, but there has also been no systematic exploration even of this topic.

The considerable lack of a gerontologic focus (i.e., on aging per se) in the ethnogerontologic literature may be attributed both to (1) the widespread use of cross-sectional studies and (2) the overwhelming or predominant concern of many ethnogerontologic investigators with the documentation of social inequities between dominant and minority aged that were due to legally impermissible discrimination on the basis of race or national origin. But, in light of the general lack of concern of many gerontologists about this issue, despite their growing concentration on improving the quality of life of older people in the United States, an ethnogerontologic concentration on public policies was and is sorely needed. Some ethnogerontologists have argued convincingly for public policies that could reduce the social inequities between dominant and minority aged. A few of them who have functioned effectively as advocates for aged minorities have also documented well many of those social inequities. They have also made some public officials more aware of those inequities.

Much of the literature that compares the sociocultural patterns of the dominant and minority aged, or of the aged of different ethnic groups, is inconclusive or confusing. This inconclusiveness or confusion is often due to conceptual and methodological differences, such as the inappropriate groupings of research subjects by racially heterogeneous, culturally heterogeneous, or minority-heterogeneous groups (see, e.g., Holley, 1978; Eve and Friedsam, 1982), divergent methods of statistical analyses (as suggested in the earlier discussion about black and white life satisfaction scores), the use of nonrepresentative or geographically localized samples that prohibit the generalization of sample findings to their populations, and inadequate knowledge about the validity and reliability of survey or other instruments that are used to measure subjective conditions, including the often used self-report measure of health status, where subjects are asked to rank their health on a scale ranging from very poor or poor to excellent.

This confusion may be further illustrated by simply noting the differential findings about the comparative health statuses of blacks and whites over 65 years of age, where such researchers as Shanas (1977), Ferron (1981), Harris and Associates (1981), and Manuel and Reid (1982) tend to believe that the health status of aged blacks is inferior to that of aged whites, a position that is not generally accepted globally by such investigators as Ostfeld et al., (1971), Nowlin (1977, 1979), and Jackson (1981, 1982). One problem that is often overlooked is that there may be a tendency for low-income people to judge their health status differently from higher-income people (see especially Kadushin, 1964, 1967). We believe that the differential judgment of one's health status represents a research problem when inadequate controls for measures of functional ability do not include, for example, the racial differences in access to mobility aids that reduce the climbing of many steps, or the extent to which the older person's survival needs are related directly to his employment status. Better data about the actual correspondence between at least the objective or medically determined and the subjective health statuses of aged minorities are yet needed, a problem that may, but should not, be complicated greatly by the inclusion of recent minority immigrants who were long accustomed to a health system that differed substantially from that of the American mainstream health system.

THE PROSPECTIVE STATUS OF ETHNOGERONTOLOGY

As indicated earlier, ethnogerontology is the study of the causes, processes, and consequences of race, national origin, and culture on individual and population aging. Ethnicity is a concept that is best restricted to culturally homogeneous groups. Thus, for example, it should not be used to refer to any group categorized only by race. The prospective status of ethnogerontology may be bright and productive scientifically if the major issues related to its scope, theory, and methodology are resolved satisfactorily in the future. These major issues include, but are not limited to, the following six points.

1. The research groups used by ethnogerontologists need to be identified precisely by the variables of race, national origin, or ethnicity. Further, the identification of a minority group or of an individual holding membership in a minority group should be based upon appropriate scientific or political criteria, depending upon the nature of the research problem. The current admixture between these different kinds of groups only leads to continued confusion about at least their changing social statuses, roles, and structures during their processes of aging, and provides little or no data about the sequence of age changes in those statuses, roles, and structures.

2. Ethnogerontologists should distinguish

clearly between their scientific and advocatory roles, recognizing full well that their scientific roles require the accumulation of theories and facts about the causes, processes, and consequences of aging, including the differences in aging that may and probably do exist between people grouped on the basis of race, national origin, or ethnicity. But their scientific generalizations about those differences, if any, should be adequately controlled by all relevant variables, including the influence of social class, sex, and immigration. Further, in this connection, ethnogerontologists should reevaluate carefully the concept of double jeopardy, probably relegating it to a politically useful concept.

3. Ethnogerontology should be expanded feasibly to include interdisciplinary investigations of biological, psychological, and social aging that will permit cross-cultural comparisons, a goal that will require the appropriate identification of ethnic groups. For example, ethnogerontologists must remember that blacks in the United States constitute a racial, not an ethnic, group.

4. Ethnogerontologists need to expand their methodological procedures to include not only longitudinal or longitudinally related studies, but also ethnographic studies that will foster the acquisition of knowledge about the causes, processes, and consequences of aging within sociocultural settings. Above all, the goal is to concentrate upon age changes that are affected by race, national origin, or culture. The ethnogerontologic goal is not simply the acquisition of data about age differences or about social inequities. Thus, ethnogerontologists must remain not only cognizant of the effects of age, cohort, and period on aging (especially in minority groups), but also of the need to advocate (if they so desire) public policies that are based upon reasonable judgments about the current and future statuses and needs of the aged, as well as the extent to which the public meeting of those needs will impact upon the working non-aged.

5. Ethnogerontologists who focus upon public policies for the aged must try to help balance the constitutional and statutory provisions that relate to equal employment opportunities and the adequacy of the provision of services to the aged of different racial, national origin, or ethnic groups, without placing much (if any) of their emphasis upon their own vested interests.

6. Finally, progress in ethnogerontology requires the infusion of highly competent and objective investigators who will concentrate heavily upon basic, as opposed to applied and evaluative, research, so as to foster our knowledge about the effects of race, national origin, and ethnicity upon the causes, processes, and consequences of individual and population aging. This is an important caveat, inasmuch as most of the current literature in ethnogerontology provides little or no information about age changes.

CONCLUSION

This chapter, which was ultimately concerned with the current and the prospective status of ethnogerontology (or the study of the causes, processes, and consequences of race, national origin, and culture on individual and population aging) concentrated mostly upon the emergence of ethnogerontology and its key concepts, sociodemographic comparisons of black, Hispanic, and white aged, and research related to the concepts of double jeopardy and the racial crossover in mortality between blacks and whites in the United States. The largely descriptive and atheoretical state of the ethnogerontologic literature, weighted heavily with inconclusive and confusing findings that may be attributed most often to theoretical and methodological weaknesses, made it impractical to provide a truly comprehensive review of the existing literature in ethnogerontology.

An analysis of the existing literature in ethnogerontology that was undertaken in order to pen this chapter, however, suggested that ethnogerontologists need to define more sharply the scope, theory, and methodology of their field, largely because ethnogerontological investigations could be extremely fruitful in uncovering the effects of race, national origin, and ethnicity on aging. Despite the inconclusive, confusing, and fragmented state of the existing literature, it is quite clear that the social statuses, roles, and structures of aged persons are affected in various and sometimes draconian ways by their race, national origin, ethnicity, or a combination thereof. Moreover, it is also clear that membership within a minority group also affects aging. Consequently, a current problem with the existing literature is its impreciseness about minority group or ethnic group identification as measured by scientific or political criteria, as well as its heavy concentration upon double jeopardy. Double jeopardy is a relatively useless concept scientifically for ethnogerontology, largely because it focuses too heavily upon social inequities without regard to age changes. It is, however, an important concept for the study of racial and ethnic relations or of social stratification.

The prospective status of ethnogerontology may be extremely promising if certain major issues that now affect it are resolved adequately. Among those issues are the inappropriate grouping of research subjects by racially or culturally heterogeneous groups, inappropriate statistical methods, inadequate samples, and inadequate attention to basic theoretical (see, e.g., Lipman, 1982) and methodological questions, including especially, once again, a concentration upon age changes that are affected by race, national origin, and ethnicity. The further accumulation of valid descriptive data should lead to the development of effective theories of ethnogerontology, which, in turn, would function as appropriate guides for ethnogerontologic research.

Given especially the new influx of immigrants of color to the United States and the considerable ethnic variation among blacks in the United States, there is every reason to hope that ethnogerontologists will obtain and disseminate necessary knowledge that could be used by public officials who have a mandate to improve the quality of life for all older people residing within their jurisdictions. Thus, it could be argued that ethnogerontologists have a scientific or professional *and* a moral responsibility to provide valid and reliable data about the effects of race, national origin, and ethnicity on aging, with emphasis on the additive or interactive patterns or processes of biological, psychological, and social aging.

Finally, ethnogerontologists should always remain concerned about the extent to which their proposed policies for the aged may foster or hinder the social and cultural integration into the mainstream of the United States, of older people who are distinguishable from the dominant group on account of their race, national origin, or ethnicity.

REFERENCES

Abbott, Julian. 1977. Socioeconomic characteristics of the elderly: Some black–white differences. *Social Security Bulletin* 40:16–42.

Aiken, Michael, and Ferman, Louis A. 1966. The social and political reactions of older Negroes to unemployment. *Phylon* 27:333–346.

Anderson, Peggye D. 1975. The black aged: Dispositions toward seeking age concentrated housing in a small town. Unpublished doctoral dissertation, Evanston, Ill.: Northwestern University.

Anderson, Peggye D. 1978. Support services and aged blacks. *Black Aging* 3:53–59.

Bailey, Shirley B. 1975. A study of selected factors related to the social satisfaction of the residents of a facility for senior citizens—The Roosevelt for senior citizens. Unpublished master's thesis, Washington, D.C.: Howard University.

Ball, Mercedes E. 1967. Comparison of characteristics of aged Negroes in two counties. Unpublished master's thesis, Washington, D.C.: Howard University.

Ball, Richard E. 1983. Marital status, household structure, and life satisfaction of black women. *Social Problems* 30:400–409.

Barg, Sylvia K., and Hirsch, Carl. 1972. A successor model for community support of low-income minority group aged. *Aging and Human Development* 3:243–251.

Barnett, Milton L. 1960. Kinship as a factor affecting Cantonese economic adaptation in the United States. *Human Organization* 19:40–46.

Barron, Milton L. 1953. Minority group characteristics of the aged in American society. *Journal of Gerontology* 8:477–482.

Barron, Milton L. 1960. Kinship as a factor affecting Cantonese economic adaptation in the United States. *Human Organization* 19:40–46.

Bastida, Elena. 1979. Family integration in later life among Hispanic Americans. *Journal of Minority Aging* 4:42–49.

Beard, Virginia H. 1976. A study of aging among a successful urban black population. Unpublished doctoral dissertation, St. Louis: St. Louis University.

Bechill, William. 1979. Politics of aging and ethnicity. *In* Donald E. Gelfand and Alfred J. Kutzik (eds.), *Ethnicity and Aging, Theory, Research, and Policy*, pp. 137–148. New York: Springer Publishing Company.

Bell, Duranm, Kasschau, Patricia, and Zellman, Gail. 1976. *Delivering Services to the Elderly Members of Minority Groups: A Critical Review of the Literature*. Santa Monica, Calif.: Rand Corporation.

Benedict, Robert A. 1971. A profile of Indian aged. *In* Robert A. Benedict (ed.), *Minority Aged in America*, pp. 51–57. Ann Arbor: Institute of Gerontology, University of Michigan and Wayne State University.

Bengston, Vern L. 1979. Ethnicity and aging: Problems and issues in current social science inquiry. *In* Donald E. Gelfand and Alfred J. Kutzik (eds.), *Ethnicity and Aging, Theory, Research, and Policy*, pp. 9–31. New York: Springer Publishing Company.

Bengston, Vern L., Cuellar, Jose B., and Ragan, Pauline K. 1977. Stratum contrasts and similarities in attitudes toward death. *Journal of Gerontology* 32:76–88.

Berger, Peggy S. 1983. The economic well-being of elderly Hispanics. *Journal of Minority Aging* 8:36–46.

Berrien, F. K., Arkoff, A., and Iwahara, S. 1967. Generational differences in values: Americans, Japanese Americans, Japanese. *Journal of Social Psychology* 71:169–175.

Berry, Brewton. 1958. *Race and Ethnic Relations*. Boston: Houghton Mifflin Company.

Biegel, David E., and Sherman, Wendy R. 1979. Neighborhood capacity building and the ethnic aged. *In* Donald E. Gelfand and Alfred J. Kutzik (eds.), *Ethnicity and Aging, Theory, Research, and Policy*, pp. 320–340. New York: Springer Publishing Company.

Bielefeld, Alvin U. 1974. Selected aspects of retirement as envisioned by groups of adult males partitioned according to age, ethnic background, educational achievement, and income. Unpublished doctoral dissertation, Tulsa, Okla.: University of Tulsa.

Blau, Zena S., Oser, George T., and Stephens, Richard C. 1979. Aging, social class and ethnicity: A comparison of Anglo, Black, and Mexican-American Texans. *Pacific Sociological Review* 22:501–525.

Blum, Zahara D. 1972. A developmental study of time perception and time perspective in three cultural groups: Anglo-American, Indian American, and Mexican American. Unpublished doctoral dissertation, Baltimore, Md.: Johns Hopkins University.

Bourg, Carroll J. 1975. Elderly in a southern metropolitan area. *The Gerontologist* 15:15–22.

Boykin, Lorraine S. 1975. Soul foods for some older Americans. *Journal of the American Geriatric Society* 23:380–382.

Bradburn, N. M. 1969. *The Structure of Psychological Well-Being*. Chicago: Adline Publishing Company.

Brand, Frederick N., and Smith, Richard T. 1974. Life adjustment and relocation of the elderly. *Journal of Gerontology* 29:336–340.

Bremer, Teresa H., and Ragan, Pauline K. 1979. The empty nest: A comparison between older Mexican American and white women. *Sociological Symposium* 26:64–82.

Butler, Frieda R. 1982. *A Resource Guide on Black Aging*. Washington, D.C.: The Institute for Urban Affairs and Research, Howard University.

Butler, Robert N. 1975. *Why Survive? Being Old in America*. New York: Harper & Row.

Cain, Leonard. 1978. Prospects for determining old age status by counting backward from projected death. Paper presented at the annual meeting of the Society for the Study of Social Problems, San Francisco, Calif.

Cain, Leonard. 1983. Personal communications to the author.

Calloway, Nathaniel O. 1967. Personal communication to the author.

Candy, Sandra G. 1979. Neighborhood concerns in an urban area: An analysis of age differences. *Journal of Minority Aging* 4:25–33.

Cantor, Marjorie H. 1975. Life space and the social support system of the inner city elderly of New York. *The Gerontologist* 15:23–27.

Cantor, Marjorie H. 1979. The informal support system of New York's inner city elderly: Is ethnicity a factor? *In* Donald E. Gelfand and Alfred J. Kutzik (eds.), *Ethnicity and Aging, Theory, Research, and Policy*, pp. 153–174. New York: Springer Publishing Company.

Cantor, Marjorie H., and Mayer, Mary, 1976. Health and the inner city elderly. *The Gerontologist* 15:17–25.

Cantor, Marjorie H., Rosenthal, Karen, and Wilker, Louis. 1979. Social and family relationships of black aged women in New York City. *Journal of Minority Aging* 4:50–61.

Carp, Frances M. 1968. *Factors in Utilization of Services by the Mexican-American Elderly*. Palo Alto, Calif.: American Institute for Research.

Carp, Frances M. 1969. Housing and minority-group elderly. *The Gerontologist* 9:20–34.

Carp, Frances M. 1971. Walking as a means of transportation for retired people. *The Gerontologist* 11:104–111.

Carp, Frances M., and Kataoka, Eunice. 1976. Health care problems of the elderly in San Francisco's Chinatown. *The Gerontologist* 16:30–38.

Carpenter, Karen and Bollman, Stephan R. 1980. The family life educator and culturally different families. *Family Perspective* 14:119–124.

Carter, James H. 1978. The black aged: A strategy for future mental health services. *Journal of the American Geriatrics Society* 26:553–556.

Carter, James H. 1982. The significance of racism in the mental illnesses of elderly minorities. *In* Ron C. Manuel (ed.), *Minority Aging, Sociological and Social Psychological Issues*, pp. 89–94. Westport, Conn.: Greenwood Press.

Chapman, Sabrina C. 1979. A social-psychological analysis of morale in a selected population: Low-income elderly black families. Unpublished doctoral dissertation, University Park: The Pennsylvania State University.

Chen, L., June, E., and Tu, A. 1973. The elderly Chinese in Los Angeles. Unpublished master's thesis, Los Angeles: University of California, Los Angeles.

Chen, Pei-Ngor. 1978. Continuity–discontinuity of life patterns among minority elderly in nutrition programs. Unpublished doctoral dissertation, Los Angeles: University of Southern California.

Chen, Pei-Ngor. 1980. Life patterns of minority elderly in nutrition programs. *Journal of Minority Aging* 5:201–208.

Cheng, Eva. 1978. *The Elder Chinese*. San Diego, Calif.: San Diego State University, The Campanile Press.

Clark, Margaret. 1959. *Health in the Mexican-American Culture*. Berkeley: University of California Press.

Clark, Margaret, and Anderson, B. G. 1967. *Culture and Aging: An Anthropological Study of Older Americans*. Springfield, Ill.: Charles C. Thomas.

Clark, Margaret, and Mendelson, Monique. 1969. Mexican-American aged in San Francisco: A case description. *The Gerontologist* 9:90–95.

Clark, Margaret, Kaufman, Sharon, and Pierce, Robert C. 1976. Explorations of acculturation: toward a model of ethnic identity. *Human Organization* 35:231–238.

Clemente, Frank, and Sauer, William J. 1974. Race and morale of the urban aged. *The Gerontologist* 14:342–344.

Clemente, Frank, Rexroad, Patricia A., and Hirsch, Carl. 1975. The participation of black aged in voluntary associations. *Journal of Gerontology* 30:469–472.

Cohler, Bertram J. 1982. Stress or support: relations between older women from three European ethnic groups and their relatives. *In* Ron C. Manuel (ed.), *Minority Aging, Sociological and Social Psychological Issues*, pp. 115–120. Westport, Conn.: Greenwood Press.

Cohler, Bertram J., and Lieberman, Morton A. 1979. Personality change across the second half of life: Findings from a study of Irish, Italian, and Polish-American men and women. *In* Donald E. Gelfand and Alfred J. Kutzik (eds.), *Ethnicity and Aging, Theory, Research, and Policy*, pp. 227–245. New York: Springer Publishing Company.

Colen, John N. 1979. Critical issues in the development of environmental support services for the aged. *Allied Health and Behavioral Sciences* 2:77–90.

Colen, John N. 1982. Using natural helping networks in social service delivery systems. *In* Ron C. Manuel (ed.), *Minority Aging, Sociological and Social Psychological Issues*, pp. 179–183. Westport, Conn.: Greenwood Press.

Colen, John N., and Soto, David. 1979. *Service Delivery to Aged Minorities: Techniques of Successful Programs*. Sacramento: School of Social Work, California State University.

Coles, Robert. 1974. *The Old Ones of New Mexico*. Albuquerque: University of New Mexico Press.

Cooper, Anna J. 1892. *A Voice from the South by a Black Woman of the South*. Xenia, Ohio: Aldine Printing House.

Crandall, Richard C. 1980. *Gerontology, A Behavioral Science Approach*. Reading, Mass.: Addison-Wesley Publishing Company.

Creecy, Robert F., and Wright, Roosevelt. 1979. Morale and informal activity with friends among black and white elderly. *The Gerontologist* 19:544–547.

Crocker, Mary W. 1968. An analysis of the living arrangements and housing conditions of old age assistance recipients in Mississippi. Unpublished doctoral dissertation, Tallahassee: Florida State University.

Crouch, Ben M. 1972. Age and institutional support: Perceptions of older Mexican Americans. *Journal of Gerontology* 27:524–529.

Cuellar, Jose B. 1977. El oro de Maravilla: An ethnographic study of aging and age stratification in an urban Chicano community. Unpublished doctoral dissertation, Los Angeles: University of California, Los Angeles.

Cuellar, Jose B. 1978. El Senior Citizens' Club: The older Mexican American in the voluntary association. *In* B. Meyerhoff and A. Simic (eds.), *Life's Career-Aging: A Cross-Cultural Investigation of Growing Old*, pp. 207–230. Beverly Hills, Calif.: Sage Publications.

Cuellar, Jose B., and Weeks, John R. 1980. *Minority Elderly Americans: A Prototype for Area Agencies on Aging, Executive Summary*. San Diego, Calif.: Allied Home Health Association [Administration on Aging Grant No. 90-A-1667 (01)].

Curran, Barbara W. 1978. Getting by with a little help from my friends: Informal networks among older black and white urban women below the poverty line. Unpublished doctoral dissertation, Tucson: University of Arizona.

Daly, Frederica Y. 1976. To be black, poor, female and old. *Freedomways* 16:222–229.

Dancy, Joseph, Jr. 1977. *The Black Elderly: A Guide for Practitioners*. Ann Arbor: Institute of Gerontology, University of Michigan–Wayne State University.

Davis, Abraham, Jr. 1966. Selected characteristic patterns of a southern aged rural Negro population. Unpublished master's thesis, Washington, D.C.: Howard University.

Davis, Delores J. 1974. Guide for minority aging program at the Institute of Gerontology, University of Michigan: Student perception approach. Unpublished doctoral dissertation, Ann Arbor: University of Michigan.

Davis, Frank G. 1939. The effects of the Social Security Act upon the status of the Negro. Unpublished doctoral dissertation, Iowa City: University of Iowa.

Davis, Lenwood G. 1980. *The Black Aged in the United States: An Annotated Bibliography*. Westport, Conn.: Greenwood Press.

Davis, Richard H. (ed.), 1973. *Health Services and*

Mexican-American Elderly. Los Angeles: University of Southern California Press.

DeGeynot, W. 1971. Health behavior and health needs in urban Indians in Minneapolis. *Health Service Reports* 88:360–366.

Delgado, Maria, and Finley, Gordon E. 1978. The Spanish-speaking elderly: A bibiliography. *The Gerontologist* 18:387–394.

Demeny, Paul, and Gingrich, Paul. 1967. A reconsideration of Negro–white mortality differentials in the United States. *Demography* 4:820–837.

Dhaliwal, S. S. 1967. A sociological description and analysis of a non-random sample of low-income, Washington, D.C., aged Negroes. Unpublished master's thesis, Washington, D.C.: Howard University.

Dilworth-Anderson, Peggye. 1981. Family closeness between aged blacks and their adult children. *Journal of Minority Aging* 6:56–66.

Dollard, John B. 1937. *Caste and Class in a Southern Town.* New Haven, Conn.: Yale University Press.

Dominick, Joan R., and Stotsky, Bernard A. 1969. Mental patients in nursing homes: IV. Ethnic influences. *Journal of the American Geriatrics Society* 17:63–85.

Dovenmuehle, Robert H., and McGough, W. Edward. 1965. Aging, culture and affect: Predisposing factors. *Journal of Social Psychiatry* 11:138–146.

Dowd, James J., and Bengtson, Vern L. 1978. Aging in minority populations: An examination of the double jeopardy hypothesis. *Journal of Gerontology* 33:427–436.

Ellis, N. K. 1962. Spanish surname mortality differences in San Antonio, Texas. *Journal of Health and Human Behavior* 3:125–127.

Eribes, Richard A. 1977. A microanalysis of the housing system within East Los Angeles. Unpublished doctoral dissertation, Los Angeles: University of Southern California.

Eribes, Richard A., and Bradley-Rawls, Martha. 1978. The underutilization of nursing home facilities by Mexican-American elderly in the Southwest. *The Gerontologist* 18:363–371.

Estel, Leo. 1956. Race as an evolutionary concept (abstract). *American Journal of Physical Anthropology* 14:378.

Evans, Ron L., and Northwood, Lawrence K. 1978. The utility of locality based social networks. *Journal of Minority Aging* 3:199–211.

Eve, Susan B., and Friedsam, Hiram. 1979. Ethnic differences in the use of health care services among older Texans. *Journal of Minority Aging* 4:62–75.

Eve, Susan B., and Friedsam, Hiram J. 1982. Use of tranquilizers and sleeping pills among older Texans. *In* David M. Petersen and Frank J. Whittington (eds.), *Drugs, Alcohol, and Aging,* pp. 55–63. Dubuque, Iowa: Kendall Hunt Publishing Company.

Fandetti, Donald, and Gelfand, Donald E. 1976. Care of the aged: Attitudes of white ethnic families. *The Gerontologist* 16:544–549.

Farris, C. E. 1976. American Indian social work advocates. *Social Casework* 57:494–503.

Faulkner, Audrey O. 1975. Life strengths and life stresses: Explorations in the measurement of the mental health of the black aged. *American Journal of Orthopsychiatry* 45:102–110.

Federal Council on Aging. 1979. *Mental Health and the Elderly, Recommendations for Action.* Washington, D.C.: U.S. Government Printing Office [DHEW Publication No. (OHDS) 80-20960].

Fenz, Walter D. 1962. Comparative need patterns of five ancestry groups in Hawaii. Unpublished master's thesis, Honolulu: University of Hawaii.

Ferrara, Peter J. 1980. *Social Security, The Inherent Contradiction.* San Francisco, Calif.: Cato Institute.

Ferron, Donald T. (compiler). 1981. *Disability Survey 72, Disabled and Nondisabled Adults, A Monograph.* Washington, D.C.: U.S. Government Printing Office (Research Report No. 56, SSA Publication No. 13–11812).

Finley, G. E., and Delgado, M. 1979. Formal education and intellectual functioning in the immigrant urban elderly. *Experimental Aging Research* 5:155–161.

Fisher, Joel. 1970. Negroes and whites and rates of mental illness: Reconsideration of a myth. *Psychiatry* 32:428–446.

Fox, William S., and Faine, John R. 1973. Trends in white–nonwhite income equality. *Sociology and Social Research* 57:288–299.

Fujii, Sharon M. 1976a. Older Asian Americans victims of double jeopardy. *Civil Rights Digest* (Fall):24–25.

Fujii, Sharon M. 1976b. Elderly Asian Americans and use of public services. *Social Casework* 57:202–207.

Gaitz, Charles M., and Scott, Judith. 1974. Mental health of Mexican-Americans: Do ethnic factors make a difference? *Geriatrics* 29:103–110.

Garcia, John A., and Juarez, Rumaldo Z. 1978. Utilization of dental health services by Chicanos and Anglos. *Journal of Health and Social Behavior* 19:428–436.

Garn, S. M., and Coon, C. S. 1955. On the number of races of mankind. *American Anthropologist* 57:996–1001.

Gelfand, Donald E., and Kutzik, Alfred J. (eds.). 1979a. *Ethnicity and Aging, Theory, Research, and Policy.* New York: Springer Publishing Company.

Gelfand, Donald E., and Kutzik, Alfred J. 1979b. Introduction: Focuses and issues. *In* Donald E. Gelfand and Alfred J. Kutzik (eds.), *Ethnicity and Aging, Theory, Research, and Policy,* pp. 1–3. New York: Springer Publishing Company.

Gerber, Dan, Snow, David, Frum, Miriam, and McMillin, Diane. 1978. Interorganizational and political obstacles to providing low cost supportive services to the elderly poor. *Black Aging* 3:142–146.

German, Pearl S., Shapiro, Sam, Chase, Gar A., and Vollmer, Mary. 1978. Health care of the elderly in a changing inner city community. *Black Aging* 3:122–132.

Gibson, Rose C. 1982a. Race and sex differences in the

work and retirement patterns of older heads of households. *In* Timothy H. Brubaker and Mildred M. Seltzer (eds.), *Proceedings, Minority Research Associate Conference, February 9–11, 1982* (Capital Hilton Hotel, Washington, D.C.), pp. 138–184. Oxford, Ohio: Scripps Foundation Gerontology Center, Miami University (Administration on Aging Grant #90AT0004102).

Gibson, Rose C. 1982b. Blacks at middle and late life: Resources and coping. *The Annals of the American Academy of Political and Social Science* 464:79–90.

Gitelman, Paul J. 1976. Morale, self-concept and social integration: A comparative study of black and Jewish aged, urban poor. Unpublished doctoral dissertation, New Brunswick, N. J.: Rutgers University.

Glenn, Norval D. 1977. *Cohort Analysis. Series: Quantitative Applications in the Social Sciences,* Number 07–005. Beverly Hills, Calif.: Sage Publications.

Gobetz, Giles E. 1972. Racial differences in attitudes and ability among the geriatric blind. *Journal of Negro Education* 41:57–61.

Golden, Herbert M. 1977. Life satisfaction among black elderly in the inner city. *Black Aging* 2:21–43.

Gordon, Barbara, and Rehr, Helen. 1969. Selectivity biases in delivery of hospital social services. *Social Service Review* 43:35–41.

Gordon, Milton M. 1964. *Assimilation in American Life.* New York: Oxford University Press.

Gray, Cleo J. 1977. Attitudes of black church members toward the black elderly as a function of denomination, age, sex, and level of education. Unpublished doctoral dissertation, Washington, D.C.: Howard University.

Green, Vera M. 1981. Levels of diversity among U.S. blacks. *In* Paul L. Wall (ed.), *Diversity in the Non-Farm Rural Population,* pp. 38–41. Tuskegee Institute, Ala.: Division of Behavioral Science Research, Carver Research Foundation.

Gregory, Robert J. 1970. A survey of residents in five nursing and rest homes in Cumberland County, North Carolina. *Journal of the American Geriatrics Society* 18:501–506.

Guttmann, David. 1979. Use of informal and formal supports by white ethnic aged. *In* Donald E. Gelfand and Alfred J. Kutzik (eds.), *Ethnicity and Aging, Theory, Research, and Policy,* pp. 246–262. New York: Springer Publishing Company.

Guttmann, David. 1980. *Perspectives on Equitable Share in Public Benefits by Minority Elderly. Executive Summary.* Washington, D.C.: Catholic University of America (Administration on Aging Grant #90–A–1617).

Hamlett, Margaret L. 1959. An exploratory study of the socioeconomic and psychological problems of adjustment of 100 aged and retired Negro women in Durham, North Carolina, during 1959. Unpublished master's thesis, Durham: North Carolina College at Durham.

Harper, Dee Wood, Jr. 1967. Socialization for the aged status among the Negro, French, and non-French subcultures of Louisiana. Unpublished doctoral dissertation, Baton Rouge: Louisiana State University.

Harris, Louis, and Associates. 1975. *The Myth and Reality of Aging.* Washington, D.C.: The National Council on the Aging.

Harris, Louis, and Associates. 1981. *Aging in the Eighties: America in Transition.* Washington, D.C.: The National Council on the Aging.

Harwood, Alan. 1981. Introduction. *In* Alan Harwood (ed.), *Ethnicity and Medical Care,* pp. 1–36. Cambridge, Mass.: Harvard University Press.

Hawkins, Brin D. 1976. A comparative study of the social participation of the black elderly residing in public housing in two communities: The inner city and the suburbs. Unpublished doctoral dissertation, Waltham, Mass.: Brandeis University.

Hawkins, Brin D. 1980. The role of caregivers in the black community. Unpublished report for the Administration on Aging (Grant #90–A–1375).

Hawkins, Brin D. 1982. Impact of health and social service delivery systems on the black elderly. *In* Timothy H. Brubaker and Mildred M. Seltzer (eds.), *Proceedings, Minority Research Associate Conference, February 9–11, 1982* (Capital Hilton Hotel, Washington, D.C.), pp. 12–35. Oxford, Ohio: Scripps Foundation Gerontology Center, Miami University.

Henderson, George. 1965. The Negro recipient of old-age assistance: Results of discrimination. *Social Casework* 46:208–214.

Herskovits, Melville J. 1928. *The American Negro: A Study in Racial Crossing.* New York: Alfred A. Knopf.

Heyman, Dorothy, and Jeffers, Frances C. 1964. Study of the relative influence of race and socio-economic status upon the activities and attitudes of a southern aged population. *Journal of Gerontology* 19:225–229.

Hill, Robert B. 1978. A demographic profile of the black elderly. *Aging* Nos. 287–288:2–9.

Himes, Joseph S., and Hamlett, Margaret L. 1962. The assessment of adjustment of aged Negro women in a southern city. *Phylon* 23:139–147.

Holden, Karen C. 1978. Comparability of the measured labor force of older women in Japan and the United States. *Journal of Gerontology* 33:422–426.

Holley, Mary R. 1978. Components of life satisfaction of older Texans: A multidimensional model. Unpublished doctoral dissertation, Denton: North Texas State University.

Holmes, Douglas, Holmes, Monica, Steinbach, Leonard, Hausner, Tony, and Rocheleau, Bruce. 1979. The use of community-based services in long-term care by older minority persons. *The Gerontologist* 19:389–397.

Huling, William E. 1978. Aging blacks in suburbia. Unpublished doctoral dissertation, Los Angeles: University of Southern California.

Hunt, Thomas L. 1978. The equity and impact of Medicare and Medicaid with respect to Mexican Americans in Texas. Unpublished doctoral dissertation, Austin: University of Texas at Austin.

Hunter, K., Linn, M. W., and Pratt, T. C. 1979. Minority women's attitudes about aging. *Experimental Aging Research* 5:95–108.

Hutchinson, Ira W., III. 1975. The significance of marital status for morale and life satisfaction among lower-income elderly. *Journal of Marriage and the Family* 37:287–293.

Ishikawa, Wesley H. 1978a. *The Elder Guamanian*. San Diego, Calif.: San Diego State University, The Campanile Press.

Ishikawa, Wesley H. 1978b. *The Elder Samoan*. San Diego, Calif.: San Diego State University, The Campanile Press.

Ishikawa, Wesley H., and Archer, Nikki H. (eds.). 1975. *Service Delivery in Pan Asian Communities*. San Diego, Calif.: San Diego Pacific Asian Coalition.

IRS Newsletter, 1982. Maintaining a group culture, pp. 7–8. Ann Arbor: Institute for Social Research, University of Michigan.

Jackson, Hobart C. 1965. Overcoming racial barriers in senior centers. *National Conference on Senior Centers* 2:20–28.

Jackson, Jacquelyne J. 1967. Social gerontology and the Negro: A review. *The Gerontologist* 7:168–178.

Jackson, Jacquelyne J. 1968. Aged Negroes: Their cultural departures from statistical stereotypes and selected rural–urban differences. Paper presented at the annual meeting of the Gerontological Society, Denver, Colo.

Jackson, Jacquelyne J. 1970. Aged Negroes: Their cultural departures from statistical stereotypes and selected rural–urban differences. *The Gerontologist* 10:140–145 (reprinted in Bill D. Bell, ed., 1976. *Contemporary Social Gerontology*, pp. 328–334, Springfield, Ill.: Charles C. Thomas).

Jackson, Jacquelyne J. 1971a. Aged blacks: A potpourri towards the reduction of racial inequities. *Phylon* 32:260–280 (reprinted in Beth B. Hess, ed., 1976, *Growing Old in America*, pp. 390–416, New Brunswick, N. J.: Transaction Books).

Jackson, Jacquelyne J. 1971b. The blacklands of gerontology. *Aging and Human Development* 2:156–171 (reprinted in Virginia M. Brantl and Mollie R. Brown, eds., 1973, *Readings in Gerontology*, pp. 78–97, St. Louis: C. V. Mosby).

Jackson, Jacquelyne J. 1971c. Sex and social class variations in Negro older parent–adult child relationships. *Aging and Human Development* 2:96–107.

Jackson, Jacquelyne J. 1971d. Quadruple jeopardy: Old, black, female, and poor. Paper presented at the annual meeting of the Gerontological Society, Houston, Tex.

Jackson, Jacquelyne J. 1971e. But where are the men? *The Black Scholar* 3:30–41.

Jackson, Jacquelyne J. 1972a. Marital life among aging blacks. *The Family Coordinator* 21:21–27.

Jackson, Jacquelyne J. 1972b. Social impacts of housing relocation upon low-income black aged. *The Gerontologist* 12:32–37.

Jackson, Jacquelyne J. 1976. The plight of older black women in the United States. *The Black Scholar* 7:47–55.

Jackson, Jacquelyne J. 1979. Aging patterns in black families. *In* Allan J. Lichtman and Joan R. Challinor (eds.), *Kin and Communities, Families in America*, pp. 145–154. Washington, D.C.: Smithsonian Institution Press.

Jackson, Jacquelyne J. 1980. *Minorities and Aging*. Belmont, Calif.: Wadsworth Publishing Company.

Jackson, Jacquelyne J. 1981. Urban black Americans. *In* Alan Harwood (ed.), *Ethnicity and Medical Care*, pp. 37–129. Cambridge, Mass.: Harvard University Press.

Jackson, Jacquelyne J. 1982. Death rates of aged blacks and whites, United States, 1964–1978. *The Black Scholar* 13:36–48.

Jackson, Jacquelyne J. 1983. The politicalization of aged blacks. *In* William P. Browne and Laura K. Olson, *The Politics of Growing Old*, pp. 67–102. Westport, Conn.: Greenwood Press.

Jackson, Jacquelyne J. in press. Poverty and Minority Status. *In* Marie R. Haug, Amasa B. Ford, and Marian Sheafor (eds.), *The Physical and Mental Health of Aged Women*. New York: Springer Publishing Company.

Jackson, Jacquelyne J., and Walls, Bertram E. 1978. Myths and realities about aged blacks. *In* Mollie R. Brown (ed.), *Readings in Gerontology*, 2nd ed. pp. 95–113. St. Louis; C. V. Mosby Company.

Jackson, James S., Bacon, John, and Peterson, John. 1977. Life satisfaction among the black urban elderly. *Aging and Human Development* 8:169–179.

Jackson, James S., Chatters, Linda M., and Neighbors, Harold W. 1982. The mental health status of older black Americans: A national study. *The Black Scholar* 13:21–35.

Jackson, Maurice, and Wood, James L. 1976. *Aging in America: Implications for the Black Aged*. Washington, D.C.: The National Council on the Aging.

Jackson, Maurice, Kolody, Bohdan, and Wood, James L. 1982. To be old and black: The case for double jeopardy on income and health. *In* Ron C. Manuel (ed.), *Minority Aging, Sociological and Social Psychological Issues*, pp. 77–82. Westport, Conn.: Greenwood Press.

Jacobson, Solomon G. 1982. Equity in the use of public benefits by minority elderly. *In* Ron C. Manuel (ed.), *Minority Aging, Sociological and Social Psychological Issues*, pp. 161–170. Westport, Conn.: Greenwood Press.

Jenkins, Mercilee M. 1971. Age and migration factors in the socioeconomic conditions of urban black and urban white women. *Industrial Gerontology* 9:13–17.

Jericho, Bonnie J. 1977. Longitudinal changes in religious activity subscores of aged blacks. *Black Aging* 2:17–24.

Kadushin, Charles. 1964. Social class and the experience

of ill health. *Sociological Inquiry* 24:67–80 (reprinted in Reinhard Bendix and Seymour M. Lipset, eds., 1966, *Class, Status, and Power,* pp. 406–412, New York: Free Press).

Kadushin, Charles. 1967. Social class and ill health: The need for further research. A reply to Antonovsky. *Sociological Inquiry* 37:323–332.

Kalish, Richard A. 1971. A gerontological look at ethnicity, human capacities, and individual adjustment. *The Gerontologist* 11:78–87.

Kalish, Richard A., and Moriwaki, Sharon. 1973. The world of the elderly Asian American. *Journal of Social Issues* 29:187–209.

Kalish, Richard A., and Reynolds, David K. 1976. *Death and Ethnicity: A Psychocultural Study.* Los Angeles: The University of Southern California Press.

Kaplan, Jerome. 1975. The family in aging. *The Gerontologist* 15:385.

Kart, Cary S., and Beckham, Barry L. 1976. Black–white differentials in the institutionalization of the elderly: A temporal analysis. *Social Forces* 54:901–910.

Kasschau, Patricia. 1977. Age and race discrimination reported by middle-aged and older persons. *Social Forces* 55:728–742.

Kent, Donald P. 1971. The elderly in minority groups: Variant patterns of aging. *The Gerontologist* 11:26–29.

Kent, Donald P., and Hirsch, Carl. 1971. *Needs and Use of Services Among Negro and White Aged,* Vols. 1 and 2. University Park: The Pennsylvania State University.

Kim, B. C., and Condon, M. E. 1975. *A Study of Asian Americans in Chicago: Their Socioeconomic Characteristics, Problems, and Service Needs.* Washington, D.C.: National Institute of Mental Health and the Department of Health, Education, and Welfare.

Kitagawa, Evelyn M., and Hauser, Philip M. 1973. *Differential Mortality in the United States: A Study in Socioeconomic Epidemiology.* Cambridge, Mass.: Harvard University Press.

Kivett, Vira R. 1982. The importance of race to the life situation of the rural elderly. *The Black Scholar* 13:13–20.

Kivett, Vira R. 1983. Older rural displaced homemakers: perspective on status and morale. *Journal of Minority Aging* 8:17–25.

Koenig, Ronald, Goldner, Norman S., Kresojevich, Ralph, and Lockwood, Gary. 1971. Ideas about illness of elderly black and white in an urban hospital. *Aging and Human Development* 2:217–225.

Korte, Alvin O. 1978. Social interaction and morale of Spanish-speaking elderly. Unpublished doctoral dissertation, Denver, Colo.: University of Denver.

Lacayo, Carmela G. 1982. Findings from the first national study to assess the service needs of the Hispanic elderly in the U.S. *In* Timothy H. Brubaker and Mildred M. Seltzer (eds.), *Proceedings, Minority Research Associate Conference, February 9–11, 1982* (Capital Hilton Hotel, Washington, D.C.), pp. 77–

137. Oxford, Ohio: Scripps Foundation Gerontology Center of Miami University (Administration on Aging Grant #90AT0004102).

Lambing, Mary L. 1969. A study of retired older Negroes in an urban setting. Unpublished doctoral dissertation, Gainesville: University of Florida.

Lambing, Mary L. 1972. Social class living patterns of retired Negroes. *The Gerontologist* 12:285–288.

Lindsay, Inabel M. 1971. The multiple hazards of age and race: The situation of aged blacks in the United States, a preliminary survey for the U.S. Senate Special Committee on Aging. Washington, D.C.: U.S. Government Printing Office.

Lipman, Aaron A. 1965. The Miami concerted services baseline study. *The Gerontologist* 5:256–278.

Lipman, Aaron A. 1982. Minority aging from the exchange and structural-functionalist perspectives. *In* Ron C. Manuel (ed.), *Minority Aging, Sociological and Social Psychological Issues,* pp. 195–202. Westport, Conn.: Greenwood Press.

Lipman, Aaron A., and Marden, Philip W. 1966. Preparation for death in old age. *Journal of Gerontology* 21:426–431.

Lopata, Helena Z. 1975. Support systems of elderly urbanites: Chicago of the 1970's. *The Gerontologist* 15:35–41.

Lopata, Helena Z. 1979. *Women as Widows: Support Systems.* New York: Elsevier.

Maldonado, David, Jr. 1979. Aging in the Chicano context. *In* Donald E. Gelfand and Alfred J. Kutzik (eds.), *Ethnicity and Aging, Theory, Research, and Policy,* pp. 175–183. New York: Springer Publishing Company.

Manson, Spero M., Murray, Carolyn B., and Cain, Leonard D. 1981. Ethnicity, aging, and support networks: an evolving methodological strategy. *Journal of Minority Aging* 6:11–37.

Manton, Kenneth. 1980. Sex and race specific mortality differentials in multiple cause of death data. *The Gerontologist* 20:480–493.

Manton, Kenneth. 1982. Differential life expectancy: Possible explanations during the later ages. *In* Ron C. Manuel (ed.), *Minority Aging, Sociological and Social Psychological Issues,* pp. 63–68. Westport, Conn.: Greenwood Press.

Manton, Kenneth, and Poss, Sharon S. 1977. The black/white mortality crossover: Possible racial differences in the intrinsic rate of aging. *Black Aging* 3:43–53.

Manton, Kenneth, Poss, Sharon S., and Wing, Steve. 1979. The black/white mortality crossover: Investigation from the perspective of the components of aging. *The Gerontologist* 19:291–300.

Manuel, Ron C. 1980. Leadership factors in service delivery and minority elderly utilization. *Journal of Minority Aging* 5:218–232.

Manuel, Ron C. 1982a. The study of the minority aged in historical perspective. *In* Ron C. Manuel (ed.), *Minority Aging, Sociological and Social Psychological Issues,* pp. 3–12. Westport, Conn.: Greenwood Press.

Manuel, Ron C. 1982b. The minority aged: Providing a conceptual perspective. *In* Ron C. Manuel (ed.), *Minority Aging, Sociological and Social Psychological Issues,* pp. 13–25. Westport, Conn.: Greenwood Press.

Manuel, Ron C. 1982c. The dimensions of ethnic minority identification: An exploratory analysis among elderly black Americans. *In* Ron C. Manuel (ed.), *Minority Aging, Sociological and Social Psychological Issues,* pp. 231–247. Westport, Conn.: Greenwood Press.

Manuel, Ron C., and Reid, John. 1982. A comparative demographic profile of the minority and nonminority aged. *In* Ron C. Manuel (ed.), *Minority Aging, Sociological and Social Psychological Issues,* pp. 31–52. Westport, Conn.: Greenwood Press.

Markides, Kyriakos S. 1980a. Correlates of life satisfaction among older Mexican Americans and Anglos. *Journal of Minority Aging* 5:183–190.

Markides, Kyriakos S. 1980b. Ethnic differences in age identification: A study of older Mexican Americans and Anglos. *Social Science Quarterly* 60:659–666.

Markides, Kyriakos S., Martin, H. W., and Sizemore, M. 1980. Psychological distress among elderly Mexican Americans and Anglos. *Ethnicity* 7:298–309.

Markides, Kyriakos S., Costley, D. S., and Rodriguez, L. 1981. Perceptions of intergenerational relations and psychological well-being among elderly Mexican Americans: A causal model. *International Journal of Aging and Human Development* 13:43–52.

Markson, Elizabeth W. 1979. Ethnicity as a factor in the institutionalization of the ethnic elderly. *In* Donald E. Gelfand and Alfred J. Kutzik (eds.), *Ethnicity and Aging, Theory, Research, and Policy,* pp. 341–356. New York: Springer Publishing Company.

Martinez, M. 1979. Family policy for Mexican Americans and their aged. *The Urban and Social Change Review* 12:16–19.

Matsumoto, G. M., Meredith, G. M., and Masuda M. 1970. Ethnic identity: Honolulu and Seattle Japanese-Americans. *Journal of Cross-Cultural Psychology* 1:63–76.

McCaslin, Rosemary, and Calvert, Welton R. 1975. Social indications in black and white: Some ethnic considerations in delivery of service to the elderly. *Journal of Gerontology* 30:60–66.

McCoy, John L., and Brown, David L. 1978. Health status among low-income elderly persons: Rural-urban differences. *Social Security Bulletin* 41:14–26.

McMurray, Harvey. 1981. Criminal victimization of the elderly. Unpublished master's thesis, Washington, D.C.: Howard University.

McPherson, Judith R., Lancaster, Doris R., and Carroll, Jack C. 1978. Stature change with aging in black Americans. *Journal of Gerontology* 33:20–25.

Messer, Mark. 1968. Race differences in selected attitudinal dimensions of the elderly. *The Gerontologist* 8:245–249.

Mindel, Charles H., and Hays, William C. 1973. Extended kinship relationships in black and white families. *Journal of Marriage and the Family* 35:51–57.

Miranda, Porfirio. 1978. Perceptions of locus of control among three multigenerational Chicano/Mexican families. Unpublished doctoral dissertation, Los Angeles: University of California, Los Angeles.

Montero, Darrel. 1979. Disengagement and aging among the Issei. *In* Donald E. Gelfand and Alfred J. Kutzik (eds.), *Ethnicity and Aging, Theory, Research, and Policy,* pp. 193–205. New York: Springer Publishing Company.

Moore, Joan W. 1970. The death culture of Mexico and Mexican Americans. *Omega* 1:271–291.

Moore, Joan W. 1971. Mexican Americans. *The Gerontologist* 11:30–35.

Morgan, Leslie A. 1981. Economic change at mid-life widowhood: A longitudinal analysis. *Journal of Marriage and the Family* 43:899–907.

Morgan, Robert F. 1968. The adult growth examination: Preliminary comparisons of aging in adults by sex and race. *Perceptual and Motor Skills* 27:595–599.

Moriwaki, Sharon Y. 1972. Correlates of mental health in an aged population: An analysis of supported self-disclosure. Unpublished doctoral dissertation, Los Angeles: University of Southern California.

Moriwaki, Sharon Y. 1973. Self-disclosure, significant others and psychological well-being in old age. *Journal of Health and Social Behavior* 14:226–232.

Mostwin, Danuta. 1979. Emotional needs of elderly Americans of central and eastern European background. *In* Donald E. Gelfand and Alfred J. Kutzik (eds.), *Ethnicity and Aging, Theory, Research, and Policy,* pp. 263–276. New York: Springer Publishing Company.

Murdock, Steve H., and Schwartz, Donald F. 1978. Family structure and the use of agency services: An examination of patterns among elderly Native Americans. *The Gerontologist* 18:475–481.

Murphy, Gerald J. 1978. The family in later life: A cross-ethnic study of marital and sexual satisfaction. Unpublished doctoral dissertation, New Orleans, La.: Tulane University.

Myers, George C. 1983. Personal communication.

Myers, Robert J. 1983. Personal communications (Mar. and Apr.).

Nam, Charles B., and Ocay, Kathleen A. 1977. Factors contributing to the mortality crossover pattern. Paper presented at the 18th General Conference of the International Union for the Scientific Study of Population, Mexico City.

National Commission on Social Security Reform. 1983. *Report of the National Commission on Social Security Reform.* Washington, D.C.: U.S. Government Printing Office.

National Council on the Aging. 1971. *Employment Prospects of Aged Blacks, Chicanos, and Indians.* Washington, D.C.: National Council on the Aging.

National Tribal Chairmen's Association, Inc. 1976. *Summary Report on the National Indian Conference on Aging.* Phoenix, Ariz.: National Tribal Chairmen's Association.

National Urban League, Inc. 1964. *Double Jeopardy—The Older Negro in America Today.* New York: National Urban League.

Newton, F. C. 1980. Issues in research and service delivery among Mexican American elderly: a concise statement with recommendations. *The Gerontologist* 20:208–212.

Niebank, Paul L., and Pope, John B. 1965. *The Elderly in Older Urban Areas.* Philadelphia: Institute for Environmental Studies, University of Pennsylvania.

Nowlin, John B. 1977. Successful aging: Health and social factors in an interracial population. *Black Aging* 2:10–17.

Nowlin, John B. 1979. Geriatric health status: Influence of race and economic status. *Journal of Minority Aging* 4:93–98.

Orchowsky, Stan J., and Parham, Iris A. 1981. Life satisfaction scores of blacks and whites: A lifespan approach. *Journal of Minority Aging* 6:38–55.

Ostfeld, Adrian M., Shekelle, R. B., Tufo, H. M., Wieland, A. M., Kilbridge, J. A., Drori, J., and Klawans, H. 1971. Cardiovascular and cerebrovascular disease in an elderly poor urban population. *American Journal of Public Health* 61:19–29.

Ozawa, Martha N. 1982. SSI recipients in Mississippi and California: A comparative study. *Journal of Social Service Research* 6:31–45.

Pacific Asian Elderly Research Project. 1977. *Understanding the Pacific Asian Elderly: Census and Baseline Data.* Los Angeles: Pacific Asian Elderly Research Project.

Palmore, Erdman B. 1969. Physical, mental, and social factors in predicting longevity. *The Gerontologist* 9:103–108.

Palmore, Erdman B., and Whittington, Frank. 1970. Differential trends toward equality between whites and nonwhites. *Social Forces* 49:108–117.

Petrowsky, Marc. 1976. Marital status, sex, and the social networks of the elderly. *Journal of Marriage and the Family* 38:749–756.

Pieper, Hanns G. 1981. Regression analysis of selected demographic and social factors related to the life satisfaction of the black and white aged. *Journal of Minority Aging* 6:67–78.

Pollard, Leslie J. 1978. The Stephen Smith Home for the Aged: A gerontological history of a pioneer venture in caring for the black aged, 1864 to 1953. Unpublished doctoral dissertation, Syracuse, N. Y.: Syracuse University.

Ragan, Pauline K. 1977. Crime against the elderly: Findings from interviews with blacks, Mexican Americans, and whites. *In* M. A. Y. Rifai (ed.), *Justice and Older Americans,* pp. 324–326. Lexington, Mass.: D. C. Heath.

Ragan, Pauline K., and Simonin. M. 1977. *Black and Mexican-American Aging: A Selected Bibliography.* Los Angeles: University of Southern California, Andrus Gerontology Center.

Red Horse, J. G. 1980. American Indian elders: Needs and aspirations in institutional and home health care. *In* E. Percil Stanford (ed.), *Minority Aging: Policy Issues for the '80s,* pp. 61–68. San Diego, Calif.: University Center on Aging, San Diego State University, The Campanile Press.

Red Horse, J. G., Lewis, R., Feit, M., and Decker, J. 1978. Family behavior of urban American Indians. *Social Casework* 59:67–72.

Register, Jasper C. 1981. Aging and race: A black–white comparative analysis. *The Gerontologist* 21:438–443.

Register, Jasper C., and Mitchell, Jim. 1981–82. Black–white differences in attitudes toward the elderly. *Journal of Minority Aging* 7:34–46.

Reilly, John T. 1977. The first shall be last: A study of the pattern of confrontation between old and young in the Afro-American novel. Unpublished doctoral dissertation, Ithaca, N. Y.: Cornell University.

Reynolds, David K., and Kalish, Richard A. 1974. Anticipation of futurity as a function of ethnicity and age. *Journal of Gerontology* 29:224–231.

Reynoso, C., and Coppelman, P. 1972. *Availability and Usefulness of Federal Programs and Services to Elderly Mexican-Americans: Proposals to Eliminate the Legal Barriers.* San Francisco: California Rural Legal Assistance Program.

Richeck, Herbert G., Chuculate, Owen, and Klinert, Dorothy, 1971. Aging and ethnicity in healthy elderly women. *Geriatrics* 26:146–154.

Rives, Norfleet W., Jr. 1977. The effect of census errors on life table estimates of black mortality. *Public Health Briefs* 67:867–868.

Roberts, R. E. 1964. Ethnic and racial differences in the characteristics and attitudes of the aged in selected areas of rural Lousiana. Unpublished master's thesis, Baton Rouge: Louisiana State University.

Rodriguez, Rafaela Rivers. 1970. Social aspects of aging in the northeast region of the Department of Health and Welfare in Puerto Rico. Unpublished doctoral dissertation, New York: Columbia University.

Rogers, C. Jean, and Gallion, Teresa E. 1978. Characteristics of elderly Pueblo Indians in New Mexico. *The Gerontologist* 18:482–487.

Rorick, Marvin H., and Crimshaw, Nevin S. 1979. Comparative tolerance of elderly from differing ethnic backgrounds to lactose-containing and lactose-free dairy drinks: A double-blind study. *Journal of Gerontology* 34:191–196.

Rosow, Irving. 1976. Status and role change through the life span. *In* Robert H. Binstock and Ethel Shanas (eds.), *Handbook of Aging and the Social Sciences,* 1st ed., pp. 457–482. New York: Van Nostrand Reinhold.

Rubenstein, Daniel I. 1971. An examination of social participation found among a national sample of black and white elderly. *Aging and Human Development* 2:172–188.

Rubenstein, Daniel I. 1972. The social participation of the black elderly. Unpublished doctoral dissertation, Waltham, Mass.: Brandeis University.

Ryder, Norman. 1975. Notes on stationary populations. *Population Index* 41:3–26.

Salber, Eva J. 1983. *Don't Send Me Flowers When I'm Dead, Voices of Rural Elderly.* Durham, N.C.: Duke University Press.

Sauer, William J. 1977. Morale of the urban aged: A regression analysis by race. *Journal of Gerontology* 32:600–608.

Sauer, William, Seelbach, Wayne, and Hanson, Sandra. 1980. Rural–urban and cohort differences in filial responsibility norms. *Journal of Minority Aging* 5:299–305.

Schaie, K. Warner, Orchowsky, Stan, and Parham, Iris A. 1982. Measuring age and sociocultural change: The case of race and life satisfaction. *In* Ron C. Manuel (ed.), *Minority Aging, Sociological and Social Psychological Issues*, pp. 223–230. Westport, Conn.: Greenwood Press.

Schermerhorn, Richard A. 1970. *Comparative Ethnic Relations: A Framework for Theory and Research.* Chicago: University of Chicago Press.

Schneider, Robert L. 1979. Barriers to effective outreach in Title VIII Nutrition programs. *The Gerontologist* 19:163–168.

Seelbach, Wayne. 1977. Filial responsibility and morale among elderly black and white urbanites: A normative and behavioral analysis. Unpublished doctoral dissertation, University Park: The Pennsylvania State University.

Seelbach, Wayne C. 1980. Filial responsibility among aged parents: A racial comparison. *Journal of Minority Aging* 5:286–292.

Seelbach, Wayne C., and Sauer, William J. 1977. Filial responsibility expectations and morale among aged parents. *The Gerontologist* 18:492–499.

Shanas, Ethel. 1962. *The Health of Older People: A Social Survey.* Cambridge, Mass.: Harvard University Press.

Shanas, Ethel. 1977. *National Survey of the Aged, Final Report.* Baltimore, Md.: Office of Research and Statistics, Social Security Administration (Grant #57823).

Shanas, Ethel, Townsend, Peter, Wedderburn, Dorothy, Friis, Henning, Milhøj, Poul, and Stehouwer, Jan. 1968. *Old People in Three Industrial Societies.* New York: Atherton Press.

Sherman, Eugene G., Jr. 1955. Social adjustment of aged Negroes of Carbondale, Illinois. Unpublished master's thesis. Carbondale: Southern Illinois University.

Shock, Nathan W. 1977. Biological theories of aging. *In* James E. Birren and K. Warner Schaie (eds.), *Handbook of the Psychology of Aging*, p. 103. New York: Van Nostrand Reinhold.

Smith, Alicia D. 1978. Life satisfaction and activity preferences among black inner city center participants: An exploratory study. Unpublished doctoral dissertation, Amherst: University of Massachusetts, Amherst.

Smith, Stanley H. 1967. The older rural Negro. *In* E.

Grant Youmans (ed.), *Older Rural Americans*, pp. 262–280. Lexington: University of Kentucky Press.

Snyder, Donald C. 1979. Elderly poor: Effects of public transfers. *Journal of Minority Aging* 4:109–112.

Solomon, Barbara. 1970. Ethnicity, mental health and the older black aged. *Proceedings of the Workshop on Ethnicity, Mental Health and Aging.* Los Angeles: Andrus Gerontology Center, University of Southern California.

Stephens, Richard C., Blau, Zena S., Oser, George T., and Miller, Melanie D. 1978. Aging, social support systems, and social policy. *Journal of Gerontological Social Work* 1:33–45.

Stewart, Arleen. 1973. Las mugeres de Aztlan: A consultation with elderly Mexican-American women in a socio-historical perspective. Unpublished doctoral dissertation, San Francisco: California School of Professional Psychology.

Stojanovic, Elizabeth J. 1970. Morale and its correlates among aged black and white rural women in Mississippi. Unpublished doctoral dissertation, State College: Mississippi State University, State College.

Stone, Virginia. 1959. Personal adjustment in aging in relation to community environment, a study of persons sixty years and over in Carrboro and Chapel Hill, North Carolina. Unpublished doctoral dissertation, Chapel Hill: University of North Carolina, Chapel Hill.

Streib, Gordon F. 1965. Are the aged a minority group? *In* A. W. Gouldner and S. M. Miller (eds.), *Applied Sociology*, pp. 311–328. Glencoe, Ill.: The Free Press.

Streib, Gordon F. 1976. Social stratification and aging. *In* Robert H. Binstock and Ethel Shanas (eds.), *Handbook of Aging and the Social Sciences*, 1st ed., pp. 160–185. New York: Van Nostrand Reinhold.

Sue, Stanley, and Kitano, Harry H. L. 1973. Asian Americans: A success story? *Journal of Social Issues* 29:218–219.

Suzuki, P. T. 1975. Minority group aged in America: A comprehensive bibliography of recent publications on blacks, Mexican-Americans, Native Americans, Chinese, and Japanese. Monticello, Ill.: Council of Planning Librarians.

Talley, T., and Kaplan, Jerome. 1956. The Negro aged. *Newletter* (Dec.), Gerontological Society, p. 6.

Taylor, Robert J., Jackson, James S., and Quick, Alida D. 1982. The frequency of social support among Black Americans: Preliminary findings from the National Survey of Black Americans. *Urban Research Review* 8:1–4, 11.

Taylor, S. P. 1980. Simple models of complexity: Pragmatic considerations in providing services for minority elderly. *In* E. Percil Stanford (ed.), *Minority Aging: Policy Issues for the '80s*, pp. 91–94. San Diego, Calif.: University Center on Aging, San Diego State University, The Campanile Press.

Taylor, Sue Perkins, 1982. Mental health and successful coping among aged black women. *In* Ron C. Manuel (ed.), *Minority Aging, Sociological and Social Psy-*

chological Issues, pp. 95-100. Westport, Conn.: Greenwood Press.

Thornton, R. J., and Nam, Charles B. 1968. The lower mortality rates of nonwhites at the older ages: An enigma in demographic analysis. Tallahassee, Fla.: Research Reports in Social Science (Vol. 11, No. 1), Institute for Social Research, Florida State University.

Thune, Jeanne M. 1967. Racial attitudes of older adults. The Gerontologist 7:179-182.

Torres-Gil, Fernando. 1976. Political behavior: A study of political attitudes and political participation among older Mexican-Americans. Unpublished doctoral dissertation, Waltham, Mass.: Brandeis University.

Torres-Gil, Fernando, and Becerra, Rosina M. 1977. The political behavior of the Mexican-American elderly. The Gerontologist 17:392-399.

Trela, James E., and Sokolovsky, Jay H. 1979. Culture, ethnicity, and policy for the aged. In Donald E. Gelfand and Alfred J. Kutzik (eds.), Ethnicity and Aging, Theory, Research, and Policy, pp. 117-136. New York: Springer Publishing Company.

U.S. Bureau of the Census. 1973. Census of Population: 1970, Detailed Characteristics, Final Report PC(1)-D1, United States Summary. Washington, D.C.: U.S. Government Printing Office.

U.S. Bureau of the Census. 1980a. Supplementary Reports, 1980 Census of Population, "Age, Sex, Race, and Spanish Origin of the Population by Regions, Divisions, and States: 1980," PC80-S1-1. Washington, D.C.: U.S. Government Printing Office.

U.S. Bureau of the Census. 1980b. Current Population Reports, Series P-20, No. 356, "Educational Attainment in the United States: March 1979 and 1978." Washington, D.C.: U.S. Government Printing Office.

U.S. Bureau of the Census. 1982a. Current Population Reports, Series P-25, No. 917. "Preliminary Estimates of the Population of the United States by Age, Sex, and Race: 1970 to 1981." Washington, D.C.: U.S. Government Printing Office.

U.S. Bureau of the Census. 1982b. Current Population Reports, Series P-60, No. 133, "Characteristics of the Population Below the Poverty Level: 1980." Washington, D.C.: U.S. Government Printing Office.

U.S. Bureau of the Census. 1982c. Current Population Reports, Series P-20, No. 372, "Marital Status and Living Arrangements: March 1981." Washington, D.C.: U.S. Government Printing Office.

U.S. Bureau of the Census. 1983a. Current Population Reports, Series P-60, No. 138, "Characteristics of the Population Below the Poverty Level: 1981." Washington, D.C.: U.S. Government Printing Office.

U.S. Bureau of the Census. 1983b. Current Population Reports, Series P-20, No. 381, "Household and Family Characteristics: March 1982." Washington, D.C.: U.S. Government Printing Office.

U.S. Commission on Civil Rights. 1982a. Minority Elderly Services, New Programs, Old Problems, Part I. Washington, D.C.: U.S. Commission on Civil Rights.

U.S. Commission on Civil Rights. 1982b. Minority Elderly Services, New Programs, Old Problems, Part II. Washington, D.C.: U.S. Commission on Civil Rights.

U.S. House of Representatives, Committee on Education and Labor. 1982. Compilation of the Older Americans Act of 1965 and Related Provisions of Law as Amended through December 29, 1981. Washington, D.C.: U.S. Government Printing Office (#89-668 0).

University Center on Aging, San Diego State University. 1981. Minority Aging Codification Project Bibliography, Administration on Aging Grant #0090-AR-0022. San Diego, Calif.: University Center on Aging, San Diego State University.

Votau, Thomas E. 1974. Death anxiety in black and white elderly subjects in institutionalized and non-institutionalized settings. Unpublished doctoral dissertation, Auburn, Ala.: Auburn University.

Walker, Gloria V. 1970. The relationship between socioeconomic status and chronic ailments of the aged in Nashville, Tennessee. Unpublished master's thesis, Nashville, Tenn.: Fisk University.

Walls, Bertram E., and Jackson, Jacquelyne J. 1977. Factors affecting the use of physicians by menopausal black women. Urban Health 6:53-57.

Ward, Russell A., and Kilburn, Harold. 1983. Community access and life satisfaction: Racial differences in later life. International Journal of Aging and Human Development 16:209-219.

Waring, Mary L., and Kosberg, Jordan I. 1980. Life conditions and the use of social welfare services among aged blacks in Northern Florida. Journal of Minority Aging 5:233-240.

Warner, W. Lloyd. 1936. American caste and class. American Journal of Sociology 42:234-237.

Warner, W. Lloyd, and Srole, Leo. 1945. The Social Systems of American Ethnic Groups. New Haven, Conn.: Yale University Press.

Washington, Harold T. 1976. A psycho-historical analysis of elderly Afro-Americans: An exploratory study of racial pride. Unpublished doctoral dissertation, Amherst: University of Massachusetts, Amherst.

Watson, Allen J., and Kivett, Vira R. 1976. Influences on the life satisfaction of older fathers. The Family Coordinator 25:482-488.

Weaver, Eyvette M. 1984. Attitudinal perceptions of the Old-Age and Survivors Insurance Program (OASI) among residents of Washington, D.C., 1983. Unpublished master's thesis, Washington, D.C.: Howard University.

Weinstock, Comilda, and Bennett, Ruth. 1968. Problems in communication to nurses among residents of a racially hetereogeneous nursing home. The Gerontologist 8:72-75.

Wellin, E., and Boyer, E. 1979. Adjustments of black and white elderly to the same adaptive niche. Anthropological Quarterly 52:39-48.

Wershow, Harold J. 1976. Inadequate census data on black nursing home patients. *The Gerontologist* 16:86–87.

White House Conference on Aging, 1972. *Aging and Aged Blacks, Special Concerns Report of the White House Conference on Aging 1971.* Washington, D.C.: U.S. Government Printing Office.

White House Conference on Aging. 1981. *Final report of the 1981 White House Conference on Aging,* Vols. 1, 2, and 3. Washington, D.C.: U.S. Government Printing Office.

White, Theodore H. 1982. *America in Search of Itself, the Making of the President, 1956–1980.* New York: Harper & Row, Publishers.

Williams, Fanny Barrier. 1898. The present status and intellectual progress of colored women. Address delivered at the Congress of Representative Women, World's Congress Auxiliary of the World's Columbian Exposition, Chicago, May, 1893.

Williams Lois, L. 1977. Analysis of social and community needs of black senior citizens in inner city Detroit. Unpublished doctoral dissertation, Ann Arbor: University of Michigan.

Wirth, Louis. 1945. The problem of minority groups. *In* Ralph Linton (ed.), *The Science of Man in the World Crisis,* p. 347. New York: Columbia University Press.

Woehrer, Carol E. 1978. Cultural pluralism in American families: The influences of ethnicity on social aspects of the aged. *The Family Coordinator* 27:329–340.

Wu, Frances Y. 1974. Mandarin-speaking aged Chinese in the Los Angeles area: Needs and services. Unpublished doctoral dissertation, Los Angeles: University of Southern California.

Wylie, Floyd. 1971. Attitudes toward aging and the aged among black Americans: Some historical perspectives. *Aging and Human Development* 2:66–70.

Wylie, M. 1976. Research on human services and delivery systems. Unpublished background paper prepared for the National Institute on Aging.

Yelder, Josephine E. 1975. Generational relationships in black families: Some perceptions of grandparent roles. Unpublished doctoral dissertation, Los Angeles: University of Southern California.

Youmans, E. Grant (ed.). 1967. *Older Rural Americans: A Sociological Perspective.* Lexington: University of Kentucky Press.

Zambrana, Ruth E., Merino, Rolando, and Santana, Sarah. 1979. Health services and the Puerto Rican elderly. *In* Donald E. Gelfand and Alfred J. Kutzik (eds.), *Ethnicity and Aging, Theory, Research, and Policy,* pp. 308–319. New York: Springer Publishing Company.

11
GENERATIONS, COHORTS, AND RELATIONS BETWEEN AGE GROUPS

Vern L. Bengtson
and
Neal E. Cutler
University of Southern California
David J. Mangen
Mangen and Namakkal
and
Victor W. Marshall*
University of Toronto

THE PROBLEM OF GENERATIONS IN GERONTOLOGY

The central problem of generations, from antiquity to the present, concerns social consequences of the succession of age groups—through birth, aging, death, and replacement—upon social organization and behavior. The central focus of gerontology in the social sciences concerns the social consequences of age-related contrasts and relationships.

It is logical, therefore, that gerontologists in the social sciences have become involved in four complex issues reflecting the problem of generations: (1) What are the effects of generational succession on social differentiation? (2) What are its effects on social relationships? (3) What are its effects on social change, for example, in the emergence of distinctive social or political movements? (4) To what extent are problems or processes of generational succession the same at different levels of analysis—macrosocial (the society) contrasted with microsocial (the family)?

Succession, Differences, and Relationships

The metaphor of "generations" has been used for centuries in attempts to organize social phenomena reflecting time, aging, age groups, and social structure (Marias, 1968; Feuer, 1969; Esler, 1972; Spitzer, 1973; Dowd, 1980; Hagestad, 1981; Marshall, 1983). In the *Iliad*, as in the book of Genesis,

*We wish to acknowledge helpful suggestions of several colleagues on an earlier draft: Paul Baltes, Glen Elder, Beverly Duncan, Jon Hendricks, Dennis Hogan, and Malcolm Johnson. We also wish to acknowledge the assistance of Shiela Miyazaki and Felicitas Vanderpol in completing the manuscript.

generational membership appears as a means of organizing social experience—a kind of triple bookkeeping in which the succession of generations is used in three ways: in marking the chronology of important events; in describing the social location of individual actors; and in explaining resultant collective change (Nash, 1978). To the earliest social historians, the cycle of generational emergence seemed a sensible way to account for the growth and decline of dynasties, ideologies, religions, even artistic styles. In the nineteenth and early twentieth centuries, analysts of social change turned to more elaborate models of within-generation elites as active agents of sociopolitical change [Dilthey, 1924; Mannheim, 1952 (1928); Ortega y Gasset, 1933 (1923), 1962] or to Marxist analyses of social class.

In the first edition of this *Handbook*, Bengtson and Cutler (1976) reviewed the various "generational" explanations for social differentiation and change. They identified three principal meanings that characterized the term's usage through the social science literature of the early 1970s: as membership in historically defined birth cohorts, as lineage descent position within families, and as membership in social movements in which age consciousness is a primary identification. They suggested that the different perspectives (cohort, lineage, and generational unit) had allowed distinct insights into the complex relationships among time, aging, and change in social structure—especially as major alternatives to the maturational explanation of age trends and apparent age changes that had characterized research on age differences prior to 1968.

Since 1976, much more research has been assembled pointing to the importance of examining differences between and relationships among age groups. Four developments are particularly noteworthy. First, many more social and behavioral scientists have addressed the theme of temporal placement—both in terms of life-course or developmental time and in terms of societal or historical time—as a means of better under-

standing change in behavior and social organization (see Elder 1975, 1979, 1984; Baltes, 1979; Hagestad, 1981, 1982; Hogan, 1981; Featherman, 1983). Second, a variety of empirical work has been carried out to examine the relationship among age, period, and cohort effects, with the tentative conclusion that cohort contrasts are much more predictive of differences than had been assumed (Palmore, 1978; Baltes, 1979; Baltes et al., 1979; Schaie, 1982). Third, considerable effort has been given to conceptual clarification of the terms cohort and generation and of their utility in explaining observed differences between groups (Glenn, 1977; Rosow, 1978; Kertzer, 1983; Marshall, 1983; Elder, 1984). Fourth, several important analyses of family intergenerational relations have pointed out new directions for empirical analysis, in terms of bidirectional influence between parents and children (Hagestad, 1984); the distinction between "alpha" and "omega" generations in the family (Hagestad, 1982); the effects of historical events on parent–child relations (Elder, 1978, 1984; Hareven, 1981); and a propositional inventory of results from 106 studies concerning intergenerational relations within the family (Troll and Bengtson, 1979).

The purpose of this chapter is to review recent developments in the analysis of age-group relations and in the explanation of age-group differences, at both the macro- and microsocial levels. First, we will examine age contrasts in attitudes and opinions, noting the utility of maturational, cohort, and historical period explanations in analyzing social policy and political data. Second, we will review intergenerational relations and differences within the family of aging individuals, examining existing research from the standpoint of various aspects of family solidarity. The final section presents a social conflict perspective on age relationships and age consciousness. We review evidence for the relevance of age in terms of macrosocial conflict and solidarity, as well as factors that may likely to enhance or diminish conflict between age groups.

Constructs and the Problems of Multiple Meanings

What are the most useful constructs and perspectives by which to examine problems of social succession, differences, and relations between age groups? From antiquity to today, the term "generation" has been used in attempts to answer this question, and to identify various social groupings defined by age. Unfortunately, the term has been employed so loosely as to create uncomfortably imprecise distinctions among groups; for example, describing a population living at one point in time (as Franklin Roosevelt did when he declared, "this generation of Americans has a rendezvous with history") or a particular group born during a common period (the "Depression generation"). So it was in classical Greek thought: Nash (1978) describes five common usages of the term in third-century history and poetry, ranging from "a single step in the line of descent from a common ancestor" such as the familial generation of Nestor before and after the Trojan wars, to "mutual participation in an important event" such as those who returned victorious after the sack of Troy.

The problem of multiple meanings can be traced to the Greek root of the word, *genos*. Its general meaning, reflected in the verb *genesthai*, is "to come into existence." But as Nash (1978) notes in describing Hellenistic usage of the term, there are many social realities that "come into existence": a new lineal descendant (the birth of a child into Nestor's family); a new social category (peers who joined Nestor in the sacking of Troy); and even a phase of life (those mature enough to speak to the assembly in Athens). Like the current English usage, the ancient Greek terms for generation (e.g., *genos, genesis, genus*) carry a wide scope of meanings, from birth and reproduction, to time of life, to peership. The central point involves sameness with one group; distinctiveness from another.

If, however, we remember that the fundamental significance of generation is "to come into existence," then it follows that the concept has an inherent relativity (i.e., a child forms a generation only with respect to his parents or when children are born to him). Thus, generation is a reference point for several phenomena, a metaphor for emergence of social realities. As Nash notes, "like the verb *to be,* generation requires an adjective of context, a predicate of relativity, before it takes on meaning" (1978, p. 2).

One point is that the relativity of "generations" requires specification of its context because it has been used since antiquity as a metaphor to describe the "coming into existence" of quite different social phenomena linking time and social structure. Because of the multiple meanings of "generation," social scientists in the past decade have attempted to delineate more distinctively defined concepts and perspectives to address questions of succession, differences, and relationships among age groups. This debate occasionally has been more acrimonious than constructive (see Kertzer, 1983); to state as Kertzer does that use of the term generation is "a liability to science" is extreme. One needs to recognize differences between the generic and more specific usages of the concept. There are three distinctive approaches especially as applied to three questions of special relevance in gerontology.

First, to what extent are there differences (or similarities) between older and younger members of a society, and what accounts for these differences?

The concept most often employed here is *cohort*, which may be defined as an aggregate of individuals born within the same time interval (usually five or ten years). The cohort perspective emphasizes demographic and historical age-specific attributes of age groups. Born during a given period of history, members of a particular age cohort experience the consequences of historical events similarly. This view emphasizes the role of age categories (or age groups) in macrosocial differentiation, and allows appropriate examination of hypotheses reflecting aging, cohort membership, and historical period effects to explain observed differences.

Second, to what extent are there differences (or similarities) between older and younger members of the family lineage group; what is the nature of their relationship; and what are the implications of this relationship for potential social support?

Here the term *generation* can most unambiguously be employed, referring to ranked descent within family lineages. Analyzing parent–child (and grandparent–grandchild) contrasts and relationships offers the most appropriate perspective for examining micropatterns of continuity and discontinuity through the primary socialization process, as well as patterns of handling crises of dependency in old age within the family context. The lineage approach to generations also provides one basis for discussion of relationships between age groups at the macrosocial level (however, as seen in the "generation gap" discussions of the 1970s, this approach to "generational cohorts" is imprecise).

Third, how do differences between cohorts translate into conflict or solidarity within age groups? And what are the consequences of age group conflict and/or solidarity in terms of social change?

The third orientation to generations and social organization focuses on subunits of age cohorts as potential *social movements*—self-conscious agents of social action within history. This perspective offers insight into the social construction of age categories and their role in history as sociopolitical movements. It highlights potential elements of conflict among contemporaneous age groups, both within and between birth cohorts; among alternative generation concepts this perspective attempts to deal most directly with the episodic nature of social change and the connections between social change and age groups. The term most often used in the past to index these phenomena is "generational unit" [Mannheim, 1952 (1929)]. Unfortunately, this term is ambiguous because of its confounding broader birth cohort effects with the lineage connotations of generation. Thus in discussing this question we will employ a "conflict perspective" to generations and attempt greater

specificity than the terms Mannheim originally introduced, while adhering to his original and insightful perspectives.

In the remainder of this chapter we will review each of these three perspectives as they are reflected in current gerontological research. Each offers distinctive insights on the problem of aging, succession, and change or stability over time in social organization. Each reflects a different perspective on "coming into existence" of social and behavioral phenomena linked to time at birth.

THE COHORT PERSPECTIVE: AGE CONTRASTS IN ATTITUDES AND OPINIONS

The cohort approach to contrasts between age groups focuses attention on aggregates of individuals who, having been born in the same period, are socialized within a common segment of social history (Ryder, 1965). As they age, they carry with them the impact of their early historical experiences—and consequently their interpretations of and orientations toward a variety of social issues.

But since individuals of a particular birth cohort change as they move through life, the central question becomes: Do their attitudes and behavior represent the effect of N years of aging, or do they represent the longstanding beliefs of those born N years ago (cohorts), that is, the attitudes and behaviors reflecting social experiences during adolescence or early adult socialization, or even later for those now elderly? Similarly, the scholar must consider the possibility that historical events affect the attitudes of all age groups the same way, that is, that neither aging nor cohort differences may be operative in a particular configuration of attitudes (historical period effects).

Competing Hypotheses. To be sure, these three constructs—maturation, cohort, and period effects—are surrogates for broad and elusive experiential phenomena (Hobcraft et al., 1982). Maturation, for example, is a surrogate for a range of social and biological processes of maturation that do not affect all individuals in the same way or at the same time in their lives. Cohort is a surrogate for the influence of past events (conceptualized in terms of socialization) on attitudes or behaviors (as structured by life chances). Period is a surrogate for the influence of contemporary events on attitudes. While we cannot easily measure the effects of all the experiences of maturation or past and current events, it is evident that these influences have an impact upon, and do leave traces within, the contemporary attitudes and behaviors of men and women.

In short, the assessment of differences between individuals who differ by age must consider a *maturational* or developmental aging hypothesis, a generational or *cohort* hypothesis, and finally, a contemporary events or *period* hypothesis.

Until recently, the prevalent approach in social scientific analysis involving age differences was to examine a given pattern of attitudes in the context of just one of the above three competing hypotheses. In many cases, the single hypothesis fails to be disconfirmed simply because the investigator did not have evidence of the competing substantive hypotheses for comparison. Studies focusing only on aging or cohort differences cannot by themselves provide conclusive evidence validating a maturational or generational hypothesis unless evidence for the competing hypotheses are included in the analysis.

In addition, it should be pointed out that the cohort dimension of generational phenomena is not the same thing as the family of data reduction research techniques commonly known as cohort analysis (see Glenn, 1977). This suggests two cautionary notes: (1) the analysis of birth cohorts within a particular substantive domain may reveal that the cohort effect is not the main influence on the behavior of the individuals or aggregates under study; and (2) the analysis of the cohort dimension of the generation concept does not require just the use of the formal cohort analysis techniques.

Intracohort Differentiation. A significant aspect of research on cohorts is that we may be concerned with either the individual or societal level of analysis. (This aspect will in fact become evident in the examples presented in this section.) Of even greater importance is the interaction between these two levels, which can be revealed through the cohort construct. As derived from demographic analysis, "a cohort may be defined as the aggregate of individuals (within some population definition) who experienced the same event within the same time interval. In almost all cohort research to date the defining event has been birth" (Ryder, 1965). However, not all individuals within an aggregate such as a birth cohort are equally influenced by their common historical experiences and exposures [Mannheim, 1952 (1928)].

The differential impact of common sociological–historical events on the members of a birth cohort reflects, by analogy, the contrast between "touch" and "saturation." Some individuals are barely touched by the cohort influences surrounding them. On the other hand, some of their contemporaries may be saturated by the same cohort influences. Distinctions along a continuum from "touched" to "saturated" vary in response to personal attributes. Personality, family circumstances, social class, and psychological resources affect the degree to which an individual is cognizant of, responsive to, and affected by external stimuli. This suggests that the results of empirical cohort studies must be interpreted cautiously because some members of a demographically defined birth cohort may be unaffected by the events the researcher identifies as the cohort-defining event or experience. Birth cohorts are only proxies in the absence of more refined measures of social differentiation.

Similarly, there is variation not only in how individuals respond to cohort stimuli, but also in the magnitude of cohort-defining stimuli in different historical periods. Some periods, such as those characterized by economic or military crisis, seem to have a greater potential for a saturating cohort effect; (e.g., the 1960's); the events of other periods (the 1970's) appear to barely touch the birth cohorts that pass demographically through those events.

Cohorts can easily be identified as statistical aggregates, as in census reports. It is less easy, however, to determine the extent to which the individuals within those aggregates identify themselves in terms of their cohort; or whether their common cohort experiences, in fact, affect their attitudes, orientations, and behavior.

Cohort Flow and Demographic Change. We have primarily been discussing the individual or microlevel aspect of the cohort perspective. But there is an important macrosocietal dimension as well. This macro perspective focuses on social change as a consequence of the inevitable demographic dynamics of population turnover. Here, our concern is not so much with how an individual's attitudes and orientations are caused by his or her being touched or saturated by cohort influences, but rather with the societal-level effects of the aggregation of these individual generational-cohort influences.

Macrosocietal aspects of the analysis of cohorts have been labeled "population aging" or "demographic succession" (Cowgill and Holmes, 1972). The basic observation is that old cohorts die out of society as new cohorts enter—continuously and inevitably (Easterlin, 1962; Ryder, 1965; Riley et al., 1972). Observation of this cohort flow, even in the absence of evidence of individual attitude change, suggests the possibility of social change, if not eventual societal transformation. The flow of cohorts through society can bring with it change, whether or not change at the individual level has taken place. The Republican presidential defeat of 1964 was followed 16 years later by a Republican presidential victory in 1980, in both cases, it has been argued, by margins of "landslide" proportions. Did a massive conversion of the American electorate take place, in which masses of voters changed from one party to another? Or, even in the absence of such individual-level conversion or change, might the cohort turnover within the political system (e.g., the baby boom entering the electorate between 1964 and 1980) account for the variant outcomes? Both hypotheses are plausible, and each illustrates the utility of the cohort concept.

The purpose of this section is to illustrate the facility of cohort analysis in resolving conflict among the three alternative age-related hypotheses. In doing so, we will confine our presentation to three case-examples well represented in extant research: political party identification, attitudes toward governmental involvement in the provision of medical care, and the decline of partisanship. A more general and comprehensive review of the relationship of age factors to society and politics is found in Chapter 20 of this volume; a discussion of methodological and statistical models relevant to cohort analysis can be found elsewhere (Schaie, 1965, Baltes, 1968; Hyman, 1972; Mason et al., 1973; Glenn, 1977).

Generations and Political Party Affiliation

Competing hypotheses. It has popularly been believed that aging brings about a more conservative perspective in social and political orientations. An interesting controversy in recent studies of political attitudes is based upon this assumption of age-induced conservatism and focuses on age patterns of public support for the Republican and Democratic parties in the United States. Each of the three competing hypotheses of cohort, maturation, and period effects, taken by itself, could be supported by available data. When evidence for just one of the explanations is presented, it is possible to conclude that it is *the* appropriate explanation of age-based patterns of party identification.

Some analyses have concluded that *maturation* is the primary underlying factor and have presented evidence pointing to life-cycle maturational changes favoring the Republican party. Crittenden (1962), for example, examined data from a series of national Gallup surveys taken in the 1940s and 1950s. In every year, more people in the older age groups were seen to be Republican than those in the younger age groups. Crittenden concluded that the explanatory hypothesis was that of maturational aging: "Aging seems to produce a shift toward Republicanism in the period 1946 to 1958. . . . The pattern appears to be linear (p. 331).

The *cohort* explanation, by contrast, is stressed in a study examining the contemporary party identifications of young voters who entered the political system during the Depression/New Deal era. Campbell et al. (1960) found that this cohort of voters maintained a Democratic party identification of a much stronger nature than would be predicted from such variables as age change and socioeconomic factors. Campbell et al. concluded that the events of the early 1930s had precipitated the creation of a heavily Democratic generation of voters whose identifications were, in the aggregate, substantially maintained throughout the life cycle of members of that group (p. 155).

Historical or *period* effects have been noted in trend studies that have found various historical alterations of patterns in party identifications in the United States in recent years (e.g., Scammon and Wattenberg, 1970; Pomper, 1975). The results of recent presidential and congressional elections clearly document changes in the popularity of the two major American parties. Political analysts have noted dozens of political, economic, social, and psychological factors that plausibly account for at least some of these changes in the structure of partisan attachments over past elections (e.g., Converse et al., 1969; Axelrod, 1972; Pomper, 1972; Scheider, 1981).

Of particular relevance is the role that cohort trends might play in this sequence of political changes. Aside from the attractiveness of particular candidates or party platforms, to what degree are changes in patterns of attitudes attributable to the entrance of new birth cohorts of citizens into the electorate (Abramson, 1975; Cutler 1983)? Certain elements of contemporary politics might strongly affect the orientations of these new cohorts but might not affect the firmly held opinions and party attachments of older voters so strongly (Carlsson and Karlsson, 1970). The basic point is that any analysis of these possibilities must take all three hypotheses into account because each one by itself potentially offers a plausible explanation of social trends.

Evidence of Multiple Effects. The issue of trends in partisan attachments has received substantial scholarly attention in recent years, and the question of the measurement and meaning of age differences has represented an interesting area of controversy. Indeed, the generational perspective on patterns of party identification has played a major role in recent reviews (Spitzer, 1973; Cutler, 1975) and in textbooks on research methods (Hyman, 1972, Ch. 7; Kirkpatrick, 1974, Ch. 5).

Crittenden's (1962) analysis supporting the maturational explanations represents a single-hypothesis analysis of age influences on patterns of party identification. As noted, Crittenden concluded that the relatively greater portions of Republicanism among the older groups was the result of the maturational dynamics of aging. A subsequent study, however, reanalyzed the same data using a formal cohort analysis approach (Cutler, 1969). By examination of the pattern of aging longitudinally across cohorts, rather than by the cross-sectional comparison of old and young within each year, Cutler identified a different pattern of Republicanism over the period 1946–58. He concluded that there is no evidence of a consistent trend *associated with aging* favoring the Republican Party during this period; if anything, the data modestly supported a cohort effect.

A subsequent analysis of the same issue employed a more expansive data base (1945–69) and a statistically more controlled application of cohort analysis (Glenn and Hefner, 1972). In analyzing their data, the investigators examined each cohort across time (and aging), rather than examining different age groups at one or more cross-sectional points in time. They found no general movement toward Republicanism associated with aging. The dominant pattern is that of differences *between* the modal responses of the successive cohorts rather than of noticeable age changes *within* cohorts. On the basis of this evidence and other aspects of their study, the investigators conclude: "Therefore, the thesis that cohorts experience an absolute increase in Republicanism as a consequence of aging receives no support. . . . The cross-sectional data gathered at various times during the past 30 years or so reflects intercohort (or 'generational') differences, rather than the effects of aging" (Glenn and Hefner, 1972, p. 35).

Generations and Social Policy Attitudes: Government Involvement in Medical Care

Competing Hypotheses. The degree to which attitudes toward specific areas of social policy are related to age phenomena may depend primarily upon the nature of the issue. Many issues concern financial allocations that grant specific benefits (or liabilities) to identifiable age groups. In such circumstances, it might be expected that age of individuals responding to a questionnaire will prove to be a significant variable in the analysis of changes or trends in the attitude.

One such policy orientation concerns government involvement in medical care programs (the issue of costs and financing) and the role the government ought to play in this area of public policy. Because poverty and poor health are correlated with advancing age in today's society, it might initially be expected that an individual's support for federal programs aimed at lowering the cost of medical care or providing medical care insurance will increase as a function of age.

As before, we must consider all of the plausible competing hypotheses by which age may be related to trends in a given attitude. The *maturational* explanation appears justifiable because we might expect support for medical care programs to increase as the individual matures into a life-stage characterized by increasing medical bills and decreasing financial resources. On the basis of studies of the national electorate in 1956 and 1960, Campbell (1962) concludes that older voters are more supportive of federal medical care programs than younger voters. He further concludes that the pattern of support represents an instance of a group-benefits orientation—an orientation toward political issues framed in terms of whether

or not the policy or program will benefit a particular group of which the individual is a member.

A more formal analysis of this hypothesis (Schreiber and Marsden, 1972), using a sequence of similarly worded items from presidential election year surveys spanning the years 1956–68, concludes that support for governmental involvement in medical care financing is associated with increasing age. The study indicates that although there are some period shifts in the electorate's overall support for such governmental involvement, from a low of 64 percent in favor (1964) to a high of 75 percent in favor (1960), the age pattern is relatively consistent within each of the survey years: in each year surveyed the younger age groups exhibited lower support, and the oldest age group (65 and over), the highest amount of support.

The *cohort* hypothesis may also provide a plausible interpretation of any age-connected patterns in this area. Evidence of this interpretation is found in a cohort analysis of the traditional dimension of liberal–conservative ideology in domestic American political attitudes: federal involvement in economic and welfare programs, including the federal medical care issue. The analysis found cohort differences both in the support of the ideology and in the degree of ideological constraint or homogeneity across several discrete policy issues (Kirkpatrick, 1974).

Finally, *period* effects must also be considered because the United States has seen substantial changes over the past three or four decades in many areas of social policy. Twenty-five years ago, government-sponsored medical aid was dismissed as socialized medicine and supported only by a minority of the nation's population. But, as with other social welfare issues, government involvement in the financing of medical care came to be inevitable, with the enactment of Medicare in 1965 (Marmor, 1973). Thus, period effects in attitude change on the issue of medical care must be considered as a plausible hypothesis, to be comparatively evaluated with the maturational and cohort hypotheses.

Evidence of Multiple Effects. One recent investigation examines the impacts of all three effects upon attitudes toward the medical care issue (Cutler and Schmidhauser, 1975). The results of a cohort analysis, spanning the years 1956 through 1972, are summarized in Table 1. Unlike the analysis of party identification reviewed above, the purpose of this presentation of data is not to trace opinion patterns across the entire life cycle, but to isolate patterns in a small segment of the aging process and to examine that segment, in a replicative fashion, across successive cohorts.

If the maturational hypothesis suggested by Campbell (1962) and by Schreiber and Marsden (1972) is valid (because of a self-interest or group-benefits orientation, aging leads to increasing support of governmental involvement in medical aid programs), then support for the issue should increase *within* a cohort because the cohort is examined at the older end of *its own* life cycle. Convincing evidence of the maturational hypothesis would require that: (a) the *level* of support among aged cohorts should be greater than that for youthful cohorts; (b) the amount of age-related *increase* in support should be greater for the cohorts observed in early adulthood; and (c) this pattern of old age support should be found *consistently* in differing periods or contexts.

The data in Table 1 substantially confirm the maturational hypothesis: (a) In general, each cross-sectional survey tends to show that respondents in their sixties more strongly endorse governmental involvement in the financing and provision of medical care than do respondents in their twenties. (b) The cohorts observed in their sixties display greater *increase in support* (or less diminution of support in those years where the historical trend was downward) than do the cohorts in their twenties. (c) Even in the context of the 1956–72 fluctuations, when the entire electorate decreased its support of government medical aid programs in 1964, the older cohorts exhibited less decrease than did the younger cohorts. The clearest confirmation of the maturational hypothesis is seen between the years 1964 and 1968, when the difference for the whole electorate was negligible (an increase of two percentage points). In this period the older cohort increased its endorsement of the issue by 12 percentage points, while the younger cohort in the same

TABLE 1. Attitudes Toward Federal Government Medical Aid Programs (Percent in Favor).*

Age Group	1956	1960	1964	1968	1975
21–24	70	77	67	67	
25–28		69	62	56	56
Change		−1	−15	−12	−11
61–64	69	84	64	72	
65–68		85	73	76	69
Change		+16	−11	+12	−3
Total sample	70	77	65	67	61
Change		+7	−12	+2	−6

* The question read for 1956 and 1960: "The government ought to help people get doctors and hospital care at low cost." For 1964 and 1968 it was: "Some people say the government in Washington ought to help people get doctors and hospital care at low cost; others say the government should not get into this. Have you been interested enough in this to favor one side or the other?" For 1972 it was: "There is much concern about the rapid rise in medical and hospital costs. Some feel there should be a government insurance plan which would cover all medical expenses. Others feel that medical expenses should be paid by individuals through private insurance like the Blue Cross. Which side do you favor?" The data, which were made available by the Inter-University Consortium for Political Research, were originally collected by the Center for Political Studies, Institute for Social Research, University of Michigan, with partial support from a grant from the National Science Foundation. Neither the original collectors of the data nor the Consortium bears any responsibility for the analysis on interpretation presented here.
SOURCE: Cutler and Schmidhauser, 1975, p. 386.

period exhibited a decrease of 12 percentage points. The more general point, however, is that only an analysis structured to simultaneously examine the maturational, cohort, and period effects can validly conclude something about the dynamics that underlie the pattern of responses.

Cohort Succession and Macrosocial Change

Competing Hypotheses. Our third example illustrates the macrosocial consequences of cohort succession. The analysis of cohorts can provide an explanation of differences in the social and attitudinal characteristics of a population independent of the attitudinal change of individuals who survive from an earlier to a later point in time. Macrosocial changes due to cohort succession between 1982 and 1984 were minimal because relatively few people died or entered the population; by contrast, between 1880 and 1980 cohort turnover within the population was virtually total.

While the decline of partisanship in the United States has been noted by political observers for several years, recent research has attributed this trend not to changes in individual partisanship but to the generational dynamics of cohort difference and succession (e.g., Abramson, 1975; Jennings and Niemi, 1981). While it is likely that the actual trend reflects a combination of both individual change and cohort succession, the example presented here demonstrates how the cohort mechanism alone theoretically could account for the societal-level change.

The example focuses on the decline of American partisanship in 1956 and 1972, two election years exhibiting partisan defection (i.e., elections in which Democrats voted for the Republican candidate). Where Eisenhower's landslide reelection yielded results almost identical to his election in 1952, Nixon's landslide reelection showed an increase in partisan defection (because Republican votes in the largely Democratic electorate increased from a 50–50 division of the two-party vote in 1968 to a 60–40 division in 1972). Examination of the 1956 and 1972

electorates in terms of the political behavior of their component cohorts illustrates the macrosocial impact cohort succession can have upon a population.

Figure 1 reflects a cohort succession model to illustrate these phenomena. The electorate of each year may be conceptualized as having two cohort components. Cohort A is 21–70 years old in 1956 and survives to 1972—16 years later—when its age is 37–86. (For illustration we assume that all voters "age out" of the electorate after age 86.) Cohort B, aged 71–86 in 1956, is part of the electorate in 1956, but has completed aging out of the political system by 1972. Finally, Cohort C was too young to be part of the 1956 electorate but comes of age politically by 1972.

In sum, even if the surviving members of Cohort A have not changed, a society-wide change in partisanship between 1956 and 1972 could take place if incoming Cohort C is substantially different from exiting Cohort B. To the degree that such a difference does exist, the population differences between 1956 and 1972 would reflect cohort succession, independent of any micro-change within Cohort A.

Evidence of Multiple Effects. In a study of this question, partisan defection was measured as the percentage within each component cohort of self-identified partisans who voted for the candidate of the other party plus those who said they were independents (Cutler and Mimms, 1977). Table 2 presents the results of the analysis for each of the component cohorts identified above and suggests the following observations:

(1) The overall level of partisan defection plus independence has increased from 1956 to 1972 across all the cohorts in the analysis, a likely period effect. (2) Despite the expectation by some observers that aging leads to strengthening of partisanships (e.g., compare the conclusion in Hudson and Binstock, 1976, with the discussion in Jennings and Niemi, 1975), these data suggest that, for whatever reason, Cohort A has become less partisan after 16 years of aging (i.e., from

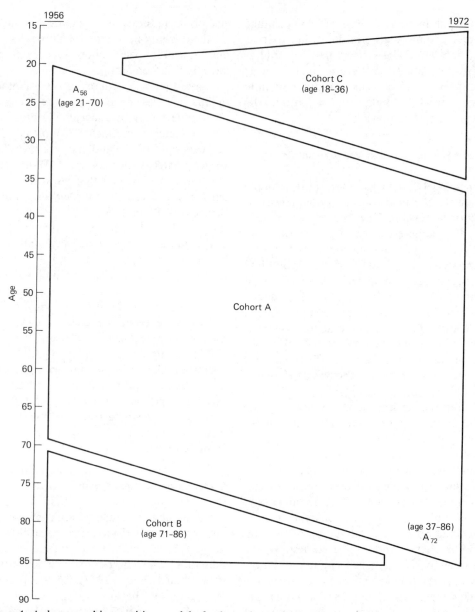

Figure 1. A demographic transition model of cohort change in the 1956 and 1972 electorates. SOURCE: Neal E. Culter and Georgeana Mimms, "The Birth and Death of Political Cohorts: A Demographic Transition Approach to the Decline of Partisanship in the United States." Adapted from a paper delivered to the Western Political Science Association, 1977.

26% defectors and independents to 42%). (3) Most directly relevant to the primary analytic question of this research, the incoming cohort (Cohort C) exhibits substantially weaker partisanship than the older cohort, which aged out of the political system (Cohort B), by a margin of more than three to one (46% vs. 13%).

On balance, the data suggest that a combination between cohort and period effects combines to make the 1972 electorate different from the 1956 electorate. Of course, nothing in these data ensures that the incoming Cohort C will not undergo further changes. The primary inference, however, is that at the macrosocietal level, the popula-

**TABLE 2. Cohort Patterns
of Defectors and Independents.**

	1956	1972	
Cohort A	26%	46%	Cohort C
Cohort B	13%	42%	

Notes: (1) Format of this table is based upon the model in Figure 1. (2) Table entries are the percent of each cohort who were either partisan defectors or independents. (3) All percentages reflect Multiple Classification Analysis adjustments for cohort differences in sex, education, and income.
SOURCE: Adapted from Cutler and Mimms, 1977, Table 3.

tion has changed from 1956 to 1972, in large part owing to the substantial differences between the entering and the exiting cohorts.

Finally, it should be noted that this analysis has thus far ignored the population sizes of the component cohorts. That is, in identifying the impact of Cohort B and Cohort C upon the 1956 and 1972 electorates, we have only mentioned their partial differences as if the two cohorts were of equal size. In fact, the overall impact of the partisan differences between the cohorts would be much greater if the cohorts were of significantly different sizes.

Consider, for example, the application of the model in Figure 1 to a different pair of elections separated by a 16-year interval but with dramatically different outcomes: the Goldwater Republican defeat of 1964 versus the Reagan Republican victory of 1980. The same analytic question is relevant: Did massive individual-level attitude conversion take place, from Democratic to Republican, or was the entering cohort substantially different from the cohort that aged out of the electorate? In this instance, the relative sizes of the cohorts may well prove to be crucial. Using the identical age definitions for Cohort C in Figure 1, 18–36, applied to 1980, yields a birth cohort defined by the years 1944–62—which is close to the usual definition of the postwar baby boom. Hence, if historically influenced cohort differences are found within an unusually large birth cohort, the macrosocietal impact of that cohort on the

political or social system as a whole will be that much more dramatic.

Implications of the Cohort Perspective for Theory and Research

This section has presented a sequence of case studies of public attitudes to demonstrate the three competing hypotheses describing age effects—the maturational or aging effect, the birth cohort effect, and the period effect. While cross-sectional descriptive studies can provide evidential support for any one of the hypotheses, our discussion has endeavored to demonstrate that for the attitudes investigated, all three hypotheses are plausible. Only studies in which the design permits the three competing hypotheses to be *simultaneously* examined can offer the most compelling explanations from among the three.

In reviewing the cases presented here, several summary points should be acknowledged as a guide for future studies employing generations as cohorts:

1. In each case, plausible maturational, cohort, and period explanations can be defended; this is true in most initial analyses of cohort-generation contrasts.

2. The cases resulted in the validation of different explanatory hypotheses. The party-identification analysis provided some evidence that a birth cohort effect describes recent Republican-Democrat differences in the United States. By contrast, in the case of attitudes toward government involvement in medical aid programs, it appears that aging leads to an increase in support for such programs.

3. The various cohort analyses present a mixed pattern of confirmation and disconfirmation of the evidence of cross-sectional studies. For party identification, the cross-sectional analysis supported the maturational hypothesis, whereas the cohort analysis supported the generational hypothesis. For attitudes toward governmental medical aid programs, the cohort analysis confirmed the interpretations reported by cross-sectional analysis.

4. Finally, discussion of the 1964–1980

elections illustrates the important connection between the microlevel characteristics of cohort members (e.g., political attitudes or voting behavior) and the macrolevel characteristics of demographic dynamics. This is a crucial connection, often ignored in analysis.

Thus, the cohort perspective on age-group differences represents an analytic approach to the systematic evaluation of the three competing age-related hypotheses. Depending upon the attitude or behavior orientation being investigated, the analytic approach is capable of either confirming or rejecting any of the three hypotheses, as these case examples have demonstrated. The fundamental lesson is that studies focusing only on one of the three hypotheses to the exclusion of the others produce incomplete and potentially misleading results. Even if one hypothesis, by itself, is confirmed rather than rejected, the investigator cannot evaluate the power of the others. Comparative analysis of age groups, across time periods and birth cohorts, must be undertaken to understand the dynamics of aging and age-related phenomena.

THE LINEAGE PERSPECTIVE: FAMILY INTERACTION AND INFLUENCE

At the level of microsocial analysis, the issue of differences between age groups involves a qualitatively different set of issues from the cohort perspective, translating most directly into questions concerning intergenerational relations within the family. A great deal of research in the past two decades has examined issues of interaction, influence, and consensus or disagreement between youth and parents (see the propositional inventory of Troll and Bengtson, 1979). A broader perspective, derived from the work of Durkheim [1964 (1983)], suggests examination of *solidarity and conflict* throughout the life course, especially between aging parents and their middle-aged children (Bengtson and Treas, 1980; Bengtson and Schrader, 1982). Gerontologists can learn much about older persons and the social processes of aging by

employing the focus of lineage generational relationships at either the microsocial or microstructural level (specific family relations) or at the macrolevel (relations between cohort-based generational aggregates). We will examine recent research from two perspectives: first, the perception of generational differences, from both cohort and lineage considerations, and second, intergenerational solidarity in the aging family.

Perception of intergenerational Relations: Cohort and Lineage Attributions of "Closeness"

Attributions or perceptions are extremely important in the analysis of relationships across generations within the family or between age cohorts within broader social groupings. On the one hand, attributed differences may be seen in the attitudes or stereotypes held by one cohort or age group of another (McTavish, 1971, 1982), as well as in generalized desirability of traits for one age group as contrasted to another (Ahammer and Baltes, 1972). On the other hand, these differences may be evidenced in the evaluation of interaction between age groups: the "closeness" or "distance" one feels from a member of another generation from the perspective of the social psychology of person perception.

Little research has examined this perceptual dimension of interage interaction or has studied the content of such contrasts systematically. One survey, however, affords the only data yet obtained regarding perceptions across generational boundaries in both cohort and lineage terms (Bengtson, 1971). In this three-generation study, three parameters of person perception were examined: (a) age of the *perceiver*; (b) age of the *referent* or *target group*; (c) *social context* of the perceiver-referent relationship (primary group vs. generalized collectivity). Respondents were asked to evaluate the closeness of various referent groups (youth-middle-aged, middle-aged-elderly, youth-elderly) in two social contexts: the "broader society" (cohort) and "your own family" (lineage).

Three conclusions are indicated. First, the "cohort gap" perceived between generations in the broader society is considerably larger than the "lineage gap" perceived within the respondent's own family. Second, the age of the perceiver makes some difference in the degree to which a "gap" is seen: the youngest age group (in this study, 16–26 years of age) perceives the least closeness, particularly at the family level (at the cohort level, the old and the young attribute similar levels of distance), whereas grandparents see the greatest degree of closeness within the family. Third, the age of the referent constitutes a considerable difference: a greater "gap" is perceived in the youth–elderly than in the other dyads (paraphrased from Bengtson, 1971).

The principal suggestion of this study, which should be tested in future research, is that the nature of cross-generational perceptions concerning social distance varies depending on several factors, the primary one being the context of the referent group (primary relationship vs. broader collectivity). For the older family member, this contrast is particularly pronounced: "Yes, there *is* a generation gap, but not in *my* family." This may be an example of "stereotypic misattribution" between family members (Acock and Bengtson, 1980).

Intergenerational Solidarity and Older Family Members

Within the family, the problem of generational relations has very practical implications. Especially for gerontologists, considering the expectable dependencies of an aged family member, the family relational context is an important consideration. Much has been written lately about "family support systems" and aging (e.g., Robinson and Thurnher, 1979; Zarit et al., 1980; Treas, 1977; Dunkle-Schetter and Wortman, 1981; Turner, 1981; Thoits, 1982). From this literature, and from more theoretical writings concerning family solidarity (Bengtson et al., 1976), it is possible to identify six critical issues in the analysis of family integration reflected in research, practice, and intervention, as listed by Bengtson and Schrader (1982, p. 79):

1. The who, what, and where of structure: Who is *available* as a resource for the older individual? What is the relationship? Where do they live?
2. How much *contact* is there between the older individual and his/her family? What do they do together, and how often?
3. What is the *quality* of the interaction? How does the older individual feel about the relationship with specific members of the family?
4. How much *consensus* is there among members of the family? Does the older individual feel conflict or similarity in terms of opinions and values?
5. How much *assistance* or help does the older person receive from the potential support system of his/her family? How much does he/she give? What is the balance of power that is reflected by such exchange?
6. What norms or *expectations* does the older person have concerning his/her family as a social system? How much filial obligation is perceived, by the elder parent and by the middle-aged child?

Research on the social aspects of aging almost always includes some information concerning the relations of aged parents and their adult children. Unfortunately, such data are usually treated as descriptive only; conceptual bases for examining parent–child relations in old age are underdeveloped. In reviewing the diverse literature addressing this topic, we detect an implicit conceptual ordering reflecting various dimensions of what Durkheim termed "solidarity," which may overlaid onto the existing research literature. These dimensions can be termed, following the six questions listed above: (1) family structure; (2) associational solidarity; (3) affectual solidarity; (4) consensual solidarity; (5) functional solidarity; and (6) normative solidarity. The operational measurement of these dimensions, as reflected in several dozen surveys concerning aging and families, is categorized by Bengtson and Schrader (1982).

Family Structure. Structure refers to the descriptive characteristics of the lineage being examined. Characteristics of family structure are important to include in any analysis of lineage generations because they provide important information about the *potential* for mobilizing the family as an interpersonal support system in old age. Three types of characteristics appear most relevant for understanding the structure of families: (1) the *number* of living grandparents, children, and grandchildren; (2) the *geographic proximity* of these lineage members; and (3) the *composition* of the households containing these members (e.g., is three-generational co-residence characteristics of lineage?).

Other rarely examined structural characteristics of the lineage include: (1) lineage typologies (e.g., are there differences between same-sex and cross-sex lineage relations?), and (2) the number and type of "fictive kin"—those who have been raised by or psychologically adopted into the lineage (see also our discussion in the next section of "lineage consciousness" as a variation on Mannheim's generational consciousness). Stepchildren may be an important component of the defined lineage, especially for some ethnic subpopulations (Jackson, 1970; Cantor, 1976; Bengtson and Burton, 1980). Children-in-law may assume important roles in "kin-keeping" (Rosenthal, et al., 1981). In both practical and theoretical terms, gerontologists should examine the social rather than the biological definitions of kinship.

The substantive findings regarding family structure clearly suggest that children do constitute a viable resource for the majority of aged family members. Over 90 percent of the elderly have been married at least once (U.S. Bureau of Census, 1973; Shanas, 1978), and approximately 80 percent of those over age 65 have at least one living child (Shanas, 1980). Furthermore, national survey data indicate that a majority of the older

persons in the United States are members of three-generation (38%) or four-generation (36%) families (Shanas, 1978). Table 3 presents Shanas's findings concerning the change over time in this aspect of family structure. From 1962 to 1975, the percentage of older people who reported only three-generation families decreased, while the percentage of older people reporting four-generation families increased. Table 3 also reveals an increase in the percentage of one-generation families, usually consisting of unmarried (widowed, divorced, or never-married) persons (18% to 21%).

Rarely do the generations share living quarters; rather, "intimacy at a distance" (Rosenmayr and Kockeis, 1965) appears to predominate. Only 17 percent of the unmarried elderly and 12 percent of the married lived with a child in Shanas's 1975 nationwide American survey (Shanas, 1978). For those relatively few elderly who do live with one of their offspring, most live with an unmarried child (Shanas, 1978). Despite the large amount of geographic mobility in American society, most older people are not isolated physically from their children. Approximately 75 percent of the elderly who have children live within one-half hour of one of them (Shanas, 1979a). These patterns clearly suggest that the elderly are not without families, at least on the level of family structure.

Family structure describes the resource context of the family for the older person; as such, it is a crucial aspect of a family support system. However, the presence of children and grandchildren only indicates the existence of these family role relationships; it does nothing to describe the nature of the relationship (Rossi, 1980).

Association. The most frequently studied dimension of intergenerational family solidarity is *associational solidarity*: "the degree to which members of a lineage are in contact with one another, engage in shared behaviors, and interact in common activities" (Bengtson and Schrader, 1982). Associational solidarity is indicated by several in-

TABLE 3. Number of Generations in the Family and Presence of Near Relatives, Persons Aged 65 and Over: 1962 and 1975 (Percentage Distribution).

Number of Generations in Family and Presence of Near Relatives	1962	1975
One	18	21
Childless, unmarried, no siblings	3	3
Childless, unmarried, with siblings	8	10
Childless, married, no siblings	2	2
Childless, married, with siblings	5	6
Two	6	4
One son only, no grandchildren	2	2
One daughter only, no grandchildren	2	2
More than one child, no grandchildren	2	1
Three	44	38
One son only, with grandchildren	4	5
One daughter only, with grandchildren	6	7
More than one child, with grandchildren	35	27
Four	32	36
One child only, with grandchildren and great-grandchildren	3	5
More than one child, with grandchildren and great-grandchildren	29	31
TOTAL	100	100
N =[a]	(2436)	(5728)

[a] The N (number) of cases for 1962 is unweighted; the numnber of cases for 1975 is weighted.
SOURCE: Shanas, 1978, Table 5–2A.

dices, including the overall *frequency* of intergenerational interaction. While the primary concern of this dimension is on the frequency of contact, another relevant factor to consider is the type of interaction. *Formal and ritualistic* contact (such as family reunions and ceremonies) versus *informal* interaction (brief visits or discussions) may have qualitatively different effects upon lineage members. A further distinction of associational solidarity may be seen in the mode of contact. Contact between generations may be "face-to-face"; or indirect communication (e.g., the telephone or letters) may be the primary vehicle for maintaining social ties. In a highly mobile industrial society, those family members who are not geographically close may still maintain relatively close contact through the use of indirect contact mechanisms (Wilkening et al., 1972).

A substantial amount of research has looked at the associational solidarity of aged parents. On the whole, adult generation members are in frequent contact with one

another. Shanas (1973) found that in 1961 about 80 percent of American elderly were in contact with at least one of their children on a regular basis. National survey data from a 1975 follow-up (Shanas, 1980) indicate a similar pattern. Approximately one-half of all old people with children saw one of those children on the day of the interview or the day immediately prior to the interview. If the time-frame for contact is expanded to one week before the interview, three-quarters of the elderly parents had been in contact with one of their children. In short, the finding that most older persons are *not* isolated from their children is well supported in the existing literature (Brown, 1960; Litwak, 1960; Rosow, 1967; Adams, 1968; Shanas et al., 1968; Shanas, 1978, 1979a,b; Rosenberg, 1970; NCOA, 1975; and see also Riley and Foner, 1968, Ch. 23; Troll, 1971; Abu-Laban, 1978; Troll et al., 1979; Lee, 1980; Streib and Beck, 1980; and Rossi, 1980, for summary reviews of the literature).

Figure 2 illustrates lineage association pat-

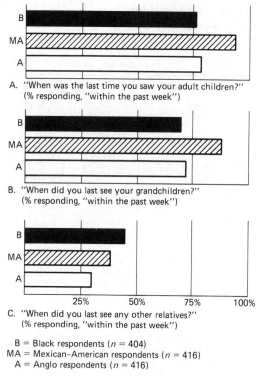

A. "When was the last time you saw your adult children?"
(% responding, "within the past week")

B. "When did you last see your grandchildren?"
(% responding, "within the past week")

C. "When did you last see any other relatives?"
(% responding, "within the past week")

B = Black respondents (n = 404)
MA = Mexican-American respondents (n = 416)
A = Anglo respondents (n = 416)

Figure 2. Family interaction for blacks, Mexican-Americans, and Anglos (age 60-74).

terns in a study of three ethnic groups (Bengtson and Burton, 1980). In this study, contact between aged parents and their adult children was quite high, with blacks and Anglos approximating the national survey data from Shanas (1978). The Mexican-Americans, however, were much more likely than the other two groups to have had contact with their children within the past week (88%). These and other data (Cantor, 1976) point to the intracohort differentiation that exists between subgroups (e.g., between ethnic American subpopulations of approximately the same birth cohort).

While the research of intergenerational solidarity has emphasized the linkage of older parents with their adult children, Figure 2 illustrates two added facets of lineage relations. Grandparent–grandchildren contact also is quite common—at least in these data—with 71 percent of the blacks, 86 percent of the Mexican-Americans, and 74 per-

cent of the Anglos reporting weekly contact. Contact with other relatives is less frequent, with only 34 percent of the Anglos reporting weekly contact. Extended family interaction, however, is more prevalent among blacks (47%) and Mexican-Americans (41%) than among Anglos.

That grandparent–grandchild interaction is frequent is generally supported by other studies. According to Hill et al. (1970, p. 62), approximately one-third of the geographically proximal grandparents and grandchildren in their three-generation study reported weekly contact. Hays and Mindell (1973) reported this contact to be greater for blacks compared with Anglos, thus suggesting a greater importance of the grandparent role for blacks. Others (e.g., Hill et al., 1970; Rossi, 1980; Hagestad, 1984; Gronvold and Bengtson, 1982; Mangen and Westbrook, 1982) have suggested that the parent generation serves as a bridge between the grandparent and grandchild generations, thus providing continuity to the passage of the generations through the family.

Affect. While the frequency of intergenerational contact is indeed an important dimension of solidarity, contact cannot be equated with quality. *Affectual solidarity* refers to the degree of positive sentiment present in the intergenerational relationship. Often this has been treated as a global concept (Adams, 1968; Cantor, 1976), although a more specific measure may be indexed by feelings of trust, understanding, respect, fairness, affection, and warmth (Bengtson and Black, 1973; Gronvold and Bengtson, 1982). Still another perspective is to examine satisfaction with the amount of intergenerational contact (Bengtson and Burton, 1980) or feelings of concern for other lineage members (Marshall et al., 1983). Finally it is important to assess both the respondent's own definition of the relationship and the definitions attributed to the other member of the intergenerational relationship.

Relatively little research has assessed directly the quality of the intergenerational relationship. In general it may be said that both aged parents and their adult children express high levels of regard for one another (Brown, 1960; Bengtson and Black, 1973); this regard may be a continuation of lifelong patterns of positive affect (Lowenthal et al., 1975). Complete satisfaction regarding the amount of contact was expressed by over two-thirds of the cross-ethnic Los Angeles sample reported by Bengtson and Burton (1980), though Anglos expressed the lowest satisfaction (56%). Interestingly, there appears to be little relationship between the frequency of intergenerational contact and the quality of the relationship (Adams, 1968; Angres, 1975), but this weak relationship may be a function of the very high level of affect present in most intergenerational relationships.

Consensus. A fourth aspect of solidarity in lineage relationships concerns the degree of consensus or conflict in beliefs or orientations external to the family. Political issues, religious practices or ideologies, global value orientation—these are often sources of family traditions on the other hand or of protracted disagreements and conflict on the other. To what extent are elderly family members similar to their middle-aged children and to their grandchildren in matters of opinion and orientation? Are the attributed differences greater than or less than the actual differences? How do such intrafamily congruences or differences compare with intercohort contrasts, given the popular literature concerning the "generation gap"? This is the area in which the contrast between lineage generations and cohort-based generations is most clear, and where the majority of empirical research has been conducted.

While many studies have focused on the real or attributed contrasts between cohorts in opinions and orientations, few analyses have addressed the issue of lineage or parent–child continuities in the face of cohort contrasts (for exceptions, see Connell, 1972; Bengtson, 1975; Jennings and Niemi, 1975). Fewer still have focused on differences between the elderly and their descendants (for exceptions, see Streib, 1965a; Hill et al., 1970; Fengler and Wood, 1972; Kalish and

Johnson, 1972; Bengtson, 1975). From the empirical evidence to date, however, several tentative observations concerning consensus in lineage generations can be made.

The first observation concerns "selective continuity" (Bengtson, 1970) in contrasts and similarities between elderly parents and their middle-aged children. On some issues the similarities between the two generations predominate, for example, in values regarding fatalism and optimism (Hill et al., 1970) and global value orientations concerning materialism versus humanism (Bengtson, 1975). These findings suggest the existence of consensus within families. For other variables, however, parent–child contrasts were marked: Values regarding child rearing (Hill et al., 1970) and value orientations toward collectivism versus individualism (Bengtson, 1975) suggest substantial differences between generations related by lineage membership.

Whether the similarities evidenced can be attributed to transmission or socialization effects operating long into adulthood is, of course, equivocal. They may be due to common location within the social structure or to the impact of commonly experienced historical or period effects; that is, the similarities may have developed in parallel rather than in series (Connell, 1972). Similarly, it is not possible to determine whether the contrasts are reflective of life-cycle (maturational) or cohort (generational) effect that outweigh similarities that result from socialization influences or other correlates of family lineage.

A second observation concerns contrasts or continuities evidenced among nonadjacent generations: grandparents and grandchildren. Some surveys have pointed to surprising similarities between youth and their grandparents, for example, in orientations toward materialism versus humanism (Bengtson, 1975) and in norms regarding expressive behavior (Kalish and Johnson, 1972). Such considerations have caused several observers to consider the young and the old as "generation gap allies" (Kalish, 1969) or as representing a potential coalition against the middle generation. However, in the three-generation study of values (Bengtson, 1975), the similarities between grandparents and grandchildren could not be explained unequivocally as lineage effects; rather, grandparent–grandchild similarities appear to be the result of common situational variables, perhaps reflecting period effects.

A third implication that can be derived from the literature on consensual solidarity addresses the relative importance of perceived (attributed) similarity versus objective similarity. Evidence (Acock and Bengtson, 1980) suggests that the beliefs attributed by children to their parents are more predictive of the child's beliefs than are the actual beliefs of the parents. While this research was conducted with middle-aged children and their young adult offspring, it is plausible to suggest that the perceived consensual solidarity in the lineage may be more important to the elderly (grandparent) generation, given their "developmental stake" in attributing continuity to lineage relationships (Bengtson and Kuypers, 1971).

The assessment of consensual solidarity usually is developed within the context of studies focusing on socialization. Thus, emphasis is on the microsocial level of analysis, where individual-level concepts are interrelated within lineages. Consensus, however, is an aggregate (microstructural) property, so that socialization processes yield varying degrees of consensus; therefore, inquiries about the determinants and consequences of this variation within a lineage should be the focus of future research. Are consensus-oriented lineages more emotionally supportive of their aged family members and thus predictive of their mental health? Can a cohesive lineage more rapidly marshal its forces to provide instrumental assistance to the aged? These and other questions are suggested by the microstructural approach to the study of lineages. Unfortunately, research at present is lacking in this area. It remains an important agenda for future studies.

Functional Solidarity. A fifth dimension of family solidarity refers to the degree to which financial assistance and service exchanges occur among family members. It is within this context that much of the recent concern for family support systems (Fengler and Goodrich, 1979; Lopata, 1979; Zarit et al., 1980; Brody, 1981; Crossman et al., 1981; Treas, 1977; Thoits, 1982) is found. Mutual aid and assistance is an important aspect of the modified extended family structure; it appears from previous research that aged parents will turn to their children for assistance before they will ask for help from their siblings (Sussman and Burchinal, 1962; Shanas, 1978).

A number of different studies have examined the exchange aspect of intergenerational relationships. Contrary to the belief of an asymmetric pattern of exchanges between the generations, the available evidence indicates that assistance is given and received by both aged parents and their adult offspring (Schorr, 1960; Sussman, 1965; Streib, 1965a; Adams, 1968; Shanas et al., 1968; Hill et al., 1970; Troll, 1971; Lopata, 1979; Shanas, 1979b). Table 4, reprinted from Shanas's (1978) national survey of the aged, suggests that family assistance to the elderly in times of health-related crisis is especially important. Immediate family members, especially the spouse (if present) and children, provide "the major social support of the elderly in time of illness" (Shanas, 1979b, p. 173).

Assistance between the generations is not restricted to times of crisis, however. Table 4 documents the change from 1962 to 1975 in patterns of exchange evident in Shanas's (1978) surveys. These data clearly suggest that older persons have become more integrated into their families over time. While 60 percent of the 1962 aged sample assisted their children, by 1975 this figure had increased to over 70 percent. An even greater increase is noted with help to grandchildren. The kinds of help given by older people to their children most frequently consist of gifts (69%), help with grandchildren (36%), and housekeeping (28%) (Shanas, 1978; higher estimates presented by NCOA, 1975, pp. 74–75). During this same period of time, however, virtually no change in the overall receipt of assistance by older persons is noted, and re-

TABLE 4. Percentage of Persons Aged 65 and Over Who Give Help to Children, Grandchildren, and Great-grandchildren, and Who Receive Help from Children, by Sex.

| | | 1962 | | | 1975 | |
Help Patterns	Men	Women	All	Men	Women	All
Gives help to children	59	60	60	72	69	71
N = [a]	(901)	(1111)	(2012)	(1850)	(2701)	(4551)
Gives help to grandchildren	50	49	50	73	69	71
N = [a]	(826)	(1025)	(1851)	(1734)	(2603)	(4337)
Gives help to great-grandchildren	—[c]	—	—	40	50	46
N = [a]	—[c]	—	—	(678)	(1413)	(2091)
Receives help from children[b]	61	75	69	62	72	68
Regular money help	1	7	4	2	4	3
Occasional money gifts	25	43	35	10	16	14
Makes medical payments	—[c]	—	—	*	2	2
Makes medical payments	—[c]	—	—	(1847)	(2703)	(4549)

* Less than 1% after rounding.
[a] The N (number) of cases for 1962 is unweighted; the number of cases for 1975 is weighted.
[b] Includes help from relatives in 1962.
[c] Data not reported in 1962.
SOURCE: Shanas, 1978, Table 7–17A.

ports of financial assistance to the elderly have substantially declined (Shanas, 1978).

While it is apparent that some degree of reciprocity characterizes exchanges between the generations (Shanas, 1978), some evidence also points to an imbalance (Hill et al., 1970), with the older generation receiving more than they give and the middle-aged parent generation being squeezed with demands from above and below in the generational hierarchy. Troll et al. (1979, p. 90), in summarizing these data, suggest that aged parents "continue to give to their children one way or another for as long as they are able." Given the operation of the norms of reciprocity (Gouldner, 1960) and distributive justice (Homans, 1961) in American society, together with the cultural value of independence, it is not surprising that aged parents continue in exchange relationships with their children and grandchildren for as long as possible. The exchanges may be symbolic, or they may represent crucial elements of the financial or service supports for the recipient generation.

A slightly different perspective on functional solidarity involves the analysis of exchanges between the generations as represented in inheritance and explicit legacy-making (Rosenfeld, 1979a,b). Elderly individuals often invest a considerable amount of energy in arranging disposition of their estate after death. The analysis of Sussman et al. (1970) suggests that these intergenerational transfers often follow carefully considered norms of reciprocity and equity by the families involved. Sussman et al. note that there is a conscious effort to effect a smooth continuity with minimal hassles among descendants over claims and priorities (p. 291). Their study of inheritance patterns of 659 family systems suggests a great deal of care is given to the just distribution of intergenerational property inheritance. Rosenfeld's (1979a) analysis of inheritance patterns suggests that the will is often used as a form of social control, especially among middle- and lower-income families. Thus, the disposition of family wealth does not necessarily lead to greater family cohesion;

rather, the disinherited may well dispute the will through the courts, thus leading to a deterioration in the solidarity of the family.

Normative Solidarity. A sixth dimension of intergenerational family solidarity addresses the norms of familism held by members of the family. To what extent are children expected to live proximal to and provide support and assistance to their aged parents? In a similar vein, to what extent do aged parents expect this of their children? Much of the early work addressing this dimension focused on the nature of extended kin relations in a modern industrialized society (e.g., Litwak, 1960), with the conclusion that American society is characterized by a modified-extended family with expectations of assistance but without the expectation of geographic proximity (see, e.g., Kerckhoff, 1966a,b). Indeed, as Kerckhoff points out, aged parents who hold norms favoring a fully extended family are likely to be disappointed because attainment of these expectations may not be realistic.

Blenkner (1965) discussed normative solidarity in the context of filial *maturity*, a characteristic hypothesized to develop during middle age, which permits the middle-aged child to see his/her parents as legitimate recipients of assistance. Filial maturity is analogous to normative solidarity in that it suggests a greater involvement of the middle-aged child in the life of the parent.

Three observations are germane to the relatively unexplored issue of normative solidarity between aged parents and middle-aged children. First, Lozier and Althouse (1974) show that norms may be adhered to for a variety of reasons, including an aversion to the negative community opinion which could obtain from violations of the normative content. Thus, the matter of sanctions, which are used to enforce the norms of familism, is an important consideration (Hagestad, 1981, 1982; Emerson, 1981). The techniques of norm enforcement await further examination in the gerontological literature.

Second, in a manner analogous to the discussion of consensual solidarity above, research must distinguish between the normative content (i.e., what are the expected behaviors in an intergenerational relationship) and the consensus regarding the normative content. A child who adheres to strong norms of familism while his/her aged parent seeks autonomy will likely provide little emotional comfort to the parent.

Third, there may be important within-cohort (subcultural) variations regarding norms about filial obligations in old age. In the Los Angeles survey of three ethnic groups (Bengtson and Burton, 1980), for example, almost 70 percent of Mexican-Americans agreed with the statement, "It is the obligation of adult children to care for their parents." By contrast, only 2.3 percent of the blacks, and 27 percent of the Anglo respondents, indicated agreement with this norm.

The entire area of normative solidarity deserves greater attention in the gerontological literature (see Rossi, 1980). Typically, research has assumed that intergenerational interaction was obligatory. This assumption is questionable, however, in light of evidence suggesting that the normative expectations tend to be greater for daughters than for sons (Hagestad, 1977).

Implications of the Lineage Perspective for Theory and Research

From this review on the lineage perspective of intergenerational relations, seven points appear especially relevant when considering the older generation in the family:

1. It must be noted continually that the nature of family intergenerational relations changes over time. Not only does the structure of the family change, but so do the interpersonal relationships in terms of association, affect, exchanges, and consensus. Both members of the parent–child dyad are in continuous and bilateral negotiation concerning the issues at stake. Not only do the individuals in the dyad change with aging, but the relationship itself is continuously altered over time (Bengtson and Black, 1973. Nowhere does the dynamic and processual quality of social systems become more evident than when one is examining the situational responses of a particular family unit

over time, whether months, years, or decades (Elder, 1984).

2. The general level of solidarity indices between generations in contemporary American families appears to be quite high, contrary to popular assumptions.

3. The perception of intergenerational solidarity, however, varies between generations. For example, the elderly perceive slightly more affection, while the younger see more exchanges of services. These differential perceptions of intergenerational interaction can be accounted for by an awareness of contrasting "developmental stakes": personal investments in the relationship that are a function of developmental concerns and that color the assessment of them (Bengtson and Kuypers, 1971).

4. The patterns of similarity and contrast in attitudes and values are complex; but it seems safe to say that there is no marked indication of conflict in orientations between aged parents and their children or grandchildren. In short, the "generation gap"—perceived at both cohort and lineage levels—turns out, upon careful inspection, to be a dubious set of contrasts reflecting more consensus than cleavage (Acock, 1984; Bengtson, 1975).

5. The family constitutes a viable resource in the support systems of older adults. However, researchers and practice-oriented professionals need to locate the family within the total network of possible alternative caregivers, thus enabling the development of a balanced, multifaceted convoy of social support (Kahn and Antonucci, 1981).

6. Research addressing intergenerational relations within the family requires further conceptual explication and theoretical development. Greater attention and concern for measurement is needed (Mangen et al., 1982), as is an explicit program of theory construction. In part, this program will require an expansion of our definition of the intergenerational relationship. Simply examining aged parents and their adult children is not sufficient; attention must be given to in-law relations and the role they play in lineage generations. Furthermore, we will better understand the family if we view it

within the context of alternatives (e.g., friendship, church organizations, etc.). In part, this examination of alternatives suggests a network theory approach to studying the microstructure of the family.

7. Many principles and concepts in macrosocial analysis must be taken into account and are particularly useful in understanding the microlevel concerns of generational inquiry. The historical setting of intergenerational interaction (Elder, 1984), the facts of differential birth cohort composition and characteristics (Easterlin, 1980), the availability of roles (Riley et al., 1972), and the nature of institutions and values in the surrounding culture (Rossi, 1980)—these contextual issues influence relations between generations and place boundaries around the ongoing processes of transmission and interaction. For these reasons we emphasize the need for a more historical, as well as macrostructural, examination of generational interaction within the families.

THE SOCIAL CONFLICT PERSPECTIVE: AGE RELATIONSHIPS AND CONSCIOUSNESS

The traditional cohort and lineage conceptualizations discussed above provide ways to describe different bases of social and behavioral differentiation between individuals and groups. But in addition, differences based on age, birth cohort, or ranked descent within lineage may form the basis for structuring the social relationships among individuals and between groups. Examination of such social bonding on the basis of age suggests two important questions. First, to what extent are the social relationships so structured mediated by awareness or by what may be termed "consciousness"? That is, if, age, as expressed in birth cohort or lineage generations, affects social relationships in a systematic way, is it because of a conscious recognition of relative position or group affiliation based on these criteria? Second, to what extent does consciousness relate to conflict between groups?

Much recent policy and research attention has focused on the possibility of cohort or age-based conflict. Some commentators note an implicit social contract between the generations—between young, middle-aged, and elderly cohorts—governing transfer payments and obligations (Torrey, 1979). This implicit contract may or may not involve conflict over its negotiation or fulfillment. Almost inevitably, however, there will be at least the possibility of conflict in interests as population contrasts affect the numbers and proportions of young and old dependents or the fertility of cohorts of varying sizes.

The perspective that most directly addresses the issue of age groups as dynamic, change-producing collectivities arising at certain points of time is that of Karl Mannheim [1952 (1928)]. For Mannheim, the basis for human behavior is an awareness of consciousness of positions and expectations and of the possibility for collective action to alter existing social institutions. The point at which an individual entered the historical experience reflects one such positional basis, and Mannheim explored this generational phenomenon with particular reference to the political realm [1952 (1928), 1956].

If an individual's encounter with history contains the possibility for structuring a generational experience, then an individual's experience of commonality based on age grouping or relative age has a similar potential for the development of age-based experiences. To each age group might pertain a consciousness of kind, of distinctiveness from others who differ in their historical location or in their age. Thus, it is useful to explore generational conflict in a variety of settings with differential awareness or consciousness. We begin by examining age-set phenomena in some relatively nonmodernized societies and then turn to more modern contexts exhibiting generational cohort-based differentiation.

Age-Sets and Age-Grades

Anthropological analyses of social organization often have noted the importance of age-sets, age classes, age-grades, and genealogical levels (see Ch. 9. by Keith in this *Handbook*). As early as 1929, Radcliffe-

Brown sought to regularize the terminology by distinguishing between an *age-set* and an *age-grade*. He defined the former as "a recognized and sometimes organized group consisting of persons (often male persons only) who are of the same age." He pointed out that "once a person enters a given age-set, whether at birth or by initiation, he remains a member of the same set for the remainder of his life" (Radcliffe-Brown, 1929).

In contrast, an age-grade refers to ". . . recognized divisions of the life of an individual as he passes from infancy to old age. Thus each person passes successively into one grade after another, and, if he lives long enough, through the whole series—infant, young boy, youth, young married man, elder, or whatever it may be" (Radcliffe-Brown, 1929). He pointed out that in East Africa, "where the age-organization is highly elaborated, each age-set normally passes from one grade to another as a whole." That is, in contrast to age-grade membership, which changes with aging, age-set membership is retained throughout life.

It is important to recognize the interaction of age-set and age-group membership as they structure life experiences. In this terminology, all age-sets are cohorts. However, Stewart (1977, p. 21, n. 11) has noted that "not all cohorts are age-sets, for an age-set—in contrast to a cohort—is by *definition* an entity created and recognized by the society in which it exists." In this sense an age-set is similar to a sociological generation as defined by Mannheim [1952 (1928)], in being nonarbitrary (Needham, 1974). It is not an observer's analytical category, but a category with a reality in a society.

Foner and Kertzer (1978) examined the dynamic relationship between these two organizing principles, as the members of an age-set collectively progress through the age grades. In most age-set societies prestige and power generally increase with progression to older age grades, at least up to the oldest such age grade. Inauguration of people into an age-set is only roughly correlated with chronological age. Their induction, as well as the timing of the age-set's transitions through age grades, is affected by power imbalances, and the process is fraught with tensions and conflicts: "Age sets which stand to lose prestige and power through the transition often do what they can to delay the ceremonies; those who stand to gain exert pressure to expedite the rites (Foner and Kertzer, 1978; p. 1089).

If the passage of age-sets through the age-graded social structure is frequently accompanied by tension and conflict, it is also the case that these tensions and conflicts are mitigated in many instances by other aspects of social organization. First, the cross-cutting of age-set and age-grade differentiation can weaken the basis for antagonistic group formation based on one principle alone. In more modernized societies, the age-grade system is much more flexible than in the age-set societies described by Foner and Kertzer, Stewart, Needham, and others. Second, there is some socialization for transitions between age-grades, and much role rehearsal for the important transitions (perhaps akin to inauguration into an age-set) into full-time labor-force participation and into marriage (Foner and Kertzer, 1978, p. 1097). There also is flexibility in age-grading through such devices as skipping grades in elementary school, early or "mature" entry into college, and flexible retirement. Third, transition processes themselves can undergo collective changes in timing, formality, extent of role-discontinuity, and scope of role involvement. Examples would be changes in legal ages for voting, drinking, driving, marriage, and retirement.

A significant source of change in transition processes is the fact that successive cohorts differ from one another in size. Waring (1976) has noted that transition points are adjusted to accommodate changes in the size of cohorts. People may be encouraged to prolong schooling if the labor market cannot accommodate a large cohort of entrants. Successive cohorts then, can, make their way through age transitions in a manner quite different from preceding cohorts (Cain, 1964, 1967; Elder, 1978, 1979). But it is important to note that the transition processes are always potential sources of tension, if not conflict, between age groups.

The Relevance of Age-Grades in Industrialized Societies: Conflict and Solidarity

In relatively modernized societies, there does not appear to be a great deal of overt conflict based on age groupings, birth cohorts, or lineage rank position. However, from a gerontological perspective, it might be argued that age-related conflict is reflected by a decline in the status of the aged with industrialization, as it is unlikely that the aged would voluntarily accept a loss of status. A number of theorists have asserted that the aged have lost status with modernization. It is noteworthy that, in developing their arguments, they have relied variously on age, generational cohort, or lineage as the unit of analysis and explanation.

Perhaps the earliest statement of the "aging and modernization thesis" was presented by Emile Durkheim in 1893. He related the decline in the status of the aged in large measure to changes in lineage relationships as a consequence of geographical dispersion of the family. In traditional society, Durkheim argued, old people "enjoy a prestige with generations reared under their eyes and their direction which nothing can replace. The child, indeed, is aware of his inferiority before the older persons surrounding him" [Durkheim, 1964 (1893), p. 293]. Urbanization, however, leads a male child to migrate away from his parents to the city where, "to be sure, there are men older than himself as well, but they are not the same as those he obeyed in his infancy. The respect he has for them is then less, and by nature more conventional, for it corresponds to no reality, present or past . . . he can then respect them only by analogy" [Durkheim, 1964 (1893), p. 294]. Durkheim concluded that this conventional respect is reinforced by a cohort effect: the fact that the "worship of age is steadily weakening with civilization."

Burgess (1960) implicated *changing lin-*

eage relationships as a cause of the declining status of the aged in a different way, suggesting that the change from the extended to the conjugal family deprived the older person of meaningful roles. As a result of "modern economic trends," Burgess says the aged "lost their former favored position in the extended family. No longer were the grandfather and the grandmother the center of the absorbing social life of their descendants but often became unwanted hangers-on, taking part by sufferance in the activities of their children and grandchildren" (Burgess, 1960, p. 20).

Cowgill's (1974) more systematic explication of a theory of aging and modernization postulates a lineage-relevant change similar to that argued by Burgess. Cowgill saw urbanization leading to migration followed by neolocal marriage and residential segregation. However, he also postulated a cohort effect similar to that argued by Durkheim, by suggesting that increased literacy, the movement of the younger cohorts into new urban areas, high-technology occupations, and intergenerational social mobility all would conspire to segregate the young from the old morally and intellectually. This segregation would serve, within and outside of families, to create a status inversion and increased social distance between old and young, parents and children. Finally, Cowgill's theory of aging and modernization draws on a third basis of age-related social differentiation. Advances in health technology, he argues, lead to greater longevity and facilitate protracted labor-force involvement of older people, thereby establishing a basis for intergenerational competition. This argument rests on a notion of age-based solidarity arising at different points in the age structure of society, pitting different age groups against each other.

In these formulations the status or relative power of the aged is postulated to decline at the same time that there are increased bases for competition or conflict between the young and the old and increased alienation between them. Elaboration and critique of the modernization thesis have focused on the error of assuming uniform and linear societal modernization or age-status declines (Palmore and Whittington, 1971; Palmore and Manton, 1974; Bengtson et al., 1975; Dowd, 1980). Critics have presented evidence that older people were not highly integrated into the family (or at least the household) and society in the premodern period (Laslett, 1976, 1977; Fisher, 1977, p. 23; Stearns, 1981), or they have questioned the direct link between modernization and declining status, suggesting that modernization and industrialization affected different social classes and industrial sectors in different ways (Dowd, 1980; Quadagno, 1983).

In general, however, it is agreed by most gerontologists that the status of the aged has decreased as a function of increased competition among age groups. There are several factors suggesting that such conflict will increase in the future, and other considerations indicating a diminution of potential age-related conflict.

Factors Increasing the Likelihood of Conflict. The major cause postulated to increase age-related conflict concerns the economic implications of population aging, especially as related to persistent small sizes of new birth cohorts and the aging of the large birth cohorts of the years 1945–60 (Easterlin, 1962, 1968, 1978). Bergman (1979) has suggested that the growing dependency ratio may lead to "intergenerational conflicts around the problem of a growing leisure group, of relatively non-old retirees versus a working population that has to bear a considerable share of the transfer of resources to the elderly" (p. 45).

Second, the actual reallocation of resources from one age group to another is not likely to be a smooth process. Different constituencies may balk at budget cuts in their sector of interest in order to finance transfer payments or health and hospital care for the aged (Hudson, 1978, p. 30; Marshall, 1983). Evidence of intergenerational tension along those lines has already been observed (Gustaitis, 1980). Also, as the aged come to be perceived as less deprived than they were formerly, pressures will mount against allocation of extensive societal resources to them (Hudson, 1978, p. 80). If the "young-old" come to be viewed as a leisure class, they may become the target of increasing resentment by the young, especially if they increase their demands for age-based services (Neugarten, 1970, p. 17).

Third, it has been suggested that the future aged increasingly will come to represent a minority group or a subculture. From one perspective, real differences between the aged and others in the society will lead to their formation into a conscious, self-identifying, politically relevant group vis-à-vis the rest of society. Rose (1962, 1965) envisioned a vigorous group of the aged developing collective concerns in fighting for adequate health care, and he argued that the increasing geographical separation of the young from the old, as well as segregation of the old through retirement, would contribute to such development. Other social scientists have argued that the aged are generally viewed stereotypically by the young (Barron, 1953; Butler, 1969; McTavish, 1971); that they are a highly visible minority target group for such views (Breen, 1960; Jarvis, 1972; Newman, 1973); that they continue to be discriminated against in the labor market (Breen, 1960; Palmore, 1969; Sheppard 1970; Palmore and Whittington, 1971); and that they are segregated increasingly through housing patterns (Breen, 1960; Lofland, 1968; Palmore and Whittington, 1971; Shulman, 1980). These factors, if exacerbated by future demographic trends, might lead to increasing age differentiation, which protrays the old as a relatively devalued and nonproductive group in the eyes of younger generations (Ragan, 1977; Davis and Van den Oever, 1981; Kutza, 1981, p. 133; and for reviews of this literature, see Streib, 1965b, and Abu-Laban and Abu-Laban, 1980).

Common social location does not, of course, automatically lead to a common recognition of this location. Consciousness does not follow inexorably from position. However, the bulk of the evidence suggests a fourth consideration: that age consciousness is in fact on the rise, recognized by older people and the young and officially by the state and the administrative bureaucracy, as it faces a "fiscal crisis" (O'Connor, 1973; Guillemard, 1980; Marshall, 1980; Myles, 1980; Cutler, 1981; Townsend, 1981).

Cutler (1981, p. 151) has argued that age consciousness is itself a generational cohort phenomenon in the U.S. context: "Contemporary older persons were already in their old years when society began to develop programs and institutions for the elderly. By contrast, tomorrow's elderly are already being socialized to the potential politics of age. To put this another way, one of the most dramatic contrasts between the elderly of today and the cohorts who will constitute the elderly of tomorrow is the portion of their life-span in which they and the society in which they live have been age conscious."

Factors Diminishing the Likelihood of Conflict. At the same time, a number of arguments suggest that the basis for generational conflict will decline or that other factors will keep it in check. First is the suggestion that age may be a less important dimension of social differentiation that it has been in the past—that we are moving toward an "age-irrelevant society" (Neugarten, 1970). As successive cohorts entering the later years become more similar in income security, health, educational attainment, and general social values, the objective basis for conflict between age groups diminishes.

A second factor mitigating against intergenerational conflict arises from implications of the age-stratification perspective (see Ch. 13 by Riley in this *Handbook*). While the imagery of age-stratification theory derives from that of class theory (Riley, 1971), in practice age-stratification theorists have tended to conduct their analyses with the nominal concepts of equal-interval age strata and birth cohorts, rather than with concepts such as those of class or generation, which presume that there are potentially identifiable social groups in dynamic, conflictual relations with one another. Age strata are cross-cut by the flow of successive cohorts.

Thus, the potential for group consciousness (e.g., identification of common interests based on entry into the retirement years) is reduced by the fact that each successive cohort to enter an age group has had its unique encounter with history, thereby differing in values and interests from preceding cohorts to enter that age category (Foner, 1974). While the passing out of older cohorts from the society and the replenishment of the society with new cohorts represents a fundamental process of social change, the process is generally viewed as a smooth one. As Riley (1976) points out, aging results in mobility or cohort flow, which continually leads younger persons to see where their future interests lie, while allowing the aged to sympathize tolerantly with the frustrations of the young.

A third factor may be other, non-age memberships and identifications. From the age-stratification perspective, Foner (1974) argued that membership in non-age-graded associations provides opportunities for cross-socialization to opposing political views. Material disputes, for example, cut across generation or cohort boundaries to unite workers of all ages in a fight to protect class interests. Alternatively, it has been argued that the potential for open generational conflict has been reduced by a state-fostered ideology that individualizes the understanding of age-based differentials (Guillemard, 1977, 1980). This approach emphasizes the role of ideology, especially as fostered by the state, in reducing overt conflict based on age-group differentiation.

Fourth, gender issues may decrease the extent to which age or generation becomes a basis for collective consciousness and action. The fact that the older population, from a purely demographic point of view, overrepresents women, especially in the very old age groups, takes on great significance in light of the association of later-life poverty with being female (Collins, 1978; Economic Council of Canada, 1979; Townsend, 1979, pp. 796–797). This may lead feminists to define issues such as income security and the need for health care as women's issues rather than age-related issues, since they are, in principle, neither one nor the other exclusively.

Finally, as noted in our earlier review of "generation gap" phenomena, lineage bonds may well act to diminish the possibility of age- or generation-based conflict. The same argument may be used at microsocial levels of interaction outside the family arena (Foner, 1974).

Class and Age Group Conflict

Social class may interact with age or generational cohort issues to either reinforce or counteract pressures toward the development of consciousness and political action based on age or generational affiliation. With respect to class issues, both Dowd (1980) of the United States and Guillemard (1977, 1980) of France argue that retirement leads to a reinforcement and exaggeration of the gap between the rich and the poor. Myles (1980, p. 327) states that, by replacing a relatively small proportion of pre-retirement income in contrast to most Western pension systems, the Canadian system "has produced an elderly population which is equal but poor." One issue often ignored concerns the impact of this prospect on the decision of the young-old not to retire.

While less dramatic than the "ideational" focus on the generation gap phenomena of the late 1960s, current tensions between different age groups appear to relate to more fundamental, structurally rooted issues such as income security in later life, job security in midlife, and meeting rising health care costs. Thomas (1976) has shown how, in sixteenth- and seventeenth-century England, a low demand for labor led younger workers to support shoekeepers when they initiated a process of gradual exclusion against their older workers. A modern-day parallel exists whenever senior workers are encouraged to take early retirement (Tindale and Marshall, 1980).

Tindale (1980a,b, 1981) has recently shown how age and generational cohort differences interact with class factors around issues of job security. In a study of secondary school teachers, he found substantial evidence of tension between older and younger teachers as a result of the smaller entering cohorts that led to school closings; and also as a result of continuing political–economic factors such as tight budgets for school boards, which led to cutbacks in the boards studied. Some teachers were declared "redundant" (i.e., they lost their jobs); younger and middle-aged teachers lacked promotion opportunities; and teachers with seniority were able to "bump" those with less seniority out of their jobs in order to preserve a job for themselves within the same school board. Age is relevant for this analysis because it relates to seniority. Teachers in the middle-age category were found less likely than the young or old to perceive pressures for early retirement—a proposed solution to this dilemma—because they were old enough to be secure in seniority but not old enough to be subject to such pressures to retire early. Cohort factors are relevant because different cohorts of teachers vary in their own educational attainment and related job skills and in their labor market experience. Class is important because the way in which generational tension is manifested is shaped by the contradictory class location of the teaching profession: teachers are to some degree professionals who seek "professional" solutions and to another degree employees who are more likely to opt for "unionist" solutions. Thus, the intersection of class and generational cohort factors might exacerbate conflict between the generations (Tindale and Marshall, 1980).

To the extent that age and cohort differences can be considered the basis for collective social action (and therefore age-based or generational-based interaction), the question can be asked: What is the relationship between generational relations and class relations? In a Marxist view, the fundamental relationship of groups of individuals to the means of production describes their class situation, and class dynamics would be at the root of any other form of differentiation and relationship such as might be based on age,

generation, or even lineage. Other views give primacy to cultural factors (e.g., Stearns, 1981) and view age and generational relations as relatively independent of class relationships. However, given the importance of economic issues in structuring relationships and the debates about the possibilities of generational conflict, it is clear that class and generational issues should be investigated simultaneously in their interaction.

Implications of the Social Conflict Perspective for Research and Theory

1. Issues discussed in this section touch on the most pressing policy issues addressed by gerontologists: relations between age groups, the importance of age in the political economy, the status of the aged compared to other age groups, and the relative importance of age for all of the above compared with cohort and lineage as a basis for differentiation and interaction between groups. Not surprisingly, these issues are touched upon in many of the major theoretical domains of social gerontology: age-stratification theory, the modernization theory of aging, the aged minority group and age-irrelevance theses, and the politics and political economy of aging.

2. An important implication of age consciousness for the social conflict perspective is what might be called the "process" dimension—as proposed by Riley Johnson and Foner's (1972) earliest conceptualization of age stratification and age consciousness. That is, like the linkage between class, class consciousness, and class-based social action, there is a process inherent in age, age consciousness, and age-based social action. Age and class are the "objective" facts: all individuals have them. Under some historical circumstances, class/age membership may lead to consciousness; there is increasing evidence that older persons are becoming more age-conscious. Furthermore, under some circumstances, such consciousness—even if it "touches" many but only "saturates" a few—could lead to age-based collective social action. Thus, one implication of age

consciousness must be a continuous reconnection, on the part of social gerontologists, of cohort phenomena, age consciousness, and the events and trends of the larger society. Changes in the societal organization of the political economy (e.g., Social Security or Medicare benefits) could stimulate age-based political activity (which includes both the activity of the elderly and the backlash to such activity and claims).

3. The development of sound theory has been hampered by conceptual ambiguities, especially concerning concepts such as age group, cohort, and generation that are often used interchangeably or nonspecifically. In particular, precision of conceptualization must recognize the different analytical goals pursued by those who would describe differences between groups. The latter objective calls for a social conflict perspective, which returns us to Mannheim's insights concerning generations, age groups, and social change.

CONCLUSIONS

The purpose of this chapter has been to examine the growing volume of empirical evidence concerning differences between, and relationships across, groups and individuals of contrasting age. Our departure has been the interface between the aging of individuals and the succession of cohorts—continuous processes within the broader society and within the family that produce change in social organization.

Within the past decade, a great deal of scholarly effort has addressed differences related to aging and age groupings, as well as relations in the context of aging and succession. There are five principal conclusions that follow from our review of the literature.

First, the terminological confusion surrounding the term "generations" can be traced to its multiple meanings: "to come into existence" refers to several classes of social phenomena, each with significant but slightly different implications for issues of succession, differences, and relationships between groups of contrasting age. Thus the term "generations" should properly be used only with an adjective of relativity: "family" generations or "cohort" generations. This clarification is necessary because of the many conflicting connotations with which the term has been used in the social sciences, as well as in popular parlance. It is our belief that confusion will continue to mar generational analyses unless conceptual distinctions are maintained.

Second, there appear to be three major distinctive issues involved in the examination of differences between, and relations across, groups that differ by year of birth and therefore age. These suggest three different but interrelated conceptual approaches to issues of succession, contrasts, and relationships between age groups. Cohorts ("an aggregate of individuals who were born within the same time interval") carry with them the accumulation of both individual and collective experience, which can lead to differentiation with other cohorts born at a different time. Lineages ("ranked descent within the family") can be studied in terms of solidarity and status, cohesion and consensus, and power and influence. A social conflict perspective focusing on the implications of age-conscious aggregates—what Mannheim called "generation units"— can be useful in exploring issues of between-cohort conflict and within-cohort differentiation and solidarity, with their resulting consequences for macrosocial change.

Third, the explanation of differences between contemporaneous age groups requires the examination of three competing hypotheses simultaneously, since aging (maturation), cohort membership, and period (historical) effects are each plausible hypotheses for contrasts between age groups.

Fourth, while the nature of family intergenerational relations changes over time, available research suggests relatively high levels of solidarity between parents and children, even in the face of the multiple demands of caretaking for the young and the old. Contemporary families do, in general, constitute a viable resource in the support systems of older adults; a focus on the multiple dimensions of "family intergenerational solidarity" helps to highlight the variable resources of aging families.

Fifth, to the extent that an individual's orientations are shaped by his or her encounter with history, the experience of commonality based on age grouping or relative age has a similar potential for the development of age-based experience. To each age group or age-set may obtain a consciousness of kind, of distinctiveness from others who differ in their historical location or in their age, and of similarity with others in the age-set. Examination of age-set phenomena provides a clue to the prospect of conflict or solidarity between birth cohorts, even within industrialized societies, as appeared to exist in the late 1960s and may emerge again among the aged of the 1990s.

REFERENCES

Abramson, P. R. 1975. *Generational Change in American Politics*. Lexington, Mass.: D. C. Heath.

Abu-Laban, S. M. 1978. The family life of older Canadians. *Canadian Home Economics Journal* (Jan.):16–25.

Abu-Laban, S. M., and Abu-Laban, B. 1980. Women and the aged as minority groups: A critique. *In* V. W. Marshall (ed.), *Aging in Canada: Social Perspectives*. Toronto: Fitzhenry and Whiteside.

Acock, A. 1984. Parents and their children: The study of inter-generational influence. *Sociology and Social Research* 68 (2): 151–171.

Acock, A., and Bengtson, V. L. 1980. Socialization and attribution processes: Actual versus perceived similarity among parents and youth. *Journal of Marriage and the Family* 42(3):501–515.

Adams, B. N. 1968. *Kinship in an Urban Setting*. Chicago: Markham.

Ahammer, J. M., and Baltes, P. B. 1972. Objective versus perceived age differences in personality: How do adolescents, adults and older people view themselves and each other? *Journal of Gerontology* 27:46–51.

Angres, S. 1975. Integrational relations and value congruence between young adults and their mothers. Unpublished doctoral dissertation, University of Chicago.

Axelrod, R. 1972. Where the votes come from: An analysis of electoral coalitions, 1952–1968. *American Political Science Review* 66:11–20.

Baltes, P. B. 1968. Longitudinal and cross-sectional sequences in the study of age and generation effects. *Human Development* 11:145–171.

Baltes, P. B. 1979. Life-span developmental psychology: Some converging observations on history and theory. *In* P. Baltes and O. Brim (eds.), *Life-Span Development and Behavior*, Vol. 2. New York: Academic Press.

Baltes, P. B., Cornelius, S. W., and Nesselroade, J. R. 1979. Cohort effects in developmental psychology. *In* J. R. Nesselroade and P. Baltes (eds.), *Longitudinal Research in the Study Behavior*. New York: Academic Press.

Barron, M. L. 1953. Minority group characteristics of the aged in American society. *Journal of Gerontology* 8:477–482.

Bengtson, V. L. 1970. The "generation gap": A review and typology of social-psychological perspectives. *Youth and Society* 2:7–21.

Bengtson, V. L. 1971. Inter-age differences in perception and the generation gap. *The Gerontologist* 11 (Part II):85–90.

Bengtson, V. L. 1975. Generation and family effects in value socialization. *American Sociological Review* 40:358–371.

Bengtson, V. L., and Black, K. D. 1973. Intergenerational relations and continuities in socialization. *In* P. Baltes and K. W. Schaie (eds.), *Life-Span Developmental Psychology: Personality and Socialization*. New York: Van Nostrand Reinhold.

Bengtson, V. L., and Burton, L. 1980. Families and support systems among three ethnic groups. Paper presented at the 33rd annual meeting of the Gerontological Society, San Diego, Calif., Nov. 21–25.

Bengtson, V. L., and Cutler, N. E. 1976. Generations and intergenerational relations: Perspectives on age groups and social change. *In* R. H. Binstock and E. Shanas (eds.), *Handbook of Aging and the Social Sciences,* 1st ed., pp. 130–159. New York: Van Nostrand Reinhold.

Bengtson, V. L., and Kuypers, J. 1971. Generational differences and the developmental stake. *Aging and Human Development* 2:249–260.

Bengtson, V. L., and Schrader, S. 1982. Parent–child relations. *In* D. J. Mangen and W. A. Peterson (eds.), *Research Instruments in Social Gerontology*, Vol. 2. Minneapolis: University of Minnesota Press.

Bengtson, V. L., and Treas, J. 1980. The changing family context of mental health and aging. *In* R. B. Sloane and J. E. Birren (eds.), *Handbook of Mental Health and Aging*. Englewood Cliffs, N.J.: Prentice-Hall.

Bengtson, V. L., Dowd, J. J., Smith, D. H., and Inkeles, A. 1975. Modernization, modernity, and perceptions of aging: A cross-cultural study. *Journal of Gerontology* 30(6):688–695.

Bengtson, V. L., Olander, E., and Haddad, A. 1976. The "generation gap" and aging family members: Toward a conceptual model. *In* J. F. Gubrium (ed.), *Time, Self and Roles in Old Age*. New York: Behavioral Publications.

Bergman, S. 1979. The future of human welfare of the aged. *In* H. Orimo, K. Shimada, M. Iriki, and D. Maeda (eds.), *Recent Advances in Gerontology*. Amsterdam–Oxford–Princeton: *Exerpta Medica,* pp. 44–48.

Blenkner, M. 1965. Social work and family relationships in later life with some thoughts on filial maturity. *In* E. Shanas and G. F. Streib (eds.), *Social Structure and the Family.* Englewood Cliffs, N.J.: Prentice-Hall.

Breen, L. Z. 1960. The aging individual. *In* C. Tibbits (ed.), *Handbook of Social Gerontology.* Chicago: University of Chicago Press.

Brody, E. M. 1981. Women in the middle and family help to older people. *The Gerontologist* 21(5):471–480.

Brown, R. 1960. Family structure and social isolation of older persons. *Journal of Gerontology* 15:170–174.

Burgess, E. W. 1960. Aging in Western culture. *In* E. W. Burgess (ed.), *Aging in Western Societies.* Chicago: University of Chicago Press.

Butler, R. N. 1969. Age-ism: Another form of bigotry. *The Gerontologist* 9:243–246.

Cain, L. D., Jr. 1964. Life course and social structure. *In* R. E. L. Faris (ed.), *Handbook of Modern Sociology.* Chicago: Rand McNally and Company.

Cain, L. D., Jr. 1967. Age status and generational phenomena: The new old people in contemporary America. *The Gerontologist* 7:83–92.

Campbell, A. 1962. Social and psychological determinants of voter behavior. *In* W. Donahue and C. Tibbits (eds.), *Politics of Age.* Ann Arbor: University of Michigan Press.

Campbell, A., Converse, P., Miller, W., and Stokes, D. 1960. *The American Voter.* New York: John Wiley.

Cantor, M. H. 1976. The configuration and intensity of the informal support system in a New York City elderly population. Paper presented at the 29th annual meeting of the Gerontological Society, New York, Oct. 13–17.

Carlsson, G., and Karlsson, K. 1970. Age cohorts and the generation of generations. *American Sociological Review* 35:710–718.

Collins, K. 1978. *Women and Pensions.* Ottawa: The Canadian Council on Social Development.

Connell, R. W. 1972. Political socialization in the American family: The evidence re-examined. *Public Opinion Quarterly* 36:321–333.

Converse, P. E., Miller, W., Rusk, J., and Wolfe, A. 1969. Continuity and change in American politics: Parties and issues in the 1968 election. *American Political Science Review* 63:1083–1105.

Cowgill, D. O. 1974. Aging and modernization: A revision of the theory. *In* J. F. Gubrium (ed.), *Late Life: Communities and Environmental Policy.* Springfield, Ill.: Charles C. Thomas.

Cowgill, D., and Holmes, L. (eds.). 1972. *Aging and Modernization.* New York: Appleton-Century-Crofts.

Crittenden, J. A. 1962. Aging and party affiliation. *Public Opinion Quarterly* 36:321–333.

Crossman, L., London, C., and Barry, C. 1981. Older

women caring for disabled spouses: A model for supportive services. *The Gerontologist* 21(5):464–470.

Cutler, N. E. 1969. Generation, maturation, and party affiliation: A cohort analysis. *Public Opinion Quarterly* 33:583–588.

Cutler, N. E. 1975. Toward a political generations conception of socialization. *In* D. C. Schwartz and S. K. Schwartz (eds.), *New Directions in Political Socialization.* New York: Free Press.

Cutler, N. E. 1981. Political characteristics of elderly cohorts of the twenty-first century. *In* S. B. Kiesler, J. N. Morgan, and V. K. Oppenheimer (eds.), *Aging: Social Issues.* New York: Academic Press.

Cutler, N. E. 1983. Political behavior of the aged. *In* D. S. Woodruff and J. E. Birren (eds.), *Aging: Scientific Perspectives and Social Issues,* 2nd ed. New York: Van Nostrand Reinhold.

Cutler, N. E., and Mimms, G. E. 1977. The birth and death of political cohorts: A demographic transition approach to the decline of partisanship in the United States. Paper presented at the 9th annual meeting of the Western Political Science Association, Apr. 24.

Cutler, N. E. and Schmidhauser, J. R. 1975. Age and political behavior. *In* D. S. Woodruff and J. E. Birren (eds.), *Aging: Scientific Perspectives and Social Issues.* New York: Van Nostrand Reinhold.

Davis, K., and Van den Oever, P. 1981. Age relations and public policy in advanced industrial societies. *Population and Development Review* 7(1):1–18.

Dilthey, W. 1924. Ueber das studium der geschichte der wissenschaften vom menschen, der gesellschaft und dem staat. *In* W. Dilthey (ed.), *Gesammelte Schriften,* Vol. 5. Leipzig and Berlin: Teubner.

Dowd, J. J. 1980. *Stratification among the Aged.* Monterey, Calif.: Brooks-Cole.

Dunkle-Schetter, C., and Wortman, C. 1981. Dilemmas of social support: Parallels between victimization and aging. *In* S. Kesser, J. Morgan, and K. Oppenheimer (eds.), *Aging: Social Change.* New York: Academic Press.

Durkheim, E. 1964 (1893). *The Division of Labor in Society.* New York: The Free Press.

Easterlin, R. A. 1962. The American baby boom in historical perspective. Occasional paper #79, National Bureau of Economic Research.

Easterlin, R. A. 1968. *Population, Labor Force, and Long Swings in Economic Growth: The American Experience.* New York: National Bureau of Economic Research (Columbia University Press).

Easterlin, R. A. 1978. What will 1984 be like? Socioeconomic implications of recent twists in age structure. *Demography* 15(4):397–432.

Easterlin, R. A. 1980. *Birth and Fortune: The Impact of Numbers on Personal Welfare.* New York: Basic Books.

Economic Council of Canada. 1979. *One in Three.* Ottawa: Economic Council of Canada.

Elder, G. H. Jr. 1975. Age differentiation and the life course. *Annual Review of Sociology,* Vol. 1, pp. 165–190.

Elder, G. H. Jr. 1978. Approaches to social change and the family. *In* J. Demos and S. S. Boocock (eds.), *Turning Points.* Chicago: University of Chicago Press.

Elder, G. H. Jr. 1979. Historical change in life patterns and personality. *In* P. B. Baltes and O. G. Brim, Jr. (eds.), *Life-Span Development and Behavior,* Vol. 2. New York: Academic Press.

Elder, G. H. Jr. 1984. Family and kinship in sociological perspective. *In* R. Parke (ed.), *The Family: NSSE Yearbook.* Chicago: University of Chicago Press.

Emerson, R. M. 1981. On last resorts. *American Journal of Sociology* 87(1):1–22.

Esler, A. 1972. Youth in revolt: The French generation of 1830. *In* R. J. Bezucha (ed.), *Modern European History.* Lexington, Mass. D. C. Heath.

Featherman, D. 1983. Life-Span perspectives in social science research. *In* P. B. Baltes and O. G. Brim, Jr. (eds.), *Life-Span Development and Behavior*, Vol. 5, New York: Academic Press.

Fengler, A. P., and Goodrich, N. 1979. Wives of elderly disabled men: The hidden patients. *The Gerontologist* 19(2):175–183.

Fengler, A. P., and Wood, V. 1972. The generation gap: An analysis of studies on contemporary issues. *The Gerontologist* 12:124–128.

Feuer, L. 1969. *The Conflict of Generations.* New York: Basic Books.

Fisher, D. H. 1977. *Growing Old in America.* New York: Oxford University Press.

Foner, A. 1974. Age stratification and age conflict in politics. *American Sociological Review* 39:187–196.

Foner, A., and Kertzer, D. 1978. Transitions over the life course: Lessons from age-set societies. *American Journal of Sociology* 83(5):1081–1104.

Glenn, N. D. 1977. *Cohort Analysis.* Beverly Hills, Calif.: Sage Publications.

Glenn, N. D., and Hefner, T. 1972. Further evidence on aging and party identification. *Public Opinion Quarterly* 36:31–47.

Gouldner, A. 1960. The norm of reciprocity. *American Sociological Review* 25:161–178.

Gronvold, R., and Bengtson, V. L. 1982. Measuring the quality of parent–child relations in old age. Paper presented at the 35th annual meeting of the Gerontological Society of America, Boston, Mass., Nov. 19–23.

Guillemard, A.-M. 1977. The call to activity amongst the old: Rehabilitation or regimentation. *In* B. Wigdor (ed.), *Canadian Gerontological Collection I, Selected Papers.* Toronto: Canadian Association on Gerontology.

Guillemard, A.-M. 1980. *Le Vieillesse et l'Etat.* Paris: Presses Universitaires de France.

Gustaitis, R. 1980. Old versus young in Florida: Preview of an aging America. *Saturday Review* 16:10–14.

Hagestad, G. O. 1977. Role change in adulthood: The transition to the empty nest. Unpublished manuscript, Committee on Human Development, University of Chicago.

Hagestad, G. O. 1981. Problems and promises in the social psychology of intergenerational relations. *In* R. W. Fogel, E. Hatfield, S. B. Kiesler, and E. Shanas (eds.), *Aging.* New York: Academic Press.

Hagestad, G. O. 1982. Life-phase analysis. *In* D. J. Mangen and W. Peterson (eds.), *Research Instruments in Gerontology,* Vol. I. Minneapolis: University of Minnesota Press.

Hagestad, G. O. 1984. The continuous bond: A dynamic perspective on parent–child relations between adults. *In* M. Perlmutter (ed.), *Minnesota Symposia on Child Psychology,* Vol. 17. Princeton, N.J.: Lawrence Erlbaum.

Hareven, T. K. 1981. Historical changes in the timing of family transitions: Their impact on generational relations. *In* R. W. Fogel, E. Hatfield, S. B. Kiesler and E. Shanas (eds.), *Aging: Stability and Change in the Family.* New York: Academic Press.

Hays, W. C., and Mindel, C. H. 1973. Extended kinship relations in black and white families. *Journal of Marriage and the Family* 35:51–56.

Hill, R., Foote, N., Aldous, J., Carlson, R., and MacDonald, R. 1970. *Family Development in Three Generations.* Cambridge, Mass.: Schenkman.

Hobcraft, J., Menken, J., and Preston, S. 1982. Age, period, and cohort effects in demography: A review. *Population Index* 48:4–43.

Hogan, D. P. 1981. *Transitions and Social Change.* New York: Academic Press.

Homans, G. C. 1961. *Social Behavior: Its Elementary Forms.* New York: Harcourt Brace.

Hudson, R. B., and Binstock, R. H. 1976. Political systems and aging. *In* R. H. Binstock and E. Shanas (eds.), *Handbook of Aging and the Social Sciences,* 1st ed., pp. 369–400. New York: Van Nostrand Reinhold.

Hudson, R. B. 1978. Emerging pressures on public policies for the aging. *Society* 15(5):30–33.

Hyman, H. H. 1972. Cohort analysis. *In* H. H. Hyman, (ed.), *Secondary Analysis of Sample Surveys: Principles, Procedures, and Potentialities.* New York: John Wiley.

Jackson, J. 1970. Kinship relations among urban blacks. *Journal of Social and Behavioral Sciencies* 61:5–17.

Jarvis, G. K. 1972. Canadian old people as a deviant minority. *In* C. L. Boydell, C. F. Grindstaff, and P. C. Whitehead (eds.), *Deviant Behavior and Societal Reactions.* Toronto: Holt, Rinehart & Winston.

Jennings, M. K., and Niemi, R. G. 1975. Continuity and change in political orientations: A longitudinal study of two generations. *American Political Science Review* 69:1316–1335.

Jennings, M. K., and Niemi, R. G. 1981. *Generations and Politics.* Princeton, N.J.: Princeton University Press.

Kahn, R. L., and Antonucci, T. C. 1981. Convoys of social support: A life course approach. *In* S. Kiesler, J. Morgan, and V. Oppenheimer (eds.), *Aging: So-*

cial Change, pp. 383–405. New York: Academic Press.

Kalish, R. 1969. The young and old as generation gap allies. *The Gerontologist* 9:63–89.

Kalish, R., and Johnson, A. 1972. Value similarities and differences in three generations of women. *Journal of Marriage and the Family* 34:49–54.

Kerckhoff, A. C. 1966a. Norm-value clusters and the strain toward consistency among older married couples. *In* I. Simpson and J. McKinney (eds.), *Social Aspects of Aging*, pp. 138–159. Durham, N.C.: Duke University Press.

Kerckhoff, A. C. 1966b. Husband–wife expectations and reactions to retirement. *In* I. Simpson and J. McKinney (eds.), *Social Aspects of Aging*, pp. 160–172. Durham, N.C.: Duke University Press.

Kertzer, D. I. 1983. Generation as a sociological problem. *Annual Review of Sociology* 9:125–149.

Kirkpatrick, S. A. (ed.). 1974. *Quantitative Analysis of Political Data*. Columbus, Ohio: Charles E. Merrill.

Kutza, E. A. 1981. *The Benefits of Old Age: Social Welfare Policy for the Elderly*. Chicago: University of Chicago Press.

Laslett, P. 1976. Societal development and aging. *In* R. Binstock and E. Shanas (eds.), *Handbook of Aging and the Social Sciences*, 1st ed., pp. 87–116. New York: Van Nostrand Reinhold.

Laslett, P. 1977. *Family Life and Illicit Love in Earlier Generations*. Cambridge, Mass.: Cambridge University Press.

Lee, G. 1980. Kinship in the seventies: A decade review of research and theory. *Journal of Marriage and the Family* 42(4):923–934.

Litwak, E. 1960. Reference group theory, bureaucratic career and neighborhood primary group cohesion. *Sociometry* 23:72–84.

Lofland, J. 1968. The youth ghetto. *Journal of Higher Education* 39(3):121–143.

Lopata, H. Z. 1979. *Women as Widows: Support Systems*. New York: Elsevier-North Holland.

Lowenthal, M. F., Thurnher, M., and Chiriboga, D. 1975. *Four Stages of Life*. San Francisco, Calif.: Jossey-Bass.

Lozier, J., and Althouse, R. 1974. Special enforcement of behavior toward elders in an Appalachian mountain settlement. *The Gerontologist* 14:69–80.

Mangen, D. J., and Westbrook, G. J. 1982. Measuring intergenerational family solidarity. Paper presented at the 35th annual meeting of the Gerontological Society of America, Boston, Mass., Nov. 19–23.

Mangen, D. J., Peterson, W. A., and Sanders, R. 1982. Introduction. *In* D. J. Mangen and W. A. Peterson (eds.), *Research Instruments in Social Gerontology*, Vol. 1. Minneapolis: University of Minnesota Press.

Mannheim, K. 1952. The problem of generations (1928). In D. Kecskemeti (ed.), *Essays on the Sociology of Knowledge*. London: Routledge and Kegan Paul.

Mannheim, K. 1956. The problem of the intelligentsia: An inquiry into its past and present role. *In* E. Mannheim and P. Kecskemeti (eds.), *Essays on the Sociology of Culture*. London: Routledge and Kegan Paul.

Marias, J. 1968. Generations: The concept. *In: International Encyclopedia of Social Sciences*, Vol. 6. New York: Free Press.

Marmor, T. R. 1973. *The Politics of Medicare*. Chicago: Aldine.

Marshall, V. W. 1980. Aging in an aging society: Cohort differences, conflicts and challenges. *Multiculturalism* 4(1):6–13.

Marshall, V. W. 1983. Generations, age groups, and cohorts: Conceptual distinctions. *Canadian Journal of Aging* 2(2):109–120.

Marshall, V. W., Rosenthal, C. J., and Synge, J. S. 1983. Concerns about parental health. *In* Elizabeth W. Markson (ed.), *Older Women*. Lexington and Toronto: D. C. Health.

Mason, K., Mason, W., Winsborough, H., and Poole, W. 1973. Some methodological issues in cohort analysis of archival data. *American Sociological Review* 38:242–257.

McTavish, D. G. 1971. Perceptions of old people: A review of research methodologies and findings. *The Gerontologist* 11(4):90–102.

McTavish, D. G. 1982. Perceptions of old people. *In* D. J. Mangen and W. A. Peterson (eds.), *Research Instruments in Social Gerontology*, Vol. I, Ch. 12. Minneapolis: University of Minnesota Press.

Myles, J. F. 1980. The aged, the state, and the structure of inequality. *In* J. Harp and J. Hofley (eds.), *Structured Inequality in Canada*. Toronto: Prentice-Hall.

Nash, L. 1978. The concepts of existence: Greek origins of generational thought. *Daedalus* 107:1–28.

National Council on Aging. 1975. *The Myth and Reality of Aging in America*. Washington, D.C.: NCOA, Inc.

Needham, R. 1974. Age, category and descent. *In* R. Needham (ed.), *Remarks and Inventions*. London: Tavistock.

Neugarten, B. L. 1970. The old and the young in modern societies. *American Behavioral Scientist* 14(1):13–24.

Newman, W. M. 1973. *American Pluralism: A Study of Minority Groups and Social Theory*. New York: Harper and Row.

O'Connor, J. 1973. *The Fiscal Crisis of the State*. New York: St. Martin's Press.

Ortega y Gasset, J. 1933 (1923). *The Modern Theme*. New York: W. W. Norton.

Ortega y Gasset, J. 1962. *Man and Crisis*. New York: W. W. Norton.

Palmore, E. 1969. Sociological aspects of aging. *In* E. W. Busse and E. Pfeiffer (eds.), *Behavior and Adaptation in Late Life*. Boston: Little Brown.

Palmore, E. 1978. When can age, period and cohort be separated? *Social Forces* 57(1):282–295.

Palmore, E., and Manton, K. 1974. Modernization and the status of the aged: International correlations. *Journal of Gerontology* 29(2):205–210.

Palmore, E., and Whittington, F. 1971. Trends in the relative status of the aged. *Social Forces* 50:84–91.

Pomper, G. M. 1972. From confusion to clarity: Issues and American voting 1956-1968. *American Political Science Review* 66:415–428.

Pomper, G. M. 1975. *Voter's Choice: Varieties of American Electoral Behavior*. New York: Dodd, Mead.

Quadagno, J. 1980. *Aging in Early Industrial Society: Work, Family, and Social Policy in Nineteenth-Century England*. New York: Academic Press.

Radcliffe-Brown, A. R. 1929. Age organization—Terminology. Letter to the editor. *Man* 29:21.

Ragan, P. K. 1977. Another look at the politicizing of old age: Can we expect a backlash effect? *The Urban and Social Change Review* 10(2):6–13.

Riley, M. W. 1971. Social gerontology and the age stratification of society. *The Gerontologist* 11(1):79–87.

Riley, M. W. 1976. Age strata in social systems. *In* R. H. Binstock and E. Shanas (eds.), *Handbook of Aging and Social Sciences*, 1st ed., pp. 189–217. New York: Van Nostrand Reinhold Company.

Riley, M. W., and Foner, A. 1968. *Aging and Society*, Vol. I, *An Inventory of Research Findings*. New York: Russell Sage Foundation.

Riley, M. W., Johnson, M., and Foner, A. 1972. *Aging and Society*, Vol. III, *A Sociology of Age Stratification*. New York: Russell Sage Foundation.

Robinson, B., and Thurnher, M. 1979. Taking care of aged parents: A family cycle transition. *The Gerontologist* 19(6):586–593.

Rose, A. 1962. The subculture of the aging: A topic for sociological research. *The Gerontologist* 2:123–127.

Rose, A. M. 1965. The subculture of aging: A framework for research in social gerontology. *In* A. M. Rose and W. A. Peterson (eds.), *Older People and Their Social World*, Philadelphia: F. A. Davis.

Rosenberg, G. 1970. *The Worker Grows Old: Poverty and Isolation in the City*. San Francisco, Calif.: Jossey-Bass.

Rosenfeld, J. 1979a. *The Legacy of Aging: Inheritance and Disinheritance in Social Perspective*. Norwood, N.J.: Abbey Publishing Company.

Rosenfeld, J. 1979b. Bequests from resident to resident: Inheritance in a retirement community. *The Gerontologist* 19 (Dec.):594–600.

Rosenmayr, L., and Kockeis, E. 1965. *Umwelt und Familis alter Menschen*. Berlin: Neuwied.

Rosenthal, C., Marshall, V., and Synge, J. 1981. Maintaining intergenerational relations: Kinkeeping. Paper presented at the 34th annual meeting of the Gerontological Society of America, Toronto, Ontario, Nov. 19.

Rosow, I. 1967. *Social Integration of the Aged*. New York: Free Press.

Rosow, I. 1978. What is a cohort and why? *Human Development* 21:65–75.

Rossi, A. S. 1980. Aging and parenthood in the middle years. *In* P. Baltes and O. G. Brim (eds.), *Life-Span Development and Behavior*, Vol. 2. New York: Academic Press.

Ryder, N. B. 1965. The cohort as a concept in the study of social change. *American Sociological Review* 30(6):834–861.

Scammon, R., and Wattenberg, B. J. 1970. *The Real Majority*. New York: Coward, McCann & Geoghegan.

Schaie, K. W. 1965. A general model for the study of developmental problems. *Psychological Bulletin* 64:72–107.

Schaie, K. W. 1979. The primary mental abilities in adulthood: An exploration of the development of psychometric intelligence. In P. Baltes and O. Brim (eds.), *Life-Span Development and Behavior*, Vol. 2. New York: Academic Press.

Scheider, W. 1981. The November 4 vote for president: What did it mean? In A. Runney (ed.), *The American Elections of 1980*. Washington, D.C.: American Enterprise Institute.

Schorr, A. L. 1960. *Filial Responsibility in the Modern American Family*. Washington, D.C.: Social Security Administration.

Schreiber, E. M., and Marsden, L. R. 1972. Age and opinions on a program of medical aid. *Journal of Gerontology* 27:95–101.

Shanas, E. 1973. Family-kin networks and aging in cross-cultural perspective. *Journal of Marriage and the Family* 35 (Aug.):505–511.

Shanas, E. 1978. *A National Survey of the Aged*. Final report to the Administration on Aging. Washington, D.C.: U.S. Department of Health, Education and Welfare.

Shanas, E. 1979a. The family as a social support in old age. *The Gerontologist* 19(2):169–174.

Shanas, E. 1979b. Social myth as hypothesis: The case of the family relations of old people. *The Gerontologist* 19(1):3–9.

Shanas, E. 1980. Older people and their families: The new pioneers. *Journal of Marriage and the Family* 42(1):9–15.

Shanas, E., Townsend, P., Wedderburn, D., Friis, H., Milhøj, P., and Stehouwer, J. 1968. *Old People in Three Industrial Societies*. New York: Atherton Press.

Sheppard, H. L. 1970. Toward an industrial gerontology. *In* H. L. Sheppard (ed.), *Toward an Industrial Gerontology*. Cambridge, Mass.: Schenkman.

Shulman, N. 1980. The aging of urban Canada. *In* V. W. Marshall (ed.), *Aging in Canada: Social Perspectives*. Toronto: Fitzhenry and Whiteside.

Spitzer, A. B. 1973. The historical problem of generations. *American Historical Review* 78:1353–1385.

Stearns, P. 1981. The modernization controversy. A socio-historical analysis of retirement in nineteenth century England. Paper presented at meeting of the American Sociological Association, New York, Aug. 21.

Stewart, F. H. 1977. *Fundamentals of Age-Group Systems*. New York: Academic Press.

Streib, G. F. 1965a. Intergenerational relations: Perspectives of the two generations on the older parent. *Journal of Marriage and the Family* 27:469–476.

Streib, G. F. 1965b. Are the aged a minority group? *In* A. W. Gouldner and S. M. Miller (eds.), *Applied Sociology*. New York: Free Press.

Streib, G. F., and Beck, R. W. 1980. The family in later life: A decade review. *Journal of Marriage and the Family* 43(4):81–99.

Sussman, M. B. 1965. Relationships of adult children with their parents in the United States. *In* E. Shanas and G. Streib (eds.), *Social Structure and the Family: Generational Relations*. Englewood Cliffs, N.J.: Prentice-Hall.

Sussman, M. B., and Burchinal, L. 1962. Kin family network: Unheralded structure in current conceptualizations of family functioning. *Marriage and Family Living* 24:231–240.

Sussman, M. B., Cates, J., and Smith, D. 1970. *The Family and Inheritance*. New York: Russell Sage Foundation.

Thoits, P. A. 1982. Conceptual, methodological, and theoretical problems in the study of social support as a buffer against life stress. *Journal of Health and Social Behavior* 23:145–158.

Thomas, K. 1976. Age and authority in early modern England. *Proceedings of the British Academy* 42:206–248.

Tindale, J. A. 1980a. Generational conflict: Class and cohort reactions among Ontario public secondary school teachers. Doctoral dissertation, Department of Sociology, York University, Toronto, Canada.

Tindale, J. A. 1980b. The intersection of age and class interests in a profession facing external pressure. Paper presented at the 9th Annual Scientific and Educational Meeting, Canadian Association on Gerontology, Saskatoon, Saskatchewan, May 2.

Tindale, J. A. 1981. Contradictory location and social closure: The OSSTF is fight for occupational control. Paper presented at the 4th annual conference on Blue Collar Workers and Their Communities, McMaster University, Hamilton, Ontario, Canada.

Tindale, J. A., and Marshall, V. W. 1980. A generational-conflict perspective for gerontology. *In* V. W. Marshall (ed.), *Aging in Canada: Social Perspectives*. Toronto: Fitzhenry and Whiteside.

Torrey, B. B. 1979. The demographics of aging: Implications for pension policy. *Aging: Agenda for the Eighties*. Washington, D.C.: A National Journal Issues Book.

Townsend, P. 1979. *Poverty in the United Kingdom: A Survey of Household Resources and Standards of Living*. Berkeley: University of California Press.

Townsend, P. 1981. The structured dependency of the elderly: A creation of social policy in the twentieth century. *Ageing and Society* 1:5–28.

Treas, Judith. 1977. Family support systems for the aged: Some social and demographic considerations. *The Gerontologist* 17 (6): 486–491.

Troll, L. 1971. The family of later life: A decade review. *Journal of Marriage and the Family* 33:263–290.

Troll, L., and Bengtson, V. 1979. Generations in the Family. *In* W. R. Burr, R. Hill, F. I. Nye, and I. L. Reiss (eds.), *Contemporary Theories about the Family,* Vol. 1. New York: Free Press.

Troll, L. E., Miller, S. J., and Atchley, R. C. 1979. *Families in Later Life*. Monterey, Calif. Wadsworth Publishing Company.

Turner, R. J. 1981. Social support as a contingency in psychological well-being. *Journal of Health and Social Behavior* 22 (Dec.):357–367.

U.S. Bureau of the Census. 1973. Some demographic aspects of aging in the United States. *Current Population Reports*, Series P–23, No. 43 (Feb.). Washington, D.C.: U.S. Government Printing Office.

Waring, J. M. 1976. Social replenishment and social change: The problem of disordered cohort flow. *In* A. Foner (ed.), *Age in Society*. Beverly Hills, Calif.: Sage Publications.

Wilkening, E. A., Guerrero, S., and Ginsberg, S. 1972. Distance and intergenerational ties of farm families. *Sociological Quarterly* 13 (Summer):383–396.

Zarit, S. H., Reever, K. E., and Bach-Peterson, J. 1980. Relatives of the impaired elderly: Correlates of feelings of burden. *The Gerontologist* 20(6):649–655.

12
SOCIAL STRATIFICATION AND AGING

Gordon F. Streib
University of Florida

Social stratification is a universal process dealing with the distribution of valued things—status, esteem, wealth, privilege, and power. It has broad implications for understanding the interrelations of older people with other age groups and with their age peers within a dynamic society, for it involves the patterns of inequality present in all societies, resulting in strata or classes that are demarcated and have differential privileges. Central to the definition of stratification are the core values—the beliefs and rationalizations that justify the institutional structure of the society.

Stratification in old age has a different theoretical orientation from stratification during the adult years—the working years. Because the elderly are largely outside the labor force, their economic standing depends either on an accumulation of past assets or on income transfer payments. The economic situation of the elderly is closely linked to past behaviors—lifetime employment, savings, home ownership, investments, participation in pension plans, and so on, rather than to their present activities. Furthermore, public transfer programs such as Social Security, public housing, and tax reductions have major effects on the standing of the elderly.

Most writers on stratification give little or no attention to the elderly. Statistical materials on such matters as income, occupation, and education are presented in terms of age categories, but there is little attempt to describe and analyze the dynamics and variability of retirement, the pension system, and their importance for understanding stratification. There is no analysis of how biological aging, as a universal phenomenon, affects stratification. For these reasons, social gerontologists should devote greater attention to this subject.*

This chapter is based on three main assumptions: (1) various age groupings are differentially valued, by individuals, by aggregates, and by collectivities; (2) there is marked stratification within the aged category itself, due to the heterogeneity of older people and their previous employment status; and (3) there is continuity in stratification patterns through the life cycle.

*Since the first edition of the *Handbook* was published, there has been increasing interest in social stratification and aging as evidenced by many publications: the appearance of a textbook, *Stratification Among the Aged* (Dowd, 1980); literature reviews in the *Annual Review of Sociology* (Haug, 1977; Foner, 1979); chapters in handbooks (Ragan and Wales, 1980); and inclusion of social stratification in the five-year research plan of the National Institute on Aging.

THE BASIC DIMENSIONS
OF STRATIFICATION

Social stratification may be viewed in terms of both process and structure. The dimensions of process involve ranking and evaluation: whether people are richer or poorer, more esteemed or less esteemed, powerful or weak. The analyst of the dynamics of process must also be concerned with mobility, both upward and downward, for one of the distinguishing features of late life stratification is downward mobility. Two other forms, career mobility and generational mobility, take on special pertinence in later life.

From a structural point of view, social stratification involves the consequences of these ranking processes—the outcomes that solidify into class structures, elites, and castes.

Social stratification as process and as structure is probably as old as culture. Only within the last one hundred years has systematic attention been given to the study of the complexities of rank differentiations. Stratification analysis takes on added complexity when one adds aging as a variable.

The universality of stratification still leaves open the question of which criteria are to be employed in sorting out the strata and classes in a given society. All studies of social stratification acknowledge the primary importance of economic factors—income, wealth, and occupation—in any social rankings. This straightforward generalization requires qualification so that we may analyze more completely and more precisely the significance of economic factors.

Most studies of stratification maintain that Marxian analysts assign greater significance to economic factors than do other analysts, who see economic considerations in relation to other variables. Marx did not systematize his ideas on social class, but almost everything he wrote had implications for the understanding of social inequality (Bendix and Lipset, 1953; Bottomore, 1966; Giddens, 1973; Lane, 1976; Wolfe, 1977; Heilbroner, 1980). The core of Marx's theory of social stratification may be summarized in three statements: (1) social classes are derived from the positions people hold in the system of production; (2) a new social structure will result from inevitable class conflicts; (3) eventually a classless type of society will develop.

Marx's ideas have stimulated a vast amount of writing, some supportive and some critical. Max Weber (1946) was among the first to offer a comprehensive, focused plan for understanding social stratification. Weber used a three-dimensional approach to stratification: class, status, and power. The economic factor is the starting point for practically all discussions of the first dimension, class. Whether one views the class system from a Marxian or Weberian standpoint, or from some other orientation, most students of stratification, regardless of their ideological perspective, assign prime importance to the economic base. Other criteria of stratification may be important—race, ethnicity, religious affiliation, and kinship—but economic position forms the basic structure, and most of the other forms of stratification are derived from it.

Weber's second dimension is status. It is closely related to one's economic or class position; however, because other aspects are involved, status must be considered a distinct phenomenon analytically and empirically. When Weber made his distinction of class, status, and power groups, he emphasized that one of the major properties of status groups is "honor" (Weber, 1946, p. 186). Status also includes styles of life, prestige, social rank, and evaluations that, although related to economic position, involve other criteria as well. Status groups, or, as Weber called them, "status communities," are identified by a number of important social behaviors, such as friendship, visiting networks, marriage choices, consumption patterns, and a general style of life.

Power is the third dimension of social stratification in Weber's analytical scheme. Power, as employed here, denotes the idea of influence, particularly that manifested through governmental structures, political parties, and the political process. However, economic factors are significant determinants of power, as they are of status. In a modern democratic state, power is manifested primarily through control of the machinery of government. Because the government has the legitimate authority to pass laws, to enforce them, and to tax, those individuals and groups who exercise political and governmental power are able to influence the behavior and destiny of other people, or as Weber wrote, their "life chances."

AGE AS A DIMENSION OF RANKING

The basic position of this chapter is that economic factors are of prime importance, although they are modified, interpreted, and embellished by status, by power, and also by social-psychological considerations: perceptions, attitudes, and personality. But in discussion of social stratification and the aged, we must give attention to age itself as a component of ranking and evaluation, because various age categories are differentially valued by individuals and groups, both within societies and across cultures (Riley et al., 1972).

There are several questions derived from the study of class stratification that can illuminate age stratification. Riley (1971) has focused upon four important comparative subjects: (1) the individual's location in the class or age structure; (2) the social relationships within and between the class or age strata; (3) the issues and problems related to upward or downward mobility and the differences between mobility and cohort flow; and (4) the impact of the processes affecting individuals and their effects upon the macrostructure of a changing society.

People in most cultures affirm the unique and special qualities of the old. Folk wisdom and social science (Simmons, 1945; Cowgill and Holmes, 1972) indicate that age may be associated with characteristics that are positively valued: maturity, wisdom, compassion, spirituality, and self-acceptance. Yet, many people would claim possession of such characteristics as wisdom and compassion at an earlier stage in the life cycle, for such

traits are not the exclusive possession of the aged.

Generally, old age is not valued highly because it is associated widely with decline in physical attractiveness, vigor, health condition, sexual prowess, and perhaps some mental abilities. And most important from an actuarial basis, it is associated with the expectation of fewer years of life itself. In a fundamental sense, this is the consideration that makes the aged lose status—even though they may have many positive characteristics. The inescapable fact of human mortality forces all other aspects of ranking to fade when evaluated in relation to life itself. Stating it boldly and simply, almost all people when asked to rank the dimensions of stratification—income, possessions, education, prestige, political power, honor—would choose extension of life over these other traits. And some persons who are most hostile to the aged as a category are those who are fearful of their own eventual decline and demise. They have not come to terms with their own mortality and shun contact with anyone who might remind them of their future condition.

CLASS, STATUS, POWER, AND AGING

This section is concerned with changes in stratification associated with age according to the Weberian scheme of class, status, and power. Age and sex are considered here as intervening or modifying variables that qualify correlations or conditions reported for earlier phases of the life cycle. Most writers on stratification give little if any consideration to the way in which aging might modify the class position of individuals or members of groups or strata. Marx and Weber, in the nineteenth century, did not consider the way in which aging and the aged complicate social stratification in modern societies. They were primarily concerned with the way in which stratification issues were joined at the peak periods of life from adulthood through middle age. Their neglect of this subject is understandable, for during their lifetime the growing significance of aging and the age structures was recognized by very few.

Class Position in Aging

Occupation. An important dimension of stratification is occupational position. Many studies of stratification use this as the major criterion of classification (e.g., Porter, 1965; Shanas et al., 1968). Therefore, retirement may cause a definite lowering of social stratification ranking for some individuals. However, the retiree still retains his skills and knowledge even though he no longer exercises his occupation. His self-evaluation and society's regard for him are higher than they are for the unemployed, untrained person. Moreover, there is a definite carry-over effect of the employment situation, especially in the professions. A physician retains his prestige as a medical expert even though he has ceased to practice; a judge is often called "Judge" and considered an expert on law; a person of high military rank keeps his title and prestige.

Social class as measured by occupation has a certain stability throughout the life span. Svalastoga (1959, p. 308), for example, has made an interesting analysis of the Danes, in which he shows a gradual increase in status until about age 60, and then a decline. The sharpest status rise is from 20 to 30; the decline begins at 60, with a sharp decrease occurring after age 70.

Income. An important component of social stratification is the trend in patterns of work, retirement, and income over time. Although cross-sectional and longitudinal studies of individuals present two important perspectives on stratification, they cannot offer the insights of an aggregated time-series analysis. Pampel (1979) offers a time-series model of changes in the income of aged males and females in the United States from 1947 to 1976. He notes a marked increase of family income of those aged 65 and over in the last 15 years of the period studied, both in absolute dollars and when adjusted for inflation. He states: "Despite the positive individual-level relationship between income and labor force participation, the addition of large numbers of labor force nonparticipants to the aged population has not caused a reduction in income over time. In fact, retirement probably would not have become so common if income levels of the aged population could not be maintained. Thus, analysis of aggregate time-series data is necessary to avoid the reverse of the ecological fallacy—making inferences about changes in the aged population from individual cross-sectional data" (Pampel, 1979, p. 139).

Henretta and Campbell (1976), studying status attainment and maintenance in old age, point out that the determinants of income *in* retirement also determine income *before* retirement—namely, occupation, education, and marital status.

Clark et al. (1978) emphasize that there has been an increase in the absolute and relative income levels of families with a head of household 65 and older. Using constant dollar values the U.S. Bureau of the Census (1983) reported that the median income of elderly persons more than doubled from 1951 to 1981. The Bureau (1983) also reported that individuals 65 and over with incomes below the poverty level declined from 5.5 million in 1959 to 3.9 million in 1981, or a reduction in the proportion of the nation's elderly below the poverty index from 35.2 percent to 15.3 percent.

Despite the overall improvement in the income levels of the elderly, a basic fact remains: at retirement, there is usually a sharp reduction in money income. How does this reduction affect the individual's class position? In the years immediately following retirement, there is no evidence that the class position is drastically altered. In the Cornell Study of Occupational Retirement, it is significant that although the average person had a decline in income of 56 percent, a quarter to a third of the retirees stated that their retirement standard of living was better than during most of their lifetimes (Streib and Schneider, 1971, p. 85–86). The data show that the percentage of people who say they worry about money was essentially the same before and after retirement. In answer to the question "Do you consider your present income enough to meet your living expenses?" from 60 percent to 87 percent of the different cohorts said that it was enough, despite the fact that their income was about half of its previous level.

A longitudinal study of old age assistance recipients in California by Tissue (1972) reports that the aged poor see their hardships largely in terms of inadequate income. However, it was discovered that one-third of the respondents having an income of $200 or less per month still felt they had no significant money problems. Tissue found that current economic dissatisfaction was not related to previous socioeconomic status.

In their review of the literature, Espenshade and Braun (1981) state: "Previous research on the economic well being of older persons has been handicapped by equating it with money worth, ignoring such considerations as net worth, home equity, leisure and possession of durable goods." These writers discuss the problems in determining economic well-being in the elderly and summarize the positions of different economists and sociologists. They consider subjective perceptions of well-being to be an important consideration in any assessment of the economic situation of the elderly.

Therefore, it is clear that we must consider not only objective income, but also its subjective aspects (Bultena et al., 1971). Furthermore, a 50 percent decline in income has different meanings for different income levels. The businessman whose income drops from $50,000 to $25,000 may feel "deprived," but he suffers no real status loss or change in class position. He is still more privileged economically than 90 percent of the rest of the population. The retired teacher whose income declines from perhaps $24,000 to $12,000 may complain of feeling pinched financially, yet in comparison to a young family of four persons existing on $12,000 he is fortunate indeed. His style of life and class identification remain the same as they were in his middle years. The really deprived segment of the population, whose income may

drop, for example, from $11,316 (the median income for older families in 1979) to $5,500, may be in a critical situation. However, from the standpoint of class, if they have endured a lifetime of poverty, they experience simply a more critical situation but not a real *loss* in class position. Their circumstances are a continuation of what they have always known.

There is, however, a group that experiences "new poverty"—those who were middle class in their earlier years and have few or no resources in later years. This would include the working man who did not receive the pension he expected, the woman divorced late in life, or the widow whose husband's pension ceased upon his death—those who have only income from Social Security to live on after having received comfortable incomes in previous years. These people suffer a real decline in class and perhaps also in self-conception.

Liang and Fairchild (1979) agree that intrapersonal relative deprivation—a comparison of one's own previous circumstances with present condition—has a significant influence on an individual's appraisal of his economic well-being. These investigators analyzed six national samples of elderly persons and found that *feelings* of relative deprivation were more important in their effects on financial satisfaction than such variables as social status and current income.

Thus, in all reports on the income of the elderly, it seems obvious that sheer dollar amounts do not represent precisely the comparative adequacy or inadequacy of their income. Many elderly couples and single persons are able to exist on very small amounts and apparently feel no decline in class level. Why are the elderly able to get along on such small incomes? Are they simply keeping a "stiff upper lip" when they say their income is enough? This area needs much more research, for we do not know enough about the resiliency and adaptability of people who must cope with declining income.

However, we have several tentative explanations. First, most of the elderly have a stock of goods and equipment accumulated throughout a lifetime. They often own a house, and they need to spend less for new furniture, appliances, and equipment.

Second, the elderly often benefit from some interhousehold transfers. Children, relatives, friends, and neighbors supply food, goods, and services. Many elderly acquire their entire clothing replacements through gifts for Christmas, birthdays, Mother's Day, and so on.

In addition, they may have absorbed and internalized some of the general attitudes of society: that retired persons should receive a lower income than working persons. Rainwater's (1974) study of the social meanings of income shows this clearly. When 600 people were asked what was a fair recommended minimum income, they listed the recommended level for a retired person at two-thirds that of a worker of age 42. Schulz (1980) estimates that the appropriate replacement of income for a retired couple is about 65 to 70 percent of the gross income for a middle-income worker, because of: (1) less need for goods and services, (2) reduced income tax burden, and (3) discontinuance of the need to save for retirement.

The amount of money needed to replace a given standard of living is discussed by Espenshade and Braun (1981). Citing information from the President's Commission on Pension Policy (1980), they state: "It may seem at first glance that 100 percent replacement is needed to maintain a given standard of living. Changes in consumption patterns, tax liabilities, and savings rates of retired persons, however, reduce the necessary replacement ratios. For example, the Commission notes that an estimate of 13.6 percent is often used to show the drop in work-related expenses. Acknowledging that it is difficult to measure the adjustments in post-retirement expenses, the Commission suggests replacement ratios ranging from 51 percent to 79 percent for single persons and 55 percent to 86 percent for married couples, with the highest earners receiving the lowest replacement rates" (Espenshade and Braun, 1981, p. 77).

Applebaum and Faber (1979) have also di-

rected attention to the difficulty of determining replacement rates. According to one recent concept, the retirement income should be set at a level to represent the immediate pre-retirement standard of living. Another concept uses the highest year's earnings as the base for figuring pension benefits. However, the President's Commission on Pension Policy (1980) questions whether it is appropriate to replace the highest standard of living ever achieved by an individual. Applebaum and Faber (1979, p. 6) conclude: "The reality is that the general level of benefits under Social Security is determined by how much our society is willing to pay for this program."

Finally, a process of disengagement could be operating. The elderly often voluntarily curtail their needs, activities, and consumption patterns in accord with their declining energy, declining interests, and declining income. Disengagement occurs in varying ways; in Tissue's (1972) study of perception of economic hardship (perception of self- and income adequacy), the most significant variable was whether a person retained a younger or older self-image. Persons who are young or who feel and act young state they have more economic problems than those who regard themselves as old or actually are old. Finally, people who perceive money problems also feel frustration in satisfying consumer needs. Tissue summarizes the issue: "A youthful age image with a desire for consumer items produces the highest problem rates, whereas an older age image, matched to a lack of consumer interest, is least productive of hardship" (1972, p. 339). Thus, a person with an older self-image may manage comfortably on a smaller income because he has "disengaged from consumerism," so to speak.

Runciman's work on relative deprivation in Britain shows that the demands of the elderly are more modest than those of other poor groups. He writes: "While there is a widespread view among younger people that the elderly have done rather badly financially, the old themselves have modest demands" (Runciman, 1966, p. 271).

Moen's (1981) qualitative study of needs

assessment in rural Oregon illustrates this modesty of demands. She found that many of her respondents were too proud to ask for assistance, or even to learn about programs for which they had real need. Situational and cultural factors may have strongly influenced their attitudes and behavior. Moen found that the younger elderly perceive need more readily and utilize services more often than do the older elderly. She reports: "Within age cohorts of elders, the reluctance to admit need and use services is more a function of social class than of rural/urban residence in that the working class has the most conservative attitudes and behavior" (Moen, 1981, p. 67).

Property. Closely related to income is accumulated property. Property has not only material value but also symbolic qualities, often accentuated in old age. For the older person, the home, the furnishings, the possessions may encompass a lifetime of values, feelings, and emotions. In the calculus of old age, these may be more significant than the dollar income.

In the United States, about 80 percent of elderly couples and 40 percent of elderly single persons live in an owned home (Schulz, 1980). Schulz also reports that 80 percent of elderly homeowners own their homes free of debt. There is thus a sizable accumulation of assets, but most of it is not easily available for daily living expenses.

Home ownership is important both financially and symbolically. Kent and Hirsch (1971), in studying low-income black and white families in Philadelphia, reported that nearly half of the sample owned their own homes. When the researchers asked why some of these very low-income people did not apply for Old Age Assistance, one of the reasons frequently given was that they were afraid they would lose their homes.

Another important component of stratification, usually overlooked, is that of net worth (assets minus debts). Henretta and Campbell (1978) have drawn attention to this significant measure of social status by the use of data on white males from the National Longitudinal Studies of the Labor Force.

These authors see consumption as a component of status and emphasize that consumption decisions are made on the basis of long-term considerations, not just current income. This approach, they point out, may seem to be insensitive to the problems of the poor, but they add that poverty may be more accurately described as low net worth rather than simply low earnings. The study population was 50 to 64 years of age, essentially a middle-aged and pre-retirement population; however, the paper adds to our knowledge of old-age stratification. What is required is a more systematic and well-rounded analysis of net worth, as Townsend has presented for the United Kingdom (to be discussed later in this chapter).

Concerning stratification in later life, Henretta and Campbell (1978) show that as people age, consumption is increasingly affected by net worth. Within the category under study (50 to 64 years), there is an increase of assets with age. Among the important correlates of net worth are education, marital status, family size, and occupational status. Persons with less education, persons who are unmarried or divorced, or persons who are married with large families and with low occupational status, have a lower net worth.

These correlates of net worth are important indicators of the intercorrelations of class and status measures. Class and status benefits accumulate over time, so that late life represents the summation of one's educational attainments, occupation, lifetime earnings, and net worth.

Education. A fourth important determinant of class is education and training. This determinant is significant because these are measurable attributes that cannot be taken away from a person, and can be used as a precise indicator of rank. However, it is true that in the case of the aged, a considerable proportion have education and training that have become obsolescent in a changing society. Nevertheless, the person with higher educational attainments retains certain objective advantages that can never be removed. More highly educated people, in particular, retain attributes that help them to maintain and even increase their social standing in the community vis–à–vis less educated older people.

Empirical evidence for this thesis is provided by Myles's (1981) study of status maintenance and income equality in the last stage of the life cycle. Employing a 1976 Canadian Survey of Consumer Finances, he found: "The most important contribution to the absolute level of inequality between educational groups is the continued advantage of the more highly educated in the labor market. . . . The educated maintain their status in old age not only as a result of higher average lifetime earnings, but also by remaining in the labor force until a later age than the less educated" (Myles, 1981, pp. 136–137).

The status effects of education persist beyond the working years, for persons with higher education are more satisfied with retirement. Foner and Schwab (1981) state: "It is not only that these better-off retirees have fewer financial worries and can more easily maintain their standard of living, but also that having money permits them to engage in pleasurable and meaningful activities. Many activities require substantial outlays— travel, sports, and the like. Even participating in organizations often entails a wardrobe and transportation expenses" (p. 65).

Succeeding cohorts of persons who are 60 and older in the United States are increasingly well educated. In 1950, 10 percent of the males and 13.2 percent of the females 60 and over had four years of high school. In 1980, this figure had risen to 30.5 percent of the males and 37.4 percent of the females. The percentage who had some college roughly doubled in 30 years, rising from 10 percent to 21.8 percent for men and 9.5 percent to 17.5 percent for women from 1950 to 1980 (Uhlenberg, 1977). By the year 2000, census projections show that 33.6 percent of the men and 24.4 percent of the women aged 60 and over will have some college experience. The higher education of retired people will undoubtedly have effects on income, style of life, consumption patterns, and political activity.

The Dual Economy and Stratification in Old Age

One of the important developments in analyses of social stratification concerns the nature and consequences of the dual economy (Dowd, 1980). An appropriate starting point is the work of Robert T. Averitt (1968), who divided the American private economy into two distinct business systems: the center or core economy, and the periphery. The center economy, the heart of the industrial system, is composed of large and influential firms. Its organizations are corporate and bureaucratic; its production processes are vertically integrated through ownership and control of raw materials. Firms in the center economy serve national and international markets. Averitt states: "The center economy gives the nation its industrial might. It forms the heart of the greatest aggregation of productive potential ever known. The top 500 industrial U.S. corporations, the elite of the center economy, account for nearly three-fifths of all workers in U.S. mining and manufacturing" (1968, p. 7).

The periphery economy, in contrast, consists of small firms, often operated by a single individual or family. They provide useful and indispensable goods and services, and employment for millions of citizens. The sales of the firms are more restricted and the market tends to be local, profits and earnings are commonly lower than those in the core economy, and bankruptcy is more common.

What is the relevance of these facts to the stratification situation of older workers? The major consideration is whether an employee is covered by a pension plan and thus has an important source of income in addition to Social Security. Great stress is placed upon the importance of people having a pension from their employers, but in 1978 only about one-fourth of the retired population over 65 years of age received income from an employee pension (President's Commission on Pension Policy, 1981, p. 26).

The lack of pension plans occurs primarily in the periphery economy, in small businesses. Ninety-three percent of the noncovered persons work in firms with fewer than 500 employees. The major reason given for the lack of pension coverage is cost, for these firms operate in very competitive economic environments with small profit margins. If an employee works for a small business that has a pension plan, the probability of his collecting 20 or 30 years in the future is reduced, because most small businesses do not exist long enough for the pension plan to mature.

Another way of viewing the center-periphery pension distinction is in terms of the characteristics of the workers. Nonunion workers, women, minorities, and lower-paid persons are more apt to be employed by periphery firms and thus less apt to receive pensions.

A precise description of the way worker characteristics are manifested in pension coverage is shown by data on age category and industry in the President's Commission on Pension Policy (1981). Almost three-fourths of the workers in mining and manufacturing are covered by a pension. Less than one-half in construction, only 36 percent in services, and 19 percent in agriculture receive private pensions.

The greatest amount of coverage is not in the private sector, but in the government service: in federal government, where 91 percent of the employees are covered, and in state and local government, where 83 percent of the workers are covered.

The marked differences in both pension opportunity and income levels are related to a series of equity issues that the United States and other societies must face. How does one justify the inequities in pensions of persons who did work of equal importance, requiring the same amount of training and skill, and receiving perhaps the same wages? For example, one person may drive a truck for a governmental organization or for a center-economy corporation, and retire with a substantial pension and often Social Security also. Another trucker may work for a small business in the peripheral economy and reach old age with only Social Security benefits.

The equity issue becomes more nettlesome in relation to public policy because employees of federal, state, and local government receive their pensions primarily from general taxation. Although most of these plans are contributory, in recent years the contributory portions have been paid out rather quickly, within two or three years (Kleiler, 1978).

Among the analysts of the dual economy, there is disagreement as to how government organizations mesh into the theory of the dual economy. On the one hand, there are those who claim government is integral to the center or core economy because of the close affiliation between core and government. Others challenge that interpretation, and consider the government as a third sector of the economy. A balanced view suggests that some aspects of government structure are indeed closely interrelated with the core economy, and others are clearly neither core nor periphery. The clearest example of this interlocking relationship between the core economy and the federal government is General Eisenhower's well-known designation of the military–industrial complex in 1946 (Melman, 1970). On the other hand, there are many parts of government, such as the Department of Health and Human Services, the largest employer in the federal government aside from defense, that have only peripheral relations with the core economy.

The dual economy is important in its effect on retirement income, hence on class position, status, and life-style, because workers in the core economy are far more likely to have favorable economic situations in retirement than are workers in the periphery.

Status and Aging

The second major dimension of stratification is that of status, prestige, or esteem. What are the attributes or characteristics that contribute to high or low rank along this dimension?

Membership Groups. Status is likely to reflect one's group affiliations because these are inextricably linked to one's family and kin ties and to the evaluation of family characteristics in the local community. Obviously, these affiliations are not completely independent of economic or class characteristics. Generally, there is a correlation between class and status position, but they do not always completely correspond. Status also involves informal affiliations such as friendships and cliques, and the interactions that originate from them. The prestige of many of these affiliations persists for the older person who no longer participates actively. For example, a person who belonged to an exclusive country club will retains the aura of membership even though he may no longer attend and pay dues.

Similarly, Lipset (1968) speaks of "accorded status," the honor and prestige given to individuals, a type of status with considerable continuity and persistence. Unlike objective or material or monetary aspects, accorded status may continue throughout retirement; for example, a retired actor or sports hero still receives considerable attention because of his past fame.

Style of Life. Status is also a reflection, in part, of one's style of life. This, of course, is related to income but may also be related to education. One of the paradoxes in later life is that persons can suffer severe declines in income yet still retain essentially the same style of life—they may live in the same neighborhood, keep the same friends, and pursue the same hobbies and interests (on a reduced scale).

Their expenditures for essentials may remain the same, but their discretionary income is reduced. The individuals themselves may be keenly aware of various economies, but their reduced economic position is not readily obvious to the outside world, and they appear to retain the same class position. In addition, an aspect of the process of disengagement may "assist" in the tapering off phases, so that they may, for example, take fewer and shorter vacations, drive their cars less, and buy new models less frequently.

Research on life-styles and consumer be-havior of older Americans is reported by Schutz et al. (1979), who state: "The older consumers' interest in money is oriented toward preserving independence rather than toward acquiring possessions. They generally express a realistic view of their financial situation and shift their expenditures accordingly. While income may be less, they usually feel it is high enough to satisfy their needs" (p. 101). These investigators found that the older Americans in their study (middle-class and lower-middle-class respondents in California) are better off financially than is generally believed. "Even though they anticipate no future increases in income, they express more satisfaction with their financial circumstances than do younger persons, have fewer debts and are more careful shoppers and spenders" (Schutz, et al., 1979, p. 154). Their life-styles show continuity with their previous behavior.

Subjective Status. Finally, there is subjective status as a major dimension of stratification. This involves a person's own perception of his rank on the social hierarchy. There is a positive relationship to the two other major dimensions of stratification, objective (e.g., economic) and accorded status, although not a perfect correlation. For example, Coleman and Neugarten (1971, pp. 112–113) found a fairly high correlation between objective indicators and subjective evaluation, but there were differentials in the correlations. At the upper-class level, the objective factors were rather poor predictors of subjective positions.

Power and Aging

Turning to the power dimension, we observe that there are two major ways that age can manifest itself: first, through a disproportionate holding of important offices by older people, and, second, by the individual or collective power of older people expressed through voting, or through interest and pressure groups. The first type is illustrated by the way in which seniority operates in most legislative bodies in the United States. One can think of state legislators, congressmen, and U.S. senators who by virtue of their seniority (highly correlated with age) are able to exercise disproportionate influence on the legislative process (Mathews, 1954). Because elective officials are not subject to formal retirement, except by the voters, some aged persons are able to exercise disproportionate power.

In appointive positions, such as the judiciary, regulatory commissions, and administrative agencies, there are often formal rules for retirement. However, the normal retirement age, whether 65 or 70, may be waived in the case of exceptional persons, or those who have unusual power over the persons who appoint them. (One thinks, for example, of the late J. Edgar Hoover, who directed the Federal Bureau of Investigation for over half a century.) Generally speaking, these persons do not conceive of the elderly as their special constituency and rarely use their power in the interests of the aged. Rather, older elected officials often attempt to create the impression of being middle-aged and try to place some social distance between themselves and their age peers.

The question often arises of whether the aged could exercise enormous power at the polls if they acted as a power bloc. We agree with the interpretation of Binstock (1974): "There is no sound reason to expect the aging will gain power by voting cohesively in the future" (p. 199). While interest groups may be galvanized from time to time on a special issue, it seems unlikely that they will form a continuous pressure group. Despite the marked growth of some membership organizations (Pratt, 1974) and the emergence of new "militant" senior power groups, it does not seem likely that they will develop into one cohesive organization in the decade ahead.

Finally, there are other ways in which older persons exercise a disproportionate influence in political and economic affairs, namely, through leadership in the trade union movement (where there are no fixed retirement ages or where such retirement rules are not invoked) and through ownership and control of vast private fortunes. In these two cases, however, they do not exercise influence on behalf of their age cohort.

A discussion of power would not be complete without a mention of power on the microlevel—in the environment of the family. Throughout history, old people have exercised power because they own and control property and have the final decision as to the disposition of their wealth. We often think of the exercise of power as involving large fortunes, but even very small amounts of wealth and property can be powerful "weapons" in the family and kinship system. Although most legacies are under the taxable limits, even small amounts can be a real consideration in the treatment that older persons receive. Many elderly persons have enjoyed attention and concern from their relatives as they have kept them guessing about the provisions of their last will and testament.

STRATUM CONSCIOUSNESS

The study of social stratification offers the opportunity to bring together the traditional concept of class consciousness and the newer concept of age consciousness. In this section, we will develop these two concepts and then show how they are interrelated. We will also analyze the ways in which group solidarity stems from group consciousness and how solidarity is necessary for group action. The development of group consciousness based on class or age can, as Mannheim pointed out, provide persons with a "common location in the social and historical process" and may lead to a "characteristic mode of thought and experience" (Mannheim, 1952).

Class Consciousness

The first step in our analysis is to demarcate the concept of class consciousness, the individual's conception of his place in the stratification system. Moreover, class consciousness may vary at different points in the life cycle, and it may be influenced by community and historical contexts. Finally, class consciousness is important because it is found in different forms at different levels of the class system. The class consciousness of the top stratum, for example, may involve a variety of feelings and motivations: snobbery, exploitation, noblesse oblige, compassion, and so on. Conversely, among the most deprived class or stratum, one may also find a variety of feelings and attitudes associated with awareness of one's class identity, such as resignation, deference, or "knowing one's place."

One of the significant issues in the study of social stratification is whether one conceives of the system as composed of social classes or of social strata. A class has boundaries and involves a degree of group solidarity. Many writers use the term *social class* when they are really talking about *social strata,* which are ill-defined layers or categories in a hierarchy. Both concepts are ill defined and hard to distinguish in the United States as compared with some other industrialized societies.

This distinction is important from the standpoint of both the analyst and the person himself. Rosenberg (1970) is one of the few investigators who has given systematic attention to the images older persons hold of the class system. His study of the white working class in Philadelphia shows that lower-income persons (all respondents had family incomes of $7500 or less) see the class system as closed. These older persons believe that automation prevents advancement, and getting ahead is out of one's hands. The image of a closed class system is correlated with the neighborhood economic context, for the old men in this study living in the poorest neighborhood were most likely to have an image of a closed class system.

A number of investigators (Rosenberg, 1970; Olsen, 1974) have observed that there are always some persons who find it difficult to formulate a conception of the class system. A simple description is that class consciousness tends to be higher among those who are least rewarded by the society. Rosenberg (1970) says: "These underdogs place the blame for lack of advancement squarely on the class system and where there own ca-

reers are concerned have the least difficulty of any group of breadwinners of conceiving of the operation of the society in terms of class factors" (p. 167).

The prevailing economic conditions may be another factor involved in the degree of class consciousness present. Rosenberg's study was carried out in a postwar period of prosperity. The studies of Pope (1941) and Jones (1941), carried out during economic depression, show a higher level of class consciousness. Therefore, one would expect that the underprivileged aged might have a heightened sense of class consciousness, and their inability to work or to anticipate an imporve economic situation would increase their apathy and antagonism to the status quo. In writing about periods of economic depression, Leggett (1968) has said: "Not only the poverty of the average person but the vivid contrasts in wealth, the relative decline in workers' standards of living and the widening gap between what the worker expected and the middle class obtained were undoubtedly relevant" (p. 25).

Another issue related to class awareness is the way in which class consciousness changes over time. Schreiber and Nygreen (1970) have analyzed eight different national surveys; they conclude that working class identification increased irregularly in the United States from 1945 to 1960 and finally reached a plateau slightly higher than the original point. These data suggest that the period effect was not very great during the 15 years after World War II.

Age Consciousness

A concept analogous to class consciousness is age consciousness—the awareness and feelings of one's chronological development. Throughout human history, individuals have been aware of their own aging and the aging of others in their communities. Poets, playwrights, and philosophers have written with sensitivity and insight about age consciousness, but the phenomenon has changed in the last half century, principally in industrialized societies. Age consciousness has new meaning because of the greatly increased number of aged, the institutionalization of retirement, and the development of voluntary and interest groups concerned with the aged.

Age consciousness has two major facets. The first is awareness of one's own aging processes—primarily a psychological phenomenon. The second is more sociological—awareness of the fact that others are growing old, and that one may have something in common with them as persons who have reached a similar point in the life cycle.

The first question to ask is: Precisely who are the aged? How does the analyst demarcate the aged as a category? The simple objective way is to use a chronological criterion, as age 60, 65, or 70. This is the means usually employed for most administrative purposes—insurance, retirement, pensions, and social security. Among gerontologists (Kelleher and Quirk, 1973), and also among lay persons, there is an effort to use functional criteria rather than chronological age for determining a person's age status. But it is a minority position, and although there are valid grounds for considering such bases, it is doubtful that functional criteria will be widely used in the near future.

Another development that bears directly upon issues related to social stratification and age stratification is the division of the older population into two or three different categories (Neugarten, 1974): (1) The young-old are those who are 55 to 65 years of age. In most instances, they are still gainfully employed and at the peak of their earning power and social recognition. (2) The middle-old, aged 65 to 75, include a large proportion of the retired population. These people have experienced a substantial cut in income and have given up their lifetime occupations. However, many of them are in good health and have an abundant supply of a precious resource—time. (3) The old-old are persons over 75 and often include those who are the most frail, the sickest, the most isolated, and the most impoverished segment of the population. It is this group who constitute the core of what might be labeled the "problem population" among the elderly and are con-

sidered by those who refer to the low status of the aged.

The use of functional criteria is a process followed not only by experts but by the aged themselves in self-rating evaluations. Indeed, numerous surveys have found that a very large proportion of 65-year-old persons consider themselves "middle-aged." This tendency to identify with younger groups persists until quite late in the life cycle. Some interpreters (Rosow, 1967) have stated that this represents denial of one's true age status. In view of such interpretations and findings concerning refusal to identify with one's age mates, it would seem that old-age consciousness is a weak basis for group solidarity and group action.

In recent years, with increasing concern and publicity about the problems of the elderly, perhaps a false message has been beamed—that most elderly have grave problems. For example, Dowd (1980, p. 58) asks why the elderly are not angry about the "unfair" treatment they have received in the United States. He says perhaps it is because of their low level of age consciousness. However, recent survey data may indicate that there are other explanations. Hubert O'Gorman (1980), using data from the National Council on Aging national survey, found that the overwhelming majority of elderly respondents did not characterize any of 12 problems as "very serious" in their lives. The problems included: not enough income, poor health, loneliness, poor housing, not enough job opportunities, and so on. Fear of crime was the most common problem acknowledged. In fact, the distribution of self-reported problems was similar to those reported in respondents 18 to 64 years of age. However, the respondents grossly exaggerated the prevalence of problems of *other* elderly. They seemed to feel that they personally are exceptions, and they have accepted the image of older persons commonly portrayed by newspapers, television, articles, and books, the idea that most elderly experience very serious problems.

"The repeated documentation of these respondents' misconceptions illustrates vividly the extent to which individuals can be mistaken about the experiences of others with whom they share an important status," says O'Gorman (1980, p. 123). "The evidence attesting to the far reaching patterns of false consciousness of kind among the aged is remarkably persistent." Thus, the increasing concern and publicity about the problems of a small minority of elderly may have beamed an inaccurate picture to the elderly themselves.

The Aged as a Conscious Minority Group

The preceding discussion leads to the question of whether the aged constitute a conscious minority group in our society. Some gerontologists have maintained that the aged are discriminated against and constitute a minority group (Barron, 1953; Palmore, 1969; Palmore and Whittington, 1971). Such an approach requires careful definition and conceptualization, for it is possible to employ the term "minority group" as both a technical term and an image-producing term. The latter usage is akin to the definition of the aged as a social problem, or as "victims" of social forces or of deprivations and discriminations imposed or invoked by other categories of persons in the society. Some persons view compulsory retirement as analogous to job discrimination on the basis of sex, race, or ethnicity. They do not recognize that over half of the persons who retire say they are unable to work because of declining health. Thus, most people are "victims" of their own biology—not "victims" of society.

A sociological evaluation would conclude that the aged are not a genuine minority group, for they do not share a distinct and separate culture (Streib, 1965). Moreover, membership in the category of persons designated as the aged is not exclusive or permanent but awaits all members of a particular society who are fortunate enough to live that long. Age is not as distinguishing a social group characteristic as sex, occupation, or social class. Many of the aged do possess distinctive physical features, but these characteristics do not usually justify or result in discriminatory treatment by other persons or groups.

Furthermore, many of the aged do not identify with their age mates, and they tend to have a low feeling of group consciousness. While membership organizations of senior citizens have grown greatly in the last decade, such groups have relatively low hostility toward younger age groups.

Some persons have charged that the aged are segregated in "geriatric ghettos." However, retirement communities are joined voluntarily and can be left at any time. Furthermore, numerous surveys and qualitative evidence indicate that many of the elderly prefer to live with their age peers.

Although the aged (until about age 75) vote more frequently than some other age groups, Binstock (1974) and others (Riley et al., 1968) have pointed out that, to date, there is limited evidence suggesting strong solidarity on political matters. Ragan and Dowd (1974) believe that the aged are a *potential* political force. However, they conclude: "Age-group political consciousness—the identification by the aged of their common political interests and potential for common action—is not clearly manifest among the current cohort of older persons" (Ragan and Dowd, 1974, p. 154).

A contrasting point of view is presented by Laufer and Bengtson (1974), who believe that the need to reorganize identity at advanced stages of the life cycle raises the prospect of collective action.

Morris and Murphy (1966) proposed that stratum consciousness be viewed as a cumulative series of steps or stages: (1) stratum awareness, or perception of separateness from other age groups; (2) stratum affiliation, or sense of belonging; (3) stratum consciousness, or identification of interests in conflict with those of other strata; and (4) stratum ideology and/or action. In the case of the aged, it would appear that the first step, stratum awareness, may be more commonly perceived, but the next three steps are less likely to occur. In spite of widespread publicity given to the Gray Panther movement, for example, it involves only a minute percentage of the elderly.

Other membership groups, such as the American Association of Retired Persons, have become active in advocating issues and policies at various levels of government. One new development at the state level is the formation of self-advocacy organizations, the silver-haired legislatures (Matura, 1982). Thus, there is a growing evidence of the potential for group action of the elderly.

A different approach to the question of group consciousness and power is expressed by Dowd (1980), who focuses on exchange theory and the elderly. He asserts that alienation among the elderly has increased, and considers this as evidence of "incipient class consciousness" among old people. He regards the problem to be one of exchanges—that the elderly are devalued because they have little power in the exchange process. While exchange theory has relevance in interpersonal interaction, it is difficult to apply it in the societal area. Furthermore, it is perhaps unrealistic to contemplate an exchange process in which the most deprived elderly would be granted a measure of power. Power is not ordinarily granted—it is wrested, seized, and invoked. And the most deprived cohort—the sick, the frail, and the old-old—have little group solidarity and are not able to mount a campaign to demand power.

The analysis of identification and group consciousness needs both a national and a comparative approach. Gurin et al. (1980) offer some insightful data from a U.S. national sample on the age consciousness of persons 60 or older, the class consciousness of people with working- and middle-class occupations, the race consciousness of blacks and whites, and the sex consciousness of women. The age consciousness of older persons was higher than expected, for it approximated the discontent expressed by blacks about their influence in American life, and it was stronger than the discontent of blue-collar workers and women. Although the elderly are as discontented about their present power as American blacks, many

fewer older people (31 percent) felt their group's influence had increased in recent years compared to that of blacks (71 percent). Indeed, only half as many older people (31 percent) compared to the blacks (64 percent) thought their group could do very much to increase its influence in the future. The negative appraisal of the older people's political effectiveness was greater than the evaluations of blue-collar workers or women. Gurin et al. (1980) concluded: "Thus, while age consciousness among these older people was by no means as weak as expected, the potential for mobilizing this group did appear weak because of their marked resignation about shifts in their influence and their capacity to increase it in years to come" (p. 40).

SPECIAL CONTEXTS OF STRATIFICATION AND AGING

It has been stressed that the aged are very heterogeneous and that various age cohorts are differentially evaluated. Three subject areas have been chosen for further analysis to illustrate cohort differentiation: sex, great wealth, and residential density.

Stratification and the Aging Woman

The way in which sex differentiation is involved in the allocation of power, prestige, and other resources must be considered in studying stratification in relation to aging. The implications of considering age and sex simultaneously are starkly shown in the way in which pension and social insurance schemes discriminate against women in some societies.

The way in which sex status enters into distribution of power and privilege has until very recently been neglected in the stratification literature. Lenski (1966, pp. 402–406) is one of the few writers to have given specific attention to "The Class System Based on Sex." Haug (1973) has pointed out that a woman's class position is generally assessed on the basis of the man's position. With two wage earners in the family, the question arises as to how the female's position affects the family rank. First is the matter of the income supplementation, and second, the possibility of status inconsistency in the family if the woman's occupational status or educational attainment is different from that of her husband.

After the husband retires, the economic situation of the family is much stronger if his wife continues to work than if they depend on his pension alone. If she retires and receives a pension too, their economic situation is also favorable.

Henretta and O'Rand (1980), utilizing data from the Longitudinal Retirement History Study, report that the most consistent and strongest effect on the decision of the wife to retire is whether she has pension coverage. If a woman has a private pension, she is more likely to stop work. However, the authors add: "Although the effect of pension coverage is great, relatively few women in this cohort expect to receive a private pension" (Henretta and O'Rand, 1980, p. 45).

As women outlive men by an average of seven years, most women face widowhood at the end of their lives. The elderly widow is in a particularly vulnerable situation, for she usually faces a sharp reduction in income after her husband's death. Lopata (1979) reports that the incomes of the widows in her Chicago study were about half of what they had been before widowhood. Social security benefits are also reduced, to a lower level than those received by the couple. Schulz (1980) states that a widow who was married to a fully insured worker for at least nine months and who has reached the age of 60 is entitled to a benefit of 100 percent of the worker's pension if payments begin at age 65, or 71.5 percent if she is age 60.

A husband's private pension often stops entirely at his death. Bernstein (1980) states: "Few plans assure widows a pension. Hence, even when the retiree does win benefits, his family is usually cut off when he dies. According to one government estimate, only two percent of widows collect private pension benefits" (p. 243). He adds that even though many plans provide for "joint and survivor" pension payout provisions, most men apparently choose the larger benefit during their lifetimes rather than reduced benefits with survivor provisions.

Since the widow usually does not choose to move to less expensive housing, she has the problem of maintaining a house with greatly reduced income. Thus, many elderly widows are "house poor" (Struyk and Soldo, 1980). Lawton (1980) has pointed out that elderly women often do not have the manual dexterity, physical strength, and experience to perform the necessary maintenance and repairs on their homes. Therefore, they must pay to have such functions performed, which may adversely affect their financial position.

Other status implications of widowhood have been studied by Lopata (1973). She found that widows were often reluctant to keep up community and neighborhood friendships and associations after their husbands' deaths. Many withdrew from social life, particularly from events they would have attended as part of a couple. One woman, reflecting the lower status she experienced as a result of this withdrawal, observed that she felt like a "second class citizen" (Lopata, 1973, p. 191).

Lopata also reported that better-educated women often found widowhood very threatening to their self-identities, for their activities and world view were constructed around the lives of their husbands and their work associates. The lower-class women, in contrast, were less involved in the world of their husbands; the couples communicated less with each other, and the husband's death was not as damaging to the self-identity of the wife.

Finally, a further loss in status is experienced by older widows who have to give up their own home and share a domicile with their children. This is a loss both in the eyes of the community and in the widow's self-perception. The fact that she is no longer mistress of her own household and no longer surrounded by the accumulated possessions of a lifetime represents a severe loss of status in her microenvironment.

Not only is there reduced financial position, but the elderly widow must cope with a tremendous role change. Lopata (1979) says: "Her identity as a wife is shattered and there is no comfortable role of widow available to her as to widows in other parts of the world" (p. 31). In some other countries, such as the Soviet Union and China (Smith, 1976; Butterfield, 1982), the older woman has a role assigned to her—caretaking of grandchildren while the daughter works. Older American women, in general, have eschewed this role, preferring to live by themselves and be independent of the burden of child care, even though they may pay the price of feeling "useless." A notable exception is the black family, where the grandmother is often involved in child care (Hill, 1971).

A full picture of stratification relating to age and sex must include the fact that statistics show that half of all millionaires are women. Why are there so many women millionaires? There are no systematic answers, but one can speculate. First, the greater longevity of women typically means that the wife inherits her husband's wealth and thus controls the fortune accumulated during his lifetime. Second, because almost all men marry women younger than themselves, many women live for years as widows. Because of these life-cycle circumstances, there is a change in the sexual allocation of income and wealth from the pattern that is normative at earlier ages in which men usually control the wealth of the family.

Age and the Very Rich in the United States

Many analyses of social stratification and the aged concentrate on the fact that the aged form a disproportionate section of the poor in most societies. However, it is a paradox that the aged are also disproportionately represented in the very rich segment of the population. The average age of millionaires in the United States is about 60, and there is not much difference in the age of male and female millionaires. A study made by *Fortune* magazine some years ago of the very wealthiest persons in the United States—the 66 centimillionaires—indicated that the median age of this group was 65 years of age (Louis, 1968).

The concentration of great wealth and high income among a small number of the aged raises some important questions about how the stratification system functions: (1) How does it happen that people can accumulate large fortunes? (2) How is this wealth transmitted at death? (3) What is the relation of great wealth to class consciousness and age consciousness?

The answer to the first two questions is that the tax structure of this capitalistic society enables people to enjoy a high income and accumulate great wealth during their lifetime, and then, by means of trust funds and inheritance-tax provisions, to transfer large fortunes from generation to generation.

The third question concerns the kind and degree of age consciousness and group solidarity. A continuing controversy in the gerontological literature is whether the aged are a minority or quasi-minority group. Writers who argue for a minority-group perspective tend to concentrate their attention upon the poor and underprivileged aged. On an aggregate basis, one does not dispute the fact that some elderly must live under conditions of extreme deprivation. However, the aged are a heterogeneous group and include many who are comfortably retired, as well as a few who are extremely rich and privileged. The lack of solidarity among the aged is demonstrated by the fact that the wealthy elderly do not use their power and influence specifically to reduce the underprivileged status of their age mates. They generally do not attempt to press for the redistribution of resources or improvement in status of the victim category. They identify with their class and with their own family and kin groups, not with their age cohort. Thus, it seems that there is age solidarity and group consciousness principally if there is a shared victim status—and as soon as persons move out of the underprivileged group, their age consciousness diminishes. As they move to the most privileged segments, it seems to vanish.

Furthermore, it would seem that the underprivileged are not too critical of the desire of the wealthy to pass on their wealth to their children and kin, for this is exactly what they would want to do if they themselves were wealthy. Even very poor people desire to "leave something" to those they love. They would rather have more generous old age benefits from federal sources but still wish to maintain inheritance laws unchanged.

In a survey of homeowners in Los Angeles County, respondents were asked whether they desired to leave an inheritance to their children. Although the median income of the 65–75-year-old group was only $3,620, 72 percent said they desired to leave an inheritance. The principal reason was parental pride and tradition. "Many respondents who, apparently, could not afford it were attempting to leave something to their heirs and were thereby reducing their own comfort and enjoyment in old age," the investigator stated (Chen, 1973, p. 44).

Retirement Communities and Stratification

A new and growing trend with implications for social stratification of the aged is the development and acceptance of retirement communities. These have been regarded both positively and negatively by gerontologists and other observers. Some have labeled them geriatric ghettos for outcast older citizens; others, who think the aged should remain productive contributors in the mainstream, consider retirement communities as an unhealthy withdrawal from life; while still other critics denounce them for the hedonistic pursuit of pleasure, recreation, and other leisure activities.

However, there is a differing point of view—namely, that the retirement communities constitute a status buffer. They provide a protective environment that tends to shield the older person from an acknowledgment of downward mobility. Persons engaged in the world of production may consider that the retiree has declined in status—is no longer in the mainstream, is a "back number," as retirees often express it.

Within the retirement community, the residents interact principally with those in the same situation. They do not need to envy those who go off to work each day. They do not need to keep up with younger people who are full of ambition and vigor. They do not want pity when they slow down. They can enjoy leisure without feeling abnormal, for all of the residents are in the same situation. Generally, they have a positive viewpoint of their status when surrounded by persons who have experienced the same role losses. Their situation is reenforced by their attitudes and values. It should also be emphasized that people join such communities voluntarily and may leave if they choose. Thus, the communities are composed of people who have made a conscious choice that this style of life is their best alternative. If they stay, they are usually enthusiastic about their decision.

Bultena and Wood (1969, p. 216) report that persons who moved to retirement communities had significantly higher morale than those who moved to regular or age-integrated communities. And Neugarten (1966) has suggested that by making old age a more attractive period of life, retirement communities may raise the general prestige of the elderly.

One woman of Sun City observed, "Retired people don't belong in a busy working society because they make pests of themselves, so we came to a retirement community where everyone is at leisure. It's nice to have a place to go to have fun and maybe act a little foolish—I never learned how to ride a bike or swim until I came here—and no one will laugh at you because you're older" (Malcolm, 1974).

Such sensitivity to ridicule by younger people undoubtedly influences some who choose retirement communities. The residents are protected from the amused, condescending attitude of younger people when they attend dances, learn new skills in classes, participate in sports, and so on.

There are clear socioeconomic differentials between those who migrate to a retirement community and those who remain in their home communities. First, the residents are mainly more affluent middle-class or upper-middle-class persons who have the funds to relocate in another part of the country. Carter and Webber (1966) reported higher educational levels and above-average income for elderly migrants in their detailed Florida study. Therefore, the residential communities are a relatively homogeneous segment of the population. In terms of status and lifestyle, they follow an emphasis on leisure, friendship, and recreation. In fact, the residents of retirement communities could be called a "new leisure class" (Michelon, 1954).

The stratification system within retirement communities tends to be democratic, for people are not impressed by previous accomplishments. As Jacobs (1974) stated in his study of a retirement community of 5600 people, "This general indifference to the former status of their neighbors was, I believe, outstanding" (p. 65). However, a more longitudinal and historical approach, as reported by Streib et al. (1982) in their study of 30 communities, reveals that in some communities, a stratification system may develop that was unintended and unanticipated by both developers and residents. The growing affluence of the aging population has raised both the level of housing expectations and the ability of people to pay for more luxurious retirement homes than were anticipated 20 years earlier. Thus the new units are often larger and more expensive than the homes of the first residents, thereby creating a status hierarchy in which the new residents have status "above" that of the early residents.

There is no clear evidence of whether retirement communities exercise political power as a bloc in relation to the larger political structure. Although it has been asserted that these enclaves of older persons constitute a cohesive bloc who might adhere to conservative low-tax voting behavior on local issues, there is little evidence to date of such block voting (Osgood, 1982). There is, however, the potential for a cohesive political force in these communities, which might be crucial if mobilized and if the issues or candidates were presented in terms emphasizing the interests of the aged.

One of the few studies (Heintz, 1976) to have investigated the voting behavior of people in retirement communities reveals that there are few data to support the claim that residing in retirement villages causes changes in political behavior. Residents did not vote as a unified bloc, and they were not overwhelmingly conservative in voting against proposals that the remainder of the electorate supported. Heintz (1976) says: "Senior citizens in general do not embrace an exclusively conservative political ideology; neither do retirement village residents. . . . Of those age sixty and over, 56.7 percent do not refer to themselves as conservatives. Furthermore, the generally conservative senior citizens are often quite liberal on economic issues from which they themselves might benefit; their political ideology is largely determined by specific economic considerations, just as is that of the broader electorate" (p. 147).

Politically, retirement communities represent an interesting phenomenon because most of the residents are not employed and potentially have more time for political activity than persons in the labor force. However, impressionistic data indicate that the persons who are active politically are those who in their former occupations or communities had some involvement in the political process.

There is some evidence that age density may also act as a crucial variable and status buffer in the microenvironment of large cities. Rosow's (1967) study of Cleveland clearly shows that small environments that are age-segregated have positive social-psychological consequences for the residents. Although younger people may complain that a community with a large proportion of aged is "depressing," such an environment offers many supports for the elderly themselves. They are more apt to help each other in case of trouble, to form visiting patterns, and to offer neighboring services than in a completely heterogeneous community. Rosow (1967) says: "The common assumption in gerontology that residential proximity readily stimulates friendships between the generations is simply not borne out by the facts . . . the number of old people's local friends varies directly with the proportion of age peers" (p. 78).

Furthermore, Rosow observed class differences, for he noted that blue-collar elderly are more apt to make and maintain friendships in communities with a high proportion of aged. He found that people in preferred positions and those with less role loss are more independent of local relationships, but persons with lower statuses and with more role loss are the most locally dependent. Rosow's observations are also supported by the research of Hochschild (1973) on a public housing project and Johnson's (1971) studies of a working class mobile home community.

PERSPECTIVES ON CROSS-NATIONAL STRATIFICATION OF THE AGED

The material presented so far has been concerned mainly with stratification in the United States. Therefore, let us review stratification and aging in a cross-national perspective. Is there something different in other societies or in the nature of aging in other societies that would result in a different picture of stratification from that found in the United States?

Western Societies

A useful source of information on cross-national social stratification is *Old People in Three Industrial Societies* (Shanas et al., 1968). This genuine cross-national study of Great Britain, Denmark, and the United States offers valuable information on social class of the aged. In these three industrialized countries, income derived from the government was of basic importance for the elderly, and economic support from the family was of minor importance. In addition, there was considerable diversity of economic circumstances among the aged, but the differences were far greater in the United States than in the other countries because of the extremes of wealth and poverty in the United States.

Shanas et al. (1968) stated: "All in all, the cross-national study suggests that at this time different patterns of employment and retirement seem to be more explicable in terms of difference in pension ages, economic and social structure, relative size of incomes and asset holdings, and disability rates than in terms of individual attitudes and national personality traits or value systems" (p. 447).

The publication of Peter Townsend's (1979) *Poverty in the United Kingdom* provides a unique chance to compare the situation of old people in two highly industrialized societies that share many historical, cultural, linguistic, and economic ties. Townsend's research on poverty in the United Kingdom provides a valuable, detailed source of information on old people and stratification, as well as on other groups and strata, and an orientation to stratification issues in general. The high proportion of the elderly living in relative poverty has been a longstanding and resistant public problem in spite of social programs that are now about a century old. Townsend (1979) places poverty in old age in cross-national perspective: "Moreover, the problem is by no means peculiar to Britain and seems to be characteristic of market economies and state socialist societies alike" (p. 784). His general thesis is that poverty in old age is related to the low levels of *resources relative to younger persons*. The restriction or the adequacy of resources may be determined by different causal factors, but in the United Kingdom, as elswhere, state pensions (Social Security in the United States) and other cash benefits are the most important sources of income for the elderly.

Townsend's approach to stratification is through the study of *poverty*, which he defines through the concept of relative deprivation: "The term is understood objectively rather than subjectively. Individuals, families and groups in the population can be said to be in poverty when they lack the resources to obtain the types of diets, participate in the activities and have the living conditions and amenities which are customary, or are at least widely encouraged or approved, in the societies to which they belong. Their resources are so seriously below those recommended by the average individual or family that they are, in effect, excluded from ordinary living patterns, customs and activities" (Townsend, 1974, p. 16).

Townsend, who obtained information about family contacts in his national survey, emphasized the importance of family ties as supplements to economic security in the highly industrialized and urbanized society of Great Britain. He then correlated family integration and the ways in which family assistance brings about higher standards of living. He found that this aid is usually indirect rather than in cash. "The elderly may stay with relatives for periods of the year, visit relatives for meals, receive gifts of food, clothes and household goods and benefit from a variety of free domestic and nursing services" (Townsend, 1979, pp. 814–815).

An important stratification subject for which there are very few empirical data is the relationship of living standards of the elderly to lifelong class position. Townsend describes these relationships by sorting the United Kingdom sample into seven "classes" —controlling the present class of the elderly and the occupational position of their fathers (e.g., nonmanual father and nonmanual offspring; manual father and nonmanual offspring, etc.). Six indicators of the levels of resources were employed, such as: net disposable household income below or on margins of poverty standards; living in home not owner-occupied (outright); fewer than eight or ten durables in the home, and so on.

The data demonstrate there are marked class differences, particularly in regard to net assets. Differences in resources on all six indicators are very great between the top class (two generations of nonmanual employment) and two generations of the lower occupational classes. A privileged position for two successive generations is the best "insurance" for high levels of resources in old age.

The British data show that with continuity of class, there is persistence of privilege throughout the life cycle. Townsend summarizes the major determinants of how inequality operates over a lifetime: "People of high status were more likely to have benefitted from high earnings; to have accumulated savings and other assets, and in particular to have become outright owner-occupiers of their homes; inherited wealth; enjoyed employer welfare benefits in kind during working life; and gained rights to occupational pensions. On the other hand, people of low status were more likely to have had low earnings; experienced long spells of unemployment and more spells of illness off work; experienced insecurity of employment with no rights to occupational pensions, paid holidays and wages during sickness; had more dependents to support during working life, and lived in rented dwellings with little opportunity to enter the owner-occupied sector of housing" (Townsend, 1979, pp. 819–820).

Townsend's use of relative deprivation avoids an arbitrary dollar or pound index of poverty or inequality, but requires considerable judgment in selection of specific items. He states that his items are "customary" in Britain: taking a week's holiday, entertaining a relative or friend in the last four weeks, having a cooked breakfast, and so on. However, one of the earmarks of complex modern societies is variability in tastes and practices. Townsend presupposes a homogeneous population that chooses the same amenities and activities, and assumes that if they do not exhibit these behaviors, they are deprived. Moreover, one generalization that is widely accepted for complex societies is that the aged are heterogeneous; in fact, some gerontologists have asserted that greater diversity is probably found among the old than among younger categories of the population. Townsend's careful design using indicators of poverty is to be commended, but the cross-national validity of his indicators of relative deprivation must be questioned.

Social Stratification and Aging in the Soviet Union

It is essential to include the Soviet Union in our discussion of social stratification, so that we have comparative information and analysis on the stratification of the aged in a socialist, industrialized society where all of the means of production, the services, and facilities are owned and controlled by the government. Furthermore, the Soviet administration has the power to enforce its programs. "Objective needs" in the Soviet Union are determined by the party, not by the individual or group (Feldmesser, 1968). How does this situation affect the status of the aged?

First it is necessary to outline some general aspects of stratification. Soviet sociologists and ideologists assume (at least publicly) that their society and government is in a transitional state and eventually will reach the goal of real equality—a classless society. Concepts of lower and higher strata do not apply, it is claimed, to the Soviet socialist society. What is the *objective* situation concerning differentiation of groups in the Soviet Union? There is a scarcity of accurate and complete information on income differentials, but one can make a few observations. Lipset and Dobson (1973) state that income inequalities in the Soviet Union are probably less now than before World War II. Yet there are still considerable differences in income between people at the top of the occupational structure and those in lower positions.

Two Soviet sociologists, Gordon and Klopov, have stressed the emergence of hereditary occupational strata (Lipset and Dobson, 1973, p. 172). This is another kind of evidence suggesting that there are inequalities, even in a society structured around the goal of equality.

Another way to empirically examine occupational differences is by studies of prestige, which reveal that the occupational prestige structure in the Soviet Union is practically identical with those of nonsocialist countries like the United States (Inkeles and Rossi, 1956; Hodge et al., 1966). Thus, in the Soviet Union we have, in effect, what might be called an "ideal" and a "real" system of stratification.

Paul Sweezy (1981), a prominent Marxian analyst of modern capitalism, has clearly expressed his opinion that the rulers of the Soviet Union "are a *class* [italics his] and not a stratum, or an elite, or a bureaucracy, or some other non-class formation" (p. 55). He states: "On the basis of the limited evidence available (at least to me) I would judge that the process of class formation is substantially complete in the Soviet Union and that it is therefore justified to speak of a definite ruling class."

What clues are there to the stratification system in old age? One might speculate that in a socialist society, the aged would receive fullest honor and consideration and support in acknowledgment of their years of productivity for the benefit of the nation. Under a system where the amassing of any kind of personal wealth is disapproved and largely prohibited, one would expect generous pensions upon retirement. However, pensions were pitifully small until the 1960s (Geiger, 1968), and it was mainly the responsibility of the children to support their parents.

Article 120 of the Constitution of the Soviet Union established that "Citizens of the U.S.S.R. have the right to maintenance in old age and also in the case of sickness or disability" (Muravyova, 1956, p. 3). The Pension Law of 1956 provided that all civilian state employees were covered by the same scheme. Men were entitled to an old age pension at age 60 if they had worked for 25 years in state employment; women at the age of 55 after working 20 years (McAuley, 1979). In 1964 and 1967, laws were passed that granted collective farm workers similar benefits (Keefe et al., 1971).

McAuley (1979) reports that in 1970 the average value of an old age pension was equal to 44 percent of average earnings, implying a value of 54 rubles a month. The average value of pensions of collective farmers was considered to be 24 rubles a month.

While there has been considerable improvement in the pension situation, about a third of the elderly are not covered, according to McAuley (1979). He states: "This means that some six or seven million elderly Soviet citizens are completely dependent upon their savings or the earnings of their relatives for support in their old age (and this figure excludes the collective farm population)" (McAuley, 1979, p. 276).

There is fragmentary evidence suggesting that income differentials and better housing from earlier periods continue into later life. There is clearly a "pension elite" in the Soviet Union. Lipset and Dobson (1973) state: "There are high retirement awards made to 'persons who have rendered exceptional service . . . in the areas of revolutionary, governmental, social and economic activity . . . and in the fields of culture, science and technology'" (p. 129).

Hollander (1973) observes that old age does not appear to be a major social problem in the Soviet Union at present, for the severe housing shortage continues to hold the older and younger generations together to a far greater extent than they are in the United States. Thus, families are forced to live together because there is absolutely no alternative. In addition, the grandmothers frequently play an important role in running the household and raising the children while the mothers are at work.

The Soviet family has adapted to the lack of adequate pensions for the aged and the shortage of homes for the aged by the use of a three-generational extended family form. Geiger (1968) summarized the situation: "In the marketplace of mutually desired services it has been a good bargain; in exchange for a home, the aged have taken over, according to capacity, the functions left undone by the working wife and mother. In past years this arrangement has been such a standard practice that it was defined as desirable. . . . All benefit from this arrangement, including the Soviet regime itself, which saved itself the expense for many years of becoming a true welfare state" (p. 205).

Two Soviet gerontologists (Solovyev and Petrichenko, 1972) extol the role of the elderly in helping young couples in family planning, taking care of the children, planning the budget, and running the household. They state: "The aged play a special role in the sphere of moral relations with the view to insure the sense of duty, dignity, agreement, diligence and collectivism in the members of the family. They educate the young generation to this aim on the high moral and humane principles" (Solovyev and Petrichenko, 1972, p. 271). It is difficult to know if the elderly really have such high status as is portrayed here. It seems to mirror aging in the "ideal world" rather than in the real world. The gerontologists add that when older people help in the household duties, "the young people get more time to participate in social life, thus raising their cultural level." (This might be considered a dubious mark of status of the elderly to some observers.)

One paradoxical aspect of the Soviet situation in regard to status of the aged must be pointed out: Although the babushka (the grandmother) is often essential to the family in caring for the physical needs of the child, there is a subtle but pervading denigration of her influence in the realm of intellect or values. She is considered to represent traditional outmoded values, and there is subtle pressure for the young person to ignore her influence and form values from the peer group, the school, and the party, according to Geiger (1968).

In Sternheimer's (1981) analysis of Soviet retirement policy and future trends, he presents striking demographic data on the future. According to U.N. population projections, by 2000 there will be 54.8 million citizens over 60 years of age—a 61.2 percent increase from 33.8 million in 1975. Simultaneously, the working age population will increase by only 18.9 percent. Furthermore, the cohort of elderly will contain over twice as many women as men, a trend called the feminization of the elderly by Sternheimer. At present, women over 60 outnumber men by a factor of almost 2.1:1. Women are less inclined to work in paid employment after retirement than men.

Working pensioners are most apt to work in the first five years of retirement. About 50 percent of all men over 60 stay in the work force, and 40 percent of the women aged 55–59. However, there are no data on whether their extended work life is a matter of months or years.

In a 1972 report by Soviet gerontologists, it was stated that working pensioners were 3.9 percent of the total Soviet work force, and the percentage of over-60 males and over-55 females was smallest in the most demanding industries. In managerial personnel in all sectors, the percentage of the staff who were pensioners ranged from 4.8 percent to 7.5 percent. Sternheimer (1979) points out: "It is important to note, however, that in the early 1970's working pensioners were still most prevalent in the least prestigious, least well-paid, and most menial occupations in Soviet society . . ." (p. 9).

Some aspects of the Soviet work and retirement system tend to differ from those of other industrial countries. For example, because of a shortage of labor, there is an interest in having older workers stay in the labor force for as long as possible. Indeed, special attempts have been made to lure older citizens back into the labor force. Depending on their employment, they receive their full pension in addition to their weekly wage (Acharkan, 1972).

Between 1975 and 1980, new groups of workers were included in the category of "Wages Plus Full Pension," and provisions were made to increase the size of their pensions for every year worked past pension age, to a maximum of 40 rubles (within the overall pension ceiling of 150 rubles). However, as Ivanovna and Nikolayevna (1972) have pointed out: "The actual placement of aging workers does not always correspond to their qualifications and professions, their physical and moral status" (p. 244). They add that older men who continue to work tend to be employed in low-status occupations as janitors, watchmen, beekeepers, and so on.

In spite of the material incentives for pensioners to continue working, the attempt to keep them in the labor force has not been very effective. Existing levels of pensions allow pensioners to "scrape by," and apparently many of them prefer this course of action to continued participation in the labor force. This may seem puzzling, since Soviet society is officially devoted to the notion that "work is good for you." Sternheimer (1979)

discusses several Soviet pensioner studies focusing on reasons for retirement. He concludes that while material factors do play a role, "social factors" are probably even more important, as, for example, the length of the working day, the choice of shifts, and relations with one's supervisor. Sternheimer (1979) writes: "There is evidence in some of the Soviet studies . . . which leads us to think that the basic issue is less one of 'work versus retirement' and more a question of job 'satisfaction' versus 'dissatisfaction.' From this perspective, it may well be . . . that the young old are voting for 'freedom from work' by retiring—even though, paradoxically, both an absolute freedom from want and a commitment to leisure-as-a-value-in-itself are lacking in the Soviet Union" (p. 23).

It is not surprising that women prefer to retire when they are eligible for a pension, for Soviet working women have a double burden of working and managing the household. The problems of shopping, with long waits in queues and absence of labor-saving devices in the home, mean that women spend many more hours in household activities than men.

Sternheimer observes that the present difficulties of the Soviet regime stem from a "tendency to view the problems of retirement strictly in economic terms, to rely overmuch on material incentives, and to see older persons (as well as the young) as 'economic men' in 'vulgar Marxist' terms, rather than as social individuals." He concludes that the retirement trends in the Soviet Union are as complex, multifaceted, and relatively impervious to social engineering as in the United States.

Alienation is not particularly an issue in the Soviet Union. Persons in the United States are concerned about feelings of personal happiness and usefulness and consider alienation to be highly undesirable. As a society, Americans berate themselves for permitting citizens to be alienated. In the Soviet Union, however, according to Hollander (1973): "Neither powerlessness nor alienation is much of an issue. . . . Powerlessness is taken for granted among the population at large. Alienation is not a pressing public or private concern. There is little self-consciousness about it; a certain amount of alienation is probably taken for granted—as a more or less natural condition" (p. 399).

The Soviet Union does have one problem that is characteristic of some developed societies—namely, the increasing percentage of middle-aged and old population in rural areas. The young people are anxious to leave the farms because of the physical isolation, a 30 to 50 percent lower level of wages of farm workers in comparison to factory workers, more limited supply of consumer goods, and longer working hours (Benet, 1970; Smith, 1976). Furthermore, it is difficult for the collective-farm peasants to get passports for travel or for change of residence. One way to evade these restrictions is to leave the farm before the age of 16. Hollander (1973) observes: "There is some similarity to the vicious circle of poverty in the United States and the hopelessness of Soviet rural areas. However, in the Soviet case a move to the city is probably a more decisive improvement than similar moves are for the American poor" (p. 341). The willingness of the babushka to move in with her grown children in the city and take care of the grandchildren may be a consequence of the grim living conditions in rural areas.

Thus, inequality exists even in the Soviet Union, which has as one of its premises a classless society. Despite great efforts, ideological and structural, to create a society of greater equality for older citizens, the analyst concludes that there are differentials between the old and those in the work force. It seems a truism that in any society marked by shortages, it is the working segment of the population that receives the first consideration. Thus, despite the *intentions* of the Soviet system that each citizen is entitled to the basic necessities and a life of dignity, the workers are accorded the highest honor, and the aged must accept secondary prestige.

The description and analysis of aging and inequality in the Soviet Union can be placed in comparative perspective through the work of John F. Myles (1980) and his analysis of the facts about aging and poverty in Canada and in other advanced capitalist societies. Myles states that the economic position of older persons is dependent upon the forces found in the economy as a whole. He asserts: "The problems which appear at the level of consumption in the form of low income are ultimately rooted in the organization of production characteristics of *all advanced capitalist societies*" (Myles, 1980, p. 317, italics added).

It would appear that there is inequality in both systems: in advanced capitalist societies because the market system and private pensions reward some citizens more than others, and in the Soviet Union because pension elites receive not only higher incomes in retirement but also many benefits (housing, health care, vacations, etc.) that are publicly supported.

The basic economic sustenance for the elderly in both advanced capitalist and in Soviet-type societies is government systems of transfer payments. Myles's statement concerning advanced capitalist societies applies also to a Marxist-organized society like the Soviet Union. He says: "It is clear, therefore, that public policy, rather than market forces, is the major factor determining the structure of inequality in old age" (Myles, 1980, p. 323).

STATUS LOSS AND STATUS DISCREPANCY

The analysis of social stratification in the latter quarter of the life cycle involves complex issues that this chapter has only begun to conceptualize. Most investigators of stratification accept the multidimensional nature of stratification and have focused on a variety of observable indicators: income, occupation, education, property, ethnicity, and sex. Surprisingly, age is not included.

Researchers on stratification in the latter part of the life cycle must recognize age and aging as the strategic characteristics, linked causally to other stratification indices, and primary reasons for downward mobility. In fact, much of the literature on retirement is actually a study of the differential loss of status and its consequences, or *status discrepancy*. We use the term "status discrepancy" rather than "status inconsistency"* because the large body of literature on status inconsistency is related to earlier stages of the life cycle and does not consider the effects of aging. In order to avoid confusion with this established subfield, we employ a different term that encompasses a broader range of phenomena, and includes status losses caused by aging itself. Rosow (1974) points out that role losses are the inevitable fate of virtually everybody who survives long enough. Status discrepancy, as used here, refers to the differential *loss* of status, in contrast to status inconsistency, which refers to differential rankings on hierarchies at one point in time. Status discrepancy involves changes on different hierarchies over time, as persons become older. In other words, there is a realization that in studying old age, one must acknowledge present rankings in relation to former positions on different hierarchies.

Status discrepancy is a useful concept in studying the stratification of the aged because it recognizes the fact that older persons may experience changes in their ranking on one hierarchy but not on another. For example, most older people have a decline in income when they retire, but not all experience downward movement in style of life. Most older people eventually relinquish their work role, but their educational attainment remains the same.

Status discrepancy also occurs because of the physical and mental decrements that are frequently associated with aging. The emergence of biological factors complicates the pattern of the usual indicators of stratification—income, education, work status, eth-

nicity, and so forth. The addition of the variable of health has significant effects on status and adds a new dimension to status discrepancy. No matter how high an individual's income level, education, power, or style of life, if that person is mentally or physically disabled, his or her stratification position is altered significantly.

It is generally assumed that younger people aspire to higher status and upward mobility. Perhaps a different set of goals evolves as the aging process proceeds. The "cult of success" (Lopreato and Hazelrigg, 1972) characterizes earlier phases of the life cycle, and emphasizes upward mobility and status striving as a life goal. Aging creates a new set of priorities. The comprehensive study by Larson (1978) on 30 years of research on the subjective well-being of Americans over 60 years of age shows that health is the factor most strongly associated with well-being, for it was rated higher than income.

The literature on status inconsistency reports that it is associated with tension and stress because of the incongruence of status measures. Various studies have noted that when the aged lose some of their roles, they appear to be more accepting of the situation and more adaptable to the consequences than do persons encountering status discrepancy at other phases of the life cycle.

There is need for research on the degree to which social deprivation and psychological strain result from differential downward mobility in the elderly. We need to delineate the adaptive mechanisms for status loss. At present, it is possible to offer only speculations. For example, the aged have had a lifetime to perfect their coping mechanisms, so that they have learned to come to terms with anomalous situations. Another explanation could be that their feelings of self-identity are often more firmly established than those of persons at earlier stages of the life cycle (Lowenthal et al., 1975).

The research of gerontologists at the University of Southern California may offer another clue as to why some elderly are undisturbed by status discrepancy—namely, the development of an integrating theme of

---

*One of the major subfields of stratification has been status inconsistency, which was defined by Lenski (1966) as dissimilar ranking on different dimensions of stratification. The concept of status inconsistency deals with the horizontal or nonvertical aspects of stratification and may be viewed as the way that different components interact in relation to one another. For a review of the status inconsistency literature highlighting conceptual, methodological, and substantive issues, see, for example, Beeghley (1978).

life for some older people, that of "aging as a career" (Myerhoff, 1978). These researchers have noted that the process of survival itself can be considered a triumph. Small and ordinary routines of living that seem insignificant to younger people constitute sources of pride and accomplishment to the elderly. "Meaning is provided by the sense that each day is lived autonomously in the community, with independence, dignity, alertness and control over one's faculties and mobility" (Bengtson, 1975, p. 60).

We agree with many writers (Rosow, 1974; Foner and Schwab, 1981; Cumming and Henry, 1961) that status changes and role losses are inevitable for almost everyone who becomes old. An important question is that of how the elderly adapt to the resulting status discrepancy. A great deal of gerontological research is concerned with this subject, approaching it in different ways, but it is not considered in terms of status discrepancy. Foner and Schwab (1981) focus upon retirement as a kind of status loss, and propose that there are three major coping modes that individuals use to adapt to the loss, namely, lowering of expectations, redefinition of rewards, and the maintenace of continuity in some activities and social life.

In writing about socialization to old age, Rosow (1974) has said that the transition to late life in America has some distinctive configurations. Three of these have special relevance for stratification: (1) devalued position, (2) role discontinuity, and (3) status loss. He suggests that coping with role loss may involve new group structures and functions. His approach to status discrepancies is that socialization to new roles in old age can be facilitated by increased association with age peers, with the corollary of weakened ties to younger persons; the elderly will often concentrate in settings in which there is a higher proportion of the old. These conditions will enhance group supports, positive reference groups, insulation of members, and so on. In the discussion of retirement communities in this chapter, it was pointed out how some of these settings provide an environment in which there is a tendency for similarity of status to develop and persist.

The study of social stratification of the aged has been too long neglected. Research on the latter part of the life cycle requires a shift in analytical perspective on the part of social scientists because they have emphasized advancement and status attainment with upward mobility as the desirable norm. Instead of employing the same stratification rankings that apply to younger people, perhaps social scientists should develop new concepts and new ranking scales to measure the status of those beyond the working years. The study of the elderly requires a different perspective, focusing on status discrepancy and status loss. In mature industrial societies, with increasing proportions of older people, more attention must be paid to the distinctive aspects of social stratification of the aged, to socialization to role loss, and to downward mobility.

REFERENCES

Acharkan, V. A. 1972. Development of the law on social security of older working persons in the U.S.S.R. *Abstracts, Ninth International Congress of Gerontology, Kiev, U.S.S.R.* 3:173.

Applebaum, J. A., and Faber, J. F. 1979. The concept of replacement ratios under Social Security. *Actuarial Note Number 96.* Washington, D.C.: Social Security Administration.

Averitt, R. T. 1968. *The Dual Economy: The Dynamics of American Industry Structure.* New York: Norton.

Barron, M. L. 1953. Minority group characteristics of the aged in American society. *J. Geront.* 8:477–482.

Beeghley, L. 1978. *Social Stratification in America.* Santa Monica, Calif.: Goodyear Publishing.

Bendix, R., and Lipset, S. M. 1953. Karl Marx's theory of social class. *In* R. Bendix and S. M. Lipset (eds.), *Class, Status and Power: A Reader in Social Stratification,* pp. 6–11. New York: Free Press.

Benet, S. (ed.). 1970. *The Village of Viriantino: An Ethnographic Study of a Russian Village.* Garden City, N. Y.: Doubleday (originally published in Moscow, 1958).

Bengtson, V. L. 1975. *The Social and Cultural Contexts of Aging: Implications for Social Policy.* Progress Report to National Science Foundation. Los Angeles: Andrus Gerontology Center, University of Southern California.

Bernstein, M. C. 1980. Forecast of women's retirement income: Cloudy and colder; 25 percent chance of poverty. *In* M. Fuller and C. A. Martin (eds.), *The*

Older Woman: Lavender Rose or Gray Panther. Springfield, Ill.: Charles C. Thomas (originally published in *Industrial Gerontology*, 1974, 1:1–13).

Binstock, R. H. 1974. Aging and the future of American politics. *Ann. Am. Acad.* 415:199–212.

Bottomore, T. B. 1965. *Classes in Modern Society.* London: George Allen and Unwin.

Bultena, G. L., and Wood, V. 1969. The American retirement community: Bane or blessing? *J. Geront.* 24:209–217.

Bultena, G. et al. 1971. *Life After 70 in Iowa: A Restudy of the Participants in the 1960 Survey of the Aged.* Sociology Report 95. Ames, Iowa: Iowa State University.

Butterfield, F. 1982. *China, Alive in the Bitter Sea.* New York: Times Books.

Carter, H. W., and Webber, I. L. 1966. *The Aged and Chronic Disease.* Monograph #9. Jacksonville, Fla.: Florida State Board of Health.

Chen, Y. P. 1973. A pilot survey study of the Housing-Annuity Plan. Offset. Los Angeles: University of California, Graduate School of Management.

Clark, R., Kreps, J., and Spengler, J. 1978. Economics of aging. *J. Economic Litearture* 16:919–962.

Coleman, R. P., and Neugarten, B. L. 1971. *Social Status in the City.* San Francisco: Jossey-Bass.

Cowgill, D. O., and Holmes, L. D. 1972. *Aging and Modernization.* New York: Appleton-Century-Crofts.

Cumming, E., and Henry, W. 1961. *Growing Old: The Process of Disengagement.* New York: Basic Books.

Dowd, J. J. 1980. *Stratification Among the Aged.* Monterey, Calif.: Brooks/Cole.

Espenshade, T. J., and Braun, R. E. 1981. Economic aspects of an aging population and the material well-being of older persons. *In* B. B. Hess and K. Bond (eds.), *Leading Edges: Recent Research on Psychosocial Aging,* pp. 51–89. National Institute on Aging, U.S. Department of Health and Human Services, NIH Publication No. 81–2390.

Feldmesser, R. A. 1968. Stratification and Communism. *In* A. Kassof (ed.), *Prospects for Soviet Society* pp. 359–385. New York: Praeger.

Foner, A. 1979. Ascribed and achieved bases of stratification. *Annu. Rev. Sociol.* 5:219–242.

Foner, A., and Schwab, K. 1981. *Aging and Retirement.* Monterey, Calif.: Brooks/Cole.

Geiger, H. K. 1968. *The Family in Soviet Russia.* Cambridge, Mass.: Harvard University Press.

Giddens, A. 1973. *The Class Structure of the Advanced Societies.* London: Hutchinson.

Gurin, P., Miller, A., and Gurin, G. 1980. Stratum identification and consciousness. *Social Psychology Quarterly* 43:30–47.

Haug, M. R. 1973. Social class measurement and women's occupational roles. *Soc. Forces* 52:85–98.

Haug, M. R. 1977. Measurement in social stratification. *Annu. Rev. Sociol.* 3:51–77.

Heilbroner, R. L. 1980. *Marxism: For and Against.* New York: Norton.

Heintz, K. 1976. *Retirement Communities: For Adults Only.* New Brunswick, N. J.: The Center for Urban Policy Research, Rutgers-State University of New Jersey.

Henretta, J. C., and Campbell, R. T. 1976. Status attainment and status maintenance: A study of stratification in old age. *Am. Soc. Rev.* 41:981–992.

Henretta, J. C., and Campbell, R. T. 1978. Net worth as an aspect of status. *Am. J. Sociol.* 83:1204–1223.

Henretta, J. C., and O'Rand, A. 1980. Labor force participation of older married women. *Social Security Bulletin* 43(8, Aug.):40–46.

Hill, R. B. 1971. *The Strengths of Black Families.* New York: Independent Publishers.

Hochschild, A. R. 1973. *The Unexpected Community.* Englewood Cliffs, N. J.: Prentice-Hall.

Hodge, R. W., Treiman, D. J., and Rossi, P. H. 1966. A comparative study of occupational prestige. *In* R. Bendix and S. M. Lipset (eds.), *Class, Status, Power,* 2nd ed., pp. 309–321. New York: The Free Press.

Hollander, P. J. 1973. *Soviet and American Society: A Comparison.* New York: Oxford University Press.

Inkeles, A., and Rossi, P. H. 1956. National comparisons of occupational prestige. *Am. J. Sociol.* 61:329–339.

Ivanovna, S. E., and Nikolayevna, S. N. 1972. Demographic shifts in modern society and labour activities of the elderly population. *In* D. F. Chebotarev et al. (eds.), *The Main Problems of Soviet Gerontology,* pp. 240–251. Kiev, U.S.S.R.: Institute of Gerontology.

Jacobs, J. 1974. *Fun City: An Ethnographic Study of a Retirement Community.* New York: Holt, Rinehart & Winston.

Johnson, S. K. 1971. *Idle Haven: Community Building Among the Working Class Retired.* Berkeley: University of California Press.

Jones, A. W. 1941. *Life, Liberty, and Property.* Philadelphia: J. B. Lippincott.

Keefe, E. K. et al. 1971. *Area Handbook for the Soviet Union.* Washington, D.C.: U.S. Government Printing Office.

Kelleher, C. H., and Quirk, D. H. 1973. Age, functional capacity and work: An annotated bibliography. *Industrial Gerontology* 19:80–98.

Kent, D. P., and Hirsch, C. 1971. *Social and Economic Conditions of Negro and White Aged Residents of Urban Neighborhoods of Low Socio-Economic Status,* Vol. I. Final report submitted to the Administration on Aging. University Park, Pa.: Pennsylvania State University.

Kleiler, F. M. 1978. *Can We Afford Early Retirement?* Baltimore: The Johns Hopkins Press.

Lane, D. 1976. *The Socialist Industrial State.* London: George Allen and Unwin.

Larson, R. 1978. Thirty years of research on the subjective well-being of older Americans. *J. Geront.* 33:109–125.

Laufer, R. S., and Bengtson, V. L. 1974. Generations,

aging and social stratification: On the development of generational units. *J. Soc. Issues* 30:181–205.

Lawton, M. P. 1980. *Environment and Aging.* Monterey, Calif.: Brooks/Cole.

Leggett, J. C. 1968. *Class, Race and Labor: Working Class Consciousness in Detroit.* New York: Oxford University Press.

Lenski, G. 1966. *Power and Privilege: A Theory of Social Stratification.* New York: McGraw-Hill.

Liang, J., and Fairchild, T. 1979. Relative deprivation and perception of financial adequacy among the aged. *J. Geront.* 34:746–759.

Lipset, Seymour M. 1968. Social class. *In: International Encyclopedia of the Social Sciences,* pp. 296–316. New York: Macmillan and Free Press.

Lipset, S. M., and Dobson, R. B. 1973. Social stratification and sociology in the Soviet Union. *Survey* 19(3[88]):114–185.

Lopata, H. Z. 1973. Self identity in marriage and widowhood. *Sociol. Quart.* 14:407–418.

Lopata, H. Z. 1979. *Women as Widows.* New York: Elsevier.

Lopreato, J., and Hazelrigg, L. E. 1972. *Class, Conflict and Mobility.* San Francisco: Chandler.

Louis, A. M. 1968. America's centimillionaires. *Fortune* 77:152–157.

Lowenthal, M. F., Thurnher, M., Chiriboga, D., and associates. 1975. *Four Stages of Life.* San Francisco: Jossey-Bass.

Malcolm, A. 1974. Special to the *New York Times,* Mar. 24.

Mannheim, K. 1952. The problem of generations. *In* P. Kecskemeti (ed.), *Essays on the Sociology of Knowledge by Karl Mannheim.* London: Routledge and Kegan Paul.

Mathews, D. R. 1954. *The Social Background of Political Decision-Makers.* New York: Random House.

Matura, R. 1982. The politics of aging in Florida: A case study of the silver haired legislature. Gainesville, Fla.: University of Florida, unpublished Ph.D. dissertation.

McAuley, A. 1979. *Economic Welfare in the Soviet Union.* Madison, Wis.: University of Wisconsin Press.

Melman, S. 1970. *Pentagon Capitalism: The Political Economy of War.* New York: McGraw-Hill.

Michelon, L. C. 1954. The new leisure class. *Am. J. Sociol.* 59:371–378.

Moen, E. W. 1981. The realities of needs assessment: Rural Oregon. *In* G. F. Streib (ed.), *Programs for Older Americans: Evaluations by Academic Gerontologists,* pp. 50–72. Gainesville, Fla.: University Presses of Florida.

Morris, R., and Murphy, R. J. 1966. A paradigm for the study of class consciousness. *Sociol. & Soc. Res.* 50:297–313.

Muravyova, N. A. 1956. *Social Security in the U.S.S.R.* Moscow: Foreign Languages Publishing House.

Myerhoff, B. 1978. *Number Our Days.* New York: Simon and Schuster.

Myles, J. F. 1980. The aged, the state, and the structure of inequality. *In* J. Harp and J. Hofley (eds.), *Structured Inequality in Canada.* Scarborough, Ontario: Prentice-Hall of Canada, Ltd.

Myles, J. F. 1981. Income inequality and status maintenance: Concepts, methods, and measures. *Research on Aging* 3:123–141.

Neugarten, B. L. 1966. The aged in American society. *In* H. S. Becker (ed.), *Social Problems: A Modern Approach.* New York: John Wiley.

Neugarten, B. L. 1974. Age groups in American society and the rise of the young old. *Annals* 415:187–198.

O'Gorman, H. 1980. False consciousness of kind. *Research on Aging* 2:105–128.

Olsen, M. E. 1974. Social classes in contemporary Sweden. *Sociol. Quart.* 15:323–340.

Osgood, N. 1982. *Senior Settlers: Social Integration in Retirement Communities.* New York: Praeger Publishers.

Palmore, E. 1969. Sociological aspects of aging. *In* E. W. Busse and E. Pfeiffer (eds.), *Behavior and Adaptation in Late Life,* pp. 33–69. Boston: Little, Brown.

Palmore, E., and Whittington, F. 1971. Trends in the relative status of the aged. *Soc. Forces* 50:84–91.

Pampel, F. C. 1979. Changes in the labor force participation and income of the aged in the United States. *Soc. Problems* 27:125–142.

Pope, L. 1941. *Preachers and Millhands.* New Haven, Conn.: Yale University Press.

Porter, J. 1965. *The Vertical Mosaic: An Analysis of Social Class and Power in Canada.* Toronto: University of Toronto Press.

Pratt, H. J. 1974. Old age associations in national politics. *Annals* 415:106–119.

President's Commission on Pension Policy, 1980. *An Interim Report.* Washington, D.C.: U.S. Government Printing Office.

President's Commission on Pension Policy, 1981. *Coming of Age: Toward a National Retirement Policy.* Washington, D.C.: President's Commission on Pension Policy.

Ragan, P. K., and Dowd, J. J. 1974. The emerging political consciousness of the aged: A generational interpretation. *J. Soc. Issues* 30:137–158.

Ragan, P. K., and Wales, J. B. 1980. Age stratification and the life course. *In* J. E. Birren and R. B. Sloane (eds.), *Handbook of Mental Health and Aging.* Englewood Cliffs, N. J.: Prentice-Hall.

Rainwater, L. 1974. *What Money Buys: Inequality and the Social Meanings of Income.* New York: Basic Books.

Riley, M. W. 1971. Social gerontology and the age stratification of society. *The Gerontologist* 11:79–87.

Riley, M. W., Foner, A., Moore, M. E., Hess, B., and Roth, B. K. 1968. *Aging and Society,* Vol. 1, *An Inventory of Research Findings.* New York: Russell Sage Foundation.

Riley, M. W., Johnson, M., and Foner, A. 1972. *Aging*

and Society, Vol. 3, *A Sociology of Age Stratification*. New York: Russell Sage Foundation.

Rosenberg, G. S. 1970. *The Worker Grows Old*. San Francisco: Jossey-Bass.

Rosow, I. 1967. *Social Integration of the Aged*. New York: The Free Press.

Rosow, I. 1974. *Socialization to Old Age*. Berkeley: University of California Press.

Runciman, W. G. 1966. *Relative Deprivation and Social Justice*. London: Routledge and Kegan Paul.

Schreiber, E. M., and Nygreen, G. T. 1970. Subjective social class in America, 1945-68. *Soc. Forces* 48:348-356.

Schulz, J. H. 1980. *The Economics of Aging,* 2nd ed. Belmont, Calif.: Wadsworth.

Schulz, H. G., Baird, P., and Hawkes, G. 1979. *Lifestyles and Consumer Behavior of Older Americans*. New York: Praeger.

Shanas, E., Townsend, P., Wedderburn, D., Friis, H., Milhøj, P., and Stehouwer, J. 1968. *Old People in Three Industrial Societies*. London: Routledge and Kegan Paul.

Simmons, L. W. 1945. *The Role of the Aged in Primitive Society*. New Haven: Yale University Press.

Smith, H. 1976. *The Russians*. New York: Quandrangle.

Solovyev, N. Ya., and Petrichenko, A. E. 1972. Old age, family and society, *In: Symposia Reports,* Vol. 2, pp. 270-273. Kiev, U.S.S.R.: International Congress of Gerontology.

Sternheimer, S. 1979. Retirement and aging in the Soviet Union: Who works, who doesn't, and what can be done about it. Paper delivered at American Association for the Advancement of Slavic Studies, New Haven, Conn.

Sternheimer, S. 1981. Soviet retirement policy and working pensioners for the eighties. Paper delivered at Conference on Retirement and Aging. Bellagio, Italy, June 1981.

Streib, G. F. 1965. Are the aged a minority group? *In* A. W. Gouldner and S. M. Miller (eds.), *Applied Sociology* pp. 311-328. Glencoe, Ill.: Free Press.

Streib, G. F., and Schneider, C. J. 1971. *Retirement in American Society: Impact and Process*. Ithaca, N. Y.: Cornell University Press.

Streib, G. F., LacGreca, A., and Folts, W. E. 1982. The life history of retirement communities: Comparative studies of thirty communities. Paper delivered at the 77th annual meeting of the American Sociological Association, San Francisco.

Struyk, R. J., and Soldo, B. J. 1980. *Improving the Elderly's Housing*. Cambridge, Mass.: Ballinger.

Svalastoga, K. 1959. *Prestige, Class and Mobility*. Copehagen: Gyldendal.

Sweezy, P. M. 1981. Paul Sweezy comments. *Monthly Review* 33:55-57.

Tissue, T. 1972. Old age and the perception of poverty. *Sociol. & Soc. Res* 56:331-344.

Townsend, P. 1974. Poverty as relative deprivation: Resources and style of living. *In* D. Wedderburn (ed.), *Poverty, Inequality, and Class Structure*, pp. 15-41. London and New York: Cambridge University Press.

Townsend, P. 1979. *Poverty in the United Kingdom: A Survey of Household Resources and Standards of Living*. Berkeley and Los Angeles: University of California Press.

Uhlenberg, P. 1977. Changing structure of the older population of the USA during the twentieth century. *The Gerontologist* 17:197-202.

United States Bureau of the Census. 1983. Cynthia M. Taeuber. America in Transition: An Aging Society. Current Population Reports. Series P-23, No. 128. Washington, D.C.: USGPO.

Weber, M. 1946. Class, status and party. *In* H. H. Gerth and C. W. Mills, (eds.), *From Max Weber: Essays in Sociology*. New York: Oxford University Press.

Wolfe, A. 1977. *The Limits of Legitimacy: Political Contradictions of Contemporary Capitalism*. New York: The Free Press.

13
AGE STRATA IN SOCIAL SYSTEMS

Matilda White Riley*
National Institute on Aging

This chapter presents an overview of age stratification as a conceptual tool for understanding the dynamic interdependence between two concepts: age as a structural feature of a changing society—as in every society both people and roles are stratified by age; and the aging from birth to death of individuals and cohorts of individuals—as all of us grow up and grow old as members of an age-stratified society (Riley et al., 1972; Riley, 1976, 1980). Full understanding of the relationship between aging and social change remains a distant goal, but recent applications of the approach are serving to revise, elaborate, and expand the emerging potential of an empirically supported theory of age stratification systems.

Following a conceptual introduction, the major sections of the chapter examine particular aspects of age stratification systems, illustrating through a few selected examples how the wealth of recent multidisciplinary research, though often uninformed by the

*This revision of the 1976 *Handbook* chapter is a distillation of many intellectual interchanges both informal and through such institutions as the Center for Advanced Study in the Behavioral Sciences and committees of the Social Science Research Council. The author is especially indebted to Joan Waring for several reformulations of earlier ideas, to David L. Featherman for detailed comment and criticism, and to the following persons for review of earlier versions of the manuscript: Ronald P. Abeles, Daniel Cowell, Anne Foner, Dale Dannefer, David I. Kertzer, Robert K. Merton, John Meyer, M. Brewster Smith, John W. Riley, Jr., and Aage B. Sorensen and many others.

approach, has nevertheless been contributing to it. The foci of the several sections are: (1) on how a person is located within the changing age structure of society; (2) on how a person of a given age relates to others within and across age boundaries; (3) on how a person, in aging biologically and psychologically, is also aging socially, that is, moving through this age structure; (4) on how, as society changes, a person belonging to one birth cohort does not age in precisely the same way as persons belonging to other cohorts, and, as many people age together, collective lives influence social change. Each of these sections will consider at the macrolevel the age-stratified society (or smaller social institution) as composed, at the microlevel, of individuals growing older in social roles located at any given time in particular strata. Taken together, these sections will consider how the age strata, which shift and change as society changes, are among the bases of social organization that shape sociocultural life and the historical course of mankind (Sorokin, 1968). The chapter highlights noteworthy advances, as these lead to new understandings and new hypotheses for further research on the interplay between aging and social change.

AGE STRATIFICATION SYSTEMS

In terms of a parsimonious set of broad concepts and postulated relationships, society is conceived as an age stratification system within which important roles are age-graded and particular individuals and successive cohorts of individuals are continually aging. Use of this conceptual model in diverse and widely scattered studies in many disciplines is providing insights into significant aspects of the aging process and the place of older people in society.

Drawing initially upon central sociological conceptions, the model has brought together two previously disparate lines of classic social research and theory. First, in respect to age in society, some social scientists (Sorokin, 1941, 1947; Parsons, 1942; Linton, 1942; Eisenstadt, 1956) had focused on the societal age structure; while others (Mannheim, [1928] 1952; Cain, 1964; Ryder, 1965) paid heed to the dynamic aspects of social change, showing how each new cohort of individuals has unique characteristics because of the particular historical events undergone. Second, in respect to aging, portions of the life course had been traced by sociologists through diaries and letters (Thomas and Znaniecki, 1918) or through panel studies (Lazarsfeld, et al., [1944] 1960). Aspects of human development had been explored by Havighurst, Neugarten, and their associates

(Neugarten, 1968). In psychology, cognitive development had been set within the total life span by Schaie, Baltes, and others (discussed below). Socialization had been viewed as extending beyond early childhood into adulthood (Brim, 1966; Clausen, 1968). As part of the model of age stratification, Clausen (1972) described the sequence of social roles in which individuals over their lifetime make continuing adjustments, bringing their accumulated stores of experience and aspirations, and seeking to preserve some sense of personal continuity and identity.

The confluence in the model of these divergent intellectual strands has given fresh meaning to old concepts and has generated new and overarching insights and principles. In the past half dozen years the model (or aspects of it) has been amplified or emended through a range of studies; scattered reviews (e.g., Maddox, 1979; Foner, 1980; Riley, 1981b); and several textbooks (e.g., Ward, 1979; Hess and Markson, 1980). Interdisciplinary communication has been generated between an essentially sociological perspective, life-span psychology (Baltes, 1979; Baltes et al., 1980), and biomedical approaches (cf. Abeles, 1981; Riley and Glass, 1982).

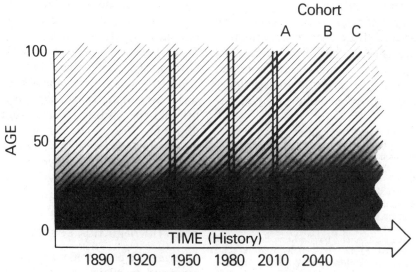

Figure 1. The age stratification system: a schematic view.

A Schematic View

Five major emphases of the model can be visualized schematically as in Figure 1, which shows a succession of diagonal bars within a social space that is bounded on its vertical axis by years of age (0 to 80 or 100 or more), and bounded on its horizontal axis by dates (e.g., 1900, 1980, 2020).

1. Each diagonal bar suggests the life course of particular individuals (or a cohort of individuals born at the same time). These individuals are *aging* over their life course. They age socially as well as biologically and psychologically: that is, they move forward across time and upward through the age strata of society (social aging is one type of social mobility). They pass through sequences of roles, selecting from available opportunities, accumulating knowledge and attitudes and experiences, developing a social self, interacting with other people of all ages who are all growing older together.

2. The series of diagonal bars suggests how *new cohorts* of people are continually being born, aging over the life course until death, and moving through historical time. Cohorts can vary in size, and composition (e.g., in the proportion of females or of foreign-born), and each cohort experiences a unique era of history.

3. At any single moment of history, such as 1979 or 1929, a cross-sectional slice through the successive cohorts divides the *people* into *age strata* (e.g., the young, middle-aged, and old), who coexist and interact within and across age boundaries.

Equally important, each cross-sectional slice denotes the age structure of *roles*. (In every society there are customs, rules, and beliefs as to which roles are open or closed at different ages—getting into school, out of school, marrying, performing military service, retiring, etc.)

Comparison of such cross-sectional slices sequentially (e.g., 1929, 1949, 1979) suggests how the age-stratified society is never static but is continually moving across time.

4. The calendar-year axis draws attention to the fact that *society itself is changing* (or remaining stable) over historical time—

through changes in people and roles within the age stratification system, and through such extrinsic changes as scientific and cultural development, wars, depressions, famines, or revolutions.

5. There is a *dynamic interplay* between two interdependent processes: individual aging and social change.

These five considerations lead inexorably to a central principle (clearly formulated by Ryder, 1964): because of social change, different cohorts cannot grow up and grow old in precisely the same way. Aging is not an immutable process. Cohorts of people born recently differ sharply from those born a century ago—in prenatal care, age of puberty, level of education, attitudes and beliefs, age of widowhood, retirement practices, exposure to chronic versus acute diseases, average length of life. Thus the persons in the older age strata today are very different from older persons in the past or in the future.

Clearly there have been enormous changes both in the age structure of society and in the process of aging. But how do such changes come about? How can the dialectical relationship between individual aging and social change be comprehended? The answers must depend on understanding both the age-stratified social structure and its changes (the cross-sectional cuts in Figure 1) and the aging patterns of successive cohorts of individuals (the diagonal bars).

Conceptual Elements

As an aid in answering such questions, the model draws attention to just a few strategically selected concepts denoting how, at any given moment of time, age is implicated in the structures of people and of roles in the changing society; and how the aging of successive cohorts of individuals, together with societal changes impinging on roles, are the dynamics that give momentum to these changing structures (see Figure 2). The model distinguishes between an age structure of people who are at varying ages from neonates to nonagenarians, and an age structure

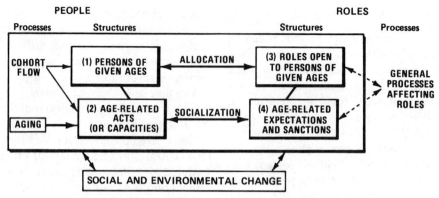

Figure 2. Age stratification system: conceptual elements.

of roles within which people are performing (e.g., as student, worker, retiree; or as child, parent, grandparent). These two structures interpenetrate: roles do not exist apart from people. Yet the role structure, with its associated definitions and norms, changes as society changes, while particular people are continually growing older and moving on into new roles.

The model also isolates three sets of underlying processes. Aging and the flow of cohorts form one set, impinging upon people, influencing where, when, and how many people are located in the several age strata, and producing age-related capacities and performances. A second set of processes, social changes coming from outside the boundaries of the age stratification system, controls and continually changes the age structure of roles to which people are allocated. A third set of processes, allocation and socialization, operates to articulate, however imperfectly, the dual structures of people and of roles.

Arrows in Figure 2 direct attention to the dynamic interconnectedness of these elements, as the ever-changing structures and processes all operate as interdependent parts of an age stratification system. Successive cohorts of individuals, as they age, move through the system to form the age structure of people; and they are allocated to, and socialized for, the age structure of roles. Meantime, as society changes, the roles are also changing. People and roles are continually

affecting and modifying one another. Thus neither the aging of individuals over the life course nor the historical course of society is fixed. Each one alters the other. Moreover, the entire system operates within a changing social, cultural, and physical environment— within history; thus a change in climate, a scientific discovery, industrial advance, or war with a neighboring society can introduce change into the system and can feed back through all the interdependent parts.

Two Dynamisms: Aging and Social Change

The essence of the age stratification model centers in this continuing interplay between these two very different dynamisms: social change and the aging of individuals. Despite the dialectical tension between them, each dynamism is distinct; neither is reducible to the other. Each has its own tempo. People as they age move along the axis of the life course (the diagonals in Figure 1 above). They are born and they die according to a rhythm that is set by the approximate length of the human lifetime. In contrast, the full set of age strata, with their age roles and the age distribution of people within them, coexist and change together as society changes (as in the vertical cross-section slices in Figure 1). And social change moves along its own axis of historical time, governed by forces that affect all age strata simultaneously (cf. Neugarten et al., 1965).

These two dynamisms of individual aging and social change, though interdependent, tend to be poorly synchronized with one another. Though particularly pronounced in modern societies, this potential for asynchrony is inherent in the age stratification system, imposing strains upon both individual and society. Thus people start their lives in one historical period, when all the age strata and people's cognitive maps of these strata are organized in one particular way; but as these people age, the full set of age strata is continually being reorganized from one period to the next. For example, people who were young earlier in this century learned societal age patterns and norms of that period; most went to school for no more than six or seven years—adequate education for the jobs then held by their fathers or older siblings. They developed images of old age from the characteristics at that time of their few surviving grandparents. But now that these people have grown old, the society is very different from that of their grandparents. Similarly, people who are young today see the entire occupational ladder before it is transformed by micro-technology; they see retirement as currently institutionalized as an entitlement. But none of these young people will themselves be old in the same society in which they began. They must move through a society that is changing. Hence there is an intrinsic pressure for readjustments between their lifelong expectations and needs and the changing exigencies of society (cf. Oppenheimer, 1981). Sorensen (1979) illustrates these two dynamisms by analyzing upward mobility as the resultant of two economic forces: the movement of persons and the availability of positions (roles) in job structures [cf. Sorokin, (1927) 1959]. As Sorensen points out, "there is no necessary relation between the timing of changes in a person's resources [ability, education, experience] and the timing of a vacancy to which the individual can gain access." The timing of vacancies, unlike the life-course changes of individuals, is related to societal fluctuations in the economy.

Selected Principles

With continuing use of the age stratification model, a number of themes and premises have been predicated (cf. Riley, 1973, 1979; Foner, 1974; Riley and Riley, n.d.; Featherman, 1981a). Several of these can now be stated as working principles and will be noted at appropriate points in this chapter:

Referring to the Age Strata. P-1) Every society is stratified by age, just as it is stratified by class and sex (and in some societies by ethnicity); but the character of age stratification varies across societies and over historical time.

P-2) Age strata are produced by the continuing interplay between (a) changes in society with its age-related roles and (b) the processes of aging and cohort flow which are unidirectional and (as long as the society endures) universal.

P-3) Age strata are interdependent, so that a change in one stratum can have repercussions on all the other strata.

P-4) *Within* a stratum, people's similarity in age and cohort membership often signals mutuality of experiences, perceptions, and interests that may lead to integration or even to age-based groups and collective movements.

P-5) Integration within age strata can foster potential cleavage *between* age strata. Moreover, differences between strata in age and cohort membership often signal differences in experiences, perceptions, and interests that can lead to indifference or divisiveness and pressures toward social change.

P-6) Within each age stratum, individuals engage actively in a complex of roles (e.g., at work, in the family) that can influence the way they grow older, their capacities and attitudes, and the other people with whom they interact; these roles set limits on, but also provide opportunity for, individual initiative and enterprise.

P-7) Individuals who are growing older in any one age stratum interact with members of other strata, allowing either for affiliation and reciprocal socialization, or for age-based tension and conflict.

Referring to Aging. P-8) Aging is a lifelong process of growing up and growing *older* from birth to death, moving through all the strata in society; it is not simply growing *old* beyond some arbitrary point in the life course.

P-9) Aging is multifaceted, composed of interdependent biological, psychological, and social processes; it is not a unitary or exclusively biological process.

P-10) The ways people age are interdependent; that is, the life-course pattern of one person will influence or be influenced by the life-course patterns of others with whom he or she is interacting.

P-11) The life-course patterns of particular individuals are affected by the character of the cohort to which they belong and by those social, cultural, and environmental changes to which their cohort is exposed in moving through each of the successive age strata.

Referring to Aging and Social Change. P-12) When many individuals in the same cohort are affected by social change in similar ways, the change in their collective lives can in turn produce further social change. That is, new patterns of aging are not only caused by social change; they also contribute to it.

P-13) Individual aging and social change involve separate dynamisms, and their intrinsic lack of synchronization with one another produces strains for both individual and society.

Misinterpretations and Fallacies

This conceptual overview of age stratification systems would be incomplete without reference to the misinformation engendered by the series of fallacies that, though clearly identified by the model (Riley, 1973, 1981a), still continue to plague much work in this area, and serve to perpetuate false stereotypes of the immutability of the aging process and the inevitable decrements of old age.

Some common types of misinterpretation include:

- The *life-course* fallacy—erroneously assuming that cross-sectional age differences, which are essential for examining age strata, refer instead to the process of aging.
- The fallacy of *cohortcentrism*—erroneously assuming that members of all cohorts will age in exactly the same fashion as members of our own cohort.
- The fallacy of *age reification*—treating chronological age in itself as a causal life-course variable (e.g., because he is 40, a person "becomes his own man").
- The fallacy of *reifying historical time*—treating historical change as a causal variable without specifying what aspects of historical change may be pertinent to understanding particular shifts in the aging process.

Despite important conceptual and methodological advances (cf. Fienberg and Mason, 1979; Winsborough et al., 1983), some researchers still fail to recognize the "identification problem" (Cohn, 1972) that arises when just two measures are used for determining the separate contributions of three different concepts called "age, period, and cohort." In the age stratification model, these three somewhat equivocal terms are reformulated, and a sharp distinction is drawn between the temporal dimensions—as age and period refer respectively to a lifetime and to history (the two axes of Figure 1) and cohort refers to the people who are aging along both these dimensions.

As empirical studies of aging multiply, still another potential pitfall, "life-span reductionism," has developed, which disregards the distinction between people and roles, and treats the changing social structure as if it were the simple converse of the aggregate of people's lives. Here the danger lies in overlooking the seemingly obvious fact that, although social structures and social roles are continually reconstructed by contemporary cohorts of people passing through them, these cohorts are antedated and may be outlived by many age-related organizational forms, customs, laws, or beliefs that are built into existing roles in the economy, the polity, the church, and other social institutions. The age strata in society cannot be fully understood by treating roles as if they were reducible to the life span of people (for implicit examples, see Featherman, 1981b), rather than as intrinsic to these social structures.

In sum, the age stratification model provides a broad framework for identifying potential misinterpretations, formulating fundamental principles, integrating miscellaneous findings into a cumulative body of knowledge, and specifying significant research objectives.

THE CHANGING AGE STRUCTURE

Selected from the model as the central concern of this chapter are the two interpenetrating and continually changing social structures that constitute the age strata: the age structure of people, and the age structure of roles (as shown in Figure 2). The people are divided roughly by age into strata with differentiated social contributions (age-related capacities, attitudes, and acts), and age criteria are used for allocating roles and specifying the expectations, facilities, and sanctions associated with particular roles. Since the age strata are understood within the broad model of the age stratification system, three of the working principles bear repetition at the outset:

P–1) Every society is stratified by age, just as it is stratified by class and sex (and in some societies by ethnicity); but the character of age stratification varies across societies and over historical time.

P–2) Age strata are produced by the continuing interplay between (a) changes in society with its age-related roles and (b) the process of aging and cohort flow which are unidirectional and (as long as the society endures) universal.

P–13) Individual aging and social change involve separate dynamisms, and their intrinsic lack of synchronization with one another produces strains for both individual and society.

Thus the people who are growing older within the age strata are viewed, not as a mere demographic aggregate or "population," but as members of society; and age roles are the smallest units in the complex and shifting networks of human relationships in the society and its institutions. These interpenetrating age structures of people and roles, at the nexus of the never-ending interplay between human aging and social change, are inherently subject to continuing strain and alteration.

These structures were initially scrutinized with reference to the model through analysis of friendship groups (Hess, 1972), the community (Starr, 1972), education (Parsons and Platt, 1972), and science (Zuckerman and Merton, 1972). Recent research amplifies scientific understanding of many aspects of these interpenetrating societal structures: how the age strata intersect with single groups and institutional spheres; how the full set of coexisting age strata move concurrently across time; how people behave, think, and relate to one another in different ways according to their ages; and how age-typical patterns develop in the routines of daily life, and age-appropriate norms and roles come to be defined and institutionalized. Recent advances have been made here in defining historical and sociocultural conditions of variability in the age strata (cf. Foner, 1980), in demonstrating the mutability of roles and performances at the oldest ages as well as in childhood (cf. Featherman, 1981a; Dannefer, n.d.), and in questioning the conditions under which age may be an important basis for stratification.

The Age Structure of People

At any given time, people are roughly divisible into age strata—from the youngest to the oldest—within which they coexist and interrelate with one another. There tend to be differences in the number, characteristics, motivations, actions, and attitudes of people at different ages.

Boundaries of Strata. The numbers of strata and their age-related boundaries are socially defined and differ from one time and place to another. For example, in an African age-set society such as the Kikuyu (Whiting, 1981) age boundaries were sharp, and people who were similar in age (circumcised together) moved together as an age set from one age stratum (age grade) to the next. In the United States today the age strata are defined only vaguely (Neugarten and Moore, 1968; Bengtson et al., 1974). Intuitively, however, one can easily distinguish between a stratum composed of infants and a stratum of old people arrived at the age when, under modern conditions of mortality control, death seems not inappropriate. Evidences of popular awareness of age divisions are omnipresent: for example, age discrimination in employment is reflected in court cases and in federal and state laws (Edelman and Siegler, 1978); in criminal cases, convictions and penalties tend to vary with the age of the defendant (Burk and Turk, 1975); subjective identification with one's own age stratum is associated with political and other behaviors (e.g., Miller et al., 1980); and older people view their own socioeconomic situations more favorably than does the U.S. public at large (National Council on Aging, 1981). In some societies only a few (perhaps three or four) age strata may be distinguished; whereas many strata (from infancy, childhood, adolescence, youth, middle age, to early old age and late old age) may be distinguished in other societies or within particular subpopulations (cf. Neugarten and Moore, 1968; Parsons and Platt, 1972; Neugarten, 1974).

Divisions among age strata in a population may be specified either precisely or approximately, and in terms either of the chronological age of the members, as in census age categories, or of life-course markers of biological, psychological, or social development. Unlike the role structure, where age is often built in as an explicit criterion

for entry or exit, age is merely an index for the population—reflecting past experiences undergone or future experiences ahead, and carrying with it varying probabilities of behavior and attitudes (just as dates are mere indexes of pertinent historical or environmental events). Use of chronological age for dividing people into age strata is largely arbitrary (cf. Maddox, 1979). Who is to say that "old age" starts at 65? or at 85? In some typically "simple" societies, age is not calculated by reference to birthdate, but is determined by generation in a family, the degree of the family's wealth, the appearance of a physical sign, the accomplishment of some feat, or the assumption of certain social roles (Stewart, 1977; Foner and Kertzer, 1978). Hence, partitions of the population by age acquire meaning as age strata only as such partitions index socially significant aspects of people or of the roles they perform.

People in the Age Strata. The several age strata differ in size and in composition (e.g., by sex or ethnicity), indicated as element 1 in Figure 2, p. 372. These strata differences reflect the melding of the underlying processes whereby people are born, grow older, engage in social roles, and interact with others within and across strata. Strata differences can vary markedly historically and cross-culturally, with important implications for both individual and society. Purely demographic changes in strata size in the United States are illustrated in Figure 3, which shows proportional declines from 1880 up to 1940 in the younger strata below age 17, and the persistent growth—most pronounced since 1930—in the proportions in the oldest strata aged 65 and over. Figure 3 makes arbitrary use of chronological age boundaries, not reflecting historical changes in designation of life-course stages, as "adolescence" first became recognized early in this century and not until midcentury was "advanced old age" differentiated from "early old age." Not shown in Figure 3 are are the kinds of people involved. For example, because women live longer than men, the sex ratio (number of

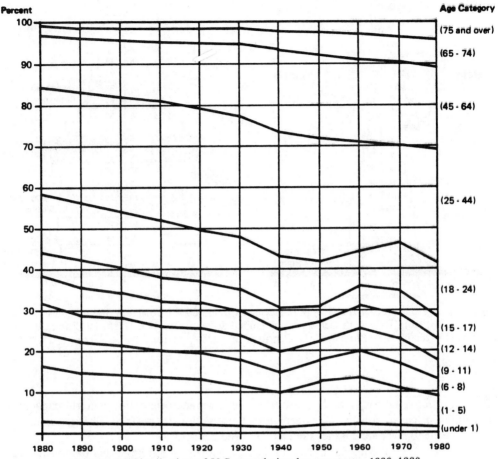

Figure. 3. Distribution of U.S. population by age strata, 1880–1980.
SOURCE: U.S. Bureau of the Census.

males per 100 females) in the stratum aged 65 and over had fallen from 102 at the beginning of the century to 68 by 1980. Figure 4 uses "age pyramids" to show the changing distribution of the population by sex within the several age strata.

Demographic and epidemiological studies have been plotting the striking changes in the age structure of people, as the "aging" of the population (the increasing percentage as well as the increasing numbers in the oldest strata) has occurred during the twentieth century in most industrialized countries. Some investigators have examined the associated societal implications: as for changing tastes or political opinions; for the feasibility of absorbing older people into occupational and other socially useful roles; for the family structure, as the middle-aged become more likely to have surviving parents and their children become more likely to have surviving grandparents and great-grandparents, and increasing proportions of old people are widows; for demands placed by the more disadvantaged old people on health and welfare services; or for increases in social security payments (cf. Maddox, 1979; Siegel, 1980).

Other studies concern, not the number and kinds of people in the older strata but their spatial redistribution (cf. Starr, 1972; Heaton, 1983). Shifts in the age strata of particular communities and regions of the country can jeopardize the local adequacy of health

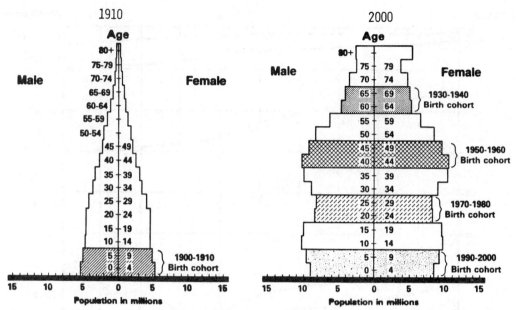

Figure. 4. Age structure of the U.S. population, 1910 and 2000 (projected) (population in millions).
SOURCE (for 1910): Thirteenth Census of the United States, 1910, Vol. I, Ch. IV, Table 29.
SOURCE (for 2000): U.S. Bureau of the Census, Current Population Reports, Series P–25, No. 704, Table 8.

care institutions, housing, and transportation, and can cause conflicts between new and old residents over local issues such as tax assessments or school budgets. Earlier in the century research had pointed to spatial concentrations of older people left behind in rural hamlets and inner cities as large numbers of young individuals and families moved. Current studies point to new trends, as during the 1960s elderly migrants pioneered the movement from metropolitan to nonmetropolitan areas; and by the 1980s some U.S. counties were experiencing rates of arrival of elderly migrants which increased more rapidly than rates of departure of younger ones (McCarthy, 1982).

Age-Related Characteristics and Performances. Not only do the age strata at any given period differ in population size, composition, and geographic distribution, but they differ also (element 2 in Figure 2) in the contributions they can make to the activities and processes of the groups and the society to which they belong. Both actual perfor-

mances and orientations and the capacity and motivation to perform are associated with the age strata.

Numerous studies either demonstrate such strata differences or explore the mechanisms explaining particular characteristics and behaviors of older people. In certain respects, many of those in the older strata are comparatively advantaged. They may have more leisure time or fewer burdensome responsibilities, and they are more likely than young adults to participate in institutionalized political processes (Foner, 1972). Some researchers are pursuing Gutmann's (1977) contention that both men and women become increasingly androgynous in their later years, that in the oldest strata each sex tends to combine the characteristics of both sexes, and that those older people who combine masculine and feminine traits may be the best able to cope positively with aging (Livson, 1980; Sinnott, 1980). If further corroborated, such a later-life generic role, replacing the traditional sex-typing of earlier life, could be important to the social adaptation of the increasing numbers of older people and the disproportionate numbers of women among them.

In other respects, however, many—though not all—older people are comparatively disadvantaged: in physiological functioning; in sensation, perception, sensori-motor coordination, memory, and learning; and in exclusion from the work force and many other social roles. Studies of people already in the older age strata, by specifying these disadvantages and seeking their antecedents and correlates, are providing the knowledge base for possible prevention or correction. For example, failure of some older people to recognize faces or to avoid oncoming street traffic may be due to environmental conditions of low contrast, and not detectable by current procedures for detecting visual acuity (Owsley et al., 1981). The nature of memory deficits is gradually being specified, and older people are found to perform as well as their younger counterparts in certain components of memory (Light et al., 1982; Dixon et al, 1982; Simon et al., 1982). Moreover, not all memory problems matter in everyday life (for details, see Perlmutter, 1983).

Other types of research address the complex processes underlying such strata differences in orientations and behavior. As the model shows, the differences cannot be traced to aging alone as a "cause" without risking a life-course fallacy; rather they reflect the confluence of aging, cohort flow, and changes in society and its age-related roles. For example, people in an older stratum may differ from the younger in being less responsive to training in technical reasoning either because they have forgotten the strategy for learning (their age), or because they have generally poorer educational background (their cohort membership), or as a self-fulfilling prophecy because their teachers offer little encouragement (their age relationships).

The Age Structure of Roles

Complementary to, but distinct from, the continually shifting age structure of people (deriving initially from the processes of cohort flow and aging) is a persistent but variable age structure of roles (deriving from societal processes of stability and change). Age, or some age-related biological or social characteristic, is used as a criterion for entering or relinquishing certain roles and for defining expectations and sanctions for role performance (elements 3 and 4 in Figure 2 above). Thus within the complex networks of society and its institutions, roles offer differential opportunities and rewards to people in the several age strata, affecting the choices available and influencing behavior and attitudes. For example, Zuckerman and Merton (1972), using the age stratification model, demonstrate the age hierarchy of powerful positions in science, showing the consequences for younger scientists and for the accumulation of scientific knowledge. Kaufman and Spilerman (1982) analyze the cross-section age distributions of workers in various types of occupations. Schlesinger and Schlesinger (1981) show how the political careers of olders people depend not only on their motivation and their share of the electorate, but also on the size, importance, and organizational arrangements of federal and local political institutions in the society.

Age as a Criterion for Role Occupancy. Many social institutions are so organized that roles are open or closed to people in particular age strata. Age criteria for role incumbency can operate directly (e.g., in the United States people cannot vote until age 18 or become President until age 35, or may be required to retire at age 70); or they can operate indirectly through association with other factors (e.g., biological stage limits motherhood, or being old enough to have completed high school limits entry into college, or the rapid reaction time required for certain occupations can exclude the aged). Age criteria can be formal, as expressed in laws and rules for entitlements and disentitlements (cf. Cain, 1976); or they can be informal, as there is an unofficial but compelling folk wisdom as to when people should marry or have children. Age norms that prescribe the timing of life events have been repeatedly documented by Neugarten and her colleagues (Neugarten et al., 1965; see Neugarten et al., 1982, for a bibliography of relevant studies). Moreover, age is a criterion that links together complexes of roles that are otherwise differentiated, as old age may place an individual simultaneously in the roles of retiree, member of a friendship group, and grandparent (cf. Rosow, 1967). Age criteria, by forming a basis for allocating persons to complexes of positions in the social structure, thereby affect the boundaries between age strata.

A central question for research here concerns the conditions associated with variations in age criteria for role occupancy (cf. Demos and Boocock, 1978). In early-nineteenth-century America, far different from today's criteria, infants were sent to school and children barely 10 labored in Pennsylvania coal mines and Massachusetts mills. Retirement, currently taken for granted in developed countries, has not always been practiced, and studies are examining varied retirement practices in early America (Vinovskis, 1982), public support for abolishing involuntary retirement today (Harris et al., 1979), lobbying efforts producing the Maine statute that prohibits mandatory retirement (Kertzer, 1981), or medical bases for disqualifying commercial airline pilots at age 60 (Institute of Medicine, 1981).

Age as a Criterion for Role Expectations and Sanctions. Age affects not only what roles are open or closed at given ages, but also how people are expected to perform in each role and how they are rewarded or punished for role performance. Obviously role expectations as to appropriate behavior will differ for the infant son and the son in his teens, for young workers and workers nearing the end of their careers, for the old person at the onset of a protracted disease and the old person in the terminal stages of it. Similarly the sanctions will obviously differ; for example, very different rewards will be given to the infant son and the teenage son when he "is good," and very different punishments when

he "is bad." Less obviously, age-graded expectations can afford (or fail to afford) important opportunities for education, work, leisure, influence over other people; age-graded rewards (or punishments) can mean income, power, esteem, or a sense of personal control.

While age-linked roles form an ordered series within the society, this ordering—though it often results in age inequalities of rewards—is not necessarily defined socially as a hierarchy. Thus, the rewards from the educational and leisure roles differentially available to the young may or may not be assessed as balancing the political and occupational role available to the mature strata. Even when a hierarchy of inequality is perceived, the ordering may not follow the chronology of the age strata. In modern societies the middle-aged strata may be considered the apex.

Recent historical and anthropological studies emphasize the variability in the social status accorded to the aged. Only in some nonindustrial societies, not in all, is access to the most highly valued roles and social rewards attached to the oldest strata (cf. N. Foner, 1982; Keith and Kertzer, 1983). In the United States, the prestige and authority once assigned to old people has declined sharply (Fischer, 1978; Achenbaum, 1978). Not only rewards but also role expectations are variable. Thus expectations for old people shifted from a nineteenth-century emphasis on "successful" aging to an early-twentieth-century emphasis on age-associated disabilties (A. Foner, 1980).

Some Bases for Age Criteria. Age criteria arise in complex ways that depend in part on whether the criteria are factual age regularities or have been normatively prescribed. Factual age criteria, such as average or modal ages of entering or leaving roles, or age patterns of role performance, are formed when society-wide conditions and changes converge upon particular age categories in the population. Thus marriage roles become closed to many old women because of high death rates among men of comparable ages; many elderly widows are enabled to live in separate households when incomes become more adequate or more houses are built; many recent high school graduates are unemployed because not enough suitable jobs are accessible.

Normative age criteria arise quite differently, often growing out of open acceptance or downright rejection of factual regularities. Normative criteria, as translated into laws, expectations, or standards, are widely based on beliefs about biological aging or age-related abilities, or on values, ideologies, and perceived exigencies of the particular society. For example, as child development into adulthood is increasingly understood as a gradual process rather than a sudden transformation, Toby (1982) proposes that juvenile courts need a doctrine of increasing fault with increasing age.

While biology sets some limits on the kind of role that can be assigned to people of a particular age, there is no biological necessity or advantage in keeping adolescents in high school, young adults unemployed, or healthy old people out of the work force. More important than biological facts in determining age criteria are beliefs about the capacities and reactions of people at particular ages, beliefs that are frequently unfounded and subject to change. Beliefs as to what children or old people can do often shade into ideological notions about what they ought to do—with similar impact on age role criteria. For example, historians describe long periods in Western history when age norms for children differed little from those for adults because no distinctive value was placed on the needs of children. Deliberate interventions are often used to bring role criteria into line with social values and ideals, as in laws preventing child labor or mandating public schools, or in arrangements prescribing that those most likely to have family responsibilities (the middle-aged) should be given the work roles, whereas those typically without families to feed (the young and the old) should be denied them.

The Interplay between People and Roles

The age structures of people and roles are not separate entities, of course, and there is a continuing interplay between social roles that are changing and individuals who are aging. At every age, as people interact with others in society, genetic makeup is expressed, personality develops, and experience accumulates. Much of this social interaction depends on the nature of the particular roles people play, the situations they meet, the others who become significant to them, and how these others in turn act, think, and feel. The power over people's lives of the usual social roles in modern society is illustrated in a study of ex-nuns, women who as teenagers had withdrawn from society into a convent (San Giovanni, 1978). As long as they were insulated from the conventional social environment, they did not age in the same way as their secular peers; only when they left the convent to return to the secular world were these grown women obliged to start from the beginning, just as if they were back at age 17, to learn such adult roles as consumer, worker, friend, or lover.

The Contingency of Interaction. The interplay between people and roles (which at the societal level can produce imbalances and pressures for change, as discussed in the final section of this chapter) can also be understood at the microlevel. In every stratum, age roles are powerful because the aging person is interacting with other people in family roles, friendship roles, work roles, or political roles. These interactions are reciprocal: what each one does is contingent upon what the others do. Figure 5 suggests a paradigm for analyzing the sequence of interactions between the *Person* who is aging and the *Other* (person or agency) who expresses the age-appropriate social expectations. The Person may or may not contribute (a) motivation and capacity to perform; the Other may or may not make clear (b) how the Person is expected (supposed) to act or feel; the Person may or may not (c) perform accord-

Contributions by the person who changes with age	Contributions by others in the role as affected by age
a) Motivations and capacities to perform (selective responses) c) Performances	b) Expectations (facilities and support) d) Rewards and punishments

Figure 5. Paradigm of interplay between person and role.

ingly; and, depending on this performance, the Other may or may not administer (d) rewards or punishments.

The paradigm draws attention to two points. First, the very complexity of contingencies in this interaction casts doubts on any view of the process of aging in a role as smooth or "normal." There can be failures of communication and perception, as nursing home staff, who presumably favor independent behavior among aged residents, nevertheless often interact with them in such ways as to reinforce expectations of dependency (Barton et al., 1980; cf. Litwak and Spilerman, 1978). There can be gaps between people's capacity and their performance, as negative sanctions in work roles may discourage older workers from maintaining their skills, or lack of facilities in leisure roles may discourage older people from vigorous exercise (cf. Fries, 1980). There can be gaps between performance and rewards. For example, Schrank and Waring (1983), finding that younger employees are promoted more rapidly than older employees, propose a "gap hypothesis": they describe organizational arrangements in the firm whereby the discrepancy between rewards and performance motivates junior members through rapid promotions, while allowing the pace of upward movement to slacken among senior employees whose commitment has already been made.

Second, the paradigm emphasizes the point that aging in a role is not mere passive compliance with the pressures exerted by society in particular strata. The person being influenced by the role is also an active participant. This active participation mediates the impact of the role on the aging process (as a nursing home resident may choose not to succumb to dependency), and it also presses to shape or reshape the role itself (as residents, by being independent, may alter the expectations and responses of their caretakers). This point is stated as one of the working principles:

P-6) Within each age stratum, individuals engage actively in a complex of roles (e.g., at work, in the family) that can influence the way they grow older, their capacities and attitudes, and the other people with whom they interact; these roles set limits on, but also provide opportunity for, individual initiative and enterprise.

Roles differ in degree of malleability. It is generally easier for most individuals to influence the expectations or sanctions in their roles in small groups as family members or friends than as civil servants, workers in a large factory, or patients in a nursing home where the structure of an entire organization is involved.

Interventions. That both people and roles are mutable is demonstrated not only by studies showing sociotemporal variability, but also by recent experimental or quasi-experimental research interventions. Interventions focused on people show, for example, that: intellectual decline with aging can often be reversed by relatively simple training (Baltes and Willis, 1982); older people can often learn to compensate for declines in reaction time, memory, and other age-related deficits (Poon et al., 1980; Horn and Donaldson,

1980); health can be promoted at every age through changes in smoking, diet, and exercise (Maccoby et al., 1977). Similarly, carefully directed interventions can change conditions and facilities for role performance. For visual impairments suffered by many older people, particular styles and sizes of type can facilitate reading, or improved environmental design can offset inability to see large objects in low contrast (Vanderplas and Vanderplas, 1980; Sekuler and Hutmen, 1980). For the serious malnutrition of many solitary older people, food can be adapted to age-related changes in taste and smell that influence eating behaviors (Schiffman and Pasternak, 1979). In nursing homes, serious disabilities of elderly residents can be reduced by rewarding activity and independence (Rodin, 1980; Barton et al., 1980). Thus even in the oldest strata, behavior, personality, health, and functioning are more malleable than is manifest in the usual contemporary social settings (Featherman, 1981a; Riley and Bond, 1983).

Lifelong Socialization. The fact that interventions can improve many types of performance among the old as well as the young (cf. Salthouse and Somberg, 1982) emphasizes three often overlooked features of socialization (see Figure 2, p. 372), conceived as the process of bringing people's capacities and performances in every stratum into alignment with age-related role expectations. First, socialization is not restricted to the early years, but continues at every stage of life (cf. Mortimer and Simmons, 1978; Brim, 1980). A person's beliefs, values, and competencies are not indelibly inprinted in childhood but can change at every age (Glenn, 1980); and every role provides opportunity for maintaining or altering current performances and for learning new ones. Second, socialization is not a one-way but a reciprocal process, in which both the socializer and the person being socialized learn from each other [as noted early by Mannheim (1928) 1953]. At every age, socialization follows the person–role interaction paradigm (Figure 5), save that additionally the aging

person must be motivated to learn, and special opportunities and resources for learning may be required. Third, the driving force in lifelong socialization may be expectations, rather than simply imitation as students of childhood socialization often claim. Indeed, if each generation were to imitate its parents precisely, there could be no social change. Studies of adolescent socialization have shown how parents, by teaching normative expectations as standards for the future, can encourage their offspring to transcend the limits of their own experience (Johnson, 1976), and Rosow (1967) notes the importance of expectations in socialization among older people.

Allocation. Parallel to socialization as an articulating process (see Figure 2), allocation operates to bring together the numbers and kinds of people at a given age with the roles available at that age (cf. Eisenstadt, 1956; Riley et al., 1972). Less well-understood than socialization, the processes of role assignment are sometimes quite explicit and apparent; often, however, they are obscure. Even when they seem clear (as in being hired or fired from a job), the visible aspects may constitute only a tiny part of much larger social, economic, or political forces of which people are largely unaware.

As allocators, diverse agencies and procedures are at work in every age stratum in the admission, retention, and extrusion of particular candidates for particular roles. On their part, candidates are involved in entering roles, staying in them for varying lengths of time, and leaving them. While allocation, like socialization, must be understood as a reciprocal process, relationships between allocators and candidates may often be asymmetrical. In many situations it is the allocators who have the resources and the power to assess the candidate's qualifications and to control the decision. To be sure, candidates can decide whether to apply for a job, to enter college, or to retire early, and they can act as their own allocators to such roles as friend or marital partner. Yet candidates have little or no control over many decisions: over being born, entering the first grade, being chosen from among competitors for scarce jobs or for scarce places in training programs, or being mandated to retire.

Recent studies of allocation deal with such issues as how the numbers of people of a given age wanting jobs may fail to match the jobs available in that stratum (cf. Sorensen, 1979); how support from older and more experienced colleagues as allocators can encourage a young salesman to remain in a job (Schrank and J. Riley, 1976); or how lack of suitable rewards in the role structure can discourage a young scientist from continuing in the role of researcher rather than becoming a teacher or an administrator (Zuckerman and Merton, 1972; Cole, 1979; Shin and Putman, 1982).

The Organization of Age Roles

Within the several age strata, people and roles are not merely differentiated by age but are organized in numerous groups and social institutions. Thus individuals of a given age participate in a complex of roles as members of families, households, communities, work organizations, educational and religious institutions, political associations, health and welfare institutions—to name just a few. Moreover, each group is itself a small social system often stratified by age, and studies following the age stratification model show how particular groups can shape the lives of people at various ages, and can in turn be shaped by these people themselves (Schrank and Waring, 1983).

Role Complexes. In addition to studies of particular groups and institutions as age stratification systems, the age stratification approach directs attention to age as a criterion that can link together complexes of roles in very different groups. In one study of age role complexes that link family structure with occupational structure, Hareven (1978, 1982) documents the active part played by kinship networks in a New England milling town both in recruiting young workers and placing

them in jobs, and in assisting older workers at the point of retirement. When role complexes make conflicting demands upon a person, they can cause problems and strains. But they can also provide complementary expectations and opportunities for a person to enact and develop differing aspects of the self (Turner, 1978; Clausen, 1972; Oppenheimer, 1981).

Relational Age. Throughout the stratification system, age can also serve as a relational criterion, affecting the gap and the nature of the interaction between a person's own age and the age of parent, friend, spouse, or other role partner. In education, for example, the youngest students have teachers older than they are; college students have many teachers close to themselves in age; while in adult education (as in the work force) older students may face teachers (or supervisors) younger than they are. In the kinship sphere, no such relational reversals can occur in a parent–child pair; offspring cannot be biologically older than their natural parents (cf. Rossi, 1980), and the gap necessarily persists over the joint lifetimes. Yet the social meaning of the chronological age gap differs with the strata involved; the power relations between a 20-year-old mother and her newborn baby are very different from those between an 80-year-old mother and her 60-year-old daughter. With step-kin, however, increasing rates of divorce and remarriage are yielding numerous anomalies in relational ages (Furstenberg, 1981).

Of particular relevance to the status of older women in modern societies is the tendency for males to marry women who are younger than they are. Anthropological inquiries emphasize the pervasiveness of the age differential between husband and wife (Keith and Kertzer, 1983). They point to the common pattern among higher nonhuman primates for males to mate at older ages than females; the characteristic role of the human male in the economic system as related to the necessity of his acquiring capital or expertise before marrying; and the widespread cultural norms and practices with regard to age at first marriage and at widow remarriage.

Age and Other Societal Divisions

Age is only one of several bases of social stratification. Members of the several age strata belong also to other subpopulations affecting social life, such as social classes, sex categories, or races. Recognition of age stratification as one of a family of stratification systems has directed attention to the intersection of age strata with other societal divisions, to certain generic properties of stratification systems, and to the conditions fostering age as a predominant basis of stratification (Sorokin, 1947, 1968; Lenski, 1966; Foner, 1979).

Cross-Cutting Strata. Within each age stratum people's lives and their patterns of aging differ widely by sex, socioeconomic status, race, and ethnicity (Neugarten and Hagestad, 1976; Streib, 1976; Ch. 12 in this *Handbook*). For the United States, Figure 4 above shows the cross-cutting of age strata by sex strata, with the tendency for women to predominate over men in the oldest strata. Another division of the population by educational level would reflect the strong negative relationship between education and age. While there are such tendencies for age lines to correspond with certain other divisions (Blau, 1974), few of these lines converge completely in any highly differentiated, pluralistic society, and individuals who are alike in age may be widely separated in other subpopulations of a matrix crisscrossed by myriad societal divisions (cf. Foner, 1980). This cross-cutting of the age strata by other divisions affects the mutuality or incongruity within each person's role complex and the societal tendencies toward age solidarity or age cleavage, as discussed in the next section of this chapter.

Social Change and the Age Strata

Endemic to the age stratification system are the continuing tendencies toward alteration. Only through increased understanding of the interplay between aging and the changing age structure of society can such system alterations be apprehended. Changes stemming from this interplay can be ephemeral or enduring. They can crystallize the age boundaries, or shift societal emphases entirely away from age-ascription and toward performance criteria for role entry and exit (e.g., for retirement). They can transform the kinds of age-related performances to which people are socialized and the complex societal and institutional networks to which people belong.

Many pressures toward change spring from within the age stratification system itself. Changes arise from conflict over the inequalities among age strata, the malintegration of values between young and old, faulty operation of allocation and socialization, and the imbalances within particular strata between roles available and numbers of people able and motivated to perform these roles. Competing demands in role complexes can cause strain, as in Oppenheimer's (1981) young adult "squeeze" between work and family roles because of low pay in entry jobs and high costs of setting up households. Still other changes derive from the processes of aging and cohort flow, as aggregates of individuals in a cohort adopt new ways of living their lives. (Only rarely does social change come from the lone individual, the "great man" or the disease "carrier," who single-handedly can affect entire regions of society.) A widespread change in the collective lives of many individuals in a cohort can permeate the society; or it can be transmitted from one generation to the next.

Changes in the age stratification system spring from sources outside as well as inside system boundaries. Famine, conquest, epidemic disease, economic growth or decline, the spread of cities, changes in governmental policies, and developments in technology or in mass culture can impinge upon the age structure of roles, or upon the demographic bases of the age structure of people, or upon the aging process. Such changes from outside, touching one part of the system, may then reverberate through the system as a whole.

Most important, changes in the age stratification system come from the basic lack of sychronization between individual aging and social change (working principle P–13). Aging individuals and age-stratified society move to different rhythms, respond to different exigencies. The lifetime of humankind has a definite rhythm from birth to death, despite wide individual variations. Cohorts ordinarily follow one another in constant succession as long as the society survives, leaving their distinctive impress upon history. But the timing of societal process has no comparable rhythm or periodicity; many early attempts to identify cyclical or "generational" rhythms of societal time were dispatched as abortive after careful analysis by both Mannheim [(1928) 1952] and Sorokin (1941). And patterns of social change differ profoundly, from short-term to long-term, and from disintegrative to reconstructive (Smelser, 1968). Thus, to repeat, underlying the age strata is an endless struggle between the demands of individuals who are growing older and the demands of the changing society, resulting in intrinsic strains, conflicts, and pressures toward further change.

Age as a Major Basis for Stratification

If age stratification is essential for understanding important aspects of human lives and of social structure and change, how essential is age as compared with other bases of stratification? And how does its importance vary as society changes? Is it true, as, for example, Banton (1965) contends, that age, like sex, becomes decreasingly likely to influence human behavior as societies advance in political and technical sophistication? While only scattered investigations have approached such questions, the predominance of age over class or other bases for stratification is affected in complex ways by differing historical and sociocultural conditions (Keith and Kertzer, 1983).

For example, in contemporary society the century-long rise in education for the masses has tended to strengthen the age stratification system. The rising educational levels, by sharpening cohort differences, have produced increasing divisions between age strata, with implications that proliferate into people's thoughts, actions, and style of life (Hyman et al., 1975). Meantime, the edu-

cational upgrading of the more recent cohorts, by providing routes for upward mobility (Featherman, 1980), has served to undermine stratification on the basis of class and ethnicity. Currently high levels of education have differing consequences for the younger and the older strata. In the younger strata, age is an integrating force, as age-graded education daily brings together major portions of the public: female and male, black and white, rich and poor. Beyond the elementary and high school levels, the decision whether or not to go on to higher education splits each cohort nearly in half (Featherman, 1980). Within each cohort those continuing in school and college tend to delay entry into work, marriage, parenthood, and the entire sequence of life course roles. The better-educated tend generally to lag behind the less-educated. Thus, depending upon educational attainment, individuals alike in chronological age can differ in life stage; and societal subdivisions based on education tend to cross-cut subdivisions based on age.

For the future, incipient changes in education and other societal domains raise many questions about the importance of age as a basis of stratification. If the secular trend in education runs its course, so that oncoming cohorts of older people become increasingly similar to young people in educational level, will the society become increasingly "age-irrelevant" (Neugarten, 1974)? If age is removed as a major basis for role allocation, will heightened competition ensue, producing an "age-diversified meritocracy" (Zuckerman and Merton, 1972)? Will increasing use of computers, robots, and telecommunication transform the age stratification of occupational and familial roles? Will biomedical advances or environmental pollution so alter genetic predispositions as to change the outer limits within which society is stratified by age?

AGE RELATIONSHIPS

Central to the operation of the age stratification system are problems of age differences, age inequalities, and age segregation as these can affect the influence of each person's life on the lives of others within and across age strata boundaries. For while people are aging and society is changing, at any given period people of all ages are simultaneously alive and interacting with one another in the same society.

Many studies have shown how strains or conflicts tend to develop between persons in different strata, while within particular strata there are tendencies for age peers to form attachments (see Eisenstadt, 1956). Within a stratum, age similarities can produce solidarity through mutual interests and ties of affection. Between strata, age differences can produce inequalities in values, in power, in worldly success. And age differences and inequalities can lead to social change: sometimes through outright conflict; sometimes through the spread from one stratum to another of age incongruities and deviance from established patterns; sometimes through shifts in the age-related imbalance of established but contradictory approaches to one's life course.

Thus age stratification systems share certain features of the more widely studied class stratification systems: involving structural social inequalities and fostering potentials for solidarity and collective action within the subordinate strata [Sorokin, (1927) 1959, 1947, 1968; Lenski, 1966]. At the same time, stratification based on age, rather than on economic position, has important unique characteristics. Unlike social mobility through the class strata, the aging process, though not immutable, is both universal and inevitable. Unlike class stratification, with its primary concentration on inequalities in material benefits, power, and prestige, age stratification draws attention also to other types of inequality as in time available for leisure pursuits, or the opportunity for accumulation of knowledge and experience.

The age stratification approach (Foner, 1972, 1974, 1979) shows how age relationships of solidarity within strata and strain between strata develop both from the nature of age roles and from the processes of cohort flow and aging. This approach points also to countertendencies toward competition among age peers and toward integration across age divisions. Moreover, the approach stresses the working principle of interdependence among age strata (Riley, 1982a), as older people coexist and continually interact with people of all ages, and as each person's later life is connected with the full life course:

P-3) Age strata are interdependent, so that a change in one stratum can have repercussions on all the other strata.

Much current research examines implications for human relationships of particular configurations in the age role structure of particular cohort differences in the people forming the age strata at given times. For example, when do "age groups" form (Pratt, 1976; Hudson, 1980)? What is the impact of increases in the percentage of old people on the burdens placed on the middle-aged or on opportunities for old people to retire early (Cohn, 1982; Espenshade and Braun, 1983)? How are changing patterns of divorce and remarriage among young adults affecting other age strata (Furstenberg, 1981; Cherlin, 1983)? How does residential segregation of old people affect the young—who have fewer models for their own later years (Rosow, 1967)? To what extent is there a gradual loosening of the age boundaries separating the three "boxes" of school, work, and retirement?

Age Integration

Within particular strata, age often operates as an integrative mechanism both for society and for its individual members. People within a stratum are similar in life-course stage, cohort membership, and many of the roles they currently occupy. And age similarities can breed mutual interests, common goals, and ties of loyalty and affection. Stated as one of the working principles:

P-4) *Within* a stratum, people's similarity in age and cohort membership often signals mutuality of experiences, perceptions, and interests that may lead to integration or even to age-based groups and collective movements.

Age Similarities. For people in a stratum, being the same age means that they share the same timing. They are all aging together. In biological and psychological development and in participation in the role structure, they tend to share a common past, present, and future. For people in the oldest strata (Marshall, 1980a), awareness of the inevitability of their own mortality can shape redefinitions of the meaning of life and of the remaining tasks to be performed. Moreover, all those within a stratum belong to the same cohort and thus also tend to share a common historical and environmental past, present, and future. Significantly, people currently in the same age stratum, though they are continually moving from one stratum to the next, have always shared, and will always share, approximately the same temporal locations in society. Cohort membership is immutable; hence people born at the same time, within the limits of their varied individual circumstances, tend to move together as they age through historical time and through the age strata. The importance of this phenomenon for understanding the age structure is apparent through contrast with the class structure, where in most societies people do not move together. Of those starting in the same class, only certain ones change to a higher or a lower class, with profound implications for values and styles of life as well as for worldly success.

Age does more than synchronize the timing of people who are in the same stratum at any given time. Age also produces similarities in roles. Unlike people, who are continually migrating through the strata, age roles are embedded in particular strata. And in special ways—entirely apart from the migrant people—age is so built into the role structure that it brings people together from otherwise separate institutional spheres, thereby integrating complexes of roles that are otherwise differentiated. For example, in the middle age strata the roles of worker, spouse, and parent of dependent offspring are often joined. Thus at a given period of history, individuals of similar age find their way into, and learn to play, roughly similar sets of roles.

Within particular strata, then, people belong together in both major dynamisms: in human aging and in the changing society. To an extent, these common positions and mutualities of experience among age peers can operate to promote age solidarity among them, tending to foster a sense of belonging together and of shared interests and goals. Under certain circumstances, cohesiveness within an age stratum can develop not only in face-to-face interaction but also in society-wide relationships.

Age Homophily. In daily living, small-group solidarity based on age, or "age homophily," can be promoted where age peers are in a position to communicate about their similar tasks, needs, and problems and about the exacerbation of these problems at stressful points in the life course. Opportunities for intimacy among age-mates are provided by the age-graded educational system, by age-homogeneity of suburbs or retirement communities, by the increasing longevity that sustains lifelong friendships into old age. Even in the family, the focal point of intergenerational solidarity, the age-heterogeneous household of a century ago (with its numerous children, other relatives, or boarders—though rarely a grandparent) has been widely replaced by several generations of related but separate households: the young couple, themselves similar in age, with their few and closely spaced dependent children; middle-aged parents of such young adults; and the aged generation of their grandparents who increasingly survive into old age together. Thus, many current tendencies toward age homogeneity in the social structure foster small-group interaction and cohesiveness within an age stratum.

Age Groups. More problematic is the formation, among members of the same age stratum, of large age groups that are based on common goals and society-wide cohesiveness. For solidarity in age groups that cut across the entire society requires that "age-consciousness" spread throughout a stratum, and that group goals and group leadership develop. Eisenstadt's (1956) monumental cross-cultural and cross-temporal study of age groups in the social system, though its details are often criticized, illustrates how age-homogeneous youth groups tend to develop where there are discontinuities between the basic values of the family and those of the larger society. In modern societies built around values of achievement, where parental socialization may be insufficient and formal education is extended, young people are especially likely to seek the protective company of age mates.

While Eisenstadt focuses on youth groups, several more recent studies focus on old-age groups, suggesting how, in the face of a role structure inadequate to their needs, older people themselves may undertake rectification of the structure through the "gray power" of age-based political movements. Pratt (1976) notes the skill of recent old-age activists "in manipulating symbols, enlarging the size and attentiveness of the relevant publics, and evolving an ideology capable of sustaining group commitment and elan." Clearly, the many and widely dispersed members of the entire old-age stratum cannot achieve solidarity through face-to-face interaction. But they are led by smaller groups who can hold meetings, communicate directly, and form a rallying point for all the others (Mannheim's "generation unit"). Moreover, knowledge of mutual interests can be obtained nowadays through the mass media, evoking similar feelings and reactions without face-to-face interaction (Foner 1975; Ward, 1979). The cohorts who will be old in the future will have spent an unprecedented proportion of their lives in an age-conscious society (Cutler, 1981). In the future the long-standing political resources of older people in the United States (their singular legitimacy as a political constituency and their utility to political actors) may be threatened because their greatly increasingly numbers will place ever-greater de-

mands on the human services budget. Nevertheless, these same demographic and budgetary pressures may themselves forge greater cohesion among the elderly in the political process (Hudson, 1978, 1980).

Consequences of Age Solidarity. When solidarity within age strata is achieved, it benefits individuals through emotional support from friends and relatives, and provides opportunities in a mass society to align oneself with others toward a common cause. For society, effective age groups can bring about social changes, sometimes salutary, sometimes detrimental to the common good. Loyalties can be pulled in diverse directions, for example, when the tastes or goals of one's age stratum conflict with the goals of one's sex, race, or socioeconomic class. Thus in Stouffer's (1955) study of political tolerance, people were pulled in one direction by their age stratum (older cohorts were less tolerant), but in the other direction by their level of education (the better-educated were more tolerant). Or in voting behavior, "cross-pressures" brought by the differing political views of a person's age, socioeconomic, and religious affiliates can discourage him or her from voting at all. Moreover, as age peers turn to each other for aid and comfort or to seek benefits for their age stratum, detriments to relationships between strata may ensue, ties between generations become attenuated, or grounds for dissension solidified. Thus formation of internally cohesive age strata can promote strain and hostility between "in-groups" and "out-groups," so that integration within strata can foster potential cleavage between strata.

Age Segregation: The Potential for Conflict

If people within age strata tend to be united by similarities of life-course stage, cohort membership, and the roles they occupy, age operates quite differently between age strata. The similarities are replaced by differences in life-course stage and in cohort membership, and the age bases for cohesiveness often give way to indifference or divisiveness, as in the working principle:

P-5) Integration within age strata can foster potential cleavage *between* age strata. Moreover, differences between strata in age and cohort membership often signal differences in experiences, perceptions, and interests that can lead to indifference or divisiveness and pressures toward social change.

Whether or not the divisive tendencies between strata erupt into open conflict (cf. Marshall, 1980b; Dowd, 1980), three sources of potential age cleavage are noteworthy: incompatability of values; abuse of power relationships; and unjust distribution of rewarding roles.

Ideational Conflicts. Age cleavages can arise because of clashes in basic values and goals, reflecting differences among the strata in standards, ideologies, and attitudes. Divergences in values can sometimes lead to outright conflict, as in the conflict in the 1960s between young and old over the goals of society.

Power Conflicts. Conflicts can arise when certain ages are felt to exercise in unjust ways their superiority or domination over other ages. The power of certain age strata to control other strata is a central and generally accepted feature of social life (N. Foner, 1982; Hammel, 1983), but in some circumstances the way in which power is exerted seems unjust. Unjust use of power can foster latent or overt hostilities of subordinates toward superordinates. For example, age is built into potential misuse of allocative positions. Once entrenched, the mature cohorts often resist, or sometimes refuse, to yield their positions to the oncoming younger cohorts.

Distributive Conflicts. In addition to age tensions and conflicts over how power is used and abused, distributive age conflicts can also develop over who gets the power, who gets the several types of valued roles in society, and which strata are deprived or assigned to devalued roles. Age strata can contend with one another over the relative share of rewards claimed by each stratum, as when the income-producing work roles go largely to the middle-aged, to the detriment of young and old. Or strata can contend over the relative share of contribution each stratum is expected to make, as when it is the young who are drafted to fight a war or the middle-aged offspring who feel an undue burden of responsibility for disabled elderly parents.

Age distribution of valued roles takes many forms. Age differentials in access to the roles that can provide economic rewards, prestige, and power are widespread. In the United States, opportunities for "success" through paid work are currently highest among people in the middle-aged strata. Current strata differences in income have derived in part from cohort succession. In the era of economic growth the recent cohorts benefitted more than the earlier cohorts from the overall rise in income. By starting later in history, they began at a higher level. Since economic trends fluctuate, however, it is not always the middle-aged who are favored. Age is also implicated in the uneven distribution of many noneconomic social desiderata including family affiliations, leisure and extended vacations, and health. Even such matters as opportunities for marriage after being widowed also vary widely by age, with the pool of possible mates far larger for younger widowed people than for older.

Certain of these age-related inequalities can be biologically legitimized. The little child is not due the same income or the same power as its parent. Nonagenarians are physically unfit for active participation in professional sports. But many of the socially structured differences between strata have no necessary counterpart in biologically grounded age differences of the people who are allotted or denied roles. Indeed, many inequalities run counter to such deep-rooted contemporary values as equality of opportunity, fair evaluation of achievement, individualism, or self-reliance. It is when inequalities are defined as inequities that age conflicts are most likely to appear. When socially valued roles are opened to certain age strata but closed to others, tensions are produced in those members of society who are denied what they think they are entitled to. To some extent, however, an age differentiation of rewards may reduce the sense of inequity, as persons in different societies, at different life-stages, and with differing cohort experiences regard different things as rewarding.

Cohesiveness across Age Boundaries

Relations between generations not only undermine the social institutions, as Sorokin put it, but also reconstruct them. For there are also diverse forms of interdependence and deference that can integrate people across the several strata, overriding their differences, as in this working principle:

P-7) Individuals who are growing older in any one age stratum interact with members of other strata, allowing either for affiliation and reciprocal socialization, or for age-based tension and conflict.

Intrinsic Bonds. Within the age stratification system itself, there are age-related aspects of the social structure and its underlying processes that operate to mitigate or prevent age conflict. The aging process in particular helps in some ways to provide harmony among the strata. Here aging contrasts with the process of cohort flow which, insofar as cohorts respond differently to social change, tends to maintain separation among the strata.

One mechanism tending to reduce conflict between strata is age-role transiency, which derives from the inevitability of the aging process itself. The particular individuals composing any given age stratum are not permanent residents in the stratum, but transients just passing through. People enter the available roles and learn to perform them. But their role occupancy is limited. Soon they must move on. New cohorts take their place. How, then, can a youth movement be sus-

tained when its leaders and its membership are continually shifting? Why should the young-old struggle against age discrimination in work, when they themselves will soon be the old-old and no longer interested? In such instances, transiency of role affiliation within an age stratum can weaken role commitment and can attenuate the power of one age group to contend against people of other ages (Foner, 1975).

Another factor that reduces the potential for age cleavage is the universality of aging, the fact that everyone ages. Though persons in the several strata differ in life stage, each can share with the others all past stages in retrospect and all future stages in anticipation. Thus the old, remembering their own adolescent problems, may sympathize with the difficulties of youth. Or the young, looking ahead, can prepare their own lives with reference to the lives of people who are old today.

Moreover, although aging is inevitable and universal, it is not immutable; and the mutability, like the inevitability and the universality, tends to prevent sharp cleavages between age strata by blurring age boundaries. Many people straddle two adjacent strata. They are "age incongruents." While they belong chronologically in one stratum, some of the roles they perform and the affiliations they make belong in a different stratum. Age incongruents who are "behind schedule" often consort with those in younger strata, while those who are "ahead of schedule" often associate with their chronological elders. When such age incongruence is widespread, it not only helps some individuals to accommodate, but also weakens the boundaries separating age strata.

Intergenerational Affiliations. Problems of age cleavage are mitigated in quite another way by group memberships that extend across the boundaries of age strata. A major source of potential cohesion between age strata is the family network. Relationships between generations in a family are tied, though loosely, to differences in age. What do these generational differences portend?

Has industrialization dealt a mortal blow to the traditional filial ties? Or are these ties fully alive and well as ever? This is a major issue in recent social science literature on the contemporary family, and there is some evidence on both sides (see Ch. 11 in this *Handbook;* Hagestad, 1981; see also studies of intergenerational relationships in different subpopulations by Bengtson, 1981; Jackson et al., 1981; Markides, 1983).

It is clear that relations of interdependence and exchange between parents and offspring are widespread and persistent. Shanas and her colleagues (1979) have shown that some three-fourths of people over 65 in the United States and several other countries have living adult children, and most, though living separately, maintain regular contact with at least one child and their grandchildren. Such linkages foster interaction and communication across age lines. The common goals of family members may become more salient than the special goals and interests of each separate age stratum (see Bengtson, 1975). Yet there are also contrary tendencies that press toward independence and thus weaken the kinship ties between generations. In the early days of the Industrial Revolution in England, the father (or grandfather) could take his children with him into the factory, training the adult sons himself and supervising the little children throughout the long workday, preserving traditional ties among the generations (cf. Smelser, 1968). If such an arrangement encouraged between-strata solidarity, subsequent changes have certainly undermined it. Save for household chores, parents and children rarely engage in paid work together today—though a coming era of "communicating to work" may perhaps reinstate the earlier pattern.

If work no longer holds generations together, the unprecedented increases in longevity have also tended to separate them. Increasingly, each generation has sought separate residence. Veroff et al. (1981) show a tension between a growing desire for independence, which cuts people off from families, and a growing expressed need to resort to families as sources of help. The con-

tinuing power of the family as a cohesive force in society, even when the older person is institutionalized (Smith and Bengtson, 1979), will depend in large part on how this tension is to be resolved.

In sum, members of the several coexisting age strata, different as they are in age and cohort experience, are continually interacting in the same society. Their interactions and interrelationships are strongly influenced by the strata to which they belong. The interdependence of the strata—as a change in any one stratum has consequences for members of the other strata—contributes to potential changes both in the social structure and in the aging patterns of individuals.

AGING AND AGE STRATIFICATION

To this point we have examined age as a component of the changing society, suggesting how individuals at every age lead their daily lives, interact with each other, and gradually grow older within an age structure of people and roles. We now turn to a consideration of aging and cohort flow, the two processes that operate in tandem to sort people into age strata and to channel people through the age-graded roles. Referring again to Figure 1, the focus now shifts from the vertical cross-sections representing the age-stratified society to the diagonals representing the lives of individuals. As people age and change biologically and psychologically, they also move diagonally up through the age strata and across historical time. While people grow older, the society with its age-stratified roles and the people in these strata are simultaneously changing.

Thus lifelong aging of individuals and cohorts of individuals is a central process in the age stratification approach (Figure 2). However, because this topic is considered in another chapter of this *Handbook* (Hagestad and Neugarten in Ch. 2; cf. also Neugarten and Hagestad, 1976; Featherman, 1981a; Dannefer, n.d.), lifelong aging is touched upon here only as it is integral to age stratification systems. The special relation of aging to the age strata may help to explain why an individual ages in particular ways, or why the life-course patterns of members of a cohort assume particular shapes or affect society in particular ways. Moreover, the location of the life-course (or the life-span) perspective within a larger social framework provides a frequently needed reminder that changes in the age strata are not ipso facto reducible to the aggregate of changing individual lives. For example, the fact that young people today have a high probability of marital disruption over their own lifetime does not replace the corresponding and equally demonstrable fact that young people today live in the same society and in patterned social relationships with other people in the older age strata whose marriages were more durable.

In the initial formulation of the model of age stratification, aging was variously scrutinized: as individuals live out their lives across the full life course (Clausen, 1972); as aging individuals experience patterned changes in their residential needs and attitudes, in their use of community facilities, and in their interaction within the community (Starr, 1972); as friendships may assume special salience at those life stages when the very young or the very old may be excluded from major social roles (Hess, 1972); or as American scientists show a steady decline during their life course in the proportion of time assigned to research and a steady increase in the time assigned to administration (Zuckerman and Merton, 1972). Subsequent research elucidates this conception of aging as mobility within an age stratification system. Recent notable advances have been made in demonstrating the interplay of social aging with biological and psychological aging (cf. Busse and Maddox, 1980; Riley, 1979; Riley and Glass, 1982); in developing models and procedures for longitudinal analysis of this interplay (Featherman, 1981a; Bielby and Hauser, 1977; Hannan and Tuma, 1979; Nesselroade and Baltes, 1979); and in defining historical and sociocultural conditions of variability in the aging process (cf. Riley et al., 1982; Keith and Kertzer, 1983).

Such advances have gone far toward transcending disciplinary barriers, and toward overcoming the difficulties of treating aging as both a complex and a lifelong process. In this overall review we allude to only three selected strands of research concerned with: (1) the mutiple facets of aging through the strata; (2) life-course transitions at the boundaries of strata as people leave former roles and enter new ones; and (3) the personal integration, or lack of integration, across the life course of the diverse role sequences, life experiences, and exigencies of growing older.

Multiple Facets of Aging

When viewed as negotiating a path through the age stratification system, aging can be apprehended as a social process, as distinct from an exclusively and putatively intrinsic biological or intra-psychic process. As people move in and out of roles from birth to death, they interact with other people, contend with the continuing processes of allocation and socialization and with the demands of social change, adapt to the social situations encountered and help to shape them, develop a social identity within which to integrate the diversity of life-course experiences, until at last they prepare for death and must accommodate to it.

At the same time, aging is by no means exclusively a social process, as in the working principle:

P-9) Aging is multifaceted, composed of interdependent biological, psychological, and social processes—it is not a unitary or exclusively biological process.

No single component of aging can be understood without reference to the others. Thus the increases in monoamine oxidase in the brains of old people may be related to depression, which may in turn lead to curtailing of social interaction. Or certain psychological predispositions (such as "Type A personality"), when brought to stressful social situations in the workplace, may be implicated in the biological changes associated with early coronary artery disease (Elliott and Eisdorfer, 1982). Or socially imposed patterns of age segregation, by undermining social stimulation and support provided in work roles or kinship roles, may be related to older people's increased susceptibility to physical and psychological deterioration (Cobb, 1979; Klerman and Izen, 1977; House et al., 1982).

Numerous psychological investigations illustrate how social structures impinge upon the course of development of individuals as organisms (ontogenetic development). For example, Horn and Donaldson (1980) hypothesize that certain types of cognitive ability ("crystallized") remain stable or even improve in later adulthood because they can be practiced and sharpened in the conventional role sequences provided in adult life (see also Schaie, 1979). Willis and Baltes (1980) demonstrate that old people's performance on intelligence tests improves with added practice, instructions about strategies for approaching the problem, and incentives that increase motivation and attention. This demonstration suggests that the observed performance on tests comes from some interplay between latent abilities and the expectations and opportunities afforded in social roles (see also Salthouse and Somberg, 1982). Making a sociological attack on this interplay, Kohn and Schooler (1978), in their ten-year longitudinal study of adult male workers, demonstrate the reciprocal relationship between changes in the demands of successive work situations (whether the jobs demand self-direction or are highly supervised; whether they call for the handling of complex novel circumstances or are substantially routinized) and changes in the intellectual capacities of workers in different occupational trajectories.

From such multidisciplinary investigations, both biosocial and psychosocial conceptions of aging are emerging that not only elaborate and clarify the age stratification approach, but also disclose important social factors in the biological and psychological processes.

Role Transitions

Scholars from several disciplines are examining not only the mutiple facets of aging but also the role transitions that punctuate the life course. As special situations at the boundaries of age strata, in which individuals not only enter new roles but must also surrender earlier ones, role transitions (much like, but no less important than, the daily experiences of growing older within particular roles) are experienced in widely varying fashion by different individuals and under different circumstances. Regardless of where they occur in the age strata, however, transitions mark points of discontinuity for the individual. Certain common features characterize, for example, both the transition from unfettered spouse to first-time parent and the transition from worker to retiree (Benedict, 1938; Riley and Waring, 1976).

Life-Course Outcomes. A good deal of current research is indicating many people's resilience in the face of life-course discontinuities, and is pointing to some possible mitigating factors and facilitating conditions. Particularly striking are recent findings on bereavement, as carefully controlled probes reexamine the reportedly high rates of mortality following the death of a spouse. In a sample of 4000 Maryland residents, Helsing and Szklo (1981; Helsing et al., 1981) find that widowed males, but not widowed females, tend to suffer excess mortality during the years following bereavement. Even widowed males, however, do not experience excess mortality if they remarry—as most of them do. Similarly the transition to retirement, as found in earlier studies by Streib and others (Riley, Foner, et al. 1968), continues to show few adverse consequences on the average (Ekerdt and Bossé, 1982, Ekerdt et al., 1983).

Facilitating Conditions. Still other studies go behind such modal patterns to examine at particular ages the wide differences in individual transition experiences, and to specify the mechanisms linking social and environmental "stress" with various negative outcomes (cf. Elliott and Eisdorfer, 1982). These studies seek to avoid the difficulties of earlier research on "stressful life events" which examined aggregate measures of role transitions, personal experiences, and historical changes without regard to their timing in the life course or their salience or meaning to the individuals involved (Holmes and Rahe, 1967; Dohrenwend and Dohrenwend, 1974; cf. the discussion by Brim and Ryff, 1980).

Stress can be greater in enduring a hated role than in transferring out of it. Whereas people are loath to lose a long-time friend, to move away from a long-familiar community, or to lose benefits accrued in a job, they may anticipate leaving an unhappy marrige, a hated job, or being an "inmate" in an institution. Studies by Lazarus and his associates (DeLongis et al., 1982) indicate that "daily hassles" are more powerful predictors of psychological and physical ill health than are major life events. Some helpless and confused old people may suffer more from their abortive struggles for survival in the community than from moving to a nursing home (cf. Frankfather, 1976).

Transitions can be eased, or the difficulties exacerbated, by the nature of the boundaries between the adjacent strata. Experienced by the individual as role sequences, the transfer from one stratum to the next can be either sharp or gradual, sometimes taking place by stages [Van Gennep (1908) 1960]. In the phasing of the transition from home to institution, Tobin and Lieberman (1976) show that it is not the phase of adapting to the new role of resident of institution, but the prior phase of relinquishing the accustomed role (the loss of independence, the sense of abandonment) that is associated with the deterioration, apathy, and helplessness widely observed among elderly residents. Moreover, age criteria for establishing boundaries between any two strata can be flexible or rigid, affecting individual freedom of choice for entering or leaving a role. Foner and Kertzer (1978) show how flexible or gradual boundaries help to minimize the discrepancies between individual inclinations and the formal rules of societal age-grade systems in Africa. Among the special problems in negotiating transitions when age boundaries are rigid, so that individuals can be ahead of (or behind) the usual or socially prescribed schedule (cf. Neugarten et al., 1965), marriages that occur earlier or later than the modal age are especially likely to end in divorce (Glick and Norton, 1977); and young widows may have more difficulty finding friends than do older widows who are surrounded by large numbers of women who themselves are widows (Z. Blau, 1961).

Other major factors facilitating role transitions are adequate strategies for coping and availability of adequate social support. Research on coping by Lazarus and colleagues indicates that people rely not on a single, but on several, strategies, depending on the nature of the problem at hand. Kahn (1979) has studied social support conceptualized as a dynamic "social convoy" of significant others that follow a person through the life course as potential moderators of stress; and House et al. (1982) in a systematic longitudinal analysis have documented the correlation between active participation in social relationships and reduced mortality.

Counterpart Transitions. As an individual moves with aging from one role to another, the significant others are also affected. Each person's transition is related to counterpart transitions in the lives of others, as in this working principle:

P-10) The ways people age are interdependent; that is, the life-course pattern of one person will influence or be influenced by the life-course patterns of others with whom he or she is interacting.

A few studies have begun to trace the consequences of such interdependent life-course patterns. Thus middle-aged men, forced into unemployment by the closing of a factory, experienced a decline in health. When the wife's counterpart transition took the form of finding employment for herself, the health of her unemployed husband either failed to improve or deteriorated (Cobb and Kasl, 1971). When many fathers were thrown out of work because of the Great Depression, there were lifelong repercussions throughout the family system (Elder, 1974). A family crisis, such as divorce, can require role transitions by all family members simultaneously, with complex consequences for the still-intertwined lives of the young adult spouses, for the socialization of their little children (Hetherington et al., 1981), and for the grandparents as well.

Such examples of counterpart life-course transitions begin to suggest their far-reaching implications for the aging of individuals and for the age strata in society as well. When age boundaries have become established so that millions of members of an entire cohort encounter particular transitions at similar ages, there are massive societal impacts through the collective conterpart transitions. Glick's (1977) studies of the family cycle show how, soon after marriage, most women become mothers and, a few years later, their youngest child starts school—transitions that ramify through the lives of husbands now become fathers, parents now become grandparents, and children moving from dependent infant in the family to entrant into the outside world. Foner and Kertzer (1978) demonstrate the power of life-course transitions as an intrinsic source of social change. Comparing contemporary American society with African societies explicitly organized on the basis of age, they illustrate how cohorts making the transitions across the age strata each continually displace the previous incumbents, usurping their opportunities and rewards. Because each new cohort must contend with the older cohorts it is displacing, societal rules of transition themselves give rise to conflicts and tensions that correspondingly press to change the norms and practices governing transitions.

Order and Timing of Transitions. Within the entire course of life, each person makes many role entrances and exits. The aging pattern is characterized by the particular order in which these occur and the particular intervals of time between them—patterns generated by the interplay between individual aging and social change (cf. Hogan, 1978; Winsborough, 1979). A postponement of an early role change or an inversion of the order has implications for the lives involved. At least one study has shown how the entire role sequence (from finishing school to the advent of the first grandchild) is pushed to later ages in the higher, as compared with the lower, socioeconomic classes (Olsen, 1969), thus producing different strata boundaries for these different subpopulations.

Life-course patterns depend on the time interval or lag between role changes, as well as on the ordering of these changes. Winsborough (1979) demonstrates that men in recent cohorts tend to move more rapidly than their predecessors through the role changes leading to adulthood. This pace has been increasing for many years (cf. Modell et al., 1976; Hareven, 1977) as, for example, the age of leaving the parental home has been declining since the late nineteenth century. Thus, much like many old people, today's young men confront a piling-up of role changes. They face a near simultaneity of entry or exit from their several overlapping roles in education, work, the military, their parental family, their own new family—complex role changes that must be negotiated in a very short span of years within a single age stratum.

Life-Course Integration

Many of these attempts to study aging as mobility through the changing age-stratified society encounter the extraordinary difficulty of treating aging as a lifelong process, as in this working principle:

P–8) Aging is a lifelong process of growing up and growing *older* from birth to death, moving through all the strata in society—it is not simply growing *old* beyond some arbitrary point in the life course.

Here the age stratification paradigm is especially useful. Even many biologists, who have traditionally studied old age as a thing apart, now seem to recognize the possible life-course linkages, as early experiences are found to have "sleeper effects" in later life (e.g., the long lag between exposure to a pollutant and eventual manifestation of a disease), or as genetic programming may affect changes in old age. And many psychologists who once described early childhood experiences as indelible, never to be erased, are beginning to question such assertions (see Brim and Kagan, 1980).

Viewed within the age stratification system, lifelong aging poses questions not only of negotiating transitions from one stratum to the next, but also of managing continuities or discontinuities throughout the life course. How do individuals incorporate within their own lives the many complex role changes they make? How do they maintain a sense of personal continuity and identity as they move across all the age strata?

"Causal" Connections. As one answer to such questions, several strands of sociological research, using longitudinal and causal modeling to trace the same individuals as they age, have provided considerable understanding of how certain early role transitions and events can affect later events in a person's life. This research provides support for the proposition that certain role changes that are observed to follow each other as a person ages follow, not purely by chance but because these successive changes are linked in some meaningful (or "causal") fashion.

One such research strand (the "status attainment" approach, summarized in Featherman, 1981b) has focused on people's socioeconomic careers (e.g., Blau and Duncan, 1967; Sewell and Hauser, 1975; Henretta and Campbell, 1978). These studies show how education and occupation in early life can lead to health and labor force participation in later life, and how these in turn can affect income and assets in old age.

Related to this research strand, which treats status rankings as attributes of individuals, is a second strand that takes roles explicitly into account—emphasizing the people/role distinction that is central to the age stratification model. For example, Kaufman and Spilerman (1982) are concerned with job sequences, that is, with "career lines" in the "sense of there existing sequences of positions with high rates of being traversed." Inferring movement through job sequences from cross-section occupational-age distributions, they show that the majority of detailed census occupations conform to one of five basic age profiles that have meaning derived from the operation of well-defined institutional forces. In another study, Sorensen (1979) develops a mathematically specified "vacancy competition model," that conceives job mobility as "the movement of persons among positions in job structures," and shows that career opportunities are less favorable for women than for men and for blacks than for whites.

This important interplay between aging of individuals and changing social roles (stated in our working principle P-13) is too frequently lost, however, in a "life-span reductionism" that, in concentrating on aging over the life course (or the life span), tends to exclude social structure from the interpretative framework (for examples, see Featherman, 1981a). Many life-span psychologists deliberately circumscribe their models to focus on ontogenetic (maturational or "normative") development (Baltes et al., 1980). They treat as error variance those deviations from the statistical norm that are of special interest to sociologists as potential clues to socioculturally patterned variations in the ways people grow older (Spanier and Glick, 1980; Dannefer, n.d.). When sociologists espouse this life-span model too literally, without questioning its psychologistic assumptions, the danger of reductionism may arise: age-graded roles are implicitly reduced to contextual characteristics of individuals, role sequences become properties of the human life span rather than of the social structure, and age strata become mere aggregates of individuals who carry their own role sequences with them as they age. For example, Featherman and Sorensen (1982), who contend that "ontogenetic development in individuals aggregates into cohort life cycles and renders to the social system its characteristic age stratification," define as "describing the same phenomenon" our two distinct concepts of the life course of individuals and the age stratification of social roles.

Such aggregative life-span models, while useful for certain research objectives, tend to obscure the independent influence of social organization on the ways in which people grow older. They overlook the separate set of dynamic processes whereby roles change as society changes (cf. Baron and Bielby, 1980; Schrank and Waring, 1983). Yet, if the total number of jobs (roles) available for the very young or the very old suddenly declines in a depression or suddenly increases in wartime, the explanation lies in societal shifts in demand for labor, not in sudden life-course changes in the aptitudes or motivations of the individuals involved. The availability of jobs for blacksmiths or computer programmers depends more on economic and technological changes in the society than on cohort differences in the aggregated lives of individuals. The age stratification model, by linking variations in life-course development to variations in social structure, alerts investigators to interpretations that recognize both human development and socioenvironmental changes as separate, but interdependent, dynamisms.

Subjective Continuities. Apprehending the subjective as well as the objective strains and discontinuities experienced by the individual growing older within the complexities of social change, philosophers and poets have long speculated on how the sense of identity can be sustained from childhood to old age throughout the many alterations in social relationships, situations, attitudes, and physical appearance (e.g., Eisenstadt, 1956; Erikson, 1968). For the person progressing through the age strata, Clausen (1972) has provided an insightful analysis of the sense of identity, as a person strives to integrate the past into the present; as her (or his) personality becomes anchored in her network of personal relationships; and as the others in

these groups, coming to expect her to act and think in established ways, continually reinforce her own sense of "being" the same person. A few studies explore the linkages as experienced through the mind between aging processes and their sociohistorical contexts. Kohn (1980) demonstrates how the complexity of a man's job can influence not only his intellectual flexibility, but also his values, self conception, and social orientation. Giele (1980) suggests how recently eroding age- and sex-role constraints can enlarge individual opportunities for growth and unification of the self. LeVine (1980) shows how the norms and social structures of the patriarchal homestead in an African tribe (the Gusii) are experienced over each individual life as three related subjective careers: reproductive, economic, and spiritual. However, the lifelong interplay between subjective experience and social relationships is a largely neglected topic, needing further systematic investigation.

In sum, aging is viewed within age stratification systems as interdependent with changing social structures and human relationships that guide daily lives, produce continuities and discontinuities over the life course, and pose problems in sustaining a sense of personal identity.

COHORT FLOW AND AGE STRATIFICATION

Cohorts form the link between individual aging and social change. As John Meyer puts it (personal communication), history is the history of society (most people know what year it is), and biography is the history of the individual (most people know their own age), but there is little about cohorts in our way of thinking about history or aging. Yet it is cohort flow that energizes the strata to which each of us belongs, ensures the changing composition of these strata, brings history into the age structure giving renewed meaning to everyday affairs, and creates pressures toward conflict and change through persistent imbalances between people and roles. If aging constitutes mobility through the age strata, influencing a person's capacities and performances at every age, the continuing flow of cohorts yields the numbers and kinds of people who form the societal age strata (as schematized in Figure 2). The size and composition, as by sex or ethnicity, of each cohort are patterned over its life course initially through demographic processes (themselves reflective of social norms and practices) of fertility, migration, and mortality. The people in the cohorts are not statistical aggregates, of course, but sentient members of society who participate in its diverse institutions and pluralistic culture, and whose individual lives share a common slice of history. Thus, as society changes, successive cohorts differ in size and composition and in the aging patterns of their individual members.

In the initial formulation of the age stratification approach, numerous studies illustrated the operation of cohort flow to affect both the process of aging and the age structure of people. The differentiation of the aging process from one cohort to the next was illustrated in the complete reversal over the past century in life-course patterns of women's labor force participation (Riley et al., 1972). When cohorts born late in the last century are compared with more recent cohorts, a woman born earlier was decreasingly likely to work outside the home as she grew older, whereas a woman born in the mid–twentieth century is increasingly likely to do so. The effect of differing sizes of successive cohorts on the age structure of people—an effect widely understood today because the population of the United States is "aging" (cf. Espenshade and Braun, 1983)—was illustrated by Zuckerman and Merton (1972), who showed how, with the rapid growth of science, the rising numbers of scientists in each new cohort had a "juvenescent effect" on the age structure of scientists, with comparatively few at the older ages and large numbers at the younger. More recent studies, including examples in other chapters of this *Handbook,* have described many other kinds of cohort differences as they relate both to the aging process and to the changing age structure of society, in line

with two of the working principles of the age stratification approach:

P-11) The life-course patterns of particular individuals are affected by the character of the cohort to which they belong and by those social, cultural, and environmental changes to which their cohort is exposed in moving through each of the successive age strata.

P-12) When many individuals in the same cohort are affected by social change in similar ways, the change in their collective lives can in turn produce further social change. That is, new patterns of aging are not only caused by social change, they also contribute to it.

Cohort Analysis

One widely used tool for exploring how cohort flow, aging, and change in the age-stratified society are interrelated is cohort analysis, or the simple mapping and direct comparison of pertinent information about the life-course experiences of successive cohorts (cf. Susser, 1969). For understanding the aging process, the comparison of an array of cohorts (the diagonals in Figure 1) is one small step toward distinguishing what "happens to be" from what "has to be." That is, cohort comparisons can aid the search for conditions under which people may age in different, or in similar, ways. Cohort differences are frequently found when changes associated with the aging process are mediated by prevailing social conditions: for example the timing of puberty seems related to the adequacy of nourishment available to successive cohorts; "reading readiness" seems affected by the pedagogical ideologies to which different cohorts of children are exposed; or the role of retiree may disappear for cohorts under the demands of war mobilization, or may arrive in life's prime for cohorts experiencing insufficient economic expansion.

The search for cohort differences also can lead to discovery of cohort likenesses. It can uncover patterns of biological and behavioral aging that persist, relatively intact, despite variations in the conditions under which people live. Such putatively intrinsic processes of aging, given expression by their repeated appearances in the life-course schedules of successive cohorts, may be determined largely by the imperatives of ontogeny, or they may be shaped by enduring features of social organization. As used by life-span psychologists primarily concerned with ontogeny (and called "cohort-sequential" analysis, cf. Nesselroade and Baltes, 1979), cohort comparisons are essential for avoiding the fallacy of cohort-centrism; as Rosow (1978) says, cohorts are not mere "statistical artifacts of a cross-sequential obstacle course."

Cohort analysis is valuable not only for exploring the variability of the aging process for which cross-cultural comparisons are also utilized, and for anticipating the future for cohorts of people whose lives have already begun (cf. Cutler, 1981; Johnston and Hoover, 1982). In addition, cohort analysis provides a map for exploring the changing age structure of society. It affords a societal view of the full set of coexisting cohorts, as they age together through time. As one example (see also Riley, 1981a), comparison of successive cohorts of women has disclosed marked changes over the past century in life-course patterns of work. By now taking cross-section slices through these cohorts (corresponding to the vertical lines in Figure 1), the changing age structure of women's working can be observed. Thus at two historical periods (1940 and 1956) percentages of women in the labor force peaked in the young adult strata, but only at the later period was there a second peak—in the middle-aged strata. Some technical principles for interpreting cross-section age differences as they reflect life-course patterns and cohort differences in these patterns are set forth by Riley (1976).

Cohort Flow and the Aging Process

Emerging from cohort analyses and related studies on a wide range of topics are many varied clues both to the age-related historical and sociocultural conditions associated with particular cohort differences in the aging process, and to the complex interplay between cohort differences in aging and societal changes.

Sociotemporal Variations in Cohort Differences. Historical studies are describing in detail how cohort differences in the ways people age are related to long-term changes in the polity, the economy, the spiritual and intellectual climate of the society, or the family. Such studies avoid reifying historical time by postulating specific aspects of social change that cut across the age strata to produce cohort differences. Vinovskis (1982) uses three cohorts of ministers to illustrate the changing status and care of the elderly in preindustrial America. The first cohort came from England early in the seventeenth century and aged under a unique set of circumstances that ensured respect, admiration, and power. The second cohort came later in the century when population growth, economic prosperity, and the spiritual ardor of their congregations had dwindled. In old age they did not receive the same veneration from their parishioners as the earlier cohort. The third cohort, who graduated from college early in the eighteenth century, fared even less well as they were confronted with inflation, disputes between ministers and congregations, and the inability to send even one son to college. Thus in their old age this cohort, and especially their widows, suffered—not because of age as such, but because of unfavorable economic and religious circumstances. In another study, Simkus (1982) focuses on the relationship between socioeconomic careers of individuals and radical historical changes in socioeconomic structures in Hungary during the past 50 years. He demonstrates how a rapid transition from agriculture to industry and a high degree of state intervention can bring substantial alterations in the aging process both through within-career shifts and through cross-cohort differences. (For a parallel Norwegian analysis, see Featherman and Sorensen, 1982.)

Other studies use systematic measures of the historical changes that are postulated to mediate the cohort differences in aging. Societal measures of economic fluctuations, for example, have been examined in relation to fertility among young women (Ogburn and Thomas, 1927), dropping out of high school by adolescents (Land and Felson, 1976), or mortality from cardiovascular diseases characteristic of later life (Brenner and Mooney, 1982; see also Pampel and Weiss, 1982).

The Interplay of Cohort Differences and Social Change. As research probes further into the mechanisms linking cohort differences in aging to social change, the feedback loops within the age stratification system are becoming clearer, and new patterns of aging are seen as not only caused by, but also contributing to, social change—as stated in working principles P-11 and P-12 of the age stratification model. Many familiar phenomena in every age stratum take on fresh meaning when viewed as processes within this interplay (Uhlenberg, 1979a; Riley, 1982a).

Consider the example of education for girls in the United States. Because of social changes in the past two centuries (industrialization, educational ideologies, increasing value attached to children), successive cohorts of children have spent increasing portions of their lives in school (the effect on aging over the life course). Such cohort differences in education have incalculable consequences, not only for the early lives, but also for the entire life course of the women affected: for experience in marrying and having children, for participation in the work force, for ranges of interests and friendships, for the sense of personal control. Meantime the interplay continues. As more and more girls in each successive cohort achieve increasingly high levels of education and lead their lives in new ways, social norms and social institutions in turn undergo still further changes (the effect on social change). Recent cohorts of women in several age strata have been recreating their roles at home, at work, in the professions, in athletics, in the arts, in science (Uhlenberg, 1979b).

Thus a social change (rising education) has left its mark on the lives of women in successive cohorts, who, in turn, have helped to restructure the institutions in which they participate.

As another example of the interplay, similar feedback processes are at work in respect to retirement for men. Long-term social changes (e.g., the changing character of occupations, the expansion of pension plans) have resulted in earlier and earlier ages of retirement. Of the cohort of men reaching age 65 in 1900, approximately two-thirds were still in the work force; but this proportion had dropped to one-third by 1960, and to only one-fifth by 1980. Combined with increases in longevity, these cohort differences in work mean many added retirement years (Torrey, 1982), with marked consequences for the aging processes in terms of income, social involvement, leisure activities, health, and effective functioning. In turn, as fewer and fewer older men in each successive cohort remain in the work force, many social norms and social institutions are affected in ways that ramify through the age strata. Laws and contracts are changing. Norms of achievement are shifting. Leisure activities are shaped by the growing numbers of retirees. Added demands to pay taxes are imposed upon the younger people still in the labor force. (See Foner and Schwab, 1983.)

Other noteworthy evidences of this continuing interplay between social change and aging derive from studies of the structure of kinship relationships. Several social changes, are involved: dissolution of parental authority, secular decline in birth rates, and—most striking of all—the dramatic increase in longevity. These changes have meant that in many families today four, even five, generations can be alive at the same time, and that the aging patterns of successive cohorts of family members have been transformed. Children coexist with their parents longer now than they used to. Indeed, there are now large numbers of 65-year-old daughters interacting with their still surviving aged mothers. Married couples live together much longer before separation by death, if not by divorce, than did their earlier counterparts. Widowhood has been postponed to the later years, usually striking in old age when the risks of ill health are greatest. All such transformations in the lives of family members, rooted in social change, in their turn have many consequences for further social change. Important among these consequences, the norm of independence is reinforced. There are increasing tendencies toward divorce and remarriage that add complexity to the aging process and contribute to the family network step-kin of varying ages. And increasing proportions of people, in particular older widows, live entirely alone (Michael et al., 1980).

Cohort Flow and the Changing Age Structure

In such fashion cohort differences in aging patterns are not only caused by social change, but, in addition, these differences in turn cause further social changes, which result in still further cohort differences in aging patterns, and so on, in a seemingly endless chain. Two aspects of the interplay between cohort flow and social structure have been given recent attention: disordered cohort flow, as cohort differences in size or composition can produce imbalances between people and roles; and cohort norm formation, as developing values and attitudes within a cohort can pervade all the age strata.

Disordered Cohort Flow. Among the unique characteristics of each cohort are its size, its composition (as by race or social class background), and the average longevity of its members. As all these differing cohorts succeed each other, there can obviously never be a perfect balance between the cohorts of people who are aging and the changing roles available for them in the stratified society. Instead there is an intrinsic imbalance between people and roles. Differences in cohort size as one source of imbalance are described in detail by Waring (1975), Easterlin (1978), and Oppenheimer (1981), who extend and elaborate the well-known exam-ple of the large numbers of people in the baby boom cohort who confronted too few places in school, too few entry jobs, too few homes to live in, thus creating a spiraling demand for many new places that, a little later on, could not be filled by the subsequent smaller cohorts. Equally disturbing to the balance between people and roles can be cohort differences in longevity. Tremendous dislocations have arisen from the persistent increase in longevity of successive cohorts over this century, as older people have outlived their traditional roles both in the work force and in the family, and new roles have not yet replaced them.

The result of such imbalances between cohorts of people who are aging and the age roles available in society can be strains and pressures for change for both individual and society, as in Oppenheimer's life-cycle "squeezes." Individuals who are underemployed, or unable to find work, or unsuccessful in finding marriage partners can feel frustrated and depressed, demand remedial action, resort to deviance. And social institutions and norms can be disturbed when there are not enough openings in the work force for young people, not enough trained soldiers in case of war, not enough people motivated to care for the elderly, or not enough jobs for highly educated women seeking to enter the labor force in midlife (cf. Uhlenberg, 1979b). These strains on both individuals and society can contribute to societal changes that, in turn, differentiate life-course patterns of successive cohorts.

Cohort Norm Formation. Another unique characteristic of each cohort is the common historical era shared by its members. Members of a particular cohort were all the same age when they experienced, for example, the Great Depression (Elder, 1979), President Kennedy's assassination, or the Iranian capture of hostages. No other cohort experienced these same events at the same age. As the members of the same cohort respond to shared experiences, they gradually and subtly develop common patterns of response, common definitions, common norms—a process called "cohort norm formation" [Riley, 1978; cf. Mannheim (1928) 1952]. Thus, in its own way, each cohort exerts a collective force as it moves through the age-stratified society, pressing for adjustments in social roles and social values. Analyses by Glenn (1980) suggest that even at the oldest ages members of a cohort still participate in major shifts in societal values.

The recent women's movement provides an example of cohort norm formation. Many individual women in the cohorts currently in young adulthood have responded to common social changes by making separate but similar personal decisions to move in new directions—to go to college, have a career, structure their family in innovative ways. While a few women in previous cohorts had made similar decisions, those women were forerunners. Only with the current cohorts of young women did such decisions become pervasive. These cohorts have burst the floodgates of custom. It is through these "floodgate cohorts" that new norms have sudenly been brought into the open and been institutionalized, as gender role attitudes and behaviors are becoming transformed (cf. Riley, 1982b).

In every stratum, as cohort norms and definitions develop and change, the meanings people attach to age have power. These meanings become age stereotypes, influencing people's personal plans, hopes, and fears. They become age constraints, built into the age structure of social roles, molding the course of human lives, directing social change. They are continually affecting the way people grow up and grow old, modifying the values attached to life and death, pressing toward societal integration or conflict.

In sum, cohort flow is a social process linked to continuing alterations both in individual aging and in the age structure of society. Gradually this interplay of processes within age stratification systems is being captured in empirical studies. For example, Seymour Spilerman and Harris Schrank are studying career and job sequences in relation to structural changes in large corporations (personal communication). Handl et al. (1979) analyze throughout the age strata of German workers the historical interplay between the consequences of World War II, which affected societal acceptance of women's working, and the more general tendency for industrial change to occur through the successive recruitment to newly developing industries of only the youngest women. Women, unlike men, are then likely to spend their entire work lives in these industries. Hareven (1982) describes historical changes in the work/retirement and family lives of individuals at various ages and the reciprocal influences of the changing lives on the nature of the family. Oppenheimer (1981) shows the adaptive behavioral responses to the economic role pressures exerted on differing age strata at differing time periods and in differing subpopulations of contemporary society. Indeed, it is beginning to appear that cohort flow through the social institutions may be a universal source of change for society and for its individual members (cf. Foner and Kertzer, 1978).

DIRECTIONS FOR THE FUTURE

This chapter has set forth recent clarifications and implementations of the age stratification approach for understanding both individual aging and social change. Not a theory but a broad conceptual framework, this approach is being used for evaluating and interpreting specific research findings, integrating the accumulating body of knowledge, identifying gaps in this knowledge, and specifying researchable hypotheses to fill these gaps.

Through this approach, seemingly disparate findings from cross-sectional versus longitudinal studies can be reconciled; numerous published research findings can be reanalyzed to yield new insights; and established concepts (such as intergenerational relationships, social stratification, socialization, allocation, or social change) can achieve new clarification. Particular studies, contributing small pieces to the vast mosaic of knowledge, have pointed to the interplay between aging persons and age-related roles, to age homophily and age consciousness; to the universality of cohort flow and cohort norm formation; to the meanings of age differences in everyday life and to cultural stereotypes attached to particular age strata; to the potential for age conflict; to the multidimensionality of the aging process and the conditions of its mutability; to the interdependent dynamisms of individual aging and social change; and to the extent to which these dynamisms are subject to personal or social control.

For the future, the chapter emphasizes two sets of implications—(1) for research and (2) for policy and practice—of the fundamental fact that, within the age stratification system, both individual lives and societal structures are not immutable but subject to change. For research, a programmatic agenda is needed so that interrelated hypotheses can be formulated and valid generalizations can cumulate under the guidance of the developing perspective. Because of continuing alterations in the age stratification system, many earlier research findings on age and aging are becoming vitiated. Thus the future agenda requires:

- Maintenance of existing longitudinal study populations from whom new information may be sought, and additions to archives of relevant computerized data for secondary analysis.
- Wider application of existing methods of longitudinal and cohort analysis (cf. Hannan and Tuma, 1979); and development of new methods of dynamic multilevel analysis for interrelating macrolevel societal changes with microlevel personal changes (cf. Riley and Nelson, 1971).
- Interdisciplinary collaboration and sustained commitment from scientists equipped to bring together from their respective fields relevant specialized knowledge and skills.
- Substantive integration, evaluation, and dissemination of accumulating research findings (as in Riley, Foner, et al., 1968).

- A stable base of research funding—recognizing the need both for long-range programmatic effort and for routine reassessment and updating of the base of knowledge.

For public policy and professional practice, indeed for daily life, fresh opportunities and fresh challenges are entailed by the fact that the age strata and the aging process itself are to an extent mutable, subject to a degree of human intervention and control. Increasingly, as weighty decisions affecting the age strata must be made by legislators, planners, professionals, and the public, these decisions can be informed by new scientific understandings of the continuing interplay between aging and social change in order to make decisions that are more precise and more humane, to dispel negative stereotypes that can become self-fulfilling prophecies, and to assess the consequences for people's lives of alternative decisions for optimizing the aging process and the place of older people in society.

REFERENCES

Abeles, Ronald P. 1981. Symposium on "Health, Behavior, and Aging: Recent Needs." Toronto, Canada: Gerontology Society of America.

Achenbaum, W. Andrew. 1978 *Old Age in the New Land.* Baltimore, Md.: The Johns Hopkins Press.

Baltes, Paul B. 1979. Life-span developmental psychology: Some converging observations on history and theory. *In* Paul B. Baltes and Orville G. Brim (eds.), *Life-Span Development,* Vol. 2. New York: Academic Press.

Baltes, Paul B., and Willis, Sherry L. 1982. Enhancement (plasticity) of intellectual functioning in old age: Penn State's Adult Development and Enrichment Project (ADEPT). *In* F. I. M. Craik and S. E. Trehub (eds.), *Aging and Cognitive Process.* New York: Plenum.

Baltes, Paul B., Reese, H., and Lipsitt, L. 1980. Life-span developmental psychology. *Annual Review of Psychology* 31:65–110.

Banton, Michael. 1965. *Roles: An Introduction to the Study of Social Relations.* New York: Basic Books.

Baron, James N., and Bielby, William T. 1980. Bringing the firms back in: Stratification segmentation, and the organization of work. *American Sociological Review* 45:737–765.

Barton, Elizabeth M., Baltes, Margret M., and Orzech, Mary Jo. 1980. Etiology of dependence in older nursing home residents during morning care: The role of staff behavior. *Journal of Personality and Social Psychology* 38:423–431.

Benedict, Ruth. 1938. Continuities and discontinuities in cultural conditioning. *Psychiatry* 1:161–167.

Bengtson, V. L. 1975. Generation and family effects in value socialization. *American Sociological Review* 40:358–371.

Bengtson, V. L. 1981. Research across the generation gap. *In* J. Rosenfeld (ed.) *Relationships: The Marriage and Family Reader.* Chicago: Scott, Foresman.

Bengtson, V. L., Furlong, Michael J., and Laufer, Robert S. 1974. Time, aging, and the continuity of social structure: Themes and issues in generational analysis. *Journal of Social Issues* 30:1–30.

Bielby, W. T., and Hauser, R. M. 1977. Structural equation models. *Annual Review of Sociology* 3:137–161.

Blau, Peter M. 1974. Parameters of social structure. *American Sociological Review* 39:615–635.

Blau, P., and Duncan, O. D. 1967. *The American Occupational Structure.* New York: Wiley.

Blau, Zena Smith. 1961. Structural constraints on friendship and old age. *American Sociological Review* 26:429–439.

Brenner, M. H., and Mooney, A. 1982. Economic change and sex-specific cardiovascular mortality in Britain 1955–1976. *Social Science and Medicine* 16:431–442.

Brim, Orville G., Jr. 1966. Socialization through the life cycle. *In* Orville G. Brim, Jr., and Stanton Wheeler (eds.), *Socialization after Childhood: Two Essays.* New York: Wiley.

Brim, Orville G., Jr. 1980. Socialization in an unpredictable society. Plenary address to the American Sociological Association, New York.

Brim, Orville G., Jr., and Kagan, Jerome (eds.), 1980. *Constancy and Change in Human Development.* Cambridge, Mass. Harvard University Press.

Brim, Orville G., Jr. and Ryff, Carol D. 1980. On the properties of life events. *In* Paul B. Baltes and Orville G. Brim, Jr. (eds.), *Life-Span Development and Behavior,* Vol. 3, pp. 368–388. New York: Academic Press.

Burk, P., and Turk, A. 1975. Factors affecting postarrest dispositions: A model for analysis. *Social Problems* 22:313–322.

Busse, Ewald, W., and Maddox, George L. 1980. *Final Report: The Duke Longitudinal Studies, An Integrated Investigation of Aging and the Aged.* Ancillary Studies and Research Support Services 1955–1980. Duke University Medical Center. Durham, N.C.

Cain, Leonard D. 1964. Life course and social structure. *In* Robert E. L. Faris (ed.), *Handbook of Modern Sociology,* pp. 272–309. Chicago: Rand McNally.

Cain, Leonard D. 1976. Aging and the law. *In* Robert H. Binstock and Ethel Shanas (eds.), *Handbook of Aging and the Social Sciences,* 1st ed., pp. 342–368. New York: Van Nostrand Reinhold.

Cherlin, Andrew. 1983. A sense of history: Recent research on aging and the family. *In* Matilda White Riley, Beth B. Hess, and Kathleen Bond (eds.), *Aging in Society: Selected Reviews of Recent Research,* pp. 5–23. Hillsdale, N.J.: Lawrence Erlbaum Associates.

Clausen, John A. 1968. *Socialization and Society.* Boston: Little Brown.

Clausen, John A. 1972. The life course of individuals. *In* Matilda White Riley, Marilyn Johnson, and Anne Foner (eds.), *Aging and Society: A Sociology of Age Stratification,* Vol. III, pp. 457–514. New York: Russell Sage Foundation.

Cobb, Sidney. 1979. Social support and health through the life course. *In* Matilda White Riley (ed.), AAAS Selected Symposium 30, *Aging from Birth to Death: Interdisciplinary Perspectives,* Vol. I, pp. 93–106. Boulder, Colo.: Westview Press.

Cobb, Sidney, and Kasl, Stanislav V. 1971. Some medical aspects of unemployment: Report to respondents. Survey Research Center, University of Michigan, Ann Arbor.

Cohn, Richard. 1972. On interpretation of cohort and period analyses: A mathematical note. *In* Matilda White Riley, Marilyn Johnson, and Anne Foner (eds.), *Aging and Society: A Sociology of Age Stratification,* Vol. III, pp. 85–88. New York: Russell Sage Foundation.

Cohn, Richard M. 1982. Economic development and status change of the aged. *American Journal of Sociology* 87:1150–1161.

Cole, Stephen. 1979. Age and scientific performance. *American Journal of Sociology* 84:958–977.

Cutler, Neal E. 1981. Political characteristics of elderly cohorts in the twenty-first century. *In* Sara B. Kiesler, James N. Morgan, and Valerie Kincade Oppenheimer (eds.), *Aging: Social Change,* pp. 127–157. New York: Academic Press.

Dannefer, Dale. n.d. The sociology of the life course. (Unpublished.)

DeLongis, A., Coyne, J. C., Dakof, G., Folkman, S., and Lazarus, R. S. 1982. Relationships of daily hassles, uplifts, and major life events to health status. *Health Psychology* 1:119–136.

Demos, John, and Boocock, Sarane Spence (eds.) 1978. *Turning Points: Historical and Sociological Essays on the Family.* Chicago: University of Chicago Press.

Dixon, R. A., Simon, E. W., Nowak, C. A., and Hultsch, D. F. 1982. Text recall in adulthood as a function of level of information, input modality, and delay interval. *Journal of Gerontology* 37:358–364.

Dohrenwend, Bruce S., and Dohrenwend, Barbara P. (eds.). 1974. *Stressful Life Events: Their Nature and Effects.* New York: Wiley.

Dowd, James. 1980. *Stratification Among the Aged.* Belmont, Calif.: Wadsworth.

Easterlin, Richard A. 1978. What will 1984 be like? Socioeconomic implications of recent twist in age structure. *Demography* 15:397–432.

Edelman, C. D., and Siegler, I. D. 1978. *Federal Age Discrimination in Employment Law: Slowing Down the Golden Watch*. Charlottesville, Va.: The Michie Company.

Ekerdt, D. J. and Bossé, R. 1982. Change in self-reported health with retirement. *International Journal of Aging and Human Development* 15:(3), 213–223.

Ekerdt, D. J., Bossé, R., and Goldie, C. 1983. The effect of retirement on somatic complaints. *Journal of Psychosomatic Research*. 27:(1), 61–67.

Eisenstadt, S. N. 1956. *From Generation to Generation: Age Groups and Social Structure*. Glencoe, Ill.: Free Press.

Elder, Glen, H., Jr. 1974. *Children of the Great Depression*. Chicago: University of Chicago Press.

Elder, Glen, H., Jr. 1979. Historical change in life patterns and personality. *In* Paul B. Baltes and Orville G. Brim, Jr. (eds.), *Life-Span Development and Behavior*, Vol. II, pp. 118–159. New York: Academic Press.

Elliott, Glen R., and Eisdorfer, Carl (eds.), 1982. *Stress and Human Health: Analysis and Implications of Research*. New York: Springer Publishing Co.

Erikson, Erik H. 1968. Life cycle. *International Encyclopedia of the Social Sciences*, Vol. 9, pp. 286–292. New York: Macmillan and Free Press.

Espenshade, Thomas J., and Braun, Rachel E. 1983. Economic aspects of an aging population an the material well-being of older persons. *In* Matilda White Riley, Beth B. Hess, and Kathleen Bond (eds.), *Aging in Society: Selected Reviews of Recent Research*, pp. 25–52 Hillsdale, N.J.: Lawrence Erlbaum Associates.

Featherman, David L. 1980. Schooling and occupational careers: Constancy and change in worldly success. *In* Orville G. Brim, Jr. and Jerome Kagan (eds.), *Constancy and Change in Human Development*, pp. 675–738. Cambridge, Mass.: Harvard University Press.

Featherman, David L. 1981a. The life-span perspective. *In* The National Science Foundations, *The 5-Year Outlook on Science and Technology*, Vol. 2, pp. 621–648. Washington, D.C.: U.S. Government Printing Office.

Featherman, David L. 1981b. Stratification and social mobility: Two decades of cumulative science. *In* James F. Short, Jr. (ed.), *The State of Sociology: Problems and Prospects*, pp. 79–100. Beverly Hills, Calif.: Sage Publications.

Featherman, David L., and Sorensen, Annemette. 1982. Societal transformation in Norway and change in the life course transition into adulthood. Paper delivered at the Population Association of America, San Diego.

Fienberg, Stephen E., and Mason, William M. 1979. Identification and estimation of age-cohort models in the analysis of discrete archival data. *Sociological Methodology*, 1–67.

Fischer, David Hackett. 1978. *Growing Old in America*. New York: Oxford University Press.

Foner, Anne. 1972. The polity. *In* Matilda White Riley, Marilyn Johnson, and Anne Foner (eds.), *Aging and*

Society: A Sociology of Age Stratification, Vol. III, pp. 115–159. New York: Russell Sage Foundation.

Foner, Anne. 1974. Age stratification and age conflict in political life. *American Sociological Review* 39:187–196.

Foner, Anne. 1975. Age in society: Structure and change. *American Behavioral Scientist* 19:144–168.

Foner, Anne. 1979. Ascribed and achieved bases of stratification. *Annual Review of Sociology* 5:219–242.

Foner, Anne. 1980. The sociology of age stratification: A review of some recent publications. *Contemporary Sociology* (Nov.):771–779.

Foner, Anne, and Kertzer, David I. 1978. Transitions over the life course: Lessons of age-set societies. *American Journal of Sociology* 83:1081–1104.

Foner, Anne, and Schwab, Karen. 1983. Work and retirement in a changing society. *In* Matida White Riley, Beth B. Hess, and Kathleen Bond (eds.), *Aging in Society: Selected Reviews of Recent Research*, pp. 71–94. Hillsdale, N.J.: Lawrence Erlbaum Associates.

Foner, Nancy. 1982. Some consequences of age inequality in nonindustrial societies. *In* Matilda White Riley, Ronald P. Abeles, and Michael S. Teitelbaum (eds.), AAAS Selected Symposium 30, *Aging from Birth to Death: Sociotemporal Perspectives*, Vol. II, pp. 71–85. Boulder, Colo.: Westview Press.

Frankfather, Dwight. 1976. *The Aged in the Community: Managing Senility and Deviance*. New York: Praeger.

Fries, James F. 1980. Aging, natural death, and the compression of morbidity. *New England Journal of Medicine* 303:130–135.

Furstenberg, Frank F., Jr. 1981. Remarriage and intergenerational relations. *In* Robert W. Fogel, Elaine Hatfield, Sara B. Kiesler, and Ethel Shanas (eds.), *Aging: Stability and Change in the Family*, pp. 115–142. New York: Academic Press.

Giele, Janet Zollinger. 1980. Adulthood as transcendence of age and sex. *In* Neil J. Smelser and Erik H. Erikson (eds.), *Themes of Work and Love in Adulthood*, pp. 151–173. Cambridge, Mass. Harvard University Press.

Glenn, N. D. 1980. Values, attitudes, and beliefs. *In* Orville G. Brim, Jr. and J. Kagan (eds.), *Constancy and Change in Human Development*, pp. 596–640. Cambridge, Mass.: Harvard University Press.

Glick, Paul C. 1977. Updating the life cycle of the family. *Journal of Marriage and the Family*, 5–13.

Glick, Paul C., and Norton, Author J. 1977. Marrying, divorcing, and living together in the U.S. today. *Population Bulletin* 32:15. Washington, D.C.: Population Reference Bureau.

Gutmann, David. 1977. The cross-cultural perspective: Notes toward a comparative psychology of aging. *In* James E. Birren and K. Warner Schaie (eds.), *Handbook of the Psychology of Aging*, pp. 302–326. New York: Van Nostrand Reinhold.

Hagestad, Gunhild O. 1981. Problems and promises in

the social psychology of intergenerational relations. *In* Robert W. Fogel, Elaine Hatfield, Sara B. Kiesler, and Ethel Shanas (ed.), *Aging: Stability and Change in the Family,* pp. 11–46. New York: Academic Press.

Hammel, E. A. 1983. Age in the Fortesian coordinates. *In* David I. Kertzer and Jennie Keith (eds.), *Age and Anthropological Theory,* pp. 141–158. Ithaca, N.Y.: Cornell University Press.

Handl, Johann, Mayer, Karl Ulrich, Mueller, Walter, and Willms, Angelika. 1979. Prozesse Sozialstrukturellen Wandels am Beispiel der Entwicklung von Qualifikations und Erwerbsstruktur der Frauen. Im Deutschen Reich und der Bundesrepublik Deutschland. Paper presented at the 19th Deutschen Soziologentag, Berlin, April 17–20.

Hannan, M. T., and Tuma, Nancy. 1979. Methods for temporal analysis. *Annual Review of Sociology* 5:303–328.

Hareven, Tamara. 1977. Family time and historical time. *Daedalus* 106:57–70.

Hareven, Tamara. 1978. The dynamics of kin in an industrial community. *In* John Demos and Sarane Boocock (eds.), *Turning Points. American Journal of Sociology,* Supplement. 84:S151–182.

Hareven, Tamara. 1982. *Industrial Time and Family Time.* Cambridge: Cambridge University Press.

Harris, L., and Associates, Inc. 1979. *1979 Study of American Attitudes toward Pensions and Retirement: A Nationwide Survey of Employees, Retirees and Business Leaders: Summary.* New York: Johnson and Higgins.

Heaton, Tim B. 1983. Geographical distribution of the elderly population: Recent trends. *In* Matilda White Riley, Beth B. Hess, and Kathleen Bond (eds.), *Aging in Society: Selected Reviews of Recent Research,* pp. 95–114. Hillsdale, N.J.: Lawrence Erlbaum Associates.

Helsing, K. J., and Szklo, M. 1981. Mortality after bereavement. *American Journal of Epidemiology* 114:41–52.

Helsing, K. J., Szklo, M., and Comstock, G. W. 1981. Factors associated with mortality after widowhood. *American Public Health* 71:802–809.

Henretta, John C., and Campbell, Richard T. 1978. Net worth as an aspect of status. *American Journal of Sociology* 83:204–223.

Hess, Beth. 1972. Friendship. *In* Matilda White Riley, Marilyn Johnson, and Anne Foner (eds.), *Aging and Society: A Sociology of Age Stratification,* Vol. III, pp. 357–393. New York: Russell Sage Foundation.

Hess, Beth B., and Markson, Elizabeth W. 1980. *Aging and Old Age: An Introduction to Social Gerontology.* New York: Macmillan Publishing Co.

Hetherington, E. M., Cox, M., and Cox, R. 1981. Effects of divorce on parents and children. *In* Michael Lamb (ed.), *Nontraditional families.* Hillsdale, N.J.: Lawrence Erlbaum Associates.

Hogan, Dennis P. 1978. The variable order of events in the life course. *American Sociological Review* 43:537–586.

Holmes, T. H., and Rahe, R. H. 1967. The social readjustment rating scale. *Journal of Psychosomatic Research* 11:213–218.

Horn, John L., and Donaldson, Gary. 1980. Cognitive development in adulthood. *In* Orville G. Brim, Jr. and Jerome Kagan (eds.), *Constancy and Change in Human Development,* pp. 445–529. Cambridge, Mass.: Harvard University Press.

House, James S., Robbins, Cynthia, and Metzner, Helen L. 1982. The association of social relationships and activities with mortality: Prospective evidence from the Tecumseh community health study. *American Journal of Epidemiology* 116:123–140.

Hudson, R. B. 1978. The "graying" of the federal budget and its consequences of old-age policy. *The Gerontologist* 18:428–440.

Hudson, R. B. 1980. Old age politics in a period of change. *In* Edgar Borgatta and Neil McCluskey (eds.), *Aging and Society: Current Research and Policy Perspectives,* pp. 147–189. Beverly Hills, Calif.: Sage Publications.

Hyman, H. H., Wright, C., and Reed, John. 1975. *The Enduring Effects of Education.* Chicago: University of Chicago Press.

Institute of Medicine, National Academy of Sciences. 1981. *Airline Pilot Age, Health and Performance: Scientific and Medical Considerations.* Washington, D.C.: National Academy of Sciences.

Jackson, J. S., Hatachett, S., and Bowman, P. J. 1981. A national survey of three generation black families. Paper presented at the annual meeting of the Gerontological Society of America.

Johnson, Marilyn. 1976. The role of perceived parental models, expectations and socializing behaviors in the self-expectations of adolescent, from the U.S. and West Germany. Unpublished dissertation, New Brunswick, N.J.: Rutgers University.

Johnston, Denis F., and Hoover, Sally L. 1982. Social indicators of aging. *In* Matilda White Riley, Ronald P. Abeles, and Michael S. Teitelbaum (eds.), AAAS Selected Symposium 79, *Aging from Birth to Death: Sociotemporal Perspectives,* Vol. II, pp. 197–215. Boulder, Colo.: Westview Press.

Kahn, Robert L. 1979. Aging and social support. *In* Matilda White Riley (ed.), *Aging from Birth to Death: Interdisciplinary Perspectives,* Vol. I, pp. 77–91. Boulder, Colo. Westview Press.

Kaufman, Robert L., and Spilerman, Seymour. 1982. The age structures of occupations and jobs. *American Journal of Sociology* 87:827–851.

Keith, Jennie, and Kertzer, David I. 1983. Age and anthropology: Introduction. *In* David I. Kertzer and Jennie Keith (eds.), *Age and Anthropological Theory.* Ithaca, N.Y.: Cornell University Press.

Kertzer, S. D. 1981. Perspectives on older workers: Maine's prohibition of mandatory retirement. *Maine Law Journal* 33:157–194.

Klerman, Gerald L., and Izen, Judith E. 1977. The effects of bereavement and grief on physical health and general well-being. *Advances in Psychosomatic Medicine* 9:63–104.

Kohn, Melvin L. 1980. Job complexity and adult personality. *In* Neil J. Smelser and Erik H. Erikson (eds.), *Themes of Work and Love in Adulthood,* pp. 193–210. Cambridge, Mass.: Harvard University Press.

Kohn, Melvin, and Schooler, Carmi. 1978. The reciprocal effects of the substantive complexity of work and intellectual flexibility. *American Journal of Sociology* 84:24–52.

Land, Kenneth C., and Felson, Marcus. 1976. A general framework for building dynamic macro social indicator models: Including an analysis of changes in crime rates and police expenditures. *American Journal of Sociology* 82:565–604.

Lazarsfeld, Paul F., Berelson, Bernard, and Gaudet, Hazel. (1944) 1960. *The People's Choice.* New York: Columbia University Press.

Lenski, Gerhardt E. 1966. *Power and Privilege.* New York: McGraw-Hill.

LeVine, Robert A. 1980. Adulthood among the gusii of Kenya. *In* Neil J. Smelser and Erik H. Erikson (eds.), *Themes of Work and Love in Adulthood,* pp. 77–104. Cambridge Mass.: Harvard University Press.

Light, L. L., Zelinski, E. M., and Moore, M. 1982. Adult age differences in reasoning from new information. *Journal of Experimental Psychology: Learning, Memory, and Cognition.* 8:435–447.

Linton, Ralph. 1942. Age and sex categories. *American Sociological Review* 7:589–603.

Litwak, Eugene, and Spilerman, Seymour. 1978. Organizational structure and nursing home policy for health care problems. Paper delivered at the World Congress of Sociology. Uppsala, Sweden.

Livson, F. B. 1980. Sex typing over the life span: His, hers, and theirs. Paper presented at the annual meeting of the Gerontological Society of America, San Diego.

Maccoby, Nathan, et al. 1977. Reducing the risk of cardiovascular disease: Effects of a community-based campaign on knowledge and behavior. *Journal of Community Health* 3:100–114.

Maddox, George L. 1979. Sociology of later life. *Annual Review of Sociology* 5:113–135.

Mannheim, Karl. (1928) 1952. The problem of generations. *In* Paul Kecskemeti (ed. and translator), *Essays on the Sociology of Knowledge,* pp. 276–322. London: Routledge and Kegan Paul.

Markides, Kyriakos. 1983. Minority aging. *In* Matilda White Riley, Beth B. Hess, and Kathleen Bond (eds.), *Aging in Society: Selected Reviews of Recent Research,* pp. 115–138. Hillsdale, N.J.: Lawrence Erlbaum Associates.

Marshall, Victor W. 1980a. *Last Chapters: A Sociology of Aging and Dying.* Monterey, Calif.: Brooks/ Cole Publishing Company.

Marshall, Victor W. 1980b. Aging in an aging society: Cohort differences, conflicts and challenges. *Multiculturalism* 4:6–13.

McCarthy, Kevin F. 1982. *The Changing Geographic Distribution of the Elderly: Patterns of Change since 1960,* R–2926–NIA. The Rand Corporation.

Michael, Robert T., Fuchs, Victor R., and Scott, Sharon R. 1980. Changes in the propensity to live alone: 1950–1976. *Demography* 17:39–56.

Miller, A. H., Gurin, P., and Gurin, G. 1980. Age consciousness and political mobilization of older Americans. *The Gerontologist* 20:691–700.

Modell, John, Furstenberg, Frank, and Hershberg, Theodore. 1976. Social change and transitions to adulthood in historical perspective. *Journal of Family History* 1:7–31.

Mortimer, Jeylan T., and Simmons, Roberta G. 1978. Adult socialization. *Annual Review of Sociology* 4:421–454.

National Council on the Aging. 1981. *Aging in the Eighties: America in Transition.* Washington, D.C.: National Council on the Aging.

Nesselroade, J. R., and Baltes, P. B. (eds.). 1979. *Longitudinal Research in the Study of Behavior and Development.* New York: Academic Press.

Neugarten, Bernice L. (ed.). 1968. *Middle Age and Aging.* Chicago: University of Chicago Press.

Neugarten, Bernice L. 1974. Age groups in American society and the rise of the young-old. *Annals of the American Academy of Political and Social Science* 415:189–198.

Neugarten, Bernice L., and Hagestad, Gunhild O. 1976. Age and the life course. *In* Robert H. Binstock and Ethel Shanas (eds.), *Handbook of Aging and the Social Sciences,* 1st ed., pp. 35–55. New York: Van Nostrand Reinhold.

Neugarten, Bernice L., and Moore, Joan W. 1968. The changing age-status system. *In* Bernice L. Neugarten (ed.), *Middle Age and Aging,* pp. 5–21. Chicago: University of Chicago Press.

Neugarten, Bernice L., Moore, Joan W., and Lowe, John C. 1965. Age norms, age constraints, and adult socialization. *American Journal of Sociology* 70:710–717.

Neugarten, Bernice L., Zweibel, Nancy R., Kramek, Lorraine M., Maines, David R., and Eglit, Howard C. 1982. Age, society and the law. Copies available from Bernice L. Neugarten, School of Education, Northwestern University, Evanston, Ill.

Ogburn, William F., and Thomas, Dorothy S. 1927. The influence of the business cycle on certain social conditions. *In* Dorothy S. Thomas (ed.), *Social Aspects of the Business Cycle.* New York: Alfred A. Knopf.

Olsen, Kenneth M. 1969. Social class and age-group differences in the timing of family status changes: A study of age-norms in American society. Ph.D. dissertation, University of Chicago.

Oppenheimer, Valerie Kincade, 1981. The changing nature of life-cycle squeezes: Implications for the socioeconomic position of the elderly. *In* Robert W. Fogel, Elaine Hatfield, Sara B. Keisler, and Ethel Shanas (eds.), *Aging: Stability and Change in the Family,* pp. 47–82. New York: Academic Press.

Owsley, C., Sekuler, R., and Culver, Boldt. 1981. Aging and low-contrast vision: Face perception. *Investigative Ophtalmology and Visual Science* 21:362–365.

Pampel, F. C., and Weiss, J. A. 1982. Economic growth, pension policies, and the labor force participation of aged males: A cross-national, longitudinal approach. Paper presented at the American Sociological Association.

Parsons, Talcott. 1942. Age and sex in the social structure of the United States. *In* Talcott Parsons, *Essays in Sociological Theory, Pure and Applied.* Glencoe, Ill.: Free Press.

Parsons, Talcott, and Platt, Gerald M. 1972. Higher education and changing socialization. *In* Matilda White Riley, Marilyn Johnson, and Anne Foner (eds.), *Aging and Society: A Sociology of Age Stratification,* Vol. III, pp. 236–291. New York: Russell Sage Foundation.

Perlmutter, Marion. 1983. Learning and memory through adulthood. *In* Matilda White Riley, Beth B. Hess, and Kathleen Bond (eds.), *Aging in Society: Selected Reviews of Recent Research,* pp. 219–242. Hillsdale, N.J.: Lawrence Erlbaum Associates.

Poon L. W., Walsh-Sweeney, L., and Fozard, J. L. 1980. Memory skill training for the elderly: Salient issues on the use of imagery mnemonics. *In* L. W. Poon, J. L. Fozard, L. S. Armak, D. Arenberg, and L. W. Thompson (eds.), *New Directions in Memory and Aging: Proceedings of the George A. Talland Memorial Conference.* Hillsdale, N.J.: Lawrence Erlbaum Associates.

Pratt, Henry J. 1976. *The Gray Lobby.* Chicago: University of Chicago Press.

Riley, Matilda White. 1973. Aging and cohort succession: Interpretations and misinterpretations. *Public Opinion Quarterly* 37:35–49.

Riley, Matilda White. 1976. Age strata in social systems. *In* Robert H. Binstock and Ethel Shanas (eds.), *Handbook of Aging and the Social Sciences,* 1st ed., pp. 189–217. New York: Van Nostrand Reinhold.

Riley, Matilda White. 1978. Aging, social change, and the power of ideas. *Daedalus* 107:39–52.

Riley, Matilda White. 1979. Introduction: Life-course perspectives. *In* Matilda White Riley (ed.), AAAS Selected Symposium 30, *Aging from Birth to Death: Interdisciplinary Perspectives,* Vol. I, pp. 3–13. Boulder, Colo.: Westview Press.

Riley, Matilda White. 1980. Age and aging: From theory generation to theory testing. *In* Hubert Blalock, Jr. (ed.), *Sociological Theory and Research: A Critical Appraisal,* pp. 339–348. New York: Free Press.

Riley, Matilda White. 1981a. Health behavior of older people: Toward a new paradigm. *In* Delores L. Parron, Fredric Solomon, and Judith Rodin (eds.), *Health, Behavior and Aging,* Institute of Medicine Interim Report No. 5, pp. 25–39. Washington, D.C.: National Academy Press.

Riley, Matilda White. 1981b. Review essay: Social gerontology and the sociology of age. *American Journal of Sociology* 86:1427–1431.

Riley, Matilda White. 1982a. Aging and social change. *In* Matilda White Riley, Ronald P. Abeles, and Michael S. Teitelbaum (eds.), AAAS Selected Symposium 79, *Aging from Birth to Death: Sociotemporal Perspectives,* Vol. II, pp. 11–26. Boulder, Colo.: Westview Press.

Riley, Matilda White. 1982b. Implications for the middle and later years. *In* Phyllis W. Berman and Estelle R. Ramey (eds.), *Women: A Developmental Perspective,* pp. 399–405. U.S. Dept. of Health and Human Services, Public Health Service, National Institutes of Health, Publication No. 82-2298.

Riley, Matilda White, and Bond, Kathleen. 1983. Beyond ageism: Postponing the onset of disability. *In* Matilda White Riley, Beth B. Hess, and Kathleen Bond (eds.), *Aging in Society: Selected Reviews of Recent Research,* pp. 243–252. Hillsdale, N.J.: Lawrence Erlbaum Associates.

Riley, Matilda White, and Glass, David. 1982. Aging from birth to death: Biosocial perspectives. Symposium at Annual Meeting of American Association for Advancement of Science, Washington, D.C., January 4, 1982.

Riley, Matilda White, and Nelson, Edward E. 1971. Research on stability and change in social systems. *In* Bernard Barber and Alex Inkeles (eds.), *Stability and Social Change: A Volume in Honor of Talcott Parsons,* pp. 407–449. Boston: Little, Brown.

Riley, Matilda White, and Riley, John W., Jr. n.d. Sociology of age and aging. (Unpublished.)

Riley, Matilda White, and Waring, Joan. 1976. Age and aging. *In* Robert K. Merton and Robert Nisbet (eds.), *Contemporary Social Problems,* pp. 357–410. New York: Harcourt Brace Jovanovich.

Riley, Matilda White, Abeles, Ronald P., and Teitelbaum, Michael S. (eds.), 1982. AAAS Selected Symposium 79, *Aging from Birth to Death: Sociotemporal Perspectives,* Vol. II. Boulder, Colo.: Westview Press.

Riley, Matilda White, Foner, Anne, and Associates. 1968. *Aging and Society,* Vol. I. New York: Russell Sage Foundation.

Riley, Matilda White, Johnson, Marilyn, and Foner, Anne. 1972. *Aging and Society, Vol. III, A Sociology of Age Stratification.* New York: Russell Sage Foundation.

Rodin, Judith. 1980. Managing the stress of aging: The role of control and coping. *In* Seymour Levine and Holger Ursin (eds.), *Coping and Health.* New York: Plenum Press.

Rosow, Irving. 1967. *Social Integration of the Aged.* New York: Free Press.

Rosow, Irving. 1978. What is a cohort and why? *Human Development,* 65–75.

Rossi, Alice S. 1980. Aging and parenthood in the middle years. *In* Paul B. Baltes and Orville G. Brim, Jr. (eds.), *Life-Span Development and Behavior,* Vol. 3, pp. 138–207. New York: Academic Press.

Ryder, Norman B. 1964. Notes on the concept of a population. *American Journal of Sociology* 69:447–463.

Ryder, Norman B. 1965. The cohort as a concept in the study of social change. *American Sociological Review* 30:843–861.

Salthouse, T. A., and Somberg, B. L. 1982. Skilled performance: The effects of adult age and experience on elementary processes. *Journal of Experimental Psychology: General* 111:176–207.

San Giovanni, Lucinda. 1978. *Ex-nuns: A Study of Emergent Role Passages.* Norwood, N.J.: Ablex Publishing Company.

Schaie, K. W. 1979. The primary mental abilities in adulthood: An exploration in the development of psychometric intelligence. *In* Paul B. Baltes and Orville G. Brim, Jr. (eds.), *Life-Span Development and Behavior,* Vol. 2, pp. 68–117. New York: Academic Press.

Schiffman, S. S., and Pasternak, M. 1979. Decreased discrimination of food odors in the elderly. *Journal of Gerontology* 34:73–79.

Schlesinger, J. A., and Schlesinger, M. 1981. Aging opportunities for elective office. *In* S. B. Kiesler, J. N. Morgan, and B. K. Oppenheimer (eds.), *Social Change.* New York: Academic Press.

Schrank, Harris T., and Riley, John W., Jr. 1976. Women in work organizations. *In* Juanita M. Kreps (ed.), *Women in the American Economy: A Look to the 1980s.* Englewood Cliffs, N.J.: American Assembly, Columbia University, Prentice-Hall.

Schrank, Harris T., and Waring, Joan M. 1983. Aging and work organizations. *In* Matilda White Riley, Beth B. Hess, and Kathleen Bond (eds.), *Aging in Society: Selected Reviews of Recent Research,* pp. 53–70. Hillsdale, N.J.: Lawrence Erlbaum Associates.

Sekuler, Robert, and Hutmen, Lucinda Picciano. 1980. Spatial vision and aging. I: Contrast sensitivity. *Journal of Gerontology* 35:692–699.

Sewell, W. H., and Hauser, R. M. 1975. *Education, Occupation, and Earnings.* New York: Academic Press.

Shanas, Ethel. 1979. Social myth as hypothesis: The case of the family relations of old people. *The Gerontologist* 19:3–9.

Shin, Ken E., and Putnam, Robert H., Jr. 1982. Age and academic-professional honors. *Journal of Gerontology* 37:220–229.

Siegel, Jacob S. 1980. On the demography of aging. *Demography* 17:345–364.

Simkus, Albert. 1982. Socioeconomic careers in the context of radical social change: Evidence from Hungary. *In* Matilda White Riley, Ronald P. Abeles, and Michael S. Teitelbaum (eds.), *Aging from Birth to Death: Sociotemporal Perspectives,* Vol. II, pp. 163–180. Boulder, Colo.: Westview Press.

Simon, E. W., Dixon, R. A., Nowak, C. A., and Hultsch, D. F. 1982. Orienting task effects on text recall in adulthood. *Journal of Gerontology.* 37:575–580.

Sinnott, J. D. et al. 1980. *Sex Roles in Mature Adults: Antecedents and Correlates.* Center on Aging, College Park, Md.: University of Maryland.

Smelser, Neil J. 1968. *Essays in Sociological Explanation.* Englewood Cliffs, N.J.: Prentice-Hall.

Smith, K. F., and Bengtson, V. L. 1979. Positive consequences of institutionalization: Solidarity between elderly parents and their middle-aged children. *The Gerontologist* 19:438–447.

Sorenson, Aage B. 1979. A model and a metric for the analysis of the intragenerational status attainment process. *American Journal of Sociology* 85:361–384.

Sorokin, Pitirim A. (1927) 1959. *Social and Cultural Mobility.* New York: Free Press.

Sorokin, Pitirim A. 1941. *Social and Cultural Dynamics: Basic Problems, Principles, and Methods,* Vol. 4. New York: American Book Company.

Sorokin, Pitirim A. 1947. *Society, Culture and Personality.* New York: Harper and Brothers.

Sorokin, Pitirim A. 1969. Social differentiation. *In* David L. Sills (ed.), *International Encyclopedia of the Social Sciences,* Vol. 14, pp. 406–409. New York: Macmillan and Free Press.

Spanier, Graham B., and Glick, Paul C. 1980. The life cycle of American families: An expanded analysis. *Journal of Family History,* 97–111.

Starr, Bernice C. 1972. The community. *In* Matilda White Riley, Marilyn Johnson, and Anne Foner (eds.), *Aging and Society: A Sociology of Age Stratification,* Vol. III, pp. 198–235. New York: Russell Sage Foundation.

Stewart, F. H. 1977. *Fundamentals of Age-Group Systems.* New York: Academic Press.

Stouffer, Samuel A. 1955. *Communism, Conformity, and Civil Liberties.* New York: Doubleday and Company.

Streib, Gordon F. 1976. Social stratification and aging. *In* Robert H. Binstock and Ethel Shanas (eds.), *Handbook of Aging and the Social Sciences,* 1st ed., pp. 160–185. New York: Van Nostrand Reinhold.

Susser, Mervyn. 1969. Aging and the field of public health. *In* Matilda White Riley, John W. Riley, Jr., and Marilyn E. Johnson (eds.), *Aging and Society,* pp. 114–160. New York: Russell Sage Foundation.

Thomas, William, I., and Znaniecki, Florian. 1918. *The Polish Peasant in Europe and America.* Chicago: University of Chicago Press.

Tobin, Sheldon S., and Lieberman, Morton A. 1976. *Last Home for the Aged: Critical Implications of Institutionalization.* San Francisco: Jossey-Bass.

Toby, Jackson, 1982. Children's own fault. *New York Times,* July 28.

Torrey, Barbara Boyle. 1982. The lengthening of retirement. *In* Matilda White Riley, Ronald P. Abeles, and Michael S. Teitelbaum (eds.), AAAS Selected Symposium 79, *Aging from Birth to Death: Sociotemporal Perspectives,* Vol. II., pp. 181–196. Boulder, Colo.: Westview Press.

Turner, Ralph H. 1978. The role and the person. *American Journal of Sociology* 84:1–23.

Uhlenberg, Peter. 1979a. Demographic change and problems of the aged. *In* Matilda White Riley (ed.), *Aging from Birth to Death: Interdisciplinary Perspectives,* Vol. I., pp. 153-166. Boulder, Colo.: Westview Press.

Uhlenberg, Peter. 1979b. Older women: The growing challenge to design constructive roles. *The Gerontologist,* 236-241.

Vanderplas, J. M., and Vanderplas, J. H. 1980. Some factors affecting legibility of printed materials for older adults. *Perceptual and Motor Skills* 50:923-732.

Van Gennep, Arnold. (1908) 1960. *The Rites of Passage,* translated by Monike B. Visedom and Gabrielle L. Caffee. Chicago: University of Chicago Press, Phoenix Books.

Veroff, Joseph, Douvan, Elizabeth, and Kulka, Richard A. 1981. *The Inner America: A Self-Portrait from 1957-1976.* New York: Basic Books.

Vinovskis, Maris A. 1982. Aged servants of the lord: Changes in the status and treatment of elderly ministers in colonial America. *In* Matilda White Riley, Ronald P. Abeles, and Michael S. Teitelbaum (eds.), AAAS Selected Symposium 79, *Aging from Birth to Death: Sociotemporal Perspectives,* Vol. II, pp. 105-137. Boulder, Colo.: Westview Press.

Ward, Russell A. 1979. *The Aging Experience: An Introduction to Social Gerontology.* New York: J. B. Lippincott Company.

Waring, Joan M. 1975. Social Replenishment and social change. *In* Anne Foner (ed.), *American Behavioral Scientist* 19:237-256.

Whiting, John W. M. 1981. Aging and becoming an elder: A cross-cultural comparison. *In* Robert W. Fogel, Elaine Hatfield, Sara B. Kiesler, and Ethel Shanas (eds.), *Aging: Stability and Change in the Family,* pp. 83-90. New York: Academic Press.

Willis, Sherry L., and Baltes, Paul B. 1980. Intelligence in adulthood and aging: Contemporary issues. *In* Leonard W. Poon (ed.), *Aging in the 1980s: Psychological Issues.* Washington, D.C.: American Psychological Association.

Winsborough, Halliman H. 1979. Changes in the transition to adulthood. *In* Matilda White Riley (ed.), AAAS Selected Symposium 30, *Aging from Birth to Death: Interdisciplinary Perspectives,* Vol. I, pp. 137-152. Boulder, Colo.: Westview Press.

Winsborough, Halliman, Duncan, O. D., and Read, P. B. 1983. *Cohort Analysis in Social Research.* New York: Academic Press.

Zuckerman, Harriet, and Merton, Robert K. 1972. Age, aging, and age structure in science. *In* Matilda White Riley, Marilyn Johnson, and Anne Foner (eds.), *Aging and Society: A Sociology of Age Stratification,* Vol. III, pp. 292-356. New York: Russell Sage Foundation.

PART 4 AGING AND SOCIAL SYSTEMS

14
THE FAMILY LIFE
OF OLD PEOPLE

Marvin B. Sussman

University of Delaware

The family and its extended kin will become more important to the elderly as a relational, caring, and economic supporting system in this and the remaining decade of the twentieth century. New political and social philosophies that espouse decreased investment in and federal institutionalization of human service programs are being effected through governmental policies and programs. A reduction in the number, and in some instances the deestablishemnt, of organized care systems is beginning. The implied alternative for such care is to return to the "problem" relative to the family for care or control.

Defining and describing families is no easy task. There are a considerable number of definitions and descriptions, largely based on differences in perceptions, institutional mandates, and intended use and treatment of family members and the family as a unit. The problems and issues of characterizing and explaining families are discussed in detail later in this chapter. Legal definitions and nonlegal descriptions, especially the latter, are plentiful.

For analytic and research purposes it is useful to use both legal and nonlegal definitions. The family legally constituted by act of marriage is the primary target of the new federalism. But, as will be evidenced subsequently, nonlegal forms such as the "every-

day" family, a living-together group who perform activities similar to those of the legally sanctioned family, have critical roles in the care, life satisfaction, and survival of elderly persons.

This chapter begins with a brief discussion of the new federalism and its potential consequence for families and aged members. This is followed by a theoretical analysis of exchange and linkage that explains the bonding of family members and connections with organizations and institutions. The next section provides descriptions and definitions of families and explains their use by human service organizations. The structure and role of kin networks, intergenerational transfer patterns, and family–aged member relationships in the 1980s are topics that complete the chapter.

THE NEW FEDERALISM

Economics is a basic component of the new federalism. Monies to support the demand and expectation for organized human services are increasingly unavailable. One example is found in the effort to make families financially responsible for dependent members whose support has come from public funds. States have been given approval to pass medicaid familial responsibility laws that can require relatives of medicaid patients in nursing homes and other private and public institutions to pay part of the costs of care (*Aging Services News,* 1983). The search for care alternatives to organized human services becomes automatic when there are limited monies for such activities. Simultaneously with this reduction in the rate of expenditures and curtailing of perquisites of elderly incumbents in such programs as social security, medicaid, and medicare, there is a turn to the notion of self-help. Self-help implies action on the local level; and, if one has to be reliant upon someone, it is the family and kin. Such an entrepeneurial and frontier stance was a prized value of our forebears.

This decade's actions to curtail the growth of human service institutions, however, has a strong value base unusual for this century. The moral imperative to return to primary groups such as the family has arisen like a phoenix out of the ashes of the unrest and upheavals of the 1960s and 1970s. Whatever the sustaining power of this swing away from support and dependence on human service institutions to individual self-reliance, and family and kin responsibility for elderly relatives, its impact is pervasive. The growing numbers of elderly in need of care for multiple chronic illnesses and disabilities will result in a shift of the focus and major responsibility for the well-being of the elderly from human service systems and their professionals to the older person's family and kin, and new family-like primary groups. It is within the context of these values and federal policy and program changes, that several basic themes and issues of the family life of older people are presented.

In complex societies if aged persons are to survive successfully they must deal with bureaucracies, especially those that provide human services. The family of these elderly persons often serves as a source of information and influence in making decisions and as a mediating link between the older individual and societal institutions and organizations.

The demography of the elderly and expected changes in age and sex distribution over the next 40 to 50 years with a diminished number of relatives to assume responsibility for day-to-day care suggest that new "like" family household forms composed of elderly persons will emerge. Economic conditions, psychologic and social needs and pressures of the elderly, and a spirit of experimentation and enlightenment will produce new forms of primary groups unlike those of today. Structures such as the extended kin family may reemerge as a feasible and highly accepted form. These arrangments will provide both new options and new problems for the elderly.

In the past, intergenerational transfers within family systems provided one basic form of economic and symbolic bonding of the elderly with their children and grandchildren. The persistance of this linkage is examined in the light of society-wide generational transfers that rely more on programs and bureaucracies than on the family and kin network to provide care, services, and economic sustenance. The current shift in values, reduced organizational support, and changing tax laws increase the significance of these inter vivos and inheritance transfers.

The new federalism, with its emphasis on self-help, neighborhood and community support, and involvement of family and kin in the lives of elderly citizens, suggests the emergence and prominence of new informal and quasi-formal groups. Such groups will function increasingly as mediating structures or substitutes for formal organizations providing human services.

The elimination of federal programs for the elderly and the returning to the community of the problems of care, service, and support of handicapped old people have particular consequences for minority and ethnic elderly and their families. Their linkages based on filial responsibility and family survival may be weakened. Even if such bondings remain because of strong cultural traditions forged over historic time, the caretaking family members, who may be experiencing unemployment or reduced income, are in danger of experiencing an even lower standard of living. The elasticity and robustness of these networks are being tested.

The particular problems and concerns of minority and ethnic aged and their families are reviewed in this chapter.

THEORETICAL BASES

Exchange and Linkage

Social exchange and linkage are the theoretical constructs most appropriate to bonding of aged persons, family units, and bureaucratic organizations. Exchange theory (Kelley and Thibault, 1954; Blau, 1955, 1964; Homans, 1961; Bengtson and Black, 1973; Bengtson et al., 1975; Dowd, 1975) provides the most viable explanation of primary group relationships. Filial responsibilities—characterized as protective, care, and financial *duties* (Brody, 1970), those "required by law, by custom, or by personal attitude" (Schorr, 1960)—provide boundaries and conditions for interaction based on a profit/cost, reward/punishment, "developmental stake" equation (Black and Bengtson, 1973).

The components of exchange—cost, reward, profit, reinforcement—have roots in hedonistic doctrine, utilitarian economics, and the psychological theory of reinforcement. Avoidance of pain and obtaining pleasure is the objective of interaction. Profit is also an object of human activity, and profit is reward minus the cost. Profit making leads to repetitive behavior, with reinforcement of the profit-making endeavor. If the quest is satiated, coupled with severely diminished drives and motivation, contributory responses emerge—costs outweigh rewards, and efforts are made to extinguish the unprofitable interaction.

Studies on the formation and structural properties of small groups (Kelley and Thibault, 1954; Thibault and Kelley, 1959; Sherif, 1966) have indicated that rewards for members in interaction may be unequal, and that individuals stay in the group because the relationships provide some reward despite the uneven exchange, and are perceived to be more satisfactory than other alternatives. This perception may be the "tension line," an invisible boundary of acceptable dyadic and group relationships (Shaw and Costanzo, 1970; Rapoport and Rapoport, 1975).

The tension line for elderly and family member exchanges may extend beyond the usual contractual arrangement of individuals unrelated by blood or marriage. Strong feelings of familial responsibility, high intensities of face-to-face interaction, rituals of sharing, and exchanges of services and information, especially by those living close by, may result in behavior not in consonance with that expected according to the exchange model. The persistence of giving much and receiving little may be observed. The binding of individuals as a consequence of blood or marriage is strong. One interpretation is that serial reciprocity is effected. According to the rules of exchange theory, the individual who is giving so much and receiving in return so little should opt out of the relationship.

Staying in the exchange relationship, however, is a function of expectations. The caring person, providing the care or service, rationalizes it as a family duty. When problems, handicaps and chronic ailments, and disabilities beset the caretaker, family members of the generation succeeding the caretaker will in turn provide the services. This generational transfer of looking after one's elderly members is assumed to occur automatically, a delayed exchange involving actors of different generations. Serial reciprocity is a generational expectation.

Inequality in any exchange means that individuals in exchanges that result in unequal rewards are said to be in a *power* relationship. There are dependence, compliance, and subordination on the part of Actor A and independence, command, and superordination by Actor B (Weber, 1947; Blau, 1964). Social interaction is a continuous process of losing or gaining power credits or resources for use in subsequent transactions. As Dowd (1975) indicates, "the problems of aging are essentially problems of decreasing power resources. . . money, approval, esteem or respect, and compliance." Esteem and compliance are the most often used credits in exchange relationships among the aged. Esteem is a short-lived commodity because of the decreasing utility of expressing past achievements repeatedly in the fact of group needs. The pressures on the elderly person to comply are exerted by societal norms and reflected in the superordinate postures of institutions and organizations and in the increasing dependency of the elderly person on the family.

Another important proposition of exchange theory is distributive justice. Individuals should be rewarded in proportion to their costs and receive profits in proportion to their investment. The pervasiveness of this conceptual element is discussed later in this chapter in relation to family inheritance patterns. The "sense" of distributive justice is a family property. It not only guides an individual's presentation of self and interaction but is a behavioral expectation. Those children who provide affection, attention, association, and services, that is, "generational solidarity" (Bengtson and Kuypers, 1971; Black and Bengtson, 1973; Brody, 1977; Bengtson and Treas, 1980; Bengtson and deTerre, 1980), to elderly members are expected to receive more than their legal share of any inheritance. This is a value shared by adult children and a viable expression of distributive justice (Sussman et al., 1970a; Cates and Sussman, 1982).

Family, Bureaucracy and Elderly Linkages

Despite industrialization and modernization, the connectedness of most elderly members with their families and kin networks is unbroken (Paillat, 1977; Munnichs, 1977; Rosenmayr, 1977; Piotrowski, 1977; Shanas and Sussman, 1981). Societal complexity with its differentiated occupational structure, social segregation, and accelerated geographical mobility may automatically constrain linkages of generationally and bilaterally linked kin. Concomitant "role exit" (Blau, 1973) of elderly persons exacerbates the feelings of alienation and isolation among many of them. However, for those aged persons who have had substantial involvement in kin family networks over the life span, there is a "pull" factor to restore

and reinforce such ties in the later years. Such older persons have more options in their exchanges than their less-involved peers; they may be wanted for themselves and the services they can potentially perform.

For elderly individuals with a poor record of kin network activities there may be a "push" to reconstitute close family relationships. With fewer options, the older person, in turning to other family members, especially children, becomes dependent upon and committed to the exchange relationship (Blau, 1964). The individual, in this circumstance, has few or no other choices. The family linkage is thus of critical importance to the elderly person and one that has extreme influence on the elderly member's relationship with nonfamily individuals and organizations. If the elderly increase their dependence on the family, there is likely to occur a lessening of the older individuals' autonomy and independence in dealing with bureaucratic organizations.

Since World War II the ideology of pluralism in family structures of complex societies has been espoused, and varied family forms and life-styles, if not legitimized, are at least tolerated (Sussman et al., 1970b; Sussman, 1972; Libby and Whitehurst, 1973; Smith and Smith, 1974; Sussman et al., 1975). It would be expected, or at least hoped, that these new optional structures and styles would provide a large number of elderly persons with environmental alternatives to living alone or with children or in institutions. This has not occurred.

This conclusion is derived from a review of extensive studies of emergent new and variant family forms and life-styles such as communal households, group marriages, and intimate networks—those that differ from traditional nuclear and kinship forms (Cogswell and Sussman, 1972; Ramey, 1972; O'Neill and O'Neill 1972; Sussman, 1975). None of these variant forms provide evidence that they are willing to handle the crises, dependencies, disabilities, and deviances of their members, regardless of age. Their ideologies and practice presume that each participant has the ability to contribute to the group and thus to achieve highly desired parity relationships and near-equal reciprocities. Self-actualization is achieved through group interaction. The potential presence of an individual who cannot contribute fully and who is identified as a liability for any reason is counter to the new ideology. Moreover, members who are not sound in mind and body and competent to carry their fair share of the load in exchanges can jeopardize group survival.

Such new family forms as communal or group marriage households have a great need of initial screening and, if error is found, need to segregate potential deviants; for the new family form is unsanctioned, usually unpopular, and has no institutional roots. When in need or trouble, it cannot call upon outside sources for help. Moreover, many of the volunteers in such groups have left traditional family forms because of their wish to escape dependent and obligatory relationships. The existentialist philosophy of these new forms requires optimal role performance to achieve self-actualization via interaction and group achievement.

It appears that "family and kin," however defined, will continue to be those primary groups who will respond in service and kind when members ask for help or are in need. The extended nuclear family is an all-purpose caretaking system. The traditional nuclear family form may have its greatest rationale for universality and continuity because of its function in taking care of its sick, disabled, deviant, and deficient members.

The state, through its massive structure of institutions and bureaucratized agencies, has created multitudinous support programs for its dependent citizens. The necessity to deal with them is obvious if aged members are to obtain even a partial share of their entitlements. The legally constituted and franchised family found in complex societies is continuously engaging in linkage activities with bureaucratic organizations in behalf of its elderly members. The "family" of the aged individual often is found to be in an interstitial position between the elderly individual and the organization. Old people use their children and relatives both as a means of reentry into the social order and as a buffer against the pressures of bureaucracy. The extended family seems to be the mediator between the aged and formal organizations. Children and relatives act as information resources for the elderly, informing them about housing, pensions, medical care, and other available options and entitlements. At the same time, it is the children and relatives who assist the aged in dealing with the bureaucratic structure of housing authorities, pension schemes, and hospitals and clinics.

As long as the elderly person can function to meet the tasks of housekeeping, transportation, social interaction, food preparation, and grocery shopping—measures of social functioning—and can perform the activities of daily living such as walking, eating, dressing, grooming, climbing stairs, and transferring from chair to bed unaided, dependence on the family is lessened (Rosow, 1967; Shanas, 1979b; Branch and Jette, 1981; Jette and Branch, 1981). While there is some relationship between increasing physical disability and age, the magnitude is less than popularly believed. Seventy-two percent of the cohort, age 65 to 84, in the Framington study of disability, had mild or no difficulty in performing one or more physical activities measured by a nine-item difficulty index developed by the investigators (Branch and Jette, 1981; Jette and Branch, 1981). These findings are similar to those of a University of Delaware study (Barnekov, 1980).

When difficulties in functioning arise, family members are usually located and called upon for help. Human service professionals indicate that many adult children and kin of the elderly are unable to cope with the emergent problem, which may be a crisis accompanied by maladaptive stress for both the elderly person and potential caretakers.

Human service professionals, aware of this problem, have begun educational and training programs for family members. One model combines didactic and therapeutic approaches (Silverman, 1978). Its objectives are:

1. To increase knowledge of participants about the aging process.
2. To develop awareness of the response of their own parents to the aging process.
3. To increase their understanding of emotional reactions of older people.
4. To initiate group problem solving to cope more effectively with the concerns of their parents.
5. To provide them with wider access to community supports.
6. To facilitate the development of support systems within the group (Silverman et al., 1977).

The participants in this program are individuals who have relatives living in community settings. The researchers indicate that they have been successful in increasing knowledge about the aging process and increasing the ability of the participants to cope with parental problems. Almost nine of every ten participants planned to use or had used ideas generated from group discussions related to more effective and greater utilization of community resources.

The significance of this project lies in its policy implications. If family support systems are to be effective, families have to be prepared to take on these effective roles. Any extensive use of family networks will require programs like these. The individuals who volunteered for the programs described above faced a variety of psychological, social, and physical difficulties in their relationships with elderly family members. Another possible significant outcome of such programs is the emergence of mediating and facilitating roles of family members acting in behalf of their elderly members. This is a further extension of the experience of family members both in achieving competence in interpersonal relationships and in serving as mediators or brokers in negotiations with both formal organizations and informal social support networks.

Demography, Connectedness, and Linkages

The connectedness of aged members, 65 years or older, to family, is corroborated by statistics regarding their living arrangements. In 1976 in the United States only 1.6 percent of the men and 1.5 percent of the women ages 65–74 were institutionalized. For ages 75 and over, 6.8 percent of men and 10.3

TABLE 1. Living Arrangements of Population 65 and Over, by Age and Sex, 1976.

Type of living arrangement	Men		Women	
	65–74	75 and over	65–74	75 and over
Total (in 1,000s)	6,038	3,186	8,898	5,541
Percent	100.0	100.0	100.0	100.0
		In households		
Head of household	95.9	85.5	44.4	51.8
Head of family household	85.1	66.4	8.6	8.0
Head of nonfamily household	0.7	0.7	0.8	0.9
Living alone	12.4	18.4	35.0	42.8
Spouse of household head	—	—	45.7	19.2
Other relative of head	0.7	6.7	7.5	17.7
Nonrelative of head	1.8	1.0	0.9	1.3
		In institutions		
Patient or resident	1.6	6.8	1.5	10.3

SOURCES: U.S. Bureau of the Census, *Current Population Reports,* Series P-20, No. 306, "Marital Status and Living Arrangements: March 1976," pp. 15, 31, and 33; and tabulations from the 1976 *Survey of Institutionalized Persons* prepared by the Center for Population Research, Georgetown University, for the Administration on Aging, Grant No. 90-17-1681. Taken from Beth J. Soldo, "America's Elderly in the 1980's" *Population Bulletin,* Vol 35, No. 4, Population References Bureau, Washington, D.C., 1980, p. 26.

percent of women are in institutions (see Table 1).

Persons living alone (one-person households) comprised 23 percent of all households in the United States in 1980. Of all single-person households in 1980, 40 percent consisted of a person 65 years or over. Widowed persons made up the largest group living alone (U.S. Bureau of the Census, 1980b, P-20-365, p. 4).

The living arrangements of women over age 65 differ from those of men. At age 75 and over, women are twice as likely as men to be living alone or living in a household of a relative other than spouse, 18 percent versus 7 percent. The linkages of these women tend to be generational rather than bilateral. For this widowed population, economic, service, social, and emotional supports are largely forthcoming from adjacent generations, primarily daughters or mothers, in the vertical time-bounded chain with little assistance from the extended kin network (Lopata, 1978). In sum, in complex societies elderly women, because of their greater longevity and fewer available potential mates for remarriage, are more likely than men to live alone, as widows and divorcees. Thus, they are most active in linkage activities along generational lines. When living alone becomes untenable because of diminished health and mobility, the factors of age and number of children ever born seem to be the most important predictors of the move into a family member's household (Chevan and Korson, 1975). The older the person, the less likely it is that his or her health and mobility status is adequate for solo living. The more offspring the person has, the more likely it is that he or she will take up residence in a child's household.

These data indicate that the linkages of elderly persons with their families are of two types: those that occur in the majority of cases, among members living in separate households; and those that exist between members of the same household, an arrangement for a minority of elderly persons. Meaningful family linkages do not require living in the same household but do require a network involving productive exchanges of reciprocal benefits for all family members. Contact and relationships at discrete times may be preferable to continuous face-to face interaction. Rosenmayr and Köckeis (1965) have referred to this desire of elderly persons to live close to relatives but not with them as "intimacy at a distance."

Propinquity is the primary condition supporting the feasibility of maintaining network and intergenerational family connectedness while preserving the autonomy and independence of elderly persons and their families. In urban as well as rural areas the vast majority of elderly persons live near relatives.

A survey conducted by Shanas (1979a) indicates that three-fourths of all elderly persons in a randomly selected national sample had a surviving child, and 75 percent of those with children lived within 30 minutes' travel time of one another. Fifty-three percent of the elderly had visited with their child the day of the survey or the previous day.

Geographic proximity and visitation between relatives and elderly persons does not guarantee that supportive behaviors are provided to keep the elderly person in independent living. In fact, visitation may invoke or be for the purpose of mental or physical violence (Steinmetz, 1981). Quality of relationships is the issue here, and those who experienced good relationships with senior relatives early in their lives are top candidates as caregivers (Sussman et al., 1977, 1979). At best, being close to relatives optimizes the prospects of reciprocal exchanges and caregiving when required—if the "chemistry" is right between the individuals. As Shanas's data suggest, one can live in close proximity to, but not be guaranteed informal support from family, friends, and neighbors.

There continues to be considerable interest in determining to whom an individual turns when help with some problem is needed. Formulations by Riley (1971) and Seelbach (1978) hypothesized that some variation existed by age cohorts in the willingness of individuals to call upon family members when in need of assistance. Other studies, however, (Sanders and Seelbach, 1981), suggest that filial responsibility is a persistent and meaningful norm internalized in the value system of person of all ages.

Blacks more than whites express preference for non-family care alternatives (Sussman, 1977). Most blacks will use available resources of human service organizations if possible. This conserves the limited resources of family and kin and simultaneously permits agencies to implement their objectives. When the option to link into agency resources is gone, then family and kin sharing and exchanging of goods, food, and services begin.

As a result of limited economic opportunities and resources, increasing numbers of blacks have become experienced in utilizing human service systems. Their use of these non-family services for sustenance and care results in a *complementarity* of processes: individuals can maintain their linkages with family and kin without being economic burdens to them while obtaining assistance from a fragmented human service system (Wylie, 1971; Hays and Mindel, 1973; Hall, 1974; Palmore and Maddox, 1977, Jackson, 1980).

Another indication of the desire for family connectedness is the preference of family members to have aging relatives living nearby in their own households rather than in the potential caretaker's residence. This preference was investigated in a study concerned with economic and social supports to families that would enable them to provide a creative home environment for elderly relatives (Sussman, 1979). Even though 80 percent of the respondents interviewed were willing to take an older person into their homes under some circumstances, over 79 percent expressed a preference for having the older person live in the same neighborhood rather than in the home. This suggests a desire to maintain closeness, solidarity, and intimacy along with autonomy and independence of household units.

One way to maintain closeness and household autonomy is to use the "granny annex" concept of house construction. The "annex" is an addition to the larger domicile, usually for an elderly parent. It was initially developed in England, New Zealand, and Aus-

tralia (Tinker, 1976). Separate entrances make for privacy. In some arrangements there may be a connecting door between households that can be used in emergencies or during inclement weather.

In early America, attaching a wing to the main house or building a cottage on nearby acreage for the retired couple or new family was common. There were space and skills readily available to do this, and some level of intergenerational continuity was maintained. In urban areas, construction of the two-family house, a favorite in some ethnic groups, provided for intergenerational linkages. Such activities were not considered to be social interventions. In the United States today, some consideration is being given to the creation of less permanent structures than two-family homes. The so-called granny annex is a detached module unit that can reconstitute families by having elderly relatives nearby (see Duffy, 1978). It is movable and may be resold when no longer needed. This housing concept has been adopted extensively. It can be an important arrangement for sustaining generational continuity in the coming period of limited numbers of family caretakers.

Family and kin members are developing complex systems of supports and exchanges with each other based on notions of gain and cost, responsibility and commitment. These behaviors result from a blending of traditional values of filial identity and responsibility and the choice to participate in family and kin network systems. Feelings of obligation can be diffused if participants in a family exchange network can experience some profit from the experience. Thus gain in anything, whether knowledge, improved self concept, material things, or just "feeling good," is the key to sustenance, nuturence, and perpetuation of these primary groups—families and their networks.

TYPES OF FAMILIES AND THE ELDERLY

Describing Families

Restructuring the living arrangements of elderly persons who feel the need for "family" and attendant behaviors, feelings, and identities for survival and enjoyment of life should not be a capricious activity. Rather, it should be a carefully planned option. Fundamental to an educational program or social intervention to keep "family" as part of the continuous life experience of elderly persons is an understanding both of what makes a group of persons a family and of the diversity of forms of family in today's society.

Describing a family is not easy. Defining a family is even more difficult. There is a lack of consensus because scholars, professionals, administrators, and others who deal with families perceive, conceptualize, and describe according to their ideology, posture, and relationship to their own families. Definitions and associated descriptions are made on the principle of utility as determined by bureaucracies with some reference to the canons of statutory and common law. Society's organizations and institutions, especially those concerned with the provision of human services, have definitions that fit their mandate, ones usually rooted in legislation that expresses social policies determined by those who govern, elected as the people's representatives.

Program implementation involves establishing guidelines for determining eligible populations, and procedures for disbursement of services and funds and for data collection and evaluation. In time definitions of family are established, usually based on some idealization of what the family is or ought to be. Once a definition is established, bureaucratic norms require rigid adherence to that definition, whether or not it is descriptive of reality, and despite the fact that it may have unanticipated negative consequences for those so labeled.

Professionals in human service systems begin with a mandate for the provision of various services to eligible clients and then proceed to develop a description of "family." If the service being provided is rehabilitation, the basic rationale is that when disability occurs to one family member, it has a "domino effect" upon all others in the household unit. In this case an effort is made to treat the whole family (Nau, 1973).

In Nau's example, designers of the program accepted a societal image that a whole family is a unit composed of a legally married father and mother with dependent children, although the legislation supporting the funding of this program did not insist upon these definitions. In limiting the selection of families in this manner the rehabilitation team excludes other forms such as single-parent, dual-work, three-generation, and communal families, where the need for creative rehabilitation programs may be as great as in intact families (Sussman and Cogswell, 1972; Sussman, 1975).

Using a definition of family that fits one's personal predilections or the requirements of an organization intrinsically may not be bad. In communications and encounters with bureaucracies, there is pressure to comply with the organization's particular definition in order either to stay out of trouble or to receive a reward. One possible cost of such compliance is a limitation in options for role development, identification, and expression within the family. Role taking by members, then, is dictated by the demands of non-family structures. A cost of such compliance that may turn out to be a gain is that varied definitions and concomitant demands require families to become experts in adaptation and in developing the competence of their members to handle these requisites of bureaucracies.

Workable Family Definitions and Applications

A clarification of family terms and forms should provide a perspective on the proper use of such designations. Terms such as household, domestic functions, family, and marriage are often used interchangeably (Bender, 1967). A household is a physical structure whose residents may share common facilities, economic resources, domestic functions; and may or may not be related by blood or marriage. A household need not be a legally defined family, although the majority of groups classified as families live in households. Domestic functions, those related to meeting the needs of everyday living, do not have to be performed in a household or by family members; they can be performed in several locations by nonrelated persons or extended kin members who do not live in the household. A legally defined family can have more than one household (e.g. those who have a commuter marriage and maintain residences in different locations); or separated spouses, or separated parents and children (Gerstel and Gross, 1982).

For purposes of further discussion of older people and families and on the assumption that commitment, attachment, love, solidarity, and emotional exchange are basic processes or needs for individual and group survival (Ball, 1972; Hall, 1974; Bowen, 1978; Reiss, 1981), the following definitions are proposed. The first is a living-together group. Such a family may be defined as any cohabitating domestic relationship that is (or has been) sexually consequential, that is, for the gratification of members or the production of offspring. "These are the relationships most often associated with the emotions of love and the home" (Ball, 1972). This argues for abandonment of a kinship-based definition of family with its legal and religious sanctions regarding relationships and behavior and the obligations of kinship because of marriage and blood ties. The advantage of a living-together definition is the inclusion of sanctioned or unsanctioned variant family forms involved in domestic functions, expressions of love, shared responsibilities, economic activities, and sexual cohabitation.

A variant of this definition of the family does not require participants to live together. It is the "everyday family." It consists of persons who may or may not be related by blood or marriage, with whom one interacts on a regular basis and from whom one receives love, and solidarity. Sexual intimacy may occur but is not requisite. Such individuals usually reside in the same community or neighborhood, which permits frequent face-to-face interaction. It is a family to which one turns when one has a problem, and it is with those family members that one likes to spend work or leisure time. The notion of an everyday family as a support system for the elderly is viable and potentially useful.

There are efforts under way in several parts of the country to develop the everyday family for the elderly, including those individuals with varying degrees of disability. In one demonstration a neighborhood (everyday) family was created in Miami, Florida with membership in the age range from 25 to 90, in a neighborhood of mixed ethnic and social characteristics.

In this demonstration, interpersonal bonding is emphasized. Caring and deeply felt concerns over one another's physical and mental well-being transcend the help and exchange patterns often perfunctorily performed by legally related family members. Members of all age groups chose to become involved. The new surrogate family provides the usual services and exchanges of the biological family and the acceptance of idiosyncratic behavior of members. The "acting-out" of members is handled with compassion and understanding. This family develops effective linkages with community institutions for the services required by its members. It implements these connections by making certain that its members keep appointments, obtain the contracted service, and return safely to their homes. Neighborhood family staff are the facilitators for these activities. This neighborhood family of 27 members respresented a cost-effective complementarity of functions between a primary group and a service organization. The main factors contributing to the low cost of this program were the volunteer labor of 27 members of the family, and the fact that the communal household where family members congregated had rent-free and electricity-free facilities (Ross, 1978).

It is possible to create or reconstruct families by appropriate interventions, producing at low cost a consumer-based and controlled unit with minimal and effective use of organizational professionals. This model has potential as a basic family form, with its blend of primary group and agency resources.

The "everyday" family is likely to form in a natural fashion as a consequence of life-cycle changes and life-course transitions.

Support from organizational functionaries may or may not be present during genesis. In fact there may be considerable agency and community opposition to such family experiments. If, however, the new family form and its self-help activities take hold, it is highly likely that organizations will become interested, involved, and even controlling. The danger to the new family form is potential takeover by a more powerful organized service bureaucracy. An appropriate philosophical posture is to anticipate such takeovers as a normal occurrence with a continuous spawning of new forms.

Elderly persons sharing a household have the potential to create a new "peer" family form. Share-A-Home came to public view in Florida when 12 senior citizens moved into a large house and hired a manager to handle household chores and finances (*Orlando Sentinel,* 1971). A self-generated communal family of elderly persons sharing a household may be short-lived if some institutional support is not provided. The loss of members because of death and disability reduces the prospects of achieving a stable infrastructure that can handle crises, succession, and continuity. At this stage of later adulthood, continuity of a structure (e.g., a communal share-a-home arrangement) may be unrealistic and unnecessary.

Another type of family is one that may fully or partially share domestic functions, but whose members live in separate households. Members are scattered within the metropolitan area or county, yet have frequent access to one another. More friends than kin members are in this primary network. Friends whose relationships are characterized by trust and openness are everyday family members. Such true friends who like one another and share points of view have reciprocal access to each other's home, larder, and most intimate secrets. The exchanges in this type of family are contracted voluntarily and are not circumscribed by legal or cultural prescriptions governing blood and marriage ties. The major test and appeal of this everyday family is the response of members in crisis situations. For the elderly, this primary

group, this everyday family of "fictive," nonrelative kin, epitomizes survival in the coming decades when blood and marriage kin may be few.

Since the 1970s more and more older persons, out of desire or necessity, have been finding communes increasingly attractive (Ramey, 1972, 1975; Kanter, 1972; Somerville, 1972; Conover, 1975). Reciprocal socialization between older and younger generations is a possible explanation. Middle-aged elderly are "experiencing" the experimentation of their young in alternative forms of family. Some, in living independently of their children in new groupings that do not require remarriage and its concomitant obligations, are sustaining the desired "intimacy at a distance" with their grown children (Somerville, 1972; Rosenmayr, 1977).

Communal and other forms are all too frequently labeled "deviant" because of the traditional description and definition given to "the family." The family of procreation—husband, wife, and offspring living in a household apart from either set of parents—is viewed as the ideal from which emanates all that is good in family life. The meaning of relationships for human beings is often confused with structure. It is presumed further that one form of structure will provide, if not the optimal condition for fulfilling human experience, than the most significant one.

The conjugal family form, referred to as nuclear, "consisting of a nucleus of spouses and their offspring surrounded by a fringe of relatives" (Linton, 1936, p. 159), emphasizes that the core of the family is the husband and wife, around which all life functions. This unit is easy to establish by contract; it is the most visible; and the obligations, as well as instrumental and affectional bonds and ties with other kinship units, can be more readily ascertained than in the consanguinal form, where "we can picture the authentic family as a nucleus of blood relatives surrounded by a fringe of spouses" (Linton, 1936).

Conventional kin are units with whom conjugal families relate and interact. They consist of various relatives or kinsmen such as grandparents, uncles, aunts, nieces, nephews, grandchildren, and cousins obtained by marriage or tied to one another by blood. Discretionary kin are those distant relatives with whom one develops close and intimate relationships, ones not normally expected because of the person's location in the kin network (e.g., a spouse's sister-in-law or cousin). Fictive are those "non-kin," usually friends (Ball, 1972), whose relationships with the members of the conjugal unit are "as family." They are adopted members who take on obligations and instrumental and affectional ties similar to those of conventional kin.

There are no legal requirements or cultural traditions in American society to make this kin network of conventional, discretionary, or fictive members functional. It is an optional system in competition with society's organizations and institutions for the participation and loyalty of family members. Conjugal family members—supported by some concern for their familial responsibilities—enter voluntarily into economic, help, and emotional exchanges with kin members. The selection and intensity of these bondings are based on personal selection and on the real and perceived values attached to the exchange by kin members.

There are no legal requirements or cultural traditions in American society to make this kin network of conventional, discretionary, or fictive members functional. It is an optional system in competition with society's organizations and institutions for the participation and loyalty of family members. Conjugal family members—supported by some concern for their familial responsibilities—enter voluntarily into economic, help, and emotional exchanges with kin members. The selection and intensity of these bondings are based on personal selection and on the real and perceived values attached to the exchanges by kin members.

One concern is a possible shift in the coming decades from these values and behaviors that currently call for the legally defined family to care for its own to a reliance on voluntarily formed primary groups for such services. The empirical data are as yet insufficient to indicate that voluntarily formed family structures and commitments are sufficiently robust to assume responsibilities for caring for dependent members without legal edicts. The issue is whether a voluntary family form such as one composed of fictive kin has or will develop the bonds and moral and ideological bases to ensure responsible behavior when the elderly person is in need.

The legally ordered and culturally sanctioned nuclear family persists as a basic caretaking unit for elderly relatives and will continue to do so in the foreseeable future. It is a changed family unit from yesteryear, however, in regard to men's and women's roles; the sharing of decision making, and household and other work responsibilities; and parenting and caring functions. Its persistence is pragmatic. Our legal system, cultural norms, and institutional practices give ultimate responsibility to the nuclear family for the behavior and care of individual members. When society and bureaucracies "give up" on the individual, the family takes over. Family members not confined to total care institutions because of their condition or believed dangerous to themselves or the public are given back to the family. "It is all up to you" is a much too often used expression in the exit interview between a professional caretaker and a family representative, at the discharge from a treatment center of a family member who is ailing, chronically disabled, or suffering from a life-threatening disease (Sussman, 1975). This turning to the nuclear unit, this transition of responsibility to such units with a reversal of the process only when the nuclear family is incapable and debilitated, suggests the persistence and universality of the nuclear family.

The response pattern of members of new family forms to the care needs of an elderly member is problematic. Relationships with almost equal sharing and exchange are presumed. The ability to perform, to "carry one's weight" is expected. Individuals are attracted to these voluntary family forms because of the potential for self-fulfillment through shared experience and expressive interaction. While the historic experience of these forms is too limited to reach empirically based conclusions, it is unlikely that the bonds between group members will persist when long-term care of a group member is required.

Blood and marriage ties of members of nuclear units form kin networks. Some are "paper" networks devoid of relationships except where responsibility for one's relatives is legally established or culturally sanctioned. Other networks are active systems providing reciprocal supports for economic, psychological, and social well-being. Functioning networks are primary systems for sharing the support and care of elderly members (Bild and Havighurst, 1976; Shanas, 1979b). A detailed analysis of kinship structure and its aged members follows.

KIN FAMILY NETWORKS

Definitions, Functions, and Usages

The meaning of family and kin family networks is found in the answer to the question "Whom do you consider to be family?" The response to this question is far more critical in evaluating the meaning, significance, and probabilities of family relationships of older persons than those estimates made by organizational functionaries or described by social scientists. This self-definition of family is a prelude to any study of kinship structure that employs as principal measures residential propinquity; type and frequency of interaction; mutual aid; familism, affectional bonds, and value transmission (Sussman, 1960; Adams, 1968; Troll, 1971; Cicirelli, 1981). Structural analysis of kinship systems is a complicated and time-consuming process because of a multi-descent pattern in the United States where one can claim up to four lineages (Schneider, 1968). In this sense one "chooses" a generational line or lines, that is, the relatives with whom one wishes to be identified. This comparative freedom to relate to those kin with whom one is reciprocally compatible or whom one finds attrac-

tive—there being no legal statutes, common laws, or cultural prescription to obligate one to be connected with relatives—indicates the major relevance of self-descriptions of family and kin and the need to tap these descriptions in empirical work to obtain meanings for kinship behavior and the voluntary nature of the kin network.

The kin structure in most complex societies is composed of household units each containing a family form (e.g., intact, single-parent, dual-career) whose members are related by blood or marriage and who in some instances may be fictive kin. The network is a voluntary system characterized by reciprocal exchanges. There are no legal rules or cultural ideologies as requirements for belonging. Moreover, one can opt out of the network; but, if one remains a member, then in time there develop expectations of interpersonal exchange, emotional support, and forms of aid and assistance under various conditions. Mutual expectations of reciprocity evolve to encompass the whole system. This network, similarly to other organizations, competes for the time, interest, and investment of its members. It cannot "demand" adherence to norms of filial piety. However, it has a distinct advantage over other human-built social structures in that kin loyalty and identification, buttressed by general societal expectations of appropriate behavior where "family" is involved, have powerful attractions. The adage that "blood is thicker than water" seems to hold even in this post-industrial period. In societies undergoing rapid changes from a rural to an industry-based economy, such as Egypt, Kenya, and Pakistan, family bondings are the primary structures vis-à-vis mechanisms for making bureaucracies functional and tolerable.

Describing the "functionality" of the kin network in terms of specific structural properties is an initial step in establishing the meaning and significance of the kin network for aged members. The suggestion of Kerckhoff (1965) is to use proximity and help exchanges as principal components of a structural kin network taxonomy. He proposes three measures of functionality: "nuclear isolated" where member units are in close proximity but have no or very few contacts; "modified extended" where families are spatially dispersed but have high scores on contacts, interaction, and exchanges; and "extended" where units are residentially propinquitous and high in functionality.

It is obvious that mapping of the network using this simplified set of categories, fully recognizing the operational issues in determining "functionality," can ascertain the relevance as well as the quality of such involvements for the older person. The test of relevance is whether the network provides intimate human interaction and empathetic reciprocal response on the emotional level, conditions critical to survival, the sustenance of mental and physical health, and "a more meaningful existence" (Lowenthal and Haven, 1968; Jourard, 1971; Moriwaki, 1973; Noelker, 1975). While other forms of structure can provide this social interaction that results in intimacy and empathy, and it has been suggested that friendship among peers is a possible solution (Rosow, 1967), the viability of the network as an optional system for handling the primary emotional needs of the elderly is at test. Relevance rests in whether it is actually achieved. If the outcome is intimacy and empathy, then quality has been obtained.

Shanas (1979a) echoes the theme of functionality of kin for elderly members in presenting four myths regarding elder–family relationships and data to refute them. These myths are: (1) high geographic mobility has separated older persons from their families, especially their children; (2) contacts between elders and their children are limited if not rare because of the generation gap and alienation; (3) elders are excluded from the predominent nuclear family; and (4) social services provided by organizations usurp the family's traditional care and interpersonal functions.

Shanas refutes these myths with the following arguments, based primarily on her national studies spanning several decades: (1) Approximately eight out of ten elders who have children report seeing at least one child during the week before their interview, and this statistic is stable throughout 20 years of research. The emotional content, perceived helpfulness, and length of these meetings between elders and their adult children are unknown, but are important components of their meaning or functionality. (2) In 1975, one-third of all elders with living siblings had seen at least one brother or sister during the week before they were interviewed, and one-half had seen a sibling during the month before the interview. (3) Two of every ten respondents indicated that they had seen some relative in the previous week and that this relative was not an adult child, grandchild, brother, or sister. (4) In 1962 only 2 percent of noninstitutionalized elders were totally bedfast at home, and 6 percent were housebound. However, 1975 research indicates a slight increase in home care with 3 percent of noninstitutionalized elders being totally bedfast at home and 7 percent housebound. Family members assumed the care of these people. Another 4 to 5 percent of elders nationwide were institutionalized.

The relative network responds more completely and, presumably more effectively, in certain task and problem areas than in others. Cantor and associates report that elderly persons select kin primarily for assistance with health and family problems and hesitantly for financial matters or in doing daily tasks. Preference is given to "working out by oneself" the financial problems and activities of daily living. Non-kin are used primarily to work through loneliness (Cantor, 1975, 1979, 1980).

Maintaining mental well-being in later adulthood involves finding persons who can and will reciprocate affection, love, intimacy, and caring. Hence, relationships that are voluntary, discretionary, and mutual, those most likely found in the creation and maintenance of friendships, are preferred for mental well-being (Rosow, 1967; Lee and Ellithorpe, 1978). One explanation is that when relationships with kin are perceived as ascribed, the mutuality of choice, a critical dimension of friendship relationships, is missing (Furstenberg, 1979). If, on the other hand, kin relationships are viewed to be voluntary, discretionary, and reciprocal with the possibility to opt out if either party desires, then the emotional well-being of the elders is a likely outcome of activity among kin members.

Intergenerational Linkages

Intergenerational linkages have proved to be the most salient component (and most researched) of the kin network. Stage of the life cycle, sex of individuals, presence of generational kin, and propinquity are related to interactional patterns, intimacy, and empathy.

Parents and young married couples are closely linked in interaction communication, and systems of mutual aid involving services and financial help, the flow being generally from parents to children, especially among the middle classes (Sussman, 1953; Litwak, 1960a,b; Aldous and Hill, 1965; Feldman, 1965; Adams, 1968, 1970; Klatzky, 1973; Arling, 1976; Lee, 1979a, b; Mancini, 1979; Shanas, 1979b). With increasing economic and psychological independence of the young married exacerbated by geographical separation and buttressed by ideologies that attempt to reconcile the contradictions of the ideal and real, independence and dependence in human relationships induce some hiatus in generational relationships until the retirement of parents, which is perceived as old age, the period of decreasing vigor and health (Troll, 1971; Troll et al., 1979).

Support for this cyclical shift in closeness and interaction is derived from clinical evidence of role reversal of children and older parents regarding dependability and dependence and from statistical data regarding residency patterns. Maturation of married children ("filial maturity"—Blenkner, 1965, 1969) is demonstrated by a competence and capability to take on supportive and, if necessary, caretaking roles with one's parents as the latter become less independent (Silverman and Brahce, 1979). The reciprocal of this is the older person's comfortable feeling

that children can be "counted on" when needed, which lessens the pervasive pathological concern of "being a burden" to children.

Data from several studies report high levels of intergenerational activities between married children and older parents (Sussman, 1960; Cumming and Henry, 1961; Youmans, 1963; Kerckhoff, 1966; Shanas, 1962, 1967, 1968, 1979). The majority of older persons, over 85 percent in most studies, live less than an hour's distance away from a child, and approximately 50 percent are living in a child's household or within 10 minutes' distance from a child (Shanas, 1979b). The separation between households of parents and children sustains the elderly in their need to be independent, to live in a separate residence as long as possible. Complementary to this perception is the desire and need to interact with family members, to know that there is someone to call on, someone who cares. Not all relationships are loving or harmonious, and intergenerational abuse is becoming too frequent an occurrence. This topic is treated briefly subsequently.

Some middle-aged (40–60) children are in key "orchestrating" positions for multiple activities and functions within generationally linked kin networks (Shanas, 1962, 1980). They may be providing a home for an aged parent; looking after a divorced daughter and her child; seeing their children through college; providing guidance and sometimes a home to other relatives who migrate in for jobs, school, marriage; and running a "boarding" house for families of married children who never seem to leave home, and, if women, try to be very supportive of their spouses. The significance of these exacting adult socialization roles of middle-generation parents for maintaining the essential emotional network of the most primary of groups is unappreciated and unresearched.

Response in case of illness involves the kin network with little differentiation according to social class or type of relative, with the major exchanges taking place among propinquitous kin (Sussman, 1959; Croog et al.,

1972). In cases of critical or long-term illness, some additional assistance may come from distantly located relatives. With both near and distant relatives care of kin is largely the work of female members. This especially holds in generationally linked families (Litman, 1971). In a linked three- or four-generation network, the mother of a middle generation will be the main provider of comfort to both her parents and her married children. Elderly family members in times of crisis were more likely to turn to their daughters than to any other family member.

The willingness to respond in the event of illness and the actual response should not be equated with feelings of competence to take care of an ill relative for any long period of time. Today's families do not have the structural, organizational, and economic resources to provide such care (Parsons and Fox, 1952). Litman reports that while four-fifths of families in his three-generation study feel convalescent care at home is most desirable, about one-third could not furnish such care under any circumstances. About 75 percent of the younger generation families state that a family member has a "right" to such home care, whereas the grandparent generation express some misgivings regarding the taking of such care (Litman, 1971).

The ideology of "taking care of one's own—familial responsibility" persists among the youngest generation, even though they allow the hospital and other health care systems to take on the major responsibility. The older generation's traditional response, "I do not want to be a burden to my children or grandchildren," is one that evokes a healthy skepticism. The need for emotional support is basic to survival, and one prominent feature of a family is its emotional network. Those elderly who cannot find emotional comfort among peers and in other primary groups may indeed crave family involvement.

A possible explanation for the attitude of the elderly and the willingness of the younger generation to use organized health care systems is that in highly differentiated societies where specialization of function is a fact of life and the economy is built around such complexities, one becomes conditioned to use such available systems. If a society shifts its policies and programs to encompass a national health insurance system with emphasis on entitlement rather than eligibility, one can anticipate greater use of nonfamilial systems not only in the area of health but in other societal sectors.

Kin Networks and Ethnicity

The functionality of the extended family system is so extensive among blacks that its existence is essential for the survival of the individual as well as black culture and tradition (Shimkin, Louie, and Frate, 1973; Shimkin, Shimkin, and Frate, 1975). A review of reported researches on family systems in black societies indicates that the extended family system is the primary one among blacks and is found in urban as well as in rural environments (Shimkin et al., 1975). The Shimkins' synthesis of black extended family systems resulted in 12 conclusions on black family structure, values, and behavior. Two are especially germaine to this presentation: "A widespread and functionally important institution of black society in the United States is a bilateral descent group with more loosely related spouses and with extensions to various kinds of fictive relatives, which is called 'family'; and characteristically, this family is centered, perceptually and in terms of action initiatives, on its representatives of the oldest living generation, who are symbols of unity, objects of respect and moral authority, sources of fosterage and objects of care for all members" (Shimkin and Shimkin, 1975). The readiness of extended families to commit their total resources to help the elderly person, including the social and economic costs of terminal care, is both alarming and amazing to researchers and policy makers, both because it is nonmodal according to the value system and experience of the latter, and because, in the long run, it may be devastating in its consequences for the economic stability of the extended family.

Similar patterns of connectedness and support of black aged members on all socioeconomic levels are reported by Jackson (1971a,b, 1972a,b, 1973). Elderly members have legitimate claims for help, and extended kin will "squeeze blood from a turnip" to provide assistance (Jackson, 1972a; McAdoo, 1982a). Generational ties are strong and are reinforced through adult-to-adult interaction where wisdom and experience are shared and where a parity model replaces the usual superordinate–subordinate model of parent–child relationships.

The economic situation of the older black is so precarious that linkage with a functional kin network is absolutely necessary to avoid institutionalization. The low level of education of elderly blacks acts as an obstacle in self-help efforts and in linking with bureaucratized human service systems that control resources. The kin network also functions as a haven for its members, especially elderly ones who are under heightened stress as a consequence of difficulties and failures in obtaining economic and service supports (McAdoo, 1982b). Reliance on family and extended kin is the one salient available option for aged blacks.

Economic status, however, is an insufficient explanation of the interdependence and reliance of members upon one another in the black family. There is a pervasive cultural tradition of reaching to parents, siblings, and other relatives as "significant others" (Billingsley, 1968; Angelou, 1969; McAdoo, 1977; Martin and Martin, 1978; Manns, 1981). Such individuals provide modeling for appropriate familial and social roles, as well as caring and caretaking; they serve as consultants for educational achievements and job placement, and as facilitators and mediators in the use of community resources.

Significant others are not limited to family and kin members. In one study of 20 middle-aged adult educated blacks with 212 identified significant others, 64 percent were non-

relatives (Manns, 1981). The majority were college or university colleagues and mentors. These nonrelatives, members of a reference group, were reported to be "like" family in their modeling and influencing behavior. For this purposively selected black group, compared to whites, nonrelative significant others were greater in number than relatives.

In addition to blacks who require the kin network as an economic safety net, Hispanics have developed a high degree of interfamily interdependency mandated by both cultural heritage and economic realities (Torres-Gil, 1976). In a study of 200 older Mexican-Americans living in San Jose, California, the Hispanic male, the "breadwinner," was reported to be the family's center. He facilitates most family–bureaucratic organizational relationships, especially in communications and economic matters. The homemaker-wife coordinates the activities of the support network. The older woman (grandmother) functions as a socialization agent and source of knowledge for support functions. The elder man (grandfather) is a respected authority, provider of information derived from a lifetime of experience, consultant to his children and kin, and facilitator of family relationships with organizations and institutions (e.g., the church). Individuals of Hispanic families identify themselves as members of groups bound by tradition and economic necessity rather than as separate units.

Intergenerational solidarity has long been hypothesized as a basic ongoing condition within ethnic groups, one that contributes to the psychological well-being and life satisfaction of its elderly members (Bengtson and Cutler, 1976). The quality of life satisfaction among the elderly is highly correlated with health, social participation, and socioeconomic status (Cutler, 1973; Edwards and Klemmack, 1973; Palmore and Kivett, 1977; Larson 1978; Markides and Martin, 1979; Markides et al., 1981).

Kin and intergenerational ties remain important to the well-being of the ethnic elderly (Greeley, 1971; Johnson, 1978; Woehrer,

1982). Guttman et al. (1977, 1978) investigated this phenomenon in a study that included eight white ethnic groups in the Washington/Baltimore area: Estonians, Greeks, Hungarians, Latvians, Italians, Lithuanians, Jews, and Poles. Approximately 720 elderly and 180 spokespersons were interviewed on family and kinship relationships and related problems of functioning in a society where human services are highly organized. Almost 84 percent of the elderly respondents were between the ages of 60 and 79 years. This sample of ethnic elderly seemed to be problem-free: 83 percent reported no important physical problem; a little over 94 percent claimed to have no important psychological one. In fact, 22 percent of the elderly stated that their health was better than that of other people in their age group. The impression is that ethnic elderly do not report their problems to investigators.

Elderly family members vary in their perceptions, in feelings of satisfaction with life, in use of community resources and government support programs, and in social participation because of different ethnic identities. In such matters one cannot talk about the "ethnic response." Each group responds differently, and this has implications for policy and program development and for service delivery.

Where there is some consensus is in the overall view that the family is the major support of the elderly. In fact, over one-third consider their greatest achievement to be a "happy family life and success of various family members." Family and kin members play a very important role in decision-making regarding the utilization of community service providers. It would appear that the major function of families in ethnic communities is to provide the elderly with information, and to act as an agent for the elderly in their dealings with service providers and government agencies such as Social Security. In functioning as a buffer for the elderly, families also provide protection by controlling information. Relatives, in this sense, "cover up" the inequities and incompeten-

cies of service providers. Thus, relatives determine what existing services and community supports are "safe."

Continuity, Care, and Abuse

The increasing incidence of persons surviving to late adulthood has created a new life course transition for both the elder and her or his adult child. The adult child's transition is to become a parent to the elderly, now dependent, parent. The loss of autonomy, mobility, and independence of the elder as a consequence of mental or physical disability results in dependence on the child. For many elders this transition is emotionally excruciating. Radical internal transformation of perception of self, questing to live or die, and evaluating the purpose of being—these are agonizing experiences for elderly persons who are thrust from independence to dependence.

This is also a highly stressful period for the adult child caretaker. Out of overwhelming and overpowering fear, anger, bewilderment, and depression, adult child caretakers of elderly parents may respond as authoritarians. Acting-out violently and abusively is one consequence of depression. Using control to bring order out of chaos, with the objective of returning the elderly person to her or his former state of functioning, may produce frustration rather than the desired outcome. Violence and abuse easily accompany these efforts.

Studies on violence within the family have encouraged a stream of research regarding the abuse of older parents by their children (Lau and Kosberg, 1978; Steinmetz and Straus, 1978; Block and Sinnott, 1979; Steinmetz, 1981; Rathbone-McCuan and Hashimi, 1982). The genesis of such violence is unclear, and few investigators have offered empirical data that support a hypothesis of the intergenerational transmission of violence. Studies on this subject tend to be surveys relying heavily on retrospective recall. None are longitudinal in design and thus able to answer the question of whether an abused child becomes an abuser as an adult and uses violence in marital, child, and parent relationships.

While causal connections of generational transmission of abusive behavior are lacking, there are a few studies indicating that adolescents are abusing their parents, especially mothers (Cornell and Gelles, 1982); that adult children are committing acts of violence against elderly parents (Rathbone-McCuan, 1978; Steinmetz and Straus, 1978; Steinmetz, 1981); and that elderly parents abuse their caretaking children (Steinmetz, 1981). Abuse takes a variety of forms and is used to effect control by one or more family members over another person.

Steinmetz (1981) reports on the first 60 families of a projected 200-family study population. From in-depth interviews it was deduced that child caretakers used abusive methods to control their elderly parents. The specific number of the caretakers interviewed who used violence is not reported, but 40 percent screamed and yelled, 6 percent used physical restraint, 6 percent used forced feeding or medication, 6 percent threatened to send the parent to a nursing home, 4 percent threatened to use physical force, and 3 percent hit or slapped their parent.

Elderly parents drew from a repertoire of tactics to control or neutralize the behavior of their children, according to Steinmetz. The form of abuse and identifying the abusers is less relevant than its apparent rise in incidence. If the incidence is not increasing, then the prevalence of abusive behavior involving parent–child relationships is now being identified.

INTERGENERATIONAL TRANSFERS AND FAMILY PATTERNS

Society-Wide Transfers

In complex societies characterized by differentiation in work, service, and occupational systems, the financial and service supports provided by such society-wide programs as social security and health care have eclipsed the importance of the single family's modus operandi for guaranteeing the well-being of older members because of the latter's control of wealth and the testamentary process (Kreps, 1962). A study of inheritance patterns in modern times reveals, however, that inheritance patterns reflect the web of the emotional fabric that links members of family networks together.

While society-wide economic transfers will be more fully discussed in Chapters 16 and 23 of this *Handbook,* a brief analysis will provide the base for discussing inheritance transfers and family relationships. In the modern period the development of society-wide welfare, social security, educational, and health care systems provides the very young and the aged with basic economic support and services that in the past were provided by the family or kinship group. A universal system of taxation provides for the old and young who are not gainfully employed and is the basis of society-wide economic transfers from one generation to the next. It is apparent that such economic transfers and income redistribution have been largely a function of governmental and political superstructures of modern societies and have overshadowed the family's efforts to arrange for the economic maintenance of its own members. One consequence is the reduced importance of the economic function of inheritance in providing the family with the necessary assets to sustain its members over generational time, educate its dependent young, and care for its ill or aged members.

While the importance of inheritance to the economic maintenance of the family in modern times has diminished, and property holdings of families, kinship groups, or lineages have very little effect upon the workings of the economic market, the transfer of property is still a vital function, especially in modern industrial countries. Inheritance may be viewed as an individually based or society-wide transfer. Support of social security, welfare, and education by persons in their middle years may be interpreted as a legacy for the younger and older generations; they are society-wide transfers. Bequeathing one's property to another in a will is an individually based transfer.

Intergenerational Inheritance Transfers

Inheritance patterns of 659 family systems, randomly selected from a court jurisdiction of approximately 2 million in the United States, were examined (Sussman et al., 1970a). The findings are relevant to the family and its aging members.

Dual patterns of serial service and reciprocity are established as existing coterminously. Transfers from one generation to the next take place in the normal course of events as evidenced by the relatively small number of gifts given to charities, friends, and distantly related family members. With the bulk of transfers occurring within generational lines, it is obvious that serial service is a dominant pattern; parents help their young children, and when these children reach maturity, they assume responsibility, doing what they can for their now aged parents. The cycle continues indefinitely over generational time.

Serial reciprocity complements this process of generational transfer. Specific allocations are made according to notions of distributive justice and actual exchanges of care, service, and material goods between members of the older and middle generations. Testators will their estates to designated children or other individuals according to the testators' perception of their needs, emotional ties with them, and services exchanged among family members over the years. Serial service—the transfer of worldly goods from parents to lineal descendants—which occurs in due course, exists side by side with serial reciprocity, which specifies the giver–taker relationship based on exchanges of goods and services and patterns of interaction.

Related to serial reciprocity and service is the occurrence of role reversals in which children begin to take care of their parents, a phenomenon previously described. These role reversals require new learning and place upon the middle generation potentially anxiety-provoking responsibilities. This generation, in addition to caring for the young, now has to care for the old parents.

Sibling members of the middle generation are sensitive to the problems they have in raising their own families. Therefore, they generally accept the notion that the sibling who has rendered the greatest amount of service to an aged parent should receive a major portion of the inheritance upon the death of that parent. If the sibling takes the parent into his home, other siblings usually expect that almost all of the parent's estate should go to that child. On the other hand, if the child went to live in the parent's home during the latter's declining years, then the payoff should be more equally distributed among the children, since the one child has already profited from living in the parent's home. The data indicate general agreement that the child who performs the greatest amount of service should receive the greatest part of the estate. Where disagreements occur, they focus on differences in perception among children concerning the amount of service actually rendered by the sibling who was left with the largest share of the estate.

Children feel that they should maintain intimate contact with aged parents in order to provide them with emotional support and social and recreational opportunities, and that such contact maintenance is requisite for obtaining a share of inheritance. Exchanges may be of different orders. Children provide parents with physical care, emotional support, affection, and the niceties of social interaction in their declining years; in return they receive financial compensation. What is suggested here is that the pattern of distribution to a particular child is based upon services rendered, even among those who live in households apart from the aged parent. The child who provides the most physical and social services generally receives the largest reward.

The pattern of exchange of care for eventual financial reward does not function when the decedent does not require special attention. The normal testate pattern of distribution is for the decedent to leave his estate to the spouse if the spouse is still living. By leaving the estate to the spouse, the testator provides the widow or widower with the means to continue an independent or nearly independent financial existence. This lateral transfer, identified as a "spouse-all" pattern, takes place prior to a vertical estate distribution from parent to child. It occurs even under intestate conditions, where there is no will. Most beneficiaries, children for the most part, who stand to share under the law of descent and distribution, at least one-third of the estate in most jurisdictions, favor the spouse-all pattern. In the majority of cases studied, the testator's spouse was an aged parent, and such a transfer enabled that individual to maintain independence for a longer period of time while still physically capable and alert.

An implication of this orderly process is the reduction of potential turbulence which usually accompanies the loss of a network member. This is a conscious effort to effect a smooth continuity of relationships within the emotional network with minimal disagreements among descendants over claims and priorities. A less desirable option is to take over the financial and moral responsibility for the aged person if, by taking one's fair share that allowed by the law governing intestacy, one has increased the dependency of this person. Respondents proved to be very sanguine in harmonizing societal expectations of filial piety and the costing-out of economic gains and losses. Knowledge that the equity, usually a nonmortgaged home, would eventually be passed on to them made the decision to keep things "as is" easy to reach.

In this analysis of generational transfers within family systems, the dynamics of the bonding relationship between adult children and their older parents have been mentioned only in passing. Significant research on intergenerational bonding and value transmission establishes that commonality of location of children and parents which increases opportunities for interaction increases value congruity for members of both generations. Direct transmission of value orientations of parent to child via the traditional model of agent–novice socialization does not occur (Hill et al., 1970; Bengtson et al., 1975; Bengtson, 1975; Bengtson and deTerre, 1980).

Differences between the generations, commonly labeled as the "gap," are not as great as popularly portrayed. This is the case even though parents tend to minimize the differences between themselves and their children, while children do the reverse. Older members in linkages with adult children report high levels of affective relationships, while children perceive these ties more in terms of service and various exchanges of help (Bengtson and Black, 1973; Bengtson and Treas, 1980). These perceptual differences should not inhibit the potential solidity of the intergenerational complement of the kin network. They imply complementary needs. Affection, real or otherwise, is desired and needed by the elderly and is sought in the exchanges with children. Children, in turn, who must invest in other affectual relationships such as their marriages, can best handle the "demands" of respect, understanding, and trust of their parents by providing very specific services. The dynamics of specific parent–child relationships will influence specific testamentary transfers.

Three developments are likely to modify the normal pattern of intergenerational transfers of equity along biological lines. The first is the rising marriage rate since 1977, which includes yearly consecutive increases in the incidence of remarriage with a new national record for 1981. The second is the high rate of divorce since 1962, which reached a record level in 1981. The third is the variety of life-styles now becoming available to the aged (U.S. National Center for Health Statistics, 1983). In the face of the changes in the rates of divorce and marriage, in 1978 three of every four individuals lived in married-couple households (U.S. Bureau of the Census, 1980b). This represents a 10 percent decline from 1960 (85 % to 75 %) but suggests that remarriage is a well used option.

These trends suggest a potential redistribution of family-acquired assets to pay for the costs of these new family formations, and distributions to heirs of a second marriage or a combination of first- and second-marriage heirs and legatees. Ante-nuptial agreements have been useful legal contracts for middle-aged and older persons entering a second marriage. Contractees agree not to claim their allowable share under state intestate laws, thus permitting inheritance transfers to biological issues of the first marriage. Even with such an arrangement, the testator can designate as beneficiaries a spouse and offspring of second marriages, and this often occurs. The ante-nuptial agreement does not reduce the autonomy of the testator to freely will assets but nullifies a spouse's usual legal entitlement to a fair share of the estate when there is intestacy (no will).

The increased incidence of divorce along with a high rate of remarriage suggests that traditional legal rulings governing generational transfers may have to change to provide for multiple beneficiaries from more than one marriage. It is anticipated that ante-nuptial agreements will be employed less frequently among remarrying middle-aged individuals. Also, some elderly persons, especially those in the upper socioeconomic brackets, who have had more than one marriage may benefit from this shift away from the usual inheritance pattern which legally protects first-marriage family members. Similar to the elderly progenitor of a large-sized family, the remarried older person has a larger number of relatives, especially children, with whom to develop linkages. The promise of an inheritance may provide motivation for family members to invest in a relationship with the elderly person, while at the same time the latter has a greater field of available relatives from whom to choose.

Alternative Life-Styles and Future Transfers

Alternative life-styles and the prospects of elderly persons' adopting these styles provide potentially divergent patterns of testamentary exchange in the future. The increased incidence of singlehood and child-free marriages will modify for those without issue the traditional pattern of transmission of property from the older to the younger generation within family lines (Stein, 1978; Veevers, 1979; Houseknecht, 1982). It is hypothesized that more bequests will be given to friends, cohabitees, charities, and bilateral relatives, for example, brothers and sisters and their descendants (Dunham, 1963; Browder, 1969; Brooks, 1979; Rosenfeld, 1979, 1980).

From 1970 to 1980 the number of unmarried couple households more than doubled. While the largest percentage of such householders were under 34 years of age, the third highest percentage was in the cohort 65 and older (U.S. Bureau of the Census, 1980b). One reason to cohabitate was the fear of losing social security survivor's benefits if they remarried. Maintenance of survivor's benefits upon remarriage after age 60, however, was assured, effective January 1979, by new legislation. Two other major reasons for the increased incidence of cohabitation in this age group are to avoid the forced share of the estate for the surviving spouse; and acquiescence to adult children's fears that their share of the estate will be diminished because of the remarriage. Judicial decisions, however, regarding the rights and responsibilities of cohabitees have viewed cohabitation as similar to marriage when a separation occurs (Weitzman, 1981). The courts are treating cohabitees increasingly as if they are legally married. Unless a will and "ante-cohabitation agreement" exist, the usual pattern of inheritance transfer to lineal kin will be dramatically altered.

The increasing number of elderly of all class levels moving into and living in age-segregated housing may modify traditional patterns of testamentary behavior (Carp, 1966; Sherman, 1975; Teski, 1981). Higher morale and feelings of greater well-being are reported by elderly persons living in age-segregated housing compared to their peers in age-integrated housing estates and communities (Bultena and Wood, 1969; Lawton and Cohen, 1974; Brody, 1978; Harel and Harel, 1978). The prediction is that in the foreseeable future there will be increased bequests to non-kin, those who provide love, care, and intimacy, and to institutions providing total care with parallel disinheritance of kin (Rosenfeld, 1980).

Each day approximately 1600 persons are added to the roles of 65 and older. More of these individuals are likely to be better educated than the previous year's cohort for any specific day (Jones, 1980). Such educated individuals are more aware of their options and the use of the will as a testamentary device than less educated peers (Sussman et al., 1970a; Simos, 1973). The well-informed will increasingly use inter vivos transfers, will substitutes, and other means to avoid high taxes on death (Dacy, 1980; Stern, 1980). Such persons will be seeking ways to remain autonomous and in control of their lives even during periods of dependency. These elders will use their resources to live the good life with diminished concern to conserve and transmit resources to the next generation.

The new political ideologies and economic conditions of the 1980s indicate that there will be an eroding of the bases for society-wide transfers, the provision of income and services to the old by those in gainful employment. Intrafamily transfers to non-kin will become more significant in reciprocity of services and caring for the individuals in later adulthood. The major transformation of the traditional inheritance transfer will be from automatic and eventual acquisition of the property and other equities of parents to one of "those who do, will receive." The new federalism with its emphasis on self-help, independence, autonomy, and the family taking care of its own suggests that testamentary freedom will be exercised more vigorously in selecting deserving beneficiaries.

FAMILY–AGED MEMBER RELATIONSHIPS IN THE 1980s

Basic Issues

One major theme of this chapter is concern with the actual and potential role of family structures and networks in providing aging members with a hedge against the control-ling demands of organizational and institutional bureaucracies. Through network linkage activities, interaction and human warmth are provided. Both are requisites for the survival and quality living of aged members. Various forms of the family, as distinct from neighborhood peer groups and friends and acquaintances in institutionalized settings, may provide a more desirable option for older persons in obtaining physical, social, and psychological well-being.

These varied family structures, some created by societal conditions and others formed in the quest for more meaningful relationships than those found in the traditional nuclear family, have the potentiality for "humanizing" the aging process. The aged person can be in a family environment where his or her contributions are highly prized. The reasons are that the circumstances surrounding the beginnings of these varied family structures and the requisite activities for effecting survival indicate that these structures require reciprocal exchanges rather than one-sided dependencies, parity over superordinate–subordinate relationships, and effective utilization of individual and organizational resources.

Society-wide transfers in the form of financial support for health care, social service, medical service, nutrition, housing, and other living accoutrements up until 1980 were obviously lessening the importance of the individual family generational transfer of equities through inheritance. The intergenerational relational system was more significant for its expression of family ties and intimacy but less than adequate as a total support system. The problem of economic and service support of the aged is exacerbated by the current abandonment of the quest to establish a universal right to available support systems, to have entitlement as the policy and law of the land. Consequently, too many older citizens and member units of family networks will have insufficient resources to provide a quality home environment for themselves.

The provision of alternatives to the institutionalization of services and people in complex societies is difficult because of its potential effects upon all societal systems, institutions, and organizations. For example, to move to a client-centered human service system requires radical changes in the current professional–client model regarding the dispensation of services. To meet the needs and demands of aged individuals and families for health and social services, for example, may require bringing such activities into the home, or utilization of a decentralized organizational model with the provision of services at the client's call. Such proposed "business irregularities" from conventional practices immediately create linkage, rational, and communication problems; resistance from human service staffs; and if not reluctance, at least controlled ambivelance from government and community elites. The threat of unknown consequences prevents a wholesale transformation of the current institutionalized patterns for doing business with aged members and their families.

Yet, the search for alternatives to institutionalization and service options continues because there are neither enough institutions nor trained people to staff them to meet the expanding need for health and custodial care for the growing aged population. During the 1970s, federal health, welfare, and rehabilitation agencies implicitly followed policies of reversing the trend of providing care and treatment for the chronically ill and aged in isolated, highly bureaucratized, and impersonal institutions. Providing services in the communities of those who require them is now being advocated, and comprehensive community health facilities are but one example of implementation of such a new policy. Whether community service systems will have the resources to effect locally based care is highly problematic. A logical extension is to carry the services one step further, to the family.

Breslau and Haug (1972) concluded as a result of a demonstration project on the delivery of paraprofessional services to the elderly that "the needed social service would be more effective if it elicited the cooperation of the family and were perceived and formulated as a family enterprise. In other words, social service, instead of being an independent and alternative agent of intervention, ought to attempt to be a family ally that offers assistance when caring for the aged member is too great a burden." To effect this recommendation requires a basic modification of current models of service and their financial support.

Some of the funds currently used for services can be channeled directly to the families of the elderly who can provide more personalized general care at perhaps less cost. In some societies with family-centered traditions, this "reversal" of the bureaucratic mode is not overly traumatic. For highly professionalized provider systems, however, the impact is potentially devastating. Experiments and demonstrations have yet to be tried. The savings and benefits thus derived can mean improved resources for the short-term treatment in general hospitals of acute illness and injury among the aged, and for the total care institutionalization that is essential for a very small proportion of the elderly.

If circumstances facilitated the care of the elderly within a unit of the family network, the options available to the aged members of the society could be increased. Many aged persons cling tenaciously to their independence and participation in social activities as continuous support for their self-images as productive self-sufficient individuals. The institution represents for such persons the abandonment of many of these personal goals. Residence with a family member, however, could ease the burden—physical and economic—on the old person of the total maintenance of a household, yet provide the opportunity to carry on accustomed extrafamilial activities.

A role for the family network in the care of the elderly, especially as a back-up system for the custody and treatment of those between independence and dependence in mental and physical functioning, is inevitable. All research findings and policy declarations maintain that in the remaining decades of this century:

1. There will be insufficient manpower for the training of professional personnel to meet the continuous demands and needs for quality health care and rehabilitation.

2. The United States has reached its "absorptive capacity" insofar as professionalization is concerned and cannot continue its current rate of expenditure for professional and quasi-professional training.

3. Skyrocketing hospital and rehabilitation costs are draining family and third-party resources, and some way for providing quality care and treatment more economically must be found.

4. Payoffs in improved functioning, if any, of elderly persons as a consequence of extended hospitalization for treatment of chronic disabilities are insufficient to warrant the high cost.

5. Further expansion or building of new centralized care institutions will vitiate current efforts to develop a client-centered program of care therapy where the elderly relate to their families and communities and have some say regarding what is being done to and for them.

6. There is a rediscovery of the family as the primary group in society; and self-help, taking care of one's own, with minimal involvement of bureaucratized human service systems, is a virtue.

7. The elderly and middle-aged ("new" elderly in 2010) are demanding increasingly new options in addition to existing traditional living arrangements, delivery of services, economic supports, and institutional care. Voting and the mass media are vital means to express these concerns.

In many areas, a chipping away of archaic structural forms is occurring, and this may be the only tolerated process of institutional innovation. One fascinating alternative is the creation of new forms of family, "fictive kin," by having one group of self-sufficient aged persons share an apartment with a second group of less mentally and physically capable elderly individuals, all residing together in a boarding house. A team of counselor and activity therapist play supportive roles to facilitate reaching the objectives of self-responsibility and independence of the competent and less competent participants (Streib and Hilker, 1980). Another alternative is the day hospital, a "grown-up" ambulatory-care clinic, where patients who do not require 24-hour in-hospital care come to the facility in the morning and return to their households in the evening after receiving medical care, rehabilitation, and social services as required (U.S. Department of Health, Education, and Welfare, 1972). A modification of the day hospital is the day care center whose major aim is to maintain in the community with their families aged persons who are not capable of independent functioning because of physical or psychosocial limitations (Cohen, 1973). The leadership of such programs has been vested in health professionals, although program components are geared to effect interaction, foster intimacy, and overcome isolation associated with long-term illness and impairment in the aged (Robins, 1974).

All these experimental programs of alternatives to dependency and total care have yet to be evaluated in relation to their costs compared to other forms of care, participant and family satisfaction, relieving inpatient bed demand, staff interest and gratification, and maintenance of level of functioning of the elderly. Still, they are exciting in their potential as interstitial quasi-institutionalized care systems, between the family and bureaucratized human service systems, with the prospect of being people-oriented and controlled.

These "halfway to institutionalization" programs, especially day care, with their short-term restorative, maintenance, and psychosocial activities for high risk elderly and post-hospitalized patients, cannot provide a long-term living environment for non-ambulatory or impaired elderly persons. The mandates of these programs at best can supply backstopping services to families that have elderly members in their households (Streib and Penna, 1982).

Considering that human beings require nurturance as well as health care, intimacy as well as privacy, interaction as well as isolation, emotional support as well as physical rehabilitation, and that these requisites are more critical to individuals as they become less sufficient and independent, the essential question is, where can these things be found in a society?

Family networks still persist in the face of organizational bureaucratization with its endemic structural properties and norms that result in treating people as commodities rather than as human beings. The simple and undeniable fact, so obvious that it is overlooked, is that family networks are pervasive as functional systems for large numbers of individuals in the United States, and, for that matter, in societies worldwide.

What is suggested here is to investigate the utility and viability of using the family network as an alternative or complementary living environment for its aged members. In this discussion, of course, family network refers to those persons who are "perceived" to be family and includes those who may be somewhat distantly related by blood or marriage such as second cousins and uncle- and aunt-in-law. Family network does not imply only members of the immediate family, for example, children and parents of the nuclear (conjugal) family of procreation.

Living Arrangements and Care Alternatives

It is anticipated that the proffering of economic and service incentives to units of family networks for the care of the aged under a contractual arrangement will make a difference. These supports, it is hypothesized, will increase the receptivity and willingness to provide an enhancing environment for the aged family member. The finding that the provision of support does not make a difference in the willingness of member units to

provide creative environments for elderly members—they will provide in any case—should not diminish the potential significance of the support package. The availability of service and economic options should facilitate and buttress the family's efforts in such endeavors.

The contract provision supplies a family with a set of expectations for a given time period and in a real sense frees its members to develop the bonding relationship, the emotional components of family linkages. Expected benefits—such as (a) a direct monthly allotment of funds; (b) specific tax write-off for expenses incurred; (c) a low-cost loan to renovate or build an addition to the home in which the elderly person can maintain independence in a physical setting with few architectural barriers; (d) the provision of income tax relief for assuming this responsibility; (e) availability of specific services, especially quality medical care, from established agencies that are necessary and convenient to the well-being of the family unit taking on the care–therapeutic role; and (f) property tax waiver with some formula proportional to dwelling usage, given singly or in combination to prospective providers of living environments for the elderly—reduce the possibility of economic devastation and enhance family self-fulfillment.

The dumping of impaired and frail elderly upon families by professionals has resulted in a mutually disastrous experience. The family sees its resources rapidly dwindling and is handicapped in its means to do things for its other members. It becomes guilt-ridden or neglectful; the thin rubber band of filial piety becomes stretched to the breaking point. By removing sacrifice and deficit living from the elderly member/family linkage, a modern version of filial responsibility can be effected. Removing the economic liabilities, and in their place offering a reward, and making available human service systems more responsive to the relief needs of families, such as the provision of day care and homebound services, provide motivation and time to develop mutually satisfactory interpersonal relationships. This is a prime function of family networks, the expressive component of filial responsibility.

Empirical Study of An Alternative

Recently two major studies were completed on the feasibility of providing economic and social supports to member units of extended families so that they could invite an elderly relative to live with them or nearby without any loss in their own efforts to achieve their goal of a quality existence (Sussman, 1977; Sussman, 1979). A few major findings are:

1. Over 80 percent of respondents in both studies were willing to take in an older person under some circumstances.

2. Respondents were asked to rank-order a number of economic and social supports that would provide "incentive" resources to the family. Economic supports were: rental or property tax deduction; food stamps; monthly check; income tax deduction; and low-cost home-improvement loan. The most preferred economic support was a monthly check of $200 for use by the family when the elderly relative lives in the household or nearby in the same community. The monthly check was preferred over any service support.

The service supports were: general services (chores including assistance in household, meals on wheels, homemaking, escort, and transportation); medical care; homemaker service (community planning agency to evaluate needs of family, elderly person, and service agencies and develop a coordinated plan); and a social center for older persons. The preferred service support was available quality medical care if the elderly relative lived as part of the respondent's household.

3. The statistical procedures of multivariate and multiple classification analyses were used to determine if the willingness to care for an elderly relative could be attributed to demographic and sociologic variables such as race, social class, or life cycle stage. These variables cannot explain willingness, or even preference for a particular support program. Rather, important correlates of willingness to take in an older person are perceptual and experiential variables. These include perception that the spouse is in agreement with the arrangement and whether the household will be crowded; the presence of relatives living sufficiently close by in the community to provide help when called on; and such personal factors as positive experiences with older people as a child or young adult and favorable attitudes toward the elderly. Of all the background variables only age and duration of marriage, both highly correlated, are related to having an elderly person live with the respondent. The younger the person is, the greater the expressed willingness for such a living arrangement.

4. Preference is overwelming to have the elderly relative live nearby in her or his own household rather than in the respondent's household (75% to 25%) with the same program of social and economic supports being provided. While this high preference is expressed, there is no diminution of willingness to care for the elderly relative in one's own household.

The conclusions of the research on social and economic supports for families have application for other types of informal support systems, those consisting of persons who are not related by blood or marriage but are viewed "like family." Such groupings provide not only services but comfort—the requisite love, intimacy, and solidarity. The research emphasis is not on the immediate family where children looked after aging and failing parents, but on a larger group, the family network. The family network consists of those persons who are perceived to be family by the respondent and to include those distantly related by blood or marriage such as second or third cousins or uncles- or aunts-in-law.

This suggested late-twentieth-century living environment for the elderly is an untested formulation. Research and demonstrations, one building on the other, can determine the viability of the approach. First, *we have determined* the condition and circumstances under which members of varied family networks are willing to care for the elderly.

Reports of a person's willingness to develop a creative living arrangement with older relatives are not the same as doing it. Consequently there is a need for quasi-experimental field demonstrations using experimental and control groups, national income maintenance and housing allowance studies to establish actual participation and test its consequences. These demonstrations will also determine definitively the social and economic cost/benefits for varied types of family network–home care arrangements.

Such demonstrations, after appropriate evaluation, should also consider the possible changes in service agencies that would result in the adjustment of services to the needs of home care. Returning the elderly to the care of the family would be compatible with recent efforts to reduce the inefficiency and the red tape that have come to characterize the operation of health, social, and welfare institutions and to return the responsibility for care to the community and ultimately to the family where it naturally resided in the past.

Serious attention should be given to the development of this auxiliary care system. This would require a reevaluation of current policies and programs of institutional care of the elderly. Supportive activities to help the family in maintaining the elderly member in the home will undoubtedly increase. Currently, interest is greater in the beginnings of a movement to develop more responsive client care systems around individuals (bringing services into the home) instead of requiring clients to enter large-scale bureaucratized care and custodial systems. Discovering ways to combine family and professional labor power should auger well for existing human service systems. It provides rationale for a new policy and changed functions, the basis for their continued existence in the future.

In a 1978 survey completed by The National Opinion Research Center, University of Chicago (U.S. Bureau of the Census, 1980a) attitudes on the issue of older persons sharing a home with their grown children were investigated. Approximately 48 percent of respondents said it was a bad idea, 35 per-

cent a good idea; and 17 percent said that "it depends" (U.S. Bureau of the Census, 1980a). The almost 50 percent rejection of the notion of having elderly parents live in one's household is not surprising, since the prospects of receiving various forms of assistance from support systems were not presented as options. What is encouraging is the almost 10 percent drop in the "bad idea" perception; a 4 percent increment in the view that it is a "good idea" over the five-year period; and a steady increase in the "it depends" group from 11 percent in 1973 to 17 percent in 1978 (see Figure 1).

Provisions of appropriate economic and social supports to families would transform the majority of the hesitant group—those in the "it depends" category—into home providers. Such back-up supports would likely increase the public perception that providing a healthful environment for elderly relatives and all household residents is neither a bad idea nor an impossible task.

Not to be overlooked in the search for empirical data are the lobbying efforts of professional administrators for more institutionalized human service systems and

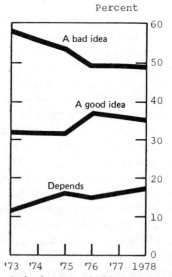

Figure 1. Attitudes toward older persons sharing home with their grown children. SOURCE: U.S. Bureau of the Census, *American Families and Living Arrangements,* Current Population Reports, Special Studies, Series P-23, #104, 1980.

larger budgets. The misperceptions of many practioners and researchers about the bases for a family's involvement with elderly members are further indications of the need for empirical data on alternative care systems for the elderly. The lack of familism and nucleated family structure are major reasons given for the American family's inability to "care for its own." Incentives in the form of economic or social benefits are considered appropriate behaviors of non-family organizations and institutions, but these same rewards have been considered disconsonant with the ideology and ethos of the family and demeaning of its values.

We do not accept this posture and find that rewards, incentives, reciprocity, exchange, and contracts are basic processes and products of everyday life. Families are not immune to them but, in fact, need them in order to survive. The proposed alternative to institutionalization of the aged in the remaining decades of this century integrates the normative, rational demands of a bureaucratic society for fiscal responsibility and cost-effectiveness with the more idiosyncratic norms of family networks where "blood is thicker than water" and where emotions are more powerful bonds than contracts.

SUMMARY

In this chapter I have presented a number of analyses that explain historic and ongoing changes in family structure, the behavior of family members, and the factors that impinge on the survival and the quality of life of elderly persons. These analyses have been organized around themes, each with its own set of assumptions, concepts, and hyptheses with clinical and empirical data to support them. The stance assumed was to select specific themes and then to elaborate, thus providing the most robust explanation of family-elderly member life-styles and relationships.

The first of these themes was family-bureaucratic organization linkages, and how family members function as facilitators, protectors, and mediators for elderly members in efforts of the latter to handle the normative demands of institutional and organizational bureaucracies. This is a critical modern-day issue, since the bureaucratization of provider systems is a worldwide phenomenon.

The task, therefore, is for the family to develop competence for handling and changing such bureaucratized social systems, largely human service ones that essentially control the life-styles of old people. To understand the potentialities of developing competencies in dealings with nonprimary groups through resocialization and other processes, exchange theory was indicated. Exchange theory components such as cost, reward, reciprocation, profit, reinforcement, power, and distributive justice provide logical explanations of family–elderly, family–organizational, and elderly–organizational linkage.

Understanding linkages, especially their conditions and processes, requires knowledge of what is a family, how best to describe it, and ways the family is perceived and used by functionaries of bureaucratized systems in their dealings with clients, patients, or customers. Suggested is a bipartite definition: the conjugal family form, spouses and their offspring, established by contract, the most visible and legitimized form in relation to rights and responsibilities; and the "everyday family," a non-kinship-based structure, composed of individuals in a cohabitating domestic relationship that provides love and emotional bonding and is sexually consequential. The "everyday family," therefore, includes sanctioned and unsanctioned variant forms such as group marriage and communal, lesbian, and homosexual life-styles.

On the assumption that families are basic emotional networks and the search for such interactional support, especially by elderly members, is continuous, the emergence of forms of family that differ from the nuclear family of procreation and may provide alternative emotional and economic supports is detailed. Special emphasis is on the kin family network and its potentialities for support of aged members living in their own households. For elderly individuals unwilling or unable to live independently, new forms of family such as communal and everyday families consisting of non-relatives are examined. Black, Hispanic, Puerto Rican, Vietnamese, and other ethnic and racial minority elderly are more likely than non-minority elderly to be connected into extended kin networks because of cultural traditions and limited economic resources.

Abuse and violence are found in a substantial number of intergenerational households and relationships. Such behaviors are bidirectional. There are reported child and elder abuses. The incidence of this behavior is likely to increase as families are given more responsibilities for the care of their aged members.

Intergenerational linkages and inheritance transfers along family lines have historically been basic processes of generational continuity and in the provision of emotional support for aged members. Patterns of serial reciprocity have characterized these transfers where equities controlled by the elderly testator are eventually conveyed to the young with implicit understanding that the latter will care for their aged parents. The historic trend toward universal and society-wide support and care systems diminished the importance of inheritance for sustaining the economic well-being of the family. Federal initiatives that emphasize the primacy of the family and one's heritage, promulgation of the notion of self-help and caring for one's own kith and kin, and reduction in federal expenditures for human services now make intergenerational linkages and transfers extremely critical processes for the well-being of elderly and family members. This situation is examined, and the functions of inheritance for emotional bonding and economic sustenance of families and their elderly members over generational time are discussed.

Also considered in this chapter are the increasing incidence of divorce and remarriage and the plethora of life-styles that may modify the normal pattern of intergenerational transfers along blood lines. The current pattern of intergenerational transfers may be modified with equities bequeathed to non-relatives who care for the elderly, with an increasing incidence of disinheritance litigation.

While societies worldwide are increasingly assuming control over their members through the bureaucratization of their social systems and concomitantly are providing for those who are not producers, the ability of these societies to continue such support is problematic. Elites are asking whether their societies have reached the "absorptive capacity" to handle further development and organization of services for their citizens.

While claimants of this view of economic insufficiency can be challenged, what is more salient from a humanistic perspective of aging with dignity is the prevention of too early an institutionalization of the elderly. Consequently, in the final section of this chapter, alternatives to institutionalization were discussed, and the feasibility of providing economic and human service supports for member units of kin family networks was examined. Such recommendations fit the proposed exchange model: harmonizing the rational demands and decreasing efficiency of bureaucratic organizations with the more idiosyncratic norms and emotional bondings of family and friendship networks. Such an accommodation is mandatory if the elderly are to be given increased options and autonomy in relation to roles, life-styles, and living arrangements.

REFERENCES

Adams, B. M. 1968. *Kinship in an Urban Setting.* Chicago: Markham Publishing Company.

Adams, B. N. 1970. Isolation, function, and beyond: American kinship in the 1960's. *Journal of Marriage and the Family* 32:575-597.

Aging Services News. 1983. States give ok to pass medicaid familial responsibility laws. 137 (Apr. 29):P1.

Aldous, J., and Hill, R. 1965. Social cohesion, linkage type, and intergenerational transmission. *Social Forces* 43:471-482.

Angelou, M. 1969. *I Know Why the Caged Bird Sings.* New York: Random House.

Arling, G., 1976. The elderly widow and her family,

neighbors and friends. *Journal of Marriage and the Family* 38:757–768.

Ball, D. W. 1972. The family as a sociological problem: Conceptualization of the taken-for-granted as prologue to social problem analysis. *Social Problems* 10:295–307.

Barnekov, T. K. 1980. *An Assessment of the Social Service Needs of the Elderly in Group Subsidized Housing.* Newark: University of Delaware, College of Urban Affairs and Public Policy.

Bender, D. R. 1967. A refinement of the concept of household: Families, co-residence and domestic functions. *American Anthropologist* 69:493–504.

Bengtson, V. L. 1975. Generation and family effects in value socialization. *American Sociological Review* 40:358–371.

Bengtson, V. L., and Black, K. D. 1973. Intergenerational relations and continuities in socialization. *In,* P. Baltes and W. Schaie, (eds.), *Personality and Socialization,* Ch. 9. New York: Academic Press.

Bengtson, V. L., and Cutler, N. E. 1976. Generations and intergenerational relations: Perspectives on age groups and social change. *In* R. H. Binstock and E. Shanas (eds.), *Handbook of Aging and the Social Sciences,* 1st ed. New York: Van Nostrand Reinhold.

Bengtson, V. L., and deTerre E. 1980. Aging and family relations: A decade review. *Marriage and Family Review* 2:51–76.

Bengtson, V. L., and Kuypers, J. A. 1971. Generational difference in the developmental stake. *Aging and Human Development* 2:249–260.

Bengtson, V. L., and Treas, J. 1980. Intergenerational relations and mental health. *In* R. B. Sloane and J. E. Birren (eds.), *Handbook of Mental Health and Aging.* Englewood Cliffs, NJ: Prentice-Hall.

Bengtson, V. L., Olander, E., and Haddad, A. 1975. The "generation gap" and age family members. *In* J. Gubruim (ed.), *Late Life: Recent Developments in the Sociology of Age.* Springfield, Ill.: Charles C. Thomas.

Bild, B. R., and Havighurst, R. 1976. Senior citizens in great cities: The case of Chicago. *The Gerontologist* 16:1–88.

Billingsley, A. 1968. *Black Families in White America.* Englewood Cliffs, N.J.: Prentice-Hall.

Black, K. D., and Bengtson, V. L. 1973. Solidarity across generations: Elderly parents and their middle aged children. Paper presented at annual meeting of the Gerontological Society.

Blau, P. M. 1955. *The Dynamics of Bureaucracy.* Chicago: University of Chicago Press.

Blau, P. M. 1964. *Exchange and Power in Social Life.* New York: John Wiley.

Blau, Z. S. 1973. *Old Age in a Changing Society.* New York: New Viewpoints.

Blenkner, M. 1965. Social work and family relationships in later life with some thoughts on filial maturity. *In* E. Shanas and G. Streib (eds.), *Social Structure and the Family: Generational Relations,* pp. 46–59. Englewood Cliffs, N.J.: Prentice-Hall.

Blenkner, M. 1969. The normal dependencies of aging. *In* R. Kalish (ed.), *The Dependencies of Old People.* Ann Arbor, Mich.: Institute of Gerontology.

Block, M., and Sinnott, J. D. (eds.), 1979. *The Battered Elder Syndrome: An Exploratory Study.* College Park: Center on Aging, University of Maryland.

Bowen, M. 1978. *Family Therapy in Clinical Practice.* New York: Jason Aronson.

Branch, L. G., and Jette, A. M. 1981. The Framingham disability study: Social disability among the aging. *American Journal of Public Health,* 71:1202–1210.

Breslau, N., and Haug, M. R. 1972. The elderly aid the elderly: The senior friends project. *Social Security Bulletin* 35:9–15.

Brody, E. 1970. The etiquette of filial behavior. *Aging and Human Development* 1:87–94.

Brody, E. 1978. The formal support network: Congregate treatment setting for residents with senescent brain dysfunction. Paper presented at the Conference on Clinical Aspects of Altzheimer's Disease and Senile Dementia, sponsored by the National Institutes of Mental Health, Bethesda, Md., Dec. 6–8.

Brody, E. 1977. *Long-Term Care of Older People: A Practical Guide.* New York: Human Sciences Press.

Brooks, D., 1979. Where there is a will there's a way. Masters thesis, Virginia Polytechnic Institute and State University.

Browder, O. L. 1969. Recent patterns of testate succession in the United States and England. *Michigan Law Review* 67:1303–1360.

Bultena, G., and Wood, V. 1969. The American retirement community: Bane or blessing. *Journal of Gerontology* 24:209–217.

Cantor, M. H. 1975. Life space and the social support system of the inner city elderly of New York City. *The Gerontologist* 15:23–27.

Cantor, M. H. 1979. Neighbors and friends: An overlooked resource in the informal support system. *Research on Aging* 4:434–463.

Cantor, M. H. 1980. Caring for the frail elderly: Impact on family, friends, and neighbors. Paper presented at the annual meeting of the Gerontological Society of America, San Diego.

Carp. F. M. 1966. *A Future for the Aged: Victoria Plaza and Its Residents.* Austin: University of Texas Press.

Cates, J. N., and Sussman, M. B. 1982. Family systems and inheritance. *In* J. N. Cates and M. B. Sussman (eds.), *Family Systems and Inheritance Patterns,* pp. 1–24. New York: Haworth Press.

Chevan, A., and Korson, J. H. 1975. Living arrangements of widows in the United States and Israel, 1960 and 1961. *Demography* 21:505–518.

Cicirelli, V. G. 1981. *Helping Elderly Parents: The Role of Adult Children.* Boston, Mass.: Auburn House Publishing Company.

Cogswell, B. E., and Sussman, M. B. 1972. Changing family and marriage forms: Complications for human service systems. *Family Coordinator* 21:505–516.

Cohen, M. G. 1973. Alternative to institutional care of the aged. *Social Casework* 54:447–452.

Conover, P. W. 1975. An analysis of communes and intentional communities with particular attention to sexual and genderal relations. *Family Coordinator* 24:453–464.

Cornell, G. P., and Gelles, R. 1982. Adolescent to parent violence. *Urban Social Change Review* 15:8–14.

Croog, S. H., Lipson, A., and Levine, S. 1972. Help patterns in severe illness: The role of kin networks, non-family sources. *Journal of Marriage and the Family* 34:32–41.

Cumming, E. N., and Henry, W. 1961. *Growing Old.* New York: Basic Books.

Cutler, S. J. 1973. Voluntary association participation and life satisfaction: A cautionary research note. *Journal of Gerontology* 28:96–100.

Dacy, N. 1980. *How to Avoid Probate—Updated.* New York: Crown Publishers.

Dowd, J. J. 1975. Aging as exchange: A preface to theory. *Journal of Gerontology* 30:585–594.

Duffy, E. J. 1978. Grandparent's cottages, pp. 1–7. Rockville, Md.: Department of Community Development and Housing Assistance, mimeographed.

Dunham, A. 1963. The methods, process and frequency of wealth transmission at death. *University of Chicago Law Review* 30:241–285.

Edwards, J. N., and Klemmack, D. L. 1973. Correlates of life satisfaction: A re-examination. *Journal of Gerontology* 33:497–502.

Feldman, H. 1965. Development of the husband–wife relationship. A research report of the National Institute of Mental Health (mimeographed). Ithaca, N.Y.: Department of Human Development and Family Studies, Cornell University.

Furstenberg, F. F. 1979. Recycling the family: Perspectives for a neglected family form. *Marriage and Family Review* 3 (1):12–22.

Gerstel, N., and Gross, H. E. 1982. Commuter marriages: A review. *In* H. E. Gross and M. B. Sussman (eds.), *Alternatives to Traditional Family Living.* New York: Haworth Press.

Greeley, A. M. 1971. *Why Can't They Be Like Us.* New York: Dutton.

Guttmann, D., et al. 1977. *The Impact of Needs. Knowledge, Ability and Living Arrangements on Decision Making of the Elderly.* Washington, D.C.: The Catholic University of America.

Guttmann, D. et al. 1978. Informal support utilization by white ethnic aged. Paper presented at the 31st annual Gerontological Society Meeting, Dallas, TX.

Hall, C. M. 1974. Variant family process. Draft paper.

Harel, Z., and Harel, B. 1978. On-site coordinated services in age-segregated and age-integrated public housing. *The Gerontologist* 18:153–158.

Hays, W. C., and Mindel, C. H. 1973. Extended kin relations in black and white families. *Journal of Marriage and the Family* 35:51–57.

Hill, R., Foote, N., Aldous, J., Carlson, R., and MacDonald, R. 1970. *Family Development in Three Generations.* Cambridge, Mass.: Schenkman.

Homans, G. C. 1961. *Social Behavior: Its Elementary Forms.* New York: Harcourt, Brace & World.

Houseknecht, S. 1982. Voluntary childlessness in the 1980s: A significant increase? *Marriage and Family Review* 5:51–70.

Jackson, J. J. 1971a. Sex and social class variations in black aged parent–adult child relationships. *Aging and Human Development* 2:96–107.

Jackson, J. J. 1971b. The blacklands of gerontology. *Aging and Human Development* 7:168–178.

Jackson, J. J. 1972a. Marital life among aging blacks. *Family Coordinator* 21:21–27.

Jackson, J. J. 1972b. Comparative life-styles and family and friend relationships among older black women. *Family Coordinator* 21:477–485.

Jackson, J. J. 1973. Family organization and ideology. *In* K. Miller and R. Dreger (eds.), *Comparative Studies of Blacks and Whites.* New York: Academic Press.

Jackson, J. J. 1980. *Minorities and Aging.* Belmont, Calif.: Wadsworth.

Jette, A. M., and Branch, L. G. 1981. The Framingham disability study: 11 Physical disability among the aging. *American Journal of Public Health* 71:1211–1216.

Johnson, C. L. 1978. Family support systems of elderly Italian Americans. *Journal of Minority Aging* 3:34–41.

Jones, L. Y. 1980. *Great Expectations.* New York: Ballantine Books.

Jourard, S. M. 1971. *The Transparent Self,* rev. ed. New York: John Wiley.

Kanter, R. M. 1972. *Commitment and Community: Communes and Utopias in Sociological Perspective.* Cambridge, Mass.: Howard University Press.

Kelley, H. H., and Thibault, J. W. 1954. Experimental studies of group problem solving and process. *In* G. Lindzely (ed.), *Handbook of Social Psychology,* Vol. II. Cambridge, Mass.: Addison-Wesley.

Kerckhoff, A. C. 1965. Nuclear and extended family relationships: Normative and behavioral analysis. *In* E. Shanas and G. Streib (eds.), *Social Structures and Family: Generational Relations,* pp. 93–112. Englewood Cliffs, N.J.: Prentice-Hall.

Kerckhoff, A. C. 1966. Family and retirement. *In* I. H. Simpson and J. C. McKinney (eds.), *Social Aspects of Aging.* Durham, N.C.: Duke University Press.

Klatzky, S. R. 1973. *Patterns of Contacts With Relatives.* Washington, D.C.: American Sociological Association.

Kreps, J. M. 1962. Aggregate income and labor force participation of the aged. *Law and Contemporary Problems* 27:52–66.

Larson, R. 1978. Thirty years of research on subjective well-being of older Americans. *Journal of Gerontology* 33:109–125.

Lau, E., and Kosberg, J. 1978. Abuse of the elderly by informal care providers: Practice and research issues, pp. 1–7, 31st annual meeting of the Gerontological Society of America, mimeographed.

Lawton, M., and Cohen, J. 1974. The generality of housing impact on the well-being of older people. *Journal of Gerontology* 29:194–200.

Lee, G. R. 1979a. Children and the elderly: Interaction and morale. *Research on Aging* 1:335–360.

Lee, G. R. 1979b. The effects of social networks in the family. *In* W. R. Burr et al. (eds.), *Contemporary Theories About the Family*, pp. 27–56. New York: Macmillan.

Lee, G. R., and Ellithorpe, E. 1978. Intergenerational exchange and subjective well-being among the elderly. *Journal of Marriage and the Family* 44:217–224.

Libby, R. W., and Whitehurst, R. N. (eds.), 1973. *Renovating Marriage: Toward New Sexual Life-Styles*. Danville, Calif.: Consensus Publishers.

Linton, R. 1936. *The Study of Man*. New York: Appleton-Century-Crofts.

Litman, T. J. 1971. Health care and the family: A three-generational analysis. *Medical Care* 9:67–81.

Litwak, E. 1960a. Occupational mobility and extended family cohesion. *American Sociological Review* 25:9–21.

Litwak, E. 1960b. Geographic mobility and extended family cohesion. *American Sociological Review* 25:385–394.

Lopata, H. S. 1978. Contributions of extended families to the support systems of metropolitan area widows: Limitations of the modified kin network. *Journal of Marriage and the Family* 40:355–364.

Lowenthal, M. F., and Haven, C. 1968. Interaction and adaptation: Intimacy as a clinical variable. *American Sociological Reveiw* 33:20–30.

Mancini, J. A. 1979. Family relationships and morale among people 65 years of age and older. *American Journal of Orthopsychiatry* 292–300.

Manns, W. 1981. Support systems of significant others in black families. *In* H. P. McAdoo (ed.), *Black Families*, pp. 238–251. Beverly Hills, Calif.: Sage Publications.

Markides, K. S., and Martin, H. W. 1979. A causal model of life satisfaction among the elderly. *Journal of Gerontology* 34:86–93.

Markides, K. S., Costley, D. S., and Rodriguez, L. 1981. Perceptions of intergenerational relations and psychological well-being among elderly Americans: A causal model. *International Journal of Aging and Human Development* 13:43–52.

Martin, E. P., and Martin, J. M. 1978. *The Black Extended Family*. Chicago: University of Chicago Press.

McAdoo, H. P. 1977. The impact of extended family variables upon the upward mobility of black families. Final report to Office of Child Development, The Department of Health, Education and Welfare, Washington: D.C..

McAdoo, H. P. 1982a. Stress absorbing systems in black families. *Family Relations* 31:479–488.

McAdoo, H. P. 1982b. Levels of stress and family support in black families. *In* H. McCubbin, A. Cauble,

and J. Patterson (eds.), *Family Stress, Coping and Social Support*. Springfield, Ill.: Charles C. Thomas Publications.

Moriwaki, S. Y. 1973. Self-disclosure, significant others and psychological well-being in old age. *Journal of Health and Social Behavior* 14:226–232.

Munnichs, J. 1977. Linkages of older people with their families and bureaucracy in the Netherlands. *In* E. Shanas and M. B. Sussman (eds.), *Older People, Family and Bureaucracy*. Durham, N.C.: Duke University Press.

Nau, L. Y. 1973. Why not family rehabilitation? *Journal of Rehabilitation* 39(3):14–17.

Noelker, L. S. 1975. Intimate relations in a residential home for the elderly. Ph.D. dissertation, Case Western Reserve University.

O'Neill, N., and O'Neill, G. 1972. Open marriage: A synergic model. *Family Coordinator* 21:403–409.

Orlando Sentinel, 1971. (July 21 and Aug. 20)

Paillat, P. 1977. Bureaucratization of old age: Determinants of the process, possible safeguards and reorientation. *In* E. Shanas and M. B. Sussman (eds.), *Older People, Family and Bureaucracy*. Durham, N.C.: Duke University Press.

Palmore, E., and Kivett, V. 1977. Change in life satisfaction: A longitudinal study of persons aged 46–70. *Journal of Gerontology* 32:311–316.

Palmore, E., and Maddox, G. 1977. Sociological aspects of aging. *In* E. Busse and E. Pfeiffer (eds.), *Behavior and Adaptation in Late Life*, 2nd ed. Boston: Little, Brown.

Parsons, T., and Fox, R. 1952. Illness and the modern American family. *Journal of Social Issues* 8:31–34.

Piotrowski, J. 1977. Old people in Poland: Family and bureaucracy. *In* E. Shanas and M. B. Sussman (eds.), *Older People, Family and Bureaucracy*. Durham, N.C.: Duke University Press.

Ramey, J. W. 1972. Emerging patterns for innovative behavior in marriage. *Family Coordinator* 21:435–456.

Ramey, J. W. 1975. Intimate groups and networks. Frequent consequences of sexually open marriage. *Family Coordinator* 24:515–520.

Rapoport, R., and Rapoport, R. N. 1975. Men, women, and equity. *Family Coordinator* 24:421–432.

Rathbone-McCuan, E. 1978. Intergenerational family violence and neglect: The aged as victims of reactivated and reverse neglect. Speech before the International Congress of Gerontology, Japan.

Rathbone-McCuan, E., and Hashimi, J. 1982. *Isolated Elders*, Ch. 8, pp. 177–210. Rockville, Md.: Aspen Systems Corporation.

Reiss, D. 1981. *The Family's Construction of Reality*. Cambridge, Mass.: Harvard University Press.

Riley, M. W. 1971. Social gerontology and the age stratification of society. *The Gerontologist* 11:79–87.

Robins, E. G. 1974. Therapeutic day care: Progress report on experiments to test the feasibility for third party reimbursement. Paper presented at 27th Annual Scientific Meeting of the Gerontological Society, Portland, Oreg.

Rosenfeld, J. 1979. *The Legacy of Aging: Inheritance and Disinheritance in Social Perspective.* Norwood, N.J.: Ablex Publishing Company.

Rosenfeld, J. 1980. Benevolent disinheritance. *Psychology Today* 3:48bb.

Rosenmayr, L. 1977. The family-source of hope for elderly of the future. *In* E. Shanas and M. B. Sussman (eds.), *Older People, Family and Bureaucracy.* Durham, N.C.: Duke University Press.

Rosenmayr, L. and Köckeis, E. 1965. *Unwelt und Familie Alter Menschen.* Berlin: Luchterland-Verlag.

Rosow, I. 1967. *Social Integration of the Aged.* New York: Basic Books.

Ross, H. R. 1978. *How to Develop a Neighborhood Family, an Action Manual.* Miami, Fla.: Northside Neighborhood Family Service, Inc.

Sanders, L. T., and Seelback, W. C. 1981. Variations in preferred care alternatives for the elderly: Family versus non-family sources. *Family Relations* 3:477.

Schneider, D. 1968. *American Kinship.* Englewood Cliffs, N.J.: Prentice-Hall.

Schorr, A. 1960. *Filial Responsibility in the Modern American Family.* Washington, D.C.: Social Security Administration, Department of Health, Education and Welfare.

Seelbach, W. C. 1978. Correlates of aged parents' filial responsibility expectations and realizations. *Family Coordinator* 4:341-350.

Shanas, E. 1962. *The Health of Older People: Social Survey.* Cambridge, Mass.: Harvard University Press.

Shanas, E. 1967. Family help patterns and social class in three countries. *Journal of Marriage and the Family* 29:257-266.

Shanas, E. 1968. A note on restriction of life space: Attitudes of age cohorts. *Journal of Health and Social Behavior* 9:86-90.

Shanas, E. 1979a. Social myth as hypothesis: The case of the family relations of old people. *The Gerontologist* 19:1-9.

Shanas, E. 1979b. The family as a social support system in old age. *The Gerontologist* 19:169-174.

Shanas, E., and Sussman, M. B. 1981. The family in later life: Social structure and social policy. *In* R. Fogel, E. Hatfield, S. B. Kessler, and E. Shanas (eds.), *Aging: Stability and Change in the Family.* New York: Academic Press.

Shaw, M. E., and Costanzo, P. R. 1970. *Theories of Social Psychology.* New York: McGraw-Hill.

Sherif, M. 1966. *In Common Predicament.* Boston: Houghton Mifflin.

Sherman, S. 1975. Patterns of contacts for residents of age-segregated and age-integrated housing. *Journal of Gerontology* 30:103-107.

Shimkin, D. B., and Shimkin, E. M. 1975. The extended family in United States black societies: Findings and problems. Unpublished paper. Urbana-

Champaign, Ill.: Department of Anthropology, University of Illinois.

Shimkin, D. B., Louie, G. J., and Frate, D. 1973. The black extended family: A basic rural institution and a mechanism of urban adaptation. Paper presented at IX International Congress of Anthropological and Ethnological Sciences, Chicago.

Shimkin, D. B., Shimkin, E. M., and Frate, D. A. (eds.). 1975. *The Extended Family in Black Societies.* The Hague: Mouton.

Silverman, A. G. 1978. As parents grow older: An intervention model. Paper presented at the 31st annual meeting of the Gerontological Society of America, Dallas, Tex.

Silverman, A. G., and Brahce, C. 1979. As parents grow older. *Journal of Gerontological Social Work, 2.*

Silverman, A. G., Kahn, B. H., and Anderson, G. 1977. A model for working with multigenerational families. *Social Case Work,* 131-135.

Simos, B. 1973. Adult children and their aging parents. *Social Work* 18:78-85.

Smith, J. R., and Smith, L. G. (eds.), 1974. *Beyond Monogamy: Recent Studies of Sexual Alternatives in Marriage.* Baltimore: The John Hopkins Press.

Soldo, B. J. 1980. America's elderly in the 1980's. *Population Bulletin,* Vol. 35, No. 4, p. 26. Washington, D.C.: Population References Bureau.

Somerville, R. M. 1972. The future of family relationships in the middle and older years. *Family Coordinator* 21:487-498.

Stein, P. 1978. The life-styles and life chances of the never married. *Marriage and Family Review* 1:1-11.

Steinmetz, S. K. 1981. Elder abuse. *Aging,* 6-10.

Steinmetz, S. K., and Straus, M. J. 1978. *Violence in the Family.* New York: Dodd, Mead and Company.

Stern, P. M. 1980. *Lawyers on Trial.* New York: Times Books.

Streib, G. F., and Hilker, M. 1980. The cooperative "family": An alternative life-style for the elderly. *Alternative Lifestyles* 3:167-184.

Streib, G. F., and Penna, M. H. 1982. Anticipating transitions: Possible options in family forms. *Annals* 464:104-119.

Sussman, M. B. 1953. The help pattern in the middle class family. *American Sociological Review* 18:22-28.

Sussman, M. B. 1959. The isolated family: Fact or fiction. *Social Problems* 6:333-340.

Sussman, M. B. 1960. Intergenerational relationships and social role changes in middle age. *Journal of Gerontology* 15:71-75.

Sussman, M. B. 1960. Intergenerational relationships and social role changes in middle age. *Journal of Gerontology* 15:71-75.

Sussman, M. B. (ed.). 1972. *Non-traditional Family Forms in the 1970's.* Minneapolis, Minn.: National Council on Family Relations.

Sussman, M. B. 1975. The four F's of variant family forms and marriage styles. *Family Coordinator* 24:563-576.

Sussman, M. B. 1979. Social and economic supports and family environments, for the elderly. Washington, D.C.: Administration on Aging, Grant #90-A-316, final report.

Sussman, M. B. 1977. *Incentives and Family Environments for the Elderly,* Washington, D.C.: Administration on Aging. Grant 90-A-316. Final report.

Sussman, M. B. and Cogswell, B. E. 1972. The meaning of variant and experimental marriage styles and family forms in the 1970s. *Family Coordinator* 21:375–381.

Sussman, M. B., Cates, J. N., and Smith, D. T. 1970a. *The Family and Inheritance.* New York: Russell Sage Foundation.

Sussman, M. B., et al., 1970b. Changing families in a changing society. *In: Report to the President: White House Conference on Children,* pp. 227–238. Washington, D.C.: U.S. Government Printing Office.

Sussman, M. B., Cogswell, B. E., and Marciano, T. D. (eds.). 1975. The second experience: Variant family forms and life-styles. *Family Coordinator,* 24.

Teski, M. 1981. *Living Together: An Ethnography of a Retirement Hotel.* Washington, D.C.: University Press of America.

Thibault, J., and Kelley, H. 1959. *The Social Psychology of Groups.* New York: John Wiley.

Tinker, A. 1976. *Housing the Elderly: How Successful are Granny Annexes?* Occasional paper. London: Department of Environments.

Torres-Gil, F. M. 1976. Age, health and culture: An examination of health among Spanish-speaking elderly. Paper presented to the First National Hispanic Conference on Health and the Human Services, Los Angeles.

Troll, L. E. 1971. The family of later life: A decade review. *Journal of Marriage and Family* 33:263–290.

Troll, L. E., Miller, S., and Atchley, R. 1979. *Families in Later Life.* Belmont, Calif.: Wadsworth Publishing Company.

U.S. Bureau of the Census. 1976. *Current Populations Reports,* Series P-20, No. 306, Marital status and living arrangements (Mar.). Washington, D.C.: U.S. Government Printing Office.

U.S. Bureau of the Census. 1980a. *Current Population Reports,* Series P-23, No. 104, American families and living arrangements. Washington, D.C.: U.S. Government Printing Office.

U.S. Bureau of the Census. 1980b. *Current Population Reports,* Series P-20, Nos. 349, 365, Marital status and living arrangements (Mar.). Washington, D.C.: U.S. Government Printing Office.

U.S. Department of Health, Education and Welfare. 1972. *Aging,* No. 215–216 Sept.–Oct.).

U.S. National Center for Health Statistics. 1983. Births, marriages, divorces and deaths for 1981. *Monthly Vital Statistics Report,* Vol. 30, No. 12. Hyattsville, Md.: Public Health Service.

Veevers, J. E. 1979. Voluntary childlessness: A review of issues and evidence. *Marriage and Family Review* 2:3–26.

Weber, M. 1947.*The Theory of Social and Economic Organization.* New York: Oxford University Press.

Weitzman, L. J. 1981. *The Marriage Contract,* Ch. 15. New York: Free Press.

Woehrer, C. E. 1982. The influence of ethnic families on intergenerational relationships and later life transitions. *Annals* 464:65–78.

Wylie, F. M. 1971. Attitudes toward aging and the aged among black Americans: Some historical perspectives. *Aging and Human Development.* 2:260–269.

Youmans, E. G. 1963. *Aging Patterns in a Rural and Urban Area of Kentucky.* Lexington: University of Kentucky Agricultural Experiment Station.

15
HOUSING AND LIVING ENVIRONMENTS OF OLDER PEOPLE

M. Powell Lawton
Philadelphia Geriatric Center

The development of concern among social and behavioral scientists for the environments where older people live is reflected in the succession of treatments of this topic given in various handbooks of aging. Kleemeier's (1959) pioneering contribution served to define this major subject area of gerontology. Another 16 years passed before the next major effort (Carp, 1976), but two more followed in quick succession (Lawton, 1977; Kasl and Rosenfield, 1980). One must also mention an extremely rich annotated bibliography in housing services for the aged up to 1981 (Taylor, 1981). Literature reviews from Australia (Kendig, 1981) and England (Tinker, 1981) have appeared recently.

The body of empirical and theoretical literature grows regularly at a pace that demands frequent updating of efforts to understand the import of these new contributions in relation to earlier environmental research and to other areas of gerontology. Thus this present chapter will build upon earlier efforts and incorporate the newer literature regarding residential arrangements of the elderly. It will examine current knowledge and relate it to policy issues. Residential decisions, planned housing, housing in ordinary neighborhoods, the residential environment, and housing policy will be discussed. The central theme of the discussions will be the older person's taking either a proactive or a passive stance in relation to the environment.

Issues in the Earlier Literature of Housing Older People

While few issues related to this topic can be considered settled, some have been dealt with at length in the gerontological literature. For instance, earlier research on planned housing for older persons showed favorable effects on older tenants (Carp, 1966) and some advantages of age density (Roscow, 1967). It led to a rich variety of descriptive studies of planned housing types, such as retirement villages (Burgess, 1961), mobile home parks (Johnson, 1971), or congregate housing (Lawton, 1969). The "discovery" of environment by behavioral scientists led to enthusiam over the possibilities of using gerontological knowledge in designing housing, institutions, and even neighborhoods for older users (Howell, 1980; Koncelik, 1976; Lawton, 1975).

A major effort was devoted to the study of the effects of involuntary relocation of institutional residents (reviewed by Coffman, 1981; Schulz and Brenner, 1977). The conclusions regarding this issue are far from settled at present.

Research at the neighborhood level concentrated on how older people construed their local environments (Regnier, 1976) and used the resources in these environments (Cantor, 1979; Carp, 1976; Newcomer, 1976).

Several theoretical approaches to understanding these and other phenomena have been advanced (recently published in Lawton et al., 1982). While a quiescent period characterized research on these subjects in the latter half of the 1970s, renewed concern over the interpretation of our person–environment knowledge in theoretical terms has begun to occur (Carp, 1983; Golant, 1984; Moos and Igra, 1980; Parr, 1980; Windley and Scheidt, 1980). In overview, most of these theoretical approaches (notably excepting Carp) have emphasized environment as a determinant of older people's behavior. Thus the search for ways of improving the environment through good design and planning is typically justified in terms of their favorable "effect" on older people's well-being.

Newer Concerns in the Environment and Aging Literature

While all the issues mentioned continue to be addressed, others have developed and in some cases have assumed a dominant position. Where the economics of housing the elderly and its policy implications were originally treated very lightly, recent years have seen public programs analyzed in terms of cost, equity, and acceptability within various frameworks (Rabushka and Jacobs, 1980; Struyk and Soldo, 1980).

With such a macro view predominating, the realization has grown that planned housing and institutions constitute only a small portion of the residential settings where older people live. The emphasis has thus turned strongly to questions of how older people deal with their existing unplanned housing in ordinary neighborhoods (Lawton and Hoover, 1981; Struyk, 1977).

Earlier migration studies described the gross aspects of residential relocation. Newer research has turned to subleties such as return migration (Longino, 1979), sun-belt migration (Biggar, 1980a), and urban-to-rural migration (Beale, 1975).

Neighborhoods have been increasingly recognized as sources of social as well as physical support (Abrams, 1981; Gottesman and Saperstein, 1981; Ruffini and Todd, 1981). The specific social problem of criminal victimization of older people and their fear of crime has concerned many recent writers (Lawton, 1980/81; Liang et al., in press; Yin, 1980).

The varieties of housing alternatives have increased and caught the attention of service planners as well as researchers: the single-room-occupancy hotel (Eckert, 1980), the mobile home (Haley, in press), accessory apartments (Carlin and Fox, 1981), home sharing (Streib, Folts, and Hilker, in press), and owner–renter match-up services (Dobkin, 1980).

These newer research emphases have in common their implication that one's residence is a dynamic component of the total behavioral space. One chooses one's environment, adjusts to it, modifies it, or decides to move to a new environment. The older person as an active agent (Lawton, 1980d), and residential adjustment as a continuing series of decisions, have thus become highlighted as an overall focus for new research in environment and aging. Carp (1983) in particular presents the view. In the primary ecological process, the person responds to environmental pressure; in the more active view, the person has needs and preferences that lead her to search the environment for means of satisfying these needs.

RESIDENTIAL DECISIONS

The study of residential decisions has usually been concerned with such changes of resident as migration, purchase of a new home, or institutionalization. The approach taken in this chapter is to look at a residential status as being constantly determined by a series of ongoing decisions that include the decision to remain in place. This broad definition highlights the fact that residential change, when it comes, is usually the result of an extended series of personal and environmental events, each involving a set of decisions. Some decisions lead to change but not moving—repairs or remodeling, for example. Some lead to remaining in an unchanged condition. All decisions in turn may have consequences for well-being. Social policies, implicit or explicit, can have profound effects on all magnitudes of residential choice and their outcomes. The fact that remaining in place is by far the most frequent decision made by older people should lead us to look more closely at the complex of factors that contribute to residential immobility and consider more carefully than has been done to date what some of the consequences of this decision may be for both the individual and society.

Theoretical Approaches to Residential Decision-Making

It may well be that one of the thickest nodes formed by the intersection of the concerns of multiple disciplines lies in residential decision making. Theories of residential behavior have posited as central elements: "push-pull" factors (Lee, 1966); family life cycle (Rossi, 1980); social role (Speare, 1970); environmental stress and personal inertia (Wolpert, 1966); psychological attachment (O'Bryant, 1982), and economic costs and personal benefits (Struyk, 1980).

Perhaps the most comprehensive model of residential behavior among the aged was articulated by Wiseman (1979, 1980), a model tht incorporates most of the important elements from all of the intellectual perspectives listed above. As shown in Figure 1, the model distinguishes the decision to move from the decision as to where to move ("destination selection"). It posits "triggering mechanisms" (life events) and both personal and environmental characteristics as determinants of these decisions. It also is equally applicable to remaining in place ("no move").

Moving and Staying

Overall, older people typically resolve the residential decision in favor of remaining in place. In the United States less than 6 percent of the aged moved between 1975 and 1976 (U.S. Bureau of the Census, 1978). While the residential movement of the general population in most other countries is less than in the United States, it is consistently greater than that of the elderly. For example, older people move only half as often as the young in France (Cribier, 1975).

It is necessary, however, to distinguish between long-distance moving (often referred to as "migration") and local moving, which appear to have quite different determinants and outcomes. Between 1975 and 1978 in the United States, for example, 61 percent of the moves made by older people were within the same county, and only 17 percent between states (U.S. Bureau of the Census, 1978).

Wiseman (1980) suggested a typology of moving that allows us to analyze some of the dynamics of residential relocation: amenity moves, environmental push, and assistance moves.

Amenity Moves. The motivation for amenity moves seems to be an active, self-chosen search for an improvement in quality of life. Sun-belt migration is the prototype of the amenity move. Chevan and Fischer (1979) demonstrated that interstate migration was linked to retirement. The new freedom associated with retirement is probably the major explanation for a "bulge" around age 65 in the interstate (but not local) migration rate, especially for men. Almost 20 percent of interstate moves made by those ages 55 + were reported in the Annual Housing Survey (AHS) as being due to retirement, while 12 percent "wanted a change of climate" (Long and Hansen, 1979). Not surprisingly, interstate migration is more likely among the more affluent (Biggar, 1980b). Among those who move, those who move greater distances are more likely to be married than those who do not (Flynn, 1980). So are those moving to sun-belt states as compared to others (Biggar, 1980a). Sun-belt migration was seen to

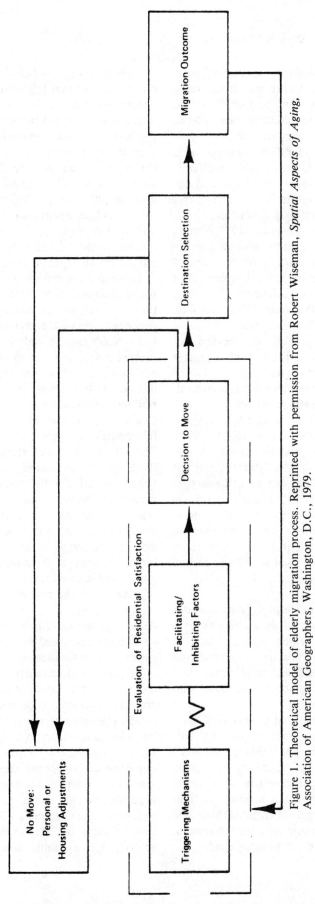

Figure 1. Theoretical model of elderly migration process. Reprinted with permission from Robert Wiseman, *Spatial Aspects of Aging*, Association of American Geographers, Washington, D.C., 1979.

result in highly significant streams of older people moving to California from seven noncontiguous states and to Florida and to Arizona from 5 noncontiguous states (Flynn, 1980). These three states account for 37 percent of all elderly interstate in-migration in the United States. Other clearly identifiable recreation areas such as the Ozarks and upper Michigan also attract older migrants (Beale, 1975; Fuguitt and Tordella, 1980).

Return migration (Longino, 1979; Serow, 1978), that is, an interstate move back to the state where one was born, is often an amenity move. Although the subjective aspects of such moves have been infrequently studied, one study showed that retired Parisians who moved back to the provinces where they were born were clearly seeking remembered satisfactions from earlier life as well as greater simplicity and quiet (Cribier, 1979). Half of all French retirement migration is return migration (Cribier, 1980). In contrast, in Great Britain a plurality of longer-distance migrants retire to seashore areas (Karn, 1977).

Some local moves may be amenity moves. A phenomenon that is clearly identifiable but not as yet studied consists of affluent suburbanites who move to some city centers after children leave home. Local moves to retirement communities and other planned housing may be made in search of an anticipated increase in level of social and recreational life (Peterson et al., 1973).

Environmental Push. Despite the voluminous literature on residential dissatisfaction as a function of deteriorated housing, lack of neighborhood goods and services, crime, and other environmental characteristics, the place of these forces in the decision to move is incompletely understood.

Struyk (1980) analyzed longitudinal (i.e., 1973 and 1974) data from the national Survey of Low-Income and Disabled (SLIAD) in the United States, separately for people who were owners and those who were renters at the first survey wave. In general, few first-wave characteristics differentiated those who would move from those who were to remain. First-wave measures of housing quality did

not significantly predict who would move during the year that followed. Analysis of the consequences of moving showed that renters who moved reported more housing deficiencies after the move, while owners who moved experienced a decrease in deficiencies. Using the same data set, Ferraro (1981) found that such variables as neighborhood appearance, neighborhood location, neighborhood safety, and perceived community sociability, and even overall housing satisfaction, were not associated with moving, though all were related to the expressed wish to move.

These findings reflect the great disjunction between objective condition and outcome, on the one hand, and an incomplete correspondence between wish and residential outcome. In Ferraro's sample, only 16 percent who expressed a wish to move in 1973 had done so within a year, while 6 percent of those who did not wish to move had done so. These findings corroborate earlier findings of low mobility fulfillment rates for older people (Goldscheider, 1966; Lawton et al., 1973). The "classical" motivations for moving (housing dissatisfaction, housing deficits, neighborhood dissatisfaction) thus strongly predict the wish to move, but not the actuality of moving. The environmental push does not have to result in a move. The push may be expressed as a frustrated urge to move or through an involuntary move; in either case it could tend to reinforce a sense of passivity in the person.

Assistance Moves. Moves that are presumed to be due to personal impairments or deprivations are assistance moves. Health is the most obvious determinant of this kind of move (Patrick, 1980). A common reason given for applying to planned housing is to escape the onus of home maintenance and housekeeping (Longino, 1982; Sherman, 1971), a reason that implies some form of impairment. Suggestive cross-sectional evidence of a tendency for poor health to lead to residence in another person's household is seen from Health Interview Survey data (National Center for Health Statistics, 1976), showing activity limitations to be far more prevalent among older people living in the household of a non-spouse relative or a non-relative than among those living alone.

Direct evidence supports the assertion that poor health leads to a move to a more dependent living arrangement. Newman (1976) obtained retrospective residential data on a national sample of older people who had experienced a major long-term illness. Almost half of them had relocated, and the most common relocations were to nursing homes or to the homes of relatives. Another study (Struyk, 1980) that might support this assertion showed that when homeowners moved, a decrease in physical capacity was reported between the pre- and the post-move occasions. Even for long-distance return migration, Longino (1979) suggested that reverse streams from Florida back to northern states might be related to a post-migration decline in health. The evidence reviewed thus underlines the relationship between health and residential relocation: good health facilitates amenity moves, whereas poor health leads to assistance moves.

Income is a potent factor in living arrangements. Older people in poor economic circumstances are more likely than their higher-income peers to live with younger family members in industrialized societies (Shanas et al., 1968), and such coresidence is greater in less economically developed countries (reviewed in Lawton, 1982). Local moving has been shown to be more common among people with low, rather than high, incomes (Aizenberg and Myers, 1977). Economic vulnerability of local movers was seen in Struyk's (1980) finding that renters who moved had higher post-move housing-expense burdens than nonmovers. A similar economic disadvantage associated with moving was found among owner-movers, in that their income was lower following the move, perhaps because some moves are precipitated by an anticipated decrease in income. Still missing is any direct estimate of the prevalence of older people's moving from independent to nonindependent households primarily for economic reasons.

Change in marital status, both death of a spouse and divorce, can be the occasion for an assistance move, as indicated by both Ferraro's (1981) and Struyk's (1980) different analyses of the same longitudinal data set. The specific extent to which bereavement triggers relocation is not yet known, nor is the time relationship to bereavement known.

To summarize what is known about assistance moves, both formal services (institutions, supportive housing) and family support may be obtained by residential relocation. These moves are typically made by older people whose functional independence and economic resources diminish. Although these moves are more likely to be local, there may also be long-distance moves. Making an assistance move obviously may involve a decision by the older person, but the decision is apt to be made within a broader context of diminishing personal autonomy.

Involuntary Relocation. Limited information is available on the prevalence of involuntary relocation by the community-resident elderly. An analysis of the data tapes from the 1976 Annual Housing Survey (AHS) of 13,000 elderly-headed households in the United States indicated that 8 and 9 percent of central-city and suburban elderly movers, respectively, reported having been "displaced by private action," which included evictions, property turnovers of various kinds, and condominium conversions (Gutowski and Feild, 1981). By contrast, only 4 percent of the under-65 central-city movers and an insignificant proportion of suburban movers reported such displacement. In a national telephone survey of 112 elderly movers, Turner and Mangum (1982) found only five people who claimed displacement as a primary reason for having moved.

The consequences of involuntary moves for community residents have also been inadequately studied. Some information is available on two types of displacement, however. "Gentrification," the repopulation of older but presently desirable areas of a city by affluent people, is a phenomenon that has many positive functions for the maintenance of the social and economic health of urban areas. On the other hand, the poor, minorities, and the aged may experience stress and dislocation as a result (Myers, 1978). Henig (1981) estimated the extent and location of elderly displacement by analyzing city-directory population change data by census tract and centrality for nine cities. He found that gentrification did occur more frequently where the percentage of older residents was higher. Moreover, there was, in fact, a positive correlation between younger in-movement and older out-movement, especially in the most central portion of the city. The aged were selectively subject to this type of displacement, as compared to younger female-headed and "blue-collar" households.

A second type of displacement is condominium conversion where older renters are offered the choice of either buying their units or having to find a new place to live (Stegman, in press). A study of converted buildings in 11 metropolitan areas of the United States revealed that while the elderly were not at higher risk of conversion than were people of younger ages, the outcomes of conversion were related to age (Office of Policy Development and Research, 1980). Of all elderly preconversion households, 49 percent moved, 23 percent purchased, and 28 percent continued to rent. These rates are much higher than the national renter mobility rate (9 percent) or renter-to-ownership change rate (6 percent) (Annual Housing Survey, 1977). Thus older renters faced with conversion behaved quite differently from older renters in general. While older movers experienced only small increases in rental costs, these people reported considerable difficulty in locating new shelter, and three-quarters moved to different neighborhoods.

The Effects of Residential Relocation

Struyk's (1980) longitudinal analysis of older movers showed a strong net change from owner to renter status but hardly any net improvement in objective housing quality indicators. Corroborative cross-sectional evidence was seen in the 1977 AHS data: neither objective housing quality, housing satisfac-

tion, nor neighborhood satisfaction discriminated between recent movers and others (Lawton, 1980c). An important distinction may be ignored when all movers are grouped. Ferraro (1981) showed that the SLIAD movers who had wished to move at the time of the first (1973) survey wave perceived significant improvement in six out of seven subjective housing and neighborhood characteristics. Those who moved but had not expressed the wish to move in 1973 perceived improvement in only two of these attributes. It is perhaps expected that those who moved most voluntarily would perceive more positive results. Regrettably, a similar analysis was not performed for objective housing-quality variables. Nonetheless, these findings emphasize the importance for the outcome (at least in psychological terms) of whether the move is proactively or responsively motivated. When the health consequences of the moves were examined, both voluntary and involuntary moves were associated with a decline in health, however (Ferraro, 1983).

With the above exceptions, research dealing with the effects of moving has addressed either the mass relocation of people in institutions or the apparently voluntary relocation involved in moving to planned housing (see reviews by Rowland, 1977, and Schulz and Brenner, 1977). It is clearly time for a prospective study of voluntary relocation that could examine a full range of both personal and environmental variables.

The Search for Housing

Information on the manner in which older people search for most new housing is difficult to locate. Informal communication through friends and relatives is known to account for some moves to planned housing (Longino, 1982). Virtually the only attempt to study the search process itself was made by Howell (1982). People who considered moving at the time of retirement, widowhood, the last child's leaving home, or a decline in health were found to have considered a number of alternatives and to have discussed the possibilities with family, friends, and others. However, 54 percent reported that they had looked at no housing unit other than the one into which they had moved, and only 19 percent looked at four or more different units. Still missing is more detailed information on the amount of search activity and on the subjective processes by which people locate sources of information, obtain it, weigh alternatives, and finally select a dwelling.

Remaining in Place

The great majority of older people remain where they are. In 1976, for instance, 59 percent of older owner-occupants in the United States had lived in the same dwelling for 16 or more years (Lawton et al., 1981). Although only 15 percent of renters had maintained their residences that long, 55 percent of them had been in place for six years.

The disinclination to move is a highly complex phenomenon. If we accept at face value the high level of housing satisfaction indicated in the AHS—83 percent rated their housing as "excellent" or "good" (Lawton, 1980c)—one may ascribe the lack of movement simply to the achievement over a lifetime of an ideal match of needs and domicile. However for a variety of reasons, such rosy interpretations should be viewed with skepticism (Carp, 1975; Campbell et al., 1976). Ego defensiveness leads people to adapt their perceived needs to the realm of the possible; a change in what is possible may easily restructure need. The advent of every new housing program or other environmental opportunity has uncovered a latent demand for residential change in some older people. Thus we must be careful not to interpret the magnitude of remaining in place as an absolute indicator of present demand. Some unknown proportion of persons who are presently staying in place would probably move if existing financial, housing-market, and psychological barriers were to be removed.

A factor that may influence older persons to remain in place, and which is just beginning to receive research attention, is the intrapsychic phenomenon of attachment to the home as a symbol and as the touchstone for reminiscence, past affects, and past relationships (Rowles, 1978). Rowles (1980) speaks of "physical insideness," a state of familiarity with the local environment that is very helpful to the person in coping with the environment on the sensory, cognitive, and affective levels: "The old person comes to wear the setting like a glove" (Rowles, 1980, p. 2). O'Bryant (1982) designed a scale to represent attitudes toward the home. Several of its factors signify symbolic attachment: a feeling of competence in a familiar environment, traditional family orientation and memories, the status value of home ownership, and a "cost-versus-comfort tradeoff" factor. In O'Bryant's study these attitudes were substantially related to generalized housing satisfaction. Howell (1982) found that older interviewees who were not considering moving expressed the strongest attachment (57 percent), recent movers a less strong attachment (46 percent), and those who had recently considered moving but had not succeeded in doing so the least attachment to their present housing (28 percent). Owners were more attached than renters, and those in stable health more attached than those whose health had recently declined.

It is apparent that home as both a personal and cultural symbol and an affective link to self, family, and the outer world has far more significance than has yet been explored. Psychological attachment as a factor in residential decisions may well be as important as economic and social factors. Remaining in place involves a decision, or, rather, a series of decisions revised over time, as awareness of changes in personal and environmental situations is processed internally. The number of instances in which the decision is out of the person's hands because of public or private actions of others, or because family are making the decision, is very small (see Longino, in press, for a discussion of this issue). The bulk of the evidence suggests that remaining in place is actively chosen and selected above other alternatives most of the time.

PLANNED HOUSING

In addition to the types of residential relocation just discussed, moves to planned housing constitute the most obvious kind of self-chosen relocation decision. The term "planned housing" is used to refer to both publicly assisted and nonsubsidized housing that is designated explicitly for older people. The term includes public housing, nonprofit housing, retirement communities, life-care communities, and other types that meet the criteria for planned housing. Earlier detailed studies of people in this kind of housing (Carp, 1966; Lawton, 1980b; Sherman, 1972) are unanimous in indicating that these tenants are active in seeking out, applying for, and becoming tenants in this type of housing. The same studies attest to the generally favorable outcomes associated with the move to planned housing. Descriptions of the government-subsidized programs in the United States and numbers served by each may be found in Struyk and Soldo (1980).

Further proof that active choices are being made by older people is seen in the success of the many varieties of unsubsidized planned housing, usually populated by people with sufficient economic resources to be able to choose among a variety of planned and unplanned housing. Mangum (1982) made a conservative estimate that, in the United States, there were around 582,000 people living in privately developed "retirement villages" and another 83,000 in "life-care communities" (purchased residential care with a monthly fee that does not change if a move is made from residential to skilled nursing care). Added to the nearly 1.5 million people occupying the 1.25 million units of federally assisted housing, more than 2 million or about 8 percent of the older population in the United States now live in planned age-segregated housing, as compared to 92 percent who live in unplanned housing in ordinary communities.

The obvious appeal of planned housing is not a phenomenon limited to the United States. The level of governmental involvement of some western European countries in subsidizing housing appears to be higher than that of the United States. For example, half of new units in France and one quarter in the Netherlands are governmentally aided; a high proportion is available to people with low incomes and managed by nonprofit organizations (Nusberg et al., 1984). In England in 1978, more than one-third of persons 65 years of age and older lived in locally subsidized housing (Tinker, 1981). However, only a minority of these units were designed specially for the aged; only about 6 percent of older people live in such age-designated units. The Federal Republic of Germany had a relatively small number living in such housing in 1969: 0.5% of all those 65 and over (Dieck, 1980). Italy (Florea, 1980), Japan (Mori, 1979), and most eastern European countries (reviewed variously in Palmore, 1980, and Teicher et al., 1979) have reported only beginning construction activity in planned housing for older people. Activity has also been reported in some countries with levels of industrialization below those already mentioned (see Lawton, 1982, for a review), and there is every reason to feel that the level of activity in planned housing throughout the world can only increase in the future.

One of the first issues to have been raised regarding planned housing was the desirability of the age segregation that has been an integral part of this housing form in the United States (though not necessarily in all countries; for example, on the situation in France, see Nusberg et al., in press). It is well established by now that interaction with one's age peers is actively sought and preferred by most people who live in planned housing (Lawton et al., in press), and that favorable social and other types of consequences result from high age density (Teaff et al., 1978). Still unresearched is the question of the effect of age-segregated living on those who prefer age mixing or on society at large, including its attitudes toward the aged.

An issue central to the transactional view of person and environment is the intensity of supportive services that are desirable in planned housing. No question better illustrates the complementarity of the active and passive stances of the person in relation to environment. It has been demonstrated that there is a tendency for older people with some early impairments to choose housing with services ("congregate housing" in the United States), whereas the more competent choose housing without services (Lawton, 1969). Clearly this behavior involves searching the local housing market, assessing one's own competence and needs and deciding whether the congruence between person and housing environment is sufficient to warrant a move. This is decision making at its most active. The service-rich environment is highly supportive, providing proximate resources such as meals, housekeeping services, and even personal care to those whose competence is marginal. In congregate housing, environmental demands on the more competent may become reduced to the point where their skills are not sufficiently exercised. For example, a study of "warden housing" (housing with a live-in caregiver) in England found that tenants in this type of housing used more services than people of comparable health not living in housing with wardens (Tinker, 1983). The question was thus raised of whether the sheltering function of the housing is acting to increase dependency. The housing environment, because it establishes a limit on individual behavior in either providing or not providing easily obtainable services, may be viewed as exercising an effect on the person (Donahue et al., 1977).

There is a wide range of matches between environment and personal needs and competence. For example, many people enter congregate housing because they enjoy the comfort of having meals provided. Demand for high-quality congregate housing, as in some high-income life-care communities, is very high. However, there is evidence that such people are buying security at a time when their competence is still adequate. Thus they actively plan and decide less for the present than for the future.

The planned housing environment provides an excellent instance of the dynamic character of the person–environment trans-action, since tenants in planned housing are likely to change over time, as is the housing environment. The "accommodating environment" (Lawton et al., 1980) adds services and physical changes necessary for service delivery as tenant health declines over time. In these settings management is also accommodating in allowing tenants to remain as their independence wanes, and sometimes relaxes admission standards so that the overall secular decline in tenant competence is substantial. In contrast, a "constant" environment requires strict control of admission and discharge policies to maintain a healthy tenant population. Although some instances of extreme accommodation have been described (Lawton et al., 1980), most housing change falls somewhere between (Ehrlich et al., 1982). Moss and Lawton (1981) studied five housing sites at the time of their opening, and again 12 to 14 years later. While declines in well-being were found, they were more marked with respect to such matters as use of the local neighborhood and subjective well-being than in ability to perform activities of daily living. Housing management had accommodated to the extent of being one of several actors in the establishment of a "patchwork of services"—primarily services delivered by local community-based agencies, and highly targeted to a small proportion of tenants who required them.

The patchwork system is geared to identifying those at highest risk and offering only them the service. Traditional congregate housing, on the other hand, usually strives to serve as high a proportion of all tenants as possible, because of the cost advantages of such broadcast service. However, the broadcast service risks overserving competent tenants. Recent congregate demonstrations in housing sponsored by both the Department of Housing and Urban Development and the Farmers Home Administration, in the United States, offer services to less than the total tenant population and thus may be better able to match individual needs with the appropriate amount of support.

Study of social processes in planned housing has continued. Longino et al. (1980)

found some evidence among retirement community residents of increased perceived social integration and high self-concept, but no difference in activity level or age consciousness as compared to the general population. They also suggested that an aged subculture characterized by "retreatism" rather than activism was the preferred mode of adaptation in the rehoused group. Moos and others (David et al., 1981; Lemke and Moos, 1980; Moos, 1980; Moos and Lemke, 1983) have studied the complexities of the social and physical environments in supportive residential environments. Their work has highlighted the importance of such social processes as degree of personal control, and the differentially positive use of opportunities for control by more functionally capable persons.

Retirement Communities

As distinguished from the assisted planned housing types, the privately developed planned housing commonly referred to as a "retirement community" is very difficult to define (Marans et al., 1984). Such a community is clearly physically separate from its surrounds, age-segregated, and noninstitutional. However, these attributes cover most planned housing arrangements. Additional attributes that frequently, but not always, define a retirement community must be specified: they are often purchased, rather than rental units; they frequently are for-profit rather than nonprofit undertakings; they frequently cater to the middle and affluent economic group of elderly; they are frequently in the sun belt, retirement areas, or peripheries of urban areas; and they frequently support at least a minimum retail goods and services economy separate from those of the larger community in which they are located. Such nonassisted housing has grown in the past decade and shows every sign of continued growth capability, including the life-care community form as defined above.

Older research (reviewed by Mangum, 1982) attests to the favorable responses of the residents to retirement-community living, as measured by such indicators as housing satisfaction and amount of activity. Recent data deal with the relationships of retirement communities to their local communities (Streib, LaGreca, and Folts, in press). Heintz (1976) demonstrated that a group of New Jersey retirement communities had a generally favorable impact on the economic life of their municipal settings and did not make extraordinary drains on their service capabilities. Duncan et al. (1978) found considerable variability among such communities in their speed of development, their absoluteness of age segregation, and the distinctness of their differentiation from their surrounding communities. They measured the degree of autonomy of the retirement community from the larger community in which it was located. The more autonomous the community, the better it could survive when forces such as rising taxes or attempts to integrate by age threatened its political or economic autonomy. These studies illustrate the potential for future research that deals with the community as a unit interacting with the macrosocial structure; the effects of this interaction on the individual also deserve study.

Alternative Planned Housing

Alternative housing includes housing types that are relatively rare by comparison with the single-family home or not among the types discussed above as planned housing. Most of them involve unrelated people sharing a housing unit or structure. Some forms of alternative housing have developed as planned environments. The most independent varieties of planned alternative housing have simply remodeled existing large single-family homes or apartments and have provided several private dwelling units, with a minimum of services (Brody and Liebowitz, 1981). One of the best-known forms of alternative housing is Share-A-Home, which often provides some services but generally houses still moderately independent people, who live in separate bedrooms but share other facilities (Streib, Folts, and Hilker, in press). Streib et al. found that both "push" factors of declining independence and "pull" factors of social relationships were motivating factors for entering this kind of living, as seen by both residents and interested non-residents. Thus this model lies clearly toward the supportive side of the independent–supportive environment continuum. Another form of home sharing is the "accessory apartment" (Hare et al., 1982), where major remodeling of a single-family home provides a second independent apartment. One such example was done under a local public housing authority (Carlin and Fox, 1981). Still another form is simple house sharing, where a room is rented and often other portions of the home are made available to the renter. In practice, this pairing has often matched an older and perhaps security-seeking owner who takes a younger tenant whose primary aim is the low rent (Dobkin, 1980). "Match-up" agencies have been started to bring together owners and renters. "Echo housing," or the "granny flat," has been implemented in England (Tinker, 1976) and Australia (*Ageing International,* 1981). This housing attaches a small self-contained unit for an older person to a family housing unit, usually occupied by a relative of the older person. Other models provide personal care and surveillance in addition to meals and housekeeping and are thus quasi-institutional. Finally, formalized foster-care programs (Sherman and Newman, 1977) serve very impaired people within a small-scale familistic setting.

Home sharing has become very successful in England, where a network of large private homes has been purchased by local non-profit groups to provide relatively independent group living that affords more support than that provided in council or warden housing (Streib, Folts, and Hilker, in press; Tinker, 1981). Similar ventures have been reported in many industrialized nations.

More complete reviews of alternative housing may be found in Eckert and Murrey (1984). Lawton (1981b), Peace (1981), and Streib, Folts, and Hilker (in press). The positive aspect of many forms of alternative housing is that they provide one more choice for people who, because of financial or other constraints, have limited residential alternatives. For some, the support offered by these types of residences may delay institutionalization; for others, the housing simply provides a lower-cost alternative at some sacrifice to needs for privacy and autonomy. In the aggregate, however, this type of housing probably forces too many compromises with the ideal of independent residence to be able to serve any substantial percentage of housing needs of older persons.

OLDER PEOPLE IN ORDINARY COMMUNITIES

If we subtract all those living in institutions and in housing of all the types discussed previously, we should still have about 87 percent who live in housing that has been individually selected at some point by the elder occupant from the pool of all open-market housing available at that time. These older people are thus scattered among people of all ages.

The residential decision to select a particular housing unit, made at some time in the past, is likely to be reviewed periodically and the decision to remain affirmed. Other decisions involving environmental change short of relocation are possible: to take in another member of the household (e.g., a family member, helper, or roomer); to change the use of a room or group of rooms; to remodel; to make repairs; to redecorate or change furnishings. Existing research informs us relatively little about some of these forms of residential adjustments. In considering the current housing situation of older people, it is important to keep in mind, however, that each of these decisions and the active behavior that follows is an instance of the person acting on the environment. This portion of the chapter will examine the quality of housing occupied by the elderly, how they assess their housing, and how they maintain their housing; and will end with consideration of some programs designed to help them to remain in their homes.

General Housing Characteristics

Older people live in housing that is older than the housing occupied by younger people

(Struyk and Soldo, 1980; U.S. Bureau of the Census, 1974–77). For example, in 1976 the median age of housing occupied by the elderly was about 36 years, as compared to about 24 for younger owners and 31 for younger renters. Whether owner or renter, the elderly live in housing of lower value or rent than do the young.

The elderly also pay a larger proportion of their incomes for their housing. In 1976, about 48 percent of older renters, as compared to 27 percent of people of all ages, paid more than 30 percent of their incomes for housing (Struyk and Soldo, 1980). Among owner-occupants with mortgages, older persons paid 38 percent of their incomes for housing, as compared with 12 percent for younger owners.

Housing Quality

The picture concerning quality of housing, as it varies by age of occupant, is less clear. Depending on which indicators of quality are used, the elderly are seen to live in notably inferior housing (Lawton, 1980a, p. 57; Mayer and Lee, 1981), or in housing whose quality is almost the equal of that occupied by younger people (Office of Policy Development and Research, 1979). The absolute level of obvious housing deficiencies is relatively low among people of all ages, however; and the proportion decreased significantly even during the few years from 1970 to 1976 (Struyk and Soldo, 1980). The estimate by Mayer and Lee (1981) from the 1976 Annual Housing Survey is representative: by those authors' selected indicators, the rate of "housing inadequacy" was 7.8 percent for older homeowners and 4.3 percent for non-elderly homeowners; greater frequency of deficits, but a comparable age difference, was noted for renters.

Defining housing quality is problematic, of course (see Goedert and Goodman, 1976; Marcuse, 1971; Struyk and Soldo, 1980, for further discussion). The problem is even greater in the case of elderly housing. One approach to resolving it is the ecological model of aging (Lawton and Nahemow,

1973). It suggests that the adequacy of a behavioral outcome is a function of the transaction between environmental demand and personal competence. A housing deficit places a constraint on behavioral outcome, but if the resident of the housing is personally limited (e.g., mobility, perceptual ability), the effect of environment on behavior is proportionately greater than in the case of a fully competent person. Since such limitations are more frequent among older people, the effect of any physically defined deficit is potentiated. Thus a "deficit" is defined partly by the user of the environment. Estimates of the aggregate quality of the housing occupied by the elderly must be "discounted" in proportion to the number of impaired elderly who must cope with the deficits.

Physical housing quality varies considerably more among subgroups of older people than it does between age groups, at least in the United States. Rental housing for older persons had 2.5 times as many inadequate units as did owner-occupied housing (Office of Policy Development and Research, 1979). Older people living in rural areas live in the poorest-quality housing (Bylund et al., 1979; Struyk, 1977), while suburbanites live in the best housing (Gutowski and Feild, 1981). Housing in the South has the most deficits, housing in the West the fewest (Struyk and Soldo, 1980). Older Hispanics, and particularly older blacks, live in housing of poorer quality than older whites (Hoover, 1981). Older blacks living in nonmetropolitan areas of the South lived in distressingly poor housing. Deficiencies have been seen in such indicators as presence of rodents (42%), incomplete plumbing (37%), incomplete kitchen (26%), and leaking roof (23%) (Lawton and Benner, 1981).

Housing quality for older persons varies even more radically among nations. For example, in England, 12 percent of the elderly use bathrooms outside the living unit (Tinker, 1981). In the Federal Republic of Germany, 43 percent have no central heating, and half live in units of less than 360 square feet (*Ageing International,* 1982–83).

In developing countries, of course, older people share the intense deprivations of the populations at large; for example, in India, 94 percent of rural households have no bathroom (Centre for Human Settlements, 1982).

Households shared by an older couple or by an older person and younger family member showed relatively few deficiencies as compared to those of older people living along, especially men (Lawton, 1981a). Several factors might account for the paradoxical situation that women living alone, with the lowest income of all household types, have housing superior in quality to that of men living alone. Women may search more carefully for better housing, be willing to allocate a greater proportion of resources to housing, obtain more help from others, and value home in a symbolic sense more than men. Also, older women living alone are more likely to be widowed than are older men living alone. An older woman's housing may benefit from her joint maintenance efforts with her former spouse. Poorer housing is apt to be occupied by people in poorer health (Rabushka and Jacobs, 1980). Thus the "excess disability" resulting from housing deficiencies may be compounded in the aggregate by a more selective residence of impaired elderly in poor-quality housing.

Subjective and Objective Deficits

The difference between the occupant's view of housing quality and quality as determined by an expert has been documented and is of potential policy relevance. Rabushka and Jacobs (1980) reported a study of 1575 older homeowners in one rural and six urban areas where estimates of adequacy were obtained from both the household ("subjective problems") and an expert housing evaluator ("objective problems"). Experts judged deficits to be more frequent than did occupants by factors that ranged from 2 for roof and gutter and house exterior to 9 for the electrical system.

One interpretation of these results, offered by Rabushka and Jacobs (1980), is that experts, as they judged "objective" quality,

were using ideal standards that in real life are rarely applied by users; the users themselves indicated by their low perception of deficits that they were not actively bothered by most of the problems seen by the experts. Rabushka and Jacobs refer to this set of findings as the "needs/preference mismatch," and conclude that occupants' evaluations constitute the more appropriate basis for estimating the magnitude of the social problem of home maintenance needs.

Counterarguments to this conclusion are many. Certainly some subset of expert-identified problems were those very difficult for any layperson to recognize, problems that nonetheless were risks to safety or long-term maintenance. Moreover, while data are not at hand to relate the perceptual problems of aging directly to the reporting of deficits, this factor probably does make the elderly selectively likely to underreport. Finally, the positive response style of older people (Carp, 1975) may have blocked the expression of dissatisfaction with any feature of the environment, especially those that they feel would be difficult to change (Campbell et al., 1976; Carp, 1975). There is thus ample reason to conclude that the judgments of deficits by the occupant afford as much of a minimum estimate as those by the experts afford a maximum estimate.

Home Repairs and Maintenance

Since a substantial proportion of the total housing stock is owned by older people, the extent to which these dwellings are maintained is a factor of great import in preserving the quality of both neighborhoods and the housing that is turned over to future generations of homeowners. Since elderly-owned homes are older and of somewhat lower quality than those owned by younger people, one might expect more maintenance activity among the older group. In fact, small repairs occur about as often, or slightly less often, in older households, while major home improvements are reported much less often (Struyk and Soldo, 1980). When major repairs are made, the price paid by older people is greater than for younger people, probably a reflection of the higher costs associated with repairing older systems or making up for deferred maintenance.

The major deleterious effect of poorly maintained and low-quality homes on individuals is on the most vulnerable segment of the elderly—the physically and mentally impaired, the low-income, and the renter dependent on the landlord for improvements. These people are the ones whose well-being is most likely to be determined by environmental quality and who are least likely to be in a position to shape their environments to suit their needs. Thus the resources available to assist them in home maintenance are of great importance.

The most proactive home-maintenance behavior is to perform the task oneself. Not surprisingly, younger and healthier older owners are more likely to repairs for themselves, while family are likely to do them for the less-healthy (Rabushka and Jacobs, 1980).

Types of Home-Maintenance Programs

The United States and most northern European countries offer some form of assistance to income-tested individual owner-occupants for the most costly kinds of major home rehabilitation (Nusberg et al., 1984). In the United States, the Department of Housing and Urban Development's (HUD's) major assistance program (Section 312 of the 1964 Housing Act) showed substantial underuse by older people, who resist taking on a new debt (Lawton and Benner, 1981). Grant programs, such as the now-defunct Section 115 program, the Farmers Home Administraton's (FmHA's) Section 505 program, and a Swedish loan program in which debt is forgiven after five years (Nusberg et al., 1984), show much greater use. In the United States it has been estimated that an average of about 8000 owner-occupied elderly homes per year were government-assisted for major rehabilitation over a period of years in the 1970s, with average level of assistance between $3000 and $5000 per household (Mayer and Lee, 1981), which constitutes an insignificant number of all those in need.

If level of assistance is poor for major repairs, it is even worse for minor repairs. There is no such program in the United States for which all poor elderly are eligible. Programs funded by the Community Development Block Grant (CDBG) program are locally elective and available only in certain urban areas. The Older Americans Act Title III program does not have a program in every area, and its total scope is very small. Home repair services under the social services block grant (formerly Title XX) are also optional by locality and have no special outreach to the aged. The FmHA Section 504 grant program for rural elderly poor has grown recently but still is small in coverage. Reviews and estimates of the aggregate number served under these programs suggested that around 107,000 older clients were served in 1978, as compared to the almost one million poor elderly households that required assistance with minor home maintenance (Lawton and Benner, 1981; Mayer and Lee, 1981).

The one home maintenance program in the United States developed and managed by HUD was a six-city demonstration project. The HUD funding ended in 1983 (the evaluation has not been published), and there are no plans to continue or extend the projects. The administrative cost per unit of service delivered is undoubtedly relatively high, and legitimate questions remain as to how localities can best be assisted to offer such services. Other countries such as the England (Wheeler, 1982) have managed to provide some publicly funded maintenance assistance, but little information is available on the specifics of such programs.

Income Support Housing Assistance

A basic form of housing assistance for renters is the rent supplement, in which an income-tested tenant pays a portion of her income and a government subsidy pays the owner the difference between this amount and an established fair market rent. Germany, France, and the Scandinavian countries, among others (Nusberg et al., 1984), have such a program.

In the United States, this approach has been taken in the major rental-assistance program, known as the Section 8 (existing) program. This program had as one goal the improvement of housing by earmarking assistance for units that met or could be brought to meet at least a minimal set of physical standards. In the case of older users, however, the great majority who received a subsidy stayed in their units rather than moving to a unit that met the standards (Struyk and Soldo, 1980). Thus the subsidy had only a small impact on the quality of housing lived in by older persons.

A social experiment in the United States, the Experimental Housing Allowance Program, used a similar subsidy. One major advantage was claimed for the housing allowance as compared to the rent subsidy: the supplement is given to the renter, therefore enhancing her feeling of competence and de-emphasizing the implied "welfare" stigma of paying the subsidy directly to the landlord. The results of the evaluation were similar to those for the Section 8 evaluation, in that older people neither tended to move nor to press landlords to improve current dwellings (Connell, 1981; Struyk and Soldo, 1980). The same basic idea is used in the housing voucher program, a currently proposed successor to most of the federal housing assistance programs.

Another income mechanism tied to housing is property tax relief. Although all states have some form of property tax relief (Abt Associates, 1977), and it is popular with local politicians because of its high visibility, its financial benefit to low-income older persons is small (Heiser, 1980), and at least in one large state its benefits went selectively to the socioeconomically privileged (Buczko, 1981).

Returning to this chapter's concern over housing decisions and choices, it is clear that a complex set of personal and environmental factors determine whether efforts are made to repair and maintain homes, and the type and means used if the work is begun. Many older people have little economic freedom currently, and this is reflected in the low probability that small contemporary increases in income will be directed toward home maintenance. For example, Struyk and Soldo (1980) found that an increase in income showed a very weak tendency to be associated with making home repairs—a 20 percent increase in income might increase by only 1 percent the probability that repairs would be done. Rabushka and Jacobs (1980) argue that older homeowners are thus demonstrating that their priorities lie elsewhere; since their housing satisfaction is high in spite of their lower housing quality, these authors suggest that the need for publicly aided repair assistance is much lower than most gerontologists have argued.

This point of view does not adequately account for a series of forces that selectively reduce the *ability* of the older person to continue home maintenance. The major environmental deterrent is economic. However, other deterrents are related to personal factors such as failure to receive relevant knowledge about the condition of the home or the availability of external assistance. Lack of practice in performing work oneself or in locating and trusting contract services is another personal deterrent.

Specialized Housing Options on the Open Market

Included within the universe of housing in ordinary normal communities are several specialized settings that are important because their unique characteristics may enable them to meet particular needs of some users—condominiums, cooperatives, hotels, rooming houses, and mobile homes. Their existence at the very least extends the range of choices available, in some cases in such a way as to benefit selectively those whose options are particularly limited by economic constraints. The literature is notably lacking in information regarding these types of residences outside the United States.

Condominiums. The condominium, a multiunit structure in which individual units are purchased outright, is a relative newcomer to the housing scene in the United States, but a form of living that is likely to become more prevalent for all ages. According to the 1976 AHS, 176,000 people 65 and over lived in condominiums. Little else is known on a national scale about the household or housing characteristics of condominiums occupied by the aged. Nationwide, older people constitute 28 percent of all condominium owners (author's unpublished tabulations from 1976 AHS public-use data tapes), slightly higher than the elderly's percentage of all owner-occupied units (22 percent). It is unlikely that the disproportionate number of older people among condominium owners is fully accounted for by involuntary condominium conversion from rental apartments. It may be that for those older people able to afford the purchase price, condominium living is selectively attractive.

Cooperatives. In 1976, the AHS indicated that 167,000 older people lived in units classed as "cooperatives," that is, a multiunit structure owned jointly by shareholders, who are also usually occupants. These units are likely to be in large projects with hired management, rather than in small-scale self-managed units. The only significant information on older people in cooperatives is the very surprising fact that they constitute 41 percent of all cooperative owner-occupants (AHS, 1980). One factor explaining their high present use by the aged may be that the peak of cooperative building came a decade or so ago, and a segment of the original population has aged in place. Thus cooperative populations may have been notably stable. Further research would be most illuminating on how such stable tenant groups have been maintained. Even more interesting would be knowledge on how they have coped with the demands of ownership and participation as they have aged, and how those who do sell their units have fared.

Hotels. The literature of the past decade has been relatively rich in description of life in one form of hotel, the single-room-occupancy (SRO) hotel. This term has come to imply also low-cost, central-city location, and a clientele likely to consist of socially marginal people (Eckert, 1980; Ehrlich and Ehrlich 1976; Stephens, 1976). In England the elderly are overrepresented in shelters and hostels, which have some similarity to SROs (Tinker, 1981). These residences contain large numbers of older people, primarily males, though in some cases younger discharged mental hospital patients and substance abusers are also present in sizable numbers. The unanimous conclusion from all studies is that the SRO hotel provides a niche for its clientele that would be very difficult for them to find elsewhere—a low-cost haven where privacy is easily attained and tolerance for personal deviations is high. A series of studies by Sokolovsky and Cohen (Cohen and Sokolovsky, 1980; Sokolovsky and Cohen, 1981) has probed the social structures of the SRO and found not an absence of social interaction (as often connoted by the SRO) but, rather, a carefully metered amount of social integration, including some contact with people outside the hotel and contact of acceptable amount and intensity with fellow residents. Clearly an active effort should be made to preserve this resource in the face of pressure from municipal and business interests to rid the central cities of such environments.

The SRO hotel is not the only variety of hotel living important to the elderly, however. For example, some hotels have high-income inhabitants. There are many women among hotel residents, more hotel residents are employed than is true for older people in general who live alone, and in one recent study only 10 percent were on welfare in metropolitan areas (Haley et al., 1981). This information suggests that some hotels provide congenial environments for those who are not deprived.

A substantial decline in number of elderly in SRO units has occurred in the past decade (Haley et al., 1981). The demand may grow, however, if the economic squeeze continues and the housing supply fails to keep pace with demand.

Another unplanned alternative is the "rooming house," a familiar residential type during earlier historical periods (Hareven, 1976) but relatively rare now [the 1976 AHS showed about 50,000 older people living in rooming houses (Goode et al., 1979]. The lines dividing the roomer, the boarder, and the home sharer are barely perceptible, and the amount of information is scant.

Mobile Homes. In 1973, 4.0 percent of housing units occupied by older people in the United States were mobile homes. Three years later this proportion had grown to 4.9 percent, an increase of 23 percent (Annual Housing Survey, 1980). Not unexpectedly, the great concentration of mobile homes is in rural nonfarm areas, where this form of housing accounted for 10 percent of all elderly-headed units (Struyk, 1977). There is thus every reason to conclude that mobile home living will continue to be an important option for some older people (Haley, in press). The AHS informs us that most older mobile-home residents own their units (92 percent), and that just over half are located in groups of six or more, most of them no doubt in mobile home parks. Some parks are limited to older people, others have evolved that way, while still others are fully age-integrated. However, except for an ethnographic study of one such park (Johnson, 1971), we know almost nothing about the social organization of everyday life or how services, if any, are managed in such environments.

Physical standards for mobile homes have improved over the years (reviewed by Rausch and Hoover, 1980; Struyk and Soldo, 1980). Struyk and Soldo (1980) have suggested the mobile home as an alternative to the shortage of acceptable-quality units in rural areas. They discuss Weitzman's (1976) analysis of the long-term financial aspects of mobile-home ownership; the move-in cost of a conventional home is far greater, monthly charges are about the same, but equity after 15 years is also much greater in a conventional home than in a mobile home. If a 15-year life is the maximum needed, this type of residence would be feasible and cost-effective. The 1978 Housing and Community Development Act allows mobile-home occupants to be assisted in rent payments under Section 8.

In summary, these alternative forms of residence are notable for allowing diverse needs to be met. While the essential appeals of condominiums and cooperatives are incompletely understood, they at least offer the security of an owned home with fewer maintenance problems. Research is needed to determine whether these forms also offer gains in perceived security or in social relations. Rooming houses, some hotels, and most mobile homes offer options to those who must live under financial constraints. A sense of personal autonomy may be gained in each of these residential types, yet it has been shown that each can support social structures as well.

NEIGHBORHOODS AND THE RESIDENTIAL ENVIRONMENT

The neighborhood is perhaps the best example of environment as a potential multifaceted service system. It has physical, personal, and social aspects and is the source of a substantial variety of resources for both challenge and support.

Several reviews of how older people use their local environments have appeared (Cantor, 1979; Carp, 1976; Lawton, 1977; Newcomer, 1976; Regnier, 1976). One conclusion has been that amount of use is a function of the person's characteristics, the type of resources, and environmental factors such as proximity to services, and threat of crime (Regnier, 1982; Regnier and Hamburger, 1978). It is not firmly established, however, that proximity or ease of access to local services and amenities is related to more distal indicators of well-being such as life satisfaction (reviewed in Lawton, 1977).

Neighborhood Age Mix

Conceptual reviews of the effects of neighborhood age mix have been provided (Golant, 1979; Ward, 1979), together with some new empirical data (though this research has been done primarily in the United States). Ward notes potentially positive outcomes in some age-graded settings because of increased social opportunities with age peers, the likelihood of mutual assistance, paths of communication regarding the availability of services, and their provision of socialization mechanisms for old age as a social role. He also identifies limitations to these generalizations. For example, much of the research supporting the above conclusions was gained from people living in multiunit housing (Rosow, 1967; Teaff et al., 1978), which may work differently from more dispersed, unplanned neighborhood environments. More important, individual differences will be major moderators of the effects of age concentration. From the point of view of society and its attitudes toward aging, the physical clustering of older people may act as a stigmatizing cue.

Thus more knowledge is required about the specific causal effects of neighborhood age mix. Unlike the situation with age-segregated planned housing, people are unlikely to choose a neighborhood because of its age mix; thus higher person–environment incongruency may be present.

Ward et al. (1981) provided some empirical evidence of the effects of neighborhood age structure on older people living in census tracts of differing age concentration. Higher age concentration was associated with having more age-peer neighbor friends, but neither age segregation, interaction with neighbors, nor age-peer interaction affected morale to any great extent. Nonetheless, neighbors were the resource favored for instrumental assistance in the absence of family. Perhaps the most significant finding was that interaction frequency was associated with morale and a measure of "mastery" for a number of vulnerable groups, such as those who are in poorer health, live alone, are widowed, or are recent movers into the area. This set of findings constitutes another validation of the "environmental docility hypothesis" (Lawton, 1970), which states that the more vulnerable are more subject to the influence of the environment (in this case, social interaction frequency). Finally, the most direct result of age-peer neighbor relationships was the greater knowledge of services exhibited by those whose closest relationships were with age peers. This research indicates that there may be substantial differences resulting from the variation in age density in ordinary neighborhoods as compared with the total age segregation in planned housing.

Social-Area Characteristics of Neighborhoods

Analyses of recent data (Cowgill, 1978; LaGory et al., 1980; Pampel and Choldin, 1978) have affirmed the earlier conclusions (Sclar, 1976; Smith and Hiltner, 1975) that census tracts within metropolitan areas and entire metropolitan areas tend to differ in their degree of residential age segregation.

Processes that might account for the occurrence of age-segregated areas were studied by LaGory et al. (1981), who structured three models that might lead to areal patterns of age segregation. The *ecological* model suggests that urbanization causes young populations to move in search of space, causing property values to rise and leaving older people immobile in low-cost housing areas, while the young go to areas where they can compete successfully for the more expensive newer housing. The *cultural* model points to active choices being made to maximize the similarity of one's background and life-style to one's neighborhood. The *political* model suggests that market-place competition is greatly altered by political forces exerted by the cultural majority, as in the case of race (or in this case, age) segregation. They tested these models by multivariate analyses using census-tract-level variables to represent forces presumed to be active in the several models. Support for the ecological model was strongest (e.g., population growth and age of housing stock strongly affected rental values, a proxy for market competition, which in turn increased age segregation). Mild support for the cultural model was seen in that regional differences were associated with different causal patterns. There was no support for the political model. One might, of course, find very different processes in other countries, for example, the Netherlands, where a policy of age segregation in housing has resulted in substantial age differentiation by neighborhood. On the other hand, developers in France are given incentives to mix the generations (Nusberg et al., 1984). These national policies thus are added to the population dynamics of the type investigated by LaGory et al. (1981) as determinants of neighborhood age mix.

Other research has examined the characteristics of age-concentrated areas. Metropolitan tracts high in average age tended also to have older housing, more multiunit housing, more female-headed and single-person households, and low property value rates (Chevan, 1979; Struyk and Soldo, 1980).

Rural Neighborhoods

This chapter cannot do justice to the topic of variations in life-style associated with the rural–urban continuum. Only very recently has research appeared with any regularity on aging in rural areas, and to date there has still been no satisfactory conceptual treatment of this topic. The ecology of social relationships and service organizations in rural areas was reviewed by Lawton (1980a, pp. 26–35) for the United States, and by Lehr (1977) for West Germany. Since that time integrative works have appeared on rural aging (Lee, in press; Lee and Lassey, 1980). In addition, results from a major environmental study of older people in Kansas small towns have begun to appear (Scheidt, 1982; Windley and Scheidt, 1982). Physical environmental attributes (dwelling-unit satisfaction and

environmental constriction) and psycho-social environmental attributes (community satisfaction and community involvement) made important contributions to the psychological well-being of these older residents. The causal effects of a number of person-community transactional variables and the uses made by people of local resources were determined in great detail, and widen our knowledge of life in the small town considerably. However, without the ability to contrast similar processes among central-city, suburban, small-town, and rural aged, such findings leave large gaps in our knowledge.

The Ward et al. (1981) study of age concentration provided some urban, suburban, and rural contrasts. Suburbs showed more neighbors available to give instrumental assistance; while suburbs and rural areas, in that order, yielded a higher prevalence of neighbor-confidants than did the urban tracts. The same order characterized a number of other indicators of both instrumental and affective functions of neighbors. These findings add to the body of research that underlines the greater extensiveness of relationships with non-kin in small communities (Lawton, 1980a).

Crime and the Well-being of Older People

It may well be that "safety on the streets" is today's major environmental concern of older people in the United States. For example, the 1981 Harris Survey (National Council on the Aging, 1981) showed that crime was the major concern of older persons (25% said that crime was a personal problem). Evidence is very clear that older people are victimized least often, but the rate for "larceny with contact" (which includes purse snatching and wallet stealing) is selectively high for older people (reviews appear in Lawton, 1980/81; Liang et al., in press; and Yin, 1980).

Fear of crime is much more prevalent than victimization. There is widespread recognition of how deeply this anxiety can cut into the quality of everyday life. However, aside from residential age segregation (Lawton and

Yaffe, 1980) or living in the least urbanized areas of the country, no effective counter-measures have been reported in the literature. While there is no lack of crime-prevention programs, none has been evaluated, and the anxiety over personal safety continues unabated. The problem is clearly less severe in many other countries, and little research literature has appeared outside the United States.

To conclude this section on neighbor-hoods, the major proactive stances available to the older person with respect to neigh-borhood may be the simple decision to re-main or to relocate and the exercise of the choice to use or not to use elements of the neighborhood environment. While evidence is clear that neighborhood characteristics may affect well-being, the major avenues for changing neighborhood conditions lie at the macrosocial rather than the individual level. Except in unusual instances, the passive stance of being "affected by one's environ-ment" typifies the older person in the given neighborhood environment.

ENVIRONMENTAL GERONTOLOGY AND PUBLIC POLICY

The issues discussed thus far are long-range in the sense that research-based knowledge accumulates slowly, does not become dated overnight, and has some validity across con-texts and national boundaries. By contrast, nothing becomes dated more quickly than national policy. Policies that work in one country are notably difficult to apply in an-other. Thus a section on the policy applica-tions of research knowledge must search out broad areas where there is relative consensus in research findings, and suggest how these areas might strengthen long-term policy de-velopment, rather than a particular contem-porary policy. Literature dealing with immediate issues is particularly difficult to locate outside its country of origin. Thus, references to current policy debates for the interested reader are primarily from the United States (e.g., Rabushka and Jacobs, 1980; Newman et al., 1984; Struyk, in press; Zais et al., 1982; White House Conference

on Aging, 1982), though a few treatments dealing with other countries have been re-ferred to (Centre for Human Settlements, 1982; Kendig, 1981; Nusberg et al., 1984; Pinker, 1980; Tinker, 1981). For present purposes, however, more generic housing needs will be discussed. Needs will be listed first; then the major constraints; and finally suggestions regarding the possible imple-mentation of specific policies.

General Housing Policy Needs

1. The major need of older people is to remain in their homes in the commu-nity.
2. For a minority, a move to improved housing is the major need.
3. High-quality housing is a high-priority need both for those who remain and for those who move.
4. For those who move, the range of choice needs to be widened.

Constraints on Fulfillment of Housing Needs

The major social constraints are:

1. Limitations on public funds available for subsidy.
2. Limited supply of high-quality hous-ing, both in the present and projected for the near future.
3. Competing demands of other target groups for equitable distribution of scarce housing resources.

Constraints inherent in the aging as a group are:

1. A higher proportion with higher rent burdens than in other age groups.
2. A higher probability of functional im-pairment than in other age groups.
3. More tenuous social integration with reduced connectedness to housing-mar-ket opportunities.

Feasible Policy Directions

The past several years have seen some ques-tioning of the appropriateness of an age-spe-cific housing policy (Rabushka and Jacobs,

1980). Thus the major issue that overrides all those listed above is whether older people need to be singled out for special attention in programs for either renters or homeowners. Since the two major constraints are personal—financial and health-related—it makes some inherent sense to think of whether age entitlements should be superseded by means testing that includes both income and health. The major barrier to such a move is the infinitely difficult problem of measuring and implementing a health criterion, in addition to the already troublesome income–assets criterion. A second barrier is that neither of these criteria subsumes the third personal constraint, socially influenced problems with knowledge acquisition, marketplace expertise, and risk management that affect many elderly people even if they are in good health. Unless some much-improved technique for identifying what might be called "biopsychoeconomic need" is developed, age targeting will continue to be necessary. If the existence of a consensus may be used as an indicator, old-age targeting appears to be an invariable marker as nations proceed toward full economic and social development (see Lawton, 1982).

Housing Services in Place. The evidence reviewed overwhelmingly supports the assertion that the great majority of older people would prefer to remain where they are, if housing and neighborhood quality were adequate. While there are many reasons for wishing to remain, psychological attachment to home is frequently a neglected pull factor in remaining, and needs continued emphasis in policy consideration. Direct policy initiatives need to be pursued as "cushioning" measures that both limit the conditions of enforced relocation and require active support for those who are relocated, whether through gentrification, condominium conversion, mortgage foreclosure, or other external pressures. Public initiatives in these matters are constrained less by high program costs than by the resistance of the free real estate market to restraining influences.

Remaining in place is encouraged by maintaining housing and neighborhood quality, an effort that is clearly to the advantage of all age groups. Home maintenance programs for the poor of all ages may be needed, but age-specific expertise is required for their delivery. Active outreach to older homeowners who do not recognize maintenance problems and to those who feel inadequate to cope with them is as necessary as outreach for purely economic assistance. Uncertain at the present time is the optimal structure for such programs—they could be structured at a national level, through a national-to-local funding pipeline, or by purely local initiative.

Physical neighborhood-improvement programs may function best as age-irrelevant efforts. However, social organizational neighborhood efforts whose primary purposes are to strengthen communication, identify need, and target community-based services to the marginally competent must be tailored to the needs of the elderly. The natural tendency for "hard" housing services and "soft" social programs to pursue separate paths needs to be countered by conscious local efforts to coordinate.

Relocation Assistance. While the percentage who feel locked into an undesirable housing situation may be relatively small, a substantial number of individuals require some facilitation of their desire to make a change, in line with their needs and preferences. One major barrier is financial; as the public capacity to extend assistance to the poor of any age expands, the elderly will benefit proportionately.

The supply of housing for lower-income people is limited. One estimate indicates that a minimum of 136,000 replacement (new or rehabilitated) units per year will be needed to supply the elderly in the United States over the next 20 years (Handler, 1983). National public efforts to stimulate such building are necessary, especially in times of sluggish construction activity. Because of both the demand for age-segregated living and the market naiveté of some segments of the older population, age targeting will continue to be necessary. Increased attention to the preservation, rehabilitation, and reuse of the existing housing stock can only benefit every national economy. Adequate representation of the interests of older people in the planning, design, marketing, and management phases needs to be ensured.

A technology for assisting older people in negotiating the total market needs to be developed, whether in the form of housing counseling or as a specific module in the local service agency for the aged.

Housing Choices. The total percentage for whom housing choice is an issue is also small. However, preservation and enlargement of available choices is a goal toward which every society aspires. It is essential that existing supplies of precious commodities like the SRO hotel be protected and that barriers to the growth and accessibility to the elderly of other alternative housing types (manufactured homes, home sharing, accessory apartments, condominiums) be decreased, within the limits of the general welfare.

The housing choice that has typified the average American is home ownership, and the trend is in this direction in other countries [e.g., England (Tinker, 1981)]. Can this situation be perpetuated? The tax incentives that have encouraged home ownership are extremely expensive for the public treasury. Struyk and Bendick (1981) estimated that the potential cost of a nationwide open-enrollment housing allowance program for income-eligible people of all ages in the United States would be about 4 billion dollars; it would add 6 million to the present 3.2 million people presently served by all assisted housing programs. They estimated that the cost of this phenomenal increase in assistance would about equal the tax loss occasioned by the deductions of interest payments from income taxes by homeowners of all ages. It would seem to be time to consider whether such a heavy subsidy to home buyers during their peak working years can be justified. The abolition of this subsidy would, of course, over the long range reduce the proportion of owned units, an effect that would be difficult for any government to ra-

tionalize to a populace that had become used to the owned home as the norm.

Where planned housing is concerned, choices for the economically privileged have grown as education and income have increased, as is seen in the way expensive retirement and life-care communities have developed. Congregate housing [adapted housing in the Netherlands, pensioners' hotels in Sweden, foyer-logements in France (Nusberg et al., 1984)] and other service-rich housing for the income-limited elderly is in very short supply in most countries. It is unlikely to grow in major way unless a cost evaluation now in process at HUD shows it to be highly effective as a substitute for institutional care. Nonetheless, it is important that this model be retained as an alternative to independent housing, just as the continued pursuit of alternative and less expensive ways of producing the same kind of support for the marginally independent is also important.

One final point is that methods of uniting public and private effort need to be explored continually. The level of public financial support for housing for the elderly, in terms of the total percentage of governmentally assisted housing units, is less in the United States than in other Western industrialized countries (Nusberg et al., 1984). Moreover, all of these other nations have such plans as tax benefits, low interest rates, and mixed financing within the same development, thus encouraging the involvement of the private sector in housing for low-income people. It is difficult to find such incentives on the housing scene in the United States at this time.

The major problems lie in housing for the poor and others who require assistance. When national resources are limited, it is very tempting to focus attention on more achievable minor housing goals. Despite their value for people with special needs and limited resources, such programs as home equity conversion, the many forms of alternative housing, condominium-coversion protection, pension-fund investment in housing, Section 202 housing, congregate housing, and a proposed family subsidy for caregiving, together can have only a relatively small impact on the totality of housing problems. The danger lies not in espousing any of these problems but in allowing the focus on them to substitute for the larger goal of homeowner and renter assistance, a goal that can be reached only with a national commitment of private and public funds.

REFERENCES

Abrams, P. (ed.) 1981. Action for care: A review of good neighbour schemes in England. Berkhamsted, England: The Volunteer Centre.

Abt Associates. 1977. *Property Tax Relief Programs for the Elderly.* Cambridge, Mass.: Abt Associates.

Ageing International. 1981. Australia's "granny flats" capture U.S. interest. *Ageing International* 8(4):11–12.

Ageing International. 1982–83. Housing. *Ageing International* 9:9.

Aizenberg, R., and Myers, G. C. 1977. Residential mobility and living arrangements. Paper presented at the annual meeting of the Gerontological Society, San Francisco.

Annual Housing Survey. 1976, 1977, and 1980. Unpublished tabulations from data tape. Philadelphia Geriatric Center.

Beale, C. L. 1975. The revival of population growth in nonmetropolitan America. Economic Research Service No. ERS-605. Washington, D.C.: U.S. Department of Agriculture.

Biggar, J. C. 1980a. Reassessing elderly sunbelt migration. *Research on Aging* 2:177–190.

Biggar, J. C. 1980b. Who moved among the elderly, 1965 to 1970. *Research on Aging* 2:73–91.

Brody, E., and Liebowitz, B. 1981. Some recent innovations in community living arrangements for older people. *In* M. P. Lawton and S. L. Hoover (eds.), *Community Housing Choices for Older Americans.* New York: Springer.

Buczko, W. 1981. Utilization of property tax relief provision by the elderly. Paper presented at the annual meeting of the Gerontological Society of America, Toronto, Canada.

Burgess, E. W. 1961. *Retirement Villages.* Ann Arbor: University of Michigan Press.

Bylund, R. A., Crawford, C. O., and LeRag, N. L. 1979. Housing quality of the elderly: A rural–urban comparison. *Journal of Minority Aging* 4:14–24.

Campbell, A., Converse, P. E., and Rodgers, W. L. 1976. *The Quality of American Life: Perceptions, Evaluations, and Satisfactions.* New York: Russell Sage Foundation.

Cantor, M. H. 1979. Life space and social support. *In* T. O. Byerts, S. C. Howell, and L. A. Pastalan (eds.), *The Environmental Context of Aging,* pp. 33–61. New York: Garland STPM Press.

Carlin, V. F., and Fox, B. 1981. An alternative for elderly housing: Home conversion. *In* M. P. Lawton and S. L. Hoover (eds.), *Community Housing Choices for the Elderly,* pp. 259–266. New York: Springer.

Carp, F. M. 1966. *A Future for the Aged.* Austin: University of Texas Press.

Carp, F. M. 1975. Ego defense or cognitive consistency effects of environmental evaluation. *Journal of Gerontology* 30:707–716.

Carp, F. M. 1976. Housing and living environments of older people. *In* R. Binstock and E. Shanas (eds.), *Handbook of Aging and the Social Sciences,* 1st ed., pp. 244–271. New York: Van Nostrand Reinhold.

Carp, F. M. 1983. A complementary/congruence model of well-being or mental health for the community elderly. In I. Altman, J. Wohlwill, and M. P. Lawton (eds.), *The Elderly and the Physical Environment.* New York: Plenum.

Centre for Human Settlements. 1982. Human settlements and the aging. Report A/CONF 113/25. Nairobi, Kenya: United Nations.

Chevan, A. 1979. Age, housing choice, and neighborhood age structure. Paper presented at the annual meeting of the Gerontological Society, Washington, D.C.

Chevan, A., and Fischer, L. R. 1979. Retirement and interstate migration. *Social Forces* 57:1365–1380.

Coffman, T. L. 1981. Relocation and survival of institutionalized aged: A re-examination of the evidence. *The Gerontologist* 21:483–500.

Cohen, C., and Sokolovsky, J. 1980. Social engagement versus isolation: The case of the aged in SRO hotels. *The Gerontologist* 20:36–44.

Connell, T. L. 1981. An overview of the elderly experience in the experimental housing allowance program. *In* M. P. Lawton and S. L. Hoover (eds.), *Community Housing Choices for Older Americans,* pp. 299–313. New York: Springer.

Cowgill, D. O. 1978. Residential segregation by age in American metropolitan areas. *Journal of Gerontology* 33:446–453.

Cribier, F. 1975. Retirement migration in France. *In* L. A. Kosinski and R. M. Prothero (eds.), *People on the Move,* pp. 360–373. London: Methuen and Company.

Cribier, F. 1979. Retirement migration of Parisian workers. Duplicated report. Centre National de la Recherche Scientifique, University of Paris.

Cribier, F. 1980. A European assessment of aged migration. *Research on Aging* 2:255–270.

David, T. G., Moos, R. H., and Kahn, J. R. 1981. Community integration among elderly residents of sheltered care settings. *American Journal of Community Psychology* 9:513–526.

Dieck, M. 1980. Residential and community provisions for the frail elderly in Germany. *The Gerontologist* 3:260–272.

Dobkin, L. 1980. Under one roof. Status report of homesharing for seniors. Seattle, Wash.: Stevens Housing Improvement Program.

Donahue, W. T., Thompson, M. M., and Curren, D. J. 1977. *Congregate Housing for Older People.* Washington, D.C.: U.S. Government Printing Office.

Duncan, C. J., Streib, G. F., LaGreca, A. J., and O'Rand, A. M. 1978. Retirement communities: Their aging process. Paper presented at the annual meeting of the Gerontological Society, Dallas, Tex.

Eckert, J. K. 1980. *The Unseen Elderly.* San Diego, Calif.: The Campanile Press.

Eckert, J. K., and Murrey, M. 1984. Alternative modes of living for the elderly. *In* I. Altman, J. Wohlwill, and M. P. Lawton (eds.), *Human Behavior and the Environment: The Elderly and the Physical Environment.* New York: Plenum.

Ehrlich, I., and Ehrlich, P. 1976. The invisible elderly. Washington, D.C.: National Council on the Aging.

Ehrlich, P., Ehrlich, I., and Woehlke, P. 1982. Congregate housing for the elderly: Thirteen years later. *The Gerontologist* 22:399–403.

Ferraro, K. F. 1981. Relocation desires and outcomes among the elderly. *Research on Aging* 3: 166–181.

Ferraro, K. F. 1983. The health consequences of relocation among aged in the community. *Journal of Gerontology* 38:90–96.

Florea, A. 1980. Italy. *In* E. Palmore (ed.), *International Handbook on Aging* pp. 234–252. Westport, Conn.: Greenwood Press.

Flynn, C. B. 1980. General versus aged interstate migration, 1965–1970. *Research on Aging* 2:165–176.

Fuguitt, G. V., and Tordella, S. J. 1980. Elderly net migration. *Research on Aging* 2:191–204.

Goedert, J. L., and Goodman, J. L. 1976. *Indicators of Housing Quality.* Washington, D.C.: Urban Institute.

Golant, S. M. 1979. Rationale for geographic perspectives on aging and the aged. *In* S. M. Golant (ed.), *Location and Environment of Elderly Population,* pp. 1–14. Washington, D.C.: V. H. Winston and Sons.

Golant, S. M. 1984. The effects of residential and activity behaviors on old people's environmental experiences. *In* I. Altman, J. Wohlwill, and M. P. Lawton (eds.), *Human Behavior and the Environment: The Elderly and the Physical Environment.* New York: Plenum.

Goldscheider, C. 1966. Differential residential mobility of the older population. *Journal of Gerontology* 21:102–108.

Goode, C., Lawton, M. P., and Hoover, S. L. 1979. Elderly hotel and rooming-house dwellers. Duplicated report, Philadelphia Geriatric Center.

Gottesman, L. E., and Saperstein, A. 1981. The organization of an in-home seervicesnetwork. *In* M. P. Lawton and S. L. Hoover (eds.), *Community Housing Choices for Older Americans,* pp. 170–179. New York: Springer.

Gutowski, M. and Feild, T. 1981. *The Graying of Suburbia.* Washington, D.C.: Urban Insitute.

Haley, B. A. In press. Mobile home elderly: A 1980 profile. *In* R. J. Newcomer, M. P. Lawton, and T. O. Byerts (eds.), *Housing an Aging Society.* Stroudsburg, Pa.: Hutchinson and Ross.

Haley, B. A., Pearson, M., and Hull, D. A. 1981. Urban elderly residents of single-room occupancy housing. Paper presented at the annual meeting of the Gerontological Society of America, Toronto.

Handler, B. 1983. *Housing Needs of the Elderly: A Quantitative Analysis.* Ann Arbor: University of Michigan, National Policy Center on Housing and Living Arrangements for Older Americans.

Hare, P. H., Connor, S., and Merriam, D. 1982. *Accessory Apartments: Using Surplus Space in Single Family Houses.* Chicago: American Planning Association.

Hareven, T. K. 1976. The last stage: Historical adulthood and old age. *Daedalus* 105:13–27.

Heintz, K. M. 1976. *Retirement Communities.* New Brunswick, N.J.: Rutgers University, Center for Urban Policy Research.

Heiser, C. 1980. Property tax postponement. *In* K. Scholen and Y.-P. Chen (eds.), *Unlocking Home Equity for the Elderly,* pp. 96–99. Cambridge, Mass.: Ballinger.

Henig, J. R. 1981. Gentrification and displacement of the elderly: An empirical analysis. *The Gerontologist* 21:67–75.

Henig, J. R. 1981. Gentrification and displacement of the elderly: An empirical analysis. *The Gerontologist* 21:67–75.

Hoover, S. L. 1981. Black and Spanish elderly: Their housing quality. *In* M. P. Lawton and S. L. Hoover (eds.), *Community Housing Choices for Older Americans* pp. 65–89. New York: Springer.

Howell, S. C. 1980. *Designing for Aging: Patterns of Use.* Cambridge, Mass.: MIT Press.

Howell, S. C. 1982. Determinants of housing choice among elderly: Policy implications. Final Report, Grant 90-AR-2116. Cambridge Mass.: Architecture Department, Massachusetts Institute of Technology.

Johnson, S. K. 1971. *Idle Haven: Community Building among the Working-Class Retired.* Berkeley: University of California Press.

Karn, V. 1977. *Retiring to the Seaside.* London: Routledge and Kegan Paul.

Kasl, S. V., and Rosenfield, S. 1980. The residential environment and its impact on the mental health of the aged. *In* J. E. Birren and R. B. Sloane (eds.), *Handbook of Mental Health and Aging,* pp. 468–498. Englewood Cliffs, N.J.: Prentice-Hall.

Kendig, H. 1981. Housing and living arrangements of the aged. *In* A. L. Howe (ed.), *Towards an Older Australia,* pp. 85–101. St. Lucia: University of Queensland Press.

Kleemeier, R. W. 1959. Behavior and the organization of the bodily and the external environment. *In* J. E.

Birren (ed.), *Handbook of Aging the Individual,* pp. 400–541, Chicago: University of Chicago Press.

Koncelik, J. 1976. *Designing the Open Nursing Home.* Stroudsburg, Pa.: Dowden, Hutchinson, and Ross.

LaGory, M., Ward, R., and Juravich, T. 1980. Explanations of the age segregation process in American cities. *Urban Affairs Quarterly* 16:59–80.

LaGory, M., Ward, R., and Mucatel, M. 1981. Patterns of age segregation. *Sociological Focus* 14:1–13.

Lawton, M. P. 1969. Supportive services in the context of the housing environment. *The Gerontologist* 9:15–19.

Lawton, M. P. 1970. Ecology and aging. *In* L. A. Pastalan and D. H. Carson (eds.), *Spatial Behavior of Older People,* pp. 40–67. Ann Arbor: University of Michigan, Institute of Gerontology.

Lawton, M. P. 1975. *Planning and Managing Housing For the Elderly.* New York: Wiley-Interscience.

Lawton, M. P. 1977. The impact of the environment on aging and behavior. *In* J. E. Birren and K. W. Schaie (eds.), *Handbook of the Psychology of Aging,* pp. 276–301. New York: Van Nostrand Reinhold.

Lawton, M. P. 1980a. *Environment and Aging.* Monterey, Calif. Brooks/Cole.

Lawton, M. P. 1980b. *Social and Medical Services in Housing For the Elderly.* National Institute of Mental Health. Washington, D.C.: U.S. Government Printing Office.

Lawton, M. P. 1980c. Residential quality and residential satisfaction among the elderly. *Research on Aging* 2:309–328.

Lawton, M. P. 1980d. Environmental change: The older person as initiator and responder. *In* N. Datan and N. Lohmann (eds.). *Transitions of Aging,* pp. 171–193. New York: Academic Press.

Lawton, M. P. 1980/81. Crime, victimization, and the fortitude of the elderly. *Aged Care and Services Review* 2 (1):20–31.

Lawton, M. P. 1981a. An ecological view of living arrangements. *The Gerontologist* 21:59–66.

Lawton, M. P. 1981b. Alternative housing. *Journal of Gerontological Social Work* 3:61–80.

Lawton, M. P. 1982. Environments and living arrangements. *In* R. H. Binstock, W.-S. Chow, and J. H. Schulz (eds.), *International Perspectives on Aging,* pp. 159–192. New York: United Nations Fund for Population Activities.

Lawton, M. P., and Benner, T. 1981. Federal housing services for community-resident elderly. Final report, AoA Grant 90A1660. Philadelphia Geriatric Center.

Lawton, M. P., and Hoover, S. L. (eds.). 1981. *Community Housing Choices for Older Americans.* New York: Springer.

Lawton, M. P., and Nahemow, L. 1973. Ecology and the aging process. *In* C. Eisdorfer and M. P. Lawton (eds.), *Psychology of Adult Development and Aging,* pp. 619–674, Washington, D.C.: American Psychological Association.

Lawton, M. P., and Yaffe, S. 1980. Victimization and fear of crime in elderly public housing tenants. *Journal of Gerontology* 35:768–779.

Lawton, M. P., Kleban, M., and Carlson, D. 1973. The inner-city resident: To move or not to move. *The Gerontologist* 13:443–448.

Lawton, M. P., Greenbaum, M., and Liebowitz, B. 1980. The lifespan of housing environments for the aging. *The Gerontologist* 20:56–64.

Lawton, M. P., Hoover, S., and Yeh, T.-M. 1981. How the elderly were housed in 1976. Tables from the Annual Housing Survey. Philadelphia: Philadelphia Geriatric Center.

Lawton, M. P., Windley, P. G., and Byerts, T. O. (eds.), 1982. *Aging and the Environment: Theoretical Approaches.* New York: Springer.

Lawton, M. P., Moles, E., and Moss, M. S. In press. The suprapersonal neighborhood context of older people. *Environment and Behavior.*

Lee, E. 1966. A theory of migration. *Demography* 3:47–57.

Lee, G. R. In press. Rural issues in elderly housing. *In* R. J. Newcomer, M. P. Lawton, and T. O. Byerts (eds.), *Housing an Aging Society.* Stroudsburg, Pa.: Hutchinson and Ross.

Lee, G. R., and Lassey, M. L. 1980. Rural–urban differences among the elderly: Economic, social, and subjective factors. *Journal of Social Issues* 36:62–74.

Lehr, U. 1977. Aging in cities and in the country. *Aktuelle Gerontologie* 7:197–204 (German, English abstract).

Lemke, S., and Moos, R. H. 1980. Assessing the institutional policies of sheltered care settings. *Journal of Gerontology* 35:96–107.

Liang, J., Sengstock, M. C., and Hwalek, M. A. In press. Environment and criminal victimization of the aged. *In* R. J. Newcomer, M. P. Lawton, and T. O. Byerts (eds.), *Housing an Aging Society.* Stroudsburg, Pa.: Hutchinson and Ross.

Long, L. A., and Hansen, K. A. 1979. Reasons for interstate migration. *Current Population Reports,* Series P-23, No. 81. Washington, D.C.: Bureau of the Census.

Longino, C. F. 1979. Aged return migration in the United States. *Journal of Gerontology* 34:736–745.

Longino, C. F. 1982. American retirement communities and residential relocation. *In* A. M. Warnes (ed.), *Geographical Perspectives on the Elderly,* pp. 239–262. London: John Wiley.

Longino, C. F. In press. Personal determinants and consequences of independent housing choices. *In* R. J. Newcomer, M. P. Lawton, and T. O. Byerts (eds.), *Housing an Aging Society.* Stroudsburg, Pa.: Hutchinson and Ross.

Longino, C. F., McClelland, K. A., and Peterson, W. A. 1980. The aged subculture hypothesis. *Journal of Gerontology* 35:758–767.

Mangum, W. P. 1982. Housing for the elderly in the United States. *In* A. M. Warnes (ed.), *Geographical Perspectives on the Elderly.* London: John Wiley and Sons, pp. 191–221.

Marans, R. W., Hunt, M. E., and Vakalo, K. L. 1984. Retirement communities. *In* I. Altman, J. Wohlwill, and M. P. Lawton (eds.), *Human Behavior and the Environment: The Elderly and the Physical Environment.* New York: Plenum.

Marcuse, P. 1971. Social indicators and housing policy. *Urban Affairs Quarterly* 1:193–217.

Mayer, N. S., and Lee, O. 1981. Federal home repair programs and elderly homeowners' needs. *The Gerontologist* 21:312–322.

Moos, R. H. 1980. Specialized living environments for older people: A conceptual framework. *Journal of Social Issues* 36:75–94.

Moos, R. H., and Igra, A. 1980. Determinants of the social environments of sheltered care settings. *Journal of Health and Social Behavior* 21:88–98.

Moos, R. H., and Lemke, S. 1983. Supportive residential settings for older people. *In* I. Altman, J. Wohlwill, and M. P. Lawton (eds.), *Human Behavior and the Environment: The Elderly and the Physical Environment.* New York: Plenum.

Mori, M. 1979. Services to the aged in Japan. *In* M. I. Teicher, D. Thursz, and J. L. Vigilante (eds.), *Reaching the Aged: Social Services in Forty-four Countries,* pp. 189–200. Beverly Hills, Calif.: Sage Publications.

Moss, M. S., and Lawton, M. P. 1981. Tenant competence over 12 years: Does it change? Paper presented at the annual meeting of the Gerontological Society of America, Toronto, Canada.

Myers, P. 1978. *Neighborhood Conservation and the Elderly.* Washington, D.C.: The Conservation Foundation.

National Center for Health Statistics. 1976. Health characteristics of persons with chronic activity limitation, United States, 1974. Vital and Health Statistics, Series 10, No. 112. Rockville, Md.: U.S. Department of Health, Education, and Welfare.

National Council on the Aging. 1981. *Aging in the Eighties: America in Transition.* Washington, D.C.: National Council on the Aging.

Newcomer, R. J. 1976. An evaluation of neighborhood service convenience for elderly housing project residents. *In* P. Suedfeld and J. A. Russell (eds.), *The Behavioral Basis of Design,* Vol. 1, pp. 301–307. Stroudsburg, Pa.: Dowden, Hutchinson and Ross.

Newman, S. J. 1976. Housing adjustments of the disabled elderly. *The Gerontologist* 16:312–317.

Newman, S. J., Zais, J., and Struyk, R. J. 1984. Housing older America. *In* I. Altman, J. Wohlwill, and M. P. Lawton (eds.), *Human Behavior and the Environment: The Elderly and the Physical Environment.* New York: Plenum.

Nusberg, C., Gibson, M. J., and Peace, S. 1984. *Innovative Ageing Programs Abroad: Implications for the United States.* Westport, Conn.: Greenwood Press.

O'Bryant, S. L. 1982. The value of home to older persons. *Research on Aging* 4:349–363.

Office of Policy Development and Research. 1979. How well are we housed? 4. The elderly. Washington, D.C.: U.S. Department of Housing and Urban Development.

Office of Policy Development and Research. 1980. The conversion of rental housing condominiums and cooperatives. Washington, D.C.: U.S. Department of Housing and Urban Development.

Palmore, E. 1980. (ed.). *International Handbook on Aging.* Westport, Conn.: Greenwood Press.

Pampel, F., and Choldin, H. 1978. Urban location and segregation of the aged: A block-level analysis. *Social Forces* 56:1121–1139.

Parr, J. 1980. The interaction of persons and living environments. *In* L. W. Poon (ed.), *Aging in the 1980s,* pp. 393–406. Washington, D.C.: American Psychological Association.

Patrick, C. H. 1980. Health and migration of the elderly. *Research on Aging* 2:233–241.

Peace, S. 1981. "Small group" housing in the community. *Ageing International* 8(1):13–16 and (2):16–20.

Peterson, J. A., Hamovitch, M., and Larson, A. E. 1973. *Housing Needs and Satisfactions of the Elderly.* Los Angeles: University of Southern California, Ethel Percy Andrus Gerontology Center.

Pinker, R. A. 1980. Facing up to the eighties: Health and welfare needs of British elderly. *The Gerontologist* 20:273–283.

Rabushka, A., and Jacobs, B. 1980. *Old Folks at Home.* New York: Free Press.

Rausch, K., and Hoover, S. L. 1980. Mobile home elderly: Structural characteristics of their dwellings. Unpublished manuscript. Philadelphia Geriatric Center.

Regnier, V. A. 1976. Neighborhoods as service systems. *In* M. P. Lawton, R. J. Newcomer, and T. O. Byerts (eds.), *Community Planning for an Aging Society,* pp. 240–259. Stroudsburg, Pa.: Dowden, Hutchinson, and Ross.

Regnier, V. A. 1982. Urban neighborhood cognition: Relationships between functional and symbolic community elements. *In* G. D. Rowles and R. Ohta (eds.), *Aging and Milieu,* pp. 63–82. New York: Academic Press.

Regnier, V. A., and Hamburger, J. L. 1978. Comparison of perceived and objective crime against the elderly in an urban neighborhood. Paper presented at the annual meeting of the Gerontological Society, Dallas.

Rosow, I. 1967. *Social Integration of the Aged.* New York: Free Press.

Rossi, P. H. 1980. *Why Families Move,* 2nd ed. Beverly Hills, Calif.: Sage Publications.

Rowland, K. F. 1977. Environmental events predicting death for the elderly. *Psychological Bulletin* 84:349–372.

Rowles, G. D. 1978. *Prisoners of Space?* Boulder, Colo.: Westview Press.

Rowles, G. D. 1980. Growing old "inside": Aging and attachment to place in an Appalachian community.

In N. Datan and N. Lohmann (eds.), *Transitions of Aging,* pp. 153–170. New York: Academic Press.

Ruffini, J. L., and Todd, H. F. 1981. "Passing it on": The senior block information service of San Francisco. *In* M. P. Lawton and S. L. Hoover (eds.), *Community Housing Choices for Older Americans* pp. 135–145. New York: Springer.

Scheidt, R. J. 1982. A taxonomy of well-being for small-town elderly: A case for rural diversity. Manhattan, Kans.: Department of Family and Child Development, Kansas State University.

Schulz, R., and Brenner, G. F. 1977. Relocation of the aged: A review and theoretical analysis. *Journal of Gerontology* 32:323–333.

Sclar, E. D. 1976. Aging and residential location. *In* M. P. Lawton, R. J. Newcomer, and T. O. Byerts (eds.), *Community Planning for an Aged Society,* pp. 266–281. Stroudsburg Pa.: Dowden, Hutchinson, and Ross.

Serow, W. J. 1978. Return migration of the elderly in the USA: 1955–1960 and 1965–1970. *Journal of Gerontology.* 33:288–295.

Shanas, E., Townsend, P., Wedderburn, D., Friis, H., Milhøj, P., and Stehouwer, J. 1968. *Old People in Three Industrial Societies.* New York: Atherton.

Sherman, S. R. 1971. The choice of retirement housing among the well elderly. *Aging and Human Development* 2:118–138.

Sherman, S. R. 1972. Satisfaction with retirement housing: Attitudes, recommendations, and moves. *Aging and Human Development* 3:339–366.

Sherman, S. R., and Newman, E. S. 1977. Foster-family care for the elderly in New York State. *The Gerontologist* 17:513–520.

Smith, B., and Hiltner, J. 1975. Intra urban location of the elderly. *Journal of Gerontology* 30:473–478.

Sokolovsky, J., and Cohen, C. 1981. Measuring social interaction of the urban elderly: A methodological synthesis. *International Journal of Aging and Human Development* 12:233–244.

Speare, A. 1970. Home ownership, life cycle state, and residential mobility. *Demography* 7:449–458.

Stegman, M. A. In press. Urban displacement and condominium conversion. *In* R. J. Newcomer, M. P. Lawton, and T. O. Byerts (eds.), *Housing an Aging Society.* Stroudsburg, Pa.: Hutchinson and Ross.

Stephens, J. 1976. *Loners, Losers, and Lovers.* Seattle: University of Washington Press.

Streib, G. F., Folts, W. E., and Hilker, M. A. In press. *Old Homes, New Families: Shared Living for the Elderly.* New York: Columbia University Press.

Streib, G. F., LaGreca, A. J., Folts, N. E. In press. Retirement communities: People, planning, prospects. *In* R. J. Newcomer, M. P. Lawton, and T. O. Byerts (eds.), *Housing an Aging Society.* Stroudsburg, Pa.: Hutchinson and Ross.

Struyk, R. J. 1977. The housing situation of elderly Americans. *The Gerontologist* 17:130–139.

Struyk, R. J. 1980. Housing adjustments of relocating elderly households. *The Gerontologist* 20:45–55.

Struyk, R. J. In press. Future housing assistance policy for the elderly. *In* R. J. Newcomer, M. P. Lawton, and T. O. Byerts (ed.), *Housing an Aging Society.* Stroudsburg, Pa.: Hutchinson and Ross.

Struyk, R. J., and Bendick, M. (eds.), 1981. *Housing Vouchers for the Poor.* Washington, D.C.: Urban Institute Press.

Struyk, R. J., and Soldo, B. J. 1980. *Improving the Elderly's Housing.* Cambridge Mass.: Ballinger.

Taylor, P. S. (ed.), 1981. Research on housing and related services for the elderly: An annotated bibliography. Contract Report HC-5204 for U.S. Department of Housing and Urban Development Gerontological Society of America, Washington, D.C.

Teaff, J. D., Lawton, M. P., Nahemow, L., and Carlson, D. 1978. Impact of age integration on the wellbeing of elderly tenants in public housing. *Journal of Gerontology* 33:126–133.

Teicher, M. I., Thursz, D., and Vigilante, J. L. (eds.), 1979. *Reaching the Aged: Social Services in Forty-four Countries.* Beverly Hills, Calif.: Sage Publications.

Tinker, A. 1976. Housing the elderly: How successful are Granny Annexes? HDD Occasional Paper 1/76. London: Department of the Environment.

Tinker, A. 1981. *The Elderly in Modern Society.* London: Longmans.

Tinker, A. 1983. Recent research on housing the elderly in the United Kingdom. Paper presented at Conference on Housing and the Elderly, International Exchange Center on Gerontology, University of South Florida.

Turner, L. F., and Mangum, E. 1982. The housing choices of older Americans. Washington, D.C.: National Council on the Aging.

U.S. Bureau of the Census. 1974–77. Annual Housing Survey, 1973–1976. Washington, D.C.: U.S. Government Printing Office.

U.S. Bureau of the Census. 1978. Geographical mobility: March 1975 to March 1978. *Current Population Reports* Series P-20, No. 331. Washington, D.C.: U.S. Government Printing Office.

Ward, R. A. 1979. The implications of neighborhood age structure for older people. *Sociological Symposium* 26:42–63.

Ward, R. A., LaGory, M., Sherman, S., and Traynor, D. 1981. Neighborhood age structure and support networks. Paper presented at the annual meeting of the Gerontological Society of America, Toronto.

Weitzman, P. 1976. Mobile homes: High-cost housing in the low-income market. *Journal of Economic Issues* 10:582–593.

Wheeler, R. 1982. Staying put: A new development in policy? *Ageing and Society* 2:299–329.

White House Conference on Aging. 1982. *Final Report,* Vol. 3. Committees' recommendations from the White House Conference. Washington, D.C.: WHCOA.

Windley, P. G., and Scheidt, R. J. 1980. Person-environment dialectics: Implications for competent functioning in old age. *In* L. W. Poon (ed.), *Aging in the 1980s*. Washington, D.C.: American Psychological Association.

Windley, P. G., and Scheidt, R. J. 1982. An ecological model of mental health among small-town elderly. *Journal of Gerontology* 37:235–242.

Wiseman, R. F. 1979. Spatial aspects of aging. Resource Paper No. 88–4. Washington, D.C.: Association of American Geographers.

Wiseman, R. F. 1980. Why older people move: Theoretical issues. *Research on Aging* 2:141–154.

Wolpert, J. 1966. Migration as an adjustment to environmental stress. *Journal of Social Issues* 22:92–102.

Yin, P. P. 1980. Fear of crime among the elderly. *Social Problems* 27:492–504.

Zais, J., Struyk, R. J., and Thibodeau, T. 1982. *Housing Assistance for Older Americans*. Washington, D.C.: Urban Institute Press.

16
THE ECONOMY AND THE AGED

Jack Habib

Brookdale Institute of
Gerontology and Adult
Human Development in Israel
and
Hebrew University, Jerusalem

I. INTRODUCTION

One of the most difficult problems in writing on aging and the economy is to frame the issues in a useful way. The issues involved lie at the point of intersection among several complex sets of factors: (1) how people are affected by and respond to the aging process; (2) change in demographic structure and in economic conditions; and (3) the social and economic policies that impinge upon individual behavior and that attempt to influence aggregate conditions. The interrelationships among these three sets of factors are a complex set of simultaneous rather than recursive or unidirectional causal links. Individual responses to the aging process are influenced by the context, as defined by economic conditions or a society's age structure. Economic conditions are themselves influenced by the manner of response to lifecycle decisions (when to retire, how much to save). The processes of population aging (an upward shift in the age structure) depend crucially on individual decisions with respect to fertility, which are in turn influenced by economic conditions.

The literature on aging and the economy has grown at a rapid rate. One small indicator is the growing number of reviews of this literature. As the literature develops, there is increasing emphasis on a broader view of the implications of changes as they ripple through the economic and social structure. Economists refer to these as the general equilibrium consequences. Moreover, many of these changes are viewed as endogenous rather than exogenous, and there is a vigorous search for their sources within the system.

Despite the simultaneous links between behavioral patterns, macroeconomic or societal change, and public policy, each may serve as a source of impetus for change. A shift in preferences with respect to retirement may emerge in a given set of economic conditions or policy parameters. The extent to which actual retirement patterns change, however, will depend on the response of the economic system and public policy to the change in preferences. Developments in world commodity markets may lead to economic stagnation, yet the actual effects on the elderly depend on the sensitivity of employment behavior and of patterns of intergenerational transfers to economic conditions. As ideological shift may start new policies in given economic and social conditions, but the individual and aggregate response will condition the consequences of

479

the policy. Public policies may attempt to moderate the effects of deteriorating economic conditions on the elderly or try to improve economic conditions by imposing sacrifices on them. These alternative policy thrusts reflect disparate concerns with the welfare of society as a whole (i.e. with economic growth, avoiding unemployment, and restraining inflation) and with the status of the elderly.

Changes in the age structure are tied to changes in overall population growth, and both derive from the same underlying factors: fertility rates, age-specific life expectancy, and immigration patterns. Populations may age in a number of different ways, depending upon the specific values and interaction among these three factors. The economic significance of population aging will correspondingly vary with the details of the pattern (Clark and Spengler, 1980b). In order to contrast alternative patterns of age structure change, we define four groups: the percentage of elderly (65+), the old-old as a percentage of the elderly, the old-young as a percentage of the young (15–18/0–18), and the percentage in the prime working age group (18–65). These groups represent the potential size of the retired, of the high-need groups among the retired (old-old) and among the young (old-young), and of producers. The translation of these groups into specific age ranges varies in practice.

Table 1 contrasts three patterns: Pattern 1 reflects the consequences of a decline in fertility in the range above the replacement level at which the population would become stationary. Pattern 3 represents a further decline in fertility to a rate below the re-

placement level. Pattern 2 is consistent with a rise in life expectancy at the upper end of the age spectrum. In all three patterns the proportion of those over age 65 and of the old-old increases; yet, the proportion in the prime age range increases in pattern 1, whereas it falls in patterns 2 and 3. This implies that the dependency ratio, defined as the ratio of children and elderly to those of working age, rises in patterns 2 and 3. Pattern 2 has the advantage that the old-young do not increase as a percentage of the young as a whole; however, it leads to the most serious increase in the old-old. Although the share of the elderly among total dependents rises in all three patterns, this increase is particularly acute in pattern 2.

To evaluate the overall consequences of an upward shift in the age structure and the differences among the various possible patterns, estimates are required of the magnitude of the differences in needs of the different age groups whose relative proportions change. Section II of this chapter reviews the literature on this topic. Similarly, the size of the productive group consistent with a given age structure depends on the ages of entry to and retirement from the labor force and on additional aspects of labor force participation rates. These variables may themselves change in response to population aging. The capacity to support the dependent population will also depend on changes in productivity per worker. Section III examines the links between population aging, the rate of labor force participation, the range of factors affecting productivity per worker, and total output. Taken together, the analyses of Sections II and III provide us with insight on

TABLE 1. Patterns of Change in Age Structure.

	% Elderly	Old-old / Elderly	% Prime Age	Old-young / Young
Pattern 1	rises	rises	rises	rises
Pattern 2	rises	rises sharply	falls	constant
Pattern 3	rises	rises	falls	rises

the extent to which dependency needs rise or fall in relation to total output, or output per person.

The bodies of literature dealing with needs and productive capacity generally focus on goods produced in the market (see overviews in Russell, 1979; Clark and Spengler, 1980a, Ch. 9; Espenshade and Braun, 1981). But market output does not reflect the full output of a society. Growing attention has been paid in the economic literature to the home production of goods and services, to the time invested by the family in the human capital of children (better health, values, knowledge and skills), to the care of dependent relations, and to the value of organized volunteer activities. This broadened concept of output is of direct importance in evaluating the implications of population aging for national output, which we shall attempt to incorporate into our subsequent discussion.

As noted, changes in the age structure are also associated with changes in the rate of population growth. The declines in fertility that generated patterns 2 and 3 also lead to a slower rate of population growth. By contrast, in pattern 2 the rate of population growth will increase somewhat as life expectancy rises. The rate of population growth in itself has implications for resource requirements, as it affects the level of required investment. This has been emphasized by modern growth theory, and Section IV reviews the implications of that theory for the economic consequences of population aging.

Aside from the consequences of population aging for the overall relationship between needs and productive capacity, this chapter is concerned with the implications of population aging for the well-being of the elderly population and for the nature of public policies toward the elderly that affect their well-being. A number of trends or factors have combined to bring the question of policies with respect to the elderly into sharp focus. Recent declines of fertility levels in developed nations, which approach or even fall below replacement, have raised the specter of a continued rise in the percentage who are elderly and of possible increases in dependency ratios as well. There is increased awareness of the rise in the old-old population, with all its implications for health and welfare expenditures and for the care demands made upon families. This has special significance at a time when the traditional caregivers—married daughters—are increasingly seeking paid employment. Recent and unexpected advances in life expectancy after age 65 have further enhanced the rate of increase in the old-old (Myers, 1981; Taubman, 1981). Aside from the effects of life expectancy on age distribution, every additional year of post-retirement life expectancy can seriously affect social security systems. It has, for example, been estimated that the expected long-term social security deficit in the United States would increase substantially if the retirement period were to be increased by one year (Boskin and Robinson, 1980, p. 44). The effect of the changes in fertility rates and life expectancy on the ratio of dependent to employed persons has been exacerbated by a strong trend toward earlier retirement. Changes in economic conditions, rapid inflation, high unemployment, low rates of growth in output and productivity, have all led to further difficulties in financing social welfare expenditures in general and for the elderly in particular. Finally, there has been increasing questioning of the appropriateness of pay-as-you-go systems for financing social welfare expenditures for the elderly (Feldstein, 1975).

These developments (changes in fertility rates and life expectancy, retirement patterns, and the questioning of financing systems) have tended to shift the balance of concern more to restraining rather than maintaining the living standards of the elderly. The word "crisis" (with respect to financing their needs) has crept into more and more book and article titles (e.g., *The Crisis in Social Security,* Boskin, 1978; *The Welfare State in Crisis,* OECD, 1981).

Sections V and VI consider the nature of the policy issues arising from population aging and the changing economic conditions. The sense in which there may be a crisis in our ability to meet the growing needs of the elderly is explored. Building on the evaluation that Sections II, III, and IV provide of the consequences of population aging for dependency needs and output, we contrast the way in which alternative regimes for providing for the needs of the elderly in retirement may adjust to changes in the age structure. Specifically, we attempt to evaluate the policy dilemmas that arise in a public pay-as-you-go system by contrasting the adjustment process with what might happen in a pure system of private savings. Section VI integrates the implications of changes in macro-economic conditions, and Section VII provides a summary.

II. AGING AND ECONOMIC NEEDS

Relatively few studies have attempted to evaluate the changes in the net support costs associated with population aging. Two conceptual distinctions are important. There is a need to distinguish between public costs financed through taxation or government debt, and private expenditures financed out of disposable income and private savings. Further, one must distinguish between actual expenditures and those required to achieve a given level of well-being or equivalent levels of well-being between household units.

One of the conclusions reached in the previous discussion is that while the overall rate of dependency may decline in some patterns of population aging, within the dependent population there will always be a shift to a larger share of elderly relative to children. The economic significance of this shift depends on the relative needs of children versus the elderly.

Much economic and demographic modeling has assumed that there is no difference in the cost of supporting an aged person or a child. More recent theoretical models of population change (Lee, 1980) have tried to allow for differences, and there have been several attempts to measure them directly.

Clark (1976) estimates that public expenditures in the United States are three times as high for elderly as for children. Wander (1978) focuses on total public and private expenditures in Germany and concludes that, on average, a child absorbs one-fourth to one-third more resources than an old person. As no details of Wander's calculations are provided, one cannot fully ascertain whether it is the inclusion of consumption expenditures that accounts for the difference, or whether Germany spends relatively more on children. Both studies focus on actual rather than on required expenditures. These patterns reflect decisions on the level of public services, and the distribution of responsibility between the public and private sectors. The relative consumption expenditures that enter into Wander's calculations reflect not only needs but also the relative incomes of the elderly and of families with children.

There is an extensive literature that deals with required private consumption expenditures where these refer to the relative expenditure levels demanded for the welfare equivalence of households of different size and age composition (as summarized in van der Gaag, 1981). The findings suggest that the economic needs of children are less than those of adults, and that they rise with the age of the child. Moreover, relative needs decline rapidly as the number of children in a given household increases. Much less research has focused on relative needs of the elderly.

It has been a common assumption in policy debates over pension adequacy to assume that the needs of the elderly are lower than those of nonretired adults (see Meier et al., 1980 for a detailed review). Work is in progress to apply the most advanced techniques for estimating equivalence scales to the question of the relative needs of the elderly. Preliminary results suggest that older households require less total consumption to reach a given utility level than do younger households (van der Gaag and Smolensky, 1980). The comparison to children is, however, more complex because both age and family size enter the equation. On the basis of the estimated equivalence scale, the needs of an aged person living alone far exceed those of a child in a two-parent family. None of the studies has provided separate estimates for the needs of an aged person living in a multigenerational household so as to isolate the effects of age and economies of scale.

The findings from studies of equivalence scales must be treated with considerable caution. There are fundamental assumptions about welfare equivalence that cannot generally be justified, and that underlie the estimation of these scales (Habib, 1980). An approach now gaining acceptance and recognition is that of Kapteyn and van Praag (1980), which uses self-reported happiness (ranging from very bad to excellent) to estimate the impact of family size and compensation on relative needs. The key assumption in this approach is that each point on the verbal scale has equivalent welfare significance across a population. No matter what assumptions are made and techniques are employed, however, it is important to note that the age pattern of needs for private expenditure is a function of the extent to which the needs of various age groups are met through direct public provision or are publicly subsidized.

There would not seem to be any conceptual basis for arriving at a single relative needs measure that encompasses public and private expenditure. In this sense there is no one simple answer to the question of whether a decline in the proportion of children might offset the impact of a rise in the share of the elderly. However, two questions may be raised in its stead, assuming a given distribution and level of public expenditures in terms of the extent and quality of the services provided: (1) How much does a decline in the number of children per family or a change in their age composition increase real family income? This question may be answered on the basis of estimated equivalence scales. (2) To what extent will changes in the population's age structure increase the share of national income required to maintain the same level of public services over time? The rise in the tax rate required to finance public services may be compared to the percentage

increase in real disposable income arising from reduced needs of children in order to obtain some notion of the increased pressure on per capita consumption standards.

Research on equivalence scales should pay more attention to the living arrangements of the elderly, and research on public expenditures should attempt to refine the age breakdown. None of the available studies has separated out the old-old from the old (e.g., Denton and Spencer, 1978), with the exception of the analysis of health care needs by Russell (1981). Health expenditures among the old-old are particularly high, and there is a rapid increase in the size of this group in many countries.

Sheppard and Rix (1977) use the estimates made by Clark to examine the predicted public dependency burden over the next 50 years in the United States. They show that despite the rise in the population over age 65 and the sharp increase in the expenditure burden of this group, the total expenditure burden rises very little (for similar results for Canada, see Denton and Spencer, 1978). The implication is that even large age-related differences in expenditure may not generate significant aggregate changes. It would be interesting to see how a more detailed age breakdown of the elderly would affect these results.

Finally, there is a third dimension of needs that has been largely ignored in evaluating age structure changes. Families not only spend money on their children, but they devote time to their children and their elderly parents as well. Further, both children and grandparents contribute time to each other and to the common needs of the family. In theory one could raise the question of the relative net consumption of "other's" time required to establish welfare equivalence between children and grandparents. As the population ages, is there a rise or fall in the amount of total time input by prime age adults required to maintain the welfare of their children and parents? If the net amount of time required by children exceeds that required by grandparents, the families may be better off as the population ages even if they must allocate more of their incomes to finance public expenditures. Similarly, changes in the age composition of children and the elderly will affect the amount of time required for each generation. Among children, the expenditures and time needs may be offset as older children demand more market goods but less time. Among the elderly, the two effects are likely to reinforce each other, as the old-old may require more of both.

III. AGING AND THE NATIONAL PRODUCT

The links between population aging and the national product take a number of forms. We begin by considering the implications for the extent of employment. We go on to consider the implications of population aging for the range of factors determining the productivity of the labor force, and conclude with a discussion of the rate of savings and investment.

Age Structure and Employment Rates

The employment rate is the percentage of a population or age group that engages in market activity. It is influenced by both the rate of labor force participation and the unemployment rate. The labor force participation rate is itself influenced by the rate of unemployment, as discouraged workers drop out of the labor force. We consider whether changes in age structure should reduce the overall employment rate by considering in turn the effects on unemployment and on participation. We also consider the implications of fertility-related changes in female labor force participation and the nature of the links between changes in market output and production within the home.

Several authors have argued that age structure shifts may substantially affect the noninflationary rate of full employment (see, e.g., Easterlin, 1978). This argument is based on the fact that should unemployment rates vary by age and demographic groups, there may be considerable unemployment at a time when the rate for prime age males is very low.

If age and sex groups are not perfect substitutes in production, further increases in demand will be inflationary. Unemployment rates are highest among younger age groups, so that the thrust of their argument is that as populations age and the weight of groups with high unemployment rates declines, the achievable rate of full employment should increase. In her review of the literature, Russell (1979) indicates that the evidence is mixed and this argument cannot as yet be fully substantiated.

Rates of labor force participation are subject to two contrasting influences as populations age. Fertility-induced declines in age structure will increase the percentage of the population in the prime age range. On the other hand, the aging of the prime age group itself could reduce this group's rate of participation. Clark and Spengler (1980b, pp. 68–70) note that this first effect is very sensitive to the ages of labor force entry and of retirement. They point out that the difference in labor force participation rates associated with changing age structure is greater as the ages of entry and retirement rise. As the age of entry has tended to rise and age of retirement to decline, the sensitivity of the participation rate to age structure changes has not increased and probably has even declined.

Clark and Spengler (1980c, pp. 160–161) focus attention on the size of the 55–60 age group which borders the official retirement age. A rise in the proportion of prime age workers in the near-retirement ages could lead to a decline in the overall rate of labor force participation among prime age workers. The lower the retirement age, the less sensitive to age structure changes will be the rate of participation below that age. This sensitivity will tend to offset the relationships suggested by Clark and Spengler. Thus one cannot easily generalize about the degree of sensitivity of participation rates to the age structure. At the same time, both a decline in the retirement age and the aging of the prime age group contribute to an absolute decline in labor force participation rates for any given age structure. Non-participation by prime age males of this age group has a particular impact on public budgets, as it is relatively easy to establish eligibility for unemployment (and in some countries for disability benefits) that provides high levels of wage replacement and leads to eligibility for a full retirement pension at age 65. This contrasts with those who retire early and who are forced to accept actuarially reduced pensions. Both early retirement and disability pensions have grown rapidly in most developed countries (see Tracy, 1979, for international trends in early retirement; see Copeland, 1981, for trends in disability).

In some countries the tendency of labor force participation to fall has been offset by rising rates of female labor force participation. Recent empirical work has emphasized that these changes may in part be inherent in the process of fertility decline (Schultz, 1978; Fleisher and Rhodes, 1979). In addition to the effects of declining fertility on female labor force participation, there is evidence that husbands' hours of work may substantially increase (Cramer, 1980), and that older workers may find work more attractive if a labor shortage emerges.

Offsetting increases in age-specific labor force participation rates may not represent net gains in the overall social product. It is unclear how much of the gain would be at the expense of leisure, and how much at the expense of other productive activities. Specifically, increased female labor participation may reduce home production, care of children and grandparents, or voluntary activities. Alternatively, market employment may reduce leisure more than these other types of productive activities. There is evidence that working wives do not reduce their time spent in household activities (Gronau, 1976). There is no evidence on the tradeoff between women's labor force participation and the extent of their involvement in informal assistance to relatives and friends outside the household unit or organized volunteer activities. The time allocation studies have not even provided a clear picture of the possible quantitative importance of these activities. Increased labor force participation

by women, even if it is offsetting in terms of total man/woman-hours, does not offset the state budget impact, inasmuch as these women would not have received public pensions if they had remained at home. On the contrary, more of the cost of informal care is shifted to the public sector.

Children and the elderly are in themselves sources of in-kind services. As the population ages, the flow of services from these two groups potentially could increase or decrease. Looked at from another perspective, the total adult time available per child (parents plus grandparents) will rise as the population ages, as will the amount of elderly time per adult. The availability of elderly parents' time may constitute the enabling factor that allows their adult daughters to participate in the labor force. It has been well established that despite the decline in common intergenerational living arrangements, there is still an active exchange of assistance between the elderly and their adult children. The informal caregiving rate among the young, prime age adults, and the elderly could thus be an important element in determining the overall consequences of age structure changes for the supply of productive man-hours.

Age Structure and Productivity

Age structure may affect labor productivity either because productivity in specific jobs changes with age or through the efficiency with which labor is deployed. The latter is related to age differences in the degree of labor mobility.

There are a number of important distinctions that must be made in trying to evaluate the relationship between age and worker productivity. One needs to distinguish between the average productivity of an age group were they all to remain employed and the productivity of those who choose employment because they are healthy enough to work and want to do so. The relationship between age and productivity may vary with the type of work and the dimension of productivity. One must also distinguish possible productivity differences that arise from physiological and mental processes and those that arise from the aging of a stock of knowledge acquired through earlier education. The organization of work and choice of technology further influence the link between age and productivity, making it an area that is subject to policy manipulation. Spengler (1971) argues that while capacities may decline throughout most of the work-life, productivity need not, as one's ability far exceeds the demands of the job.

The findings with respect to these issues vary with the different types of evidence that have been considered. There have been attempts to examine worker productivity through direct observation of workers and through ratings by supervisors or co-workers.

Every author who has summarized the direct studies of productivity has concluded that productivity on the average does not decline with age (Riley and Foner, 1968; Clark et al., 1978; U.S. Department of Labor, 1979). Whereas specific attributes have been found to decline, it is usually argued that there are often compensating increases. However, to the extent that there is a rapid increase in technology and new knowledge, the importance of the older worker's experience is diminished, and retraining capacity becomes a key element in the preservation of productivity. The existing evidence regarding the relative retraining capacities of the elderly is minimal and inconclusive.

Labor costs per unit of output are related to attendance and injury rates. Here too the evidence suggests that older workers are not at a disadvantage. Attendance patterns are found to be equal or better among older workers compared to younger workers (e.g., Welford, 1958). The age pattern of work injuries has been examined by a number of authors and most recently by Dillingham (1981). The most prominent finding is that the aged have fewer but more serious or lengthy injuries. The net implications for unit labor costs have not been evaluated.

A second type of evidence relates to age-earnings profiles. To the extent that wages reflect productivity, differences in relative earnings by age may be used to evaluate the effects of changes in the age structure on productivity. Studies of age–earning profiles have consistently found that relative earnings rise with labor force or job experience and decline after peaking at ages 45–50. They still tend to remain above those of younger workers. Absolute earnings levels may continue to increase with age owing to inflation or productivity growth in the economy. This literature has attempted to distinguish the effects of experience (assumed to be positive) and of age (assumed to be negative); however, this distinction is not very important from the point of view of evaluating the consequences of changes in the age structure, as an older labor force can be expected to have greater experience as well.

Non-economists (and some economists) have always been skeptical about the assumption that wages reflect the marginal product of labor. A critique of this assumption has recently emerged as part of new approaches to the conceptualization of the labor market. In one such approach, wages at any point in time are viewed from the perspective of an implicit lifetime contract. Lazear (1979) attempts to explain mandatory retirement rules in this framework and argues that wages systematically underestimate productivity at younger ages and overstate them at older ages. If this is the case, productivity declines with age would be greater than those implied by wage–earnings profiles.

A third approach estimates production functions of a firm, a sector, or an overall economy where labor inputs are differentiated by age. Very few studies have estimated production relations with labor inputs disaggregated by age. Anderson (1977) found that workers of different ages were imperfect substitutes, thus implying productivity differences.

On the whole there would seem to be only a limited empirical basis for establishing the direction or magnitude of age-related productivity differences. Yet the assumption that older workers are less productive persists and even finds expression in some of the more sophisticated attempts to model and simulate the consequences of aging on the economy (Lesthaeghe, 1979; Denton et al., 1980; Anderson, 1980). Much more convincing research is required before much confidence can be placed in the results.

Age Differences in Mobility. Labor mobility is viewed as a prerequisite for the efficient functioning of labor markets. The willingness of workers to take advantage of differences in the return to jobs is essential to maximizing output. This is particularly important at times of rapid change in the structure of demand or in technology. The utilization of available opportunities may also imply residential relocation, and the willingness of workers to relocate may affect the ability of multi-regional firms to make an optimal allocation of their labor force.

A number of authors express concern with the effects of age structure on mobility (Sauvy, 1948, p. 194; Wander, 1978), and there is clear evidence that the extent of mobility declines with age (Leigh, 1978; Klinov, 1978). The decline in voluntary mobility (quits as opposed to layoffs) is even greater with age (Habib and Spilerman, 1981).

Analyses of mobility have been limited in a number of respects. Parnes et al. (1975, Ch. 3) make the important distinction between the propensity for mobility and actual rates of movement. Propensity is measured by the size of the gain required to induce a move, while actual movement reflects the distribution of opportunities as well. The degree of opportunity, not only the propensity, could easily decline with age. The meaning for differential mobility rates also needs to be examined against the background of different types of mobility.

In addition to job shifts associated with capturing the opportunities created by new or shifting sources of demand, mobility is related to the exploration of job preferences or advancement along hierarchical job ladders. The decline in job mobility with age could reflect a declining need to learn about tastes and skills, diminished opportunities for those near the peak of their career ladders, or age discrimination in job offers. These issues remain largely unexplored in the literature. Several authors have noted that job shifts frequently are not rewarded by increased pay (Andrisani, 1977; Klinov, 1978; Habib and Spilerman, 1981), so that it is not clear to what extent lower mobility rates represent forgone income and input.

As noted by Keyfitz (1973) and others, opportunities for occupational advancement themselves change with changes in age structure. The progress of the representative individual from a lower to a higher position slows mainly because of the slower population growth associated with older age structures. At the same time, wage profiles may flatten in response (Freeman, 1978). The implications of these two related phenomena are quite controversial. They are hypothesized to affect economic performance either because they may lead to worker disgruntlement with negative consequences for labor productivity, or because the flattening of wage differentials will weaken incentives for advancement. Yet as Espenshade and Braun (1981) note, there are equally plausible arguments in the other direction. Nor is there much notion of the possible severity of these problems.

The implications of age structure changes for labor productivity, or even labor force participation, may be considerably more significant if changes in age structure are also associated with large structural changes in the economy. Thus if there are large effects of age on the patterns of consumption, population aging would imply large-scale structural changes. If older workers have less of a propensity for mobility, there will be a higher probability of their staying on in situations in which they have become redundant or their productivity has declined, owing to structural change. Forced displacement may lead more to early retirement than to reemployment in a new job or sector. The changes in the age structure simultaneously increase the need for job mobility while decreasing the likelihood that it will occur.

Pension policies that deter or facilitate

mobility and retraining play an important role in shaping the nature of the response (Schiller and Weiss, 1979). The degree of pension portability and policies with respect to severance pay vary considerably between countries. Some countries, such as Germany, offer the older worker extensive retraining programs (Rohrlich, 1980, p. 92). In other countries, the link between structural change in the economy and early withdrawal or non-mobility may be institutionalized in the norms governing eligibility for unemployment, disability, or early retirement benefits. The norms of what is expected of older workers in terms of employer or occupational shifts vary a great deal across countries. Older workers may thus have the opportunity to retire with full benefits rather than face the need to adjust to a new job.

Age Structure and Demand

How large will be the structural changes in demand associated with changes in the age structure of the population? The major studies of consumption patterns have confirmed the existence of statistically significant age effects (e.g., Parks and Barten, 1973). However, when consumption demand equations are used to quantify the potential overall effect on the structure of consumption, the aggregate effects prove to be small.

The most recent and extensive study of demographic effects on the composition of demand was conducted by Musgrove (1980). His study estimates detailed demand equations that allow for the age of the head of the household and the age of a number of family members. He finds that the effects of population composition on the composition of demand are small, and concludes that "what principally changes the composition of spending is the growth of income per person, and that growth is largely independent of the population path the society takes."

Age Structure and the Rate of Savings and Investment

The link between aging and the level of savings and investment has been one of the most studied and controversial issues addressed by the literature on aging. There are two major issues:

1. What is the effect of the age structure on the aggregate societal rate of savings? This issue has at times been addressed in the broader context of the effect of population growth and dependency ratios on savings.
2. What is the effect of alternative forms of financing retirement incomes on the rate of savings for a given population and age structure?

We begin with the question of how changes in the age structure affect the aggregate saving rate. The life-cycle theory of savings (Modigliani and Brumberg, 1975) gives rise to the prediction that families have positive savings up to retirement and dissave after retirement. In the simplest versions of the model, savings rates are expected to be constant up to retirement. More elaborate versions, such as that of Tobin (1967), postulate a variable rate of savings related to the stages of the family life cycle and the timing of needs, such as for investment in education. According to this model, savings will be lowest at about age 40, when college expenses must be met, and will peak in the years prior to retirement. Friedman (1980) presents evidence that the larger part of retirement saving occurs in the period immediately preceding retirement.

The simplest versions of the life-cycle theory imply a reduction in the aggregate savings rate as the population ages. Yet changes in the age structure also lead to an aging of those in the labor force. If savings rates rise over the working-age years, there will possibly be an offsetting effect (Clark and Spengler, 1980a, Ch. 9). Furthermore, with low fertility, the lifetime number of expected births and the average number of children per worker in any given age group should be lower. This should have an additional effect on savings rates and has been generally overlooked in empirical attempts to relate age structure and savings rates. (An exception is Denton and Spencer, 1975.) If, as in traditional societies, children are viewed as a source of support in old age or in times of special need, then the more children people have, the less the need for personal savings. In addition, children reduce the level of real income so that some of this could be expected to come at the expense of savings. On the other hand, if families plan to leave bequests, the more children the greater the required savings rate.

A large body of literature has attempted to empirically validate the life-cycle theory. Few studies have found either that the elderly dissave or that they save at a lower rate. There are many reasons why the elderly may not behave according to the prediction of the life-cycle model. In addition to providing for consumption in retirement, wealth may be held as a precaution against emergency needs, to provide bequests, and for its psychological utility. Illiquidity and the indivisibility of major assets may inhibit dissaving behavior. While a nondeclining wealth pattern might disprove the life-cycle hypothesis, a declining pattern does not necessarily support it. Wealth could decline if emergencies occur and if there are significant inter vivo gifts. Thus not all observed dissavings should be attributed to life-cycle considerations. As Mirer (1980) notes, savings motives may vary with age. The middle-aged might save primarily for retirement (consumption), while the old may continue to save or dissave at low rates out of habit, or a misperceived life expectancy, or because they become more aware of the nature of emergency needs in old age.

There may also be methodological reasons why the life-cycle theory has not been substantiated; indeed, most studies have been subject to limitations. Russell (1979) and Danziger et al. (1982) emphasize the failure to include the imputed value of the services from durable goods. Diamond and Hausman (1980) and Friedman (1981) emphasize that cross-section data, which have been the major basis of the existing studies, may have a serious bias inasmuch as the cross-section pattern may reflect cohort effects or a positive correlation between wealth and time

since retirement. Finally, the theory predicts that total savings rates should be negative or that total wealth should decline where both private wealth and the wealth embodied in social security and private pension entitlements is included. Most of the findings have focused only on private savings and wealth.

Espenshade and Braun (1981) note that it has generally been assumed that increased numbers of children reduce savings. Yet most of the empirical evidence has failed to find a significant impact (Espenshade, 1975; Kelley, 1976). Blinder et al. (1981) examined the link between the number of children and wealth at ages 60–67, holding lifetime income and a number of other relevant factors constant. They find that asset holdings do not rise or fall with the number of children, implying that there is no effect on savings.

A number of studies have used age-related savings rates to simulate whether population aging will effect the overall savings rate. As Russell (1979) indicated in her review, the findings have been mixed, and the degree of detail in the age breakdown has been too broad to capture the full process. The state of present knowledge would not seem to justify conclusions about the relationship between age structure and savings. There is a need to arrive at a much better understanding of the effects of age and family size on savings before we proceed to simulate the future with any degree of certainty.

The Effect on Savings of Alternative Mechanisms for Financing Income in Retirement. There is an additional way in which age structure could affect aggregate savings. With an older population, contribution rates to public or private programs for financing retirement income would be higher. If public pension programs financed on a pay-as-you-go basis reduce aggregate savings, a view championed by Feldstein (1974), then the rise in contribution rates would contribute to a decline in aggregate savings. The work of Feldstein has given rise to an extensive debate involving questions of the appropriate theoretical conceptualization of human behavior over the life cycle, as well as the significance and meaning of various empirical findings. There has been an outpouring of research on this issue, and several recent attempts have been made to review the debate (Danziger et al., 1981; Cartwright, 1981; Munnell, 1981).

Within the context of this chapter we shall not be able to review all the dimensions of this debate. The reader is referred to the review articles cited above. We would, however, emphasize two conceptual points that have come to the fore.

Kurz and Arvin (1979) and Hymans (1981) have stressed the importance of the distinction between past (start-up) and present cohorts entering a mature system. They argue that a social security system may have a one-time effect on consumption during its start-up period, but not necessarily an ongoing effect once the system matures. If they are correct, pay-as-you-go financing of increases in total pensions paid to the elderly should not contribute to any further reduction in aggregate savings.

Moreover, it does not necessarily follow that a decline in the savings rate will reduce investment. Eisner (1979), for example, points to the importance of the macroeconomic conditions. The level of investment may be restrained by demand factors or by balance-of-payment considerations rather than by a shortage of savings.

Age Structure and the Rate of Investment. The level of investment may be affected by population aging as a consequence of any changes in the aggregate savings rate. However, it has been argued that aging brings about systematic biases in the structure of investment as well. These arguments rely on the assumption that the aged are risk-averse or more resistant to innovation than younger people (Sauvy, 1948). Simon (1981) argues that people are the major source of new ideas, so that in a population that is growing at a slower rate there will be fewer people and fewer new young people to spawn these ideas. While these scenarios are based solely on conjecture, they convey a concern that has an important place in the literature on aging.

The implications of population aging for investment cannot be evaluated without also taking into account the fact that with slower population growth, the need for investment may also be lower. This link is a major focus of the next section.

IV. THE ROLE OF POPULATION AGING IN THEORIES OF ECONOMIC GROWTH

Modern growth theory has had both a positive and a normative thrust. What is the long-run steady state growth path (constant and sustainable) along which the economy can evolve? What is the optimal steady state growth path, and under what conditions will an economy be likely to move toward its optimal long-term path? In a parallel fashion, the implications of age structure and age-related behavior for the nature of growth have been considered, along with the question of optimal rates of population growth and, as a corollary, the optimal age structure.

Does a decline in the rate of population growth lead to a higher or lower sustainable level of capita consumption? The early neoclassical growth models led to the conclusion that a decline in the rate of population growth raises the long-run level of per capita income (Solow, 1956). These models had several limiting features. It is of particular relevance that there was no allowance for differential work and retirement periods, and consequently there was no allowance for the effects of population growth on age structure and labor force participation. Yet these models provided the important insight that lower population growth reduces the level of investment per worker required to maintain a given level of capital per worker over time. This is what makes possible a certain degree of capital widening in the sense that the steady state path along which the economy evolves is characterized by a higher capital/labor ratio and higher per capita consumption than required with higher rates of population growth.

The results contradict the implications of another theoretical tradition (consumption-loan models) that focused on the possible gains from intergenerational transfers in overlapping generation models (Samuelson, 1958). Such models generally assume that individuals live and consume for two periods, but work only in the first. In pure consumption models where there is no capital, it was found that the faster the rate of population growth the better, since having more children means better support for retired parents.

Each of these traditions has had its separate development within the theoretical literature. Samuelson (1975) made an attempt to integrate them in a model that allows for the effects of population growth both on age structure and on the required levels of investment. His results were corrected and clarified in an exchange with Deardorff (Deardorff,1976; Samuelson, 1976). Samuelson conjectured that he could prove the existence of an intermediate level of population growth at which benefits and costs balance. The analysis did not support this position. Rather, as stated by Deardorff, "the old result of neoclassical growth theory, that economies benefit from low or negative population growth, still stands."

Recently there has been renewed interest in these theoretical results, and they have been extended by Arthur and McNicoll (1978), Lee (1980), and Willis (1981) to include more of the factors we identified in Sections II and III. They extend the Samuelson model to allow for a childhood period in which there are intergenerational transfers to children (Arthur and McNicoll) and to allow for household units in which the needs of children may be less than those of adults (Lee). Lee, as well as Willis, incorporates an effect of the fertility level on the labor force participation of women. The thrust of these later works is that the desirability of slower population growth depends on whether both direct expenditures on children and subsequent cash transfers are considered, and whether there is a net lifetime flow of resources from older to younger or from younger to older generations.

Willis summarizes the development of this argument as follows:

Following Samuelson (1976), they noted that an increased rate of population growth reduces the amount of output available for consumption in steady state because more resources must be devoted to investment in order to equip each worker with a given amount of capital equipment. Because this "capital widening effect" is always negative, a lower rate of population growth would always increase individual welfare in a population without an age structure in which there is no generational overlap. When there is a generational overlap, however, an increase in n might lead to a positive "intergenerational transfer effect" which, in principle, might outweigh the negative capital widening effect; alternatively the intergenerational transfer effect might be negative so that it reinforces the capital widening effect. (1981, pp. 15–16)

When the pattern of transfers is to children, the intergenerational transfer effect will also favor slower population growth. The dominant view in this literature is that the direction of transfers is most likely to be from parents to children. Caldwell (1980) argues that the direction of transfers has shifted with economic development from transfers to parents to transfers toward children. This shift, he continues, has been accompanied by a change in fertility motivations, from economic (support in old age) to psychic motivations, that has contributed to sustained fertility decline. Willis (1981), building on Caldwell's approach, extends the optimal growth models and allows for direct utility from children so that the fertility rate becomes endogenous. He argues that if parents adopt an altruistic approach to their children in the sense that they value their children's utility as much as their own, one can demonstrate that they will always choose a fertility level such that net direction on intergenerational transfers over the life-cycle flows from parents to children. In his model, the more technologically advanced the society, the more likely bequests and transfers in old age are to be positive. These arguments suggest that the intergenerational effect will be positive, so that the overall effects of a decline in population growth and the associated aging of the population will be to raise living standards. However, insufficient weight has been given in this discussion to the rate of productivity growth. Arthur and McNicoll (1978, p. 245) note that rapid productivity growth could generate transfers to older generations and possibly offset the gains from slower population growth. Feldstein (1978) argues that with real income growing between generations, many would like to leave negative bequests (be supported by their children), which are not enforceable and hence leave nothing. But there is little direct evidence on the extent and direction of intergenerational flows, and how they vary with the rate of productivity growth.

The assumptions underlying the optimal population growth literature are much too restrictive to permit the discussion to be viewed as conclusive. In addition to the many assumptions made in defining the basic behavioral and technological functions, they describe what is essentially a long-run steady state response to the aging process in a world where the rate of saving remains at an optimal level. Yet dramatic steps have been taken to incorporate more and more of the phenomena associated with population aging. This literature brings attention to the intriguing links between fertility and patterns of intergenerational transfer on the one hand, and between female labor force participation and fertility on the other. It also suggests that exogenous shifts in work preferences, in the desired number of and quality of care for children, and in intergenerational support patterns, could each play an important role in shaping fertility and, hence, the extent of population aging and its consequences. These links will certainly be of major concern in future research on aging and the economy. We would add that there is a need to supplement this analysis by incorporating the link between fertility, female labor force participation, and the extent and direction of intergenerational transfers of time (informal support).

V. ECONOMIC ADJUSTMENT TO POPULATION AGING UNDER ALTERNATIVE RETIREMENT FINANCE SYSTEMS

In the discussion in previous sections the concern was with the level of sustainable consumption per capita. In this section we shall deal with possible changes in the relative share of the elderly in overall consumption and the implications for their standard of living. In the broader discussion of age structure changes that will now follow, the lessons of the above theoretical models will be referred to, but without their simplifying assumptions. We shall consider not only the long-run consequences after full adjustment, but problems of transition as well. The discussion will emphasize the ways in which changes in the age structure require public policy responses.

There has been a tendency to associate the difficulties posed by population aging with the pay-as-you-go system and to suggest that no difficulties would arise under a system that relies on private savings or on a fully funded (defined contributions) compulsory system. Any system faces the basic problem of real resource transfers. As Rosen states: "The basic economic problem that must be solved is a mechanism for transferring resources from 'productive' nonretirees to sustain the consumption of 'nonproductive' retirees" (1981, p. 7). This requires both that retirees somehow establish claims on current economic output and that non-retirees be induced to forgo sufficient consumption and investment in future consumption to make possible a given level of consumption by the elderly.

Outside the context of the optimal growth literature, there has been no discussion of how private systems adjust. Therefore we first consider the nature of the response in private savings systems to population aging. The characteristics of the adjustment process in a private system will serve as a basis for evaluating public systems.

Private Savings for Retirement

Broadly, a private savings system is the equivalent of a fully funded system of private pensions (defined contributions). Rosen describes the workings of this system as follows:

> Retirees must somehow establish claims on current output and income of the economy, even though they are not working. In a fully-funded system this is accomplished by retirees having accumulated claims to productive capital assets prior to the period of retirement, often through the intermediary of the employer. Abstention from consumption while young through private acts of savings are accumulated (invested) at market rates of interest and converted to annuities at the date of retirement. The income flows guaranteed by these annuities are met by successively selling off previously accumulated claims to the then younger generations, who in turn accumulate them in anticipation of *their* retirement, and so forth. The ownership of capital therefore rolls over among successive generations of workers and retirees in the economy. (1981, p. 7)

In almost all cases, population aging requires a transfer of resources to the elderly in response to the increase in their population share. Only if the elderly's share of total income rises in proportion to the increase in their population share will the relative income levels of the young and the elderly remain constant. In the eventuality of a decline in output per capita, the loss will be shared by both groups.

In a private regime, a rise in the share of the elderly in income happens automatically, inasmuch as the elderly own a greater share of the capital stock than do the young. However, the level of consumption consistent with that capital is a function of the terms on which the elderly can sell off their assets. It is through these terms that the real resource uses of the old and the young are reconciled.

Rosen (1981) suggests that one response to population aging should be a rise in the interest rate, inasmuch as the elderly are net dissavers and the redistribution of income to them should reduce the savings rate, thereby creating an excess supply of assets and driving down their price. This implies that the incomes of the elderly would decline. He argues that the pressure arising in the pay-as-you-go system to reduce the benefits of the elderly has its parallel in a private system in the declining value of the elderly's assets. Any resultant decline in output would reduce savings even further and aggravate the decline in asset values.

Rosen's prediction may be subject to a number of criticisms. First of all, it is not clear that the aged are net dissavers, as our review of the literature of the life-cycle theory has indicated. Moreover, even if the elderly do dissave, his analysis ignores many of the concomitants of the aging process discussed in the previous sections. These include the reduction in required investment associated with slower population growth or the possible rise in the savings rates of the young as the number of children declines. These factors could moderate or eliminate the reduction in the value of assets. A decline in output that arises from a drop in the percentage of the population gainfully employed would lead to an immediate rise in the capital/labor ratio. The extra capital could allow investment to decline still further and possibly offset the fall in savings. The net impact of these factors on the demand for assets will determine whether there is a transfer of resources from the young to the old. What is important to note is that the change in the terms on which the elderly dissave varies in direct relation to whether population aging leads to a rise or fall in feasible levels of total consumption and output. Therefore, when there is a decline in per capita consumption, the elderly will generally share in this decline.

We have indicated in earlier sections how per capita output could decline as a result of population aging. This decline would, however, be only temporary in a system in which there is secular growth in productivity because of technological change. How would the benefits from productivity growth be distributed? First, productivity growth will generate increased savings. Savings serve to reduce pressure on interest rates. As a result, losses to the elderly due to population aging may be avoided, or there may be gains. They will also benefit from the effect of profits on asset values. Such gains to those who are dissaving could be offset in part if technological change is embodied in investment. Under these circumstances, investment demand would rise, and equilibrium interest rates would be higher.

In summary, in a system of private savings there is an automatic transfer of resources claims to the elderly and an adjustment mechanism that assures that real resources are available. This mechanism has a number of noteworthy features:

1. The mechanism is influenced by the full range of possible offsets to the rise in the resource needs of the elderly as a group.
2. The mechanism will impose real income losses on the elderly in relation to declines in per capita consumption.
3. No public decisions need be taken in order for the adjustment to occur.
4. The benefits of technological change are shared by the elderly, and as a result, losses associated with population aging may be avoided.

The above characteristics may be viewed as advantages of a private system. However, the implied link of the fortunes of the elderly and the savings of the young with the demand for investment may be viewed as a disadvantage as well. If the young were to decide to consume more and set aside less for their retirement, then interest rates could rise, and the present generation of elderly would find themselves forced to finance in part the consumption of the young at the expense of their own consumption. Similarly, if investment demand were to rise, the elderly would again find that they are being asked to help finance that investment although only the young may live to reap the

benefits. Depending on the range within which interest rates vary, there is considerable uncertainty associated with retirement planning in a private system.

Public Provision in a Pay-As-You-Go-System

We now consider the nature of the response to population aging in a public system of provision in which the elderly's consumption is financed through pay-as-you-go and general revenue financing.

In a public system the claims of the elderly are granted through legislative enactment, and the adjustment of resource demands is achieved through direct taxation of the nonretired. The designation of an increased share of the national income for the elderly generally cannot be achieved without increasing the rate of taxation. The consequences of population aging will emerge directly within the pay-as-you-go components. If no policy parameters are changed, the systems will not be able to meet their commitments. The pay-as-you-go systems will enter a "crisis" that will raise the question of whether taxes should be raised or benefits reduced. There is no self-correcting mechanism in this type of system. Population aging imposes the need for a public policy response. The response may take one of three forms: reduce benefits, raise contribution rates, or provide supplementary finance from other sources. Ideally, the resolution of this issue should be related to what has happened to the overall capacity to maintain per capita consumption. In a private system the factors offsetting the rise in the needs of the elderly find expression in the flow of demand for assets. The offsets take a variety of forms in a public system and so are less direct and often overlooked. The public debate has consistently failed to consider these offsets, with the result that the positions taken have often been misleading.

The most direct offset is the reduced need for public expenditures on the young, allowing a shift of revenues to finance higher benefits for the elderly. This shift may be implemented in a number of ways. Surplus funds can be used to increase general expenditures on the elderly or to supplement contributions to pay-as-you-go programs. Partial general revenue financing is quite common in many social security systems, although there are still ideological objections to it. Another possibility is to fully finance increased costs by raising the contribution rate within the pay-as-you-go system, but to moderate the overall increase in the tax burden by reducing other forms of taxation.

A second offset is the reduced burden on families for child care. This reduction is in part translated directly into higher tax payments as dependents' deductions decline. Families are left with higher real incomes for a given level of money income,* and may therefore be viewed as having a greater capacity to sustain a tax increase. It is not clear that the families will subsequently recognize that they are better able to bear taxation. A two-child family might be better off, despite the higher taxes, than the average family that had more children in the past, but it will pay a higher rate than a family in the past paid with the same income and number of children.

Still another offset is the lower level of investment that is required to maintain a given capital/labor ratio, as has been emphasized by the growth theories reviewed in Section IV. Some of the reduction is reflected directly in reduced public investment needs. It is less obvious how the decreased need for private investment eases the burden of financing expenditures on the elderly. This can lead to a lower rate of interest and less savings by the family. In this way they would be encouraged to maintain consumption despite any tax increase. The government might impose this solution directly by discouraging investment through increased taxes on capital. But again, it is unclear to what extent the willingness to bear taxes would be increased under such circumstances. Lower savings and investment will not reduce the capacity for future consumption. In this sense the young

*This assumes that child deductions do not finance the full cost of a child, as is almost universally the case.

will be able to enjoy higher consumption in the present and the future (or, at least, a reduction in consumption that is less than the tax increase). They will reap the benefits when they dissave assets at a higher price in the future. More important is that the public sector could forge a direct link with the decline in investment needs (or any increase in private savings). The government may choose to finance increased expenditures on the elderly by running a deficit that would absorb any excess of savings over investment and prevent a fall in interest rates, thus avoiding some or all of the tax increase.

While the positive factors associated with population aging work in indirect ways in a public system, the negative factors have a more immediate impact. A decline in output per capita will reduce total tax revenues. Declines in the wage bill will be felt directly in the social security system.

Summary

As a population ages, both potential output and needs are affected in a number of ways. We illustrated how a private system might adjust to these factors and link the fortunes of the elderly directly to the net impact on per capita consumption. The factors affecting the capacity to maintain consumption are no different in a public pay-as-you-go as opposed to a private system. Public systems of finance operate on a logic that is parallel to that of private systems, yet public systems must rely on policy decisions rather than automatic adjustment mechanisms.

In a public system the links among the various factors are much more tenuous. Whereas the unseen hand in the private system will incorporate the various factors and give each its appropriate weight, public policymakers have to make the link between the impending social security deficits and possible surpluses in other government programs and to evaluate the implications of reduced child care needs and lower levels of required investment. Because of the difficulties in measuring and adding up these factors, policymakers can be guided by them only in general terms and are not provided with explicit, quantified amounts that can be used in deciding whether to lower benefits to the elderly or to raise taxes and by how much. If the belief is that consumption must decline, then there may be justification in imposing some of the losses on the elderly. However, in making the decision whether to impose such losses the possible growth in productivity and incomes of future generations must also be considered, just as in the case of the private system.

A comprehensive policy requires a broad view of the needs for public expenditures, private consumption, and investment and requires flexibility in adjusting tax rates, social security contribution rates, and even the government deficit. The adjustment process that emerges from this perspective sharply contrasts with the nature of the debate over the implications of aging for social security systems. This debate confines itself in the main to the deficits within social security as determined by the ratio of retired persons to workers, while ignoring the nature of the overall age structure shift and the decline in investment needs associated with slower population growth.

VI. THE EFFECTS OF MACROECONOMIC CONDITIONS ON THE ELDERLY

This section considers the possible implications of inflation and unemployment for the elderly and for societal adjustment to population aging.

Unemployment

The general rate of unemployment may affect the rate of employment among the elderly both by discouraging labor force participation and by increasing their unemployment. A number of studies have examined fluctuations in participation (Wachter, 1977; Perry, 1977) or in unemployment by demographic groups (Feldstein, 1973; Feldstein and Wright, 1976). Of the greatest interest are those studies that have tried to relate the two (Smith, 1977; Clark and Sum-

mers, 1980). Clark and Summers find that two groups are particularly affected by the aggregate unemployment rate: youths aged 16–19 and the male elderly. The employment of those over age 65 is very sensitive to the unemployment rate, mainly because their participation rate is very sensitive. This may be due in part to forced retirement of the elderly in conditions of high unemployment.

Another way in which the elderly are affected by unemployment is through the more general consequences for dependency ratios and public expenditures. Unemployment reduces the wage base for financing benefits, and pressures on pension systems will increase with more induced early retirement. Further, increased social expenditures on unemployment and disability benefits will add more pressure to the level of public spending. These problems might be allayed to the extent that high unemployment created the basis and the justification for fiscal expansion. However, this recourse is not so attractive when accompanied by rapid inflation. Permanently higher unemployment rates imply permanently lower employment rates among the elderly and a permanent increase in the dependency burden. This aggravates the pressure on the tax rate required to finance the burden.

Inflation

As noted above, concern with inflation indirectly affects the elderly by preventing the adoption of policies to reduce unemployment. In addition, the elderly will be directly affected if inflation serves to reduce the real value of their savings and public benefits. This gives rise to the further question of what indexing arrangements, if any, should be made to reduce the uncertainty associated with future inflation rates.

It is frequently noted that while social security programs generally provide for the indexing of pensions, private pension schemes typically do not. There has been some controversy concerning the extent to which these schemes provide de facto protection against inflation and whether the indexing of such pensions is feasible or even desirable. This issue overlaps, although it is not identical with, the question of the vulnerability of the elderly's private savings to inflation.

Public and private pensions systems have several differences that affect their ability to provide indexed benefits. Clark and Spengler (1980b) point out that in a pay-as-you-go system the value of contributions rises with money wages, which should keep pace with inflation. Thus the pool to be distributed to retirees will expand sufficiently to support indexed benefits to the elderly. But in a funded system, Clark and Spengler (1980c) and Munnell (1980) argue that the government must guarantee the purchasing power of private pensions and annuities purchased by the elderly through the sale of bonds or annuities linked to the cost of living, to pension funds or directly to retirees. This is the procedure in a number of countries.

The argument with respect to the difference between the two systems ignores two key points. First, if high inflation is accompanied by unemployment, the growth in the total wage base is retarded. Second, real wages may fall if inflation is rooted in exogenous changes in the terms of trade that impose real income losses on a society. In either case, the wage base will decline, and the problem of maintaining real benefits in a pay-as-you-go system will arise along with the question of who should bear the real losses. In other words, the question inevitably arises of the conditions under which indexed benefits are desirable. Second, private pensions may be less vulnerable to inflation than is generally believed.

Munnell emphasizes that the extent to which indexing is implicit in existing pension formulas, even if not explicit, depends on several of a plan's major features: Is the plan a defined contribution or defined benefit? To what extent is it funded? What is the wage base definition within the benefit program? What are the nature of the investments in defined contribution programs?

If the plan is a defined benefit plan and the wage base for calculating pensions is based on earnings in the years near retirement, then there is an implied indexing of the wage base for initial determination. The benefits in a defined contribution plan will be fully impervious to inflation only if the real rate of return is itself impervious to the inflation rate.

In a recent paper, Feldstein (1981) addresses this issue of changes in the net return to assets under inflationary conditions. He emphasizes the need to distinguish between certain inflation and uncertain inflation. If the rate of inflation is known and expected, he concludes that:

> On balance, it is clear that a positive expected rate of inflation would not be a problem for the private pension system. The real net return earned by pension funds is relatively insensitive to inflation and might actually increase. (Feldstein, 1981, p. 426)

With uncertain inflation, one finds different responses for different types of assets. How well a pension fund does depends on where it invests its assets. Moreover, there is a tradeoff between the return or yield associated with the asset and how well it is protected against inflation. Bodie (1980) finds that a portfolio with a minimum-variance real return would provide only a zero yield (this portfolio would include short-term debt with a small amount in commodity futures). Higher yields could be obtained at the price of more susceptibility to inflation.

This analysis contains two important implications. The first is that at a low enough return, private pensions could largely be protected against inflation. The second implication is that the desirable degree of protection against inflation is a matter of the weighing of costs and benefits. Feldstein (1981, p. 427) notes that "the optimal extent of pension indexing depends on the risk aversion of employees and the cost, in terms of the reduction in the expected yield, of investing pension assets to produce a constant real return."

In defined contribution plans, this tradeoff is reflected in the way in which the funds are invested. In defined benefit programs of the type described earlier, a tradeoff exists between the degree of indexing and either initial benefit levels or the increase in contribution rates. Feldstein illustrates how the tradeoff could be significant even if inflation is moderate.

VII. INTEGRATION AND SUMMARY

Much of the policy oriented literature on the economic consequences of fertility related changes in age structure has emphasized the expected difficulties. We have emphasized how tentative the empirical base is for evaluating the consequences of population aging for needs or output. The theoretical growth literature that we reviewed provides a much more sanguine perspective. This literature emphasizes that it is inappropriate to resolve the issue of future benefit levels and contribution rates in public retirement programs exclusively on the basis of their long-run actuarial deficits and without regard for the reduced needs of other population groups and for investment. We also considered the argument that the adjustment to population aging is an issue only in pay-as-you-go public programs. All systems must deal with the real resource and redistributive challenges posed by population aging. Private systems were shown to automatically adjust in a way that linked the fortunes of the elderly directly to the net impact of population aging on potential per capita consumption. The analysis of how private systems adjust provides a possible guide to policy decisions in public systems and to an understanding of the sense in which population aging leads to a "crisis" in the ability to maintain the living standards of the elderly.

We have argued that the major difference between pay-as-you-go and funded private systems is that resource transfers to the elderly, even when identical in substance, are achieved through different mechanisms. Whereas asset ownership and values self-adjust in private systems, much of the burden of resource transfers may require increases in taxes or the government deficit in public systems. In this sense, public systems face a crisis that may be unique. The constraints on implementing these adjustments may be more ideological than real. Another distinct difference between private and public systems is that public systems require information about the net implications of population aging so that appropriate decisions may be made. This information is not generally available and is difficult to obtain (see Schulz, 1977, for additional points of comparison).

There are conditions in which the implications of population aging are likely to be more severe than in others. It has been claimed that pay-as-you-go systems of retirement finance induce a large initial, as well as an ongoing reduction in the capital stock. If this is true, these losses might be aggravated if tax rates in pay-as-you-go programs increase with population aging. Our review of the funding controversy indicated how different authors have expressed diametrically opposed views even at the theoretical level. The recent theoretical discussion is characterized by increasing polarization on these issues, rather than by any approach toward a consensus.

Population aging has the most serious implications when it emerges simultaneously with macroeconomic conditions of high unemployment, a high rate of inflation, and slow productivity growth. Prognoses of long-run economic performance are critical therefore in formulating policy responses to population aging. Macroeconomic conditions, particularly high long-run unemployment rates, impinge on the ability to maintain high consumption levels by the elderly, both through their encouragement of early retirement and by reducing the wage base. Inflation discourages the adoption of policies to reduce unemployment and may indirectly undermine the real value of savings. Section IV emphasized that the appropriate response to population aging is related to the expected rate of productivity growth, and, as some have argued, this rate may itself be affected by population growth and per capita investment levels. It will be less appropriate and more politically difficult to impose short-run adjustments in real income levels on the younger generation alone if there is also a slowdown in the rate of growth in future income. If productivity growth is retarded, then there will be increased justification for imposing some of the real income losses on the current elderly generation.

This illustrates one of the basic questions that come to the fore about the principles that should guide public policies with respect to intergenerational transfers. Moreover, the direction, extent, and timing of intergenerational transfers repeatedly emerge as critical unknowns in the resolution of a range of issues: life-cycle savings patterns, the effects of social security and other public programs, and optimal rates of population growth. The direction, extent, and form of intergenerational transfers in cash or kind constitute an area in which the quality and availability of data remain a major obstacle to further progress, which deserves priority. This would also seem to be an area in which economists and non-economists could fruitfully collaborate, both in establishing the empirical patterns of exchange and in developing realistic models of the underlying intergenerational utility functions.

Recent and unexpected advances in longevity have focused attention on the possibility that changes in mortality rates may play a central role in future age structure changes (pattern 2 in Table 1). The economic impact of aging at the apex may be much more serious, as there is no corresponding decline in the rate of population growth or in the number of children, and the old-old especially may increase their population share. The literature on the economics of population aging has hardly begun to come to terms with this phenomenon and its implicatons, not only for public budgets but also for the direct care burdens on families for their elderly relatives.

REFERENCES

Anderson, Joseph M. 1977. An economic–demographic model of the United States labor market. Ph.D. dissertation, Harvard University.

Anderson, Joseph M. 1980. *Modeling Analysis for Retirement Income Policy: Background and Overview.* Washington, D.C.: Employee Benefits Research Institute.

Andrisani, Paul. 1977. The effects of aging and experience on productivity. *Industrial Gerontology* 4:13–17.

Arthur, W. Brian, and McNicoll, Geoffry. 1978. Samuelson, population and intergenerational transfers. *International Economic Review* 1:241–246.

Blinder, Alan S., Gordon, Roger, and Wise, Donald. 1981. Life cycle savings and bequests: Cross-sectional estimates of the life-cycle model. Princeton, N.J.: Princeton University. (Unpublished.)

Bodie, Zvi. 1980. An innovation for stable real retirement income. *Journal of Portfolio Management* 1:5–13.

Boskin, Michael J. (ed.) 1978. *The Crisis in Social Security: Problems and Prospects.* San Francisco: Institute for Contemporary Studies.

Boskin, Michael J., and Robinson, Marc. 1980. Social security and private saving: Analytical issues, econometric evidence, and policy implications. *In* U.S. Congress, Joint Economic Committee, *Special Study on Economic Change,* Vol. 8, *Social Security and Pensions: Programs of Equity and Security,* pp. 38–64. Washington, D.C.: U.S. Government Printing Office.

Caldwell, John C. 1980. Mass education as a determinant of the timing of fertility decline. *Population and Development Review* 6:225–555.

Cartwright, William S. 1981. *Technical Paper Review: Social Security, Pensions and Savings.*

Clark, Kim B., and Summers, Lawrence, H. 1980. *Demographic Differences in Cyclical Employment Variation.* Working Paper Series No. 514, New York: National Bureau of Economic Research.

Clark, Robert, L. 1976. *The Influence of Low Fertility Rates and Retirement Policy on Dependency Costs.* Washington, D.C.: American Institutes for Research in Behavioral Sciences.

Clark, Robert L., and Spengler, Joseph J. 1980a. *The Economics of Individual and Population Aging.* New York: Cambridge University Press.

Clark, Robert L., and Spengler, Joseph J. 1980b. Dependency ratios: Their use in economic analysis. *In* Julian L. Simon and Julie de Vanzo (eds.), *Research in Population Economics,* Vol. 2, pp. 63–76. Greenwich, Conn.: JAI Press.

Clark, Robert L., and Spengler, Joseph J. 1980c. Economic responses to population aging with special emphasis on retirement policy. *In* R. L. Clark (ed.). *Retirement Policy in an Aging Society,* pp. 156–166. Durham, N.C.: Duke University Press.

Clark, Robert, Kreps, Juanita, and Spengler, Joseph J. 1978. Economics of aging: A survey. *Journal of Economic Literature* 3:919–962.

Copeland, Lois S. 1981. Trends in invalidity pension programme growth from an international perspective. *International Social Security Review* 3:238–258.

Cramer, James. 1980. The effects of fertility on husband's economic activity: Evidence from static dynamic and nonrecursive models. *In* Julian L. Simon and Julie DaVanzo (eds.), *Research in Population Economics,* Vol. 2, pp. 151–182. Greenwich, Conn.: JAI Press.

Danziger, Sheldon, Haveman, Robert, and Plotnick, Robert. 1981. How income transfers affect work, savings and the income distribution. *Journal of Economic Literature* 19:975–1028.

Danziger, S., van der Gaag, J., Smolensky, E., and Taussig, M. K. 1982–1983. The life cycle hypothesis and the consumption behavior of the elderly. *Journal of Post-Keynesian Economics* 5:208–227.

Deardorff, A. V. 1976. The growth rate for population: Comment. *International Economic Review* 17:510–515.

Denton, Frank T., and Spencer, Byron, G. 1975. *Population and the Economy.* Lexington, Mass.: Lexington Books and D.C. Heath.

Denton, Frank T., and Spencer, Byron G. 1978. *Population Change and Public Expenditures.* Working Paper No. 78-04. Ontario: Department of Economics, McMaster University.

Denton, Frank T., Spencer, Byron, G., and Feaver, Christine H. 1980. OASI and the U.S. economy: A model and some long-run projections. *In: Special Study on Economy Change,* Vol. 8, *Social Security and Pensions: Programs of Equity and Security.* Prepared for the Joint Economic Committee, U.S. Congress. Washington, D.C.: U.S. Government Printing Office.

Diamond, Peter A., and Hausman, Jerry. 1980. *Individual Savings Behavior.* Cambridge, Mass.: Massachusetts Institute of Technology. (Unpublished.)

Dillingham, Alan E. 1981. Age and workplace injuries. *Aging and Work* 1:1–10.

Easterlin, Richard A. 1978. What will 1984 be like? Socioeconomic implications of recent twists in age structure. Presidential address, annual meeting, Population Association of America.

Eisner, Robert. 1979. Social Security and capital formation. Chicago: Northwestern University. (Mimeo.)

Espensade, Thomas J. 1975. The impact of children on household savings: Age effects versus family size. *Population Studies* 29:123–125.

Espenshade, Thomas, J., and Braun, Rachel Eisenberg. 1981. Economic aspects of an aging population and the material well-being of older persons. *In* Beth B. Hess and Kathleen Bond (eds.), *Leading Edges: Recent Research on Psychosocial Aging.* U.S. Department of Health and Human Services. NIH Publication No. 81-2390.

Feldstein, Martin S. 1973. Lowering the permanent rate of unemployment. Study prepared for the use of the Joint Economic Committee, U.S. Congress, Washington, D.C. (Sept.).

Feldstein, Martin 1974. Social security, induced retirement, and aggregate capital accumulation. *Journal of Political Economy* 82:905–926.

Feldstein, Martin. 1975. Toward a reform of Social Security. *The Public Interest,* 40: 75–95.

Feldstein, Martin. 1978. Reply. *In* Robert Barro (ed.), *The Impact of Social Security on Private Saving: Evidence from U.S. Time Series,* pp. 37–47. Washington, D.C.: American Enterprise Institute for Public Policy Research.

Feldstein, Martin. 1981. Private pensions and inflation. *American Economic Review* 71(2):424–428.

Feldstein, Martin, and Wright, Brian. 1976. High unemployment groups in tight labor markets. Harvard Institute for Economic Research. Dicussion paper No. 448 (June).

Fleisher, B., and Rhodes, G. 1979. Fertility, women's wage rates, and labor supply. *American Economic Review* 69 (Mar.): 14–24.

Freeman, Richard B. 1978. The effect of the youth population on the wages of young workers. Testimony before the U.S. House of Representatives Select Committee on Population (June 2).

Friedman, Joseph. 1980. Patterns of private wealth accumulation and liquidation: Evidence from the retirement history study. Cambridge, Mass.: Abt Associates, Inc. (May).

Friedman, Joseph. 1981. Private assets accumulation and decumulation in a retirement policy microsimulation model. Paper presented to the Brookings Institution Conference. Cambridge, Mass: Abt Associates, Inc.

Gronau, Reuben. 1976. The allocation of time of Israeli women. *Journal of Political Economy* 4:5201–5221.

Habib, Jack. 1980. The determination of equivalence scales with respect to family size: A theoretical reappraisal. Research paper 116. Jerusalem: Maurice Falk Institute for Economic Research.

Habib, Jack, and Spilerman, Seymour, with Wittman, Laura, and Factor, Haim. 1981. The elderly worker and quality of work life in Israel. Report to the Ministry of Labor. Jerusalem: Brookdale Institute of Gerontology and Adult Human Development.

Hymans, Saul. 1981. Saving, investment and Social Security. *National Tax Journal* 1:1–8.

Kapteyn, A., and van Praag, B. M. S. 1980. Family composition and family welfare. *In* Julian L. Simon and Julia de Vanzo (eds.), *Research in Population Economics,* Vol. 2, pp. 77–97. Greenwich, Conn.: JAI Press.

Kelley, Allen C. 1976. Savings, demographic change, and economic development. *Economic Development and Cultural Change* 24 (July):683–693.

Keyfitz, Nathan. 1973. Individual mobility in a stationary population. *Population Studies* 27:335–352.

Klinov, Ruth. 1978. Occupational mobility—Some findings. Jerusalem: Maurice Falk Institute for Economic Research. Discussion paper No. 7814.

Kurz, Mordechai, and Arvin, Marcy. 1979. The funding issue and modern growth theory. Working paper.

Washington, D.C.: President's Commission on Pension Policy.

Lazear, Edward P. 1979. Why is there mandatory retirement? *Journal of Political Economy* (6):1261–1284.

Lee, Ronald. 1980. Age structure, intergenerational transfers, consumption and economic growth. *Revue Economique* (Nov.):1129–1156.

Leigh, D. 1978. *An Analysis of the Determinants of Occupational Upgrading.* New York: Academic Press.

Lesthaeghe, Ron J. 1979. Demographic change, social security and economic growth: Inferences from the Belgian example. *Schweiz Zeitschrift fur Volkswirtschaft und Statistik* 3:225–255.

Meier, Elizabeth L., Dittmar, Cynthia C., and Torrey, Barbara Boyle. 1980. *Retirement Income Goals.* Washington, D.C.: President's Commission on Pension Policy.

Mirer, T. W. 1980. The dissaving behavior of the retired aged. *Southern Economic Journal* 46:1197–1205.

Modigliani, Franco, and Brumberg, R. 1954. Utility analysis and the consumption function: an interpretation of cross-section data. *In* K. Kurihara (ed.), *Post-Keynesian Economics,* pp. 388–436. New Brunswick, N.J.: Rutgers University Press.

Munnell, Alicia H. 1980. The impact of inflation on private pensions. *In* R. L. Clark (ed.), *Retirement Policy in an Aging Society,* pp. 167–183. Durham, N.C.: Duke University Press.

Musgrove, Phillip. 1980. *Effects of Income and Demographic Change on the Structure of Household Consumption, 1975–2025.* Washington, D.C.: Resources for the Future.

Myers, George C. 1981. *Mortality Declines, Life Extension and Population Aging.* Durham, N.C.: Center for Demographic Studies, Duke University.

Organization for Economic Cooperation and Development (OECD). 1981. *The Welfare State in Crisis.* Paris.

Parks, Richard W., and Barten, Anton P. 1973. A cross-country comparison of the effects of prices, income and population composition on consumption patterns. *Economic Journal* 83:834–852.

Parnes, Herbert S., et al. 1975. *The Pre-Retirement Years,* Vol. 4, *A Longitudinal Study of the Labor Market Experience of Men.* U.S. Department of Labor, Manpower Research and Development Monograph No. 15. Washington, D.C.: U.S. Government Printing Office.

Perry, George L. 1977. Potential output and productivity. *Brookings Papers on Economic Activity.* Washington, D.C.: Brookings Institution.

Riley, Matilda, and Foner, Anne. 1968. *Aging and Society,* Vol. 1. New York: Russell Sage Foundation.

Rohrlich, George F. 1980. International perspectives on social security. *In: Special Study on Economy Change,* Vol. 8, *Social Security and Pensions: Programs of Equity and Security.* Prepared for Joint Economic Committee, U.S. Congress. Washington, D.C.: U.S. Government Printing Office.

Rosen, Sherwin, 1981. Some arithmetic of Social Security. Presented to the Conference on Controlling the Cost of Social Security. Washington, D.C.: American Enterprise Institute for Public Policy Research.

Russell, Louise B. 1979. The macroeconomic effects of changes in the age structure of the population. *In* Maurice B. Ballabon (ed.), *Economic Perspectives: An Annual Survey of Economics,* Vol. 3. Amsterdam: OPA.

Russell, Louise B. 1981. An aging population and the use of medical care. *Medical Care* 19 (16):633–643.

Samuelson, Paul. 1958. An exact consumption-loan model of interest with or without the social contrivance of money. *Journal of Political Economy* 66:467–482.

Samuelson, Paul A. 1975. The optimum growth rate for population. *International Economic Review* 16:531–538.

Samuelson, Paul A. 1976. The optimum growth rate for population: Agreement and evaluations. *International Economic Review* 17:516–525.

Sauvy, Alfred. 1948. Social and economic consequences of the ageing of Western European populations. *Population Studies* 2:115–124.

Schiller, Bradley, and Weiss, Randall. 1979. The impact of private pensions on firm attachment. *Review of Economics and Statistics* 61 (Aug.):369–380.

Schultz, T. P. 1978. The influence of fertility on labor supply of married women: Simultaneous equation estimates. *In* R. Ehrenberg (ed.), *Research in Labor Economics,* Vol. 2, Greenwich, Conn.: JAI Press.

Schulz, James H. 1977. Public policy and the future role of public and private pensions. *In* G. S. Tolley and Richard V. Burkhauser (eds.), *Income Support Policies for the Aged.* Cambridge, Mass.: Ballinger.

Sheppard, Harold L., and Rix, Sara E. 1977. *The Graying of Working America.* New York: Free Press.

Simon, Julian L. 1981. World population growth. An anti-doomsday view. *The Atlantic Monthly* (Aug.):70–76.

Smith, Ralph E. 1977. A simulation model of the demographic composition of employment, unemployment and labor force participation. *In* Ronald G. Ehrenberg (ed.), *Research in Labor Economics,* Vol. 1. Greenwich, Conn.: JAI Press.

Solow, R. M. 1956. A contribution to the theory of economic growth. *Quarterly Journal of Economics* 70:65–94.

Spengler, Joseph J. 1971. Introductory comment: Work requirements and work capacity. *In* Juanita M. Kreps, *Lifetime Allocation of Work and Income,* pp. 3–9. Durham, N.C.: Duke University Press.

Taubman, Paul. 1981. Pensions and mortality. Presented at the Private and Public Pension Conference, Martha's Vineyard, Mass.

Tobin, James. 1967. Life cycle saving and balanced

growth. *In* William Fellner et al. (eds.), *Ten Economic Studies in the Tradition of Irving Fisher,* pp. 231–256. New York: Wiley.

Tracy, Martin. 1979. Trends in retirement. *International Social Security Review* 32:131–159.

U.S. Department of Labor. 1979. *Employer-Related Problems of Older Workers: A Research Policy.* Research & Development Monograph 73. Office of Research & Development of the Office of Policy Evaluation & Research, Employment & Training Administration. Washington, D.C.: U.S. Government Printing Office.

van der Gaag, J. 1981. *The Cost of a Child—A Review of the Literature.* Madison, Wis.: Institute for Research on Poverty. (Mimeo.)

van der Gaag, J., and Smolensky, E. 1980. Consumer expenditures and the evaluation of levels of living. Madison, Wis.: Institute for Research on Poverty. (Unpublished.)

Wachter, Michael L. 1977. Intermediate swings in labor force participation. *Brookings Papers on Economic Activity.* Washington, D.C.: Brookings Institution.

Wander, Hilda. 1978. Zero population growth now: the lessons from Europe. *In* Espenshade and Serow (eds.), *The Economic Consequences of Slowing Population Growth.* pp. 41–70. New York: Academic Press.

Welford, Alan T. 1958. *Ageing and Human Skill.* London: Oxford University Press.

Willis, Robert J. 1981. The direction of intergenerational transfers and demographic transition: The Caldwell hypothesis re-examined. Discussion paper 81-3. Chicago: Economic Research Center/NORC.

17
WORK AND RETIREMENT

Pauline K. Robinson,
Sally Coberly,
and
Carolyn E. Paul
Andrus Gerontology Center
University of Southern California

The participation of older persons in the labor force and retirement have taken on added significance in studies of aging owing to recent policy developments and national concerns. The timing of retirement, for example, is a crucial consideration in the policy debate about retirement benefit financing for older persons who are retiring early and living longer. A second area of public concern involves age discrimination in employment and forced retirement, and the effects of unemployment and retirement on the income, health, and well being of the older population. A third set of problems, which has drawn the attention of policymakers in the public and private sectors, is related to "the aging workforce." (Although the workforce is often described as "aging," i.e., having a higher proportion of older individuals, this chapter will show that it is in fact becoming more "middle-aged.") Concerns about aging in the workforce are related to the effects of aging on job performance and labor costs, and to the possibility of future shortages of entry level workers due to the changing age structure of the labor force.

Theoretical perspectives on aging continue to assign importance to work and retirement (Atchley, 1982). Social stratification studies,

for example, stress the differential distribution according to age grades of resources such as employment, leisure time, and retirement income (Riley et al., 1972; Streib, 1976; Ragan and Wales, 1980). Similarly, the emerging social institutionalization of retirement is important in understanding aging in the individual life cycle (Blau, 1973; Bengtson, 1973; Neugarten and Hagestad, 1976). In the aging of the individual the retirement event has been viewed as a symbolic boundary and a rite of passage between the middle years and old age (Maddox, 1968). At the psychological level of analysis of individual aging, research on cognitive changes in the later adult years has found significant application in the area of job performance (Welford, 1976b; Baugher, 1978).

The study of aging in the context of work and retirement, in contrast to other topics, draws attention to aspects of aging in the middle and pre-retirement years and to the work as well as the retirement stages of the life cycle. The older worker as discussed in this chapter, and in the literature generally, may be as young as 40 or even younger in certain occupations. Since age discrimination, obsolescence, burnout, and physiological decline can be work-related problems in the middle years, it is appropriate to focus research on aging on this period (Sonnenfeld, 1978). In considering national patterns of early retirement and the retirement decision, workers in their fifties and early sixties are the focus of attention.

The objectives of this chapter are to provide information about work and retirement that is relevant to crucial policy issues, and to highlight the importance of employment and retirement in the understanding of the individual life cycle and of aging in society. The first part of the chapter describes the current and projected labor force participation of various age segments of the population and the changes that are occurring in the employment pattern of older adults. The problems of unemployed and discouraged older workers in their late fifties and early sixties are considered here. The decline in labor force participation rates of males over the age of 55 in the last several decades is the major phenomenon to be noted in the employment status of older persons.

The second part of the chapter shifts from the macro to the micro level of analysis and deals with the place of leisure in the work and retirement stages of the life cycle, the retirement decision, and the impact of retirement on the individual. The analysis of factors in the retirement decision includes both individual characteristics and institutional factors. In many cases transition from work to retirement is not so much a complete severing of ties with the workforce as it is a dynamic process involving partial retirement or reentry into the workforce. The line between work and leisure life stages is thus becoming less distinct.

Organizational aspects of work and retirement are then considered, with a discussion of the importance of the employer's role in shaping individual aging and patterns of aging in society. Concerns of employers about skills shortages, productivity, and retirement age policy are identified. These employer dilemmas stem from current trends of early retirement, age discrimination legislation, and demographic shifts in the age structure of the workforce.

Most of the data and examples in this chapter are drawn from the United States, because of the complexities of compiling comparable information from a number of countries and because so much of the recent published material on older workers is based on the U.S. experience. Nevertheless, concerns about aging in the workforce are shared in many countries, most notably in England, other European countries, and Japan (Bruche and Casey, 1982; Morrison, 1982; Sekimoto, 1982). A decreasing ratio of persons under age 65 in the labor force to persons 65 and over has forced attention in many countries to policies affecting retirement age. A review of trends in social security policies in England, Europe, Japan, and other countries has been provided by Rosa (1982) and Zeitzer (1983). The cross-national studies by Shanas et al. (1968), the Organization for Economic Cooperation and Development (1979), Rix and Fisher (1981), and Bruche and Casey (1982) have examined patterns of work and retirement in the United States and Europe.

EMPLOYMENT STATUS OF OLDER PERSONS

This section presents information about the current employment status of older persons, trends in the employment status of older persons over time, and projections of future labor force participation. (All references to the labor force are to the civilian labor force.)

Size and Composition of the Labor Force

As seen in Table 1, the total U.S. civilian labor force was estimated at just over 106 million in 1981. Workers aged 16 to 24 represented 23 percent of the total labor force, while persons aged 25 to 54 accounted for 63 percent. Workers age 55 and older made up just under 14 percent of the labor force; less than 3 percent of the labor force was age 65 or older.

Despite increases in the numbers of persons in the population age 55 or older, the

TABLE 1. Civilian Labor Force by Sex and Age: 1981, 1985, 1990, and 1995.

Percent

	Actual	Middle-growth Projections		
	1981	1985	1990	1995
TOTAL (000s)	106,393	114,985	122,375	127,542
Men				
16–24	12.2	10.9	9.2	8.3
25–54	36.4	36.5	37.7	38.2
55–64	6.7	6.2	5.4	5.1
65+	1.7	1.6	1.5	1.3
55+	8.4	7.8	6.9	6.4
Women				
16–24	10.7	10.3	9.2	8.8
25–54	26.8	29.3	32.2	33.7
55–64	4.4	4.1	3.6	3.5
65+	1.1	1.0	1.0	1.0
55+	5.5	5.1	4.6	4.5
Both Sexes				
16–24	22.9	21.3	18.5	17.1
25–54	63.2	65.8	70.0	72.0
55–64	11.0	10.3	9.1	8.6
65+	2.8	2.6	2.5	2.3
55+	13.8	12.9	11.6	10.9

Totals may not add to 100% owing to rounding.

DATA SOURCES: Fullerton, H., Jr., "The 1995 labor force: A first look," *Monthly Labor Review,* Dec. 1980; and U.S. Department of Labor, Bureau of Labor Statistics, *Employment and Earnings January 1982,* Washington, D.C.: U.S. Government Printing Office, 1982.

proportion of the labor force in this age group has declined steadily. This drop is due in part to continued declines in the labor force participation of older persons, particularly males, and in part to the growth of the prime age segments of the work force.

Within the age 55 and older labor force in 1981, approximately 60 percent were men and 40 percent women. Nine in ten workers age 55 and older were white. Among workers age 65 and older, three out of five were aged 65 to 69; persons age 75 and older represented just under 14 percent of the total 65 and older labor force in 1981.

As shown in Table 1, the age composition of the labor force will change significantly over the next few decades, largely as a result of the aging of the World War II baby boom generation. Under middle growth projections prepared by the Bureau of Labor Sta-

tistics (Fullerton, 1980), the prime working group aged 25 to 54 will grow 27 percent, and will account for 70 percent of the total labor force in 1990. In contrast, owing to the low fertility levels experienced after the baby boom peak, the number of young workers aged 16 to 24 will decline. Workers in this age group will account for only 17 percent of the labor force in 1995 compared to 23 percent in 1981, potentially creating a scarcity of labor for entry level jobs. The size of the labor force age 55 and older will also decline after 1985 owing to continued falling labor force participation rates. By 1995, workers age 55 and older will represent 11 percent of the labor force compared to nearly 14 percent in 1981. Blacks and other minorities will make up a slightly larger proportion of the age 55 and older workforce in 1995 than they did in 1981, as will women.

Labor Force Participation

As shown in Figure 1, the most dramatic indicator of change in the employment status of older persons over time is the declining labor force participation rate of older men. In 1955, nearly 88 percent of males aged 55 to 64 and nearly 40 percent of men age 65 and older were in the labor force. By 1981, these participation rates had dropped to 70.6 percent and 18.4 percent, respectively. Within the age 55 to 64 group, declines in labor force participation have been most pronounced for those men aged 62 to 64. Census and Current Population Survey data reported by Clark and Barker (1981) show, for example, that while the labor force participation rates of men age 55 declined only 2.1 percent between 1950 and 1979, the rates of men age 62, 63, and 64 declined 25, 31, and 34 percent, respectively, during the same time period. The participation of women aged 55 to 64 in the labor force, on the other hand, actually increased during the 1960s and

early 1970s before leveling off at around 41 percent. Between 1970, when the labor force participation of this group was at its peak, and 1979, the rates of women aged 55 to 60 continued to rise while the participation of women aged 60 to 64 declined slightly (Clark and Barker, 1981). Participation rates of women aged 65 and older have also dropped since 1955, although less dramatically than those of older men.

With some exceptions, the labor force participation rates of older white males have been higher than those for blacks and other men. Rones (1978) notes that the participation rates of blacks are influenced by two counteracting factors: poor health, leading to labor force withdrawal; and low career earnings, encouraging continued work. The net effect has been a continued decline in the labor force participation rates of older black and other minority men.

In contrast to the patterns observed for white and nonwhite men, the labor force participation rates of older white women

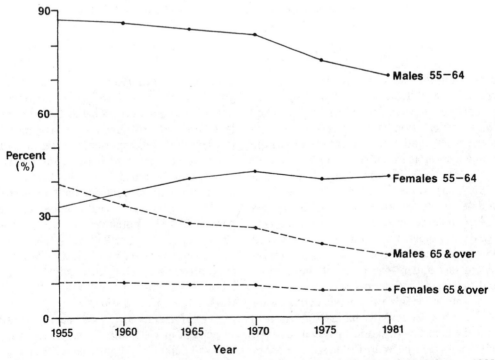

Figure 1. Labor force participation trends of males and females aged 55–64, and 65 and over: 1955–1981.

tend to be lower than those of nonwhite women. Since the participation rates for minority women aged 55 to 64 have been relatively stable, it appears that the overall increase in labor force participation of women in this age group is primarily a result of increased participation of older white women (Kingson, 1982).

The declining labor force participation rates of older workers are manifested in the early-retirement trend. In 1980, 56.2 percent of all male and 69.2 percent of all female social security beneficiaries were receiving benefits reduced for early retirement before age 65 (U.S. Department of Health and Human Services, Social Security Administration, 1982).

Declines in labor force participation among older persons have occurred despite passage of the 1978 Amendments to the Age Discrimination in Employment Act, which raised the mandatory retirement age from 65 to 70, and despite continued high inflation (Parnes, 1981). One possible explanation for the continued drop in labor force participation rates is that the oldest segments within the elderly population are growing as a proportion of the total elderly population, and are receiving correspondingly greater weight in the calculations of labor force participation rates. In examining data from the Current Population Survey, however, Rones (1982) found that the changing age distribution of the civilian noninstitutional population explained very little of the decline in labor force participation rates of older persons. This finding suggests that factors such as the availability of pension income, poor health, and unemployment are more important than age distribution in explaining labor force participation trends.

Under the Bureau of Labor Statistics' middle growth projections of the future labor force, the early retirement trend will continue into the 1980s and 1990s (Fullerton, 1980). The labor force participation rates of *all* persons age 65 and older are assumed to continue to decline. Within the group aged 55 to 64, the participation rates of men are projected to decline, whereas toward the year 2000 slight increases in the participation of women in this age group are expected. The participation rates of white and minority men are projected to continue to diverge, whereas the opposite is projected for the participation rates of minority and white women.

Full-time/Part-time Status. The incidence of working part-time increases with age. While only 22 percent of all workers age 16 or older worked at a part-time job in 1981, just over half of the age 65 and older segment of the labor force did so. Not surprisingly, higher proportions of older women in the labor force worked part-time than men; nearly three times as many women aged 60 to 64 worked at a part-time job in 1981 as men in this age group in the labor force. Among those aged 65 and older, approximately 52 percent of the male labor force and 60 percent of the female labor force were employed at a part-time job. For those working at a full-time job, the incidence of working only part of the year also increases with age.

Several national surveys of the older population (Louis Harris and Associates, Inc., 1979; National Council on the Aging, Inc., 1981) have reported preferences for part-time work, particularly among those persons still employed full-time but interested in continuing to work after retirement. While some older persons may prefer and voluntarily choose part-time work, others may be forced into taking part-time jobs because of illness, disability, family responsibilities, and the impact of the social security retirement test. Additionally, fluctuations in the economy or the business cycle that limit full-time work opportunities also play a role in determining the incidence of part-time and part-year work among older persons. Analyzing data from the 1980 Current Population Survey, Axel and Brotman (1982) note that unemployment, disability, and illness are much more important reasons for part-year work among blacks than whites, particularly after age 65. Men aged 60 to 61 are also more likely to give unemployment or layoff or disability or illness than retirement as their reason for part-year work (Rones, 1978), whereas the

majority of men age 65 and older cite retirement as the reason for their part-year work.
For women age 65 and older, taking care of
the home is another important reason for
part-year work. Thus, while part-time or
part-year work is the preferred choice of
some older persons, many minorities and
pre-retirement-age men may work part-time
because their opportunities for securing full-
time employment are limited.

It should also be noted that part-time jobs
are concentrated in the services and trade
sectors where wages tend to be low and the
fringe benefits for part-time workers minimal or nonexistent.

Unemployment and Discouragement. In 1981,
approximately 533,000 men and women age
55 and older were officially classified as unemployed. Another half million persons age
60 and older were discouraged workers—
persons out of the labor force who wanted a
job but had given up looking for work (U.S.
Department of Labor, Bureau of Labor Statistics, 1982). While the official unemployment rates experienced by older persons have
historically been lower than the rates for
younger age groups, critics argue that when
the discouraged worker and involuntary early
retiree are added to the official count of the
unemployed, the problem of unemployment
among older workers is much more serious
than the official unemployment statistics
would suggest (Sheppard, 1976).

Studies of social security beneficiaries receiving reduced benefits suggest that unemployment may be the first step to early
retirement for as many as one in five men
(Lauriat and Rabin, 1976; Reno, 1976). Another study found that early retirees who had
not expected to be retired experienced a
greater incidence of unemployment preceding their retirement than those individuals
who expected to be retired (Bould, 1980).
Additionally, several researchers have found
a relationship between unemployment rates
and early retirement or declining labor force
participation rates among older persons
(Stafford, 1979; Clark and Barker, 1981).
Thus, it would appear that at least some re-

tirements, particularly early retirements, are
retirements from unemployment rather than
from jobs.

In 1981, the official unemployment rates
for older nonwhite men were nearly two and
three times those of white men: 6.1 percent
for those aged 55 to 64 and 8.1 percent for
those age 65 and older, compared to 3.4 and
2.4 percent, respectively, for whites. The gap
in unemployment rates between older white
and nonwhite women was much smaller, but
nonwhite women still experienced higher
rates than their white counterparts (U.S. Department of Labor, Bureau of Labor Statistics, 1982).

While the absolute numbers of officially
unemployed older persons are relatively
small, these individuals usually experience a
higher average duration of unemployment
than younger age groups. For example, the
mean duration of unemployment for persons
aged 55 to 64 was 18.4 weeks in 1981, compared to 14.8 weeks for those aged 25 to 34.
Additionally, a higher proportion of unemployed persons in the 55 to 64 age group were
unemployed 15 weeks or more—36.8 percent
compared to 30.4 percent of unemployed individuals aged 25 to 34 (U.S. Department of
Labor, Bureau of Labor Statistics, 1982).

Longer spells of unemployment experienced by older workers may be due to a
number of factors, including job discrimination, skills obsolescence, low educational
and/or skills levels, poor health, lack of mobility, and inadequate job search skills (U.S.
Department of Labor, Employment and
Training Administration, 1979). Regardless
of its cause, unemployment, especially unemployment of long duration, may result in
serious negative consequences for the older
worker, including skills atrophy, health deterioration, loss of family income, and reduced future pension benefits (Cobb and
Kasl, 1972; Parnes and King, 1977; Kahn,
1981).

Employment of Older Workers by Industry and Occupation

A variety of factors, such as physical demands of the job, pension coverage, self-

employment opportunities, the rate of employment growth, wages, and the availability of flexible work schedules, influence the way in which older persons are distributed among industries and occupations (Rones, 1978). Gender is also important in explaining distribution patterns within the older workforce. The differences in distribution patterns of older men and women, for example, reflect historical differences in work opportunities or choices available to each that have in turn been determined by educational and physical requirements and by societal norms about the work roles of the sexes. As a result, older women, as described below, are concentrated in industries and occupations characterized by low wages and limited pension coverage that exacerbate the problem of ensuring adequate retirement income for this population.

In 1980, nearly three out of five employed men age 55 to 64 worked in manufacturing, services, and trade sectors. Three out of five employed women in this age group worked in only two sectors—services and trade. Employed men age 65 and older were concentrated in services, trade, and agriculture, whereas the vast majority of employed women in this age group worked in services and trade. The concentration of workers age 65 and older in the services and trade sectors is not surprising because these sectors offer numerous self-employment, part-time, and easy-entry opportunities. Moreover, in comparison to manufacturing, these industries have fewer mandatory retirement provisions (Rones, 1978). Additionally, flexible work schedules preferred by many older workers are more prevalent in the trade and service sectors (Coberly, 1982; Nollen, 1982).

Sex differences are more pronounced when the occupational distribution patterns of older workers are examined. In 1980, just over one in five employed men aged 55 to 64 held jobs in craft and kindred occupations; another 19 percent worked as managers and administrators. In contrast, approximately one-third of employed women aged 55 to 64 worked in clerical occupations, only 2 percent were in the crafts, and the proportion

in managerial and administrative occupations was approximately half of that of older men.

The occupational distribution patterns of both men and women shift somewhat for individuals above age 64. Smaller proportions of men age 65 and older compared to those aged 55 to 64 were employed in craft occupations, for example, whereas the proportion employed as farmers and farm laborers and in service occupations increased. The proportion of women employed in clerical positions at age 65 and older compared to ages 55 to 64 also declined, whereas increased proportions were employed in service and private household jobs. What is not clear is the extent to which these differences in occupational distribution patterns at age 65 and older compared to ages 55 to 64 can be attributed to variations in retirement patterns, and the extent to which they are due to the incidence of retired workers becoming reemployed in new occupations after retirement. For example, the high proportion of men age 65 and older employed in agriculture is undoubtedly due to the fact that retirement is less common in this sector. The increase in the proportion of men employed in the services sector at age 65 and older, however, probably reflects the reemployment in this sector of some workers who retired from manufacturing and other sectors. Additional research is needed for a clearer understanding of the role that delayed retirement and reemployment after retirement play in determining the occupational and industrial distribution patterns of workers age 65 and older.

Firm Size. Not only are workers age 65 and older concentrated in certain specific industries, but they are also concentrated in smaller firms. The March 1979 Current Population Survey revealed that 42 percent of workers aged 55 to 64 who reported the size of the firm for which they worked were employed by firms with 1000 or more employees; only 12 percent of workers age 65 and older were employed in firms that size. In contrast, 52 percent of workers age 65 and older worked in firms with fewer than 25 employees, compared to only 25 percent of workers aged 55 to 64. Even allowing for substantial error in employee reports of firm size, it is clear that the vast majority of workers age 65 and older work for smaller firms. This is not surprising given the fact that both men and women in this age group are concentrated in the service and trade sectors, which include large numbers of small businesses. Small employers are also less likely than large firms to mandate retirement at age 70 and can more easily accommodate the scheduling preferences of older persons. Pension coverage among small employers tends to be low, however, suggesting that older persons employed in small firms may work past normal retirement age because retirement income sources are inadequate.

Future Employment Opportunities and the Older Worker

The uncertainty surrounding future economic conditions makes it difficult to determine what kinds of employment opportunities will be available to older workers in the future. Projections of future employment prepared by the Bureau of Labor Statistics (Personick, 1981) suggest that older workers will benefit from continued growth in the services and trade sectors of the economy, sectors that traditionally offer flexible work arrangements and currently employ large numbers of older persons. Older men aged 55 to 64 may be adversely affected, however, by future declines in employment growth in durable goods manufacturing sectors, although they are likely to enjoy greater protection against job loss than younger workers due to seniority.

Employment opportunities for older workers may also be affected by the changing age structure of the labor force. The size of the younger workforce will shrink during the 1980s, leading some observers (Olson, 1982) to conclude that employers will turn to older workers to fill entry level positions. Whether employers will choose this solution and whether older workers will actively seek,

successfully compete for, or even accept these positions remains to be seen. If the labor force participation rates of older workers projected by the Bureau of Labor Statistics for the 1990s do in fact occur, however, many industries would need to employ greater numbers of older workers in 1990 than are likely to be available if they wish to maintain an age distribution similar to that observed today.

THE INDIVIDUAL

Whereas the emphasis in the first part of this chapter has been on trends in labor force participation, the discussion turns next to the individual: to the place of leisure in the work and retirement stages of the life cycle; factors in the retirement decision; and the impact of retirement on the individual.

Leisure, Work, and Retirement in the Life Cycle

The factor of leisure in the work/retirement equation is important because of the substantial overlap in the concepts of retirement and leisure; in fact, the terms are almost interchangeable in the literature. Adult leisure time is concentrated in the retirement period; and retirement has been seen to consist mostly of leisure activities. Leisure becomes more important and more abundant in affluent, developed society, because of fewer hours devoted to work (in some occupations), earlier retirement, and longer life expectancy (Kreps, 1972; Osgood, 1982). The concept of the life cycle itself rests in part upon the predominance of work or leisure in various life stages (Riley et al., 1972; Havighurst, 1973). Leisure, or free time, is distributed differentially through the life cycle, depending on the individual's tradeoffs of wages for time off. During the early and middle adult years, leisure takes its importance mainly from its contrast to the major role of work. The retirement years represent the phase of the life cycle in which leisure becomes the predominant role.

Critical analyses of the institutionalization

of work and leisure through the life cycle have often advocated a more even or flexible distribution of leisure (Havighurst, 1962; Kaplan, 1975; Kreps, 1976; Morrison, 1978). Best (1980) has described the prevalent "linear life plan" in which whole sectors of the life cycle are devoted to education, to work or child rearing, and finally to leisure. He argues for a more flexible scheduling, a "cyclic life cycle," through such strategies as work-scheduling flexibility, educational leaves throughout the life span, and variations on the theme of complete retirement from work.

Some aspects of the current social situation suggest that the line between work and leisure is becoming blurred. Retirement is difficult to operationalize because individuals move in and out of work roles or engage in modified work schedules. Atchley (1980) points out that many people mix work and leisure (defined as preferred activity satisfying in its own right) on the job. Some workplaces are becoming sites of leisure activities as more companies provide facilities and time for fitness activities. Leisure in retirement, in turn, often takes on aspects of employment; for example, through volunteer work and through hobbies that earn income (Miller, 1965; Shanas et al., 1968).

Leisure in Retirement. The greatest difficulty in dealing with leisure in retirement stems from the lack of consensus on its definition (Voss, 1967; Parker, 1971; Kreps, 1972; Kaplan, 1975; Gordon et al., 1976). Sometimes the definition rests simply on the distinction between work and non-work activities (Kleemeier, 1961; Kreps, 1972), in which case retirement becomes synonymous with leisure. Another common definition is based on a three-fold distinction among work, other obligations (or maintenance activity), and leisure, which is specified as unobligated, discretionary time (Dumazedier, 1967; Kabanoff, 1980). Some definitions of leisure can be heavily value-laden, in that leisure must be valuable (developmental, creative, and renewing) in order to be considered as leisure (DeGrazia, 1962).

More recently, conceptualizations are more objective; Gordon et al. (1976), for example, include relaxation (sleeping, doing nothing) and passive entertainment (watching television). Atchley (1971), on the other hand, distinguishes leisure from recreation, leisure activities being pursued as ends in themselves, unplanned, and characterized by action.

Perspectives on leisure in relation to the work/retirement transition fall into several categories. The most common is a problem approach, which is concerned with adjustment to the substitution of leisure activity for the work role (Parker, 1971). Burgess (1960) contributed the now familiar notion of the "roleless role" of leisure in retirement. Miller (1965) was concerned with the loss of occupational identity and the lack of cultural values to support leisure except as a respite for those who work. The research of Pfeiffer and Davis (1971) lent support to the contention that leisure is not as satisfying as work.

Much of the effort in gerontology to analyze retirement has been typified, explicitly or not, by activity theory approaches, as tested by Lemon et al. (1972) and Longino and Kart (1982). The problem of occupational and other role losses is met with the prescription of leisure activity, which is held to be positively associated with morale and adjustment in retirement. An age stratification conceptualization includes the allocation of the scarce resource of discretionary time (as well as employment) differentially among age strata, involving the emergent institutionalization of leisure among the retired (Ragan and Wales, 1980).

Retirement is generally thought of as a period of leisure, but the research by Gordon et al. (1976) shows a direct relationship between older age and lower levels of participation in general leisure activity. Although leisure activity in general was found to be lower among older adults, certain forms of leisure, such as solitary activities, increased sharply in old age.

In the future, the adult life cycle may be less compartmentalized into work and leisure segments, and leisure may be less problematic for retirees for several reasons. First, in some industries, there is a trend toward the development of programs that allow for a rehearsal of leisure before retirement (i.e., phased retirement). Second, the changing nature of work, that is, the movement from physically demanding to cognitive-based work, may make it more feasible for individuals to extend work into the period that has been considered their retirement years. Third, cohort differences in values and expectations suggest that the future middle-aged and older population will demand more intrinsic satisfaction from their work experience on the one hand, and will more positively value leisure relative to work on the other (Cherrington, 1980).

Although the retirement decision has sometimes been viewed as the complete and final tradeoff of wages for leisure, the following discussion of this decision will present a more dynamic view of the leisure, work, and retirement aspects of the "retirement" phase of the life cycle.

The Retirement Decision

The decision to retire is one of the most important decisions made during the life course. It results in a separation from the world of work and a new commitment to leisure time. Given the significance of the work ethic in many cultures, the decision to forfeit the work role holds importance not only for the individual, but also for his or her community and society.

The Retirement Decision: Conceptual Perspectives. Social scientists have conceptualized the retirement decision as a process by which the older worker weighs the consequences of continuing to work against the consequences of electing retirement. For the most part, this conceptualization has developed out of the empirical work conducted independently by economists and sociologists in the field. Labor economists have viewed the retirement decision as a "work-leisure tradeoff" in which the older person makes a conscious choice between work and leisure in response

to his or her individual wealth and the amount of time believed important to allocate to the workplace and to the home. Clark and Barker (1981) present this perspective in their description of the retirement decision as being made on the basis of assessing present and future opportunities for spending time and resources. Increases in wealth, for example, are said to reduce the individual's desire to continue working, while changes in the value of time spent at work and at home can result in a reallocation of time. Individual variation in personal characteristics, preferences, and labor market opportunities thus leads to retirement at different ages.

Similarly, sociologists have described the decision to retire as an exchange of the role and status of worker for the role and status of retired person. Retirement is viewed as an event denoting the end of employment and the beginning of a time period without a job. Atchley (1979) outlines this perspective in his model of the decision-making process that describes (1) how older workers arrive at the point of considering retirement, (2) the factors that influence the consideration of the retirement alternative, and (3) the variables that affect the actual timing of retirement. In considering retirement, Atchley suggests that two comparisons are made by aging workers. First, financial needs in retirement are compared with financial resources available at the time of retirement. Then the person anticipates what his or her social situation will be in retirement in comparison to what it was while working. Atchley indicates that different factors, such as attitudes toward work and retirement and social support pressures, influence the results of these comparisons. In effect, the person will be motivated to retire if the rewards of retirement appear greater than the rewards of work or job search. The actual timing of retirement is said to be dependent upon the amount of anticipated retirement income. If the economic needs in retirement are perceived to be greater than the resources available to meet them, then the person is expected to continue working or to pursue employment if physically able to do so.

TABLE 2. Factors in the Decision to Retire.

Individual	Institutional
Financial resources	Workplace conditions and employer policies
Health status	Public policy regulations
Attitudes toward work and retirement	Economic conditions
Social support pressures	Societal events and values

Factors in the Decision to Retire. The majority of empirical studies of the retirement decision have focused on the identification of factors that directly influence the decision-making process. As outlined in Table 2, two major types of factors have been reported in the literature. Individual factors are intrinsic to the person and to his or her immediate social environment. Institutional factors are external variables over which the person has minimal or no control.

Research on the retirement decision began with the exploration of individual determinants that influenced the decision to retire early, that is, retire before age 65 (Barfield and Morgan, 1969; Pollman, 1971; Streib and Schneider, 1971; Schulz, 1980). This research revealed that health and retirement income are the two major factors contributing to early retirement. In effect, older workers in poor health are more likely to elect early retirement than workers in good health, and those persons who expect their retirement income to be adequate to live on show a greater likelihood of retiring early than those who do not anticipate their income in retirement to be sufficient for their needs (Boskin, 1977; Burkhauser and Turner, 1980). Recent studies suggest that there is an interactive effect between these two variables in contributing to the early retirement decision. Quinn (1977) found that while eligibility for Social Security reduced the probability of labor force participation in a sample of older workers both with and without health limitations, the estimated effect was approximately five times larger for the former group; while the difference was smaller, this same effect was found to exist when he examined the influence of private pension plans. The U.S. House of Representatives Select Committee on Aging (1981b) has reported that older workers with health problems who expect low replacement rates from their pension income are more likely to continue working and not retire than individuals expecting high replacement rates. The committee concluded that because males who withdraw from the labor force before age 62 cannot receive Social Security, the interaction between health and retirement income is not as significant for the below-62 group as for the 62–64 age group.

Studies of the effect of attitudes toward work and retirement on the decision to exit from the labor force have tended to report that the preference for early retirement is based on a desire for less work and a positive image of retirement (Barfield and Morgan, 1969; Orbach, 1969). Cohn (1979) suggests that there is a decline in the importance of work with age, an attitude change that encourages early retirement. What remains an unresolved issue is whether an inverse relationship exists between a person's negative attitude toward work and his positive attitude toward retirement (Fillenbaum, 1971; Goudy et al., 1975; Glamser, 1976).

Empirical investigation of the ways in which social support pressures influence the decision to retire has principally concentrated on the influence exerted by the spouse. Anderson et al. (1980) have discovered that the retirement decision of the husband will be directly influenced by his wife's labor market decisions. Their findings support the notion of concurrent retirement in the dual-career family, suggesting that retirement patterns in this type of household may be different from those in the traditional one-earner family. Given the increase in the number of dual-career households, this type of research warrants further investigation.

More recent studies in the field have concentrated on institutional determinants of retirement with emphasis on the decision to continue working and postpone retirement past age 65, that is, the decision to elect late retirement. In part, this shift in research focus represents a response to the public discussion about possible federal retirement policies that would encourage older workers to remain in the labor force beyond the time when many are currently retiring (Paul, 1982).

Illustrative of studies assessing the influence of workplace factors on the decision to retire is the research on the interest of older workers in innovative work options. Among retirement-age workers surveyed in two large organizations, McConnell et al. (1980) found that one-half of all the workers would remain employed beyond their planned retirement ages if alternatives to the normal working day were available. Part-time schedules were the most desired of the work options. This interest in employment alternatives was revealed to be contingent, however, upon the compensation and fringe benefit conditions associated with the options. If the workers were unable to receive a portion of their pension benefits while utilizing the options, the majority reported that they would elect to retire; nearly one-half indicated they would then seek employment with another employer. In particular, job modifications and job transfers were desirable only if they were not accompanied by salary reductions. In effect, this research points to the importance of attractive work conditions and employee benefit plans in the decision to elect late retirement.

Pension policies represent another important workplace factor affecting older workers' decision to retire. Employers tend to use pensions as a tool to deal with shifts in demand for their goods and services and in coping with cyclical economic problems (Graebner, 1980; Kingson, 1982; Schulz, 1983). For example, a recent phenomenon has been the development of pension policies in the form of attractive severance plans that encourage older workers to retire when a company's financial status is deteriorating.

Public policy regulations have been found to affect the retirement decision in different ways. Yet very little research has been conducted in this area until recently. The 1978 Amendments to the Age Discrimination in Employment Act barring mandatory retirement before age 70 were found to have a weak short-run impact on worker retirement plans (U.S. House of Representatives, Select Committee on Aging, 1981b). Moreover, it has been estimated that if mandatory retirement were eliminated, older males who are not yet of the mandatory retirement age would be only modestly affected; but for men who reach the ages of 68 to 70 in the future, labor force participation would increase 26 percent in 1985 and 21 percent in the year 2000 (U.S. House of Representatives Select Committee on Aging, 1981b). These findings, however, must be considered tentative and preliminary.

The influence that the social security program has upon the decision to retire has been debated for some time. Studies examining the effect that the size of benefits has upon the decision tend to report that high benefit levels contribute to the decision to retire early (Bowen and Finegan, 1969; Boskin, 1977; Fraker, 1983). Conversely, the effect that the delayed retirement credit has had upon encouraging older workers to postpone retirement and continue working has been estimated to be negligible (Clark and Barker, 1981).

The availability of jobs can influence the older person's retirement status. The U.S. Congressional Budget Office (1982) has reported that the higher the rate of unemployment, the less likely it is that older individuals will find jobs, a situation often leading to "retirement" among "discouraged workers." Clark and Barker (1981) estimate that a 1.0 percentage point increase in the overall unemployment rate results in a 1.2 percentage point decline in labor force participation of workers between the ages of 55 and 64. Although it is also conventionally assumed that a high rate of inflation may influence older workers to stay in the workforce longer, no research has established evidence to this effect. Indeed, it has been suggested that when high inflation is accompanied by high unemployment, it is unlikely that older worker participation rates increase (Schulz, 1983).

Finally, with regard to societal influences on the retirement decision, Barfield and Morgan (1978) have pointed to a "period of history" effect dominating changes in plans to retire early. In repeating core questions asked ten years earlier on retirement plans, their national personal interview survey revealed that a cohort entering the labor force at an economically favorable time in history may have a greater than average proportion of their members electing to retire early, presumably because they can afford it. Similarly, other research has described the early retirement phenomenon as a recently established norm in American society, a norm recognized by current retirement-age cohorts (Goudy et al., 1980). What remains unknown is the extent to which this norm will continue to influence older working Americans in the future.

Emerging Issues in the Literature. What is currently known about the retirement decision is primarily based on cross-sectional studies of older white males, studies that have treated retirement as a permanent exit from the labor force. Attention is being drawn to the methodological issues that characterize this body of research (Ekerdt et al., 1980; Palmore et al., 1982). These issues center upon the manner in which retirement has been defined and measured in the past.

Palmore et al. (1982) have found that determinants of retirement vary with different definitions of retirement, that is, early retirement (retirement before age 65), late retirement (retirement after age 65), and retirement as defined by the number of hours worked in a given year. In using longitudinal data from seven studies and multiple definitions of retirement, it was revealed that the predictors of early and late retirement differed. The strongest predictors of early retirement were factors such as self-reported health status and attitudes toward retirement. In contrast, the strongest predictors of late retirement were factors related to socioeconomic status and job characteristics. When retirement was defined by the number of hours worked per year, job characteristics became the most important predictors.

Ekerdt et al. (1980) point out that survey questions asking older workers about their retirement age take several forms. These questions tend to solicit either the age at which the workers believe they will retire, (i.e., their planned retirement age) or the perceived ideal age or preferred age of retirement. Individual changes in planned retirement age have been found to represent a response to changes in pension policies and economic conditions. For example, during poor economic times, the older worker will often plan to retire during a period when the economy is perceived as improving. In contrast, fluctuations in the preferred age of retirement have been accounted for by advancing age. In other words, as the individual grows older, the age at which he prefers to retire tends to be pushed back to a later age. In a longitudinal study of workers who were asked both their planned and preferred retirement ages, Ekerdt and his colleagues found that these two ages changed simultaneously over time. It was concluded that older workers' willingness to retire is a phenomenon sensitive to forces beyond their control.

These studies suggest the need for social scientists to acknowledge that the decision to retire is subject to change over the individual's work career and does not always imply a complete severing of ties with the workforce. The work of Quinn (1981) exemplifies the attention being given to what is referred to as "partial retirement." Using the 1969 Retirement History Study data, he found that partial retirement was more common than full retirement among the self-employed. Among the wage and salary workers, however, this form of retirement was discovered to be far less common.

In summary, a sizable amount of the research conducted in the work and retirement area has been devoted to the retirement decision. Early studies in the field have pointed to the importance of personal factors in affecting a person's decision to retire early. More recent research has revealed the significance of institutional forces in electing late retirement. Taken together, this body of knowledge contributes to the emerging perspective that the retirement decision involves a dynamic process sensitive to changes in the individual's need for work, retirement, and leisure.

The Impact of Retirement

Research on the impact of retirement on the individual has often stressed the negative consequences for income, psychological adjustment, health, and mortality (Miller, 1965; Maddox, 1968; Blau, 1973). This emphasis may be viewed in contrast to earlier concepts of retirement as the welcome reward for a lifetime of hard work (Graebner, 1980). It is possible that a negative emphasis reflects an interest among academic and professional gerontologists in correcting injustices and solving problems of old age, as noted by Streib and Schneider (1971). There are in fact wide individual differences in the experience of retirement, and an attempt to balance the emphasis on the negative consequences is not a denial of the severe problems of some individuals due to retirement.

The most obvious and most easily documented change that occurs for most individuals with retirement is a reduction in income level, although there is variability in the effect of retirement on income. Retirement usually results in a one-half to two-thirds reduction in income and moves many retired persons into a low income category (U.S. Senate Special Committee on Aging, 1982). Parnes and Nestel (1981) compared total family income in the year prior to retirement to income in 1976 (in constant dollars) and found decreases ranging from 33 to 45 percent. Questions of adequacy come into play in assessing levels of income in retirement, and these assessments need to take into account different demands on income as a function of retiring from the labor force, along with many other complex considerations (U.S. Senate Special Committee on Aging, 1980). The reduction in work-related expenses, such as transportation, may not be

so significant a factor as it appears to be, and is balanced by increases in other expenditures such as leisure activities (Schulz, 1980). At a subjective level, nevertheless, the Harris poll for the National Council on the Aging (1981) found that "not having enough money to live on" was reported as a serious problem for more adults under the age of 65 (22 percent) than for adults 65 and over (17 percent).

The literature on psychological adjustment to retirement often stresses retirement as a loss, of social status and occupational identity crucial to self concept (Miller, 1965); of role (Burgess, 1960; Bengtson, 1973); of a daily structuring of time and activities (Blau, 1973); and of associates (Lowenthal and Robinson, 1976). Other studies, however, have challenged assumptions of discontinuity, crisis, and problems of adjustment in the retirement period (Atchley, 1971, 1980; Streib and Schneider, 1971; Parnes, 1981). Atchley (1976), for example, has suggested that adjustment varies during successive periods following retirement; these periods are conceptualized as the honeymoon, disenchantment, reorientation, stability, and termination phases. Furthermore, Parnes and Nestel (1981) found that when they compared retirees and comparable nonretired men, expressions of satisfaction with various aspects of life were favorable among the retirees, if they first eliminated from the comparison those individuals who had retired because of poor health. The relationship between retirement and psychological adjustment depends on many variables, including not only health, but also occupation, gender, income, personality, morale before retirement, and attitudes toward work and retirement (Maddox, 1970; Streib and Schneider, 1971; Eisdorfer, 1972; Lowenthal et al., 1975; Bengtson, et al., 1976; Schaie and Geiwitz, 1982).

It is commonly believed by both lay persons and professionals that the event of retirement contributes to health problems and the probability of premature death (American Medical Association, 1972; Bradford, 1979; Bernard, 1982). The effects of retirement on morbidity and mortality are ascribed to the psychological trauma of the loss of the work role, or to stress related to change and its somatic disturbances (Minkler, 1981). Although these observations are sometimes based on involuntary retirement, they are often generalized to retirement per se. The major difficulty in analyzing the effects of retirement on health lies in the fact that failing health and precursors of mortality may be the cause rather than the effect of retirement; but it is of course difficult to manipulate retirement as an experimental variable (Myers, 1954; Carp, 1972). The causal sequence therefore cannot be ascertained, nor can the effects of retirement be distinguished from the effects of aging per se (Streib and Schneider, 1971).

Arguments for the negative effect of retirement on mortality have often been based on clinical impression only (Portnoi, 1981), but have been influential in policy deliberations, for example, in the 1977 hearings on the amendments to the Age Discrimination in Employment Act (U.S. Senate Special Committee on Aging, 1967; U.S. Senate Committee on Human Resources, 1977b; U.S. House of Representatives Select Committee on Aging, 1977). During the 1977 hearings, data from the Haynes et al. (1978) research were widely cited as supporting the mortality effect, although this conclusion does not bear up under closer scrutiny of that study. Statements maintaining the retirement–morbidity–mortality link thus prevail in spite of research and reviews that offer contradictory evidence (Shanas, 1970; Streib and Schneider, 1971; Friedmann and Orbach, 1974; Palmore et al., 1979; Menefee, 1980).

Studies of the impact of retirement on income, psychological adjustment, and mortality suffer from several limitations. First, they do not fully account for the great variability among individuals due to the many factors on which the effects of retirement depend and the various stages of adjustment over time. Second, methodological difficulties interfere with attempts to isolate the impact of retirement. Third, objectivity may be

hampered in assessments of the impact of retirement, since they are often made in a context of policy discussions concerning the raising or lowering of retirement age and the elimination of mandatory retirement.

THE EMPLOYER

The employing organization has not received as much attention in studies of aging as other social institutions and organizations, although its importance is apparent. The employer plays a key role in determining the outcomes of individual aging and in contributing to national patterns and trends in the labor force participation, unemployment, and retirement of the older population. The employer's role in shaping the course of aging of the individual is significant because the employer's policies are crucial in determining the probability, at successive career stages, of the individual's earning income, maintaining a productive role with opportunities for training and promotion, identifying him- or herself with a certain occupational status, and receiving a retirement income.

Employer practices in regard to age in the workforce can also have a substantial bearing on a number of national problems related to an aging population. First, discrimination against older workers affects the unemployment and poverty of the older working age population (Sheppard, 1976). The 1981 Department of Labor study has traced age discrimination in employment in the United States to the late 1800s and concluded that substantial age discrimination in hiring continued almost unabated until the 1967 Age Discrimination in Employment Act (U.S. House of Representative Select Committee on Aging, 1981b; U.S. Senate Special Committee on Aging, 1981). The illegality of the practice now makes estimates of its prevalence difficult, but most observers would agree that it is a serious problem facing older workers. Second, failure to provide updating and retraining opportunities for employees in their middle years is a factor in the obsolescence and reduced productivity of some older workers (Dalton and Thompson, 1971; Dubin et al., 1980). Third, private pensions are significant in the income adequacy of retired annuitants, but private pensions are paid currently to only one out of five persons over 65 (U.S. Social Security Administration, 1980; President's Commission on Pension Policy, 1981).

Employers in turn face certain dilemmas in dealing with the age factor in the workplace, dilemmas that can be traced quite broadly to a number of trends discussed in this chapter: current early retirement trends versus pressures at the national policy level to raise retirement age; legislation barring chronological age as a personnel decision criterion, with a related increase in age discrimination litigation (Edelman and Siegler, 1978); and demographic trends that will limit the number of younger workers and increase the number of middle-aged (and eventually older) workers. The dilemmas and concerns facing employers pose a challenge to social scientists in the study of aging (Work in America Institute, 1980; Copperman and Keast, 1983; Robinson, 1983). A discussion of some of these concerns follows.

Skill Shortages

Even under conditions of high unemployment, labor shortages in certain occupations persist and are projected for the future. A complex combination of factors is responsible, two of which are age-related. First, employers frequently offer early retirement for several reasons; for example, under pressure of unions, as a recruitment incentive, or as a method of reducing the workforce. Owing to fluctuating labor demands and skill shortages, some employers who have encouraged their employees to retire at an early age then rehire them, thus incurring the simultaneous costs of salary and pension due to their policy of early retirement. A second factor, which may increasingly contribute to labor shortages, is the dramatically reduced number of young entry level workers, as discussed above (Drucker, 1979; Olson, 1982). Some employers have successfully experi-

mented with recruiting older workers for both unskilled and technical entry level jobs in the face of these shortages. Employers in some industries are thus experiencing an uncertain transition to viewing older individuals as an important source of labor in the future (Jacobson, 1980).

Functional Assessment

Chronological age is not a useful predictor of individual performance, because of the great variability on performance among individuals of the same age, especially at higher ages. Furthermore, using age as a factor in personnel decisions is prohibited by legislation (within the protected age class). Employers therefore are increasingly challenged to measure performance and potential more directly, without using the proxy measure of chronological age, and with measurement procedures that are not biased against older employees (Sonnenfeld, 1978; Walker and Lazer, 1978). Here experience in research on aging is relevant because the concept of "functional age" has appeared to offer a substitute criterion for chronological age (McFarland, 1973; Birren and Renner, 1977), and because investigators have attempted to devise tests free of age bias (Schaie, 1977).

The concept of functional age is based on the assumption that it is feasible to take a single index measurement of an individual on a cluster of work-relevant functions that are highly correlated with chronological age. It would thus be possible to take advantage of the common knowledge that, for example, certain individuals aged 60 function as well as typical 50-year-olds, and decisions about them should be made on the basis of their level of functioning rather than their actual age. One problem in the development of a single functional age measure, however, is that the rate of individual aging on one function (e.g., vision) may be quite different from the rate on another function (e.g., physical strength); to index an individual's overall "functional age" can thus be misleading. In addition, relevant functions are specific to particular jobs. The measure of functional age has a number of serious conceptual and methodological difficulties, and has not become practically useful (Heron and Chown, 1967; Schaie and Gribbin, 1975; Krauss, 1980; Salthouse, 1982; Avolio et al., in press).

Neither has the assessment of individuals for specific jobs, according to a system of functional job analysis, become widespread (Fine, 1971; Koyl, 1974; U.S. Senate Special Committee on Aging, 1982). Nevertheless, an important principle remains, namely, that direct observation of individual job-related performance and potential must be substituted for the use of chronological age in hiring, selection for training and transfer, promotion, and termination. (It should be noted that the Age Discrimination in Employment Act provides an exception for occupations in which age is a bona fide occupational qualification.) Personnel systems of performance appraisal and testing systems for skills assessment are the necessary tools, and attention to potential interactions of age with assessment and testing methods becomes increasingly important.

Productivity

The effects of age on individual employee output, performance, and productivity have been a long-standing concern of employers (Fox, 1951; Welford 1976b; Robinson, 1983). These concerns range from the speed and accuracy of units produced in manufacturing to the creativity and innovation of the highly placed executive, and they extend to a broader set of issues such as intelligence, ability to learn, interpersonal relations, absenteeism, accident rates, and disability. Decisions on age-related questions in business are often based on unwarranted negative age stereotyping (Rosen and Jerdee, 1977), but research results minimizing age differences in task performance have not been sufficient to counteract discriminatory beliefs and practices.

The results of laboratory research demonstrating age effects are not always transferable to the workplace (Fozard and Carr, 1972). Salthouse (1982), for example—in a review of laboratory research findings on age differences in cognition, reasoning and decision making, memory, spatial abilities, perceptual-motor and cognitive speed, and sensory factors—concludes that there are age declines in cognitive functions in laboratory tests. He observes, however, that these age effects are noticeably absent from on-the-job performance, perhaps because of the minimal demand level of most activities (compared to laboratory tests) and the advantage of experience that is usually associated with increasing age. He also notes that age-related gains (e.g., judgment) are not generally captured in laboratory research. In addition, it has often been observed that employees tend to leave positions when their level of functioning falls short of the demands of the job (Welford, 1976b; Sonnenfeld, 1978).

A number of reviews of research on occupational performance with age are available (Kelleher and Quirk, 1973; Meier and Kerr, 1976; Baugher, 1978; Fleisher and Kaplan, 1980; United States Senate Special Committee on Aging, 1982). The overall conclusions of these and other reviews and research reports can be summarized as follows: (1) While some productivity declines with age have been observed in certain industries (e.g., manufacturing), in others there were no significant age differences, and in some occupations (e.g., clerical, manufacturing, sales) older workers were more productive than younger workers. (2) There are wide differences in productivity within age groups. (3) There are some declines with age in physical capacity, but environmental conditions are important in mitigating the effects of decline, and chronological age is not necessarily a limiting factor in physically demanding work even through the sixties. (4) Age differences manifest themselves in a slowing of reaction time and speed of performance, but older employees score as well as or better than younger employees on creativity, flexibility, facility of information processing, absenteeism, accident rates, and turnover. (5) Although some older employees may be reluctant to undergo retraining, with appropriate training methods and environment they can usually learn as well as younger employees.

Some reservations need to be stated in reviewing research on productivity and age. Much of the literature is polemical in that it argues for the value of older workers, and therefore must be scrutinized for objectivity. There are also serious problems in generalizing about age and productivity; the most serious stems from the finding of great variability in productivity within age groups, variability that is even higher with older age groups. A second limitation in making simple generalizations is that the definition of "older workers" ranges in the published research from over 40 to over 65. Furthermore, both measures of productivity and age effects vary substantially from one industry and occupation to another.

Many of the findings on age and productivity reflect not so much the effects of aging per se but rather cohort differences, lower expectations of and opportunities for older workers, and (in the case of higher performance levels at other ages) the advantages of survivorship, experience, and optimization. Greater attention to on-site research on age differences in job performance is needed in order to address the employer's uncertainties about the effects of age and to redesign the work environment to maximize the productivity of middle-aged and older workers. In spite of the limitations of the available research on the effects of age on job performance, the overall findings have important implications for business policy on recruitment, training, job redesign, and retirement age. The implications for termination and retirement are especially pertinent, as reflected in retirement age policy.

Retirement Age Policy

Closely related to concerns about skill shortages, assessment, and productivity is the question of an optimal retirement age policy. Pressures to offer early retirement as an attractive option come from many directions: (1) most union policies; (2) employee pref-

erences for and thus competition in offering early retirement as a fringe benefit in recruitment; (3) workforce redundancy in periods of economic downturn and the need to terminate some segment of the workforce (with older employees sometimes perceived as the most costly in terms of compensation and fringe benefits); (4) the perceived need for retirement incentives in order to avoid legal challenges to forced retirement or termination, if they should become necessary; (5) perception by younger employees of blocked opportunities; (6) perception of the obsolescence and reduced productivity of the older workforce; and (7) interest of manipulating the age structure of institutions through the continual succession of cohorts, for example in the case of tenured university faculty succession (Sonnenfeld, 1978; Work in America Institute, 1980; Patton, 1981). The *perception* of these pressures is stressed in this discussion because organizational policy reflects such perceptions, whether accurate or not.

The problems employers face with early retirement are related to costs, inflexibility, and unforeseen outcomes. Costs of early retirement policies need to be calculated, not only in terms of increased pension benefit costs but also in the costs of turnover due to recruitment and training needs and due to the loss of continuity. Early retirement provisions built into company pension policy are difficult to retract when changed economic and human resources circumstances call for a reversal. Some organizations thus get caught with a policy of early retirement during labor shortages, and incur the additional costs of hiring retirees back.

Problems that result from early retirement policies in turn create pressures for a flexible retirement policy. The employer's concerns about manipulating retirement age vary according to the particular industry and occupation involved, labor supply and demand, and fluctuating economic conditions. In addition, pressure to delay retirement is beginning to be felt from the federal government. These considerations are discussed in the following section on public policy.

✗ PUBLIC POLICY ON EMPLOYMENT AND RETIREMENT

The approach to retirement age on the part of the federal government in the United States is in transition. Recent policies have encouraged early retirement and limited the labor force participation of older persons; developing policies aim to delay retirement (Clark and Barker, 1981; U.S. House of Representatives Select Committee on Aging, 1981b; U.S. Congressional Budget Office, 1982). Two features of the Social Security Act have functioned to limit participation. First, individuals drawing social security retirement benefits are penalized for earnings from employment, over a given limit and up to a given age (with year-by-year variations in both factors). This earnings limitation feature serves to restrict the labor force participation of older persons (Burkhauser and Turner, 1980). Second, men have been able to draw reduced early retirement benefits at age 62 since 1961 (women, since 1956); this provision has contributed substantially to the early retirement trend (Schulz, 1980; Kingson, 1982). There have been no major federal policies that would similarly encourage early retirement practices by *employers*, but on the other hand there is a notable absence in public policy of significant efforts to encourage the training and placement of older workers by employers (U.S. Senate Special Committee on Aging, 1981).

Recent changes in the Social Security Act are intended to extend the labor force participation of older workers of the "baby boom" generation by gradually raising the age for full retirement benefits from 65 to 67 between 2000 and 2027 and by reducing early retirement benefits. Other countries (e.g., Japan) are also instituting policies to encourage later retirement (Sekiguchi, 1980; Sekimoto, 1982). In western Europe, on the other hand, the pressures of high unemployment have resulted in a trend to lower the retirement age even further (Zeitzer, 1983).

The major legislation directed to employer behavior and aimed at extending employment opportunities has been the Age Discrimination in Employment Act of 1967, and its 1978 amendments that raised the permissible age of mandatory retirement to 70 in most employment (U.S. Senate Committee on Human Resources, 1977a). The impact of the legislation on actual labor force participation rates has been only moderate (U.S. Department of Labor, 1981). (It should be noted, however, that the main stated purpose of the legislation was to prohibit inequitable and unjust practices against individuals, rather than to increase labor force participation.) Currently proposed policies directed to employer behavior include lifting the age lid on mandatory retirement altogether; mandating pension accrual after normal retirement age; providing incentives to employers to hire, train, and retain older workers; and educating employers regarding the value of older workers (U.S. Senate Special Committee on Aging, 1980; Coberly, 1983; Rappaport, 1982).

Pressures to extend the working years of older individuals come from several directions (U.S. Senate Special Committee on Aging, 1980; *Final Report of the 1981 White House Conference on Aging, 1982*). The chief concern is that the greatly increased number of individuals over the age of 65 after the turn of the century, in proportion to the number of individuals of working age, will add to the costs of retirement unless retirement age is delayed. It has been estimated that the ratio of retired persons and children to persons of working age will be the same in 2025 as it is today only if retirement age increases to 70 (President's Commission on Pension Policy, 1981). Arguments in favor of raising the retirement age are sometimes based on the thesis that improving longevity is an indication that the older population is healthier than older cohorts in the past, and thus can continue to work to later ages. The contrary view is that reductions in mortality are not necessarily accompanied by reductions in chronic illness and disability, and in fact may be offset by the phenomenon of survival, with reduced mortality but increased disability (Covez and Blanchet, 1981; Wilson, 1981).

SUMMARY

Public policy developments have drawn increased attention to the labor force participation and retirement decisions of older workers. Private sector policy is also undergoing reexamination in regard to the most productive employment of the middle-aged and older population. Theoretical perspectives, as well, assign importance to the sequencing of work and retirement roles in the life cycle, the social institutionalization of retirement, and age effects on performance.

A continuing trend in labor force behavior is the early retirement of males in their late fifties and early sixties. Labor force participation patterns of middle-aged and older men and women are quite diverse, however, and women aged 55 to 64 have shown increasing labor force participation in the last two to three decades while the participation rates of men of the same age have been showing a marked decline.

The decision to retire is based on two sets of factors, individual (primarily income and health) and institutional (such as part-time work options and labor market conditions). It is the individual characteristics that are the main determinants of the decision to retire early.

Work and leisure stages of the life cycle are becoming less distinct as persons of retirement age move in and out of the workforce and seek working arrangements that provide an optimal mix of work and leisure. Individual preferences for early retirement, partial retirement, or continued employment, however, operate within the constraints of public policy pressures for early or delayed retirement and within the constraints of fluctuating employer policies and practices.

A review of current knowledge of employment and retirement as they relate to aging reveals a number of gaps in knowledge that need to be addressed through further research. From the employer's point of view, techniques of directly assessing functional abilities, instead of relying on chronological age, are still undeveloped. In addition, research on the effects of age on job performance is generally out of date and limited in generalizability. Regarding individual behavior, despite a great deal of research on the retirement decision, further research is needed to understand the interaction in this decision among the factors of health and employer pensions and other benefits. With the dramatically increased labor force participation of married women, more needs to be known about how husbands and wives will decide on their ages of retirement. Research on employment and retirement patterns has in the past been focused largely on men, and needs to expand in the future to include information about women in the labor force.

REFERENCES

American Medical Association, Committee on Aging. 1972. *Retirement: A Medical Philosophy and Approach.* Chicago: AMA.

Anderson, Kathryn, Clark, Robert L. and Johnson, Thomas. 1980. Retirement in dual-career families. *In* Robert L. Clark (ed.), *Retirement Policy in an Aging Society,* pp. 109–127. Durham, N.C.: Duke University Press.

Atchley, Robert C. 1971. Retirement and leisure participation: Continuity or crisis? *The Gerontologist* 2:13–17.

Atchley, Robert C. 1976. *The Sociology of Retirement.* Cambridge, Mass.: Schenkman.

Atchley, Robert C. 1979. Issues in retirement research. *The Gerontologist* 19:44–54.

Atchley, Robert C. 1980. *The Social Forces of Later Life: An Introduction to Social Gerontology,* 3rd ed. Belmont, Calif.: Wadsworth.

Atchley, Robert C. 1982. Retirement as a social institution. *Annual Review of Sociology* 8:263–287.

Avolio, Bruce J., Barrett, Gerald V., and Sterns, Harvey L. In press. Recapitulating the origin of a concept: Considerations for functional age measurement and alternative assessment strategies. *Experimental Aging Research.*

Axel, Helen, and Brotman, Herman B. 1982. Demographics of the mature work force. *In* Dorothy Bauer (ed.), *Significant Segment—Employment and Training of the Mature Worker: A Resource Manual,* pp. 14–42. Washington, D.C.: National Council on the Aging, Inc.

Barfield, Richard E., and Morgan, James N. 1969. *Early Retirement: The Decision and the Experience.* Ann Arbor: The University of Michigan.

Barfield, Robert E., and Morgan, James N. 1978. Trends in planned early retirement. *The Gerontologist* 18:13–18.

Baugher, Dan. 1978. Is the older worker inherently incompetent? *Aging and Work* 1:243–250.

Bengtson, Vern L. 1973. *The Social Psychology of Aging*. Indianapolis, Ind.: Bobbs-Merrill.

Bengtson, Vern L., Kasschau, Patricia, and Ragan, Pauline K. 1976. The impact of social structure on aging individuals. *In* James E. Birren and K. Warner Schaie (eds.), *Handbook of the Psychology of Aging*, pp. 327–353. New York: Van Nostrand Reinhold.

Bernard, Kenneth. 1982. The first step to the cemetery. *Newsweek* (Feb. 22):15.

Best, Fred. 1980. *Flexible Life Scheduling*. New York: Praeger.

Birren, James E., and Renner, V. J. 1977. Research on the psychology of aging: Principles and experimentation. *In* James E. Birren and K. Warner Schaie (eds.), *Handbook of the Psychology of Aging*. New York: Van Nostrand Reinhold.

Blau, Zena S. 1973. *Old Age in a Changing Society*. New York: New Viewpoints.

Boskin, Michael. 1977. Social Security and the retirement decision. *Economic Inquiry* 15:1–25.

Bould, Sally. 1980. Unemployment as a factor in early retirement decisions. *American Journal of Economics and Sociology* 39:123–136.

Bowen, William G., and Finegan, T. Aldrich. 1969. *The Economics of Labor Force Participation*. Princeton, N.J.: Princeton University Press.

Bradford, Kenneth. 1979. Can you survive your retirement? *Harvard Business Review* (Nov.–Dec.):103–107.

Brotman, Herman. 1982. Summary table A. Middle series projections, all ages and 65+, by race and sex, 1982–2050. (Mimeo).

Bruche, Gert, and Casey, Bernard. 1982. *Work or Retirement: Labour Market and Social Policies for Older Workers in France, Great Britain, the Netherlands, Sweden, and the USA*. Berlin: International Institute of Management.

Burgess, Ernest W. 1960. Aging in Western culture. *In* Ernest W. Burgess (ed.), *Aging in Western Societies*, pp. 3–28. Chicago: University of Chicago Press.

Burkhauser, Richard V., and Turner, John A. 1980. The effects of pension policy through life. *In* Robert L. Clark (ed.), *Retirement Policy in an Aging Society*, pp. 128–141. Durham, N.C.: Duke University Press.

Carp, Frances M. 1972. *Retirement*. New York: Behavioral Publications.

Cherrington, David J. 1980. *The Work Ethic*. New York: AMACOM, A Division of American Management Association.

Clark, Robert L., and Barker, David T. 1981. *Reversing the Trend Toward Early Retirement*. Washington, D.C.: American Enterprise Institute.

Cobb, Sidney, and Kasl, Stanislav. 1972. Some medical aspects of unemployment. *In* Gloria M. Shatto (ed.), *Employment of the Middle-Aged*, pp. 87–98. Springfield, Ill.: Charles C. Thomas.

Coberly, Sally. 1982. Alternative working arrangements. *In* Dorothy Bauer (ed.), *Significant Segment—Employment and Training of the Mature Worker: A Resource Manual*, pp. 85–104. Washington, D.C.: National Council on the Aging, Inc.

Coberly, Sally. 1983. Incentives for hiring older workers in the private sector—are employers interested? *Aging and Work* 6:37–47.

Cohn, Richard M. 1979. Age and the satisfaction from work. *Journal of Gerontology* 34:264–272.

Copperman, Lois F., and Keast, Frederick D. 1983. *Adjusting to an Older Work Force*. New York: Van Nostrand Reinhold.

Covez, Alain, and Blanchet, Madeleine. 1981. Disability trends in the United States population, 1966–1976: Analysis of reported causes. *American Journal of Public Health* 71:464–471.

Dalton, Gene W., and Thompson, Paul H. 1971. Accelerating obsolescence of older engineers. *Harvard Business Review* (Sept.–Oct.):127–137.

DeGrazia, Sebastian. 1962. *Of Time, Work, and Leisure*. Garden City, N.Y.: Anchor Books.

Drucker, Peter F. 1979. After fixed age retirement is gone. *In* Max Ways (ed.), *The Future of Business: Global Issues in the 80's and 90's*, pp. 37–47. New York: Pergamon Press.

Dubin, Samuel S., Farr, James L., Enscore, E. Emory, Kozlowski, Stephen W. J., and Cleveland, Jeanette N. 1980. Relationships among individual motivation, work environment, and updating in engineers. Final report to the National Science Foundation. (Mimeo.)

Dumazedier, Joffre. 1967. *Toward A Society of Leisure*, translated by Stewart E. McLure. New York: Free Press.

Edelman, Charles D., and Siegler, Ilene C. 1978. *Federal Age Discrimination in Employment Law: Slowing Down the Gold Watch*. Charlottesville, Va.: The Mitchie Co.

Eisdorfer, Carl. 1972. Adaptation to the loss of work. *In* Frances M. Carp (ed.), *Retirement*, pp. 245–265. New York: Behavioral Publications.

Ekerdt, David J., Bosse, Raymond, and Mogey, John M. 1980. Concurrent change in planned and preferred age for retirement. *Journal of Gerontology* 35:232–240.

Fillenbaum, Gerda G. 1971. On the relation between attitude to work and attitude to retirement. *Journal of Gerontology* 26:244–248.

Final Report of the 1981 White House Conference on Aging. 1982. Washington, D.C.: Department of Health and Human Services.

Fine, Sidney A. 1971. *An Introduction to Functional Job Analysis*. Washington, D.C.: W. E. Upjohn Institute.

Fleisher, Dorothy, and Kaplan, Barbara H. 1980. Characteristics of older workers: Implications for restructuring work. *In* Pauline K. Ragan (ed.), *Work and Retirement: Policy Issues*, pp. 140–163. Los Angeles: University of Southern California Press.

Fox, Harland. 1951. Utilization of older manpower. *Harvard Business Review* 29:40–54.

Fozard, James L., and Carr, Gordon D. 1972. Age differences and psychological estimates of abilities and skills. *Industrial Gerontology* 13:75–96.

Fraker, Thomas M. 1983. The effects of social security wealth on the resolution of unemployment spells of older men. *In* Christopher Garbacz (ed.), *Economic Resources for the Elderly: Prospects for the Future,* pp. 53–80. Boulder, Colo.: Westview Press.

Friedmann, Eugene A., and Orbach, Harold L. 1974. Adjustment to retirement. *In* Silvano Arieti (ed.), *American Handbook of Psychiatry,* Vol. 1, 2nd ed. New York: Basic Books.

Fullerton, Howard N., Jr. 1980. The 1995 labor force: A first look. *Monthly Labor Review* 103:11–21.

Glamser, Francis D. 1976. Determinants of a positive attitude toward retirement. *Journal of Gerontology* 31:104–107.

Gordon, Chad, Gaitz, Charles M., and Scott, Judith. 1976. Leisure and lives: Personal expressivity across the life span. *In* Robert H. Binstock and Ethel Shanas (eds.), *Handbook of Aging and the Social Sciences,* 1st ed., pp. 310–341. New York: Van Nostrand Reinhold.

Goudy, Willis J., Powers, Edward A., and Keith, Patricia. 1975. Work and retirement: A test of attitudinal relationships. *Journal of Gerontology* 30:193–198.

Goudy, Willis J., Powers, Edward A., Keith, Patricia, and Beger, Richard A. 1980. Changes in attitudes toward retirement: Evidence from a panel study of older males. *Journal of Gerontology* 35:942–948.

Graebner, William. 1980. *A History of Retirement.* New Haven, Conn.: Yale University Press.

Havighurst, Robert J. 1962. The nature and values of meaningful free-time activity. *In* Clark Tibbitts and Wilma Donahue (eds.), *Social and Psychological Aspects of Aging,* pp. 899–904. New York: Columbia University Press.

Havighurst, Robert J. 1973. Social roles, work, leisure, and education. *In* Carl Eisdorfer and M. Powell Lawton (eds.), *The Psychology of Adult Development and Aging,* pp. 598–618. Washington, D.C.: American Psychological Association.

Haynes, Suzanne G., McMichael, Anthony J., and Tyroler, Herman A. 1978. Survival after early and normal retirement. *Journal of Gerontology* 33:269–278.

Heron, Alistair, and Chown, Sheila. 1967. *Age and Function.* London: Churchill.

Jacobson, Beverly. 1980. *Young Programs for Older Workers: Case Studies in Progressive Personnel Policies.* New York: Van Nostrand Reinhold.

Kabanoff, B. 1980. Work and nonwork: A review of models. *Psychological Bulletin* 88:60–77.

Kahn, Robert L. 1981. *Work and Health.* New York: John Wiley.

Kaplan, Max. 1975. *Leisure: Theory and Policy.* New York: John Wiley.

Kelleher, Carol H., and Quirk, Daniel A. 1973. Age, physical capacity and work: An annotated bibliography. *Industrial Gerontology* 1:80–98.

Kingson, Eric. 1982. Current retirement trends. *In* Malcolm Morrison (ed.), *Economics of Aging: the Future of Retirement,* pp. 98–135. New York: Van Nostrand Reinhold.

Kleemeier, Robert W. (ed.). 1961. *Aging and Leisure.* New York: Oxford University Press.

Koyl, Leon F. 1974. *Employing the Old Worker: Matching the Employee to the Job.* Washington, D.C.: National Council on the Aging.

Krauss, Iseli. 1980. Assessment for retirement. *In* Pauline K. Ragan (ed.), *Work and Retirement: Policy Issues,* pp. 111–126. Los Angeles: University of Southern California Press.

Kreps, Juanita M. 1972. Lifetime tradeoffs between work and play. *In* Gloria M. Shatto (ed.), *Employment of the Middle-Aged,* pp. 31–41. Springfield, Ill.: Charles C. Thomas.

Kreps, Juanita M. 1976. The economy and the aged. *In* Robert H. Binstock and Ethel Shanas (eds.), *Handbook of Aging and the Social Sciences,* 1st ed., pp. 272–285. New York: Van Nostrand Reinhold.

Lauriat, Patience, and Rabin, Wiliam. 1976. Characteristics of new beneficiaries by age at entitlement. *In* U.S. Department of Health, Education and Welfare, Social Security Administration, *Reaching Retirement Age: Finding from a Survey of Newly Entitled Workers 1968–1970.* Washington, D.C.: U.S. Government Printing Office.

Lemon, Bruce W., Bengtson, Vern L., and Peterson, James A. 1972. An exploration of the activity theory of aging: Activity types and life satisfaction among in-movers to a retirement community. *Journal of Gerontology* 27:511–523.

Longino, Charles F., and Kart, Cary S. 1982. Explicating activity theory: A formal replication. *Journal of Gerontology* 37:713–722.

Louis Harris and Associates, Inc. 1979. *1979 Study of American Attitudes Twoard Pensions and Retirement.* New York: Johnson and Higgins.

Lowenthal, Marjorie F., and Robinson, Betty. 1976. Social networks and isolation. *In* Robert H. Binstock and Ethel Shanas (eds.), *Handbook of Aging and the Social Sciences,* 1st ed., pp. 432–456. New York: Van Nostrand Reinhold.

Lowenthal, Marjorie F., Thurnher, Majda, and Chiriboga, David. 1975. *Four Stages of Life: A Psychosocial Study of Women and Men Facing Transition.* San Francisco: Jossey-Bass.

Maddox, George L. 1968. Retirement as a social event in the United States. *In* Bernice L. Neugarten (ed.), *Middle Age and Aging,* pp. 357–365. Chicago: University of Chicago Press.

Maddox, George L. 1970. Adaptation to retirement. *Gerontologist* 10:14–18.

McConnell, Stephen R., Fleisher, Dorothy, Usher, Carolyn E., and Kaplan, Barbara H. 1980. *Alternative Work Options for Older Workers: A Feasibility Study.* Los Angeles: Ethel Percy Andrus Gerontology Center.

McFarland, Ross A. 1973. The need for functional age

measurements in industrial gerontology. *Industrial Gerontology* (No. 19):1–19.

Meier, Elizabeth L., and Kerr, Elizabeth A. 1976. Capabilities of middle-aged and older workers: A survey of the literature. *Industrial Gerontology* 3:147–156.

Menefee, John A. 1980. The demand for health in retirement. *In* Robert L. Clark (ed.), *Retirement Policy in an Aging Society*, pp. 18–51. Durham, N.C.: Duke University Press.

Miller, Stephen J. 1965. The social dilemma of the aging leisure participant. *In* Arnold M. Rose and Warren E. Peterson (eds.), *Older People and Their Social World*, pp. 77–92. Philadelphia: F. A. Davis.

Minkler, Meredith. 1981. Research on the health effects of retirement: An uncertain legacy. *Journal of Health and Social Behavior* 22: 117–130.

Morrison, Malcolm H. 1978. Flexible distribution of work, leisure, and education: Potentials for the aging. *In* Barbara Herzog (ed.), *Aging and Income*. New York: Human Sciences Press.

Morrison, Malcolm H. 1982. Flexibility in retirement: U.S. and international experience. *In* Malcolm H. Morrison (ed.), *Economics of Aging*, pp. 261–279. New York: Van Nostrand Reinhold.

Myers, Robert J. 1954. Factors in interpreting mortality after retirement. *Journal of the American Statistical Association* 49:499.

National Council on the Aging, Inc. 1981. *Aging in the Eighties: America in Transition*. Washington, D.C.: National Council on the Aging.

Neugarten, Bernice L., and Hagestad, Gunhild O. 1976. Age and the life course. *In* Robert H. Binstock and Ethel Shanas (eds.), *Handbook of Aging and the Social Sciences*, 1st ed., pp. 35–55. New York: Van Nostrand Reinhold.

Nollen, Stanley. 1982. *New York Schedules in Practice*. New York: Van Nostrand Reinhold.

Olson, Larry. 1982. Dynamic labor shortage in the offing. *Aging and Work* 5:15–21.

Orbach, Harold L. 1969. *Trends in Early Retirement*. Ann Arbor: University of Michigan, Wayne State University Institute of Gerontology.

Organization for Economic Co-operation and Development. 1979. *Socio-Economic Policies for the Elderly*. Paris: OECD.

Osgood, Nancy J. 1982. Work: Past, present and future. *In* Nancy J. Osgood (ed.), *Life after Work: Retirement, Leisure, Recreation, and the Elderly*. New York: Praeger.

Palmore, Erdman B., Cleveland, William P., Nowlin, John B., Ramm, D., and Sieger, Ilene C. 1979. Stress and adaptation in later life. *Journal of Gerontology* 34:841–851.

Palmore, Erdman B., George, Linda K., and Fillenbaum, Gerda G. 1982. Predictors of retirement. *Journal of Gerontology*, 37:733–742.

Parker, Stanley. 1971. *The Future of Work and Leisure*. London: MacGibbon and Kee.

Parnes, Herbert S. 1981. Inflation and early retirement: Recent longitudinal findings. *Monthly Labor Review* 103:27–30.

Parnes, Herbert, and King, Randy. 1977. Middle-aged job losers. *Industrial Gerontology* 4:77–95.

Parnes, Herbert S., and Nestel, Gilbert. 1981. The retirement experience. *In* Herbert S. Parnes (ed.), *Work and Retirement: A Longitudinal Study of Men*, pp. 155–197. Cambridge, Mass.: The MIT Press.

Patton, Arch. 1981. The coming promotion slowdown. *Harvard Business Review* (Mar–Apr.):46–56.

Paul, Carolyn E. 1982. Public policy and the work life of older women. *In* Nancy J. Osgood (ed.), *Life After Work: Retirement, Leisure, Recreation, and the Elderly*, pp. 119–131. New York: Praeger.

Personick, Valerie A. 1981. The outlook for industry output and employment through 1990. *Monthly Labor Review* 104 (Aug.):28–41.

Pfeiffer, Eric, and Davis, Glenn C. 1971. The use of leisure time in middle life. *Gerontologist* 11:187–195.

Pollman, A. William. 1971. Early retirement: A comparison of poor health to other retirement factors. *Journal of Gerontology* 26:41–45.

Portnoi, Valery A. 1981. The natural history of retirement. *Journal of the American Medical Association* 245:1752–1754.

President's Commission on Pension Policy. 1981. *Coming of Age: Toward a National Retirement Income Policy*. Washington, D.C.: PCPP.

Quinn, Joseph F. 1977. Microeconomic determinants of early retirement: A cross-sectional view of white married men. *Journal of Human Resources* 12:329–346.

Quinn, Joseph F. 1981. The extent and correlates of partial retirement. *The Gerontologist* 21:634–643.

Ragan, Pauline K., and Wales, Jeffrey B. 1980. Age stratification and the life course. *In* James E. Birren and Bruce Sloan (eds.), *Handbook of Mental Health and Aging*, pp. 377–398. Englewood Cliffs, N.J.: Prentice-Hall.

Rappaport, Anna M. 1982. *An Analysis of the Costs of Pension Accrual after Age 65*. An information paper prepared for the Select Committee on Aging, House of Representatives (Comm. Pub. No. 97-323). Washington, D.C.: U.S. Government Printing Office.

Reno, Virginia. 1976. Why men stop working before age 65. *In* U.S. Department of Health, Education and Welfare, Social Security Administration, *Reaching Retirement Age: Findings from a Survey of Newly Entitled Workers 1968-70*. Washington, D.C.: U.S. Government Printing Office.

Riley, Matilda W., Johnson, Marilyn, and Foner, Anne. 1972. *Aging and Society*, Vol. 3, *Sociology of Age Stratification*. New York: Russell Sage.

Rix, Sara E., and Fisher, Paul. 1981. *Retirement-Age Policy: An International Perspective*. Washington, D.C.: American Institute for Research.

Robinson, Pauline K. 1983. *Organizational Strategies for Older Workers*. New York: Pergamon Press.

Rones, Philip L. 1978. Older men—the choice between

work and retirement. *Monthly Labor Review* 101 (Aug.):3–10.

Rones, Philip L. 1982. The aging of the older population and the effect on its labor force rates. *Monthly Labor Review* 105:27–29.

Rosa, Jean-Jacques (ed.). 1982. *The World Crisis in Social Security*. Paris: Fondation Nationale d'Economie Politique.

Rosen, Benson, and Jerdee, Thomas H. 1977. Too old or not too old. *Harvard Business Review* (Nov.–Dec.):97–106.

Salthouse, Timothy A. 1982. *Adult Cognition: An Experimental Psychology of Adult Cognition*. New York: Springer-Verlag.

Schaie, K. Warner. 1977. Quasi-experimental research designs in the psychology of aging. *In* James E. Birren and K. Warner Schaie (eds.), *Handbook of the Psychology of Aging*, pp. 39–58. New York: Van Nostrand Reinhold.

Schaie, K. Warner, and Geiwitz, James. 1982. *Adult Development and Aging*. Boston: Little, Brown.

Schaie, K. Warner, and Gribbin, Kathy. 1975. Adult development and aging. *Annual Review of Psychology* 261:69–96.

Schulz, James H. 1980. *The Economics of Aging,* 2nd ed. Belmont, Calif.: Wadsworth.

Schulz, James H. 1983. Private pensions, inflation, and employment. *In* Herbert S. Parnes (ed.), *Issues in Work and Retirement*. Kalamazoo, Mich.: W.E. Upjohn Institute for Employment Research.

Sekiguchi, Shiro. 1980. How Japanese business treats its older workers. *Management Review* 69:15–18.

Sekimoto, Masahide. 1982. *Japanese Human Resources Management in Transition*. Tokyo: Edward and Kyoto Jones.

Shanas, Ethel. 1970. Health and adjustment in retirement. *Gerontologist* 10:19–21.

Shanas, Ethel, Townsend, Peter, Wedderburn, Dorothy, Friis, Henning, Milhøj, Paul, and Stehouwer, Jan. 1968. *Old People in Three Industrial Societies*. New York: Atherton.

Sheppard, Harold L. 1976. Work and retirement. *In* Robert H. Binstock and Ethel Shanas (eds.), *Handbook of Aging and the Social Sciences,* 1st ed., pp. 286–309. New York: Van Nostrand Reinhold.

Sonnenfeld, Jeffrey. 1978. Dealing with the aging workforce. *Harvard Business Review* (Nov.–Dec.):81–92.

Stafford, Frank. 1979. Unemployment and labor force participation of older workers. *In* T. Gustafson (ed.), *Work, Income and Retirement of the Aged: Report of a Workshop*, pp. 78–91. Washington, D.C.: U.S. Department of Health, Education and Welfare.

Streib, Gordon. 1976. Social stratification and aging. *In* Robert H. Binstock and Ethel Shanas (eds.), *Handbook of Aging and the Social Sciences,* 1st ed., pp. 160–185. New York: Van Nostrand Reinhold.

Streib, Gordon F., and Schneider, Clement J. 1971. *Retirement in American Society: Impact and Process*. Ithaca, N.Y.: Cornell University Press.

U.S. Congressional Budget Office. 1982. *Work and Retirement: Options for Continued Employment of Older Workers*. Washington, D.C.: U.S. Government Printing Office.

U.S. Department of Health and Human Services, Social Security Administration. 1982. Table Q-5. *Social Security Bulletin* 45:67.

U.S. Department of Labor, Employment and Training Administration. 1979. *Employment Related Problems of Older Workers: A Research Strategy*. (R. & D. Monograph 73). Washington D.C.: U.S. Government Printing Office.

U.S. Department of Labor. 1981. *Abolishing Mandatory Retirement: Implications for America and Social Security of Eliminating Age Discrimination in Employment* (Pub. No. 97–283). Washington, D.C.: U.S. Government Printing Office.

U.S. Department of Labor, Bureau of Labor Statistics. 1982. *Employment and Earnings,* January, 1982. Washington, D.C.: U.S. Government Printing Office.

U.S. House of Representatives Select Committee on Aging. 1977. *Retirement Age Policies* (Part II). Washington, D.C.: U.S. Government Printing Office.

U.S. House of Representatives Select Committee on Aging. 1981a. *The Early Retirement Myth: Why Men Retire Before Age 62* (Pub. No. 97–298). Washington, D.C.: U.S Government Printing Office.

U.S. House of Representatives Select Committee on Aging. 1981b. *Abolishing Mandatory Retirement* (Comm. Pub. No. 97–283). Washington, D.C.: U.S. Government Printing Office.

U.S. Senate Committee on Human Resources. 1977a. *Age Discrimination in Employment Amendments of 1977*. Washington, D.C.: U.S. Government Printing Office.

U.S. Senate Committee on Human Resources. 1977b. *Age Discrimination in Employment Amendments*. Hearings before the Subcommittee on Labor, July 26–27. Washington, D.C.: U.S. Government Printing Office.

U.S. Senate Special Committee on Aging. 1967. *Retirement and the Individual*. Hearings before the Subcommittee on Retirement and the Individual, June 7–8. Washington, D.C.: U.S. Government Printing Office.

U.S. Senate Special Committee on Aging. 1980. *Emerging Options for Work and Retirement Policy*. Washington, D.C.: U.S. Government Printing Office.

U.S. Senate Special Committee on Aging. 1981. *Toward a National Older Worker Policy*. Washington, D.C.: U.S. Government Printing Office.

U.S. Senate Special Committee on Aging. 1982. *Aging and the Work Force: Human Resource Strategies*. Washington, D.C.: U.S. Government Printing Office.

U.S. Social Security Administration. 1980. *Income and Resources of the Aged*. Washington, D.C.

Voss, Justin. 1967. The definition of leisure. *Journal of Economic Issues* 1:91–106.

Walker, James W., and Lazer, Harriet L. 1978. *The End of Mandatory Retirement: Implications for Management.* New York: John Wiley.

Welford, Alan T. 1976a. Motor performance. *In* James E. Birren and K. Warner Schaie (eds.), *Handbook of the Psychology of Aging,* pp. 450–496. New York: Van Nostrand Reinhold.

Welford, A. T. 1976b. Thirty years of psychological research on age and work. *Journal of Occupational Psychology* 49:129–138.

Wilson, Ronald W. 1981. Do health indicators indicate health? *American Journal of Public Health* 71:461–463.

Work in America Institute. 1980. *The Future of Older Workers in America: New Options for an Extended Work Life.* Scarsdale, N.Y.: Work in America Institute.

Zeitzer, Ilene R. 1983. Social security trends and developments in industrialized countries. *Social Security Bulletin* 46:52–62.

18
AGE AND THE LAW

Howard Eglit
Illinois Institute of Technology
Chicago-Kent College of Law

Social scientists have amply documented the pervasive cross-cultural use of age within societies, from the simple to the complex, as a critical determinant of individuals' statuses, rights, and responsibilities (Riley et al., 1972, p. 402). Cain (1976) has detailed the incorporation of age criteria in legal charters, codes, and statutes ranging from ancient Greece and Rome to eighteenth-century England and nineteenth-century France. Thus, it is hardly surprising that today in the United States, to note one example, age distinctions are extensively utilized in the constitutions, laws, and regulations that order political, economic, and social relationships (Eglit, 1981a).

What *is* perhaps surprising is that it is only in recent years that American lawyers and legal scholars, for whom these formal charters are professional grist, have begun to take note of this phenomenon. Indeed, their earlier inattention is aptly demonstrated by the primary compilation of United States legal journals (the *Index to Legal Periodicals*), which until late 1973 contained among its hundreds of subject headings no separate listing for age or the aged.

Paralleling the legal community's past apparent lack of interest or awareness regarding the uses of age distinctions has been the typically casual employment by U.S. legislators and administrators of age lines in enacting and implementing statutes. Cohen

(1957, pp. 17–18), for example, has written of the absence of deliberation involved in selecting age 65 as the critical eligibility benchmark in the Social Security Act of 1935.

It is not the aim of this chapter to record specific incidences of age criteria in formal legal documents in the United States. Rather, their commonality being taken as a given, the focus here is on the relatively new, and still growing, awareness on the part of legislators and lawyers that there are real and potential abuses involved in too ready use of age distinctions as formalistic mechanisms of social control.

Although developments in the United States comprise the source material for this enterprise, this heightened sensitivity has international dimensions. In December 1973 the United Nations General Assembly called upon member states to "discourage, wherever and whenever the overall situation allows, discriminatory attitudes, policies and measures in employment practices based exclusively on age" (General Assembly Resolution 3137, 28 U.N. GAOR, Supp. 30, at 81). The plenary session of the 1982 United Nations World Assembly on Aging adopted as a part of its International Plan of Action on Aging a recommendation also condemning age discrimination in the employment arena: "Governments should eliminate discrimination in the labor market and ensure equality of treatment in professional life . . ." (Oriol, 1982, p. 79). Leading scholars likewise have focused on age discrimination as an international human rights issue (McDougal et al., 1976).

In Canada there is a constitutional ban on age discrimination at the federal level, and several of the provinces have enacted bans on age discrimination in various contexts. Employment discrimination regarding age apparently is prohibited in Israel (Bergman, 1980, p. 224). The state of New South Wales, in Australia, has also adopted a law banning age discrimination in employment (Anti-Discrimination Act 1977, §119), and a state agency recommended in 1980 that that Act be amended to extend to education, accommodations, and the provision of goods and services (New South Wales Anti-Discrimination Board, 1980, p. 257).

While the methodology of this chapter is to review some of the most significant U.S. legal developments involved in a spreading rejection of age discrimination, or ageism, there is a larger aim than simple reportage. A number of problems and questions are generated by efforts to use legal mechanisms to change long-established practices. These should be of particular concern and interest to social scientists, who by training and expertise may well have much more to offer than do lawyers in understanding the dynamics of age categorization in the United States, and in societies generally.

First, it is important to note that the virtually uniform view of legislators and courts in the United States has been that age discrimination is simply not as significant a problem, in terms of the depth and breadth of its venality, as are the well-recognized vices of racism and sexism, which victimize racial minorities and women. It is worth examining the validity of this perception. Does age generate deprivation comparable to that associated with racism and sexism? Are the root sources of ageism different in quality from those that sustain race hatred or those on which the debasement of women is grounded? Is age—because it is immutable at any given point in time—more like race and "femaleness" than it is different from

them? Is this analogy at least persuasive insofar as old age is concerned, inasmuch as an old person can never grow young, just as a white cannot become a black, and a woman—save for rare instances of transsexual surgery—cannot change her sex? Is it even useful to draw analogies between racism and sexism on the one hand, and ageism on the other? Breen has observed that "[i] n many respects the aged show characteristics of a minority group" (Breen, 1960, p. 157); Streib contends that "[f]rom the standpoint of conceptual clarity and empirical fact, the notion of the aged as a minority group . . . obscures [understanding]" (Streib, 1968, p. 46).

Second, what accounts for what appears to be a growing generalized condemnation of discrimination against the old? Is it an expectable, or at least likely, feature of industrial societies in which machines replace muscle power and thus older people retain economic utility more so than they do in agrarian societies? Is it due to particular social currents of egalitarianism unique to certain societies? Is it simply the product of political power exercised by growing numbers of old people in democratic societies, as expressed through the efforts of organized lobbying groups that offer both the gift of support and the threat of opposition to elected politicians?

Third, what uses, if any, of age are appropriate, and when, and why? If some are, how does one separate condemnable age discrimination from tolerable age distinctions? Neugarten (1979) espouses not total abolition of age as a relevant criterion in social programs, but at least diminished use of this criterion, with need to be substituted in lieu of it. Competency is another alternative basis for decision making. What social and political costs might ensue from heavier reliance on these criteria? Does the efficiency of basing decisions on individuals' ages outweigh the unfairness of ignoring a given individual's particular need or competence and treating him or her only in terms of the attribute of age? Do the dangers of abuse in discretionary systems—ostensibly designed to facilitate fairness by allowing for individualized assessments of people's particular needs or competencies—justify using the easily established, clear-cut factor of age, even if some individual unfairness results for those whose ages are indeed not accurate proxies for their needs and abilities?

Fourth, can a movement grounded in part on an egalitarian ideal—taking the form of like treatment for people who are similarly situated in terms of ability or need, rather than differential treatment based solely on differences in age—continue to survive and grow while those who most actively protest ageism at the same time profit in some settings because of their ages? In other words, can the elderly, who typically praise and often promote anti-age discrimination laws, successfully justify their being beneficiaries of the large number of laws and programs that exclude the too-young from eligibility (Select Committee on Aging, 1979; Longman, 1982)? Or must rejection of ageism, to be intellectually sound and to maintain continued political palatability, include the divestiture of age-based benefits along with the destruction of age-based disadvantages?

Most of these questions, perhaps all, should be pertinent outside the context of the United States. Even though the following discussion addresses specific American statutes and judicial decisions, these laws and cases simply express, in small or large measure, efforts to respond to these questions. Accordingly, the legislative and judicial experiences in the United States also should have considerable relevance beyond their jurisdictional origins.

CONSTITUTIONAL ANALYSIS GENERALLY

There are several levels at which legal controls operate in the United States. First, the common law, that body of doctrine developed through judicial decision independent of statutory or constitutional guidance, frames private relationships in a number of settings, such as aspects of contract and tort law. Second, legal rights and responsibilities flow from statutes enacted at the local, state,

and federal levels, as well as from governmental regulations and policies. In addition, each state has a constitution, which generally speaks in broader terms than do statutory enactments. Finally, the federal Constitution sets the ultimate law of the land in many respects.

At the outset of any discussion of constitutional rights one point must be stressed, since it is so often misperceived by nonlawyers. The U.S. Constitution's most important guarantees of individual rights (i.e., the Bill of Rights and the Due Process and Equal Protection Clauses of the Fourteenth Amendment) only impose limits on what government may do vis-à-vis the individual. That these parts of the Constitution are not applicable to private acts of discrimination does not mean, of course, that no redress is available. Sometimes, albeit rarely in the individual rights arena, other provisions of the Constitution which do not require governmental perpetration of the alleged wrongdoing can be invoked. In any event, the U.S. Constitution generally only sets minimum standards for government conduct: "the state may not do X." State constitutions may secure broader (but not narrower) rights than those embodied in the federal document. Moreover, legislatures, at both the federal and state levels, can enact statutes that bestow additional rights: "the state may not do X or Y or Z." Thus, an individual victim of discrimination may be able to vindicate a claim of ageism under a given statute even if that vindication cannot be secured under the Constitution itself. This clarification becomes particularly pertinent because later discussion will address statutes that purport to secure greater protection to potential and real victims of age discrimination than does the Constitution.

In making a federal constitutional argument, the victim of age discrimination typically will claim to have been denied equal protection of the laws. Equal protection language (i.e., no person shall be denied the equal protection of the laws) is only set forth explicitly in the Fourteenth Amendment to the Constitution, but the Supreme Court has read the Fifth Amendment's Due Process Clause as embodying a like guarantee. [*Bolling v. Sharpe* (1954)]. By way of simple explanation, it is enough to say now that this is a guarantee that similarly situated people are to be treated similarly by government.

In the equal protection context the dominant judicial standard for scrutinizing governmental action is a minimum rationality test. This mode of analysis entails great deference by the courts to the legislature. It consequently is a test that in the great majority of cases results in the challenged law or regulation being sustained. Typical of the use of the minimum rationality standard is the statement by the Supreme Court in *Vance v. Bradley,* a 1979 decision in which the Court rejected a constitutional attack on a federal statute requiring the retirement of foreign service officers at age 60:

> [T]hose challenging the legislative judgment must convince the Court that the legislative facts on which the classification is apparently based could not reasonably be conceived to be true by the governmental decisionmaker. . . . [I]t is the very admission that the facts are arguable that immunizes from constitutional attack the congressional judgment represented by this statute. [*Vance v. Bradley* (1979), pp. 111–112]

Thus, rationality for the courts does not mean that a given law is the wisest, or the most efficacious, or the least burdensome, or that which is best supported by empirical data. Rather, the minimum rationality test only requires that some reasonable person— even one ignorant of the facts or possessed of misconceptions about them—could have devised the statute in question.

For the social scientist such judicial acquiescence to ill-advised, albeit "rational," legislative choices may be difficult to comprehend. The general explanation for this judicial deference is in good measure the reluctance of federal courts to substitute their judgments for those of legislators. The federal courts are staffed by life-tenured judges who, once seated, are not accountable to the electorate. If the federal courts too readily

undertake to scrutinize, and possibly strike down, any and all legislation (or regulations or policies), they run the risk of being accused of substituting their insulated predilections for the wishes of the people. This accusation is of course often made in any event. But it would be multiplied considerably were the courts to assume an actively interventionist stance.

To the contention that the courts must step in because, if they do not, victims of democratic majorities will be without recourse, there is a principled response. First, majoritarian democracy necessarily implies that there are going to be losers. Second, those who are defeated need not suffer permanent loss: they can return to the democratic fray and secure victory by doing a better job of convincing the public, and thereby the public's elected representatives, of the rightness of *their* position. This rationale has particular persuasiveness for the courts in dealing with economic and social welfare legislation. Here, the issues are complex, there is no one "truth" as to how best to order relationships and resources, and a judicial ruling may have economic consequences difficult to predict and thus may not any better bring society closer to the "right" ultimate solution than did the challenged law.

Of course, the federal courts do not always play a deferential role. In the equal protection context they will act much more aggressively when called upon to address laws that utilize what are termed "suspect" classifications. Additionally, enhanced judicial activism will arise in response to the infringement, whether in due process or equal protection terms, of what are denominated as "fundamental" rights and interests. Suspect classifications—of which race and national origin are the only two invariably recognized by the Supreme Court—are somewhat ill defined. They will be discussed below in the context of the Court's most significant treatment of an age discrimination claim —i.e., *Massachusetts Board of Retirement v. Murgia* (1976). As for fundamental rights, these are, as a general matter, not particularly clearly identifiable. The Supreme Court has defined them as rights "explicitly or implicitly protected by the Constitution" [*San Antonio Independent School District v. Rodriguez* (1973), p. 17]. The open-endedness of this characterization is illustrated, at least in the view of some students of constitutional law, by the Court's 1973 holding in *Roe v. Wade* that women have a fundamental right to seek to secure an abortion during the early stages of pregnancy. Even if one views the decision as morally or ethically correct, certainly there can be no dispute that such a right is not explicitly set forth in the Constitution. Nor is it even one whose implicit embodiment therein is readily discernible from any of the language of that document.

Should a fundamental right be infringed or a suspect classification be employed by a statute or policy or regulation, a standard of analysis very much more rigorous than the minimum rationality test will come into play. The challenged governmental body will carry the burden of establishing that a compelling interest is being served, and that the means used (i.e., the statute or regulation being attacked) is the least burdensome available. The result of application of this test is, as is demonstrated by a review of the case law, virtually a foregone one: the law almost always will fall (Gunther, 1972). For even if the state can successfully prove a compelling interest, hardly ever can the means used be shown to be the least burdensome available.

THE CONSTITUTION AND AGE DISCRIMINATION

The body of case law concerning age discrimination under the Constitution is relatively small (Eglit, 1981b). One general grouping of cases not often thought of in ageism terms, although that is what they involve, consists of decisions regarding the rights of minors. While the Supreme Court has not yet so held, it seems clear that classifications based on childhood status are not, at least from the judiciary's perspective, suspect. This is a conclusion already reached by more than one lower federal court [*Williams*

v. City of Lewiston, Me. (1981)]. Moreover, when claims are made by minors that their fundamental rights are being infringed, and that therefore the compelling interest test ought to apply, the Court has typically responded that children, while not beyond the protection of the Constitution, have lesser rights than do adults. The rationale underlying this judicial posture was put rather succinctly by Justice Powell in a case involving a statute that restricted the right to secure an abortion by requiring that minors obtain parental consent to the procedure:

> We have recognized three reasons justifying the conclusion that the constitutional rights of children cannot be equated with those of adults: the peculiar vulnerability of children; their inability to make critical decisions in an informed, mature manner; and the importance of the parental role in child rearing. [*Bellotti v. Baird* (1979), pp. 633–634 (citations omitted)]

Because in the United States the Supreme Court occupies the role of ultimate arbiter of constitutional rights, its decisions are enormously significant and thus here compel careful exposition. Constitutional challenges to age discrimination experienced by adults have been the subject of only two Supreme Court opinions—*Massachusetts Board of Retirement v. Murgia* (1976) and *Vance v. Bradley* (1979). Both cases concerned employment discrimination; more specifically, they addressed mandatory retirement laws.

The *Murgia* and *Vance* Cases

In *Murgia*, a 1976 decision, the Court addressed a state law that required the involuntary retirement of state police officers at age 50. In a 7 to 1 ruling the Court upheld the statute's constitutionality. Officer Murgia argued that his case presented a situation calling for rigorous judicial scrutiny, that is, utilization of the compelling interest test. He pursued two tacks. He contended that classifications based on age—or more specifically, older age—were suspect. Additionally, he argued that a fundamental interest, employment, was at stake. The Court rejected both contentions. As for the latter, it simply asserted, citing three earlier decisions that actually had nothing to do with mandatory retirement, that "[t]his Court's decisions give no support to the proposition that a right of governmental employment *per se* is fundamental" [*Murgia* (1976), p. 313].

The Court's reasoning regarding the suspectness claim was both more expansive and more provocative than its statement on employment as a fundamental interest. The Court first looked to an earlier ruling in which it had set forth three alternative bases for suspectness:

[A] suspect class is one "saddled with such disabilities, or subjected to such a history of purposeful unequal treatment, or relegated to such a position of political powerlessness as to command extraordinary protection from the majoritarian political process." [*Murgia* (1976), p. 313]

The Court then focused on age classifications within the parameters of this definition:

While the treatment of the aged in this Nation has not been wholly free of discrimination, such persons, unlike, say, those who have been discriminated against on the basis of race or national origin, have not experienced a "history of purposeful unequal treatment" or been subjected to unique disabilities on the basis of stereotyped characteristics not truly indicative of their abilities . . . . [O]ld age does not define a "discrete and insular" group . . . in need of "extraordinary protection from the majoritarian political process." Instead, it marks a stage that each of us will reach if we live out our normal span. [*Murgia* (1976), pp. 313–314]

It is notable—and perhaps particularly instructive regarding the arguable drawbacks of courts making decisions with social and political dimensions, where more than just legal analysis is brought to bear—that this reasoning was based on sociological and historical premises regarding the status of the elderly that the Court failed to support with any authority. There is at least room for discussion, and possibly dispute, about the Court's perhaps overly sanguine image of the

statuses, roles, and history of the aged. Moreover, the Court seemingly erred in stating that the aged have not been subjected to "unique disabilities on the basis of stereotyped characteristics not truly indicative of their abilities." At least so far as mandatory retirement is concerned, respectable commentators have documented the error of perceiving older workers as physically and mentally decrepit or devoid, at any rate, of any new ideas and thus deadwood (Baltes and Schaie, 1974; Drucker and Moore, 1977; Kutscher and Walker, 1960; Note, 1975).

The Court's observation that, unlike racially identified groups, the elderly are not a discrete and insular group needful of special protection from the majoritarian political process because all of us are going to grow old (short of the perhaps worse alternative) was not only cryptic but, even when filled out through informed interpretation, arguably somewhat obtuse. The essential perception that the Court was almost certainly articulating flows from the idea that in a majoritarian democracy minority racial groups are at a virtually insurmountable disadvantage. Simply by virtue of their very minority status they may well be unable to muster the votes, even by forming coalitions, to prevail on issues. In the United States this reality of the political process clearly has played a role in the courts' present-day emphatic resistance to race-based laws, absent extraordinary justification by their proponents. Such laws typically are the product of the majority whites (the "we's") who in the past, at least, have imposed deprivations on blacks (i.e., the minority "they's") (Ely, 1973, pp. 933–935).

Further warranting special judicial scrutiny in the typical race context is the fact that whites have, as a general matter, few close relationships with blacks. Thus, the white majority may have little compunction about imposing burdens upon those who are, in a social sense, strangers. And further involved is the perception that because race is an immutable characteristic, white lawmakers who enact laws affecting only blacks may well have diminished concerns, since they need never fear that the onus of their legislation will fall upon them. (Of course, in the context of laws concerning blacks, there are other factors further explaining enhanced judicial concern. The history of the Constitution's Fourteenth Amendment, in which the Due Process and Equal Protection Clauses are lodged, instructs that it was adopted to address and redress deprivations imposed upon blacks. The tragic history of race relations, and the general current social consensus that racism is an evil without any redeeming merit, further justify special judicial solicitude.)

In implicit contrast to racial minorities, the *Murgia* Court posed the situation of the elderly: "old age . . . marks a stage that each of us will reach . . ." [*Murgia* (1976), p. 313]. Thus, the potential for the passage of laws penalizing the "they's" is muted, since the "we's" will some day become the "they's." Moreover, as contrasted with laws geared to race classifications, most legislators do have intimate contact with older people: their parents, their supervisors on the job, their aunts and uncles, and so on. Thus, the potential for somewhat thoughtless adoption of invidious laws is mitigated inasmuch as such laws would affect the legislator's own families and social and professional confreres.

Even granting all this, it would seem that the *Murgia* Court's reasoning perhaps embodied a troubling flaw. While it is true that unless death intervenes we will all become aged, it is also true that once having become old there is no way for the individual to escape that class except by dying. In brief, age— *like* race—is an immutable characteristic, beyond personal choice and control. Yet this similitude was ignored in the *Murgia* Court's suspectness analysis.

In contrast, immutability is a characteristic that has obtained considerable currency in other settings as being relevant to the suspectness equation. In *Frontiero v. Richardson* (1973), a sex discrimination case, four Supreme Court justices argued that gender-based distinctions are particularly condemnable under the Equal Protection Clause because, as they put it:

[S]ince sex, like race and national origin, is an immutable characteristic determined solely by the accident of birth, the imposition of special disabilities upon the members of a particular sex because of their sex would seem to violate "the basic concept of our system that legal burdens should bear some relationship to individual responsibility . . . ." [*Frontiero* (1973), p. 686]

While the *Frontiero* justices were unsuccessful in securing a fifth vote to constitute a majority in support of the proposition that gender-based distinctions are suspect, the Supreme Court has since established that such classifications are at least "quasi-suspect," and thus demand more justification by the state than a mere rationality explanation [*Craig v. Boren* (1976)].

A further consideration undercutting the *Murgia* Court's apparent benign view regarding the solicitude of legislators is that while old age is the inevitable consequence of not dying, it is not so clear that "non-old" legislators really comprehend that eventuality in a direct way. Simone de Beauvoir has written: "Until the moment is upon us, old age is something that only affects other people" (de Beauvior, 1975, p. 13). If de Beauvoir's point is valid, one ought not to so casually accept the notion that young, or relatively young, legislators will refrain from harming the aged, even if they are ordinarily guided by self-interest.

Post-hoc criticism has its utility. But the undeniable ultimate fact is that *Murgia* rejected the suspectness argument. Had it not, the police officer no doubt would have won his case. For even if the state had been successful in establishing a compelling interest in assuring a competent police force, it almost certainly would have been unable to establish that the use of an age criterion was the least burdensome (i.e., the narrowest) means available to do so. Or even if it could have done that, the state certainly would have been unable to establish that age 50 was any better an age cut-off than 51 or 52 or other specific ages.

Since the Court in fact disposed of the arguments that the compelling interest test should apply, it proceeded to utilize the mere rationality test to examine the statute. The purpose of the law, the Court observed, was to protect the public by assuring the physical preparedness of the uniformed police. There was testimony in the trial court from three physicians that "clearly established," as the Court saw it, "that the risk of physical failure, particularly in the cardiovascular system, increases with age, and that the number of individuals in a given age group incapable of performing stress functions increases with the age of the group" [*Murgia* (1976), p. 311]. While the testimony also recognized that some people over age 50 could be capable of safely performing the tasks of police officers, the police officer's own witness had testified that "evaluating the risk of cardiovascular failure in a given individual would require a number of detailed studies" [*Murgia* (1976), p. 311]. Given this background, the Court concluded that the state law was rational:

> Since physical ability generally declines with age, mandatory retirement at 50 serves to remove from police service those whose fitness for uniformed work presumptively has diminished with age. This clearly is rationally related to the State's objective. There is no indication that . . . [the statute] has the effect of excluding from service so few officers who are in fact unqualified as to render age 50 a criterion wholly unrelated to the objective of the statute. [*Murgia* (1976), p. 315–316 (footnotes omitted)]

Three years after its decision in *Massachusetts Board of Retirement v. Murgia* the Supreme Court by an 8 to 1 vote rejected another challenge to a mandatory retirement law, in this instance a statute requiring the retirement of federal foreign service officers at age 60. At issue in *Vance v. Bradley* was the alleged violation of equal protection flowing from the fact that while 60 was the set age of retirement for the plaintiffs, other federal employees did not have to retire until age 70. The plaintiffs accepted the validity of mandatory retirement per se as a general practice, but they opposed the imposition of a lower age for them as contrasted with other

employees. While the case thus was because of its facts a narrower one than *Murgia,* which addressed mandatory retirement generally, the Court left no doubt that it still viewed mandatory retirement approvingly— even in the context of two different ages being used for employees of the same entity (i.e., the federal government).

More important, the *Vance* court filled in some potentially arguable gaps left by *Murgia.* For one, the case dealt with white collar employees, many of whom were engaged in sedentary work. The Court's willingness to uphold their mandatory retirement largely foreclosed the possibility of confining the *Murgia* decision to employees engaged in physically rigorous occupations, such as policing. Moreover, the *Vance* Court addressed and approved a justification for mandatory retirement that had not been considered in *Murgia* but which is commonly put forth— that it is necessary to make room for the young by pushing older people out of the job hierarchy: "[T]he compulsory retirement age assures room at the top at a predictable time; those in the ranks know that it will not be an intolerable time before they will have the opportunity to compete for maximum responsibility" [*Vance* (1979), p. 103, n. 20].

Because of *Murgia* and *Vance,* constitutionally based attacks on mandatory retirement have been rendered fruitless for now and the foreseeable future. In the American system of jurisprudence, based on the rule of *stare decisis* whereby the decision of a higher court binds courts subordinate to it, a decision of the Supreme Court sets the pattern for the lower courts. Thus, *Murgia* regularly has been followed, and even has been expanded by lower courts to uphold age classifications utilized in nonemployment settings and with regard to the nonelderly. Courts have applied the mere rationality test to virtually any claim that an age classification is constitutionally offensive (Eglit, 1981a, 1982). Thus, with only a very few exceptions [*Gault v. Garrison* (1977); *McMahon v. Barclay* (1981); *Daley v. Farm Credit Administration* (1978)], discriminatees have lost in situations ranging from the exclusion of children under age 5 from primary schools [*Hammond v. Marx* (1975)], to the barring of secondary school students over age 18 from interscholastic sports competition [*Blue v. University Interscholastic League* (1980)], to the involuntary retirement of older teachers [*Palmer v. Ticcione* (1978)], judges [*Trafelet v. Thompson* (1979)], police officers [*McIlvaine v. Pennsylvania State Police* (1973)], and psychiatrists [*Nurenberg v. Ward* (1976)].

Murgia and *Vance* in Perspective

The *Murgia* and *Vance* rulings cannot simply be dismissed as expressions of a resolutely insensitive Court. Indeed, the *Murgia* Court made what was perhaps a dutiful, but nonetheless articulated, obeisance to the plight of mandatory retirees:

> We do not make light of the substantial economic and psychological effects premature and compulsory retirement can have on an individual; nor do we denigrate the ability of elderly citizens to contribute to society. The problems of retirement have been well documented and are beyond serious dispute. [*Murgia* (1976), pp. 316–317 (footnotes omitted)]

There are, in fact, several bases for understanding *Murgia* and *Vance* as actually reflecting both neutral institutional constraints confronted by federal judges and the complexities of age discrimination, rather than as biased rulings of a benighted Court. First, as already discussed, there is the deeply embedded resistance of the federal courts in the United States to engage in reviewing the constitutionality of legislation or policies produced by democratically elected legislatures or executives. Whatever the degree of one's commitment to combating ageism, one must at least pause and assess the merits and demerits generally of an activist, life-tenured, politically insulated judiciary. One need not be a supporter of age discrimination or an undiscerning believer in majoritarian democracy to share the conclusion reached by one recent federal lower court in

rejecting a constitutional challenge to a mandatory retirement law:

> It may well be that the economic and social hardships imposed on elderly persons will require an altered view as to . . . mandatory retirement plans, but this is the type of decision with competing social interests and objectives that should be resolved by legislatures, not by courts . . . . [*Hawkins v. James* (1981), p. 916]

Second, there are significant substantive problems for courts in addressing ageism. To justify in the courts invocation of the rigorous compelling interest test, opponents of age discrimination in the United States seemingly would have to equate it with racism. And yet, as a historic matter, the case to be made for that equation does not seem strong. Slavery, lynchings, Jim Crow laws, and the like—all grim facets of U.S. history—simply are not, fortunately, a part of the picture of the treatment of those most often discretely singled out by statutes and regulations in terms of their age, e.g., the elderly and children. History aside, there is a good case to be made that the elderly (Neugarten, 1979, p. 50) and youngsters (Teitelbaum, 1981) have fared remarkably well in the American political process, as evidenced by the massive federal and state expenditures devoted to serving their needs. [Others apparently would disagree (Jones, 1977)].

Third, it could be very difficult to avert perhaps undesired expansion if courts were to start down the path of exposing age distinctions to special scrutiny. This, at least, likely would be so in a legal system such as that of the United States, in which analogical reasoning is at the core of legal analysis and argumentation. More concretely, typically the focus has been on discrimination against the old, yet children too are subjected to disadvantage because of their lack of age (Katz, 1974). If ageism is so bad, then why not condemn discrimination leveled against the young as well as the old? Or, in more legalistic terms, should not laws dealing with minors be subjected to the compelling interest test? Some people may readily respond affirmatively to this question. Many, however, likely would pause before embracing an approach that almost certainly would lead to the downfall of laws precluding those under 16 from being licensed to drive, barring those under 18 from the franchise, requiring school attendance until age 16 or 17, and so on. Granted, there may be an acceptable analytical escape from this logical trap. Discrimination against the old, it could be argued, is different in kind and quality because no one can ever become younger and thereby escape the complained-of burden. In contrast, discrimination for being too young at least can be outgrown because youth, unlike old age, is mutable (Eglit, 1981b). Nonetheless, for the judge already reluctant to enter the age discrimination fray, a rationale enabling condemnation of some instances of ageism and condonation of others would add another element of complexity to a puzzle better entirely avoided.

There could be another potentially undesirable consequence of judicial embracement of special protection under the Constitution for victims of age distinctions, namely, the destruction of age-based benefits. If distinctions based on age are to be tolerated only if the state has compelling interests for them, and no less burdensome alternatives to use to achieve those interests, might the result not be that a number of laws beneficial to older people—those most typically thought of as the victims of ageism—would fall? After all, if Congress were to enact a statute, as in fact it has, requiring federally funded mass transit systems to offer half-fare rides to those 60 and over [49 U.S.C. §1604(m)], could not the 40-year-old persuasively claim that she was deprived by virtue of being too young? If she could, the result would be the downfall of the challenged statute, a consequence that would probably be condemned by many of the very same people who oppose age-based mandatory retirement.

One must take into account, also, the social and fiscal costs involved in rejecting age distinctions as a tool for distributing resources and imposing responsibilities. The use of the age criterion is efficient and inexpensive. The substitution of alternative testing devices in many instances would generate considerably more expense and delays in decision making. Indeed, the use of the unarguable fact of age not only offers efficiency, but it may even afford some assurance of fairness by curtailing the potential for arbitrary treatment that often accompanies discretionary bureaucratic systems. Convenience and financial savings may not, in and of themselves, be compelling justifications for sanctioning discriminatory acts. Nonetheless, they may carry enough weight at least to support the conclusion that, if they are to be sacrificed, they should be sacrificed by legislatures—which are attuned to debating and balancing competing social and economic costs—rather than by life-tenured judges in the rarified, and often narrow, context of litigation.

A further difficulty in calling upon the courts to rigorously examine the constitutionality of age distinctions follows from the ambiguities that may ensue when particular age criteria are called into question, rather than all uses of age in general. For example, there have been several constitutionally based challenges to age restrictions vis-a-vis the franchise. In *Oregon v. Mitchell* (1970), in which the Supreme Court held that Congress did not have the authority by statute to lower the voting age in state elections to 18, Justice Stewart, who concurred, observed: "to test the power to establish an age qualification by the 'compelling interest' standard is really to deny a state any choice at all, because no state could demonstrate a 'compelling interest' in drawing the line with respect to age at one point rather than another" [*Oregon v. Mitchell* (1970), p. 294]. That perception obviously carries beyond the voting context. Were courts to embark upon intensive scrutiny of age lines, it would be very difficult to justify any given age line—even if there were acceptance of the general notion that some age line is tolerable and disagreement only as to the suitability of the particular one being challenged.

Compounding these problems is the fact that it may be difficult even to focus on the victims of an age-based statute challenged on equal protection grounds. This is so because some statutes speak only in general terms. For example, the federal Equal Credit Opportunity Act proscribes age discrimination generally, and accords certain special treatment to the "elderly" without identifying who fits within this grouping. Yet, as one historian of aging has noted:

[T]here has never actually been a consensus about what birthday, if any, marks the beginning of old age . . . . The ages of 55, 60, 62, 64, 70, 72, and 75 are . . . perennial favorites . . . . Some have contended that old age begins at fifty; others argued that no one is "old" before eighty. (Achenbaum, 1978, p. 2)

There is a final problem involved in the courts taking an aggressive stance. American jurisprudence involves the slow change of doctrine through the gradual development of precedent, each case laying the foundation for the next. If the Supreme Court were to have held in *Murgia* that classifications based on age, or even just on old age, were suspect, might it not have followed that soon other groups not yet identified as deserving of special judicial concern would have pressed, with persuasive reasoning by way of analogy, for like treatment? After all, the blind, the lame, and the intellectually retarded are—like the elderly—victims of conditions over which they have no control, and because of which they may suffer deprivation and even stigmatization. Perhaps it would be a good result were these groups to secure the status of suspectness. But for courts reluctant to engage in interventionist judicial review, the specter of opening the equal protection doors wide to whole new varieties of claimants certainly must provide cause for hesitation, as it should for anyone attuned to the problems involved in life-tenured courts setting standards of social justice at odds with the majoritarian consensus.

In sum, the federal courts' treatment of constitutional challenges to age discrimination generally has been disappointing from the perspective of those who would seek judicial redress. In part, this is so because these courts have generally recognized that their institutional nature (i.e., their distance from the democratic majoritarian political process) necessitates self-imposed constraints in engaging in review of legislation. In part, their lack of receptivity to age-based claims results from the arguably unimpressive plights of the complainants. And, in part, they may have concluded that the issues are too complicated to tackle—not because judges are incapable of facing up to hard problems, but rather because the answers in this setting either are unsatisfactory or just generate more problems. By use of the minimum rationality test, the courts effectively have said that whatever the quantity and quality of age discrimination, this is a problem for the other branches of government and not for the federal courts. And indeed the legislative branches, both of the states and of the federal government, have responded, as discussed below.

Jury Selection

Since the 1976 *Murgia* decision, applying a minimum rationality test to age distinctions, there has been only one area in which constitutional analysis has followed a somewhat different tack—although not one producing any more success from the perspective of discriminatees. In the context of challenges to discriminatory jury selection procedures, the courts have developed a line of cases under both the jury trial guarantee of the Sixth Amendment to the Constitution and the Equal Protection Clause which is premised on the requirement that juries represent a "fair cross-section of the community" [*Taylor v. Louisiana* (1975), p. 536]. To establish lack of a fair cross-section on the basis of the exclusion of a given group, it must be established that the group is "distinctive" [*Duren v. Missouri* (1979), p. 364] or "cognizable" [*United States v. Guzman* (1972), p. 143].

With virtual unanimity the courts have rejected arguments that groups defined by age are cognizable (Eglit, 1981a; Ziegler, 1978).

Typical is the decision in *King v. United States* (1965), in which the defendant in a criminal prosecution argued that the fair cross-section principle was violated because his jury was made up of persons selected from a list that excluded those 21 to 24 and over 70. The court stated:

> The difference in viewpoint between ages 21 and 25 would not seem to us of any great significance. Nor would there seem to be any substantial effect upon the composition of a jury as a result of eliminating persons over 70 as might be competent to stand duty. We regard it as highly speculative whether the decisional outlook of such excluded persons would be different than that of persons a mere few years older or a few years younger . . . . [*King v. United States* (1965), p. 124]

Other courts have rejected arguments that other age groups were cognizable, such as those 21–39 [*United States v. Test* (1976)], 18–20 [*United States v. Allen* (1971)], 21–30 [*People v. Hoiland* (1971)], and so on. However, the cases notwithstanding, there are social science data suggesting that, on some issues at least, young people on the one hand, and old people on the other, indeed are distinctive and different in terms of attitudes and experiences (Van Dyke, 1977, p. 39 nn.; Ziegler, 1978; Riley et al., 1972, p. 431; Rose, 1968).

STATUTORY TREATMENT OF AGE DISCRIMINATION

There are three major federal laws in the United States dealing with age discrimination. There are also several federal statutes of lesser scope, as well as a considerable number of state laws, most of fairly recent vintage. Specific federal statutes ban discrimination by air carriers [49 U.S.C. §1302(a)(3); Eglit, 1981a]; by recipients of federal revenue sharing funds [31 U.S.C. §6716(b)(1); Eglit, 1981a]; by recipients of federal funds for mass transit purposes [49 U.S.C. §1615(a)(1); Eglit, 1981a]; by recipients of federal funds distributed to assist in preparing for, and alleviating the conse-

quences of, major disasters and emergencies (42 U.S.C. §5151; Eglit, 1981a); as well as in other discrete contexts as narrow as the selection of members of United States Olympic teams [36 U.S.C. §391(b)(6); Eglit, 1981a]. In addition, a generalized civil rights guarantee embodied in a post–Civil War federal statute, 42 U.S.C. §1985(3), has been interpreted in a few instances as having applicability to age discriminatees, notwithstanding its making no mention of age discrimination (Eglit, 1982).

At the state level, statutory strictures on discrimination have proliferated. While the most commonly addressed contexts are employment (Eglit, 1982) and credit (Eglit, 1981a), states have legislated in areas ranging from housing to public accommodations to automobile liability insurance to the provision of state services (Eglit, 1981a, 1982).

Space constraints preclude review of all of these laws. In any event, their similitude averts the need for jurisdiction-by-jurisdiction examination. The major federal statutes, however, merit some discussion, not only because of their broad geographical import, but because, in addition, their substance and genesis afford insights into the complexities of attempting to deal with ageism by legislation.

The Age Discrimination Act

The Age Discrimination Act (ADA) particularly merits scrutiny, because of both its purported breadth and its failings. Analysis leads to at least two conclusions. First, the developing sensitivity to ageism that was discussed in the opening to this chapter is as yet characterized by considerable ambivalence. Second, it appears easier to deplore ageism in the abstract than it is to define it and to legislate its eradication.

Enacted into law in 1975 and amended in 1978, the ADA represents the first federal essay at addressing ageism on a broad scale. Previous efforts at dealing with ageism had focused, as discussed below, on particularized aspects of the problem, such as discrimination in the fields of employment and credit. The ADA bans any discrimination (save in employment) on the basis of age by any recipient of federal financial assistance, with loss of funding the penalty for transgression. Thus, it applies to the 100,000 direct recipients and 450,000 indirect recipients of federal assistance (Schuck, 1980, p. 70, n. 1), which has in peak years totaled in excess of $100 billion annually.

At the outset the ADA speaks in sweeping terms: "It is the purpose of this . . . [Act] to prohibit discrimination on the basis of age . . . " (42 U.S.C. §6101). Accordingly, "no person in the United States shall, on the basis of age, be excluded from participation in, be denied the benefits of, or be subjected to discrimination under, any program or activity receiving Federal financial assistance" (42 U.S.C. §6102). Having uttered the pieties with which statutes often open, the Congress proceeded to eviscerate the Act's potential effectiveness by setting forth three major exceptions to the discrimination prohibition. Subsequently, the federal enforcement agency [the then Department of Health, Education, and Welfare (HEW)] created a fourth exception in an implementing regulation.

The first exception provides that it is not a violation of the statute to take an action otherwise prohibited "if, in the program or activity involved . . . such action reasonably takes into account age as a factor necessary to the normal operation or the achievement of any statutory objective of such program or activity . . . " [42 U.S.C. §6103(b)(1)(A)]. Obviously, this language leaves room for clarification. The regulations provide that "'[n]ormal operation' means the operation of a program or activity without significant changes that would impair its ability to meet its objectives" (45 C.F.R. §90.13), but neither "significant" nor "impair" is defined. It is likewise unclear whether an age-based standard must be shown as being "necessary" to the program, or whether it is simply sufficient that the program administrator reasonably believes that such a standard is necessary. As indicated above in the discussion of constitutional adjudication, a rea-

sonableness standard is generally a test of very limited rigor. This holds true in nonconstitutional legal contexts as well. Thus, the latter possible interpretation of the ADA exception would vastly expand its scope and cripple the statute's basic prohibition.

The second ADA caveat also incorporates a reasonableness standard: the Act will not be transgressed by use of "reasonable factors other than age" [42 U.S.C. §6103 (b)(1)(B)], even if the consequence of reliance upon such a factor is a disproportionate impact in terms of age (45 C.F.R. §90.15). For example, suppose a program designed to provide computer training imposes a requirement that participants must have high school diplomas. On its face, this criterion for admission appears to be a neutral one; in other words, it is a reasonable factor *other than age*. In fact, the requirement impacts adversely upon those under 18, who have not yet finished their schooling, and upon those over 60, who as a group have a lesser number of high school graduates as a proportion of the total group than does the population at large.

The regulation interpreting this exception somewhat limits it by requiring that it must be shown that the factor employed, that is, the diploma requirement, bears "a direct and substantial relationship to the normal operation of the program or activity or the achievement of a statutory objective" (45 C.F.R. §90.15). This is a standard tougher than mere rationality. In the commentary accompanying the regulation the drafters explained their rationale:

[A] minimal scrutiny standard would permit activities that should be prohibited. The use of that standard would make it very difficult to establish that an activity is in violation of the ADA . . . . [44 Federal Register 33783 (1979)]

This observation was a sound one. However, it is dubious whether an agency as a legal matter may rectify the weakness of explicit statutory language by substituting in implementing regulations a more rigorous test than that prescribed by the legislators [*Bryan v. Koch* (1980)].

The final statutory exception legitimizes any age-geared program or activity that is "established under authority of any law" [42 U.S.C. §6103(b)(2)]. The statute itself is silent as to this phrase's meaning. The implementing regulation interprets "any law" as encompassing any federal, state, or local governmental law or ordinance enacted by an elected, general-purpose body (45 C.F.R. §90.3). This is obviously an expansive reading, since it excludes from the onus of the ADA's prohibitory language programs ranging all the way from federal activities down to the activities of cities and towns. HEW cannot be faulted, however. There had been an abortive attempt in 1978 to amend the ADA so as to limit the "any law" exception just to federal laws, and the failure of that effort really left the agency with little ability to by regulation construe the surviving statutory language that narrowly, given the Congress's rejection of such a reading.

Finally, HEW on its own initiative created still another exception. It promulgated a regulation to avert the possible jeopardizing by the Act of "special" benefits programs, such as reduced fares for students and "senior citizens" on public mass transit systems, which—even given the ADA's weaknesses—might have otherwise fallen. Inasmuch as "the Congress has consistently made clear its support for the concerns of older persons . . . ," the regulation's drafters reasoned that "[i]t is . . . unlikely that Congress intended the Act to call into question the generally accepted special benefits which are provided to older persons . . ." [44 Federal Register 33771 (1979)]. Likewise, "no one has suggested that similar benefits for children should be questioned under the Act" (ibid.). Accordingly, HEW promulgated a regulation saving these programs, with language that contorted reality to serve the end sought:

If a recipient operating a program which serves the elderly or children in addition to persons of other ages, provides special benefits to the elderly or to children the provision of those benefits shall be presumed to be voluntary affirmative action [and therefore not violative of the ADA] provided that it does not have the effect of excluding otherwise eligible persons from participation in the program. [45 C.F.R. §90.49(c)]

Thus, an impoverished 40-year-old mother of three children who unwillingly pays full fare as she daily takes public transportation in search of a job, cannot complain of age discrimination, even though if she were over 60 she could ride the buses at a reduced rate. This is so because, under the HEW regulation, she is not excluded from participation in the "program"—to wit, the mass transit system. Of course, this is a semantic game. She *is* excluded from the fare reduction program, and that is the only one of concern to her.

None of the statutory exceptions is explained in the legislative history of the ADA. Nonetheless, some explanations can be inferred. Perhaps the most significant is the fact that the Congress did not perceive ageism as a vice to be equated with racism. In the congressional conference report explaining, in general terms, the original bill which ultimately was enacted into law it was stated:

. . . Distinguishing among individuals on the basis of race for purposes of determining their eligibility to receive the benefits of, or participate in, federally assisted programs is per se unfair treatment and violative of the Constitution; in this context, race is an arbitrary distinction. But age may often be a reasonable distinction for these purposes . . . . [House Conference Report No. 94–670 (1975), at 56]

Accordingly, rather than adopting a statute devoid of caveats—which is what in fact the Congress earlier had done in enacting Title VI of the Civil Rights Act of 1964, the ADA's predecessor and analogue regarding race discrimination by recipients of federal assistance—here the Congress took a much narrower course.

Given their ambivalent position regarding the invidiousness of ageism, the legislators confronted an exceedingly difficult task. They had to devise formulae that would separate unacceptable age discrimination from tolerable age distinctions. The mechanism for accomplishing this was the incorporation into the statute of the exceptions. Those activities that can fit within one or more of the exceptions are, by definition, tolerable uses of age distinctions. Those that do not satisfy the language of the exceptions are unlawfully discriminatory.

The Congress's ambivalence explains the existence of the exceptions; it does not necessarily explain their expansiveness, however. Perhaps their breadth is due to the fact when the ADA was enacted there was little empirical support for the charge that ageism was a serious problem in federally funded programs. Even when the Congress made some changes in the law in 1978, the evidence—in the form of a study done by a government agency (U.S. Civil Rights Commission, 1977)—was of dubious probity because of methodological weaknesses (Schuck, 1980). Thus, while legislative receptivity to an aggressive assault on ageism perhaps existed, it simply was not sustained and solidified by sufficient data. Some would argue that in fact the data were not available, even if sought, because actual ageism just was not prevalent (Schuck, 1980).

Another explanation for the ADA's weakness as an effective anti-discrimination tool may lie in the fact that age discrimination is a difficult concept to identify in specific terms. At least in the areas of racism and sexism, the victims are fairly clearly identifiable: one is either black or not; one is either a woman or not. In contrast, age, the trigger for discrimination in the context of ageism, is a characteristic that all possess to a greater or lesser extent. It is comparatively easy to single out one group—say, those 40 to 70— for protection. But if all persons, of all ages, are to be protected, the task becomes much more difficult. For example, in any given program there likely is a finite number of spaces, and often age is used as a criterion to determine who may occupy them. To exclude those over, let us say, 50 is to thereby make more room for those under 50. To disallow by statute exclusion of the over-50 age group is, in turn, to make less room for those

outside the group. Thus, in the name of outlawing ageism, an assurance that 50-year-olds not be barred may result in 40-year-olds being rejected on the basis of the very characteristic—age—that the ADA purports to proscribe as an appropriate basis for decision making. This contrasts with redress accorded in the areas of race and sex. If blacks have been excluded because of discrimination, then eradication of the discrimination leads, presumably, to the enhanced participation of blacks—but typically not at the expense of others bearing the characteristic of "blackness."

A different aspect of the complexities of coping with ageism by way of legislative action arises from the fact that age discrimination as a concept may carry with it varying amounts of invidiousness, depending upon who is victimized. The Age Discrimination Act applies on its face to all persons, and the legislative history confirms that the Act is intended to apply across the age spectrum [House Report No. 94–67 (1975), at 16]. Yet it may well be that children and youths—who are subjected to a variety of restrictions defined in terms of age—do not, after all, have the same rightful claims to freedom from age-based decision making as do adults. Children—at least those under some age— are not yet fully developed physically, intellectually, emotionally, or in terms of judgmental abilities (Stodolsky, 1981), as adults presumably are. Thus, to impose upon a child the requirement of attending school— a requirement defined in age terms—is to establish a considerably different type of imposition qualitatively than, for example, a requirement that all persons ages 30 to 40 must attend heart attack prevention classes. Rather than tackling the tough task of distinguishing between the proper and improper uses of age in terms of the persons affected, the Congress erected broad statutory exceptions largely leaving the status quo unimperiled.

Finally, the Congress was caught in an internal contradiction. The legislators set out to combat age discrimination. Yet the Congress has regularly engaged in the practice of extending benefits to some (and thus denying them to others) on the basis of age. There was a certain tension, then: an unswerving statutory condemnation of age discrimination likely would lead to the downfall of laws favoring those who most vocally condemn ageism; that is, the elderly. Again the broad caveats to the ADA's ostensible prohibition were the answer, although apparently even they were inadequate, and so the implementing agency, HEW, had to step in and by regulation save the Congress from itself.

In sum, the ADA reveals that while discrimination in the abstract is easy to deplore, defining that discrimination, at least in the context of age, is a very difficult task for legislators. This is particularly so when, as the Congress acknowledged, the condemnation of ageism begins with ambivalence, with the legislators both deploring the vice and yet acknowledging that some age distinctions are useful and proper.

As a final note, it should be stated that the courts have not yet had the occasion to offer any elucidation of the ADA's substantive provisions, perhaps because, given the breadth of the statutory exceptions, there just are no claims of wrongdoing that could be pursued successfully in the courts.

The Age Discrimination In Employment Act

Certainly the most significant federal statute addressing age discrimination, in terms of cases generated, is the Age Discrimination in Employment Act of 1967, as amended (ADEA). In fiscal year 1983 (October 1, 1982–September 30, 1983) over 15,000 claims were filed with the federal enforcement agency, the Equal Employment Opportunity Commission, charging alleged violations.

The ADEA attacks age discrimination in the workplace in all contexts, including hiring, firing, demotion, promotion, withholding of benefits, and discriminatory advertising. Its prohibitions extend to employers, both public and private, that employ 20 or more employees for 20 or more weeks in a year; to labor unions with 25 or more members; and to employment agencies. The Act

is limited by age, however, as to whom it protects: while all federal employees and job applicants age 40 and over are protected, workers and applicants in private industry and in local government agencies are only covered between ages 40 and 70. Until 1978, this coverage had been more limited: the ceiling for coverage was age 65. Even subsequent to the 1978 amendment which raised the age level for coverage, some minor exceptions remained, whereby certain executives and persons in policy-making positions fall outside the statute's reach at age 65. So do federal employees to whom a specific mandatory retirement statute applies, such as law enforcement personnel.

The Act authorizes enforcement both by the federal government and by private grievants. The relief available includes damages (with some limitations to be discussed below) and injunctive remedies, such as restoration to the job, securing of a wrongfully denied promotion, and so on.

Like the Age Discrimination Act (ADA) and like most other federal and state statutes proscribing age discrimination, the Age Discrimination in Employment Act contains exceptions to its ostensibly global prohibition of discrimination. It is not a violation of the Act for an employer, union, or employment agency to use an age criterion "where age is a bona fide occupational qualification reasonably necessary to the normal operation of its business" [29 U.S.C. §623(f)(1)]. Additionally, differential treatment of persons of different ages is legal "where the differentiation is based on reasonable factors other than age" [29 U.S.C. §623(f)(1)]. Another exception legitimizes actions that might otherwise violate the statute's prohibition if they are taken in observance of the terms of a "bona fide seniority system or any employee benefit plan . . . which is not a subterfuge to evade the Act . . ." [29 U.S.C. §623(f)(2)]. Finally, disciplining for good cause is explicitly, albeit unnecessarily, approved by the statute [29 U.S.C. §623(f)(3)].

Whereas the genesis of the Age Discrimination Act, discussed above, was marked by an absence of data establishing the prevalence of age discrimination in federally assisted programs, the need for the ADEA was amply documented (Report to the Congress on Age Discrimination in Employment, 1965; Older Americans Message, 1967). And the considerable number of cases in which plaintiffs have prevailed since enactment of the statute confirm that discrimination persists. Where the ADA and the ADEA do correspond is that like the former statute, the ADEA is premised on the perception that ageism is qualitatively different from racism. In the report to the Congress that laid the groundwork for ultimate adoption of the 1967 statute, the Secretary of Labor drew a key distinction between the two:

> Employment discrimination because of race is identified, in the general understanding of it, with nonemployment resulting from feelings about people entirely unrelated to their ability to do the job. There is *no* significant discrimination of this kind so far as older workers are concerned. (Report to the Congress on Age Discrimination in Employment, 1965, p. 2)

Rather, discrimination against older workers, as explained both in the report and by the Secretary of Labor in subsequent congressional hearings, is based on employer ignorance: "It results . . . from a basic misunderstanding of fact, . . . an assumption that people lose their power to contribute to an establishment of one sort or another, as age progresses" (Statement of Secretary Wirtz, Hearings on Employment Problems of Older Workers, 1965, p. 26).

This posture helps to explain why it is that the ADEA contains the bona fide occupational qualification (bfoq) exception, whereas the statute's analogue and predecessor, Title VII of the Civil Rights Act of 1964, makes no such exception for race discrimination in employment. Race is irrelevant to ability and suitability for employment. Age, at least in some circumstances—typically physically rigorous public safety positions—may be relevant. (Paralleling the ADEA, Title VII does make the same bfoq exception applicable to gender discrimination in the workplace.)

The ADEA case law is far too extensive to review in this format. The statute is complex, and thus has generated a considerable number of questions, which in turn have spawned a wide-ranging body of often conflicting decisions. Issues that have produced particularly significant amounts of litigation include questions concerning:

- The significance of a failure to timely file an administrative complaint [*Naton v. Bank of California* (1981); *Hiscott v. General Electric Co.* (1975); Eglit (1982)].
- The substantive and formal adequacy of administrative complaints [*Reich v. Dow Badische Co.* (1978); *Woodford v. Kinney Shoe Corp.* (1973); Eglit (1982)].
- The requisite elements of a prima facie case [*Marshall v. Airpax Electronics, Inc.* (1979); *Williams v. General Motors Corp.* (1981); Eglit (1982)].
- The feasibility of pursuing class action suits [*LaChapelle v. Owens-Illinois, Inc.* (1976); Eglit (1982)].
- The availability of jury trials [*Morelock v. NCR Corp.* (1976); *Rogers v. Exxon Research & Engineering Co.* (1977); Eglit (1982)].
- The scope of the statute's bona fide occupational qualification exception [*Hodgson v. Greyhound Lines, Inc.* (1974); *Equal Employment Opportunity Commission v. City of Janesville* (1980); Malin (1981)].
- The scope of the statute's pension plan exception [Malin (1981)].
- The necessary quantum of proof to establish a violation [*Cancellier v. Federated Department Stores* (1982); *Jacobs v. College of William & Mary* (1980); Eglit (1982)].
- The availability of damages for pain and suffering [*Pfeiffer v. Essex Wire Corp.* (1982); *Pavlo v. Stiefel Laboratories, Inc.* (1979); Eglit (1982)].
- The availability of punitive damages [*Murphy v. American Motor Sales Corp.* (1978); *Wise v. Olan Mills, Inc.* (1980); Eglit (1982)].

- The quantum of willfulness necessary for recovery of liquidated damages [*Loeb v. Textron, Inc.* (1979); *Wehr v. Burroughs Corp.* (1980); Eglit (1982)].

On some issues a consensus position among the lower courts has been reached. In some instances the Supreme Court has provided final authoritative interpretation, such as in its decision regarding the question of whether a grievant must first seek relief in state proceedings in certain instances [*Oscar Mayer & Co. v. Evans* (1979)]. Amendments to the Act adopted in 1978 also clarified some previously ambiguous matters. Nonetheless, the ADEA remains a statute about which many questions remain for final authoritative resolution, either by the Supreme Court or through legislative change enacted by the Congress.

While no analysis satisfactory in legal terms can be essayed here, some generalizations regarding the statute can be made. First, it is safe to say that the ADEA affords less than optimum protection to workers. Depending on one's perspective, this can be seen as either salutary or unfortunate. The aggrieved employee or job applicant confronts a number of limitations on achieving full satisfaction. One is the expense of litigation—a problem in many aspects of the American legal process, but one that is perhaps exacerbated in this context by the nature of the typical claimant. Often, the plaintiff will be a discharged worker who suddenly finds himself in a precarious financial position by virtue of his loss of his job. He will therefore find it particularly difficult to undertake a costly lawsuit in which the prospect of success almost always will be less than certain.

The nonavailability of class actions under the ADEA (Eglit, 1982) means that the deterrent effect of potentially large liability that defendants in such suits face in other contexts is absent. Because of the wording of the statute, as well as general common law doctrine, recompense for prevailing plaintiffs is limited. The thrust of the Act is to make the wronged employee or job applicant whole by placing him in the posture he would have been in but for the discrimination. Thus, the victorious plaintiff is entitled to back pay; that is, the wages and benefits he would have received had he not been fired, demoted, or denied the promotion or job he sought. In addition, in some but not all instances the employer will be subject to the imposition of injunctive relief, taking the form of a requirement that the employee be reinstated or promoted, or that the applicant be hired (Eglit, 1982). While these remedies are unquestionably important ones for the discriminatee, they do not, after all, put the employer in any worse position than it would have been in had it not acted wrongfully. Indeed, the employer may fare better, since the back pay award must be reduced by the wages earned in any interim job, which the plaintiff has an obligation to seek so as to mitigate his employer's liability [*Fiedler v. Indianhead Truck Line, Inc.* (1982); Eglit (1982)].

Further remedies enhancing the plaintiff's position, and at the same time increasing the costs of violating the Act for the employer, are generally unavailable. Most courts have read the language of the ADEA as precluding damages for the employee's pain and suffering [*Rogers v. Exxon Research & Engineering Co.* (1977); Eglit (1982)]. Thus, the psychological and even physical problems that may result from loss of the job—problems that, while disputed, have been identified by a committee of the American Medical Association (AMA, n.d.)—are not compensable. Nor are punitive damages recoverable, according to most courts' interpretations of the Act [*Murphy v. American Motors Sales Corp.* (1978); Eglit (1982)]. Thus, the employer who does wrong by discriminating escapes punishment. This latter situation is tempered only by a statutory provision for the award of liquidated damages for willful violations of the statute. But the severity of this liability is in turn tempered by such damages being limited to no more than twice the amount of back pay recovered; so, in a situation where an employee finds alternative work and thus mitigates the back pay award, the maximum possible liability for liquidated damages diminishes. Furthermore, some courts have been reluctant to award front pay; that is, damages representing the amount the employee would have earned had he been allowed to work in his job until retirement [*Jaffee v. Plough Broadcasting Co.* (1979); Eglit (1982)].

Apart from the question of relief, there is the more basic problem for the plaintiff of even establishing liability. It is not enough that age was a factor in the employer's decision; it must have been a determinative factor [*Loeb v. Textron, Inc.* (1979); Eglit (1982)]. It typically will be very difficult for the plaintiff to establish this. Invariably, the employer will claim that the employee was not performing adequately, or that changed business conditions ruled out any further role for the employee. In brief, the employer will argue that the basis for its action was not age, but some other acceptable concern. Rarely will the truth be obvious because the driving force of employment decisions is often hard to isolate. Consequently, identification of age as the determinative factor typically is a very difficult task—more so, perhaps, than is the case in the areas of race and sex discrimination.

It should be made clear that the ADEA is not unique in its limitations. Title VII of the Civil Rights Act of 1964, which bars discrimination in employment on the bases of race, sex, national origin, religion, and color, also has been read as barring the award of damages for pain and suffering and punitive damages. While under Title VII class actions are maintainable, there are other aspects of that statute that impose limits not applicable to ADEA plaintiffs. Thus, the ADEA cannot be read as illustration of singularly low-level legislative concern. It is clear, nonetheless, that it would be erroneous to conclude that simply because the Congress passed a law making age discrimination in employment unlawful (subject to certain exceptions), a revolution in civil rights was worked. The actual application and implementation of the ADEA reveal that indeed

age discrimination is, in legal terms at least, a slippery animal to capture and identify.

The Equal Credit Opportunity Act

The third major federal statute addressing age discrimination focuses on credit transactions. The Equal Credit Opportunity Act (ECOA) prohibits discrimination, actually, on a number of other bases as well, including race, sex, marital status, and religion. For most of these, the statute erects no exceptions. However, as to age and the status of being a public assistance recipient, there are caveats to the ostensible ban on discriminatory practices. This characteristic—that is, assertion of a broad prohibition, followed by exceptions undercutting the scope of that prohibition—is of course seen as well in the Age Discrimination Act and the Age Discrimination in Employment Act.

The justification for these exceptions was offered by the Senate committee that considered the legislation. In brief, the committee perceived age, unlike race, marital status, and other individual characteristics, as being relevant to the determination of whether a person is creditworthy. By way of example, the committee observed:

> [A] creditor justifiably may inquire how close to retirement an applicant is so that he may judge whether the applicant's income will continue at a sufficient level to support the credit extension. Similarly, the creditor is entitled to ask the applicant's age to gauge the pattern or intensity of his or her credit history. (Senate Report No. 94-589, 1976, p. 5)

The ECOA and its implementing regulations are far too complicated to lend themselves to abbreviated analysis. One particular aspect of the statute, however, is of special noteworthiness, at least in part because it reveals how social science research and lawmaking sometimes merge. The statute contains an exception that authorizes the "use of any empirically derived credit system which considers age if such system is demonstrably and statistically sound . . . " [15

U.S.C. §1691(b)(3)]. The implementing regulations, issued by the Federal Reserve Board, define an "empirically derived credit system":

> The term means a credit scoring system that evaluates an applicant's creditworthiness primarily by allocating points (or by using a comparable basis for assigning weights) to key attributes describing the applicant and other aspects of the transaction. In such a system, the points (or weights) assigned to each attribute, and hence the entire score:
>
> (i) Is derived from an empirical comparison of sample groups or the population of creditworthy and non-creditworthy applicants of a creditor who applied for credit within a reasonable preceding period of time; and
>
> (ii) Determines, alone or in conjunction with an evaluation of additional information about the applicant, whether an applicant is deemed creditworthy. [12 C.F.R. §202.2(p)(1)]

The regulations further define the phrase "demonstrably and statistically sound" [12 C.F.R. §202.2(p)(2)].

In sum, if a creditor uses a qualifying statistical system for determining creditworthiness, the age of applicants can be taken into account, notwithstanding that the Act purports to abjure, in its initial prohibitory statement, the use of age as a basis for decision making. The Congress authorized this on the basis of testimony in the hearings that preceded adoption of the age ban. Witnesses representing major credit institutions testified that demonstrably and statistically sound empirically derived credit scoring systems have significant predictive value as to the creditworthiness of a given credit applicant (Senate Report No. 94–589, 1976, p. 6). There was also testimony that age is the single most significant predictor of creditworthiness (Hearings on H.R. 3386, 1975, p. 94).

Ironically, the premise for allowing explicit consideration of age—that is, its statistically verified significance as an accurate predictor—is undercut by a further provi-

sion of the same exception in the Act. This provides that in credit scoring systems "the age of an elderly applicant may not be assigned a negative factor or value . . . "[15 U.S.C. §1691(b)(3)]. The implementing regulations define "elderly" as the status of being age 62 or over [12 C.F.R. §202.2(o)]. They explain "negative factor or value" as:

> [A] factor, value or weight that is less favorable regarding elderly applicants than the creditor's experience warrants, or is less favorable than the factor, value, or weight assigned to the class of applicants that are not classified as elderly applicants and are most favored by a creditor on the basis of age. [12 C.F.R. §202.2(v)]

Suppose, for example, that in a scoring system persons ages 65 and over were assigned initially 30 points for their age. By virtue of the statute and the regulations, even if the creditor's subsequent experience warranted a reduction, that reduction could not go below a certain floor. The highest score on the basis of age given to applicants who are less than age 62 creates that floor. Accordingly, if in the statistical credit scoring system persons ages 50 to 55 now were assigned the maximum point total for the age factor—let us say, 25—based on the statistically established fact that this age group has the best record of payment of debts, then 25 would be the lowest score that could be assigned to persons age 62 and over. This would be so even if in actuality their creditworthiness record, as statistically established, would only warrant a lesser score. Thus, notwithstanding the ECOA's exception allowing the consideration of age in statistical systems because such systems are said to be accurate predictors of creditworthiness, the Act bars the honoring of such systems if they redound adversely to the elderly.

HOUSING DISCRIMINATION

Age discrimination is common in the housing market in the United States. More than its commonality makes it deserving of attention here, however. One factor that particularly distinguishes this arena in which ageism occurs is that its victims most often are not being penalized for being too old— as was the case in the *Murgia* and *Vance* decisions and as is the case with ADEA plaintiffs. Rather, it is the "too-young" who are commonly the victims in this instance (Marans et al., 1980). It is also notable that the housing decisions constitute the clearest judicial recognition thus far that the claims of one age-defined group may conflict with the interests of another group also defined in terms of age.

By way of background, it should be noted that land use control is one of the most ubiquitous forms of governmental regulation in the United States. Virtually every local community imposes restrictions, in the form of zoning requirements, on the uses of property within the community, with certain areas typically being designated for residential purposes, others for light industrial purposes, others for stores, and so on. The courts as a general matter have been very deferential to the choices made by community zoning boards, regarding land use control as a subject particularly proper for determination within the local political processes and therefore inappropriate for more than superficial supervision by the judiciary. Nonetheless, state judges have not been totally uncritical.

Relatively few courts have addressed challenges to zoning allowing retirement communities, which typically exclude anyone under age 52 or 55 save for occasional visitations by children (Eglit, 1981a). What is notable is that in none of the cases have the courts been willing to uphold the legitimacy of zoning for retirement communities in situations where there was a shortage of other housing for younger people. Indeed, most of the courts have been sensitive to the discriminatory nature of such communities. Thus, for example, a New York state court observed:

> [W]e are not unmindful of the fact that senior citizen housing may be embraced as part of an overall pattern of improper exclusion in a particular case. To put it bluntly, a municipality

could so regulate its zoning districts as to virtually exclude all but senior citizens, high income younger families, and industrial and commercial users, thereby ensuring the benefits of a large tax base. [*Campbell v. Barraud* (1977), 58 A.D.2d at 572–73, 394 N.Y.S.2d at 913]

Perhaps the leading decision is that rendered by the New Jersey Supreme Court in *Taxpayers Association of Weymouth Township, Inc. v. Weymouth Township* (1976), which involved a zoning plan allowing the establishment of mobile home parks on tracts exceeding 140 acres, with the caveat that the occupancy in such parks was to be restricted to "elderly persons" and "elderly families." The court recognized that "planned housing developments for the elderly can be exploited for . . . exclusionary purposes . . . " (*Weymouth Township,* 71 N.J. at 289, 364 A.2d at 1038). It was only willing to approve the zoning plan so long as the zoning body provided, "by their land use regulations, the opportunity for an appropriate variety and choice of housing [in the general area] for all categories of persons who may desire to live there" (71 N.J. at 289, 364 A.2d at 1040).

As it happens, in none of the retirement community cases has there been either proof or even a specific claim that housing for younger people in fact was not generally available. The discrimination argument has been made as a secondary claim by plaintiffs actually challenging the zoning on economic and aesthetic grounds, rather than on the basis of their having themselves been excluded for being too young. Thus, the courts have not been called upon to speak in more than abstract rhetoric, espousing a principle rather than applying it to particular facts. However, two recent decisions dealing with multiple-unit dwellings, rather than full-scale communities, have dramatized the potential for intergenerational conflict.

Marina Point, Ltd. v. Wolfson was decided by the California Supreme Court in 1982. At issue was the refusal of an 846-unit apartment building to rent to a family solely because the family included a minor child.

The complex had successfully convinced the trial court that "'[c]hildren are rowdier, noisier, more mischievous and more boisterous than adults'" (30 Cal.3d at 725, 180 Cal. Rptr. at 498, 640 P.2d at 117), and that accordingly exclusion was justified. The state supreme court reversed the lower court, relying upon a state law that, while not explicitly dealing with age discrimination in housing, nonetheless established a general anti-discrimination requirement. This posed a problem for the court, however, given the existence within the state of a number of seniors-only housing complexes and communities. It offered a saving rationale that was not particularly persuasive in justifying the obvious fact that such communities indeed bar individuals on the basis of age:

> Such facilities are designed for the elderly and in many instances have particular appurtenances and exceptional arrangements for their specified purposes. The special housing needs of the elderly in contemporary American society have been extensively chronicled, and both the state and federal governmental have enacted specific "age-conscious" legislative measures addressed to this problem . . . . Such a specialized institution designed to meet a social need differs fundamentally from the wholesale exclusion of children from an apartment complex otherwise open to the general public. (*Marina Point, Ltd.,* 30 Cal.3d at 742, 180 Cal. Rptr. at 509-10, 640 P.2d at 127-28)

The court went on to state that the apartment complex could not "plausibly claim that its exclusionary policy serves any similarly compelling societal interest" (*Marina Point, Ltd.,* 30 Cal.3d at 743, 180 Cal. Rptr. at 510, 640 P.2d at 128).

In brief, the *Wolfson* court recognized, but skirted, the larger problem of age-based exclusionary housing by saying that there is a qualitative difference between exclusion of the too-young from seniors-only housing and communities and exclusion of the too-young from other housing settings. But it really offered no convincing rationale for this assertion. Recognition of a need—e.g., the need of the elderly for special housing—does not necessarily constitute justification, in and of

itself, for discrimination. If it did, the claims of men to jobs could warrant excluding women in a time of scarce employment opportunities—hardly an acceptable conclusion under the very law at issue in *Wolfson.*

A 1980 decision by a lower New York state court acknowledged the discriminatory nature of seniors-only housing, did not attempt to justify it as had the *Marina Point* court, and proceeded to make the seniors "pay" for their benefit. In *Apfelbaum v. Town of Clarkstown* (1980) the town's zoning code barred the construction of more than 106 dwelling units at any one senior citizen housing site. The code further prohibited the construction of senior citizen housing complexes within less than 1500 feet of each other. The plaintiffs argued that these restrictions were unconstitutional because they discriminated against seniors, who were defined as persons over age 60, by virtue of the fact that no other multiple residence zone was limited in terms of numbers of units or minimum distances between sites. The court upheld the restrictions:

> . . . [I]t does not appear as irrational or discriminatory that . . . restrictions are [not] imposed upon other dwellings erected in multiple dwelling zones . . . because the remainder of these buildings are erected without regard to considerations of the age of the occupants and will, therefore, be available for the utilization of the entire populace, including senior citizens. (*Apfelbaum,* 104 Misc.2d at 374-75, 428 N.Y.S.2d at 389)

In brief, the *Apfelbaum* court said that the quid pro quo for toleration of discrimination by the elderly against young people was the imposition of other forms of discrimination against the old.

By training, lawyers in the United States are accustomed to generalizing from specific judicial decisions to broader principles. But generalizing should be undertaken cautiously, with awareness of the professional bias that encourages reading cases for more than they can sometimes stand. Even so, there is legitimate basis for pondering the housing cases as representing a judicial response to what the popular media have termed intergenerational conflict. Almost all the rest of the case law concerning age discrimination and virtually all of the anti-discrimination statutes have focused on claims of people victimized for being too old. [The Age Discrimination Act, discussed above, is a rare exception, but even though on its face it purports to protect persons of all ages, its legislative history makes clear that Congress really had most in mind those who were mistreated for being too old (Eglit, 1981a).] The housing case law is the singular exception, and interestingly the courts in the housing case in the main have responded sympathetically to the complaints of young persons victimized by the elderly or near-elderly— even to the extent in the *Apfelbaum* decision of imposing burdens on the elderly beneficiaries of governmental largesse. Perhaps the housing cases will remain a unique body of law. Perhaps, however, the growth of sensitivity to ageism will now, or soon, begin to manifest itself in a more generalized recognition that age discrimination does not only, or always, victimize the old. If that occurs, the courts and legislators either may then have to reject all uses of age, or to confront the full complexities of ageism and more finely tune their efforts to separate acceptable age distinctions from invidious age discrimination.

CONCLUSION

Use of age for distributing rights and privileges, and for imposing or relaxing responsibilities, has long been common in U.S. statutes and regulations. Only recently have legislators, judges, and lawyers begun to react with sensitivity to the possibility that, in some instances at least, reliance upon age as a basis for distribution of rights, responsibilities, and resources entails unfairness.

Certainly there are no studies by legal scholars attempting to explain this rising concern about the misuses of age. One factor accounting for enhanced legislative and legal concern may be the efforts of organized lobbying groups representing constituencies defined in terms of age—in brief, the so-called senior citizens' organizations. They have supported the enactment of anti-discrimination legislation, and have clearly won sympathetic ears in both the federal and state legislatures.

More likely, concern about the misuse of the age criterion flows, at least in the United States, from a heightened sensitivity generated by abuses in other contexts. The persuasive claims in the 1950s, '60s, and '70s of victims of racism and sexism have encouraged a generalized concern in the United States about equality under the law. There has been a spillover to other groups, such as elders, who—like blacks and women—are defined by a characteristic over which they have no control and which may generate real or perceived deprivation and disadvantage. While middle-aged and elderly adults have in the main failed in their constitutional attacks in the courts on statutes denying them equality, they have obtained, by way of anti-discrimination laws, a number of protections.

Whatever its driving forces, rejection of age discrimination appears to be a movement of significant strength. Even so, concrete exercises in seeking judicial and legislative redress have been marked by some ambivalence and a chariness in extending rights. It is too easy to ascribe this situation to ignorance and ineptitude. Rather, there are larger factors at work here, encapsulated in the questions set forth at the beginning of this chapter. It may well be that some of those questions are readily answered or, upon examination, do not need resolution. Clearly, not all of them can be readily dealt with. In the consideration of these questions, social scientists may offer particular knowledge, insights, and approaches that can improve the efforts of legislators, judges, and lawyers in working out a just and useful role for age categorizations as criteria for ordering social systems.

REFERENCES

Achenbaum, W. A. 1978. *Old Age in the New Land.* Baltimore: The John Hopkins Press.

Age Discrimination Act of 1975, as amended, 42 U.S.C. §§6101-6107.

Age Discrimination in Employment Act of 1967, as amended, 29 U.S.C. §§621-634.

American Medical Association. (n.d.) *Employment of Older People.* American Medical Association.

Anti-Discrimination Act (New South Wales).

Apfelbaum v. Town of Clarkstown, 104 Misc.2d 371, 428 N.Y.S.2d 387 (1980).

Baltes, P. B., and Schaie, K. 1974. Aging and I.Q.: The myth of the twilight years. *Psychology Today* (Mar.): 35-40, 86, 95.

Bellotti v. Baird, 443 U.S. 622 (1979).

Bergman, S. 1980. "Israel." *In* E. Palmore (ed.), *International Handbook on Gerontology,* pp. 209-232. Westport, Conn.: Greenwood Press.

Blue v. University Interscholastic League, 503 F. Supp. 1030 (N.D. Tex. 1980).

Bolling v. Sharpe, 347 U.S. 497 (1954).

Breen, L. Z. 1960. "The aging individual. *In* C. Tibbitts (ed.), *Handbook of Social Gerontology,* pp. 145-162. Chicago: The University of Chicago Press.

Bryan v. Koch, 492 F. Supp. 212 (S.D. N.Y. 1980), *affirmed,* 627 F.2d 612 (2d Cir. 1980).

Cain, L. 1976. Aging and the law. *In* R. H. Binstock and E. Shanas (eds.), *Handbook of Aging and the Social Sciences,* 1st ed., pp. 342-368. New York: Van Nostrand Reinhold.

Campbell v. Barraud, 58 A.D.2d 570, 394 N.Y.S.2d 909 (1977).

Cancellier v. Federated Department Stores, 672 F. 2d 1312 (9th Cir. 1982), *cert. denied,* 103 S Ct 131 (1982).

Civil Rights Act of 1964, Title VII, 42 U.S.C. §§2000e-2000e-17.

Cohen, W. 1957. *Retirement Policies Under Social Security.* Berkeley: University of California Press.

12 C.F.R. §202.2(p)(1) (1983).

12 C.F.R. §202.2(p)(2) (1983).

12 C.F.R. §202.2(o) (1983).

12 C.F.R. §202.2(v) (1983).

45 C.F.R. §90.3 (1983).

45 C.F.R. §90.13 (1983).

45 C.F.R. §90.15 (1983).

45 C.F.R. §90.49(c) (1983).

Craig v. Boren, 429 U.S. 190 (1976).

Daley v. Farm Credit Administration, 454 F. Supp. 953 (D. Minn. 1978).

de Beauvoir, S. 1975. *The Coming of Age.* New York: Warner Paperback Library.

Drucker, G., and Moore, L. Mandatory retirement: Past, present, and future of an anachronism. 5 *Western State University Law Review* 1-44 (1977).

Due Process Clause, United States Constitution, Amendment V.

Due Process Clause, United States Constitution, Amendment XIV, §1.

Duren v. Missouri, 439 U.S. 357 (1979).

Eglit, H. 1981a. *Age Discrimination,* Vol. 1. Colorado Springs, Colo.: Shepard's/McGraw-Hill.

Eglit, H. Of age and the Constitution. 57 *Chicago-Kent Law Review* 859-914 (1981b).

Eglit, H. 1982. *Age Discrimination,* Vol. 2. Colorado Springs, Colo.: Shepard's/McGraw-Hill.

Ely, J. The wages of crying wolf: A comment on *Roe v. Wade.* 82 *Yale Law Journal* 920-949 (1973).

Equal Credit Opportunity Act, as amended, 15 U.S.C. §§1691-1691f.

Equal Employment Opportunity Commission v. City of Janesville, 630 F.2d 1254 (7th Cir. 1980).

Equal Protection Clause, United States Constitution, Amendment XIV, §1.

44 Federal Register 33771 (June 12, 1979).

44 Federal Register 33783 (June 12, 1979).

Fiedler v. Indianhead Truck Line, Inc., 670 F.2d 806 (8th Cir. 1982).

Frontiero v. Richardson, 411 U.S. 677 (1973).

Gault v. Garrison, 569 F.2d 993 (7th Cir. 1977), *cert. denied,* 440 U.S. 945 (1979).

General Assembly Resolution 3137, 28 U.N. GAOR, Supp. 30, U.N. Doc. A/9030 (1973).

Gunther, G. Foreword: In search of evolving doctrine on a changing court: A model for a newer equal protection. 86 *Harvard Law Review* 1-48 (1972).

Hammond v. Marx, 406 F. Supp. 853 (D. Me. 1975).

Hawkins v. James, 525 F. Supp. 914 (M.D. Ala. 1981).

Hearings on Employment Problems of Older Workers, on H. Rep. 10634 etc., Subcommittee on Labor, Committee on Education and Labor, U.S. House of Representatives, 89th Cong., 1st Sess. (1965).

Hearings on H.R. 3386, a Bill to Amend the Equal Credit Opportunity Act to Include Discrimination on the Basis of Race, Color, Religion, National Origin, and Age, and for Other Purposes, Subcommittee on Consumer Affairs, Committee on Banking, Currency and Housing, U.S. House of Representatives, 94th Cong., 1st Sess. (1975).

Hiscott v. General Electric Co., 521 F.2d 632 (6th Cir. 1975).

Hodgson v. Greyhound Lines, Inc., 449 F.2d 859 (7th Cir. 1974), *cert. denied,* 419 U.S. 1122 (1975).

House Conference Report No. 94-670, Older Americans Amendments of 1975, Committee on Education and Labor, U.S. House of Representatives, 94th Cong., 1st Sess. (1975).

House Report No. 94-67, Older Americans Amendments of 1975, Committee on Education and Labor, U.S. House of Representatives, 94th Cong., 1st Sess. (1975).

Jacobs v. College of William & Mary, 517 F. Supp 791 (E.D. Va. 1980), *affirmed without opinion,* 661 F.2d 922 (4th Cir. 1981), *cert. denied,* 454 U.S. 1033 (1981).

Jaffee v. Plough Broadcasting Co., 19 Fair Employment Practices Cases 1194 (D. Md. 1979).

Jones, R. 1977. *The Other Generation.* Englewood Cliffs, N.J.: Prentice-Hall.

Katz, S. N. (ed.). 1974. I *The Youngest Minority.* Chicago: American Bar Association.

King v. United States, 346 F.2d 123 (1st Cir. 1965).

Kutscher, R. E., and Walker, J. F. 1960. Comparative job performance of office workers by age. *Monthly Labor Review* 83:39–43.

LaChapelle v. Owens-Illinois, Inc., 513 F.2d 286 (5th Cir. 1976).

Loeb v. Textron, Inc., 600 F.2d 1003 (1st Cir. 1979).

Longman, P. 1982. Taking America to the cleaners. *The Washington Monthly* (Nov.): 24–30.

Malin, M. 1981. Employment discrimination: The Age Discrimination in Employment Act—protections, prohibitions and exceptions. *In* H. Eglit, *Age Discrimination,* Vol. 1, pp. 16-1-16-119. Colorado Springs, Colo.: Shepard's/McGraw-Hill.

Marans, R. W., Colten, M. E., Groves, R. M., and Thomas, B., 1980. Measuring restrictive rental practices affecting families with children: A national survey. Ann Arbor: Survey Research Center, The Institute for Social Research, University of Michigan.

Marina Point, Ltd. v. Wolfson, 30 Cal.3d 721, 180 Cal. Rptr. 496, 640 P.2d 115 (1982), *cert. denied,* 103 S. Ct 129 (1982).

Marshall v. Airpax Electronics, Inc., 595 F.2d 1043 (5th Cir. 1979).

Massachusetts Board of Retirement v. Murgia, 427 U.S. 307 (1976).

McDougal, M. S., Lasswell, H. D., and Chen, L. The human rights of the aged: An application of the general norm of nondiscrimination. 28 *University of Florida Law Review* 639–654 (1976).

McIlvaine v. Pennsylvania State Police, 454 Pa. 129, 309 A.2d 801 (1973), *appeal dismissed,* 415 U.S. 986 (1974).

McMahon v. Barclay, 510 F. Supp. 1114 (S.D.N.Y. 1981).

Morelock v. NCR Corp., 546 F.2d 682 (6th Cir. 1976), *vacated,* 435 U.S. 911 (1978).

Murphy v. American Motor Sales Corp., 570 F.2d 1226 (5th Cir. 1978).

Naton v. Bank of California, 649 F.2d 691 (9th Cir. 1981).

Neugarten, B. 1979. Policy for the 1980s: Age or need entitlement? *In: Aging: Agenda for the Eighties,* National Journal Issues Book, pp. 48–52. Washington, D.C.: Government Research Corporation.

New South Wales Anti-Discrimination Board, *Discrimination and Age* (1980).

Note. The constitutional challenge to mandatory retirement statutes. 49 *St. John's Law Review* 748–791 (1975).

Nurenberg v. Ward, 51 A.D.2d 1022, 381 N.Y.S.2d 412 (1976).

Older Americans Message of January 23, 1967, by President Lyndon Johnson, 113 Congressional Record 34743–44 (1967).

Oregon v. Mitchell, 400 U.S. 112 (1970).

Oriol, William. 1982. A special report on the United Nations World Assembly on Aging. Washington, D.C.: National Council on Aging.

Oscar Mayer & Co. v. Evans, 441 U.S. 750 (1979).

Palmer v. Ticcione, 576 F.2d 459 (2d Cir. 1978), *cert. denied,* 440 U.S. 945 (1979).

Pavlo v. Stiefel Industries, Inc., 22 Fair Employment Practices Cases 489 (S.D.N.Y. 1979).

People v. Hoiland, 22 Cal. App.3d 530, 99 Cal. Rptr. 523 (1971).

Pfeiffer v. Essex Wire Corp., 682 F.2d 684 (7th Cir. 1982), *cert. denied,* 103 S Ct 453 (1982).

Reich v. Dow Badische Co., 575 F.2d 363 (2d Cir. 1978), *cert. denied,* 439 U.S. 1006 (1978).

Report to the Congress on Age Discrimination in Employment Under Section 715 of the Civil Rights Act of 1964, U.S. Department of Labor (1965).

Riley, M. W., Johnson, R., and Foner, A. 1972. *Aging and Society,* Vol. 3. New York: Russell Sage Foundation.

Roe v. Wade, 410 U.S. 113 (1973).

Rogers v. Exxon Research & Engineering Co., 550 F.2d 834 (3d Cir. 1977), *cert. denied,* 434 U.S. 1022 (1978).

Rose, A. M. 1968. The subculture of the aging: A topic for sociological research. *In* B. Neugarten (ed.), *Middle Age and Aging,* pp. 29–34. Chicago: The University of Chicago Press.

San Antonio Independent School District v. Rodriguez, 411 U.S. 1 (1973).

Schuck, P. The graying of civil rights law. 60 *Public Interest* 69–93 (1980).

Select Committee on Aging, U.S. House of Representatives, Federal Responsibility to the Elderly, Comm. Pub. No. 95-167, 95th Cong., 2d Sess. (1979).

Senate Report No. 94–589, Equal Credit Opportunity Act Amendments of 1976, Committee on Banking, Housing and Urban Affairs, U.S. Senate, 94th Cong., 2d Sess. (1976).

Stodolsky, S. Age related changes in the individual: Childhood and adolescence. 57 *Chicago-Kent Law Review* 851–857 (1981).

Streib, G. F. 1968. Are the aged a minority group? *In* B. Neugarten (ed.), *Middle Age and Aging,* pp. 35–46. Chicago: The University of Chicago Press.

Taxpayers Association of Weymouth Township, Inc. v. Weymouth Township, 71 N.J. 249, 364 A.2d 1016 (1976), *cert. denied,* 430 U.S. 977 (1977).

Taylor v. Louisiana, 419 U.S. 522 (1975).

Teitelbaum, L. The Age Discrimination Act and youth. 57 *Chicago-Kent Law Review* 969–1008 (1981).

Trafelet v. Thompson, 594 F.2d 623 (7th Cir. 1979), *cert. denied,* 444 U.S. 906 (1979).

United States v. Allen, 445 F.2d 849 (5th Cir. 1971).

United States v. Guzman, 337 F. Supp. 140 (S.D. N.Y. 1972), *affirmed,* 468 F.2d 1245 (2d Cir. 1972), *cert. denied,* 410 U.S. 937 (1973).

United States v. Test, 550 F.2d 577 (10th Cir. 1976).

15 U.S.C. §1691(b)(3).

29 U.S.C. §623(f)(1).

29 U.S.C. §623(f)(2).

29 U.S.C. §623(f)(3).

31 U.S.C. §6716(b)(1).

36 U.S.C. §391(b)(6).

42 U.S.C. §1985(3).

42 U.S.C. §5151.

42 U.S.C. §6101.

42 U.S.C. §6102.

42 U.S.C. §6103(b)(1)(A).

42 U.S.C. §6103(b)(1)(B).

42 U.S.C. §6103(b)(2).

49 U.S.C. §1302(a)(3).

49 U.S.C. §1604(m).

49 U.S.C §1615(a)(1).

United States Commission on Civil Rights. 1977. *Age Discrimination Study.* Washington, D.C.: United States Government Printing Office.

Van Dyke, J. 1977. *Jury Selection Procedures.* Cambridge, Mass.: Ballinger.

Vance v. Bradley, 440 U.S. 93 (1979).

Wehr v. Burroughs Corp., 619 F.2d 276 (3d Cir. 1980).

Williams v. City of Lewiston, Me., 642 F.2d 26 (1st Cir. 1981).

Williams v. General Motors Corp., 15 Fair Employment Practices Cases 411 (N.D. Ga. 1976), *affirmed,* 656 F.2d 120 (5th Cir. 1981), *cert. denied,* 455 U.S. 943 (1982).

Wise v. Olan Mills, Inc., 485 F. Supp. 542 (D. Colo. 1980).

Woodford v. Kinney Shoe Corp., 369 F. Supp. 911 (N.D. Ga. 1973).

Ziegler, D. H. Young adults as a cognizable group in jury selection. 76 *Michigan Law Review* 1045–1110 (1978).

19
AGING AND POLITICAL SYSTEMS

Robert B. Hudson
Fordham University
and
John Strate
University of Massachusetts at Boston

This chapter looks at aging and political systems from two perspectives. The first perspective examines the effects of aging on the political orientations and participation of individuals and the consequences of these effects for political systems. The second examines reasons why aging has become a concern of political systems and the factors accounting for the manner in which political systems have responded to that concern. The aging of populations throughout the industrial world and the growing share of national resources directed toward older persons have made these issues of increasing interest and importance in recent years.

POLITICAL ORIENTATIONS AND POLITICAL PARTICIPATION OF AGING PERSONS

A large body of literature now exists on the effects of aging on political orientations and participation. Political orientations refer to the content, intensity, and stability of the attachments individuals have to political objects. Most research covering these dimensions of political orientations has focused on the following areas: political interest; attitudes toward self, politics, and political institutions; political values and ideology; party attachments; and policy positions and

preferences. Political participation refers to the ways in which individuals attempt to influence or take part in governmental activity. It is generally understood to range along a continuum from less intensive to more intensive activity. Most research on the subject concentrates on voting, more active forms of influencing governmental personnel and actions, and elite/leadership activity within the political system.

In order to understand the political orientations and participation of older persons, it is necessary to disentangle the effects of aging understood in chronological or life-cycle terms from the effects associated with birth cohorts and historical periods. The analytical problems of doing this are complex, with researchers seeking to determine the nature and magnitude of these effects by using longitudinal data and ruling out one or more effects (or their interactions) on theoretical grounds (Mason et al., 1973). Apart from the intrinsic interest in better understanding attitudes and behaviors of particular age groups, sorting out life-cycle, cohort, and period effects can be important for understanding and predicting different patterns among them.

Explanations stressing life-cycle effects associate attitudes and behavior with chronological aging and the biological, social, and economic patterns that may be intrinsic to it. Thus, a life-cycle effect often cited as accounting for declines in levels of political participation among the very old is loss of physical vigor and the lessened social interaction that may result. Cohort or generational explanations see the legacy of common experiences of particular age clusters as determining attitudes and behaviors. Age cohort effects result from the distinctive and lasting impact exposure to common schools, family structures, political regimes, and economic cycles may have on individuals in the same cohort. Historical or period effects are environmental changes that simultaneously alter attitudes or behavior of all or most individuals. Included here are events such as wars, depressions, or a salient instance of political corruption, such as the Watergate affair in the United States, that color the perceptions of individuals across age groups.

Political Orientations

Political Interest. Studies that have examined the relationship between aging and expressed interest in political affairs find that interest increases markedly between young adulthood and middle age, and that the interest of persons over 60 is roughly the same as the middle-aged (Curtis and Lambert, 1976; Glenn, 1969). However, a study by Glenn and Grimes (1968), which controlled for differences in the sex and educational composition of different age groups, found that there was a steady increase in political interest throughout life, with the highest levels of reported interest at age 60 or higher. A panel study by Jennings and Niemi (1981) of high school seniors and their parents over the period 1965 to 1973 also found that political interest increased with age. Numerous media studies have reported the elderly being more attentive to political campaigns and devoting more time to news and public affairs programming than younger groups (Comstock et al., 1978; Schramm, 1969).

There are many possible explanations for the general increase in political interest with age. The relatively low interest on the part of the young may be due to their distraction with age-related concerns such as obtaining an education, establishing a career, finding a mate, and taking care of young children (Glenn and Grimes, 1968). By way of contrast, the middle-aged have fewer such distractions and also a greater perceived stake in political matters because of higher incomes and longer residency within a community. The elderly may be seen as having even fewer distractions because of the more limited social contacts that may come with retirement (Glenn and Grimes, 1968). There is, however, little indication that the elderly "disengage" from political matters (Glenn, 1969).

Cross-national data suggest that age cohort rather than life-cycle effects may also lie behind age-related variations in political interest. In countries that have experienced major changes in political regimes, the turmoil associated with those changes may have discouraged the age cohorts who experienced them from developing a strong interest in politics. Lower levels of interest among the elderly in countries where that generation experienced severe political turmoil has been reported for West Germany (Almond and Verba, 1965; Baker et al., 1981), Italy (Almond and Verba, 1965), and Japan (Richardson, 1974).

Attitudes Toward Self, Politics, and Political Institutions. Cross-national data indicate that older persons have a marginally lower sense of efficacy in politics than do younger groups. Even these differences are more the result of cohort and period effects than life-cycle effects. Today's older persons have less education and may lack the skills associated with education that would enhance their feelings of efficacy in political matters (Almond and Verba, 1965; Edinger, 1983). In certain countries, such as West Germany, the quite low levels of political efficacy found among the older cohorts may be due to their negative political experiences at earlier points in their lives (Baker et al., 1981).

In their evaluation of political processes and institutions, older persons do not differ in their responses from other groups. Concerning overall trust in what government does, data collected in the National Election Study series in the United States show a substantial decline in trust in government among every age group since 1964 (Tropman et al., 1979). While it is possible to attribute such a decline to aging processes, it is far more likely that the decline in trust was due to the salient political events of the period, such as urban riots, the Vietnam war, and the Watergate scandal.

In regard to more specific evaluations, such as of candidates, political parties, legislatures, and so on, the importance of period effects is revealed through the greater temporal variability in responses found among all age groups. The classic study by Campbell et al. (1960) found that the public's image of the Republican Party improved during the 1950s as memories of the depression associated with President Hoover faded in the face of relatively prosperous times under President Eisenhower. The Jennings and Niemi (1981) study found a uniform decline in the ratings given by both parents and their children to eight different sociopolitical groups. They attribute this decline to the events of the 1960s and 1970s, which resulted in a general malignment of societal institutions among all age groups.

A common theme in political literature is that a greater sense of attachment to political institutions and to the nation (patriotism) is found among the older age groups. It is often further assumed that this pattern suggests a life-cycle explanation. However, data reported by Baker et al. (1981) on support for political institutions in West Germany show increases among all cohorts during the 30 years of postwar democratic stability. Data reported by Edinger (1983) on patriotic sentiments in the United States, Japan, and West Germany show that support for patriotic citizenship increases with age, although large differences among younger and older groups in Japan and West Germany suggest the presence of age cohort as well as life-cycle effects.

Political Values and Political Ideology. These more fundamental orientations refer to the beliefs that individuals hold about government's proper place in society. Political values consist of the goals, standards, and criteria that individuals bring to bear in evaluating governments and their actions. Political ideologies are sets of beliefs about government's proper place in society that can be considered to be coherent, structured, and shared by others. As in other areas, the effects of aging and the magnitude of those effects have been subject to considerable debate.

During the past decade, interest in political values has increased substantially owing largely to the pioneering work of Inglehart (1971, 1977, 1981), who contrasted the political values of different western European age cohorts and found substantial intercohort differences. Older cohorts in these countries place great emphasis on the "materialist" values of economic well-being and physical security, whereas younger age cohorts, socialized during a period of relative economic prosperity and peace, put more emphasis on post-materialist values such as the satisfaction of social, aesthetic, and intellectual needs.

One consequence of these age cohort differences is that the political agendas of these countries have become crowded. As argued by Inglehart, older cohorts, with more materialistic orientations, focus on the "old politics" issues of inflation, unemployment, old age benefits, taxes, law and order, and national security. In contrast, the younger age cohorts are more concerned with the "new politics" issues of nuclear disarmament, nuclear power, environmental protection, women's rights, abortion, homosexual rights, and relations with foreign countries. These differences in concerns are reflected in voting behavior. The emphasis that middle class members of these younger age cohorts give to new politics issues has resulted in a decline of class-based voting and in the appearance of new parties on the left, such as the Greens of West Germany, who gained representation in the West German parliament in the 1983 elections.

Several analysts have criticized Inglehart's thesis, contending that the probable impact on politics of post-materialistic values is less than he suggests. For example, Dalton (1977) argues that, as postwar cohorts come to dominate the electorates of western European countries, the possibility for further growth in the number of post-materialists due to generational replacement will diminish. And, as acknowledged by Inglehart (1981), constraints on economic growth may compel all age groups to pay greater attention to materialistic concerns.

A more basic critique of Inglehart's thesis centers on whether economic growth always has the uniform effect of promoting the spread of post-materialistic values. Survey data from Japan show that economic growth is associated with value changes that are difficult to classify within the materialist/post-materialist framework. Ike (1973) found that value changes in Japan are best explained by a trend toward individuation and privatization at the expense of family ties and the public interest. Similarly, Flanagan (1979, 1982) has argued that the basic value cleavage in Japan is traditional versus libertarian. Older age cohorts in Japan hold traditional values that are distinctively Japanese: frugality, piety, self-discipline, conformity, dependency, and devotion to authority. Younger cohorts of Japanese, rebelling to some extent against such traditional values, more often hold libertarian values: self-indulgence, secularism, permissiveness, independence, self-assertiveness, and cynicism. It thus seems that economic growth may have different effects on the values of the same age cohorts in different cultures (cf. Inglehart, 1982). Flanagan (1980) also found that the youngest and the oldest cohorts in Japan place the most emphasis on nonmaterialistic values, raising further doubts about any simple interpretation of the relationships of age and age cohorts to political values.

Turning to political ideologies, it is important at the outset to stress that only a small proportion of individuals in mass publics, young or old, possess views about government's proper role in society that are coherent and structured enough to be called ideological (Converse, 1964; Klingemann, 1973). The ability to think about politics in a highly abstract and analytical way is a skill that is largely restricted to those with higher education or active involvement in politics. For most of those with less education and involvement, ideology has little content beyond familiarity with labels such as conservative and liberal (or left and right) and very general ideas about the meaning of such labels.

Nonetheless, the content of these ideas and how they may be associated with age, variously understood, is interesting. Campbell and Strate (1981) looked at the meaning attached by the middle-aged and elderly in the United States to the labels conservative and liberal and found substantial differences in the ways that these age groups think about politics. To older people, the conservative label reflects a preference for sound fiscal policy, limited spending, and a balanced budget; to the middle-aged, the conservative label reflects a preference for free enterprise and limited government, and a resistance to change and new ideas. To older people, the liberal label reflects a preference for big government and socialism; to the middle-aged the liberal label reflects an acceptance of change, new ideas, and progressive policy. The greater attention given by older persons to such long-standing partisan issues as spending and the size of government is probably a legacy of their experiences during the depression and the New Deal. It also seems that older people, more than the middle-aged, give political rather than purely social content to the labels conservative and liberal.

A related question of long-standing interest is whether individuals are more likely to identify themselves as conservative as they grow older. Unfortunately, there is surprisingly little research tied directly to this question. An early study by Evan (1965), reproduced by Foner (1972), used cohort analysis and found a small increase within each cohort in the proportion of individuals identifying themselves as conservative over the period 1938 to 1957. Campbell and Strate (1981) looked at the placement of older and middle-aged people on a seven-point liberal–conservative scale over the period 1972 to 1980 and found that older people were only slightly more likely than the middle-aged to identify themselves as conservatives on "feeling thermometers" indicating the degree of warmth (or coldness) toward conservatives and liberals. The results of these studies suggest that the effect of aging on the tendency to identify as a conservative, if it exists at all, is probably small.

Indirect evidence concerning the relationship between age and ideology comes from the literature addressing party attachments. These data show contemporary older populations to identify to a somewhat greater extent with conservative parties than younger groups, but analysis suggests this patterning is more the result of cohort than life-cycle effects. The most convincing evidence to this effect comes from research on the United States. An early study by Crittenden (1962) seemed to show that individuals shifted from the Democratic to the Republican Party as they grew older. Subsequently, however, studies that applied cohort analysis to longitudinal cross-sectional data found that there was no tendency for individuals to become Republicans as they grew older (Cutler, 1969; Glenn and Hefner, 1972; cf. Knoke and Hout, 1974). A panel study of Jennings and Niemi (1981) that followed adults over the period 1965 to 1973 substantiated this conclusion. There is thus good evidence that the disproportionate Republicanism of older cohorts in the United States is due to formative socialization during the era prior to the depression dominated by the Republican Party. Furthermore, cross-sectional data on the acquisition and maintenance of partisan attachments discussed in the following section strongly suggest that cohort rather than life-cycle effects account for older persons' disproportionate support for parties based on traditional values and cleavages.

Party Attachments. Party attachments are important because of their impact on the political behavior of individuals and the political stability of systems. A very large

literature shows that party attachments affect individual attitudes on domestic and foreign policy, evaluations of candidates, interest and involvement in election campaigns, split ticket voting, and partisan regularity in voting. Widespread and strong party attachments also contribute greatly to the stability of political systems in those countries where such attachments are found.

Party attachments include both a direction and a strength component. Although controversy continues to exist about the relationship between aging and party attachments, it is generally agreed that the direction of party attachments (e.g., Democratic, Republican, Independent) in any particular age group results from age cohort effects; while it appears that the strength of party attachments (e.g., strong, not very strong) results from a mix of life-cycle, age cohort, and period effects.

The directional component is attributed to age cohort effects in large part because most individuals in countries with stable party systems acquire party attachments during childhood from their parents (Dennis and McCrone, 1970; Kubota and Ward, 1970; Jennings and Niemi, 1975). Furthermore, those children who do not acquire party attachments from their parents, and enter the electorate without such attachments, are especially susceptible to salient political events that may favor one party over another, such as the depression, which favored the Democratic Party in the United States. Thus, the distribution of party attachments of any particular age cohort reflects the stamp of the parental generation and the particular historical events that it experienced during the period when it first entered the electorate.

A major consequence of these processes of acquiring party attachments is that a somewhat larger proportion of older cohorts hold attachments to long-established parties based on traditional or class cleavages. In most countries, older cohorts give stronger support (in terms of party attachments and/or votes) to parties on the right and right/center: the Gaullists of France (Inglehart and Hochstein, 1972); the Christian

Democrats of West Germany (Edinger, 1983; Urwin, 1974); the Conservative Party of Great Britain (Butler and Stokes, 1971); the Christian Democrats of Italy (Barnes, 1972); the Liberal Democrats of Japan (Kubota and Ward, 1970); the Catholic parties of Belgium (Hill, 1974); and the Republicans of the United States (Campbell and Strate, 1981). The Netherlands is an exception to this pattern, with older cohorts giving stronger support to that country's Socialist Party (Lijphart, 1974).

The weakening of *some* of these traditional parties' support in recent years is due partly to shifts and abandonments. It also results from the process of "generational replacement" due to the deaths of members of older cohorts with attachments to traditional parties and their replacement by young adults either without attachments or with attachments to smaller, less traditional parties. This replacement is a potent source of political change that has benefited many of the new ideological, single-issue, and linguistic parties that appeared in western Europe during the 1970s (Inglehart, 1977). However, because of their small size, the temporal or topical specificity of their appeal, and the provisions of electoral laws in many countries, the continued survival and growth of these parties must be considered problematical.

The strength of party attachments has also been a major area of investigation. Strength of attachments is important because strong party attachments are likely to be durable and to be associated with consistent party voting. For this reason, the overall strength of party attachments in a country is thought to affect the stability of its political system (Converse, 1969).

Survey research from the countries of western Europe and the United States has found a uniform tendency for a disproportionate number of old people to hold strong party attachments. Campbell et al. (1960), who first observed this pattern in the United States, argued that party attachments become stronger through processes of reinforcement: the longer that an individual

associates with a party and the more times he votes for it, the easier it becomes for him to believe complex political events reflect favorably on his own party.

The relationship between age and strength of party attachments is most prominent in countries with stable party systems, such as Great Britain and the United States; but it is often modified or weakened in countries that have undergone major changes in regimes, such as Japan (Richardson, 1975) and West Germany (Baker et al., 1981), or that have not experienced stable party politics, such as France (Converse and Dupeux, 1962; Inglehart and Hochstein, 1972). To explain these anomalies, Converse (1969) has argued that the overall strength of party attachments within any particular age cohort is the net result of four processes: the acquisition of party attachments from parents (transmission); the strengthening of party attachments as a result of reinforcement processes (learning); the weakening and loss of party attachments as a result of the suspension of party politics (forgetting); and the difficulty of middle-aged and older persons just entering the electorate, such as women who recently gained the franchise, in acquiring attachments (resistance).

Although Converse's theory about the strength of party attachments is elegant and consistent with a variety of cross-national survey data (e.g., Norpoth, 1978, for West Germany), there are instances it may not be able to explain. In India (Eldersveld, 1973), a country with a relatively new political system, and in France (Inglehart and Hochstein, 1972), a country that experienced major political changes with the advent of the Fifth Republic, the proportion of individuals with party attachments is much higher than Converse's theory would predict. It would seem that intense periods of partisan politics can result in rapid alignment and strengthening of party attachments.

Interesting data from the perspective of Converse's theory come from the United States. Data from the National Election Studies show a strengthening of party attachments within age cohorts over the period 1952 to 1964, but no strengthening over the period 1964 to 1976. Converse (1976) has argued that the period 1952 to 1964 was a normal "steady state" period. Thereafter, the strong support by the Democratic Party for civil rights and ensuing domestic and foreign problems were a period effect that weakened party attachments, disrupting the normal pattern of strengthening with age. Abramson (1976, 1979) has vigorously challenged this view, arguing that the strengthening of party attachments that occurred from 1952 to 1964 was not an aging effect but rather occurred only among blacks and was due to increased enfranchisement and the advocacy of civil rights by the Democratic Party.

A study by Claggett (1980) seems to support Converse's interpretation of the U.S. data. Previous studies, he argued, had confounded the processes by which attachments are acquired with the processes by which they are strengthened. Looking only at the strengthening process, he found a strong aging effect over the entire 1952 to 1976 period and a somewhat weaker age cohort effect. Thus, while there is considerable support for Converse's original theory, it does need to be modified to account for instances in which other effects modify the rate of strengthening (or weakening) of party attachments.

Whatever the final resolution of this controversy, however, it is clear that a disproportionate number of the old have strong party attachments. A major consequence of this is that the voting predispositions of the old are not easily influenced by the candidates and issues of particular elections. For example, old people in the United States gave less support than other age groups to George Wallace in 1968 and to John Anderson in 1980 (Campbell and Strate, 1981). The old are much less likely than the young to vote against their party attachment. They are also less likely to vote a split ticket. As a consequence, they contribute less than do other age groups to shifts in party vote totals.

Issue Positions and Policy Priorities. Three initial points must be made in discussing the positions of older persons on specific social, economic, and political issues. First, people of all ages possess more loosely structured opinions on specific issues than they do on more general orientations such as political values or ideologies. This difference between the fundamental and the specific or the ideological and the operational has been demonstrated by Prothro and Grigg (1960), Free and Cantril (1968), and Douglass et al. (1974).

Second, the opinions of older people with respect to most policy areas are much like those of other groups (Campbell, 1971; Campbell and Strate, 1981). The cause of this similarity is the importance of self-interest in determining positions on specific issues combined with the linkage of self-interest to non-age characteristics such as party attachments, religion, race, region, income, and language. The heterogeneity of age groups in these characteristics ensures that differences of opinion within age groups on public policy issues generally equal or exceed differences between age groups.

Third, this general finding needs to be qualified in that there is considerable though not uniform evidence that older people in the United States take what are generally considered to be more conservative positions on a number of contemporary political issues than do the middle-aged or young adults. The pattern is clear and consistent in "new politics," civil rights, and law-and-order issues. It is more mixed in domestic economic and social welfare issues, especially where the benefits and costs of a particular policy, such as pension benefits and health care, are presumed to be closely related to age. Although the literature on this topic is substantial, it lacks a comprehensive theoretical perspective that would link age, birth cohort, and period effects to issue positions.

On "new politics" issues such as abortion, the roles of women, the use of marijuana, birth control, pornography, and homosexuality, older people are substantially more conservative than other age groups and especially more so than young adults (Epstein and Browne, 1979; Fengler and Wood, 1972;

Heilig, 1979). The conservatism of today's older people on these issues seems to reflect their socialization in an earlier and more conservative era—they grew up at a time when these were "non-issues" because of social conformity.

However, the opinions of older cohorts generally do change in the same direction and at much the same rate as the opinions of younger cohorts (Evan, 1965; Glenn, 1974). A recent cohort analysis of attitudes about legalized abortion conducted by Cutler et al. (1980), using Gallup Poll data, found that older cohorts followed much the same trend as other cohorts—toward more favorable attitudes between 1965 and 1972, but a leveling-off of favorable opinion thereafter. There is little evidence, therefore, to support the notion that the attitudes of middle-aged and older persons on "new politics" issues become more rigid with age. The old, just as the young, find it important to adapt to changing social conditions.

On issues of "law and order" such as protection of the rights of the accused, methods of law enforcement, capital punishment, and gun control, older people are substantially more conservative than the middle-aged and the young. The greater conservatism of the old in this area may reflect their greater vulnerability to and concern with crime (National Council on the Aging, 1975). It may also reflect differences in educational levels between age cohorts. Older cohorts have less education than younger ones, and less education is consistently associated with less tolerance of deviancy (Cutler and Kaufman, 1975; Glamser, 1974), as well as with a tendency to blame individuals rather than social conditions for crime (Gergen and Back, 1965).

In regard to racial issues, older people have higher levels of prejudice than other age groups (Campbell, 1971; Hyman and Sheatsley, 1964; Killian and Haer, 1958). Such opinions are most pronounced on issues that affect their daily lives such as open housing, desegregation in hotels and restaurants, and general desegregation; and less so on issues that do not affect them so directly, such as school desegregation, school busing, fair employment, and preferential treatment of minorities (Campbell and Strate, 1981).

The major factor behind the more prejudiced opinions of today's older people is the legacy of growing up in a culture that condoned and often institutionally acknowledged racism and other forms of discrimination. Such opinions have adjusted over time in a less prejudiced direction, but not sufficiently fast to keep pace with overall changes of opinion caused by the entry of younger cohorts with more tolerant attitudes on racial issues (Campbell, 1971). Also, it is important to note that opinion on racial issues depends more on individual characteristics such as race, region, and education than on either early socialization or later life-cycle developments.

In the area of foreign policy, older people are more isolationist than the middle-aged and young adults (Campbell, 1971; Campbell and Strate, 1981; Cutler, 1968; Gergen and Back, 1965). They are also more inclined to support greater defense spending (Campbell and Strate, 1981; Epstein and Browne, 1979; Heilig, 1979). The reason for these differences of opinion is differential cohort experience (Inglehart, 1977). Individuals who were born prior to World War II and lived through the war and the Cold War period that followed experienced and perceived serious threats to their physical security from disparate ideologies and nations. Individuals born after World War II did not experience these immediate threats, and as a consequence did not come to perceive the outside world in such nakedly hostile terms. As in other issue areas, however, the opinions of older people on issues of foreign policy do change over time in the same direction as changes in overall opinion (Cutler, 1968).

On domestic policy issues, the opinions of older people and other age groups show clearly how self-interest can supersede political values and ideology. Although there is considerable similarity in the opinions of older people and other age groups, differences do exist, especially in policy areas where there are age-related differential costs and benefits. Older people are substantially more favorable than other age groups to governmental action in the area of health care (Weaver, 1976) and to governmental action that promotes employment and a good standard of living (Campbell and Strate, 1981). They also express greater support for and confidence in the social security program (Johnson & Higgins, 1979; National Commission on Social Security, 1980). In policy areas where older people's self-interest is more difficult to isolate or where programs disproportionately favor the non-aged, however, the pattern reverses itself. Thus, older people give less support than other age groups to federal aid to education (Campbell and Strate, 1981; Clemente, 1975). Older people are also less concerned with high taxes than other age groups and would prefer more services to a tax cut (Campbell and Strate, 1981).

Finally, it is important to note that the positions older people hold on issues are probably of little consequence for voting or other forms of political participation if they do not regard the issues as being very important. An intriguing question is whether older people are "age conscious" and whether this consciousness is expressed in the priorities they assign to issues (Cutler, 1977). It is difficult to see how older people (or more than a small fraction of them) could be effectively mobilized on "old age issues" if they lacked this consciousness and did not have issue priorities that differed from those of other age groups.

There is, however, little research on the policy priorities of older people and how they differ from other age groups. A survey conducted by the National Council on the Aging (1981) found that in 1981 older people felt that the most serious problem was the cost of energy; the second most serious problem was crime; and the third most serious problem was poor health. Those aged 18 to 64 felt much the same, although they placed less emphasis on poor health and somewhat greater emphasis on not having enough money to live on, poor housing, and insufficient job opportunities.

Campbell and Strate (1981) contrasted the responses of older people and the middle-aged to multiple-response questions about the most serious national problems and found that, overall, there was remarkably little difference between the age groups. Only two sizable differences were found. Older people gave somewhat greater emphasis to problems of race, law and order, and civil liberties; the middle-aged gave somewhat greater emphasis to economic problems. There is little evidence, therefore, that the policy priorities of older people differ substantially from those of other age groups, and this suggests the general absence of policy-relevant age consciousness.

Political Participation

Citizenship Activity. In democratic political systems citizen participation includes "legal acts by private citizens that are more or less directly aimed at influencing the selection of governmental personnel and/or the actions that they take" (Verba et al., 1978). Studies ordinarily distinguish between the following forms of political participation: voting; campaign activities such as working for candidates, attending political meetings or rallies, encouraging people to vote in particular ways, making campaign contributions, and displaying signs or bumper stickers; communal activities, which involve working through groups to contribute to the community or public good; particularized contacting such as telephoning or writing political officials; interest group activity; and protest behavior (Rusk, 1976).

A consistent cross-national finding is that overall levels of political participation (measured by indices that include all forms of participation except interest group activity and protest behavior) increase with age through late middle age and then gradually drop off in old age (Milbrath and Goel, 1977; Nie et al., 1974; Verba and Nie, 1972). In the absence of any additional controls, the consistency of these findings supports the hypothesis that the "curvilinear" relationship between age and overall levels of political participation is due to aging or life-cycle effects.

In this understanding, low levels of overall participation among young adults are a result of the "start-up" problem (Verba and Nie, 1972). The nonpolitical concerns of young adults, as argued above, distract them from political matters. In addition, owing to high geographical mobility, young adults often lack roots in the communities in which they live (Milbrath and Goel, 1977) and, furthermore, are often confronted by legal obstacles to participation such as registration and residency requirements for voting. The increase in political participation that comes with passage into middle age results from marriage, increased resources such as money and time, and increased integration within the local community as indicated by home ownership, length of residency, and organizational involvement (Milbrath and Goel, 1977; Verba and Nie, 1972).

The drop-off in participation that may be associated with old age (or, in the case of voting, very advanced age) can be attributed to retirement, which is associated with decrements in income, and physical infirmities, which make the very act of participating more difficult (Nie et al., 1974). Another phenomenon of old age is differential mortality between men and women. Since men tend to die at a younger age than women and because men's overall participation rate is greater than women's (Milbrath and Goel, 1977), some of the drop-off in participation rates among older cohorts may be due to the high ratio of women to men within those cohorts.

In any event, these findings regarding the bivariate relationship between age and overall political participation must be qualified. Considerable evidence shows that much of the drop-off in overall participation that is imputed from cross-sectional studies actually reflects the lower socioeconomic status (i.e., education and income levels) of older people (Glenn and Grimes, 1968; Verba and Nie, 1972). Also, in countries with relatively new democratic political systems (e.g., Austria and Japan), the drop-off prob-

ably reflects a persisting reluctance among older cohorts to participate rather than their lower socioeconomic status (Nie et al., 1974).

Voting-turnout studies have explored the place of these different factors in considerable detail. Glenn and Grimes (1968) found that controls for sex and education virtually eliminated the difference in turnout between people in their fifties and older people up to age 80. Verba and Nie (1972) found that a control for education resulted in a less severe drop-off in turnout, and that a control for income eliminated the drop-off entirely. Hout and Knoke (1975) analyzed change in voter turnout over the period 1952 to 1972 and, using controls for sex, occupation, region, race, and social class, they found that participation dropped off in late age (73 and older) and also that turnout was less among successively younger cohorts. Nie et al. (1974) found that controls for education reduced the drop-off in turnout for the over-60 group completely in India, to a great extent in Nigeria and the United States, but only somewhat in Austria and Japan. These studies show that voting turnout, in the absence of counteracting period effects that depress turnout (Abramson and Aldrich, 1982), increases throughout life until advanced age when there is some decline.

Almost all forms of political participation require a greater personal effort than does voting. The study by Verba and Nie (1972) constructed an overall participation index. Six clusters of participants were devised, ranging from those who engaged in no political activities ("inactives") to those who engaged in voting, communal activity, campaign activity, and personalized contacts ("complete activists"). The authors found that the elderly were overrepresented on lower-intensity modes of participation and increasingly underrepresented moving toward the most active forms of participation.

Other evidence shows that older people are much less conspicuous than other age groups in political activities that require a great deal of effort. Milbrath and Goel's (1977) review concludes that participation in unconventional forms of political activity is a youth phenomenon. A study by Jennings and Beck (1979) found that both middle-aged and old people were less involved in protest activities than young adults.

There has been increasing interest in recent years in the effects of periods on rates of political participation among age groups. Jennings and Beck (1979) found that the normal curvilinear relationship between age and participation was altered in the late 1960s and early 1970s, owing mostly to the protest activity of young adults. In the 1972 presidential election, for example, when George McGovern opposed Richard Nixon, far more liberals than conservatives were involved in campaign activities. The campaign activity of the elderly in that year was virtually nil and less than that for any other age group. The large number of young adults, their disproportionate liberalism, and the disproportionate participation by liberals due to the political stimuli during this period contributed to the impression of a leftward bias in participation. The authors conclude that there is no constant relationship between age and participation because some political issues may be much more salient to some age groups than to others.

There has also been increasing attention to the effects of actual life-cycle traits on political participation. Most research has used chronological age as a surrogate for these traits rather than using actual measures such as marital status, parental status, length of residency, employment status, health status, and physical mobility. Jennings (1979) argues that research on the life cycle and political participation should use measures of these traits rather than only chronological age. Further, theory in this area should incorporate the finding that individuals will participate in politics given adequate resources (e.g., income and education), a clearly perceived stake, and an opportunity structure that is reasonably well-defined, accessible, and penetrable.

Although life-cycle events are clearly related to rates of overall participation, the impact of these events should not be exaggerated. Most of the variation in rates of overall participation between individuals is not explained by life-cycle events but rather by individual motivation and resources associated with such factors as education, income, and group involvement (Verba et al., 1978). It is likely that habits of political participation (or non-participation) become established when individuals are young adults and that these habits tend to endure into middle and old age. Those who have voted regularly, engaged in campaign activities, or written public officials will continue to do so; those who have not will not. The tendency for habits of political participation to persist throughout life greatly attenuates the impact on individuals of transition through the life cycle. The forms and volume of participation in the future of young adults who contributed to the liberal bias in participation in the late 1960s and early 1970s will further inform the debate over the relative importance of life-cycle, age cohort, and period effects.

Leadership Activity. Persons in late middle age and early old age, as widely believed, disproportionately occupy positions of leadership in most industrialized societies, although in the wake of revolutionary change, leadership tends to be younger. A positive relationship between older ages and the importance of leadership positions continues well into old age, although recent data show a decline in the absolute ages in question. It is not entirely clear from the existing data that older leaders are more conservative than younger ones, but different belief patterns can be found between leadership generations.

The proposition that political leadership positions are held by relatively old persons is supported in a number of settings. Lehman's (1953) data show this general pattern for a variety of political contexts—American presidential candidates, members of the British cabinet, "chief ministers" in early England, American ambassadors and Supreme Court justices, and cabinet members. Schlesinger's (1966) study found, in addition, that the importance of an office (house, governor, senate, president) is positively correlated with the age of those first attaining it. The general relationship between old age and high political office is found throughout history and across types of political systems, the most notable contemporary examples being the United States, the Soviet Union, and China.

Analyses of the most recent period suggest, however, that age is becoming somewhat less a factor in accounting for career patterns among leadership cadres in the Western nations. The data of Lammers and Nyomarkay (1980) on cabinet members in the United States, Germany, France, Great Britain, and Canada show a consistent and marked fall-off during the 1960s and 1970s in the proportion of ministers over age 65, and a somewhat lesser fall-off rate for those over 60. They cite the greater bureaucratization of politics in the Western nations, and specifically the greater routinization of careers, as responsible for the reduction.

Similar findings are reported by Aberbach et al. (1981) in addressing the career paths of politicians (legislators) and bureaucrats in the United States, Great Britain, Germany, France, Italy, and the Netherlands. The study grouped these two leadership groups by age and tenure in national government and found a clear congruence of career paths among the politicians of all six countries (midforties to midfifties in age; six to ten years in government) and an even more remarkable congruence among the bureaucrats of all six (early fifties in age; 20 to 30 years in government). Moreover, legislators in these countries have spent roughly 70 percent of their adult lives outside of national government, while the corresponding figure for the bureaucrats is only 20 percent. The higher variation in the age of the politicians indicates a more varied recruitment pattern than for the bureaucrats. It suggests, as well, that career routinization is not only less marked for politicians than bureaucrats, but less for legislators than for the cabinet-level political officials discussed by Lammers and Nyomarkay (1980).

Evidence on whether older members of political elites tend to be conservative and whether individuals become more conservative as they age while in office is inconclusive. Lehman (1953) suggests a conservative bias among older elites by contending that "elderly leaders are more likely to be chosen by groups long established, firmly entrenched, and relatively complacent or satisfied with the status quo." However, Fishel (1969) did not find that younger challenging candidates are necessarily more liberal than older ones. In responses to questions on the domestic economy, civil rights, and foreign policy, candidates under 40 of both major parties who were nominated for the first time proved to be more conservative than older candidates.

Putnam's (1971) study of legislators in Great Britain and Italy addressed itself explicitly to two different meanings of ideology. He found that, while older legislators were much like their younger counterparts in viewing politics through a coherent set of beliefs ("ideological style"), they did exhibit greater "interparty hostility" than younger legislators. The causes underlying the age relationships in Putnam's findings are not definite (he emphasizes cohort over life-cycle effects). Nonetheless, his data do show that older legislators have tended to retain the hostility of earlier partisan divisions in the face of an overall lessening of interparty ideological divisions in the last half century, whereas younger legislators have not. Aberbach et al. (1981) also found consistent ideological differences among younger and older political elites in the six countries they studied. The younger individuals were significantly more favorably inclined toward "pluralist" and "populist" ideas than were the older elite members. Aberbach et al. see these differences as generational in origin, downplaying period influences and dismissing life-cycle ones.

The relationship between elite age patterns and the age and stability of political systems has been carefully reviewed in both historical and cross-national contexts. The sense of much of this literature is stated by North and Pool (1966): "It is only in times of revolutionary change . . . that one finds an elite whose average age is in the thirties or early forties." In the post-colonial revolutionary America of 1799, the average age of senators was 45; by 1925, it had risen to 57 (Lehman, 1953). In the case of the Soviet Politburo, the average age of members has been continually increasing since 1917, with only three exceptions over that period (Schueller, 1966). North and Pool (1966) document the relatively young ages of both the Kuomintang and Chinese Communist elites starting with the 1920s, and observe that, even by 1945, none of the Kuomintang Central Executive Committees had an average-age membership above 45. Rigby (1972) notes the resistance of those early members of the Politburo to recruitment of younger generations, one obvious factor being their concern with self-preservation. In the case of China, Butterfield (1979) observes that all prestige and power flows from political position, which accounts for the reluctance of today's elderly Chinese leadership to relinquish their offices.

Modern Germany may represent the clearest case of aging and generations linked to questions of regime stability and change. In studying the Nazi elite, Lerner, et al. (1966) found relative youth to be associated with centrality of revolutionary role. Party propagandists—the captains of persuasion who "spearheaded" the movement—were the youngest of all leaders; Nazi administrators were somewhat older; and the average age of all Nazi members was older yet. In contrast, the postwar leadership in West Germany has, until recently, been relatively old. Whereas the average age of the Nazi elite was under 50, 61 percent of the postwar West German political elite was over 50, and 27 percent was over 60 years of age (Edinger, 1968). As reported by Lammers and Nyomarkay (1980), a new pattern of career routinization may have set in more recently, since the percentage of cabinet members in West Germany age 60 or more declined from 26.1 percent in the 1960s to only 9.2 percent in the 1970s.

Summary

The principal conclusion of this review of political orientations and behaviors is that older persons are more notable for their similarities to other age groups than their differences. These similarities result from the heterogeneity of all age groups and from period effects acting upon all age groups simultaneously. Where differences are found between age groups, they are often rather small and due to cohort rather than life-cycle effects.

In terms of their political interest and participation, older persons are very similar to the middle-aged, with both groups being considerably more attentive and active than young adults. These similarities stem from shared and accumulated life experiences. There are similarities among all age groups in their evaluations of political leaders and institutions, this patterning being largely due to period effects.

Data related to aging and political ideology show that contemporary older persons are slightly more likely to think of themselves as conservative, and there are more substantial data documenting the somewhat greater likelihood of older persons to identify with conservative parties. Considerable debate has taken place about why older persons have aligned themselves somewhat to the right of younger ones. Early studies suggesting that conservatism came with aging have been refuted by cohort analyses revealing strong generational effects on political identification. The importance of differential cohort experiences is further underscored by studies showing different age groups assigning different meanings to the terms liberal and conservative and by evidence from the United States and western Europe showing that different political values—materialist and post-materialist—are found between older and younger generations.

Closely tied to the question of ideology has been party attachment, which involves both directional and strength components. The direction of one's preference is, at least in stable democracies, directly related to the preference of one's parents. On the matter of the strength of partisanship, the old have stronger attachments than the middle-aged and young adults. The reinforcement hypothesis suggests that this characteristic is due to experience, although major events may disrupt the normal strengthening associated with "steady state" periods.

In the area of issue preferences, major discrepancies between age groups are uncommon. The largest differences are found on "new politics" issues where older persons tend to be more conservative. Lesser differences are found in older persons' favoring strong law-and-order measures, being more isolationist on foreign policy questions, and being more opposed to civil rights measures that affect them or are perceived to affect them negatively. On self-interest grounds, older persons give stronger endorsement than the middle-aged and young adults to public policies related to pensions and health care. Overall, however, individuals of all ages show little ideologically based consistency in many of their issue-specific preferences.

In the case of political leadership, older persons occupy a disproportionate number of leadership positions, and this pattern is most marked among the higher offices. This relationship can vary, however, depending on the leadership positions in question and the career patterns that may be associated with them. The only clear exception to the general relationship is in the wake of revolutionary change, where leadership figures are much younger than those found in stable systems.

The important remaining question concerns the impact of older persons upon political systems. Owing to their marginally conservative orientation and their relatively strong and enduring party attachments, older persons may have a stabilizing effect on political systems. However, the importance of social and economic factors in shaping political orientations and behaviors results in limited cohesion within any particular age cohort, including the elderly. Cohort differences do exist and are introducing new strands and strains into Western political systems, but these changes are gradual and may be altered by period effects, such as continuing economic problems. In their orientations and behaviors, contemporary older persons are fully integrated into national political systems and their differential impact remains modest.

FACTORS ACCOUNTING FOR OLD-AGE POLICY

This section turns from an examination of the forms and levels of older persons' involvement in the political process to the factors accounting for how public policies for the elderly have developed to the present period. This is but one piece of the larger topic of public sector responses which is explored in other chapters of this *Handbook,* most notably those included in the book's final section.

In looking at the evolution of these policies, the material here isolates factors that social scientists have argued are responsible for contemporary old-age policies. Concern with these factors is found in works that look broadly at the array of contemporary welfare state programs and their development (Kaim-Caudle, 1973; Rimlinger, 1971; Wilensky, 1975); in works that look at the development of age-based or age-related policies (Estes, 1979; Olson, 1982; Williamson et al., 1982); and in works that focus on single policy areas, such as Social Security (Derthick, 1979), long-term care (Vladeck, 1980), and age discrimination and retirement (Graebner, 1981). Although these studies vary in both substance and method, there is substantial agreement that a limited constellation of factors is particularly important for contemporary old-age policies. These factors do not constitute any grand theory explaining aging policy, but being "rigorously eclectic" (Achenbaum, 1980) in the application of these and related factors may yet have considerable theoretical payoff.

Overview of Relevant Factors

The review groups factors associated with aging policy developments under six headings. In addition to itemizing and enumerating the factors, the discussion sets forth the reasons why each has been considered critical to aging policy developments and the manner in which each has operated in the policy-making process. These vary from the deep-seated effects of economic development and political culture to more immediate effects such as activities of interest groups and critically placed elite actors. Also included is policy itself, a factor that a number of analysts see as having important independent effects on the policy-making process. The factors and the ways in which they have been seen as affecting aging policy are as follows:

1. *Economic and ecological developments*—industrialization generating economic resources and social dislocations that lead the state to take on social welfare functions.
2. *Political culture and political structure*—prevailing values concerning appropriate governmental roles and levels of institutional development that critically affect the legitimacy and scope of policy and program options.
3. *Public input and demands*—the coherence, direction, and strength of citizen and organizational demands that induce or force decision makers toward certain options and away from others.
4. *Political elites*—the power and expertise of highly placed actors affecting the timing and direction of policy initiatives.
5. *Existing policies and programs*—the state of policy at any point in time framing subsequent policy debates and creating access and opportunities for strategically placed interests.
6. *Concentrated capital*—policies affecting the aging being largely determined by the workings of capitalist market economies and allied social control mechanisms resulting in socially marginal roles for the elderly.

The import and interplay of these factors will differ, depending on the policy in question, the time period under consideration, and the setting where the decisions are being made. The respective role of each is discussed in turn.

Economic and Ecological Developments

A major contributing factor to the origins and development of the modern welfare state lies in the economic growth and social modernization that came with industrialization of the Western world. Through the resources it generated and the dislocations it brought, industrialization made welfare state development both possible and necessary. This combination of needs plus resources affected nineteenth- and twentieth-century life to a sufficient degree that theorists refer to the economic and social imperatives that were at the root of the development of the contemporary welfare state.

Studies that trace social policy development cross-nationally find that economic and ecological factors are necessary to that development if not sufficient to account for all aspects of it. Researchers consistently find positive correlations between indices of economic development and measures of domestic welfare spending. Cutright (1965) finds a large, positive correlation between economic development and social security coverage; Aaron (1967) reports that per capita income is the best predictor of social security outlays; and Pryor's (1968) time-series data show that level of economic development is a better predictor of "public consumption expenditures" than the type of political system. Wilensky (1975) concludes that contemporary welfare state development results from the interrelated effects of economic development, age of the public welfare system, and age of population, and sees them playing out in the following manner:

> Over the long pull, economic level is the root cause of welfare-state development, but its effects are felt chiefly through demographic changes of the past century and the momentum of the programs themselves, once established. With modernization, birth rates declined, and the proportion of aged was thereby increased. This increased importance of the aged, coupled with the declining economic value of children, in turn exerted pressure for welfare spending. (p. 47)

The role of age of the public welfare system and age of population are also reported by Pryor (1968) and Scharf (1981). Age of system is actually a surrogate for the workings of more proximate factors, including the development of bureaus and their politics. Because it is associated with numbers of would-be recipients and pressures for benefits, age of population has a strong and direct effect on welfare expenditures (Wilensky, 1975). There are, however, limits to the continuance of this pattern. Scharf (1981) finds that there is a strong negative relationship between the pension burden (i.e., the percentage of the adult population aged over 65) and relative pension expenditures. "States with especially unfavorable demographic profiles (German Democratic Republic, Austria) are unable to overcome this burden, even though their resource commitment may be very high."

Aside from the effects of industrialization on economic development and demography, it also brought major changes in the makeup and obligations of the family and other social groups. Most important is the shift in caretaking responsibility from the family to the state (Cowgill and Holmes, 1972). Changes in modes of production upset family structure, pressing the state into a larger role. Giele (1982) argues that a new functional explanation is necessary to explain why national governments came to sponsor programs (a) that are virtually the same throughout the industrial world, and (b) that are remarkably congruent with traditional functions of the family: economic, nurturance, residential, and legal/cultural, that is, ones that define identities and structure activities. Giele argues, "certain basic human needs, traditionally those met by the family, but now in danger of going unfulfilled, become subject to a new public consciousness." The common forms these programs take cross-nationally—covering old-age security, sickness and disability, unemployment, housing, and family needs—derive "from their correspondence not only to traditional functions of the family but to basic human needs."

These functions are critical everywhere, but the manner in which the response is in-stitutionalized in different countries may differ. An instance is Japan, where governmental provision of pension benefits is decidedly lower than that of other nations at comparable levels of development (International Labor Office, 1979), largely because intergenerational households have survived industrialization and urbanization to a greater extent than elsewhere. Thus, data reported by Palmore (1975) show roughly 80 percent of Japanese over age 65 living with children as contrasted with a range of 14 to 40 percent of persons of similar age in Britain, the United States, or Denmark. In China, a variety of public policies—especially the emphasis on the collective (Davis-Friedman, 1978)—yield a similar result. Prevailing attitudes toward the individual, the state, and society can fundamentally alter the Western presumption that near-universal and comprehensive packaging of benefits will be made available through state auspices.

Although not totally determinative, economic factors play a fundamental role in aggregate welfare state development. Through various means, the modern nation-state sees to it that at least some minimal standard of living is available to its members. Resources make it possible, levels of need make it essential, and cultural traditions sanction its occurrence. As Giele (1982) observes, the well-being of the elderly (and other dependent persons) becomes the responsibility of multiple social institutions: economic organizations, the family, and the state. All welfare state societies provide at least a minimal level of subsistence to their members through the efforts of one or more of these social groupings.

Political Culture and Political Structure

Although economic and ecological factors account for much of the growth of welfare state programs, they do not explain all aspects of that growth, and they may obfuscate important cross-national distinctions. In the words of Ashford (1981):

> The macro-level data easily conceal important intra-systemic variations, much of which may

elude aggregate measurement. While these essentially statistical explanations help us avoid some obvious pitfalls of comparative policy analysis, they may also generate new and no less damaging distortions by eliminating institutional and political features that in fact operate in different ways within each system. (p. 2)

The timing and processes leading to welfare state programs have been subject to other influences. Of these, the most fundamental is political culture or the prevailing national norms toward the role of the state. The independent effects of prevailing norms are clearly revealed in both historical and contemporary developments.

In this regard, one notes first that Germany inaugurated the modern welfare state in the 1880s, although its economic development still lagged well behind that of Britain. In accounting for the early developments in the case of Germany, one notes as well a traditional deference to central authority and a politically anemic middle class that lacked any firm attachment to the tenets of classical liberalism. These confluent factors—in combination with the political skills of Bismarck directed against the Social Democrats—were sufficient to generate those early programs (Dahrendorf, 1967). In Britain, introduction of analogous programs was delayed until the turn of the century when classical liberal attachments waned among the upper and middle classes. In France, adherence to liberal beliefs and the associated opposition to state intervention lost out to the growing forces of the left (Rimlinger, 1971). The early developments in Denmark, Belgium, and New Zealand must also be considered anomalous in the developmental context because significant population aging did not occur until later.

It is in the American social welfare experience, however, that the role of both culture and structure have had their most distinctive impact. A large proportion of the early immigrants came to America fleeing state intrusions on what they felt to be individual rights and prerogatives (Hartz, 1955). This was the first stage in the development of a political culture that prevented the growth of the corporatist and collectivist politics that was central to welfare state development elsewhere (Beer, 1965). Instead, there developed a pervasive fear of concentrated governmental power, with the institutions put in place being "strong enough to harness but not strong enough to act" (Hofstadter, 1948).

The response of "the fragment culture" (Hartz, 1955) to industrialization was very different from that found elsewhere. National governments of European nations were deeply involved in the promotion of industrialization and the amelioration of its consequences. The United States, on the other hand, responded with a series of disjointed steps consonant with the traditional American values of individualism, the small community, and the belief in progress associated with the pursuit of rational self-interest. Widespread antipathy to interventionist government was found in the business community's adherence to the tenets of laissez-faire economics and in organized labor's commitment to voluntarism (Lubove, 1968; McConnell, 1966). It is significant in this context that the one area of social welfare activity where the United States became a leader, public education, was undertaken in the name of individual initiative and betterment and has long remained very much a function of local government (Heidenheimer, 1973).

The interplay of cultural and structural factors has continued to impede welfare state developments in the United States to the present day. The impact of prevailing political orientations, in the estimation of King (1971), has been nothing less than determinative: "the state plays a more limited role in America than elsewhere because Americans, more than other people, want it to play a limited role." The existence of this consensus, according to Huntington (1966), has allowed the country to persist with the least developed political institutions in the Western world. The ease of modernization within

American society precluded the modernization of the country's political system. "The United States thus combines the world's most modern society with one of the world's most antique politics" (Huntington, 1966).

These interrelated factors are central not only to understanding the delayed development of social policy in the United States, but also the particular place occupied by older persons when welfare state initiatives finally did come about. Because the United States conformed to what Zetterberg (1979) terms a residual model of social policy development, the notion of deservingness took on an import not to be found in countries where "social citizenship" rights (Marshall, 1963) were more broadly established. As a result, the special vulnerability of the elderly to a variety of life circumstances has been featured in social welfare politics in the United States through what Binstock (1983) refers to as "compassionate ageism." This has been sufficiently striking that, in the American context, the elderly can properly be considered to be a stalking horse or "ideological loss leader" (Hudson, 1978a) for programs to which there is substantial opposition.

In terms of policy, the special standing of the elderly was seen for the first time in the treatment afforded veterans in the decades after the Civil War (Kutza, 1981). It has been seen repeatedly since then, and in ways that highlight the particular legitimacy and utility of the elderly in the American context (Hudson, 1978b): the timing and placement of old-age provisions in the original social security legislation (Altmeyer, 1968); the calculated choice of the bureaucratic proponents of national health insurance to focus exclusively on the elderly during the Medicare struggle (Marmor, 1970); and the truncated outcome of the Family Assistance Plan proposal in the form of Supplemental Security Income for the "adult categories" (Burke and Burke, 1974). These episodes are important not only for what they say about America's concern for the elderly, but also because they show that classical liberal values and the politics and institutions associated with them persist in the United States.

Public Input and Demands

In all political systems, whatever their capabilities, imperatives, and presumed predilections, it is the input and demands of individuals and groups that transform situational factors into public policies. The role of aging-based groups in the policy-making process has been a central concern of the politics of aging literature. Three themes have been of special interest: the organizational bases and development of aging-based groups; the type and degree of influence of those groups on the policy process; and the constituencies of those groups and the benefits they have sought.

There is now a considerable literature on aging-based organizations in the United States. These accounts devote much of their attention to the mass-membership aging-based organizations, most notably the American Association of Retired Persons (AARP) with over 14 million members, and the National Council of Senior Citizens (NCSC) with over 4 million members. Attention is also given to aging-based organizations whose existence depends in large measure on the presence of older persons as consumers, clients, or subjects of research and scientific investigation (Hudson and Binstock, 1976).

What is most notable about these organizations in historical perspective is their relatively high levels of organizational development and sophistication. In this regard, current groups differ markedly from the pension reform organizations prominent some decades ago. As argued by Carlie (1969), these early organizations are better understood as social movements than interest groups, the principal difference being that they were an expression of broad-based and time-bound discontent rather than an expression of enduring interests and concerns associated with old age. As seen by students of these early organizations (Holtzman, 1963; Messinger, 1955; Pinner et al., 1959; Pratt, 1976), social dislocations intensified the deprivation of an already marginal group and, in doing this, increased their group consciousness. In such circumstances, energetic figures—Francis Townsend of the Townsend Movement, George McLain of the California pension movement—catalyzed the widespread discontent, put forth far-reaching if simplistic solutions, and unsettled elected officials at all levels of government. At its peak in 1936, the Townsend Movement may have had as many as 1.5 million members, and the McLain organization attained a level of about 70,000 members during the 1950s (Pinner et al., 1959).

The appearance and growth of these early social movements depended on highly personalized leadership and particular sets of circumstances. As a result, these movements failed to institutionalize and maintain themselves once the leadership and circumstances changed. The membership and influence of the Townsendites declined rapidly during the 1940s and 1950s, and the McLain organization withered following the death of its founder (Putnam, 1970). There has been considerable interest in the actual effect the Townsendites may have had on the passage of the original social security legislation during the 1930s, but a number of participants and scholars have tended to dismiss the movement's role (Altmeyer, 1968; Schlesinger, 1958; Witte, 1962).

The aging-based organizations that have grown up in more recent years have attained a level of organizational development typical of modern political interest groups generally. Unlike the early social movements, contemporary aging interest groups are marked—in the words of the organizational development literature—by secularized leadership, differentiated structures, and regularized resource flows. These organizations have increased the size and professionalism of their staffs and have expanded their resource base to include a greater proportion of non-membership support such as government grants and private philanthropy. They have also become highly skilled at gaining

access to and recognition from both governmental officials (Pratt, 1976) and political parties (Reimer and Binstock, 1978).

The membership figures of the two mass-based organizations, in particular, provide them with a formal legitimacy that few other organizations can equal (Pratt, 1976). Whether the positions taken by the groups actually reflect membership preferences and whether the groups, in fact, carry political weight commensurate with their numbers is less clear. Binstock (1972) notes that these groups have not demonstrated an ability ''to deliver'' their members' support on policy issues; he adds, however, that this is not essential so long as groups can convince political actors of their potency and representativeness. Fortunately for these groups, they have not yet been tested, although ongoing political and budgetary attacks on aging programs may eventually do this.

These perceptions notwithstanding, Olson (1965) suggests a theoretical basis for questioning the claims of these groups to both representativeness and influence. On the first point, Olson argues that most individuals do not join mass-membership organizations to pursue collective goals but rather to obtain the material benefits that are available only through membership. In the case of AARP, this line of reasoning led J. Walker (1981) to conclude that:

> the secret to [its] phenomenal growth, however, was not the attractiveness of the policies being advocated by the group; rather, it was the special medical insurance policies available to older people only through membership, the tours and vacation trips . . . and many useful personal services available for retired persons through membership. (p. 22)

While this assertion is difficult to verify, the popularity of material benefits that these organizations offer and the ease of joining and belonging to them given their nominal membership fees do raise a question about the members' commitment to the groups and their goals.

In claiming to be influential in the policy

process, the mass-membership groups emphasize the size of their membership and the presumed concerns of their members. For the two principal groups, AARP and NCSC, the claim is a striking one. However, the older population is so heterogeneous that lack of cohesion is almost a foregone conclusion on any but the most salient age-based issues such as significant cuts in Social Security or Medicare benefits. Certainly, the groups have been most vocal where older persons share common interests and have a strong stake in policy: retirement income, health benefits, and increased availability of home care benefits. Even here, however, the salience to older persons of specific programs and their views about them vary widely. The absence of cohesion has served to lessen the collective impact the aging-based groups might have, as illustrated in the early reluctance of AARP to endorse the Medicare legislation and the later reluctance of NCSC to stand at the forefront of the battle to eliminate mandatory retirement provisions.

The most hotly contested issue in the study of aging politics has been the political power of aging-based interest groups. While several studies of a few years ago credited aging groups with considerable influence or potential (Cottrell, 1971; Rose, 1965), more recent analyses have been more modest and selective in their assessments. Thus, while Pratt (1976) finds the aging groups, particularly NCSC, to have been particularly effective in the early and mid-1970s, he is cautious in attributing influence ot these groups during other periods. Williamson et al. (1982) see different authors as having either overestimated or underestimated "senior power," and argue that the aging groups have been most effective when they have been part of a broader coalition of interest groups, such as organized labor.

An even more restrained view of the influence of these organizations is found in studies of particular legislative histories. Most noteworthy, in fact, is that these studies tend to minimize the import of organized groups in the policy formation process, whereas books devoted to the workings, structures, and histories of interest groups tend to credit them with a variety of policy developments. Accounts of policy-making in Social Security (Derthick, 1979), age discrimination (Schuck, 1980), Supplemental Security Income (Burke and Burke, 1974), and even Medicare (Marmor, 1970) have attributed only marginal influence to aging interest groups.

There are some policy areas, however, in which aging-based groups have been decisive. These successes say much about the paramount interests of the groups as well as the kinds of politics in which the groups can be influential. Several observers have highlighted the key role of the aging-based groups in the enactment of various in-kind benefit programs in the areas of social services (Armour et al., 1981; Binstock, 1972; Hudson, 1973), long-term care (Mendelson and Hapgood, 1974; Vladeck, 1980), and research (Olson, 1982). In promoting in-kind benefits, the groups create a middleman role for themselves (Binstock, 1972), obtain concrete benefits for the elderly, and generate "disagreeable" constituency benefits for electorally oriented politicians (Lowi, 1969; Mayhew, 1974). Since the individual programs are relatively small (e.g., the Older Americans Act or Section 202 of the Housing and Community Development Act), they are viewed in distributive or positive-sum terms. Other constituencies and groups are unlikely to feel deprived by virtue of what the elderly or those serving them are receiving.

One criticism of such policies is that they serve the special interests of aging-based groups as much as they do their formally designated clients. A more substantial criticism holds that aging-based groups, in pursuing in-kind benefits in small packages for a small number of older persons, are neglecting issues and problems that are much more fundamental to the well-being of large numbers of other older persons. Binstock (1972) emphasizes the failure of the aging-based groups to press for reforms that would in any way redress the economic and social conditions of the severely disadvantaged aged;

Estes (1979) sees these small programs as piecemeal and remedial efforts that only reinforce the marginal status of the elderly in American society.

These activities may also reveal that aging-based groups have a greater concern for organizational autonomy and security than they do for the pursuit of political power. In the words of Williamson et al. (1982), "politics is not only the struggle for power and influence but autonomy and the desire to free oneself of constraints." There is a substantial sociological literature dating back to Michels (1949) stressing the primacy of these organizational concerns. Organizations pursue activities that will secure regular sources of external financial and political support and, toward those ends, create and maintain relationships that are symbiotic, reciprocal, and positive-sum.

The new "policy domains" of aging (Pratt, 1976) are based on relationships of this type. Domains formed on a triangular basis (Davidson, 1977) include aging-oriented executive branch agencies, aging-based interest groups, and legislative committees dealing with aging issues. Each party to the policy domain has a political commodity to offer the others (money, programs, visibility, contacts, support). So long as members are able to keep their relations with others free of outside influence or pressure, the members can proceed in a cooperative and mutually advantageous way. These policy domains have enabled aging-based groups to voice and represent at least some of the concerns of older persons. In doing so, aging-based groups have gained legitimacy and access as well as the organizational resources central to their own well-being.

Recent pressures on governmental spending appear, however, to be altering the environment that has allowed the symbiotic public/private relationships to prosper. In turn, this is altering the policy orientation of the aging-based groups. Policy domains survive in an environment of outside indifference, and successive rounds of budget cuts and program consolidations are dislodging these domains across the policy landscape. A response to this new turbulence in the aging policy environment is the birth and increasing influence of the 26-member Leadership Council of Aging Organizations which now represents the collective interests of previously uninvolved or quarrelsome aging-based groups (Pratt, 1982). This broad-based group is voicing the organized aging community's recent concerns about larger issues such as Social Security and restrictive spending targets and budgetary ceilings.

These new outside political threats will have important organizational consequences for aging-based groups. These groups, to varying degrees, have always claimed to represent the general interests of all older persons. As observed by Binstock (1974) and Pratt (1976), groups making such a claim significantly enhance their organizational legitimacy. For groups to maintain the credibility of this claim under the present political circumstances, they must devote greater attention and resources to defending the broad benefit base of all older persons. At this point, it is not clear whether these groups will be successful in staving off cuts and restructurings. It will be important for them, however, to adopt and maintain positions that tie them to reforms their constituents can be convinced to support.

The aging-based groups have been particularly influential in policy areas that are closely tied to their own survival and well-being. Their influence is more suspect with regard to larger policy areas that have benefited large numbers of older persons, such as income and health policies (Lammers, 1983). So long as these outside pressures remain, these groups will face two problems: preserving small programs for which they are responsible and on which some of them are largely dependent; and defending large programs for which they are less responsible but which are central to their claims to representativeness. These problems, in fact, serve to update the earlier observations of Binstock (1974) and Estes (1979), who asked whether any disadvantaged group in society can gain access to the resource system without itself becoming a special interest.

Political Elites

The actions of political elites have been central in the formulation of age-related social policies. Both historically and cross-nationally, political elites have served frequently as the initiators, architects, and engineers of policy enactments and programs for the elderly. In looking at the impact of elites on aging policy, it is necessary to focus attention on key individuals whose ideas and positions placed them at the center and/or in control of major policy developments. These individuals impact on policy in a manner distinct from that associated with the push and pull of interest groups. Elite actors may or may not predicate their actions on visions of a better society, but even their more strategic calculations extend beyond the more purely organizational concerns associated with interest group activity.

Three types of elites have played central roles in aging policy developments: national leaders, reformers, and policy professionals. National leaders have played a central role in the initiation and enactment of aging policy. Among those leaders are found, most notably, Bismarck, Lloyd-George, and Franklin Roosevelt. Here as well one finds most clearly displayed the latent functions of social policies. In Germany, early welfare state programs owed their origins to Bismarck's political calculations and preemptive strategies employed against the Social Democrats; in Britain, these programs were partially a response by Lloyd-George to the nascent Labor party growing up on his left. In the United States, dire economic circumstances generated the opportunity to save the capitalist system (Olson, 1982), reduce unemployment among the young (Graebner, 1981), and bring American social policy into the twentieth century (Schlesinger, 1958).

Reformers of various persuasions have played a central role in supplying ideas for social change and the arguments for why it is needed. The accounts and proposals of Booth, Rowntree, the Webbs, and Beveridge in Great Britain, and of Addams, Rubinow, Epstein, and Commons in the United States forced the issue of reform and provided guidance for going about it. In the case of the United States, Lubove (1968) has argued:

> To understand the emergence of the aged as a major source of social politics in the 1920s it is not enough to cite long-term demographic, economic, and familial trends, or figures demonstrating the scope of old-age dependency. The appearance of a new social insurance leadership, which adopted old-age pensions as the primary objective, was equally important . . . (p. 137)

In the case of these reformers, in contrast with age-based interest groups or leadership figures, rational explanations link the life circumstances of categories of individuals to prevailing economic, social, and political conditions. The reforms proposed varied widely depending on the values and diagnosis of the reformer, as noted by Williamson et al. (1982) in their discussion of individualist, corporatist, and collectivist reformers in the United States. For all the reformers, however, there is a positive regard for some version of the public interest that both allowed and compelled political elites to justify the initiation and enactment of policy on those grounds.

An important development in recent years is the "professionalization of reform" (Moynihan, 1965), a change that is strikingly similar to that which occurred earlier within age-based interest groups. The tendency to rely on resident experts to initiate policy changes began with the social security proposals of the 1930s and the Committee on Economic Security. The tendency has grown in importance since then. The "brain trust" of the 1930s is now understood to be—and in hundreds of different settings—"the community of policy professionals" (Campbell, 1978). This transition has been gradual but inexorable. In the United States, the resident expert is best personified by Wilbur Cohen, who joined the Committee on Economic Security as a young staffer, worked to expand governmental obligations and coverage, and completed his governmental career as secretary of health, education, and welfare, working until midnight of his last day in office on finalizing liberal regulations (Burke and Burke, 1974; Derthick, 1975).

The "elite ideas," entrepreneurial activities, and altruistic motivations of resident experts serve not only to frame debate but also to generate and determine concrete policy outcomes (Campbell, 1978). The role of resident experts has been given particularly heavy emphasis in Derthick's (1979) account of American social security development. In her words:

> Policy has been made by a relatively constricted and autonomous set of actors with a strong sense of proprietorship in the program. Decisions about social security were generally made in isolation from decisions about other governmental activities, both structurally and financially. Within the proprietary group, there was a high level of consensus about guiding principles. Initiatives and choices generally followed paths well defined by programmatic doctrines and were treated as if they were technical matters. Major alternatives were hardly considered. The dominant mode was maintenance and enlargement of the program. (p. 7)

Heclo (1974) also emphasizes the role of bureaucratic and allied experts, and argues that, if forced to choose "one group among all the separate political factors as most consistently important . . . , the bureaucracies of Britain and Sweden loom predominant in the policies studied."

This phenomenon of bureaucratic dominance is particularly evident in less important policy areas. A study by Campbell (1978) of policy innovation in Japan looks at "small-new" aging policies and singles out the importance of bureaucrats and their ideas and activities. In the case of the American states, Epstein and Browne's (1978) analysis concludes that the involvement of prominent elites lends a critical ingredient of legitimacy that activates and expands agendas. Conversely, they found little evidence that those items reaching the agenda required widespread public support or even the interest of those directly affected.

Where the political system allows it, elites and their ideas can create a perception of need where it did not exist before, propose "resolutions" that frame the policy debate (if not the outcome), and generate policies that "take on a life of their own." It is to this last tendency that discussion now turns.

Existing Policies and Programs

The state of public policy at any given point is an important factor in shaping and constraining subsequent policy activity. First, existing policies serve as an unequivocal point against which all actors must base future actions. Second, those involved in formulating, implementing, and evaluating policy enhance their own positions and influence by gaining access to the resources that existing policies generate—dollars, legitimacy, and domains. In these two senses a longitudinal perspective of the policy process typically shows that policy at one point in time is the best predictor of policy at a later time.

Policy serving as a base point affecting future activity is closely tied to the theory of incrementalism. In the incremental understanding, existing policy represents the commitments and sunk costs of involved parties who are further constrained in their efforts by limited time, money, and information. Incrementalism weighs the current state of policy heavily in stressing that policy-making is a process of small adjustments to what already exists rather than a comprehensive review of all that might be done.

Derthick (1979) and Heclo (1974), among others, have argued that policy-based incrementalism is a core ingredient of the decision-making process in the aging policy area. Derthick concludes that adopting the "incremental mode" was probably the most important adjustment made by policy elites involved with Social Security; they learned not to ask for the whole pie at once but rather for "one piece at a time." Heclo develops a "political learning" model to explain the seemingly disjointed decision-making processes and uneven influence of various policy elites and institutions involved in pension policy developments in Britain and Sweden. He argues that politics and policy are often not so much about power and influence as they are about uncertainty and "puzzlement." This puzzlement results in an indirect form of "collective learning" as institutions and actors wend toward interim solutions that manifest themselves in programs, provisions, and regulations. These solutions, in whatever way they are brokered and negotiated, come to serve as benchmarks that define a new, if only modified, policy reality. At any point in time existing policy is a snapshot that makes fixed and singular a process that has been continuous and multifocused.

Another form of policy-based incrementalism is policy imitation and diffusion across nations. General commentaries on pension and welfare developments note the spread of similar policy provisions across Europe or to the British Commonwealth countries (Collier and Messick, 1975; Kaim-Caudle, 1973). The study by Collier and Messick modifies the economic development hypothesis presented earlier in two important ways. They note, first, that among the nations first developing social security systems, diffusion is from nations with a lower level of modernization to those with higher levels. Second, nations adopting systems at later dates tend to do so at levels of economic development considerably lower than was the case with the earliest adopters. Coupled with historical material showing leaders and officials in different nations openly imitating previous interventions, Collier and Messick call for greater attention to the innovation and diffusion process. Leichter's (1979) cross-national investigation in health policy-making stresses both how policy-makers were constrained by their predecessors' choices and the ways in which policy imitation took place across nations. Imitation was clearly at work in Britain and the Soviet Union and, in the case of Japan, Leichter sees it as having been

practically compulsive. In keeping with these arguments, Scharf (1981) believes that the "age of system" variable found in the economic development literature may actually be a partial surrogate for the likelihood of one system emulating and imitating another.

The second general point concerning the role of policy is that existing policy not only frames the debate but also generates pressures and incentives directed toward that policy's expansion and liberalization. When policy is formally enacted with its attendant provisions and appropriations, opportunities for interested parties are created, and self-interest becomes a key ingredient.

The case of public policies pertaining to nursing homes in the United States is perhaps the most stark example of policy provisions permitting the creation of an entire industry. This happened as service providers were able to broker open-ended public appropriations with a broad-based need for institutional care in the absence of other care alternatives. In this case, Heclo's notion of puzzlement is captured by Vladeck's (1980) observation that "the purposiveness in the behavior of those who have made public policy for nursing homes over the past forty years should not be overestimated" (p. 30). Vladeck goes on to detail the interplay of policy provisions and vested interests, noting in particular that it is difficult for decision-makers at some later point to unmake past mistakes and the patterns of behavior they have generated. Feder (1977) makes an analogous argument in the case of Medicare, arguing that hospital and medical interests have successfully resisted policy reforms in the areas of cost containment and quality assurance.

A study by J. Walker (1981) analyzed the ways in which policy enactments were at the heart of the rapid growth in the numbers and size of interest groups in the United States during the 1960s and 1970s. These groups were unable to rely on public goods as incentives to recruit and retain members; they also found that there were limits to the utility of ancillary benefits. As a result, these groups sought out and found funds from beyond their ranks, most notably private donors, foundations, and government. For nonprofit interest groups—one of the four types of groups investigated by Walker—government funding supplanted foundation grants as the largest single source of outside resources in the period after 1960. Moreover, Walker's data show that for groups brought into existence with the aid of a "patron," there is a continued pattern of dependence on that source.

Walker also finds that reliance on government for support results in greater dependency than reliance on any other outside source. While government agencies have a long history of close working relations with private sector counterparts, the enactment of new domestic policies in the United States during the 1960s added the ingredient of policy itself. Nowhere has this been more notable than in the case of aging, with Walker finding that more than half of the groups in his sample have come into existence since the watershed year of 1965. In aging as in other areas, policies have spawned new groups, and the policies and the groups have become interdependent.

There are important normative implications if policy-making actually does occur in accordance with policy-based incrementalism. The first, addressed by Walker, is that, procedurally, the democratic model in which decision-makers respond to the demands of citizens is often an incomplete or partially inverted understanding of what is actually transpiring. Policies can build on themselves, as policy elites act to protect and expand policy domains rather than acting in the interest of broader publics or the groups they represent.

The substantive consequences of a closed policy-making process are also serious. Since decision-making is restricted to a relative few, those individuals have the incentive and the ability to put forth options in keeping with their own professional skills and interests. Thus, Estes (1979) argues that the problem addressed by the Older Americans Act continues, after a decade, to be one of "organizational and technical management, re-

solvable by technocrats, planners, and administrators" (p. 57). Other examples are found in the areas of health care, education, and mental health, where policy has resulted in special forms of privilege and control (Lowi, 1969).

Finally, policies have a double-edged effect on groups. In addition to spawning groups, policies can both destroy old ones and preclude new ones. Enactment of Social Security in 1935 stole the organizational thunder of the Townsend Movement, resulting in its steady decline in the 1940s (Messinger, 1955; Williamson et al., 1982). In the case of in-kind policies, the close linkages between policies and groups often comes to mean that a group without "its" policy is in serious difficulty. In the United States, the fate of the Gray Panthers is problematic because its raison d'être is to a considerable degree based on its standing above and beyond the organization of contemporary social service programs.

Concentrated Capital

The appearance of several analyses employing the perspective of political economy is a major addition to the literature addressing factors behind the development of old-age legislation. This perspective focuses on the workings of the social and economic institutions of capitalist market economies of the Western world. Authors using this approach find the organization and shortcomings of contemporary aging policies grounded in the imperative and logic of market economies. Additionally, they argue that dire predictions about the future of aging policies reflect the deep-seated contradictions of capitalism rather than the demographic and economic changes identified by most "liberal accommodationists" (Olson, 1982). To political economists, these accommodationists see problems of the elderly, such as isolation and lack of community supports, as special or unique. The political economist sees the elderly as one social aggregation among many whose welfare is a function of a political system dominated by concentrated capital and class politics (Guillemard, 1977; Estes et al., 1982).

Political economists who analyze the social situation of the elderly argue that contemporary social gerontology accepts existing economic and social institutions as given and proposes reforms that are either trivial or irrelevant. Townsend (1981) refers to the individualistic approach adopted by "most social gerontologists" as one borrowed from an admixture of neoclassical economic theory, functionalism in sociology, and the more descriptive traditions of social work and social administration. In this view, social gerontologists, like others writing in the pluralist tradition, place heavy emphasis on political process variables, and in so doing have divorced politics from underlying social and economic structures.

A major defect of the field of gerontology has been the tendency to segregate analysis of the aged and their problems from the same problems suffered by other have-not groups throughout society. Whereas the liberal may see age segregation as a problem best addressed through such remedial activities as services integration, the political economist finds the phenomenon more pernicious. Politics, programs, and research based on age distinctions obfuscate the more fundamental divisions based on class (A. Walker, 1981). They are thus understood to be part of the problem rather than the solution, since they hinder the development of more fundamental and far-reaching policies taking cognizance of social and economic realities.

Olson (1982) argues that monopoly capital and the state, in the interests of accumulation and profits, have fostered dependency and subjugation on older persons. Then, in designing remedies for the problems they have created, they have further enhanced their own dominant position. Income programs better serve the needs of capital than of older persons, since they reinforce racial and sexual stratification and increase rather than reduce income inequalities among older persons and between older and younger generations. In the case of housing, the dominance of capital is shown through higher prices, tight credit, and gentrification. In health care, professional and corporate interests have continued to control the medical marketplace while the state has poured massive funds into the Medicare and Medicaid systems, the result being rampant inflation and excessive profits. In the social services, programs have little more than incidental impact on the problems at hand, and they tend, in any event, to foster dependence.

Estes (1979) and Townsend (1981) place a somewhat greater emphasis on social structure than does Olson. Estes, invoking the social construction of reality perspective of contemporary sociology, sees the marginal status of the elderly and the remedial orientation of public policy to be largely the result of America having defined the aging process and aging itself to be "a problem." The American response has not addressed a different reality that sees older persons as systematically disadvantaged and constituting a status group whose legitimate economic and social needs go unmet. Public policy, as seen by Estes, helps individuals adjust to their inferior status but does not reform institutional patterns that create and perpetuate that status. Both Townsend and Estes stress the ways in which older persons as well as society more generally come to view the elderly as unable to promote their own interests and well-being. Forced from the workplace, housed in age-segregated facilities, and served by age-based legislation, the elderly become in both perception and reality a distinct and second-class population.

A major element of the structural interpretation is that "aging legislation" is not really about aging at all. The function of much aging and other social legislation is preserving existing institutional arrangements by controlling and coopting those whose interests are nominally being addressed. Graebner's (1981) study of retirement in America deals with this theme. In his view, Social Security was retirement legislation initiated to solve particular labor market problems; it was not social legislation designed to provide a pension or "security."

That retirement has come to be viewed as a separate, distinct, and normatively acceptable status represents the ascendancy of a collective consciousness that varies considerably from the early history and rationale behind Social Security. He sees other public and private pension legislation in America as also designed to deal primarily with labor market problems. A. Walker (1981) makes a similar argument in the case of Great Britain.

Graebner's study, however, goes beyond a purely structural interpretation to meld these elements with the Progressive legacy in the United States. He recounts the early stages of age discrimination in America, noting the overriding concern of the Progressives with efficiency, stamina, and expertise. The Progressive mentality, combined with economic imperatives associated with labor market conditions, yielded public policy about retirement. As retirement came to be economically viable, it also came to be normatively sanctioned through popular application of the disengagement and activity theories that Estes and Townsend argue lie at the heart of contemporary age segregation. In Graebner's view, however, the underlying economic and political factors reasserted themselves in the late 1970s. Demographic and labor force trends and the condition of the social security trust funds generated concern for what he calls "the new efficiency," which "resembles nothing so much as the old efficiency of the Progressive era."

Authors adopting the political economic perspective have enriched the policy and aging literature by reintroducing economic and structural variables. This broader perspective raises important policy-related issues. Was the Townsend Movement radical in origins and purpose, or was it almost slavishly devoted to the preservation of American economic, social, and political institutions? Are the weak redistributive effects of Social Security the result of monopoly capital extending itself to accommodate the presence of an older population, or are they the result of the weak political institutions that were all that America's "fragment culture" made necessary? And the political economy perspective has reinvigorated a debate that has been central to comparative political analysis since World War II. Do welfare state policies control the destinies of working populations through concentration, manipulation, and quiescence, or do such policies provide the programmatic basis for maintaining democratic stability in the industrial nations?

Summary

The factors reviewed above account in large part for the origins, development, and current status of age-related policies in the Western industrial nations. Their application may vary by nation and by policy, and there is no larger theoretical consensus as to why responses have taken their present form.

What can be said, however, is that aging policy will continue to depend on the role and makeup of these different factors and will be affected by changes in them. Economic growth has provided an underlying ability for systems to make benefits available, and demographic patterns made necessary those benefits. Contemporary concerns about the ability of systems to maintain and expand benefits in the face of aging populations highlight the possibility that the requisite resources may not be fully available in the years ahead. Such conditions could, in turn, weaken the widespread political consensus that has supported development of aging policies across nations, although there is very little current evidence that popular support is eroding. However, questions about the distribution and magnitude of aging policy benefits have been raised by political elites. The relative priority many elite actors have given to aging policies and allocations as contrasted with those of the unemployed and children, among others, may lessen. It seems certain that elite actors will not be able to invoke the needs and legitimacy of the aging in their desire to promote expansive social welfare initiatives generally as they have in the past. Finally, changes such as these will undo the workings of policy-based incrementalism through which programs gradually expanded and those associated with them were able to solidify their spheres of influence.

Should these underlying factors be altered, the pressures, demands, and cohesiveness of the organized aging will play a more central role than has been necessary to this point. Because of the other factors discussed above, it has not been possible to accurately assess the power or even the importance of the aging-based groups and their political activities. Should traditional resources, norms, agendas, and expectations about aging policy and benefits shift in line with the comments here, the ability of the aging and their groups to press and lobby for programs and allocations will be more important than before, and assessments about their power will be more accurate. The roles of the elderly as actors in political systems and as recipients of benefits generated by those systems may become less distinct in the years ahead.

REFERENCES

Aaron, H. J. 1967. Social security: International comparisons. *In* O. Eckstein (ed.), *Studies in the Economics of Income Maintenance,* pp. 13–48. Washington, D.C.: Brookings Institution.

Aberbach, J. D., Putnam, R. P., and Rockman, B. A. 1981. *Bureaucrats and Politicans in Western Democracies.* Cambridge, Mass.: Harvard University Press.

Abramson, P. R. 1976. Generational change and the decline of party identification in America, 1952–1974. *American Political Science Review* 70:469–478.

Abramson, P. R. 1979. Developing party identification: A further examination of life-cycle, generational, and period effects. *American Journal of Political Science* 23:78–96.

Abramson, P. R., and Aldrich, J. H. 1982. The decline of electoral participation in America. *American Political Science Review* 76:502–521.

Achenbaum, W. A. 1980. Did Social Security attempt to regulate the poor? Historical reflections on Piven and Cloward's social-welfare model. *Research on Aging* 2:470–488.

Almond, G., and Verba, S. 1965. *The Civic Culture.* Boston: Little, Brown.

Altmeyer, A. J. 1968. *The Formative Years of Social Security.* Madison: University of Wisconsin Press.

Armour, P. K., Estes, C. L., and Noble, M. L. 1981. The continuing design and implementation problems of a national policy on aging: Title III of the Older Americans Act. *In* R. B. Hudson (ed.), *The Aging in Politics,* pp. 199–219. Springfield, Ill.: Charles C. Thomas.

Ashford, D. E. 1981. The British and French social security systems: Welfare states by intent and by default. Paper delivered at the 1981 annual meeting of the American Political Science Association, New York.

Baker, K., Dalton, R., and Hildebrandt, K. 1981. *Germany Transformed.* Cambridge, Mass.: Harvard University Press.

Barnes, S. 1972. The legacy of Fascism: Generational differences in Italian political attitudes and behavior. *Comparative Political Studies* 5:41–58.

Beer, S. 1965. *British Politics in the Collectivist Age.* New York: Alfred A. Knopf.

Binstock, R. H. 1972. Interest-group liberalism and the politics of aging. *The Gerontologist* 12:265–280.

Binstock, R. H. 1974. Aging and the future of American politics. *The Annals* 415:199–212.

Binstock, R. H. 1983. The aged as scapegoat. *The Gerontologist* 23:136–143.

Burke, V., and Burke, V. 1974. *Nixon's Good Deed.* New York: Columbia University Press.

Butler, D., and Stokes, D. 1971. *Political Change in Britain.* New York: St. Martin's Press.

Butterfield, F. 1979. Aging and leadership is worrying Peking. *New York Times,* Nov. 26. 7.

Campbell, A. 1971. Politics through the life cycle. *The Gerontologist* 11:112–117.

Campbell, A. Converse, P. E., Miller, W. E., and Stokes, D. 1960. *The American Voter.* New York: John Wiley.

Campbell, J. C. 1978. Entrepreneurial bureaucrats and programs for old people in Japan. Paper delivered to the 1978 annual meeting of the American Political Science Association, New York.

Campbell, J. C., and Strate, J. 1981. Are old people conservative? *The Gerontologist* 21:580–591.

Carlie, M. K. 1969. The politics of age: Interest group or social movement? *The Gerontologist* 9:259–263.

Claggett, W. 1980. The life cycle and generational models of the development of partisanship: A test based on the delayed enfranchisement of women. *Social Science Quarterly* 60:643–650.

Clemente, F. 1975. Age and the perception of national priorities. *The Gerontologist* 15:61–63.

Collier, D., and Messick, R. E. 1975. Prerequisites vs. diffusion: Testing alternative explanations of social security adoption. *American Political Science Review* 69:1299–1315.

Comstock, G., Chafee, S., Katzman, N., McCombs, M., and Roberts, D. 1978. *Television and Human Behavior.* New York: Columbia University Press.

Converse, P. E. 1964. The nature of belief systems in mass publics. *In* D. E. Apter, (ed.), *Ideology and Discontent,* pp. 206–261. Glencoe, Ill.: Free Press.

Converse, P. E. 1969. Of time and partisan stability. *Comparative Political Studies* 2:139–171.

Converse, P. E. 1976. *The Dynamics of Party Support.* Beverly Hills, Calif.: Sage.

Converse, P. E., and Dupeux, G. 1962. Politicization of the electorate in France and the United States. *Public Opinion Quarterly* 26:1-23.

Cottrell, W. F. 1971. *Government and Non-Governmental Organizations.* Washington, D.C.: White House Conference on Aging.

Cowgill, D. O., and Holmes, L. D. 1972. *Aging and Modernization.* New York: Appleton-Century-Crofts.

Crittenden, J. 1962. Aging and party affiliation. *Public Opinion Quarterly* 26:648-657.

Curtis, J. E., and Lambert, R. D. 1976. Voting, election interest and age: National findings for English and French Canadians. *Canadian Journal of Political Science* 9:293-307.

Cutler, N. E. 1968. The alternative effects of generations and aging upon political behavior: A cohort analysis of attitudes toward foreign policy, 1946-1966. Oak Ridge National Laboratory, Oak Ridge, Tenn.

Cutler, N. E. 1969. Generation, maturation, and party affiliation: A cohort analysis. *Public Opinion Quarterly* 33:583-588.

Cutler, N. E. 1977. Demographic, social-psychological, and political factors in the politics of aging: A foundation for research in "political gerontology." *American Political Science Review* 71:1011-1025.

Cutler, S. J., and Kaufman, R. L. 1975. Cohort changes in political attitudes: Tolerance of ideological nonconformity. *Public Opinion Quarterly* 39:69-81.

Cutler, S. J., Lentz, S. A., Muha, M. J., and Riter, R. N. 1980. Aging and conservatism: Cohort changes in attitudes about legalized abortions. *Journal of Gerontology* 35:115-123.

Cutright, P. 1965. Political structure, economic development, and national social security programs. *American Journal of Sociology* 70:537-550.

Dahrendorf, R. 1967. *Society and Democracy in Germany.* Garden City, N.Y.: Doubleday.

Dalton, R. J. 1977. Was there a revolution? A note on generational versus life cycle explanations of value differences. *Comparative Political Studies* 9:459-473.

Davidson, R. H. 1977. Breaking up those "cozy triangles": An impossible dream? *In* S. Welch and J. Peters (eds.), *Legislative Reform and Public Policy,* pp. 30-53. New York: Praeger.

Davis-Friedman, D. 1978. Welfare practices in rural China. *World Development* 6:609-619.

Dennis, J., and McCrone, D. J. 1970. Pre-adult development of political party identification in western democracies. *Comparative Political Studies* 3:243-263.

Derthick, M. 1975. *Uncontrollable Spending for Social Services Grants.* Washington, D.C.: Brookings Institution.

Derthick, M. 1979. *Policymaking for Social Security.* Washington, D.C.: Brookings Institution.

Douglass, E., Cleveland, W., and Maddox, G. 1974. Political attitudes, age, and aging: A cohort analysis of archival data. *Journal of Gerontology* 29:666-675.

Edinger, L. 1968. *Politics in Germany.* Boston: Little, Brown.

Edinger, L. 1983. Politics of the aged: Orientations in major liberal democracies. New York: Brookdale Center on Aging and Adult Human Development, Columbia University.

Eldersveld, S. J. 1973. Party identification in India in comparative perspective. *Comparative Political Studies* 6:271-295.

Epstein, L. K., and Browne, W. P. 1978. The social and political conditions of issue credibility: Public policy and the elderly. Paper delivered to the 1978 annual meeting of the American Political Science Association, New York.

Epstein, L. K., and Browne, W. P. 1979. Public opinion and the elderly: An exploration of the "sometimes it's this way and sometimes it's that way" principle. Paper presented for delivery at the annual meeting of the Midwest Political Science Association, Chicago.

Estes, C. L. 1979. *The Aging Enterprise.* San Francisco: Jossey-Bass.

Estes, C. L., Swan, J. H., and Gerard, L. E. 1982. Dominant and competing paradigms in gerontology: Toward a political economy of aging. *Ageing and Society* 2:151-164.

Evan, W. M. 1965. Cohort analysis of attitude data. *In* J. M. Beshers (ed.), *Computer Methods in the Analysis of Large-Scale Social Systems,* pp. 117-142. Cambridge, Mass.: Joint Center of Urban Studies of the M.I.T. and Harvard University.

Feder, J. 1977. *Medicare: The Politics of Federal Hospital Insurance.* Lexington, Mass.: D. C. Heath.

Fengler, A. P., and Wood, V. 1972. The generation gap: An analysis of attitudes on contemporary issues. *The Gerontologist* 12:124-128.

Fishel, J. 1969. Party ideology and the congressional challenger. *American Political Science Review* 63:1213-1232.

Flanagan, S. C. 1979. Value change and partisan change in Japan: The silent revolution revisited. *Comparative Politics* 11:253-278.

Flanagan, S. C. 1980. Value cleavages, economic cleavages, and the Japanese voter. *American Journal of Political Science* 24:177-206.

Flanagan, S. C. 1982. Changing values in advanced industrial societies: Inglehart's silent revolution from the perspective of Japanese findings. *Comparative Political Studies* 14:403-444.

Foner, A. 1972. The polity. *In* M. W. Riley, M. Johnson, and A. Foner (eds.), *Aging and Society,* Vol. 3, pp. 115-159. New York: Russell Sage Foundation.

Free, L., and Cantril, H. 1968. *The Political Beliefs of Americans: A Study of Public Opinion.* New York: Simon and Schuster.

Gergen, K., and Back, K. 1965. Aging, time perspective, and perferred solutions to international conflicts. *Journal of Conflict Resolution* 9:177-186.

Giele, J. Z. 1982. Family and social networks. *In* R. H. Binstock, W. S. Chow, and J. S. Schulz (eds.), *In-*

ternational Perspectives on Aging: Population and Policy Challenges, pp. 41–74. New York: United Nations Fund for Population Activities.

Glamser, F. 1974. The importance of age to conservative opinions: A multivariate analysis. Journal of Gerontology 29:549–554.

Glenn, N. D. 1969. Aging, disengagement and opinionation. Public Opinion Quarterly 33:17–33.

Glenn, N. D. 1974. Aging and conservatism. The Annals 415:176–186.

Glenn, N. D., and Grimes, M. 1968. Aging, voting, and political interest. American Sociological Review 33:563–575.

Glenn, N. D., and Hefner, T. 1972. Further evidence on aging and party identification. Public Opinion Quarterly 36:31–47.

Graebner, W. 1981. A History of Retirement. New Haven, Conn.: Yale University Press.

Guillemard, A. M. 1977. A critical analysis of governmental policies on aging from a Marxist sociological perspective. Paris: Center for the Study of Social Movements.

Hartz, L. 1955. The Liberal Tradition in America. New York: Harcourt Brace.

Heclo, H. 1974. Modern Social Politics in Britain and Sweden. New Haven, Conn.: Yale University Press.

Heidenheimer, A. J. 1973. The politics of public education, health and welfare in the U.S.A. and western Europe: How growth and reform potentials have differed. British Journal of Political Science 3:315–340.

Heilig, P. 1979. Self-interest and attitude patterns among the elderly. Paper prepared for delivery at the annual meeting of the Midwest Political Science Association, Chicago.

Hill, K. 1974. Belgium: Political change in a segmented society. In R. Rose (ed.), Electoral Behavior: A Comparative Handbook, pp. 29–107. New York: Free Press.

Hofstadter, R. 1948. The American Political Tradition. New York: Knopf.

Holtzman, A. 1963. The Townsend Movement: A Political Study. New York: Bookman.

Hout, M., and Knoke, D. 1975. Change in voting turnout, 1952–1972. Public Opinion Quarterly 39:52–68.

Hudson, R. B. 1973. Client politics and federalism: The case of the Older Americans Act. Paper delivered at the 1973 annual meeting of the American Political Science Association, New Orleans.

Hudson, R. B. 1978a. Emerging pressures on public policies for the elderly. Society 15:30–33.

Hudson, R. B. 1978b. The "graying" of the federal budget and its consequences for old-age policy. The Gerontologist 18:428–440.

Hudson, R. B., and Binstock, R. H. 1976. Political systems and aging. In R. H. Binstock and E. Shanas (eds.), Handbook of Aging and the Social Sciences, 1st ed., pp. 369–400. New York: Van Nostrand Reinhold.

Huntington, S. P. 1966. Political modernization: America vs. Europe. World Politics 18:378–414.

Hyman, H. H., and Sheatsley, P. B. 1964. Attitudes toward desegregation. Scientific American 211:16–23.

Ike, N. 1973. Economic growth and intergenerational change in Japan. American Political Science Review 67:1194–1203.

Inglehart, R. 1971. The silent revolution in Europe: Intergenerational change in post-industrial societies. American Political Science Review 65:991–1017.

Inglehart, R. 1977. The Silent Revolution: Changing Values and Political Styles among Western Publics. Princeton, N.J.: Princeton University Press.

Inglehart, R. 1981. Post-materialism in an environment of insecurity. American Political Science Review 75:880–900.

Inglehart, R. 1982. Changing values in Japan and the West. Comparative Political Studies 14:445–479.

Inglehart, R., and Hochstein, A. 1972. Alignment and dealignment of the electorate in France and the United States. Comparative Political Studies 5:343–372.

International Labor Office. 1979. The Cost of Social Security, 1972–1974. Geneva: International Labor Office.

Jennings, M. K. 1979. Another look at the life cycle and political participation. American Journal of Political Science 23:755–771.

Jennings, M. K., and Beck, P. A. 1979. Political periods and political participation. American Political Science Review 73:737–750.

Jennings, M. K., and Niemi, R. G. 1975. Continuity and change in political orientations: A longitudinal study of two generations. American Political Science Review 69:1316–1335.

Jennings, M. K., and Niemi, R. G. 1981. Generations and Politics. Princeton, N. J.: Princeton University Press.

Johnson & Higgins. 1979. 1979 Study of American Attitudes toward Pensions and Retirement. New York: Johnson & Higgins.

Kaim-Caudle, P. R. 1973. Comparative Social Policy and Social Security. London: Martin Robertson.

Killian, L., and Haer, J. 1958. Variables related to attitudes regarding school desegregation among white Southerners. Sociometry 21:159–164.

King, A. 1971. Ideologies as predictors of public policy patterns: A comparative analysis. Paper delivered at the 1971 annual meeting of the American Political Science Association, New York.

Klingemann, H. D. 1973. Dimensions of political belief systems: Levels of conceptualization as a variable, some results for USA and FRG 1968/1969. Comparative Political Studies 5:93–106.

Knoke, D., and Hout, M. 1974. Social and demographic factors in American political party affiliations, 1952–1972. American Sociological Review 39:700–713.

Kubota, A., and Ward, R. E. 1970. Family influence and political socialization in Japan. Comparative Political Studies 3:140–175.

Kutza, E. A. 1981. *The Benefits of Old Age.* Chicago: University of Chicago Press.

Lammers, W. W. 1983. *Public Policy and the Aging.* Washington, D.C.: Congressional Quarterly Press.

Lammers, W. W., and Nyomarkay, J. L. 1980. The disappearing senior leaders. *Research on Aging* 2:329–349.

Lehman, H. 1953. *Age and Achievement.* Princeton, N. J.: Princeton University Press.

Leichter, H. M. 1979. *A Comparative Approach to Policy Analysis: Health Care Policy in Four Nations.* Cambridge: Cambridge University Press.

Lerner, D., Pool, I. de S., and Schueller, G. 1966. The Nazi elite. *In* H. Lasswell and D. Lerner (eds.), *World Revolutionary Elites: Studies in Coercive Ideological Movements,* pp. 194–318. Cambridge, Mass.: The M.I.T. Press.

Lijphart, A. 1974. The Netherlands: Continuity and changing voting behavior. *In* R. Rose (ed.), *Electoral Behavior: A Comparative Handbook,* pp. 227–268. New York: Free Press.

Lowi, T. J. 1969. *The End of Liberalism.* Boston: Norton.

Lubove, R. 1968. *The Struggle for Social Security.* Cambridge, Mass.: Harvard University Press.

Marmor, T. R. 1970. *The Politics of Medicare.* London: Routledge and Kegan Paul.

Marshall, T. H. 1963. *Class, Citizenship and Social Development.* Garden City, N. Y.: Doubleday.

Mason, K., Mason, W., Winsborough, H. H., and Poole, W. K. 1973. Some methodological issues in cohort analysis of archival data. *American Sociological Review* 38:242–258.

Mayhew, D. R. 1974. *Congress: The Electoral Connection.* New Haven, Conn.: Yale University Press.

McConnell, G. 1966. *Private Power and American Democracy.* New York: Knopf.

Mendelson, M. A., and Hapgood, D. 1974. The political economy of nursing homes. *The Annals* 415:95–105.

Messinger, S. L. 1955. Organizational transformation: A case study of a declining social movement. *American Sociological Review* 20:3–10.

Michels, R. 1949. *Political Parties.* Glencoe, Ill.: Free Press.

Milbrath, L. W., and Goel, M. L. 1977. *Political Participation.* Chicago: Rand McNally.

Moynihan, D. P. 1965. The professionalization of reform. *The Public Interest* 1:6–16.

National Commission on Social Security. 1980. *A Nationwide Survey of Attitudes toward Social Security.* Prepared by Peter D. Hart Research Associates. Washington, D.C.: National Commission on Social Security.

National Council on the Aging. 1975. *The Myth and Reality of Aging in America.* Washington, D.C.: The National Council on the Aging.

National Council on the Aging. 1981. *Aging in the Eighties: America in Transition.* Washington, D.C.: The National Council on the Aging.

Nie, N., Verba, S., and Kim, J. 1974. Political participation and the life cycle. *Comparative Politics* 6:319–340.

Norpoth, H. 1978. Party identification in West Germany: Tracing an elusive concept. *Comparative Political Studies* 11:36–61.

North, R., and Pool, I de S. 1966. Kuomintang and Chinese communist elites. *In* H. Lasswell and D. Lerner (eds.), *World Revolutionary Elites: Studies in Coercive Ideological Movements,* pp. 319–455. Cambridge, Mass.: The M.I.T. Press.

Olson, L. K. 1982. *The Political Economy of Aging.* New York: Columbia University Press.

Olson, M. 1965. *The Logic of Collective Action.* Cambridge, Mass.: Harvard University Press.

Palmore, E. 1975. *The Honorable Elders.* Durham, N. C.: Duke University Press.

Pinner, F. A., Jacobs, P. , and Selznick, P. 1959. *Old Age and Political Behavior.* Berkeley: University of California Press.

Pratt, H. J. 1976. *The Gray Lobby.* Chicago: University of Chicago Press.

Pratt, H. J. 1982. The "gray lobby" revisited. *National Forum* 62:31–33.

Prothro, J., and Grigg, C. 1960. Fundamental principles of democracy: Bases of agreement and disagreement. *Journal of Politics* 22:276–294.

Pryor, F. L. 1968. *Public Expenditures in Communist and Capitalist Nations.* Homewood, Ill.: Irwin.

Putnam, J. K. 1970. *Old-Age Politics in California: From Richardson to Reagan.* Stanford, Calif.: Stanford University Press.

Putnam, R. 1971. Studying elite political culture: The case of "ideology." *American Political Science Review* 65:651–681.

Reimer, Y., and Binstock, R. H. 1978. Campaigning for the "senior vote": A case study of Carter's 1976 campaign. *The Gerontologist* 18:517–524.

Richardson, B. 1974. *The Political Culture of Japan.* Berkeley: University of California Press.

Richardson, B. 1975. Party loyalties and party saliency in Japan. *Comparative Political Studies* 8:32–57.

Rigby, T. H. 1972. The Soviet Politburo: A comparative profile, 1951–1971. *Soviet Studies* 24:3–23.

Rimlinger, G. 1971. *Welfare Policy and Industrialization in Europe, America, and Russia.* New York: John Wiley.

Rose, A. M. 1965. Group consciousness among the aging. *In* A. M. Rose and W. M. Peterson (eds.), *Older People and Their Social World.* Philadelphia: Davis.

Rusk, J. 1976. Political participation in America: A review essay. *American Political Science Review* 70:583–591.

Scharf, C. B. 1981. Correlates of social security policy: East and West Europe. *International Political Science Review* 2:57–72.

Schlesinger, A., Jr. 1958. *The Politics of Upheaval.* Boston: Houghton Mifflin.

Schlesinger, J. A. 1966. *Ambition and Politics: Political Careers in the U.S.* Chicago: Rand McNally.

Schramm, W. 1969. Aging and mass communications. *In* M. W. Riley, J. W. Riley, Jr., and M. E. Johnson (eds.), *Aging and Society,* Vol. 2, pp. 352–375. New York: Russell Sage.

Schuck, P. 1980. The graying of civil rights law. *The Public Interest* 60:69–93.

Schueller, G. 1966. The Politburo. *In* H. Lasswell and D. Lerner (eds.), *World Revolutionary Elites: Studies in Coercive Ideological Movements,* pp. 97–178. Cambridge, Mass.: The M.I.T. Press.

Townsend, P. 1981. The structured dependency of the elderly: A creation of social policy in the twentieth century. *Ageing and Society* 1:5–28.

Tropman, J. E., Achenbaum, W. A., and Tice, T. 1979. Final report: American values and the elderly. Ann Arbor: University of Michigan.

Urwin, D. W. 1974. Germany: Continuity and change in electoral politics. *In* R. Rose (ed.), *Electoral Behavior: A Comparative Handbook,* pp. 109–170. New York: Free Press.

Verba, S., and Nie, N. H. 1972. *Participation in America.* New York: Harper and Row.

Verba, S., Nie, N. H., and Kim, J. 1978. *Participation and Political Equality.* Cambridge: Cambridge University Press.

Vladeck, B. 1980. *Unloving Care.* New York: Basic Books.

Walker, A. 1981. Towards a political economy of old age. *Ageing and Society* 1:73–94.

Walker, J. L. 1981. The origins and maintenance of interest groups in America. Paper delivered at the 1981 annual meeting of the American Political Science Association, New York.

Weaver, J. L. 1976. The elderly as a political community: The case of national health policy. *Western Political Quarterly* 29:61–69.

Wilensky, H. 1975. *The Welfare State and Equality.* Berkeley: University of California Press.

Williamson, J. B., Evans, L., and Powell, L. A. 1982. *The Politics of Aging.* Springfield, Ill.: Charles C. Thomas.

Witte, E. 1962. *The Development of the Social Security Act.* Madison: University of Wisconsin Press.

Zetterberg, H. 1979. Maturing of the Swedish welfare state. *Public Opinion* 2:42–47.

PART 5 AGING AND SOCIAL INTERVENTION

20
POLITICAL DILEMMAS OF SOCIAL INTERVENTION

Robert H. Binstock
Case Western Reserve University
Martin A. Levin
Brandeis University
and
Richard Weatherley*
The University of Washington

The fundamental notion that governments should intervene in the social conditions of aging persons has long been firmly established in industrialized societies, and has begun to receive attention from developing nations (Binstock et al., 1982; Oriol, 1982). For many decades the policies of industrialized nations toward issues of aging expanded in scope and size within a more general context of social program growth (Flora and Heidenheimer, 1981). But in recent years this expansionist mode of public intervention has eroded in the context of declining national economies.

Political leaders, confronting what appear to be "zero-sum" economies rather than sustained and substantial economic growth, presently subscribe to the notion that governmental expansion in one area necessarily requires reductions in other areas (Thurow, 1980). Consequently, even as nations experience rapid population aging (Myers, 1982),

they are attempting to cut back or at least curtail the rate of growth in expenditures on aging.

Ironically, both those who would curtail government intervention with respect to aging and other social conditions, and those who still press for incremental or radical expansion, lament the failures of public policies to achieve their respective objectives. Conservatives criticize the wastefulness of social programs (Stockman, 1975; Lilley and Miller, 1977), and often find it difficult to execute their policies for eliminating and cutting back selected social programs (Greider, 1981). Similarly, proponents of government activism are critical of existing public policies because they are ineffective and poorly focused for ameliorating the conditions of the most severely disadvantaged among the elderly population (Binstock, 1978, 1983; Crystal, 1982) and other population groupings. Critics of the prevailing social order in industrial democracies interpret governmental interventions toward older persons and others as instruments for social control (Guillemard, 1977; Williamson et al., 1982)

*We wish to express our appreciation to Professors Paula Dressel and James Schulz for their critical comments on a draft; the authors, of course, are solely responsible for the contents of this chapter.

and would prefer to see a fundamental redistribution of power in society (Olson, 1982).

Whether nations are in a mode of retrenchment or aggressiveness in expenditures for social programs, most segments of the spectrum of political ideology share a viewpoint regarding the conditions of severe economic deprivation, ill-health, and social dependency (see Chs. 22, 24, and 26) that can be found among the aging. The viewpoint is that the amount of public resources devoted to social intervention toward aging—relatively scarce or bountiful—should somehow be more efficiently and effectively employed for achieving intended policy objectives (Selby and Schecter, 1982).

The purpose of this chapter is to provide perspectives on the politics of public policy through which social scientists and their professional colleagues—interested in aging and other social issues—can be somewhat more realistic and optimistic in their outlooks toward policy interventions, and more effective as participants in policy processes. We will assume for purposes of this discussion that social science is capable of developing intervention models (see Ch. 21) that would be effective if political processes did not "interfere" with the adoption and implementation of those models. We will also assume that fundamental changes in political systems *might* bring about more effective policies without sacrificing democratic values. Although such assumptions may warrant extended examination, they are not considered in this chapter.

The central issue of this chapter is: If social scientists and other professionals explicitly confront what is known about the contemporary political contexts in which policies are adopted and implemented, what can they do within those contexts to optimize social intervention efforts?

In order to treat this issue within a single chapter it will be necessary to emphasize certain political structures and processes to the exclusion of others. Although we will make a few general observations about the politics of public policy in modern democratic systems, as American political scientists we have chosen to deal with the American political system as a context for most of the discussion. A great deal of what we will say is germane in some degree, however, to other political systems. If one conceives of modern democratic systems arrayed on a continuum ranging from centralized to fragmented or dispersed power, the American system is located among those characterized by dispersion. The dispersion of power, exemplified in American politics, is a characteristic that is central to the difficulties of adopting and implementing effective policies for social intervention.

The scope of this chapter also makes it necessary to eschew a number of intriguing theoretical and definitional issues. Among them is the problem presented by the very word "policy." Neither scholarly definitions (e.g., Friedrich, 1963; Lasswell and Kaplan, 1970) nor popular conceptions of the term are adequate, since they imply that policies are relatively clear, authoritative expressions of public goals that provide a fundamental context within which other governmental decisions and activities can be viewed and interpreted. The implication is unrealistic because any attempt to reify "policy" disintegrates when political behavior is examined. The language of a legislative act (and "the intent" behind it) is no more or less a policy than the decisions made by the bureaucrats who implement it (and their intentions in doing so). As Pressman and Wildavsky (1979) have observed, one cannot work with a definition of policy that excludes implementation. The full range of governmental actions that one can observe—executive decisions, referenda, and many other kinds of activities—are important for understanding the politics of social intervention. Also important, moreover, are the failures of a government to act, which obviously can have consequences equal to or even surpassing the results of action (Bachrach and Baratz, 1963). In short, the definition and organization of a discussion of policy must largely be a function of the phenomena and issues one chooses to examine.

The two kinds of political phenomena that will receive attention in this discussion of policy are: those involved in processes of legislative decisions and those that legislative decisions set in motion. Accordingly, the discussion will be facilitated by a simple distinction between *policy adoption*—the enactment of national legislation (other than appropriation bills)—and *policy implementation*—the variety of activities set in motion by the adoption of legislation. In choosing to focus on the enactment of legislation as a type of policy adoption, we are excluding from consideration many other forms of public action to which this term can be properly applied, such as executive orders, court decisions, referenda, and constitutional amendments. One reason for this choice is that in all democratic political systems, legislative decisions are among the most important initiatives for domestic social intervention. Furthermore, the significance of power fragmentation in shaping policy adoption is most readily perceived and illustrated in the context of national legislative behavior.

The balance of this chapter is organized into four major sections. In the first section we will briefly examine some of the sources and manifestations of political limitations on effective policy intervention. The second section will consider how political limitations endemic to the American system tend to limit intervention policies that are adopted through legislation. The third section will discuss some of the ways in which these political characteristics also limit the efficiency and effectiveness of policy implementation. And a final section will suggest means through which social scientists and other professionals can optimize policy adoption and implementation by actively confronting the political dilemmas that limit the effectiveness of policy intervention.

SOURCES AND MANIFESTATIONS OF POLITICAL LIMITATIONS

The adoption of a social policy not only requires politicians to choose among policy proposals, but it also characteristically re-quires them to sacrifice some of the substance of the proposal that they choose. In the United States, as in all nations that have some form of representative government, an ongoing concern of politicians is their prospects for reelection. Because of this concern they are eager to be identified with policies that are regarded favorably by the electorate, and by financial contributors to their election campaigns. Accordingly, they seek to espouse and support policies that evoke favorable reactions even if they do so at the expense of alternative policies that may be more effective for solving problems, but viewed less favorably. There is an "electoral rhythm" in national economic performance, for instance, that may reflect the efforts of political leaders to produce economic conditions they believe will enhance their chances for reelection. Through transfer payments, and fiscal and monetary policies, they attempt to reduce unemployment before presidential elections. As Tufte (1978) has demonstrated:

> . . . the electoral-economic cycle from 1948 to 1976 (other than the Eisenhower years) has consisted of:
> —A two-year cycle in the growth of real disposable income per capita, with accelerations in even-numbered years and decelerations in odd-numbered years.
> —A four-year presidential cycle in the unemployment rate, with downturns in unemployment in the months before the presidential election and upturns in the unemployment rate usually beginning from twelve to eighteen months after the election. (p. 27)

While this pattern may best serve the needs of incumbent politicians, its value for the economy is problematic.

The desire of politicians to be identified with policies favored by their constituents and financial contributors is reflected in a number of more specific tendencies. First, politicians prefer to espouse and support policies that are immodest—dramatic and ambitious—in promise, whether they are operating within a climate of governmental expansionism or one of retrenchment. Rather than announcing policies for getting more and better qualified personnel in nursing homes, they will declare policies that promise to older Americans "The best possible physical and mental health which science can make available . . ." and "Immediate benefit from proven research knowledge which can sustain and improve health and happiness" (Older Americans Act, 1981, 101, 2 & 9). Rather than announcing that they are curtailing intervention by the national government and cutting back expenditures on social programs, they will proclaim an era of New Federalism and claim that they are directing programs to "the truly needy" (Palmer and Sawhill, 1982; Achenbaum, 1983).

Second, regardless of the immodest terms in which policies may be couched, politicians want those policies to lend themselves to tangible, particularly quantifiable results, for which they can take credit in reelection campaigns. For example, a policy proposed to improve nutrition among older persons would not lend itself to the kinds of tangible outcomes preferred by politicians if its design were such that reports of results could only be expressed in terms of an assessment of the nutritional status of aging persons. In contrast, the Congregate Nutrition program for the elderly designed in Title III of the Older Americans Act is very suitable politically. Since it lends itself to reports from each Congressional district on the number and location of nutrition programs in operation, and on the number of meals served to older persons, assessments of either the nutritional value of the meals or the nutritional status of those who have eaten them are not politically necessary.

Third, because the time span between elections is relatively short, policies that embody goals that can be achieved quickly are preferred to policies that may require a generation, a decade, or perhaps just five years to be effective. This preference is especially unfortunate in its implications for some of the possible policies that could be undertaken in relation to aging. Many of the characteristics of persons who will join the ranks of the aged

each year between now and the early years of the twenty-first century will be different from those of the contemporary aged (Neugarten, 1974). Since these future aged are already well along in their life courses, it is possible to make use of our knowledge about them to undertake policy initiatives to deal with some of the social issues that their continuing maturation may involve (Binstock, 1975). But the tendency of politicians to favor policies that quickly show results of some kind makes the adoption of such initiatives difficult.

There are notable exceptions, of course, to each of these three patterns. One could argue, for instance, that: the Age Discrimination in Employment Act is undramatic and modest in its prohibitions and enforcement objectives; the research objectives of the National Institute on Aging do not easily lend themselves to reports of tangible results; and the private pension reform law, the Employee Retirement Income Security Act, is designed for effectiveness in the mid- to distant future. While these are possible exceptions, the preference of legislators for policies that are immodest, and that lend themselves to tangible and quick results, is generally at work in shaping the outcomes of policy adoption processes.

A desire to appeal to the electorate and campaign contributors, however, is but one of the elements at work in shaping the behavior of politicians as they engage in policy processes. Far more important are their struggles to cope with the peculiar fragmentation of power that is a predominant characteristic of the American political system. Power is dispersed among innumerable private entities—economic, social, professional, and religious elites; commercial, industrial, and trade organizations; political parties, political action groups, and organized citizen constituencies—that not only have influence in nongovernmental spheres of activity but also have influence on governmental structures and decisions. In addition, public power (authoritative or official power) is dispersed among tens of thousands of units of government, semi-autonomous structures within these units, and a number of quasi-public entities.

In any given effort to adopt or to implement a policy, numerous fragments of private and public power come into play. A political leader desiring to have a legislative proposal adopted must usually concert power by securing the support and neutralizing the opposition of those who control relevant power fragments. The same need is confronted by those who implement policy. But the price of concerting or neutralizing these fragments is often paid by sacrificing the substance of what might be regarded as an "ideal proposal" for policy adoption, or an "ideal policy" for implementation.

Before we examine the patterns through which power fragmentation leads to modifications in proposed and adopted policies, it is worth considering briefly the sources and manifestations of public power fragmentation in the United States. It is important to note that the dispersion of public power that is a central impediment to effective policy intervention is also an expression of central values in American political culture.

The fragmentation of public power that characterizes the American political system can be accounted for by a number of factors in the nation's early history and its subsequent 200 years of development. Given the prenational development of distinct colonies, a virtual precondition of union was the choice of a federal structure of government in which each state retained sovereignty. Moreover, most of the framers of the national and state governments were wary of consolidated power because of their colonial political experiences. Their fears of centralized authority, reinforced by the political philosophies of Locke and Montesquieu, were expressed in structures that separated powers within the national and state governments. In part this was done to make it more difficult for informal factions—"a number of citizens, whether amounting to a majority or minority of the whole, who are united and activated by some common impulse of passion or of interest"—to assemble sufficient influence to tyrannize through controlling the powers of government (Madison, 1937). The prospect of political leadership sufficiently powerful to be able to adopt and implement its version of an ideal policy was and remains for most Americans a fear, not an aspiration.

In the two centuries of the United States' existence, the proliferation of public fragments of power has been exponential. In the contemporary United States there are 80,000 distinct units of government—counties, townships, municipalities, special district governments, metropolitan governments, and school districts, as well as the states and the national government. Most overlap in jurisdiction. Each has a specific set of formal powers, and within a substantial proportion of these units that power is divided among executives, legislatures, and judiciaries. In addition, during the last two decades the national government has sponsored and financed thousands of local and regional entities—regional and area planning units, community action agencies, coordinating councils, citizen committees, technical commissions—and delegated to many of them independent authority affecting local policies that draw on federal resources. The federal government's role in proliferating such entities can be grasped by simply noting the impact of one piece of national legislation, and Older Americans Act. In accordance with this legislation some 600 Area Agencies on Aging (AAAs) have been created through the distribution of federal funds (Older Americans Act, 1981).

In addition to this proliferation of governments and governmental entities, public power has been further fragmented due to the persistent influence of a major tenet of American political culture: the belief that public decisions, whenever feasible, should be based on the widest possible participation of the governed and not left to a governing elite. Under the influence of the Progressives of the late nineteenth and early twentieth centuries, this tenet became expressed in constitutional provisions requiring that many important state and local policy decisions be made through direct popular referenda. It has also become manifest since the early 1960s through federal legislation mandating establishment of mechanisms for citizen participation in a variety of programs that are designed for implementation by local community agencies.

This highly fragmented and overlapping distribution of public power—among governments, governmental entities, and the public at large, as well as within governments and between governments—in the larger societal context of a dispersion of private power among elites, interest groups, political parties, political action groups, and organized citizen constituencies, makes the challenges involved in exercising policy leadership seem overwhelming. Not only does policy leadership require a general capacity to concert and/or neutralize fragments of public and private power, but the sets of fragments involved may vary substantially from one policy to another, each set comprising an ad hoc system defined by the policy proposal to be adopted or by the policy to be implemented.

When the difficulties of overcoming power fragmentation are added to some of the difficulties engendered by politicians' desires to espouse appealing policies, the possibilities of adopting and implementing effective social intervention policies are considerably limited. In the next two sections we will examine some of the ways in which these political difficulties influence policy adoption and implementation.

THE POLITICS OF POLICY ADOPTION

The need to overcome power fragmentation in order to undertake public initiatives for social intervention poses one of the central dilemmas of policy leadership in American politics. To overstate somewhat for purposes of clarification, policy leadership is typically carried out in either a "power-costly" or "power-costless" pattern. Through one pattern the policy leader expends his or her store of political resources in order to obtain the support of some persons and entities who control fragments of power (or "requisite

actions") and to neutralize the opposition of some others. In this pattern the leader's power-costly proposal is adopted at the expense of the political power he or she has managed to acquire as well as at the cost of opportunities to maintain and enhance power. The other prototypical approach is for the political leader to bargain away the substance of a policy proposal, or let it be altered, until it is a power-costless proposal, providing a distribution of rewards to "requisite actors"—persons and entities controlling requisite actions—that is sufficient to obtain necessary support and neutralize opposition. The leader's store of political power tends to be maintained and often enhanced through this pattern, but at the cost of substantive goals (see Banfield, 1961).

While these two characteristics may represent the extremes of the situation, they capture a central dilemma of policy leadership within the American political system and, to greater or lesser degrees, within many other political systems. Only rarely will politicians expend sufficient power to have a proposal for intervention adopted as policy without alterations in its substance. More commonly, the adoption of a proposal for intervention is achieved because elements of the proposal itself are modified in return for the supporting actions requisite to the enactment of a policy.

Adoption of policy through legislation is especially susceptible to this dilemma. The President and Congress share the authority to make legislation become law but derive, maintain, and seek their power from different electoral bases. Within Congress individual legislators cannot and do not rely wholly on a party organization to keep them in office. They tend to develop legislative voting patterns that are based on their own conceptions of what is necessary to maintain the support of their constituencies and electoral campaign contributors. Similarly, the major legislative committees within Congress develop behavioral patterns that are keyed to groupings of organized interest constituencies both within the bureaucracy and outside the government (Davidson, 1977).

In addition, it is an article of faith in American politics that interest groups should participate in the legislative process (Lowi, 1969), certainly on proposals affecting the aging (Vinyard, 1972; Pratt, 1976), by helping to shape and criticize legislation in both formal hearings and informal sessions with members of Congress and Congressional staff. This faith is so central to contemporary American political culture that if interest groups do not seek to participate in the legislative process, the President and Congress recruit their active participation in order to legitimate the process and products of policy-making (Binstock, 1974).

To have a policy proposal adopted in such a legislative context, its proponent must act as a broker among members of Congress and Congressional committees, among bureaucracies and interest groups, and between Congress, the President, and bureaucracies and interest groups. He or she may be willing and able to expend a sufficient store of power to obtain enough support for the policy to be adopted in a form that closely resembles the initial or ideal proposal. But more often than not, the costs of building adequate support for the adoption of a policy are a number of changes in the policy proposal itself, and, as will be considered in a later section of this chapter, a concomitant reduction in the probability that the policy adopted will be effectively implemented.

President Reagan's appointment of a National Commission on Social Security Reform in 1982 was an example of a policy leader choosing an exceptionally power-costless approach to resolve the political dilemmas of concerting power fragments for the adoption of legislation. Due to a sustained period of relatively high unemployment, accompanied by high rates of inflation, the financing mechanism of the Social Security program was not yielding sufficient revenues to pay scheduled Old Age benefits. Some new legislative policy had to be enacted in 1983 in order to increase revenues and/or curtail benefits. All of the proposals that were being put forward to solve this problem were unpopular with at least one significant political

faction. After several decades in which amendments to the Social Security Act had been relatively uncontroversial, "easy votes" on Social Security legislation had come to an end (Derthick, 1979).

Within this controversial context Reagan did not push forward his own Presidential policy proposal, and he avoided expending his store of political power in an attempt to get his preferred solution enacted. Rather, he assembled leaders from a variety of different public and private power bases—Democrats and Republicans from both houses of Congress, business, organized labor, and professional elites—as members of an ad hoc commission, and charged them with the responsibility of putting forth their proposal to solve the problem. The recommendations that the commission reported—the bargained outcome of conflicts and accommodations among the interests represented by its members—were adopted by Congress without much difficulty and only minor modifications as the Social Security Amendments of 1983. This precompromised legislation did not appear to resemble any interest's ideal policy for reforming Social Security (Cohen, 1983).

Policy proposals that call for allocations of public resources to be highly concentrated in relatively few specific geographic areas or electoral constituencies often become legislatively modified to distribute those resources widely among legislative districts. The development of the Model Cities Program was a striking case of this. It started with the original proposal by a leader of organized labor to rebuild two cities, Detroit and any other, through a massive infusion of federal funds. The proposal was modified by a Presidential task force to obtain broader political support by expanding it to 66 neighborhoods distributed among a number of cities. By the time the Presidential proposal had been subjected to brokering in Congress to obtain adequate legislative support, the policy adopted provided $212 million for 150 cities (Banfield, 1973).

The tendency toward a wide distribution of resources made available through national social policies is often expressed in an explicit formula, stated in legislation, that allocates funds among state and local implementing agencies. Title III of the Older Americans Act is one of the typical legislative provisions spelling out such a formula for distribution. It provides funds to all state implementing agencies through a formula that uses the population 60 years of age and older in each state as a proportion of the national total of persons 60 years and older; the resulting proportions are then modified to ensure that a minimum level of funds is distributed to each state (Older Americans Act, 1981, Title IIIA). For certain types of social legislation the use of such formulas became routine (Wright, 1968) several decades ago. They eliminate the need for ad hoc processes of brokering, and are the results of bargained accommodations among regions and legislative districts in their competition for what each considers its fair share of federal funds.

Also typically modified to obtain support are proposals that call for focusing expenditures of resources upon a social program or social grouping that is defined in relatively narrow terms. This takes place through several characteristic patterns.

One pattern is to *add* to the initial target problem or group several other narrowly defined targets that have an apparent relationship to the initial target. The apparent relationship may not bear up to careful scrutiny, but close examination may be fended off through the use of a legislative title that is broad enough to cloud the picture. In the late 1960s, for example, the National Association for Retarded Children sought federal legislation to provide funds to the states to develop services and facilities for the mentally retarded. Sufficient political support to enact legislation, however, was only obtained through the development of a coalition that added organized advocates of public initiatives for the epileptic and the cerebral palsied. The policy adopted, dealing with three specific and generally unrelated problems—mental retardation, epilepsy, and cerebral palsy—was symbolically rational-

ized by the use of broad language; it was labeled the Developmental Disabilities Act of 1970 (Cherington, 1972). In a similar fashion the 1974 Education for *All* Handicapped Children Act (emphasis added) was the response to a broad-based coalition of interest groups (Weatherley, 1979).

In another classic pattern broader support is obtained not by including several additional narrowly defined targets, but by broadening the definition of the initial target. Examples of this phenomenon are the uses of the terms "older American," "senior," and "elderly" in many policies that have been adopted, and particularly the official applicability of many such policies to the largest possible categories of citizens implied by these names. The authorization of supportive services and senior centers under the Older Americans Act (1981, Title IIIB), for instance, does not even restrict client eligibility on the basis of age. Although many of the social issues associated with aging apply to relatively small proportions of the older population, the need to obtain legislative support exerts a pressure for broadening policies toward aging so that they apply to the largest possible aggregate constituency of citizens (see Ch. 19).

Through still another pattern, the target or problem is not added to or broadly redefined, but the nature of what is to be done about the problem is changed to directly provide benefits to interest groups and constituencies so that they will support legislation. A classic illustration of this is provided by the evolution of various proposals for "senior employment programs" that ultimately became embodied in Title V of the Older Americans Act. When a bill for such a program was sponsored in Congress in 1967, conflicts among interest groups over which of them would share in the benefits of administering the policy killed the legislative proposal and also delayed by a year the reauthorization and amendment of the Older Americans Act. Only when an accommodating pattern of resource distribution among aging-based interest groups was finally achieved, were they able to join in supporting senior employment legislation (Binstock, 1972). These political compromises arrived at in 1969 were still maintained in the Older Americans Act in the 1980s, even though the legislation had been amended a number of times in the interim. As late as 1983, Title V, Community Service Employment for Older Americans, was the only portion of the legislation not administered by the Administration on Aging (AoA) or the Department of Health and Human Services. Rather, it was administered by the Department of Labor, which was authorized to implement it by directly funding public and private organizations that are not part of AoA's network of State and Area Agencies on Aging (Older Americans Act, 1981, Title V).

Which of these several patterns of legislative modification come into play, singly or in combination, can often be traced to the specific nature of the proposal under consideration. Even within the same area of concern, the distribution and intensity of support, opposition, and indifference among and between sets of requisite actors—individual legislators, committee chairpersons, bureaucrats, organized interests, elites, and citizen constituencies—can vary from one proposal to another. In relation to policies affecting the aging, Binstock (1972) has illustrated that the kinds of reactions among aging-based interest groups shift in relation to the substance of the legislation proposed. The patterns of legislative modification that are used to secure sufficient support for the adoption of a policy seem to parallel the shifts in interests, accordingly.

A number of schemes for classifying proposed and adopted policies have been developed that are of some value for identifying recurring patterns of political brokering in the legislative process (e.g., Lowi, 1964; Wilson, 1973; Brown, 1983). Such typologies are useful for examining many issues relating to political behavior and public policy. But it is neither necessary nor of any special value to choose a particular scheme for making certain generalizations about the central issue under consideration here, namely: What can be said about the cumulative impacts of the various patterns of legislative modifications that take place as domestic social policies, particularly those of relevance to the aging, are adopted?

One generalization that clearly emerges from the literature is that very few, if any, policy proposals are adopted without undergoing modifications that are made to secure legislative support and to neutralize opposition. To be sure, it is plausible to argue that the greater the sense of crisis that pervades the nation, the less a proposal to deal with that crisis is likely to be modified through legislative brokering, and the more it is likely to be effective as an instrument for social intervention. Proponents of this thesis argue that an underlying American liberal consensus (Hartz, 1955) makes it possible for differences to be transcended through effective mobilization of powerful, if temporary, coalitions while opponents are placed at a severe disadvantage. Frequently cited to support this thesis is the New Deal legislation enacted during the Great Depression, especially the Social Security Act of 1935. However, if one compares the Social Security program and its contributory "insurance" rubric with more radical schemes of the era such as the Townsend Plan (Holtzman, 1963), both the efforts to secure widespread support for the legislation through compromise (Achenbaum, 1983) and the relatively moderate character of the intervention it authorized become evident.

Indeed, there are many notable examples of legislatively brokered social policies that have been enacted within the context of so-called crises in the American political system. A case in point is the Social Security Amendments of 1983, referred to earlier. Enacted in the midst of a widely publicized "crisis in Social Security," this policy was an exemplary model of highly brokered legislation (Cohen, 1983), and did little to reform long-standing issues of equity and income adequacy under the Social Security system (Lawlor, 1983). Similarly, the legislative response to the "urban crisis" in the 1960s was the adoption of a series of highly compromised policies, including the Model Cities program described earlier in this chapter. Of course, as Banfield (1970) has pointed out, the declaration of a crisis by politicians and the media does not necessarily mean that a deep and broad sense of crisis is experienced within the society.

Another generalization that emerges is that even policy proposals that are relatively uncompromised when enacted, perhaps in the context of a mood of crisis, tend to become modified in substance over time much as if the process of securing political support and neutralizing opposition were being carried out longitudinally rather than cross-sectionally. Organized interests and constituencies whose powers may have been neutralized by a public sense of crisis or some other contextual factor at the time when a policy was intitially adopted are often afforded a new opportunity for legislative brokering through the process of amendment. Several years later in the different context of a deadline for reauthorization of legislation, new patterns of support, opposition, and indifference often emerge, and organized interests may be able to extract substantive policy changes in return for their support. "Community action" policies adopted in an atmosphere of urban rioting in 1967, for instance, were modified later in legislation responsive to the interests of big city mayors and middle income constituencies (Sundquist and Davis, 1969).

A third generalization is that many policies are legislated primarily as symbolic responses (Edelman, 1964) to public and interest group demands, and thereby engender subsequent problems of implementation. This phenomenon helps to explain why a number of scholars of public policy have directed their attention to issues of policy implementation.

Regulatory legislation, for instance, is frequently an excellent symbolic response to popular outrage at abuses against the public. But such policies are commonly vitiated because the parties to be regulated are later able to exercise power to effectively neutralize or capture the machinery of regulatory implementation. One need only consider, for instance, the familiar cycle through which media exposure of nursing home conditions engenders a sense of public outrage, a commission is appointed to investigate conditions and to recommend legislation to deal with them, and reasonably strong regulatory standards are legislated. Nonetheless, the nursing home industry is able to remain remarkably immune to regulation (Mendelson and Hapgood, 1974; Vladeck, 1980).

A form of symbolic response particularly favored by Congress since World War II is what might be termed "circuit breaker" legislation—a political mechanism that has enabled it to cope with an overload of popular and interest group demands for adopting policies of social intervention. From the New Deal to the 1980s the American political system continually broadened the scope of activities that it considered legitimate for intervention by the federal government.

Particularly in the 1960s and '70s—a period of economic growth in which the proportion of Americans with middle incomes, white-collar occupations, and college educations increased—there were fewer debates than before over the wisdom and propriety of public initiatives to solve social problems. Clearly such debates have been reinvigorated on economic if not philosophical grounds, as resources have become scarcer (Thurow, 1980). But the tendency of the 1960s and '70s was toward a presumption that if a social problem could be identified, it required a governmental response. Many important political changes were taking place. Legal barriers to the participation of Blacks in the political system were removed, particularly through voting rights measures; consequently, their needs as constituents received more attention from politicians. Effective articulation of issues concerning the status of women (Friedan, 1963) served to broaden the agenda of social needs that might be addressed by government. And as television became a major source of political information, the number of issues that could be politicized as "crises," if only temporarily, was limited by little more than the reformer's imagination.

The circuit breaker that Congress developed for coping with the overload of demands for public initiatives was a legislative pattern through which specific substantive issues of policy implementation are notably avoided in legislative adoption of policies. An exemplary case is the provision in the Older Americans Act that requires implementing agencies, State Units on Aging (SUAs) and Area Agencies on Aging (AAAs), to "provide assurances that preference will be given to providing services to older individuals with the greatest economic or social needs. . . . " (1981, Title III). But the controversial issues of how to determine who these individuals are, and how to treat them preferentially, are not dealt with in the legislation. These issues, as one analyst suggests (Cutler, 1981), were deliberately avoided in the legislative process.

The circuit-breaker approach became especially manifest in the 1960s and '70s in the enactment of policies for the development of social services and facilities. Many phrases—such as President Lyndon Johnson's "The Great Society Programs"—have been used to describe these policies which mandate a number of complex implementing actions to be undertaken by federal, state, and local agencies. However, since such phrases are associated with specific political eras, and because this type of policy has persisted through several decades, we will employ the term Social Development policies. The term Social Development is intended to represent a full range of social policies—the Older Americans Act, Employment Development, Model Cities, Community Action, and so on—that mandate implementing agencies to initiate and change social services and facilities within a legislative context that is outlined below.

The central ingredient in the Social Development legislative pattern is distribution of funds to state and local entities, with only the most general rules about what should be done with the distributed resources. Sometimes the funds are to be distributed to existing entities, but often the legislation calls for the designation and creation of new entities that can be directly identified with the issue to which the legislation is responding. In either case, the composite nationwide administrative apparatus is a hybrid comprised of whatever entities may exist, or be designated and created, in the various state and local jurisdictions (Binstock et al., 1974). The substantive responsibilities of these implementing entities are usually described in the most general terms: develop services and comprehensive plans; coordinate; undertake advocacy. And a flexible, competitive process is usually established for distributing funds to organizations that are directly engaged in operating programs.

Title III of the Older Americans Act, as originally enacted in 1965 and amended through 1981, is a classic example of Social Development legislation. It provides funds for services, planning, coordination, evaluation and administration to each state that designates a State Unit on Aging (SUA). These SUAs, in turn, subdivide their respective states into Planning and Service Areas (PSAs), and designate an Area Agency on Aging (AAA) as an administrative entity for each PSA. The legislation authorizes AAAs, in accordance with plans submitted to SUAs, to expend federal funds on nutrition services, senior centers, and a broad range of supportive services—including more than 30 services explicitly described in the statute, and "any other services . . . necessary for the general welfare of older individuals" (1981, Title IIIB, 321). The choice of programs and services to be provided is almost entirely left to the state and local implementing agencies. Funds for nutrition services are separately authorized and appropriated from those for supportive services and senior centers, but the legislation permits each state to transfer up to 20 percent of its allotment from one category to another. The only other statutory restriction on state and local choices is a provision that "an adequate proportion" of an AAA's allotment of funds be spent on access, in-home, and legal services (1981, Title III, 306).

The ingredients of Social Development

legislation, so well illustrated by this omnibus Title III of the Older Americans Act, comprise a recipe for political triumph, if not one for effective social intervention. Through the adoption of legislation based on this recipe, national politicians can maintain and reinforce their legitimacy as public leaders. The cadres of state and local entities that receive federal funds, as well as their associated participating constituencies and interest groups, are grateful supporters of the policy although they inevitably regard as inadequate the amount of funds made available to them. Citizen constituencies and interests that are unable to gain access to the resources distributed by such policies may complain, but national politicians (expressing sympathetic concern) can refer all complaints back to the semi-autonomous state and local implementing agencies. Moreover, constituencies that feel excluded can always be accommodated through inclusion in subsequent amendments. For instance, a 1978 amendment to the Older Americans Act created a special Title VI, "Grants for Indian Tribes," in response to pressures from Native Americans. While legislation is vague about the social outcomes to be achieved through this policy, it is relatively specific about the allocation of funds to implementation entities and their need, in turn, to expend effort and to distribute money for developing programs. Consequently, "successful results" can ensue relatively quickly and in tangible form. Virtually all that is required is to report on the number of entities and programs that have been established, the number of dollars that have been widely distributed among constituencies throughout the nation, and the estimated number of clients served.

Although the Social Development recipe has provided Congress with an excellent means of responding symbolically to a variety of politicized issues, it also leaves policy effectiveness highly dependent upon the agencies that implement it—the federal bureaucracy that must interpret the vague responsibilities described in legislation to make them somewhat operational, and the state

and local entities that receive the funds and the broad mandates to develop programs and services, to plan comprehensively, to coordinate, and to advocate. The effectiveness of these implementing agencies is partly limited by the amount of funds that policies provide to them. But the agencies are more severely limited because their efforts at implementation encounter problems of power fragmentation and other political dilemmas characteristic of the American political system. As we will see in the next section, the success of Congress in evading these dilemmas through the enactment of highly symbolic circuit-breaker legislation passes these dilemmas along to the agencies expected to implement policy.

THE POLITICS OF POLICY IMPLEMENTATION

All policies require implementation, and most implementation efforts encounter political difficulties. As indicated earlier, for instance, even very clear and specific regulatory policies are often vitiated by the capacity of powerful private interests to neutralize or capture the implementing machinery. Social Development policies, however, mandating initiation or changes in social services and facilities, inevitably seem to encounter more of the political difficulties of implementation than other kinds of policies. Consequently, our examination of the politics of policy implementation in this section will emphasize Social Development policies. In the next section of the chapter we will draw upon this examination for a comparative discussion of the challenges involved in implementing different types of policies.

The implementation of Social Development policies has unquestionably provided benefits to citizen constituencies, as well as to interest groups (Binstock, 1972; Estes, 1979) and to state and local governments. Health services have been greatly expanded, some educational programs have improved, structural barriers against women and minorities have been reduced, and mechanisms for protecting the rights of the poor have been established (Haveman, 1977). Implementation of the Older Americans Act has provided many older persons benefits through a great variety of social and supportive services (Coombs, 1982).

At the same time, Social Development policies have not made a substantial dent in *aggregate* social problems. As an evaluation of the Older Americans Act reported by the U.S. House of Representatives Select Committee on Aging, Subcommittee on Human Services expressed it:

> Such fragmentation, duplication, and total lack of coordination exact a price—a price that is paid by the loss of needed services to their would-be beneficiaries. Only a fraction of those eligible for services benefit from them. Many are unaware of the services that are available; others are excluded from participation by statutory inconsistencies. (1980, p. 31)

Some of the disappointment with such programs can be traced to their relatively small, symbolic levels of funding (U.S. House of Representatives, Select Committee on Aging, 1977). For instance, of the $234 billion in federal expenditures on benefits for the elderly estimated for fiscal year 1984, only $1.5 billion or six-tenths of one percent (.006) were for Social Development policies, as contrasted with over 96 percent for income and health policies such as Social Security, Medicare, and Medicaid (U.S. Senate, Special Committee on Aging, 1983, pp. 49–50). But, in addition, a number of policy studies that examine Social Development initiatives show that policy ineffectiveness—delays, exorbitant cost–benefit ratios, and goal displacement—can be traced to a variety of political dilemmas that are endemic to American politics.

In the expansionist era of the 1960s and '70s, federal agencies and Congressional oversight committees routinely funded "independent evaluations" of Social Development interventions, thereby stimulating an outpouring of policy implementation studies. But as noted earlier, the politics of policy adoption often produce programs that are not designed to achieve outcomes that can be assessed in terms of technical rationality (Wildavsky, 1979a). Not surprisingly then, evaluation studies of Social Development programs—assessing the outcome of policies in terms of their stated ambitions for social intervention—emphasize program failures. As Elmore (1982) notes: "The first round of implementation studies consisted largely of documenting the failures of ambitious social programs initiated by the federal government in the mid-1960s . . . . What this generation of studies demonstrated more than anything else was that proving the absurdities and failures of implementation was like shooting fish in a rain barrel, easy and fun at first, but boring and dissatisfying with practice . . . " (pp. 105–106). Nonetheless, these studies yielded valuable insights and generalizations about conditions that influence success and failure in policy implementation.

The major contribution of this generation of studies has been a recognition that although policy adoption and implementation might be separated conceptually, in reality they are inextricably joined. Some policies may have far-reaching unintended consequences for other policies. The legislative politics of policy adoption may tend to preclude effective implementation. The structural need to rely upon multiple public and private organizations for implementation may pose obstacles. The response of service workers to pressures they confront may, in effect, change the initial intent of a policy. And the perpetuation of a policy is largely dependent upon continuing political support, regardless of its effectiveness as an intervention effort.

The Interconnectedness of Policies

A condition that frequently undermines the effectiveness of a single intervention effort is the contemporary proliferation of interconnected policies, both public and private, that bear upon any specific social problem. An effort to deal with a problem through any one policy can be canceled out by another existing policy, or can have far-reaching, unforeseen consequences that create other related problems.

A policy change raising an individual's Old Age benefit under Social Security can automatically reduce that same person's private pension benefits, because many pension plans have "integration mechanisms" that use Social Security benefits to reduce the level of private pensions (Schulz et al., 1983). Health cost-containment policies are adopted to limit the amount of governmental funds that Medicare will reimburse for charges billed by hospitals that serve patients 65 years of age and older. But this leads hospitals, in turn, to raise their general price levels in order to recapture—through additional out-of-pocket payments from individuals and payments from private insurance companies—the portion of charges not reimbursed by Medicare (Finkler, 1982). There are also signs that such policies may have the unintended consequences of lower levels and qualities of care for Medicare patients (Altman, 1982). This lesson of policy-interconnectedness has also been learned from analyses of welfare policies (Moynihan, 1973), urban policies (Wilson, 1966), tax reform policies (Levin, 1979), and many other arenas of social intervention.

To be sure, the probability of far-reaching consequences of proposed interventions can be estimated through computer simulations, field experiments, and other analytical techniques. For instance, a Technical Committee for the 1981 White House Conference on Aging attempted to project the probable costs and aggregate economic effects of an expanded public income transfer program that would be used as a direct measure for addressing income-adequacy problems of the elderly through the year 2005 (U.S. White House Conference on Aging, 1981). But the techniques used for such estimates are far from infallible. Indeed, the complex linkages they reveal often lend credence to the viewpoints of both those who seek sweeping and comprehensive policy reforms and those who would prefer no reform at all.

The Consequences of Policy Adoption Politics

A number of implementation problems can be traced to the patterns in the legislative politics of policy adoption that were discussed earlier. The tendency of politicians to exaggerate goals and expectations often sets unrealistic standards for judging successful implementation. The Public Welfare Amendments of 1962 declared, much to the subsequent embarrassment of social work professionals, that the social services which the legislation authorized and funded would lead to strengthened family life, self-support and self-care, and the prevention of dependency (Derthick, 1975). Legislative compromises made to secure enactment of a proposed intervention can so dilute it that the basic intervention concept becomes undermined and unviable, as was the case with the Model Cities proposal (Banfield, 1973). A sure formula for failure, as in the Education for All Handicapped Children Act of 1974, is circuit-breaking legislation that requires major changes in state and local practices without an accompanying allocation of major new federal funds to implement those changes (Weatherley, 1979). And President Johnson's New Towns program provided the lesson that policies enacted in the context of legislative disinterest, without commitment or attachment from any interest group, bureaucracy, or local constituency, are highly likely to fail (Derthick, 1972).

Fragmentation through Federalism and Private Sector Participation

Most national social intervention policies, with the exception of some income transfer and regulatory policies, are implemented by a plethora of state and local jurisdictions, as well as nongovernmental organizations. This is so because central values in American political culture, discussed earlier, emphasize fragmentation of power within the public sector's structure of federalism, and between the public and private sectors. This fragmentation, regardless of the politics of legislative policy adoption, sets the stage for a series of implementation difficulties. The very multiplicity of decision points involved in programs tends to increase probabilities that the manifest or intended goals of a policy will be thwarted, displaced, or only achieved after long delays and adaptation, with much larger expenditures than initially planned, and with a smaller impact than envisioned (Pressman and Wildavsky, 1979).

Many policies depend upon the efforts of professional and proprietary interests as well as state and local public bureaucracies. Analyses focusing on such policies—for example, examinations of the network of agencies and professionals implementing the Older Americans Act (Estes, 1979) and the health care professionals and industries sustained by Medicare and Medicaid (Alford, 1976; Vladeck, 1980; Starr, 1982)—have argued that social program expenditures may provide substantial benefits to implementing professionals and proprietary interests, but may leave the intended beneficiaries, on the whole, little better off.

A central dilemma in implementation of such policies is that implementing agencies do not have sufficient power resources of their own to deal effectively with the dispersion of public and private power that they must confront if they wish to accomplish anything at all. They are rarely armed with more than their dedication, some amount of technical expertise, an official mandate to implement, and a relatively small amount of funds that can be expended at their discretion. Yet, as an early study of public and private agency efforts in "community organization for the aging" showed, virtually any attempt to develop or change service programs and facilities requires, at some point, obtaining the support and neutralizing or overcoming the opposition of public organizations—county, municipal, and state agencies; special district and metropolitan governments; regional planning authorities; advisory commissions, committees, and councils—as well as private organizations, interest groups, organized citizen constituen-

cies, and local elites that control relevant fragments of power. To the extent that the implementing agencies are unable to exercise some form of power to secure support and to neutralize or overcome opposition, the results are that initial objectives are substantially altered and attenuated, success in implementation is greatly delayed, and many efforts at implementation are unsuccessful, even with altered and attenuated objectives (Morris and Binstock, 1966).

Analyses of efforts to implement a variety of Social Development policies reinforce these findings, regardless of whether there is initial consensus (Pressman and Wildavsky, 1979) or substantial conflict (Derthick, 1972) among the relevant parties. A generalization that emerges from such studies (Bailey and Mosher, 1968; Murphy, 1971; Williams and Elmore, 1976; Bardach, 1977) is that the greater the number of parties that are involved and need to be dealt with in an implementation effort, the greater the probability of failure, delay, and goal alteration and attenuation. But even if comparatively few parties are involved, perhaps two or three target organizations or constituencies, implementation is still likely to deviate from initial policy objectives. Such deviation is likely because the state and local bureaucracies responsible for implementation often do not have the organizational capacities or intra-organizational incentives to carry out the necessary tasks (Murphy, 1971, 1974).

The tendency of public and private bureaucracies to resist innovations, whether generated externally or internally, has received extensive treatment in scholarly literature. In the context of considering organizations as targets of implementation efforts, it is sufficient to note a major reason for this tendency. An "organization does not search for or consider alternatives to the present course of action unless that present course is in some sense 'unsatisfactory' " (March and Simon, 1958). Or, to state it another way, an organization's "existing pattern of behavior has qualities of persistence; it is valuable in some way or it would not be maintained" (Simon et al., 1961). Since implementation efforts almost always pose some change in a target organization's existing pattern of behavior, an implementing agency needs to be able to exercise some form of power in an attempt to overcome or at least neutralize the target's resistance.

Organized citizen constituencies and other political action groups also may often be relatively unsusceptible to the exercise of power by an implementing agency because such groups are primarily maintained through purposive incentives (the attainment of political objectives), rather than through material or associational incentives (Wilson, 1973). Because of the stress that American political culture exerts in favor of participatory processes (Lowi, 1969), many of the Social Development policies adopted in the 1960s and '70s explicitly required local citizen participation in the processes of implementation.

Skeptics assume that citizen participation has been pro forma. Some social scientists have argued that participation requirements are a strategy employed by elites to preempt potential citizen opposition (Lipsky, 1968; Piven and Cloward, 1977). Nevertheless, there is some indication that genuine participation by citizen constituencies can shape policy to meet local circumstances and desires. In a study of the initial implementation of the General Revenue Sharing program, for instance, Nathan and Adams (1977) reported evidence that citizens' groups had leverage on resource allocation at the state and local levels. At the same time, authentic participation by such constituencies may result in delay and goal attenuation (Crain et al., 1969; Riedel, 1972; Greenstone and Peterson, 1973). An early study of advisory commissions, councils, and committees of State Units on Aging identified patterns of association between the participation of various constituencies in those bodies and selections of state and local goals that were comparatively noninnovative (Binstock et al., 1974).

If the objectives of implementation are not vitiated and frustrated by the tradeoffs of citizen participation requirements, an implementing agency may have opportunities to exercise power for securing support and neutralizing or overcoming opposition from other relevant parties. But as indicated earlier, few implementing agencies have an impressive stock of resources for exercising power, and Social Development legislation adds little to that stock—relatively small amounts of funds, and vague official mandates from Washington to carry out implementation missions. Although the funds and the importance of the missions may be greater under some policies than others, in few cases are there sufficient resources for efficiently and effectively coping with state and local fragments of public and private power—certainly not, for instance, in the case of the Older Americans Act (U.S. House of Representatives, Select Committee on Aging, 1977).

The classic solutions proposed for the problems engendered by the multiplicity of implementing parties may cause more difficulties than the problems themselves. One recurring proposal is to have federal legislation and regulations sufficiently detailed to anticipate and counter the tendencies of implementing agencies and vested interests to thwart or attenuate intended policy results (Lowi, 1969). The likelihood of such tightly drawn provisions is small, however, because of the basic circuit-breaker pattern of policy adoption politics discussed earlier in this chapter. Moreover, as Lipsky (1980) and others have pointed out, detailed and complex legislative and regulatory provisions can become a major source of administrative difficulties in the process of implementation. For instance, federal regulations require all service providers under the Older Americans Act to "provide each older person with a free and voluntary opportunity to contribute to the cost of the service . . . " (Federal Register, 1980, pp. 21157–58). Attempts to operationalize this regulation, particularly at the sites of congregate nutrition programs, cause a great many difficulties for administrative agencies. On the one hand, some older persons who are economically well off come forward to receive free meals and do not contribute; tales are commonly heard in which the older person drives an expensive automobile up to a nutrition site and comes in for a free meal, but refuses to contribute. On the other hand, administrators and staff express concern that relatively low-income older persons are making contributions when they should not feel obligated to do so (Binstock et al., 1984).

Another recurring proposal is to let state and local agencies have virtual autonomy in the determination of policy goals (Anderson, 1978). This policy strategy, by definition, reduces the problems of implementation engendered by federalism. But, of course, it also fundamentally undermines the premise that intervention and funding by the national government are needed at all.

In the 1960s and early '70s it was recognized that some implementing agencies with substantial power at their disposal used it to thwart new Social Development initiatives. This led to a number of policies that called for bypassing established bureaucracies and creating new agencies for implementation such as the Area Agencies on Aging (AAAs) under the Older Americans Act. The theory behind this approach was that newly created bureaucracies would be unfettered by organizational stasis, committed to the innovations of the policy that created them, and willing to expend what power they had directly for the goals of implementation (Marris and Rein, 1969). But this device did not solve the underlying dilemmas of implementation. The advantages of being a new implementing structure tend to vanish quickly over time. And as Hudson (1974) observed in analyzing the creation of AAAs, the incentives leading new bureaucratic agencies to work for their political survival are likely to be in conflict with implementation effectiveness.

Another device that has been frequently put forward as a panacea for dealing with the fragmentation of power that impedes implementation is a mandate for coordination. However, legislation and administrative regulations that charge implementing agencies with a mission to coordinate are simply restating the underlying dilemma of policy implementation in a somewhat misdirecting and confusing fashion. Coordination is a euphemism for exercising power to secure support and to neutralize or overcome the opposition of organizations, constituencies, and other parties that control relevant fragments of power (Binstock, 1971). Efforts to coordinate are frustrated by the customary difficulties of implementing policies in a political system characterized by a dispersion of power. An analysis of 184 coordination objectives sought by 48 State Units on Aging, for instance, found a remarkable degree of goal displacement and attenuation (Hudson and Veley, 1974).

Pressures on Service Providers

Still another issue uncovered in implementation studies is the critical role played by the front-line workers or "street-level bureaucrats"—professionals and other staff members—who are expected to deliver (but sometimes do not deliver) policy to the public. As Vladeck (1980) has pointed out, it is far more difficult to implement regulations that pertain to the interactions between staff and nursing home patients than those that apply to the physical structure of nursing homes because the characteristics and behavior of staff are not easily controlled.

Nursing home aides, police, hospital workers, and social workers face the difficult challenge of reconciling the often conflicting demands of policy directives, clients, co-workers, and formal and informal performance criteria within their own organizations. And they face this challenge within a context of limited time and resources available for an appropriately individualized response. The informal coping mechanisms that workers develop to accommodate to these conflicts (Dressel, 1984) often result in a level and quality of services that fall far short of stated policy objectives (Weatherley and Lipsky, 1977; Weatherley, 1979; Lipsky, 1980). At the same time, the wide discretion that some street-level bureaucrats have in making case-by-case decisions means that they often, in effect, determine policy. Such insights about the critical role played by street-level bureaucrats have led to reconceptualizations of the implementation process for certain types of policies, starting with an emphasis on the behavior of service providers and the conditions they confront in attempting to deliver policy to the public (Lipsky, 1978; Elmore, 1979–80; Weatherley, 1979).

The Politics of Policy Perpetuation

Many Social Development policies, in their very nature, need to be sustained for a substantial period of time if they are to have any chance of achieving their stated social intervention goals. For example, the achievement of a comprehensive, coordinated service delivery network through the Older Americans Act—involving the establishment and operation of some 600 Area Agencies on Aging—obviously requires, even in an era of social program expansion, many years of nurturing and development. Program survival is part of the implementation process for such policies.

The survival of a Social Devlopment policy appears to rest largely with its capacity to maintain political support, regardless of its effectiveness as an intervention effort. One source of support is the cadres of implementing agency personnel, consumer constituencies, and organizations that directly receive the benefits distributed through implementation. When the issue of continuing the policy through legislative reauthorization is at stake, such cadres are well-equipped and prepared to pursue their interests effectively in the legislative arena. Throughout the two decades since the Older Americans Act was first enacted, more than 24 aging-based interest groups have been effective in extending, expanding, and shaping the legislation in accordance with their various interests (Coombs, 1982).

Another reason Social Development policies have tended to survive is that they meet the requirements of political symbolism for instant and quantifiable "success." The ex-

ecutive and legislative branches of government along with implementing agency staff and beneficiary groups all have an interest in keeping programs going at some level, no matter how limited they may be in addressing underlying problems (Kaufman, 1976). Political leaders can point to existing programs as evidence that something is being done; sympathetic bureaucracies and constituencies can hope that even weak programs may someday be improved incrementally.

For these reasons many Social Development policies have been perpetuated despite the implementation dilemmas that render them inefficient and ineffective as measures of social intervention. To be sure, some of them have been abandoned as federal programs; but the overwhelming majority of the initiatives of the expansionist period of the past two decades have survived, in one form or another, despite their widely acknowledged limitations as ameliorative policies.

Even a new President who is strongly inclined to curtail Social Development programs finds it politically difficult to repeal existing policies outright. For instance, when President Reagan took office in 1981 he initially aspired to consolidate some 500 specific categorical grant-in-aid programs into six unrestricted block grants—two for education, two for health, one for energy and emergency aid, and one for social services. By the end of the year, however, he had to settle for consolidating only 57 programs into nine block grants.

On the other hand, policies can be maintained in form but eviscerated in content through the appointment of agency administrators who are willing to curtail or redirect programs through budget reductions, new regulations, selective enforcement, and the articulation of new intitiatives. In the Reagan Administration, for example, such appointments were made in the Department of Education, the Environmental Protection Agency, the Department of the Interior, the Legal Services Corporation, and the Office of Civil Rights Enforcement.

The American political system tends to reward its national politicians for the causes they espouse and the policies they adopt; but it does not tend to punish them for failures of implementation. Neither the American public nor the media demand that members of Congress give continuous oversight to policy implementation. Responsibility for implementation failure tends to be placed upon federal, state, and local bureaucrats and attributed to their administrative inadequacies. For Social Development policies to be legislatively sustained in some ongoing fashion, it is sufficient that they be relatively noncontroversial, and that members of Congress receive reports that the amount of money appropriated has been used to establish program units and serve clients in their separate constituencies, as well as throughout the nation.

SOCIAL SCIENTISTS AND THE POLITICS OF INTERVENTION

Despite the political dilemmas that limit the effectiveness of governmental intervention policies, social scientists and reformers across the spectrum of political ideologies have managed to maintain some degree of optimism regarding the prospects for social amelioration. Some of this optimism is sustained by looking for alternatives to the mechanisms of the existing political system.

An enduring approach of conservatives has been an assumption that the economic market, relatively unfettered by governmental interference, is the best available mechanism for the allocation of resources and for determining what should be produced and how it should be distributed (Schultze, 1977; Wolf, 1979; Friedman, 1981). Yet, the experience of recent decades has repeatedly pointed up the inequities, inefficiencies, redundancies, and unanticipated consequences of the private market (Liebman, 1974; Lindblom, 1977), as well as the flaws in theories of market behavior (Thurow, 1983).

Another classical optimistic approach is to focus upon forces through which basic features of a system may change. Liberals tend to search for underlying social and economic

trends that may have a gradual, inexorable impact over time (Heclo, 1981). Radicals look to fundamental changes in the locus of power within society (Carnoy and Shearer, 1980). The possibilities for such changes and whether they would be desirable are issues beyond the scope of this analysis.

Within the context of the existing political system, however, it is possible to have a reasonably optimistic perspective. The political structures and processes that limit policy effectiveness also present opportunities to reformers through which the effectiveness of policy initiatives may be somewhat improved. The final portion of this chapter considers some of the ways available to social scientists and other professionals for influencing choices in processes of policy adoption and implementation so that social interventions may be optimized.

Optimizing Policy Adoption

An exponential growth in the amount of social information used in public policy processes took place between the Great Depression and the 1960s, leading to a "professionalization of reform" in which many social scientists and other professionals have become heavily involved in the development of policy proposals (Moynihan, 1965). In addition to generating data that are used to develop and justify policy proposals, social scientists are able to offer their policy advice and ideas, and are listened to, in a variety of public and private settings: through Congressional testimony, service on commissions and task forces, and articles and speeches; and by working directly with politicians and their staffs, bureaucrats, political parties, and organized interests.

Despite the political dilemmas that make it difficult for effective social policies to be legislatively adopted, the substance of policy advice and proposals put forward can make a difference. There are some considerable differences in content and strategy among approaches that can be chosen as proposals for coping with a particular social problem or set of problems. The choice proposed, though customarily altered and diluted in the legislative process, is usually reflected to some extent in the policy ultimately adopted. Aggressive advocacy of proposals by social scientists and other professionals can optimize legislative outcomes by emphasizing basic approaches to intervention that, given the nature of American politics, seem to work better than others. Even if social scientists are not the source of a proposal that may come into political fashion, they at least can choose to play a role in legitimating it (Wilson, 1981).

One choice that is clearly indicated by our earlier analysis of the political limitations on policy implementation is to deemphasize approaches that require complex strategies of implementation and to emphasize approaches that come closest to approximating "self-implementing" or "self-executing" policies. No policy, of course, is wholly self-implementing. Yet there can be substantial contrasts in the degree and complexity of implementation required to carry out different types of policies.

A good example of a relatively self-implementing policy is the Old Age benefits program under Social Security, through which legislated policy states clear, specific objectives and the means for achieving them. To be sure, the administrative machinery and discretionary operations required to distribute predictable and tangible Social Security income benefits to older persons do seem quite complex when viewed in isolation, and are hardly immune to fraud, error, sabotage, and confusion (Fialka, 1981). When contrasted, however, with the machinery and operations required to distribute health care benefits through Medicare and Medicaid, and service benefits under the Older Americans Act, the implementation of Social Security seems comparatively simple and direct.

An emphasis on policies that are relatively self-implementing would seem to imply that cash income transfer policies—such as Social Security, Supplemental Security Income, and various proposals for a guaranteed minimum income—should be chosen for advocacy when issues such as the severe economic, social, and health care problems of older persons are considered for legislative attention. They avoid most of the problems of administrative discretion because they specify benefit levels and relatively clear-cut eligibility requirements. Although implementation of such policies involves some decentralization and a certain number of administrative problems, the *political difficulties* of state and local implementation through public and private agencies are minimized if not totally eliminated.

In contrast, noncash or in-kind policies entail relatively complex administrative machinery and do involve substantial political difficulties of implementation. In-kind policies—such as Medicare, Medicaid, and housing subsidies—restrict income transfers to purchasing power for a particular category of goods, services, and facilities, and require the participation of a variety of jurisdictions, agencies, administrators, and providers that receive reimbursement from the federal government. These policies necessitate substantially greater administrative discretion than Social Security and other cash transfer policies, certainly encounter far more political difficulties in the implementation process, involve excessive financial costs, and lead to goal alteration and attenuation (Altman and Sapolsky, 1981).

Social Development policies are also discretionary, complex, politically difficult to implement, and uncertain in outcome. They pass on to a complicated, costly, and hybrid administrative apparatus of state and local implementing agencies the responsibility of clarifying policy through the process of spending money and assembling and coordinating programs. As indicated earlier, implementation of these policies not only tends to be inefficient in financial terms; it also tends to alter and attenuate the objectives of policy, vague as they may be.

Although an emphasis on cash income policies is indicated by the far greater political difficulties of implementing in-kind transfer and Social Development policies, it is not at all clear that we can do without the latter two types of policies. In debating the prudence of income versus in-kind transfer and Social Development policies on the basis of considerations other than the built-in political limitations of effective implementation, proponents of both views have acknowledged that something needs to be done to improve the quantity and quality of health and social services and facilities. Some proponents of cash income policies argue that needed services and facilities should and can be developed by the private sector, as an alternative to government in-kind transfer and Social Development policies (Solomon, 1974). However, this argument rests on problematic assumptions about market elasticity, speed, and information; moreover, it sidesteps issues concerning quality control in proprietary operations (Greene and Monahan, 1981; O'Brien et al., 1983).

Regardless of the relative merits of these policy approaches, it is highly likely that in-kind transfer and Social Development policies will continue to be legislatively renewed and initiated for the foreseeable future, even in the context of curtailed government spending on social intervention. What can social scientists advocate in the policy adoption process for optimizing the effectiveness of such interventions?

Pressman and Wildavsky (1979) recommend an emphasis on in-kind transfer and Social Development policies that are simple and direct rather than those that require an extensive sequence of numerous interdependent steps. This is fine in principle. But most in-kind transfer policies, particularly those dealing with health care, inherently involve a plethora of interconnected organizational and individual providers, bridging the public and private sectors; and most Social Development policies must rely upon the structure of federalism for implementation. Hence, the principle of simplicity and directness is difficult to realize in terms of specific policy proposals.

The problems of implementation can be reduced somewhat, however, by emphasizing certain types of in-kind transfer and Social Development policy approaches rather than others. In dealing with the financing and delivery of acute and long-term health care, for instance, there is an extraordinary variety in the range of policy options available (Callahan and Wallack, 1981; Altman and Sapolsky, 1981). In evaluating them with respect to problems of implementation, a policy advocate or analyst should be generally skeptical toward policy options that must rely upon *cooperative* and *coordinated* planning, development, and execution from a variety of organizational entities and cadres of personnel, either within the public sector or between the public and private sectors—Health Systems Agencies, Professional Standards Review Organizations, block grants to the states for long-term care, case management, and so on. In contrast, a somewhat more favorabe view can be taken in evaluating policies that are directed toward just one type of organizational structure, set of service providers, or consumers—vouchers, prospective reimbursement mechanisms, Health Maintenance Organizations, compulsory insurance programs—and have objectives that are not premised upon a complicated, interdependent series of steps and relationships. These latter kinds of policies, of course, do usually engender a series of new relationships among numerous organizations, personnel, and consumers; and they often have far-reaching consequences. But in any sound policy analysis an estimation of the permutations of probable consequences is involved (Wildavsky, 1979b). The comparative advantage in policies of this kind is that the immediate objectives, themselves, are not built upon unrealistic expectations regarding cooperation and coordination.

Another useful approach is to emphasize policies that are both designed to meet politicians' needs for tangible and quick results, and intended to achieve relatively intangible and longer-term social objectives. This combination of ingredients is particularly needed to maintain political support for Social Development policies so that they can be sustained long enough to have an effective impact.

A reasonably good example of such a policy is the Congregate Nutrition Services program authorized by the Older Americans Act. Among its stated goals when it was initially enacted in 1972 were: promotion of "better health among the older segment of our population through improved nutrition," and reduction of the social "isolation of old age, offering older Americans an opportunity to live their remaining years in dignity" (Older Americans Act, 1972, Title VII). Conditions such as better health, social integration, and dignity are neither amenable to swift achievement nor easily measured. But congregate nutrition program sites can be established, and free meals can be served within a matter of months. Measurements of the number and location of operating programs and meals served in each congressional district are easily obtainable for continuing reports to Congressional staff. Hence, the nutrition program has survived politically for more than a decade, distributing very specific benefits to older persons and, perhaps, improving their nutritional health, social integration, and dignity. Alternative nutrition policies—for example, nutritional counseling services for retirees and preretirees, or a series of educational television and radio programs—might or might not have been better for achieving the intended social objectives. It is probably safe to say, however, that they would not have maintained comparable political support for long-term survival.

Some social issues—such as age discrimination in employment; private pension funding, management, and eligibility for benefits; and the quality of care and safety conditions in nursing homes—lend themselves rather naturally to the adoption of regulatory policies. In theory, strict compliance with the standards set forth in such policies—the Age Discrimination in Employment Act, the Employee Retirement Income Security Act, and Medicaid regulations—may be the best predictors of the desired social outcomes. However, as indicated earlier, the implementation of regulatory policies is frequently ineffective because the targets of regulation are often able to neutralize or capture the regulatory machinery. Nonetheless, even the existence of regulatory policies expressing societal standards for desired outcomes—elimination of discrimination; adequate, equitable, and reliable sources of retirement income; and humane nursing home care—is to be preferred to no such policies at all. Advocates of regulatory policies should, however, be wary of unintended consequences. Rigid enforcement of strict nursing home regulations, for instance, may result in the shutdown of facilities and a reduction in the supply of badly needed nursing home beds. Tradeoffs of this kind need to be carefully weighed.

An alternative to regulatory policies that social scientists can advocate is an approach in which the federal government directly develops and continues to operate a model service or facility. The classic example of this kind of policy, which has been termed "yardstick regulation," is the Tennessee Valley Authority (TVA). A program operated directly by the federal government, the TVA was supported by reformers as a means of displaying to the American citizenry that electric power could be produced with better service and lower costs than private firms had claimed was possible (Selznick, 1966; Derthick, 1974).

Following this approach it would not be unreasonable to suggest as an alternative or complement to nursing home regulatory policy, for instance, that the federal government begin to undertake direct development and operation of a small number of model nursing homes or community-based long-term care programs. Perhaps the Veterans Administration would be an appropriate vehicle for such model operations, since for the foreseeable future it will be called upon to use its appropriations to provide care to an enormous number of veterans who will be reaching the age of 65, regardless of whether their disabilities are service-connected (Mather, 1984).

Development and operation of such model programs by the federal government would bypass some of the political difficulties encountered in implementation of contemporary service and regulatory policies that require securing cooperation and operational compliance from assembled networks of existing public and private organizations over which the implementing agency has little or no control. If an avoidance of some of the political difficulties of implementation were to yield results that were even moderately efficient and effective, public recognition of what could be done might produce the "yardstick regulation" effect. That is, the political pressures generated by public approval of the model operation might act as a countervailing force to the power of nursing home and other long-term care interests. This might, in turn, reduce the political difficulties of implementing existing long-term care regulations and services.

Although federally developed and operated model programs are likely to evade many political difficulties of implementation, it is a matter for conjecture whether a yardstick regulatory effect can take hold. Much depends on the larger societal context within which such a policy is implemented. Public attitudes toward a model federal operation might be clouded by ideological and practical concerns about government eventually taking over direct operation of all long-term care programs. On the other hand, such concerns have often tended to erode when it has become widely apparent that the mechanisms of the market, even when combined with public regulation, are inadequate for coping with severe problems of service provision.

In any event, even if a policy for direct federal operation of model long-term care programs did not result in a moderately efficient and/or effective program mode, and/or did not turn out to have some kind of yardstick regulation effect, the financial costs of this approach are not great, and the policy would provide some citizens with care. As is the case with the nutrition program discussed earlier, neither consumers nor society would be harmed.

Some social scientists and related professionals may find the notion of federally operated models, and other policy emphases that we suggested earlier in this discussion,

to be unsatisfactory on ideological or other grounds. Perhaps we would agree with them on some such considerations. However, our attention has been primarily directed to one consideration, namely, that the particular type of policy *adopted* substantially determines conditions of implementation. Accordingly, our suggestions regarding the types of policies to be advocated for adoption have been based upon criteria for reducing the inefficiency and ineffectiveness of subsequent implementation. However, some of the conditions of implementation can, in fact, be improved *after* a policy is adopted.

Optimizing Policy Implementation

The implementation studies of Social Development policies in the 1960s and '70s, emphasizing the failures of social intervention, spawned a second generation of analysis focused on overcoming the problems of implementation. This newer literature has suggested some conceptual models of the implementation process and prescribed conditions and checklists for successful implementation. But these models and prescriptions are hardly panaceas. Since policy adoption and implementation are inextricably linked, the larger contexts that shape social intervention efforts—the interconnectedness of policies, the politics of legislative adoption, and the dispersion of public and private power within the structural context of federalism—limit the efficacy of remedies focused upon the implementation process per se.

Distinctions have been drawn between "macro-implementation" and "micro-implementation" (Berman, 1978). Elements of macro-implementation have been illustrated by an analysis of bargaining between the federal government and states in the grant-in-aid process (Ingram, 1977). A study of micro-implementation has focused on "the process of strategic interaction among numerous special interests all pursuing their own goals, which might or might not be compatible with the goals of the policy mandate" (Bardach, 1977). Conditions contributing to effectiveness in both macro- and micro-implementation have been analyzed by Levin (1981).

Less theoretically oriented analyses have attempted to identify prerequisites for effective implementation (Van Horn, 1979), and develop elaborate checklists of resources to be marshaled and obstacles to be overcome in the process of implementation at the local level (Chase, 1979). A summary prescriptive listing of five conditions needed for effective implementation has been presented by Sabatier and Mazmanian (1979):

1. The program is based on a sound theory relating changes in target group behavior to the achievement of the desired end-state (objectives).
2. The statute (or other policy decision) contains unambiguous policy directives and structures the implementation process so as to maximize the likelihood that target groups will perform as desired.
3. The leaders of the implementing agencies possess substantial managerial and political skill and are committed to statutory goals.
4. The program is actively supported by organized constituency groups and by a few key legislators (or chief executive) throughout the implementation process, with the courts being neutral or supportive.
5. The relative priority of statutory objectives is not significantly undermined over time by the emergence of conflicting public policies or by changes in relevant socioeconomic conditions that undermine the statute's technical theory or political support. (pp. 484–485)

This prescriptive framework exemplifies both the strengths and weaknesses of much of the implementation literature. The five "conditions" capture much of what implementation case studies suggest are necessary, if not sufficient, prerequisites for effective implementation of intervention policies. At the same time, one can know that these conditions are necessary but not be able to bring them about; in reality they rarely exist. Theories on which policies are based tend to be chosen from among a range of competing theories reflecting different ideological positions; indeed, theories often serve simply as after-the-fact rationalizations for political coalitions and accommodations. The legislative process generally produces ambiguous statutes. Consequently, public and private agencies have some freedom to implement them selectively. Constituent groups are frequently divided in their views of how policies should be carried out. Managerial commitment and skills are, in themselves, insufficient to overcome these obstacles, and resources are rarely commensurate with the statutory task. Even when some favorable conditions exist, their contributions are significantly limited because politics pervades implementation as well as policy adoption (Levin, 1981).

Nonetheless, social scientists and their professional colleagues can have some influence on the process of implementing policies that have already been adopted, particularly in relation to what we have termed Social Development policies. Federal, state, and local implementing agencies, of course, will tend to adapt the advice given to them in order to meet the political conditions of their survival and enhancement. Yet, such advice can be reflected in agencies' decisions and need not, in any event, always be at odds with the political pressures they confront.

Our earlier analysis of the political difficulties that limit efficient implementation has several implications for giving advice to federal bureaucrats who interpret the implementing conditions set forth in legislation. First, to the extent that legislation does not spell out complicated, interdependent steps and procedures for implementation, federal officials should be advised to avoid the creation or elaboration of complications through their own interpretive decisions.

Federal regulations under the Older Americans Act provide excellent illustrations of both an unnecessarily complicated approach to implementation and a sensible approach. On the one hand, the Title III mandate that "preference will be given to providing services to older individuals with greatest economic or social need" is interpreted by pages of federal regulations that are internally contradictory (Binstock et al., 1984). These regulations not only apply to the behavior of State Units on Aging (SUAs), Area Agencies on Aging (AAAs), and service-providing organizations, but range in content from definitions of "economic need" and "social need" to provisions regarding "specialization in the types of services most needed by such persons" (Federal Register, 1980). As a consequence, a great many political issues of implementation have been engendered (Cutler, 1981; Parrish and Omarzu, 1984). On the other hand, federal officials have sensibly refrained from interpreting the legislative provision that "an adequate proportion" of an AAA's allotment of Title III funds be spent on access, in-home, and legal services, even though this provision is a tempting opportunity for bureaucratic proliferation of regulations.

A second strategy for advising federal administrators is to emphasize the need to provide implementation agencies with every possible chance for building power that will facilitate their capacities to implement. For instance, under Title III of the Older Americans Act, each SUA is required to designate Planning and Service Areas within the state, for which, in turn, AAAs are designated. Some SUAs, in submitting their designations to the federal Commissioner on Aging for review and approval, choose to tailor their proposals in a fashion that makes it possible for them to use as power bases the existing councils on aging, home care corporations, and other organizations that they have previously nurtured and developed. The Commissioner has a choice, within the language of the legislation, to review and approve these submissions in terms of relatively rigid demographic considerations or in terms of strategic considerations reflected in some of the SUA submissions. A social scientist concerned with optimizing implementation would advise the commissioner to choose the latter course. Federal officials should generally be encouraged to enhance the power stock of implementing agencies whenever they can because the resources available to

most implementing agencies are inadequate for coping with the difficulties of power dispersion that they must confront at the state and local levels.

Advice to state and local implementing agencies, of course, should generally follow the same lines. That is, they should be urged to use every chance they can to build their stocks of power, and to keep their processes as simple and as direct as possible.

Since state and local implementing agencies usually have limited resources for exercising power, however, what advice can be given to them for minimizing the attenuation of policy goals? Morris and Binstock (1966), using a theoretical framework of political influence, have argued that it is often possible for an implementing agency with limited resources to avoid failure and to minimize goal adaptation and attenuation by reformulating the immediate strategic objectives of its efforts. In this way, they suggest, the agency can make an effective match between the limited kinds of power it has for neutralizing opposition and securing support from among the particular situational array of targets with which it must deal, without sacrificing the substance of policy objectives. They cite a case, for example, in which an implementing agent was unsuccessful in attempting to bring about a formal agreement for coordinating the services of two mutually hostile private sector agencies. Instead of futilely persisting, the agent developed an appealing proposal for the two organizations to merge, which was accepted. Consequently, the threat posed to their respective organizational identities by the proposed agreement for coordination was eliminated by the merger, yet effective coordination of service resources for older persons was achieved.

One further important issue confronting many implementing agencies, especially those that are relatively new entities engendered by federal policy, is whether to use what power they have for political survival and maintenance in their state and local environments or for the implementation of federal policy. The implementation requirements of federal policy can tend to make these two objectives mutually exclusive (Hudson, 1974). Advising an implementing agency on this issue, however, is probably pointless. Even if one were disposed to urge an agency to risk its survival in a vigorous attempt to implement the goals of national policy, it could hardly be expected to heed such advice. This is especially so in view of a frequently demonstrated pattern in which minimal efforts to implement national policy—observance of federal regulations and expenditure of funds—and mobilization of vested interests seem sufficient to maintain continuing federal support.

The suggestions that can be made to social scientists and other professionals for optimizing implementation are limited because, as noted earlier, the few models and prescriptions that have been developed for successful policy implementation only serve to illustrate the constraints endemic to the American political system. We have already suggested, however, a number of approaches that can be emphasized in the processes of policy adoption for avoiding some of the subsequent problems of implementation. And we have also suggested a few approaches for optimizing implementation efforts. Still to be addressed is the issue of whether efforts to optimize policy intervention are worth the struggle to do so in view of the inherent political limitations on policy effectiveness.

Social Scientists and the Decision to Intervene

Americans tend to view politics as a process for resolving value differences through compromise and accommodation, rather than through the triumph of some values over others. But the difficulty with this view is that political resolutions characteristically tend to accommodate some interests more than others (Schattschneider, 1960), especially those interests that control some of the larger fragments of private power. The weighting of values and interests that reflect concern for the severity of social ills expe-

rienced by some members of society is not heavy.

In view of the deprivation and suffering experienced by millions of older persons, and by many other Americans, social scientists and other professionals have a special responsibility to be actively concerned with social intervention policies—regardless of the state of the economy and/or the inherent political constraints on policy effectiveness. Policy initiatives, even if ineffective and inefficient, provide some benefits to those in dire need. And although the rate of growth in social intervention efforts may be curtailed, at least for the time being, existing policies can be modified to provide greater benefits by reducing their ineffectiveness and inefficiencies. Moreover, an important debate is emerging, at least in the United States, on the issue of whether intervention policies toward older persons in an aging society should be designed on the basis of chronological age or according to specifically identifiable needs (Neugarten, 1982). Social scientists who have been concerned with the phenomena of aging should have a great deal to contribute to discussions of this fundamental issue.

The costs of inadequate intervention policies rarely occur in terms of social harm, but are largely in terms of time, money, and effort. Perhaps the maxim "do no harm" should govern social scientists contemplating advocacy in policy processes; they should be guided by feasibility assessments that give extra weight to potential harmful impacts through unintended consequences. The social scientist can enter into processes of policy adoption and implementation with greater aggressiveness and optimism than he or she customarily employs in evaluating scientific evidence (Levin and Dorbusch, 1973). Certainly policy initiatives entail the risk of failure. But even as the failure of some business enterprises are not treated as condemnations of capitalism, the limitations of policy effectiveness should not be treated as evidence that social intervention should be abandoned.

The period of social program expansion

that began in the United States during the Great Depression, and accelerated with the post–World War II economic boom, may be over, at least for a while. Yet social policy retrenchment offers opportunities both to renew advocacy for fundamental reforms and to minimize harm that may be incurred by social program reductions. Persistent problems of economic insecurity, illness and incapacity, and social isolation and dependency are likely to be found among older persons and other population groupings regardless of macroeconomic conditions. Solutions to many aspects of these problems exist; the obstacles to their adoption and implementation are more political than economic or technical. Basic changes in fiscal, tax, transfer, and development policies to meet the needs of vulnerable persons and reassessments of national priorities regarding social intervention remain important issues for advocacy on the agenda of policy issues. While social intervention efforts are being curtailed, social scientists and others would do well to contemplate, develop, and advocate policy approaches that may become politically feasible regardless of economic conditions.

REFERENCES

Achenbaum, W. A. 1983. *Shades of Gray: Old Age, American Values, and Federal Policies Since 1920.* Boston: Little, Brown.

Alford, R. 1976. *Health Care Politics.* Chicago: University of Chicago Press.

Altman, S. H. 1982. The larger context of Medicare financing: Issues confronting both government and the private sector. *Proceedings of a Symposium on Income Maintenance,* pp. 36–46. Waltham, Mass.: National Aging Policy Center on Income Maintenance, Brandeis University.

Altman, S. H., and Sapolsky, H. (eds.). 1981. *Federal Health Programs.* Lexington, Mass.: D. C. Heath.

Anderson, M. 1978. *Welfare.* Stanford, Calif.: Hoover Institution, Stanford University.

Bachrach, P., and Baratz, M. 1963. Decisions and nondecisions. *American Political Science Review* 57:632–642.

Bailey, S. K., and Mosher, E. K. 1968. *ESEA: The Office of Education Administers a Law.* Syracuse, N.Y.: Syracuse University Press.

Banfield, E. C. 1961. *Political Influence.* New York: The Free Press of Glencoe.

Banfield, E. C. 1970. *The Unheavenly City.* Boston: Little, Brown.

Banfield, E. C. 1973. Making a new federal program: Model Cities, 1964–68. *In* A. Sindler (ed.), *Policy and Politics in America,* pp. 125–158. Boston: Little, Brown.

Bardach, E. 1977. *The Implementation Game: What Happens After a Bill Becomes a Law.* Cambridge, Mass.: The M.I.T. Press.

Berman, P. 1978. The study of macro- and micro-implementation. *Public Policy* 26:157–184.

Binstock, R. H. 1971. *Planning.* Washington, D.C.: 1971 White House Conference on Aging.

Binstock, R. H. 1972. Interest-group liberalism and the politics of aging. *The Gerontologist* 12:265–280.

Binstock, R. H. 1974. Aging and the future of American politics. *Annals of the American Academy of Political and Social Science* 415:199–212.

Binstock, R. H. 1975. Planning for tomorrow's urban aged. *The Gerontologist* 15:42–43.

Binstock, R. H. 1978. Federal policy toward the aging—its inadequacies and its politics. *National Journal* 10:1838–1844.

Binstock, R. H. 1983. The aged as scapegoat. *The Gerontologist* 23:136–143.

Binstock, R. H., Cherington, C. M., and Woll, P. 1974. Federalism and leadership planning: Predictors of variance in state behavior. *The Gerontologist* 14:114–121.

Binstock, R. H., Chow, W.-S., and Schulz, J. H. 1982. *International Perspectives on Aging: Population and Policy Challenges.* New York: United Nations Fund for Population Activities.

Binstock, R. H., Grigsby, J., and Leavitt, T. 1984. Targeting Strategies under Title III of the Older Americans Act. Waltham, Mass.: Working Paper No. 16 of the National Aging Policy Center on Income Maintenance, Brandeis University.

Brown, L. 1983. *Politics and Health Care Organization.* Washington, D.C.: The Brookings Institution.

Callahan, J. J., Jr. and Wallack, S. S. (eds.). 1981. *Reforming the Long-Term Care System.* Lexington, Mass.: D. C. Heath.

Carnoy, M., and Shearer, D. 1980. *Economic Democracy.* White Plains, N.Y.: M. E. Sharpe.

Chase, G. 1979. Implementing a human services program: How hard will it be? *Public Policy* 27:385–435.

Cherington, C. M. 1972. Interest groups in the evolution of the Developmental Disabilities Act of 1970. Waltham, Mass.: unpublished paper, Brandeis University.

Cohen, W. J. 1983. Securing Social Security. *The New Leader* 66:5–8.

Coombs, S. R. (ed.). 1982. *An Orientation to the Older Americans Act.* Washington, D. C.: National Association of State Units on Aging.

Crain, R., Katz, E., and Rosenthal, R. 1969. *The Politics of Community Conflict.* Indianapolis, Ind.: Bobbs-Merrill.

Crystal, S. 1982. *America's Old Age Crisis: Public Pol-

icy and the Two Worlds of Aging. New York: Basic Books.

Cutler, N. E. 1981. Approaches and Obstacles to the Definition of "Greatest Economic or Social Need." Washington, D.C.: Report submitted to the Federal Council on the Aging.

Davidson, R. H. 1977. Breaking up those "cozy triangles": An impossible dream. *In* S. Welch and J. G. Peters (eds.), *Legislative Reform and Public Policy.* New York: Praeger.

Derthick, M. 1972. *New Towns In-Town.* Washington, D.C.: Urban Institute.

Derthick, M. 1974. *Between State and Nation.* Washington, D.C.: The Brookings Institution.

Derthick, M. 1975. *Uncontrollable Spending for Social Service Grants.* Washington, D.C.: The Brookings Institution.

Derthick, M. 1979. *Policymaking for Social Security.* Washington, D.C.: The Brookings Institution.

Dressel, P. 1984. *The Service Trap.* Springfield, Ill.: Charles C. Thomas.

Edelman, M. 1964. *Symbolic Uses of Politics.* Urbana, Ill.: University of Illinois Press.

Elmore, R. 1979-80. Backward mapping: Implementation research and policy decisions. *Political Science Quarterly* 94:601-616.

Elmore, R. 1982. Implementation of federal education policy: Research and analysis. *In* R. Corwin (ed.), *Research in the Sociology of Education and Socialization,* Vol. 3, pp. 97-119. Greenwich, Conn.: JAI Press.

Estes, C. L. 1979. *The Aging Enterprise.* San Francisco, Calif.: Jossey-Bass.

Federal Register. 1980. *Grants for State and Community Programs on Aging. Final Rule, Vol. 45, No. 63.* Washington, D.C.: Department of Health, Education and Welfare.

Fialka, J. J. 1981. Botched benefits. *Wall Street Journal,* Oct. 5, pp. 1 and 12.

Finkler, S. A. 1982. The distinction between costs and charges. *Annals of Internal Medicine* 96:102-109.

Flora, P., and Heidenheimer, A. 1981. *The Development of Welfare State Programs in Europe and America.* New Brunswick, N.J.: Transaction Books.

Friedan, B. 1963. *The Feminine Mystique.* New York: Dell.

Friedman, M. 1981. *Free to Choose.* New York: Harcourt, Brace, Jovanovich.

Friedrich, C. J. 1963. *Man and His Government.* New York: McGraw-Hill.

Greene, V. L., and Monahan, D. J. 1981. Structural and operational determinants of quality of patient care in nursing homes. *Public Policy* 29:399-415.

Greenstone, D., and Peterson, P. E. 1973. *Race and Authority in Urban Politics.* New York: Russell Sage Foundation.

Greider, W. 1981. The education of David Stockman. *The Atlantic* 248:27-54.

Guillemard, A. M. 1977. *A Critical Analysis of Governmental Politics on Aging from a Marxist Per-*

spective. Paris: Center for the Study of Social Movements.

Hartz, L. 1955. *The Liberal Tradition in America.* New York: Harcourt, Brace.

Haveman, R. H. 1977. *A Decade of Federal Anti-Poverty Programs: Achievements, Failures, and Lessons.* New York: Academic Press.

Heclo, H. 1981. Toward a new welfare state? *In* P. Flora and A. Heidenheimer (eds.), *The Development of Welfare State Programs in Europe and America,* pp. 383-406. New Brunswick, N.J.: Transaction Books.

Holtzman, A. 1963. *The Townsend Movement.* New York: Bookman Associates.

Hudson, R. B. 1974. Rational planning and organizational imperatives: Prospects for area planning in aging. *Annals of the American Academy of Political and Social Science* 415:41-54.

Hudson, R. B., and Veley, M. B. 1974. Federal funding and state planning: The case of the state units on aging. *The Gerontologist* 14:122-128.

Ingram, H. 1977. Policy implementation through bargaining: The case of federal grants-in-aid. *Public Policy* 25:499-526.

Kaufman, H. 1976. *Are Government Organizations Immortal?* Washington, D.C.: The Brookings Institution.

Lasswell, H. D., and Kaplan, A. 1970. *Power and Society.* New Haven, Conn.: Yale University Press.

Lawlor, E. F. 1983. Perspectives on Reform of Income Security Policy for the Aged. Waltham, Mass.: Working Paper No. 8 of the National Aging Policy Center on Income Maintenance, Brandeis University.

Levin, M. A. 1979. The department of unintended consequences. *Taxing and Spending* 2:12-15.

Levin, M. A. 1981. Conditions contributing to effective implementation and their limits. *In* J. Crecine (ed.), *Research in Public Policy Analysis and Management,* Vol. I, pp. 65-111. Greenwich, Conn.: JAI Press.

Levin, M. A., and Dornbusch, H. D. 1973. Pure and policy social science. *Public Policy* 21:383-423.

Liebman, L. 1974. Social intervention in a democracy. *The Public Interest* 34:14-29.

Lilley, W., III and Miller, J. C., III. 1977. The new "social regulation." *The Public Interest* 47:49-61.

Lindblom, C. E. 1977. *Politics and Markets.* New York: Basic Books.

Lipsky, M. 1968. Protest as a political resource. *American Political Science Review* 62:1144-1158.

Lipsky, M. 1978. Standing the study of public policy implementation on its head. *In* W. D. Burnham and M. W. Weinberg (eds.), *American Politics and Public Policy,* pp. 391-402. Cambridge, Mass.: The M.I.T. Press.

Lipsky, M. 1980. *Street-Level Bureaucracy.* New York: Basic Books.

Lowi, T. J. 1964. American business, public policy, case studies and political theory. *World Politics* 16:677-715.

Lowi, T. J. 1969. *The End of Liberalism.* New York: W. W. Norton.

Madison, J. 1937. The federalist no. 10. *In: The Federalist,* pp. 53–62. New York: Random House.

March, J. G., and Simon, H. A. 1958. *Organizations.* New York: John Wiley.

Marris, P., and Rein, M. 1969. *Dilemmas of Social Reform: Poverty and Community Action in the United States.* New York: Atherton Press.

Mather, J. H. 1984. Long term care issues in aging. *In* W. Kelly (ed.), *Current Issues in Geriatrics.* Springfield, Ill.: Charles C. Thomas. (In press.)

Mendelson, M. A., and Hapgood, D. 1974. The political economy of nursing homes. *Annals of the American Academy of Political and Social Science,* 415:95–105.

Morris, R., and Binstock, R. H. 1966. *Feasible Planning for Social Change.* New York: Columbia University Press.

Moynihan, D. P. 1965. The professionalization of reform. *The Public Interest* 1:6–16.

Moynihan, D. P. 1973. *The Politics of A Guaranteed Income.* New York: Vintage Books.

Murphy, J. 1971. Title I of ESEA: The politics of implementing federal education reform. *Harvard Educational Review* 41:35–63.

Murphy, J. 1974. *State Education Agencies and Discretionary Funds.* Lexington, Mass.: D. C. Heath.

Myers, G. C. 1982. The aging of populations. *In* R. H. Binstock, W.-S. Chow, and J. H. Schulz (eds.), *International Perspectives on Aging: Population and Policy Challenges,* pp. 1–39. New York: United Nations Fund for Population Activities.

Nathan, R. P., and Adams, C. F., Jr. 1977. *Revenue Sharing: The Second Round.* Washington, D. C.: The Brookings Institution.

Neugarten, B. 1974. Age groups in American society and the rise of the young-old. *Annals of the American Academy of Political and Social Science* 415:187–198.

Neugarten, B. (ed.). 1982. *Age or Need?* Beverly Hills, Calif.: Sage Publications.

O'Brien, J., Saxeberg, B. O., and Smith, H. L. 1983. For-profit or not-for-profit nursing homes: Does it matter? *The Gerontologist* 23:341–348.

Older Americans Act, As Amended Through 1972 (Public Law 89–73).

Older Americans Act, As Amended Through 1981 (Public Law 89–73).

Olson, L. K. 1982. *The Political Economy of Aging.* New York: Columbia University Press.

Oriol, W. 1982. *Aging in All Nations.* Washington, D.C.: The National Council on the Aging.

Palmer, J. L., and Sawhill, I. V. (eds.). 1982. *The Reagan Experiment.* Washington, D.C.: The Urban Institute.

Parrish, C., and Omarzu, C. 1984. Implementation of the mandate for an intrastate funding formula. San Francisco, Calif.: Paper presented at the 36th Annual Scientific Meeting of the Gerontological Society of America.

Piven, F. F., and Cloward, R. A. 1977. *Poor People's Movements: Why They Succeed, How They Fail.* New York: Pantheon Books.

Pratt, H. J. 1976. *The Politics of Old Age.* Chicago: Unversity of Chicago Press.

Pressman, J. L., and Wildavsky, A. B. 1979. *Implementation: How Great Expectations in Washington Are Dashed in Oakland.* Berkeley: University of California Press.

Riedel, J. A. 1972. Citizen participation: Myths and realities. *Public Administration Review* 32:211–220.

Sabatier, P., and Mazmanian, D. 1979. The conditions of effective implementation: A guide to accomplishing policy objectives. *Policy Analysis* 5:481–504.

Schattschneider, E. E. 1960. *The Semi-Sovereign People.* New York: Holt, Rinehart & Winston.

Schultze, C. L. 1977. *The Public Use of Private Interest.* Washington, D.C.: The Brookings Institution.

Schulz, J. H., Leavitt, T. D., Litkouhi, S., and Strate, J. M. 1983. The Impact of Pension Integration on the Income of Minority Persons in Later Years. Waltham, Mass.: Working Paper No. 11 of the National Aging Policy Center on Income Maintenance, Brandeis University.

Selby, P., and Schechter, M. 1982. *Aging 2000: A Challenge for Society.* Boston: MTP Press Limited.

Selznick, P. 1966. *TVA and the Grass Roots.* New York: Harper & Row, Torchbook.

Simon, H. A., Smithburg, D. W., and Thompson, V. A. 1961. *Public Administration.* New York: Alfred A. Knopf.

Solomon, A. P. 1974. *Housing the Urban Poor.* Cambridge, Mass.: The M.I.T. Press.

Starr, P. 1982. *The Social Transformation of American Medicine.* New York: Basic Books.

Stockman, D. A. 1975. The social pork barrel. *The Public Interest* 39:3–30.

Sundquist, J. L., and Davis, D. W. 1969. *Making Federalism Work.* Washington, D.C.: The Brookings Institution.

Thurow, L. 1980. *The Zero-Sum Society.* New York: Basic Books.

Thurow, L. 1983. *Dangerous Currents.* New York: Random House.

Tufte, E. R. 1978. *Political Control of the Economy.* Princeton, N.J.: Princeton University Press.

U.S. House of Representatives, Select Committee on Aging. 1977. *Fragmentation of Services for the Elderly.* Washington, D.C.: U.S. Government Printing Office, Comm. Pub. No. 95–93.

U.S. House of Representatives, Select Committee on Aging, Subcommittee on Human Services. 1980. *Future Directions for Aging Policy: A Human Service Model.* Washington, D.C.: U.S. Government Printing Office, Comm. Pub. No. 96–226.

U.S. Senate, Special Committee on Aging. 1983. *Developments in Aging: 1982, Volume 1.* Washington, D.C.: U.S. Government Printing Office, S. Report. 98–13.

U.S. White House Conference on Aging, Technical

Committee on an Age-Integreated Society—Implications for the Economy. 1981. *Economic Policy in an Aging Society*. Washington, D.C.: White House Conference on Aging, 1981.

Van Horn, C. E. 1979. *Policy Implementation in the Federal System*. Lexington, Mass.: D. C. Heath.

Vinyard, D. 1972. The Senate Special Committee on Aging. *The Gerontologist* 12:298–303.

Vladeck, B. 1980. *Unloving Care: The Nursing Home Tragedy*. New York: Basic Books.

Weatherley, R. 1979. *Reforming Special Education*. Cambridge, Mass.: The M.I.T. Press.

Weatherley, R., and Lipsky, M. 1977. Street-level bureaucrats and institutional innovation: The case of special education reforms. *Harvard Educational Review* 47:171–197.

Wildavsky, A. 1979a. *The Politics of the Budgetary Process*. Boston: Little, Brown.

Wildavsky, A. 1979b. *Speaking Truth to Power*. Boston: Little, Brown.

Williams, W., and Elmore, R. 1976. *Social Program Implementation*. New York: Academic Press.

Williamson, J. B., Evans, L., and Powell, L. A. 1982. *The Politics of Aging*. Springfield, Ill.: Charles C. Thomas.

Wilson, J. Q. 1966. The war on cities. *The Public Interest* 1:27–44.

Wilson, J. Q. 1973. *Political Organizations*. New York: Basic Books.

Wilson, J. Q. 1981. "Policy intellectuals" and public policy. *The Public Interest* 64:31–46.

Wolf, C., Jr. 1979. A theory of non-market failures. *The Public Interest* 55:114–133.

Wright, D. 1968. *Federal Grants-in-Aid: Perspectives and Alternatives*. Washington, D.C.: American Enterprise Institute.

21
STRATEGIES OF RESEARCH FOR PROGRAM DESIGN AND INTERVENTION

Robert J. Newcomer
Carroll L. Estes
and
Howard E. Freeman*
University of California
San Francisco and Los Angeles

In the field of aging, as in other areas of human concern, methodologies must be developed and research conducted as a basis for designing intervention. The purpose of this chapter is to direct attention to some of the issues and requirements for the design, implementation, and evaluation of social interventions for older persons. In this discussion intervention is broadly defined to include both programmatic and structural alterations that aim at social change (Baltes, 1973).

Our premise is that the application of social science knowledge and perspectives can improve understanding of the root causes of social problems and conditions, and that such knowledge can be useful in developing ideas about the prevention, treatment, and management of the problems affecting society. The analytical approaches discussed are applicable in the development of both

public and nonpublic interventions, and are relatively universal with respect to societies throughout the world. The major concern is to obtain a clear problem definition and to select a course of action that responds to the root issues. In discussing the methodological strategies for accomplishing this we have drawn examples from the evaluation research literature to give tangible illustration to these concepts. While this literature is largely from the United States, we believe the examples themselves reflect broader experience.

KNOWLEDGE AS A BASIS FOR INTERVENTION

It is important to remember that what is done for and about the elderly is to some degree a product of our conceptions of aging. In an abstract philosophical sense, the aged have only the problems we "create" for them as a result of such conceptions. Therefore, a consideration of the determinants of such

*We gratefully acknowledge the editorial and research assistance of Lenore Gerard, Associate in Research, Aging Health Policy Center, University of California, San Francisco.

conceptions and the knowledge and opinions on which they are based is necessary.

The Social Construction of Problems of the Aging

For the past 30 years much of the social gerontological research has focused on the individual and the adjustment of the individual to circumstances that in large part are externally determined (Freeman, 1978; Estes, 1979; Tindale and Marshall, 1980; Dowd, 1980). Knowledge is socially generated; it emerges from the ordering and interpretation of facts (Gouldner, 1970). Based upon empirical demonstrations of proof or upon the judgments of proclaimed experts and authorities with status and power, knowledge may be accepted as factually legitimate. The less the knowledge base is empirically developed, the greater the influence of social and political factors in the interpretation and acceptance of data as knowledge.

As definitions of reality become widely shared, they are institutionalized as part of the "collective stock of knowledge" (Berger and Luckman, 1966, p. 67), or what Lindblom and Cohen (1979) term "ordinary" knowledge. Although socially generated, such knowledge and expert opinion take on the character of objective reality, whether or not they are valid. This "knowledge," in turn influences both the perception of social problems and ideas about how to deal with them (i.e., social interventions). Thus, social researchers and others involved in the design and implementation of intervention programs are, themselves, actively engaged in modifying and structuring social reality for the aged through their research and generation of "knowledge."

The essential point is that theories and perspectives in the field of gerontology are versions of reality that are also socially constructed. Current conceptions of the aged and aging, as well as appropriate intervention strategies in the aging field, are not determined solely by objective facts but by (1) the interpretation and ordering of perceptions of those facts into paradigms or ways of perceiving and explaining the world (Kuhn 1970), and (2) the power and influence of the perceivers and interpreters (Gouldner, 1970). Thus, in an important sense, the aged do not have social problems other than the ones we have "given" them.

To assert that reality is socially constructed is not to deny phenomena associated with chronological aging and structural conditions that may be said to be objectively real, regardless of how they are perceived. Social action, however, is indivisible from the socially constructed ideas that define and provide images of these phenomena. These ideas, in turn, are affected by the dominant ideologies and paradigms, as well as by the organizational and interorganizational political resources of advocacy and interest groups for the elderly. All these elements influence the definition of social problems and the prescribed solutions.

The development of intervention strategies is intertwined, then, with the "societal reaction" to the phenomenon of aging, including that of professionals in the field (Lemert 1951, 1973; Coser, 1965).

CONCEPTUAL AND OPERATIONAL FRAMEWORKS FOR INTERVENTION

It is clear that a complex mosaic of political views, values, professional and research interests, funding agencies, and priorities determines the scope and nature of intervention. Even when there is readiness for change, or at least a climate that allows it to be accomplished, it can be difficult. For example, while it is recognized that social structural changes are important, the power of interest groups to modify their own positions limits the applicability of this framework. This is as true of social agency practitioners as it is of members of the general community (Estes, 1973).

Three general orientations guide most of the intervention efforts in the field of aging. They involve efforts aimed at change at the individual, social psychological, and social structural levels.

Individual Change

The functioning of an individual within any environmental setting depends in part on the individual's capabilities. Important factors contributing to these capabilities are such physical and mental health conditions as sensory perception and adaptive skills and functional status. Other forms of individual capability are reflected in material resources such as income levels and social networks (Lawton and Nahemow, 1973).

This perspective reflects interactions among biological processes, stress, trauma, disease, various life-style patterns, and a number of other social, cultural, economic, and environmental conditions (Kasl and Berkman, 1981).

Many programs emphasize the individual as the focus of intervention. This is done through such procedures as treating specific diseases, providing prostheses for physical impairments and psychotherapy for mental conditions, and efforts designed to change the behavior of individuals.

A framework that focuses on the individual offers a number of attractions. Problems are often manifest on the individual level, and many problems can be prevented or ameliorated by such a focus. A limitation of a singular focus on this level of intervention is that it may concentrate on symptoms of a condition and not necessarily the cause. The selection of an intervention strategy should involve consideration of whether the problem is being addressed in fundamental ways or just treated. However, it should also be recognized that not all problems can be resolved by a single or even a complex set of interventions. This is particularly true if the causal factors lie outside the control of the individual experiencing the problem.

Social Psychological Change

Many programs are based on the viewpoint that, in one way or another, it is essential to change the thinking, values, and attitudes of one group or another. Some of these programs focus directly on the aged; they often

include efforts to provide information on nutrition and opportunities for participation in social activities, as well as to modify the value stances of different groups. Such programs may be directed toward the elderly, toward others in the community, and sometimes toward an entire community population (Cohen, 1970). Some may be essentially political in character, to provide popular support for various actions believed appropriate by politicians and politically appointed administrators. It is absolutely necessary, of course, that such activities take place if there is to be public support for programs of extended health insurance, public housing, and the like for the aged.

In addition, although less prevalent, there are programs directed toward changing the attitudes, beliefs, and values of the professionals who interact with the aged. The aged have often been regarded, regardless of what profession is involved, as "uninteresting," "disreputable," or "difficult" (Coe, 1967; Butler, 1969; Mutschler, 1971). In the medical field, there is evidence to suggest that there is an aversion to providing care to the elderly, especially to those residing in nursing homes (Sparacino, 1979; Kane et al., 1981). Long-term terminal cases in particular are frequently regarded as burdensome by health practitioners (Spence et al., 1968). The same observation holds for those engaged in a variety of social programs, including recreational activities and educational efforts (Troll and Schlossberg, 1970). Efforts to change the perspectives and interests of professionals have filtered into formal education programs of all sorts (Seltzer et al., 1978; Peterson and Bolton, 1980).

Social psychological interventions attempted in fields such as race relations and mental health provide important lessons for gerontology. A generalization supported by research is that "knowledge" is relatively easy to modify through a variety of communication methods. Most studies of efforts to modify values and deep-seated attitudes, however, have not proved particularly successful. Many argue that these more fundamental changes occur only when the social environment is modified and are subsequent rather than antecedent to major modifications in the values held by individuals (Rose, 1965; Scott and Freeman, 1966).

Social Structural Change

The idea that important modifications in the lives of individuals and in their environments require intervention at a social structural level is not a new viewpoint; it can be traced to religious movements throughout history and to numerous social, political, and economic philosophers who have stressed the need to modify the outlines of society.

Social structural change may be directed to altering opportunity structures in the social environment in specific areas such as work, health, housing, or income. The economic well-being of older persons is an example of a complex causal model problem influenced by macroeconomic trends and political events at the national and international levels (U.S. Department of Health, Education, and Welfare, 1978). Factors such as the rate of economic growth, inflation, labor force trends, and productivity are critical in shaping the economic climate, which in turn influences the quality of life for older persons (Kingson and Scheffler, 1981). Interventions designed to stimulate social structural change may represent a wide range of options, including raising the age of mandatory retirement, encouraging workers to stay in the labor force longer by creating real employment opportunities, and providing tax incentives for individual savings and retirement accounts.

Social structural change, however, need not be aimed only at the general level of the community. Although modifications in the service delivery system may appear to be too narrow to be regarded as social structural change, such modifications can represent important incremental change. For example, one could speculate that legislation requiring all agencies and organizations to have 10 percent of their client caseloads consist of persons 60 years of age or older, or requiring all hospitals and outpatient clinics to have

special geriatric units, would undoubtedly result in improvement of service delivery access. In addition to changes in the health and social service delivery systems, it is also important to consider changes in the methods by which public support is given to old people. For example, a federally guaranteed minimum income program might well have less social stigma than a welfare system of transfers for medical care, food stamps, and the like (Williamson, 1974, 1982).

Chapters 19 and 20 of this *Handbook* present discussions of legislation and programs designed for such forms of change, and also consider alternative explanations for the emergence of policies toward older persons.

REQUIREMENTS FOR POLICY RESEARCH

A basic assumption of this chapter is that social science research can and does produce results with policy and program relevance. There is evidence, however, to show how infrequently specific research findings are translated into policy (Weiss, 1977a). The traditional schism between research and application is at least as evident in gerontology as in other fields. It is found at all levels of research, from the formulation and design of research to the translation of research findings for practical application.

As described by Scott and Shore (1974), policy relevance is determined by the policy salience and tractability of the variables assumed to be associated with the outcome variables. Tractability is related to the potential for manipulation or change in an operating program or policy.

An orientation to policy-tractable measures, it can be concluded, is a necessary factor in explaining the relevance of a study for policymakers. But is tractability by itself sufficient? It has been argued that social research at best only supplements other inputs into social problem solving, and that it rarely produces independent authoritative knowledge (Lindblom and Cohen, 1979). Research findings in this context are thought to be useable when they confirm or are confirmed by "ordinary" knowledge. In other words, the value of the research is dependent upon the points of view, common sense, or other informal bases of knowledge (e.g., experience or interest group discussion) among decision makers.

How then does one reconcile this disparity between scientific approaches to problem analysis and the more politically negotiated approaches? Is one inherently more valid than the other? Lindblom (1980) has characterized this tissue as one of image. On the one hand there are analysts and others who desire more scientific information as a basis for social problem solving. At the extreme, these individuals would argue for analysis as an alternative to politics. Others, like Lindblom, recognize the limitations of all research (e.g., measurement, scope, depth, conceptualization) and the fact that participants in a decision-making process are informed by their own experts. This expertise may be in the form of scientific studies, practical experience, or simply logical arguments. Analysis in this context, therefore, is viewed as one of many contributions to the political interaction that produces policy choices.

The perspective underlying our assumptions about the usefulness of research is based on several givens. First, policy research, while addressing many of the same issues and employing the same theories, concepts, and variables as research on social phenomena and social problems, is generated by specific policy concerns and concentrates on studying tractable input variables (Coleman, 1972). This research is also pragmatic, political, and value-laden (Lindblom, 1980). There is an obvious tension in the conduct of policy research between adhering to the canons of science and the rules of social research and also attempting to satisfy the demands and expectations of policymakers. This strain is most evident in a pressure to do the best work possible, given the limited time and information available, and the need to be explicit with regard to the values and assumptions that influence one's conclusions. Unless social research meets such conditions and is otherwise usable by policymakers, the latter are likely to use inadequate research or none at all. This suggests that the policy researcher has a special responsibility to meet a dual commitment to policymakers and to academic peers in the conduct of research for intervention.

PERSPECTIVES ON CAUSATION

Despite the plea for orderly development of intervention models, there is no inevitable sequence to their development. As in the case of the genesis of most research problems in the social sciences, a number of inputs—including extant theoretical notions, visibility of social concerns, political considerations, and availability of funding—play a role in the development of particular interventions. Sometimes specification of the target population and choice of a level of intervention are early steps; at other times they occur subsequent to the formulation of other elements in an intervention design. In general, it is reasonable to think of three causal models as guiding the development of intervention models in the aging field: proximal, multicausal, and epidemiological.

Proximal Cause

Continuing scientific investigation into the human condition provides ample evidence against the simplistic idea that single causes can be isolated to explain any of the individual, interpersonal, or social ills that confront us. The "A causes B" model, the single cause view, in most cases neither provides a sufficiently satisfying explanation nor allows full development of interventions to prevent, restore, or manage the problems confronting the aged or any other population.

At the same time, specific interventions, for purposes of the design of programs and their evaluation, often must take an economical approach. Such intervention concentrates upon a single determinant hypothesized to directly affect a given condition. It is theorized that modification of the single determinant will result in a change in the condition. This is the idea of proximal cause.

At all levels of intervention in which biological phenomena are involved, the concept of proximal cause is clear. For example, while a complex causal model is necessary to explain diabetes, control of sugar intake by either diet or drugs provides the means of managing this illness. At first glance, it seems reasonable to argue that proximal causes should be given priority in developing interventions; but there are reasons in many studies or conditions as well to argue against taking this view of causation.

From a practical standpoint, as we have noted, in addition to assessing the proximal relevance of a cause or determinant, it is essential to consider the opportunities for modification and tractability. For example, the proximal cause of unhappiness among older persons may be feelings of estrangement from their children. Remedying this situation may require changing the general community's concept of aged persons, rather than merely counseling the parties directly involved. The proximal cause, in some cases at least, must remain unattended until more distant conditions are attended to.

Finally, attention to proximal causes may direct activities unduly to interventions at the level of management of social and medical problems to the neglect of preventive types of intervention. This is not always the case, but often interventions addressed to proximal causes do not touch the underlying etiological problems. Social as well as medical concerns among the aged are more likely to be "chronic" than acute, and long-term rather than short-term. Dealing with proximal causes often can be likened to holding one's finger against a spigot rather than replacing the faucet washer.

Multicausal Models

There are two conceptions of multicausal models that are often used as a basis of intervention programs. One view holds that many different determinants exist for a particular behavior or condition. Inadequate housing for the aged, for example, is believed to be a function of lack of interest on the part of architects and physical planners, a shortage of public funds, the residential mobility of families, inflation rates in housing, and tax laws affecting housing investment. Correction or modification in any one of these areas may have an impact on housing available to the elderly. This is an example of a causal model in which the various determinants may be *independent* of each other.

The second multicausal model is one in which a series of determinants are thought to be *interrelated*. Depression among the aged, for example, may be related to geographic distance from relatives and friends, the social commitments of these people, and lack of adequate transportation. In these circumstances, modification of any one of these interrelated determinants is unlikely to have a significant impact on the mental health of older persons. Rather, a program that seeks the remedy of all of the explanatory phenomena would be required.

In fact, rarely are the various determinants of particular social concerns in any area, and particularly in the field of aging, either entirely independent or completely interdependent. Rather, there usually is a partial connection between various determinants of particular problems. The dilemma is that one must begin many intervention programs without having knowledge of causation; at the same time, however, one needs a hypothetical model of causation in order to design a program and provide proper evaluation of it.

Evaluation research complexities that ensue as a consequence of multiple causation are well recognized. First, the recognition of multicausality leads to complex intervention programs. Second, if needed, such complex programs make rigorous evaluation research difficult. There is no ready solution to this situation. On the one hand, highly simplistic intervention programs, particularly with interdependent determinants, are clearly doomed to failure. On the other hand, overly complex programs become almost impossible to administer consistently and are also exceedingly difficult to evaluate.

An illustration of one condition presently in the forefront of policy development is the organization and delivery of long-term care services. Although historically in the United States, nursing home policy was de facto the long-term care policy, there has been concerted effort to establish a broader concept of long-term care. Such a conception refers to a "continuum of interrelated health and social services" (Koff, 1982, p. 1). This includes a full range of services offered in institutional and community-based settings such as nursing homecare, hospital and physician services, adult day health, home health, homemaker services, health screening, and health promotion (Koff, 1982). The service industry in the United States is characterized by a dichotomy between the health and social spheres, in terms of financing, administration, organization, and delivery of services. Efforts to find a rational solution to linking health and social services, however, have received attention of an international scope (Hokenstad and Ritvo, 1983). Working within this fragmented system, some have advocated an age-based service strategy; others have argued for a functionally-based strategy. One main strategy in the United States has been directed toward developing alternatives to institutionalization such as homemaker/chore service, adult day health, and client or case management services. This activity has culminated in the development of a number of demonstration programs intended to identify persons in the community who, because of their physical or mental frailty, are seen as being at risk of institutionalization (Quinn et al., 1982). Adult day health care and case management programs to assess individual needs and match people to existing resources are the primary examples of these efforts. While the results of these activities are far from conclusive, the providers of these services nevertheless have established a strong visible constituency (Kane and Kane, 1980). The factors contributing to the individual need for assistance and the alternative methods of providing this assistance still require careful delineation.

The Epidemiological View

A third way of thinking about cause is derived from work in the field of epidemiology and public health. In many respects, the epidemiological view is a subset of the multicausal model. Nevertheless, it articulates a range of alternative actions that go beyond the individual as the source of problems and the sole target for intervention. In efforts to control epidemics, public health physicians observed that there were often three sets of related conditions that might be modified, and that it made little difference in outcome, except in expediency, which set was modified. These sets of conditions are often labeled "host," "agent," and "environment." The classic illustration is the eradication of malaria, a disease carried by a germ in mosquitoes living in swamps. One approach is to provide a vaccination against the germ; a second is to develop a means of killing the mosquitoes that carry the germ; and the third is to contaminate the swamps in which mosquitoes live by placing oil on them, so that the environment is no longer compatible for the insects.

Epidemiological research that directs intervention strategies to modifying individual behavior and life-style is particularly relevant in the field of aging (Fries and Crapo, 1981). This is evident in a large body of research discussing the etiology of disease and the design of more effective preventive health strategies for the elderly (Cassel, 1974; Syme, 1974; Eisdorfer and Wilkie, 1976; Shanas and Maddox, 1976; Antonovsky, 1979; Lin et al., 1979; Minkler, 1981). The relationship between aging and illness may be elucidated by studying life changes, social networks, and social support. Future research should include the study of a socially heterogeneous and noninstitutionalized population to determine the effects of social class, ethnicity, sex, and age on social relations and health, measures of general health status, impairment, and disability, as well as the independent and joint effects of different life changes and social supports on health status (Satariano and Syme, 1981).

Chronic illness is a physical or mental illness or disability caused by disease that persists over a long period of time (Koff, 1982). This type of illness, in particular, requires an approach that treats the social, environmental, and psychological, as well as the biological aspects of disease. Interventions aimed at increasing social support in this context may be as effective as strategies aimed at a specific chronic impairment in improving functional levels of health. Butler and Newacheck (1981) argue, for example, that the biomedical model with its emphasis on short-term acute care is both costly and ineffective for poor aged and disabled persons suffering from chronic illness. The challenge, from their point of view, is to identify the resources potentially available in health and social service delivery systems that could be redirected to strengthen social supports, rather than to rely exclusively on biomedical intervention. Defining the problem in these broader terms, they also assess the factors that presently prevent public and private financing systems from underwriting the cost of these alternative support services.

EVALUATION RESEARCH AND PROGRAM FEEDBACK

Evaluation research is an important component of any intervention strategy. It represents the feedback mechanism that enables those responsible to assess the effects of intervention programs. In gerontology, as in other areas, evaluation is useful to decision making regarding the design and refinement of program operations. For example, it is important to assess the relative merits of nursing home versus independent home care, retirement communities versus age-integrated living arrangements, and categorical versus noncategorical medical and rehabilitation programs.

Evaluative research differs from "basic research" primarily in terms of purpose rather than method; that is, general canons of good methodology apply to both types of research, and the research question can be said to determine the most appropriate design. However, the purpose of evaluative research is determined by policy questions residing in legislative mandates, the requirements of the persons awarding grants, and planners and practitioners administering and implementing policies and programs. The researcher designing and implementing an evaluation study must, to a greater degree than is necessary with basic research, work directly with those persons overseeing the project or program being evaluated in order to institute appropriate measurement criteria and to assure utilization of the results by the staffs concerned.

Evaluation research is often contracted for by a specific group or agency to provide information to be used for internal purposes. Consequently, evaluation data all too often fail to reach the public domain. Contracting agencies are reluctant to lay bare the faults that evaluation may reveal; therefore, the dissemination of results is likely to be characterized by a limited and self-serving release of evaluation data (Rossi and Freeman, 1982). The researcher, as a member of the scientific community, has the responsibility to see that the information gained in the research reaches the public domain in the form of conference papers, journal articles, and other reports. Evaluation research adds to the empirical data base of the social sciences primarily in this manner. However, even when evaluation research results are published and available, the problems of utilization are still great. For example, the objectives of researchers and those of policymakers and practitioners may differ widely regarding the use and presentation of the research data; the scientific community may be more interested in testing theories than in the effectiveness of specific program input.

Also, because of the multidisciplinary character of social gerontology, location and integration of completed investigations is difficult; research results may appear in specialized gerontological journals, single-discipline publications, or monographs that have narrow audiences and distribution. The problem of access to studies and data is widely recognized in the aging field. The "Research Utilization" section of this chapter (see below) offers some potential solutions to problems of access.

Evaluation Research Perspectives

As with methods utilized for basic research, appropriate methodologies for evaluating specific types of major programs and individual projects within them are controversial. There is disagreement on (1) the advantages and disadvantages of experimental, quasi-experimental, and nonexperimental designs, and on the more qualitative process-oriented methods (Campbell and Stanley, 1966; Weiss, 1972; Rossi and Williams, 1972; Cook and Reichardt, 1979; Cook and Campbell, 1979); (2) whether such research should document only program inputs or program outputs—or whether it is essential to compare inputs and outputs in some formal way, as in cost–benefit analysis (Boruch and Riecken, 1975; Patton, 1978; Schulberg and Jerrell, 1979); and (3) the extent to which the research should assess impact on individuals (attitudinal or behavioral), organizations, institutions, or processes of decision making (Weiss and Rein, 1969; Caro, 1971; Attkisson et al., 1978). These issues are further complicated by the extent to which the research is focused on immediate, intermediate, or long-run objectives and effects (Freeman, 1964; Rich, 1979).

In spite such disagreement, there is concurrence regarding the basic elements requiring investigation in evaluation research, although the emphasis given to one element or another will vary depending on the needs of the agency commissioning the evaluation. As stated by Suchman (1967), there are five components relevant to evaluation: (1) the effort expended (amount of activity or input), (2) the effect (results of the effort), (3) the adequacy of impact, (4) efficiency (the effect in relation to cost), and (5) the process (how the effect was achieved).

Steps in Research Evaluation

The evaluation of social intervention has been the topic of a large number of recent papers and monographs (see Cook and Reichardt, 1979; Kimmel, 1981; and Rossi and Freeman, 1982, for bibliographies). Although space prohibits detailed discussion of evaluation procedures, it is important to note that sound evaluation requires the development of an impact model and an empirical testing of the research hypotheses that make up the model. It also involves a number of "steps," including specific identification of the target population, the measuring process, the impact assessment, and benefit costs.

The Impact Model. In all fields, including gerontology, decisions must be made regarding which particular evaluation research strategy is most practical and efficient for studying a specific intervention (Boruch and Riecken, 1975). In general, most evaluation researchers argue for experimental or quasi-experimental designs (Campbell and Stanley, 1966; Attkisson et al., 1978). Such designs impose a useful type of specification on the investigator, for he or she must develop an impact model. Impact models are not only essential for experimentally designed evaluations but for rational and systematic program development as well.

Ideally, the development of an impact model is inherent in the design of an intervention program. The impact model is a statement about the expected relationship between the intervention program and movement toward the goal it hopes to achieve. The impact model delineates the hypotheses to be tested by the evaluation research.

Unfortunately, in many social service programs the intervention is implemented without consensus as to outcome goals, that is, without an impact model being developed (Lind and O'Brien, 1971). When this is the case, the researchers must attempt to construct an ex post facto impact model in order to evaluate the intervention program. The absence of an explicit model prevents the extension of programs on a general basis and limits opportunities for confirming the implementation and the effectiveness of intervention programs through evaluation research. Impact models are predicated not only on conceptual and experiential knowledge but also on some view of cause and effect.

Concerning the expected relationship between program activities and the movement required to obtain the goal, the impact model is a statement of strategy for closing the gap between the standard or goal specified during the design of the intervention and the behavior or condition currently existing. An impact model must contain, at a minimum, three hypotheses: a causal hypothesis, an intervention hypothesis, and an action hypothesis.

The Causal Hypothesis. Central to any impact model is a hypothesis about the influence of one or more characteristics or processes (as independent variables) on the condition of behavior whose modification is the object of the program. An assumed relationship between the extent of social isolation and suicide among the aged illustrates this point. In the development of the causal hypothesis, it is necessary that it be stated in a way that permits testing. A restatement of the suicide illustration in operational terms might be: suicide is most likely among persons who have minimal participation in the community's political activities and voluntary associations and whose contacts with their families are intermittent and limited in both number and intensity. The specification of both the independent or causal variable (social integration) and the dependent or outcome measure (suicide reduction) in measurable form has another utility beyond hypothesis testing: it also aids in the design of the intervention program.

The Intervention Hypothesis. The intervention hypothesis is the statement that specifies the relationship between the program and the behavior or condition to be modified, changed, or eliminated. One intervention hypothesis, in our example of suicide reduction, might be that knowledge of com-

munity resources and organizations by the aged is related to their participation in political and voluntary groups. A program could then be specified to increase knowledge of resources and organizations. Thus, the impact model for the reduction and prevention of suicide would specify that a program increasing the knowledge of available resources and organizations would increase social and political participation and lead to a reduction in suicide. In more complex programs, multiple intervention hypotheses may be necessary.

The Action Hypothesis. This third hypothesis is necessary because events that occur in vivo may not be duplicated when they are brought about by an intervention. To continue the example considered before, increasing older persons' participation in community activities by giving them information about voluntary associations may not make them any less prone to suicide than before. Older persons may learn about associations and not join them, or alternatively they might join but be stressed and depressed by their failure to develop additional interpersonal experience. Thus, the action hypothesis and its testing are as important as the other two hypotheses in evaluations of intervention.

Identifying the Target Population. The characteristics of the population to be subjected to an intervention should be specified prior to the development and execution of the intervention program. Intervention evaluation attempts to estimate the extent to which the program actually was directed at those identified as the target population. This may be done by means of surveys, analysis of agency records, or observation of persons served.

It is important to develop refined procedures for estimating the congruence between the persons or units actually included in a social intervention and those for whom the intervention was intended. The reasons are twofold. First, most social interventions are small-scale experiments, and the major basis for their implementation and study is applicability to larger populations. Extension of programs is possible only if the characteristics of the study group in the experiment are well documented. The second reason for carefully identifying the population is to have measures available on which to distinguish those who are willing to participate in programs, and those who are not, from the pool originally defined as the target population. Similar analyses also are necessary if one is to understand the differential impact of programs on subaggregates within the study population.

The factors affecting participation in a program can present major problems in an evaluation design because of the self-selection bias of the study sample. Random assignment of clients into a program is an obvious, though often impractical, means of minimizing this problem. Quasi-experimental designs through some form of matched sampling or statistical control are the procedures more commonly used (Cook and Campbell, 1979).

While the reasons for precise and explicit identification of the target population may appear fairly obvious, in practice the matter is subject to numerous constraints. From the standpoint of the design of innovations, on the one hand, study groups should comprise a representative sample of a known population, one for which there is evident concern. On the other hand, from the standpoint of the evaluation of the impact of social innovations, the study group should be as homogeneous as possible. Even in cases where classical experimental designs are used, minimal subject heterogeneity reduces the risk that internal differences within the study group will obscure the results (Hanushek and Jackson, 1977).

There are political problems in restricting study groups when either potential participants or community leaders are convinced of the benefits and desirability of participation in programs. It may be seen as immoral to exclude anyone in need of either a treatment or service although it might be beneficial to do so from the research perspective. Thus, for example, although it may be sensible for program implementation and evaluation

purposes to limit the target population by age, race, sex, role, socioeconomic status, mobility, or geographic location, the actual choice is a compromise between program needs, research aspirations, and political considerations. When the evaluation of the intervention requires assignment of some subjects to "control groups" or competing programs, the political problems and the strains of taking into account the characteristics of the study group are often greatly intensified (Rossi and Freeman, 1982).

Further, the inclusion of cases on the basis of identifiable characteristics is often resisted by practitioners who wish, or insist, that clinical judgment about "amenability for treatment," "responsiveness to therapy," "cooperativeness," and the like are valid requirements for inclusion in programs. Since it is difficult to reliably reproduce such judgments, taking them into account and restricting participants in such ways limits generalizability of the findings regarding the effects of the interventions (Rossi and Freeman, 1982).

The design contraints also may involve excessive costs and problems of case finding. Programs limited by some condition of the study group (e.g., mental health problems requiring protective services intervention) and by a set of personal characteristics (e.g., ethnic or economic) often require considerable surveying and outreach in order to secure the required study group, particularly in providing a systematic sample of the population to ensure representativeness.

Moreover, there is the legal and moral concern that persons involved in any intervention program be fully informed about the requirements, procedures, and anticipated outcomes of participation. Since most intervention programs involve sustained and frequent participation, interest and motivation can lag with consequent attrition of the target population. Knowledge of the properties of the study group is necessary in estimating bias resulting from such losses.

There is, of course, a limit to the quality of data that can be collected about a study group. Selection must be based upon a framework providing guidelines for "what counts." Also, it is sometimes difficult to develop valid and reliable measures of characteristics. Issues such as life satisfaction, morale, and service need have traditionally been among the more perplexing measurement problems within gerontology. Economical selection of measures rather than choosing excessively broad batteries of tests and instruments is important for methodological development.

A final complexity is the task of providing identifying data when the targets are not persons but geographical, ecological, or organizational units. For example, a program may be concerned with modifying the procedures and activities in nursing homes by shifting the character of the organization. The target population in this case is organizations with selected characteristics such as number of beds, staff to patient ratio, and source of funding. If interventions are to be extended and are to provide efficacious alternatives to current programs, specification of both level of intervention and the characteristics of the target population is critical.

The Measuring Process. Equally critical is the knowledge of whether the program was executed in a format similar to that described in the impact model. As previously discussed, it is important that programs be specifically described in terms of procedures, practices, and personnel arrangements. Unless one knows that programs were actually undertaken in ways consistent with the program design, there is no point in being concerned about the efficacy of the intervention. The examination of operating programs usually requires a combination of research approaches. Agency reports of what takes place are often the most convenient (though not necessarily most reliable or valid) means for determining congruence between program design and implementation (Weiss and Rein, 1969; Attikisson et al., 1978). Ideally, direct observation and interviews with clients should be used to augment or verify agency reports.

In part, studying the process of social in-

tervention is a quality control function. It serves to alert planners and program developers to what is actually taking place. But this is only one purpose of what is commonly called "process research." If programs are to be expanded to different locations or situations, and if larger numbers of individuals are to be used as agents of social change, it is necessary to be able to tell practitioners with clarity and specificity what they are supposed to do. Only if there is a process evaluation of the actual implementation content of a program can this occur.

Assessing Impact. Impact assessment involves a "before and after" comparison of control (no treatment) and experimental (treatment) groups to which subjects have been assigned. Analysis is greatly strengthened in an experimental design that randomly assigns subjects to these groups. This enables the researcher to infer equivalence of the two groups in all respects except the treatment (i.e., the program) and thus to distinguish the effects of the program from those attributable to other factors. The randomization requirement is often difficult to fulfill completely in action programs because program agencies are reluctant to deny service to persons in the control group.

In response to these and other problems, a variety of alternative quasi-experimental designs have been suggested. In one way or another, quasi-experimental designs involve attempts to adjust statistically for differences between experimental and control or comparison groups. There have been numerous warnings about the extent to which such an approach may lead to faulty conclusions regarding the effect or effectiveness of programs (Riecken and Boruch, 1974), and many strategies have been suggested to minimize these problems (Cook and Campbell, 1979).

Experimental and quasi-experimental designs may not be appropriate or applicable in all types of evaluation. Programs focused on altering participation in decision making or planning rather than on altering individual behavior or attitudes present experimental difficulties. Weiss and Rein (1969) discuss the research problems that occur when the aim of a program is primarily to make an impact on a situation, and only secondarily an impact on individuals. In such cases, researchers often study individuals because they cannot decide how to assess the broader types of impact that the program attempts to make.

Another criticism of experimental and quasi-experimental designs is that they do not permit consideration of the more dynamic aspects of programs, in which many variables are essentially uncontrolled. Cook and Reichardt (1979), Weiss and Rein (1969), and many others suggest that such programs must be studied with more descriptive and inductive methodologies then has been customary. The focus in such studies may be on the details of interrelationship between programs and surroundings, on the reactions of individuals and institutions to programs, or on the consequences for individuals and the larger community. Studies using field methods combined with interviewing to evaluate the impact of action programs in a number of communities (Vanecko, 1969; Trend, 1979; Newcomer et al., 1982) illustrate the use of a process-oriented qualitative method for comparative community studies.

In addition to the question about appropriateness, there are numerous difficulties with implementing true experiments because of ethics and political concerns regarding the denial of treatment (see, e.g., Fox, 1959). Further, there are administrative difficulties in undertaking experiments. Nevertheless, there is little doubt that, with adequate cooperation of action groups and sufficient resources from funding agencies, the proportion of social intervention that could be appropriately studied by means of true experiments could be increased. At the same time, there are legitimate concerns about the amount of time evaluation experiments take and the problems this poses when quick results are needed.

These and other limitations (for more examples, see Lindblom, 1980) on experimental and quasi-experimental research constrain the investigator's ability to measure impact scientifically. While many programs can be effectively evaluated in terms of their impact, others cannot. Whether this is perceived as a problem or an accepted reality for the researcher depends, in some degree, on the problem being studied and the potential role that research findings might have in the policy-making process.

From a practical standpoint, the design of an evaluation should consider from the outset whether or not an experimental or quasi-experimental design can be maintained, the cost (human, political, and dollars) of undertaking it, and the timeliness of the results. When the conditions of maintainability, cost, and timeliness can be adequately met, an impact study is appropriate. When they cannot be met, the study, if needed at all, would likely have its greatest utility in assessing only the process of program implementation. In this context the evaluation would strive to improve program operation rather than test its fundamental assumptions.

Many scholars may find it unsatisfactory and inappropriate to abandon or avoid experimental or quasi-experimental designs simply because of practical considerations. For them knowledge about a program (or problem) is desirable regardless of its timing or salience to a decision process. While we endorse this concern, it is important to distinguish between what Coleman (1972) has termed "decision-oriented" or policy research and "conclusion-oriented" or discipline research. The former aims to provide information for policy decisions that are likely to be made, while the latter is designed to contribute to knowledge in a scholarly area—perhaps even to theory. The usefulness of a study depends on the intended target user of the information. The audience for policy research is political actors. Discipline research, for whatever reason (including lack of timeliness), does not have an audience of political actors; instead, it is more appropriate for other researchers and educators and the more evolutionary development of "ordinary knowledge."

The distinctions between policy research

and discipline research emphasize the importance of research utilization by decision makers, without which a program evaluation fails to serve its primary purpose. This is not to say that decisions necessarily follow research findings, but only that findings should be available and appropriate for decision making.

Choosing a Process or Impact Analysis Model

The major purpose of program evaluation is providing logical, informed analyses of the presenting problem or program and determining the effective and ineffective elements of a social intervention. It is desirable to correct ineffectiveness and that studies be designed to contribute to this end. It is equally desirable that evaluation be undertaken only when the results are needed and appropriate to the decision at hand. In general, this rule of thumb suggests that process evaluation is almost always appropriate, while impact analyses may be more selectively applied.

An example may illustrate this point. A county agency desires to assess a meals program it is administering. It can elect to consider program operation issues such as per-meal cost, staff morale, program participation rates, and food quality. Changes in operation that affect each of these dimensions are within the authority of the county agency. Such issues would be appropriate concerns for a process evaluation. On the impact side, the intended purpose of the program may be to affect the daily nutrition levels of the elderly, and their level of social interaction. Should the county analyze these issues? The answer to this question lies in what the county decision makers can and would do if the programs were found not to be effective in improving either nutrition or social interaction. While this agency might terminate the program and refuse acceptance of the program funds from the state, assume for this example that no such action would be taken. From our point of view, if the county would not terminate this program when faced with negative impact evaluation results, then it should not undertake an impact analysis. On the other hand, the state or federal government financing this county program might be prepared to act on negative impact findings. If this were true, then the impact analysis would be appropriately conducted for decision makers at that level of government.

In short, whether an impact analysis should be undertaken is largely dependent upon the ability and willingness of the appropriate decision makers to use this information. All decisions do not require or use such fundamental information.

RESEARCH UTILIZATION

Strengthening the utility and applicability of social science research for decision making about social interventions has been an underlying theme of this chapter, and a considerable body of social science literature traces the history of transferring research into knowledge utilization. (For representative examples and bibliographies see Weiss, 1977a, and Larsen, 1980). We have discussed the varying ways in which the quest for relevance leads policy researchers away from the ordered and circumscribed discipline of traditional research into the world of political pressure, historical tradition, hunches, and the like. Such actions have been described as attempts to make the research relevant and thus utilizable. Several fundamental questions about utilization, however, have remained elusive. How is utilization defined? Is it always the same, or does it change? What factors impede or facilitate the impact of research? In this section attention is given to answering these questions and discussing means of strengthening research utilization.

Traditionally, a basic assumption of researchers was that research was used if it led directly to some decision or course of action as part of a program or policy. This is the principal definition of utilization implied throughout most of this chapter. However, a variety of alternative utilization forms have been suggested, and they are further elaborated within this section.

Instrumental and Conceptual Utilization

One of the first attempts to define utilization included the idea of differentiating between intended and unintended outcomes (Merton, 1949; Rogers and Shoemaker, 1971). Further definitions have differentiated between instrumental and conceptual levels of utilization. Instrumental utilization refers to cases in which respondents can cite and document the specific ways in which knowledge was used (Caplan et al., 1975; Rich, 1977). Conceptual utilization refers to the influence on a policymaker's thinking that has not been put to a specific documentable use. Weiss (1977b) suggests the term "enlightenment" to describe this general and broad impact of knowledge. Lindblom and Cohen (1979) further elaborate on the import of this generally unrecognized contribution of research.

The many studies and commentaries attempting to chronicle the use or nonuse of research have typically employed the narrow instrumental utilization definition (Larsen, 1980). Partly because of this perspective, early findings, including those cited in recent compendia (see, e.g., Weiss, 1977a), have tended to find few examples of strong direct utilization. As the sophistication and volume of policy research has expanded, however, it has become more and more difficult to accept these earlier measures of usefulness.

It has been found with social programs, for example, that recommendations may be partially used, used in alternative ways, or justifiably not used at all. The user, in other words, was discovered to select the appropriate portions of knowledge and disregard the others (Berman and McLaughlin, 1977; Campeau et al., 1978). Caplan et al. (1975) state that the extent of utilization hinges on the conceptualization of use and of research. If use was defined as direct influence on programs or decisions, it was not common. If it included the consideration of research-based concepts and generalizations in formulating questions, setting goals, and planning activities, then it was not uncommon. This perspective has been further refined to acknowledge that consideration, but non-utilization, of information is a legitimate dimension of knowledge transfer and can be a preferable alternative to inappropriate instrumental utilization (Larsen et al., 1976).

Another aspect of utilization's receiving attention is the effect of time on the nature and extent of use. Although the literature presents studies (Larsen et al., 1976; Rich 1977; Peterson and Leinbach, 1981) with time-span intervals measured only over a matter of months (rather than years), identifiable patterns of use appear to occur. The first wave of utilization is likely to involve instrumental use. The second wave is typically conceptual.

One of the major problems in judging the utility of policy research, then, is defining utilization. Those concerned with instrumental utilization can continue their pessimism about the low use rate of research. Those more willing to accept conceptual utilization have reason for optimism.

Overcoming Barriers to Nonutilization

Regardless of the definition of utilization, a consensus has emerged among evaluation researchers about the major factors contributing to non-utilization. Weiss (1972) has organized them into five major areas:

1. The evaluator's perception of his/her role in the utilization process.
2. The organization's resistance to change in its program.
3. Inadequate dissemination of results.
4. The gap between evaluation findings and clear courses for future action.
5. The tendency of much evaluation to show little or no positive effect.

The latter two are relevant as factors adversely affecting instrumental rather than conceptual utilization.

Various strategies have been suggested for overcoming these barriers. Lindblom and Cohen (1979) and Lindblom (1980) articulate a practical approach for resolving both the problem of the evaluator's role perception and the organization's resistance to change. They contend, as noted at the outset of this chapter, that researchers must view their role as one of supplementing other inputs into social problem solving. In other words, research should not be seen as the rational, systematic, authoritative, and value-free perspective on a problem or issue. They argue that research into complex social issues rarely can meet such standards even if the standards are desirable. Instead, they urge that research be explicit as to its values, perspectives, and limitations; and that the findings be included in a pluralistic partisan debate surrounding decision making. This argument is a major departure from the more rationalistic perspective of researchers who tend to view research findings as authoritatively indicating the correct decisions that should be made by policymakers.

Affecting an organization's willingness to change requires a somewhat more complex approach. Again, Lindblom and Cohen (1979) provide a reasonable strategy. First, they suggest that policy research be limited to those issues that are within the purview of the organization to change. Second, it is useful to devote a major emphasis in policy research to testing existing propositions growing out of the common or ordinary knowledge used by the organization. With this technique policy research becomes largely focused on refining "ordinary" knowledge. Last, Lindblom and Cohen suggest that analysis of new knowledge significance for social problem solving be limited to a small number of propositions. These combined strategies are geared largely to imparting conceptual rather than instrumental utilization, but their merit lies in their recognition of the incremental decision process characteristic of most organizations. This approach seems to meet the requirement that to be useful, research must meet the needs and capabilities of the intended consumer.

The inadequate dissemination of results, the third major problem area, is generally viewed as arising from two causes: poor or inappropriate communication by researchers (this usually includes a criticism of writing or presentation style) and poor publicity about the information available. One solution proposed to this first problem is the creation of a new profession of translators sufficiently trained in the techniques of research to interpret and translate data into recommendations for those who plan and conduct action programs (Clark, 1969). Variations on this theme would be to train research consumers to be better able to synthesize and translate findings for themselves, or to train researchers in the art of communication. These approaches are evolving and will be intensified by the competition for research funds, particularly as such funds diminish. Experience and competence in adequate communication by both researchers and funding sources can be expected to play a decisive role in the selection of researchers.

Additional strategies for general information dissemination include conferences, publications, and indexing and abstracting of reports. These approaches have built-in lag time and consequently are more useful in conceptual than instrumental utilization. A number of other efforts attempt to reduce the lag time and inconvenience of procuring material, and, in some cases, even to promote instrumental utilization.

Efforts over the past 15 or so years to bring existing knowledge in the aging field into an organized framework are exemplified by such works as Neugarten (1968), Riley and Foner (1968), Riley et al. (1972), Binstock and Shanas (1976), Finch and Hayflick (1977), and Birren and Schaie (1977). These references review, categorize, and organize research, as well as conceptualize various problem domains. Additionally, the Administration on Aging (AoA) sponsored an inventory of past and present federally supported research covering the period 1966–1975 (U.S. National Clearinghouse on Aging, 1977) and an inventory of the products and uses of research sponsored by the Administration on Aging (Peterson and Leinbach, 1981).

A number of excellent information resources have also developed; for example: the National Archive of Computerized Data on Aging at the University of Michigan; the Andrus Gerontological Exchange Data Base

(AGEX) at the University of Southern California; the Quarterly Index to Periodical Literature on Aging edited at Wayne State University; the National Gerontology Resource Center sponsored by the American Association of Retired Persons; the National Council on the Aging Current Literature on Aging; Project SHARE of the Department of Health and Human Services; and the publications of the U.S. Senate Special Committee on Aging and the House Select Committee on Aging.

These data sources are important starting points for the development of intervention efforts, for selecting methods of intervention, and for designing evaluations to assess both process and impact. The Administration on Aging, in an attempt to enhance the instrumental utilization of research, established a network of long-term-care gerontology centers for the express purpose of developing and testing alternative models of service delivery. AoA also established a limited number of national policy centers, each with a policy focus on one substantive area (e.g., employment, health, and income maintenance). These national centers conduct policy research and analysis and provide technical assistance to AoA.

The remaining two research utilization issues—the gap between evaluation findings and a clear course of action, and the frequent absence of positive program findings—received attention earlier in this chapter under the heading "Steps in Research Evaluation." Success in these areas begins with the program itself—in its perspective on problem causation and program impact in the selection of policy- and program-tractable measures for analysis; in the formulation of causal intervention and action hypotheses; in identifying the target population; and in differentiating those aspects of the study appropriate for impact and/or process analyses. The greater the clarity of these dimensions, the easier it is to design a study to measure and test the program perspectives and outcomes. When the program has not been explicit in these areas, it is necessary for the evaluation to articulate

a set of problem perspectives and hypothesized impacts for testing. This can be done either in isolation from the program providers and recipients or with their advice. While every investigator and every situation require unique consideration, it is our opinion that input from those involved with the program will generally enhance the analytic design and provide a strong reality base.

In short, practical interpretation of and confidence in evaluation research findings depend on obtaining agreement on the objectives of the program, the program elements expected to contribute to their attainment, and the information needs of the decision makers. After these steps, the complex but basic research procedures common to any study are all that remain in conducting a successful evaluation project. Examples of these basic procedures are developing appropriate measures, maintenance of sample design, and maintenance of data quality throughout program implementation.

THE CHALLENGES IN INTERVENTION RESEARCH

The discussion in this chapter of designs and research for intervention assumes that the contribution of such strategies to decision making and enlightenment occurs in a democratic setting allowing fair debate. In its ideal form this implies that results are made available to all parties having an interest in the decision, and that these parties use the results as they desire.

This perspective with its clear focus on the political debate raises questions concerning the information development and dissemination process. In discussing the potential misutilization of evaluation research findings, Cook et al. (1980) are concerned both with the "generation of inaccurate findings and the biased dissemination of results" (p. 481). Operationally defining and correcting these potential problems is, in our view, the first of the major challenges for intervention research.

Defining accuracy entails at least these considerations: appropriate and correctly implemented research procedures, problem definitions that reflect alternative interpretations of the possible causal factors influencing program consequences, valid measurement, and controlling for the varying processes by which programs are administered. Among solutions suggested to the accuracy dilemma are that less reliance be put on single study results and that more emphasis be given to multiple replications preferably with different investigators, and to the synthesis of multiple evaluation results (Cook et al., 1980).

These approaches have important implications for the present practice and funding of evaluation research. One consideration relevant to practice is that replications and synthesis generally lengthen the evaluation process. Moreover, this process will virtually eliminate the instrumental use of any *one* study and explicitly assign most of the value of evaluation research to conceptual or enlightenment use (Patton et al., 1977).

Recognizing that funds available for research are not unlimited, we can expect that there will also have to be a narrowing of research priorities and resulting studies if replication investigations are to go forward. The scarcity of research dollars may also necessitate the coordination of research priorities with program activities. Better conceptualization and coordination in the selection and financing of research as suggested by these actions can be expected to have a positive influence on facilitating coordination, synthesis, and dissemination of the research findings.

These advantages do not come without cost or risk. Tighter coordination in research priority selection will reduce the latitude of the research community to generate and investigate the important problems they themselves define through investigator research strategies. Narrowed priorities might constrain investigation of the fundamental assumptions implicit in public policy. A balance in funding is needed to assure that a social construction of reality is not perpetuated in pursuit of better-coordinated research and policy priorities.

The second challenge to intervention research stems from the mechanisms of information dissemination and its use in policy debates. It is rare for the major actors in debates to obtain their information directly from research reports. Instead, it might come from memoranda, verbal briefings, media reports, or anecdotal accounts from colleagues. Whatever the source, information can be summarized or transmitted inaccurately. Even if the information is transmitted accurately, there is the possibility that the bias of the persons or institutions receiving it might lead to misinterpretation, or that the actors most in need of the information will not receive it at all.

The research utilization approaches characteristic of the field, and summarized earlier, have dealt primarily with enlightenment among the research community and the instrumental use of single study results. Recent knowledge utilization studies are beginning to recommend informed approaches for reaching policymakers (Weiss, 1977a; Alkin et al., 1979; Cook et al., 1980). Current methods of theory regarding information use suggest, for example, that disseminators adapt to the way decision makers use information, rather than expect users to adapt to the mechanisms by which researchers typically disseminate their findings.

For example, it may be unrealistic to expect decision makers to read reports. The reading of summaries or memoranda is more likely; and oral briefings would be perhaps even more useful. Thus it seems appropriate to continue exploring means by which researchers might become more involved in developing appropriate summaries, or even in conducting briefings. All these processes would be further facilitated in a context in which multiple research findings were synthesized, and any ambiguity and contradictions also addressed. The organization and financing of these dissemination efforts cannot be the responsibility of individual investigators, but could be a function of the agency or agencies sponsoring the research, or interested in its results. Newspaper and other media accounts of research findings also need to be recognized for their critical importance in dissemination. Researchers should take more responsibility in working with the media to review and sharpen the accuracy of the information reported.

Finally, Cook et al. (1980) have suggested an area in which research is needed—the process by which research findings are disseminated within agencies. It is possible that the weaknesses in dissemination of research results to policymakers could be corrected if better communication were established with those responsible for implementing the knowledge. When this process is ignored, as it is now, dissemination at the top level may be ineffective and may fail to produce the desired results within an organization.

CONCLUSION

There is obviously much to be done before the various objectives delineated throughout this chapter can be accomplished. Within the federal government alone there are numerous agencies financing programs affecting the aged. Further complicating planning are simultaneous policy shifts, such as reductions in federal research allocations and national data base resources (Stanfield, 1981) and decentralization of the federal system of health and human service programs. Any one or all of these actions would affect the ability to carry out policy analysis and program evaluation.

For example, the Omnibus Budget Reconciliation Act of 1981 (U.S. Public Law 97–35, 1981) and cost-cutting efforts initiated at the federal government level raised important and critical issues for evaluation research. One of these was a widespread concern over the impact of present and future budget reductions on the utility and quality of federal statistics (U.S. House of Representatives, 1982). The effects of the budget reductions range from a loss of geographic detail and comparable data across jurisdictions and sectors to a loss of ability to measure economic and social conditions and to ascertain the effects of policy changes (U.S. House of Representatives, 1982).

The block grant program consolidated under this act (U.S. Public Law 97–35, 1981) shifted most of the responsibility for program evaluation to the state level. These evaluation activities must compete for resources with other state activities. Consequently, it is expected that there will be "substantial variation in the scope and nature of evaluation activities from state to state" (U.S. General Accounting Office 1982, p. 72). In addition, the emphasis of responsibility for program evaluation at the state level makes it uncertain whether there will be an authoritative source of nationwide information on the levels and types of services available and the nature of program operations and impact (U.S. General Accounting Office 1982). These problems can be counteracted in some measure through ongoing federal data-gathering programs such as special surveys by the Bureau of the Census, the Department of Labor, and other specific program monitoring systems.

Decentralization offers the opportunity for multiple replications of programs and their evaluations. There is a strong likelihood that the learning opportunities from these efforts will be missed if there is an absence of a coordinated effort in problem definition, information collection, information sharing, and information synthesis. The federal agencies with oversight over state-administered programs, as well as national task forces, trade associations, and other groups, must work together to provide unifying leadership if we are to learn from these emerging experiences.

How can the federal bureaucracy, much less the greater complexity of states, be brought together to define priorities, debate issues, and provide input on specific research questions? The Administration on Aging in the definition of its own mission within the Department of Health and Human Services and in the establishment of National Policy Centers and the Long Term Care Gerontology Centers, has laid a base for such an effort. Among other things, these actions can help to shape the broad parameters for aging policy discussion. The ensuing discussion, at whatever level, if generally confined to these frameworks, could explore more specific issues.

The broad framework, and the specific issues, to be achievable must be selective in scope and modest in aspiration. Operationally this will require adjustments in traditional administrative approaches. The research field tends to place prime importance on the identification of problems and questions to be investigated. This quest has translated itself into a constantly churning mix of research priorities. Much agency effort is expended annually to define new research priorities.

It may be time to step back from this approach and make a more concerted attempt to connect the generation of research questions with the slower and more incremental evolution of policy and program changes. While the individual questions might change rapidly, the larger agenda likely would not. The major policy problems of escalating expenditures for long-term care and income maintenance (Clark and Menefee, 1981) illustrate topics for two of these broad agendas. Specific approaches to cost containment in the areas of health and income program spending would represent more temporal concerns.

Less urgency, greater focus in delineation, and more thoroughness in investigating policy options may do much to improve policy-making and the incorporation of research results into the decision process. At the same time, researchers should be willing to participate in and be responsive to the policy-making, research agenda debates. Accepting this constraint on the traditional autonomy of researchers may be the greatest challenge for intervention research.

REFERENCES

Alkin, M. D., Daillak, R., and White, P. 1979. *Using Evaluation: Does Evaluation Make a Difference?* Beverly Hills: Sage.

Antonovsky, A. 1979. *Health, Stress, and Coping: New Perspectives on Mental and Physical Well-being.* San Francisco: Jossey-Bass.

Attkisson, C. C., Hargreaves, W. A., and Horowitz, M. J. 1978. *Evaluation of Human Service Programs.* New York: Academic Press.

Baltes, P. B. 1973. Strategies for psychological intervention in old age. *The Gerontologist* 13:4-5.

Berger, P. L., and Luckman, T. 1966. *The Social Construction of Reality.* Garden City, N.Y.: Doubleday.

Berman, P., and McLaughlin, M. W. 1977. Federal programs supporting educational change. Vol. 7, *Factors Affecting Implementation and Continuation.* Santa Monica: Rand.

Binstock, R. H., and Shanas, E. (eds.) 1976. *Handbook of Aging and the Social Sciences,* 1st ed. New York: Van Nostrand Reinhold.

Birren, J. E., and Schaie, K. W. (eds.) 1977. *Handbook of the Psychology of Aging.* New York: Van Nostrand Reinhold.

Boruch, R. F., and Riecken, H. W. 1975. *Experimental Testing of Public Policy.* Boulder, Colo: Westview.

Butler, L. H., and Newacheck, P. 1981. Restructuring service programs for the low income and disabled. San Francisco: Institute of Health Policy Studies, University of California.

Butler, R. 1969. Age-ism: Another form of bigotry. *The Gerontologist* 9:243-246.

Campbell, D. T., and Stanley, J. C. 1966. *Experimental and Quasi-Experimental Design for Research.* Chicago: Rand McNally.

Campeau, P. L., Hawkridge, D. G., and Treadway, T. G. 1978. Evaluation of project information package dissemination and implementation. First year report. Palo Alto: American Institutes for Research.

Caplan, N., Morrison, A., and Stambaugh, R. J. 1975. The use of social science knowledge in policy decisions at the national level. Ann Arbor: Institute for Social Research, University of Michigan.

Caro, F. (ed.) 1971. *Readings in Evaluation Research.* New York: Russell Sage Foundation.

Cassel, J. 1974. An epidemiological perspective of psychosocial factors in disease etiology. *American Journal of Public Health* 64(11):1040-1043.

Clark, M. F. 1969. Creating a new role: The research utilization specialist. *Rehabilitation Record* X:32-36.

Clark, R. L., and Menefee, J. A. 1981. Federal expenditures for the elderly: Past and future. *The Gerontologist* 21:132-137.

Coe, R. 1967. Professional perspectives on the aged. *The Gerontologist* 7:114-119.

Cohen, E. 1970. Toward a social policy on aging. *The Gerontologist* 10:13-21.

Coleman, J. S. 1972. *Policy Research in the Social Sciences.* Morristown, N.J.: General Learning Corporation.

Cook, T., Levinson-Rose, J., Pollard, W. 1980. The misutilization of evaluation research. *Knowledge: Creation, Diffusion, Utilization* 1(4):477-498.

Cook, T. D., and Campbell, D. T. 1979. *Quasi Experimentation: Design and Analysis Issues for Field Settings.* Chicago: Rand McNally.

Cook, T. D., and Reichardt, C. S. (eds.) 1979. *Qualitative and Quantitative Methods in Evaluation Research.* Beverly Hills: Sage.

Coser, L. 1965. The sociology of poverty. *Social Problems* 13:140-148.

Dowd, J. 1980. *Stratification among the Aged.* Monterey, Calif.: Brooks/Cole.

Eisdorfer, C., and Wilkie, F. 1976. Stress, disease, aging and behavior. *In* J. E. Birren and K. W. Schaie (eds.), *Handbook of the Psychology of Aging,* pp. 251–275. New York: Van Nostrand Reinhold.

Estes, C. L. 1973. Barriers to effective community planning for the elderly. *The Gerontologist* 13:178–183.

Estes, C. L. 1979. *The Aging Enterprise.* San Francisco: Jossey-Bass.

Finch, C. E., and Hayflick, L. (eds.) 1977. *Handbook of the Biology of Aging.* New York: Van Nostrand Reinhold.

Fox, R. C. 1959. *Experiment Perilous.* New York: Free Press.

Freeman, H. E. 1964. Conceptual approaches to assessing impacts of large scale intervention programs. *Social Statistics, Proceedings of the American Statistical Association,* 192–198.

Freeman, M. 1978. Limits of the biological metaphor. Unpublished paper, Department of Sociology, University of California, Davis, Ca.

Fries, J. F., and Crapo, L. M. 1981. *Vitality and Aging.* San Francisco: Freeman.

Gouldner, A. 1970. *The Coming Crisis of Western Sociology.* New York: Basic Books.

Hanushek, E. A., and Jackson, J. E. 1977. *Statistical Methods for Social Scientists.* New York: Academic Press.

Hokenstad, M. C., and Ritvo, R. A. (eds). 1983. *Linking Health Care and Social Services: International Perspectives.* Beverly Hills: Sage.

Kane, R., and Kane, R. 1980. Alternatives to institutional care for the elderly: Beyond the dichotomy. *The Gerontologist* 20:249–259.

Kane, R. L., Solomon, D. H., Beck, J. C., Keeler, E. B., and Kane, R. A. 1981. *Geriatrics in the United States: Manpower Projections and Training Consideration.* Lexington, Mass.: Lexington Books.

Kasl, S. V., and Berkman, L. F. 1981. Some psychosocial influences on the health status of the elderly: The perspective of social epidemiology. *In* J. L. McGaugh and S. B. Keisler (eds.). *Aging: Biology and Behavior,* pp. 345–385. New York: Academic Press.

Kimmel, W. A. 1981. Putting program evaluation in perspective for state and local government. Washington, D.C.: Department of Health and Human Services, Human Services Monography Series, No. 18.

Kingson, E. R., and Scheffler, R. M. 1981. Aging: Issues and economic trends for the 1980s. *Inquiry* 18:197–213.

Koff, T. H. 1982. *Long Term Care: An Approach to Serving Frail Elderly.* Boston: Little, Brown.

Kuhn, T. 1970. *The Structure of Scientific Revolutions.* Chicago: University of Chicago Press.

Larsen, J. K. 1980. Knowledge utilization: What is it? *Knowledge: Creation, Diffusion, Utilization.* 1(3): 421–442.

Larsen, J. K., Norris, E. L., and Kroll, J. 1976. Consultation and its outcome: Community mental health care centers. Final report. Palo Alto, Calif.: American Institutes for Research.

Lawton, M. P., and Nahemow, L. 1973. Ecology and the aging process. *In* C. Eisdorfer and M. P. Lawton (eds.), *The Psychology of Adult Development and Aging,* pp. 619–674. Washington, D.C.: American Psychological Association.

Lemert, E. 1951. *Social Pathology.* New York: McGraw-Hill.

Lemert, E. M. 1973. Beyond Mead: The societal reaction to deviance. Presidential address, Society for the Study of Social Problems, New York.

Lin, N., Simeone, R. S., Ensel, W. M., and Kuo, W. 1979. Social support, stressful life events, and illness: A model and an empirical test. *Journal of Health and Social Behavior* 20:108–119.

Lind, S. D., and O'Brien, J. E. 1971. The general problem of program evaluation: The researchers' perspective. *The Gerontologist,* 11(4), Part II:43–50.

Lindblom, C. E. 1980. *The Policy-Making Process,* 2nd ed. Englewood Cliffs, N.J.: Prentice-Hall.

Lindblom, C. E., and Cohen, D. K. 1979. *Usable Knowledge: Social Science and Social Problem-Solving.* New Haven, Conn.: Yale University Press.

Merton, R. K. 1949. *Social Theory and Social Structure.* New York: Free Press.

Minkler, M. 1981. Research on the health effects of retirement: An uncertain legacy. *Journal of Health and Social Behavior* 22(June):117–130.

Mutschler, P. 1971. Factors affecting choice of and perseveration in social work with the aged. *The Gerontologist* 11, Part 1:231–241.

Neugarten, B. L. 1968. *Middle Age and Aging.* Chicago: University of Chicago Press.

Newcomer, R., Estes, C., Benjamin, A., and Swan, J. 1982. Funding, practices, policies and performance of state and area agencies on aging. Final report. Vol. II. San Francisco: Aging Health Policy Center, University of California.

Patton, M. Q. 1978. *Utilization—Focused Evaluation.* Beverly Hills, Calif.: Sage.

Patton, M. Q., Grimes, P. S., Guthrie, K. M., Brennan, N. J., French, B. D., and Blyth, D. A. 1977. In search of impact: An analysis of the utilization of federal health evaluation research. *In* C. Weiss (ed.), *Using Social Research in Public Policy Making,* pp. 141–163. Lexington, Mass.: Lexington Books.

Peterson, D. A., and Bolton, C. R. 1980. *Gerontology Instruction in Higher Education.* New York: Springer.

Peterson, K., and Leinbach, D. 1981. *The Products & Uses of Research Sponsored by the Administration on Aging.* Washington, D.C.: American Institute for Research.

Quinn, J., Segal, J., Raisz, H., and Johnson, C. 1982. *Coordinating Community Services for the Elderly: The Triage Experience.* New York: Springer.

Rich, R. F. 1977. Uses of social science information by federal bureaucrats: Knowledge for action versus knowledge for understanding. *In* C. Weiss (ed.), *Us-*

ing *Social Research for Public Policy,* pp. 199–211. Lexington, Mass.: Lexington Books.

Rich, R. F. 1979. *Translating Evaluation into Policy.* Beverly Hills, Calif.: Sage.

Riecken, H. W., and Boruch, R. F. (eds.) 1974. *Social Experimentation.* New York: Academic Press.

Riley, M. W., and Foner, A. (eds.) 1968. *Aging and Society,* Vol. 1, *An Inventory of Research Findings.* New York: Russell Sage Foundation.

Riley, M. W., Johnson, M., and Foner, A. 1972. *Aging and Society,* Vol. 3, *A Sociology of Age Stratification.* New York: Russell Sage Foundation.

Rogers, E. M., and Shoemaker, F. F. 1971. *Communication of Innovations.* New York: Free Press.

Rose, A. M. 1965. A current theoretical issue in social gerontology. *The Gerontologist* 4:46–50.

Rossi, P., and Williams, W. 1972. *Evaluating Social Programs: Theory, Practice and Politics.* New York: Seminar Press.

Rossi, P., and Freeman, H. E. 1982. *Evaluation: A Systematic Approach,* 2nd ed. Beverly Hills, Calif.: Sage.

Satariano, W. A., and Syme, S. L. 1981. Life changes and disease in elderly populations: Coping with change. *In* J. L. McGaugh and S. B. Kiesler (eds.), *Aging: Biology and Behavior,* pp. 311–327. New York: Academic Press.

Schulberg, H. C., and Jerrell, J. M. (eds.) 1979. *The Evaluator and Management.* Beverly Hills, Calif.: Sage.

Scott, J. F., and Freeman, H. E. 1966. A critical review of alcohol education for adolescents. *Community Mental Health Journal* 2:222–230.

Scott, R. A., and Shore, A. 1974. Sociology and policy analysis. *American Sociologist* 9(May):51–59.

Seltzer, M. M., Sterns, H., and Hickey, T. 1978. *Gerontology in Higher Education: Perspectives and Issues.* Belmont, Calif.: Wadsworth.

Shanas, E., and Maddox, G. L. 1976. Aging, health, and the organization of health resources. *In* R. H. Binstock and E. Shanas (eds.), *Handbook of Aging and the Social Sciences,* 1st ed., pp. 592–618. New York: Van Nostrand Reinhold.

Sparacino, J. 1979. Individual psychotherapy with the aged: A selective review. *International Journal of Aging and Human Development* 19(3):197–220.

Spence, D. L., Feigenbaum, E. M., Fitzgerald, F., and Roth, J. M. 1968. Medical student attitudes toward the geriatric patient. *Journal American Geriatrics Society* 16:976–983.

Stanfield, R. 1981. Numbers crunch—data funds cut just when most statistics are needed. *National Journal* (Nov. 11):2118–2121.

Suchman, E. 1967. *Evaluative Research.* New York: Russell Sage Foundation.

Syme, S. L. 1974. Behavioral factors associated with the etiology of physical disease: A social epidemiological approach. *American Journal of Public Health* 64(11):1043–1045.

Tindale, J., and Marshall, V. 1980. A generational conflict perspective for gerontology. *In* V. Marshall (ed.), *Aging in Canada,* pp. 43–50. Ontario, Canada: Fitzhenry & Whiteside.

Troll, L. E., and Schlossberg, N. A. 1970. A preliminary investigation of "age bias" in helping professions. *The Gerontologist* 10(3), Part II: 46.

Trend, M. G. 1979. On the reconciliation of qualitative and quantitative analyses: A case study. *In* T. D. Cook and C. S. Reichardt (eds.), *Qualitative and Quantitative Methods in Evaluation Research,* pp. 68–86. Beverly Hills, Calif.: Sage.

U.S. Department of Health, Education, and Welfare; Public Health Service, National Institutes of Health, 1978. *Our Future Selves: A Research Plan Toward Understanding Aging.* Washington, D.C.: U.S. Government Printing Office, Publication No. NIH 78-1444.

U.S. General Accounting Office. 1982. *Lessons Learned From Past Block Grants: Implications for Congressional Oversight.* Washington, D.C.: General Accounting Office.

U.S. House of Representatives. March 16, 1982. Committee on Post Office and Civil Service, Subcommittee on Census and Population. *Impact of Budget Cuts on Federal Statistical Programs.* Washington, D.C.: U.S. Government Printing Office.

U.S. National Clearinghouse on Aging. 1977. *A Comprehensive Inventory and Analysis of Federally Supported Research in Aging, 1966–1975.* Rockville, Md.: National Clearinghouse on Aging.

U.S. Public Law 97-35. 1981. The Omnibus Budget Reconciliation Act of 1981. Washington, D.C.: U.S. 97th Congress.

Vanecko, J. J. 1969. Community mobilization and institutional change. *Social Science Quarterly* 50(3):609–630.

Weiss, C. 1972. *Evaluation Research.* Englewood Cliffs, N.J.: Prentice Hall.

Weiss, C. (ed.) 1977a. *Using Social Research in Public Policy Making.* Lexington, Mass.: Lexington Books.

Weiss, C. 1977b. Research for policy's sake: The enlightenment function of social research. *Policy Analysis* 3:531–545.

Weiss, R. S., and Rein, M. 1969. The evaluation of broad aim programs: A cautionary case and a moral. *Annals of the American Academy of Political and Social Scientists* 385:113–142.

Williamson, J. B. 1974. The stigma of public dependency: A comparison of alternative forms of public aid to the poor. *Social Problems* 22(2):213–228.

Williamson, J. B. 1982. Public policy and regulation of the elderly poor prior to the rise of the welfare state. Paper presented at the Annual Meeting of the Society for the Study of Social Problems, San Francisco.

22
ECONOMIC STATUS
OF THE AGING

Yung-Ping Chen*

The American College at Bryn Mawr

The worldwide phenomenon of population aging has accentuated the problem of income support in old age (Binstock et al., 1982). Because of greatly diverse support mechanisms in so many different countries and because of unavailable, unreliable and, most important, noncomparable data pertaining to different countries, it is not possible to analyze and compare income support systems around the world in adequate depth within the scope of one chapter. Accordingly, we will analyze the economic status of the aged in the United States as one illustration of the worldwide phenomenon. The term "aged" and similar terms in this chapter refer to persons age 65 and over.

Section 1 points out the changing (and improving) economic status of the aged during the 1970s. Section 2 offers an analysis of their sources of income in 1980 as a new decade began. Some important issues that bear upon the future economic status of the aged are discussed in Section 3. Section 4 contains concluding remarks.

* The author is grateful to the following persons for assistance with data and discussions: Carol Fendler (poverty statistics and measurements), Edward Welniak (median income data), Helen H. Lamale (standard budgets), Susan Grad and Wayne Finegar (sources of income statistics), Robert H. Binstock and James H. Schulz (editorial).

1. IMPROVEMENT IN ECONOMIC STATUS OF THE AGED

During the decade of the 1970s, the aged in general improved their economic status as measured by four criteria: (1) the decline in the incidence of poverty; (2) the rise in real income; (3) their income distribution compared to standard budgets; and (4) the increase in holding of assets and homeownership. While the improvement in economic status is true of the aged as a group, certain subgroups among them fared relatively poorly in terms of poverty rates or money receipts. In addition, more improvement took place in the early part of the 1970s than in the latter part.

Incidence of Poverty

Poverty rates among the aged as measured by the official government indicator declined rapidly during the early 1970s from nearly 25 percent (4.7 million people) in 1970 to 15 percent (3.3 million people) in 1975. However, the poverty rate has improved little since 1975, hovering between 14 and 16 percent, and in absolute numbers the number of poor elderly was approximately 3.3 million between 1975 and 1978, and reached 3.9 million in 1980 and 1981. Moreover, from 1978 to 1981, about 620,000 aged persons were added to the ranks of the poor (Table 1).

TABLE 1. Persons Age 65-plus below the Poverty Level, 1970, 1975, and 1978 to 1981.

| Year | Numbers below Poverty Level (in Thousands) | | | |
	All Races	White	Black	Spanish Origin[1]
1970	4,709	3,984	683	—[2]
1975	3,317	2,634	652	137
1978	3,233	2,530	662	125
1979[3]	3,682	2,911	740	154
1980[4]	3,914	3,083	782	181
1981	3,853	2,978	820	146

| Year | Poverty Rate | | | |
	All Races	White	Black	Spanish Origin
1970	24.5%	22.5%	48.0%	—[2]
1975	15.3	13.4	36.3	32.6%
1978	14.0	12.1	33.9	23.2
1979[3]	15.2	13.3	36.2	26.8
1980[4]	15.9	13.8	38.1	31.2
1981	15.3	13.1	39.0	25.7

[1] Persons of Spanish origin may be of any race.

[2] Dash indicates figure is not available.

[3] Based on 1980 Census Population Controls. The poverty rate would be 15.1% and the number of persons in poverty would be 3,584,000 if based on 1970 Census Population Controls.

[4] Based on the new poverty definition. The poverty rate would be 15.7% and the number of persons would be 3,871,000 if based on the old poverty definition.

SOURCE: U.S. Bureau of the Census, Current Population Survey for various years.

Variations in the Incidence of Poverty. Poverty rates vary greatly among subgroups in the aged population by race, sex, and family status. In 1981, while the poverty rate was 15 percent for aged persons of all races, the rate for *white* aged persons was 13 percent, for *black* aged persons, 39 percent, and for aged persons of *Spanish* origin, 26 percent.

Among families headed by aged persons who were poor in 1981, the lowest poverty rate was 7 percent for aged families with *white male* heads, and the highest rate was 34 percent for aged families with *black female* heads (Table 2).

Of all aged unrelated individuals who were poor in 1981, the lowest rate was 20 percent for aged *white single men,* and the highest rate was 64 percent for aged *black single women.*

Of the nearly 3.9 million poor persons age 65-plus in 1981, almost 2.5 million or 63 percent of them were unrelated individuals. Over 2.0 million were single women; they represented 53 percent of all aged poor persons and 84 percent of all poor unrelated individuals. In other words, almost two-thirds of poor aged persons were single people, and aged single women comprised more than one-half of all poor aged persons and more than four-fifths of all poor single aged people.

More than 850,000 families with an aged head were poor in 1981. Of these, more than 25 percent were black. Of all poor aged families with a female head, more than 37 percent were black.

Poverty Rates among the Nonaged. In order to provide a comparative view of the poverty status of the aged, it would be well to examine the development of poverty rates

TABLE 2. **Poverty Rates in 1981 among Aged Families and Aged Unrelated Individuals.**

| | Poverty Rates and Numbers (in Thousands, in Parentheses) | | | |
	All Races	White	Black	Spanish Origin
All aged families	9.0%	7.2%	29.7%	25.0%
	(851)	(611)	(227)	(56)
All aged families	8.0	6.5	28.0	22.5
with a male head	(654)	(490)	(154)	(40)
All aged families	16.0	12.0	33.9	—[1]
with a female head	(196)	(121)	(73)	(16)
All aged unrelated	29.8%	26.5%	55.8%	43.2%
individuals	(2,421)	(1,929)	(466)	(58)
All aged male unre-	23.4	19.7	45.8	34.9
lated individuals	(395)	(278)	(108)	(17)
All aged female unre-	31.4	28.2	64.3	47.9
lated individuals	(2,026)	(1,651)	(358)	(42)

[1] Not available; base was less than 75,000.

SOURCE: U.S. Bureau of the Census, March 1982 Current Population Survey.

among the nonaged during the same period, 1970 to 1981. Table 3 shows persons under age 65 below the poverty level in selected years in that period.

The incidence of poverty among nonaged persons during the 1970s differed substantially from that among the elderly. While the overall poverty rate among the aged declined dramatically from nearly 25 percent in 1970 to 15 percent in 1975, the incidence of poverty among the nonaged increased slightly from 11 percent in 1970 to 12 percent in 1975. During the three years 1979 to 1981, the poverty rate among the aged remained approximately the same, between 15 and 16 percent, but the poverty rate among the nonaged grew from 11 percent in 1979, to 13 percent in 1980, and to 14 percent in 1981.

Criticisms of Poverty Measures. Families and unrelated individuals are classified as being above or below the poverty level based on the poverty index originated by the U.S. Social Security Administration in 1964. The index is based on the U.S. Department of Agriculture's 1961 economy food plan, reflecting different consumption requirements of families according to their size and composition. It was determined from the U.S.

Department of Agriculture's 1955 survey of food consumption that families of three or more persons spent approximately one-third of their income on food; the poverty level for these families was, therefore, set at three times the cost of the economy food plan. For smaller families and single persons, the cost of the economy food plan was multiplied by factors slightly higher than 3 to compensate for the relatively larger fixed expenses of these smaller households (U.S. Bureau of the Census, 1982a).

In 1981, the poverty cutoff income for one person age 65 or older was $4,359. For two-person families with one householder age 65 or older, it was $5,498. Because the official poverty thresholds represent an emergency-type food plan, some have argued that the "near-poverty" benchmarks (income at 125 percent of the chosen poverty level, or 25 percent above that level) would be a more appropriate measure. In 1981, for example, while the poverty rate was 15 percent for all aged persons using the official poverty index, the rate would have been 25 percent had near-poverty benchmarks been used. The number of persons in poverty would have risen to 6.4 million from 3.9 million, an increase of 64 percent. In other words, a very

TABLE 3. Persons under Age 65 below the Poverty Level in 1970, 1975, and 1978 to 1981.

Year	Numbers below Poverty Level (in Thousands)			
	All Races	White	Black	Spanish Origin[1]
1970	20,711	13,500	6,865	—[2]
1975	22,560	15,136	6,893	2,854
1978	21,264	13,729	6,963	2,482
1979[3]	22,390	14,303	7,310	2,767
1980[4]	25,726	16,966	7,773	3,385
1981	27,969	18,575	8,353	3,567
	Poverty Rate			
1970	11.3%	8.5%	32.2%	—[2]
1975	11.9	9.3	30.9	26.7%
1978	11.0	8.3	30.3	21.5
1979[3]	11.3	8.4	30.6	21.6
1980[4]	12.8	9.9	31.9	26.0
1981	13.9	10.8	33.8	26.5

[1] Persons of Spanish origin may be of any race.
[2] Dash indicates figure is not available.
[3] Based on 1980 Census Population Controls. The poverty rate would be 11.2% and the number of persons in poverty would be 21,759,000 if based on 1970 Census Population Controls.
[4] Based on the new poverty definition. The poverty rate would be 12.7% and the number of persons in poverty would be 25,401,000 if based on the old poverty definition.

SOURCE: U.S. Bureau of the Census, Current Population Survey for various years.

large number of aged people were clustered near the poverty lines.

By contrast, in 1981, while the poverty rate among all persons under age 65 was 14 percent, the incidence of near-poverty was 19 percent—an increase of only 33 percent. Consideration of near-poverty, therefore, would place a greater proportion of aged persons than nonaged persons in the category of poverty.

Another criticism of the official definition of poverty—one that would move the figures in the direction of less poverty rather than more poverty—is that it is based on money or cash income and does not include the value of in-kind or noncash transfers. Between 1965 and 1980, government expenditures for major noncash transfers such as food stamps, school lunches, publicly owned or subsidized rental housing, Medicare and Medicaid increased from under $2 billion to over $72 billion (U.S. Bureau of the Census,

1982b). It has been argued that the value of in-kind transfers ought to be included in counting income for the purpose of measuring poverty.

However, including the value of in-kind benefits as income presents some measurement problems. Adding the value of in-kind transfers to cash income requires that the poverty thresholds be revised to reflect both cash and noncash income (the value of in-kind benefits). Moreover, the value of in-kind transfers may be measured in many different ways.

A recent study issued by the U.S. Bureau of the Census (1982b) attempts to provide different methods for the valuation of in-kind food, housing, and medical care transfers received by the low-income population. The report, however, does not tackle the problem of how to revise the poverty thresholds.

Emphasizing the limited and exploratory

nature of its estimate, the Census Bureau report presents three different approaches to valuing in-kind benefits: (1) market value, (2) recipient or cash-equivalent value, and (3) poverty budget-share value. These three approaches are defined as follows (U.S. Bureau of the Census, 1982b):

1. The *market value* is equal to the purchase price in the private market of the goods received by the recipients; for example, the face value of food stamps.
2. The *recipient or cash-equivalent value* is the amount of cash that would make the recipient just as well off as the in-kind transfer; it therefore reflects the recipient's own valuation of the benefit. The recipient or cash-equivalent value is usually less than and never more than the market value. Even though cash equivalent value is the theoretically preferred measure, it is quite difficult to estimate, especially for medical care.
3. The *poverty budget-share value,* which is tied to the current poverty concept, limits the value of food, housing, or medical transfers to the proportions spent on these items by persons at or near the poverty line in 1960–61, when in-kind transfers were minimal. It assumes that in-kind transfers in excess of these amounts are not relevant for determining poverty status because an excess of one type of good (for example, housing) does not compensate for a deficiency in another good (for example, medical care).

The official poverty rate for the elderly was 15 percent in 1979. Under the market-value approach, adding the value of food, housing, and medical care benefits to money income reduces the poverty rate dramatically to 5 percent. Alternatively, under the recipient or cash-equivalent value approach, adding the value of these three types of benefits reduces the poverty rate to 9 percent. Finally, valuing these three types of benefits by the poverty budget-share method reduces the poverty rate to 11 percent.

The author believes that different valuation approaches may be appropriate for different in-kind benefits, and therefore questions the validity of applying one approach to all three types of transfers. Specifically, the market-value approach may be suitable for valuing food transfers, but not for housing and medical care transfers; the recipient or cash-equivalent value method may be appropriate for valuing housing transfers, but not for food and medical care benefits; and the poverty budget-share technique may be useful for valuing medical care transfers, but not for food and housing benefits. In other words, a composite approach may be necessary.

Because the Census Bureau report presents only the effects on poverty rates of using the different approaches for valuing *all* three major types of transfers together, it is not possible to estimate the effects, based on the report's data on poverty rates, of valuing different types of transfers by *separate* approaches.

Despite an inability to present quantitative results, however, we may pursue a qualitative discussion. For instance, as noted above, when the poverty budget-share approach was used to estimate the value of transfers, the poverty rate was reduced from 15 percent to 11 percent. But while the poverty budget-share approach appears suitable for valuing medical care benefits (because no specific allocations are made for medical care in the poverty "budget" and hence the value of Medicare and Medicaid received would not have replaced a specific portion of the budget), this approach seems to underestimate the contributions of food and housing transfers to the poverty budget. On the other hand, as noted, if all three types of benefits were evaluated by the market-value method, the poverty rate would be reduced to 5 percent. Therefore, it would appear that the poverty rate would be between 5 percent and 11 percent, probably close to 9 percent, if in-kind benefits were included in its calculation.

Growth in Median Income

The income of persons age 65-plus improved during the 1970s. The improvement may be shown in two ways: (1) median income levels in 1981 over those in 1970 in dollars of constant purchasing power (that is, after correcting for inflation or in real terms); and (2) median income levels of aged persons as compared to those of persons of all ages.

Between 1970 and 1981, the median income of aged persons increased in real terms. As shown in Table 4, all four subgroups by race and sex improved their income position in the decade, but the rates of improvement differed.

In 1981, the median income of aged white males was $8,586. This statistic means that one-half the aged white males had incomes above $8,586 and the other half had incomes below $8,586. While all aged persons in the race-and-sex subgroups saw increases in the decade, rates of improvement differed among the four subgroups. The highest rate of increase was 34 percent (for aged white females), and the lowest rate of increase was 10 percent (for aged black males). In-between rates of increase were 14 percent (for aged white males) and 28 percent (for aged black females).

Improvement in Relative Income Position. In the decade of the 1970s, the aged also improved their income position relative to the total population. Table 5 shows the ratios of median income of specified race-and-sex subgroups in 1970 and 1981. The statistics analyzed in this table are for persons only, because *family* income statistics are more difficult to interpret owing to the difference in family size between families headed by young and old persons.

In 1970, the median income of aged white males was 46 percent of the median income of white males of all ages. That ratio increased to 56 percent in 1975 and 1978, and then became 60 percent in 1981.

In 1970, the median income of aged white females was 70 percent of the median income of white females of all ages. That ratio grew to 80 percent in 1975, 84 percent in 1978, and 89 percent in 1981. Thus the relative income position of aged white females improved continuously throughout the period 1970 to 1981.

The relative income position of aged black females in 1970 was 57 percent of the median income of black females of all ages. That ratio rose to 68 percent in 1975 and 1978, and reached 72 percent in 1981.

In 1970, the median income of aged black males was 46 percent of the median income of black males of all ages. The ratio was 55 percent in 1970, 52 percent in 1978, and 57 percent in 1980. Therefore the relative income position of aged black males improved between 1970 and 1975, deteriorated between 1975 and 1978, and improved again, reaching 57 percent in 1981. This trend differed from that experienced by the other subgroups just described (aged white males, aged white females, and aged black females).

As with the growth in median income discussed above, aged white females experienced the greatest improvement and aged black males had the least improvement in relative income position. Aged white males and aged black males also improved their in-

TABLE 4. Rates of Increase in Median Income of Aged Persons by Race-and-Sex Subgroups, 1970 to 1981.

Subgroups	Median Income in 1981	Rates of Increase in Real Income[1] from 1970 to 1981
Aged white males	$8,586	14%
Aged white females	4,934	34
Aged black males	4,875	10
Aged black females	3,528	28

[1] Real income was calculated using annual average Consumer Price Index.

SOURCE: U.S. Bureau of the Census, Current Population Survey for various years.

TABLE 5. Ratios of Median Income of Aged Persons to Median Income of All Persons by Subgroups, 1970 to 1981.

Subgroups	Ratios of Median Income			
	1970	1975	1978	1981
Aged white males / All white males	46%	56%	56%	60%
Aged white females / All white females	70	80	84	89
Aged black males / All black males	46	55	52	57
Aged black females / All black females	57	68	68	72

SOURCE: U.S. Bureau of the Census, Current Population Survey for various years.

come position, though not as much as their female counterparts did.

BLS Standard Budgets

Another indication of the improving economic circumstances of the aged during the 1970s may be provided by the trends in the proportion of aged couples and aged single persons who had enough income for the levels of living reflected in the standard budgets estimated by the U.S. Bureau of Labor Statistics (BLS).

From 1967 to 1982, BLS annually estimated three standard budgets for city workers' families of four persons and, as well, three standard budgets for urban retired couples. These budgets serve as useful benchmarks to estimate the relative economic well-being of different groups in the population and to consider changes in living standards of the population over time.

Retired Couples' Budgets. A retired couple is defined as a husband age 65-plus and his nonworking wife. They are assumed to be in reasonably good health, self-supporting, and living in an urban area (U.S. Bureau of Labor Statistics, 1969a). In the autumn of 1980, the average annual costs for the three standard budgets (excluding personal income taxes) for an urban retired couple were estimated at these levels: the lower budget,

$6,644; the intermediate budget, $9,434; and the higher budget $13,923.

These budgets are based on standard lists of goods and services. Each budget provides for seven major consumption groups—food, housing, transportation, clothing, personal care, medical care, and other consumption— and the category "other items." Food costs (including meals away from home and guest meals) are based on quantities in the 1964 low-, moderate-, and liberal-cost food plans developed by the U.S. Department of Agriculture. Housing includes shelter, home furnishings, and household operation. Shelter costs are based on average costs for rented and owned dwellings. Rental costs include rents, utilities, and insurance. Homeowner costs include utilities, property taxes, insurance, home repair, and maintenance, but allow no mortgage payments. Medical care costs recognize "out-of-pocket" costs for Medicare and allow for items not covered by Medicare. "Other consumption" includes reading, recreation, tobacco, alcoholic beverages, and the like. "Other items" include gifts and contributions, as well as life insurance premiums (in the higher budget).

During the decade of the 1970s, the proportion of retired couples with incomes more than sufficient to meet the higher budget increased. Thus income distribution data relative to estimated hypothetical budgets indicates that the economic circumstances of the aged as a whole improved. Table 6 shows details of how the proportions of retired couples with incomes below, within, and above the three budgets changed during 1970–80. The following are some highlights of the changing proportions:

1. *Proportions of retired couples below the lower budget:* During 1970–80, the number of retired couples with income below the lower budget declined to 1.2 million in 1980 (18 percent of such couples in that year) from 1.4 million in 1970 (29 percent of such couples in that year).

2. *Proportions of retired couples below the intermediate budget:* During 1970–80, the number of retired couples with income below the intermediate budget dropped to 2.3 million in 1980 (35 percent of such couples in that year) from 2.4 million in 1970 (49 percent of such couples in that year).

3. *Proportions of retired couples above the intermediate budget:* Over the period 1970–80, the number of retired couples with incomes to meet at least the intermediate budget rose to 4.2 million in 1980 (65 percent of such couples in that year) from 2.5 million in 1970 (51 percent of such couples in that year).

4. *Proportions of retired couples above the higher budget:* During 1970–80, the number of retired couples with incomes that could more than meet the higher budget increased to 2.7 million in 1980 (42 percent of such couples in that year) from 1.4 million in 1970 (28 percent of such couples in that year).

As shown in the following tabulation, the proportion of retired couples with incomes insufficient to meet the intermediate budget declined to 35 percent in 1980 from 49 percent in 1970. Correspondingly, the proportion of such couples with incomes at least at the level of this budget increased to 65 percent in 1980 from 51 percent in 1970.

| | Proportions of Retired Couples | |
Budget Levels	1970	1980
Below the intermediate budget	49%	35%
Above the intermediate budget	51	65
	100%	100%

The preceding discussion of the proportions of retired couples falling into different budget levels was based on comparing the distribution of income as reported by the Bureau of the Census against the income levels required to meet the different budgets as estimated by the Bureau of Labor Statistics. The income data used for estimating those proportions were those for male-headed families *without* earned income, with the head age 65-plus. Such couples represented more than 80 percent of all male-headed families with male heads age 65-plus.

TABLE 6. **Percent of Retired Couples with Current Money Incomes below, within, and above the Three Standard Budgets, 1970–80.**

Budget Levels	1970	1972	1975	1978	1980
Below lower budget	29%	22%	21%	19%	18%
Between lower and intermediate budgets	20	22	21	19	17
Between intermediate and higher budgets	23	25	23	25	23
Above higher budget	28	31	35	37	42
	100%	100%	100%	100%	100%

Note: For 1970, the lower budget was $3,108; the intermediate budget, $4,489; and the higher budget, $7,114. For 1980, the lower budget was $6,644; the intermediate budget, $9,434; and the higher budget, $13,923.

SOURCE: Bureau of Labor Statistics, U.S. Department of Labor, and U.S. Bureau of the Census (*Consumer Income,* Series P-60 for various years).

| | Proportions of Single Aged Persons | | | |
| | 55% Scale | | 75% Scale | |
Budget Levels	1970	1980	1970	1980
Below the intermediate budget	63%	51%	76%	68%
Above the intermediate budget	37	49	24	32
	100%	100%	100%	100%

Single Aged Persons' Budgets. The Bureau of Labor Statistics has suggested an equivalence scale of 55 percent to convert the retired couples' budget into a comparable budget for single aged persons. Some have considered the equivalence scale of 55 percent inadequate. For example, the 1971 White House Conference on Aging recommended that for a comparable standard budget (lower, intermediate, or higher) an aged single person would require 75 percent of the dollar amount estimated for the retired couple (White House Conference on Aging, 1971). The following discussion of the trends in the changes of the proportions of single aged persons with enough income to meet the three budget levels presents the data using both 55 percent and 75 percent.

Based on either 55 percent or 75 percent of the retired couples' budget, the proportions of aged single persons with insufficient income to meet the lower budget declined, while the proportions with income (a) between the lower and intermediate budgets, (b) between the intermediate and higher budgets, and (c) above the higher budget, all increased.

The preceding tabulation summarizes the trends and also points out the differences between the equivalence scale of 55 percent and 75 percent. More details are shown in Table 7.

TABLE 7. Percent of Single Aged Persons with Current Money Income below, within, and above the Three Standard Budgets, 1970-80.

	1970	1972	1975	1978	1980
	I. Based on 55% of the retired couples' budget (55% Scale)				
Below lower budget	40%	34%	29%	25%	25%
Between lower and intermediate budgets	23	25	27	25	26
Between intermediate and higher budgets	18	20	19	21	21
Above higher budget	19	21	25	29	28
	100%	100%	100%	100%	100%
	II. Based on 75% of the retired couples' budget (75% Scale)				
Below lower budget	60%	55%	52%	48%	48%
Between lower and intermediate budgets	16	19	19	19	20
Between intermediate and higher budgets	12	13	14	16	15
Above higher budget	12	13	15	17	17
	100%	100%	100%	100%	100%

Note: For 1970, based on 55% of the retired couples' budget, the lower budget was $1,710; the intermediate budget, $2,469; and the higher budget, $3,913. For the same year, based on 75% of the retired couples' budget, the lower was $2,332; the intermediate was $3,367; the higher, $5,335.

For 1980, based on 55% of the retired couples' budget, the lower budget was $3,654; the intermediate, $5,189; and the higher, $7,659. For the same year, based on 75% of the retired couples' budget, the lower was $4,983; the intermediate, $7,076; and the higher, $10,443.

Source: Bureau of Labor Statistics, and U.S. Bureau of the Census (*Consumer Income,* Series P-60 for various years).

The percentage of single aged persons without enough income to meet the intermediate budget declined, and the percentage of such persons with income more than sufficient for the intermediate budget increased.

The income distribution data employed were for all unrelated persons age 65-plus, as reported by the U.S. Bureau of the Census. Ideally, the estimates of proportions of the single aged persons with different income who meet the various budget levels should be based on income data for aged unrelated individuals *without* earned income. Because such income distribution data are not available for all the years for which the proportions were estimated, we use the income data for all aged unrelated individuals.

Budgets for City Families of Four Persons. In order to gain some perspective, in terms of the relative position of the elderly versus the nonelderly, the improved position among retired couples may be compared to what occurred among the city workers' families. BLS has estimated three standard budgets for city families of four persons (U.S. Bureau of Labor Statistics, 1969b). In the autumn of 1980, the average annual costs for the three hypothetical budgets for such families were estimated at these levels: the lower budget, $14,044; the intermediate budget, $23,134; and the higher budget, $34,410.

During the decade of the 1970s, the percentage of city workers' families with income more than sufficient to meet the higher budget decreased, and those with income sufficient to meet the lower budget increased. While the proportions of city workers' families with income below, within, and above the three budgets during 1970–80 are detailed in Table 8, the changing proportions may be highlighted by the following tabulation:

Budget Levels	Proportions of City Workers' Families	
	1970	1980
Below the intermediate budget	44%	47%
Above the intermediate budget	56	53
	100%	100%

As shown here, the proportion of city workers' families with income insufficient to meet the intermediate budget increased from 44 percent in 1970 to 47 percent in 1980, and the proportion of such families with income more than sufficient to cover the intermediate budget decreased from 56 percent in 1970 to 53 percent in 1980. Therefore, with respect to standard budgets, city workers' families *on the average* saw their economic circumstances worsened during 1970–80, in

TABLE 8. Percent of City Workers' Families with Current Money Income below, within, and above the Three Standard Budgets, 1970–80.

Budget Levels	1970	1972	1975	1978	1980
Below lower budget	17%	15%	20%	19%	21%
Between lower and intermediate budgets	27	25	28	25	26
Between intermediate and higher budgets	29	26	27	26	29
Above higher budget	27	34	25	30	24
	100%	100%	100%	100%	100%

Note: For 1970, the lower budget was $6,959; the intermediate budget, $10,664; and the higher budget, $15,511. For 1980, the lower budget was $14,044; the intermediate budget, $23,134; and the higher budget, $34,410.

SOURCE: Bureau of Labor Statistics budgets for an urban family of four persons; and U.S. Bureau of the Census (*Consumer Income,* Series P-60 for various years).

contrast to the improvement in living standards for retired couples *as a group* during the same period of time.

Assets and Homeownership

Two relevant surveys, conducted in 1970 and 1977 by the University of Michigan Survey Research Center, used the same methodology, enabling us to review changes in asset ownership by the aged during the 1970s. Other sources of data on assets and homeownership, as in Murray (1972) and Friedman and Sjogren (1981), do not lend themselves to such comparisons over time.

According to the 1977 Survey of Consumer Credit (Survey Research Center, 1977) and its predecessor, the 1970 Survey of Consumer Finances (Survey Research Center, 1970), the proportions of aged households (family heads and single persons) owning the various forms of assets generally increased between 1970 and 1977, as shown in the table below:

From 1970 to 1977, the percentages of aged households owning savings accounts, checking accounts, and certificates of deposit increased, but the proportions of these households with bonds and stocks decreased. While rising proportions owning these assets may imply some improvement in well-being from the standpoint of participation in asset ownership, dollar amounts in

terms of median values would be a better measure. Unfortunately, as shown in the above tabulation, median values were available for 1977 but not readily ascertainable for 1970.

Homeownership was more widespread among those 65-plus in 1977 than the comparable age group in 1970. The incidence of homeownership grew to 74 percent in 1977 from 71 percent in 1970.

During the 1970s, house values rose significantly. The median value of homes occupied by aged owners was $30,000 in 1977, an increase of 35 percent from 1970 in *real* terms. The 35 percent rate of increase was higher than the rates for all other homeowning age groups except those aged 35–54.

In 1977, the average home equity among the aged homeowners was $31,600. It was higher than the average home equity of all other groups except those homeowners aged 45–64. The distribution of house equity among aged homeowners in 1977 was as follows:

House Equity	Percent Distribution
Under $5,000	6%
5,000–14,999	13
15,000–24,999	16
25,000–49,999	41
50,000 or more	14
Not ascertained	10
	100%

	Proportions of Aged Households Owning Assets		Median Value		
Type of Assets	1970	1977	1970	1977	Rate of Increase in Real Terms
Savings accounts	65%	72%	—	$6,250	—
Checking accounts	71	77	—	750	—
Certificates of deposit	17	23	—	11,250	—
Bonds	27	22	—	3,000	—
Stocks	24	22	—	8,750	—
Real estate other than owner-occupied homes	—	18	—	22,500	—
Owner-occupied homes	71	74	$14,300	30,000	35%

Note: Dashes indicate that figures are not available.

TABLE 9. Estimated Home Equity in 1978 of Poor Elderly Homeowners and All Elderly Homeowners (percent of homeowners in indicated subgroups).

Home Equity	Poor Elderly Homeowners[1]		All Elderly Homeowners	
	Aged 65–71	Age 72 +	Aged 65–71	Age 72 +
Less than $5,000	7.4%	6.9%	2.2%	2.7%
5,000–10,000	19.0	13.7	6.7	5.5
10,000–20,000	33.8	42.1	15.2	21.5
20,000–40,000	25.6	28.8	31.4	35.6
40,000–80,000	11.8	7.6	37.0	29.9
80,000 or more	2.4	0.9	7.3	4.9
All	100.0%	100.0%	100.0%	100.0%

[1] Measured by the lowest income/needs quintile, which is roughly equivalent to the official poverty standard.

SOURCE: Calculated from data in Table 10 in F. Thomas Juster. "Current and Prospective Financial Status of the Elderly Population," *Saving for Retirement:* Report on a MiniConference on Saving held for the 1981 White House Conference on Aging (Washington, D.C.: American Council of Life Insurance, 1981), p. 46. Juster's table shows percentage of elderly persons with zero home equity (nonhomeowners) as well. Basic data from the Panel Study of Income Dynamics, Survey Research Center, University of Michigan.

Table 9 shows the distribution in 1978 of home equity among all aged homeowners and poor aged homeowners: 44 percent of those aged 65–71 and 35 percent of those age 72-plus had net equity of $40,000 or more, whereas among the poor aged homeowners, 14 percent of those aged 65–71 and 8.5 percent of those age 72-plus had net equity of at least $40,000 in 1978.

The statistics quoted here indicate that assets other than homeownership are not substantial for the aged, and that many elderly homeowners are "asset-rich but income-poor." Converting assets into income is a challenging task (see discussion in Section 3).

2. CURRENT SOURCES OF INCOME OF THE AGED

Some Characteristics of Aged Units

The most comprehensive data for an analysis of the income status of the aged are tabulations for 1980 provided by the Social Security Administration, based on the March 1981 supplement to the Current Population Survey conducted by the Bureau of the Census. Statistics cited in this subsection are, however, unpublished tabulations based on the March 1981 Current Population Survey supplied by the Social Security Administration.

In 1980, there were 19,192,000 aged units. An aged unit refers to either a married couple living together or a non-married person. The aged unit is one in which at least one member is 65 years of age or older. Non-married persons are widows or widowers, divorced persons, never-married persons, or persons married but living apart. Using an aged unit as a unit of analysis permits an assessment of the income status of all aged persons regardless of their living arrangement. That is, income data pertaining to aged persons themselves are obtained and presented, whether they live together as couples, alone, or in households headed by younger persons.

Recognizing the diversity among the 19.2 million aged units is useful in considering the future income status of the aged (to be discussed in Section 3). Some of the characteristics of this aged population are pointed out below.

1. Older units predominated. One-half of all aged units were age 73-plus, and two-thirds were aged 70-plus.

Age	Number of units	Percent	
65–67	3,870,000	20.2%	32.1%
68–69	2,290,000	11.9	
70–72	3,185,000	16.6	67.9%
73 +	9,847,000	51.3	
Total (65 +)	19,192,000	100.0%	

2. Single persons predominated. Nearly 60 percent of all aged units were single people.

Marital status	Number of units	Percent
Married couples	7,804,000	40.7%
Nonmarried persons	11,388,000	59.3
Total	19,192,000	100.0%

3. Single woman-units predominated. Accounting for 47 percent of all aged units, single women comprised nearly four-fifths of all nonmarried persons.

Marital status	Number of units	Percent
Married couples	7,804,000	40.7%
Nonmarried men	2,324,000	12.1
Nonmarried women	9,064,000	47.2
Total	19,192,000	100.0%

Single persons	Number of units	Percent
Nonmarried men	2,324,000	20.4%
Nonmarried women	9,064,000	79.6
Total	11,388,000	100.0%

4. The median total money income declined with age, regardless of marital status.

	Median income		
Age	Married couple	Nonmarried men	Nonmarried women
65–67	$14,800	$6,310	$5,250
68–72	12,300	5,720	5,130
73–79	10,860	5,520	4,710
80 +	9,330	4,990	4,040
Total (65 +)	$12,020	$5,570	$4,630

5. Single women had lower median income. Single women had lower median income than did single men, and widowed women had the lowest median income of all subgroups by marital status.

	Median income	
Marital status	Nonmarried men	Nonmarried women
Widowed	$5,800	$4,620
Never married	4,830	5,340
Divorced	5,590	4,680
Total nonmarried	$5,570	$4,630

6. Black units had lower median total money income than white units, regardless of marital status.

	Median income		
Race	Married couples	Nonmarried men	Nonmarried women
White	$12,340	$5,910	$4,850
Black	7,350	4,180	3,320
All units	12,020	5,570	4,630

Relative Importance of Income Sources of the Aged

The elderly receive income from various sources. There are two ways in which the relative importance of various sources of income may be measured: (1) the percentage of aged units that derive income from those sources, and (2) the percentage of the aged units' aggregate income each source of income represents. Statistics cited in this subsection are from Upp (1983).

For 1980, in terms of the percentage of aged units that received income from them, the relative importance of income sources was as follows:

Income sources	Percent of aged units
Social Security	90%
Asset income	66
Earnings	23
Private pensions	22
Government employee pensions	12
Public assistance	10

These sources of income were not equally important, however, in providing dollar amounts of income to older persons. In terms of the percentage of aggregate income of all aged units that was represented by a particular source of income, the relative importance of various income sources was as follows:

Income sources	Percent of aged income
Social Security	40%
Asset income	22
Earnings	19
Private pensions	7
Government employee pensions	7
Public assistance	1
Other	4

The six sources of income will be discussed separately.

Social Security. Social Security is the single most important source of income to the elderly, providing, in 1980, 40 percent of the aggregate income of all aged units, with 90 percent of aged units receiving income from it (Table 10). Of those receiving Social Security, two-thirds (65 percent) relied on such benefits for at least half their income, and more than one-quarter (26 percent) relied on such benefits for 90 percent or more of their income.

In Upp (1983), aged units were divided into four income classes (1980 income): those receiving less than $5,000, $5,000 to $9,999, $10,000 to $19,999, and $20,000 or more. These four classes are referred to hereafter as the lowest, second, third, and highest income groups, respectively.

The importance of Social Security declined with increasing income level. Ninety-four percent of the aged receiving Social Security in the lowest income group relied on these benefits for at least half their income, while 78 percent of those within the second group and 36 percent of those in the third group relied on such benefits for at least half their income. Only 1 percent of aged units in the highest income group relied on such benefits for at least half their income.

Asset Income. Asset income (interest, dividends, rental income, and the like) was received widely by the elderly. In 1980, 66 percent of all aged units had income from assets (Table 11), accounting for 22 percent of the aggregate income of all aged units.

The percentage of aged units in different income groups that had asset income increased with income level. While 38 percent of those in the lowest income group had income from assets, the ratio rose to 72 percent for the second group, 89 percent for the third group, and 97 percent in the highest group.

The relative importance of asset income increased with income level as well. Whereas

TABLE 10. Relative Importance of Social Security by Income Level.

	All Units	Income Level			
		Lowest (less than $5,000)	Second ($5,000–$9,999)	Third ($10,000–$19,999)	Highest ($20,000 or more)
Percent of all aged units with Social Security	90%	87	94	92	84
Percent of aged units receiving Social Security and relying on this source for 50% or more of their income	65%	94	78	36	1

Compiled from Upp (1983).

TABLE 11. Relative Importance of Asset Income by Income Level.

			Income Level		
	All Units	Lowest (less than $5,000)	Second ($5,000–$9,999)	Third ($10,000–$19,999)	Highest ($20,000 or more)
Percent of all aged units with asset income	66%	38	72	89	97
Percent of aged units receiving asset income and relying on this source for 50% or more of their income	13%	6	8	16	28

Compiled from Upp (1983).

6 percent in the lowest income group relied on asset income for at least half of their income, the ratio grew to 8 percent in the second group, 16 percent in the third group, and 28 percent in the highest group.

Earnings. Employment was another important source of income to older persons. In 1980, 23 percent of all aged units had earnings (Table 12), and this source of income provided 19 percent of the aggregate income of aged units. As in the case of asset income, the percentage of aged units with income from employment rose with income level. Only 6 percent in the lowest income level had earnings, 19 percent in the second group, 36 percent in the third group, and 58 percent in the highest group.

Like asset income, earnings rose in importance with income level as well. The percentage of aged units in four income groups who relied on earnings for at least half their income were 24 percent, 27 percent, 45 percent, and 56 percent, respectively.

Private Pensions. Private pensions were also an important source of income to the aged. In 1980, 22 percent of all aged units received some income from private pensions (Table 13), which represented 7 percent of their aggregate income.

Receipt of private pensions was more common for higher income groups than for those with lower income. While 39 percent in the third income group and 36 percent in the highest income group received income from private pensions, only 4 percent in the lowest income group and 24 percent in the second income group did.

As to the relative importance of private

TABLE 12. Relative Importance of Earnings by Income Level.

			Income Level		
	All Units	Lowest (less than $5,000)	Second ($5,000–$9,999)	Third ($10,000–$19,999)	Highest ($20,000 or more)
Percent of all aged units with earnings	23%	6	19	36	58
Percent of aged units receiving earnings and relying on this source for 50% or more of their income	42%	24	27	45	56

Compiled from Upp (1983).

TABLE 13. Relative Importance of Private Pensions by Income Level.

		Income Level			
	All Units	Lowest (less than $5,000)	Second ($5,000–$9,999)	Third ($10,000–$19,999)	Highest ($20,000 or more)
Percent of all aged units with private pensions	22%	4	24	39	36
Percent of aged units receiving private pensions and relying on this source for 50% or more of their income	7%	16	7	7	6

Compiled from Upp (1983).

pension benefits, 16 percent of those in the lowest income group relied on private pensions for at least half their income, but the ratio became 7 percent, 7 percent, and 6 percent for those in the second, third, and highest income groups.

Government Employee Pensions. Government employee pensions, received in 1980 by 12 percent of all aged units (Table 14), provided 7 percent of their aggregate income.

Like private pensions, government employee pensions were more likely to be received by higher income groups. Whereas 20 percent and 28 percent in the third and highest groups received this form of income, only 3 percent and 10 percent in the lowest and second groups did.

Although only 12 percent of all aged units received pensions from government employee retirement programs, to those who received them, this source of income was relatively important. Between 30 and 40 percent of the aged units with such income throughout the four income groups relied on this source for more than half their income.

Public Assistance. Public assistance (means-tested welfare payments) was received in 1980 by 10 percent of all aged units (Table 15), constituting only 1 percent of the aggregate income of all aged units.

TABLE 14. Relative Importance of Government Employee Pensions by Income Level.

		Income Level			
	All Units	Lowest (less than $5,000)	Second ($5,000–$9,999)	Third ($10,000–$19,999)	Highest ($20,000 or more)
Percent of all aged units with government employee pensions	12%	3	10	20	28
Percent of aged units receiving government employee pensions and relying on this source for 50% or more of their income	35%	31	32	40	32

Compiled from Upp (1983).

TABLE 15. Relative Importance of Public Assistance by Income Level.

	Income Level				
	All Units	Lowest (less than $5,000)	Second ($5,000–$9,999)	Third ($10,000–$19,999)	Highest ($20,000 or more)
Percent of all aged units with public assistance	10%	24	5	1	0
Percent of aged units receiving public assistance and relying on this source for 50% or more of their income	30%	32	22	19	0

Compiled from Upp (1983).

Public assistance by definition was available only to the lower income groups. In the first income group, nearly one-quarter (24 percent) of the aged units received this source of income, whereas only 5 percent and 1 percent in the second and third income groups did.

To those who received welfare payments, it was a very important income support. For 32 percent of those aged units in the lowest income group, public assistance provided at least half their income, whereas for 22 percent and 19 percent of those in the second and third groups public assistance represented at least half their income.

Income Sources by Income Groups

In order to assess the relative importance of various income sources to older persons, it is necessary to analyze the contributions these sources of income make to the elderly in different income groups. As shown in Table 16, considerable variation exists in the

TABLE 16. Relative Importance of Various Income Sources in the Aggregate Income of Aged Units in Different Income Levels (1980).

	Income Level						
Lowest (less than $5,000)		Second ($5,000–$9,999)		Third ($10,000–$19,999)		Highest ($20,000 or more)	
Income Source	Percent	Income Source	Percent	Income Source	Percent	Income Source	Percent
1. Social Security	79%	1. Social Security	63%	1. Social Security	39%	1. Asset income	34%
2. Public assistance	10	2. Asset income	14	2. Asset income	21	2. Earnings	33
3. Asset income	4	3. Earnings	8	3. Earnings	17	3. Social Security	16
4. Earnings	2	4. Private pensions	6	4. Private pensions	10	4. Government employee pensions	9
5. Private pensions	1	5. Government employee pensions	4	5. Government employee pensions	9	5. Private pensions	6
6. Government employee pensions	1	6. Public asssistance	1	6. Public assistance	0	6. Public assistance	0

SOURCE: Adapted from Melinda Upp, "Relative Importance of Various Income Sources of the Aged, 1980," *Social Security Bulletin,* 46, No. 1 (Jan. 1983), Table 1, p. 5.

roles these sources play in contributing to the aggregate income of aged units in the different income groups.

Lowest Income Group. In 1980, nearly 90 percent of the aggregate income of the aged units in the lowest income group (less than $5,000) came from Social Security and public assistance. Social Security benefits were of paramount importance, providing 79 percent of the aggregate income, with public assistance payments providing another 10 percent of the aggregate income. Asset income, earnings, private pensions, and government employee pensions provided 4 percent, 2 percent, 1 percent, and 1 percent, respectively.

Second Income Group. For aged units in the second income group ($5,000–$9,999), Social Security was still a very significant contributor, accounting for nearly two-thirds (63 percent) of the aggregate income. Unlike the lowest income group, for whom public assistance was the second largest source of income, asset income was second in importance in contributing to aged units in this second group, providing slightly less than one-sixth (14 percent) of the aggregate income. In descending order of importance, after Social Security and asset income, were earnings (8 percent), private pensions (6 percent), government employee pensions (4 percent), and public assistance (1 percent).

Third Income Group. The relative importance of various sources of income for aged units in the third income group ($10,000–$19,999) was quite different. Though still important, Social Security was a less significant income source for this group than for the two groups with lower incomes; it was 39 percent of the aggregate income. More than one-fifth (21 percent) of the aggregate income came from assets. Next in importance was earnings, which provided approximately one-sixth of aggregate income (17 percent). The remaining sources of income were private pensions and government employee pensions, which

contributed 10 percent and 9 percent, respectively, to the aggregate income of aged units in this income group.

Highest Income Group. Finally, aged units in the highest income group ($20,000 or more) derived their income from essentially the same sources, but the relative importance of these income sources was very different. Interestingly, asset income, earnings, and retirement income (Social Security, government employee pensions, and private pensions) each provided approximately one-third of the aggregate income. Ranked first was asset income, which provided 34 percent; next was earnings, which accounted for 33 percent; and the remaining third came from Social Security, government employee pensions, and private pensions. For the highest income group, Social Security contributed only one-sixth (16 percent) to their aggregate income. Government employee pensions provided 9 percent, and private pension benefits contributed another 6 percent to the aggregate income.

Relative Importance of Non-earnings Income

Because earnings provided nearly one-fifth (19 percent) of income to all aged units, but more than three-fourths of them (77 percent) did not have this source of income, inclusion of earnings in the analysis of income sources tends to obscure the role non-earnings income programs played in providing income to the elderly.

Statistics cited in this subsection are from Upp (1983). The term "non-earnings income" is equivalent to Upp's term "retirement income." "Retirement income" does not include earnings, and some people consider earnings as part of retirement income. Non-earnings income refers to Social Security, private and government employee pensions, and income from assets (Upp, 1983).

In 1980, by far the most significant source of non-earnings income was Social Security, which provided nearly one-half (49 percent) of such income of all aged units. Approximately 70 percent of aged units relied on Social Security for at least half their non-earnings income.

Next in importance was assets income, which accounted for 28 percent of non-earnings income of all aged units.

After income from assets, government employee pensions and private pensions each provided 9 percent of total non-earnings income.

As shown in Table 17, Social Security was clearly the single most important source of non-earnings income. It was more important as a share of total non-earnings income among lower income levels than among higher income levels.

Assets provided three times as much non-earnings income as did either government employee pensions or private pensions. Asset income, government employee pensions, and private pensions are all more important to higher income levels than to lower income levels. For example, for aged units in the fifth quintile, asset income contributed 43 percent to their non-earnings income.

Government employee pensions and private pensions accounted for less than 1 percent of the non-earnings income for aged units in the lowest quintile. On the other hand, for aged units in the highest quintile, government employee pensions provided 14 percent and private pensions provided 11 percent to their non-earnings income.

As also shown in Table 17, 70 percent of all aged units received at least half their non-earnings income from Social Security. The proportions were 13 percent, 5 percent, and 2 percent, respectively, for asset income, government employee pensions, and private pensions.

3. FUTURE ECONOMIC STATUS OF THE AGED

Data analyzed in Section 1 indicated an improvement in the economic status of the el-

TABLE 17. Relative Importance of Various Sources of Non-earnings Income among All Aged Units by Quintiles.

| Non-earnings Income Sources | All Aged Units | | | | | |
| | Total | Quintiles | | | | |
		1st	2nd	3rd	4th	5th
Share (in percent) of income from:[1]						
Social Security	49%	86%	87%	71%	56%	29%
Government employee pensions	9	1	1	4	7	14
Private pensions	9	1	1	5	11	11
Asset income	28	7	6	13	21	43
Percent of aged units receiving 50% or more of income from:[2]						
Social Security	70	83	94	84	67	23
Government employee pensions	5	1	1	2	6	14
Private pensions	2	1	1	2	3	4
Asset income	13	13	2	5	13	34

[1] Amounts of Social Security are excluded from that item for persons receiving both Social Security and railroad retirement because the CPS questionnaire asks for the combined amount. Persons receiving only railroad retirement also are not included. Amounts of government employee pensions and private pensions are excluded from the separate items for persons receiving both sources.

[2] Units with zero or negative total income are excluded. In addition, units with negative earnings are excluded from the Social Security item, and units with a person receiving both a government employee and private pension are excluded from those items.

SOURCE: Adapted from Melinda Upp, "Relative Importance of Various Income Sources of the Aged, 1980," *Social Security Bulletin,* 46, No. 1 (Jan. 1983), Table 4, p. 8.

derly in the 1970s, while statistics in Section 2 reported the sources from which they derived their income in 1980. These materials are useful for looking into the future economic status of the aged. How healthy will the economic circumstances of the older population of the future be?

We will attempt to speculate on this question by considering a number of factors that bear on the following major income sources for the elderly: Social Security, asset income, earnings, and occupational pensions (private pension and government employee pension plans). Since some distinct subgroups among the aged did not fare as well in the 1970s as the rest of the elderly population, we will discuss the special, low-income problems faced by single women, racial minorities, and the very old among the aged.

Relative Role of Income Sources

For speculating on the future, it may be useful to review the changing importance of the various sources of income during the past two decades, as well as consider some of the more important factors that will affect the mechanisms that generate those sources of income.

Role of Social Security. During the last 20 years, Social Security has gained importance in terms of both (1) the proportion of the elderly receiving income from it, and (2) the share in the aggregate income of the elderly that Social Security represented. This twofold improvement is shown as follows:

	1962	1980
Percent of all aged units with income from Social Security	69	90
Percent of aggregate income of all aged units provided by Social Security	31	40

Social Security will continue to perform a significant role in providing income to the elderly. According to calculations provided to the author by the Office of the Actuary, U.S. Social Security Administration, Social Se-

curity is designed to provide retirement benefits, for retirees in the year 2000 and beyond, that would replace 54 percent of earnings in the year before retirement for low earners (full-time workers earning the federal minimum wage). For average earners, the replacement rate would be 42 percent, and for maximum earners, 28 percent. (Average earnings in the early 1980s were twice the low earnings. Maximum earnings refer to earnings at the taxable ceiling for Social Security purposes.) These would be replacement rates for single workers. In the case of couples, replacement rates would be one-half again as much as those for single workers. For example, since the replacement rate for a single worker as an average earner is 42 percent, the replacement rate would become 63 percent for a couple. The Social Security Amendments of 1983 did not change the projected replacement rates.

Readers interested in a technical and detailed analysis of replacement rates should consult Fox (1982). Criticisms of average replacement rate calculations may be found in Schulz (1978) and Munnell (1982).

Coverage of workers under Social Security will be expanding in the future—principally as a result of the Social Security Amendments of 1983—to new employees of the federal government, legislative branch employees, all members of Congress, the president and the vice president, all sitting federal judges, and all employees of nonprofit organizations. The 1983 legislation also prohibits state and local governments from terminating coverage under Social Security for their employees. In addition, state and local governments that had withdrawn from Social Security will be allowed to rejoin (Kollman, 1983).

Under the 1983 Amendments, a portion of Social Security benefits will be included in taxable income for taxpayers whose adjusted gross income, including otherwise tax-exempt interest income, combined with 50 percent of their benefits, exceeds $25,000 (for an individual) and $32,000 (for a married couple filing a joint return). This provision will have the effect of reducing the relative importance of this income source to Social Security beneficiaries in higher income groups.

The normal retirement age for full benefits will be gradually raised to 66 by the year 2009, and then to 67 by the year 2027. After the age for full-benefit retirement is changed to 67, early retirement benefits (at age 62) will be reduced to 70 percent of full benefits, as compared to 80 percent at present. These provisions will have some effect on the level of income the elderly in the future will receive from Social Security.

Role of Asset Income. Discussion in this subsection is based on Scholen and Chen (1980), Chen (1980), and Employee Benefit Research Institute (1982).

Even though asset income represented, as indicated earlier, an important percentage of the aggregate income of the high-income aged, and even though a large proportion of the aged had income from this source, the median amounts of asset income were quite low in 1980: $1,700 for couples, $1,010 for single men, and $740 for single women, according to an unpublished tabulation by the U.S. Social Security Administration.

One major reason for the relatively meager median asset income is that the value of liquid or financial assets in the hands of the aged is typically small or modest. Without diminishing the value of the capital, at an interest rate of 5 percent, $1,700 of interest income requires a capital of $34,000, and $740 of interest income requires a capital of $14,800.

Another problem is the illiquid nature of home equity, pointed out in Section 1. In the context of private saving, homeownership requires special attention. What is the income potential from the assets represented by home equity?

The ability and willingness of an older homeowner to use home equity for augmenting current income poses a dilemma under existing circumstances. Usually, conversion of a home into cash requires its sale—an action that often is not agreeable to older persons because of their attachment to the home and the resulting psychological and social adjustment problems related to change in residence. In addition, by selling one's home, a person becomes a renter, paying rent with the proceeds from sale. As a renter, a person may lose some measure of freedom, may be faced with uncertainty over rental charges, and must judiciously manage the proceeds from the house sale. Moving in with younger members of the family—thus avoiding rental payments—is the exception rather than the rule.

A solution to this dilemma might be to borrow against home equity. But conventional modes of financing homes would, for the most part, preclude older persons from using their homes as collateral. Home Equity Liquefying Plans (HELP) are methods—some already in limited use—that may be employed to tap the largely untapped financial resources of many elderly persons, and make liquid the illiquid savings of many millions of older people. The logic of HELP is simple: a young person who buys a house is mortgaging future income to acquire an asset (an act of saving); an elderly homeowner who uses HELP is liquefying an otherwise frozen asset to obtain income for current use (an act of dissaving).

As of 1983, only five nonprofit organizations provided information, advice, and aid in arranging such financing: (1) San Francisco (California) Development Funds; (2) the Essex County (New Jersey) Senior Cooperative; (3) the Buffalo (New York) Home Equity Living Plans; (4) the Madison (Wisconsin) Development Corporation; and (5) the Monona (Wisconsin) Senior Citizens Commission.

Although home equity plans have aroused interest and action, they present a number of complex issues for homeowner/borrower, lender/investor, and government tax/welfare/regulatory agencies. The problems are no longer statutory, however: financing remains an issue, as does consumer acceptance of a still new concept; both sides of the transaction need to understand the costs and risks involved; and there is little experience to draw upon. The potential for home equity conversion depends on such objective factors as interest rates, government policy, and consumer safeguards; and such subjective factors as desire to bequeath and attitudes of potential heirs.

There are now in existence some tax-induced mechanisms to .encourage retirement saving: the Keogh Plan and Individual Retirement Accounts (IRAs). The Keogh Plan allows self-employed persons to set aside tax-deductible savings up to $15,000 or 15 percent of income, whichever is less, and IRAs permit workers to set aside tax-deductible savings of up to $2,000 or up to $2,250 for a worker with a non-working spouse.

Keogh and IRA plans have been designed to fill the void left by the coverage gap under private pension plans. Whether these plans will become significant supplements to Social Security and private pensions for the aged population in general is an open question.

Role of Earnings. Employment as a source of income to the elderly has clearly declined during the past two decades, as shown by the following:

	1962	1980
Percent of all aged units with earnings	36	23
Percent of aggregate income of all aged units provided by earnings	29	19

Earnings may contribute less to the aggregate income of the aged in the future if the labor force participation rate among older persons continues to decline and the early retirement trend continues to accelerate. However, it is possible that earnings may become a more important income source if the elderly remain in the workplace longer as a means to enhance their income position during inflationary times. In addition, if the health status of older persons improves, with mortality improvement, then they may wish to work longer and not retire earlier. Finally, recent low birth rates and the low rates estimated for the future will result in a smaller labor force (as defined by conventional ages) in the future. The aged may well be called

upon to work longer. The change in the normal retirement age under Social Security, scheduled to begin some 20 years from now, is consistent with this possibility.

Role of Occupational Pensions. Occupational pensions refer to private pension plans and government employee pension systems (state and local government employee retirement plans, as well as the Civil Service Retirement System operated by the federal government).

Private pension benefits have gained relative importance from 1962 to 1980, but most of the increase in importance occurred between 1962 and 1976, as shown by these statistics (Upp, 1983):

	1962	1976	1980
Percent of all aged units with private pensions	9	20	22
Percent of aggregate income of all aged units provided by private pensions	3	7	7

In the case of government employee pension systems, while the proportion of older persons receiving this type of benefit increased substantially from 1962 to 1980, the aggregate income of the elderly represented by these benefits was practically unchanged at 6–7 percent, as indicated in the following tabulation (Upp, 1983):

	1962	1976	1980
Percent of all aged units with government employee pensions	5	9	12
Percent of aggregate income of all aged units provided by government employee pensions	6	6	7

The role of these pensions as a source of income in the future will be reduced by the Social Security Amendments of 1983 which mandate coverage for new federal employees beginning in 1984 (although federal pensions will continue to exist as supplements).

Although private pension plans continued to grow through the 1970s, future growth in coverage for those workers not yet covered is expected to be at a slower pace because: (1) the most accessible groups of workers (such as in manufacturing, mining, transportation industries, and large-size establishments) have already been covered; (2) industries with traditionally high pension coverage are expected to employ a declining share of workers, whereas industries with low pension coverage are expected to increase their share of workers; and (3) the large proportion of workers primarily in small- and medium-size businesses will continue to find it difficult to obtain coverage (Munnell, 1982; White House Conference on Aging, 1981).

Despite this, a recent simulation study suggested that the proportion of families headed by persons aged 65–69 receiving pension benefits in the year 2000 will double the 1979 proportion (ICF Inc., 1982). The same estimates indicate that the average annual initial pension benefits for workers in these families in the year 2000 will be at nearly the same constant level of real pension benefits as in 1979. In addition, although pensions will increase in importance, the ICF estimates suggest that Social Security will provide over one-half of all retirement program income for the majority of families.

It may be helpful to point out the relative size of Social Security benefits and private pensions at present. According to Table 18, in 1980, while the median income from Social Security for all aged household units was $4,210, the median income from private pensions was $2,420. The table also shows variations in the relative magnitudes of Social Security and private pension benefits by marital status. For example, compared to other marital status groups, private pensions

were much less important (relative to Social Security) to nonmarried women.

The relative importance of private pensions as a source of income to the elderly will be in large measure determined by the extent of future inflation. Because private pensions are seldom adjusted for inflation, continued inflation will reduce the contribution private pensions can make, vis-à-vis Social Security, toward income security in old age.

Special Income Problems for Some Subgroups

At least three subgroups of the aged now faced with special income problems require special attention: single women, racial minorities, and the very old.

Single Women. As pointed out in Section 2, in 1980, single (or nonmarried) women accounted for 47 percent of all aged units and comprised nearly 80 percent of all nonmarried persons. Single women had lower median income than did single men, and widowed women had the lowest median income of all subgroups by marital status. The median income of single women was approximately 80 percent of the median income of single men. Poverty statistics in Section 1 also indicated the special plight of single women. In 1981, aged single women comprised more than one-half of all aged poor and more than four-fifths of the poor, single, aged population.

In the future, if life expectancy continues to widen between men and women, there will be more women and more nonmarried women among the aged. If the pattern of lower income for single women persists, then they will become an increasingly serious concern for society.

TABLE 18. Median Income from Social Security and Private Pensions among All Aged Units by Marital Status, 1980.

Income Source	All Household Units	Married Couples	Nonmarried Men	Nonmarried Women
Social Security	$4,210	$6,030	$3,860	$3,520
Private pensions	2,420	2,980	2,560	1,490

SOURCE: Unpublished tabulations by Office of Research and Statistics, Social Security Administration.

The lower economic position of aged women of today has resulted from a number of factors that operated in the past and to some extent exist even now, such as: low labor force participation rate of women; intermittent pattern of employment and short job tenure; concentration in lower-paying industries and jobs; concentration in industries with low participation in private pension plans (such as trade and service), in occupations not typically covered by private pensions (such as sales, clerical, and service), in nonunionized employment, or in small- or medium-size establishments without private pension plans; and sex discrimination in compensation.

Elderly women of the future, however, may well face brighter income prospects due to some factors that have come into play in the recent past, such as: higher labor force participation, more career-oriented employment history, wider participation in occupations and jobs, greater participation in private pension plans, and less sex discrimination in compensation. Still, the lower income positions of aged women in at least the next decade or two will be a reality that requires attention.

Racial Minorities. With respect to race, poverty statistics in Section 1 and income distribution statistics in Section 2 both point to the special low-income problem faced by blacks and persons of Spanish origin. (There are no systematic data on other racial minorities). For example, in 1981, whereas the poverty rate for white aged persons was 13 percent, the rate for aged persons of Spanish origin was twice as high (26 percent), and the rate for black aged persons was three times as high (39 percent). In terms of income distribution in 1980, black aged units had lower median income than white aged units, regardless of marital status. The median income of black couples was only 60 percent of the median income of white couples. The median income of black single men and women was approximately 70 percent of the median income of white single persons.

Many of the reasons for blacks' low income were enumerated above in discussing the plight of women. For example, like women, black workers have been much less likely to have jobs with private pension coverage, and less likely to accumulate private pension rights because of shorter job tenure or lack of continuous employment. Although labor market conditions for blacks are improving, the income position of aged blacks in the next decade or two is likely to remain relatively low vis-à-vis white aged persons.

The Very Old. The aged are increasing at a faster rate than is the total population.

From 1980 to 2000, the aged will be increasing at more than twice the rate as the total population: almost 39 percent versus 17 percent. After the year 2000, the growth rate in the aged population is estimated to become between 3.5 and 4 times the growth rate of the total population (Faber and Wilkins, 1981).

The rates of increase are greater for the very old among the elderly, defined as those 75 to 84, and those 85 and over. Moreover, the oldest females (age 85-plus) are estimated to grow at a faster rate than the oldest males.

There are numerous possible implications of the growth of the very old, such as:

1. More years in retirement, hence more retirement income needed.
2. Greater effect of inflation on the purchasing power of a given amount of income at the start of retirement.
3. A greater differential between the income of the retired and the income of the active population, in those periods when workers enjoy rising wage income due to the growth rate of wages exceeding that of prices.
4. Continuation and perhaps worsening of limited employment opportunities for the very old, and thus lesser opportunity to rely on earnings as a source of income in old age.
5. Greater incidence of health problems, physical and mental.
6. Changing expenditure needs, especially for health care and housing.

7. Greater need for institutional and in-home long-term care.

8. Less reliance on care by family members when the children (especially of those age 85-plus) would themselves be retired or elderly, possibly with impaired capacity.

4. CONCLUDING REMARKS

Statistics in Section 1 demonstrated that the aged in the United States had improved their economic circumstances during the 1970s by referring to the decline in the incidence of poverty among the aged; the rise in real income; the income distribution of the aged in comparison to standard budgets; and the increase in holdings of assets and homeownership. More important, the aged improved their economic position relative to the non-aged population. In addition, this chapter described and analyzed the relative importance of six sources from which the elderly derived their income in 1980: Social Security, asset income, earnings, private pensions, government employee pensions, and public assistance. Finally, this chapter speculated on the future economic status of the aged by analyzing the changing roles of the major sources of income and by commenting on special problems facing aged single women, aged racial minorities, and the very old.

REFERENCES

Binstock, Robert H., Chow, Wing-Sun, and Schulz, James H. 1982. *International Perspective on Aging: Population and Policy Challenges.* New York: United Nations Fund for Population Activities.

Chen, Yung-Ping. 1980. Elderly homeowners may need HELP. *The Philadelphia Inquirer,* Aug. 25, p. 15-A.

Employee Benefit Research Institute. 1982. Reverse annuity mortgages: A viable source of retirement income? (EBRI issue brief.) Washington, D.C.: Employee Benefit Research Institute.

Faber, Joseph F., and Wilkins, John C. 1981. Social security area population projections. Actuarial Study No. 85. Washington, D.C.: Social Security Administration.

Fox, Alan. 1982. Earnings replacement rates and total income: Findings from the retirement history study. *Social Security Bulletin* 45 (Oct.):3–23.

Friedman, Joseph, and Sjogren, Jane. 1981. Assets of the elderly as they retire. *Social Security Bulletin* 44 (Jan.):16–31.

ICF Incorporated. 1982. Pension coverage and expected retirement benefits (final report, prepared for the American Council of Life Insurance). Washington, D.C.

Juster, Thomas F. 1981. Current and prospective financial status of the elderly population. *Saving for Retirement:* Report on a Mini Conference on Saving held for the 1981 White House Conference on Aging. Washington, D.C.: American Council of Life Insurance.

Kollman, Geoffrey. 1983. The Social Security Amendments of 1983. (Issue brief no. IB83070.) Washington, D.C.: Congressional Research Service, The Library of Congress.

Munnell, Alicia H. 1982. *The Economics of Private Pensions.* Washington, D.C.: The Brookings Institution.

Murray, Janet. 1972. Homeownership and financial assets: Findings from the 1968 survey of the aged. *Social Security Bulletin* 35 (Aug.):3–23.

Scholen, Ken, and Chen, Yung-Ping (eds.). 1980. *Unlocking Home Equity for the Elderly.* Cambridge, Mass.: Ballinger Publishing Company.

Schulz, James. 1978. Pension adequacy and pension costs. *Aging* (Feb.):279–280.

Survey Research Center. 1970. 1970 Survey of Consumer Finances. Ann Arbor: University of Michigan.

Survey Research Center. 1977. 1977 Survey of Consumer Credit. Ann Arbor: University of Michigan.

U.S. Bureau of the Census. 1982a. Money income and poverty status of families and persons in the United States: 1981 (advance data from the March 1982 Current Population Survey). *Current Population Reports, Series P-60, No. 134. Washington, D.C..* U.S. Government Printing Office.

U.S. Bureau of the Census. 1982b. Technical Paper No. 50. Alternative methods for valuing selected in-kind benefits and measuring their effect on poverty. Washington, D.C.: U.S. Government Printing Office.

U.S. Bureau of Labor Statistics. 1969a. Three budgets for a retired couple. (Release No. SF BLS 9-88.) Washington, D.C.: U.S. Government Printing Office.

U.S. Bureau of Labor Statistics. 1969b. Three standards of living for an urban family of four persons. (Release No. USDL-10-296.) Washington, D.C.: U.S. Government Printing Office.

Upp, Melinda. 1983. Relative importance of various income sources of the aged, 1980. *Social Security Bulletin* 46 (Jan.):3–10.

White House Conference on Aging, 1971. Toward a national policy on aging. Final report, Vol. II. Washington, D.C.: U.S. Government Printing Office.

White House Conference on Aging, 1981. Report of technical committee on retirement income. Washington, D.C.: Department of Health and Human Services.

23
INCOME MAINTENANCE POLICIES

Robert L. Clark
and
David L. Baumer
North Carolina State University

The economic well-being of the nation's elderly has substantially improved over the past three decades. During this time, existing income maintenance programs have been expanded and new programs established. The growth of income transfers to older persons has become one of the primary issues for federal fiscal policy because of the significant increase in the costs of these transfers and the continuing projections of higher future costs (Hudson, 1978; Samuelson, 1978). This chapter examines governmental and private income maintenance policies for their effect on the incomes of the elderly, retirement decisions, and the national economy. We begin by examining the economic and political rationale for governmental income transfer systems and regulation of private pensions. This is followed by a review of the growth and development of public transfers to the elderly in the United States; next, we examine the trend in economic well-being of the elderly over the past two decades and the role of government programs in raising the real income of older persons. Finally, the future costs of these transfers are considered and policy options for future modification of the income maintenance system are assessed.

RATIONALE FOR INCOME MAINTENANCE POLICIES

The principal public policies influencing the well-being of the elderly in most countries consist of social insurance programs, federal pensions and the regulation of private pensions, and welfare programs. The importance of these programs varies considerably among the countries of the world. Each nation develops its income transfer programs within the prevailing social and economic framework. Thus, while the structure (U.S. Social Security Administration, 1977) of income transfer programs differs, there should be great similarity in the rationale for the existence of public transfer programs, especially within the group of developed countries. In order to develop the issues related to income maintenance policies, this chapter focuses on the United States. Despite this emphasis on a single country, many of the concepts and problems that are examined are international in scope. These central themes will be indicated throughout the text.

Social Security

Old age benefit programs are common throughout the world, with some of the old-

666

est plans being those of Germany (first legislation 1889), the United Kingdom (1908), France (1910), Sweden (1913), and Italy (1919). The United States enacted social security legislation in 1935, and the U.S. system is the focus of the following discussion. All national compulsory retirement programs face the problem of taxing employers and current workers to provide benefits to retirees. Although the framework of taxes and benefits differs, the rationale for the existence of retirement income programs is similar in many countries.

The old age and survivors benefit (OASI) component of the social security system in the United States was founded on six basic principles: participation is compulsory for designated groups; benefits are based on past earnings; social security should provide a floor of protection but should not be viewed as the sole source of retirement income; funds are to come from an earmarked payroll tax; social adequacy is considered through the use of a progressive benefit formula; and a retirement test limits benefits to those who have substantially reduced work efforts (Schulz, 1980, pp. 94–95). The social insurance system was expanded to include disability insurance (DI) in 1956 and medicare or health insurance (HI) in 1965. These three programs are often considered together as the Old Age, Survivors, Disability and Health Insurance (OASDHI) system of the United States. Together they insure persons against retirement, disability, and health problems in old age.

Social security has developed in conjunction with the expansion of welfare programs that provide a minimum income for indigents of all ages, and federal encouragement and regulation of private retirement saving systems. These private methods of saving include employer pensions, individual retirement accounts, and tax-deferred annuities, all of which receive preferential tax treatment. In addition, private disability and health insurance is available. In an economic system that allows and encourages private savings and provides welfare benefits for the least fortunate, why should compulsory savings and insurance systems exist? And if such systems exist, why should they contain a redistribution component instead of being a more nearly actuarially fair system?

There are several economic rationales for social security. First, social security may enhance economic efficiency through risk pooling and the elimination of selling costs that sales of private retirement insurance would necessarily entail. Second, some analysts contend that, on average, people's expectations regarding the needs for retirement income are unrealistically low, and inadequate preparations are made for health catastrophes or long life. The resulting extreme poverty in old age creates severe personal hardships and an externality for society; in other words, the full costs of poverty are not borne by the poor person because society comes to his aid with welfare programs. Each of these contentions is examined by presenting some of the major arguments on both sides of the debate.

Most analysts view the goals and effects of social security as encompassing both social insurance and a mechanism for redistribution. With respect to the insurance function, the issue becomes whether the government or the private sector can most efficiently provide this service. Certainly from the perspective of the individual, risk pooling is often desirable. An "adequate" retirement income depends upon several factors that are beyond control of individuals. For example, while average longevity is well-known, it is of little value to the individual in planning for retirement income. By pooling risk through insurance, annuities, or pensions (public or private), the risk of long life (exhausting savings) can be reduced. Much the same argument can be made to explain the existence of health insurance (public or private). Of course, inflation is another important determinant of an adequate retirement income that is beyond control of the individual.

Both government and the private sector provide mechanisms for reducing risk. OASI benefits, which are paid as long as the recipient lives, and medicare provide essentially the same service as variable annuities and private health insurance. At present, although the private sector has no financial instrument that, like OASI, is explicitly keyed to the rate of inflation, there are annuities whose yields are indexed to interest rates that historically have been highly correlated with the rate of inflation, and there are other investments that have been good (but not perfect) hedges against inflation. Thus, it appears that the private sector is capable of providing mechanisms that can reduce the effects of the three forms of uncertainty—longevity, health, and inflation—that are the major determinants of the adequacy of an individual's retirement income. However, the individual may lack important information relevant to his choice, and the private sector may encounter substantial problems in offering a constant real level of benefits (Munnell, 1980; Feldstein, 1980).

A benefit of public insurance through social security is that the selling costs of private insurance are eliminated, and administrative cost may be reduced. These benefits are provided, however, at the expense of individual diversification. The preferences of people are clearly not identical. Some are willing to assume more risk than others. In addition, some people prefer to save more in their later years, whereas others desire the opposite. With social security a relatively constant relationship between income and savings (social security taxes) is maintained regardless of the life-cycle preferences of the individual with respect to savings. It is more accurate to say that social security may reduce selling costs, but it does so by ignoring individual preferences with respect to risk and savings. Of course, people save for retirement by means other than social security, and these transactions can be structured according to risk and saving preferences. Thus, it is improper, a priori, to contend that the public sale of retirement insurance (through social security) is more efficient than private sales because economic efficiency is partly dependent upon individual preferences. Since most

people save additional resources for retirement, this constraint on life-cycle allocation of resources may in practice not be very important.

Another argument for a mandatory social security program is that, on average, people are overly optimistic about their needs for retirement income. In other words, people will generally save too little. As noted, an "adequate" retirement income is dependent upon several factors (longevity, health, inflation) that are partially outside the control of individuals. Forecasting events is always problematic even if accurate information is available. If, on average, people have rational expectations about income needs upon retirement, there is still a problem if a significant fraction seriously underestimates these needs (see Diamond, 1977). For those who overestimate the income in retirement necessary to satisfy their desired life-styles, the private and social costs are minor. Such is not the case for those who underestimate their income requirements during retirement. Their income may significantly decline, and they may have trouble obtaining the basic necessities of food, clothing, and shelter. The plight of destitute elderly who have been productive most of their lives imposes a major social cost on society. If, on average, people underestimate their retirement needs, then the problem becomes correspondingly worse.

The presence of other social support systems means that people who have suffered adverse health events, planned poorly for late life, or chosen to consume early in life will be cared for by the state. Within this system of social welfare, mandatory savings for a minimum retirement income are a prudent social policy. Rosen (1981) argues that "this is a case of true externality that is internalized by requiring individuals to provide for themselves, which improves individual incentives and promotes efficiency" (p. 4).

As mentioned above, social security is also viewed as a mechanism to redistribute income. There are two dimensions to redistribution within social security. First, because tax revenues are used to pay current benefits instead of being accumulated to fund accrued liabilities, the retired generation must rely on intergenerational income transfers (through taxes) from those currently working. Second, intragenerational redistribution within the benefit structure of OASI implies that low income workers will receive a higher return on their taxes than middle and upper income workers.

The economic rationale for redistribution is quite straightforward. Because the existence of a population of destitute older persons is disagreeable to a civilized population, most people would be willing to contribute a fraction of their income (especially if matched by contributions from others) to alleviate the conditions of the poverty-stricken elderly. The problem with a voluntary scheme is that any one individual could refuse to contribute and still derive the benefit (alleviation of poverty). The use of a compulsory retirement income program to accomplish some income redistribution allows persons who have worked throughout their lives to receive a more nearly adequate income in retirement without the stigma attached of going on the welfare rolls.

Given these considerations, it is unclear whether the government or the private sector is more efficient in providing individual insurance for retirement income, but no private (totally voluntary) sector plan can make individuals save for retirement and thus bear the costs of financing continued income in late life. Such a compulsory retirement income program seems desirable as long as the benefit structure is not set so high as to significantly limit life-cycle allocation of resources.

When viewed as a compulsory life-cycle savings mechanism, the economic rationale for the social security system is that it requires each person to contribute a minimum amount toward his or her retirement income and the purchase of health insurance in old age. This savings by the individual requires only a small administrative expense because it is uniform across the population and should provide a minimum level of retirement income. It is only one leg of the so-

called three-legged stool of retirement income that should also include, for those who choose to save for retirement, an employer pension benefit and private savings.

Welfare Programs

Society initiates poverty programs to prevent unfortunate individuals from falling below some predetermined standard of living. This standard is typically influenced by the national per capita income and varies over time and across countries. The willingness of workers to support transfers to the poor is determined by the effect of the existence of poverty on the welfare of workers (the externality argument described above relating to social security) and the possibility that they may experience some period of low income in the future. This latter reason suggests that poverty programs contain an element of insurance for the nonpoor.

These rationales for income maintenance programs for the poor also indicate why society may place restrictions on who is eligible for benefits. Poverty programs contain economic incentives that may result in workers with low earnings leaving the labor force to accept benefits. To limit this possibility, only persons from clearly "deserving" groups may be allowed to receive benefits. Designated groups have historically included the blind, disabled, mothers with dependent children, and the elderly. Welfare programs require that eligible individuals have income and assets below a specified level. These means tests are an important factor that differentiates these programs from social insurance.

For most of the numerous programs providing benefits to the elderly, the specified objective is to provide economic assistance to persons with relatively low income. Some programs such as supplemental security income (SSI) provide cash benefits, whereas others such as food stamps, housing subsidies, and medicaid provide in-kind assistance. These programs have low income as their eligibility criterion and also award benefits to nonaged persons. Elderly recipients are eligible for benefits because of their economic status and not their age. Although low income, nonaged persons may receive SSI payments, they must be either blind or disabled to do so.

The use of in-kind assistance to the poor is an interesting issue. Economists have long argued that cash income is the most effective method of raising the welfare of the poor. This is a clear, unmistakable implication of basic economic theory. Despite this finding, many poverty programs allocate specific commodities to low income persons. The general argument for such programs is that society has a better knowledge of the minimum consumption needs of families in the areas of food, housing, and health care than the family itself. The use of in-kind programs may also be an attempt to ensure minimum consumption levels for children when the parents control the family's resources. Of course, a problem arises when secondary markets exist for the benefits, as, for example, with the sale of food stamps.

In addition to these welfare programs, there are other public transfers designed to aid the elderly directly. For example, the aged receive several types of favorable tax treatment including double exemptions from federal income tax, exemptions from capital gains in certain housing sales, and tax breaks in state and local tax systems. The prices to the elderly of certain publicly provided goods and services are sometimes reduced through the use of "senior citizens" rates (e.g., lower fares for public transportation). Some government benefit programs use age as an eligibility criterion.

In general the social welfare implications of these very specific measures to provide benefits to all older persons are less favorable as a means of income redistribution than either cash or in-kind transfers to the poor, among whom are many of the elderly. There is no basis in welfare economics for contending that the elderly qua elderly are more deserving of income than any other group. Although the cash and in-kind transfers from social security and medicare can be fully justified on the basis of social insurance and ex-

ternality rationales presented earlier, these justifications do not depend on the fact that the beneficiaries are elderly. The welfare programs described above transfer resources to those in need and are justified by society's concern for the poor. Benefit programs solely for older persons may have been justified on the grounds that once a larger proportion of the elderly were poor. However, in recent years as the poverty rate of older persons has approached the incidence of poverty for all Americans, these programs have become an increasingly inefficient method of transferring resources to the poor. In addition, some of these programs are probably more valuable to the higher income elderly. The tax deductions provide a greater net benefit to wealthier persons in higher tax brackets. High income elderly are also more likely to use the reduced fares for such items as admittance to national parks.

Pension Regulation

The economic justifications for pension regulation originate from some of the same rationales described above. One aspect of pension regulation essentially amounts to governmental encouragement of pension plans. Through preferential tax treatment of retirement savings, pension plans are encouraged. The justification for these encouragements rests on the concept of externality already developed. In addition, widespread pension coverage relieves some of the reliance on social security as a source of income for the elderly.

The federal government does more than just encourage the use of pension plans. Pension plans must comply with a number of regulations in order to retain the favorable tax treatment. Among these regulations is a requirement that the pension fund be insured by the Pension Benefit Guarantee Corporation, a public corporation within the U.S. Department of Labor. Beneficiaries of pension plans are insured against such contingencies as bankruptcy of the employer. There are also regulations regarding the type of investments allowed with pension fund monies, and who is allowed on the boards that administer the funds and decide on investments. The Employee Retirement Income Security Act (ERISA) of 1974 attempts to prevent pension plans from discriminating in favor of high-wage executives. The coordination of pension and social security benefits is also regulated through integration requirements.

It may be asked why such regulation is desirable. Economic theory suggests if such protections were valued, workers would demand them and employers would supply them. Firms that did not provide adequate safeguards would have to pay compensating wage differentials (higher wages) to attract labor. Competition should force firms to offer a mix of wage and nonwage benefits, which is preferred by typical workers.

There is, however, ample precedent for government intervention in markets where access to information may be excessively costly to obtain. In other markets where individuals face large corporate entities, government regulation requires the corporate side to disclose certain information. For example, under the Truth-in-Lending law virtually all suppliers of consumer credit are required to disclose the annual percentage rate of the interest. In the sale of securities, the corporations issuing the stock, underwriters, brokers, and dealers are all highly regulated, and certain information must be made available to investors. In both of these examples the intent is to increase the information available to the individuals and to reduce fraud.

Some of these same considerations are present in pension regulation. The information costs of evaluating a pension plan are large enough that it may be efficient to shift the burden of reliability to the sellers (employers). Prior to ERISA some companies had complicated vesting requirements that sometimes would leave workers unqualified to receive a pension after a relatively long period of service. Under ERISA, companies must choose among three relatively simple vesting standards. Such regulations undoubtedly reduce information costs to em-

ployees. However, in contrast to Truth-in-Lending and the securities laws, pension regulation does more than just require disclosure. Through the establishment of minimum standards for vesting, outcomes are altered. In several other aspects of pension regulation there are standards affecting both the information available to the employees and the content of the plan itself.

Another aspect of federal regulation of private pensions is the requirement that the plan be moving toward full funding. This full-funding requirement does not apply to social security (which is not fully funded) or state and local plans, many of which are not fully funded. The full-funding requirement is intended as protection against the risk of bankruptcy of the company. The exemption of public entities from full-funding reflects a view that the risk of public bankruptcy (default by a governmental authority) is less probable than private default. In recent years the risk of default (or at least benefit reductions) by public authorities has increased, perhaps indicating that a reexamination of the dissimilar treatment of public and private pensions is appropriate.

DEVELOPMENT OF U.S. INCOME MAINTENANCE SYSTEM

Income transfers to older Americans are provided through social insurance, employer pensions, and welfare programs along with other programs in which age is the sole criterion. This section contains an overview of the growth of the old-age income maintenance system and a discussion of the current policies.

Old Age and Survivors Insurance

The social security system has been significantly expanded and liberalized in the past four decades. Initially, only retired workers age 65 and over were to be eligible for benefits. In 1939, benefits were extended to dependents with the initiation of a 50 percent spouse benefit and a benefit for widows. Subsequent amendments permitted workers to retire between the ages of 62 and 65 at reduced benefits. The 1935 legislation required all workers in commerce and industry (except railroads) to be covered by a payroll tax to finance the system, and these workers would be eligible for future benefits. Subsequent expansions in coverage have added farm and domestic workers, farmers, and other self-employed workers. These extensions have raised social security coverage from 58 percent of the paid labor force in 1940 to approximately 90 percent. The principal groups presently outside the system are federal civilian employees and some state and local workers (for reviews of the history of social security, see Munnell, 1977; Ball, 1978; Myers, 1975). The 1983 social security legislation requires that all new federal employees be covered by social security and ended the ability of state and local governments to choose to withdraw from coverage. Thus, coverage should move gradually toward 100 percent of the labor force.

OASI benefits are determined by applying a legislated formula to a person's earnings history in social-security-covered employment. Initially this formula was liberalized by periodic adjustments. The 1972 amendments indexed the formula to changes in the consumer price index (CPI). This framework was modified in 1977 to its current structure. For new retirees, the basic benefit for those who retire at age 65 is determined by a three-tier benefit formula that replaces a portion of the average indexed monthly earnings (AIME) of the recipient. The actual calculation includes the indexing of past earnings to the rate of growth of average earnings of all covered workers to determine the AIME. For persons who were 65 in 1982, this benefit was equal to 90 percent of the first $180 of AIME, 32 percent of the next $905 of AIME, and 15 percent of AIME in excess of $1085. Current legislation holds the percentages constant but raises the dollar break points automatically to reflect increases in earnings in covered employment.

The replacement ratio is a useful measure of the adequacy of retirement benefits. It indicates the percent of pre-retirement earnings being replaced by the pension benefits. The changes in the benefit formula noted above were sufficient to raise the initial replacement ratio for a hypothetical newly retired worker aged 65 with a lifetime of median earnings from 34.1 percent in 1968 to 48.6 percent by 1976. The median actual replacement rates for married men in the Retirement History Study retiring at age 65 rose from 27 percent in 1968–70 to 35 percent in 1973–74 (Fox, 1979; also see Munnell, 1977, and Rosen, 1981).

Benefits after retirement have also been regularly raised. Prior to 1972, the level of individual benefits was raised by specific legislation enacted every few years. An automatic adjustment equal to the change in the CPI was adopted in 1972. The earlier ad hoc adjustments and subsequent automatic increases have been sufficient to raise the real level of benefits since the early 1960s. The cumulative effect of statutory and automatic increases in benefits under OASI produced a minimum increase in benefits of 210 percent between January 1965 and June 1980, compared to a 160 percent change in the consumer price index. These increases in the benefit structure and in benefits after retirement, along with a growth in real earnings, have raised the average monthly benefit of retired workers from $22 in 1940 to $386 in December 1981. In that month, over 20 million retired workers were receiving monthly benefits (*Social Security Bulletin*, Apr. 1982, p. 2).

Much of the increase in the replacement ratio after 1972 was an unintended side effect of the automatic inflation adjustment mechanism instituted in 1972. The same method of adjustment of benefits with respect to inflation was used for current retirees and to index the future benefits of current workers. Current retirees received an increase in benefits equal to the increase in the CPI. The adjustment in future benefits for current workers exceeded the rate of change in prices. As a result of this overcompensation in future benefits, the replacement ratio for retirees rose with increases in inflation (Campbell, 1976; Kaplan, 1977). Legislation in 1977 removed this overcompensation effect by changing the indexing formula used to determine initial OASI benefits. The new indexing formula, described above, indexes past wages in a manner that provides for a constant replacement ratio in the future, but the replacement ratio was left at the higher level to which it had risen during the early 1970s. (For a detailed discussion of current social security provisions, see *Social Security Bulletin: Annual Statistical Supplement*.)

Total OASI expenditures have risen owing to the introduction of new programs, expansion of coverage, and increases in the level of benefits. Payments have also increased with the maturing of the system as more people have become eligible based on their work histories. These factors have generated an income security program that has required an increasing proportion of national income to finance its benefit payments. Total expenditures for OASI have risen from $62 million in 1940 to one billion dollars in 1950, $17.5 billion in 1965, and $122 billion in fiscal year 1981. As a result, this program, which required less than one-tenth of a percent of the gross national product (GNP) in the early 1940s and only 2.7 percent in 1960, now requires over 4 percent of GNP to meet current expenditures.

OASI retirement benefits in the United States are financed by a tax on covered payroll up to a maximum taxable earnings. Although the tax is paid directly and in equal proportion by the employee and the employer, economists generally believe that much of the employer's portion of the tax is paid indirectly by the worker in the form of lower wages (Brittain, 1972). Many other countries employ tripartite funding, with the national government joining the employer and employee as funding partners. Historically, current taxes have not been used to create a large fund in order to pay future benefits, but instead have been devoted to paying current benefits. This pay-as-you-go system employs a relatively small trust fund through which revenues and expenditures flow. The purpose of the trust fund is to maintain the payment of benefits during

short periods when revenues do not exceed disbursements.

In order to finance the escalation of expenditures, the payroll tax rate has been raised rapidly in conjunction with increases in the maximum taxable earnings. Table 1 shows that the OASI tax rate rose from 1 percent paid by both the employer and employee in 1937 to 5.2 percent in 1984. During the same period, the maximum earnings subject to the payroll tax increased from $3,000 to $37,800. In the past self-employed persons have paid less than the combine tax for both the employer and employee, however, 1983 legislation raises the self-employment tax rate to 100 percent of the combined tax rate paid by wage earners and their employers. The other components of the social insurance system, disability insurance and health insurance, have also required approximately fourfold increases since their inception. These programs, which are discussed in more detail in other sections of this chapter, each have designated payroll taxes and a separate trust fund.

Despite these tax increases, social security is currently facing short- and long-range financing problems. In the short run projected deficits occur because of continuing high rates of unemployment that reduce taxable payrolls and because of prices rising faster than wages. As a result of the automatic adjustment, benefits are rising faster than average earnings. Real average weekly earnings for production or nonsupervisory workers in private, nonagricultural industries declined in 1979, 1980, and 1981 so that real earnings in 1981 were 10 percent below their 1978 level. Furthermore, Mellor and Stamas (1982) report that real median weekly earnings of full-time wage and salary workers were approximately 10 percent lower in 1981 compared to 1973 for most demographic groups. The decline in real earnings of these workers can be contrasted to the constant real value of OASI benefits. Another indicator of benefit increases exceeding wage increases is the observation that in each year during 1979–81 average wages in covered employment rose by less than the automatic

TABLE 1. Annual Maximum Taxable Earnings and Actual Contribution Rate, Social Security.

| | | Contribution Rate (percent)[b] | | | |
| | | Total | Employer and Employee, Each | | |
Beginning	Annual Maximum Taxable Earnings[a]	Total	OASI	DI	HI
1937	$3,000	1	1	—	—
1950	3,000	1.5	1.5	—	—
1951	3,600	1.5	1.5	—	—
1954	3,600	2	2	—	—
1955	4,200	2	2	—	—
1957	4,200	2.25	2	0.25	—
1959	4,800	2.5	2.25	.25	—
1960	4,800	3	2.75	.25	—
1962	4,800	3.125	2.875	.25	—
1963	4,800	3.625	3.375	.25	—
1966	6,600	4.2	3.5	.35	0.35
1967	6,600	4.4	3.55	.35	.5
1968	7,800	4.4	3.325	.475	.6
1969	7,800	4.8	3.725	.475	.6
1970	7,800	4.8	3.65	.55	.6
1971	7,800	5.2	4.05	.55	.6
1972	9,000	5.2	4.05	.55	.6
1973	10,800	5.85	4.3	.55	1.0
1974	13,200	5.85	4.375	.575	.9
1975	14,100	5.85	4.375	.575	.9
1976	15,300	5.85	4.375	.575	.9
1977	16,500	5.85	4.375	.575	.9
1978	17,700	6.05	4.275	.775	1.0
1979	22,900	6.13	4.33	.75	1.05
1980	25,900	6.13	4.33	.75	1.05
1981	29,700	6.65	4.525	.825	1.30
1982	32,400	6.70	4.575	.825	1.30
1983	35,700	6.70	4.775	.625	1.30
1984	37,800	7.00	5.200	.500	1.30

[a] The maximum taxable earnings is indexed to the average earnings in the economy and will continue to rise as nominal earnings rise.
[b] Further tax increases through 1990 are called for under existing legislation.

SOURCE: *Social Security Bulletin: Annual Statistical Supplement, 1977–79*, p. 35.

increase in OASI benefits. This occurred despite legislation that raised the maximum taxable earnings at a rate that exceeded the increases in the CPI.

A series of proposals has been considered to moderate expected short falls in OASI revenues. First, Congress has permitted borrowing between the retirement, disability, and health trust funds. Second, certain benefits have been reduced (e.g., burial benefits

and student benefits for persons over 18). An attempt was made to eliminate the minimum benefit; however, this benefit has been reinstated for current but not future retirees. The minimum benefit is the lowest allowable monthly benefit. It is awarded to individuals whose benefit based on their own earnings history falls below this specified level. Third, the Reagan Administration supported increased penalities on early retirement starting in 1982, but in the face of adverse public reaction, this proposal was abandoned. Finally, several alternatives to alter the cost-of-living adjustment have received considerable attention. Current projections indicate that further policies limiting benefits must be enacted, or additional revenues must be found—from either general revenues or higher payroll taxes—in order to finance the system through the 1980s. The long-run financial problem is primarily a demographic one and is examined later. (For a detailed review of the 1981 legislation, see Svahn, 1981, 1982.)

Any changes in OASI are reviewed in a highly politicized environment. Public reaction to his 1981 proposals forced President Reagan to withdraw the principal changes he had advocated. Instead of pressing for their passage he established the 15-member National Commission on Social Security Reform to review the system and report recommendations for modifications. Despite the ongoing deliberations of this commission, social security issues have periodically emerged in the continuing congressional budget debates. Until fundamental changes are made in the system to establish its financial integrity, social security will remain the dominant political issue of the nation's income maintenance policy for older Americans.

Medicare

Medicare, or the health insurance (HI) program, was added to the social security system in 1965. HI is a compulsory hospital insurance program financed by a payroll tax (see Table 1). This legislation also created a supplementary medical insurance program (SMI) financed through direct payment and federal subsidies from general revenues. These programs provide prepaid or subsidized health insurance to older persons (A detailed examination of HI is found in other chapters of this *Handbook*.) The rationale for health insurance was examined earlier and shown to be consistent with the social insurance approach to income security. Justification for singling out the elderly as a de-

serving group arises from their greater use of health care and the finding that many workers receive health insurance protection through their employers. This employer-provided insurance typically is not continued after retirement.

The gain in family well-being from medicare depends on the value placed on the health care benefits. Several important conceptual issues arise in the evaluation of these benefits. First, should the value of medical services actually received be counted as additions to the cash income of families? If utilization of the program is the measure of benefits, then people who are in poorer health and, therefore, consume more health services will be viewed as having more resources and higher welfare than persons with better health. To avoid this problem, an insurance value of HI and SMI is derived below. The second issue pertains to an individual's personal assessment of the value of the health insurance. If a person would not purchase this quantity of insurance at the current market price if provided with an equal amount of cash, then the implied cash value of the health insurance overstates the actual value to the individual. To determine the insurance value, the sum of annual health care payments and administrative costs is divided by the number of enrollees. Individual contributions are subtracted from this term in the case of SMI.

The value of uniform health insurance will vary among individuals on the basis of their current health, the availability of medical facilities, and the actual access to health care. The following estimates are not based on these differential values. Tables 2 and 3 estimate the nominal and real insurance values of HI and SMI. Table 2 indicates that the nominal insurance value of health insurance rose from $259.37 in 1970 to $1,093.45 in 1981. The increase in insurance value rose more rapidly than the rise in the medical component of CPI, so that real per-person insurance benefits from HI increased by 72 percent over this period. The increase in real benefits from supplementary medical insurance was 170 percent from 1970 to 1981.

TABLE 2. Health Insurance.

Year	(thousands) No. of Enrollees[a]	Disbursements Benefits	Disbursements Ad. Exp.	Disbursements Total Dis.	Nominal Insurance Value[b]	Real Insurance Value[c]
		(millions)				
1966	19,082	$ 891	108	999	$ 52.35	$ 53.86
1967	19,494	3,353	77	3,430	175.95	175.95
1968	19,770	4,179	99	4,277	216.38	203.94
1969	20,014	4,739	118	4,857	242.68	214.00
1970	20,361	5,124	157	5,281	259.37	215.07
1971	20,742	5,741	150	5,900	284.45	221.53
1972	21,115	6,318	185	6,503	307.98	232.44
1973	23,301	7,057	232	7,289	312.82	227.18
1974	23,978	9,099	272	9,372	390.86	259.71
1975	24,646	11,315	266	11,581	469.89	278.70
1976	25,312	13,340	339	13,679	540.42	292.59
1977	26,094	15,737	283	16,619	636.89	314.67
1978	26,777	17,682	496	18,178	678.87	309.42
1979	27,459	20,623	450	21,073	767.44	319.63
1980	27,500	25,064	512	25,577	930.07	348.08
1981	28,100	30,342	384	30,726	1,093.45	370.54

[a] As of July 1 of the year. Totals in 1973 and after include pre-65 disability recipients.
[b] Total disbursements divided by number of enrollees.
[c] Nominal insurance deflated by the medical component of the consumer price index, 1967 = 100.

SOURCE: Board of Trustees, Federal Hospital Insurance Trust Fund, *1982 Annual Report*, Washington, D.C., U.S. Government Printing Office, 1982, Table 6, p. 29; *Social Security Bulletin: Annual Statistical Supplement, 1977–79*, pp. 202–203; and our calculations.

The increasing benefits per person have necessitated substantial increases in total expenditures. Expenditures for HI rose by almost 500 percent from 1970 to 1981. During this same period government contributions for SMI rose from $1.1 billion to $11.3 billion. To balance the increase in HI benefits, the payroll tax rate was raised from its initial rate of 0.35 percent paid by the employer and employee in 1966 to 1.3 percent in 1982.

Despite the increase in real medical benefits, the per capita expenditures on health expenditures by the elderly rose from $300 in fiscal year 1966, the year prior to the implementation of medicare, to $698 in calendar year 1977. This represents a 25 percent increase in out-of-pocket expenditures as measured in constant 1966 dollars. Because of the rise in per capita income of older persons, personal health care expenditures declined from 15 percent of average income in 1966 to 12 percent in 1977 (U.S. Congressional Research Service, 1981).

Government Pensions

Pension benefits for federal government employees began with the payment of benefits to Revolutionary War soldiers. The Federal Civil Service Retirement System was established in 1920 and was expanded by amendments in 1942 and 1946 to include employees in the executive, judicial, and legislative branches of the government. Separate retirement systems have been developed for employees of the Federal Reserve System, TVA, and the armed services. Over time these programs have been expanded and liberalized to provide increased benefits for retirees (Greenough and King, 1976). Increased funding has also been required due to the expansion of federal employment that will in time increase the number of beneficiaries. The cost of federal pensions has been driven up due to full (and at times over-) indexation of benefits for increases in consumer prices. Expenditures for the civil service retirement

TABLE 3. Supplementary Medical Insurance.

Year	(thousands) Enrollees[a]	Total Premiums	Per Person Monthly	Disbursement (millions)			Nominal Insurance Value[b]	Real Insurance Value[c]
				Benefits	Ad. Exp.	Tot. Dis.		
		(millions)						
1966	17,736	322	$3.00	128	75	203		
1967	17,893	640	3.00	1,197	110	1,307	$ 37.28	$ 37.28
1968	18,805	832	Ap. 3/4.00	1,518	183	1,702	46.26	43.60
1969	19,195	914	4.00	1,865	196	2,061	59.76	52.70
1970	19,584	1,096	Je. 4/5.30	1,975	238	2,212	56.99	47.26
1971	19,975	1,302	5.30	2,117	260	2,377	53.82	41.92
1972	20,351	1,382	5.60	2,325	290	2,614	50.54	38.14
1973	22,491	1,550	5.80	2,526	318	2,844	57.53	41.78
1974	21,422	1,804	6.30	3,318	410	3,728	89.81	59.67
1975	23,964	1,918	6.70	4,273	462	4,735	117.55	69.72
1976	24,614	2,060	6.70	5,080	542	5,622	144.71	78.35
1977	25,364	2,247	7.20	6,038	467	6,505	167.88	82.94
1978	26,074	2,470	7.70	7,252	503	7,755	202.69	92.38
1979	26,757	2,719	8.20	8,708	557	9,265	244.65	101.90
1980	27,100	3,011	8.70	10,635	610	11,245	303.84	113.71
1981	27,600	3,722	9.60	13,113	915	14,028	373.41	127.54

[a] As of July 1 of the year. Totals include eligible disabled persons in 1973 and thereafter.
[b] (Total disbursement − total premiums) ÷ number of enrollees.
[c] Nominal insurance value deflated by the consumer price index medical component, 1967 = 100.

SOURCE: Board of Trustees, Federal Supplementary Medical Insurance Trust Fund, *1980 Annual Report*, Washington, D.C.: U.S. Government Printing Office, 1980, Table 1, p. 3, and Table 6, p. 10; *Social Security Bulletin: Annual Statistical Supplement, 1977-79*, p. 202; and our calculations.

system in fiscal year 1981 were estimated to be $17.6 billion, up from $15 billion in fiscal year 1980.

All states and most local governments also provide pensions for their employees. Coverage of these plans has grown rapidly until the proportion of full-time employees covered by such plans is 90 percent (Munnell, 1979). Most of the state plans provide limited automatic inflation increases in benefits.

Supplemental Security Income

Supplemental security income (SSI), which replaced the old age assistance program in 1974, provides an income floor for all of the nation's low income elderly who choose to participate in this program. In December 1981, SSI benefits were paid to 2.1 million aged poor at an annual cost of over $2.4 billion. The total federal cost of SSI is only

slightly higher than that of the old age assistance program during the 1960s. In addition, some states supplement these federal payments (*Social Security Bulletin: Annual Statistical Supplement 1977-79*, pp. 218-243).

SSI is a welfare program, and is financed from general tax revenues. Unlike social security, a history of work in covered employment is irrelevant in the determination of eligibility and the level of benefits. Instead, eligibility is determined by certain income and asset tests. The SSI program reduces benefits dollar for dollar for unearned income above $20.00 a month and 50 cents for every $1.00 of earned income above $65.00 per month. Despite this well-defined target population, there is a relatively low participation rate in the program. Menefee et al. (1981) estimate that only 55 percent of the eligible low income elderly population are enrolled in SSI.

In-Kind Welfare Programs

The low income aged are eligible for a variety of in-kind benefit programs along with the cash transfer programs. These programs include medicaid, food stamps, housing assistance, and a number of other programs that provide a rather small level of total benefits to the elderly. Most of these programs were introduced during President Johnson's War on Poverty years of the 1960s and were expanded during the recession years of the early 1970s. Many of them are aimed at the poor in general and do not contain age-related eligibility conditions. The aged receive benefits because of their low income status. Medicaid is the most significant of these programs to the elderly. Low income elderly are eligible for medical assistance through medicaid, which was instituted in 1965. This program can pay for charges not covered by medicare for those eligible for low income assistance.

Employer Pensions and Government Regulations

Although pension benefits are a major source of retirement income for many older Americans, pension plans are a relatively recent form of employee compensation. The existence and growth of pension plans is closely tied to government policy. Federal regulations determine, in part, the cost and benefits of pension compensation. In addition, the demand for pension benefits is influenced by the level of social security benefits.

Private pension coverage grew rapidly in the post–World War II era until the mid-1960s. This growth is clearly shown in Tables 4 and 5. The proportion of private, non-agricultural workers participating in a pension plan rose from 25 percent in 1950 to 43 percent in 1965. The coverage rate continued to expand for the next decade and peaked in 1975 at 48.7 percent. Since that time, the estimated participation rate has fallen slightly. Table 5 shows that the net creation of new plans (new plans minus plans terminated) grew rapidly until 1973–74 and then dropped

sharply, before a recent upturn (Schieber, 1982). This is especially true of defined benefit plans, which cover 65 percent of total participants in private pensions (Munnell, 1982, p. 213).

What factors explain the growth of employer pensions, the sharp decline in the rate of growth in the mid-1970s, and the subsequent upturn in new plan formations? Several have been cited as the principal determinants of the trend toward increased utilization of pensions. Three events in the 1940s may have prompted greater use of pensions. First, 1942 amendments to the Internal Revenue Code clarified and expanded tax treatment of pensions and precluded the establishment of pension funds for corporate officers only (Greenough and King, 1976). Second, wartime stabilization policy made it easier to increase less observable fringe benefits rather than cash wages. Third, in 1949 the National Labor Relations Board ruled in the Inland Steel decision that pensions were a proper subject for collective bargaining. This action may have altered union attitudes toward seeking pension benefits (Melone and Allen, 1972).

The preferential tax treatment of pensions implies that workers covered by these plans can receive greater total compensation for the same cost to the firm if they are covered by pensions and other fringes, than if they receive all compensation as wages. In addition, the tax benefits are greater for those in higher tax brackets. This lower cost for pension benefits in comparison with cash wages is probably the most important reason for the growth in pensions and also helps to explain the pattern of coverage in the private sector. Table 6 briefly describes the major legislation concerning the tax treatment of pension plans (See Munnell, 1982, Ch. 3).

The sharp decline in new plan formation is partly attributable to the passage of the Employee Retirement Income Security Act (ERISA) in 1974 (Comptroller General, 1978; Paul, 1976; Meier, 1977). This legislation sets guidelines for the funding and insuring of pension plans that firms must follow if their pension is to qualify for pref-

TABLE 4. Wage and Salary Workers in Private Sector, Nonagricultural Establishments and Pension Participation, 1950-79.

Year	Private Sector Wage and Salary Workers (000's)	Workers Participating in Private Pensions (000's)	Participation Rate
1950	39,171	9,800	25.0%
1951	41,430	10,800	26.1
1952	42,185	11,300	26.8
1953	43,557	12,600	28.9
1954	42,239	13,400	31.7
1955	43,727	14,200	32.5
1956	45,091	15,500	34.4
1957	45,237	16,700	36.9
1958	43,485	17,200	39.6
1959	45,185	18,200	40.3
1960	45,836	18,700	40.8
1961	45,405	19,200	42.3
1962	46,659	19,700	42.2
1963	47,427	20,300	42.8
1964	48,687	20,900	42.9
1965	50,691	21,800	43.0
1966	53,117	22,700	42.7
1967	54,412	24,300	44.7
1968	56,058	24,800	44.2
1969	58,189	26,000	44.7
1970	58,326	26,100	44.7
1971	58,333	26,400	45.3
1972	60,342	27,500	45.6
1973	63,059	29,200	46.3
1974	64,095	29,800	46.5
1975	62,260	30,300	48.7
1976	64,511	30,700	47.6
1977	67,345	32,000	47.5
1978	71,025	33,700	47.5
1979	73,966	35,200	47.6

SOURCE: Sylvester Schieber, Trends in pension coverage benefit receipt, *The Gerontologist, 22*:6, Dec. 1982. p. 475

erential tax treatment (Greenough and King, 1976). In addition, mandatory acceptable vesting requirements were established. ERISA provides three acceptable standards for vesting. They are: (1) full vesting after ten years of service; (2) 25 percent of accrued benefits after five years of service, 5 percent additional vesting over each of the next five years, and 10 percent per year for the following five years, thereby achieving 100 percent vesting after fifteen years; (3) vesting of 50 percent of accrued benefits when age and years of service add to 45 years, with 10 per-

cent of vesting being added in each of the next five years subject to a five-year minimum service requirement. Most companies have adopted the ten-year–100 percent option (Schulz, 1980, p. 134). The ERISA regulations raised the cost to firms of providing pension plans and increased the federal reporting requirements. These cost factors and the uncertainty surrounding a change in regulatory environment probably caused the sharp decline in new plans and the increase in plan terminations between 1975 and 1978.

The decline in net new plan formations

TABLE 5. Corporate and Self-Employed Pension Plan Creations, Terminations and Net Plan Increases.

	Defined Benefit Plans			Defined Contribution Plans			
Year	Plans Qualified	Plans Terminated	Net Plans Created	Plans Qualified	Plans Terminated	Net Plans Created	Net Total Plans Created
1956	3,175	192	2,983	2,072	111	1,961	4,944
1957	3,527	180	3,347	2,898	171	2,727	6,074
1958	3,883	224	3,659	3,071	179	2,892	6,551
1959	3,824	270	3,554	3,442	204	3,238	6,792
1960	5,011	300	4,711	4,946	258	4,688	9,399
1961	4,919	374	4,545	4,468	361	4,107	8,652
1962	5,188	476	4,712	5,030	383	4,647	9,359
1963	5,840	441	5,399	5,304	453	4,851	10,250
1964	6,581	509	6,072	5,127	532	4,595	10,667
1965	7,495	512	6,983	6,037	524	5,513	12,496
1966	10,124	603	9,521	8,059	607	7,452	16,973
1967	11,292	602	10,690	9,229	705	8,524	19,214
1968	12,896	672	12,224	10,886	771	10,115	22,339
1969	14,692	868	13,824	13,383	861	12,522	25,905
1970	16,512	1,142	15,370	16,062	1,164	14,898	30,268
1971	22,493	1,605	20,888	18,171	1,730	16,441	37,329
1972	28,265	1,745	26,520	21,070	1,775	19,295	45,815
1973	33,830	2,222	31,608	25,775	1,908	23,867	55,475
1974	32,579	2,577	30,002	26,806	2,207	24,599	54,601
1975	15,319	4,550	10,769	14,720	3,558	11,162	21,931
1976	4,790	8,970	−4,180	23,334	15,660	7,674	3,494
1977	6,953	5,337	1,616	28,463	10,478	17,985	19,601
1978	9,728	4,625	5,103	55,956	10,661	45,295	50,398
1979	15,755	3,267	12,488	41,122	7,574	33,548	46,036
1980	18,849	4,297	14,552	50,493	8,982	41,511	56,063

SOURCE: Sylvester Schieber, Trends in pension coverage and benefit receipt, *The Gerontologist, 22:*6 Dec. 1982. p. 476.

may prove to be a one-time reduction in the growth trend as employers learn to adapt to the ERISA constraints. Recent increases in new plans provide some support for this view; however, the future growth of pension coverage is likely to be slow. This pessimism stems from the fact that most high-wage workers in large firms are already participating in pension plans. Uncovered workers are mainly in small, nonunion plants. They are also more likely to be part-time or low-wage workers. These workers and firms have less incentive to institute a pension plan. The benefits of increased government incentives would probably go to existing pension plans. For this reason, the President's Commission on Pension Policy (1981) advocated man-datory universal pensions. This recommendation from a commission appointed by President Carter is unlikely to receive much support in the 1980s.

In the 1978 Amendments to the Age Discrimination in Employment Act, the federal government outlawed the use of mandatory retirement prior to the age of 70 in most private employment and abolished its use in federal employment. While this action is unlikely to result in large numbers of older persons remaining in the labor force (Barker and Clark, 1980), some firms may find a high percentage of their workers wishing to remain on the job. This legislation will also force firms to reconsider employment and pension contracts (Lazear, 1979). Pensions

TABLE 6. History of Major Legislation Regarding the Tax Treatment of Pension Plans.

Act	Provisions
Revenue Act of 1921	Employer contributions to a trust created as part of a stock-bonus or profit-sharing plan were tax-deductible for the employer and were not taxable to the employee until benefits were received. Taxes on the earnings of the trust were also deferred.
Revenue Act of 1926	The provisions of the Revenue Act of 1921 were extended to pension trusts.
Revenue Act of 1928	The provisions of the Revenue Act of 1921 were extended to employer contributions to trusts made on behalf of an employee's past service.
Social Security Act of 1935	The Social Security System was established.
Railroad Retirement Act of 1935	The Railroad Retirement System was established.
Revenue Act of 1938	A "no diversion" rule was enacted. This provided that the income of a pension trust could not be used for, or diverted to, purposes other than the exclusive benefit of employees or their beneficiaries.
Revenue Act of 1942	Limited the deductibility of employer contributions to a pension plan or plans that were irrevocable and did not discriminate in favor of selected personnel. A limitation was placed on the amount of allowable deduction. Integration of private plans with social security was allowed.
Self-Employed Individual's Retirement Act of 1962	Allowed self-employed individuals to make tax-deferred contributions to a Keogh Plan.
Employee Retirement Income Security Act of 1974 (ERISA)	Increased the maximum deductible contribution to a Keogh Plan and established Individual Retirement Accounts (IRAs). Expanded regulation of pension plans in areas of function, vesting, and insurance.

SOURCE: President's Commission on Pension Policy, Taxation of retirement savings, unpublished staff paper, 1981, p. 7.

that were developed around the concept of compulsory retirement at age 65 must now be adjusted. Firms may now attempt to entice workers to retire by altering the gain in pension benefits from continued work (Clark and McDermed, 1982).

INCOME OF OLDER PERSONS AND THE ROLE OF GOVERNMENT TRANSFERS

The economic well-being of the elderly is determined by their ability to purchase and consume goods and services. The purchasing power of older persons is influenced by their personal wealth, continued earnings, government cash and in-kind transfers, and family assistance. This section examines the income of the elderly and indicates significant improvements in the economic status of older persons during the past two decades. In addition, the responsiveness of the income of the elderly to increases in the price level is assessed.

Rising Real Cash Incomes

During the past two decades, the standard of living of the nation's elderly as measured by their cash income has substantially improved. Several comparisons serve to illustrate this trend toward improving economic well-being. For example, the number of individuals 65 and over with incomes below the Social Security Administration's poverty level declined from 5.5 million in 1959 to 3.9 million in 1980, a reduction in the proportion of the nation's elderly below this poverty index from 35.2 percent to 15.7 percent. The rate of decline in the poverty rate of older persons has exceeded by far the reduction in the poverty rate of younger persons (U.S. Bureau of the Census, 1981). For example, the poverty rate for persons 65 and older declined from 24.5 percent in 1970 to 15.7 percent in 1980. By contrast, the poverty for all persons remained fairly stable, with its 1980 rate of 13 percent slightly higher than the 1970 poverty rate. Rising real earnings have increased savings, both personal and through pension plans, so that the private resources available during retirement have risen. The long-term decline in the incidence of poverty among the aged is also due to the expansion in coverage and liberalization of benefits in both public and private pension systems, as well as the initiation of additional income transfer programs described earlier in this chapter.

The median income of families in which the head of the household is 65 years old or older has more than tripled since 1965, increasing from $3,514 to $12,881 in 1980. This rise represents an increase in real income (income adjusted for increases in the consumer price index) of approximately 40 percent. The relative income position of the aged also has shown gradual improvement over the last decade as the ratio of median income of elderly families to the median income of all families has risen from 49.3 percent in 1965 to 61.3 percent in 1980. (U.S. Bureau of the Census, 1981; see also Torda, 1972, and Bridges and Packard, 1981). During this period, elderly families along with unrelated older individuals, both male and female, enjoyed growth rates in real income above the national average.

In-Kind Transfers

The significant reduction in the incidence of poverty among older persons reported above underestimates the improvement in the purchasing power of the elderly because there has been a simultaneous expansion of in-kind benefit programs over the last two decades. Moon (1977) estimates that in-kind transfers to the aged average more than 10 percent of the mean current money income for aged families. Borzilleri (1980) attributes even greater importance to in-kind transfers. He concludes that the value of medicare, medicaid, housing, and food stamp benefits increases the mean income of families whose head is aged 65 or older by 14.4 percent and the mean income of single older persons by 32.2 percent. In assessing the contribution of in-kind benefits to family welfare, one must

be careful not to overestimate these payments. This problem arises because individuals may not value in-kind payments at the market price for these goods (Moon, 1979). The problem of evaluation of in-kind benefits is especially important in attempts to determine their effect on the number of people below the poverty level (Moon, 1979).

The inclusion of in-kind transfers in measures of the total resources of older persons significantly reduces the degree of inequality among the elderly (Moon, 1977). Since the in-kind transfers are primarily poverty programs, they are targeted toward the low income population. Borzilleri (1980) finds that accounting for in-kind benefits raises the mean total income of older families with less than $7,000 of cash income by 68 percent.

Adequacy of Income of the Elderly

Several standards are available by which to judge the adequacy of the income of older persons. The most widely recognized measure is the official poverty index developed by the Social Security Administration in 1963 and adjusted every year to reflect increases in the consumer price index. Other indicators are three budgets derived by the Bureau of Labor Statistics (BLS) each year for retired couples. These budgets—low, intermediate, and high—show progressively increasing living standards for older couples (U.S. Bureau of Labor Statistics, 1970; see also Ch. 22 of this *Handbook*).

Using only cash income, 8 percent of older families are below the poverty level, while 17 percent are below the lower BLS budget (see Table 7). The rates are much higher for unrelated individuals. Including the value of in-kind benefits decreases the proportion of families below each of these indicators of low income. Borzilleri (1980) adjusts the BLS budgets to include the value of medicare and concludes that "virtually the entire aged family population had sufficient income to purchase the lower living standard."

Government transfer programs play a major role in insuring the income of older persons. The effect of these programs on

TABLE 7. Proportion of Older Persons with Cash Income Below Various Indices, 1978.

Index	Families, Head 65 or Older		Single Individuals	
	Cash Value of Index	Proportion with Income below Index	Cash Value of Index[a]	Proportion with Income below Index
Poverty Level	$ 3,944	8	$ 3,127	24
Lower Budget	4,514	17	3,673	35
Intermediate Budget	7,846	36	5,244	60
High Budget	11,596	55	7,868	81

[a] The BLS calculates budgets only for couples. These values are Borzilleri's estimates.

SOURCE: Thomas Borzilleri, In-kind benefit programs and retirement, paper prepared for the President's Commission on Pension Policy, 1980.

consumable income of the elderly is shown in Table 8, with public tax and transfer programs lowering the observed poverty rate from 59.9 percent to 6.1 percent in 1976. Of course, in the absence of these programs we would expect that people would adjust life-cycle income and increase work effort. In addition, older persons would probably receive increased transfers from family and charitable organizations. Thus, it is unlikely that the poverty rate of older persons would in fact be almost 60 percent without these programs.

Another measure of income adequacy is comparison of an individual's disposable income in the immediate pre-retirement years with earnings prior to retirement. As noted earlier, this concept of retirement income compared to earnings is called a replacement ratio. For any individual, the decline in income at retirement may represent a form of relative impoverishment. The replacement ratio measures the extent of the decline in income with retirement. Adjusting gross pre-retirement income for federal and state income tax, OASDHI tax, and any decline in work-related expenditures provides a measure of the tax-free income that enables retirees to continue receiving the same level of disposable income. These replacement rates range from 80 percent for low-wage workers to 65 percent for those with higher incomes (Schulz et al., 1974).

On the basis of hypothetical earnings records, some people contend that social security provides sufficient benefits to enable low and middle income couples to maintain their pre-retirement living standards (Munnell, 1977). The validity of this conclusion has been questioned because few if any workers follow the lifetime earnings pattern implied by the hypothetical earnings profile, and

TABLE 8. Families Aged 65 and Over Below the Poverty Level Under Alternative Definitions, Fiscal Year 1976.

	Families below Poverty Level	
	Number (000)	Percentage
Pretax/Pretransfer income	9,647	59.9
Pretax/Post–social insurance income	3,459	21.5
Pretax/Post–money transfer income	2,686	16.7
Pretax/Post–money and in-kind transfer income	977	6.1
Post tax/Post–money and in-kind transfer income	982	6.1

SOURCE: U.S. Congressional Budget Office, *Poverty Status of Families Under Alternative Definitions,* background paper No. 17 (revised), Washington, D.C.: U.S. Government Printing Office, 1977, p. 12.

earnings of the spouse are frequently ignored in these calculations (Schulz, 1978; Fox, 1979). Thus, many workers with relatively low earnings will suffer declines in disposable income if only social security benefits are available. This finding, along with the probability that these persons are not covered by employer pensions, led the President's Commission on Pension Policy (1981) to advocate a system of mandatory employer pensions.

Inflation and the Real Income of the Elderly

An old myth concerning the income of the elderly is that older persons are one of the most vulnerable demographic groups to losses in real income due to inflation. An example of this belief is a statement by Arthur Okun (1970, p. 14), in which he concluded that the "retired aged are the only major specific demographic group of Americans that I can confidently identify as income losers," in response to inflation. The 1981 White House Conference on Aging helped to perpetuate this belief when it concluded that "the elderly are particularly vulnerable to loss from inflation" (White House Conference, Vol. 1, p. 27). If this vulnerability did exist, the growth of income maintenance programs described in this chapter has created a new reality concerning the real income of older persons.

The principal sources of income for the elderly are OASI benefits, other government transfers, employer pensions, income from personal wealth, and earnings. A review of these sources of income indicates considerable responsiveness to price changes. OASI benefits are fully indexed so that annual adjustments equal the change in the CPI. The value of government in-kind transfers is generally fixed in terms of a flow of goods and services. Periodic legislative adjustments have been more than sufficient to offset price increases. Employer pensions are far from being fixed in nominal terms. Public pensions are typically indexed, although most state and local pensions provide less than full adjustment (Tilove, 1976). Also many private employers provide ad hoc adjustments to the benefits of their retirees (King, 1982).

Income from personal wealth depends on the composition of one's investment portfolio. Many older persons hold a substantial portion of their wealth in their home. During the 1970s, the average value of homes rose at a more rapid rate than prices. Counteracting this favorable effect, many older people have savings accounts and life insurance policies that are declining in real terms. The real return of various assets is determined by changes in their relative prices as influenced by the demand for and supply of the asset. One should not expect any asset to continuously rise or fall in real value. Real earnings depend on the growth rate of productivity. Without a detailed model of labor markets, there is no reason to expect the earnings of the older worker to be adversely affected relative to other workers in the presence of inflation. Positive real productivity growth is necessary for real earnings increases.

This brief review indicates that most of the sources of income of the elderly are insulated from losses in real income due to inflation. This is especially true for the poorest of the elderly who receive most of their income from social security and other public transfer programs that are indexed with inflation. The greatest potential for real income loss is through employer pension benefits. In contrast to Okun's statement, the evidence of the 1970s suggests that older persons fared better than other groups during this inflationary decade (see Clark et al., 1982).

CURRENT ISSUES AND POLICY OPTIONS

The development of income maintenance programs in the United States has been a major force in the improvement of the economic status of older persons. Although the various programs previously examined have different objectives, these programs transfer substantial resources to the elderly and have been one of the principal reasons for the sharp decline in the incidence of poverty among the aged. This section reviews the increasing cost of these programs and projections of their future financial requirements. Policy options for the social security programs are examined for their ability to reduce cost and their effect on the welfare of older persons.

Growth in Federal Expenditures: 1960–81

Federal expenditures on behalf of persons age 65 and over have risen dramatically since the early 1960s in response to legislative initiatives and growth in the older population. Benefit payments to the elderly are estimated to have totaled $12.8 billion dollars in 1960, whereas expenditures in 1982 reached $196.2 billion, a 15-fold increase. By contrast, the number of people 65 and over increased by only 57.5 percent, from 16.7 million in 1960 to 26.3 million in July 1981. These expenditures included federal retirement programs (civil service, railroad, military, and veteran's benefits), OASDI, HI, SMI, federal medicaid, and SSI. Also included in the totals are benefits to the elderly from housing subsidies, food stamps, and social and employment services (Califano, 1978; Torrey, 1982; U.S. Congressional Budget Office, 1982).

Because the consumer price index more than tripled between 1960 and 1982, real expenditures measured in 1967 dollars were $14.4 billion in 1960, and real spending on these programs in 1982 was five times the 1960 level. Thus, two-thirds of the growth rate in annual spending on the elderly is due to increases in nominal spending to maintain the real value of benefits. After accounting for the inflation effect, there has been a significant increase in the real resources allocated to these programs. Reflecting this increase is the growth in the proportion of the federal budget necessary to finance these programs, from 13 percent in 1960 to 26.6 percent in 1982. A similar increase is noted in the proportion of the gross national product allocated to these benefit programs, from 2.5 to 5.9 percent (see Califano, 1978; Torrey, 1982).

The average benefit per person 65 and over increased from $768 in 1960 to $7,948 in

1982. If benefits had been increased only to reflect price increases, the average benefit would have been $2,516, whereas if benefits had risen in accordance with the growth in per capita disposable income, the transfer per elderly person would have been $3,663 in 1982. Therefore, the expansion in federal spending per older American since 1960 has significantly exceeded the growth of per capita income. This increase is the result of the introduction of new programs, higher benefits under existing programs, and less restrictive eligibility conditions.

An examination of the relevant data reveals that increases in the aged population have been a significant factor in the rise in aggregate spending on the nation's elderly. However, expenditures have not been driven up uncontrollably by a graying of the population. Instead, most of the increase is due to the government's responding to the perceived needs and/or the growing political power of the elderly with improvements in these transfer programs. As a result, many new programs have been introduced during the past two decades. Benefits under existing programs have been liberalized and coverage expanded. Thus, much of the past graying of the federal budget has occurred due to explicit policy changes by the federal government (Clark and Menefee, 1981).

Federal Expenditures for Older Persons: Projections to 2035

The growth and development of income maintenance programs for the elderly has become one of the most important issues in public policy. The preceding section noted the growth in total expenditures on these programs over the last two decades and attributed much of the growth in benefits to new legislation liberalizing benefits and instituting new programs. As public scrutiny of these developments has become more prevalent, considerable attention has focused on future cost of income transfers as the population continues to age. (For a more detailed discussion of the economic effects of population aging, see Clark and Spengler, 1980b.)

In a widely publicized speech before the American Academy of Political and Social Science, then Secretary of Health, Education and Welfare, Joseph Califano (1978) estimated that real spending (1978 dollars) on the major aged-related program described earlier would total $350 billion in 2010 and $635 billion in 2025. The figures for 2025 represent more than 10 percent of projected GNP. This increase occurs due to higher prices, real economic growth, and continued population aging. These projections also assume that public policy relating to expenditures for the elderly is unchanged. The maintenance of current rules coupled with expected high rates of price increases for medical services results in the health insurance and supplemental health insurance programs accounting for 42 percent of the expected total real cost increase of these programs between 1980 and 2025. These estimates are quite sensitive to the assumptions concerning the rate of growth of medicare (O'Neill, 1978; Torrey, 1982). A reduction in the rate of increase in health care costs would lower these cost estimates.

Torrey (1982) compares these projections to those by O'Neill (1978) and more recent projections of her own that also assume that the conditions for benefits in the transfer programs are unchanged. Table 9 shows these projections and contrasts them with projections by Clark and Menefee (1981) that

TABLE 9. Outlays for Persons 65 and Older as a Percent of Total Federal Outlays.

Year	Clark Menefee	O'Neill	Califano	Torrey
1982				26.6
1990		29.8		32.4
2000	29.5	31.6	33.9	34.1
2010	30.5	33.2	36.4	36.2
2025	41.5	46.3	50.8	49.6
2035				49.3

SOURCE: Barbara Torrey, Guns vs. canes: The fiscal implications of aging population, *American Economic Review*, May 1982, p. 310.

assume that average benefits to the elderly from all programs remain a constant percent of per capita income. In order to compare these studies, Torrey assumes that the federal budget will remain 20 percent of GNP throughout the period. The rise in expenditures for the elderly from 26.6 percent of the budget in 1982 to almost half of federal expenditures by 2025 is primarily a function of expected increases in OASDI and medicare spending. A comparison of the projections by O'Neill, Califano, and Torrey to those of Clark and Menefee indicates that current legislation will likely produce benefits that rise more rapidly than per capita income. Much of this difference is due to the assumption that health care prices will continue to rise more rapidly than all consumer prices and average wages. Each of these studies also indicates significant increases in the proportion of GNP required to finance transfers to older persons. For example, Torrey estimates that the percent of GNP allocated to income transfers to the elderly rises from 5.6 percent in 1980 to 9.9 percent in 2030.

OASDI Financing

Most projections of required spending for the old age survivors and disability insurance program indicate that the cost as a percent of payroll will rise substantially in the coming years. The Social Security Administration is required by law to make 75-year cost projections for OASDI. These projections indicate the expected cost of the program under current law using alternative demographic and economic assumptions. Table 10 shows the four projections made in 1982. In general, the projections become increasingly pessimistic moving from I to III. The fertility assumptions, which play a major role in determination of future cost, are overly optimistic in I and would require a 30 percent increase in fertility rates. By contrast, alternative III has fertility rates falling only slightly relative to 1980 levels. The intermediate projections assume that the fertility rate rises by 14 percent from 1.84 births per

TABLE 10. Tax Rates[a] and Estimated Cost Rates[b] of the OASDI System Under Alternatives I, II-A, II-B, and III, Calendar Years 1982–2060.

Calendar Year	Tax Rate	Cost Rate by Alternative			
		I	II-A	II-B	III
1982	10.80	11.55	11.51	11.78	11.83
1983	10.80	11.29	11.46	11.65	12.02
1984	10.80	11.00	11.41	11.63	12.32
1985	11.40	10.74	11.20	11.70	12.40
1986	11.40	10.51	11.00	11.71	12.51
1987	11.40	10.30	10.81	11.71	12.62
1988	11.40	10.12	10.66	11.68	12.71
1989	11.40	9.82	10.55	11.66	12.77
1990	12.40	9.79	10.47	11.64	12.85
1991	12.40	9.61	10.39	11.59	12.86
1992	12.40	9.57	10.37	11.54	12.86
1993	12.40	9.62	10.37	11.51	12.90
1994	12.40	9.58	10.35	11.46	12.91
1995	12.40	9.52	10.32	11.42	12.97
1996	12.40	9.44	10.25	11.35	12.98
1997	12.40	9.38	10.20	11.27	12.93
1998	12.40	9.32	10.15	11.19	12.88
1999	12.40	9.25	10.10	11.10	12.82
2000	12.40	9.16	10.03	11.03	12.82
2001	12.40	9.06	9.96	10.96	12.81
2002	12.40	9.01	9.93	10.90	12.78
2003	12.40	8.99	9.94	10.87	12.80
2004	12.40	9.00	9.97	10.87	12.84
2005	12.40	9.06	10.06	10.95	12.97
2006	12.40	9.08	10.11	10.99	13.09
2010	12.40	9.49	10.69	11.53	13.92
2015	12.40	10.49	11.96	12.82	15.76
2020	12.40	11.67	13.53	14.44	18.17
2025	12.40	12.64	14.96	15.97	20.70
2030	12.40	12.96	15.75	16.83	22.63
2035	12.40	12.69	15.89	17.02	23.94
2040	12.40	12.10	15.64	16.80	24.80
2045	12.40	11.61	15.48	16.66	25.80
2050	12.40	11.39	15.53	16.72	26.93
2055	12.40	11.28	15.63	16.81	27.87
2060	12.40	11.18	15.63	16.81	28.49
25-year averages:					
1982–2006	12.01	9.75	10.46	11.37	12.73
2007–2031	12.40	11.30	13.15	14.08	17.84
2032–2058	12.40	11.88	15.85	16.81	25.66
75-year average:					
1982–2056	12.27	10.98	13.09	14.09	18.74

[a] Tax rates as fixed by existing legislation are the sum of the employer and employee taxes; i.e., the tax paid by each party after 1990 is 6.2 percent.

[b] The costs are represented by a percent of covered payroll required to fund projected benefits. The implied tax rate the employer and the employee each pay is one-half the percent of payroll.

SOURCE: *1982 Annual Report,* Board of Trustees, Federal Old Age and Survivors Insurance and Disability Insurance Trust Funds, Apr. 1982, pp. 67–68.

woman in 1980 to 2.1 births per woman starting in 2005.

The intermediate or the "best guess" projections (II–A and II–B) indicate that the proportion of payroll required to finance OASDI rises by 36 to 43 percent between 1982 and 2030. The implied payroll tax rate to support the system is approximately 8 percent paid by the employee and an additional 8 percent paid by the employer. This compares to current tax rates for OASDI of 5.4 percent that are scheduled to rise to 6.2 percent in 1990. If fertility remains low and the III case emerges, tax rates would have to rise to 14 percent each paid by the employer and the employee. By contrast, the optimistic alternative has projected costs rising by less than the currently legislated tax increases.

The principal force behind these projections is the changing age structure of the population. Declining fertility rates produce an older population that requires a higher tax rate on current workers to sustain any given level of benefits. In this framework, the options facing society are limited. Either taxes are raised, or benefits are lowered.

All projections of future events, including these, require that specific assumptions be made concerning important determinants of the projected values. Thus a brief review of the assumptions and the sensitivity of the results is useful. Because some people believe that the intermediate assumptions imply a continuation of today's poor economic conditions, these assumptions are reviewed and changes in individual assumptions are made while maintaining the other requirements of alternative II–B.

In the II–B alternative, real wage growth is assumed to rise during the 1980s and eventually stabilize at 1.5 percent increase per year. This is an improvement relative to the 1970s but is below the 2.0 percent growth rate of the 1960s. Sensitivity analysis in the *1982 Annual Report* of the Board of Trustees indicates that an increase in the real wage growth rate to 2.5 percent within the framework of other II–B assumptions would lower the average OASDI cost rate for 2032–2056 from 16.81 shown in Table 10 to 14.72. Thus,

an increase of 67 percent in the rate of growth of productivity would mean that the OASDI payroll tax would only rise to 7.36 percent paid by the employer and by the employee. This decrease in future required taxes is due to the lag between the time workers pay taxes on the higher projected earnings and the time when they receive benefits based on these earnings. In addition, positive real wage growth requires that wages rise faster than prices. This reduces the cost of OASDI because payments to current retires are adjusted with price increases, not wage gains.

Alternative II–B has the rate of growth of consumer prices falling over the next two decades before stabilizing at a 4 percent rate of inflation. Holding real wage growth constant, slowing inflation actually slightly increases the required tax rate. This seemingly perverse effect occurs because taxable income is assumed to rise in conjunction with price increases, while benefits are raised with a lag of approximately a half year.

As noted earlier, the fertility assumption requires fertility to rise to 2.1 births per woman. Retaining other II–B assumptions but increasing the fertility rate to 2.4 lowers the proportion of payroll necessary for OASDI from 16.81 to 15.04 percent during the period 2032–2056.

Increases in the rate of improvement in mortality raise the cost of this program. The II–B assumptions allow for 37 percent improvement in mortality during the 75-year projection period. If mortality gains were 59 percent (as specified in alternative III) the proportion of payroll needed during 2032–2056 would rise to 19.53 percent. Thus, greater improvements in the life expectancy of older persons substantially increase the projected cost of OASDI.

All of these assumptions are subject to debate and criticism (Morrison, 1982). In general, the II–B assumptions have fertility rising, inflation moderating, real growth increasing, and mortality improving relative to current conditions. Whether these forecasted conditions actually occur can only be determined after the fact. These assumptions seem reasonable given today's information and should be used along with the other projections to form the basis of prudent planning for future income maintenance policy. Changes in economic and demographic conditions should be carefully monitored to provide evidence for updating projections and planning modifications in the governmental transfer programs.

Medicare Financing

The hospital insurance program was instituted at a cost of less than 1 percent of taxable payroll. Expenditures as a percent of payroll more than doubled by 1982 to 2.39 percent. Table 11 shows that expenditures under this program are expected to grow more rapidly than earnings. As a result, the intermediate assumptions indicate almost a threefold rise in the cost of the program to between 6 and 7 percent of payroll. This compares to a currently legislated total tax (employer plus employee tax) of 2.90 percent in 2005.

The rising cost of medicare is due to medical prices rising faster than all other prices and wages and the continued aging of the population. Without reductions in benefits or a slowing of health price increases, substantial new tax increases will have to be enacted. These figures do not include general fund expenditures for supplementary medical insurance, which totaled $7.5 billion in 1980. A reduction in the rate of growth in

TABLE 11. Cost and Tax Rates of Hospital Insurance Program as a Percent of Taxable Payroll.

Year	Cost of Program[a]	Legislated Tax Rate[b]	Difference
1967	0.95		
1970	1.21		
1975	1.69		
1980	2.21		
1981	2.39		
Alternative II-A			
1982	2.69	2.60	−0.09
1985	3.03	2.70	−0.33
1990	3.77	2.90	−0.87
1995	4.68	2.90	−1.78
2000	5.49	2.90	−2.59
2005	6.27	2.90	−3.37
Alternative II-B			
1982	3.08	2.60	−0.48
1985	3.16	2.70	−0.46
1990	4.03	2.90	−1.13
1995	5.10	2.90	−2.20
2000	6.11	2.90	−3.21
2005	7.13	2.90	−4.23

[a] The costs are represented by a percent of covered payroll required to fund projected benefits. The implied tax rate paid by both the employer and employee is one-half the percent of payroll.

[b] Tax rates as fixed by existing legislation are the sum of the employer and employee taxes; i.e., the tax rate paid by each party after 1990 is 1.45 percent of payroll.

SOURCE: *1982 Annual Report,* Board of Trustees, Federal Hospital Insurance Trust Fund, p. 37.

health care prices could significantly lower projected costs for HI and as a result total federal spending on transfers to the elderly.

Policy Reforms for Social Security

The preceding discussion indicates that if the current benefit structure is maintained, large tax increases will be required. These new taxes obviously would be in addition to the taxes necessary to finance the other operations of federal, state, and local governments. If fertility rates remain low and alternative III becomes a reality, combined payroll tax rates for OASDHI under current legislation would have to rise to 35–40 percent of taxable payroll by the middle of the next century. Even alternatives II–A and II–B necessitate total tax rates of 22–24 percent of payroll.

Some have proposed supplementing payroll tax revenues from, or completely transferring the funding of social security to general tax revenues. Of course, this change would not affect average tax rates in the aggregate. It would raise marginal tax rates even more for the high income person because federal income tax rates are progressive, whereas social security taxes are proportional or regressive. In addition, such a change would weaken the link between social security contributions (taxes) and receipt of benefits. The program would be made more explicitly to resemble a welfare program. Such a connotation would probably not be popular among retirees, who see themselves as much different from welfare recipients because of their previous contributions. The welfare connotation of a huge income transfer program such as social security would probably increase its political vulnerability, especially as taxes were raised. A possible exception to this would be the general fund financing of medicare. The level of medicare benefits is not related to past earnings.

Regardless of the method of financing, social security will probably entail major tax increases if benefit levels are maintained, although the necessary tax increases may be disguised somewhat if social security comes from general revenues. The major issue is whether the current benefit structure is sustainable. Politically, significant tax increases may polarize relations between workers and retirees. The chance is increased of a worker/taxpayer revolt that might jeopardize the program. Very high taxes on earned income decrease labor supply and discourage saving, thus lowering economic growth. The projected tax rates necessary to sustain the current level of benefits through the next 50 years are so high that the program is politically vulnerable, and the economic consequences may be severe. Despite this rather gloomy long-term assessment, several recent Harris polls reveal considerable public support for the system and indicate a willingness of people to pay somewhat higher taxes to sustain existing benefits. The fundamental question is whether this support will continue if tax rates rise by 60 percent or more.

Obviously one way to avoid major tax increases is to reduce the benefit structure. Rosen (1981) suggests that as a society becomes wealthier, the reliance people place on government income transfer programs such as social security should diminish. Since one of the primary economic justifications of social security is based on the potential poverty of the aged, it follows that reductions may be acceptable as people on average become wealthier.

Several options are available to reduce future expenditures of the social security system. First, replacement rates could be lowered. Second, the age of eligibility for benefits could be raised. A final strategy is to selectively eliminate parts of the program. The Reagan Administration began by advocating the first and third policy options; however, only provisions costing relatively small amounts were eliminated (i.e., minimum benefits for future retirees, burial benefits, and student benefits). (These options are discussed more fully in following paragraphs.)

Heretofore, the history of social security has been one of sharing the risk of unforeseen events. Eliminations of specific programs represent a radical departure from this philosophy. Even though the current economic justifications for some aspects of the program are tenuous, many people have placed great reliance on these benefits. If social security does not perform one of its major functions, social insurance—that is, if people's expectations regarding benefits are defeated by abrupt rule changes—then the economic justification for the program is undermined. If benefits are reduced in the future, it will be very important how the cuts are made.

It may be difficult to measure the social costs of stability, but it is well-established in economics that reducing uncertainty is a benefit. Consider which of the following alternatives you would prefer: a lifetime annuity of $16,000 a year with no chance of default, or a $20,000 annuity with a 10 percent chance that it will terminate completely before death. Although the annual dollar value of the latter alternative is higher, many people would prefer the annual income that they know will continue throughout their life. People value certainty, and much of the value of social security is that it reduces uncertainty. The benefits to each retiree depend on a number of factors including age, marital status, number of dependents, and so on, but the retiree is usually able to determine his or her benefits, and to include them in financial planning. With specific cuts the plans of some people are dashed completely, while with across-the-board cuts most people have to make relatively minor adjustments. As a result, the aggregate harm by across-the-board cuts is likely to be less than the harm caused by specific cuts.

Two principal methods for reducing benefits across the board are available (see above). The raising of the age of eligibility for full benefits reduces the annuity value of social security benefits by decreasing the years a person expects to receive benefits. Similar reductions could be achieved by lowering the replacement ratio and maintaining existing eligibility standards. Of course, some combination of the two could also be adopted.

Raising the age of eligiblity is a desirable option because it reflects the increasing longevity of Americans and could continue to provide a relatively high replacement ratio. This policy option has been advocated by numerous recent study commissions (National Commission on Social Security, 1981; President's Commission on Pension Policy, 1981; Committee for Economic Development, 1981; Business Roundtable, 1981; see Greenough, 1982, for a review of these reports). Available evidence indicates this option would have a greater effect of keeping people in the labor force when compared to comparable reductions in the replacement ratio (Clark and Barker, 1981, pp. 25-40). Torrey illustrates the significance of raising the age of eligibility when examining total federal expenditures (see Table 12). An increase in the age of eligibility to 68 reduces the proportion of the budget for these programs by over 15 percent, while an age of 70 lowers this share by approximately 25 percent (also see Clark and Spengler, 1980a). If similar reductions were achieved in social security, the required increase in the payroll tax during the next 75 years would be substantially moderated. Similar reductions in ex-

TABLE 12. Projected Share of the Federal Budget Devoted to Eligible Elderly Population (in percentages).

Age of Eligibility	1990	2000	2010	2020	2030
65	32.4	34.1	36.2	43.8	49.5
68	26.5	29.0	29.8	35.6	41.7
70	23.4	26.1	26.6	31.5	37.3

SOURCE: Barbara Torrey, Guns vs. canes: The fiscal implications of an aging population, *American Economic Review*, May 1982, p. 312.

penditures could be achieved by lowering the replacement ratio, an option that enables future workers to maintain greater flexibility in the timing of initial benefits.

The aging of the population necessitates that significantly higher taxes will be required to maintain current replacement rates, or that future benefits will be reduced in comparison to what they currently are projected to be. It is very important to emphasize that future benefits continue to rise with real wage gains, and what is being suggested is a slowing in the growth rate of benefits. No matter which option is chosen, people should be given time to adjust and plan for the changes. For example, 1983 legislation raises the age for receiving full benefits to 67 by the year 2027. This increase is accomplished by raising the age by two months each year between 2003 and 2009 and again between 2020 and 2027. This amendment does much to reduce the future tax increase, and does not affect anyone now over the age of 46, and gives younger workers almost two decades to adjust to new social security policy. This plan should eliminate much of the current uncertainty over the viability of social security, for it is an across-the-board reduction in benefits that does not dismantle the basic promise of social security. Other more drastic proposals to reduce future taxes such as the use of government retirement bonds (Buchanan, 1968) or the elimination of the progressive benefit formula (Munnell, 1977, pp. 38–52) have not received any popular or political support.

Income Maintenance Policies and Retirement

Income maintenance policies influence the retirement decision by altering the gains from continued work and by providing a flow of income if persons leave the labor force. Since Ch. 17 of this *Handbook* focuses directly on the retirement decision, this examination is relatively brief. First, consider the effect of social security on the net compensation from employment. The most visible effect is the earnings test, which reduces OASI benefits by one dollar for every two dollars of earnings when earnings exceed an exempt

amount. This tax encourages people to alter their labor supply in order to avoid the penalty. Early in 1981, President Reagan as part of his social security reforms recommended that the earnings test be eliminated. This modification would encourage delayed retirement; however, the benefits would accrue to the healthier and higher income elderly (Schulz, 1978). Gordon and Schoeplein (1979) have estimated cost of removal of the earnings test for persons 65–69 in 1978 would have been $2.1 billion; however, this increased expenditure is largely offset by increased payroll and income taxes.

Offsetting the earnings test are two forms of recalculation of benefits that increase the total compensation. When benefits are deferred, the future monthly benefit is increased. This increase is greater between 62 and 65 than after 65. In addition, current earnings are used to recalculate a person's earnings history. If earnings exceed the lowest previous year used in the formula, then future benefits rise. (See Clark and Barker, 1981, for a more detailed discussion of these effects. For a debate on the relative magnitude of these effects, see Burkhauser and Turner, 1981, and Blinder et al., 1980). President Reagan has proposed increased reductions for early retirement and a liberalized earnings test. These changes would encourage delayed retirement.

Employer pensions have similar effects except that the gain from continued work may be substantially less. This occurs because firms do not necessarily continue to count employment service after age 65. Also, pensions can be thought of as having a 100 percent earnings test; that is, if you continue working for the same employer, your entire pension benefit is withheld for that pay period. Regulations requiring firms to allow their employees to accumulate pension credits would encourage later retirement.

Women and Retirement Policy

Until recently, personal retirement was not a major decision among the life-cycle choices of many women. Most women married, raised a family, and worked intermittently.

Within this family framework, the retirement of the husband was the dominant labor market event as the family aged. The rapid growth of married women in the labor force has significantly altered this life-cycle pattern. During the past three decades, women have entered the labor force at earlier ages, had fewer children, spent less time out of the labor force, and become increasingly career-oriented (Kreps and Clark, 1975). This new emphasis on market work raises questions concerning the treatment of women by existing retirement programs.

Older women respond to the same incentives that influence retirement decisions of men (see Cain, 1966; Bowen and Finegan, 1969; Oppenheimer, 1969). Clark and Johnson (1980) show that retirement of each spouse is a family decision, and that the value of each person's time and pension variables of both are important determinants of the work decisions by the husband and the wife. Thus, the earlier discussion is applicable to females.

Most of the programs that provide income to older persons treat men and women equally under the law. For several years, considerable attention has been focused on de-sexing provisions of social security that had explicit gender orientation. Most government retirement programs favor women as a group because they provide equal annual benefits for the same work history. The longer life expectancy of females results in their receiving a greater annuity value for their contributions or taxes. Since women on average have lower lifetime earnings histories, they benefit more from the progressive benefit structure of the system.

With regard to the treatment of women, the social security issue that has received the most attention is the relationship between one- and two-earner families and the gain in benefits due to the wife's working. Current legislation provides that a woman who has never worked is eligible for a spouse benefit equal to 50 percent of her husband's benefit. If she works, her total benefit is not affected until her earnings record is sufficient to generate a benefit in excess of the spouse benefit (Burkhauser, 1979). Most people agree that this is an undesirable aspect of the benefit structure. It has become increasingly unpopular as the number of working women has grown. The spouse benefit was instituted because it was believed that a couple needed more resources in retirement than a single person. Obviously, its elimination would cut the benefits for families in which the wife does not work. Although a number of proposals to alter the structure of family benefits have been made, none has yet produced a legislative consensus (Flowers, 1977; Holden, 1979; Burkhauser and Holden, 1982).

SUMMARY

Federal income maintenance policies are an important determinant of the well-being of older Americans. These policies are centered primarily in the OASDHI program, federal regulation of private pensions and federal pensions, and welfare programs that provide cash and in-kind benefits to the elderly. This chapter has indicated the significant influence these policies have on the income of older persons and the rising cost associated with them. Federal transfers have contributed to the decline in the incidence of poverty among the aged. They have also done much to insulate older Americans from declines in real income associated with inflation. This is a result of the explicit and implicit indexation of most of these programs (U.S. Congressional Research Service, 1981).

The primary income maintenance issue today in the United States and in other developed countries is the prospect of significant future tax increases or benefit reductions resulting from continued population aging. The demographic pressures vary across these countries, and the implied tax increases depend on the structure of social security programs. However, the basic problem of providing adequate resources to the elderly is similar throughout much of the world. Even the developing countries have growing aged populations and face the financial pressures of resource transfers to retirees. Policy decisions made in the 1980s will likely determine the future of income maintenance programs for many years to come. This chapter has described the options that are currently available. It seems likely that fundamental changes in income maintenance programs will be made during the next five years. Large reductions in these programs may reverse the trend toward the improving well-being of older persons.

REFERENCES

Ball, Robert. 1978. *Social Security: Today and Tomorrow.* New York: Columbia University Press.

Barker, David, and Clark, Robert. 1980. Mandatory retirement and labor force participation of the respondents in the retirement history study. *Social Security Bulletin* (Nov.):20–29.

Blinder, Alan, Gordon, Roger, and Wise, Donald. 1980. Reconsidering the work disincentive effects of social security. *National Tax Journal* (Dec.):431–442.

Board of Trustees, Federal Hospital Insurance Trust Fund. 1981. *1981 Annual Report* (July).

Board of Trustees, Federal Old-Age and Survivors Insurance and Disability Insurance Trust Funds. 1981. *1981 Annual Report* (July).

Borzilleri, Thomas. 1980. In-kind benefit programs and retirement. Paper prepared for the President's Commission on Pension Policy.

Bowen, William, and Finegan, T. A. 1969. *The Economics of Labor Force Participation.* Princeton, N. J.: Princeton University Press.

Bridges, Benjamin, and Packard, Michael. 1981. Price and income changes for the elderly. *Social Security Bulletin* (Jan.):3–15.

Brittain, John. 1972. *The Payroll Tax for Social Security,* Washington, D.C.: The Brookings Institution.

Buchanan, James. 1968. Social insurance in a growing economy: A proposal for radical reform. *National Tax Journal* (Dec.):386–395.

Burkhauser, Richard. 1979. Are women treated fairly in today's social security system? *The Gerontologist* (June):242–249.

Burkhauser, Richard, and Holden, Karen. 1982. *A Challenge to Social Security: The Changing Roles of Women and Men in American Society.* New York: Academic Press.

Burkhauser, Richard, and Turner, John. 1981. Can twenty-five million Americans be wrong? *National Tax Journal* (Dec.):467–78.

Business Roundtable. 1981. *Statement of Social Security Policy Positions of the Business Roundtable* (Feb.).

Cain, Glen. 1966. *Married Women in the Labor Force.* Chicago: University of Chicago Press.

Califano, Joseph. 1978. The aging of America: Questions for the four-generation society. *Annuals of the American Academy of Political and Social Science* (July):96–107.

Campbell, Colin. 1976. *Over-Indexed Benefits: The De-*

coupling Proposals for Social Security. Washington, D.C.: American Enterprise Institute.

Clark, Robert, and Barker, David. 1981. *Reversing the Trend Toward Early Retirement,* Washington, D.C.: American Enterprise Institute.

Clark, Robert, and Johnson, Thomas. 1980. Retirement in the dual career family. Final report for Social Security Administration, Grant No. 10-P-90543-4-02.

Clark, Robert, and McDermed, Ann. 1982. Inflation, pension benefits, and retirement. *Journal of Risk and Insurance* (Mar..):19–38.

Clark, Robert, and Menefee, John. 1981. Federal expenditures for the elderly. *The Gerontologist* (Apr.):132–137.

Clark, Robert, and Spengler, Joseph. 1980a. Economic responses to population aging with special emphasis on retirement policy. *In* Robert Clark (ed.), *Retirement Policy in an Aging Society.* Durham, N. C.: Duke University Press.

Clark, Robert, and Spengler, Joseph. 1980b. *The Economics of Individual and Population Aging.* New York: Cambridge University Press.

Clark, Robert; Maddox, George; Schrimper, Ronald; and Sumner, Daniel. *Inflation and the Economic Well-being of the Elderly.* Baltimore: Johns Hopkins University Press, 1984 forthcoming.

Commitee for Economic Development. 1981. *Reforming Retirement Policies.* (Sept.).

Comptroller General. 1978. *Effect of the Employee Retirement Income Security Act on the Termination of Single Employer Defined Benefit Pension Plans* (Apr.).

Diamond, Peter. 1977. A framework for social security analysis. *Journal of Public Economics* (Dec.):275–298.

Feldstein, Martin. 1980. Inflation and the stock market. *American Economic Review* (Dec.):839–847.

Flowers, Marilyn. 1977. *Women and Social Security: An Institutional Dilemma.* Washington, D.C.: American Enterprise Institute.

Fox, Alan. 1979. Earnings replacement of retired couples. *Social Security Bulletin* (Jan.):17–39.

Gordon, Josephine, and Schoeplein, Robert. 1979. Tax impact from repeal of the retirement test. *Social Security Bulletin* (Sept.):22–32.

Greenough, William. 1982. Pensions, what now? *Journal of Risk and Insurance* (Mar.):104–113.

Greenough, William, and King, Francis. 1976. *Pension Plans and Public Policy.* New York: Columbia University Press.

Holden, Karen. 1979. The inequitable distribution of OASI benefits among homemakers. *The Gerontologist* (Oct.):250–256.

Hudson, Robert. 1978. The graying of the federal budget and its consequences for old-age policy. *The Gerontologist* (Oct.):428–440.

Kaplan, Robert. 1977. *Indexing Social Security,* Washington, D.C.: American Enterprise Institute.

King, Francis. 1982. Indexing retirement benefits. *The Gerontologist* (Dec.):488–92.

Kreps, Juanita, and Clark, Robert. 1975. *Sex, Age and Work*. Baltimore, Md.: The Johns Hopkins Press.

Lazear, Edward, 1979. Why is there mandatory retirement? *Journal of Political Economy* (Dec.):1261–1284.

Meier, Elizabeth. 1977. ERISA and the growth of private pension income. *Industrial Gerontology* (Summer):147–157.

Melone, Joseph, and Allen, Everett. 1972. *Pension Planning*. Homewood, Ill.: Richland D. Irwin.

Mellor, Earl, and Stamas, George. 1982. Usual weekly earnings: Intergroup differences and basic trends. *Monthly Labor Review* (Apr.):15–24.

Menefee, John, Edwards, Bea, and Schieber, Sylvester. 1981. Analysis of nonparticipation in the SSI program. *Social Security Bulletin* (June):3–21.

Moon, Marilyn. 1977. *The Measurement of Economic Welfare: Its Application to the Aged Poor*. New York: Academic Press.

Moon, Marilyn. 1979. The incidence of poverty among the aged. *Journal of Human Resources* (Spring):211–221.

Morrison, Peter. 1982. Demographic links to social security. *Challenge* (Jan.):44–49.

Munnell, Alicia. 1977. *The Future of Social Security*. Washington, D.C.: Brookings Institution.

Munnell, Alicia. 1979. *Pensions for Public Employees*. Washington, D.C.: National Planning Association.

Munnell, Alicia. 1980. The impact of inflation on private pensions. *In* Robert Clark (ed.), *Retirement Policy in an Aging Society*, pp. 167–183. Durham, N. C.: Duke University Press.

Munnell, Alicia. 1982. *The Economics of Private Pensions*. Washington, D.C.: Brookings Institution.

Myers, Robert. 1975. *Social Security*. Homewood, Ill.: Richard D. Irwin.

National Commission on Social Security. 1981. Final report, *Social Security in America's Future*. Washington, D.C. (Mar.).

Okun, Arthur. 1970. Inflation: The problems and prospects before us. *In* Arthur Okun, Henry Fowler, and Milton Gilbert (eds.), *Inflation: The Problems it Creates and Policies it Requires*. New York: New York University Press.

O'Neill, June. 1978. Unpublished data prepared for the Congressional Budget Office. Estimates summarized in James Storey and Gary Hendricks, *Retirement Income Issues in an Aging Society*, Urban Institute Paper, Dec. 1979.

Oppenheimer, Valarie. 1969. *The Female Labor Force in the United States*. Berkeley: University of California.

Paul, Robert, 1976. The impact of pension reform on American business. *Sloan Management Review* (Fall):59–71.

President's Commission on Pension Policy. 1981. *Coming of Age: Toward A National Retirement Income Policy* (Feb.).

Rosen, Sherwin. 1981. Some arithmetic of social security. Unpublished paper presented to Controlling the Costs of Social Security, American Enterprise Institute Conference (June).

Samuelson, Robert. 1978. Busting the U.S. budget: The cost of an aging America. *National Journal*, Feb. 18, pp. 256–260.

Schieber, Sylvester. 1982. Trends in pension coverage and benefit receipt. *The Gerontologist* (Dec.):474–481.

Schulz, James. 1978. Liberalizing the social security retirement test: Who would receive the increased pension benefits. *Journal of Gerontology* (Mar.):262–268.

Schulz, James. 1980. *The Economics of Aging*. Belmont, Calif.: Wadsworth.

Schulz, James, et al. 1974. *Providing Adequate Retirement Income*. Hanover, N. H.: University Press of New England.

Svahn, John. 1981. Omnibus Reconciliation Act of 1981: Legislative history and summary of OASDI and medicare provisions. *Social Security Bulletin* (Oct.):3–24.

Svahn, John. 1982. Restoration of certain minimum benefits and other OASDI program changes. *Social Security Bulletin* (Mar.):3–12.

Tilove, Robert. 1976. *Public Employee Pension Funds*. New York: Columbia University Press.

Torda, Theodore. 1972. The impact of inflation on the elderly. *Federal Reserve Bank of Cleveland Economic Review* (Oct.):3–19.

Torrey, Barbara. 1982. Guns vs. canes: The fiscal implications of an aging population. *American Economic Review* (May):309–313.

U.S. Bureau of the Census. 1981. Money income and poverty status of families and persons in the United States, 1980 (advance data from the Mar. 1981 current population survey). *Current Population Reports,* Series P-60, No. 127, Washington, D.C.: U.S. Government Printing Office.

U.S. Bureau of Labor Statistics. 1970. *Three Budgets for a Retired Couple,* Bulletin No. 1570-6. Washington, D.C.: U.S. Government Printing Office (May).

U.S. Congressional Budget Office. 1977. *Poverty Status of Families under the Alternative Definitions,* background paper No. 17 (revised). Washington, D.C.: U.S. Government Printing Office.

U.S. Congressional Budget Office. 1982. *Work and Retirement: Options for Continued Employment of Older Workers*. Washington, D.C.: U.S. Government Printing Office (July).

U.S. Congressional Research Service. 1981. *Indexation of Federal Programs*. Washington, D.C.: U.S. Government Printing Office.

U.S. Social Security Administration. 1977. *Social Security Programs Throughout the World 1977,* SSA Research Report No. 50. Washington, D.C.

U.S. Social Security Administration. 1979. *Social Security Bulletin: Annual Statistical Bulletin, 1977–79*. Washington, D.C.

White House Conference on Aging. 1981. *Final Report,* Vol. 1.

24
HEALTH, HEALTH RESOURCES, AND THE UTILIZATION OF CARE

Ethel Shanas
University of Illinois at Chicago
and
George L. Maddox
Duke University

Physical and psychological well-being are matters of social as well as personal concern. Health and illness affect an individual's performance of basic personal tasks of daily living and of expected social roles. Impairment and disability increase the probability of failure in carrying out personal tasks and social roles; and such failures in turn increase dependency, which, particularly for adults, challenges widely shared personal and social expectations and preferences for independence. Moreover, loss of autonomy tends to have a negative effect on self-evaluation and life satisfaction. Illness also exacts social and economic costs in terms of both lost opportunities for productive work and charges for the health services required to restore functioning. Health is thus both a key personal resource for any individual and a social concern because performance of social roles in economic, kinship, and community organizations requires individuals who can function competently.

A complex relationship exists among disease, impairment, disability, and illness. Both lay and professional observers know from experience and understand, at least intuitively, what epidemiologists mean by "the

iceberg phenomenon." The real prevalence of disease and impairment is always higher than the estimate of such prevalence based on clinically identified disease or impairment. This is so because disease and impairment do not automatically lead to a demand for or utilization of health services. Individuals who are equally well or equally unhealthy can and do behave quite differently. Some are the "worried well" who respond anxiously to the possibility of disease. Others deny illness and inappropriately resist seeking care. The symptoms of disease are not always obvious, understood, or urgent. Further, the availability of and access to help affect the response of an individual to illness. Health clinicians are also very familiar with processes of compensation that influence the experience of illness and how individuals respond to it.

These considerations suggest why it is important to take account of the societal and behavioral aspects of illness. All societies develop definitions of illness that provide their members with guidelines both for being ill and for responding to illness. Social groups have an obvious investment in ensuring that illness is not used to achieve inappropriate exemptions from social expectations and the performance of usual social roles and obligations. Illness is not only socially disruptive; it is also costly.

HEALTH AND ILLNESS AS SOCIAL CONCERNS

Aging, Health, and Illness

The relationship between chronological age and health and illness is well known and well documented in life tables and epidemiological reports on the distribution of disease and impairment. Chronological age is a basic and the best single general predictor of mortality as indicated by death rates; age is also associated with morbidity as indicated by age-related incidence and prevalence of disease and disability. These observations will be documented in some detail later in this chapter. Whether as a result of intrinsic biological mechanisms inherited at birth, exposure to hostile environmental factors, or both, the older the biological organism, the greater its risk of disease, impairment, and death (Lasagna, 1969; Fries and Crapo, 1981). As we will see, factors other than chronological age must be considered in understanding observed patterns of mortality and morbidity. Nevertheless, the middle and later years of life are characterized by a series of biological changes, usually gradual ones, that result in a decreased capacity for functioning and survival. We are not surprised therefore to see reports on health and illness that summarize findings by age categories such as 45 to 64, 65 to 74, 75 and older, and that demonstrate repetitively the expected changes in health with age (National Center for Health Statistics, 1980a,b).

A variety of disciplines are interested in understanding illness and responses to illness among older persons. Scientists are interested in charting human performance over the life span and the factors that affect functioning and survival. One aspect of this interest is the possibility and probability of interventions that might lengthen the currently observed life span and enable more individuals to achieve the longer-than-average life now enjoyed by an increasing number of persons in their eighties and nineties (e.g., Fries, 1981). Scientists also wish to understand how human performance is affected by the complex relationship between the physical and psychological aspects of health and illness and between the objective and subjective aspects of these states. Furthermore, there is interest in the complex and imperfect way in which illness and the need for health care are translated by individuals into demand for and utilization of health services (Haug, 1981b).

While social administrators are interested in scientific issues related to health and illness, they have special concerns of their own. They are likely to note, for example, that older persons have high rates of illness and disability and generate high demand for health services, and that this older age category is increasing at a higher rate than other age categories in developing as well as in developed countries. Health practitioners, in turn, take special note of older persons not only because they are at high risk for disease and disability and generate demand for services at a high level, but also because particular kinds of health problems are observed in late life. The health problems most frequently observed among older persons tend to be chronic, degenerative, and multiple (including physical, psychological, and social components in a complex mixture).

Further, it appears that the particular manifestation of illness and disability in late life does not mesh well with modern systems of health care. Health care tends to be organized primarily to concentrate on the specialized management of acute disease in hospital settings, which, in turn, are not well linked to community-based primary, preventive, or rehabilitative care (McKeown and Cross, 1969; U.S. Department of Health, Education and Welfare, 1971b). This mismatch between the health care needs of older persons and the organization of resources to meet those needs has become increasingly obvious. The increasing proportion of older persons in the populations of all societies, especially the growth of their numbers at later ages, as well as the escalating cost of their health care, underlie a general widespread sense of urgency in the devising of more efficient and effective health care systems.

Improved social conditions, coupled with advances in medical technology and sanitation, have ensured the survival of increasing numbers of persons into the later decades of life. Increasing longevity has also encouraged expectations that health care, because it is perceived to be beneficial, ought to be available as a social right. As a result, all societies currently share a set of common basic problems in the provision of health care. According to Somers (1971), these are: control of expenditures; development of adequately comprehensive care systems; manpower development; and achievement of consensus about the equitable distribution of basic services. Any discussion of these common problems in the provision of health care inevitably involves consideration of the relationship betwen aging and illness. The risk of illness and impairment increases with age, and, correspondingly, the personal and social costs of illness in late life are very high.

Economic Aspects of Health Care

In recent decades modern industrial societies have invested an increasingly large proportion of their economic resources in developing and maintaining organizations designed to control illness and to restore sick individuals to maximum functioning. In western European societies, for example, the capital investments, manpower development, and operating expenses committed to health constituted about 7 percent of the gross national product (GNP) in the early 1970s; in the United States the annual investment in health services in 1972 was 7.7 percent of the GNP and exceeded 93 billion dollars (Somers, 1971; Cooper et al., 1974). By 1980 the percent of the GNP devoted to health had risen to 9.4 ($247 billion) (U.S. Department of Health and Human Services, 1981a). Unlike western European countries that have tended to consider health care pri-

marily as a societal responsibility to be insured with public funds, the United States has stressed health care as a personal responsibility to be insured by private funds. Consequently, the private share of national health expenditures has been large, although decreasing from 72.8 percent in 1950 to 57.8 percent in 1980. Concomitantly, public expenditures for health have increased steadily in the last three decades, reaching 42 percent in 1980 (Freeland and Schendler, 1981; U.S. Department of Health and Human Services, 1981a). Over half of 20 billion dollars paid annually for nursing home care in the United States is from public sources (Fox and Clauser, 1980; U.S. Department of Health and Human Services, 1981a).

The personal economic costs of health care in late life are high. The personal health care costs of older persons are between two and three times higher than the amount that might be expected on the basis of chance alone (Andersen et al., 1973; Cooper and Piro, 1974; Zook and Moore, 1980). Recent experience in the United States provides an illustration: The average annual medical bill of persons 65 years of age and older tends to be 2.5 times higher than for persons aged 19 to 64 and about 7 times as high as that for persons under the age of 19. Moreover, the average physician's bill for older persons tends to be three times greater than the average bill for other adults. Comparable estimates of the high cost of health care in late life have been made in Great Britain, where older persons comprise 14 percent of the population but consume about 40 percent of the resources of the National Health Service (Logan, 1966).

In the United States where, unlike Britain, health care bills are considered to be primarily a private responsibility, public expenditures in 1978 covered about two-thirds of the total expenditures for health services to older persons. Despite this high level of public expenditures, older persons themselves paid a large portion of their health bills out-of-pocket. In 1978 per capita health care cost in the United States for older persons was $2,026, of which 37 percent was out-of-pocket. Over the past decade, rates of utilization of nursing homes and mental health services by older adults as well as the median number of days spent in all types of hospitals by older persons have increased (Federal Council on Aging, 1981). Payment under Medicare, a national health insurance reimbursement program for the aged, however, is severely restricted for both nursing homes and mental health services.

Forecasting either the health of older persons or their utilization of health care must be done with caution. The proportion of the GNP devoted to health care in the United States is expected to continue upward. While a substantial factor in this estimated increase is attributable to cost inflation and a growing number of older persons, the observed 16.6 percent annual rate of national expenditures for health between 1965 and 1980 also reflects real increases in the services used (Freeland and Schendler, 1981; see also Federal Council on Aging, 1981). We know that death rates among older adults have declined consistently from 1940 to 1980—by 18 percent for those 65–74; 14 percent for those 75–84; and 25.5 percent for those 85 and older. Further, we know that heart disease and neoplasm are the major causes of death for both older and younger adults (Siegel, 1980). What we do not know, but need to know, is whether the lengthening of life and the prevalence of disabling disease will combine to ensure increased need and demand for health services. Fries (1981; see also Fries and Crapo, 1981) argues that the incidence of chronic disabling disease might be lowered in the future, its onset delayed, and the degree of disablement reduced. Such optimistic speculation may be reasonable and plausible, but, at this stage, it does remain speculation.

The recognized costs of health care significantly understate the real cost of illness borne by sick individuals and the kinsmen on whom they depend for informal care and support. An estimated 5 to 10 percent of older individuals living outside institutions require home care, which, to a substantial degree (perhaps 70 percent), is provided by private sources (Duke Center, 1978; Health Care Financing Administration, 1981). The psychological and social burden of such care has received little attention (Grad and Sainsbury, 1968), and the real economic cost of such care has not been systematically studied. For example, we do not know the economic cost implicit in having an adult family member forgo employment in the interest of remaining at home to care for a disabled individual. Generally, home care provided by family members has been treated as though it had no economic cost, although the cost of publicly financed home health care programs is demonstrably high (Stiefel, 1967). A United States General Accounting Office study (Duke Center, 1978) estimates that for perhaps 17 percent of impaired older adults living in the community, the need for compensatory care is so great that the cost of maintaining them in the community is actually higher than the cost of institutional care. This finding is masked in part by another fact; about 80 percent of the cost of the care for these very disabled persons is provided from private, not public, sources.

As noted above, inflation of health care cost plus uncertainty about levels of demand for services among high utilizers of services, such as older persons, have made projections of the cost of health services quite difficult, whether for the aged or the total population. For example, in 1965, at the inception of the Medicare government insurance program for older persons in the United States, the projected 1970 cost of Part A (hospital care) of that program was $3.1 billion; the actual cost for services in this program in 1970 proved to be $5.8 billion. Similarly, in 1965 the projected 1990 cost for hospital services under Medicare was $8.8 billion; by 1969 the revised cost estimate for 1990 was $16.8 billion. Comparable underestimations of cost were intitially made for Part B (supplemental medical insurance): a fivefold increase in the cost of this program was observed between 1965 and 1970 (U.S. Senate Committee on Finance, 1970). Between 1967 and 1975 the rate of utilization for Parts A and B among Medicare enrollees increased from

367 per 1000 to 528 per 1000. There was an average annual increase of 4.7 percent in reimbursement and 7.5 percent in the total cost of the program (Ruther, 1981).

In an analysis of the probable effects of various policy options for organizing and financing health care in the United States, Newhouse et al. (1974) provided an extensive review of evidence related to three interrelated issues of considerable relevance in considering alternative approaches to health insurance: (1) How do various options affect demand for services and the total health bill? (2) How does a health care system adapt under pressure? (3) What is the expected return on various health care investments? Using evidence from a number of small experiments in health care organizing and financing, they concluded that a publicly financed total health care program would increase inpatient demand between 5 percent and 15 percent, and that a program that required 25 percent co-insurance might increase inpatient demand not at all or no more than 8 percent. On the other hand, they anticipated that ambulatory care would be dramatically and differently affected by these two options. The total care option was projected to increase demand for ambulatory care by as much as 75 percent, and 25 percent co-insurance was projected to increase demand by as much as 30 percent.

While increased demand for health services potentially could generate additional resources and personnel to meet the demand, other responses tend to be more probable, according to Newhouse et al. These more likely responses include, at least in market economies, increased prices for services; and in all types of economies, a probable increase in the time required to receive services. Newhouse et al. conclude somewhat pessimistically that "even a substantial investment in delivery of more health services is not likely to produce any clearly measurable changes in any dimension of health, whether length of life or physical well-being." There is no other convincing evidence to the contrary from economically developed countries.

Such a conclusion sheds some light on why the organization and financing of health care for older persons is increasingly a matter of public discussion in all societies. If the best available health care for all individuals is a right ensured by removing price as a barrier and equilibrating supply and demand, the total health bill of a society will be predictably high. In the United States, as a case in point, a health system designed to cover *total* cost of care would require an investment well above the 10 percent of the GNP currently observed. Most national health insurance options under discussion at the beginning of the decade of the 1980s included various provisions for co-insurance and a wide range of exclusions from coverage (Feder and Holahan, 1979).

MEASURING HEALTH AND THE DEMAND FOR HEALTH CARE

Problems Inherent in Defining Health

Our discussion has focused on health and illness as social concerns. We will now consider some of the problems inherent in measuring "health." A definition of health is essential for describing the status of a population or individual, for allocating resources for health care, and for organizing services to meet health needs (Sullivan, 1966; Andersen, 1968; Fanshel and Bush, 1970; Maddox, 1972, 1980; Aday and Eichorn, 1972; Patrick et al., 1973). Definitions of health may focus on individuals, their disease state, and/or their ability to function; or they may be global definitions of the extent of a given disease state or disability in the population.

If one focuses on the disease states of individuals, attention is typically directed to the medical diagnosis, the treatment plan, and its impact on the person who is ill. If one concentrates on the ability of the individual to function, one observes the behavior of an individual. Illness must be distinguished from both disease and illness behavior: with a given complaint persons may or may not go about their usual activities; they may or may not spend time in bed because of illness. The global statistic of the extent of disease or disability, in contrast, presents a summary of the experience of the population, for example, all persons with a given disease or all persons who spend time in bed because of illness.

In practice, health in the aged is usually defined in one of two ways: in terms of the presence or absence of disease, or in terms of how well the older person functions or his general sense of "well-being." A definition of health in terms of pathology or disease states is commonly used by health personnel, particularly physicians. This definition illustrates what we call a medical model or perspective on health. A judgment of health based on the presence or absence of pathology is the result of observation, examination, and the findings of laboratory tests. Such a judgment is often described as "objective." However, the achievement of a truly objective measure of health is difficult if not impossible. The skills of technicians administering laboratory tests vary. The findings of such tests for a given individual may differ from day to day. Physiological measures such as blood pressure or glucose levels, for example, are known to differ radically within a short time period in an individual. Further, even though the physician may be careful in the use of indications of pathology as a basis for judgment, diagnosis is influenced by attitudinal set and the conditions the physician expects in a person of a given age and sex. While a condition may worsen with age, this fact does not establish a causal relationship with aging (Kannel and Gordon, 1980; Costa and McCrae, 1980).

The health professional's overall assessment of and response to the older patient characteristically reflects the social climate of the time (Haug, 1981b). The introduction of health insurance for the aged (Medicare) in the United States, for example, was followed by a sharp increase in the proportion of older persons admitted to hospitals; presumably the health status of older persons did not change in response to the enactment of Medicare, but medical judgments about hospitalization did. Physicians, like laymen, are the product of their cultures, and in American society "the centralized medical facility that features inpatient service and high technology is the hallmark of contemporary medical care" (Maddox, 1981a).

An alternative way to define health among the elderly is based not on pathology or disease states but on level of functioning (Haber, 1967, 1969, 1970; Katz et al., 1970; Harris et al., 1971; Lawton, 1971; Shanas, 1971, 1974; Branch, 1980; Ferraro, 1980; Kane and Kane, 1981; Williams and Williams, 1982). This perspective was summarized by a World Health Organization advisory group more than a generation ago (1959). This group states: "health in the elderly is best measured in terms of function; . . . degree of fitness rather than extent of pathology may be used as a measure of the amount of services the aged will require from the community." Thus the things that old persons can do, or think they can do, are useful indicators of both how healthy they are and the services they will require or seek. The implications of a functional perspective for the development of health resources will be discussed in greater detail below; but, in effect, a functional approach assumes that both the individual and the physician may have relevant and possibly conflicting information about health status (Williams, 1978). Patients and their physicians may see the same event from different perspectives. The patient may not report environmental factors considered unimportant or irrelevant, although such factors may influence the disease or its symptoms. Symptoms may be attributed to disease by the patient and to aging by the doctor, or vice versa (Kart, 1981).

Functional definitions of health tend to deemphasize global statistics of prevalence or incidence of disease states among the elderly as predictors of their demand for services, and tend to stress individual assessments. Shanas et al. (1968), in their three-country study of the elderly in Denmark, Britain, and the United States, developed an index of incapacity that focused on the ability of the older person to perform those tasks that made the person independent of others for personal care. The rationale for the index is "that the presence of a particular disease does not necessarily indicate the inhibition of activity which results from it" (Townsend, 1963). In a study of the elderly in Manitoba, Canada, a modification of this index proved to be a reliable and valid measure of function for both old people in the community and those in institutions (Chappell, 1981). High index scores were related to known disabilities and the use of medical care.

An important forward step in the use of a functional assessment instrument for both clinical intake of individuals and epidemiological surveys that yield population data has been undertaken at Duke University (Maddox and Dellenger, 1978; Duke Center, 1978). Using a Multidimensional Functional Assessment Questionnaire designed to rate five levels of functioning—social, economic, mental, physical, and activities of daily living—the Duke studies indicate that different service settings (e.g., institutions or mental health clinics) attract elderly patients with differing assessment profiles.

The points of view of those who prefer the medical model of health needs and of those who prefer the functional model are not irreconcilable, and efforts have been made to assess the two models by comparing the self-reports of old people with the findings of physical examinations (Sachuk, 1963; Maddox, 1964; Sullivan, 1966, 1971; Van den Heuvel, 1974; LaRue et al., 1979). Piotrowski (1970) and his colleagues in Poland demonstrated the value of the functional model in assessing health needs, by comparing old people's responses to a standardized set of questions widely used in cross-national studies to assess the functioning of the elderly with the results of physician examinations of these old people. The greatest disparities between self-reports of health and medical examinations in the Polish sample occur between the overall global judgments of health made by an elderly individual and judgments made by his physician. The overall judgment of old persons that their health

is "good" or "poor" is most likely to differ from the physician's comparable overall assessment. When actual behavior of an old person in each of the areas investigated is compared with the medical evaluation of the possibility of such behavior, the degree of convergence in judgment of the physician examiner and the elderly subject is quite high.

Fillenbaum (1979) compared the health self-assessment of men and women community residents with both the number of their health problems and their disabilities, and their illnesses both as individually reported and as verified by a knowledgeable informant. For persons living in the community she found that self-assessment of health was a useful indicator of health status. However, Fillenbaum also reported that the assessments of institutional residents, in contrast to community residents, are not related in a consistent manner to objective measures of their health. She pointed out that, since institutions are places for the sick and infirm, institutional residents may emphasize their dependency and sickness.

Maddox and Douglass (1973), in their discussion of the findings of the Duke University longitudinal study of the elderly, compared the medical and functional evaluation of an initial sample of 270 elderly persons in a study that covered 15 years and six observations. Over time, the old person's and the physician's rating of health tended to be congruent. From one observation to the next, the self-health rating of the individual was a "better predictor of future physicians' ratings than the reverse." Thus, while self-reported health is not a substitute for clinical diagnosis, it is useful as well as reliable information.

Branch (1980), in a panel study of the needs of the elderly in Massachusetts, in which a sample of old people were re-interviewed after 15 months, isolated three characteristics of original interviewees with the greatest likelihood of dying within the period. These persons were: (1) individuals no longer self-sufficient in personal care; (2) individuals no longer able to do heavy work around the house; (3) male respondents.

Moreover, respondents who were unable to undergo the 45-minute original interview also had a high probability of dying. If a person reported that she or he was no longer self-sufficient in personal care and no longer able to do heavy work around the house (widely used questions in functional assessment studies), then the likelihood of mortality within the 15-month period was one in four (24 percent). Branch also found that, irrespective of gender, those elderly persons reporting that they were able to do heavy work around the house had only a 3 percent mortality rate in the short term, compared to a 7 percent rate for the total sample.

Specialists in geriatrics, that branch of medicine dealing with older people, largely have accepted a position that represents a compromise between the view of health in the elderly as the presence or absence of pathology and the view that defines health in terms of functional abilities. A World Health Organization (1974) report on the planning and organization of geriatric services stated: "It is now accepted by the medical profession that morbidity should be measured not only in terms of the extent of the pathological process but also in terms of the impairment of the function in the person affected by a pathological condition. . . . Functional diagnosis is one of the most important elements that has been introduced in geriatrics. In this approach a distinction is made between an impairment and a disability caused by a pathological condition."

The expert committee then defined impairment and disability, the first as a physiological or psychological abnormality that does not interfere with the normal life activities of the individual, and the second as a condition that results in partial or total limitation of the normal activities of the individual (see also World Health Organization, 1982a). Harris et al. (1971), in their study of the impaired in Britain, also pointed out that a person may be impaired but not necessarily disabled.

In the United States a distinction is made between short-term and long-term disability. Short-term disability is usually measured by the number of days during the year that a person has had to modify his or her usual behavior because of illness. Three measures of short-term disability are commonly used: days of restricted activity, days in bed, and days lost from work. Kovar (1977) indicated that the level of the first two of these measures for older persons remained unchanged between 1965 and 1975, about 39 days of restricted activity, and about 13 days in bed; while time lost from work declined by half, from 8 days per person in 1965 to 4 days in 1975. A lesser proportion of older persons were working in 1975 than in 1965, and the decline in the days lost from work may reflect the fact that those persons in better health have continued in the work force, whereas those in poorer health have left it.

Persons who are limited in their normal activity or in their mobility because of chronic conditions or impairments are described as having long-term disability. The proportion of persons limited in their usual activity, that is, those with long-term disability according to the previous definition, increased from 42 percent in 1965 to 47 percent in 1975. Kovar stated that this change reflects the fact that a higher proportion of the aged population itself in 1975 compared to 1965 was 75 years of age and over.

People report feeling impaired or handicapped only when some condition causes restriction of their activity (Kovar, 1977). In 1972 about one-fifth (18 percent) of the noninstitutionalized elderly were unable to move about freely owing to chronic conditions or impairments. According to Kovar (1977), "if one assumes that residents of nursing homes are also limited in mobility, then 22 percent of the total elderly population were in some degree limited in mobility, and 16 percent were unable to get around alone."

There is now growing consensus among health professionals and program planners regarding the desirability of functional assessment of the health of the elderly (World Health Organization, 1974). The measurement of health, once considered solely a prerogative of physicians and their interpretation of objective laboratory tests, has now been broadened to include some measure of how well the individual copes with his impairments and the extent to which such impairments interfere with life routines. Such measures of the health status of the aged become increasingly important as one attempts to forecast the demand for health services, facilities, and health manpower.

Measuring Health Status and Forecasting Utilization

Older persons will likely make greater demands on health resources in the future than they do now. It is likely that in addition to an increase in the numbers of older people, the average demand of older individuals for health care will increase. Older people will require more physicians' care, more places in hospitals and nursing homes, and more home health services. Both developed and developing countries will show substantial increases in their numbers of older persons (U.S. Bureau of the Census, 1979a,b; Siegel, 1981; Myers, 1982). While a 41 percent increase in the number of persons age 65 and over is expected between 1975 and the year 2000 in the more developed countries, the number of persons age 65 and over in the less developed regions will more than double.

In the United States, for instance, persons age 65 and over, about 25 million in 1980, are expected to increase almost 30 percent to a projected 32 million by 2000. Even more important in terms of the demand for health services is the expected change in the "population mix" among the elderly. The proportion of younger aged (65 to 69) in the total older population is decreasing, while the proportion of those 75 years of age and over is increasing. Of the estimated 7 million increase in the elderly expected between 1980 and 2000, about three-fourths will be in the age group 75 years and over (Soldo, 1980). This "aging" of the elderly population will likely mean an increase in the use of health services. Should there be improvements in mortality and extension of length of life, further demands on the health services may be expected (Myers, 1978).

The changing ratio of men to women

within the older population also suggests an increase in the demands for services. Women are more likely to utilize health services than men (Shanas, 1962; Maddox, 1975; Hing and Cypress, 1981; Verbrugge, 1981). Among the very old in the United States, those 85 years of age and over, where there were about 45 men for every 100 women in the year 1980, there are expected to be about 39 men for every 100 women in the year 2000. As the older population becomes increasingly a population of widowed, divorced, single women, these persons are likely to have no one who can serve as surrogate trained nurse or household helper. The increase in the proportion of women in the older population, like the aging of the population itself, predicts a rise in the demand for health services, whether such services are delivered in or out of institutions.

Some (e.g., Fries and Crapo, 1981) argue that, as physiological aging is slowed, by both life-style changes and the positive contributions of aging research, most older persons will die after relatively short-term illnesses. Fries and Crapo see the aged of the future as filled with vigor, and their demands on the health services as substantially less. This view of the health of the aged is speculative, not demonstrated.

The question has been raised whether the availability of services in and of itself increases the utilization of medical care by the elderly. Shanas (1978) compared the findings of a 1975 national survey of the noninstitutionalized elderly with the findings of a 1962 survey, the latter four years before Medicare (health insurance for the aged) went into effect. In both 1962 and 1975 about twice as high a proportion of old people were bedfast and housebound at home as were in institutions of all kinds. In both surveys, between eight and nine of every ten elderly persons could go outdoors without help, and about seven of every ten reported no restrictions on their physical functioning. There was no difference between the two surveys in the proportion of the elderly who reported that they had spent some time in bed because of illness during the preceding year, or who said they had seen a doctor during the past month.

What did change betwen 1962 and 1975 was the proportion of the elderly with severe functional limitations who reported seeing a doctor recently. A higher proportion of these people in 1975 than in 1962 reported visits to the doctor. This change in the use of physicians by persons with functional limitations undoubtedly is in part a result of the availability to the elderly of payment schemes. It also may reflect changes in the expectations of the elderly between 1962 and 1975. New cohorts of old people may have been educated to "see a doctor" for symptoms and conditions that earlier cohorts may have ignored.

While demographic indices point to a future increase in the utilization of medical care by the elderly, at the same time some among the elderly are now assuming more responsibility for medical self-care both as individuals and as members of self-care groups. Old people are now being urged to follow good health practices and to learn how to make self-care judgments wisely. They are urged to participate in patient self-help groups that teach skills that can make daily living easier for persons suffering from chronic diseases (U.S. Department of Health, Education and Welfare, 1977).

The Predictors of Health Status and the Utilization of Medical Care

The development of prediction models for the utilization of medical care is a long-time and continuing interest among both physicians and social scientists. (For relevant early papers see Chiang, 1965; Rosenstock, 1966; Andersen, 1968; Moriyamo, 1968.) The available models range from those that predict the utilization of medical care in the population from the estimated prevalence of a disease, to mathematical models, to psycho-social analyses of why people use health services. Currently, studies of the characteristics of people using health services have yielded very little definitive information on the basis of which sound predictions about health care utilization can be made. An individual's perception of physical illness and of the appropriate time for physician inter-

vention in such illness is part of a dynamic behavioral process that incorporates his value orientations, life-time experiences, level of stress, level of education, and income level, as well as his immediate needs. It is difficult to tap all these areas and to relate them to one another in large-scale studies of health care utilization (Mechanic, 1979). Some investigators believe an intensive study of a single life event may be more useful in predicting health outcomes than global measures that combine a variety of past experiences (Kasl et al., 1980). Despite their admitted limitations, however, findings of certain of the psycho-social studies of health and illness seem relevant to understanding patterns of health care utilization among the elderly.

Kasl and Cobb (1966) distinguish *health behavior,* activity undertaken for the purpose of preventing disease by a person who believes himself well; *illness behavior,* activity undertaken by a person who feels ill for the purpose of diagnosis; and *sick-role behavior,* activity engaged in for the purpose of cure by a person who considers himself ill. According to Kasl and Cobb, whether an individual engages in one of these behaviors or not is a function of whether he or she feels threatened by disease or illness, and of the perceived value of taking action. Haug (1981a) raised the question of whether the utilization patterns of the elderly are appropriate to the symptoms they experience. Haug's analysis emphasized the complicated intermix of factors that influence the utilization of health care by older people. Using survey data, she reported that the elderly (those over 60) are more likely than younger persons to suffer from serious complaints, but are like younger persons in underutilizing medical care for such complaints. At the same time, the elderly report overutilization of physicians for nonserious complaints. Haug pointed out that the utilization of physicans for nonserious complaints may not always be patient-initiated but may result from physicians advising their patients to come in for "check-ups" or other treatments.

Aday and Andersen (1975) evaluated families' use of health services in terms of three categories: *predisposing factors,* in which they include family attitudes, social structure, and health beliefs; *enabling factors,* including family and community resources; and *need,* which they divided into *perceived* need and *evaluated* need. *Perceived* need would include illness, reported symptoms, and self-perception of general state of health. *Evaluated* need is the extent to which a physician believes a patient should see a doctor for the symptoms reported and the physician's rating of the severity of medical diagnosis reported in the interviews. In a Swedish study using the framework of predisposing factors, enabling factors, and need, Andersen et al. (1968) found that the social class and income of an individual were more important in predicting use of health services than either age or sex, both demographic factors that have been widely used to predict need. A Canadian study to determine whether there was a difference between persons under age 75 and those over 75 in their use of health services reported similar findings (Snider, 1981a). Age differences as well as other predisposing factors turned out not to be significantly related to the use of services. Monthly family income, however, as well as the older person's education and knowledge of available services, were related to the use of services. Shuval et al. (1970) also demonstrated that while diagnosed medical need is an important predictor of services, a position also taken by Kasl and Cobb and Andersen, medical care has other functions for the individual. The user of medical care may be seeking general reassurance, or even, as Shuval et al. found in their study in Israel, may be seeking a physician's excuse for being absent from work.

Shanas (1962, 1978; Shanas et al., 1968) analyzed both the predictors of health status among the elderly and the use of medical care by this age group. She stated that many old people in the United States probably do not seek medical care for reasons that are primarily psychological, not financial. Such older people, despite their health complaints, believe that a doctor cannot help them, or that they are not really sick enough to require medical attention. In a 1975 national study, one of every eight elderly Americans living in the community said that they needed care or treatment from a doctor, but that they were not seeking such care. One-third of these persons said lack of money was the reason for putting off needed care. The remaining two-thirds gave other reasons, such as fear of or lack of trust in doctors, or belief that a doctor could not help them, or that their illness was not severe enough to require a doctor's attention. These data from the mid-1970s suggest that substantial numbers of old people in the United States tend to accept aches, pains, and other symptoms of physical distress as being the usual accompaniments of advanced years.

Changes in social policy, as indicated earlier, also affect the use of health services. With limitations in services for whatever reason—whether reduction in funds or lack of personnel—need is defined more rigidly and service utilization declines. Svane (1972), in a Danish study, and Harris and Clausen (1968), in Britain, both show that the use of medical care by the elderly rises in response to how need is defined by those offering services. As services increase, the definition of need for the service is often broadened. In the United States the changes in the proportion of the elderly using home health services under Medicare have risen and fallen with the application of differing criteria for service (Gornick, 1976). Some investigators have argued that whatever the amount of health services available, they will tend to be utilized (Raskin et al., 1978). This is an important observation. Subjective and objective assessments of need for service actually translate differently into utilization of services, depending on the availability of services.

STUDIES OF THE PHYSICAL AND MENTAL HEALTH STATUS OF ELDERLY PERSONS

In preparation for the 1971 White House Conference on Aging in the United States, the National Center for Health Statistics (1971b) produced a particularly useful profile on physical health in the later years of life. In addition to the collection of vital statistics from which annual life tables are constructed, the Center uses continuing surveys of national probability samples to obtain data that can only, or best, be obtained through household interviews (e.g., social factors related to illness, injury, disability, and cost and uses of medical services); data from direct examination regarding the prevalence of illness in the population by disease category, including previously undiagnosed illness; and data on health facilities and their utilization, including nursing homes. Several characteristics of the United States National Health Survey reports are worth noting. The age categories used in data presentation distinguish those who might be called the middle-aged (45–64), the young old (65–74), and the very old (75 and over). Moreover, these reports give specific attention to functional definitions of health status.

The origin, program, and operation of the national health surveys are described in a continuing series of reports of the National Center of Health Statistics (1965), and numerous substantive reports by the National Center or other agencies on particular topics are identified in cumulative annual listings and topical indexes (e.g., National Center for Health Statistics, 1973; Federal Council on Aging, 1981). We have chosen in this section to give only limited attention to detailed reports of the distribution of health and disability among older persons; to indices of the utilization of health resources by older persons; and to trends in health and health care indicators. While it is important to provide the reader with some sense of the relevant current evidence, it is equally important to emphasize that such evidence goes out of date quickly. We will provide illustrations of types of data available and direct the reader to the best source of relevant data. Internationally, the United Nations, the World Health Organization, and various countries collect and report data on the health status and health services utilization patterns of older adults (e.g., Mahler, 1980; Siegel, 1981; Evans et al., 1981; Binstock et al., 1982).

We will begin by reviewing the most recent profile of the physical health status of older persons in the United States available and then introduce some cross-national comparisons. We suggest that, while the health profile of older persons in the United States may differ in detail from the profile of similar persons in other industrial societies, the profile will probably be generally applicable to such societies.

Life Expectancy

Average length of life is a traditional measure of health status in a population. Age-specific estimates of average remaining years of life illustrate both the use of chronological age as a predictor of mortality and cohort differences in life expectancy. In 1978, for example, the average future lifetime for an individual born in the United States was 73.3 years; the expectation of life was 70.2 years for a white male, 77.8 for a white female, 65.0 for a nonwhite male, and 73.6 for a nonwhite female. Sweden, with an average life expectancy of 72.5 years for males and 79.0 for females, ranked first among the nations of the world (U.S. Department of Health and Human Services, 1981a). By 1968 individuals 45 years of age in the United States (cohort born in 1923) had already lived almost as long as the average person born in 1900 could have expected to live, and the white 45-year-old still had on the average about 30 years of life remaining, specifically 26.8 years for men and 32.5 years for women. Similarly, men and women who had survived to age 65 could expect 12.8 and 16.3 years of life remaining, and those who had survived to age 75 could expect 8.2 and 9.9 years.

In interpreting such data, one should keep in mind the distinction between life expectancy at birth and age-specific life expectancy. Variations in average life expectancy at birth are to a considerable degree a function of infant mortality. Hence increasing average life expectancy at birth reflects substantial decreases in infant mortality in developed countries. Decreasing death rates in the adult and later years of life affect average remaining years of life at particular ages; age-specific life expectancy has been increasing in recent years, even for very old persons. However, these increases have been small. The sex difference in life expectancy illustrated in Table 1 are characteristic of all developed countries. For males and females, from 1940 through 1978, the trend in average remaining years of life at ages 45, 65, and 75 was upward, with females exhibiting the larger increases.

Currently, major causes of death in late life in the United States are diseases of the heart, malignant neoplasms (cancer), and cerebrovascular disease (mainly strokes). These three conditions account for 70 percent of deaths of persons 45 years of age and older; 40 percent of these deaths are accounted for by disease of the heart alone. Similar patterns, with minor variations, are observed in other industrial societies (Siegel, 1981). In general, the lower the socioeconomic position of an individual, the higher the prevalence of disease and the higher the age-specific death rate. These commonly observed associations between socioeconomic position, illness, and life expectancy have a complex explanation. Indices of socioeconomic status usually include measurements of income, occupation, and education. Such factors, singly or in combination, are reflected in different styles of life and differential access to and use of health resources. For instance, in all industrialized countries, low income, a manual occupation, and minimal education generally predict a high prevalence of disease and elevated death rates (Kitagawa and Hauser, 1973).

Patterns of Morbidity

The prevalence of chronic disease increases markedly with age (National Center for Health Statistics, 1971b). Of individuals 65 years of age and older living outside institutions, 85 percent report at least one chronic disease, and about 50 percent report some limitation of normal activity related to chronic health conditions. Dental problems also increase with age. Over one-fourth of persons aged 45–64 have lost all their teeth, and almost nine out of ten have diseases of the tissues supporting or surrounding remaining teeth.

Poor vision is increasingly common after age 45, particularly among women. Good vision (20/20+) without correction is demonstrated for 39.2 percent of men and 30.9 percent of women aged 45–64 in contrast to 7.5 percent of men and 2.7 percent of women aged 65–79. Correspondingly, the proportion of moderate to severe visual defects among those aged 65–79 is twice as high as that observed among those aged 45–64. Even with corrected vision, 5 percent of the younger age category still exhibit severe visual impairments, and this triples in the older age category. Hearing impairments also increase with age. Among individuals aged 65–79, about one-third have significant impairment of hearing in the frequencies essential in the range associated with normal speech. The rate of impairment in this age category is 40 times greater than that found among

TABLE 1. Average Remaining Years of Life at Ages 45, 65, and 75, by Sex and Color: United States, 1968, 1978.

| Sex and Color | Average Remaining Years of Life | | | | | |
| | At Age 45 | | At Age 65 | | At age 75 | |
	1968	1978	1968	1978	1968	1978
White						
Men	26.8	29.1	12.8	14.0	8.2	8.6
Women	32.5	35.2	16.3	18.4	9.9	11.5
All Other						
Men	24.6	26.5	12.7	14.1	10.3	9.8
Women	29.4	32.7	15.8	18.0	12.0	12.5

Source: National Center for Health Statistics, *Health in the Later Years of Life,* 1971, p. 4; Metropolitan Life, *Statistical Bulletin* 61:4 (Oct.–Dec. 1980); see also Metropolitan Life, 1981, for revised estimates.

individuals aged 18–24 and 4 times greater than among those 45–64.

Although chronic conditions are the most frequent health problems in late life, acute episodes of illness and injury that occasion restriction of activity or medical attention are also common. In recent years older persons have reported on the average at least one acute episode of illness each year, most commonly respiratory disease.

Following this brief review of morbidity statistics, we wish to again emphasize that the pattern of disease and impairment observed in old persons currently is not necessarily an accurate indication of the health profile of subsequent cohorts of older people (see, e.g., Brody, 1982).

Some Social and Social-Psychological Implications of Illness

Observed patterns and trends in the distribution of disease and disability are substantially a function of age, and hence are relevant for understanding factors that affect the total as well as average length of the human life span. Disease and disability also affect economic costs for individuals and society in terms of both income and productivity forgone and the expense of health care, as noted above. We wish to stress here the social and social-psychological implications of disease and disability, particularly as they result in handicaps or restricted social functioning.

Illness affects the energy available to individuals and their capacity to direct the energy at their disposal toward the achievement of personal goals and the meeting of social obligations. Disability and related illness handicap an individual in the role performances required in everyday life and reduce the social space effectively available to that person. An individual who is ill, for example, loses days at work and may be forced into early retirement. A large proportion of males (43 percent) who have retired prior to age 65 report that poor health was involved in some way with their decision to give up work (Palmore, 1971; Shanas, 1978). Illness

and disability also affect the capacity to play marital roles. And, since body image is an important aspect of self-concept, and social involvement and integration contribute positively to life satisfaction, illness and disability predictably and demonstrably have a negative effect on self-esteem and on sense of well-being. From these arguments we would expect physical impairment and disability to be correlated negatively with intellectual functioning, with the correct perception of and adaptive responses to environmental stimuli, and hence with mental health. We will see subsequently that this is, in fact, the case. The reports of the surveys of the United States National Health Survey, therefore, appropriately concentrate not only on disease, impairment, and disability but also on associated limitations of activity and inability to carry out important social roles.

Since illness and impairment increase with age, so predictably does limitation of activity and disability. Table 2 indicates the extent and seriousness of limited activity associated with age. In the United States in 1968, for example, from a detailed table presented in full in the earlier edition of this volume, about one in five males aged 45–64 reported some limitation of activity. One in ten reported a restriction in amount or kind of major activity, and one in sixteen indicated an inability to carry on major activity. For males age 65 and over, over two in five reported restricted activity, and one in four indicated an inability to carry on major activities. The extent of disability experienced by nonwhite men and women was somewhat higher than that observed among whites. Comparable analyses by socioeconomic status and race are not available for 1978. Age and sex differentials in degree of limitation for 1978 presented in Table 2, however, follow a predictable pattern. Females and older adults of both sexes report relatively more restricted activity. A general increase in limitation of activity due to chronic illness from 1968 to 1978 for both sex and age categories is observed. However, a majority of persons in every category report no significant limitation of activities.

TABLE 2. Degree of Limitation of Activity Due to Chronic Conditions at Ages 45–64 and 65 and Over, by Sex: United States, 1968 and 1978.

Sex and Age	No Limitation		Total with Limitation		Limited in Major Activity[a]	
	1968	1978	1968	1978	1968	1978
	Percent of Specified Category					
Males						
45–64	79.3	75.7	20.7	24.3	17.6	19.7
65 & over	54.2	51.8	45.8	48.2	41.8	43.2
Females						
45–64	82.2	77.0	17.8	23.0	14.5	17.5
65 & over	60.1	57.3	39.9	42.7	34.3	34.9

[a] Major activity refers to ability to work, keep house.

SOURCE: National Center for Health Statistics, 1979a, 1981.

Brody (1982) commented on the rise in reports of limitation of activity: "we must temper our optimism about a prolonged healthy life in the face of these as yet uncontested data describing a rise in childhood, midlife and late life morbidity."

Illness and Functional Capacity

As we noted earlier, from the standpoint of a health professional, an individual is considered to be diseased, impaired, or ill if the signs and symptoms presented by the individual deviate significantly from prevailing professional judgments of physiological, psychological, or social normalcy. From a layman's point of view, individuals are ill if they feel ill or experience signs and symptoms usually associated with illness. In fact, there is typically substantial congruence between professional and lay views of illness (Maddox and Douglass, 1973); among older persons realistic assessments of health and illness predominate. While it is known that disease is not automatically translated into disability, the rates at which adults discount or accentuate illness are not known. Both denial of illness and hypochondriacal accentuation of illness are observed among older persons, but only limited evidence shows such discounting or accentuation to be a function of age (Haug, 1981a).

These observations are important for understanding the use of reported disability and

limitation of activity data in the United States National Health Survey home interview study. A report of illness, disability, or limitation is not to be simply equated in an epidemiological sense with underlying disease or impairment. Nonetheless, so far as social consequences are concerned, individuals are ill if they believe they are ill and behave as though they are ill.

The data in Table 3 reflect succinctly the typical and expected patterns of reported disability days in relation to age and gender. As noted in regard to limitations of activity, disability days have tended to increase over the last decade. Restricted-activity days and bed-disability days increase with age, tend to be higher for women than men, and are highest among those with the lowest socioeconomic position. Older men and women who are currently employed on the average report fewer days lost from work than younger workers, although after age 65 only a small proportion of individuals remain in the work force.

Disease and impairment clearly increase in the later years of life and, by any standard, are quite common. It is equally important to point out, however, that a very substantial majority of older individuals continue to function in a community setting. Most function reasonably well in carrying out the activities of daily living.

The pattern of disease and impairment and related limitation of activity and disability in

TABLE 3. Average Number of Disability Days per Person at Ages 45–64 and 65 and Over, by Sex: United States, 1969 and 1978.

Sex and Age	Restricted-Activity		Bed-Disability		Work-loss, Currently, Employed	
	Average number of days per person per year					
	1969	1978	1969	1978	1969	1978
Men						
45–64	19.1	23.2	7.4	7.3	6.5	6.2
65 & over	30.9	35.1	11.9	14.2	6.7	2.9
Women						
45–64	20.9	28.1	7.7	10.1	6.1	5.9
65 & over	35.5	43.9	13.7	14.8	4.0	6.5

SOURCE: National Center for Health Statistics, 1971a, 1979a.

developed countries can reasonably be presumed to be similar to that decribed in the United States. We also have direct evidence from a cross-national study of health status among older persons in the United States, Great Britain, and Denmark (Shanas et al., 1968). An index of incapacity was used in this survey to assess the ability of older individuals to be ambulatory, to negotiate stairs, and to carry out personal acts such as washing, dressing, and trimming toenails. The findings indicate comparable patterns of capacity and incapacity in the three societies. When individuals in the three societies were asked to assess their health status in terms of "good," "fair," or "poor," again comparable patterns of response were found. In the United States, 18 percent considered their health to be poor; 16 percent responded in this way in Denmark, and 14 percent in Great Britain.

In a study of the handicapped and impaired in Great Britain, Harris et al. (1971) documented the expected association between age and disability. The probability of being appreciably or severely handicapped was found to increase with age. Those 65 years of age and older comprised more than half the handicapped persons 16 years of age and over in this study. Moreover, among the very severely handicapped adults, almost six in ten were 65 or older. Similarly, in a Fininsh survey (World Health Organization,

1982b), one-third of the men and one-fifth of the women above the age of 65 considered themselves unable to do any physical work.

Aging and Psychological Impairment

Disease and disordered behavior vary in the degree to which their etiology, natural course, and a definitive therapy are known. Some disorders, particularly those that are traceable to a particular pathological agent, have clearly recognizable symptoms and a well-known natural course, and are amenable in predictable ways to prevention, amelioration, or cure. Common disorders, particularly those that involve complex malfunction of organ systems, such as disorders of the heart or lungs, tend to have multiple etiologies, variable natural courses, and less than definitive therapies. Still other human disorders appear to be quite unspecific; etitology is debatable, natural course is highly variable, and nothing approximating a definitive therapy exists. For these phenomena, such as obesity or alcoholism, there is likely to be a debate over whether "behavior disorder" is a more appropriate designation than "disease."

On a continuum of specificity/nonspecificity, mental illness (or disorder) is relatively nonspecific. Predictably, what we call nonspecific diseases or disorders present difficulties for diagnosticians as well as laypersons. Problems in classifications make it difficult for the epidemiologist to identify reliably the incidence and prevalence of various types of psychological impairments.

Riley et al. (1968, Part 3, Ch. 16) provide a useful introduction to the conventional terminology of mental health research and illustrate typical findings. The classification "psychosis" refers to impairment of mental processes and a related inability to evaluate reality in a socially tolerable way. Psychosis is usually distinguished from neurosis or psychoneurosis, which refers to an impairment of psychological functioning but without a sharp break with conventionally defined reality. Another distinction of special relevance for understanding psychological impairment in late life relates to the presumed organic or nonorganic (or functional) etiology of the impairment. Useful general introductions to mental health theory and research related to the later years are provided by Busse and Blazer (1980) and Birren and Sloane (1980).

A number of useful summaries of comparative epidemiological research on the prevalence of psychological impairment in late life exist (e.g., Lowenthal et al., 1967; Busse and Pfeiffer, 1969; Kay, 1972; Federal Council on Aging, 1981; Blazer, 1982). In spite of differences in detail, the picture that emerges from this research is quite consistent. Among persons 65 years of age and older living in a community setting, an estimated 15 to 25 percent display symptoms of significant mental illness; the lower estimate is for the relatively young older adult and the higher estimate for the oldest adults. Estimates of the prevalence of senile dementia range from 5 per 100 for all persons 65 years of age and older, to 20 per 100 for those 80 and older. Estimates of the prevalence of depressive disorders, a relatively common problem in later life, vary considerably for different categories of older adults. Evidence from population registers in Europe and community surveys in the United States, for example, indicate the prevalence of depressive disorders among older adults to be in the range of 4 to 7 percent, with a lifetime prevalence for all adults of 18 percent. Estimated prevalence of older adults receiving ambulatory care for depressive disorders tends to be in excess of 30 percent. The prevalence of depressive disorders in institutionalized populations of persons age 65 and over in the United States and Europe ranges from 50 percent to over 60 percent (Blazer, 1982). Depressive symptoms among older adults living in the community, as distinct from diagnosed depressive disorders, however, are on the order of 14 percent.

In nursing homes in the United States, a primary diagnosis of mental disorder or senility is recorded for slightly over 20 percent of residents. Chronic and significant cognitive impairment is estimated for 56 percent of residents (National Center for Health Statistics, 1979b; Federal Council on Aging, 1981).

The rate of hospitalization for mental disorders increases with age. Older persons account for about one-fourth of the new admissions to state mental hospitals and constitute a high proportion of the long-term residents in such institutions (Kramer et al., 1973; Munnichs, 1973). Attempts to reduce long-term hospitalization in the United States have resulted in a decrease in the number of older residents in mental hospitals. But as the populations of mental institutions have decreased, there has been an increase both in the number of older persons treated for psychiatric disorders in general hospitals and the mentally ill elderly residents in nursing homes (Kramer et al., 1973).

The association between physical illness and mental disorder is especially marked among older persons. Of a sample of older persons in the San Francisco Geriatric Screening Clinic, 87 percent were reported to be in need of full-time psychiatric care at the time they were seen; and 42 percent were found to be seriously impaired physically. The seriousness of the physical impairments exhibited is indicated by a very high death rate following institutionalization. Twenty-five percent of the institutionalized older persons in the San Francisco study died within one year, and 44 percent within two years (Simon et al., 1970).

In the absence of appropriate longitudinal data, the association between age and functional mental disorders remains somewhat ambiguous. It is possible that the relationship is curvilinear, with the highest rates appearing in the middle adult years and lower rates in late life. However, the association between aging and organic brain diseases is quite clear.

Kay (1972) reviewed the evidence on aging and organic brain disease and concluded that, of all mental and physical handicaps of the old, chronic organic brain disease is the most disabling and the most costly. Acute or subacute forms of this problem, which is characterized by a clouding of consciousness and confusion or delirium, have multiple causes and are potentially reversible. Chronic forms of the problem, however, usually reflect widespread organic damage and are both degenerative and progressive. A high proportion of first admissions to state and county mental hospitals in the United States were diagnosed as presenting chronic brain syndrome, according to Kay: for first admissions aged 65–74, about 75 percent presented this problem; for those 75 and older, 90 percent. Kay noted a similar trend in Great Britain. In many parts of the world an estimated 4 to 6 percent of all persons 65 years of age and older have chronic brain disease, and a larger proportion experience acute confusional states at one time or the other. Studies in Japan, England, and Denmark indicate that at age 65 about 2 percent of all individuals manifest chronic brain disease; at age 70, 4 percent; and at age 80, 20 percent.

Current interest in chronic dementing illness among older persons focuses on Senile Dementia of the Alzheimer's Type (SDAT). Alzheimer's disease, which is estimated to account for 50 to 60 percent of all dementing illness in the later years, is a progressive, currently irreversible brain disorder with unknown etiology. In SDAT the nerve endings of the brain deteriorate, interrupting electrochemical signals between cells. Symptoms of the disease include severe short-term memory loss, lack of judgment, progressive confusion, and mood and behavior changes. The disease both disturbs and places heavy demands on families and health personnel who care for SDAT patients at home or in institutions (U.S. Department of Health and Human Services, 1981b; Warshaw, 1982).

THE ORGANIZATION OF HEALTH CARE AND ITS UTILIZATION BY OLDER PERSONS

Sites of Health Care Facilities

Health care for older persons may be delivered to them as outpatients or as inpatients. Outpatient care may be given in a doctor's office or clinic, as day care in adult day care centers or day hospitals, or in the old person's home. Inpatient care is given in a hospital or a nursing home. Long-term care is provided within special hospital units, within nursing homes, or in other residential institutions, or it may be provided to the older person while he or she remains at home. Different countries place differing emphases on the site of health care for the elderly, taking into account their allocation and organization of available resources for the delivery of health services (Kozak, 1980; Kane and Kane, 1976).

Outpatient/Home Care. The decade of the seventies saw an expansion in the United States of the types of ambulatory care facilities available to the elderly. Adult day care centers and day hospital programs were developed as supplementary services to traditional home nursing care. At the same time, there was an increase in the use of hospital outpatient clinics and emergency rooms by the elderly, and a decline in the average number of visits made to doctors' offices. For example, in 1974, for every 100 noninstitutionalized persons age 65 and over, 509 visits were made to doctors' offices and 59 visits to hospital outpatient departments. By 1979, visits to doctors' offices had declined to 459 for every 100 persons, and those to hospital outpatient facilities had risen to 71 for every 100 persons (U.S. Department of Health and Human Services, 1981a). Four of every ten visits to doctors' offices by old people involved 10 minutes or less of direct face-to-face contact with a physician; in seven of every ten visits the doctor scheduled a future return visit; and in three of every ten visits the doctor felt that the principal problem presented by the elderly patient was not serious (U.S. Department of Health and Human Services, 1980).

An emphasis on home care for the elderly was a dominant theme of the 1970s. A World Health Organization (1980) report included this pertinent comment: "While governments, professionals and pressure groups (for a variety of good and bad reasons) have newly discovered the concepts of self-care and family care, old people have continued doggedly to care for themselves within their familiar environments." Similarly, it has been pointed out that in the United States only the emphasis on home care is new, since care at home is the traditional form of care for most persons (Warhola, 1980).

Both family members and professionals may provide home health care. Home health services include an array of services: skilled nursing and home health aide care; occupational and physical therapy; and even podiatry and home dental care, in addition to physician visits. Trager, in a report prepared for the United States Senate Special Committee on Aging (1972), described three types of home health services: *concentrated* or intensive service, *intermediate* service, and *basic* service. Concentrated services are needed for patients who otherwise would require admission to institutions. Such service could include frequent physician visits, daily nursing visits, physical and occupational therapy, social services, the provision of special equipment such as a hospital bed, and the services of a homemaker–home health aide. The designation intermediate implies a lesser number of home health services. This range of service is most often applicable to those persons who are temporarily disabled. Basic home health service is the least elaborate and refers to medical supervision, home nursing visits, and perhaps the services of a homemaker or home health aide. Although this basic package of services is described as simple, the organization and delivery of such services is still very complex and involves the integration and cooperation of a variety of health professionals, as well as policymakers and planners.

In the United States, the passage of Medicare in 1965 greatly influenced the development of home health services. Between 1966 and 1979 the number of agencies certified to deliver such services and to receive Medicare reimbursement increased from 1275 to nearly 2800. In the fiscal year 1977 home health services were used by 530,000 Medicare beneficiaries, most of whom were elderly, and by 208,000 low income persons qualified for Medicaid, many of whom were elderly. In addition, services were provided to the elderly and disabled at home under Title XX of the Social Security Act, which allows each state to offer eligible populations a variety of social services including home health aides, aides to assist with personal care and home chores (Warhola, 1980).

A 1966–68 survey by the National Center for Health Statistics (1971a) (U.S. Department of Health, Education and Welfare, Monthly Vital Statistics Report) estimated that about 499,000 persons aged 65–74 and 886,000 persons age 75 and over received some type of health care at home. About 30 percent of the younger group and 24 percent of the older group received medical care, such as changing bandages, receiving injections, and related treatments. Four of every five persons, however, had personal care, ranging from having meals served in bed to help with bathing. Most of this home care was given by family household members. About 7 percent received care from a registered nurse, and about 34 percent had care provided by other sources.

Shanas (1978) reported data from a national survey indicating that about 3 percent of the noninstitutionalized elderly were bedfast at home. Two of every three among the bedfast neither were visited regularly by a doctor nor had a regular doctor they could call on. Only about one in five was regularly visited by a nurse.

Day care as a mode of ambulatory care for the elderly encompasses both day hospitals that provide therapy and the usual hospital services by day but do not provide custodial services at night, and day centers that usually provide some health services together with various social services (Lorenze et al., 1974). Weissert (1976, 1978) divides geriatric day centers into two models: the day hospital model and the day center multipurpose model. Weissert and his associates (Weissert et al., 1980a,b; Wan et al., 1980) have further analyzed whether day care and/or homemaker services can delay or retard institutionalization. The effect of day care on institutionalization of infirm program participants was described by them as "inconclusive," and their findings suggested that day care may not be cheaper than nursing home care, since most of the participants used the services as an "add-on" to existing health care services (Weissert et al., 1980a). The findings in four cities indicated that day care that serves infirm patients with health as well as social services may have prolonged life for some patients, but the diagnostic condition of the old person rather than the treatment explained most of the differences between the experimental and control groups in their research.

In contrast to the United States, Great Britain has an organized home health service that includes—in addition to physician visits—health visitors, nursing care, chiropody, homemakers, home-delivered meals, and social services. There are wide variations from area to area in the provision of these services, however, because of differences in the allocation of funds, difficulties in recruiting staff, and the differing criteria adopted by local bodies in assessing an elderly person's need for help (Wroe, 1973; Kane and Kane, 1976; Pinker, 1980; Davis and Challis, 1980; Godlove and Mann, 1980). Sweden and other Scandinavian countries have made an effort to maintain the elderly in their own homes, but again the provision of services varies from one municipality to another (Kane and Kane, 1976).

It is argued, in the United States and other countries, that ambulatory or outpatient care in combination with home health care can keep some older people in their own homes and out of institutions. But ambulatory care assumes that the services of a physician will be available, whether that physician be an individual practitioner, a member of the staff of a neighborhood health center or family care center, or a representative of a hospital outpatient department. Ambulatory care as an alternative to institutional care also assumes that transportation is available to bring the patient from his home to the health center or hospital and back again when required. Most important of all, ambulatory care means either that the old person can manage by himself with such care, or that someone is available to look after him. This emphasis on avoiding institutionalization and on keeping frail and sick people in the community assumes, often inappropriately (as Maddox, 1975, has noted), the availability of a family unit that can be mobilized in the care of the old person (*The Gerontologist,* 1980).

Inpatient Care. Inpatient care is available to older persons in short-stay and long-stay hospitals and in nursing homes. In the United States, the proportion of older persons using hospitals has risen steadily since the introduction of Medicare. The rise in discharge rates from short-stay hospitals is particularly impressive, from 264 per 1000 noninstitutionalized elderly peesons in 1965, to 381 per 1000 elderly persons in 1978 (Kovar, 1977; U.S. Department of Health and Human Services, 1980). The average length of stay in short-term hospitals decreased, however, from 11.9 days in 1968 to 8.8 days in 1978. Forty percent of the elderly had stays in short-term hospitals of one week or less in 1968, compared to 49 percent in 1978 (Kopstein, 1980).

Chronic disease hospitals, Veterans

Administration hospitals, state and county mental hospitals, private hospitals, and nursing homes all provide long-term inpatient care to the elderly. A comprehensive survey of nursing homes in the United States was conducted by the National Center for Health Statistics (Van Nostrand et al., 1979). All types of nursing homes were included in the survey, irrespective of the amount of service they gave and whether or not they participated in the Medicare or Medicaid programs. The survey identified 18,900 nursing homes, containing 1,402,400 beds and 1,303,100 residents. About 5 percent of the population age 65 and over, 10 percent of the population 75 and over, and 22 percent of the population 85 and over were residents of nursing homes for at least a single night during the data collection period, May through December 1977. Three-fourths of these residents were women.

The turnover of patients in nursing homes is substantial. In 1977 nursing homes admitted 1,367,400 persons. Discharges in 1976 totaled 1,117,500 persons, of whom about eight of every ten were live discharges (persons discharged either to go into institutional settings, such as hospitals or homes for the aged, or to return to their own homes). Since sick people may move back and forth between the hospital and the nursing home, admission figures for both hospitals and nursing homes tend to overstate the actual number of individuals who use such facilities. The National Health Survey, using survey data, estimated that about one-fifth of all older persons in short-stay hospitals in 1976–77 had more than one hospital episode that year (U.S. Department of Health, Education and Welfare, 1979).

Goldfarb's (1969) studies of the elderly in New York demonstrated that many sick old people are living in homes for the "well" aged. The population using nursing homes and long-stay hospitals and those using other kinds of institutions may be quite similar. The decision to place an older person in a nursing home, a long-stay hospital, or in another kind of congregate housing setting primarily reflects medical custom, the availability of facilities, and the ability to pay for services rather than any careful decision on the part of the old person, his family, and his attending physician. The decision tends to be not whether to institutionalize but where to institutionalize.

The Role of the Family in Health Care

Recent research interest in the family and family responsibility for the aged sick in part represents an emotional reaction to long-term institutional care and a search for other care options. It also represents an effort to develop possibly cheaper alternatives to costly institutional care (Maddox, 1975). The family is still the major caretaker for the sick old person. The average individual to whom an older person would turn in a health crisis is a middle-aged woman (Shanas, 1962). Brody (1981) has called these resource persons "women in the middle." In a 1975 national study the main source of help for bedfast persons living at home was found to be the husband or wife of the invalid. Adult children, usually women, either in the same household or outside the household, were the next most important source of help. Men, who were more likely to be married, were taken care of by their wives; women, who were more likely to be widowed, were taken care of by their children (Shanas, 1979). Similar findings have been reported by other American investigators (Comptroller General of the United States, 1977; Brody, 1977; Brody et al., 1978; Laurie, 1978; Johnson and Catalano, 1981).

A World Health Organization Expert Group (1980) reported comparable findings from all parts of Europe: "the major, the most immediate and continuous support of the elderly comes from their relatives. . . . they also give personal bodily care not readily available from friends and neighbors and, through their mere existence, a sense of personal psychological security." (See also Piotrowski, 1968; Nathan, 1970; Nedeljkovic, 1970.)

Old people in institutions are far more likely than the community elderly to have never married, or if once married, to be widowed. These persons without close family are more likely to be institutionalized when they are ill. Wan and Weissert (1981), in a one-year panel study at six sites in the United States, found that married persons, as might be expected, had more sources for social supports than unmarried persons and that those persons who lived alone were the least likely to have social support networks. In their summary of findings they state, "Institutionalization, as measured by the length of stay in a skilled nursing facility and by the length of hospitalization in a short-term stay hospital, was found to have a strong relationship to 'living alone'." (See also Townsend, 1965.)

The National Nursing Home Survey (Van Nostrand et al., 1979) indicated that families continue to provide care for their elderly members even after institutional placement. One-third of all persons discharged alive from nursing homes in 1976 returned to a private or semiprivate residence.

Despite the findings from national studies that when an older person with children is in poor health, he will live with or close to the children so that they can take care of him (Shanas, 1962; Shanas et al., 1968; Shanas and Hauser, 1974; Snider, 1981b; Treas, 1977), the increasing proportion of women in the labor force, the decline in family size, and increased urbanization all indicate sources of continuing strain in efforts to maintain the family as caretaker for the sick aged (Sussman et al., 1979). Kramer (1969) suggested that the proportion of men and women who are single, widowed, and divorced may be a more important factor affecting future demand for health care than changes in the age structure of the population. A somewhat similar position was taken by a World Health Organization Expert Group (1972) dealing with mental illness: "sociological studies of various types of family structure and kinship and their association with the emotional well-being of the elderly, might prove more useful than the traditional studies of social class, economic status, and isolation as assessed by the usual criteria."

In any decision concerning the assumption of care for their aged parents, children of aged parents have to consider the welfare of their own families. They have to evaluate the sacrifices and stress that their own children might experience with a sick old person in the home. The childless relatives of many older people would also be faced with difficulties if they were called upon for help. Many of them are age contemporaries of the old person. Their incomes are equally limited; their health may be equally precarious. The capabilities of families to cope with impaired and disabled members are very limited, and the real costs to family caretakers in terms of physical and psychic stress have yet to be determined (Maddox, 1975).

SOME KEY RESEARCH ISSUES

In the past decade, increasing worldwide attention has been given to the health characteristics of older adults. There has been an expansion of data collection relevant to the older population, a development of more sophisticated methods of data analysis, a consideration of differences and similarities among subgroups of the aged, and efforts to reduce mortality and to improve the quality of life in old age. These activities have involved scientists and clinicians from a variety of disciplines (see, e.g., National Academy of Sciences, 1978). In this chapter we focus primarily on behavioral and social scientific research, providing illustrations of research on important issues rather than exhaustive summaries of published work. Convenient overviews may be found in Hickey (1980), Haynes and Feinleib (1980), and Somers and Fabian (1981). (See also National Center for Health Statistics, 1980a,b.)

In the United States a number of government agencies have instituted systematic, large-scale, continuing studies that provide not only current estimates of longevity, disease, impairment, disability, care utilization, and related cost, but also provide estimates of trends in key indicators over time. Similar sources of data are available in most Western nations and are supplemented by publications of the United Nations and the World Health Organization, both of which have shown increasing interest in population aging. Cumulatively, such information provides the basis of some important generalizations. For instance, average expected longevity is increasing worldwide. Already half of the world's older adults are in developing countries (Myers, 1982). Comparative research indicates that, while the total health care costs are high and increasing in all Western nations and the patterns of disease are similar, how geriatric health care is organized and used is quite different, as reflected in the utilization of physicians, hospitals, and community care (Maddox, 1982).

Given increased concern about the growing cost of health care and about the lack of essential information about efficient and effective strategies for controlling cost without compromising quality of care and access to care, one might expect to find a substantial and increasing investment in health research. In the United States this expectation is partially realized. Between 1965 and 1979, expenditures for health research increased from $1.4 to $4.6 billion, reflecting an average annual growth rate of 8.6 percent. In real dollars, however, per capita expenditures for health research increased annually on average by only 1.3 percent in contrast to a real per capita gross national product increase of 2.3. Most of the support (85 percent) for health research was from the federal government.

Differences in Health Characteristics and Behavior

Progressively, all research on health and health care is stressing the differentiation in the health characteristics and behavior of older adults. References to "the elderly" are increasingly replaced by references differ-entiating older adults by age, as 65–74, or 75–84, or 85 and older, and frequently further differentiating them by sex, education, economic status and ethnicity (Federal Council on Aging, 1981). Whatever the indicator being used (morbidity, disability, functional limitations, care utilization, mortality), these indicators are substantially different for various categories of older adults.

Multivariate analysis techniques and attention to the interaction of individuals with changing social environments at different periods of time will increasingly assist in differentiating aging effects from cohort and situation effects in explaining the various responses of older adults to disease and impairment (see, e.g., Kohn and White, 1976; Snider, 1980; Ferraro, 1980; Minkler, 1981; Fenwick and Barresi, 1981). Manton (1980) has applied multivariate analysis techniques to clarify a puzzling observation about the age-specific mortality and survival rates of whites and blacks in the United States. At younger ages, blacks have higher mortality rates and fewer expected remaining years of life than whites. Just the reverse is true at later ages. Manton concludes that the observed age-related differentials in survival to age 65 reflect better medical treatment and management of chronic disease experienced by whites compared with blacks. Blacks who survive to age 65, on the other hand, appear to be a select category of individuals who have a proportionately lower prevalence of chronic disease at advanced ages. In any case, from age 65 onward older blacks and older whites have increasingly similar life expectations, with very old blacks, in fact, having favorable life expectancy.

The relationship between gender and health in later life also illustrates the importance of differentiation of the health characteristics of older adults. Two apparent observations about gender and health are well established. First, females have a substantial, continuing advantage in longevity, in both life expectancy at birth and age-specific remaining years of life. Second, indicators of health care utilization are consistently higher for females. This apparent contradiction underlies the conclusion that "women get sick but men die." The explanation of these observations has produced continuing controversy. A multivariate analysis by Gove and Hughes (1979) suggests a possible resolution. They conclude that all research on gender differences indicates that the rates of poorer health for women are predominantly in milder forms of disease. The higher rates of complaints about illness and the use of care resources, therefore, reflect the fact that women have more occasions to complain and seek help. (See also Fillenbaum, 1979; Haug, 1981a; Haug and Lavin, 1981; Kessler and McRae, 1981).

The necessity and usefulness of differentiating the health characteristics, experience, and behavior of older adults is reflected in a new perspective on the factors that explain health over the life course. There is a differential risk of morbidity and mortality over the entire life cycle, and this differential for many years has been related not only to age, gender, and ethnicity, but also to socioeconomic status (Kitagawa and Hauser, 1973; see also Kulka and Douvan, 1979; Rundall and Wheeler, 1979; Mahler, 1980; Snider, 1980). But even when these factors are accounted for, individual differences in morbidity and mortality rates exist.

The Concept of Risk Factors

The concept of risk factors has added a new dimension to the discussion of differences in health. Stimulated by research on cardiovascular disease (see Kannel and Gordon, 1980), risk factor analysts moved beyond assessment of possible genetic differences and differences in health care to differences in behavior and life-style such as diet, weight, smoking, drinking, and stress management. In contrast to genetic factors, behavior and life-style factors appear to be amenable to modification in a favorable direction throughout the life cycle. A dramatic statement of the new perspective was presented in the Surgeon General's (United States) (1979) report on health promotion and dis-

ease prevention; for a similar observation from Canada, see LaLonde (1974). Both reports concluded that the variance in each nation's observed morbidity was attributable substantially (as much as 50 percent) to modifiable behavior and life-style factors.

Systematic demonstration of the potential and limitations of beneficial behavior and life-style modification in later life is not yet available. However, this new perspective that stresses the possibility of modification has generated considerable interest, specifically among investigators in aging (see, e.g., Fries, 1981; Fries and Crapo, 1981). The optimistic conclusion of Fries that morbidity can be compressed into fewer years prior to death and the disabling effects of morbidity reduced has not been convincingly demonstrated and is controversial (Manton, 1982). For example, recent analyses indicate that declines in cardiovascular and cerebrovascular mortality for females since 1945 and for males since the early 1960s are apparently independent of modern medication or the emphasis on better health habits (Brody, 1982). But the idea of beneficial modifications of behavior and life-style has obviously generated a new interest in experiments designed to test its validity. Further, documentation of current preventive health behavior among older adults is beginning to appear (National Center for Health Statistics, 1980c; Rundall and Wheeler, 1979).

Long-Term Care

Another contemporary health and health care issue of considerable importance is the organization and role of long-term care for the elderly. The increased public visibility of this issue has been prompted by the demonstrably high cost of institutionalization and by evidence that a substantial proportion of older persons is inappropriately and ineffectively institutionalized (Maddox, 1977, 1980, 1981a; Congressional Budget Office, 1977; Kane and Kane, 1978; Health Care Financing Administration, 1981). These factors have stimulated a search for "alternatives to institutionalization" and hope that, among these alternatives, long-term care can be based in the community, preferably in the home (Fox and Clauser, 1980; Health Care Financing Administration, 1981).

Conceptualization of problems in the area of long-term care has remained imprecise, and there is a lack of definitive information. The current debate on returning institutionalized older adults to the community often misses the point that most of the care of impaired and disabled older adults has remained in the community. There is no question, however, that public policy in the United States (e.g., Medicare) generated a flourishing nursing home industry increasingly dependent on public funds (National Center for Health Statistics, 1979b). Further, public funding was so designed that it ensured that compensatory care financed by public programs would have an institutional rather than a community emphasis. Medicare funds, for example, restrict the use of community and home care. In 1977, less than 2 percent of Medicare funds was spent on noninstitutional services.

Advocates of more community care for older adults have argued that such care is preferred by older persons (it is), has beneficial outcomes (it probably has), and is cheaper (it is not necessarily). Responding to the challenges of providing community care depends on improved procedures for assessment of the functional capacity of older adults, identification of appropriate compensatory care, and demonstration of the efficiency and effectiveness of alternative ways of providing appropriate care (Maddox and Dellinger, 1978; Maddox, 1980). Progress is being made on the development of adequate functional assessment procedures (Kane and Kane, 1981; Kane et al., 1982) and conceptualization of units of care services to which economic cost can be assigned (Maddox, 1981b; see also Young and Fisher, 1980).

Further discussion of public policy regarding health care for older persons will concentrate increasingly on the currently fragmented, relatively uncoordinated system of care that is skewed toward medical and institutional care. If the high cost of inadequacies of health care for older persons are in fact the result of the way the health care system is organized and financed, as some observers believe (e.g., Enthoven, 1980; Luft, 1981), then social values and political preferences will be central in identifying and selecting alternative organizational and financial arrangements that promise a more satisfactory outcome.

REFERENCES

Aday, L., and Andersen, R. 1975. *Development of Indices of Access to Medical Care.* Ann Arbor, Mich.: Health Administration Press.

Aday, L. A., and Eichorn, R. 1972. *The Utilization of Health Services: Indices and Correlates, A Research Bibliography.* Washington, D.C.: The National Center for Health Services, Research and Development.

Andersen, R. 1968. *A Behavioral Model of Families' Use of Health Services.* Chicago Center for Health Administration Studies, Research Studies No. 25. Chicago: University of Chicago Press.

Andersen, R., Anderson, O. W., and Smedby, B. 1968. Perceptions of and response to symptoms of illness in Sweden and the United States: *Medical Care* 6 (Jan.-Feb.):18–30.

Andersen, R., Kravits, J., Anderson, O. W., and Daley, J. 1973. *Expenditures for Personal Health Services: National Trends and Variations, 1953–1970.* Rockville, Md.: Public Health Service.

Binstock, R. H., Chow, W. S. , and Schulz, J. H. (eds.). 1982. *International Perspectives on Aging: Population and Policy Challenges.* New York: United Nations Fund for Population Activities.

Birren, J., and Sloane, R. (eds). 1980. *Handbook of Mental Health and Aging.* Englewood Cliffs, N.J.: Prentice-Hall.

Blazer, D. G. 1982. *Depression in Late Life.* St. Louis: The C. V. Mosby Co.

Branch, L. 1980. Functional abilities of the elderly: An update on the Massachusetts health care panel study. *In* S. G. Haynes and M. Feinleib (eds.), *Epidemiology of Aging.* NIH Publication No. 80–969. Washington, D.C.: U.S. Government Printing Office.

Brody, E. M. 1977. *Long-Term Care for Older People.* New York: Human Sciences Press.

Brody, E. M. 1981. "Women in the middle" and family help to older people. *The Gerontologist* 21:471–480.

Brody, J. A. 1982. Life expectancy and the health of older persons. *J. Am. Geriat. Soc.* 30:681–683.

Brody, S. J., Poulshock, S. W., and Masciocchi, C. F. 1978. The family caring unit: A major consideration in the long-term support system. *The Gerontologist* 18:556–561.

Busse, E. W., and Blazer, D. G. (eds.). 1980. *Hand-*

book of Geriatric Psychiatry. New York: Van Nostrand Reinhold.

Busse, E. W., and Pfeiffer, E. 1969. Functional psychiatric disorders in old age. *In* E. W. Busse and E. Pfeiffer (eds.), *Behavior and Adaptation in Late Life.* Boston: Little, Brown.

Chappell, N. L. 1981. Measuring functional ability and chronic conditions among the elderly: A research note on the adequacy of three instruments. *J. of Health and Soc. Behavior* 22:90–102.

Chiang, C. L. 1965. An index of health: Mathematical models. *Vital and Health Statistics,* Series 2, No. 5 (May). Washington, D.C.: U.S. Government Printing Office.

Comptroller General of the United States. 1977. Report to the Congress: *The Well-Being of Older People in Cleveland, Ohio.* Washington, D.C.: General Accounting Office.

Congressional Budget Office, U.S. Congress. 1977. *Long Term Care for The Elderly and Disabled.* Washington, D.C.: U.S. Government Printing Office.

Cooper, B. S., and Piro, P. A. 1974. Age differences in medical care spending, fiscal year 1973. *Social Security Bulletin* 37(5) (May):3–14.

Cooper, B. S., Worthington, N., and Piro, P. A. 1974. National health expenditures, 1929–1973. *Social Security Bulletin,* 37(4) (Apr.):3–40.

Costa, T., and McCrae, R. R. 1980. Functional age. *In* S. G. Haynes and M. Feinleib (eds.), *Epidemiology of Aging.* NIH Publication No. 80–969. Washington, D.C.: U.S. Government Printing Office.

Davis, B., and Challis, D. 1980. Experimenting with new roles in the domiciliary service: The Kent community care project. *The Gerontologist* 20(3) (June), Part I:288–299.

Duke Center. 1978. *Multidimensional Functional Assessment: The OARS Methodology,* 2nd ed. Durham, N.C.: Duke University Center for the Study of Aging and Human Development.

Enthoven, A. 1980. *Health Plan.* Reading, Mass.: Addison-Wesley.

Evans, J., Hall, K., and Warford, J. 1981. Health care in the developing world: Problems of scarcity and choice. *New Engl. J. Med.* 305(19) (Nov.):1117–1127.

Fanshel, S., and Bush, J. W. A. 1970. A health status index and its application to health services outcome. *Operations Res.* 181:1021–1066.

Feder, J., and Holahan, J. 1979. *Financing Health Care for the Elderly: Medicare, Medicaid, and Private Health Insurance.* Washington, D.C.: The Urban Institute.

Federal Council on Aging. 1981. *The Need for Long Term Care: Information and Issues.* Washington, D.C.: U.S. Government Printing Office.

Fenwick, R., and Barresi, C. 1981. Health consequences of marital-status change among the elderly: A comparison of cross-sectional and longitudinal analyses. *J. Health and Soc. Behavior.* 22 (June):106–116.

Ferraro, K. R. 1980. Self-ratings of health among the old and the old-old. *J. of Health and Soc. Behavior* 21(4):377–382.

Fillenbaum, G. G. 1979. Social context and self-assessments of health among the elderly. *J. of Health and Soc. Behavior* 20(1):45–51.

Fox, P., and Clauser, S. 1980. Trends in nursing home expenditures: Implications for aging policy. *Health Care Financing Review* 2:65–70.

Freeland, M., and Schendler, C. 1981. National health expenditures: Short-term outlook and long-term projections. *Health Care Financing Review* 2(3) (Winter):97–138.

Fries, J. F. 1981. Aging, natural death, and the compression of morbidity. *In* A. Somers and D. Fabian (eds.), *The Geriatric Imperative,* pp. 105–116. New York: Appleton-Century-Crofts.

Fries, J. F., and Crapo, L. M. 1981. *Vitality and Aging.* San Francisco: W. H. Freeman and Company.

The Gerontologist. 1980. *Alternatives to Nursing Home Care for the Frail Elderly: An International Symposium* 20(3) (whole issue).

Godlove, C., and Mann, A. 1980. Thirty years of the welfare state. *Aged Care and Social Services Review* 2(1) (whole issue).

Goldfarb, A. I. 1969. Institutional care of the aged. *In* E. W. Busse and E. Pfeiffer (eds.), *Behavior and Adaptation in Late Life.* Boston: Little, Brown.

Gornick, M. 1976. Ten years of medicare: Impact on the covered population. *Social Security Bulletin* 39(7):3–21.

Gove, W., and Hughes, M. 1979. Possible causes of the apparent sex differences in physical health: An empirical investigation. *Am. Soc. Rev.* 44 (Feb.):126–146.

Grad, J. C., and Sainsbury, P. 1968. The effects that patients have on their families in a community care and a control psychiatric sample, a two year follow-up. *British Journal of Psychiatry* 114:265–278.

Haber, L. D. 1967. Identifying the disabled: Concepts and methods in the measurement of disability. *Social Security Bulletin* 30(12) (Dec.):17–35.

Haber, L. D. 1979. *Epidemiological Factors in Disability: I. Major Disabling Conditions.* Social Security Survey of the Disabled, Report No. 6 (Feb.). Social Security Administration.

Haber, L. D. 1970. *The Epidemiology of Disability: II. The Measurement of Functional Capacity Limitations.* Social Security Survey of the Disabled, Report No. 10 (July). Social Security Administration.

Harris, A. I., assisted by Clausen, R. 1968. *Social Welfare for the Elderly, 1 and 2.* Government Social Survey. London: Her Majesty's Stationery Office.

Harris, A. I., with Cox, E., and Smith C. R. W. 1971. *Handicapped and Impaired in Great Britain, Part I.* Social Survey Division, Office of Population Censuses and Surveys. London: Her Majesty's Stationery Office.

Haug, M. R. 1981a. Age and medical care utilization patterns. *J. Geront.* 36(1):103–111.

Haug, M. R. 1981b. *Elderly Patients and Their Doctors*. New York: Springer Publishing Co.

Haug, M., and Lavin, B. 1981. Practitioners or patient: Who's in charge? *J. of Health and Soc. Behavior* 22: (Sept.):12–29.

Haynes, S. G., and Feinleib, M. (eds.). 1980. *Epidemiology of Aging*. NIH Publication No. 80–969. Washington, D.C.: U.S. Government Printing Office.

Health Care Financing Administration. 1981. *Long Term Care: Background and Future Direction*. Washington, D.C.: Department of Health and Human Services.

Hickey, T. 1980. *Health and Aging*. Belmont, Calif.: Wadsworth.

Hing, E., and Cypress, B. K. 1981. Use of health services by women 65 years and over. *Vital and Health Statistics,* Series 13, No. 59. Washington, D.C.: U.S. Goverment Printing Office.

Johnson, C. L., and Catalano, D. J. 1981. Childless elderly and their family supports. *The Gerontologist* 21(6):610–618.

Kane, R. L., and Kane, R. A. 1976. *Long-term Care in Six Countries: Implications for the United States*. DHEW Publication No. (NIH) 76–1207. Washington, D.C.: U.S. Government Printing Office.

Kane R. L., and Kane, R. A. 1978. Care of the aged: Old problems in need of new solutions. *Science* 200(4344):913–918.

Kane, R. L., and Kane, R. A. 1981. *Assessing the Elderly: A Practical Guide to Measurement*. Lexington, Mass.: Lexington Books.

Kane, R., Riegler, S., Bell, R, Potter, R., adn Koshland, G. 1982. *Predicting the Course of Nursing Home Patients: A Progress Report*. Santa Monica, Calif.: Rand.

Kannel, W. B., and Gordon, T. 1980. Cardiovascular risk factors in the aged: The Framingham Study. *In* S. G. Haynes and M. Feinleib (eds.), *Epidemiology of Aging*. NIH Publication No. 80–969. Washington, D.C.: U.S. Government Printing Office.

Kart, C. 1981. Experiencing symptoms: Attribution and misattribution of illness among the aged. *In* M. R. Haug (ed.), *Elderly Patients and Their Doctors*. New York: Springer Publishing Co.

Kasl, S. B., and Cobb, S. J. 1966. Health behavior and sick-role behavior. *Arch. Environ. Health* 12 (Feb.):246–266.

Kasl, S. B., Ostfeld, A. M., Brody, G. M., Snell, L., and Price, C. A. 1980. Effects of "involuntary" relocation on the health and behavior of the elderly. *In* S. G. Haynes and M. Feinleib (eds.), *Epidemiology of Aging*. NIH Publication No. 80–969. Washington, D.C.: U.S. Government Printing Office.

Katz, S., Downs, T. D., Cash, H. R., and Grotz, R. C. 1970. Progress in development of the index of ADL. *The Gerontologist* 10 (Spring), Part I:20–30.

Kay, D. W. K. 1972. Epidemiological aspects of organic brain disease in the aged. *In* C. M. Gaitz (ed.), *Aging and the Brain*. New York: Plenum.

Kessler, R., and McRae, J. A. 1981. Trends in the relationship between sex and psychological distress: 1957–1976. *Am. Soc. Rev.* 46 (Aug.):443–452.

Kitagawa, E. M., and Hauser, P. 1973. *Differential Mortality in the United States*. Cambridge, Mass.: Harvard University Press.

Kohn, R., and White, K. (eds.). 1976. *Health Care: An International Study*. London: Oxford University Press.

Kopstein, A. 1980. Length of hospital stays. *In* Department of Health and Human Services, *Health United States 1980*. DHHS Publication No. (PHS) 81–1232. Washington, D.C.: U.S. Government Printing Office.

Kovar, M. G. 1977. Elderly people: The population 65 years and over. *In* Department of Health, Education and Welfare, *Health United States 1976–1977*. DHEW Publication No. (HRA) 77–1232. Washington, D.C.: U.S. Government Printing Office.

Kozak, L. J. 1980. International utilization of hospital services. *In* Department of Health and Human Services, *Health United States 1980*. DHHS Publication No. 81–1232. Washington, D.C.: U.S. Government Printing Office.

Kramer, M. 1969. Statistics of mental disorders in the United States, some urgent needs and suggested solutions. *Journal of the Royal Statistical Society* 132:353–407.

Kramer, M., Taube, C., and Redick, R. 1973. Patterns of use of psychiatric facilities by the aged: Past, present and future. *In* C. Eisdorfer and P. Lawton (eds.), *The Psychology of Adult Development and Aging*. Washington, D.C.: American Psychological Association.

Kulka, R., and Douvan, E. 1979. Social class and the use of professional help for personal problems: 1957 and 1976. *J. of Health and Soc. Behavior* 20 (Mar.):2–17.

LaLonde, M. 1974. *A New Perspective on the Health of Canadians*. Ottawa: Department of National Health and Welfare.

LaRue, A., Bank, L., Jarvik, L., and Hetland, M. 1979. Health in old age: How do physicians' ratings and self-ratings compare? *J. Geront.* 34(5):687–691.

Lasagna, L. 1969. Aging and the field of medicine. *In* M. W. Riley, J. W. Riley, Jr., and M. E. Johnson (eds.), *Aging and Society*, Vol. 2, *Aging and the Professions*. New York: Russell Sage Foundation.

Laurie, W. F. 1978. Employing the Duke OARS Methodology in cost comparisons: Home services and institutionalization. *Center Reports on Advances in Research,* 2. Durham, N.C.: Duke University Center for the Study of Aging and Human Development.

Lawton, M. P. 1971. The functional assessment of elderly people. *J. Am. Geriat. Soc.* 19:465–481.

Logan, R. F. L. 1966. The burden of the aged in society and on medical care. *In* J. N. Agate (ed.), *Medicine in Old Age*. London: Pittman Medical.

Lorenze, E. J., Hamill, C. M., and Oliver, R. C. 1974. The day hospital: An alternative to institutional care. *J. Am. Geriat. Soc.* 22:316–320.

Lowenthal, M. F., Berkman, P. L., and associates.

1967. *Aging and Mental Disorder in San Francisco: A Social Psychiatric Study.* San Francisco: Jossey-Bass.

Luft, H. 1981. *Health Maintenance Organizations: Dimensions of Performance.* New York: Wiley.

Maddox, G. L. 1964. Self assessment of health status: A longitudinal study of selected elderly subjects. *J. Chronic Diseases* 17:449–460.

Maddox, G. L. 1972. Social determinants of behavior. *In* F. Hine, E. Pfeiffer, G. L. Maddox, and P. Hein (eds.), *Behavioral Science: A Selective View.* Boston: Little, Brown.

Maddox, G. L. 1975. The patient and his family. *In* Sylvia Sherwood (ed.), *Long-Term Care.* New York: Spectrum Publications.

Maddox, G. L. 1977. The unrealized potential of an old idea. *In* A. N. Exton-Smith and J. Grimley Evans (eds.), *Care of the Elderly: Meeting the Challenge of Dependency.* London: Academic Press.

Maddox, G. L. 1980. The continuum of care: Movement toward the community. *In* E. W. Busse and D. G. Blazer (eds.), *Handbook of Geriatric Psychiatry.* New York: Van Nostrand Reinhold.

Maddox, G. L. 1981a. Assessing the functional status of older patients: Its significance for therapeutic management. *In* M. R. Haug (ed.), *Elderly Patients and Their Doctors.* New York: Springer Publishing Co.

Maddox, G. L. 1981b. Measuring the well-being of older adults: Conceptualization and applications. *In* A. Somers and D. Fabian (eds.), *The Geriatric Imperative.* New York: Appleton-Century-Crofts.

Maddox, G. L. 1982. Challenge for health policy and planning. *In* R. H. Binstock, W. S. Chow and J. H. Schulz (eds.), *International Perspectives on Aging: Population and Policy Challenges.* New York: United Nations Fund for Population Activities.

Maddox, G. L. and Dellinger, D. C. 1978. Assessment of functional status in a program evaluation and resource allocation model. *Annals of the Am. Acad. of Pol. and Soc. Sc.* 438:59–70.

Maddox, G. L., and Douglass, E. B. 1973. Self-assessment of health. A longitudinal study of elderly subjects. *J. of Health and Soc. Behavior* 14:87–93.

Mahler, H. 1980. People. *Scientific American* 243(3):67–77.

Manton, K. 1980. Sex and race specific mortality differentials in multiple cause of death data. *The Gerontologist* 20(4):480–492.

Manton, K. 1982. Changing concepts of morbidity and mortality in the elderly population. *Milbank Memorial Fund Quarterly, Health and Society* 60:183–244.

McKeown, T., and Cross, K. 1969. Responsibilities of hospital and local authorities for elderly patients. *Brit. J. Prevent. and Social Med.* 23:34–39.

Mechanic, D. 1979. Correlates of physician utilization: Why do major multivariate studies of physician utilization find trivial psychosocial and organizational effects? *J. of Health and Soc. Behavior,* 20(4):387–396.

Metropolitan Life Insurance Company. 1980. Expec-

tation of Life in the United States at new high. *Statistical Bulletin* 61(4) (Oct.–Dec.):13–15.

Metropolitan Life Insurance Company. 1981. Decline in life expectancy. *Statistical Bulletin* 62(2) (Apr.–June):14–15.

Minkler, M. 1981. Research on the health effects of retirement: An uncertain legacy. *J. Health and Soc. Behavior* 22 (June):117–130.

Moriyamo, I. M. 1968. Problems in the measurement of health status. *In* E. B. Sheldon and W. E. Moore (eds.), *Indicators of Social Change.* New York: Russell Sage Foundation.

Munnichs, J. M. A. 1973. Linkages of older people with their families and bureaucracy in a welfare state, the Netherlands. Paper prepared for a Conference on Family, Elderly and Bureaucracy, Quail Roost, N.C. (May).

Myers, G. C. 1978. Cross-national trends in mortality rates among the elderly. *The Gerontologist* 18(5):441–448.

Myers, G. C. 1982. The aging of populations. *In* R. H. Binstock, W. S. Chow, and J. H. Schulz (eds.), *International Perspectives on Aging: Population and Policy Challenges.* New York: United Nations Fund for Population Activities.

Nathan, T. 1970. Health needs and health services. *In* United Nations, *Symposium on Research and Welfare Policies for the Elderly.* New York: United Nations.

National Academy of Sciences. 1978. *Aging and Medical Education.* Report of a study by a committee of the Institute of Medicine. Washington, D.C.: National Academy of Sciences.

National Center for Health Statistics. 1965. *Vital and Health Statistics Programs and Collection: Procedures,* Vol. 1, No. 1. Washington, D.C.: U.S. Government Printing Office.

National Center for Health Statistics. 1971a. Current estimates from the health interview survey, U.S.—1969. *Vital and Health Statistics,* Series 10, No. 63. Washington, D.C.: U.S. Government Printing Office.

National Center for Health Statistics. 1971b. *Health in the Late Years of Life: Data From the National Center for Health Statistics.* Washington, D.C.: U.S. Government Printing Office.

National Center for Health Statistics. 1973. *Current Listing and Topical Index to the Vital and Health Statistics Series, 1962–1972.* Washington, D.C.: U.S. Government Printing Office.

National Center for Health Statistics. 1979a. Current estimates from the health interview survey: U.S.—1978. *Vital and Health Statistics,* Series 10, No. 130. Washington, D.C.: U.S. Government Printing Office.

National Center for Health Statistics. 1979b. The National Nursing Home Survey: 1977 Summary for the United States. *Vital and Health Statistics,* Series 13, No. 43. Washington, D.C.: U.S. Government Printing Office.

National Center for Health Statistics. 1980a. Basic data

on health care needs of adults ages 25-74 years, U.S.—1971-1975. *Vital and Health Statistics,* Series 11, No. 218. Washington, D.C.: U.S. Government Printing Office.

National Center for Health Statistics. 1980b.The National Ambulatory Medical Care Survey. *Vital and Health Statistics,* Series 13, No. 44. Washington, D.C.: U.S. Government Printing Office.

National Center for Health Statistics. 1980c. Health Practices among Adults: United States, 1977. *Vital and Health Statistics, Advance Data,* 64 (Nov.).Washington, D.C.: U.S. Government Printing Office.

National Center for Health Statistics. 1981. Prevalence of selected impairments, United States, 1977. *Vital and Health Statistics,* Series 10, No. 134. Washington, D.C.: U.S. Government Printing Office.

Nedeljkovic, Y. 1970. *Old People In Yugoslavia.* Analytical tables. Belgrade: Institute of Social Policy.

Newhouse, J. P., Phelps, C., and Schwartz, W. 1974. Policy options and the impact of national health insurance. *New Engl. J. Med.* 290(24):1345-1359.

Palmore, E. 1971. Why do people retire? *Aging and Hum. Devel.* 2:269-283.

Patrick, D. L. Bush, J. W., and Chen, M. M. 1973. Toward an operational definition of health. *J. of Health and Soc. Behavior* 14(1):6-23.

Pinker, R. A. 1980. Facing up to the eighties: Health and welfare needs of British elderly. *The Gerontologist* 20 (June), Part I:273-283.

Piotrowski, J. 1968. *Report to the Social and Rehabilitation Service,* U.S. Department of Health, Education and Welfare. Warsaw.

Piotrowski, J. 1970. *Old People in Poland and their Vital Capacity.* Warsaw.

Raskin, I. E., Coffey, R. M., and Farley, P. J. 1978. Cost containment. *In* United States Department of Health, Education and Welfare, *Health United States 1978.* DHEW Publication No. (PHS) 78-1232. Washington, D.C.: U.S. Government Printing Office.

Riley, M. W., Foner, A., Moore, M. E., Hess, B., and Roth, B. K. 1968. *Aging and Society: An Inventory of Research Findings, I.* New York: Russell Sage Foundation.

Rosenstock, I. M. 1966. Why people use health services. *Milbank Memorial Fund Quarterly* 44(3), Part 2:94-124.

Rundall, T., and Wheeler, J. 1979. The effect of income on use of preventive care: An evaluation of alternative explanations. *J. Health and Soc. Behavior* 20 (Dec.):397-406.

Ruther, M. 1981. *Medicare: Health Insurance for the Aged and Disabled, 1975.* Washington, D.C.: Health Care Financing Program Statistics.

Sachuk, N. N. 1963. Some general studies of the health of the aged. *In* World Health Organization, *Seminar on the Health Protection of the Elderly and the Aged and on the Prevention of Premature Aging.* Copenhagen: World Health Organization.

Shanas, E. 1962. *The Health of Older People: A Social Survey.* Cambridge, Mass.: Harvard University Press.

Shanas E. 1971. Measuring the home health needs of the elderly in five countries. *J. Geront.* 26:37-40.

Shanas, E. 1974. Health status of older people, cross-national implications. *Am. J. Public Health* 64:261-264.

Shanas, E. 1978. National survey of the aging. A report to the Administration on Aging. Typescript.

Shanas, E. 1979. The family as a social support system in old age. *The Gerontologist* 19(2):169-174.

Shanas, E., and Hauser, P. M. 1974. Zero population growth and the family life of old people. *Journal of Social Issues* 30(4):79-92.

Shanas, E., Townsend, P., Wedderburn, D., Friis, H., Milhøj, P., and Stehouwer, J. 1978. *Old People in Three Industrial Societies.* New York: Atherton Press; London: Routledge & Kegan Paul.

Shuval, J. T., in collaboration with Antonovsky, A., and Davis, A. M. 1970. *Social Functions of Medical Practice.* San Francisco: Jossey-Bass.

Siegel, J. 1980. Recent and prospective demographic trends for the elderly population and some implications for health care. *In* S. Haynes and M. Feinleib (eds.), *Epidemiology of Aging.* NIH Publication No. 80-969. Washington, D.C.: U.S. Government Printing Office.

Siegel, J. S. 1981. Demographic background for international gerontological studies. *J. Geront.* 36(1):93-102.

Simon, A., Lowenthal, M. F., and Epstein, L. 1970. *Crisis and Intervention: The Elderly Mental Patient.* San Francisco: Jossey-Bass.

Snider, E. 1980. Factors influencing health services knowledge among the elderly. *J. Health and Soc. Behavior* 21 (Dec.): 371-377.

Snider, E. 1981a. Young-old versus old-old and the use of health services. Does the difference make a difference? *J. of the Am. Geriat. Soc.* 29(8):354-358.

Snider, E. 1981b. The role of kin in meeting the health care needs of the elderly. *Canadian Journal of Sociology* 6(3):325-336.

Soldo, B. J. 1980. American elderly in the 1980's. *Population Bulletin* 35(4)(Nov.).3-47.

Somers, A. R. 1971. The nationalization of health services: A universal priority. *Inquiry* 8(1):48-60.

Somers, A., and Fabian, D. (eds.). 1981. *The Geriatric Imperative: An Introduction to Geronotology and Clinical Geriatrics.* New York: Appleton-Century-Crofts.

Stiefel, J. B. 1967. Use and cost of AHS coordinated home care programs. *Inquiry* 4(1) (Oct.):61-68.

Sullivan, D. F. 1966. Conceptual problems in developing an index of health. *Vital and Health Statistics,* Series 2, No. 17. Washington, D.C.: U.S. Government Printing Office.

Sullivan, D. F. 1971. Disability components for an index of health. *Vital and Health Statistics,* Series 2,

No. 42. Washington, D.C.: U.S. Government Printing Office.

Surgeon General, U.S. 1979. *Healthy People: Report on Health Promotion and Disease Prevention.* Washington, D.C.: U.S. Department of Health, Education and Welfare.

Sussman, M. B., and associates. 1979. Social and economic supports and family environments for the elderly. A report to the Administration on Aging. Typescript.

Svane, O. 1972. *Vurdinger af aeldres behov for pleje og omsorg.* Copenhagen: The Danish National Institute for Social Research.

Townsend, P. 1963. Measuring incapacity for self-care. *In* R. H. Williams, C. Tibbitts, and W. Donahue (eds.), *Processes of Aging.* New York: Atherton Press.

Townsend, P. 1965. On the likelihood of admission to an institution. *In* E. Shanas and G. F. Streib (eds.), *Social Structure and the Family: Generational Relations.* Englewood Cliffs, N.J.: Prentice-Hall.

Treas, J. 1977. Family support systems for the aged: Some social and demographic considerations. *The Gerontologist* 17(6):486–491.

U.S. Bureau of the Census. 1979a. Social and economic characteristics of the older population, 1978. *Current Population Reports,* Series P-23, No. 85 (Aug.). Washington, D.C.: U.S. Government Printing Office.

U.S. Bureau of the Census. 1979b. Population of the world to the 21st century. *Current Population Reports,* Series P-23, No. 79. Washington, D.C.: U.S. Government Printing Office.

U.S. Department of Health, Education and Welfare. 1971a. Persons 55 years and over receiving care at home, July, 1966–June, 1968. *Monthly Vital Statistics Report* 19(10) (Jan.), Supplement.

U.S. Department of Health, Education and Welfare. 1971b. *Toward a Comprehensive Health Policy for the 1970's.* Washington, D.C.: U.S. Government Printing Office.

U.S. Department of Health, Education and Welfare. 1977. *A Guide to Medical Self-Care and Medical Self-Help Groups for the Elderly.* NIH Publication No. 80–1687. Washington, D.C.: U.S. Government Printing Office.

U.S. Department of Health, Education and Welfare. 1979. *Health United States 1979.* DHEW Publication No. (PHS) 80–1232. Washington, D.C.: U.S. Government Printing Office.

U.S. Department of Health and Human Services. 1980. *Health United States 1980.* DHHS Publication No. (PHS) 81–1232. Washington, D.C.: U.S. Government Printing Office.

U.S. Department of Health and Human Services. 1981a. *Health United States 1981.* DHHS Publication No. (PHS) 82–1232. Washington, D.C.: U.S. Government Printing Office.

U.S. Department of Health and Human Services. 1981b. *Progress Report on Senile Dementia of the Alz-*

heimer's Type. NIH Publication No. 81–2343. Washington, D.C.: U.S. Government Printing Office.

U.S. Senate Committee on Finance. 1970. *Medicare and Medicaid Problems, Issues, and Alternatives.* Washington, D.C.: U.S. Government Printing Office.

U.S. Senate Special Committee on Aging. 1972. *Home Health Care Services in the United States.* 92nd Congress, 2nd session. Washington, D.C.: U.S. Government Printing Office.

Van den Heuvel, W. J. A. 1974. *Older People and Their Health.* Some notes on health measurement in gerontology. Nijmegen: Gerontologisch Centrum.

Van Nostrand, J., Zappolo, A., Hing, E., Bloom, B., Hirsch, B., and Foley, D. J. 1979. *The National Nursing Home Survey: 1977 Summary for United States. Vital and Health Statistics,* Series 13-1, No. 43. U.S. Department of Health, Education and Welfare, DHEW Publication No. (PHS) 79–1794. Washington, D.C.: U.S. Government Printing Office.

Verbrugge, L. M. 1981. Women and men: Sex differences in mortality and health of older people. *In* B. B. Hess and K. Bond (eds), *Leading Edges: Recent Research on Psychological Aging.* NIH Publication No. 81–2390. Washington, D.C.: U.S. Government Printing Office.

Wan, T. H., and Weissert, W. G. 1981. Social support networks, patient status and institutionalization. *Research on Aging* 3(2):240–256.

Wan, T. H., Weissert, W. G., and Livieratos, B. 1980. Geriatric day care and homemaker services: An experimental study. *J. Geront.* 35(2) (Mar.):256–274.

Warhola, C. F. R. 1980. *Planning for Home Health Services: A Resource Handbook.* DHHS Publication No. (HRS) 80–14017. Washington, D.C.: U.S. Government Printing Office.

Warshaw, Gregg. 1982. Cognitive Impairment and its Treatment in Later Years: Delirium, Dementia and Depression. *Center Reports on Advances in Research.* Vol. 6, No. 2 (Nov.) Durham, N.C.: Duke University Center for the Study of Aging and Human Development.

Weissert, W. G. 1976. Two models of geriatric day care: Findings from a comparative study. *The Geronotologist* 16(5) (Oct.):420–427.

Weissert, W. G. 1978. Long-term care: An overview. *In* U.S. Department of Health, Education and Welfare, *Health United States 1978.* DHEW Publication No. (PHS) 78–1232. Washington, D.C.: U.S. Government Printing Office.

Weissert, W. G., Wan, T. H., Livieratos, B., and Katz, S. 1980a. Effects and costs of day-care services for the chronically ill. *Medical Care* 18(6) (June):567–584.

Weissert, W. G., Wan, T. H., Livieratos, B., and Pellegrino, J. 1980b. Cost-effectiveness of homemaker services for the chronically ill. *Inquiry* 17 (Fall):230–242.

Williams, T. F. 1978. Assessment of the geriatric patient in relation to needs for services and facilities. *In* W.

Reichel (ed.), *Clinical Aspects of Aging*. Baltimore, Md.: Williams and Wilkins.

Williams, T. F., and Williams, M. 1982. Assessment of the elderly for long term care. *J. Am. Geriat. Soc.* 30:71-75.

World Health Organization, Regional Office for Europe. 1959. *The Public Health Aspects of the Aging of the Population*. Report of an advisory group. Oslo, 28 July–2 August 1958. Copenhagen: World Health Organization.

World Health Organization. 1972. *Psychogeriatrics*. Technical Report, Series 507. Geneva: World Health Organization.

World Health Organization. 1974. *Planning and Organization of Geriatric Services*. Technical Report, Series 548. Geneva: World Health Organization.

World Health Organization, Regional Office for Europe, 1980. *Appropriate Levels for Continuing Care of the Elderly*. Report of a WHO Working Group. Berlin (West) ICP/ADR o26 4566B.

World Health Organization, Regional Office for Europe. 1982a. *Preventing Disability in the Elderly*. Report of a WHO Working Group. Cologne: EURO Reports and Studies, 62. ISBN 92 890 1231 S. Copenhagen: World Health Organization.

World Health Organization, Regional Office for Europe. 1982b. *Medical and Social Problems of the Disabled*. A report based on the technical discussion at the thirty-first session of the Regional Committee for Europe, 73. ISBN 92 890 1239 0. Copenhagen: World Health Organization.

Wroe, D. C. L. 1973. The elderly. *In* Muriel Nissel (ed.), *Social Trends,* No. 4. London: Her Majesty's Stationery Office.

Young, K., and Fisher, C. 1980. Medicare episodes of illness: A study of hospital, skilled nursing facility and home health agency care. *Health Care Fin. Rev.* 2(2) (Fall): 1–24.

Zook, C., and Moore, F. 1980. High-cost users of medical care. *New Engl. J. Med.* 302(18) (May):996–1002.

25
HEALTH CARE POLICIES AND THE AGED: OBSERVATIONS FROM THE UNITED STATES

Karen Davis*

Johns Hopkins University

A dramatic increase in the size of the aged population will occur in the United States and most other major industrialized countries over the next 50 years. This demographic change will place increasing pressure on governments to formulate public policies responsive to the demands on society generated by this shifting age composition of the population. Many countries will be forced for the first time to articulate a comprehensive public policy for the aged, encompassing income security, housing, health, and social services.

This chapter attempts to aid the process by delineating some of the major health problems of the aged in the United States and outlining major principles that should guide policy formulation for the aged. It begins with a review of the rationale for the role of public policy and the special justification for emphasis upon the aged population. An overview follows of major health problems faced by the aged and current policies dealing with them. Particular attention is given to the problems of the severely impaired elderly and their service needs. Options for future

*The author wishes to thank Diane Rowland for research assistance and Evelyn Waltz for editorial assistance.

directions are offered in accord with basic principles for shaping public policy.

Health and long-term care services for the aged in the United States are used as an illustration of the organization and delivery of such services in a developed country. Although modern societies can learn much about options for future directions from the experiences of other countries, health care policy is typically incremental in nature and builds on current programs and the historical experience of a particular country. Different countries face very different problems with regard to access, financing, and organization of health and long-term care services. What is appropriate for one society may be totally inapplicable to another. The political, social, and economic forces shaping each society will inevitably shape the response of that society to changes in the age structure. The experience of the United States in providing long-term care and health care services is presented here to show how the public policies and cultural values of the United States have influenced the development of services for the elderly, and how they guide future directions. The American approach is offered as an example of a mixed public–private approach to care of the elderly.

ROLE OF PUBLIC POLICY

In the next 50 years, the population over age 65 will increase markedly in the United States, as well as in many other developed countries. Especially rapid increases are predicted in the numbers of very old, those over 85 years of age. An increase in the number of people over age 65, and especially a major increase in the very old age groups, means more resources will be required to care for the aged.

As the aged population grows, the allocation of budgetary resources among policy priorities is likely to generate severe strains. Society must grapple with whether limited resources are to be increasingly committed to those in the twilight of life. Funding for maternal and child care or transportation or defense will be weighed against additional spending for the elderly through Social Security and pensions as well as health and long-term care programs. Resolution of these tensions will depend upon a host of political, economic, and social factors. Some insight into this conflict can be found by examining the rationale for public policy emphasis on the needs of the aged (for a discussion of alternative justifications for age-based programs, see Kutza, 1981). Although this rationale derives from the American experience, it embodies a public policy perspective shared by most capitalist countries.

Rationale for Public Policy Action

Traditional economic theory asserts that private perfectly competitive markets lead to an efficient allocation of resources. In such an economy consumers seek out and obtain that bundle of goods and services that maximizes their utility within the constraints of their income. Producers of goods and services must produce items valuable to consumers in an efficient manner. Competition for consumers leads firms to set prices at a level just adequate to cover costs including a return to capital.

In such a utopian world, the role for public policy and governmental intervention is quite limited. Government is responsible for the provision of public goods and services, such as national defense, police, and fire protection, where provision for one is provision for all. Government is also responsible for assuring that producers do not possess monopoly powers, block new firms from entering markets, collude in setting prices, or interfere with the functioning of a perfectly competitive market. In industries where only one firm can efficiently provide goods or services (e.g., utilities), government may intervene to provide or regulate the private provision of a service.

In reality, most societies do not single-mindedly desire consumption of goods and services to the detriment of all other objectives. Other goals such as sustaining a humane and just society are important. Nor are societies limited in their horizon to a single generation. Many wish to leave a rich cultural, intellectual, and social heritage, an unspoiled environment, and economic resources to future generations. Requirements for a perfectly functioning private market are rarely met in practice, and in some vital areas such as health care, imperfect information and limited competition among providers of services are the norm.

These departures from the assumptions of traditional economic theory lead to the following specific rationales for a public policy for the aged:

- To maintain minimum standards of human decency.

One of the objectives of most people is to live in a humane and just society. Such a society ensures that all of its citizens live with dignity. As stated by the late Arthur Okun: "the case for a right to survival is compelling. The assurance of dignity for every member of society requires a right to a decent existence—to some minimum standard of nutrition, health care, and other essentials of life. Starvation and dignity do not mix well" (Okun, 1975).

Since old age often brings with it the inability to continue to work and earn an income, many aged cannot maintain a minimum standard of existence without assistance. Assurance of adequate nutrition and health care is basic to human decency and therefore to public policy. None should die, or suffer desperation or avoidable pain because they cannot afford food, shelter, or health care. Opinion may vary about the boundary between dignity and luxury, but a minimum standard of living for all is essential to the preservation of social order and justice.

For the aged a minimum standard of living cannot be guaranteed merely by assuring a minimum level of income. With advancing age comes increasing incidence of infirmity and disease, causing large unexpected expenses. Action is required to assure that these expenses do not undermine a minimum standard of living for the aged. Provision of health and long-term care services to needy elderly is an important component of a strategy to protect a minimum standard of living for the elderly.

• To repay past contributions to society.

A second rationale for public policy is that the aged have made contributions to society for which they should be repaid. The aged have supported the education and investment in human resources of their children and other members of society. They have forgone consumption to permit the accumulation of capital that serves to improve productivity and the standard of living of today's younger generation. They have contributed as taxpayers to the creation of a social infrastructure, including highways, rail beds, dams, bridges, sewer systems, schools, and hospitals that all serve the younger generation. They have fought in wars to assure freedom for succeeding generations. This debt owed by the younger generation is one rationale for a public policy that repays the aged as a group with programs that assure a decent old age.

• To correct the failures of the private market.

Perhaps the most obvious rationale for public action to assist the aged is the failure of the private market to enable the aged to plan for and handle their own needs. Who could have anticipated the double-digit in-

flation of the late 1970s and the vastly reduced purchasing power of savings set aside for old age? How can any individual predict a life in good health versus a life that ends in a nursing home?

The private market does not facilitate adequate planning and saving for old age, nor does it assist the aged in dealing with the uncertainties of inflation, health, and life expectancy. Private insurance companies have been reluctant to write comprehensive health insurance policies for the aged for fear of excessive risks. The policies that are available limit coverage, exempt preexisting conditions, rarely cover nursing home care for infirmity or senility, and generally fail to protect the aged from the crushing financial burden of medical catastrophe (Meiners, 1982).

Whereas the majority of aged are vigorous and mentally alert, a fraction are quite frail. Physical and mental disabilities and/or limited education make it impossible for many elderly to function as fully informed and rational consumers in a competitive private market. Some have children who can act as their agents, but others have outlived their offspring or are childless. This level of dependency requires governmental assistance through public policies for the special needs of the aged. Even less severely disabled aged require assistance with the health system because of its complexity, increasing sophistication, and rapidly changing technology.

The theoretical model of a perfectly informed consumer in a perfectly competitive health market is far from reality, and has led some countries to abandon the model as an allocator of health resources. While this conclusion is debatable, it is clear that the aged need assistance with their health care problems. A private market solution with no role for public policy appears untenable, even in the United States.

The Role of Policy Analysis

The need for public policy affecting the aged is clear; a more difficult question is determining the nature and degree of public policy intervention. In part this depends upon the extent of need for assistance among the aged. But in a world of competing needs for scarce resources, improvements for the aged may mean fewer goods and services for younger members of society—including the poor and disabled, infants, and young children. Because of government budget limits, greater assistance to the aged may mean less investment in education, highways, sewer systems, parks, national defense, police, and fire protection; and, for the poor and other disadvantaged groups, less assistance with housing, employment training, nutrition, and health care.

Few analytical methods help in choosing among competing policy priorities. Cost–benefit analysis provides a theoretical basis for choices. But quantifying and measuring benefits are problematical, and decisions based on such analyses often are difficult to justify and implement because benefits are valued in strictly economic terms. For example, in cost–benefit analysis a life is valued by that person's future earning potential, and thus the analysis discriminates against both the poor and the aged.

Given the inadequacy of current economic analytical tools, decision making inevitably becomes a political process, where competing priorities are weighed and judgments made on the basis of a politically determined social consensus. Society's value for a given good or service can be measured indirectly through the political process. In the United States, voter responses to candidates and issues coupled with historical patterns of choice offer evidence of societal preferences. Thus, in the absence of quantitative measures of alternative policy strategies, political determinations appropriately fill the gap. In the United States, elected officials determine the priorities for public funding and resource allocation.

Public policy analysis assists in this process by delineating the nature and extent of problems to be addressed, and by analyzing major alternatives for action in terms of their benefits, costs, and consequences. Cost-effectiveness analysis estimates which alternatives achieve the greatest benefit per dollar ex-

pended. Take, for example, the objective of enabling the aged to function independently in a home environment. Cost-effectiveness analysis compares alternative methods of achieving this objective such as home health care assistance, housing assistance, meals on wheels, and a comprehensive package of health care and social services. Economic analysis can also identify ways of improving the efficiency of any given public program or approach. Such economic analysis makes its greatest contribution in evaluating alternative courses of action to achieve a single objective.

A more difficult problem is evaluating alternative courses of action to pursue multiple objectives. If health care for the nonaged is part of the policy agenda, should universal programs for all age groups be established, or should separate programs be created for the unique needs of the aged? Should health care be separated from other forms of support, or should an integrated approach be developed? Should public policy be directed toward designing an idealized system of assistance, or should it build incrementally on current policies and programs? Again, final decisions may reflect political forces, administrative feasibility, and a host of economic and social factors. The role of policy analysis is to lay out systematically the decisions to be made, the choices available, and the considerations bearing on these choices.

CURRENT HEALTH POLICIES FOR THE AGED

The health of the elderly is a good measure of how well a health system works. Health promotion and disease prevention throughout the life span contribute to a long life and a healthy vigorous old age. Because the need for health care increases markedly with age, the way in which a nation organizes, finances, and delivers health services also will be reflected in the health care received by the elderly. Assessing the health situation of the elderly can point the way to improving services for the entire population.

Different countries have used different means to provide health care to their population. Britain, Canada, Germany, Japan, and the United States, for example, employ widely differing models of health care financing and delivery. Each country has evolved a health system based on unique historical, social, economic, and political forces within that society (see Maxwell, 1974).

Approaches to meeting the health care needs of the aged also differ among countries. Differences exist in the organization and financing of services. Some countries, such as Britain, provide comprehensive health care for all age groups. Others offer a mix of publicly and privately provided and financed services. Some countries choose to define health care broadly to include medical care, social services, nutrition, and housing. Others take a narrow medical care focus, and separately address housing, income support, and social needs of the aged. Finally, some countries provide special assistance for the aged, whereas others provide universal services to all age groups (Kane and Kane, 1976).

The experience of the United States is instructive as an example of a mix of public and private services, often provided through multiple providers and financed by several sources. The United States targets some special assistance for the aged, while, for the most part, keeping health services separate from income support, housing, and social services.

The following sections examine current approaches in the United States for providing health care for the aged. The U.S. experience highlights many of the universal health problems of the aged and the array of policy choices for meeting the needs of older people.

Health Care Needs of the Aged

With advances in age, disabilities become more common. The acute illness episodes of youth are replaced by the more enduring discomfort of chronic illness. Treatment of these chronic conditions assumes a large share of the medical services used by the elderly. Thus, by examining the prevalence of chronic disease and disability among the elderly in the United States, we can assess current efforts and identify areas for improvement. We will discuss in turn mortality trends, disability, functional independence, health service utilization, and health expenditures as they relate to the health care needs of the elderly.

Mortality Trends among the Aged. Reduction in death rates among the aged in the United States in the last few decades has been virtually without precedent. The resulting growth in the size of the aged population has altered the nature and demand for social and health services.

Three distinct periods of mortality rate decline have occurred in the United States in the last 40 years. During the period 1940-54, mortality rates declined moderately. The age-adjusted death rates for those 65 years of age and older decreased at an average annual rate of 1.1 percent for males and 2.0 percent for females. The period 1955-67 brought stabilization of mortality rates. The age-adjusted death rate increased slightly for males (0.2 percent annually) and decreased by 1.0 percent annually for women. Beginning in the mid-1960s, death rates for the aged showed sharp reductions. Between 1968 and 1978 the age-adjusted mortality rate for males declined at an annual rate of 1.5 percent, and the female rate declined at an annual rate of 2.3 percent (U.S. Department of Health and Human Services, 1981a).

Most of the decrease in mortality for the aged is attributable to substantial declines in heart disease and cerebrovascular disease as a cause of death. From 1950 to 1975, the death rate for heart disease, the leading cause of death for the aged, declined by 16 percent, and cerebrovascular disease declined by 21 percent. The decline in deaths from heart disease alone accounted for 55 percent of the overall decline in mortality rates for the aged between 1950 and 1975 (U.S. Department of Health, Education and Welfare, 1977).

Canada and western European countries have also experienced declines in mortality rates for the aged over this period. These countries had greater declines in aged death rates than the United States in the 1955–67 period, and substantially smaller, but nonetheless important, declines in the 1968–77 period (U.S. Department of Health and Human Services, 1981a).

The improvement in life expectancy for the aged has led to dramatic demographic shifts. The size of the aged population is increasing, and within the aged population the proportion of the very old is also increasing. In 1940, there were 9 million persons age 65 and over in the United States. By 1979 there were 25 million persons in this age group. As a proportion of the total population, the aged increased from 7 percent in 1940 to 11 percent in 1979. In 1940, 13 percent of the aged were over age 80; by 1979, 21 percent of the aged were over 80 (U.S. Department of Health and Human Services, 1981a).

Disability among the Aged. The increasing numbers of the elderly, especially of the very old, have led to an increase in the absolute numbers of aged persons with serious health care problems.

The number of persons age 65 and over residing in nursing homes in the United States has increased from fewer than 500,000 in 1963 to 720,000 in 1969, to over 1.1 million in 1977. This represents an increase in the proportion of the aged population residing in nursing homes from 2.5 percent in 1963 to 4.8 percent in 1977 (U.S. Department of Health and Human Services, 1981a). This rise in institutionalization may reflect an increased frailty; it may also reflect the increased financial coverage and available supply of nursing home care.

Among the noninstitutionalized aged population, the prevalence of disabling conditions does not appear to have changed markedly. In 1963 the aged averaged 38 restricted-activity days per person per year; in 1979 this had increased slightly to 42 days per year. Bed-disability days per aged person stayed constant over this period at 14 days per person annually (U.S. Department of Health and Human Services, 1981a; U.S. Department of Health, Education and Wel-

fare, 1965). While the rate of disability among the aged noninstitutionalized population has not worsened over time, it is important to remember that disability among the aged is markedly more severe than for younger age groups (see U.S. Department of Health and Human Services, 1981a, Table 27). Restricted-activity days occur almost three times more frequently among the aged than among adults 17 to 44 years of age. Nearly three-fourths of the restricted-activity days of the aged are related to chronic conditions, while virtually all of the activity restriction among the young is linked to acute conditions (U.S. Department of Health and Human Services, 1981a, Tables 28 and 29). Conditions such as heart disease, arthritis, diabetes, and high blood pressure limit the ability of many older persons to enjoy a vigorous life (U.S. Department of Health, Education and Welfare, 1977).

Functional Independence and the Aged. Loss of functional independence is a special problem for the elderly, particularly for those over age 85. Nursing home placement is much more common in this age group. For example, while 1.5 percent of all persons age 65 to 74 are in nursing homes, 22 percent of all persons over age 85 are in nursing homes (U.S. Department of Health and Human Services, 1981a, Table 45).

Nearly all of the 1.1 million aged in nursing homes have some limitation in their ability to carry out the basic activities of daily living without assistance. These activities have been summarized as bathing, dressing, using the toilet room, mobility, continence, and eating. Nearly all persons in nursing homes require assistance with bathing, and at least half with dressing, toileting, and moving about, as well (U.S. Department of Health and Human Services, 1981b). Among the aged outside of nursing homes, many require similar kinds of assistance. Nearly 0.9 million aged require assistance with at least one of the six basic activities of daily living. Dependence is closely linked to age. Ten percent of those over age 85 are dependent in one or more activities of daily living, compared with 2.3 percent of those aged 65 to 74 (National Center for Health Statistics, unpublished tabulations).

Loss of functional independence is a particularly serious problem for older women. Since women outlive men, more older women are widowed or single, whereas older men tend to have a spouse to assist them. Married persons or persons living with family members are far less likely to be placed in a nursing home than are persons living alone (U.S. Department of Health and Human Services, 1981a, Table 45). Support from families is not always possible. Many of the very old have outlived their children, or are childless. For others, their children may themselves be experiencing health problems with advancing age.

Loss of functional independence when accompanied by lack of support from close family members greatly increases the health needs of the aged.

Health Services Utilization by the Aged. The greater health care problems of the aged outlined above are reflected in their greater use of a wide range of health care services. The aged visit physicians an average of 6.3 times annually, compared with 5.2 physician visits per person aged 45 to 64, and 4.5 physician visits per person aged 17 to 44 (U.S. Department of Health and Human Services, 1981a, Table 34).

The total annual days of hospital care per aged person are more than four times greater than for the nonaged (U.S. Department of Health and Human Services, Table 41). Those age 65 and over average 39 hospital discharges per 100 persons annually, compared with 20 per 100 persons for persons aged 45 to 64. The most common ailments for which the aged are hospitalized are: heart disease, malignant neoplasms, cerebrovascular disease, fracture (aged women), and hyperplasia of prostate (aged men). Serious conditions in the aged, as indicated earlier, are more commonly chronic conditions that require ongoing medical attention, whereas serious conditions in the nonaged adult population are acute and episodic in nature.

Health Expenditures and the Aged. The greater needs of the aged and their greater utilization of service is reflected in the expenditure of funds on care for the aged (Butler and Newacheck, 1981). In 1978, the average expenditure for personal health care services for persons age 65 and over in the United States was $2,026, compared with $764 for nonaged adults, and $286 for children.

Much of this difference in expenditures reflects greater use of hospital and nursing home care by the aged. For example, the average annual per capita hospital expenditures of the aged were $869 in 1978, compared with $369 for nonaged adults. Nursing home expenditures averaged $518 per aged person, compared with $23 for the nonaged. Differences also exist in expenditures for ambulatory care services. Physician expenditures per aged person were $366 in 1978, compared with $164 for nonaged adults (Fischer, 1980).

Other Indicators of Need. If health is defined broadly to include physical, mental, and social well-being, then additional indicators point to the need for assistance to the aged. The aged are more likely to be poor. In 1981, 15.3 percent of the aged, compared with 14 percent of the population as a whole, had family incomes below the poverty income threshold (U.S. Bureau of the Census, 1982). Malnutrition, poor housing with inadequate heating or cooling, lack of transportation, all may increase the health care needs of certain groups of aged. Minorities among the aged face additional problems. Hispanic aged may not understand the care prescribed for them and thus may find the health care system especially confusing. Blacks face discrimination in obtaining services; few patients admitted to nursing homes are black (White House Conference on Aging, 1981).

If health encompasses physical, mental, and social well-being, then a comprehensive public policy for the aged should include the entire range of conditions affecting the health of the aged, including income support, housing and environment, nutrition, employment, transportation, social services, and the need for social interaction and contact with others. All these factors play an important role in determining the health and well-being of the aged population.

Meeting the Health Care Needs of the Aged

The United States differs from most industrialized countries in that it finances health care services for the aged without a national health insurance plan for the total population (Davis, 1976). Medicare (Title XVIII of the Social Security Act) is the largest program providing health care assistance for the aged. This program, enacted in 1965, finances acute care for nearly all aged. The Medicaid program (Title XIX) provides additional health care insurance coverage for low-income aged persons (Davis and Schoen, 1978). Additional health services are provided the aged through other programs. Health-related programs—social services, housing assistance, income security, and some rehabilitation services for the aged—are also provided under separate programs (Lowy, 1980). The following sections outline the major features and experiences of the health and health-related programs.

Medicare. The primary objective of Medicare is to protect the aged against large medical outlays. The program also seeks to eliminate financial barriers that discourage the aged from seeking medical care. Medicare covers persons age 65 and over who are entitled to receive social security or railroad retirement benefits (for a history of Medicare and future policy options, see Davis, 1982). As a result, about 95 percent of all aged persons are covered. Beginning in July 1973, Medicare coverage was also extended to individuals who have been permanently and totally disabled for two years or more and to persons with end-stage renal disease.

Medicare consists of two parts: Part A covers hospital, nursing home, and home health services; Part B covers physician, outpatient hospital, home health, and some ambulatory services. The program does not cover prescription drugs, preventive services, dental care, routine eye examinations, eyeglasses, hearing aids, or long-term institutional services. Part A covers all eligible persons; those covered under Part A may voluntarily enroll in Part B by paying a premium. Part A is financed by a payroll tax on employers and employees; Part B is financed by general tax revenues and premium contributions.

Part A covers inpatient hospital care for 90 days of any illness (a new illness is defined to begin when the beneficiary has not been in a hospital or a nursing home for 60 continuous days), plus a 60-day lifetime reserve. The beneficiary pays a deductible for the first day of care set at a level indexed to the cost of one day of hospital care ($304 in 1983, up from $40 in 1966 when the program began). In addition the beneficiary pays an amount equal to one-fourth of the hospital deductible for the 61st through 90th days of hospital care, and an amount equal to one-half of the deductible for each day of the lifetime reserve.

The premium for Part B as of July 1983 is $13.50 per month, up from $3 in July 1966. The beneficiary is responsible for the first $75 of Part B services, 20 percent of all allowable charges, and any physicians' charges beyond those allowable by Medicare. On about half of Medicare claims, physicians charge more than the allowable rate (Ferry et al., 1980).

Medicare expenditures have risen rapidly throughout the last 15 years. Reimbursement for services under Medicare increased from $4.5 billion in 1967, the first full year of the program, to $29.3 million in 1979. Enrollees over this period increased from 19.5 million in 1967 27.9 million aged and disabled individuals in 1979 (U.S. Department of Health and Human Services, 1981c).

Growth in Medicare expenditures is caused by some of the same factors that affect the total health care system: inflation in costs, expanding technology, and increased demand for care. Medicare payments per enrollee have increased more markedly than health care expenditures per capita, with reimbursements per enrollee increasing from $233 in 1967 to $1,053 in 1979, reflecting increased hospital admissions of the aged and increased services to hospitalized aged patients (Davis, 1982).

No slowdown in expenditure growth is expected at this time. Medicare budget outlays are projected to increase from $35 billion in FY1980 to $50 billion in FY1982 and to $75 billion in FY1985. This projected growth is generating political pressure to curb outlays under the program (Office of Management and Budget, 1982).

Medicare expenditures pay primarily for hospital and physician services. In 1980, 72 percent of Medicare expenditures paid for hospital care, a little over 20 percent went to physicians' services, and 1 percent of payments supported nursing home care, with administrative expenses taking 3 percent of total expenditures under the program (Gibson and Waldo, 1981).

Variability among the aged in their need for and use of health care services is masked by average statistics for the program as a whole. Medicare enrollees are far from homogeneous. Many are healthy and rarely use health care services. Others have multiple chronic health conditions requiring extensive care and treatment. Nine percent of the aged account for 70 percent of all Medicare payments for the aged. At the other extreme, 40 percent of the aged receive no Medicare-reimbursed services, and another 37 percent account for only 5 percent of Medicare payments (Davis, 1982). It is clear that Medicare provides assistance primarily to those with serious health care problems. While it is undoubtedly important for the elderly with routine medical problems, the bulk of expenditures is concentrated on a minority of the aged with life-threatening or serious chronic conditions.

The burden of heavy medical expenses on the aged and their families created the impetus behind Medicare. Before Medicare's passage, about half of the aged had no private health insurance. As individuals retired, they usually lost their employer group insurance. Insurance companies in turn were re-

luctant to write individual comprehensive health insurance policies for the aged for fear of an excessive number of poor risks. Available policies often limited coverage, exempted preexisting conditions, and offered inadequate protection. Thus, remedying the private sector's failure to provide adequate health insurance became the chief goal of the Medicare program. It has succeeded.

Medicare has extended comprehensive health insurance coverage to virtually all of the aged. Without it, medical bills for the 10 to 20 percent with serious health problems would be a devastating financial burden on aged patients and their families.

A major increase in hospital utilization by the aged has resulted since the enactment of Medicare. This usage has been among the aged traditionally identified as most in need of care—individuals living alone with low incomes, members of minority groups, residents of the South and of nonmetropolitan areas (Lowenstein, 1971).

Dramatic increases in certain types of surgery occurred with the introduction of Medicare. Cataract operations doubled between 1965 and 1975, and arthroplasty nearly tripled. The increase in these types of surgery has led some analysts to conclude that the quality of life for the aged has improved as a result of Medicare (Donabedian, 1976; Drake, 1978).

Medicare's objectives were to ease the financial burden of medical care and to assure access to health care for the elderly. Studies confirm that for many of the elderly the promise of Medicare has been partially fulfilled—nearly all the elderly have some protection against health care costs, and availability of care has improved more dramatically for the elderly than for other population groups without comparable coverage. Medicare may also have been a contributing factor in the improved health of the elderly reported in the last 15 years.

Despite significant improvements in health care for the aged, notable gaps remain. Medicare does not cover preventive services to help alleviate the need for chronic care. No national financing program assures the nonaged adequate access to care that will prevent the development of, or deterioration from, chronic conditions.

Medicare has virtually no long-term care coverage. For those frail aged who are unable to function independently, Medicare provides no social services to enable them to remain in their own homes. Nor does Medicare provide nursing home care except under the most limited and time-restricted circumstances.

Many health care bills must still be paid by the aged patient. Medicare's benefit package excludes prescription drugs, dental care, eyeglasses, hearing aids, and many other health care services. In 1978, only 44 percent of the bill for aged health care was paid by Medicare. The remainder was paid by the aged out-of-pocket or indirectly through private health insurance premiums (Fischer, 1980).

For the aged poor, benefit limitations and the substantial deductible and co-insurance requirements of Medicare deter access to adequate care. Some of the cost-sharing requirements and benefit gaps under Medicare are filled by other public programs, most notably Medicaid. But despite the myriad of public programs designed to assist the aged, services such as community care are often unavailable to those without the ability to purchase them privately.

Medicaid. Medicaid finances a wide range of health care services for some of the poor and the medically needy (those who would be on welfare if their incomes were a little lower) (Davis and Schoen, 1978). It is not focused specifically on the elderly, but persons aged 65 and over account for 15.6 percent of all beneficiaries and 37.4 percent of all expenditures (U.S. Department of Health and Human Services, 1981c). Thus, Medicaid is an important form of health care assistance for the aged poor.

Unlike Medicare, Medicaid is a federal-state program. Administrative responsibility and about half the financial burden of the program are borne by state and local governments. Eligibility for Medicaid is linked to eligibility for welfare and shares the complexity of that system (Rowland and Gaus, 1981). In the case of the aged, most states cover under Medicaid all persons receiving federal income assistance from the Supplemental Security Income program. In addition to covering cash-assistance recipients, states may provide Medicaid coverage to those described as medically needy, persons whose income is slightly above the limit for welfare. Over half of the states elect to provide this coverage.

States are required to cover several basic services, including inpatient and outpatient hospital care, physicians' services, laboratory and X-ray, and skilled nursing facility and home health care. States may choose to cover a wide range of optional services with federal matching assistance, including drugs, eyeglasses, private duty nursing, intermediate care facility services, inpatient psychiatric care, physical therapy, dental care, and other services. Forty-one or more states and jurisdictions add clinic services, prescribed drugs, prosthetic devices, emergency hospital services, and intermediate care facility services. States may also impose limits on services covered, such as limits on the number of covered hospital days or co-payment charges for prescription drugs. Thus, the benefits covered vary from state to state.

States may buy Medicare coverage for the low income aged on Medicaid, and most states choose to do so. States that choose to buy into Medicare pay the premium and beneficiary cost-sharing under Medicare for individual enrollees as well as providing any benefits, such as prescription drugs, not covered by Medicare.

Like Medicare, Medicaid has experienced a tremendous growth in expenditures since it began operations in 1966. Combined federal, state, and local government expenditures under the program have increased from $3.5 billion in 1968 to $25 billion in 1980. Expenditures are projected to increase to $34 billion in 1982 and to $48 billion in 1985 (Health Care Financing Administration, unpublished statistics).

Most of the increase in costs results from

three causes: general inflation in health care costs, increased numbers of persons covered, and the high cost of institutionalization. There is little indication that the program is less efficient than private health insurance, or that high costs in the program indicate fraud or abuse. Per capita costs for acute care services under Medicaid are comparable to those for privately insured individuals. It is the inclusion of nursing home costs in the per capita calculation that drives Medicaid expenditures above the private insurance levels. However, since private insurance does not cover nursing home care, comparisons with private insurance inappropriately overstate the cost of Medicaid.

Medicaid has substantially assisted the low income aged covered by the program. First, as indicated, Medicaid pays for Medicare's premiums, deductibles, and co-insurance for 3.5 million aged (U.S. Department of Health and Human Services, 1981c). This reduces barriers to care and permits the use of physician and hospital services by low income aged at a rate comparable to the use of care by high income aged with supplemental private health insurance.

Second, Medicaid expands Medicare's limited benefit package to cover services that the aged poor cannot afford to purchase directly. These include prescription drugs, dental care, eyeglasses, hearing aids, and preventive services such as flu shots. While states vary in their coverage of such services, most cover some of these options.

Third, Medicaid covers some poor aged who are not covered under Medicare. This includes some domestic workers and immigrants not covered by Social Security.

Finally, and most important, Medicaid covers long-term care services excluded by Medicare. Both nursing home care and home health services are financed for impoverished aged. Medicaid also covers many aged persons who, while not poor to begin with, impoverish themselves because of either the costs of chronic illness or the expense of nursing home care.

While Medicaid has done much to remedy some of the gaps in the Medicare program, it contains several inequities and deficiencies (Davis and Schoen, 1978). Medicaid is by law a program for poor people. Its long-term care benefits are available only to those who are poor or who become poor after placement in a nursing home. Its eligibility requirements, reimbursement methods, and administrative procedures frequently treat beneficiaries as second-class citizens who receive second-class care.

Further, Medicaid benefits are limited and subject to rules established at the state government level. Personal care services, chore services, homemaker aid services, and other types of social services were recently added to services eligible for Medicaid reimbursement, but only at the request of each state government and only if such benefits are shown not to increase total expenditures under the program. Income eligibility levels require some individuals to enter institutions for long-term care because their incomes do not qualify them for those services that would enable them to remain in their homes.

While Medicaid for the aged functions largely as a long-term care program, it also provides important care benefits not covered by Medicare. However, many of these benefits such as prescription drugs, eyeglasses, dentures, hearing aids, and so on, are needed by a much larger group of the elderly than is now covered by Medicaid.

Long-Term Care Demonstrations. As of this writing (1983) the United States has yet to formulate a national long-term care policy. In place of major reforms in existing policy, numerous demonstrations and research projects to test alternative approaches for improving long-term care services for those aged who are unable to function independently have been tried. These demonstration efforts have been aimed at overcoming the major problems of the present long-term care system—resource fragmentation, multiplicity of funding sources, and a dearth of community-based alternatives to institutional care. (For a background on long-term care and problems of the existing system, see U.S.

Department of Health and Human Services, 1981d; Callahan and Wallack, 1981.)

The Medicare and Medicaid demonstration projects initiated during the 1970s sought to address these problems. The purpose of the demonstrations was to identify the range of services necessary to maintain individuals in the community and to assess the utilization and cost of such services (Lowy, 1980). The development and use of needs assessment screening to divert at-risk individuals from institutionalization to community-care was an integral component. Each person's service needs were evaluated, and a plan of care tailored to his or her requirements and family situation was established. A care coordinator implemented the plan by finding and arranging appropriate services in the community, monitoring the individual's health and social needs, and adapting the service package to meet changing needs.

Medicaid or Medicare reimbursement and coverage requirements were waived to permit the coordinator to authorize payment for needed services that are normally excluded from coverage such as transportation, homemaker and chore services, and home repair and maintenance. The care coordinator in the early demonstrations did not serve as a care provider. More recent demonstration efforts are now testing this approach. Evaluation of the care coordinator's role in these demonstration projects has been inconclusive because none of these projects used a care coordinator independent of an expanded range of services (U.S. Department of Health and Human Services, 1981d).

Comparisons across sites in the early demonstration projects could not be made because of differences in research design and data collection. Most projects, however, reported that patients could be treated at lower costs in the community than in a nursing home. Although the cost per individual was lower, the cost of expanding services to provide comprehensive commuity-based services expands the user population. Many aged people, even if severely impaired, are unwilling to enter a nursing home but are willing to use services offered in the community.

These early demonstration projects could not answer the policymakers' questions on the cost and effectiveness of various alternatives to long-term care delivery. The empirical evidence desired was not obtained. The unanswered research questions led to another long-term care demonstration effort by the federal government. The new effort, known as the National Long-Term Care Channeling Project, was initiated in 1980 by the Department of Health and Human Services.

Employing a more rigorous quasi-experimental multi-site research design, the new demonstration was intended to test the care coordination and expanded services model in ten sites. A common evaluation framework and standard data collection were to be employed at each site. Two approaches were to be tested. Five sites would employ a basic model using both care coordination and expanded services to provide families with needed comprehensive medical and social services not currently covered by Medicare. The other five sites would use a care coordinator to provide assessment and service coordination, but provide no services beyond those traditionally available under Medicare, Medicaid, or other social and health services programs. The evaluation of the ten sites would assess the effectiveness of care coordination with and without expanded benefits. By distinguishing the impact of expanded benefits from the impact of existing services coordination, the new channeling projects should help to answer questions raised by the first-generation demonstrations. Researchers are hopeful that the cost-effectiveness of the alternate models can be assessed from the study results. However, as with many quasi-experimental research projects, the findings may have limited generalizability.

Health Services Delivery Programs. The United States supplements its major health care financing programs with selected health service delivery programs (Davis and Schoen,

1978). These include community health centers, rural health clinics, the National Health Service Corps, and community mental health centers. These programs provide health care services to underserved rural and inner-city areas and address the problems of disadvantaged population groups.

Health service delivery programs are modestly funded. Total expenditures for the above-named programs averaged less than $1 billion in 1980, less than $100 million of which provided services to aged persons (Office of Management and Budget, 1982).

While small in scope, these programs are quite effective in improving access to care and health status of the individuals served. They fill important gaps left by the financing programs. For example, community health centers in medically underserved poor communities enable many isolated aged to obtain care by providing a comprehensive range of services including outreach and transportation. Some centers use home health nurses and outreach workers to deliver and administer medications and change dressings for the homebound aged.

Because the health service delivery programs are funded at a modest level, they reach only a small fraction of those in need. Most services are for children and women of childbearing age. The potential for addressing the special problems of homebound and frail aged remains unrealized. Where home care services are unavailable, nursing home placement may be unavoidable.

Health-Related Programs. Federal, state, and local governments support a range of complementary health-related programs. Long-term care services are available through the Older Americans Act, Title XX of the Social Security Act, the Veterans Administration Program, and the Vocational Rehabilitation program. Additional services can include congregate meals, meals on wheels, social services, day care, homemaker/chore services, and attendant care. Rent subsidies, congregate living facilities, and home maintenance and repair services are also covered (U.S. Department of Health and Human Services, 1981e).

A comprehensive policy providing all available services to the needy elderly is difficult, and often impossible to arrange. Services are financed by multiple agencies and programs at the federal, state, and local level. Each program has its own eligibility requirements, making some people eligible for one service and ineligible for a complementary service. Benefit packages, types of providers covered, reimbursement procedures, administrative structures, and service delivery mechanisms all differ substantially among programs. Each tends to operate independently of the other. The elderly are left alone to cope with a complex and confusing service system.

Summary. Numerous programs exist and large expenditures are made to assist the aged. Important gaps remain. These are reflected in out-of-pocket expenditures by the aged for their health care. In 1978, 44 percent of such care was paid out-of-pocket or through privately purchased health insurance (Fischer, 1980).

Inadequacy is particularly marked in the case of long-term care. Half of all nursing home expenditures for the aged are met privately.

But the basic problem is that the aged are unable to assure themselves a life of dignity. Inflation eats away at the value of their savings. The specter of catastrophic illness hangs over them, without their having the security of adequate insurance protection against expensive acute, chronic, or long-term care.

PRINCIPLES OF A NATIONAL HEALTH CARE POLICY FOR THE AGED

Public policy to promote health care for the aged has had notable success. Mortality rates have declined dramatically. Much of the heavy financial burden of medical bills has been lifted from the shoulders of the aged and their families. Yet, many problems remain. Programs are neither coordinated nor comprehensive, and are lacking in guiding principles or policy. Current programs fall far short of assuring the aged that they can live out their lives with dignity without worrying about choosing between medical care and other necessities of life such as food and adequate housing.

The Older Americans Act of 1965 is currently the centerpiece of U.S. commitment to the aged. Under the policy objectives of the Older Americans Act, the elderly are deemed to be entitled to an adequate income, the best possible physical and mental health, suitable housing, full restorative services, employment without age discrimination, and retirement with health and dignity.

In order to implement these objectives with regard to health of the elderly, we must scrutinize our efforts and formulate an overall policy. The following principles reflect the objectives of the Older Americans Act and can serve as a basis for such a health care policy:

1. Adequate health care throughout life is essential to a healthy old age. Health policy for the aged must also ensure the health of the future aged through assurance to children and nonaged adults of access to preventive and acute care services.
2. As one enters old age, health care financing should continue to be universal and comprehensive, with additional benefits tailored to the needs of old age. All aged regardless of income, race, or prior work history should be covered.
3. Comprehensive benefits should include preventive services, treatment for acute and chronic conditions, and assistance in coping with functional limitations. The scope of services covered should be flexible enough to enable the aged to meet their health care needs without incurring heavy financial burdens.
4. Choice of care alternatives and maximum independence should be promoted. Choice of living arrangements with supportive services from family, friends, and community should be available.

5. Services should be financed from federal, state, and local tax revenues, philantropy, and individual contributions. Any financial requirements should not consititute an undue burden on the aged.
6. Cost controls must be included in any comprehensive health care scheme. Incentives should encourage low-cost, high-quality care and program administration.
7. Access to quality care must be assured through minitoring efforts of the existing network of voluntary agencies, senior citizen groups, and community organizations.

The principles stated above reflect the current policy discussions in the United States with respect to health care of the aged and reform in long-term care. These principles draw upon the positive experiences of other countries that have taken innovative approaches to assist their elderly populations. The experiences of these other countries demonstrate that these principles can in fact be embodied in an overall health care and long-term care policy for the elderly.

INSIGHTS FROM ABROAD

The experience in the provision of health care of other developed countries is difficult, and often impossible, to transfer directly to the United States. However, the innovative approaches being tried in other nations play a valuable role in the pilot testing of ideas for future trial in the United States. The lessons from abroad help spark new approaches for the United States as well as offering warnings about which options to avoid.

Several nations have implemented innovative approaches to promote health and disease prevention through improved services to the elderly and their families in the home setting. This emphasis on primary care is often an inexpensive and especially humanitarian approach to care of the aged. For example, the Volkssolidaritat program in the German Democratic Republic encourages volunteers to help the elderly by conducting home help visits to administer medications to homebound elderly. Denmark attempts to keep people active, fit, and involved in their communities through pensioner clubs, educational programs offered in high schools, and access to gymnasia and physical fitness programs. Denmark also uses youth sports clubs and music organizations to provide services to elderly people in exchange for community purchase of needed sports or musical equipment.

Several nations are pursuing or planning strategies that would provide support to families who care for their aged relatives by educating families in coping with the health problems of the old and providing day hospital care and respite services to permit working people to care for their relatives during nights and weekends. Denmark is experimenting with 24-hour nursing services to help even seriously impaired aged persons remain at home. Scotland and the province of Manitoba in Canada have instituted comprehensive assessment programs to determine the health and social needs of frail elderly people. Based on these assessments, services, including hot meals, alarm systems, and day centers, can be provided to the aged in their homes.

Other developed countries have made strides in providing new forms of housing to meet the social needs of elderly people. Evidence from Norway suggests that if the burden of maintaining their own homes is excessive, people are willing to move to apartments in the community. Scotland provides a continuum of housing settings depending on the functional capacity of aged persons. Sheltered housing staffed by auxiliaries is available for those with minimal impairments who are largely able to care for themselves, while residential homes are available for those with more serious impairments. Increasingly, these homes are located in the center of town to keep older persons active in the community.

Elements of these innovative approaches in other industrial countries also exist in the United States today. The demonstration activities described earlier reflect U.S. efforts to test new approaches in health care, but much more needs to be learned about how best to prepare the elderly for an active old age.

FUTURE POLICY DIRECTIONS FOR THE UNITED STATES

Specific policy proposals building on the principles enumerated earlier will differ from country to country depending upon current programs, experience, and needs. The lessons from other countries can be studied, but any application to the United States must take account of the existing health and long-term care system in the United States. Health care financing programs in the United States historically have given favorable treatment to the aged. Future policy must assure early access to care for the entire population. The neglect of preventive and primary care at an earlier age has led to an emphasis upon treatment of acute and chronic conditions in old age that perhaps could have been prevented or ameliorated by earlier intervention.

A second major gap in U.S. health care programs is the absence of adequate long-term care for the frail aged. The frail aged must have long-term care available through a spectrum of options from home care to institutionalization.

Finally, given major economic and budgetary concerns, effective cost constraints must be built into existing programs as well as any future program of expanded benefits for the aged.

National Health Plan

The foundation of health policy for the aged must be a health care financing plan encompassing the entire population. The United States stands alone among industrialized nations in basing health care on ability to pay. Nearly 25 million Americans, most with moderately low incomes, do not have health insurance. They have serious problems buying health care services. Providing access to health care through financial support is thus a major objective. Such a reform can eliminate the anomalies of separate programs for the aged and the poor.

One approach to universal insurance coverage is an incremental, phased-in national health plan. Under this plan, Medicaid would become a completely federal program. Eligibility and benefit inequities would be eliminated, and coverage would be expanded to cover all the poor and medically needy.

Medicaid and Medicare would be merged into a "Healthcare" program with comprehensive coverage and benefits, including current Medicare benefits plus prescription drugs, preventive services, hearing and vision services, and appliances. Cost sharing for the poor would be eliminated, and for others a ceiling would guarantee freedom from financial hardship. Long-term care benefits would be provided as described below.

This national health plan has two objectives: access to care for everyone and freedom from financial hardship. The aged would benefit in at least two ways: more would be enabled to reach age 65 in good health, and their financial security would be enhanced through the expansion of benefits and improved coverage for catastrophic illness.

Long-Term Care

Improved long-term care coverage is a natural component of the "Healthcare" national health plan. Alternatively, however, these expanded benefits could be incorporated into Medicare. Funds from existing programs could be pooled to assist with financing.

In a phased-in approach, coverage would begin first with those frail aged at risk of institutionalization. Eligibility would be contingent upon assessment and certification of need for services.

Benefits would include:

- Nursing home care
- Home health benefits
- Home assistance benefits, e.g.:
  - Homemaker services
- Chore services
- Repairs and modifications
- Transportation
- Nursing-home-alternative services, e.g.:
- Respite care
- Day care
- Attendant care in the home

In contrast to the existing programs, Medicare and Medicaid, all aged meeting physical or mental dependency criteria would be eligible. Contributions by the aged toward the cost of care would be held to modest levels, and each would be guaranteed a manageable lifetime maximum contribution. This plan would remove the distinction between skilled nursing facilities and intermediate care facilities. Preadmission assessments would be required and conducted by an independent team. Reimbursement would vary with the complexity of care required.

Similarly, many of Medicare's restrictions on home health benefits would be removed. Coverage would be available for those with chronic deteriorating conditions and those not yet homebound. Certification of need to establish eligibility for extended home health benefits would be based on assessment of physical and mental functioning.

Coverage of home assistance benefits would represent the greatest departure from existing benefit programs. Phased-in coverage would be particularly appropriate for home health benefits, and initially the program could be limited to those at risk of institutionalization. Cost-sharing provisions or a fixed monthly benefit would provide additional utilization controls until benefit–cost experience could be obtained. Title XX of the Social Security Act and the Older Americans Act funds could help support this benefit.

Nursing home alternative services could also be phased in, with participation contingent upon determination of risk of institutionalization.

The expansion of benefits for long-term care requires several funding sources and cost control provisions. Medicare and Medicaid long-term care funds could be diverted to the plan. Income and payroll taxes could be earmarked for long-term care. Contributions by the aged would further offset costs and limit potential abuse. A guaranteed maximum lifetime contribution should preclude economic hardship for the aged. Tight prospective reimbursement rates and careful monitoring of returns to providers should be designed.

Cost Containment and Reimbursement Rates

Even with tight cost controls on new benefits, expansion of current Medicare and Medicaid benefits would only be fiscally feasible if coupled with strong controls on health care costs. Annual rates of increase for hospital care have reached almost 20 percent in recent years. The most promising cost containment approach is a prospective payment system limiting hospital cost increases for all patients. At this time, six states in the United States have enacted such plans. Experience indicates that using a prospective payment plan results in a three- to six-percentage-point slower rate of increase in hospital costs.

Other cost containment elements include promotion of prepaid groups practices and other health care delivery organizations that are reimbursed on a capitation basis, comprehensive health planning with rigorous review of new capital expansions in health facilities, and utilization review of the necessity and quality of health care services provided under public and private health insurance plans. The assessment process for long-term care services suggested in this chapter would provide an even stronger means of utilization review in this component.

CONCLUDING COMMENTS

A positive policy agenda encompassing a national health plan, long-term care reform, and cost containment and reimbursement reform would result in the elimination of many of the current gaps in coverage and inappropriate incentives in existing long-term care and health care programs. Pursuit of the steps outlined above would provide the elderly of this and coming generations the assurance that their health and long-term care needs would be met, allowing them to live out their lives with dignity.

REFERENCES

Butler, Lewis, and Newacheck, Paul. 1981. Health and social factors relevant to long term care policy. *In* J. Meltzer, F. Farrow, and H. Richmond (eds.), *Policy Options in Long Term Care.* Chicago: University of Chicago Press.

Callahan, J., and Wallack, S. 1981. *Reforming the Long Term Care System.* Lexington, Mass.: Lexington Books.

Davis, Karen. 1976. *National Health Insurance: Benefits, Costs, and Consequences.* Washington, D.C.: Brookings Institution.

Davis, Karen. 1982. Medicare reconsidered. Paper prepared for Duke University Medical Center Seventh Private Sector Conference on Financial Support of Health Care for the Elderly and Indigent, Durham, North Carolina, Mar. 14-16.

Davis, Karen, and Schoen, Cathy. 1978. *Health and the War on Poverty: A Ten Year Appraisal.* Washington, D.C.: Brookings Institution.

Donabedian, Avedis. 1976. Effects of Medicare and Medicaid on access to and the quality of health. *Public Health Reports* 91(4)(July-Aug.):322-331.

Drake, David. 1978. Does money spent on health really improve U.S. health status? *Hospitals,* Oct. 16, pp. 63-65.

Ferry, Thomas, Gornick, Marian, Newton, Marilyn, and Hacherman, Carl. 1980. Physicians' charges under Medicare: Assignment rates and beneficiary liability. *Health Care Financing Review* 3, (Winter):49-75.

Fischer, Charles. 1980. Differences by age groups in health care spending. *Health Care Financing Review* 1(4) (Spring):65-90.

Gibson, R., and Waldo, D. 1981. National health expenditures, 1980. *Health Care Financing Review* 3(1)(Autumn):1-55.

Kane, Robert L., and Kane, Rosalie. 1976. *Long Term Care in Six Countries: Implications for the United States.* U.S. Department of Health, Education and Welfare (PHS) Publication No. 76-1207. Washington, D.C.: U.S. Government Printing Office.

Kutza, Elizabeth Ann. 1981. *The Benefit of Old Age: Social Welfare Policy for the Elderly.* Chicago: University of Chicago Press.

Lowenstein, Regina. 1971. The effects of Medicare on health care of the aged. *Social Security Bulletin* 34 (Apr.):3-20.

Lowy, Lewis. 1980. *Social Policies and Programs for the Aging.* Lexington, Mass.: Lexington Books.

Maxwell, Robert, 1974. *Health Care: The Growing Dilemma.* New York: McKinsey and Company.

Meiners, Mark R. 1982. Shifting the burden: The potential role of the private sector in long-term care insurance for the elderly. *American Health Care Association Journal* (Mar.). 20–22.

National Center for Health Statistics. Unpublished tabulations.

Office of Management and Budget. 1982. *Budget of the U.S. Government,* FY1983. Washington, D.C.: U.S. Government Printing Office.

Okun, Arthur M. 1975. *Equality and Efficiency: The Big Tradeoff.* Washington, D.C.: Brookings Institution.

Rowland, D., and Gaus, C. 1982. Reducing eligibility and benefits: *In* R. Blendon and T. Moloney (eds.), *New Approaches to the Medicaid Crisis,* New York: Frost and Sullivan. p. 19–46.

U.S. Bureau of the Census. 1982. Money income and poverty status of families and persons in the United States: 1981. *Current Population Reports,* Series P-60, No. 134. Washington, D.C.: U.S. Government Printing Office.

U.S. Bureau of Health, Education and Welfare. 1965. Disability days, United States, July 1963–June 1964. National Center for Health Statistics, *Vital and Health Statistics,* Series 10, No. 24. Washington, D.C.: U.S. Government Printing Office.

U.S. Department of Health, Education and Welfare. 1977. *Health United States, 1976–1977.* DHEW Publication No. (PHS) 77-1232. Washington, D.C.: U.S. Government Printing Office.

U.S. Department of Health and Human Services. 1981a. *Health United States 1981.* DHHS Publication No. (PHS) 82–1232. Washington, D.C.: U.S. Government Printing Office.

U.S. Deapartment of Health and Human Services. 1981b. *Characteristics of Nursing Home Residents, Health Status, and Care Received, National Nursing Home Survey, United States, May–December, 1977.* National Center for Health Statistics, Series 13, No. 51, PHS 81-1712 (Apr.).

U.S. Department of Health and Human Services. 1981c. *Medicare and Medicaid Data Book, 1981.* Health Care Financing Administration. Washington, D.C.: U.S. Government Printing Office.

U.S. Department of Health and Human Services. 1981d. *Long Term Care: Background and Future Directions.* Health Care Financing Administration Publication No. 81-20047. Washington, D.C.: U.S. Government Printing Office.

U.S. Department of Health and Human Services. 1981e. *Working Papers on Long Term Care.* Prepared for the 1980 Under Secretary's Task Force on Long Term Care, Office of the Assistant Secretary for Planning and Education (Oct.).Washington, D.C.: U.S. Government Printing Office.

White House Conference on Aging. 1981. *Chartbook on Aging in America.* Washington, D.C.: U.S. Government Printing Office.

26
AGING AND SOCIAL CARE

Marjorie Cantor
Fordham University
and
Virginia Little
University of Connecticut

A major objective of supportive services for the elderly is "maintenance of the quality of life." Although this goal is rarely defined as such, a reading of the gerontological and related literature suggests that the principal components related to the preservation of a positive quality of life for older people include adequate income and health care; suitable housing and environmental conditions (including personal and household safety and accessible transportation); the existence of meaningful roles and relationships; and sufficient social supports. Most often discussions concerning the quality of life emphasize the ability of the elderly to remain independent in the community. However, persons involved in institutional care of older people are equally concerned with the quality of life.

This chapter will focus on but one contributor to quality of life: the provision of social supports or social care to older people, whether by formal organizations or by the extensive informal support networks of family, friends, and neighbors. Such a delimitation is, of course, artificial. In any given situation, it is the unique interaction of several components that determines an older person's quality of life. However, the other factors are addressed in other chapters of this book. An adequate understanding of social supports, as they presently exist in the United States and other parts of the world, requires a separate examination of this critical component and the current state of the art regarding it.

This chapter builds on the Beattie (1976) chapter in the first edition of this *Handbook*. It is indicative, however, of how far we have come in our knowledge of the role of family and "significant others" as service providers for older people, that our concept of social services has been broadened to include both informal and formal support providers.

In line with this enlarged conceptualization, this chapter will attempt to do several things. First, it will comment on the need for social care and the parameters of social supports required by older people. Next it will present a theoretical model of social care from a systems perspective. Included therein will be a delineation of the major informal and formal supports and how they relate to a continuum of care and a continuum of frailty. The next two sections will examine in greater detail the nature of the informal and formal support systems of older people. Although major emphasis will be placed on the U.S. experience, references will be made to other countries as well. The chapter will conclude with an overview of current issues in social care that deserve further research and policy consideration in the decades ahead.

CONCEPTUAL FRAMEWORK OF SOCIAL CARE

The Duality of Informal and Formal Supports

Human beings are by nature interdependent; their functional capacities and even survival depend on what they derive from their fellows (Clark, 1969). Acceptance of this concept of mutual interdependence has varied from society to society depending on the society's particular history, culture, and state of economic development. Since American pioneering days the emphasis has been on the ability of the individual to survive and prosper with a minimum of assistance. Although the United States may have carried the theme of independence to its furthest extreme, this general notion of self-sufficiency as a sign of maturity and ego integrity is shared by most western European countries.

From the life cycle perspective, however, there are two significant stages in which most cultures are more accepting of dependency needs—at the beginning and the end. It is considered appropriate, therefore, for infants and children to be nurtured by parents and "significant others" as they are socialized into the culture. And again as persons grow older and frailer most societies look with greater tolerance on their needs for assistance and support. Dependency in these contexts is normal, not pathological, "a state of being not a state of mind . . . in which to be old as to be young is to be dependent" (Blenkner, 1969).

However, in the case of old age, as the balance shifts from independence to dependency, the potential for individual normative conflicts increases. Thus an older person is often caught in a dilemma, on the one hand, between adherence to the cultural norms of self-sufficiency and independence characteristic of adulthood and, on the other hand, the concrete needs for assistance as health, physical strength, mobility, and economic resources decline with age (Cantor, 1978).

How older people attempt to deal with this conflict can be best understood within the context of modern kinship structure and the relationship between informal support networks and formal organizations. Research suggests that older people perceive the informal network of kin, friends, and neighbors as the most appropriate source of social support in most situations of need. (Townsend, 1968; Valle and Mendoza, 1978; Gurian and Cantor, 1978; Sussman, 1979; Adams, 1980; Dukippo, 1980; Connelly, 1980; Horowitz and Dobrof, 1982). Family and other informal network members are seen by older people as natural extensions of themselves. Reciprocal helping patterns often rooted in earlier phases of the life cycle are activated in times of crisis. Such a preference minimizes psychological damage to ego systems based upon norms of self-sufficiency and self-reliance.

Thus it is to the informal system that older people turn first and most frequently (Cantor, 1975a,b, 1980; Shanas, 1979a,b; Horowitz and Dobrof, 1982). Only when assistance from the family is unavailable, or kin and "significant others" can no longer absorb the burden of assistance (because of excessive time and/or money commitments, or lack of requisite skill) do older persons and their families turn to formal organizations for help. Cantor (1980) has characterized this manner of selecting assistance as the hierarchical compensatory theory of social supports. Kin, particularly spouse and children, are preferred as the cornerstone of the support system; they are followed next in preference by friends, neighbors, and eventually formal organizations in a well-ordered hierarchical selection process.

However, the primacy of the kin network in assisting older people does not mean that formal social services are without a role. Litwak, in his theory of shared functions and balanced coordination, postulates that the dependency needs of the elderly are best met if there is a proper balance between formal services and informal supports, with each system performing the tasks for which it is most suited. Ideally an older person should be able to access the element most appropriate for the particular time and function (Litwak, 1965, 1978; Litwak and Meyer, 1966; Sussman, 1977). Thus, the social support system of the elderly can be viewed as an amalgam of kin, friends and neighbors, and societal services, each having different roles and differing relative importance at various phases in the dependency continuum of old age.

Social Care—Definitions and Derivations

Before describing in greater detail how the social care system operates, some definitions are in order. Three decades of gerontological research and practice have shown that the conditions of the elderly that require support are usually ongoing, calling for sustained assistance. Although purely medical or health-related services are sometimes involved, in the main the supports required are of a social nature (Brody and Brody, 1981). Such assistance is most usually directed toward enabling older people to fulfill three critical needs: the need for socialization and personal development; the need for help in carrying out the tasks of daily living; and the need for personal assistance during times of illness or other crisis (Cantor, 1981a). The social supports provided can be of an instrumental nature involving direct tangible assistance or material aid, or of an affective nature involving emotional support and sustenance (Lopata, 1975; Tolsdorf, 1976; Kahn and Antonucci, 1980).

Although the term social care has tended to be used to describe formal social services, it is actually a broader concept encompassing both informal and formal social support activities, which in fact exist side by side. In this chapter the terms social care and social support system will be used interchangeably to delineate the entire spectrum of helping, access, socialization and development activities, and support services, both formal and informal, that assist older people to maintain themselves in their environment. Basic to the concept of a social support system is the idea that the assistance provided is a

means of augmenting individual competency and mastery over environment rather than increasing dependency.

In this context, the social support system of older people can be viewed as a pattern of continuous ties and interchanges of assistance that play a significant role in maintaining psychological, social, and physical integrity over time. For such a system to function, consistency and availability of relationships are required to meet a variety of needs, both ongoing and time-limited (Cantor, 1981a). Although the concept of a social support system originally stressed supports necessary for independent living in the community, it is equally applicable to institutional life (Dobrof and Litwak, 1977). Excluded from such a conceptualization of social care are those activities and programs dealing specifically with income support and employment, health, formal education, and the provision of housing (Cantor, 1981a).

The notion of a social support system is derived from the work of network theorists such as Mitchell (1969), Barnes (1972), and from mental health and social service literature that stresses the importance of informal or helping networks in sustaining an individual's psychological and physical equilibrium in a rapidly changing and often stressful environment (Collins, 1973; Lowenthal and Robinson, 1976; Snow and Gordon, 1980; Swenson, 1981).

Caplan (1974) postulates the positive health and ego effects of a support system for an individual. For Caplan, a support system involves three elements, all pertinent to the social care needs of older people: significant others help the individual mobilize psychological resources and master emotional burdens; they share his/her tasks; and they provide the extra money, materials, skills, and guidance necessary to improve the handling of a given situation.

Given older people's needs for social supports, how does the system operate to provide the necessary assistance? In the following model, the United States is used as an example, but the approach is equally applicable to other developed countries. Furthermore, it is likely that a similar model of social supports will emerge in less developed countries as formal services for the aged are instituted alongside family care.

The Provision of Social Care—
A Systems Model

Social services currently provided to older people can be categorized in a variety of ways including the type of service (Kamerman and Kahn, 1976), the locale of the service (Little, 1982a), the nature of the service provider (e.g., public, not-for-profit, proprietary), and the source of funding. Our preference is to view services from a system approach. Such a model emphasizes the ever changing, interactive nature of the support system from both the individual and ecological perspectives.

Inasmuch as the social care system of older people has both formal and informal components, any attempt to understand the operation of the system requires an examination of both individual and institutional forces and their interactive effects. In line with this approach, Cantor (1977, 1978, 1980) has conceptualized the social support system of the elderly as a series of concentric circles each containing a different type of support element or subsystem (see Figure 1). In this model, the older person is at the center and the sources of support radiate outward according to the degree of social distance from the older person (i.e., nearest to farthest) and the degree of bureaucracy of the support element (i.e., informal to formal). The older person interacts with the several subsystems, which in turn may interact with each other.

At the outermost reaches of such a system are the political and economic entities that determine the basic entitlements available to older people. Such entitlements impact significantly on well-being in all areas but are particularly germane to income supports, health, housing, safety, and transportation.

Somewhat closer to older people in terms of social distance, though still far from playing a central role in the support system, are public and voluntary service organizations.

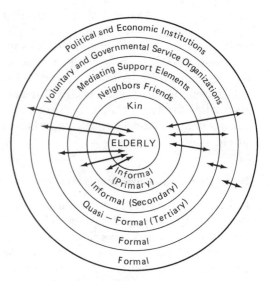

Figure 1.   Schematic model of the social support system of the elderly.
←→ Interaction between systems.
Note: In this model it is possible to start from the center and proceed outward or from the outer ring, the macro system, inward to the microlevel. The direction chosen depends on whether one is concerned with describing the support system of individuals or whether one's interest lies more with issues of social distance and the impact of macrolevel social policies on individuals and families. From: Cantor, M. 1977. Neighbors and friends: An overlooked resource in the informal support system. Paper presented at the symposium: Natural Support Systems for the Elderly: Current Research Implications for Policy, 30th Annual Meeting of the Gerontological Society, San Francisco.

Such organizations carry out the economic and social policies and programs mandated by public laws, such as the Social Security Administration and the Administration on Aging in the United States. The institutions or agencies in the two outer rings are clearly part of the formal support system. In line with the characteristics of bureaucratic organizations, they are expected to function instrumentally and objectively according to an ideology of efficiency and rationality. Thus, formal organizations are best able to provide services requiring the application of technical knowledge uniformly and impartially to large aggregates of people (Litwak and

Mayer 1966; Litwak and Szelenyi, 1969; Litwak, 1978).

Still closer, somewhere between formal organizations and informal networks, are the non-service formal organizations or quasi-formal service organizations. Often referred to as mediating structures, these include religious organizations and racial/cultural, social, block, and neighborhood groups, as well as individuals such as postmen, shopkeepers, bartenders, and building superintendents. Such groups or individuals often serve as a link between the individual and society, as well as offering informal assistance (Berger and Neuhaus, 1977). They have great potential for assisting elderly people and their families to determine, plan, and obtain services (New York State Health Planning Commission, 1981). In the model this circle has been labeled as tertiary support.

Finally, closest to and most involved in the daily life of an older person are the individuals who comprise the innermost circles—the informal support system of kin, friends, and neighbors. It is precisely these "significant others" with whom older people have the most frequent interaction, both instrumentally and affectively; and who provide the broad base of social care in countries throughout the world (U.S. General Accounting Office, 1977; Gibson, 1981).

Caregivers in the informal support system are distinguished from formal service providers in several significant ways. Perhaps most important, they are chosen by the older people on the basis of intimacy and personal involvement. In general, informal assistance is nontechnical in nature (e.g., housekeeping, bathing, feeding, as compared with specialized medical procedures), and is more tailored to the unpredictable and idiosyncratic needs of the individual. Informal supports can, in addition, usually respond more quickly with assistance, and be more flexible with respect to time commitment and task specification. Assistance tends to be based on a system of mutual reciprocity. In the case of kin, such reciprocity stretches over the life cycle; with respect to neighbors and friends, it may have more recent origins. And finally

the role of informal supports in providing affective, emotional support is often crucial and can be as important as the provision of instrumental assistance (Litwak, 1965; Litwak and Szelenyi, 1969; Dobrof and Litwak, 1977; Cantor, 1979a; Dono et al., 1979; Wentowski, 1981).

Although the model (Figure 1) shows each support element as separate and distinct, the subsystems interact considerably, illustrating the dynamic nature of the system. The most common helping interactions are the direct reciprocal exchanges between older people and members of the informal system. Not uncommon, however, are examples of indirect reciprocal interactions in which parents help children, who in turn are involved with neighbors, who may assist the older person in the children's absence. Only among the frailest, most impaired elderly does the pattern of assistance tend to be asymmetrical, flowing in only one direction, usually from younger to older. Yet even in the most difficult caretaking situations involving impaired elderly, there is a suggestion of important psychological benefits to those providing assistance, again underscoring the interactive nature of social supports.

Still another way of viewing the model, holistically, involves the services provided. Certain services may be provided by only one subsystem; in other cases, similar services may be offered by more than one sector. For example, recent studies in Cleveland (U.S. Comptroller, 1977; U.S. GAO, 1977) and New York (Gurland et al., 1978) report that many of the same types of services are being provided by nursing homes and by families in the community. This tendency for overlap is illustrated in Figure 2, where services provided by the informal and formal sectors are related to varying levels of functional impairment.

THE NEED FOR SUPPORTIVE SERVICES

Growth in Aged Population

The growth in the need for aging services, whether formal or informal, is directly related to changes occurring in the world's

		Informal System	Mediating and Formal Systems
Frail impaired, 10%	Low	Co-residence Total money management Assistance in home—extensive, light and heavy housekeeping, meals, shopping, etc. Personal care—washing, bathing supervision of medical regimes, etc.	Institutional care Protective service Case management Counseling—older person and/or families, self-help groups Respite service—day hospital, day care, special set-aside beds Homemaker service Home health aides, visiting nurse Meals on wheels
Moderately impaired, 30%	Level of Competency	System negotiation Help with financial management Accompanying to medical appointments Assistance in home—more frequent, wider array of tasks, i.e., shopping, occasional meal preparation, light housekeeping	Linkage to services, counseling older person Escort, transportation Friendly visiting Congregate housing Chore service—limited in time and amount
Well elderly 60% of population	High	Assistance when ill—short term Assistance in home—short term Escort, transportation Advice Gifts, money Visiting, providing affective support	Reduced-fare programs on public transportation Information and referral Assistance with entitlements, Cultural and spiritual enrichment programs, Socialization, recreation opportunities, i.e., senior center, nutrition, parks

Provider of Service

Note: The services shown are cumulative, and it is assumed that any services shown in a prior level will continue to be available if appropriate.

Figure 2.   Major tasks performed by informal, mediating and formal systems according to level of functional impairment of elderly.

population. Demographic projections presented to the United Nations World Assembly on Aging, Vienna, July 1982, indicated that the fastest-growing population group in the world continues to be the elderly (Oriol, 1982). In 1980, there were an estimated 258 million aged persons 65 and over with the number expected to rise to 396 million by the year 2000 (Myers, 1982).

Although at the present time there is a relatively even division between the number of older people in less developed regions and those in developed regions, a radical shift in the distribution of the world's aged population has been occurring. This trend will be even more pronounced by the year 2000, when approximately 60 percent of the aged will reside in developing countries. However, it is in the already developed regions that the

more rapid graying of the population is occurring; thus 11.4 percent of the total population in developed regions is aged, as compared with 3.9 percent in less industrialized areas. This difference is a reflection of the fact that the younger population in less industrialized regions far exceeds that in more industrialized regions (Myers, 1982).

The preponderance of aged females over males is a well-established fact in the developed countries and is true, although to a lesser degree, in developing countries as well. Inasmuch as women tend to outlive men, the majority of older people are women, and they make up an increasingly larger proportion of the extreme old, 80+ (e.g., in the United States women comprise 57 percent of persons 65 to 74, 63 percent of those 75 to 84, and 70 percent of those 85 and over). This sex imbalance has serious implications for social care because women are more likely than men to be widowed and limited in financial resources.

Equally significant in terms of need for social supports is the rapid increase occurring all over the world in the proportion of elderly 80 and over. In 1980, 14 percent of the world's aged population was in this extreme age category, with the percentages greater in the more developed regions than in the developing regions of the world. The percentage of such persons is expected to increase by the year 2000 in all countries, especially in the more developed; and in nearly all nations 10 percent of the aged population will be 80 years and older (Myers, 1982). For developing countries this will mean still another burden; not only will there be extensive growth in numbers of older people, but that population will become older as well (Myers, 1982). For developed countries, the continued increase in the old-old coincides with the expanded involvement of women in the labor force and the resultant reduction in the pool of persons potentially available to provide family care (Treas, 1981).

The worldwide demographic trends are, of course, reflected in the United States. The 1980 census indicates that there are approximately 25.5 million persons 65 and over, or slightly over 11 percent of the total population. The majority, over 60 percent, are between the ages of 65 and 74 (the young-old); 30 percent are 75 to 84 (moderately old); while approximately 9 percent are 85 years of age or older (the old-old). It is this old-old group that is growing fastest and expected to double by the year 2000, as compared with a 23 percent increase in those 65 to 74 (Brotman, 1982).

Degree of Disability and Service Need among Older People

Although most older people suffer from one or more chronic illnesses, the majority are not sufficiently limited in activities to be considered disabled or dependent. Brody (1981) notes that "most older people do not need any more help than the normal garden variety of reciprocal services that family members of all ages need and give each other on a day to day basis and at times of emergency or temporary illness."

A survey of the data on disability and the need for services in the United States supports this view and suggests that there are three variations in chronic illness and disability rates. Most important is the age factor in impairment, with three distinct groups discernible within the older population. The younger old, 65–74, can be characterized as relatively fit and active (i.e., 61 percent are without any major functional limitation). The moderately old, 75 to 84, have increasing rates of illness and disability—yet even among this group, half are without limitations in their ability to carry out the major activities of daily living. It is the oldest elderly, 85 and over, who are the most vulnerable and in need of assistance. The majority of this group are limited in either the kind or amount of major activity they can undertake, or are totally unable to carry out the major activities of daily living (U.S. Department of Health, Education, and Welfare, 1978; American Council of Life Insurance et al., 1982).

In addition to age, there are sex and socioeconomic differences. Women have higher rates of illness than men, both acute and chronic, and are more likely to suffer limitations in their ability to perform normal routines. However, the diseases associated with women tend to be less life-threatening than those more prevalent among males, suggesting one reason why women tend to outlive men. Furthermore, the burden of illness and chronic disability falls heaviest on those of lowest socioeconomic position and minority status (American Council of Life Insurance et al., 1982).

Most older people in need of social care are found living in the community. The U.S. General Accounting Office (1977) estimated that 10 percent of the total elderly population of the United States could be classified as "extremely impaired" and dependent on the help of others to carry out the basic activities of daily living (ADL) such as bathing, dressing, eating, and toileting. Of this group only 37 percent were in institutions. The remainder were in the community and represented 7 percent of all noninstitutionalized elderly.

In another large health survey, Shanas (1977) found that among community-based elderly about 8 to 10 percent were bedfast or homebound, and as functionally impaired as those in institutions. Thus, there were twice as many bedfast or homebound elderly at home as in institutions (estimated to be 4 to 5 percent of the elderly population at any given time). In addition, another 7 percent of these community residents were able to go outside only with difficulty.

While the amount of help needed by the elderly living in the community in the United States varies greatly, estimates of overall proportion requiring some kind of supportive services range from 12 to 40 percent (depending on the services included). The majority of opinions cluster around the one-third mark, or about 8 million people (Brody, 1981).

Soldo (1980a,b), analyzing the data from a national probability sample of community residents, found certain groups of elderly most likely to be in need of assistance: women, those over 85, widowed persons, and those living with relatives other than spouse. The lower levels of impairment found among persons living alone are probably accounted for by the tendency of older persons with severe health problems to move in with children and other relatives or to be institutionalized if they have no family.

Gurland et al. (1978) introduced a concept of "personal time dependency" (PTD) to measure the time-consuming help required by an older person from others in order to cope with environmental demands. Findings from a random sample of New York City elderly indicated that the proportion of each age group characterized as "personal time dependent" increases steadily with age. However, the majority in each age group remain independent until age 85. Of the total sample, 30 percent were judged to be "personal time dependent" subjects, a figure in line with other estimates regarding the proportion of elderly who require some assistance in order to remain independent in the community.

The demonstrated differences in level of disability and need for assistance among the young-old, the moderately impaired middle-old, and the most vulnerable old-old suggest the appropriateness of using age as an organizing variable in discussions of service provision, whether informal or formal.

THE INFORMAL SUPPORT SYSTEM OF THE ELDERLY

Preceding sections have described the social care system, including its informal and formal components, and the need for care of different groups of older people. We now examine in detail the nature of the social supports provided to older people and the major sources of such help. Inasmuch as the informal sector provides the majority of care and is perceived by the elderly as the first avenue of assistance, we will begin with informal supports.

Three distinct components make up the informal system: kin, close friends or intimates, and neighbors. In turn, six separate support elements are involved. Four are part of the primary or kinship network: spouse, children, siblings, and other relatives (e.g., cousins, grandchildren, etc.). Two elements, friends and neighbors, comprise the secondary support network of significant others (Cantor, 1975b, 1979a).

Family, friends, and neighbors can help only to the extent that they are available and functional. Before describing the assistance provided by informal supports, a brief overview of the living arrangements of older people and the nature of their family–friend relationships will place informal supports in perspective.

Living Arrangements of Older People

Although co-residence between the elderly and an adult child is still found in a few industrialized countries such as Japan and in South Africa among the Coloured, in most developed nations older people tend to maintain their own residences (Gibson, 1981; Lawton, 1982). Research indicates that there is a preference on the part of both generations to live near but in separate quarters, a state Rosenmayr (1977) has called "intimacy at a distance". Even in somewhat less industrialized transitional societies (e.g., Austria, Hungary, Poland, Yugoslavia), joint living is becoming less common and is not the most important factor governing the relationship between old people and their grown children, and whether or not kin provide informal supports (Shanas, 1979b). A reasonable hypothesis to account for the trend away from co-residence is that the attainment of economic independence by older people allows the majority the option of remaining in their own households (Lawton, 1982).

However, the availability of assistance during periods of illness or growing frailty is affected by whether one lives alone or with someone else. In the United States, for example, the 1980 census indicated that 30 percent of the elderly live alone. Among those living with others, the largest proportion (53 percent) live with spouse, while 15 percent live with children or other relatives, and 2 percent living with non-relatives. The proportion living alone increases to 39 percent among persons 75 and over. There is, in addition, a definite sex difference in the proportion of older people living alone; 41 percent of older American women in 1980 were living alone as compared with only 15 percent of men (Crystal, 1982).

Studies from a number of nations indicate that co-residence with other than spouse is more common among older women, lower socioeconomic level families, persons of minority and/or recent immigrant status, and those living in rural areas of the world (Shanas, 1967; Shanas et al., 1968; Cantor, 1975a; Cantor et al., 1979; Rapport Fedéral, 1979; Ciuca, 1979; Simeone et al., 1980; Bengtson et al., 1981; Weeks and Cuellar, 1981; Weihl, 1981; Hörl and Rosenmayr,

1981). Moving in with children is also clearly related to degree of frailty, and older people living with children more commonly suffer from poor health and limited functional ability than those who live independently (Soldo, 1980a,b).

Who Provides Informal Supports?

Research Overview. A review of research with respect to informal supports indicates that the family has received far more attention than have friends, neighbors, and mediating structures. Emphasis on the family, particularly adult children, arises from both the family's centrality in providing social care and its primacy in the lives of the elderly.

Family-oriented research has taken several paths. Initially there was the crucial research that empirically refuted the myth of the dissolution of the family and the isolation of the elderly. Researchers such as Shanas et al. (1968), Sussman (1977, 1979), and Rosenmayr (1977) showed that most older people in industrialized Western countries have children and are in contact with their children on a regular basis; and that substantial assistance is exchanged between generations. Subsequent studies by Bengtson (1979), Bengtson et al. (1981), Cantor (1975a,b; 1979a; 1980; 1981a), Cantor et al. (1979), Hill (1972), and Guttman (1979) indicated that even in America's largest cities, known for their alienation, there were strong familial ties and patterns of mutual assistance between generations. The importance of family was evident among all socioeconomic classes and ethnic groups, although there were variations in the frequency and forms of interaction.

A second and more recent avenue of research focuses more specifically on the role of the family as a support system, particularly in providing long-term care to the frailer, more dependent elderly. Important contributions to an understanding of what the family does have been made by Streib and Shanas (1965), Shanas (1979b), Brody (1978, 1981), Lopata (1975), Gurland et al. (1978),

Rosenmayr (1977), Cantor (1981b, 1982), Branch and Jette (1983), Horowitz and Dobrof (1982), Senior Citizens Provincial Council (1981), Hörl and Rosenmayr (1981), and Maeda (1981), among others. In the beginning it was assumed that children, mainly daughters, were the main supportive element, but recent research by Shanas (1979a,b), Cantor (1981b, 1982), Lewis et al. (1980, 1981), Horowitz and Dobrof (1982), and Lurie (1981) suggest that spouses play a significant and underestimated role in the care of the impaired elderly and require more attention from both a research and a service perspective.

Most recently, research interest in many countries has expanded to documenting the impact on family life of providing care for the frail elderly. Questions of stress and strain and pathways to institutionalization have been explored by Sussman (1979), Gurland et al. (1978), Branch and Jette (1982), Brody (1978, 1981), Horowitz and Dobrof (1982), Cantor (1981a, 1982), Soldo and Myers (1976), Poulshock and Noelker (1982), and Nardone (1980) in the United States; Sanford (1975), Gilleard et al. (1981), Abrams (1978), and Agate (1979) in England; Shimizu and Honma (1978) and Maeda (1981, 1982) in Japan; and Lüders (1981) in Germany, among others. This research has coincided with public policy and practice concerns regarding the nature of assistance required by families to maintain impaired elderly in the community and the appropriate role of formal organizations and government in providing such assistance (Moroney, 1976; Friis, 1979; Sussman, 1979; Callahan et al. 1980; New York State Health Planning Commission, 1981; Steinitz, 1981; Hörl and Rosenmayr, 1981; New York State Office for the Aging, 1983).

Finally, the growing world attention to the role of families and other informal efforts in providing social care for older people was explicitly articulated in the Plan of Action adopted by 98 countries at the United Nations–sponsored World Assembly on Aging, Vienna, 1982 (Oriol, 1982).

Spouses. As indicated above, family members—especially spouses, daughters, and daughters-in-law—provide the bulk of care received by chronically ill elderly in most parts of the world, and the care provided by family resources far outweighs that provided through public and voluntary sectors combined (Gibson, 1981). For older people who are still married, the spouse is usually the primary support element (Shanas, 1979a,b; Cantor, 1982; Horowitz and Dobrof, 1982; Stoller and Earl, 1983). Children in such families are more apt to play a secondary social and/or respite role (Fengler and Goodrich, 1979).

In the United States, according to the 1980 census, 53 percent of all older people are married; this proportion has remained relatively stable for the past few decades. With increasing age the likelihood of having a spouse decreases. Thus, those most in need are least likely to have a spouse (e.g., in the United States four-fifths of those 85 and over have no spouse). Furthermore, differences in longevity and marital patterns mean that older women of all ages are less likely to be married than men. As a result, women are more apt to be cared for by children, while men most usually look to their wives for support (Horowitz and Dobrof, 1982).

Socioeconomic status is also related to the likelihood of spouse support. Among the predominantly lower income elderly in the inner city of New York, only 36 percent had a living spouse as compared with the national average of 53 percent (Cantor, 1975a).

Children. A second and most critical element in the informal support system of older people is children. All major studies of kinship structure in all parts of the world suggest that the adult child–aging parent relationship is special within the family constellation with respect to emotional bonds and interactions as well as service exchanges.

The fact that co-residence is decreasing in most industrialized countries, including Japan, does not mean that ties with children are weakened. A survey of family support patterns in developed nations by Gibson (1981) indicates that most older people have one or more living children, that there is usually at least one child who resides nearby, and that there is generally frequent interaction and bonding between parents and children (Gibson, 1981). Recent European and Canadian studies even suggest that children may more frequently than parents initiate family face-to-face contacts (Roussel, 1976; Teeland, 1978). Studies in United States indicate a similarly high level of interaction and cohesion between generations (Harris et al., 1974; Cantor, 1975a,b, 1981a; Shanas, 1979a,b, 1980; Bengtson et al., 1981).

Older people in the United States, for example, see their children more frequently than other kin, most usually weekly or biweekly, and children serve as the main providers of social care, assuming a less important role only when there is a functional spouse (Harris et al., 1974; Brody, 1966, 1977; Shanas, 1979a,b; Tobin and Kulys, 1980; Cantor, 1981a; Horowitz and Dobrof, 1982).

As in the case of marital status, social class influences the likelihood of having a child, the number of children, and the distance children live from parents. In Britain and the United States, middle class elderly are more likely than working class persons to have only a few children and live at a greater distance from their children (Shanas et al., 1968).

One final consideration in the role of children as support elements concerns the sex of the adult child providing the major amount of assistance. Every study points to the preponderance of daughters as providers of direct day-to-day care with sons playing a less active role except with regard to financial and other family decision making (Hendricks and Hendricks, 1977; Nye, 1976; Troll et al., 1979; Cantor, 1981b; Brody, 1981; Horowitz, 1981; Jacobson and Hawkins, 1982).

Although most older people have children, a sizable number of elderly in all countries are without living children. In United States and Denmark for example, one-fifth nationally are childless, while in Britain almost one-quarter of the elderly are without children (Shanas et al., 1968; Shanas, 1979a,b). The higher proportion of older persons without children reported in studies of the elderly in New York City (ranging from 36 to 44 percent depending on the neighborhood) suggests that big cities may contain a greater concentration of elderly who never married or who have lost contact with families and are therefore without the potential support of close kin. (Cantor, 1975a; Mayer et al., 1981).

While childless elderly form a small proportion of all older people (e.g., less than 20 percent nationally in the United States), they represent a potentially at-risk group for whom formal services may be required. Data on the social profile of the institutionalized elderly indicate that the never married are much overrepresented (Crystal, 1982), and that the fewer children an older person has, the greater the chance of institutionalized placement (Townsend, 1965; Soldo and Myers, 1976; Brody et al., 1978; Brody and Brody, 1981; Branch and Jette, 1982).

Siblings and Other Relatives. The research regarding the informal support role of siblings and other relatives is relatively limited.

According to Townsend and his colleagues, the principle of structured compensation or substitution applies to siblings and other relatives with such kin more likely to be involved when spouse or children are absent or unavailable (Shanas et al., 1968). Similarly, in Cantor's hierarchical compensatory model of social supports, other relatives, friends, and neighbors are preferred sources of assistance in serial order following spouse and child, with formal organizations the least preferred and least likely to be called upon for assistance (Gurian and Cantor, 1978; Cantor, 1979a).

Although four-fifths of the elderly in the United States, Denmark, and Britain have siblings (Shanas et al., 1968; Shanas, 1979a), brothers and sisters are often old themselves and may not be readily accessible either geographically or as caregivers. Those studies that have looked at the full range of informal supports suggest that siblings are less likely than spouse and children to be involved in primary caregiving. Perhaps their most important contribution lies in the area of affective support (Branch and Jette, 1983; Shanas, 1979a,b; Cantor, 1982; Lurie, 1981; Gurland et al., 1978; Horowitz and Dobrof, 1982; Morris and Sherwood, 1984).

However, in the case of elderly who are widowed, childless, or never married, the importance of siblings increases. Shanas et al. (1968) note that "old people who have never married tend to maintain much closer relationships with their brothers and sisters than those who marry and have children." Similar findings are reported by Johnson and Catalano (1981). For many widowed persons, siblings assume some of the responsibilities of a deceased spouse (Shanas, 1979a). In those cases in which two siblings live together and one is homebound or bedfast, the other sibling tends to take on the characteristics of an elderly spouse caregiver with regard to extensive time involvement, kinds of tasks performed, and the degree of emotional and physical strain experienced in the caregiving role (Cantor, 1981b, 1982).

Friends and Neighbors. Friends and neighbors are generally thought to be important in the informal support network of the elderly. The limited evidence regarding their role suggests that they are of particular importance in the lives of the well and mildly impaired elderly and persons without functional family networks. In general, friends and neighbors can not be counted upon to the same degree as family in the long-term care of the frail elderly. Brody et al. (1978) note that informal supports other than those of family become unavailable in proportion to the increasing severity of the older person's impairment. In the few cases in which they are reported as the principal caregiver, they are usually less involved and perform more limited tasks (Gurland et al., 1978; Cantor, 1981b; Lurie, 1981; Horowitz and

Dobrof, 1982; Jacobson and Hawkins, 1982; Branch and Jette, 1983).

However, in the case of "familyless elderly," functional friend/neighbor networks often act in a compensatory manner assuming many of the functions of family (Cohen and Rajkowski, 1982; Stoller and Earl, 1983). For example, among the inner city elderly of New York, "familyless elderly" interacted more frequently with friends and neighbors, and the number of shared activities and level of assistance was much higher than among elderly with families (Cantor and Johnson, 1978). Johnson and Catalano (1981) suggest that unmarried elderly use a process of anticipatory socialization in order to build up a storehouse of resources in the extended family and among friends and neighbors.

With changing life-styles and family patterns, including the increase in numbers of individuals with incomplete ties to a nuclear family (e.g., divorced, never married, migrated), friends and neighbors may be expected to increase in importance in the future, and more research is needed with respect to their role as informal supports.

Functionality of Informal Supports

Merely having a living child, spouse, or other relative does not, however, guarantee having someone willing or in a sufficient position to assist in times of crisis. In an article critical of the current claims about the viability of kinship structures, Gibson (1972) suggests the need for more careful study of the subdimensions of family interaction relevant to support provision, including the availability of kin, the frequency of interaction, and the functionality of kin. In line with this approach, Cantor, (1977, 1979a,b) introduced the concept of "functional support" in examining the support system of New York City's elderly. In this construct, the mere presence of a support element is not considered sufficient to assure meaningful assistance from those around. Rather, for a support element to be considered "functional," there must be evidence of an ongoing and steady-enough relationship to make meaningful assistance possible. Utilizing this stricter definition of functionality considerably reduced the number of children, relatives, and so on, in the social network of the respondents (e.g., 64 percent of the sample had a living child, but only 54 percent had at least one functional child; 65 percent reported having a sibling, but only 29 percent had a functional sibling; etc.) (Cantor, 1977, 1979a).

It would seem that to assess realistically the level of informal supports in a given population, researchers need to use more precise criteria than the number of respondents who report having children, friends, and neighbors or even the number of such persons who live nearby.

Nature of Social Supports Provided by the Informal System

In earlier sections, it was noted that the need for social support varies among different groups of older people, and that there is a clear age gradient with respect to chronic illness and dependency. It was suggested that an examination of patterns of assistance should follow this age continuum and attempt to distinguish between assistance to the younger well-elderly, the moderately impaired middle elderly, and the most vulnerable old-old. The types and amount of assistance and the degree of reciprocity between helper and helped is usually quite different among these groups.

Assistance Patterns Among the Well Elderly. Among younger, more functionally able elderly, assistance between generations and interactions with friends and neighbors follow patterns established in earlier years. In most countries support is generally two-directional, and older people are not passive members of the family or other informal networks. Parents help children with babysitting and gifts (both nonmonetary and monetary), socialize with them, and assist during times of illness. Direct assistance with chores of daily living (e.g., shopping, meal preparation, housekeeping), and the giving of advice are somewhat less frequently reported but are still important aspects of intergenerational relationships. In turn, children respond to parents as the need arises. Again crisis intervention and gift giving far outweigh direct assistance, and there is considerable evidence of affective support through frequent visiting, telephoning, and expressions of closeness between generations (Shanas et al., 1968; Shanas, 1979a; Hill, 1972, 1978; Cantor, 1975a; Roussel, 1976; Gibson, 1981; Hörl and Rosenmayr, 1981). Children also play an important role as intermediary and advocate, supplying information and linkage with the bureaucracies responsible for entitlements and with appropriate formal services (e.g., information and referral services, senior centers, and congregate meal programs) (Sussman, 1965, 1979). Research from eastern European countries indicates that patterns of help and interaction between the elderly and their children in socialist countries are similar to those in the West (Amann, 1980).

Intergenerational exchanges occur in all socioeconomic strata, but the nature and extent of help from children is influenced by class, culture and ethnicity (Shanas et al., 1968; Hill, 1972; Lopata, 1975; Cantor, 1979a; Fry, 1980; Weeks and Cuellar, 1981; Gibson, 1981). In working and lower-middle class families in the United States and Europe, children are more apt to be involved in the direct provision of in-home assistance to parents, while more affluent families rely more heavily on emotional support and gifts and/or monetary assistance (Rosow, 1967; Cantor, 1976, 1979b; Cantor and Brook, 1982).

A noteworthy aspect of the helping patterns in the case of the well elderly is the high degree of reciprocity between generations and between the elderly and their friends and neighbors. Townsend (1968) notes that in Britain and the United States roughly half of the elderly reported receiving help from children during the past month, while 50 to 60 percent of the elderly provided help during the same time period. Among New York City's predominantly low income elderly, 75 percent reported helping children, while a somewhat greater proportion of children, 87 percent, helped parents (Cantor, 1975a). The Harris et al. (1974) study and Bengtson and DeTerre (1980) also showed that a balanced reciprocity between generations characterized the helping patterns in old age.

As in the case of children, relationships between elderly and friends/neighbors tend to be reciprocal. Older people and their friends and neighbors visit together, escort each other to doctors, help out during emergencies, and assist with shopping. Above all, friends/neighbors provide important sources of socialization and affective supports, including tension reduction, over and above that supplied by the kinship system (Cantor, 1975a, 1979a; Cantor and Johnson, 1978; Collins and Pancoast, 1976; Dono et al., 1979; Wentowski, 1981).

Assistance to the Moderately and Severely Impaired Elderly. As older people become frailer and more dependent, a shift occurs in the kinds of social supports needed and the patterns of assistance. Kin respond with more help. Symbolic of alterations in the nature of the help is a change in the nomenclature employed by researchers in describing the helping relationships: caregiver and care-receiver replace the parent–child or friend–friend dyads. An examination of the studies involving the impaired elderly (ranging from persons with moderate functional limitations to the homebound and bedfast) indicates that the helping patterns are altered in the following areas:

1. The time frame of assistance changes from intermittent and crisis-oriented to continual and long-term.
2. The degree of family involvement in the day-to-day lives of the elderly increases from relatively minimal to considerable.
3. Assistance is no longer balanced and

reciprocal but flows more clearly from children to parents.
4. The nature of the tasks changes from peripheral to more central, including direct intervention in housekeeping, personal care, and total management of affairs.

For the family member of a frail older person, caregiving now goes beyond socialization contacts and involves a substantial time commitment in order to provide the needed services. Although estimating time is difficult, Horowitz and Dobrof (1982) found that three quarters of the primary caregivers studied were able to give some approximation, with the estimates varying considerably by type of caregiver. Spouses devote the most time and perform the widest array of tasks—usually a minimum of 35 hours per week (i.e., the equivalent of a full-time job). Children reported spending an average of 18 hours. Other relatives were less frequently designated as primary caregivers, and less involved both timewise and taskwise; 45 percent spent less than 5 hours per week, while the average for the group was 10.8 hours per week in care-related services.

In all studies involving caregiving to frail older people, the array of tasks performed is similar. Providing affective assistance and emotional sustenance (e.g., visiting, sitting and talking, keeping company, watching TV together) clearly emerges as a universal caregiving role involving all types of caregivers (kin and non-kin) and is considered by many to be the most important way in which caregivers help care-receivers (Lewis et al., 1980, 1981; Lurie, 1981; Cantor, 1981b, 1982; Horowitz and Dobrof, 1982).

With respect to instrumental assistance, it is possible to construct a hierarchy of tasks. Frail older people require, at a minimum, assistance with shopping, errands, escort/transportation, and some financial management. These tasks represent the basic level of support provided by most informal caregivers. In addition, many caregivers of even the mildly impaired are involved with obtaining formal services and "negotiating the system" on behalf of the older person (Cantor, 1981b; Lewis et al., 1981; Lurie, 1981; Cantor and Donovan, 1982; Horowitz and Dobrof, 1982; Branch and Jette, 1983).

With somewhat greater functional incapacity comes the next level of tasks performed by somewhat fewer caregivers. These include care of the home (light and heavy housecleaning, laundry) and preparation of meals. Such tasks are labor-intensive services requiring more regular and extended time commitments (Lewis et al., 1980; Horowitz and Dobrof, 1982; Cantor, 1982).

And last there is the most difficult and emotionally draining level of assistance involving the provision of personal care (washing, bathing, toileting) and health maintenance (including supervision of medical regimes, giving of medicine, and performing some medical procedures). Because these services involve very sick elderly with considerable physical and/or mental impairment, such tasks are least frequently reported by informal caregivers. However, studies indicate that anywhere from 25 to 40 percent of the primary caregivers are involved in these arduous responsibilities (Lurie, 1981; Cantor, 1982; Horowitz and Dobrof, 1982). When heavy housekeeping, personal care, and medical assistance are required, there is a greater likelihood that formal support services will be called upon to supplement the informal (Lewis et al., 1981).

The giving of gifts, both monetary and non-monetary was seen to figure heavily in the reciprocal helping patterns of the well elderly. When long-term care is involved, to what extent do families provide financial assistance? Children play an important role in caring for the sick or impaired elderly, but most of this help is provided in kind, and in the United States rarely extends to paying for care provided by someone else, either in the home or in an institution (Crystal, 1982). However, in two studies that inquired into the financial involvement of caregivers in long-term care situations in the community, approximately half of the children and one-quarter of relatives (other than spouse) bore some financial burden, while virtually none

of the friends or neighbors were so involved. Financial assistance provided was more likely to be in the form of groceries and gifts rather than regular monthly allowances, and the dollar value reported was usually in the $1,000–2,000 per year range (Cantor, 1982; Horowitz and Dobrof, 1982). More needs to be known about the financial involvement of family caregivers, in both the United States and other countries, particularly those where filial responsibility is the law. However, it would appear that in the United States at the present time the primary needs of the elderly for food, shelter, and health care are covered by government entitlement programs, with caregivers supplying supplemental assistance according to the needs of the older person and the ability of the family to pay. It is therefore not surprising that in most studies to date, financial strain ranks far behind emotional and physical strain according to the caregivers of frail and dependent elderly (Cantor, 1982; Horowitz and Dobrof, 1982; Poulshock and Noelker, 1982).

Effects of Ethnicity and Class on Informal Social Supports

A general theoretical perspective with respect to the ethnic contrasts in family life emphasizes the uniqueness of minority cultures and their greater potential for family support systems (Frazier, 1957; Bernard, 1967; Stack, 1974; Mindel and Habenstein, 1981). It has been hypothesized that the elderly will receive more social care from the informal support system in minority and immigrant cultures where the traditional extended family pattern is more dominant (Cantor, 1979b; Cantor et al., 1979; Bengtson, 1979; Maldonado, 1979; Jackson, 1980; Weeks and Cuellar, 1981).

Scholars have theoretically viewed ethnicity in several ways, each of which can be related to a companion model of aging in ethnic families. Those who conceptualize ethnicity as culture, particularly immigrant culture, stress assimilation, with variations in family support expected to diminish from generation to generation. Another related view of ethnicity stresses issues of traditional versus modern, with minority and immigrant families seen as following traditional family patterns and majority families as modern in their family relationships. In still another view, ethnicity is associated with minority status and differential societal rewards, with variations in ethnic support patterns arising in response to poverty, discrimination, and social class (Rosenthal, 1982).

Large-scale empirically based research comparing different ethnic groups regarding family roles and the aged remains limited to relatively few studies. The findings suggest that differences due to ethnicity and/or race may be less than presumed, particularly when controls for class and age are introduced.

In an extensive cross-cultural study of the elderly in inner-city New York, Cantor and associates compared life-styles among black, Hispanic, and white elderly (Cantor, 1975a, 1976, 1979b; Mayer, 1976). With regard to patterns of family assistance and evidence of family solidarity, ethnicity was a predictor only with respect to the Hispanic elderly and did not differentiate between blacks and whites when controls were exercised for class and other relevant variables. Compared to blacks and whites, Hispanic elderly were more likely to have a greater number of children available to help (i.e., functional children), saw children more often, and in general received more help from offspring. Among blacks and whites there were no significant differences in these areas. However, with respect to the giving of financial assistance to children, blacks and Hispanics were more similar to each other and gave greater financial assistance compared to white elderly. Cantor et al. (1979) suggest that this greater sharing of more limited economic and social resources on the part of Hispanic and black elderly is a positive adaptation to the pressures of poverty within a functioning family structure.

In another large study of Chicanos, blacks, and Anglos, in Los Angeles County, Bengtson and associates (Bengtson, 1979; Bengtson et al., 1981; Manuel and Bengtson, 1976) had similar findings. Even with controls for relevant variables, Chicanos evidenced the

highest degree of structural, interactional, and normative family solidarity, while blacks and whites evidenced the least and were more similar to each other. Bengtson concluded that contrary to the study's initial hypothesis, "race is not a uniformly predictive variable in indicating family patterns and allocation of responsibility for meeting the needs of the aged. Moreover, although some distinct differences were found, no consistent ethno-minority patterns were indicated with Blacks and Chicanos in some respects being as different from each other as they were from their white counterparts" (Bengtson et al., 1981).

It should be noted that because of sampling limitations and a tendency to conceptualize ethnicity as a minority issue, in most comparative "ethnic" research, including the New York and Los Angeles studies, there has been a tendency to combine white elderly of different national origins into a single "white" category. This has tended to minimize cultural differences among the great variety of groups of European extraction (Holzberg, 1982a,b).

The importance of controlling for class in determining the role of ethnicity as an explanatory variable, is further suggested by Weihl (1981) in a longitudinal study of elderly Israelis of European and non-European origins. Differences in patterns of intergenerational support were found, suggesting a cultural explanation. But when class (i.e., income) controls were introduced, those differences disappeared, leaving income as the underlying explanatory variable.

In discussing the importance of class and culture, Markides (1982) cautions that, in most situations, class and ethnic–minority status are not totally independent of each other. Thus, ethnic or cultural factors may be present, even though significant ethnic differences are not found after controlling for the effects of class. Rather, as Solomon (1981) has noted, it is important to be aware of the cultural nuances that influence the daily life of older people, particularly those that represent a variance from the dominant majority experience.

The impact of ethnicity on the provision

of informal as well as formal supports is an area in which much more research is needed (Gelfand and Kutzik, 1979). The findings, to date, however, suggest caution in the assumption of distinct and overriding minority differences in family assistance patterns or norms regarding family responsibility for the care of the aged. Strong helping networks within families exist among many different ethnic groups, among immigrant populations as well as those who have been in the United States for some time, and among minorities of color (Stack, 1974; Fandetti and Gelfand, 1976; Gelfand and Olsen, 1979; Osako, 1979; Guttmann, 1979; Jackson, 1980; Weeks and Cuellar, 1981; Watson, 1982). There is evidence that over time and generations the effects of dominant socialization are causing the disappearance of many ethnic and minority differentials arising from traditional extended family patterns (Cantor, 1979b; Maldonado, 1979). Thus, it may be that, in the future, ethnic minorities will be as likely as, but no more likely than, majority populations to provide social care for their elderly. Furthermore, the effect of class may prove to be more important than ethnicity in determining the nature and level of informal caregiving. Rosenthal (1982) correctly notes that, to date, scholars studying ethnicity and the family have not been able to move beyond equivocal answers to the question, does ethnicity matter? To do so, it will be important to conceptually clarify the role of culture and successfully disaggregate the effects of culture/ethnicity and class.

Stress and Strain in the Caregiving Role

The rewards of giving care to an older person are primarily interpersonal (Horowitz and Dobrof, 1982). In addition to deep affectional ties, positive values of family continuity and feelings about moral obligations frequently underlie visiting and assistance (Troll et al., 1979). Cultural, religious, and childhood experiences also undoubtedly influence the degree of involvement and commitment. Persons evidencing a strong sense of familism are not only more likely to provide care but are more likely to be affected by the role (Cantor, 1982).

However, despite the warmest feelings and best intentions, caring for a frail dependent elder frequently involves considerable strain as well as family disruption. Because so many caregivers are women, particularly middle-aged women, with responsibilities for parents on the one hand and their own families on the other, Brody has referred to them as "the women in the middle" (Brody, 1981). For many such women there is still a third point of pressure, as more and more return or continue to work (Treas, 1977). Findings suggest that such women respond not by giving up the care of the elderly but by curtailing to a minimum their own personal lives to meet the added responsibilities (Brody, 1981; Horowitz and Dobrof, 1982; Cantor, 1981b, 1982).

It is not surprising, therefore, that emerging research from many nations (including the United Kingdom, Japan, and Germany as well as the United States) is documenting the considerable stress and strain involved in providing long-term care to elderly relatives (Gibson, 1982). Most pervasive and often expressed is the emotional strain, followed next by physical strain and to a lesser degree financial strain (Mellor and Getzel, 1980; Cantor, 1982; Horowitz and Dobrof, 1982; Gibson, 1982). The level of strain differs for different types of caregivers according to the centrality of the relationship and the amount of involvement. As a result, spouse and children are more likely to suffer strain than other relatives, while friends and neighbors experience the least amount of strain (Cantor, 1981b). Strain appears to be more severe in situations involving mental impairment and disruptive behavior (e.g., senile dementia) than functional limitations (Zarit et al., 1980; Moryez, 1980; Poulshock and Deimling, 1982; Poulshock and Noelker, 1982; Gibson, 1982).

Because strain and personal dislocation are so endemic to long-term caregiving, there is considerable interest in methods to ease the burdens of families. While the development of services targeted to family caregivers does not seem to be keeping pace with evidence indicating their need for assistance, there are some encouraging examples in several nations (Gibson, 1982). Most widespread is the provision of supplementary in-home services. In addition, however, other types of respite services are slowly developing, including day care, day hospitals, and the provision of beds for short-term stays in nursing homes or other residential settings. In New Zealand, for example, those caring for disabled elderly are entitled to four-week holidays through the Disabled Relief Scheme, which places impaired elderly in suitable residential accommodations or provides alternative care in the home (Gibson, 1982). In the United Kingdom and other countries where beds are not easily available, special short-stay residential establishments have been developed, often under voluntary auspices with the assistance of public funds (Hobman, 1981). Yet another alternative to institutional short-term care is to provide temporary placements for elderly persons in private homes of qualified individuals, a program that has proved successful in the United Kingdom (Thornton and Moore, 1980). Finally, several other forms of respite care are provided under voluntary auspices in Britain, including a program called "crossroads care attendant," which provides volunteers as part-time care attendants to support families and disabled elderly (Osborne, 1981).

Growing in popularity as a means of strengthening family networks and supplying needed emotional and informal aid and assistance to caregivers, are group support programs for families of the frail elderly. Such programs have been directed to relatives of community-based elderly, those in institutions, and most recently relatives of mentally impaired elderly suffering from Alzheimer's disease. Reports from a variety of countries (e.g., Denmark, Germany, the United Kingdom, Canada, the United States, the Netherlands) suggest that such groups lessen the sense of isolation of family members and help them to cope with their tasks (Crossman et al., 1981; Gibson, 1982). In the United States, the group support movement recently evolved into a new phase, that of social action (Mellor et al., 1981).

Provision of special allowances to disabled persons and/or financial incentives for families providing long-term care for older people is also an emergent trend. Forty-seven countries (but not including Canada, the United States, or the Federal Republic of Germany) have some form of constant attendance allowance for eligible disabled persons who need assistance from another adult. Although geared primarily to working populations, these payments have also been extended to non-work-related conditions in some countries (Great Britain). The sums are not sufficient to purchase costly care but enable such persons to compensate a relative or friend or purchase some form of assistance (Morris and Leavitt, 1982).

In the United States, three states (California, Florida, and Maryland) have experimented with cash allowances for family members (but not spouse) who care for impaired elderly in their own homes (State of Maryland, 1977; Whitfield, 1982; New York State Office for the Aging, 1983). In the Soviet Union, Bulgaria, Poland, and Hungary, individuals providing long-term care for older family members are eligible for the same type of privileged pension treatment as workers in arduous occupations (e.g., earlier retirement, shorter service requirements) (Chebotarev et al., 1982). Given the increase in numbers of old-old and rising costs of institutional care, much more needs to be known about ways of helping informal caregivers and the appropriate combination of service and financial incentives for families involved in long-term care of the elderly.

THE FORMAL SUPPORT SYSTEM

As discussed in the previous section, mutual aid between adult children and their aging parents is a norm as well as common practice in nations throughout the world (United Nations, 1982). Even in the case of the more impaired elderly requiring intensive and extensive care, the major source of nonmedical supports comes from family, friends, and neighbors. Callahan et al. (1980) suggest that the family role in the provision of care to all impaired persons in the United States, regardless of age, is significant for between 60 percent and 85 percent of the disabled in the society. Collins and Pancoast (1976) postulate that without informal supports formal services would be overwhelmed, a position supported by the U.S. General Accounting Office (1977) findings that families provide up to 80 percent of all home health care for elderly individuals in the United States.

Although a considerable body of literature attests to the significance of the informal system in the lives of older people, this in no way minimizes the role of formal social services. It is important to reiterate that there are sizable numbers of older people without living children and some elderly without other kin or friends/neighbors to act as compensatory informal supports [e.g., 8 percent of the 400,000 elderly living in inner-city New York were without any formal supports, while in another study 10 percent of the respondents named a "responsible other" who performed neither affective nor instrumental functions (Cantor, 1975a; Tobin and Kulys, 1980)]. For such elderly the formal system is the principal source of social care.

Furthermore, the findings on the nature of caring for impaired elderly and the resultant stresses and strains illustrate the crucial backup and respite role of formal social services in enabling families to maintain their elderly in the community. Also some types of services can best be performed by the formal sector, from both a societal and an individual perspective.

The Role of Formal Services

Given the extensive data on the role of the informal support system, as well as its limitations, what responsibilities are assumed by the formal sector of public, not-for-profit voluntary, and proprietary agencies, and which groups of elderly do they serve? Using the age continuum employed in previous sections, we find that formal social services are utilized by all three groups of elderly: the

well, generally younger, elderly; the moderately impaired older elderly; and the often very frail old-old.

The formal support system, in all countries where it exists, provides services that supplement, complement, and in some cases substitute for family care. As with informal supports, there is a relationship between the nature of services and the level of dependency of the older person. The extent of formal services, however, is a product of macrolevel factors such as the stage of social and economic development of the country, the proportion of elderly in the population, and the dominant value system regarding the appropriate roles of the individual and society in providing care for dependent persons.

In the case of the younger well elderly, formal services are mainly important in the area of socialization and personal development. Thus, well elderly are involved in senior centers, congregate meal programs, adult education, volunteer services, and other formal sector programs with activity and socialization as the core components. The moderately frail elderly may take part in some of the same programs, but in addition may need help from formal organizations with housekeeping chores, shopping, transportation, and other aspects of daily living. For the frail old-old, the importance of formal social services markedly increases including a wide range of in home services and personal care. Where the family is an active caregiver, formal services may act as a backup or respite. In the absence of a functional informal network, the formal sector acts as a substitute for family and is expected to assume surrogate responsibility through the provision of either in-home services or institutional care. In addition, all three groups of elderly sometimes require information and referral services, assistance in securing or retaining entitlements, and help in completing application, tax, and insurance forms. Some elderly and their families also require counseling or legal services. (For a summary of formal services by target population, see above, Figure 2.)

The Continuum of Care

A value that seems to be expressed in every society, regardless of ideology or stage of development, is that older people should remain "at home" and "in familiar surroundings" as long as possible. Although this is the value preference, it is accompanied by wide variations in resource allocation and service delivery patterns between countries and even among local authorities within the same country. In fact, there is evidence suggesting that most countries react initially to perceived needs of physically dependent elderly in terms of institutional care and/or specialized independent housing (Little, 1974, 1975a,b, 1978, 1979, 1982a; Morris and Leavitt, 1982). Thus, Lawton (1982) found that the first institutions available in a developing country are local hospitals or private old age homes, often sponsored by a religious or fraternal group. With less family support and more older people to care for, authorities usually think in terms of more beds, as in Egypt today (Fadel-Girgis, 1982).

However, the continuum of care needed to meet the needs of the well, moderately frail, and very frail elderly involves a variety of personal care services in the community, the home, and institutions. On the basis of studies sponsored by the European Center for Social Welfare Training and Research, Little (1979, 1982a) and others have conceptualized social care for the elderly as having three components: open care, closed care, and unorganized care. *Open care* is care in the community provided by the formal sector, and encompasses all of the formal social services aimed at supporting independent living in one's home and forestalling premature or unnecessary institutionalization. *Closed care,* by contrast, is formal care in institutions behind closed doors including both medical and social facilities such as shelters or homes for the aged, nursing homes, and other forms of congregate living. These two forms of care comprise the formal system in the model set forth in Figure 1, above. *Unorganized or nonorganized care* is the term reserved for the informal caregivers (i.e., the first, second, and third circles in Figure 1).

From the 24 developed and developing countries studied by Little (1979, 1982a), and the seven European countries studied by the Amann (1980) group, certain generalizations about social care can be drawn. All types of care are found side by side, with a substantial amount of the care being provided by families supplemented by neighbors and friends. Most societies have some institutions (i.e., closed care), and public funding for institutional care always exceeds that for open care services. While most countries agree on the value of community living, there is a serious deficit in home-delivered open care services to supplement informal care.

The Development of Closed and Open Care

Comparative research on social care systems in different countries suggests that closed care typically develops before open care. In the development of closed care, six stages have been identified; the first three are more characteristic of developing countries, and the latter three of developed countries (Little, 1982a). Figure 3 shows these six stages with an indication of representative countries at each stage.

Widespread attention to open care, even in developed countries, has only occurred in the past 50 years as the cost of medical care has escalated, and as personal expectations for independent living have increased (Morris and Leavitt, 1982). In the development of open care, like closed care, different stages may be distinguished, providing a useful analytic tool for examining the open care system or non-system of a given country. Four stages of open care have been identified by Little (1982a) and are shown in Figure 3, with examples of countries at each stage. It should be noted that with respect to both open and closed care, development does not necessarily progress in a linear fashion.

Level of Effort

Although it is possible to assess the level of development of a country with regard to open and closed care, precise quantitative and qualitative indicators to measure and

Closed Care			Open Care		
Stage of Development	Characteristics	Example	Stage of Development	Characteristics	Example
Stage 1	One or more privately sponsored old age homes, often by church/religious groups	Western Samoa	Stage 1	Embryonic, essentially unorganized, no public assistance, no or few private agencies	Western Samoa
Stage 2	Beginning regulation and nationalization of private homes	Singapore Hong Kong	Stage 2	Emergent, largely private sector, limited public funding to private sector	Hong Kong
Stage 3	Establishment of model old age homes Semipublic auspices Public In national capital In different regions	Burma Philippines Thailand	Stage 3	Rapid transition and expansion of services emanating from public welfare offices	Japan
Stage 4	Public reimbursements to private institutions and attendant regulation	United States	Stage 4	A highly developed public system with services extended to entire country, including rural areas	Sweden
Stage 5	A mix of public and private-for-pay institutions	Japan			
Stage 6	A highly developed public system of institutions of specialized types and varying levels of care	Great Britain Sweden			

Countries studied: Afghanistan, Indonesia, Western Samoa, Burma, Pakistan, Kenya, Iran, India, Philippines, Greece, Singapore, Hong Kong, New Zealand, Australia, Austria, Germany, Netherlands, United States, Japan, Israel, Canada, Great Britain, Denmark, Sweden.

Figure 3.   Typology of the development of closed and open care in 24 selected countries. (Constructed from information in Little, 1982a, pp. 17–18).

compare resource allocations to formal programs for older people are in their infancy (Little, 1982a; Morris and Leavitt, 1982). The most commonly used measures have been the rate of institutionalization and the rate of co-residence with adult children. Rates of institutionalization vary widely from a low of 1 to 2 percent in countries such as Poland and Japan where co-residence is relatively widespread, to 3 to 4 percent in Great Britain and Austria, to 5 percent in the United States, Western Germany, and France, to a reported high of 6 percent in Denmark and 10 percent in the Netherlands (Little, 1979). However, to evaluate these figures properly one needs to know exactly what is included in institutional care as well as the level of co-residence and the allocation of resources to open care.

With respect to open care, the best data are those that cover home helpers, since most countries consider home help the core of open care. The actual number of home helpers reported by the 16 developed-country members of the International Council on

Home Help Services showed a steady rise from 1970 to 1976 (i.e., 118, 718 in 1970 to 209,000 in 1976 (Morris and Leavitt, 1982)). An even better measure of comparative effort than sheer numbers of helpers is the ratio of home helpers per 100,000 total population as proposed by Little (1974). Table 1 shows the number of home helpers and the ratio per total population for the 16 developed countries in 1976/77. Although growth in absolute numbers of home helpers has occurred, the ratios of home care per 100,000 population suggest that open care for the elderly at home is still very thin and uneven, even in the most developed countries (Morris and Leavitt, 1982). As can be seen in Table 1, there is a sharp drop from a high ratio in Sweden, Norway, and the Netherlands, to a moderate ratio in Great Britain, to token coverage in most other countries. The relatively low availability of formal sector help in the home only underscores the previously noted importance of family care in the lives of frail or impaired elderly.

TABLE 1. Number of Home Helpers and Ratio PER 100,000 Persons in Total Population in Selected Countries.

Countries	Total Population (000 omitted)	Number of Home Helpers	1976/77 Rates per 100,000 Pop.
Australia*	12,500	2,747	22.0
Austria*	7,525	340	4.5
Belgium	9,823	9,953	101.0
Canada*	22,000	3,290	15.0
Finland	4,700	6,943	148.0
France	53,000	51,062	96.0
W. Germany*	60,000	12,685	22.0
Gt. Britain*	49,000	129,724	265.0
Israel	3,500	500	14.0
Italy	54,000	50	0.1
Japan	115,276	11,369	9.8
Netherlands	13,500	101,057	748.0
Norway	4,054	41,184	984.0
Sweden	3,000	77,550	946.0
Switzerland	6,000	3,760	63.0
United States*	209,000	60,000	28.7

* Dec. 1976 = latest figures available. For the other countries figures are Dec. 1977.

SOURCE: Adopted from Little (1982a, p. 92).

Delivery of Formal Services
in the United States

In the United States, the federal government's major strategy with regard to older people has been to provide income or income supplementation, either directly through cash programs or indirectly through the payment of hospital and medical care, tax benefits, and other non-cash benefits such as food or subsidized housing (Kahn and Kamerman, 1978). The health programs that affect the elderly (Medicare, Medicaid) have in the main encouraged the expansion of closed care institutions and institutional care. Federal expenditures for open care programs, on the other hand, have been relatively small and experienced further reductions in funding in fiscal years 1981 and 1982.

The Subcommittee on Human Services, Select Committee on Aging, U.S. House of Representatives estimated in a 1980 report that for every dollar allocated to older people, 71.4 cents was for retirement benefits, 22.7 cents for health benefits, 2.8 cents for income maintenance (SSI), .7 cent for employment services, and only 1.5 cents for community-based social services and nutrition programs combined (U.S. Congress, 1980). Furthermore the retirement benefits and health care are partially self-funded. If expenditures for all partially self-funded programs had been excluded from 1982 federal spending estimates, less than 4 percent of the federal budget would have been directed to programs assisting the elderly (U.S. Congress, 1982a). In addition to federal monies, funds also come from states, localities, and private philanthropy, but such monies play a relatively minor role in open care service funding for older Americans.

Ideally, a social service delivery system translates resources into assistance. Unfortunately, fragmented policy over time has created not one but several service systems in the United States, making for considerable fragmentation and sometimes duplication of effort (U.S. Congress, 1980).

Social services for older people are mainly provided under two auspices: the Social Services Block Grant (Title XX) of the Social Security Act (Public Law 93–647), and the Older Americans Act (Public Law 89–73). Each of these mechanisms has a different service delivery system and different eligibility criteria, although in some localities similar services are provided under both (e.g., senior centers funded by Title XX and nutrition programs by the Older Americans Act). A third funding mechanism, revenue sharing, which distributes federal tax revenue on a formula basis to states and localities, may also affect older people. However, it is generally agreed that very few of these funds go to support services for seniors (U.S. Congress, 1980).

Title XX, now the Social Services Block Grant, is a 2.5-billion-dollar federal program that provides funds to states on a 75 percent federal–25 percent state formula for costs incurred in providing social services to low income people of all ages. The program operates as a block grant to states, which determine what services to provide under broad federal guidelines. However, at least three services must be directed toward the aged, blind, or disabled receiving Supplemental Security Income. Under Title XX (Social Service Block Grant) the designated state agencies (usually the Department of Social Services) contract with social service providers to deliver services outlined in a state plan. Title XX programs are means-tested, except that information and referral and protective services may be provided to anyone regardless of income. Because Title XX covers all ages and the number of elderly served varies according to state plans, it is hard to identify the number of elderly covered by Title XX. It was estimated (U.S. Congress, 1982a) that in fiscal 1981 about 21 percent of the total program dollars benefited the elderly.

The current Title XX Social Services Block Grant represents a consolidation of several existing categorical programs. The funding level in 1981 at the time of consolidation was set lower than the combined totals of the individual programs, and the 1982 authorization constituted a further 20 percent reduction from the already reduced 1981 level (U.S. Congress, 1982a). This has precluded any expansion to meet the needs of a growing population, particularly the increasing number of frail elderly. The U.S. government in its report on aging to the United Nations World Assembly therefore noted that "not all older persons with unmet needs are eligible for block grant financed services" (U.S. Department of State, 1982).

The other major legislation providing formal social services for older people is the Older Americans Act (OAA) of 1965. To channel federal, state, and local resources to older people and service providers, the Act mandated the establishment of a three-tiered aging network. The network includes the federal Administration on Aging (Department of Health and Human Services) and, in each state, a State Office on Aging (SOA) having administrative, advocacy, coordination, and evaluation responsibilities. In turn, under the 1973 amendments, each state is divided into planning and service areas headed by Area Agencies on Aging (AAAs). The commissioner of aging awards grants to each State Agency on Aging according to that state's elderly population. The states in turn reallocate the funds to the AAAs.

Congress reaffirmed strong support for the OAA programs in 1981. However, in 1982, the programs suffered a 4.3 percent cut in funding from the fiscal 1981 level, with total 1982 funding at about $900 million (U.S. Congress, 1982a). The Act's major service provisions are found in Title III, which provides funds for the development of a comprehensive and coordinated state and local delivery system of supportive social services, senior centers, and nutrition and home-delivered-meal programs. The other titles of the Act, mainly federally administered, cover training, research, and demonstrations (Title IV), senior community service employment programs (Title V), and grants to Native American ("Indian") tribes (Title VI). Although the goals of the Act are broad, the funding is limited and tends to be spread thin (less than one billion for all titles). Critics have questioned how much impact the OAA

can have on any one problem or on system change (U.S. Congress, 1980).

At the local level, AAAs are responsible for needs assessment and service planning within their jurisdictions. AAAs develop area plans that in turn are approved and coordinated into the state plan outlining how Older Americans Act monies are to be allocated statewide. In general AAAs do not deliver services themselves (with the exception of information and referral assistance). Rather they act as administrative, planning, and advocacy units identifying gaps in service and contracting with local agencies to provide the authorized nutrition services and the locally identified gap-filling services.

Thus the current service delivery system in the United States is a purchase-of-service system with few public services as such. Units of service are delivered by contract under the Social Services Block Grants (Title XX, Social Security Act) and by grantees under Title III of the Older Americans Act. In the main, the providers of service are voluntary not-for-profit social agencies, community groups, or religious organizations that respond to "requests for proposals" to provide services specified in various area or state plans.

As would be expected given the diverse funding mechanisms and service criteria, programs and services vary widely from state to state and among localities. At best, localities have information and referral services, nutrition and home-delivered-meal programs, and usually a minimal level of in-home services, possibly targeted only to elderly with low income (U.S. Congress, 1982a). However, Title XX Social Services Block Grant services have mandated income elgibility criteria, while in general Title III programs have none. Except through demonstration programs or in a few states, such as Massachusetts, there is no single entry point into a single service delivery system. Even when one has successfully accessed the system, there may be few or no services for which one is eligible, and those that are available may be fragmented and uncoordinated (U.S. Congress, 1980).

Social Care Delivery Models
in Countries Outside the United States

International comparisons are possible today as reflected in such recent publications as: the first four volumes of the *Meeting Human Needs* series (Thursz and Vigilante, 1975–79); the work of Kahn and Kamerman (1977, 1978), in which social care systems in eight countries were compared; Amann's (1980) studies of open care systems in European countries; Little's (1979, 1982a) studies of closed and open care development in selected European and Asian nations; and Nusberg's (1972–present) comprehensive reporting on worldwide developments in *Ageing International.*

A look at the literature on social care, however, indicates that there are really only a few models, most of which originate in western Europe and Great Britain. The world's largest Communist societies—the Union of Soviet Socialist Republics and the People's Republic of China—have no models and few formal programs, other than a small number of closed care institutions and limited pension systems. Instead, these countries have opted to give top priority to promoting universal health care, beginning at the commune level with *feldschers* or barefoot doctors. Social care remains in the informal sector. There is no recognized profession of social work, nor are there training programs as such (Madison, 1968, 1975; Sidel, 1972, 1976).

The most developed social care programs are found in the advanced welfare states such as the Scandinavian countries and Britain. Other western European countries have their own variants of the basic model. Certain characteristics typify the welfare systems of these countries. There is usually a strong public welfare base with responsibility lodged in district offices; a national health system; and an older and more comprehensive system of social insurance. Such countries usually have a variety of institutions, medical and nonmedical, and a sizable investment in public housing, including variations of sheltered housing for older people. As a rule, they have more adequate public transportation than is found in many parts of the United States, with its greater dependence on private automobiles.

Kahn and Kamerman (1978), in their comprehensive cross-national study of social welfare systems in eight countries, suggest that there are, in fact, six basic subsystems that comprise human services. The first five are income transfers, health, housing, education, and employment training. The sixth emerging system is social services or personal services (both open and closed), and is akin to social care as we have defined it herein.

Focusing on personal social services, Kahn and Kamerman (1978) identified four basic patterns of service delivery, and noted countries that best typify each pattern as follows:

- A free-standing comprehensive, integrated, personal social service system with a delivery outlet in each locality (United Kingdom).
- Personal social services based in many societal institutions (e.g., schools, factories, social security offices) and integrated locally as needed by *polyvalents de secteur,* social workers who cover geographic area (France).
- Parallel public and voluntary systems, often subdivided into child welfare and "other" services—the "other" theoretically including the family, young and single, and aged. However, in practice, only services to the aged have seen expansion in recent years (Germany).
- The life-cycle approach in which the social institution most critical to a life phase is the base for services for all six service subsystems—i.e., health is the base through age 6, education until employment, workplace and union for work life, and health again after retirement (Poland).

In addition to these more generalized models of service delivery, there are countries such as the United States and Canada that have a multiple system model characterized by regional variations and a variety of systems and outlets (e.g., Title XX and the OAA).

Within these broad service delivery patterns, countries have interesting variations—some for the system as a whole, some pertaining only to the older frailer citizens. The Netherlands, for example, resembles other western European countries in having a highly structured public welfare system. However, actual service delivery is handled by a parallel structure of organized private providers, making it closer to the purchase of service model common in the United States. The "life cycle" approach in Poland has a variation unique only to that country: almost all social services are delivered by volunteers. Thus retired teachers and civil servants are largely responsible for serving older people, thereby supplementing the heavy support provided by family.

Another variation among countries is the focus of services and whether they are individual or collective (to use Swedish terminology). Tobin (1977) suggests that time and cost vary according to whether services are delivered individually or in a congregate setting.

Experimentation with congregate service delivery is widespread in European countries. Sweden, for example, has a new kind of housing called residential hotels or service houses with 24-hour coverage and a built-in staff of home helpers. Swedish old age homes are being phased out in favor of this newer modality (Little, 1978a). In Britain's sheltered housing, the so-called wardens link residents to community open care systems and at the same time supply all kinds of personalized individual attention themselves (Heumann, 1980). Israel's long-range planning for the aged includes remodeling closed care institutions and training their staff to look outward and serve the surrounding community (Bergman, 1973).

The delivery system for older people in West Germany has recently been augmented by the establishment of separate local service offices for the elderly (*Sozialstationen*), principally set up to provide home nursing and home help. Because Germany has dual public and private social services, each "Land" (province) was given the right to decide where and under whose auspices the *Sozialstationen* should be established. *Sozialstationen* are also found in Vienna, Austria, which previously had instituted a citywide system of *Pensioninstenheime* or homes designed principally for pensioners still able to live independently (Little, 1982a).

Looking at other parts of the world, most British Commonwealth countries have followed Western models of social care. Japan has borrowed deliberately from abroad, especially from Britain and Sweden and to a lesser extent from the United States. City-states such as Singapore and Hong Kong have their own particular combination of Western and Asian elements. Since both have a Council of Social Services to organize the private sector, the major issues concern the extent to which public funds will be made available to subsidize emerging services. Meanwhile, populous countries like India and Indonesia have virtually no programs or provisions for formal public social care and rely primarily on the informal support system (Little, 1982a,b).

Issues in Service Delivery

In any country, certain service delivery issues require consideration. Among the most pressing for older persons and their families is whether the system has one or multiple points of entry. Another question facing older persons is what services are available and whether they meet needs.

At the macrolevel, most Western countries have chosen to emphasize local government responsibility with respect to needs assessment and resource allocation within a broad framework of national policy. However, the degree of decentralization varies: in Western Germany and the United States, considerable autonomy is given to states, provinces and localities; in Britain, national guidelines are clearly set but local variance is allowed; while in Sweden, a required basic core of in-home services is in place throughout the country (Kahn and Kamerman, 1977; Little, 1978a). Although decentralized organizational strategies have many advantages, there is always the possibility of considerable variation among neighboring communities, and what British home help studies have termed "territorial inequity" (Davies, 1971; Goldberg and Connelly, 1978).

From the individual point of view, the questions of which services are needed and how to procure them present multiple difficulties. As noted previously, in the United States, for example, this may mean accessing different formal services from different providers with different eligibility requirements and different workers. Usually this involves going to several offices; sometimes there may be a number of different formal helpers coming into the home at different times. According to the Federal Council on Aging (1975–80, 1978), frail older Americans require either professional counselors or helping relatives to guide them through the maze.

In analyzing the difficulties in obtaining social services in a highly fragmented "non-system," Lowy (1979) and Tobin (1977) have highlighted the lack of three A's: access, availability, and adequacy. Other, more medically oriented analysts have stressed the absence of three C's: comprehensiveness, continuity, and coordination (Kane and Kane, 1976). All agree, however, on the centrality of the related problems of access and service integration and coordination.

Eschewing broad system change as such, the United States has tended, in recent years, to concentrate efforts on a series of demonstration projects aimed at achieving access through a single entry point and coordination of service through the case management approach (i.e., a single person or team coordinates the case for an older person and acts as an advocate to obtain needed services) (Steinberg, 1979; Little, 1981; Steinberg and Carter, 1982). There is a widely shared consensus that a major weakness of the U.S. non-system is its lack of a universal gateway or doorway to service. Unlike the European or Japanese older client who knows exactly where to go (i.e., the local public welfare office or local authority (Little, 1979)), the older American is faced with many private providers who may or may not

be known to the individual and may or may not relate to each other. Providing a single entry point was one of the achievements of the first Massachusetts local Home Care Corporations (Somerville-Cambridge Home Care Corporation, 1975), and of a series of other demonstration projects such as Triage in central Connecticut, On Lok in San Francisco's Chinatown, AGE in Minneapolis, and statewide projects in Illinois and Oregon (Minneapolis Age and Opportunity Center, 1975; Kalish and Lurie, 1975; Little, 1976; Taber et al., 1980, Hodgson and Quinn, 1980; special issue of *Gerontologist,* June 1980; Quinn et al., 1982).

Establishing a single entry point is, of course, much simpler when one is setting up a new demonstration program. A far more complicated task is to achieve service coordination among a group of existing agencies with different funding sources in an urban or county area. One demonstration project, ACCESS in Monroe County, New York, was able to bring together a complex system of medical and social care by doing the initial assessments and providing ongoing case management (Eggert et al., 1980).

Several other demonstration projects attempting various aspects of service coordination, integrated case planning, and case management are still in the early stages—notably the "Channeling Projects" for the frail elderly under the aegis of the Health Care Financing Administration, Department of Health and Human Services; and the new Social Health Maintenance Organizations in which social and health services will be provided in a single agency on a capitation payment basis (Diamond and Berman, 1979). However, to date, there are virtually no empirical data suggesting that successful service coordination and integration, either within the formal social care system or between social and health care systems, is achievable beyond the demonstration phase. Even countries like Sweden and the United Kingdom, with more extensive service systems, have grappled with how to coordinate their health and social care systems without outstanding success (Kahn, 1979; Flynn, 1980;

Little, 1982a); although a single entry point may be more easily attainable, service coordination, particularly between the health and social care systems, would at best appear to be far in the future.

CONCLUSIONS AND FUTURE DIRECTIONS

This chapter has been devoted to a discussion of social care of the elderly in the United States and in other parts of the world. The availability of adequate social care or social supports (used interchangeably herein) is seen as an important factor in the maintenance of quality of life for older people whether living in the community or in institutions. Basic to the discussion is the conceptualization of social care as going beyond traditional social services to include both informal and formal supports in a single broad-based social care system. Social supports seen from such a systems perspective involve several separate but interacting subsystems—the informal, mediating, and formal—each with distinguishing attributes and distinct although sometimes overlapping roles. Because of cultural norms of independence and self-sufficiency, many older people are reluctant to seek assistance; but when they do, their preference is to involve those with whom they are socially closest—family, friends, and neighbors. At any given time, the nature and amount of assistance provided by family and significant others is related to the age and degree of frailty of the older person. In addition, family structure, socioeconomic status, and ethnicity influence caregiving patterns. With increasing age there is some evidence of a shift from total reliance on the informal to greater involvement of formal services. Assistance in the case of the frail and impaired elderly changes from the normal "garden variety" of reciprocal assistance characteristic of intergenerational relationships to more protracted levels of care involving the tasks of daily living and even personal care. Issues of family strain become more paramount, and both informal and formal interventions may be required. Eventually as one reaches the outer limits of the age-impairment continuum, the formal system tends to assume a more important role in the provision of social care to the frailest elderly.

In line with the preferences of older people and their families, in all parts of the world, kin, principally spouse and children, are the main providers of social care, supplemented by friends, neighbors, and other informal community helpers. However, the role of formal care can be of critical importance. Formal care, in those countries where it exists, provides services that supplement, complement, and in some cases substitute for family care. Countries vary in the pattern of service delivery and the extent to which formal social care services are organized into a single or multiple delivery system. In the United States, social services tend to be fragmented, with diverse funding sources and eligibility criteria, and there is rarely a single entry point to services. The formal system in the United States has often been referred to as a non-system. In contrast, western European systems are better developed, have a stronger public welfare base, and tend to have clearly defined gateways to services, known to both older people and their families.

Given this overview of the current state of social care, both informal and formal, what are some of the important issues that will require research and policy attention in the decades ahead? First are the questions pertaining to the ability of families and other informal supports to continue as the principal providers of social care.

The number of older people in the population relative to younger adults is expected to increase worldwide; and the fastest-growing segment of the elderly population, particularly in developed countries, is the aged over 75. These are the very people who will need the greatest amount of assistance. Thus, there will be more, not less, need for social care in the coming decades.

At the same time, women, presently the major providers of informal care, are increasingly entering the labor market and remaining even during the years of child rearing. Particularly significant is the increase in working women aged 45-64, the very group who have traditionally contributed many hours to volunteer service and informal support of the elderly. As yet there is no indication that today's women, even those who work, are abandoning their filial responsibilities. These "women in the middle" appear to be assuming multiple roles of caring for their own families, for aged parents, and for parents-in-law in addition to working. How long this pattern will continue is unknown. However, the strain involved is considerable and has implications for both younger families and older people.

Furthermore, spouses as well as friends and neighbors are also involved as informal caregivers. Compared to the "women in the middle," much less is known about the difficulties these people face and the extent to which they can reasonably be expected to continue as viable sources of long-term care. More attention needs to be directed to such persons as well as the appropriate involvement of other neighborhood helpers such as churches, block associations, postmen, and so on.

If informal supports are to continue to be a principal mode of social care for older people, serious consideration must be given to methods of assisting family, friends, neighbors, and other informal groups in their efforts. Many forms of assistance merit consideration, including home care, respite service, and counseling, training, and self-help groups for caregivers. Is support best given in the form of direct services, vouchers for service, cash allowances, or a combination thereof? Throughout the world there is a growing awareness that methods of assisting informal networks are essential, but widespread and comprehensive family-oriented policy in this area has yet to emerge.

With informal care such a crucial part of the social care system, the question of the proper interface between informal and formal subsystems becomes critical. We need to know more about the appropriate balance between individual, family, and societal responsibility for the care of dependent elderly. Futhermore, formal helpers of all disciplines must learn to appreciate the role of family, friends, and neighbors, and to take the time to work with them and include them in care planning for older persons. Such an interface probably involves radical reexamination of and changes in attitudes about professionalism, status, and the importance of technical expertise. Shortage of resources may force such a reappraisal, but it is hoped that the new working relationships that must emerge can be built upon a positive appreciation for the respective roles of each sector, formal and informal.

If we accept the premise that both informal social care and formal social care have unique value and that the welfare of older persons is advanced by cooperative efforts, we must be careful not to upset the delicate ecological balance between the two subsystems. The tendency to formalize the informal system, regulate it, and bureaucratize it in our desire to enhance and support poses a real and serious threat. Does filial responsibility under law really promote informal support, or is the widely accepted moral imperative of caring for parents the more important motivating force? How does a society help mediating structures such as churches and neighborhood groups to play a role in social care without interfering with them? Even the granting of modest sums for development costs involves issues of accountability and regulation. In a similar vein, although direct or indirect financial incentives may require less regulation, can frail elderly realistically assume responsibility for obtaining and supervising home services without the oversight assistance of a case manager or younger family member? These are complex issues requiring more study. Solutions will differ, depending on the mix of public and private services and value systems in particular countries. But the basic issue of how to strengthen informal networks without transforming them into formal entities and creatures of government is applicable everywhere.

Turning to the formal social service system, there are equally challenging questions requiring future consideration. Some have been with us for a long time and were discussed fully by Beattie (1976) in the first edition of this *Handbook*. Others are made newly urgent because of pressure of limited resources and the emergence in the United States of the "New Federalism," with its emphasis on local responsibility and deregulation.

Given the problem of service fragmentation, what is the best way to organize services to assure accessibility and coordination of effort? It would appear that coordination efforts need to go on simultaneously at the individual, community, and systems levels. For the consumer of services there is still the need to find the best method or methods of providing a single entry point into the service delivery system. Such a gateway requires at a minimum high visibility and a staff capable of assessing need and accessing the system. Perhaps, in addition, there is a need for case planning and case management. How and where this is best accomplished is not yet clear. The professional case management approach would appear to offer possibilities. At the same time greater attention is needed to the use of families as case managers, another as yet unstudied alternative. However, the current demonstration route so prevalent in the United States has limited value unless procedures assessed as workable have a chance of being institutionalized once the demonstration ceases.

Equally important is systems coordination, both within the formal social care system and between systems, particularly health and social care. No country has yet found answers to this ongoing problem. Perhaps the new Social Health Maintenance Organizations in the United States will find a way to combine formal health and social care services effectively within a reasonable cost frame. Certainly for the frail elderly requiring long-term care a more holistic approach is essential, even if the actual delivery of services is not lodged in a single agency or service system.

The special needs of vulnerable populations—ethnic, racial, rural, low income—continue to require attention. Particularly in service provision for minorities, a dual perspective should be considered, consciously relating the unique history and experience of minority groups to the value systems and behavior of the larger society.

However, accessing services and entering systems assumes that services are available. Here issues of resource allocation, territorial inequity, and distributive equality must be faced. At present most countries assign a relatively low priority to formal social services in the community. Should all communities be required to provide a minimum base of services as in Sweden, or is local autonomy the answer to ensure that local needs are met? To what extent should services be targeted, to what groups, and according to what criteria?

Current demographic projections for the decade ahead suggest the need for an expansion of formal services, particularly long-term care assistance in the home. Yet, home care throughout the world is in short supply. How can such an expansion occur and be financed? A variety of in-home services are essential as backup to informal supports and as a substitute when they are absent. Without such services the so-called continuum of care is an empty phrase. In the United States the very affluent may be able to purchase service from the increasing number of proprietary vendors. The very poor have some protection under existing legislation. What about the vast majority of elderly between the two extremes? Their need for home care can be expected to increase at the same rate, and some method must be found to make home care available for all in need. Perhaps the answer lies in making home care universally available like a public utility financed out of public revenues. Or it might be paid for on an insurance basis—for example, expanded coverage under Medicare with the government paying for the poor. Still another widely discussed approach is the institution of sliding fee scales according to individual means. Clearly more needs to be known about the implications of these and other alternatives to service provision in the decades ahead.

Perhaps the most important difference between European and American approaches to social care is a philosophical difference best expressed by the title of Kahn and Kamerman's (1975) book: *Not for the Poor Alone*. Students of social policy have talked of a new social wage to call attention to the fact that in modern society standards of living depend not only on income (wages or retirement benefits) but on accessibility of a range of public services including health care, education, and social care (Kahn, 1979). Although each society decides for itself what rights go with citizenship, rising expectations suggest broadened definitions of basic needs. In a climate of service retrenchment and economic constraint, it is particularly important that the role of community-based, publicly supported social care services be reaffirmed. It is clear that the family and other informal supports have a unique role to play with regard to assistance to the elderly. It is the system to which older people turn naturally, and there is little indication that the moral responsibility to care for the old will be eroded in the coming period. But, the informal system in highly industrialized societies cannot function adequately without a floor of comprehensive social care entitlements and services in place in the community. Only with such a floor of services can we ensure, on the one hand, that older persons without kin are adequately cared for; and, on the other, that assistance will be readily available when the need for care is beyond the capacity of the informal network. There is always the danger in periods of presumed limited resources that the informal care system will be offered as an alternative to community-based formal services. Such an approach would not only destroy the balance between informal and formal but result in a serious reduction in care for older people. Only when both systems are in place and functioning at optimum levels will the increasing number of the world's elderly be assured the social care they need and desire.

REFERENCES

Abrams, M. 1978. *Beyond Three Score and Ten.* London: Age Concern.

Adams, J. 1980. Service arrangements preferred by minority elderly; a cross cultural study. *The Gerontologist* 3(2):39–57.

Agate, J. 1979. *Taking Care of Older People at Home.* London: George Allen and Unwin.

Amann, A. 1980. *Open Care for the Elderly in Seven European Countries: A Pilot Study in the Possibilities and Limits of Care.* London: Pergamon Press.

American Council of Life Insurance and Health Insurance Association of America. 1982. *Population Aging: Some Consequences for Social Institutions and Human Service Organizations.* Washington, D.C.: American Council of Life Insurance.

Barnes, J. A. 1972. *Social Networks.* Reading, Mass.: Addison Wesley Modular Publications, Module 26.

Beattie, W. 1976. Aging and the social services. *In* R. Binstock and E. Shanas (eds.), *Handbook of Aging and the Social Sciences,* 1st ed., pp. 619–642. New York: Van Nostrand Reinhold Company.

Bengtson, V. 1979. Ethnicity and aging: Problems and issues in current social science inquiry. *In* D. Gelfand and A. Kutzik (eds.), *Ethnicity and Aging,* pp. 9–31. New York: Springer.

Bengtson, Vern, and DeTerre, E. 1980. Aging and family relations. *Marriage and Family Review* 3:51–76.

Bengtson, V., Burton, L., and Mangen, D. 1981. Family support systems and attribution of responsibility: Contrasts among elderly Blacks, Mexican-Americans and Whites. Paper presented at 34th Annual Meeting of the Gerontological Society, Toronto.

Berger, P., and Neuhaus, R. 1977. *To Empower People.* Washington, D.C.: American Enterprise Institute.

Bergman, S. 1973. Facilitating living conditions for aged in the community. *The Gerontologist* 13(2):184–188.

Bernard, J. 1967. *Marriage and Family among Negroes.* Englewood Cliffs, N. J.: Prentice-Hall.

Blenkner, M. 1969. The normal dependencies of aging. *In* R. Kalish (ed.), *The Dependencies of Old People,* pp. 27–37. Ann Arbor: University of Michigan/Wayne State University, Institute of Gerontology.

Branch, L., and Jette, A. 1982. A prospective study of long-term care institutionalization among the aged. *American Journal of Public Health* 72(12):1373–1379.

Branch, L., and Jette, A. 1983. Elders' use of informal long-term care assistance. *The Gerontologist* 23(1):51–56.

Brody, E. M. 1966. The aging family. *The Gerontologist* 9:187–196.

Brody, E. M. 1977. *Long-Term Care of Older People.* New York: Human Sciences Press.

Brody, E. M. 1978. The aging of the family. *Annals of the American Academy of Political and Social Science* 438:13–27.

Brody, E. M. 1981. Women in the middle and family help to older people. *The Gerontologist* 21(5):471–480.

Brody, E. M., and Brody, S. J. 1981. New directions in health and social supports for the aging. *In* M. A.

Lewis (ed.), *The Aging: Medical and Social Supports in the Decade of the 80's,* pp. 35–48. New York: Fordham University, Center on Gerontology.

Brody, S. J., Poulshock, W., and Masciocchi, C. 1978. The family caring unit: A major consideration in the long-term support system. *The Gerontologist* 18(6):556–561.

Brotman, H. 1982. *Every Ninth American.* Special report prepared for U. S. Senate Special Committee on Aging.

Callahan, J., Jr., Diamond, L., Giele, J., and Morris, R. 1980. Responsibility of families for their severely disabled elders. *Health Care Financing Review* (Winter):29–48.

Cantor, M. 1975a. Life space and the social support system of the inner city elderly of New York. *The Gerontologist* 15(1):23–27.

Cantor, M. 1975b. The formal and informal social support system of older New Yorkers. Paper presented at the 10th International Congress of Gerontology, Jerusalem, Israel.

Cantor, M. 1976. The configuration and intensity of the informal support system in a New York City elderly population. Paper presented at the 29th Annual Meeting of the Gerontological Society, New York.

Cantor, M. 1977. Neighbors and friends: An overlooked resource in the informal support system. Paper presented at the symposium, Natural Support Systems for the Elderly: Current Research and Implications for Policy, 30th Annual Meeting of the Gerontological Society, San Francisco, Calif.

Cantor, M. 1978. The informal support system in the lives of the elderly. Unpublished paper, New York: Fordham University.

Cantor, M. 1979b. The informal support system of New York's inner city elderly, is ethnicity a factor? *In* D. Gelfand and A. Kutzik (eds.), *Ethnicity and aging* New York: Springer. pp. 153–174.

Cantor, M. 1979a. Neighbors and friends: an overlooked resource in the informal support system. *Research on Aging,* Vol. 1, pp. 434–463.

Cantor, M. 1980. The informal support system, its relevance in the lives of the elderly. *In* E. Borgotta, and N. McCluskey (eds.), *Aging and Society.* Beverly Hills: Sage. pp. 111–146.

Cantor, M. 1981b. Factors associated with strain among family, friends and neighbors caring for the frail elderly. Paper presented at 34th Annual Meeting of the Gerontological Society, Toronto.

Cantor, M. 1981a. The extent and intensity of the informal support system among New York's inner city elderly. *In, Strengthening Informal Supports for the Aging.* N. Y.: Community Service Society. pp. 1–11.

Cantor, M. 1982. Caring for the frail elderly-impact on family, friends and neighbors. *In* C. Snyder (ed.), *Financial Incentives for Informal Caregiving-Directions from Recent Research.* New York: Community Council of Greater New York. pp. 5–12.

Cantor, M. and Brook, K. 1982. Life space and the social support systems of the suburban elderly. Paper presented at the 35th Annual Meeting of the Gerontological Society. Boston, Mass.

Cantor, M. and Donovan, R. 1982. *Enriched Housing. A viable alternative for the frail elderly.* Final report. New York: Third Age Center, Fordham University.

Cantor, M. and Johnson, J. 1978. The informal support system of the familyless elderly—who takes over? Paper presented at the 31st Annual Meeting, Gerontological Society, Dallas, Tx.

Cantor, M., Rosenthal, K., and Wilker, L. 1979. Black women in New York City. *Journal of Minority Aging* III and IV, 1–3; 50–61.

Caplan, G. 1974. *Support Systems and Community Mental Health,* New York: Behavioral Publishers.

Chebotarev, D. F., Sachuk, N. N., Verzhikouskaya, N. V. 1982. Status and condition of the elderly in Socialist countries of Eastern Europe. *Ageing International,* Vol. IX, (3), Autumn, pp. 23.

Ciuca, A. 1979. The elderly and the family. *In* G. Dooghe and J. Melander (eds.), *Family life in Old Age,* pp. 49–54. The Hague: Martinus Nijhoff.

Clark, M. 1969. Culture values and dependency in later life. *In* R. Kalish (ed.), *The Dependencies of Old People,* pp. 59–72. Ann Arbor: University of Michigan/Wayne State University, Institute of Gerontology.

Cohen, C., and Rajkowski, H. 1982. What's in a friend? Substantive and theoretical issues. *The Gerontologist* 22(3):261–266.

Collins, A. 1973. Natural delivery systems: Accessible sources of power for mental health. *American Journal of Orthopsychiatry* 43:46–52.

Collins, A. H., and Pancoast, D. L. 1976. *Natural Helping Networks. A Strategy for Prevention.* Washington, D.C.: The National Association of Social Workers.

Connelly, J. R. 1980. An expanded outline and resource for teaching a course on the Native American elderly. *In* G. Sherman (ed.), *Curriculum Guidelines in Minority Aging.* Part VI. Washington, D.C.: National Center on Black Aging.

Crossman, M. S., London, C., and Barry, C. 1981. Older women caring for disabled spouses; a model for supportive services. *The Gerontologist* 21(5):464–470.

Crystal, S. 1982. *America's Old Age Crisis.* New York: Basic Books.

Davies, B. P. 1971. *Variations in Services for the Aged: A Causal Analysis.* Occasional papers in Social Administration. London: G. Bell & Sons.

Diamond, L., and Berman, D. 1979. The social health maintenance organization: A single entry, prepaid, long-term care delivery system. Discussion paper. Boston, Mass.: University Health Policy Consortium, Brandeis University.

Dobrof, R., and Litwak, E. 1977. *The Maintenance of Family Ties of Long-Term Care Patients: Theory and Guidance of Practice.* Washington, D.C.: U.S. Government Printing Office, N.I.M.H., Fall.

Dono, J., Falbe, G., Kail, B., Litwak, E., Sherman, R.,

and Siegel, D. 1979. Primary groups in old age: Structure and functions. *Research on Aging* 1:403–433.

Dukippo, F. 1980. *The Elder American Indian.* San Diego, Calif.: The University Center on Aging, San Diego State University.

Eggert, G. M., Bowlyow, J., and Nichols, C. 1980. Gaining control of the long-term care system: First returns from the Access experiment. *The Gerontologist* 20(3), Part I:356–364.

Fadel-Girgis, M. 1982. The family as a source of elderly support. Paper prepared for International Family Symposium, First World Assembly on Aging, Vienna, Austria, July.

Fandetti, D. V., and Gelfand, D. E. 1976. Care of the aged: Attitudes of white ethnic families. *The Gerontologist* 16:544–549.

Federal Council on Aging. 1975–1980. *Annual Report to the President.* Washington, D.C.: U.S. Government Printing Office.

Federal Council on the Aging. 1978. Public policy and the frail elderly: A U.S. staff report. DHEW Pub. No. OHDS 79-20959. Washington, D.C.: U.S. Government Printing Office.

Fengler, A., and Goodrich, N. 1979. Wives of elderly disabled men; the hidden patients. *The Gerontologist* 19:175–183.

Flynn, M. 1980. Coordination of social and health care for the elderly. The British and Irish examples (U.K.). *The Gerontologist* 20(3):300–308.

Frazier, E. F. 1957. *The Negro in the United States.* New York: Macmillan.

Friis, H. 1979. The aged in Denmark: social programs. *In* M. Teicher, D. Thursz, and J. Vigilante (eds.), *Reaching the Aged: Social Services in Forty-four Countries.* Vol. 4, Social Service Delivery Systems: An International Annual. Beverly Hills, Calif.: Sage.

Fry, C. (ed.). 1980. *Aging in Culture and Society: Comparative Viewpoints and Strategies.* New York: Bergen.

Gelfand, D., and Kutzik, A. 1979. Conclusions. The continuing significance of ethnicity. *In* D. Gelfand and A. Kutzik (eds.), *Ethnicity and Aging: Theory Research and Policy,* pp. 357–361. New York: Springer.

Gelfand, D. E., and Olson, J. 1979. Aging in the Jewish family and the Mormon family. *In* D. Gelfand and A. Kutzik (eds.), *Ethnicity and Aging: Theory, Research and Policy,* pp. 206–221. New York: Springer.

Gibson, G. 1972. Kin family network: Overheralded structure in past conceptualizations of family functioning. *Journal of Marriage and the Family* 34:13–23.

Gibson, M. J. 1981. Family support patterns, policies and programs in developed nations. Paper presented at the 34th Annual Meeting of the Gerontological Society, Toronto.

Gibson, M. J. 1982. An international update on family care for the ill elderly. *Ageing International* IX(1):11–14.

Gilleard, C. J., Watt, G., and Boyd, W. D. 1981. Problems of caring for the elderly mentally infirm at home. Paper presented at the 12th International Congress of Gerontology, Hamburg, July.

Goldberg, E. M., and Connelly, N. 1978. Home help services for the elderly: A review of recent research. London: Center for Policy Studies (mimeo).

Gurian, B., and Cantor, M. 1978. Mental health and community support systems for the elderly. *In* G. Usdin and C. Hofling (eds.), *Aging: The Process and the People,* pp. 184–205. New York: Brunner/Mazel.

Gurland, G., Dean, L., Gurland, R., and Cook, D. 1978. Personal time dependency in the elderly of New York City: Findings from the U.S.-U.K. cross national geriatric community study. *In: Dependency in the Elderly of New York City,* pp. 9–45. New York: Community Council of Greater New York.

Guttmann, D. (ed.). 1979. *Informal and Formal Support Systems and Their Effects on the Lives of the Elderly in Selected Ethnic Groups.* Washington, D.C.: School of Social Service, Catholic University of America.

Harris, L., and associates. 1974. *The Myth and Reality of Aging in America.* Washington, D.C.: National Council on the Aging.

Hendricks, J., and Hendricks, C. D. 1977. *Aging in Mass Society: Myths and Realities.* Cambridge, Mass.: Winthrop Publishing Co.

Heumann, L. F. 1980. Sheltered housing for the elderly: The role of the British warden (England). *The Gerontologist* 20(3):318–331.

Hill, R. B. 1972. *The Strength of Black Families.* New York: Emerson Hall.

Hill, R. B. 1978. Excerpts from *The Black Elderly. In* M. Seltzer, S. Corbett, and R. Atchley (eds.), *Social Problems of the Aging: Readings,* pp. 273–277. Belmont, Calif.: Wadsworth.

Hobman, D. 1981. Caring for the caregivers of the elderly. Paper presented at the 12th International Congress of Gerontology, Hamburg.

Hodgson, J. H., and Quinn, J. L. 1980. The impact of the triage health delivery system on client morale, independent living and the cost of care. *The Gerontologist* 20(3), Part I:364–372.

Holzberg, C. 1982a. Ethnicity and aging: Anthropological perspectives on more than just the minority elderly. *The Gerontologist* 22(3):249–257.

Holzberg, C. 1982b. Ethnicity and aging: Rejoinder to a comment by Kyriakos S. Markides. *The Gerontologist* 22(6):471–473.

Hörl, J. and Rosenmayr, L. 1981. Assistance to the elderly as a common task of the family and social service organizations. Paper presented at the 12th International Congress of Gerontology, Hamburg.

Horowitz, A. 1981. Sons and daughters as caregivers to older parents: Differences in role performance and consequences. Paper presented at the 34th Annual Meeting of the Gerontological Society, Toronto.

Horowitz, A., and Dobrof, R. 1982. The role of families in providing long-term care to the frail and chronically ill elderly living in the community. Final report. Submitted to the Health Care Financing Administration, Grant #18-P-97541/2-02. New York: Brookdale Center on Aging of Hunter College.

Jackson, J. 1980. *Minorities and Aging.* Belmont, Calif.: Wadsworth.

Jacobson, S., and Hawkins, B. 1982. The role of caregivers in the black community. Final Report to the Administration on Aging, Grant #90-A-1375. Columbia, Md.: The Institute for the Study of Human Systems, Inc.

Johnson, C., and Catalano, D. 1981. Childless elderly and their family supports. *The Gerontologist* 21(6):610–617.

Kahn, A. 1979. *Social Policy and Social Services,* 2nd ed. New York: Random House.

Kahn, A., and Kamerman, S. 1975. *Not for the Poor Alone.* Philadelphia: Temple University Press.

Kahn A., and Kamerman, S. 1977. *Social Services in International Perspective.* HEW/SRS 76-05704. Washington, D.C.: U.S. Government Printing Office.

Kahn, A., and Kamerman, S. 1978. Options for delivery of social services at the local level: A cross-national report. *In* D. Thursz and J. Vigilante (eds.), *Reaching People—The Structure of Neighborhood Services,* Vol. 3, Social Service Delivery Systems. An International Annual. pp. 95–113, Beverly Hills, Calif.: Sage.

Kahn, R., and Antonucci, T. 1980. Convoys over the life course: Attachment roles and social supports. *In* P. Baltes and O. Brim (eds.), *Life Span Development and Behavior,* pp. 254–283. New York: Academic Press.

Kalish, R. A., and Lurie, E. 1975. On Lok senior health services: Evaluation of a success. San Francisco (Mimeo.)

Kamerman, S. 1976. Community services for the aged: The view from eight countries. *The Gerontologist* 16(6):529–537.

Kamerman, S., and Kahn, A. 1976. *Social Services in the United States,* pp. 313–386. Philadelphia: Temple University Press.

Kane, R., and Kane, R. 1976. *Long-Term Care in Six Countries: Implications for the U.S.* Washington, D.C.: U.S. Government Printing Office, #DHEW Pub. #76-1207 (NIH).

Lawton, M. P. 1982. Environments and living arrangements. *In* R. H. Binstock, W.-S. Chow, and J. H. Schulz (eds.), *International Perspectives on Aging,* pp. 159–193. New York: United Nations Fund for Population Activities.

Lewis, M. A., Bienenstock, R., Cantor, M., and Schneewind, E. 1980. The extent to which informal and formal supports interact to maintain older people in the community. Paper presented at 33rd Annual Meeting of the Gerontological Society, San Diego.

Lewis, M. A., Mclauchlan, W., and Cantor, M. 1981.

Impact on informal supports of the entrance of the formal organization in a homemaker population. Paper presented at 34th Annual Meeting of the Gerontological Society, Toronto.

Little, V. C. 1974. Social services for the elderly: With special attention to Asia and the West Pacific region. Paper presented at the 27th Annual Meeting of the Gerontological Society, Portland, Oreg., Oct. 1974.

Little, V. C. 1975a. *In: Home Help Services for the Aging Around the World,* edited by C. Nusberg. pp. 16–23; 32–43, Washington, D.C.: International Federation on Aging.

Little, V. C. 1975b. Factors influencing the provision of in-home services in developed and developing countries. Paper presented at the 10th International Congress of Gerontology, Jerusalem, Israel.

Little, V. C. 1976 (rev. 1977). Coordinating services for the elderly. Paper presented at the Governor's Bicentennial Conference, Honolulu, 1976.

Little, V. C. 1978a. Open care for the aged: Swedish model. *Social Work* 23(4):272–278.

Little, V. C. 1978b. A comparison of the impact and effect of home help services in Japan and homemaker–home health aide services in the United States. Paper presented at the 11th International Congress of Gerontology, Tokyo, Japan, Aug. 1978.

Little, V. C. 1979. For the elderly: An overview of services in industrially developed and developing countries. *In* M. Teicher, D. Thursz, and J. Vigilante (eds.), *Reaching the Aged: Social Services in Forty-Four Countries,* Vol. 4, pp. 149–173, Social Service Delivery Systems: An International Annual. Beverly Hills, Calif.: Sage.

Little, V. C. 1981. The art of case management: Some preliminary international comparisons. *In* J. T. Bost (ed.), *Social Work and the Elderly: The Growing Callenge,* pp. 97–113. University of Connecticut School of Social Work Career Training Program in Aging.

Little, V. C. 1982a. *Open Care for the Aging: Comparative International Approaches.* New York: Springer.

Little, V. C. 1982b. Aging in the Third World. *In: Aging: An International Perspective: Proceedings of a Conference, March 11, 1982,* pp. 46–60. New York: Columbia University.

Litwak, E. 1978. Agency and family linkages in providing services. *In* D. Thursz and J. Vigilante (eds.), *Reaching People: The Structure of Neighborhood Services,* Vol. 3, pp. 59–95, Social Service Delivery Systems: An International Annual. Beverly Hills, Calif.: Sage.

Litwak, E. 1965. Extended kin relations in an industrial democratic society. *In* E. Shanas and G. Streib (eds.), *Social Structure and the Family,* pp. 290–325. Englewood-Cliffs, N. J.: Prentice-Hall.

Litwak, E., and Meyer, H. 1966. A balance theory of coordination between bureaucratic organizations and community primary groups. *Administrative Sciences Quarterly* 11:31–58.

Litwak, E., and Szelenyi, I. 1969. Primary group structures and their functions: Kin, neighbors and friends. *American Sociological Review* 34:465–481.

Lopata, H. 1975. Support systems and elderly urbanites: Chicago of the 1970's. *The Gerontologist* 15(1):35–41.

Lowenthal, M. F., and Robinson, B. 1976. Social networks and isolation. *In* R. Binstock and E. Shanas (eds.), *Handbook of Aging and the Social Sciences*, 1st ed., pp. 432–456. New York: Van Nostrand Reinhold.

Lowy, L. 1979. *Social Work With the Aging: The Challenge and Promise of the Later Years*. New York: Harper and Row.

Lüders, I. 1981. Social work for the elderly and family support. Paper presented at the 12th International Congress of Gerontology, Hamburg, July.

Lurie, E. 1981. Formal and informal supports in the post-hospital period. Paper presented at the 34th Annual Meeting of the Gerontological Society, Toronto, Canada.

Madison, B. 1968. *Social Welfare in the Soviet Union*. Stanford, Calif.: Stanford University Press.

Madison, B. 1975. Social services administration in the U.S.S.R. *In* D. Thursz and J. Vigilante (eds.), *Meeting Human Needs*, Vol. 1, pp, 244–281. Social Service Delivery Systems: An International Annual. Beverly Hills, Calif.: Sage.

Maeda, D. 1981. The cultural forces encouraging and supporting caregivers in Japan. Paper presented at the 12th International Congress of Gerontology, Hamburg, July 1981.

Maeda, D. 1982. The family as a source of elderly support. Paper presented at the International Symposium, First World Assembly on Aging, Vienna, Austria, July 1982.

Maldonado, D., Jr. 1979. Aging in the Chicano context. *In* D. Gelfand and A. Kutzik (eds.), *Ethnicity and Aging: Theory, Research and Policy*, pp. 175–183. New York: Springer.

Manuel, R. C., and Bengtson, V. L. 1976. Ethnicity and family patterns in mature adults: Effects on race, age, socioeconomic status and sex. Paper presented at the Annual Meeting of the Pacific Sociological Association, San Diego, Calif.

Markides, K. 1982. Ethnicity and aging: A comment. *The Gerontologist* 22(6):467–471.

Mayer, M. 1976. Kin and neighbor: Differential roles in differing cultures. Paper presented at the 29th Annual Meeting of the Gerontological Society, New York.

Mayer, M., Engler, M., and Lepis, B. 1981. The support systems of participants in home-delivered meals programs in New York City. Report of New York City Department for the Aging. (Mimeo.)

Mellor, M. J., and Getzel, G., 1980. Stress and service needs of those who care for the aged. Paper presented at the 33rd Annual Meeting of the Gerontological Society, San Diego, Calif.

Mellor, M. J., Raffel, R., and Barkley, F. 1981. A partnership of caring: A blueprint for social action. Paper presented at the 34th Annual Meeting of the Gerontological Society of American and the Canadian Association of Gerontology, Toronto, Nov.

Mindel, C., and Habenstein, R. (eds.) 1981. *Ethnic Families in America: Patterns and Variations*, 2nd ed. New York: Elsevier.

Minneapolis Age and Opportunity Center, Inc.: Daphne A. Krause, Ex. Dir. 1975. Nothing happens unless first a dream. Testimony presented to U.S. House of Representatives, Committee on Aging, Sub-committee on Health and Long-Term Care, July 8, 1975.

Mitchell, J. C. (ed.) 1969. *Social Networks in Urban Situations*. Manchester, U.K.: University Press.

Moroney, R. M. 1976. *The Family and the State: Considerations for Social Policy*. London: Longmans.

Morris, J. N., and Sherwood, S. 1984. Informal support resource for vulnerable elderly persons: can they be counted on, why do they work? *International Journal of Aging and Human Development*. 18(1):1–17.

Morris, R., and Leavitt, T. 1982. Issues of social service delivery. *In* R. H. Binstock, W.-S. Chow, and J. H. Schulz (eds.), *International Perspectives on Aging, Population and Policy Challenges*, pp. 193–216. New York: United Nations Fund for Population Activities.

Moryez, R. 1980. An exploration of senile dementia and family burden. *Clinical Social Work Journal* 8(1) (Spring):16–27.

Myers, G. 1982. The aging of populations. *In* R. Binstock, W.-S. Chow and J. H. Schulz (eds.), *International Perspectives on Aging, Population and Policy Challenges*, pp. 1–39. New York: United Nations Fund for Population Activities.

Nardone, M. 1980. Characteristics predicting community care for mentally impaired older persons. *The Gerontologist* 20(6):661–668.

New York State Health Planning Commission. 1981. *Enhancing and Sustaining Informal Support Networks for the Elderly and Disabled*. Conference proceedings and recommendations. Albany: New York State Health Advisory Council.

New York State Office for the Aging. 1983. Family caregiving and the elderly. Report. Albany: New York State Office for the Aging.

Nusberg, C. 1972–present. *Ageing International*. Washington, D.C.: International Federation on Ageing.

Nye, F. I. 1976. *Role Structure and Analysis of the Family*. London: Sage.

Oriol, W. 1982. *Aging in All Nations*. Washington, D.C.: The National Council on the Aging.

Osako, M. 1979. Aging and family among Japanese Americans: The role of ethnic tradition in the adjustment to old age. *The Gerontologist* 19(5):448–455.

Osborne, P. 1981. Crossroads care for the carers. *Geriatric Medicine* (May):59–62.

Poulshock, S., and Deimling, G. 1982. Families caring for elders in residence: Measurement issues in the

Cleveland study. Paper presented at 35th Annual Meeting of the Gerontological Society, Boston.

Poulshock, W., and Noelker, L. 1982. *The Effects of Families of Caring for Impaired Elderly in Residence.* Cleveland, Ohio: The Benjamin Rose Institute.

Quinn, J., Segal, J., Raisz, H., and Johnson, C. (eds.). 1982. *Coordinating Community Services for the Elderly.* New York: Springer.

Rapport Fedéral. 1979. *Vieillir en Suisse,* p. 242. Berne: Office Fédéral des assurances sociales.

Rosenmayr, L. 1977. The family—a source of hope for the elderly. *In* E. Shanas and M. Sussman (eds.), *Family, Bureaucracy and the Elderly,* pp. 132–157. Durham, N.C.: Duke University Press.

Rosenthal, C. 1982. Family supports in later life: Does ethnicity make a difference? Paper presented at the 11th Annual Meeting of the Canadian Association on Gerontology, Winnipeg, Manitoba.

Rosow, I. 1967. *Social Integration of the Aged.* New York: Free Press.

Roussel, L. 1976. *La famille après le mariage des enfants.* P.V.F. Paris.

Sanford, J. R. A. 1975. Tolerance of debility in elderly dependents by supporters at home: Its significance for hospital practice. *British Medical Journal* (3):471–473.

Senior Citizens Provincial Council. 1981. *Regina Social Support Study.* Saskatchewan, Canada.

Shanas, E. 1967. Family help patterns and social class in three countries. *Journal of Marriage and the Family* 29(2): 257–266.

Shanas, E. 1977. The national survey of the aged. Final Report. AoA Grant #90–A–369. Chicago: University of Illinois at Chicago Circle.

Shanas, E. 1979a. Social myth as hypothesis; the case of the family relations of old people. *The Gerontologist* 19(1):3–9.

Shanas, E. 1979b. The family as a social support system in old age. *The Gerontologist* 19(2):169–174.

Shanas, E. 1980. Older people and their families: The new pioneers. *Journal of Marriage and the Family* (Feb.):9–15.

Shanas, E., and Sussman, M. 1977. Family and Bureaucracy: Comparative analysis and problematics. *In* E. Shanas, and M. Sussman (eds.), *Family Bureaucracy and the Elderly.* pp. 215–229. Durham, N. C.: Duke University Press.

Shanas, E., Townsend, P., Wedderburn, D., Friis, H., Milhøj, P., and Stehouwer, J. 1968. *Old People in Three Industrial Societies.* New York: Atherton Press. (Reprinted Arno Press, 1980.)

Shimizu, Y., and Honma, M. 1978. Difficulties of families living with and caring for impaired old people. Paper presented at the 11th International Congress of Gerontology, Tokyo, Japan, Aug.

Sidel, R. 1972. *Women and Child Care in China: A First-hand Report.* New York: Hill and Wang.

Sidel, R. 1976. People serving people: Human services in the People's Republic of China. *In* D. Thursz and

J. Vigilante (eds.), *Meeting Human Needs,* Vol. 2, pp. 163–197. Beverly Hills, Calif.: Sage.

Simeone, I. 1980. The evolution of the family and the health of elderly people. Paper presented at the WHO Preparatory Conference for the U.N. World Assembly on Aging, Mexico City, Dec. 8–11.

Snow, D., and Gordon, J. 1980. Social network analysis and intervention with the elderly. *The Gerontologist* 20(4):463–467.

Soldo, B. 1980a. Family caregiving and the elderly: Prevalence and variations. Final report. AoA Grant #90–AR–2124. Kennedy Institute of Ethnics, Georgetown University.

Soldo, B. 1980b. Family caregiving to the elderly. Prevalence and variations. AoA Grant #90–AR–2124/01. Based on special tabulation from the 1976 survey of income and education (SIE), prepared by the Center for Population Research, Kennedy Institute of Ethics, Georgetown University.

Soldo, B., and Myers, G. C. 1976. The effects of lifetime fertility on the living arrangements of older women. Paper presented at the 29th Annual Meeting of the Gerontological Society, New York.

Solomon, B. B. 1981. The delivery of mental health services to Afro-American individuals and families: Translating theory into practice. *In* B. Bass, G. Wyatt, and G. Powell (eds.), *The Afro-American Family: Assessment, Treatment and Research Issues,* pp. 165–181. New York: Grune & Stratton.

Somerville-Cambridge Home Care Corporation. 1975. A profile of home care. (Mimeo.)

Stack, C. 1974. *All Our Kin: Strategies for Survival in a Black Community.* New York: Harper & Row.

State of Maryland, Office on Aging and Office of the Comptroller. 1977. Tax credits to families who care for elderly relatives. A report to the General Assembly.

Steinberg, R. M. 1979. Alternative designs for comprehensive delivery through case service coordination and advocacy. Progress report. AoA Grant #90–A–1280, Nov. 1979. Social Policy Laboratory: Andrus Gerontology Center.

Steinberg, R. M., and Carter G. 1982. *Case Management.* Lexington, Mass.: Lexington Books.

Steinitz, L. 1981. Informal supports in long-term care: Implications and policy options. Paper prepared for the Administration on Aging and the National Conference on Social Welfare, Cooperative Agreement, 90–A1–0008/01.

Stoller, E., and Earl, L. 1983. Help with activities of everyday life: Sources of support for the non-institutionalized elderly. *The Gerontologist* 23(1):64–70.

Streib, G. F. and Shanas, E. 1965. Social structure and the family: generational relations: an introduction *In* E. Shanas and G. F. Streib (eds.), *Social Structure and the Family: Generational Relations.* Pp. 2–9. Englewood Cliffs, N. J.: Prentice-Hall.

Sussman, Marvin. 1965. Relations of adult children with their parents. *In* E. Shanas and G. Streib (eds.), *Social Structure and the Family: Generational Rela-*

tions pp. 62–92. Englewood Cliffs, N. J.: Prentice-Hall.

Sussman, M. B. 1977. Family, bureaucracy and the elderly individual. *In* E. Shanas and M. Sussman (eds.), *Family, Bureaucracy and the Elderly,* pp. 2–20. Durham, N. C.: Duke University Press.

Sussman, M. B. 1979. Social and economic supports and family environments for the elderly. Final report to Administration on Aging. AoA Grant #90-A-316 (03).

Swenson, C. 1981. Using natural helping networks to promote competence. *In* A. Maluccio (ed.), *A New/Old Approach to Social Work Practice,* pp. 125–150. New York: Free Press.

Taber, M., Anderson, S., and Rogers, Jean C. 1980. Implementing community care in Illinois: Issues of cost and targeting in a statewide program. *The Gerontologist* 20(3) Part 1: 380–388.

Teeland, L. 1978. Keeping in touch: The relation between old people and their adult children. Gothenburg: University of Gothenburg, Monograph 16.

Thornton, P., and Moore, J. 1980. The placement of elderly people in private household. Leeds, England: Department of Social Policy and Administration Research Monograph.

Thursz, D., and Vigilante, J. 1975–79. *Meeting Human Needs Series.* Social Services Delivery System: An International Annual. Beverly Hills, Calif.: Sage.
Vol. 1, *Meeting Human Needs: An Overview of Nine Countries.*
Vol. 2, *Meeting Human Needs: Additional Perspectives from Thirteen Countries.*
Vol. 3, *Reaching People: The Structure of Neighborhood Services.*
Vol. 4, *Reaching the Aged: Social Services in Forty-four Countries* (also edited by Morton L. Teicher).

Tobin, S. 1977. *Effective Social Services for Older Americans.* Detroit: University of Michigan/Wayne State Gerontology Center.

Tobin, S., and Kulys, R. 1980. Older persons and their responsible others. *Social Work* 25(2):138–145.

Tolsdorf, C. C. 1976. Social networks, support and coping: An exploratory study. *Family Process* 15:407–417.

Townsend, P. 1968. The structure of the family. *In* E. Shanas, P. Townsend, D. Wedderburn, H. Friis, P. Milhøj, and J. Stehouwer, *Old People in Three Industrial Societies.* New York: Atherton Press. (Reprinted Arno Press, 1980, pp. 132–176.)

Townsend, P. 1965. The effects of family structure on the likelihood of admission to an institution in old age. *In* E. Shanas and G. Streib (eds.), *Social Structure and the Family,* pp. 163–187. Englewood Cliffs, N. J.: Prentice-Hall.

Treas, J. 1977. Family support systems for the aged: Some social and demographic considerations. *The Gerontologist* 17(6):486–491.

Treas, J. 1981. The great American fertility debate: Generational balance and support of the aged. *The Gerontologist* 21(1):98–104.

Troll, L., Miller, S., and Atchley, R. 1979. *Families in Later Life.* Belmont, Calif.: Wadsworth.

United Nations. 1982. *Report of the World Assembly on Aging,* Vienna July 26–Aug. 6. New York: United Nations, A/Conf/113/31.

U.S. Bureau of the Census. 1980. 1980 Census Supplementary Report, PC 80–81.

U.S. Comptroller-General. 1977. *The well-being of older people in Cleveland, Ohio.* Washington, D.C.: General Accounting Office, HCD 77-70.

U.S. Congress. 1980. *Future Directions for Aging Policy: A Human Service Model.* Washington, D.C.: Sub-Committee on Human Services of the Select Committee on Aging, U.S. House of Representatives. Committee Publication #96.226.

U.S. Congress, 1982. *Developments in Aging: 1981,* Vol. 1. Washington, D.C.: Special Committee on Aging, United States Senate. Report 97–314, Vol. 1.

U.S. Department of Health, Education and Welfare. Public Health Services. 1978. Selected chronic conditions causing limitations of activities, U.S. 1976. Table 56. *Health United States, 1978.* DHEW Publication # (PHS), 178-1232, 236–237, Dec.

U.S. Department of State. 1982. *U.S. National Report on Aging for the United Nations World Assembly on Aging,* Washington, D.C.: June.

U.S. General Accounting Office. 1977. *Home health: the need for a national policy to provide for the elderly.* Washington, D.C.: Report #HRD78-19.

Valle, R. and Mendoza, L. 1978. *The Elder Latino.* San Diego, Calif.: The Campanille Press, San Diego State University.

Watson, W. 1982. *Aging and Social Behavior.* Monterey, Calif.: Wadsworth Health Sciences Division.

Weeks, J., and Cuellar, J. 1981. The role of family members in the helping networks of older people. *The Gerontologist* 21(4):388–394.

Weihl, H. 1981. Cultural differences and situational constraints on the interaction between aged parents and their adult children. Paper presented at the 12th International Congress of Gerontology, Hamburg, Germany.

Wentowski, G. 1981. Reciprocity and the coping strategies of older people: Cultural dimensions of network building. *The Gerontologist* 21(6):600–609.

Whitfield, S. 1982. Family support demonstration project. *In* C. Snyder (ed.), *Financial Incentives for Informal Caregiving,* pp. 24–28. New York: Community Council of Greater New York.

Zarit, S. H., Reever, K. E., and Bach-Peterson, J. 1980. Relatives of the impaired elderly: Correlates of feeling of burden. *The Gerontologist* 20(6):649–655.

AUTHOR INDEX

*Italized pages are from reference list at the end of chapters.

SUBJECT INDEX